D0475144

The Case for Fewer People:

The NPG Forum Papers

Lindsey Grant, Editor

SEVEN LOCKS PRESS

Santa Ana, California

Seven Locks Press
P.O. Box 25689
Santa Ana, CA 92799
(800) 354-5348

Individual Sales. This book is available through most bookstores or can be ordered directly from Seven Locks Press at the address above.

Quantity Sales. Special discounts are available on quantity purchases by corporations, associations, and others. For details, contact the "Special Sales Department" at the publisher's address above.

Printed in the United States of America

Library of Congress Cataloging-in-Publication Data
is available from the publisher
ISBN 1-931643-51-2

This book is dedicated to

Donald Mann,

who created Negative Population Growth in 1972

and has been its President ever since.

and to

Theresa Mickendrow,

NPG's loyal and

longest-serving employee.

ABOUT THE EDITOR

Lindsey Grant writes on population and public policy. A retired Foreign Service Officer, he was a China specialist and served as Director of the Office of Asian Communist Affairs, National Security Council staff member, and Department of State Policy Planning Staff member.

As Deputy Assistant Secretary of State for Environment and Population Affairs, he was Department of State coordinator for the Global 2000 Report to the President, Chairman of the interagency committee on International Environmental Affairs, United States delegate to (and Vice Chairman of) the OECD Environmental Committee and United States member of the UN ECE Committee of Experts on the Environment.

His books include: *Too Many People: The Case for Reversing Growth, Juggernaut: Growth on a Finite Planet, Foresight and National Decisions: the Horseman and the Bureaucrat, Elephants in the Volkswagen* (a study of optimum United States population) and *How Many Americans?*

ABOUT NPG

Negative Population Growth, Inc. was founded in 1972. In the same year, thirty-four of Great Britain's most distinguished scientists, including Sir Julian Huxley, endorsed the basic principles of a landmark study called *A Blueprint for Survival.* The study warned that demand for natural resources was becoming so great that it would exhaust reserves and inevitably cause the breakdown of society and the irreversible destruction of the life-support systems on this planet. To prevent disaster they urged Britain to cut its population in half. That study greatly influenced the thinking of NPG's founders, who were convinced that a similar reduction in population was necessary for our own country.

Now, thirty-two years later, NPG is a fast-growing organization with over 30,000 members nationwide. We continue our efforts to better educate the American people and our policymakers about the devastating effects of overpopulation on our resources, environment and the quality of our lives. Our purpose, broadly stated, is, through public education, to encourage the United States, and then every country in the entire world, to put into effect national programs with the goals of first achieving a negative rate of population growth, then eventually stabilizing population size at a far lower level than today's—a size that would be sustainable indefinitely in a sound and healthy environment.

Our extensive publications are intended to both stimulate public discussion and debate, and to change the way our opinion leaders and policymakers view the issues of population size and growth, and their impact on our environment, resources and quality of life.

TABLE OF CONTENTS

INTRODUCTION

Lindsey Grant, Editor

There were remarkable changes during the twentieth century: the increase in consumption levels in the industrialized world, the dramatic increase in reliance on fossil fuels, the transformation of agriculture, the perturbation of natural systems as mankind rearranged the earth's flows of nitrogen, carbon and the other elements, and an exponential increase in the creation and manufacture of new chemicals. The most fundamental change of all, and the one that drove most of the others, was the quadrupling of the human population during that one century—a growth three times as large as the human tribe had experienced in all its previous history.

Those interconnected changes have profoundly altered the relationship of humankind to the Earth. It is astonishing how little that alteration is studied or understood in the midst of our preoccupation with secondary matters of religious and ethnic conflict, war, politics, and the pursuit of money, sex and novelty. Only occasionally is the public's attention momentarily diverted to the fundamentals of our existence, when some shocking moving picture appears, dramatizing the impacts of human crowding or climate change.

Scientists and environmentalists have attempted to understand one or another of those fundamental changes and to identify some of their consequences. However, there is very little cross-disciplinary literature relating those changes to each other and to the future of human well-being. And only a small fraction of that literature is focused on population growth, its connections with the other great changes, and the implications for present prosperity and future survival. For two decades, quite a bit of the writing directed toward that broad issue of population change and its consequences has come out of Negative Population Growth, Inc. (NPG).

The NPG studies are generally referred to as the NPG Forum papers. (Most of the papers bear that name, though I use it here to include various NPG Policy Papers, NPG Footnotes and NPG Booknotes that NPG has published from time to time.)

One problem with the reliance on short papers is their transience. The distribution of each Forum paper is now about 30,000 copies, which is fairly large by the standards of serious publishing. A much larger readership is exposed to the papers in the electronic library at the NPG website (www.npg.org). There is, however, a certain evanescent quality about an electronic document. Some readers have saved the paper copies, but such incidental papers do not usually stay long in libraries.

For that reason, I suggested recently to Donald Mann, President of NPG, that it would be useful to put those papers together in a single volume. This book has emerged from that conversation. Its principal target is a list of major American libraries. NPG plans to place copies gratis in as many libraries as it can afford, and to call other libraries' attention to its existence. Our hope is that present and future students, if they become interested in the immense issues raised by population change, will have available a single source dealing with the change itself and many of the issues it raises.

We have told NPG's membership of this project and have invited contributions to a special fund to be used solely to place the book in more libraries.

Some serious students of the issues described earlier in this introduction will, we hope, wish to have a copy in their own library. Seven Locks Press, which has published several books based originally on NPG studies, has undertaken the commercial distribution of the book.

Three notes on the contents of the volume itself:

First, in the table of contents, we have grouped together the papers published in NPG's Optimum Population series. Shortly after beginning the Forum series, we realized that it would be worthwhile to publish views by different specialists as to what an optimum population of the United States would be. That is a fundamental question raised by NPG's very title. It is not susceptible to a single, scientific answer because there are too many variables and value judgements, but we thought it valuable to get a sense of what numbers might seem reasonable from different scientific perspectives. In the end, the lowest proposed figure was 40 million people; the highest was a range of 125–250 million. From these calculations, I arbitrarily selected a range of 125–150 million as a tentative target. The important thing was that all the calculations suggested that U.S. population should be going down, not upwards—as it was then and is now, even faster. That series of essays was incorporated into the book *Elephants in the Volkswagen* (New York: W.H. Freeman, 1992). We are indebted to the experts who participated in a useful and unprecedented exercise.

Second, in putting this compilation together, we have had to leave out a few older Forum articles on secondary issues, in order to keep the collection within one volume. We apologize to the authors, but we do not believe the deletions substantially affect the usefulness of the volume.

Third, this does not mark the end of the NPG Forum series. We hope to keep producing them and, with luck, there may eventually be enough to bind together as Volume II.

We appreciate the support of NPG's members and contributors, who made the original papers and this compilation possible. Jason Smith did invaluable work in assembling the digital draft from NPG's website and organizing it into a book. Craig Lewis, NPG's Executive Vice President was as always a steady hand in making sure that things were done right, and on time.

—Lindsey Grant
Santa Fe, NM, June 2004

BEYOND FAMILY PLANNING

Anthony Wayne Smith

May 1987

This article was written early in 1985 as a review of a book by Donald J. Hernandez entitled, Success or Failure? Family Planning Programs in the Third World.

The African famine, with the probable death of hundreds of thousands of people from starvation, despite heroic efforts at food relief, points up the serious imbalance between population and resources.

Recent studies forewarn us that Sub-Saharan Africa may be going through a fundamental process of permanent desiccation as a result of over-grazing and deforestation, both stemming from catastrophic population pressures on the land.

The need for an accelerated program of population stabilization and reduction, certainly not only in Africa, becomes glaringly apparent. The warning signals were flying forty years ago and more. How can the leadership of the human race have failed so miserably?

Two schools of thought have been at war for twenty years and longer: the socioeconomic development school and the family planning school. The former has held that development brings demographic stabilization; the latter that planned parenthood does so.

The difficulty with the developmental theory is that the experience of the last decade in too many countries disproves it. In more and more nations, development has been overwhelmed by the population explosion. The cost of merely keeping people alive in abject poverty has prevented the investments in agriculture, industry. education, health, and balances of trade which are necessary to complete the demographic transition.

This is not to dispute the obvious: that the industrialized countries have low fertility rates, and that these have been associated with urbanization and industrialization by processes which are well understood. There are exceptions, of course, such as the baby boom in the United States, which suggest that something more than blind developmental economics will be needed for long-term demographic security. But the trouble is that in a rising number of the emerging nations socioeconomic development efforts have not kept pace with population growth, and the situation is going from bad to worse.

In one sense, of course, the dispute is irrelevant. Taken separately or together, development as it has been practiced and family planning as it has been practiced, have as a matter of history, failed. Famine, civil war, social conflict, poverty, political and economic instability, and environmental and ecological breakdown are among the dominant realities of our times. True, some little corners have been turned: fertility and rates of growth have declined slightly in recent years world-wide (in large part due to China), but absolute growth has accelerated as the result of generational momentum; actual population climbs and will continue to climb for a long time toward levels far beyond the carrying capacity of the planet. A greatly intensified effort at stabilization and reduction is needed.

And now comes Donald J. Hernandez with his book *Success or Failure? Family Planning Programs in the Third World,* (Greenwood Press. Westport, CT ($29.95)) to say that family planning has been but marginally successful, and that such reductions in birth rates as have occurred would have taken place anyway for the most part as the result of changes in the socioeconomic situation, and that neither family planning nor socioeconomic development as presently conducted will be sufficient. Incentives for small families, and development targeted toward family size reduction, will be necessary. The imprimatur of Kingsley Davis as editor of the series in which the book appears, *Studies in Population and Urban Demography,* helps to stamp it with authority.

The rigorous application of scientific method is always a pleasure to behold. Hernandez looks at the methodologies used in the past in judging the efficacy of family planning programs and concludes that they have been seriously flawed. He examines the potentials of controlled scientific inquiry and designs approaches better fitted to get the facts.

He then undertakes to apply the improved methodologies to the experience of four countries and to a transnational aggregate. He concludes that the family planning program in Taiwan accounted for only 11 percent of the reduction in the crude birth rate between 1965 and 1975; in South Korea between 1 and 10 percent between 1968 and 1971; in Costa Rica between 4 and 13 percent, but probably closer to 4 percent between 1968 and 1971; and in Mauritius a dubious 34 to 51 percent between 1965 and 1975. In the cross-national study of eighty-three Third World countries, family planning accounted for between 3 to 10 percent of the fall between the late 1960s and the early 1970s. In all these cases, trends were already in evidence which, if properly projected, would have indicated most of the result anyway. Conclusion: that whatever the value of family planning as a humanitarian measure, it has not been markedly successful as a means of population stabilization. One might add that population stabilization is the world's most desperate humanitarian cause.

Does this mean that the family planning effort should be relaxed or abandoned? Of course not; even the marginal contribution it makes to fertility reduction is to be welcomed. And its contribution to maternal and child health and, in terms of contraception, to the reduction of abortion and infanticide, justifies itself. If conducted with a view toward the reduction of desired family size, and not merely reproductive freedom, it can serve the necessary moral education. But it cannot be relied upon, without more, for population stabilization.

Most emphatically, on the other hand, the findings do not mean that we can fall back on generalized socioeconomic development as the solution to the population problem. The leaders of too many less-developed countries know by now full well that development, in which they trusted so implicity as recently as the Population Conference of 1974, will not take place if burdened with run-away populations. They said so at the Population Commission meetings in New York a year ago, and again in Mexico City last summer.

The answer, first of all, is to drive ahead with incentive systems to reduce desired family size. Such systems must be added to development and family planning. They must get an increasing share of domestic and international budgets. We can no longer afford reliance on either hoped-for development or planned parenthood without more. It has to be planned parenthood for sub-replacement families induced by incentive systems, and development targeted at family-size reduction. This runs against the grain of most conventional thinking about voluntary parenthood. That thinking has to change.

The customary distinction between incentives and disincentives is useful. An incentive is a benefit given to a family which keeps its family small, such as a cash payment to persons accepting voluntary sterilization. A disincentive is a penalty imposed on parents with large families, such as the loss of scholarships for the third and fourth child. Hernandez argues for incentives and against disincentives, on the ground that disincentives limit freedom. But freedom is never unlimited, and in respect to population matters, human welfare is more gravely undercut by congestion than by limits on the size of families induced by disincentives.

This is a tragic day for the family planning movement. The agencies and organizations which have carried the burden for so many years are under assault by the present American Administration, responding to the pressures of the Reactionary Right. Funds for the International Planned Parenthood Federation and the UN Fund for Population Activities have been heavily cut on the ground that programs or countries availing themselves of their support in some measure permit or support abortion (though no American funds are used for these purposes). The result will be the diminished use of contraceptives, more unwanted pregnancies, and more abortions, indeed more infanticide. And so one hesitates before the facts; that family planning has not been sufficiently successful as a program for the reduction of fertility. But the truth has to be faced.

Whether one thinks that disincentives, imposing minor burdens in comparison with the greater good, should also be employed, may depend on one's appraisal of the seriousness of the situation. The evidence runs against complacency from both the humanitarian and the ecological-point of view. Southeast Asia, Sub-Saharan Africa, the Amazon basin, all tell us that time is running out. All the non-coercive approaches—including in that category, social counter-pressures against the traditional large family, and including cash payments to acceptors—will have to be employed. Or else the result will shortly be indescribable human misery and the collapse of the global biosystem.

The necessary acceleration, in the opinion of a growing number of observers, means socioeconomic incentives and disincentives, both individual and community. It means social counter pressures to neutralize traditional pressures for large families. It means targeting for sub-replacement fertility rates; that is, for the two-child family, and in many countries, as in China, the one-child family. It means the universal availability of family planning materials and services by the year 2000 at the latest. And it should mean a crusade by religious organizations for the humane purposes of the small family.

It means expanded, not contracted, development aid, but focussed on programs useful for population stabilization; e.g., education, not dams; local food production by indigenous methods; the employment of women outside the home. It means the conditioning of loans and grants by unilateral and multilateral public and private credit institutions on the adoption and implementation of population stabilization programs, and strict reporting on compliance. It means warnings that food aid cannot go on indefinitely unless population is brought under control.

It means total fertility rates of two or less by the year 2000; if Bangladesh can set that target, others can. It means population stabilization everywhere by

2020 as a goal, not a complacent 2080 or later; but not as a goal only, but coupled with specific and realistic programs to reach the goal, with annual reports to a world agency on the measure of progress. And it means a world-wide effort directed toward individual couples to teach the morality of the small family in terms of the welfare of family members, the local community, and the nation and society as a whole. Human beings are driven by conscience no less than economics; and conscience in the end by reason; every man and woman on the planet needs to understand what the population crisis is, so that the family may adjust its conduct accordingly.

Governments everywhere should be setting up official policies and programs for the stabilization and reduction of population. The programs must be more than words, and must include schedules for implementation. They should be supported by realistic budgetary analysis; that is, they should attempt to forecast the beneficial effects of stabilization on reduced costs for health care, education, housing,. food, and welfare, and the increased ability to finance industrial growth, agricultural modernization, environmental protection, and trade-deficit reduction.

For example, the rapid adoption of payments to acceptors for voluntary sterilization, a program which has been successful in Sri Lanka and elsewhere, accompanied by thorough-going education as to practical irrevocability, and with strong safeguards against actual compulsion, could solve many national budgetary problems in a generation's time and set a country on a road to stable prosperity.

Millions of people starve and sink in poverty. The world credit structure totters. Austerity is imposed which imperils fragile democracies. Unemployment rises world-wide. American industry, pursuing cheap labor, moves abroad. American consumers, pursuing cheap goods, buy from abroad. The American trade deficit overtakes the budgetary deficit. Third World development founders in the crowding. The family planning movement demurs as to incentives. The environmental-movement avoids the issue. The labor movement slumbers in peace. New leadership is needed; it cannot come from the United States government while the present negative mood persists. Can it come from China? India? Africa?

Hernandez has contributed enormously to an understanding of the facts; his book should help launch a new epoch in the population stabilization movement.

A PROGRAM FOR NORMS AND INCENTIVES

Organized efforts to cope with the population explosion have been underway for about fifty-five years. They have not been remarkably successful.

The first efforts went to sounding the alarm. The great names we associate with those times are William Vogt, Fairfield Osborne, Robert Cook and Hugh Moore. Guy Irving Burch, founder of the Population Reference Bureau, was an even earlier pioneer. The problem of what to do about it, however, was left largely unanswered.

Research in the techniques of family limitation was obviously needed. Generous foundation funding and eventually public financing, were poured into this approach. A wide variety of contraceptive methods is now available. The difficulty is to get people to use them.

Great quantities of contraceptive materials have been produced and shipped into the less developed countries over the years. Large numbers of technicians have been trained and dispersed to teach people how to use them. Clinics have been established everywhere. The problem of acceptance remains.

The development of the sciences and institutions of demography has been another essential response to the challenge. Again the financing provided by foundations and eventually public agencies has been commendable and indispensable. While there has been a tag in the production of statistics on desired family size, the world has been provided with an admirable and necessary body of information. But without action, information is sterile.

The birth control movement, later known as voluntary parenthood or family planning, preceded the population stabilization effort. Insofar as the family planning movement works for freedom to limit family size, its purposes parallel those of the population stabilization effort. But though the family planning movement assumes and contends that family planning will result in smaller families, the movement disavows any such purpose, and substantial evidence now indicates that the necessary reduction is not taking place.

All of us are familiar with the facts and theory of the demographic transition. Urbanization, industrialization, and rising living standards have resulted in lower birth rates in many places. But there is evidence that this may not occur everywhere. There is also abundant evidence that rising population levels impede economic development and rising living standards. Population stabilization and reduction will be needed in many places if economic take-off is to be achieved.

While Vogt and Osborne warned as far back as 1948 that the planetary ecosystem could be gravely endangered if the population trends of that time were to continue, a wide recognition of the deepening crisis by conservationists and environmentalists has been relatively recent. Economists have been slow to acknowledge the impact of population pressures on resources and productivity. It is ardently hoped that economics, ecology, and demography may now be converging.

All these efforts were commendable and indispensable and must be continued, but more is necessary if the challenge of the times is to be met. A growing body of evidence indicates that birth rates, fertility rates, and population growth rates are not falling rapidly enough, if at all, nor in enough places, to result in stabilization, let alone reduction, in time to forestall planetary disaster with untold misery for millions of human beings.

The problem, as more and more people see it, is one of motivation. Warnings about famine, pollution, unemployment and economic breakdown go unheeded by couples all over the world, who see their personal security and prosperity dependent on large families. While they may make use of contraceptives and clinics for spacing, desired family size appears too often to remain four children or more, as does the total fertility rate, indicating that people are having, the number of children they want in most cases, even though four children to a couple will mean doubling of populations every generation, a growth rate the world cannot sustain.

More attention must be given to problems of ethical norms and economic and other motivation. If the facilities available for population stabilization and reduction are to be used by the people who make the crucial decisions as part of their personal lives, the desire for small families and the understanding of their importance must be achieved by the great majority of human beings all over the world. Only so, incidentally, can we avoid those changes in the weather of public opinion which often undo vital advances from generation to generation.

A number of countries have instituted motivational systems and brought fertility rates and desired family size down sharply. We know enough about these systems now to be reasonably sure that it can be done. Objectives and methods will vary from country to country. In most cases, eventually the norm will be the two-child maximum; in others, where more drastic measures are clearly needed, the one-child family will be the norm for several generations. Social pressures and economic incentives and disincentives must be applied toward these ends. Overseas aid programs should be directed toward these purposes.

There will be disagreement among private organizations about these conclusions. Many are engaged in other work from which they should not be diverted. What is needed is not the replacement of present efforts, but their supplementation. Persons and organizations free to focus in any measure on the problems of norms and incentives should undertake to do so; the others, precluded by circumstances or desire from participation, should facilitate and not impede their efforts.

THE GREATEST MERCY

Most of the factors of chaos can he mitigated in some measure by direct remedial attention. The polluting effects of industrialization can be abated to some extent by industrial development for the production of abatement equipment. The destructive effects of a polluter, like the internal combustion engine, can be mitigated by modification or abolition, or by getting the automobile under control. Even the explosion of electric power consumption might be contained in a minor measure by an inversion of rate schedules, or, for example, by going back to windows and sunlight in buildings.

But none of these measures will be adequate, alone or together, unless the population explosion can be contained. The per capita factor compounds every danger. All the signs indicate that for mere survival, let alone civilized living, this Nation and the world are already overcrowded. Population levels must be stabilized and reduced by a rapid lowering of birthrates, and in some countries, like the United States, by the curtailment of immigration.

We suggest that reliance can be placed on two essentially human characteristics: reason and morality. A rational standard of personal conduct must be created to which every individual can repair. The essence of this personal and social standard is a normal family size of not more than two children. The need for the standard must be explained in simple terms to as many human beings as possible and as quickly as possible around the planet, and their help must be obtained in adopting it in their personal lives and recommending it to others.

Step one on a world program for population stabilization and reduction would be a planetary educational effort, coupled with technical and clinical assistance, not merely with respect to the facts and dangers of overpopulation, nor the gains for society in population stabilization and reduction, nor the advantages and methods of family planning, but with respect also to the moral obligation which people owe themselves, their children; their parents, and the community, to stop at two. The need is for both telical and technical education, and the materials and services for implementation, providing not merely facts, but orientation and motivation.

An educational and operating program of this kind, or any such program which is to be realistic and effective, must be couched and practiced in terms of the distinctive cultures and subcultures and by persons closely in touch with the economic and social conditions of the people involved. The work must be done by the teachers, social workers, physicians, and ministers, who are already serving the needs of the people, and in the dialects and against the background of the customs and religions of the particular communities. The necessary technical and economic assistance must come from the world community, in large part from the more affluent nations.

Step two in a rational planetary population program would be to offer economic motivation and security to persons consenting on a completely voluntary basis to terminate fertility permanently after two children. Simple low-risk techniques of oviduct ligation or cauterization are becoming available for women, involving no external abdominal surgery, and vasectomy is available for men.

The levels at which economic rewards should be set can be determined only by experience. The compensation would be an immediate inducement, but if properly handled could afford a measure of the economic security which parents expect from children in countries without social security systems.

Not the slightest suggestion of any ethnic, economic, national, regional, or other prejudice or discrimination can be allowed to touch the program, lest it destroy itself.

. . . Mere human survival, and certainly the quality of life for all people on the planet, and even more assuredly the continuing existence of thousands of cherished forms of plant and animal life throughout the globe, hang now in substantial measure on dealing resolutely, intelligently, and with a profound moral understanding, with the basic issue of overcrowding. Let those who profess love for humanity turn their hands to the greatest mercy: toward the stabilization and reduction of human numbers.

Excerpted from an editorial that appeared in the May 1972 issue of National Parks & Conservation Magazine.

A POPULATION FOCUS FOR U.S. AID

Lindsey Grant

June 1987

At a time when AID, driven by the Kemp amendment, has just eliminated all support for the UN Fund for Population Activities (UNFPA), it may seem folly to propose that the nation make population programs a focus for its international economic development activities. Nevertheless, let me undertake to plant the seed of an idea.

U.S. developmental aid has diminished to practical irrelevance to the capital needs of the third world. Only by identifying a few key issues and concentrating on them can the nation hope for perceptible worldwide results from its assistance.

Population growth is such an issue. The United States has been a leader in developing worldwide approaches to human fertility control. It would be well advised to resume the role for the benefit, not just of others, but of ourselves and our future.

The United States could meet its share of present "unmet needs" for population assistance. It could go on to vitalize a World Bank plan to bring fertility in the third world close to replacement levels (the first step to stabilization) by 2000. This would require an annual expenditure rising 10 percent per year until 2000. Even then, it would take only 7 percent from all other U.S. foreign assistance programs—even if there is no growth in foreign aid.

THE VANISHING RESOURCE: U.S. AID

In constant dollars, U.S. economic assistance has declined by about 50 percent since 1966. As a proportion of our GNP—or as aid **per capita** in the third world—it has declined by about two-thirds.

Moreover, we have tended to concentrate the aid for immediate military or political purposes. In 1986, total U.S. economic and military assistance was $15.9 billion. Of that, $13.3 billion was bilateral assistance. Of that:

- half (47.5 percent) , went to Israel, Egypt and Jordan—i.e. to foster friendly Arab governments and assure the survival of Israel.
- one-quarter (27.6 percent) helped to assure military base rights (Greece, Philippines, Spain, Turkey) or went to two foreign policy hot spots (Pakistan and Central America.)

That leaves one-quarter for the rest of the world—or $3.3 billion.

THE NEED FOR BETTER FOCUS

The aid to Israel approximates $860 per Israeli. At that level, bilateral assistance can have considerable impact. Spread around the third world, the $3.3 billion works out to 86¢ per person. The difference makes the point: we must select our places or select our issues if the aid is to have any serious function.

As a nation, we have more and more taken the route of concentrating on specific places. In government, there is always the danger that the urgent will freeze out the important. We started with a broader ideal. "Point Four" was President Truman's proposal for widely-distributed technical assistance to the third world. Perhaps it over-simplified the process of economic modernization, but it contained some fundamental wisdom. Truman believed that a world divided between a few rich nations and many poor ones would be inherently unstable, and that both sides would benefit if we helped the poor to find the way to prosperity. There was altruism in the idea, and self-interest.

The altruism has tended to erode, but we should at least look again at our self-interest. There are now more arguments than there were for seeing the world as an interconnected organism. Truman was thinking in terms of world politics and perhaps of trade. We now know that the world is interconnected in ways more visceral than that. Europe and the United States are just beginning to find out that, if people are hungry and jobless, it is very difficult to keep them from migrating to where the jobs are. Ecology was hardly a public issue in Truman's time, but we now realize that the climate—**our** climate—is affected as deserts advance and tropical forests are cut down. All of us are impoverished when species die off and genetic diversity is narrowed.

Such profound issues deserve more attention than they get.

THE PIVOTAL ROLE OF POPULATION

Demographic change affects most issues. Its amelioration—the slowing and perhaps reversing of population growth in crowded lands—is not the only element in an effort to achieve our political, economic and environmental objectives, but it is probably (as the logician would say) the condition

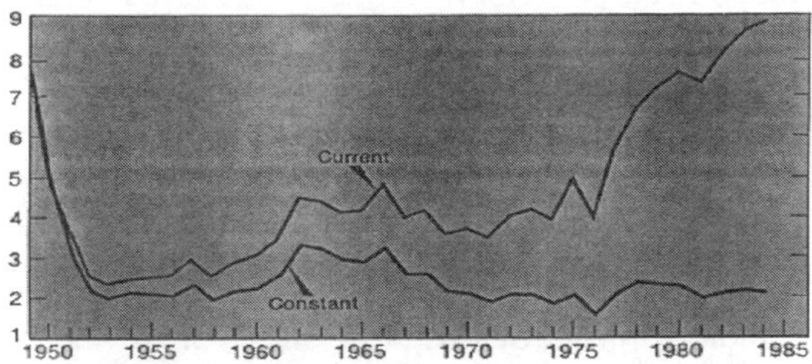

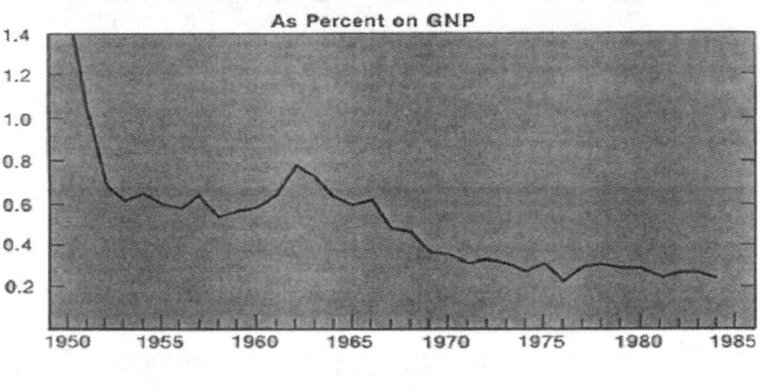

SOURCE: A.I.D., U.S. Overseas Loans and Grants and Assistance from International Organizations. Price deflator and GNP figures from The Economic Report of the President, 1986.
(Reprinted from U.S. International Development Cooperation Agency "Congressional Presentation FY1987," Washington, D.C., April 1986.)

Figure 1. U.S. Economic Assistance 1949–84 in Billions of Dollars and as Percent on GNP

precedent. Without it, you may not be able to reach those other objectives.

Let us relate population change to just three major indicators that tell us a great deal about the way the world is heading.

First, Income per Capita

This is the argument most frequently heard, although it is the least important.

In this brief paper, perhaps the best argument is simply to document what has been happening. This graph is from the World Bank's **World Development Report 1984.**

In 1972 and again in 1982, a lower fertility rate correlated with a higher per capita income. Moreover, during that decade, most countries with declining fertility enjoyed increasing incomes.

Like most macroeconomic analysis, this table reflects correlation, not rigorous causation. Perhaps, in part, prosperity leads to lower fertility. There are, however, causation studies documenting the tendency of rapid population growth to slow or imperil economic growth. There are various reasons: the diversion of capital from productive investment to maintaining infrastructure; the effect of driving the supply of labor to a point where labor productivity is declining markedly; the impaired performance when children are born too fast, without adequate nutrition and attention; the vicious spiral of population growth degrading the resource base, in turn leaving fewer resources to support more people.

At the UN Population Conference in Mexico City in 1984, the third world representatives generally argued the benefits of family planning for economic development. The U.S. delegation, influenced by a pro-natalist faction within the Reagan administration, found itself isolated. It argued that the effect of population growth on development was moot, and that the real need is for the third world to free its economies and allow the free market to work its miracles.

There was no need to set those ideas in opposition, and there is no reason for any administration to assume that fertility control is antithetic to a free economy. It might even help the move toward one. Couples with two children are more likely to have the wherewithal to go into business than those with eight.

If third world prosperity is an object of aid, then assistance in limiting human fertility is a good way of contributing to that goal.

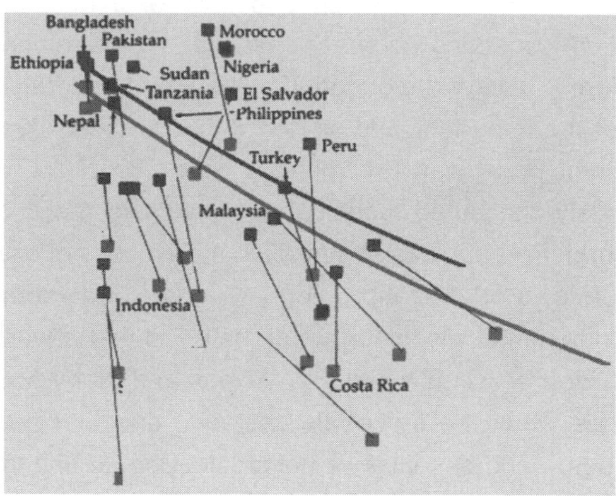

Figure 2. Fertility in relation to income in developing countries, 1972 and 1982; Total fertility rate

Second, Unemployment and Migration

National income figures are complex abstractions, but unemployment is a wrenchingly important experience to the person suffering from it. Unemployment and underemployment are endemic in the third world. Rough estimates for Mexico, for instance, run at 40 to 50 percent. To an existing problem is added the present burst of population growth. By conservative estimate, the third world labor force will expand by 850 million in this quarter century. Only the most dynamic economies (which as we have seen tend to have had lower fertility and consequently fewer entrants to the labor market) have any hope of generating the necessary jobs. Foreign aid is simply not of the scale to provide the capital to make much difference to the others.

Moreover, the problem is no longer even theoretically soluble simply by trying to provide jobs for more people. When does the point come at which finding the raw materials for so many workers, and dealing with the industrial effluents and pollutants they would generate, make the concept of solution by expansion untenable?

When agriculture is glutted with workers and there is nothing to be done in the village, the young men begin to migrate to the cities, or directly to countries with job opportunities if they are accessible (e.g. Mexicans to the U.S., Moroccans and Algerians to France, Turks to Germany, and so on). Europe and the U.S. are beginning to feel the pains of this process, but the numbers moving to third world cities are greater by orders of magnitude. We are living in an era of exploding cities with collapsing urban services (water, sewage, roads, power, education, police protection). Mexico City is the nearest example. Having trebled its population since 1960, it is—if the people can live through the process—on the way past 30 million by the turn of the century. Thirteen years away.

Limiting human fertility cannot do much for the existing problem. Those people are already born. It can, however, offer a long-term hope by slowing the growth of the labor force. And, for the unemployed, it can make the immediate problem a little less desperate if it offers a way to limit the number of children he or she must feed.

Third, the Destruction of Natural Resources

When the farmland cannot be subdivided any more, those who don't leave for the cities go into the woods or climb the mountain to hack out some new land to plant. In the tropical forest, the slash-and-burn farmer plants lands on a shorter cycle, cutting the time for the land to revive. The herdsman runs more animals on a landscape already too heavily grazed. These things are happening now. Deserts are expanding at the expense of pasture and cropland, and tropical forests are being cut down. There are arguments as to exactly how fast, but it is happening very fast.

The immediate consequence is obvious: in each generation, more people must be supported on a diminishing resource base. The secondary result is that rivers become more erratic, affecting irrigation on the remaining lands. Local climate becomes harsher and crops suffer without the buffering effects of the forests.

The worldwide impact is becoming better understood. It is a *Catch-22* situation. If the poor stay poor, they cut down the forests for fuel and to clear the land. In the process, they release carbon dioxide to the atmosphere, intensifying the "greenhouse effect." If the poor get rich, they use fossil fuels and release more carbon dioxide, and the industries and automobiles that support them contribute to acid precipitation.

The National Academy of Sciences (NAS) and the Smithsonian Institution recently sponsored a national forum on what was described as a global crisis: the possibility that perhaps one-half the world's species of animals and plants are threatened with destruction, mainly through deforestation. Science magazine, reporting the Conference, described the prospect as "A Mass Extinction without Asteroids." There are various programs to save tropical forests, to protect African wildlife, and so on. Most of the programs call for technical fixes, and most ignore the engine driving the problem: population growth. The central problem may not be the poacher but rather the farmer moving in and destroying the habitat. Man has been damaging Earth's ecology for centuries, but he simply did not have the numbers and the tools to do it on the present scale. Those interested in wildlife, or biological diversity, or the climate, or acid rain, should be making common cause to insist upon an attack on the common element in all their problems: population growth.

Tunnel vision is apparently an ingrained human weakness. All of us make our own plans without considering how we may be affected by others' plans. The UN Food and Agriculture Organization (FAO), for instance, conducted a study of the Earth's agricultural carrying capacity in which they assumed that all the land that could be farmed would be farmed, forgetting that some of that land is presently in forests. They did not project what would happen to timber and cellulose supplies, how the food would be cooked, or what would happen to rainfall and climate as the result of such an epochal shift.

We all seem to regard the Earth as though it consisted of so many yards of space, so many barrels of resources, to be manipulated at our will. In fact, it is an extraordinarily complex, interconnected set of systems that we as yet understand only imperfectly. As a race, we are undertaking to manage a machine that we do not understand.

At the NAS/Smithsonian conference, one ecologist estimated that humans, directly or indirectly, already consume about 40 percent of the world's "net terrestrial primary productivity," which is roughly the total solar energy trapped on land by photosynthesis. Such a calculation is necessarily rough, but if one thinks in terms of a further doubling of world population (as shown in World Bank and UN projections), we are entering an era when we expect to engineer substantially all the Earth's production for our own uses. History and current performance offer no assurance that we can do it without wrecking the system.

Let me cite just one example. Some attention has been paid to scientists' reports that acid precipitation is beginning to cause substantial damage to northern hemisphere temperate forests. No attention has been paid to a 1983 warning by the President's Acid Rain Peer Review Panel as to possible effects of soil acidification on soil microorganisms: " . . . it is just this bottom part of the biological cycle that is responsible for the recycling of nitrogen and carbon in the food chain. The proper function of the denitrifying microbes is a fundamental requirement upon which the entire biosphere depends. The evidence that increased acidity is perturbing populations of microorganisms is scanty, but the prospect of such an occurence is grave. It may take years . . . before measurable consequences would be observed. Such an effect is "long-term" or "irreversible . . . "

Here is a way in which human activities may be threatening the future of the Earth's biosphere. Including us. Will we have the political will to pay the costs, save the forests and perhaps head off the sterilization of that tiny layer of soil on which terrestrial life depends? Man's role on Earth has changed so swiftly—the modern industrial world with its population, energy output and chemicals is really just two or three generations old—that we have no experience.

One thing is certain: acid precipitation is intertwined with energy consumption. There are technical fixes, but at any level of per capita use and technology employed—the size of the problem is proportional to the number of people being served. Population growth multiplies the problem. The successful third world countries are industrializing and joining the industrial world in its high-energy consumption habits. In this situation, success could lead to destruction. Nobody, so far as I am aware, has dared to speculate on the size of the acid precipitation problem if world population were to double, and if the war on poverty were to be won.

That is just one example.

The issues come together here. Fertility control should help aid recipient nations to mobilize the capital for their own economic betterment. It will ease the crushing problem of unemployment, and it offers the prospect of a population stabilized at a level that can enjoy prosperity without endangering us all.

THE SIZE OF THE PROBLEM

The press periodically dismisses the "population bomb." In fact, it is live and ticking in the third world. The efforts to do something about it have been just successful enough to suggest that it can be influenced by deliberate human policy.

China apparently is having dramatic success in fertility limitation. Because it is one-quarter of the third world, its success tends to skew the apparent performance for the rest of the third world. With China not counted, annual population growth in the third world was about 2.4 percent in the 1960s. A doubling time of twenty-nine years. It is still 2.4 percent. Fertility has been corning down in many countries, particularly where population programs are in place, but death rates have been declining, too.

Where will it lead?

The standard projections show another doubling of the world' s population, stabilizing toward the close of the next century at around 10–12 billion.

Those projections are based upon current demographic trends, and on hope, rather than on any estimate of the Earth 's ability to support so many people. They assume low mortality—i.e. that conditions in the third world will continue to improve.

They assume that fertility everywhere in the third world will decline to around 2.0 (i.e. replacement level in a low-mortality economy) within a generation or two. This is a highly optimistic estimate when only Barbados, Cuba, Hong Kong and Singapore had achieved that level by 1986 (with China coming very close). Most women in Africa are still having six to eight children, and much of Central America, Western and Southern Asia are close behind.

If fertility does not come down in time, it does not necessarily mean that population will reach or surpass those projections. More likely, mortality will rise. The countries that do not get their fertility down will encounter problems so serious as to push them back toward the pre-modern trap of high birth rates and high death rates. In the process, they will have substantially damaged their agricultural and forest resources. They will have lost the golden opportunity that technology has provided: a civilization where there is enough to eat for all, where disease is controlled and people do not die unnecessarily.

Voluntary family planning has brought this ideal very close to reality for the industrial countries. It is frequently proposed that we should let the same thing happen for the third world.

There are two answers to that argument: first, population growth itself is robbing the most prolific countries of the chance to escape their poverty; second, there is not enough time. There have never been population growth rates comparable to the present ones. There has never been a generation that could buy an entire new health technology "off the shelf" and thereby bring death rates down as they have come down in the past generation. There have never been so many little girls surviving to adulthood and having babies of their own. This has generated an extraordinary population momentum, and every year lost in bringing fertility down brings closer the specter that the imbalance will be addressed by rising mortality—that the little girls will start dying again.

By way of example: theoretically, according to UN projections, if Africa should reach replacement fertility by 2030, the population would eventually stabilize at about 1.4 billion—more than twice the present population. If it takes another forty years to reach replacement level fertility, the ultimate theoretical population would be 3.4 billion—the size of the world's population in 1965. Two billion people for a forty year delay.

Civilizations have made technological breakthroughs before, and then have eaten up the increased production through population growth. The principal difference this time is the speed, and the scale. There are no new frontiers when one's homeland is impoverished, and the activities associated with this particular technological revolution—the energy production, the introduction of chemicals—are themselves generating perturbances to the Earth's system that are in turn complicated by population growth. We may not have the luxury of ignoring a population boom and bust in Africa or Latin America.

WHAT CAN BE DONE?

Given their importance, family planning and fertility programs are a low-cost investment. The World Bank, on the basis of rather dated information, estimates total annual governmental expenditures at about $2 billion, half of it by China. In no case cited did population programs absorb more than 0.5 percent of the country budget. Foreign assistance has provided about one-quarter of that $2 billion, and the United States provides about one-half of that assistance, though the proportion has been diminishing. The U.S. AID Population Program totalled $288 million in FY1985 and $239 million in FY1986.

Except for China and India, most funding comes from external aid, though the proportion of self-help has tended to rise as programs are put in place.

The World Bank notes that only about 1 percent of official aid now goes for population assistance. A 50 percent increase in all population programs would take care of today's unmet needs (i.e. all requests for birth control assistance that cannot presently be met because of lack of funds). To meet an ambitious target of 2.4 total fertility by 2000, total public spending (donor and recipient) on population programs would have to rise to $7.6 billion in constant dollars by 2000. That involves a rise of 7 percent per year. The assumptions needed for such calculations are heroic, but they represent a ballpark figure based upon the experience so far. They demonstrate that, in this specific but limited sector, a relatively modest increase in expenditure could have a remarkable impact upon the future.

Let me make a proposal:

- the United States should increase its population program by 50 percent over FYI985 in FY1988, to meet its share of the "unmet need" described by UNFPA and the World Bank. It should challenge other donors to do the same.
- propose to increase the program annually by 10 percent per annum until 2000, soliciting a comparable effort from donor and recipient countries, and calling upon the World Bank to take the lead in the population program that it has envisaged.
- be prepared to raise our contribution and urge others to do the same, if third world population programs can effectively use more than this.

This would bring our annual population aid up to $1.356 billion by 2000, which is 18 percent of the world total needed for the World Bank's "rapid fertility reduction" program. That proportion is only slightly larger than the present U.S. role in worldwide programs.

Because population aid is so small relative to our other aid programs, this could be achieved with only a very slight redirection of the total U.S. effort. If the aid budget is projected to remain constant and the population aid increase were distributed equally among other programs, it would require only a 7 percent reduction in those programs. Given the contribution that effective population control could make to many programs, this diversion is more bureaucratic than real. (If we dare to think of an aid budget increasing in step with real GNP growth, and if, that growth is 2 percent per annum, the increased population budget could be absorbed within the increase, and still leave most of the increase for other programs.)

We are presently putting 1.6 percent of our foreign aid budget into population programs. We are putting more than twice that into El Salvador and Honduras, more than twice that into the Philippines and Spain, more than twice that into Pakistan, and thirty times that much into the eastern Mediterranean.

Isn't it time to do a bit of thinking about our priorities?

Let me leave the reader with one cautionary note. As Americans, we enjoy providing moral instruction to the world, along with our aid. Perhaps we should relax a little and recognize that the recipient countries have to make their own decisions about the trade-offs between pressing demographic problems and the policies needed to deal with them. In the curve of human history, we have just arrived at the stage of recognizing that human success in affecting mortality imposes an obligation to regulate fertility .We are still learning how to do it with minimal interference with human freedom. We do not have time for leisurely experimentation. The most successful crash programs in the third world have involved the manipulation of group pressures and incentives and disincentives. We should not automatically turn against those programs simply because we have the luxury of not sharing their problem, here at home.

And finally, to those in the "right to life" movement who would scuttle U.S. population aid programs: you may be caught in a dangerous confusion. Making contraception less accessible is more likely to increase abortions than to decrease them.

Desperate people who have not practiced contraception will turn to abortion.

NOTES:

1. For a detailed discussion of world population trends and programs, and for the World Bank proposal to accelerate the programs, see the World Bank **World Development Report 1984**, Oxford University Press, New York, 1984.
2. The description of the current U.S. aid program is taken from Agency for International Development, **FY1988 Summary Tables**, Washington, January 1987.

The estimate as to mankind's monopolization of terrestrial productivity is derived from a study reported in BioScience, Vol. 36, No.6, June 1986: "Human Appropriation of the Products of Photosynthesis," by P.M. Vitousek, P.R. & A.H. Ehrlich and P .A. Matson.

NPG COMMENTS:

NPG, Inc., publishes from time to time in the **NPG Forum** articles of exceptional merit in the population/resources/environment field. Our own views on the subject of Mr. Grant's excellent paper are summarized as follows:

1. The projected increase in the population of third-world countries is mind boggling (828 million between 1990 and 2000 alone). Such an increase represents a grave threat to the already abysmally low living standards of most citizens of third-world countries, as well as to the global environment and resource base. It represents, also, a very real threat to the national security of the United States, and to our vital strategic interests around the world, since such

population growth cannot fail to bring in its wake economic chaos and political instability.

2. Faced with this unprecedented situation, the United States must realize that a "business as usual" approach is hopelessly inadequate. We must adopt extraordinary, although entirely reasonable, measures to help third-world countries prevent their populations from reaching projected levels.
3. The goal of our international population assistance programs should be, not replacement level fertility, but sub-replacement fertility by the year 2000, with a view toward halting, and eventually reversing, population growth just as soon as it is humanely possible to do so. Replacement level fertility is an inadequate goal, since, once this level is reached, the populations of most developing nations would still double in size because of the momentum of their past growth.
4. Our population assistance programs should be increased now to more than ten times current levels, to at least 3 billion a year. This amount would still be only 25 percent of our total foreign aid program.
5. In addition, the basic thrust of our program should be changed from an emphasis on family planning to family limitation. We should encourage recipient nations to make the small family goal (not more than one child per couple, but not more than two at most) the central focus of their national population policies. We should further encourage them to promote non-coercive social and economic incentives in pursuit of that goal.
6. With loans to third-world countries of about 16 billion a year, The World Bank is in a position to have a tremendous influence on the population policies of those countries. The United States should do all in its power to change The World Bank policy so that no loans would be made to countries that do not have effective population policies with the goal of sub-replacement fertility within the next decade or so.

FAMILY RESPONSIBILITY

Anthony Wayne Smith

August 1987

The dedication of the family-planning and socio-economic development movements as humanitarian efforts during the past forty years has been highly commendable. But viewed as instruments of population stabilization, these efforts have thus far failed.

Recurrent famine, abject poverty, soil and forest destruction, plant and animal extinction, mineral depletion, air and water pollution, hideous urbanization, financial collapse, civil unrest, a world in chaos, all testify to that sad failure.

A new dimension must be added, and swiftly, to the population stabilization effort: small-family motivation. By small is meant sub-replacement; statistically, a total fertility rate less than replacement; ethically and practically, a maximum, not average, of two children per couple; in some countries one child as a target.

By motivation is meant an appeal to responsibility, and the use of socioeconomic incentives and disincentives. Incentives can be direct, like housing, equipment, educational or tax advantages, or cash payments, or indirect, like getting jobs for women outside the home, though indirect incentives will have to be supplemented by direct benefits.

Motivation can also mean rewards to communities achieving low birth targets, such as water wells or photovoltaic electric systems; reliance can be placed in such cases in part on the social pressures arising in closely-knit communities. Social pressures, better spoken of as counter-pressures against traditional big-family customs, will indeed always be essential to effective motivation. But individual incentives, administered in the case of community action by the community, will also be necessary.

Disincentives means withdrawal of advantages in housing, jobs, and so forth, from the parents of large families. This places the children in large families at a disadvantage, but nothing so great as the deprivations entailed by life in the crowded barrios and the miserable poverty of overpopulated countries.

We must free ourselves of the notion that rewards, particularly cash payments for acceptance, continuity, and voluntary sterilization, are coercive. At present, we permit payments to procurers of such sterilizations but not to acceptors. If there is coercion it is among the promoters, not the acceptors.

The problem is to get family size down to replacement or sub-replacement. Not all the access/supply efforts in the world will do that unless desired-family-size comes down rapidly. That is where the efforts of the population stabilization movement should be focused.

The Bucharest and Mexico City Declarations both contain the caveat that freedom of choice as to the number and spacing of children is limited by responsibility. Responsibility means concern for the children, parents, community, and society, or it means nothing very much. There can be no question at this late date that it means not-more-than-two, and in many cases not-more-than-one, if disaster is to be forestalled.

In terms of national plans, the targets should be universal access/supply, and replacement fertility or less, by the year 2000; population stabilization at the earliest date thereafter permitted by population momentum; and reduction thereafter by attrition to carrying capacity, which will be far below the peak populations resulting from runaway reproduction some time in the late twenty-first century. But targets will not be enough; they must be implemented by motivational systems and monitored at short intervals by thorough-going public review.

What does all this mean for action by the American population, humanitarian, and environmental movements? It means, first of all, continued vigorous support for family planning, but coupled with motivational programs. Family planning without more will not be enough.

A policy revision of that magnitude will require a sea change in conventional thinking within the birth control movement, one long overdue. It will entail a revised vocabulary; we should be talking about family responsibility and family limitation, not family planning without more.

It means that family responsibility and limitation, not merely family planning must be the theme of funding by national and international financial institutions such as USAID, UNFPA, the World Bank, and philanthropic foundations. Groups and coalitions of nonprofit organizations should re-orient their efforts toward that end.

National and international lending and granting institutions, public and private, should incorporate both environmental and demographic conditionality into their loans to industry and governments: That is, financial assistance should be conditioned on the adoption of resource management and population stabilization programs and their effective implementation. The population programs should be based on family responsibility, not merely planning. Nonprofit groups should press the point.

The famine-relief, food supply, child-care, maternal welfare, immunization, and other health movements should look at the undesirable side-effects of their devoted efforts. Valiant contributions to rescue famine victims are mocked by death from malnutrition thereafter. Lowering infant mortality means but misery if malnutrition results in impaired mental and physical health. Immunization campaigns compound the dangers of overpopulation if they are not led by population stabilization and reduction campaigns. All these movements have magnificent fund-raising skills and extensive field organizations around the globe. They should incorporate family responsibility programs into their work; nonprofit groups and coalitions should urge them to do so.

Basing population stabilization on family responsibility places it on a high moral and strategic ground from which it can readily defend itself against attack by the anti-abortionists. Big families are cruelly inhumane to the children themselves and society as a whole. Parents, whatever the seeming advantages in child labor and old-age security may be, harm themselves by destroying the social and natural world in which they live. People everywhere can and must understand this.

The organizations concerned with famine, food, medicine, health, and education should be joining forces with independent leaders to mobilize a worldwide moral campaign for small families. This has nothing to do with particular methods of family limitation. The only requirement is that limitation be effective. Couples would be free to make their own choices as to method, as between contraception, abstinence, abortion, or other means of limitation, once they have been offered the necessary knowledge, services, and supplies, the essential moral support in the community, and the appropriate incentives and disincentives. Nonprofit groups and coalitions should initiate and encourage such a campaign.

A far better working collaboration is needed between the ecological wing of the conservation movement and the environmental and population wings. Species extinction proceeds apace; it is the one irrevocable result of the population explosion. Survivalists fight desperate battles to rescue threatened or endangered species; they plead for ecological reserves in the tropical forests, in the oceans. They seldom suggest that anything should be done about the human proliferation which is crowding the other animals and plants from the earth. And demographers talk of economic productivity, population growth rates, migrations, usually without suggesting that an ecological problem exists. But the plant and animal life of this planet is worth saving for its own sake, not merely for its economic, scientific, or even pharmaceutical value. We ought to be saying so and fighting for its salvation.

In our home land, America, a revitalized population movement will seek first of all to abolish illegal immigration. One long stride has at last been taken with the new legislation imposing penalties on employers who hire illegal immigrants, a major source of present population growth, and establishing procedures for proving legal residence. As to legal immigration, a ceiling should be established for all immigration, including families and refugees, no higher than recorded emigration. This has been called Zero Net Migration. Immigration should no longer contribute to our population growth. And we should enact a formal national policy of population stabilization and reduction as a result of continued low birth rates to carrying capacity. We can then enjoy the advantages of a constantly growing per capita GNP if that is what we want.

But what of the present political impasse? It will not last forever. The pressures driving nations toward population stabilization and reduction are ponderous and ultimately irresistible. It will take time to get our own house in order: to reorientate birth-control efforts toward family responsibility and limitation, to initiate a small family moral campaign, to fight off the attack on voluntary parenthood by the anti-abortionists and to organize the legislative and political machinery which an ultimately successful population stabilization effort will require.

The law and regulations which forbid assistance to effective stabilization programs such as cash incentives to acceptors of voluntary sterilization should be rewritten with a view to changing them when the time is once more opportune. Determined efforts should be launched now to incorporate resources and population conditionality into our overseas assistance programs. Public education through the nonprofit institutions must be vastly expanded and re-directed to population reduction goals, not merely voluntary parenthood, industrial development, or ecological survival. Efforts to prepare for a turning of the tide will themselves help to turn the tide.

Proliferation is a far graver threat to civilization than the nuclear weapons, the dangers of which are visible and at long last understood. Proliferation unchanged will bring economic, social, environmental, ecological and political collapse on a planetary scale. Proliferation reversed can usher in a great civilization such as before was only the stuff of dreams.

A GLOBAL SMALL FAMILY CAMPAIGN

The following letter to the editor by Anthony Wayne Smith appeared in the August 20, 1986 issue of the National Catholic Reporter.

The *Reporter* is to be commended warmly for publishing Steve Askin's articles on the population problem in Kenya and Father Arthur McCormack's concurring note. The tragic situation in Kenya is largely typical of much of the Third World. The article did well to highlight the differences among religious leaders in Kenya on birth control methods.

The UN Conferences on Population in Bucharest (1974) and Mexico City (1984), asserted the right of every couple to decide freely and responsibly on the number and spacing of children. Far too little emphasis has been placed in practice on responsibility which these conferences stressed.

We are dealing here with the responsibility of parents to their children already born, to themselves, and to their community, country, and society in general. Responsible conduct as to family size is moral; irresponsible conduct is immoral; this is surely within the domain of the churches.

The overcrowding of our planet has reached the place where population must be reduced by lowering birth rates to the carrying capacity of the earth as rapidly as possible in high rate countries, mainly in the Third World. This can be done only by reducing family size to lower levels (or increasing the death rate!). That means smaller families to each couple. In other words, in the situation of the world today, such reduction is responsible and moral; larger families are irresponsible and actually immoral though people may not realize this.

Family planning, meaning the provision of contraceptive information and supplies, by themselves, and socio-economic development, which is often frustrated by population growth, cannot do the reduction job. Motivation toward smaller families must also be provided. Socio-economic rewards and penalties, incentives and disincentives, have been found to be necessary and effective. But moral education and persuasion could be an ecumenical crusade for the small family and responsible parenthood to rescue the hundreds of millions of people throughout the world who will otherwise die of malnutrition or starvation during the next few decades.

But if people are to be persuaded toward small families, they must also be taught how to limit family size. They must have access to information as to the effectiveness of the full range of birth control methods. They should be encouraged to use contraception, not discouraged from it. In this situation, it is profoundly disturbing to find Catholic authorities in Kenya denouncing contraception as immoral.

Grant, if you wish, that periodic abstinence, referred to as natural family planning, may be one method of birth control, as are total abstinence and celibacy. But experience and common sense tell us that it will not be effective. Pope John Paul II conceded as much (in Acapulco 1982) when he said that natural family planning methods were not possible for vast sectors of the developing countries and pastoral compassion should be shown if they used other methods; that is, the practice of contraception by them should not be condemned for them. But compassion for the misery of hundreds of millions calls for advocacy not merely acceptance.

Grant, again, that the Catholic clergy may not be in a position to advocate contraception; they should step aside on that issue, avoiding denunciation, and join in the advocacy of smaller families. President

Moi of Kenya has set a target of an average of four children for the year 2000. This will be impossible, the present average being eight, without an ardent moral campaign for smaller families, nor indeed without socio-economic incentives and disincentives and effective birth control methods. He needs help, not hindrance, from all concerned with the welfare of the people of Kenya. Let me comment that I am not a Catholic; my background is Protestant; but I am strongly sympathetic toward the humanitarian efforts of all the churches. The churches should take the lead in a global small-family crusade. They should enlist the support of humanitarian organizations engaged in famine and food relief, maternal and child care, and health and immunization, whose work is constantly defeated, whether they recognize it or not, by population growth; of the family-planning, population, environmental, and ecological organizations, all of which have been negative toward motivational systems, and indifferent in many cases to the population issue itself; and of the powerful lending and granting institutions, public and private, which are struggling to manage an international debt crisis which cannot be managed without resolute attention to the underlying population issue. No clergyman has a right to stand in the way of such an effort; nor does any church doctrine authorize or require him to do so.

Reprinted by permission of the National Catholic Reporter

"A SLOWLY FALLING POPULATION IS GOOD"

The following letter by Anthony Wayne Smith appeared in the May 10, 1986 issue of the Washington Post.

Allen Carlson had the story backward in his article on depopulation (*Outlook,* April 13). He seemed to be recommending a breeding competition between the developed and the less developed countries. The developed countries would certainly lose that race.

But why try? A slowly falling population is good, not bad. There are fewer bodies to feed, clothe, shelter and care for. Per-capita gross national product can rise, not fall. In modern times, high productivity results from inventiveness, organization and the application of external energy, not manpower, and is limited only by the declining availability of resources and energy. Population contraction can and should produce affluence, spaciousness and leisure.

With stabilization or decline, no longer need we seek the eternal expansion of the supercities; the factories, office buildings, roads we have will be enough. No longer need our soils and forests be forced beyond their capacity; countryside, wilderness, wildlife can be restored. The available jobs managing the machines and maintaining the equipment can be divided up. The work day and work week can be cut and incomes increased at the same time.

There can be leisure for the arts and sciences. There can be time for the handicrafts, taking over much work from the mass-production system. There will be time for learning for its own sake, for aesthetic and erotic pursuits, for friendships and for the enjoyment of the natural world.

The limiting factor will be resources and energy, ultimately solar energy. The solar-energy/population balance will be the key.

Food, clothing, shelter, medical care, education, travel -all these will become available for the average person working short weeks and days, once the rat race of eternal growth has been called off. The advanced countries are calling it off now when they cut down on family size; they are not going to work all that much harder for another child. We might well have been horrified by Carlson's suggestion that we must maintain our populations so that we can produce weapons. We produce weapons, if we must, by automation computerization and assembly lines, not manpower. And are we to live to produce weapons?

The advanced countries are vulnerable to imported help. The oceanic pressures of population keep on pushing immigrants upon them, legal and illegal. It is tempting to hire them for what are considered the menial jobs. But farm labor and domestic service are honorable and pleasurable tasks, requiring skill and training, and if well-enough paid will be sought for by the native-born. The prosperous countries are checking immigration. What then of the less developed countries! They have been slow to recognize their predicament and their opportunities. Drastic measures to cut their birthrates are their only hope. The advanced countries have a huge stake in helping them to do it.

EUROPE IN THE ENERGY TRANSITION: THE CASE FOR A SMALLER POPULATION

Lindsey Grant

July 1988

When one has gotten used to anything, the prospect of change can be upsetting. West Europe's population has been growing, probably, since the end of the Black Plague, and some writers are disturbed at the prospect that the trend may be reversing.

The concern may be misplaced.

THE DEMOGRAPHIC FACTS AND PROJECTIONS

Europe is crowded. The sub-region of Western Europe (see Note at close for definitions) has a population of about 155 million—nearly two-thirds that of the United States—in an area about one tenth as large. Despite the surge of third world populations, it is the most densely populated sub-region of the world except Japan. In the Northern Europe sub-region, the United Kingdom is even more densely populated. The population of the two subregions grew by almost one-quarter following World War II and has stabilized since 1980 at just under 240 million.

Perhaps the best indicator of coming demographic trends is the total fertility rate (TFR), a measure of how many children a group of women may be expected to bear. In modern societies, "replacement level TFR" is just above 2.0—i.e. two children per woman, plus a small allowance for mortality and for the tendency to bear more boys than girls. At that level, a population will eventually stabilize; below it, the population will eventually decline, unless immigration makes up the difference.

In the so-called developed world, Poland, Romania and the USSR are slightly above replacement level. All the non-communist developed countries (except Ireland) are now below it. Japan and the United States have TFRs of 1.8, Canada 1.7. (By contrast, the third world—excluding China—has a TFR of 4.8 and a current population doubling time of thirty-three years.)

The lowest rates of all are in non-communist Europe. West Germany is at 1.3; Denmark, Italy and Luxembourg at 1.4; Austria, Belgium, the Netherlands and Switzerland at 1.5. It is these figures that lead to the concern about depopulation.

Why do I believe that the concern may be misplaced?

First, there is a matter of perspective: these processes take a long time. For the next generation, European populations are on a plateau, not in rapid decline. The United Nations" 1984 projections illustrate this point and also remind us of the uncertainty of predicting future TFRs. There are three projections. If fertility should stay roughly at its present levels, West Europe's population in 2025 will have declined by only one percent. Even the low variant, with fertility well below current levels for most of the period, yields a projection of 90 percent of the present population—a little higher than the population in 1960, when West Europe was hardly underpopulated. The "high variant" assumes a return to 1960s fertility and yields a population increase of 9 percent. Europe has time to think about its demographic future.

Second, and more important: Europe may be wise to aim for lower population densities. Europe exported a sizeable fraction of its population growth during its demographic transition and is probably better off for having done so. Now a rollback of population growth may benefit them.

Some day, the societies of West Europe must decide how to bring fertility back to replacement levels if they are not to die out or be supplanted by immigrants—and European governments are not very receptive to immigration. Before that, however, they would do well to decide what population densities would best serve their interests as they look into the next century.

Along with the rest of us, Europe faces an imminent energy transition away from petroleum-based economies. At the same time, it faces an environmental transition. Its own economic success has brought it face to face with resource and environmental constraints that will limit its future options. These issues are interconnected, and it will take foresight to deal with them both. My contention is that they can be better addressed with a smaller population.

THE ENERGY TRANSITION

World petroleum production will probably peak and begin to decline some time in the next generation—the exact timing probably more dependent upon demand, prices and technology than upon the discovery of new fields. For Europe, the International Energy Agency (IEA) thinks the transition has already come.

In varying degree since the industrial revolution, West European countries have been paying for net imports of food, natural fibers and energy through their possession of colonial empires, foreign investments and technological superiority. Their overall energy dependence intensified as petroleum supplanted coal. By 1973, non-Communist Europe was only 38 percent self sufficient in primary energy. Discovery of the North Sea fields gave Europe (and particularly the United Kingdom) a temporary boost, and non-Communist Europe reached 64 percent of self-Sufficiency in 1985. That boost is winding down, however, and the IEA anticipates a 28 percent decline in European petroleum production during the 1990s. The United Kingdom expects to become a net importee again sometime in the mid-90s. That may not be a happy time to be entering the market. The monopoly position of OPEC as the residual supplier will become increasingly strong, particularly if U.S. imports continue to rise.

THE ENVIRONMENTAL TRANSITION

West Europe is struggling—like the United States but in a much tighter space—with urbanization and its byproducts, with multiple byproducts of industrialization such as toxic substances, and with the pollution generated by fossil fuels and nuclear energy.

The energy-related problems are perhaps the most pressing ones: world climate change; and acid precipitation. World sea levels are rising, posing particular threats to eastern England and the low countries. The effects of climate change upon European agriculture are still unpredictable. Acid precipitation, still little understood, is damaging the continent's forest and may affect its agriculture.

Europe must change its practices to preserve its environment if it is to preserve its livability.

It starts these energy and environmental transitions with some penalties. The colonies are gone, and technology has fled to multi-national corporations seeking resiliency, but at the cost of an extremely intensive development of a small and crowded region.

In agriculture, Europe has hedged its bets—at considerable economic cost—to avoid relying on imports. The deliberate pursuit of self-sufficiency has almost succeeded. The European Community has reached self-sufficiency in major foodstuffs. Non-Communist Europe as a whole runs a $20 billion annual deficit on its overall agricultural account, but this is a modest figure in $3 trillion economics, and the import gap has been declining.

This has been achieved by subsidizing very high-yield, high-cost agriculture. In the European Community, direct subsidies constitute about 45 percent of the value of agricultural production. On top of that, consumers pay a premium of about 76 percent over world prices for agricultural products. Moreover, the system has a built-in conflict. In the European Community (EC), only Denmark, France and the Netherlands are net agricultural exporters, and they are subsidized by Germany and the UK, the principal importers.

The high yields come at the cost of very high inputs. In most of West Europe, cereal yields exceed five tons per hectare (well above the United States), but fertilizer inputs per hectare are more than double those in the U.S. France alone uses almost as many tons of insecticides and fungicides as the U.S., on one-tenth as much cropland. Italy uses more. From the scattered data available (e.g. river-borne nitrates and phosphates) Europe's agricultural pollution problems are correspondingly serious.

Consider the intensity of energy use. West Germans use 15 percent as much energy as Americans, in less than 3 percent of the U.S. land area. They drive 13 percent as many vehicle miles in that same crowded area. Individually, they don't use as much energy or drive as much, but the atmosphere has no way of knowing that.

As a result of such disparities, the zone of extremely acid precipitation (below pH 4.7) covers substantially all of West Europe, but less than one-fifth of the United States. No wonder the Germans find half their forests damaged.

One could go on with such examples. The U.S. lost about 18 percent of its wetlands between 1950–1980. West Germany and the Netherlands each lost more than 50 percent. There may be policy differences, but the driving engine is the pressure to use the land.

The point is that the energy transition will be a much more complex process than simply finding substitutes for oil. The Europeans must find environmentally benign ways of running their energy economies. They must arrest the environmental attrition generated by industry and agriculture—and all this at costs they can afford.

THE ALTERNATIVES TO OIL

West Europe faces a tougher transition than does the U.S. Its fossil fuel resources are very limited, even if it can find ways to mitigate the environmental costs of using them.

West Germany and the United Kingdom, the traditional coal suppliers, have remaining resources totaling perhaps 20 to 40 percent of U.S. resources, and they are substantially less accessible. (Fuel resource estimates are notoriously tricky.) The new Cool Water integrated coal gasification combined cycle (IGCC) technology may make it possible to exploit these reserves and still ameliorate acid precipitation, though it offers less comfort concerning carbon dioxide.

Most of the dwindling natural gas reserves are in Norway and the United Kingdom.

Biomass is the first and natural alternative to fossil fuels. Before the advent of coal, biomass was already the principal non-animal energy source. Ideally, if it is harvested on a sustained yield basis, it can be neutral with respect to carbon dioxide, since it recycles the carbon dioxide between plants and the atmosphere rather than releasing it from fossil fuels. Unfortunately, here again the Europeans are the victims of their own intense use of the environment. Where does one find the land to grow the biomass? Some 78 percent of West Germany is already in cropland, pasture land and forest, and 84 percent of France. Every hectare given to biomass production will involve trade-offs against food or forestry production—and the forests are already in trouble. The European climate will not grow crops like bagasse and corn that yield high tonnages of potential fuel. There is only limited opportunity here.

Nuclear Energy once seemed the answer, but one need hardly belabor the concerns that it has generated. France, West Germany, the United Kingdom and Sweden are the only major West European countries to go heavily into nuclear power. In Sweden, even before Chernobyl, the voters had voted to phase out of nuclear energy by 2010. The programs in Germany and the UK are in trouble, and only in France is there a major continuing commitment to the nuclear route. Already, 80 percent of its electric power production is nuclear.

As a result, France already has over one-half as many cubic meters of spent fuel and radioactive wastes to be stored or reprocessed as does the Unite States—in a country with one-quarter our population and only 6 percent of our land area.

Nuclear energy itself is only a transitional fuel, unless one goes to a breeder reactor, which is proving very expensive and which poses dangers of operating safety and plutonium diversion to weapons. Nobody can yet say whether fusion-based energy is possible—it is not easy to harness a 50 million C. explosion—and we cannot yet assess the radioactivity problems or environmental implications of using such a vast new source of energy.

Hydropower. Europe already uses 59 percent of the theoretical potential—more than any other continent—but hydropower meets only 7 percent of non-communist Europe's energy needs. The potential is marginal, and the social and economic cost of developing new sites is high.

Europe is the least favorably situated inhabited continent for direct solar energy. Almost all of Europe north of the Alps averages more than fifty percent cloud cover, and much of it is 70 percent cloudy or more, and the northerly location means the days are very short when the energy is most needed.

Wind. Think of windmills and one thinks of holland. The potential is there a (a NASA study once concluded that it is technically feasible to meet the United States' energy needs with wind power.) Since the potential energy varies with the cube of the wind speed, the cost rises exponentially where average wind speeds are low. There are some opportunities as rising fuel costs justify the investment, but West Europe with its relatively placid climate is not particularly well situated.

THE DEMOGRAPHIC CONNECTION

Daunting as this brief survey is, Europeans are educated and resilient. They will experiment and come up with some presently unpredictable mix of sources—perhaps including other exotics such as wave power and ocean thermal gradients. There will be an incentive to develop more efficient engines such as the fuel cell, and to intensify energy conservation. Back to bicycles?

However, demography is fundamental to the size of the problem. At any given levels of per capita consumption, technology and conservation, the scale of the problem is proportional to the size of the population to be served. A reduction of—let us say—20 percent in population would mitigate the pressure for high agricultural yields, in turn reducing the polluting problems, the high cost of food—savings that could be invested in the energy transition—and the political tensions within the European Community. Agriculture itself would require less energy, and land would be freed for possible biomass production for energy.

A population reduction would generate comparable benefits from reduced requirements for new energy sources, or from reduced costs in managing urban wastes and toxic substances. And so on. The benefits are not necessarily linear because the connections are complex. Europe might, for instance, choose to maintain food output to generate exports to pay for energy imports. However, the direction in which population reduction would act upon the management of the energy transition is unmistakable, and it is favorable.

The classic rebuttal is that "labor creates wealth—the more people the more wealth." Not so. A mental model for a less crowded world may not fit a crowded one. In the current technological revolution, a better model would be "capital creates wealth, with a bit of intelligent direction." It is worth noting that the Leontief-Carter UN world model tied production size in the industrial societies to investment rather than to work force. In the real world, Europe's present problem is unemployment, not labor shortages.

THE CANNON FODDER ARGUMENT

The most popular argument for a large population is that it is needed for military security. This "musket mentality" finds resonances in European countries that have been fighting each other and their neighbors for millennia.

The first answer to that argument is that it ain't necessarily so. It is momentarily beguiling but unsupported by systematic historical research. A quick mental scan of the histories of Europe, the Americans and Asia suggests that at least half of all wars have been won by the smaller adversary.

The second answer is to define the potential adversaries. Wars have been getting more costly and destructive. If one assumes a continuation of Europe's historical fratricidal behavior, it is probably foolish to waste much time speculating how they will accomplish their mutual self-destruction. The European Community is, however, the testament to a driving desire to break the historical cycle, and it seems to be succeeding.

The USSR is more often perceived as the threat, and again the question is "how do you define the adversaries?" At present, the total forces of NATO countries are 34 percent larger than those of the Warsaw Pact, but for both sides, questions of cohesiveness and will are more important than crude numbers.

At the other extreme, a single European country such as West Germany is already completely outnumbered by the USSR, and a change of 20 or 30 percent either way would not substantially alter the equation.

If the Apocalypse should come, the present assumption is that it would be nuclear exchange and that manpower would be of limited relevance. Even assuming that the Soviets would entertain the risk of a mutual and perhaps worldwide holocaust—and even assuming that they would wish to take on the management of West Europe—the enticement to attempt limited moves against West Europe depends upon the opportunities, and a stable Europe adjusting successfully to the energy and environmental transitions is less likely to offer opportunities than a Europe riven by economic and resource problems—and I have already argued that a smaller population makes a successful transition more likely. Competitive fertility justified on military grounds may be self-defeating.

The containment of the threat of war depends upon the unity and determination of the two alliances, and the problems are not all ours. With memories of the disaffection of their own Ukraine in World War II, the Soviets can hardly be confident of the support of the East European allies in some future engagement.

The "cannon fodder" argument rests in part upon the awareness that the population of the USSR is still growing. However, most of that growth is occurring among the Soviets' restive Asian minorities. Wars, as the Soviets know, regularly lead to results far different from the expectations of those who start them. The Soviets would be well advised not to put the loyalties of those minorities to an extreme test.

Moreover, in an increasingly interdependent world, autarky may be very unattractive to both sides. The USSR is now a major importer of Western grains, which it pays for in some part with energy exports, including natural gas to West Europe.

In short, Soviets' relations with Europe are now shaped by forces far different from the simplistic confrontation out of which NATO and the Warsaw Pact emerged, and strategic thinking must adjust to the change.

THE PROBLEM OF TRANSITION

There are problems of adjustment as population stabilizes, and they are more severe if there is a roll-back, particularly if it happens quickly. How does one run a prosperous "steady state economy" without the stimulus of population growth? How do you maintain innovation and creativity?

How does one manage a changing age structure? It is regularly pointed out that there will be more old people to support. It is less frequently mentioned that there will be fewer young to raise and educate, and better job opportunities for them when they enter the work force.

These issues have to be faced. Population growth cannot continue indefinitely in a finite world. You cannot avoid the energy transition or the environmental issues by ignoring them. The problems will face us all. West Europe (and Japan) have simply gotten there first.

CONCLUSION

If a sustainable society is judged by its success in living comfortably within its resources—in preserving the environmental and resource base that supports it—then Europe like the rest of the world has not yet achieved it. Fossil energy has made possible a period of very high productivity while its byproducts have been sowing the seeds of destruction of the economies it has supported. The energy transition may be a blessing if it lessens that threat and forces us all toward sustainable energy policies.

It is ironic that when West Europe has just succeeded in stabilizing population growth, controlling a potentially dangerous dependency on imported food, adjusting to the transition from the colonial era, and positioning itself to deal with the energy transition there are those who are fearful of that very success.

There is no magic about "population stability," nor is it even attainable the real world. When growth ends, there will be fluctuations, not a constant.

Europe, apparently, has entered that period, and the present demographic patterns help to meet the problems that they face. Bravo. We should be studying their experience and their solutions.

NOTES:

1. *I follow the UN usage: Western Europe includes Austria, Belgium, France West Germany, Luxembourg, the Netherlands and Switzerland. Northern Europe consists of Denmark, Finland, Iceland, Ireland, Norway, Sweden, and the United Kingdom. For convenience, I describe these two sub-regions as "West Europe." Some of the generalizations are made for all of non-Communist Europe, since OECD and some other sources present their data on the basis.*
2. The data for this article were taken from the *UN Statistical Yearbook 1986*; *World Population Prospects: Estimates and Projections as Assessed in 1984*, Population Studies No. 98 (New York: UN Dept. of International Economic and Social Affairs, 1986); 1986 and 1987 *World Population Data Sheets* (Washington: Population Reference Bureau); UN Food and Agriculture Organization 1985 *Production* and *Trade Yearbooks* and *1984 Fertilizer Yearbook*, and *1951 FAO Yearbook: Production*; *Statistical Abstract of the U.S.; Energy Policies and Programs of IEA Countries* (Paris: Organization for Economic Cooperation and Development (OECD), 1987; *OECD Environmental Data Compendium 1987; Coal Information 1987* (Paris: OECD , 1987); Luther J. Carter, *Nuclear Imperatives and Public Trust* (Washington: Resources for the Future, 1987); International Institute for Environmental and Development and World Resources Institute. *World Resources 1987* (New York: Basic books, 1987); *The Global 2000 Report to the President, Vol. Two*; WAES, *Energy: Global Prospects 1985–2000* (New York: McGraw-Hill, 1977); Paul R. Ehrlich et. al, *Ecosceince* (San Francisco: W.H. Freeman, 1977); *New York Times*, p. E3 September 27, 1987; J Goldemberg et al, *Energy for a Sustainable World* (Washington: World Resources Institute, 1987.)

TOO MANY OLD PEOPLE OR TOO MANY AMERICANS? THOUGHTS ABOUT THE PENSION PANIC

Lindsey Grant

July 1988

The country has been treated to recurrent speculation that, because the population is aging, we must encourage higher fertility or more immigration to provide workers to support the old people on Social Security.

Let me offer some reasons for thinking that the fears may be unfounded.

THE DEPENDENCY RATIO

The aged are not the only dependents. Children make demands upon society that may be higher than those made by the old. To make a somewhat imprecise comparison: total school expenditures (excluding kindergartens, nurseries and creches) in 1986 were estimated at $261.5 billion-spent, of course, overwhelmingly on the young. This is 66 percent more than total Social Security payments to the aged in that year, and it is almost identical with the estimate of total federal benefits to the aged that year, including their share of Social Security, Medicare, Medicaid, all federal military and civilian retirement programs, food stamps and subsidized housing. Beyond these statistics, there is another point to be made for the old: by and large, they are living on their savings, while the support of the young is a direct charge on parents and on society.

There are about twice as many young people (depending upon how you define them) as old ones, and the cost of rearing them is a major element of the economy. An Urban Institute study suggests that, in 1981 dollars and depending upon the education provided and whether the mother was working, it cost roughly $75,000 to $125,000 to raise a child. With 72 million children that year, this translated very roughly into something like 10–16 percent of GNP. A maturing population will mitigate these costs, as it increases the expenditures by and for the old.

As a first step, we should compare the total working age population with the total population of the young and the old—a comparison somewhat loosely called the "dependency ratio." The proportion of the population in the working ages has been rising and, barring another "baby boom," it will continue to rise for another generation. The working age population, defined rather arbitrarily as fifteen to sixty-four years old (a convention popular with demographers) has constituted the following percentage of the total population in recent decades:

1940—65 percent
1950—65 percent
1960—61 percent
1970—62 percent
1980—66 percent
1985—66 percent

If fertility stays about as it is now, that proportion is expected to rise to 69 percent by 2010 and then begin to decline to 63 percent in 2025.

The point is that the dependency ratio has moved down and up, without any clear correlation with economic well-being. If it is important to you, take comfort in the fact that the nation faces a long period with an improving ratio. In a stable population, by the way—with low mortality and after the demographic wobbles had been sorted out-about 61 percent of the population would be fifteen to sixty-four.

THE TROUBLE WITH THAT RATIO

Such an analysis offers a rather simple version of the world, in which those of working age are supporting those who are not. A look at this graph should dispel that simplicity.

The people in that central grey area are working. Those in the black stubs are unemployed-and unemployment compensation totals about $20 billion each year. At those lighter ends of the bars are other dependents: students, the discouraged workers no longer looking for work, the idle rich, housewives, retirees and family members and widow(er)s of those on retirement programs. Some of them are on AFDC (aid to families with dependent children), which costs the nation $14.5 billion per year. There are disabled workers on Social Security receiving, in total, $18 billion per year.

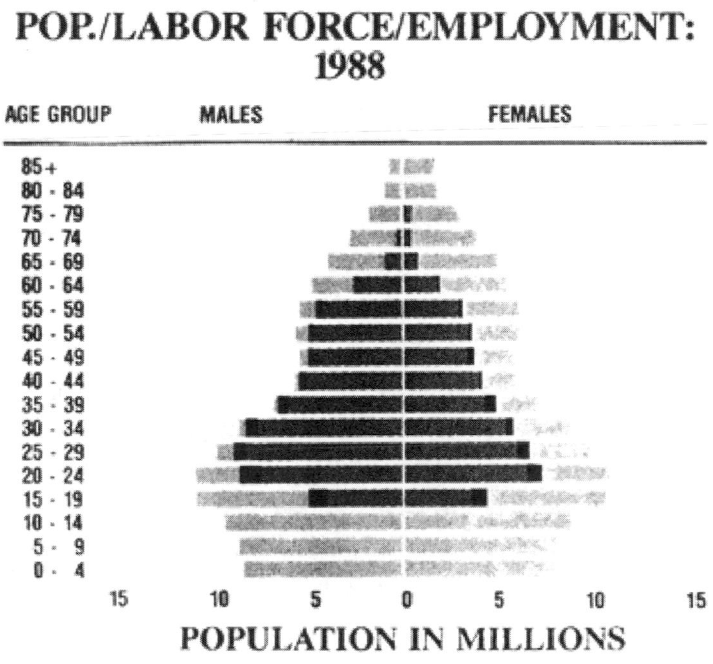

The real proportion of working to non-working is much lower than the "dependency ratio" would suggest. At present, about 45 percent of the total population works. This is the true measure of dependency. Every worker supports about 1.2 non-workers.

If indeed we need more workers, there are ways of improving the ratio. Bring unemployment down. Find ways of bringing labor and jobs together. Improve job safety. Find ways of enlisting the discouraged workers. Encourage more women to seek jobs. Employ the elderly through programs such as shared jobs.

HOW MUCH LABOR DO WE NEED?

Those who worry about dependency ratios may be worrying about precisely the wrong problem. Now and for the foreseeable future, the problem seems to be, not a shortage of labor, but rather a redundancy of labor of the wrong types, in the wrong places.

Along with the rest of the industrial world, the country is in the midst of a technological revolution. Computerization, automation, genetics, the systematic organization of production—all of these are multiplying the productivity of labor—assuming only that there is capital to mobilize the technology.

There are immense gains from this process. There are also two very apparent

POP./LABOR FORCE/EMPLOYMENT: 1988

AGE GROUP | MALES | FEMALES

85+, 80 - 84, 75 - 79, 70 - 74, 65 - 69, 60 - 64, 55 - 59, 50 - 54, 45 - 49, 40 - 44, 35 - 39, 30 - 34, 25 - 29, 20 - 24, 15 - 19, 10 - 14, 5 - 9, 0 - 4

15 10 5 0 5 10 15

POPULATION IN MILLIONS

Figure 1

penalties. One of them is unemployment, which has been inching up from 4.5 percent of the labor force in the 1950s to 8 percent so far in the 1980s.

The other result is the reappearance of the sweatshop the disenfranchised accepting third world employment conditions to compete with the better-capitalized firms. One sees an image, like multiple mirrors, of millions of John Henrys struggling to win their races against the steam hammer.

The nation that gave the "American Dream" to the world should look to its own tradition. If more labor is cheap labor, it may be leading to a two tier system of wealth and poverty that is closer to traditional societies than to any dream of the future.

If we recognize the implications of technological change, the country should be asking how much labor it needs, and of what kinds, to mobilize capital and take advantage of the new opportunities. In that society, the multiplication of entry-level labor, with the concomitant social and welfare costs, is probably an object to be avoided rather than pursued.

We have seen enough history to recognize that the "baby bust" children of the 1930s could find better jobs, with less dislocation, than could their "baby boom" successors of the 1950s.

Perhaps we should be studying how to save and invest enough to put the labor force to work rather than spending the money on raising more children to meet an imagined need some forty years away.

OUR CROWDED FUTURE

Kenneth Boulding, the economist, coined the wonderful epigram:

Anyone who believes exponential growth can go on forever in a finite world is either a madman or an economist.

How better could one dispose of the tons of garbage that have been written on the topic of growth?

To propose more children or more immigration to maintain a high proportion of the working age population to the old is—on a gigantic scale—akin to proposing a little drink to cure a hangover. We are presently working off the baby boom. I have argued that there are various ways to accommodate the aging of that cohort without resorting to population inflation. Do we want to "solve" an anticipated problem that may not materialize when the baby boomers grow old, by generating more rapid population growth?

Before World War II, demographers—looking at then current fertility figures—anticipated that the United States' population would stabilize about now, somewhere in the vicinity of 150 million. Then came the baby boom.

At some stage, one must ask the question: "How many of us do we want?" There is no precise mathematical formula that can give us the answer, but in retrospect 150 million doesn't look too bad. That was the level in 1950, before the creation of most of the huge chemical dumps, before CFCs, when carbon dioxide in the atmosphere was just beginning its rise to problem levels, before acid rain, when nuclear energy was new enough to seem wholly benign, when suburbs were within commuting distance of the cities, and when the cities themselves seemed attractive places to live. 1950 was no idyll. We were already pursuing the habits that led to the environmental issues with which we are now dealing. But wouldn't it be attractive to face our present problems with that population?

This sounds like nostalgia, but can anybody who was here then deny a certain regret at what has been lost?

Several demographers have projected the population a century from now. Using very conservative assumptions fertility does not rise despite the rising proportion of high fertility groups such as Hispanics; there is no illegal immigration, and legal immigration stops rising despite the continuing pressures forcing it up—the projections converge at about 255–259 million. A very modest allowance for illegal immigration or rising legal immigration would push the figure over 340 million. (It is presently about 245 million.) A return to "replacement level fertility" (very roughly, the two-child family) could push the figure over a half billion. The point here is that, even without deliberately stimulating immigration or fertility, the prospect is for a more crowded rather than a less crowded society.

Fertility in the United States has risen very slightly in the past decade, rather than continuing its earlier decline. This underlines the conservatism of the projections above.

If the decline should resume, it would be wise to reexamine the conclusions in this paper. However, Census "low" projections using a fertility rate about 10 percent below the present one do not lead to conclusions very different from those above. In our demographic future, immigration seems likely to be a more volatile and thus more important variable than fertility, and the present evidence all points to continued population growth.

As Kenneth Boulding reminds us, stabilize we must. The question is not whether, but when? Do we wait until the population density has reached that of India or Bangladesh? We may differ as to what population size is desirable or practicable. We need to begin the debate, and to translate the results into a population policy. It is remarkable that, on an issue so fundamental to our well-being, the nation has hardly begun the process.

FUTURE ISSUES

When we have arrived at a consensus, there are real issues to be addressed. How do we shift from the support of children, who tend to be financed by their parents, to the support of the old, which is usually a societal responsibility in this country, and whose cost is painfully evident in every worker's Social Security deductions? Medical miracles are making it possible to keep more and more of the very old alive, but the miracles are very expensive. As a society, we have an entire debate ahead of us concerning our responsibilities to the old: how much life support is the nation morally obligated to provide to the very old, and to what ends?

More generally, how can creativity be maintained in a steady-state economy that has come to the end of its physical expansion? How do we maintain employment and economic activity?

There is time for the debate. With the 1983 changes in the Social Security system, the Social Security Trust Fund is beginning to run a surplus which is expected to mount to almost unmanageable levels through the middle of the next century. The problem is not, as so many believe, that the Fund is in imminent danger of exhaustion. Rather, it is that the Fund is being used to help fund the Federal deficit rather than to make the productive investments which would support the aging when their numbers do begin to mount steeply about a generation from now.

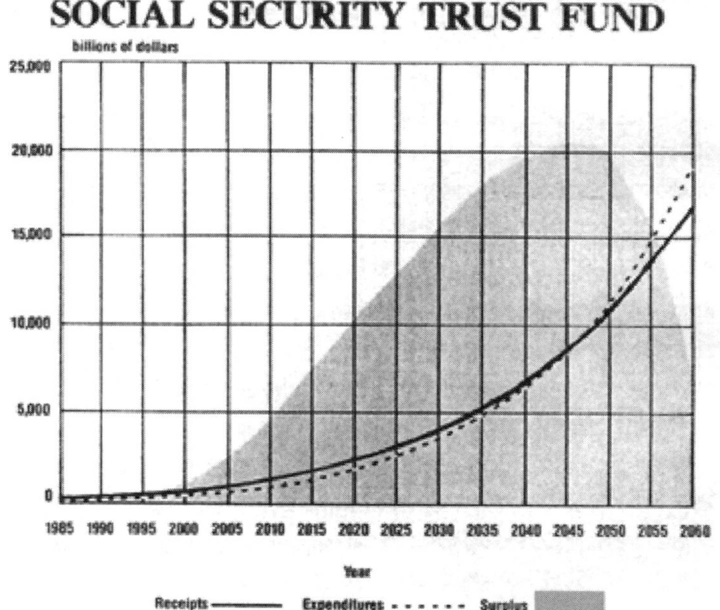

Figure 2.

THE "COUNSEL OF THE PRUDENT MAN"

The point of this brief essay is that those who argue for higher fertility or more immigration to support the aged are in effect arguing for more population growth. It would take a very sharp drop in fertility indeed to justify their fears, and such a drop is not presently in sight. Let us not buy future problems by embracing a single-track "solution" with such vast and unexamined ramifications.

Note:

1. Data for this paper were taken primarily from the Statistical Abstract of the U.S., 1987, the World Bank "World Population Projections 1985," and the United Nations' World Population Prospects: Estimates and Projections as Assessed in 1984 (New York: UN Department of International Economic and Social Affairs, 1986.) A concise summary of projections of the U.S. population is contained in Leon Bouvier, "Will There Be Enough Americans?" (Washington: Center for Immigration Studies Backgrounder No. 1, July 1987.) The estimate of the cost of raising children is from Thomas Espenshade, Investing In Children (Washington: Urban Institute Press, 1984.) The graph of the Social Security Trust Fund is from Population Today March 1985 (Washington: Population Reference Bureau.)

"NIMBYS" AND THE FENCE

Lindsey Grant

January 1995

INS (the Immigration and Naturalization Service) plans to build a four-mile ditch from the Mexican border at Tijuana to the sea, to channel the sewage-laden Tijuana River (which flows North across the border) and to interrupt the present traffic of vehicles, which simply race across the desert border carrying illegal immigrants or drugs.

In January a private citizens' group named FAIR (Federation for American Immigration Reform) proposed that, as part of a ten-point proposal to help the Border Patrol enforce the immigration law, a substantial fence be built along the most vulnerable sections of our southern border.[1]

Both proposals seem eminently practical and sane. There are some fences already, but they are in shreds and ineffective. The Border Patrol, because of some curious ambivalence that extends into the U.S. Government, is told to make bricks without straw—to prevent illegal movements but without being given the most elementary of tools.

The FAIR proposal received considerable favorable publicity, including editorials in the *Washington Post* and in two newspapers close to the action, the *San Diego Union* and the *Dallas Morning News.* It also received some bitter criticism. The Government, one hopes, will be considering the suggestion, but the fear of controversy could dissuade it. As for the INS plan to build the ditch, it has been put on hold as of this writing.

One can understand the criticism driven by self-interest, from commercial farmers, Los Angeles sweatshop operators, people needing household help, all of whom seek cheap labor. From politicians who gain by confounding border control with racism. Even perhaps from some clerics of the "sanctuary movement" who have promoted a one-dimensional view of justice into a universal right.

But **every country asserts the right to control its borders, including Mexico. We have an immigration law. Why don't we try to enforce it? Why do opponents of effective border control in the United States carry such weight?**

THE MISDIRECTED "NIMBY"

Readers may have noticed that a new word has entered the American vocabulary: "NIMBY." It is usually capitalized, as if in anger or frustration, and it means "not in MY back yard!

The exclamation is a natural reaction to a world of sudden and mysterious new threats, of increased crowding and violence, a world changing in directions that most people do not like.

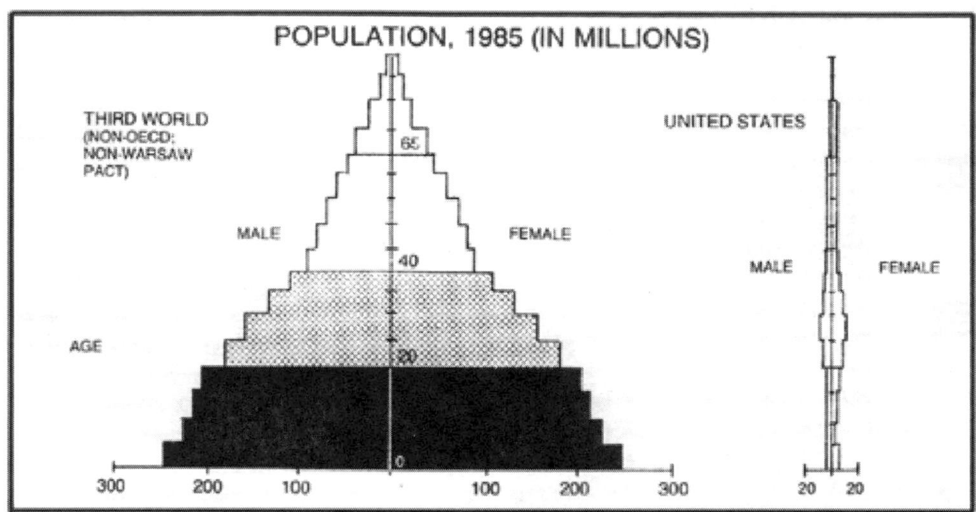

THE SHADED AREA REPRESENTS THE POPULATION PRESENTLY 20 TO 40 YEARS OLD—THE MOST LIKELY MIGRANTS. THOSE IN THE DARK AREA WILL REACH THOSE AGES THROUGH 2005.
SOURCES: Population Reference Bureau; **Statistical Abstract of the U.S., 1987.**

Figure 1.

It is usually aimed at a chemical factory, a nuclear dump, a new prison or low-income housing project, a new superhighway or a sewage disposal plant, or simply (as in the movements in California and Seattle) at state or local growth.

The anger is understandable, but usually misdirected. It erupts when people learn of a local threat, and subsides if that particular threat disappears.

We cannot just pull up the ladder and save our own back yards. Today's problems do not respect property or county lines. The "NIMBYS" cannot just deal with the problem in California or Seattle. They must address the causes, and that requires a national perspective.

IMMIGRATION AND POPULATION

Immigration is a major element in U.S. population change. **If migration were in balance (emigration equals immigration), and if the fertility of American women stayed about where it is (slightly below replacement level), our population would peak somewhere around 2020 at about 270 million, and then slowly drift downward to 220 million—the 1977 size—in 2080.** Nobody really knows how much immigration there is, because illegal immigration is by its nature hard to measure, and because the nation does not try to keep track of emigration. **If annual net immigration is 800,000 a year, then the population will be 333 million in 2080 (half again as large as with zero net migration). Double that rate, and you have a population passing 400 million.**[2]

Let us turn to another phrase that is entering the language: **sustainability.** Most simply, it means running one's country or the world, for that matter—in a way that will not degrade its capacity to support future generations. In a way, it harks back to Pericles' injunction to "leave Athens a better place than you found it."

By that standard, **the United States is overpopulated.** As a general proposition, resource and environmental problems are proportional to the population being served. Not necessarily a direct correlation; there are thresholds and non-linearities and system collapses; and there are other variables such as consumption levels and technical fixes. But it is a good rule of thumb.

We have more timber resources than we did in 1950, but fewer per capita because the U.S. population has grown by two-thirds. We have about as much prime farmland, but 40 percent less per capita, and we have kept up by using more fertilizer and more pesticides, by drawing down water tables, poisoning aquifers and wetlands, affecting not only fishery production and wildlife stocks, but our own health. In Iowa, farmers are drinking bottled water from out of state because they have poisoned their own wells.[3] As the Chairman of the National Research Council's Board on Agriculture and Chancellor of the University of California at Davis said: "We know that we just can't keep applying chemicals and pesticides to the soil the way we have."

We can conserve. We can find more benign productive processes. But at any given level of conservation or technology, the problem is proportional to the population of consumers.

Let me tick off some other issues familiar to most readers:

- urban air pollution at levels far above health standards;
- acid precipitation, with forest damage, widening acidification of the soil, some indication of direct health effects, and potentially a threat to soil micro-organisms and the terrestrial carbon cycle;
- the related problems of ozone creation at nose level and depletion in the stratosphere, with important effects on health, climate warming and potentially the entire aquatic food chain;
- the greenhouse effect, global warming and rising sea levels;
- the need to detoxify nuclear and toxic wastes already generated, and the mounting problems of disposing of toxic and urban wastes;
- the proliferation of man-made chemicals in the environment. Of the chemicals in commerce very few have been tested for direct health effects and none have been tested for secondary effects as they move through the environment and are transformed and re-combined. These things are not happening somewhere else; the chemicals are literally part of us; they are in our bodies. We are in for many unpleasant surprises like DDT, dioxin, PCBs and CFCs.

This list of problems is awesome. It is not necessarily overwhelming. We have identified other problems and solved them. Nationally, emissions of airborne particulates have declined 61 percent since 1970, carbon monoxide 29 percent, and lead 80 percent.[4] We can solve these other problems and live again within our resources.

We can move toward conservation, fuel cells, renewable energy sources. We can restructure our cities and our transportation systems. We can enforce controls on pumping aquifers, and change policies so as to discourage the kind of intensive monocultures that are poisoning the water. We can require thorough environmental impact studies on chemicals before they are introduced. If we cannot solve problems like the greenhouse effect, because of their momentum, we can find ways to accommodate them. We can build dikes and/or move coastal cities away from the lowest areas . . .

We could, but we have not been. From 1981 until President Bush's June 12th proposal to address air pollution, the Federal Government showed little inclination to begin the process.

The expense will be staggering. The Government has put a $66–100 billion tag on cleaning up the existing pollution from nuclear weapons, and another $23–100 billion to clean up just the worst of the known toxic waste sites. The President put a price tag of $14–$19 billion per year on his clean air proposals. The Government has not yet even begun to look at the total costs of redressing the problems I have described.

The National Academy of Engineering has already recommended that a stop be put to locating major facilities in low coastal areas, because the greenhouse effect cannot simply be stopped tomorrow, and sea levels are rising.[5] I know of no project within the Government to consider that recommendation and decide what needs to be done. Meanwhile, relentlessly, our national population is concentrating near the coasts. Most of Florida lies within a few feet of sea level; the population of Florida has risen 82 percent since 1970 and 347 percent since 1950.

Astonishingly, **neither the Government nor the experts take population into account when they look at such problems.**[6] Take the energy example. It is a prime source of atmospheric pollution, acid precipitation and the greenhouse effect. People are worried, and there is an endless debate as to whether to control the problems through conservation, or solar and renewable energy, or nuclear power. We may need all three, and relief from population growth as well. Reduce the projected population and you reduce the demand for energy.

Such thinking would require **foresight**—the recognition that problems cross departmental lines, and so do solutions and neither the Government nor academe have learned to practice that sort of thinking.

Let us take Los Angeles as one specific case. Los Angeles suffers the worst air pollution of any city in the country. The local Air Quality Management District has proposed a plan to clean up Los Angeles' air through a 70 percent to 80 percent reduction in sulfur and nitrogen oxide emissions. It would involve everything from new transit systems to bans on single-occupancy automobiles and on backyard barbeques. The cost has been estimated at $4 billion now, and $12 billion by 2000, **per year.**[7] There are more than 13 million people in the Los Angeles metropolitan area (CMSA). In 1950, there were fewer than five million. Los Angeles could probably meet the Federal air standards now, except for the growth in population. The population is still growing, in large part because of illegal immigration. Yet there is no sign that anybody addressing air quality thought of including, among those numerous recommendations, an endorsement of the proposal for better fences along the nearby Mexican border. It is not their department.

IMMIGRATION, LABOR AND EQUITY

If you are interested in domestic tranquility in your home town, perhaps you have a personal stake in national immigration policy, as well as a moral one.

The argument is made that immigrants work hard for little money, and they do not cause trouble. Very well for the employer, but is it good for the country?

This country and the "American dream" were built on a degree of labor scarcity, which meant that a worker could expect a decent wage for his work. The scarcity encouraged experiments with labor saving approaches and technologies, which in turn led to higher productivity, high wages, and a mass market that is still the center of world trade.

We could allow wages to be driven down to subsistence levels, because the potential labor supply is, for practical purposes, inexhaustible (see Graph on page one), and the U.S. is a powerful magnet. This would change the economic profile of the United State to that of a third world country, with perhaps half its people at the ragged edge of survival. Is that what we want?

There is a conflict of moral issues here. **We are right to feel sympathy for the world's poor, but our first obligation is to our own society.** As that graph makes clear, we cannot solve even the existing population problem in the third world (to say nothing of future population growth) by absorbing it, and no other nation except Australia and Canada has shown any inclination to try. We should, I believe, be putting more of our foreign assistance into the fundamental issue of population.[8] But we have more immediate responsibilities at home.

The nation a generation ago, in rare unity, launched perhaps its greatest moral crusade: to eliminate racism and to bring blacks into the economic mainstream. Since then, by winking at the failure to enforce our immigration laws, we have inadvertently done the one thing that could most effectively sabotage that crusade. We have allowed the almost unfettered entry of competition for entry level jobs, at which the blacks should be starting their entry into the economy. For the consequences, see the graph on this page. It is not enough to argue that the immigrant—hungry and fearful of deportation—will work harder. One must also answer the question: The blacks are Americans; how do we bring the increasingly alienated, restless and isolated ghetto blacks into the system?

The Immigration Reform and Control Act of 1986 was (except for an enormous loophole created to placate commercial agriculture) an effort to address that competition by limiting the job market to Americans and legally admitted aliens. One must wait to see whether it will be effectively enforced and whether the means will be found to identify who in fact is entitled to work. It was not meant, however, to stand alone, its success rests upon keeping the numbers controllable by having the means to enforce the law at the border.

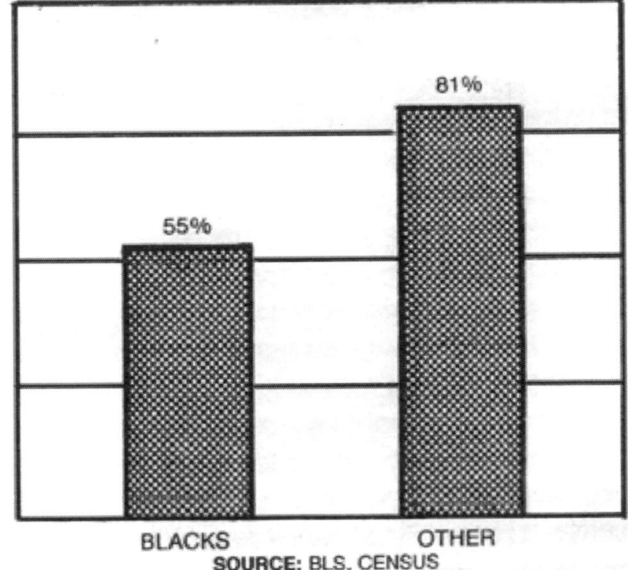

Figure 2.

BACK TO THE FENCE

The remarkable thing about the inattention to population is that, **compared with extraordinarily costly repair bills such as I have mentioned, our population future can be shaped at relatively little cost.**

Immigration should be the easiest component of population growth to address. We even have the law. We simply need to enforce it. An obvious starting point would be to make it easier for the Border Patrol to patrol the border. Begin with that fence. Add certain **technical improvements** (see the FAIR proposals, footnote 1). Proceed with the other measures such as the recent decision, spurred by Congress, to **deploy the National Guard** to help control the border.[9] Develop better ways of **identifying** who in the United States is entitled to be here.[10] The rewards are not simply demographic; they include better control of drug smuggling and crime.

Population growth must eventually stop, at some level. The control of illegal immigration would give us as a nation the opportunity to decide when and at what level. With such a consensus in view, we can adjust legal immigration levels. Then we should consider going where other nations have gone before us, but we have feared to tread: toward a national view as to what fertility levels are desirable to **achieve the demographic future we want.** It may be that a sustainable system, passing our environment and resources intact to our children, will require a smaller population than we have yet considered.

It should be popular to address illegal immigration. Polls regularly indicate that, at the mass level, Americans want better control over illegal immigration, by wide majorities. Even among Hispanic Americans, four polls showed substantial majorities who viewed illegal immigration as a serious problem. A recent Tarrance poll in California showed that 81 percent of the respondents believed border security should be improved, and 67 percent supported rebuilding and strengthening the fence south of San Diego.[11]

Apparently, it is not so simple. Among our opinion forming elite, there is a curious reluctance. Our sympathy for the world's poor, our self-image as a nation of immigrants, the Statue of Liberty and Emma Lazarus' poem all somehow come together to create a very guilty feeling about any proposal to strengthen immigration control.

I don't believe the guilt is justified or even necessarily moral, and I have made the arguments elsewhere.[12] Nevertheless, it seems to be a continuing fact of life and an impediment to reasoned policy.

NIMBYS, UNITE . . .!

Had enough? Very well. My point is that NIMBY is no answer, nor is flight. We are all in this together. The problems of environmental deterioration are national, not local, and so is the population growth that contributes to them. **Our political leadership seems incapable of looking beyond current crises toward a larger view of the future. It will begin to wrestle seriously with-the issues of sustainability only when there is a political base.** The local NIMBYs are focused on real problems, but they seek, in the Chinese phrase, to "treat the branches, not the roots." NIMBYs are needed on the national scene. The Government will hear only the special interest groups unless it hears from the people . . ."

To a nation bred on the dream of the frontier and of open spaces, it is hard to put a fence up against the Statue of Liberty as a symbol. Perhaps that is just as well. Let the unequal contest stand as a test of whether we respond to symbols or to argument, whether we are led by myth or reason.

The fence is a practical idea, stalled by a myth. And it is just a beginning.

COMMENTS BY DONALD MANN, PRESIDENT, NPG, INC.

The United States can never hope to prevent millions of illegal aliens from entering the country across its southern border unless it builds an impenetrable fence to keep them out. Our present policy, if it can be called that, borders on the insane.

It consists of allowing upwards of a million illegal aliens each year to cross our southern border virtually unimpeded, then seeking to apprehend them at great expense, then expelling the ones (perhaps one in four) that we apprehend. They are then free to try again to cross our border illegally as many times as they wish, often the same night. Could anything more ridiculous possibly be imagined?

The technology is available to build an—impassable fence on portions of our southern border. Since mountains and desert make up most of our border with Mexico, such a fence would only be necessary along some 200 miles of the border, where 90 percent of all illegal crossings occur.

We must face up to the fact that explosive population growth in the countries of the Caribbean basin, within easy reach of our southern border, will inevitably lead to massive unemployment, economic chaos, and social and political turmoil. During the decade of the 1990s it is virtually certain that tens of millions of poor and desperate people from this group of countries (their numbers swelled by political, economic and environmental refugees from most other third world countries) will seek to cross our southern border illegally, in search of jobs and a better life, and perhaps for mere survival.

They will succeed in doing so unless we build an impenetrable fence on portions of that border. It may be difficult for the American public to accept, but it is an undeniable fact: no matter how much we may sympathize with their plight, the United States simply does not have the means nor the resources to save other sovereign nations from the tragic consequences of their failure to stabilize their populations at a sustainable level.

NOTES:

1. "Ten Steps to Securing America's Borders," January 26, 1989. FAIR, 1666 Connecticut Avenue NW, Suite 400, Washington DC 20009. 202/328-7004.
2. For U.S. population projections under different assumptions, see "Projections of the Population of the United States, by Age, Sex and Race: 1988 to 2080," by Gregory Spencer. (Washington, Bureau of the Census, Series P-25, No. 10 1 8, January 1989) and "The Future Racial Composition of the United States" by Leon F. Bouvier and Cary B. Davis (Demographic Information Services Center of the Population Reference Bureau, 777 14th Street NW—Suite 800, Washington DC 20005, 202/639/8040, August 1982).
3. *New York Times*, November 22, 1987.
4. *World Resources 1987*, IIED & The World Resources Institute. (New York: Basic Books, 1987.) p. 87.
5. *Implications of Changes in Relative Mean Sea Level*, Commission on Engineering and Technical Assistance, National Research Council. (Washington: National Academy Press, 1987.)
6. Both the *Global 2000 report to the President* (Washington: GPO, 1980) and the 1972 report of the Commission on Population Growth and the American Future, chaired by John D. Rockefeller III, considered demographic change and its relevance to U.S. national interests. The "Rockefeller Commission" report concluded that no national purposes would be served by further population growth. That was seventeen years and 40 million people ago. The Global 2000 Report made no recommendations, but a follow up report (*Global Future; Time to Act*. Council on Environmental Quality and U.S. Department of State. GPO; January 1981) called for a national population policy and suggested a policy of stabilization be considered. Subsequently, there have been no comparable studies or followup.
7. *Science*, 5 May 1989, P. 5517.
8. See NPG Forum paper "A Population Focus for U.S. Aid," Negative Population Growth, Inc., June 1987.
9. *Christian Science Monitor* 3-29-89, p. 7. *New York Times* 5-21-89, p. 29. This is a test program, authorized at $300 million, aimed at drug control, but it should help to apprehend illegal entrants at the border, and it may provide experience and a precedent for more extensive use

of the National Guard in what is, after all, a primary traditional function of armies: to protect the borders.

10. See NPG Forum paper "Secure Identification: the Weak Link in Immigration Control," by David Simcox. (NPG, Inc., May 1989).
11. For the Tarrance poll and a summary of other polls, see FAIR's *Information Exchange*, May 9, 1989 (address as above.)
12. "Immigration and the American Conscience," by Lindsey Grant and John H. Tanton, in *Progress as if Survival Mattered* (San Francisco: Friends of the Earth, 1981. Reprints available from Population Environment Balance, 1325 G Street NW—Suite 1003, Washington DC 20005. 202/879-3000.)

THE SECOND GREAT WALL OF CHINA: EVOLUTION OF A SUCCESSFUL POLICY OF POPULATION CONTROL

J. Mayone Stycos

October 1989

Flushed with his victory over the Chinese nationalists, Mao proclaimed in 1949 that, "Of all things in the world people are the most precious. " On the eve of the formation of the People's Republic, he forecast a China rich in both people and material goods, explicitly attacked the pessimism of Malthus, and reaffirmed the classical Marxist theme that under communism no problem of overpopulation could ever occur. On the contrary, since labor was the basic source of wealth, more people coupled with socialist organization could only mean more wealth and power. How does it happen that less than three decades later China unveiled the most radical program of population control the world has ever seen? And in the light of the program's success, what lessons does it have for other nations struggling with problems of population?

MARX VERSUS MALTHUS

The Chinese have managed to be remarkably flexible about ideology, without losing the great advantages to the state that ideology offers. In the political sphere Marxist orthodoxy has not impeded the see-sawing of relations with Moscow; and in the economic arena, the Chinese have been willing to try everything from back yard steel smelting and collectivation to free enterprise. This same pragmatic spirit has characterized their stance on population. Current Malthusian policies have been renamed as socialist but with a Chinese twist. According to a rhetorical question raised by the Vice President of the Chinese Academy of Social Sciences in 1987, "In a society of public ownership where the production of material wealth is carried out according to plan, can there be anarchy in population?"

During a visit last summer I asked a number of Chinese family planning officials how the current Malthusian ideology could be justified in a Marxist regime. One official said that Marx lived in different times and had never dreamed that population density or growth could reach such levels. Another argued that economic development under socialism had not been as rapid as Marx had predicted and that these unanticipated circumstances demanded new policies. Virtually all persons I spoke with stressed the consistency of socialist planning with family or population planning, in the sense that neither production nor reproduction was a matter that could be left entirely to individuals. Still others essentially replied with a shrug. All of the replies seemed to be saying that when push comes to shove the ideology is bent but not discarded.

THE WINDING DEMOGRAPHIC TRAIL

Current policies are the outcome of a long and tortuous ideological controversy and crude population experiments that were themselves products of broader political and economic shifts in the People's Republic. Also influential in the development of policy has been the steady improvement in contraceptive technology.

The optimism that followed the 1949 revolution was soon dissipated by the failure of socialism to prevent food shortages, and by a 1953 census that showed there were 100,000,000 more people than had been supposed. As a consequence, local health departments were quietly ordered to set up family planning clinics, but the technology was both crude and controversial. Condoms, diaphragms, and jellies were known, but in short supply. Abortion, though theoretically favored as a socialist approach to the liberation of women, required medical expertise and septic conditions. Moreover, it was frowned on by the medical profession and, until 1957, permitted only under stringent conditions. Female sterilization was even more expensive than abortion, and required an abdominal operation. Perhaps desperate to offer the people something in the way of contraception, even folk methods (such as swallowing spring tadpoles) and acupuncture were recommended.

This campaign probably had no impact on national birth rates, and, in any event, came to a halt in 1958 with the launching of the Great Leap Forward. For the next few years, although family planning facilities, such as they were, were not removed, the promotional efforts ceased. Instead, the Great Leap produced a return of optimism concerning the benefits of socialist planning. "Surpass Britain and catch up with America" was a key slogan for the period, and attacks were renewed on pessimistic Malthusian views. People were again viewed as capital, and massive public works were organized utilizing tens of millions of laborers. The first secretary of the Communist Youth League boasted that, "The force of 600 million liberated people is tens of thousands of times stronger than a nuclear explosion. Such a force is capable of creating wonders which our enemies cannot even imagine." (Cited by Aird).

The wonders were short lived. Agricultural production plummeted, famine ensued, and birth rates dropped precipitously—not because of family planning, but because the unsettled conditions delayed and disrupted marriages. The painfully obvious failure of the new socialist policies led the government to step up both the birth control program and its promotion in 1962. A mission was quietly dispatched to Japan to discover how the Japanese had been so successful in curbing their birth rates, and in a 1964 interview with journalist Edgar Snow, Premier Zhou Enlai expressed his admiration for their achievements. Around this time two major contraceptive breakthroughs occurred. IUDs had been successfully introduced in a number of countries and a safe and simple method of inducing an early abortion, the vacuum pump, had been developed and simplified in China. Thus, two effective and relatively inexpensive methods became available for the first time. Urban fertility began to decline, dropping from about six children per woman in 1963 to about three by the late 1960s. (In the rural areas, comprising about 80 percent of the population, fertility did not begin to decline until the 1970s.) However, during the Cultural Revolution in the late 1960s the program was again suspended, and then reactivated with full force in the early 1970s when a 1971 State Council Directive announced that "comrades at every level must strengthen leadership and conduct penetrating propaganda and education, so that late marriage and birth planning become voluntary behavior. " To expedite the policy, paramedics in the cities and rural midwives and barefoot doctors in the country had "planned births" added to their responsibilities. Volunteer health workers began the detailed supervision of contraception at a neighborhood level that much later came under attack as "coercive. " Ruth Sidel, who was permitted to visit China in the early 1970s, described the procedure used in Hangchow neighborhoods: "Each month the health workers go from door to door to determine what method of birth control each woman in the block is using. A chart is kept on the wall of the health center indicating how many women use what kind of contraception."

The politicization of birth control became a major characteristic of this and subsequent campaigns. Family planning was now rationalized less in terms of the health of mothers and children, and more in terms of political goals—small families would speed world revolution, consolidate the dictatorship of the proletariat and facilitate preparation for war. The "gang of four," including Mao's wife, was accused of anti-family planning intentions later in the decade, a sure sign that family planning had achieved the highest priority.

A number of provinces began to introduce demographic targets for their cities and counties, followed by communes, brigades and production teams, many of whom created public charts of the targets, as well as lists of those who were to have births in the following year. At each of the many levels of organization family planning was introduced via "thought work" or "study." At these meetings, testimonials would be given by those who had married too early or had too many children, and the evils of the old ways of thinking would be exposed. Group leaders would highlight new thinking and tell with pride of their own contraceptive efforts. These were standard techniques for political indoctrination and for innovating whatever economic reform was current. The Chinese have always emphasized the importance of persuading, not compelling, and these techniques, though heavy handed and smacking of "brain washing" to Westerners, were simply adapted to a new theme. By the late 1970s contraceptive pills had been certified, a simpler technique for female sterilization (mini-laparotomy) was introduced, and a relatively autonomous system of service delivery was created—in contrast to the integration of family planning with other health services, the organizational form favored by international agencies.

NEW TARGETS FOR THE '80S

By the end of the decade about 70 percent of the couples of childbearing age were using effective methods of birth control, and the abortion rate (318 per 1,000 live births) was substantial. The Chinese were now confident enough to announce to the world in 1979 that they would try to stop population growth by the end of the century, and their public rationale for the program was unabashedly Malthusian. The *New York Times* cited the Deputy Prime-Minister as saying that raising a child to the age of sixteen cost $1,000 in rural areas and nearly $4,500 in big cities. "Therefore, she said, both the people and the state could save a fortune by cutting the birth rate." (August 13, 1979).

Western spokesmen may have talked this way, but rarely put their money where their mouths were. That is, they supported family planning, but not population planning. The former implies that couples decide the number they want, while government helps them to achieve that number, regardless of the demographic consequences. Population planning, on the other hand, implies not only the setting of national demographic targets, but a concrete program to achieve them. In China this means inducing couples to have the number of children the government wants them to have. By the end of the 1970s, the Chinese had taken the tough decision that this number was one, and put into motion an unprecedented system of local target setting, grass roots monitoring, financial and social incentives and disincentives, meticulous monitoring of conformity, and massive educational campaigns.

As early as 1981, the now famous "one-child certificates"—contracts by couples with zero to one children, who agree to have no more than one—had been signed by 57 percent of 20 million eligible couples. By 1982 China became the first nation in the world to build population planning into its

Constitution: "The State promotes family planning so that population growth may fit the plan for economic and social development." It also stipulates that "both husband and wife have the duty to practice family planning." In the developed countries, family planning had had a long history of battling to make family planning a human right. The Chinese moved past this, and in their new Constitution explicitly made it a duty.

That the program is working hardly seems in question. Nearly one-half of the births in 1981 were first births, as compared with one-fifth in 1970. In the latter year the average woman finished childbearing having had six births, but by the mid-1980s between two and three births was the average. A higher proportion of couples in China than in the USA are using modern family planning methods. These are incredible achievements for a huge and underdeveloped country. But what is the price, and is the payoff sufficient to justify that price?

The Chinese think the stakes are huge. Their general goals for economic development have been set high, and they are fiercely determined to achieve them. Since the revolution they have been highly successful in reducing mortality and raising educational levels, and have redistributed the nation's wealth in a highly equitable fashion. But their social program has had more dramatic successes than their economic, though by international standards growth in GNP since the revolution has been high. In 1978, just a year before the one-child policy was announced, the Chinese specified long range economic plans that were ambitious but more realistic than earlier ones. No longer trying to "catch up to America" by the end of this century, their new targets were a quadrupling of the gross national product and a tripling of the per-capita product. To do this they unleashed programs that accelerated private initiative on the one hand, and tightened up on population growth on the other. Chinese demographers calculated that if the annual population growth rate of 1.5 percent continued until the end of the century they would have 116 million more people than the 1.2 billion they targeted for the year 2,000. 116 million is the population of Bangladesh today.

The 1982 census, with heavy technical and financial assistance from the United Nations, proved beyond any doubt that China had been the world's first nation to achieve a population of one billion. Since the census, about 13 million persons—roughly the population of Afghanistan—have been added each year. The massiveness of these population figures seem to have sunk in at the highest levels, and are used to justify the tough population policies. As China's Foreign Minister put it recently, "If the United States population were five times its current size, it would be fairly easy for members of Congress to agree on China's family planning policy" (*New York Times,* March 28, 1989).

Why "members of Congress" don't agree has to do with what critics such as Nick Eberstadt term the "grave and obvious human rights abuses" (*New York Times,* February 22, 1984), or what Julian Simon calls Chinese "arm-twisting." (*Asian Wall Street Journal*, February 24, 1988). However, the Chinese are used to arm twisting—they have experienced it with respect to production quotas, health practices, political activity and ideology. In all of these areas they are accustomed to government programs and targets that. use the many administrative layers and political groupings to bring pressure for conformity. Although it is now clear that an iron fist lies under every silk glove, dissenters have traditionally been brought into line not by coercion but by peer pressure and education. "One of the proud boasts of China (has been) that even 'counter revolutionaries' were dealt with in an allegedly humane way, by 'educating' them . . . " (Richard Bernstein, *New York Times,* June

6, 1989). While this may not justify the peer pressure methods used in the case of family planning, in the Chinese setting the practice is far less extraordinary than it would be elsewhere.

A VISIT TO THE PROVINCES

Once national guidelines and demographic targets are set, provinces, cities, counties, villages, and even smaller units negotiate their own targets and devise their own ways of persuading lower administrative groups and individuals to conform. The Chinese allow considerable flexibility at each administrative level and carefully monitor the results. By encouraging competition and innovation (within narrow limits), in effect they release a multitude of trial balloons that help them determine what works and what does not. Successes are rewarded with public praise and material benefits. Failures are variously penalized.

To carry out a national guideline such as a target number of births for the coming year requires thousands of lower level decisions and a precise control of demographic statistics. This kind of statistical control is often lacking or slip-shod in other countries, and its fidelity in China in no small way accounts for a successful program.

An example can be given from Sichuan, a province with over 100 million inhabitants. The provincial program director showed me their overall birth targets, which had been negotiated with the National Office of Family Planning. They were shooting for a birth rate of eighteen per thousand population in the current five-year plan (1986–90), and sixteen for the 1996–2000 period. To translate such targets into behavior, late marriage (at least twenty-three for women and twenty-five for men) is encouraged by cash bonuses and extended honeymoon leaves. After marriage first births are generally uncontrolled, but a number of attractive incentives are put into effect if the couple signs a one-child contract. In any event the woman is expected to have an IUD inserted following the first birth. Second births are permitted only under specified conditions, which vary with geographic area and individual circumstances. The fine for an unplanned second birth is 10 percent of family income charged for a period of seven years. An unplanned third birth can increase the fine to 20 percent. Abortion is available and encouraged as a remedy for unplanned pregnancies, as is sterilization after two births.

To carry out the program the province spent about 122 million yen (about $43 million in 1987), mainly on salaries for a not-so-small army of professionals and volunteers: over 600 provincial level professionals, 22,000 full-time personnel at the county, city and township level (including 5,536 who spend full-time at information and education activities), 75,000 part-time workers at the village level, and 570,000 part-time volunteers.[1]

A visit to a township level family planning center serving an agricultural population of 20,000 revealed how the policies are carried out at a local level. The staff (a secondary level doctor and two assistants) seemed well aware of local conditions and alert to adapting the provincial policies to them: how a market every other day facilitates staff contact with the women, how family planning workers cooperate with agricultural extension workers, and how the new profit initiatives have motivated women to have fewer children. Without resorting to notes the doctor informed me that of the 3,946 women of reproductive age, 3,586 were practicing contraception and most of the remaining women were either just married or infertile. Fifty-five percent of the women were using IUDs and about one third were sterilized. Last year there were 137 abortions and 318 births, of which all but thirty-three were first births and none of which were third or higher order births. In comparative context these statistics are little short of amazing. This agricultural town in the heart of China has less than sixteen births per 1,000 population, a rate not achieved by the United States until the mid-1970s.[2] It has a contraceptive prevalence rate that exceeds that of American women, while its abortion ratio (forty-three per one hundred births) was well below that of the State of New York.[3]

THE WILL OF THE PEOPLE

"Coercion" means compelling people to do something that they do not want to do. Is it the case that the traditionally familistic Chinese, really want big families, but are being forced to have small ones? In fact, the Chinese prefer very small families under two in urban areas and about two in rural areas.[4] This is to be contrasted with the preferences of women in Asia and Latin America who want about four, or women in Southern African nations who want between six and eight (World Fertility Survey).

In one survey of 1,100 cases in Danjiang County, Hubei in 1986, the subjects were asked for the advantages and disadvantages of having more than one or two children. The expensiveness of children was seen as the major disadvantage, while economic assistance to their elderly parents was viewed as the main advantage. These financial concerns seem very plausible in the light of the last decade's economic changes, and lend credibility to the statements of desired family size. Of special interest, however, were the high proportions who cited a concern for "overpopulation" as a disadvantage in, having more children: 52 percent in the urban and 24 percent in the rural area. In most countries, family planning campaigns have de-emphasized its benefits to the nation and stressed its advantages for parents and children. The major thrust of the private family planning movement in the West has been maternal and child health and reproductive rights for women. The socialist countries of Europe have emphasized its contributions to female liberation, while the Catholic countries of Latin America stress it as an antidote for illegal abortions. China has been unusual in insisting that family planning is a patriotic duty that will accelerate the nation's economic development.

This is nowhere clearer than in the opinions of the younger generation—those who have not yet begun their reproductive lives. I visited a secondary school in Sichuan that had introduced an experimental course in population education, with assistance from the United Nations Fund for Population. The teachers were proud of their efforts, and one of them had written out his strategy, which was mainly directed at getting students to make the connection between their individual behavior and the national welfare.

> Our students must be taught the basic views of Marxist population theory, ecologic balance and population control. . . . At first they thought this subject had nothing to do with them . . . Many think that giving birth to a child is a person's private affair. So we teach that carrying out family planning is important to the construction of socialist spiritual civilization. The students ideological problem was one of putting the state's welfare before their own. Our population education is really a subject that can teach them patriotism.

I was given translations of about a dozen essays written by the eleventh grade students at the conclusion of the course. We can assume that these essays were among the better ones, stylistically and ideologically, but one would have a hard time finding anything remotely resembling them in any other country. The examples below bear no trace of Western family planning's emphasis on family welfare. Instead, they illustrate how the national interest requires personal sacrifices that the citizen should be proud to make:

—My country relatives told us about their neighbor who secretly had a second child. He was fined 2,000 yuan but he told others "In the future I'll be rich because I have two children. " I think that is absurd and one-sided. A person is a producer for part of his life but a consumer all his life. If there are too many consumers to support, it will influence the improvement of our living standards.

—We love our country. A large population is a big obstacle to our four modernizations. Being the inheritors of our country we must carry out its population policy. This is the glorious duty of every citizen and it reflects one's patriotic spirit.

—(Before) I never thought that a large population would do great harm or that population growth was closely connected with the realization of our socialist modernizations. . . . it is very necessary for young people to have only one child. I will have only one.

—When my aunt gave birth to a girl my uncle told my grandmother he could afford to have a son even if he would be fined . . . I told granny that uncle was wrong to 'buy' a son. If all the peasants try to have more children, our future life will be destroyed. I told her everything had learned in class. Then my grandma criticized my uncle and made him give up the strange idea. I feel a little proud because I have done something for my country.

This kind of zeal may be revolutionary, but is not new in China. As early as 1972 Ruth Sidel observed that, "planned birth is a direct contribution that every young couple can make to the building to China. Limiting one's family becomes a gain for society, not an individual loss, and some of the zeal attached to other revolutionary values such as working to prevent famine or studying Mao's works rubs off on the issue of birth control." Although special programs of population education will probably now be extended to all schools, the essential message seems to have been absorbed already. This is shown in a 1988 survey of 6,000 Sichuan high school students carried out by the Cornell Population and Development Program, in collaboration with the China Population Information Center. Nine-tenths of them correctly identified the size of world population on a multiple-choice question.[5] (When we asked the same question to similar national samples in Peru, Costa Rica and Colombia, in the best of the three countries only 15 percent of the students answered correctly.) Asked about the ideal number of children for a Chinese family, 57 percent said one child or no children, 39 percent said two, and only 4 percent said three or more. While considerably smaller than the preferences of adolescents in other countries, the students were not merely parroting the "party line," which, in 1988, essentially supported the one-child family. These general ideals make their own intentions even more dramatic. Asked how many children that they think they will have, six percent of the 6,000 students said none and 78 percent said one. In short, the ideal of a small family (no more than two) is clearly preferred, but an even smaller family—one child is what they expect to have. The difference, I believe, is due to the students' willingness to make sacrifices in their nation's welfare.[6] Thus, when given a multiple choice question concerning the most important reason for having a small family, two-thirds said it was for the welfare of the nation or community, while only one-third said it was for the welfare of either parents or children.

CONCLUSIONS

Since the revolution of 1949, the Chinese have followed a long and tortuous path toward effective population control, arriving at their present policy only after a great deal of controversy, trial, and error. The policy has shifted with the political winds and details of it are still under discussion; e.g., whether the population should be held at 1.2 billion, allowed to grow somewhat, or rolled back to 600 or 700 million; whether a two-child norm with longer birth intervals should be substituted for the one-child policy; whether education should be stressed over fines and disincentives.[7] No one, however, is debating the need to limit population, and no one contests that it is the business of the state to control it.

What can other countries learn from all of this? First, is the importance of technology. Even the Chinese could not make a go of the program before adequate contraceptives became available. For countries with lower motivational levels than the Chinese, technology that makes contraception even easier is still needed, and international efforts to develop a wider range of male and female methods need to be reinforced. We can also see the importance of good organization that reaches down to the village and neighborhood with contraceptive supplies, accompanied by mass media and person-to-person communication and monitoring. Few countries have the deeply penetrating political organization that makes such a program workable, but certain aspects of Chinese organization deserve experimental programs in less authoritarian nations; e.g., an independent Ministry of Family Planning, incentives and disincentives to groups and organizations as well as to individuals, the negotiation of annual population targets at all administrative levels, and the massive use of volunteers. Other countries could also learn much from how the Chinese use program statistics for motivating staffs and for continually relating achievements to goals. Finally, we have seen the importance of ideology and the linking of personal family behavior with patriotic goals. This is a lesson that all nations concerned about rapid population growth should study carefully.

What the developed nations might learn would be more tolerance toward systems unlike their own, especially systems that work. There are thin lines between information, education, persuasion, arm-twisting, and coercion; and the placement of the lines varies from culture to culture. The Reagan administration's decision to stop all contributions to the UNFPA because of Chinese "coercive abortion"[8] punishes all developing countries because of China's alleged sin. The price for such lofty ethics is high. The economic and environmental interdependence of the peoples of the world has never been so critical. We are all in the same fragile boat, and one out of every five passengers is Chinese. The other passengers should be grateful to their traveling companions for their unusual and successful efforts to curb population growth. China should be rewarded, not punished.

COMMENTS BY DONALD MANN, PRESIDENT, NPG, INC.

In his most interesting and informative paper, Dr. Stycos brings out many important points with regard to China's population policies—"the most radical program of population control the world has ever seen."

I agree wholeheartedly with his concluding sentences: "The economic and environmental interdependence of the peoples of the world has never been so critical. We are all in the same fragile boat, and one out of every five passengers is Chinese. The other passengers should be grateful to their travelling companions for their unusual and successful efforts to curb population growth. China should be rewarded, not punished."

The principal features of the Chinese population program should be adopted by other less developed countries. They must move beyond reliance on mere family planning (which asserts the absolute right of couples to decide the number of children they have, regardless of the demographic consequences) to population planning, with emphasis on family limitation and small families (one child, or two at most).

Failure to move beyond family planning will almost certainly result in economic and ecological catastrophe, as the populations of this already greatly overpopulated group of countries continue to grow to perhaps three or four times their present size.

That being said, I would like to examine briefly what China has accomplished until now, and what still remains to be done, if that huge country is to be ultimately successful in achieving a population size that is both ecologically sound and economically sustainable.

China's present population size is slightly over 1.1 billion. It is increasing by about 14 million a year, and is projected to reach nearly 1.3 billion by the year 2000, and 1.523 billion by the year 2020. The latter figure would represent an increase of about 420 million in the space of thirty-one years. By way of comparison, the combined population of the U.S., Canada, Mexico and Central America is 390 million.

China's present total fertility rate (TFR) is about 2.4 (a completed family size of 2.4 children, on average). This in itself represents a remarkable achievement. By comparison, the TFR of the less developed countries excluding China is 4.1. Nevertheless, 2.4 is still far above the below replacement level TFR that will be necessary if China is to succeed in halting and then reversing its population growth.

Furthermore, while China's TFR dropped precipitously in the 1970s, the current rate is approximately equal to that in 1981. There have been, of course, fluctuations in the rate from year to year, but it would be fair to state that during the 1980s no progress has been made in lowering it.

What, in NPG's view, should be the goals of China's population policy at this time? We believe that China should consider as an eventual goal a population size that does not exceed 500 million, and that a TFR of about 1.5 should be the goal for the next several decades. To achieve those goals, we believe that China will need to renew and continue its emphasis on the one-child family.

In order to put those views in perspective, I should like to state briefly what NPG considers to be the essential elements of any national population policy, whether it be for China or for any other country.

1. The first is a specific goal for a stabilized population size, a size that would be economically and ecologically sustainable for the very long term, and would permit an adequate standard of living for everyone. That goal could be expressed in terms of long-range carrying capacity, in terms of an optimum population size, or in terms of a maximum population size not to be exceeded. Since such a specific goal could never be determined with scientific precision, any given nation would have to decide, on the basis of the preponderance of present evidence, the goal to agree on. That goal, of course, should be subject to periodic review as new evidence comes to light. For example, the

carrying capacity of any given nation is most likely to shrink over an extended period of time as the earth's resources, including fossil fuels, continue to be depleted.

Given the many imponderables, and our lack of understanding at present of our ecosystem, it would seem obvious that prudent planning would require a large margin of error in calculations of carrying capacity.

2. Second, what total fertility rate (TFR) would be needed in order to achieve the population size decided upon, and within what time frame?

3. Third, what population programs would be necessary in order to achieve the fertility rate decided upon?

With regard to China specifically, our recommendation above that it consider a goal of not over 500 million as an eventual stabilized population size is somewhat lower than the goal of 700 million already advocated by some Chinese environmental and population experts. To its great credit, China is the only less developed country that has considered actually reducing its population size.

In order to halt and then reverse its population growth as soon as it is humanely possible to do so, a TFR substantially below the long-term replacement rate would be necessary. Nothing short of that is sufficient to break the momentum of past population growth. Because of that momentum, the populations of most less developed countries would double even after replacement level fertility is reached, a doubling the world's environment might not withstand.

For the admittedly herculean task for China to achieve a TFR substantially below the long-term replacement rate, I see no alternative to a renewed and then continued emphasis on the one-child family. If about half of all couples had only one child, and half had two children, the resulting TFR would be around 1.5.

No one familiar with China's experience until now could underestimate the difficulties of implementing a one-child policy. Such a program must inevitably result in some personal sacrifice, and carry with it a considerable burden in social costs. We should bear in mind, however, that such a program would only need to last for several decades at most.

In addition, even the sacrifices and social costs involved with a one-child policy would be relatively minor when compared to the vast and probably permanent state of human suffering and misery that continued population growth would bring in its wake.

In trying to halt its population growth, China is faced with a gargantuan task. Great progress has already been made, but a great deal more remains to be done. It is very much in our own national interest, and in the interest of all nations, that China succeed in its efforts.

The United States, and-all the other developed nations, should extend to China whatever technological and financial assistance is necessary in order to help it succeed.

NOTES:

1. The volunteer effort is another phenomenal aspect of the Chinese program, an aspect that dwarfs the efforts of private family planning organizations in the West or in other LDCS. Half the nation's 2,300 counties and 115,000 of the nation's 970,000 villages have Family Planning Associations, with nearly six million members. The volunteers do everything from agricultural

extension (combined with a family planning message) to distributing pills and condoms. The plan is to have one volunteer for each half dozen couples by 1990, and a membership of 40 million. The Association has 2,500 full-time and 36,000 part-time paid workers. See *People*, 16, 1, 1989.

2. The U.S. birth rate was thirty as late as 1910, dropped to nineteen during the height of the depression, peaked at twenty-five in 1955, and has leveled out at about fifteen since the 1970s.
3. For China as a whole the abortion ratio was forty-eight per 100 births in 1987. In the State of New York it was seventy-five in 1985, and 43 for the U.S. (*Statistical Abstract of the United States*, 1988: 69.)
4. A review of sixteen such studies carried out between 1983 and 1985 found the mean preferred number to range from 1.2 to 1.8 in six urban surveys, and from 1.6 to 2.5 in ten rural surveys. (Whyte and Gu, 1987: 475.)
5. The current generation of Sichuan high school students is within easy reach of the mass media. 81 percent of their homes have radios, and 71 percent have television sets.
6. A survey conducted in a traditional fishing village asked an adult sample how many children they would want if the present government policy did not exist. Nearly nine out of every ten said they would want three or more. (Freedman and Guo, 1988: 133)
7. The new head of the National Family Planning Commission, tleng Peiyun, said recently that "a much greater reliance . . . must be placed on 'education' in family planning activities . . . to convince the masses of the need to control population growth in macro-economic terms."
8. The number of abortions per 100 live births has declined from fifty-nine in 1985 to forty-eight in 1987, not far from the U.S. rate of forty-two. (*Outlook*, 1989: 2)

REFERENCES:

The following references have been quoted or have been especially helpful:

1. John S. Aird. 1972. "Population Policy and Demographic Prospects in the People's Republic of China" National Institutes of Health.
2. R. Freedman and Shenyand Guo. 1988. "Response of a Traditional Fishing Community to China's Family Planning Program." *International Family Planning Perspectives*, 131–36.
3. Guoguang Liu, et al. 1987. *China's Economy in 2000.* Beijing: New World Press.
4. Ruth Sidel. 1973. *Women and Child Care in China: A Firsthand Report*. Penguin Books.
5. H. Yuan Tien. 1983. "China: Demographic Billionaire." *Population Bulletin* Vol. 38, No. 2.
6. World Fertility Survey. 1984. *Fertility in the Developing World.*
7. M. K. Whyte and S. J. Gu. 1987. "Popular Responses to China's Fertility Transition." *Population and Development Review* 471–93.

SECURE IDENTIFICATION: THE WEAK LINK IN IMMIGRATION CONTROL

David Simcox

May 1989

Immigration control rests on a precarious paper structure of certificates, affidavits and identification documents.

The public servants who distribute the complicated rewards and penalties of our immigration system must decide on the basis of documents with a dizzying diversity of origins and degree of reliability. These are the documents that attest to your identity and nationality, your occupation and education, and importantly—because our immigration system confers special rewards for kinship—your family ties.

This dependence on questionable documents presented by interested parties compares in administrative absurdity to what would be an effort by the Internal Revenue Service to collect income taxes without W-2s or other corroboration—trusting the individual taxpayer to state honestly his taxable income.

THE PARADISE OF DOCUMENT FORGERS

The United States can do little about the quality and reliability of foreign documents. But our nation manages the vital identification documents of its own residents with a remarkable complacency. In the words of the Reverend Theodore Hesburgh, onetime chairman of the Select Commission on Immigration and Refugee Policy, the United States is a "document forgers' paradise." Basic civil documents are issued by over seven thousand jurisdictions. The lack of uniformity, uneven quality, and relaxed rules of issuance of many of these documents guarantees widespread abuse.

Falsified or stolen vital statistics records become "breeder documents" for a chain of false documents that open the doors to highly-prized entitlements-legal resident status for illegal aliens, social security, food stamps, unemployment compensation, and guaranteed student loans. The birth certificate of most citizens is easily and, in some states, legally, obtainable by imposters, even though that document can become the first big step to unearned citizenship. Immigration control is not the only national interest at risk because of the nation's insouciant approach to the security of individual identification. The 1976 Federal Advisory Commission on False Identification (FACFI) found that easy access to false identification aided broad patterns of crime and abuse, from drug smuggling and money laundering to fraudulent veterans claims and evasion of warrants.

Particularly troubling is the contamination by unreliable "breeder documents" of other identification systems that must depend on them. **Some four million social security numbers are now being used by more than one person.** With the legalization of three million illegal aliens under the 1986 amnesty, some state motor vehicle authorities have had to institute their own amnesties to reissue driver's licenses to newly legalized aliens who originally got them with false names and social security numbers.

The 1986 amnesty itself bears witness to two decades of negligence in controlling illegal immigration. Nearly one fifth of the 1.8 million applicants for general amnesty originally entered the country not by sneaking across the border, but by using documents that were altered or obtained under false pretenses. Legalization itself has stimulated further widespread abuses of documents. Officials of the Immigration and Naturalization Services (INS) estimate that half or more of the 1.2 million applicants for legal residence under the Special Agricultural Workers (SAW) program presented fraudulent information about themselves or their work histories.

ENFORCEMENT CRIPPLED BY FALSE DOCUMENTS

The central enforcement feature of the 1986 immigration reforms—penalties against employers of illegal aliens—has what could be a fatal flaw: it depends on the soundness of existing identification documents for employers to determine the job seeker's right to work in the United States. Document fraud has become a major enforcement hindrance.

INS surveys of three hundred southern California businesses in early 1988 showed that virtually every one of them employed illegal alien workers who got around the law by presenting counterfeit identification. Interviews of three hundred illegal alien workers in southern California in 1988 by immigration scholar Wayne Cornelius revealed that forty-one percent of them either purchased fraudulent documents or borrowed those of a friend or relative. Some unscrupulous employers aid prospective employees to get false documents. Even well intentioned employers are hard pressed to judge the validity of the confusing variety of ID documents they receive.

False documents are also undercutting the efforts of authorities to deny public assistance to illegal aliens under SAVE, a computer matching program to screen out the unentitled. Aliens able to present documents showing citizenship can bypass this check.

THE NATIONAL HUNGER FOR RELIABLE IDENTIFICATION

Despite our vulnerability to massive illegal immigration and citizenship fraud, the widespread perception of the threat to individual privacy from a national ID card blocks serious remedies. FACFI itself refused to endorse the concept of a national ID card. And Congress, in enacting the 1986 immigration reforms, explicitly disavowed any intent to authorize one.

Even as we hesitate about an effective national identification system, federal agencies, state governments and private companies have created far-reaching specialized identification systems linked to vast banks of data about millions of citizens. A complex society's insistence that we share more and more information about ourselves—and our vulnerability to misuse of this data—has heightened our need for reliable identification. The driver's license, though issued by the states with relatively few security precautions, has become a **de facto** national ID document—so much in demand that the states issue "non-drivers" cards to residents needing proof of their identity.

Rather than protect our privacy, our present decentralized system jeopardizes the right of citizens to protection of the privacy and security of their own identities. Each of us runs the risk of having such uniquely personal documents as his birth certificate, academic credentials, social security number, and even death certificate appropriated by others.

SCREENING OUT THE INELIGIBLE: TELEPHONE VERIFICATION AND IMPROVED SOCIAL SECURITY CARDS

In passing the 1986 reforms, Congress called for evaluations of the soundness of existing identification documents with recommendations for improvements. Following Congress's orders, INS in 1987 studied the feasibility of a system for confirming work eligibility by telephone; the General Accounting Office (GAO) evaluated the security of the social security card; and the Social Security Administration (SSA) in 1987 and 1988 tested a call-in system for validating the 210 million social security numbers now in use.

INS found telephone verification feasible and now plans a pilot project permitting employers to use touchtone phones or "point of sale" devices to check the alien registration numbers of foreign job applicants against a data base held by INS. The INS master index will ultimately be expanded to include additional identifiers on each alien, such as social security numbers and even digital fingerprint codes. (State governments will tap the same master index to verify the legal status of alien applicants for public assistance).

In its study of the social security card, the GAO concluded that the present requirement that the nation's 7 million employers judge the validity of literally hundreds of different acceptable documents cannot be made fraud-proof. GAO proposed that the social security card become the sole document for confirming work eligibility. Warning that the current social security card, with sixteen versions in use, is easily counterfeited, GAO recommended technical changes to make it secure. But GAO's study stressed the underlying dilemma in devising better identification—technical security features are of no avail if the breeder documents remain unreliable.

SSA field office employees review millions of applications for cards each year. They must determine whether each applicant is who he says he is and whether the birth certificate and other documents he submits are genuine. Social security employees are able to verify less than one percent of the documents they look at. Fifty percent of a sample of social security employees interviewed by GAO believed that fraudulent documents were getting through.

SSA concluded from its 1987–1988 study that a card validation system was technically feasible, though its high costs and the inherent shortcomings of the card as a reliable identifier would reduce its utility. SSA recommended as an alternative that all state drivers' licenses carry the bearer's social security number validated by SSA (twenty-nine states now require the number). SSA has opposed making its card a national identifier, chiefly because of the high cost of producing and issuing new cards. While it is technically possible to add security features to the card such as unique personal characteristics and biometric indicators (e.g. photos, and digitized fingerprints or signatures), civil libertarians and their allies in Congress would see much moves as steps toward a national ID card.

Meanwhile, SSA is tightening its antifraud training and procedures. INS now prepares and submits directly to SSA applicants for cards for newly legalized aliens. Registrars of vital statistics in nearly half the states now obtain cards for infants at birth.

MACHINE READABLE TRAVEL DOCUMENTS

Skyrocketing numbers of international travelers and growing concern for security have quickened movement toward more secure, machine-readable travel documents and identification cards. **In 1987, customs and immigration officials had to inspect a staggering one-third of a billion persons entering the U.S.**

Machine-readable passports, visas and border crossing cards are more difficult to counterfeit or alter, allow faster but more thorough inspection of each traveler, and permit instantaneous capture of data from each document. Abuse of visas and border crossing cards has accounted for nearly 20 percent of all illegal immigration. Until now, INS ability to check alien visitors in and out of the United States and track overstayers has been limited.

The latest version of INS' "green card," Form I-551 in official parlance, is partly machine-readable. However, various versions of the alien registration card issued before 1979 and still in circulation are easily counterfeited or altered. INS is moving toward a machine-readable card for all permanent resident aliens and a single tamper-proof card for all temporary residents with work authorization.

SAFEGUARDING AMERICA'S CIVIL DOCUMENTS

In 1979 FACFI recommended a range of federal and state actions to protect the integrity of the birth certificate. FACFI urged uniformity of format and other characteristics, centralization of issuing authority in each state, tighter controls over certificate forms, tougher penalties for fraud, recordkeeping of requests for certificates, and more training to sensitize vital statistics personnel to fraud. Concerned over the frequency of fraudulent use of birth certificates of deceased Americans, particularly infants, FACFI called for the matching of birth and death certificates.

State legislatures have considered many of these proposals since the 1970s, but change has been slow. **The United States, long in the vanguard of sophisticated information technology, approaches the twenty-first century with vital statistics recordkeeping not far removed from the era of the quill pen.**

Twelve of the fifty states—including California, with nearly half of the country's illegal alien population-persist in treating individual birth, marriage and death documents as public records. Three states continue to maintain all original records at the local level. While some twenty states at one time centralized all recording and issuance, heavy pressures from local interests in recent years have reversed this trend.

One area of progress is in the matching of births and infant deaths, now a widespread practice. Some states now match all in-state birth and adult death certificates. But concern over costs and the sheer magnitude of the task has seriously slowed movement toward a comprehensive nationwide procedure for matching births and deaths.

These basic gaps in the security of our national identification network can only be bridged not by advancing technology, but by political will. Technological advances are making feasible the low-cost issuance of tamperproof identification documents for citizens and legal residents such as passports and alien registration and social security cards. But those documents ultimately are only as reliable as the civil records from which they are derived. The birth record of a deceased American obtainable for a fee of five dollars or less, or purchased from a forger for a few hundred dollars, can open the door to the highly coveted entitlements and enhanced earnings that accompany American residence, which are worth hundreds of thousands of dollars over a lifetime.

WHAT CAN BE DONE WITHIN PRESENT POLITICAL LIMITS

Eventually Congress and the nation must come to terms with the political issues blocking creation of a secure national identification system. Our complex, information-intensive society will demand it for a host of reasons that go beyond effective immigration control. Reasoned national debate will show that such a system can help protect our liberties rather than diminish them, and that the experience of Western European democracies demonstrates that free societies can enjoy the security of sound national identification systems with full safeguards against government abuse.

But much can be done now to increase our protection short of creating a national identity card and central population register. The following actions would offer the best chances for positive results in the short term:

Stronger federal leadership in encouraging states to adopt **tighter controls on vital statistics documents**, with greater federal support for a national system of matching birth and death records.

Conversion to a **tamperproof social security card bearing unique personal identifying data** and biometric indicators. To deal with the added expense and workload, the improved card could be phased in with free issuance to all first-time registrants and issuance at cost and on request to existing cardholders. Its value as a quality identification document would ensure a heavy demand.

Alternatively, if resistance to a secure social security card is too great, evolution of the drivers' licensing systems of the fifty states into a decentralized but standardized national identification system, using digitized fingerprints, photos and validated social security numbers could be started.

Higher priority for creation of a system of **telephone verification** of work eligibility and expansion of the INS master index of alien registration data to include social security numbers, digitized fingerprints and other identifiers.

Early distribution of single **tamperproof alien registration cards** for legal permanent residents and a single counterfeit-proof card for all temporary residents authorized to work, thus easing the dilemmas of employers in hiring decisions.

Resumption of the requirement ended in 1981 that all aliens in the U.S. report their presence yearly to the INS. Besides providing valuable demographic data, **an annual inscription of the alien population** would help fill gaps in the INS master index and would permit the agency to screen out fraudulent, outdated or erroneous immigration documents.

NOTES:

Materials for this article were taken from:

1. U.S. Congress, Senate Judiciary Committee: Hearings on False Identification Documents (No. J-97-111); Washington, June 16, 1982.
2. U.S. Congress, Senate Committee on Governmental Affairs: Hearings on Computer Matching and Privacy Protection Act of 1986, 99th Congress; Washington, September 16, 1986.
3. U.S. Congress: Congressional Record, Senate, Speech of Senator Robert Dole, October 21, 1988.
4. General Accounting Office: "New Alien Identification Systems—Little Help in Stopping Illegal Aliens;" Report GGD-79-44 of May 30, 1979.
5. General Accounting Office: "Immigration Control: A New Role for the Social Security Card; " Report HRD-88-4 of March, 1988.
6. General Accounting Office: "Computer Systems: Overview of Federal Systems for Processing Aliens Seeking U.S. Entry; " Report IMTEC-88-55BR of September 1988.
7. U.S. Department of Health and Human Services: Inspector General's Report on ''False Identification: The Problems and Technological Options;" December 1982.

8. U.S. Department of Health and Human Services: Report to Congress of the Secretary of Health and Human Services: "A Social Security Number Validation System: Feasibility, Costs and Privacy Considerations;" December 15, 1988.
9. U.S. Department of Health and Human Services: National Center for Health Statistics: Model State Vital Statistics Act and Regulations, 1977.
10. U.S. Department of Justice, Federal Advisory Committee on False Identification: Report on the Criminal Use of False Identification; November 1976.
11. Interviews with officials of Departments of State, Justice, Health and Human Services and with Senate Committee Staff members; November/December 1988 and January 1989.

RECONCILING TEXAS AND BERKELEY: THE CONCEPT OF OPTIMUM POPULATION

Lindsey Grant

November 1989

Images float in the mind's eye. I recall (probably from some long ago Western) a scene of horses in deep grasses, and I remember a quotation in a history book describing the arrival of the Anglos in Arizona a century or so ago: " . . . the grass was up to the horses' bellies."

More immediately, this year, I was in the Glorieta Pass in northern New Mexico, at a National Monument surrounding the remains of the Pecos Pueblo. It sits on a low ridge partly enclosing a shallow swale. And that little flat valley was a miracle: a profusion of tall grasses and sedges and weeds, full of birds. They owed their existence to their "exclosure"—the specialists love that word—from the effects of domestic cattle grazing.

What have we lost? The ranch that surrounds that little valley is a rich man's ranch, protected from the brutal overgrazing that one sees everywhere in the West, particularly on Indian reservations but also (whatever the statistics may claim) on BLM (Bureau of Land Management) and private lands. But it bore no comparison with that little protected area, for beauty, for diversity of life, or even-for that matter-for the amount of food that it could produce for human use if only we would live within our environment rather than savaging it.

To judge from the newspapers, the nation has discovered that it cannot go on running its affairs as it has. There is a desperate gap between working class incomes and urban housing costs. We are degrading the air, making the climate worse, poisoning our water supplies, wiping out the Chesapeake Bay fishery and the Everglades' wildlife, overgrazing the land, losing soil and damaging our forest resources. We do not know what to do with radioactive wastes. Our bills for garbage are trebling and quintupling, and our cities send trucks to other states and garbage scows wandering around the world seeking a place to unload. There are reports of beaches paved with human excrement.

These problems are driven by three variables: population size, per capita consumption, and the technologies involved—the ways we produce and consume. To put the population aspect more starkly: **At any given level of conservation and technology, the problems are roughly proportional to the size of the population involved.** (I say "roughly" because there are niceties such as thresholds and non-linearities; but they generally aggravate the problem rather than ameliorating it, and the statement remains a good rule of thumb.)

Having recognized the problems, the nation seeks solutions in technological fixes and pleas for conservation. Population has been almost wholly ignored as a part of the problem and of the solutions. It is a bit like a Restoration bedroom farce, with the actors looking for the culprit in every direction but the right one; but this time it is not funny.

There are other problems linked intimately with population and population change, but in more complex ways. As an example, I will later touch upon the interconnected phenomena of growing income disparities, drugs, violence and alienation in the ghetto. These are not simply the results of Reaganite policies. They reflect underlying demographic trends. They are seldom addressed in those terms.

RECONCILING TEXAS AND BERKELEY

With injustice to some, I typify Texas as the spiritual home of the viewpoint that "I am entitled to a great big air conditioned car, and I have the right to drive it as fast as I want." (Our President is a Texan from Connecticut, and his relaxation is—or was—cruising about in a Cigarette speedboat, a vehicle designed primarily to maximize gas consumption.) I use Berkeley as proxy for believers in alternative life styles, bicycles for transport, and a vegetarian diet so as to feed corn to hungry foreigners rather than American beef cattle.

In order to disengage these two proponents from each other's throat, may I suggest that their differences are driven by a force that neither of them addresses: population growth. To repeat my homily in another form: the big automobile becomes an environmental threat and the steak an immoral diversion of resources only when the number of automobiles begins to exceed the capacity of the atmosphere to buffer the exhaust, or population outruns the capacity of the land to support a beef diet.

Texas need not fear that somebody will take away its air conditioned cars and thereby make life in Texas once again intolerable, if it will recognize that its views about them are irreconcilable with its advocacy (among employers, at least) of an unfettered supply of cheap, illegal labor from Mexico.

I choose to believe that a nation that can land men on the moon can learn the pentagonal relationship among

- consumption levels,
- population
- environmental sustainability,
- as influenced by foreseeable technologies and
- the availability of capital to apply them.

The more we incline toward the "Texas" view of consumption, the smaller the population the environment can bear.

FREEDOM, SOCIAL CONSTRAINTS AND POPULATION

Conspicuous consumption is only the subcase. The broader issue is the trade-off between freedom and social responsibility. In the land of the celluloid cowboy, the good people of Los Angeles are already being told that they must give up their backyard barbeques, and before long they will learn that they must trade in their beloved automobiles for their own good and ours.

Everywhere, industrialists and common folk alike chafe at being told by earnest environmentalists that they can no longer behave as they have been behaving. If the friction is intense, and probably rising, it is perhaps because we are traversing the fault zone between two powerful and antithetical world views.

The idea of personal freedom is very strong in this country, and it has deep roots. With a sparse population and a seemingly limitless environment, a man is worth a great deal, and a tree is not worth much. It is probably no accident that John Ball's ringing assertion of the rights of man came in the wake of the Black Plague, when labor in England was suddenly very scarce, and that it found an echo in the Declaration of Independence and Tom Paine three centuries later when this embryonic nation stood on the edge of a wilderness.

Meanwhile, science has been revising Western civilization's image of mankind's place on Earth. That image has shrunk in less than four centuries from a central role, the possessor and beneficiary of a timeless Earth itself central to the Universe—and in personal communication with an anthropomorphic deity concerned about our fate—to one recent species in the extraordinarily complex and evolving ecology of one small planet, associated with a rather ordinary star part way toward the edge of one among countless galaxies. The Earth is no longer an infinite sheltering mother. It is, in Adlai Stevenson's indelible phrase, a fragile space ship.

And we have become aware that we are managing the space ship very badly. We may be appropriating as much as 41 percent of the Earth's primary terrestrial productivity for human uses.[1] We are suddenly learning the profundity of the risks which we have recently set in motion: the greenhouse effect; an even more dire warning from the 1983 report of the President's Acid Rain Review Panel that human activities may affect "... the denitrifying microbes ... upon which the entire biosphere depends."

Those of us who hear and understand such language respond (shrilly) with demands that societies regulate human activities so as to bring such threats under control. Farewell to the heroic—the frontier—image of personal freedom. Enter the era of mutual coercion to save ourselves from the mess we are creating.

Again, there is a trade-off. If the problem is induced in part by population growth, the severity of the mutual restraints will depend on whether we choose to address that source of the environmental pressures.

—not that it will be easy, either to come to a consensus or to act on it.

MAXIMUM POPULATION, "SUSTAINABILITY" AND OPTIMUM POPULATION

This population-freedom trade-off is almost universally ignored. When scientists have dealt with population limits at all, it has generally been at the very crude stage of trying to estimate what maximum population can be fed. It seems to me that this is the wrong question. It would be better to investigate what numbers are **desirable.**

Aside from that, maximum population studies have generally been flawed in two ways:

- They deal with one variable, food, as if the complexity of the Earth could be reduced to an equation of arable land, yields and consumers. (One FAO study—by way of example—simply assumed the conversion of forests into fields wherever it was arable, without considering the likely effects: the loss of firewood to cook the food, the effects on rainfall, water supplies and agriculture itself, the disruption of the ecosystem, the loss of biodiversity, the economic impacts, the broader effects upon climate.)
- It is a one-shot concept. It does not attempt to judge whether its own assumptions would lead to a declining resource base and a decline in the maximum population itself.

"Maximum population" is a slippery number. It has moved up with the burst of agricultural technology. It can move down again as some of that technology proves environmentally unbearable, or as climate changes and fields erode. It can be driven down suddenly by a natural calamity such as drought or a volcanic explosion like the one (Agung) that created the worldwide "year without a summer" in 1816, or perhaps by disruptions such as disorder in oil producing countries.

A maximum population is a vulnerable one, since it has no slack. It cannot drop back to lower consumption levels in the wake of a disaster, except through hunger and disease and rising death rates.

The word **sustainability** has become a rallying point for environmentalists. Briefly, it is the goal of running the world's economies in a way that insures that we pass an undiminished environment to our heirs. It was a central theme of the report of the World Commission on Environment and Development or "Brundtland commission."[2]

The ecological issues facing us have been well described.[3] The reader who is not generally familiar with the evidence must either be remarkably insouciant, or perhaps have a pillow over his ears. I can envy the first and sympathize with the second. For those of us between the two extremes, however, sustainability is a good ethical guideline.

The proponents of "sustainability" have dealt only in passing with population, but they have added a new dimension to the idea of "maximum population." It should not be so large as to degrade the carrying capacity of the system.

Environmental degradation—the failure of sustainability—is eroding carrying capacity in much of the third world and already reducing theoretical maximum populations. We should not automatically assume that the United States is immune. Already, by the standard of sustainability, the **United States is overpopulated or mismanaged, or both, since we are depleting our per capita natural resources and impairing the environment.**

Environmental thinking must take the next step beyond "sustainability. " The issue is not just pollution control. We need to bring human activities into better balance with the rest of the Earth's ecosystem. Environmentalists are regularly accused of "caring more about trees than people." The environmentalists are justified; the two forms of life are interdependent, and the people/tree balance has been badly disturbed. We need a way of reconciling the concern for humanity with the broader concern for the system that supports us.

It is no wonder that, from Gaia to Earth Firsters, the era is full of people trying to work their way toward some new philosophy that relates humankind to the totality of Earth. Any such philosophy must incorporate a viewpoint as to how many of us there should be. **Population must be treated, like sulfate emissions, as a variable subject to conscious human decisions.** In some instances, technological fixes alone may be enough, but I doubt there will be many. For an extreme case, take Holland. They have announced an official goal of reducing sulfate and nitrogen oxide emissions 70 to 80 percent. I think they will find that goal simply unattainable without a dramatic decline in population or living standards, especially as global warming drives the sea higher on their dikes. They do not have a population policy. They are badly going to need one.

Thus enters the concept of **optimum population.**

POPULATION POLICY BY DEFAULT . . .

Here in the United States, there is something of an intellectual vacuum at the center of what is arguably the central issue of our time. The issue is whether and how governments should attempt to influence demographic change. The vacuum is the lack of any systematic way of deciding what the optimum population might be.

I imagine one could find agreement with the idea that Africa or Central America would be better off with smaller populations-even if the thought is dismissed as visionary. The thought is hardly even raised with respect to the United States, and yet there is no necessary reason for assuming that the only possible direction is up.

The Rockefeller commission in 1972 concluded that it saw no benefit from further population growth in the United States, and it proposed family planning and immigration policies to bring that growth gradually to a halt.[4] That was some 40 million Americans ago, and it seems to have been forgotten.

The failure to address the issue does not mean that we are avoiding it. **The United States has a population policy, or policies. We don't think we have one; and that perhaps is the most dangerous of situations.** The decisions the nation takes, about taxation—policy, welfare, urban policy and housing, transportation policies, day care for children, abortion or immigration, will all influence population change, and population change in turn will influence those policies. Perhaps it would be wise to try to understand what we are doing.

. . . OR BY DESIGN: OPTIMUM POPULATION

There is an opportunity here for new thinking. Fertility in the United States is now below replacement level, and our population growth is increasingly a function simply of immigration, which—at least in theory—is a variable more accessible to deliberate national control than is fertility. At current fertility levels, the United States would be headed for a turnaround in population growth in thirty or forty years, were it not for immigration. We—like the Europeans who are ahead of us on that curve[5]—should be thinking about the prospect and deciding whether or not we like it. And the results of that thinking should be incorporated in national policies.

The term "optimum population" seems to have originated with Sir Julian Huxley:

> The recognition of an optimum population size (of course relative to technological and social conditions) is an indispensable first step towards that planned control of population which is necessary if man's blind reproductive urges are not to wreck his ideals and his plans for material and spiritual betterment.

There were, at about the time of the Rockefeller Commission study, at least two academic efforts to define "optimum population."[6] They may seem dated now, but some of the participants argued that one must define optimum population, not in terms of whether you can get away with it, but in order to set a target that would help achieve the greatest human well-being. They did not try to agree on a definition or to propose numbers, but they suggested at least the direction for the inquiry.

Optimum population obviously must be small enough so that we do not endanger the environment that supports us, but it is not dictated by that alone. It is, presumably, **some magic point that best reconciles all the different goals that are related to demography:** prosperity; full employment; maximum productivity per person; livable housing accessible to satisfying employment; social equity and some agreed criteria as to reasonable levels of consumption; national security; open spaces and the preservation of resources; the quality of the air we breathe and the water we drink; leisure; education and cultural amenities; and indeed "liberty and the pursuit of happiness."

THE WANT OF TOOLS

The process of groping toward "optimum population" will not be intellectually rigorous. That is the fault of the state of the art rather than of the authors. The intellectual disciplines have not been developed to handle complex systems where multiple causes lead to multiple results, and everything is connected.

Keynesian/post-Keynesian economics and the scientific method are the two dominant disciplines of the era, and neither is satisfactory for our purposes. Macroeconomics hinders more than it guides the search for optimum population.

- It is a theory of equilibrium, and it does not contain the concepts for the study of growth or change or scale or limits.
- It puts an economic value upon the processes that destroy natural resources-and it puts a value on the belated efforts to correct the damage-but it does not value the natural world until it enters the economy.[7]
- It puts a value on the supply of amenities that once were free, and thus overstates the well-being of a crowded society as compared to an uncrowded one. One can think of hundreds of economic goods and services that inflate the GNP and create the illusion of prosperity, but in fact simply represent efforts to deal with problems that exist only because of crowding. Starting, perhaps, with parking meters and traffic jams.

The scientific method works best when one can study simple systems with single causes, holding all other variables constant. There is no way within these disciplines, or any others available to us, to come to or defend very precise statements as to what population size would be "optimum."

And there is the problem of value judgements. The dilemma is still with us that Jeremy Bentham encountered (but did not solve) when he stated the goal of "the greatest good for the greatest number."One cannot multiply apples and oranges, or make other than a value judgement in trying to decide which is better: one apple each for four people; or two apples each for two people? There is no scientific way of judging the tradeoffs between individual liberty, social responsibility, and the protection of the Earth. These are value judgements, but they must be made.

And there is technological change. Different technologies can support vastly different numbers of people. For the purposes of this exercise, let us assume current technology as a starting point and attempt to identify whether and in what areas technological changes may justify a change in our conclusions as to what population would be optimum. (Labor saving technology may come to seem much less important, and the critical technologies may be those that offer benign ways of increasing agricultural yields and those that reduce pollution.)

And finally, change itself, and the rate at which it occurs, will affect capital formation, employment, education, Social Security and other national interests. (I believe that this can be overstated, but I have dealt with this issue elsewhere.)[8]

This all being said, there are **now approaches that may be of help.** "Foresight" systems and "alternative futures" studies offer hope, precisely because they are intended to deal with multiple variables. The emerging methodology of "systems analysis" is an effort to bring mathematical discipline to the study of complex and interacting systems.[9]
There have been periodic journalistic exercises undertaking to measure the "livability" of cities, using nine different indices: climate and terrain; housing (stock, price, heating and cooling costs, mortgage rates and taxes); health care and environment (air and water pollution, hay fever); crime; transportation (how hard is it to get to work?); education; the arts; recreation and sports; and personal economics (living costs, incomes, taxes and jobs).[10]

The high scoring cities tend to be the smaller ones with living space, stable neighborhoods, low housing prices and low taxes. Despite its climate, a recent winner was Pittsburgh. Its population is down, and the steel industry has gone. It should be a basket case. The common wisdom holds that one must have growth for job opportunities, but Pittsburgh in May 1989 had unemployment of only 4.3 percent. There must be a lesson in this, and it would be interesting to run a population correlation with that study.

Zero Population Growth, Inc. (ZPG) has attempted such a correlation, using somewhat different indices, and has found that smaller cities tend to have better environmental and living conditions than larger ones.[11]

We should not disdain the simple approach, used in these "livability" surveys, of identifying and weighting the elements of optimum population, and coming up with a composite number.

No study is likely to result in a consensus, but it will have been a useful exercise if it suggests a range, or even a vector from the present level-and if it brings connections into focus that the nation has ignored in its population non-policy.

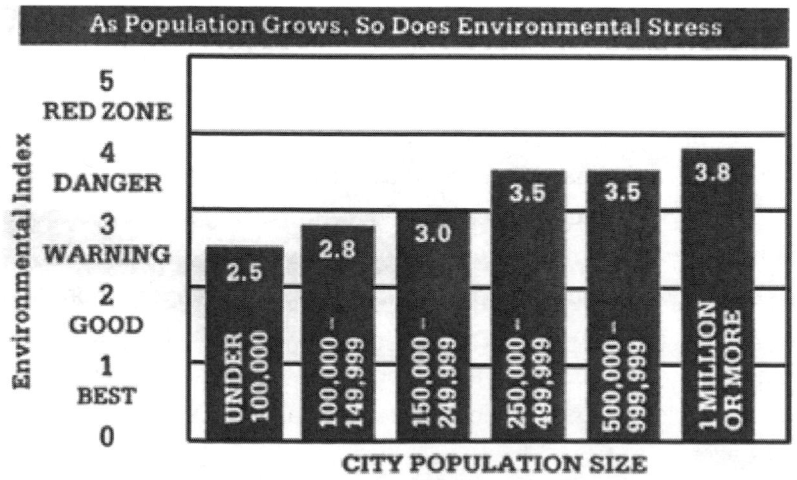

Figure 1.

These suggestions are just a beginning. We need a systematic intellectual framework for studying optimum population, but we cannot simply wait for one. Societies have seldom had the luxury of knowing all about a problem before being obliged to deal with it. We do not have that much time.

THE NO-COST SOLUTION

I have generalized about the connections between population and other issues. It will be the province of later essays in this NPG Forum series to flesh out the details, but let me give a few tentative examples.

Air Pollution, Acid Precipitation and the Greenhouse. Nationally, we are beginning to recognize that we face serious environmental problems. We are trying to deal with them in a typically American way: bull our way through the problem by throwing money at it. President Bush's proposals on clean air are a welcome change from the drought of the Reagan years, but they reflect that mindset. Eventually, we will have to face the issues of how many people? using how many cars? and using them how much? The President's proposals touch only the third of those questions, and only obliquely, and the emphasis is upon technical fixes involving alternative fuels-each of which exacts its own economic and environmental penalties.

Los Angeles' problem is the worst in the nation, and a recent regional proposal for a remedy was estimated to cost $4 billion per year now, and $12 billion per year by 2000.[12]

The scale of the problem is generally proportional to the number of people. We can, and should, practice greater efficiency and seek cleaner technologies, but these are expensive remedies.

If our present population were what it was in 1950, there would be about one-third as many people in Los Angeles, and only 60 percent as many in the United States, and our air pollution problems would be correspondingly smaller.

The same observations can be made, **mutatis mutandi,** about many other national issues.

Energy. As the petroleum era begins to wind down, the United States is crossing the line of 50 percent dependence upon foreign sources of petroleum, at the cost of a considerable addition to our foreign exchange deficit and at some risk from depending upon unstable foreign sources for a vital share of our energy budget.

If our population were still 150 million, and with current consumption patterns, we would now have the choice of a 17 percent dependency on imports, or more oil still in the ground-or more likely, both.

Unemployment and the Ghetto. If there is one clear effect of current technology upon the labor market, it has been to increase the demand for certain skills and to reduce the demand for mass labor. Our demographic non-policy and our immigration policies have been precisely the wrong ones for this situation. The baby boom and high fertility among the poor have created a large pool of unskilled labor. Immigration law has favored the immigration of the unskilled rather than the skilled. The failure to enforce the immigration law has permitted an additional influx of workers competing for the bottom level jobs. The results are visible in the impoverishment of the poor in the past decade (while the rich get richer) [13] and in unemployment in the ghetto. According to current Census and Bureau of Labor Standards statistics, only 55 percent of blacks in their twenties have jobs, compared with 81 percent for other Americans in their twenties.

If one seeks causes for the social breakdown and drug problems in the ghetto, or looks for potential sources of unrest, here is a good starting point.

It would be tempting to proceed on to agriculture and other issues, but I will leave them to the specialists who follow. Let me identify-

The Demographic Role in the Solutions. The most recent Census projections suggest that, if fertility stays where it is and immigration were to be balanced with emigration, the U.S. population would rise slightly to 270 million in the next thirty years and then decline to 220 million by 2080. With net annual immigration at 800,000 (which is a very conservative estimate of the current figure), it would be 333 million in 2080, and rising.[14] A higher immigration rate, which seems likely in view of world population pressures, would of course drive the number higher.

The capital costs of achieving a lower population would be negligible. It would require only a national resolve to limit immigration to refugees most in need of asylum and those potential immigrants who bring needed skills to our economy. Add to that a national goal of "the two child family," and shape social policies (e.g. tax, welfare, housing) to help realize the goal, and we could achieve a lower population more quickly. (If women generally "stopped at two," the total fertility rate would probably decline, since many women have no children).

The two-child family would have other advantages. It is already becoming the accepted norm for more prosperous Americans, if only because of the cost of educating their children. It would provide an equitable rationale for encouraging the poor—and particularly the proliferating unwed teenage mothers—to exercise similar restraint. Since those mothers are frequently poor and unable to provide for their children, such a change would in turn make it easier for society to help educate smaller cohorts of children to participate in the economy and exploit the new technologies. At present, the women having children are the ones who cannot raise them. Women with family incomes over $35,000 average 1.24 children; those with incomes under $10,000 average 2.53. At that rate, the poorest will have more than sixteen great-grandchildren, the most prosperous will have fewer than two.

Moreover, the policy would help to forestall an eventuality that most demographic projections ignore: that fertility and the population may rise if the poor continue to get poorer and as immigrants from high-fertility societies produce a rising proportion of the total population.

If we could forestall or deal with the problems through population policy, and if there are very few visible costs in moving toward a smaller population, why not consider such policies?

When these proposals are aired, the usual reaction is "You can't do it." The answer is "We haven't tried."

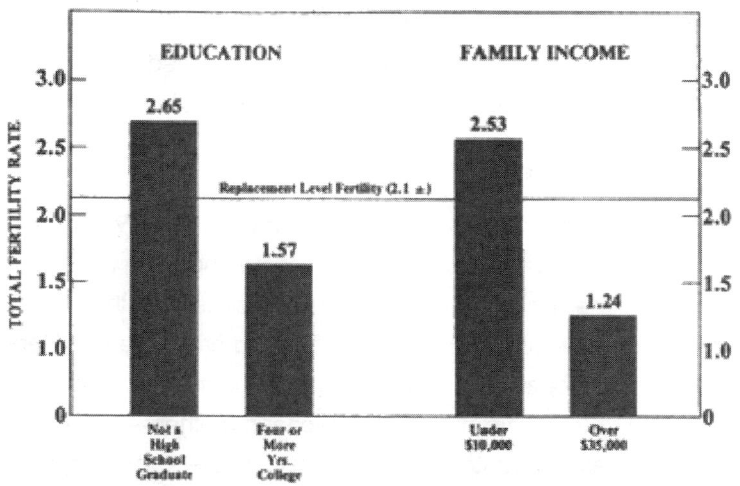

Figure 2.

THE RESISTANCES

There are deep resistances, some of them with good reasons, to the idea of a government policy on population.

"Bigger is Better" is a very deeply held feeling in the outlook of a nation that has been expanding for most of its existence, and that sees itself as a nation of immigrants.

Self Interest. As Garrett Hardin showed in "The Tragedy of the Commons," self interest can conflict with the common good. Realtors, land speculators, businessmen looking for a larger market, educators worried about shrinking school-age populations, may all believe their immediate interest is served by growing numbers, even if they recognize that it would harm the community. And private interest usually wins against the public interest when people take positions.

Putting Man in His Place. To people who like children and who were raised on the injunction "be fruitful and multiply," there is something viscerally disturbing about any proposal to consider reversing course. Perhaps this will change as we come to a shared understanding of mankind's place in the system, but the resistances are enormous.

The Fear of Coercion. We have had a tradition of governmental non-interference in personal affairs, and it is a good one. The problem here is a conflict of objectives. It would be nice to keep that pattern, but what does society do if women's choices about fertility are leading to an unsustainable population? As I said earlier, crowded societies do not leave room for the kinds of freedom that uncrowded ones do.

This issue is of course inflamed by the whole abortion debate, and its sensitivity is well illustrated by the furor that Chinese practices have generated in the United States. Lower fertility can of course be achieved without abortions, in theory, but in practice it seldom if ever happens.

We would do well to recognize at the outset that a country embarks upon a delicate course when it consciously brings fertility into social policy decisions (even though there are already inadvertent impacts.) The line between incentives and disincentives and coercion will need to be honestly and publicly debated.

There is a related problem. How does one avoid penalizing the child—who is guiltless even if it is the eighth child—in the process of trying to dissuade the mother from having more children? I think part of the answer is feeding programs directed at the children rather than welfare provided to mothers who might, in any case, be diverting it to drugs.

Finally, there is a real question as to how much governments can do in a free-enterprise society. The historical evidence is mixed. Both recent and pre-World War II efforts in Europe to encourage higher fertility have had very limited success. On the other hand, through some alchemy of incentives and disincentives and public consensus, the so-called "chopstick cultures" of East Asia have done remarkably well at bringing fertility down, and only in China have there been charges of coercion.

It will take patience and good government to thread away through these issues. Even if all the problems are successfully handled, population change takes a long, long time, as a subsequent essay in this series will make clear.

RESPONSIBILITY FOR A SMALL PLANET

The argument is regularly heard that, since natural increase is now largely a third world phenomenon, population control is important for them but not for us, and that one person is one person, whether in Peru or the United States.

That argument founders on the facts of resource use and pollution. One hears the generalization that, with 5 percent of the world's population, the United States generates one quarter of the pollution. I am not sure that this reflects a serious study, or how such a study would find common units for different kinds of pollution, but certainly with respect to air pollution and climate change, the United States with its present population is a major driving force.

This is not a question of altruism. We share the Earth and the Climate, and we cannot expect that others will reduce their pollution coefficients sufficiently to permit the United States to continue its present ways.

As to the Peruvian migrating to the United States: in so far as he shares in our national life style, he will pollute more than he did in Peru. And we may be sure that one of the first things he will buy, to get to work, is a big old cheap automobile, belching smoke.

OPTIMIZE OR MAXIMIZE

If we do not optimize, we will probably maximize at an unsustainable level, and that is not a very attractive option.

Human tribes have from time to time discovered new technologies or new lands and have prospered for a time, until population growth brought them to the edge once again. In this century **we have had, with the explosion of technology, the greatest opportunity of all to create a world in which all could live decently. And we are in the process of blowing the**

chance because we have been willing to control mortality but not fertility. We think of that as a third world process, but migration brings it home.

The United States courts that fate by its population growth. There is no assurance when we will stop growing. Fertility may rise as the population composition changes. As for immigration, Congress has been immune to the demographic implications and responsive to pressure groups. As a result, every "reform" of the past decade has increased the numbers of legal immigrants.

We in the United States still have an advantage that has been lost to Africa, or India, or China, or Bangladesh. Our range of options is much greater. We have more room for conservation, more money for technical fixes, and we can yield a bit on per capita consumption. We have not driven population up, and consumption down, to the point where the immediate issue is survival. In India, despite the journalistic reports of the "green revolution," all the production gains have not been sufficient to maintain per capita grain consumption at the level of 1900.[15] As anybody familiar with those countries can attest, "maximum" under those circumstances is grim indeed. We have been warned.

We think of our country as a bread basket, but Lester Brown has recently pointed out that the United States in 1988 for the first time in modern history consumed more grain than it produced.[16] With more bad years, perhaps connected with climate change, the first result is more expensive meat, and less of it for the poor. Then, what is the next step? A conscious population policy? another Agung? a gradual erosion?

The choice is ours, but the timing is not. If we do not foresee problems, we will have to try to live with them. If we did all the right things tomorrow, we could only slow down the global greenhouse effect; we could not avoid it. If we should come to a consensus tomorrow that the population of the United States should be smaller, it might take a century or more to reach that level. The momentum of change demands a long perspective.

On that note, we invite our readers into the joint exploration of a landscape still only dimly seen.

REFERENCES:

1. Peter M. Vitouseketal,"Human Appropriation of the Products of Photosynthesis," *Bio Science*, June 1986, pp. 368–373.
2. UN World Commission on Environment & Development, *Our Common Future*. (Oxford University Press, 1987.)
3. See, for instance, World Resources Institute *World Resources 1988–1989* (New York: Basic Books, 1988), and individual reports by the World Resources-Institute, 1735 New York Avenue, Washington DC 20006. Or Lester R. Brown et al, *State of the World 1989* (New York: Norton, 1989) and other Worldwatch papers (Worldwatch Institute, 1776 Massachusetts Avenue, NW, Washington DC 20036.)
4. The Commission on Population Growth and the American Future, *Population and the American Future*, March 27, 1972. (Washington; GPO, 1972.)
5. See Lindsey Grant, "Europe in the Energy Transition: The Case for a Smaller Population," in NPG Forum Series, July 1988.
6. See Noel Hinrichs, Ed., *Population, Environment and People*, for the National Congress on Optimum Population and the Environment, Chicago 1970. (New York:

McGraw Hill, 1971.) And S. Fred Singer, Ed., *Is There an Optimum Level of Population?*, a Population Council book (New York: McGraw Hill, 1971.)

7. To their credit, several economists have experimented with changes in the national accounts calculations to bring resource depletion or expansion into the accounts. See for instance Robert Repetto et al, *Wasting Assets: Natural Resources in the National Income Accounts*. Washington: World Resources Institute, June 1989.)
8. See Lindsey Grant, "Too Many Old People or Too Many Americans? in NPG Forum series, July 1988.
9. For a survey of the cross-sectoral processes of foresight, alternative futures studies and systems analysis, see Lindsey Grant et al, *Foresight and National Decisions: The Horseman and the Bureaucrat* (Lanham, MD: University Press of America, 1988.)
10. R. Boyer and D. Savageau, *Places Rated Almanac*, 1985. (Chicago: Rand, McNally, 1985.)
11. *Urban Stress Test*, 1988. Zero Population Growth, 1400 16th Street NW—Suite 320, Washington DC 20036.
12. *Science*, 5 May 1989, p. 5517
13. *New York Times*, July 16, 1989, p. A1.
14. Gregory Spencer, *Projections of the Population of the United States, by Age, Sex and Race: 1988 to 2080*. U.S. Bureau of the Census, Current Population Reports, Series P-25, #1018, January 1989.
15. Study cited by Robert Repetto, "Population, Resources, Environment: An Uncertain Future," p. 19. (*Population Bulletin* Vol. 42, No.2, July 1987. Washington: Population Reference Bureau, Inc.)
16. *State of the World*, op cit, p. 15.

HOW TO GET THERE FROM HERE: THE DEMOGRAPHIC ROUTE TO OPTIMAL POPULATION SIZE

Leon F. Bouvier

December 1989

OUR "LOVE AFFAIR" WITH GROWTH

During a recent episode of the popular TV game show, *Jeopardy,* the college-level participants were asked which country will "surpass China in population within the next century." Two of the three contestants properly identified India. The third replied "The United States." Such an answer from a Harvard student is surprising. But even more surprising was the comment of the host, Alex Trebek: "That is a noble thought but unfortunately it is incorrect."

In January 1989 the U.S. Census Bureau published a new set of population projections (U.S. Bureau of the Census, 1989). Its middle scenario projected an eventual decline in population starting fifty years from now. The "neodoomsdayers, " worried about population decline, jumped up in unison to sound the alarm. Journalist Ben Wattenberg, already on record as advocating more births to American women, commented in U.S. News and World Report (1989) "The surest way to break the downward momentum of the projections is through more immigration. And only more immigration can provide the stream of 'instant adults' to deal with the looming problems in a timely manner." Economist Julian Simon, another supporter of higher fertility, has argued that immigration levels should be raised to perhaps 2 million annually (*Washington Post,* 1988). The media generally viewed the prospect of declining population quite gloomily never mind that the so-called "middle range" scenario of the Census Bureau was in fact a rather low projection given current levels of fertility, mortality, and immigration. (Bouvier, 1989)

These two unrelated incidents point out the built-in bias for growth among many Americans. Texans proudly look forward to passing New York state in population, as Californians did in 1963. Chambers of Commerce hail the latest population estimates showing their metropolitan area to have climbed two places. Suburbanites are gleeful when their city's population surpasses that of the older central city in their metropolitan area. We have forgotten E.P. Schumacher's words that "Small is Beautiful." Rather, we have been convinced, particularly in the Reagan era, that "Growth is Good."

Such a turn of events is quite ironic. Twenty-five years ago most Americans who thought about population were concerned about explosive growth. The population of the United States was increasing at a rate we now associate with the Third World, one that would have yielded over 400 million inhabitants by 2050. Many felt that the United States was growing too fast. Mortality was low and immigration moderate, but fertility was high. Consequently, the goal of zero population growth gained wide acceptance. In the intervening quarter of a century the perceptions of many Americans has turned about. From its baby boom peak of 3.7 in 1957, the U.S. fertility fell below the level needed to replace the population and reached 1.8 in 1972. Baby boom had given way to baby bust. Even though the country has added 54 million people in the last two decades, a new and unfamiliar fear now troubles some Americans: population decline. Yet even the highly publicized "medium" projection of the Census Bureau shows a population of 292 million in 2080—some 40 million more than today's 248 million.

Interestingly, those agonizing about population decline and who advocate increased population growth seldom discuss the consequences of that growth. Alex Trebek is a thoughtful and intelligent individual. His comment on Jeopardy was on the spur of the moment. No doubt he would not advocate a United States population of over one billion people! Yet if our fertility reverted to that during the baby boom and if we did accept 2 million immigrants per year, the resulting 2 percent annual growth rate would yield 1 billion Americans well within the next century.

Even a more conservative set of assumptions yields a disturbing answer. **If life expectancy increased slightly, if fertility rose to a mere 2.2 live births per woman (rather than 1.8 today) and if net immigration was constant at 800,000 annually (close to current levels), the United States population would surpass half a billion in just ninety years—and still be growing fairly rapidly!**

It may be difficult for Americans to accept the fact that not all growth is beneficial. The small world of certain growth-oriented economists is just that—a small world that fails to take into account the dangers to the environment and to the quality of life of all Americans that will result from continued population growth. So, like it or not, and while we may disagree on the eventual ideal number, sooner or later, population growth must come to an end. Those advocating continued rapid growth concede privately that, eventually, growth must come to an end, perhaps at some astronomical number. Those advocating negative growth must also favor eventual stationarity at some level smaller than the current population-otherwise, the society would run out of people!

THE DEMOGRAPHIC VARIABLES

Given agreement that growth must eventually come to an end, this begs the question: "How do we get from here to there?" We get there by manipulating the three demographic variables that account for all the changes in population size. These are fertility, migration, and mortality.

Slight variations in any single demographic variable can have considerable impact on eventual population size. For example, according to the Census Bureau projections, if immigration is 800,000 per year rather than 500,000 (while holding fertility and mortality constant) there will be 41 million more people by 2080.

A gradual increase of seven years in life expectancy (holding immigration and fertility constant) means a difference of 25 million by 2080.

The impact of fertility is particularly powerful. A gradual 20 percent increase in fertility from 1.8 to 2.2 live births (holding immigration and mortality constant) means 128 million more people by 2080!

Furthermore, in 2080, in all instances the population would still be growing. Population momentum must thus be considered when looking at the three demographic variables. If an end to growth is desired, it cannot be achieved overnight. **There is a built-in momentum for growth in any young population.** A drop in the fertility rate does not necessarily mean that the **number** of births has fallen. The number of potential mothers is as important as the number of children each has. In the United States, for example, the **number** of births has climbed from 3.1 million in 1978 to 3.9 million in 1989 although the fertility rate has remained fairly constant at about 1.8 live births per woman. In the 1980s there were proportionately many women in their childbearing years-the baby boom babies had become potential mothers. Interestingly, a momentum for population decline is also possible. If American women were to average one child for the next generation, there would be very few women twenty-five to thirty years hence to have babies. If further population decline was not desirable at that time, these relatively few women would have to average at least three births for the population to stop falling. Thus momentum is an important concept to consider when trying to determine "how to get there from here."

DEMOGRAPHIC MODELS

What do we mean by "there?" This can be both a number and a date. There is general consensus that population growth must end. Other writers in this series believe that it should stop at a lower level than present United States population. Demographers are supposed simply to give the facts: what are the results of different sorts of demographic behavior? Demographers are people too, and I confess to a certain sympathy with the view that eventual moderate population decline is desirable. However, my obligation is to demonstrate just how hard such a task will be, and how long it will take. To be realistic, we limit our horizon to the next sixty to ninety years-to the years 2050 and 2080. What combinations of fertility, mortality, and migration behavior patterns will get us from "here to there, whatever 'there' is?"

We begin by examining demographic mathematical models. These are not intended to serve as projections; rather, they illustrate what would occur under certain constant demographic conditions. Perhaps the best known of such models is the stable model developed by Dublin and Lotka early in this century. (Dublin and Lotka, 1925) Essentially, the model states that, in a closed population (that is, where there is no migration), a stable condition evolves if age-specific birth and death rates remain constant over a long period of time. A stable population exhibits a constant rate of growth and has constant birth and death rates. Note that a stable population can be growing, declining, or be stationary. Herein lies the reason why demographers never use the word "stability" to mean "no growth." That is reserved for the term "stationarity."

In 1982, the stable model theory was expanded to include migration: the open, stable model. (Espenshade, Bouvier, and Arthur, 1982) If age-specific birth and death rates are fixed, if fertility is below replacement, and if the yearly number of immigrants as well as their age and sex composition are constant, then that population will evolve in the long run to a stationary state with a constant size. In other words, as long as fertility is below replacement and the level of immigration is constant, zero population growth will eventually occur.

Such models, while not appropriate for real world projections, nevertheless point us in the right direction. This is particularly true for the United States which exhibits both below replacement fertility and net immigration. For example if the current fertility remained at 1.8 live births and if immigration were limited to 400,000 annually, the eventual stationary population of the United States would be about 120 million. However, it would take two or three centuries to approach this goal. We are more concerned with the twenty-first century. Using the demographic model as a guide, what demographic patterns are needed to attain our stated goal, whatever that may be?

THE PROJECTIONS

We first accept the fact that there is a momentum for growth in the current United States population. We then assume that life expectancy will increase in future years.

Admittedly gains in life expectancy contribute to additional growth and more aging of the population and admittedly, life expectations could be depressed in the next ninety years by the environmental deterioration presently underway. Be that as it may, all of us, whether advocating massive increase or negative growth, favor extending the longevity of all Americans and we should plan on it. The United States rates near the bottom of the list of all developed nations on such measures as life expectancy and infant mortality. The rate among certain American minorities is particularly disturbing. One Census Bureau projection has life expectancy climbing gradually from seventy-five years today to eighty-eight years in 2080. This is a mere one and one-half years every decade—a reachable and desirable goal. In all further projections, such improvements in life expectancy are assumed.

It remains for us to balance fertility and immigration. Fertility has been remarkably stable over the past eighteen years. It fell to 1.8 live births per woman in 1972 and has remained at approximately that level ever since. Preliminary 1988 data indicate that the rate rose to 1.94. Similar increases have been observed in Sweden and West Germany. The fertility rate could rise in the future because of an increasing proportion of minorities in the population. Hispanics, in particular, have substantially higher fertility (about 2.8) than other groups. Gains in their share of the population could result in some increases in the nation's fertility.

Given these conditions, I feel it is unrealistic to project lower fertility in the United States for the immediate future. Americans could be encouraged to lower their fertility through more and better jobs for women, better and easier access to abortions, and wider availability of effective contraceptives. Much more could be done, through sex education, to lower the disturbingly high level of adolescent fertility. In a democratic society, specific fertility levels can never, nor should they, be enforced. However, a population policy encouraging lower fertility could prove effective.

Contrary to fertility, much can be done to determine the extent of immigration. Federal legislation limiting international movements, in one way or another, has been in effect in some form for over a century. Currently, about 650,000 legal immigrants enter the country annually. Additional hundreds of thousands enter illegally. We do not know the exact number, but conservative estimates put it at between 200,000 and 400,000. Nor do we know how many people leave the country in any given year. It could well be as high as 200,000. In balance, these figures suggest that annual net migration may be in the vicinity of 750,000 to 800,000.

A continuation of such current demographic trends (that is, fertility of 1.8 and net immigration of 800,000) would yield a population of 346 million by 2050 and 360 million by 2080 according to the Census Bureau projections. At that time the population would still be growing by about 1 million per year (see graph). Growth would eventually come to an end, as indicated by the demographic model, but only in the very distant future. This is an example of how to get from "here to there" following current trends of demographic behavior. One hundred million more people in a mere 60 years is far too many for the nation to handle, if its quality of life and its infrastructure are to remain at least at current levels, much less improve. It is not an "optimal population."

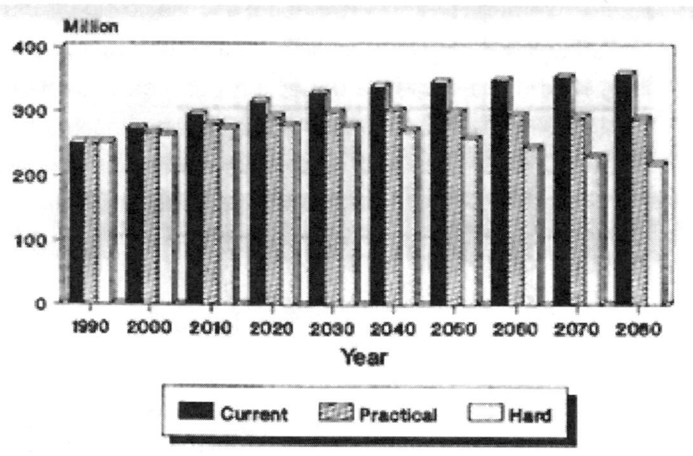

Figure 1.

The "Practical" Scenario: I think that a maximum population of 300 million with decline beginning well before 2080 is a practical and attainable goal. One of the Census Bureau's projections meets these requirements. Recall that life expectancy is assumed to increase to eighty-eight years by 2080. When that mortality is combined **with fertility at about 1.8 and net migration of 300,000 per year, the population peaks at 300 million in 2040 and falls to 289 million by 2080.** Beyond that year, the population declines slowly, reaching stationarity at about 120 million some three centuries later. But let us not concern ourselves with the twenty-second century any more than Americans of 1890 concerned themselves with our demographic problems!

The "Hard" Scenario: To those less patient with population growth, such a model may appear too high. Admittedly, adding 50 million Americans poses serious environmental problems.

Lowering fertility to 1.5 live births per woman, for example, is a possibility. Austria, West Germany, and Italy all exhibit rates below 1.5. Affluent Americans show similar fertility. It is the poor and the minorities who drive U.S. fertility up. Reductions in their fertility rates could result in an overall total fertility rate of 1.5 if government population policy encouraged such a change. With net migration reduced to 300,000, **the nation's population would still grow to 278 million in 2020 before falling to 218 million in 2080.** (See Graph) However, a majority of immigrants come from societies where fertility is high. With the resident American birth rate below replacement, the proportion of the nation's population who are minorities will increase. We have projected elsewhere that by 2060, it is likely that no racial/ethnic group will comprise a majority of the United States population. (Bouvier, forthcoming) Thus, for overall fertility to fall to 1.5, some substantial reductions in the fertility of native-born Americans will have to occur to compensate for the growing proportion of minorities in the population.

Very few Americans advocate ending immigration entirely. As a "nation of immigrants," it is doubtful if such a policy would be accepted by the American public. One possibility would be to take in only as many as leave the country in any given year. In other words, net migration of zero.* However, this would work only for as long as there was a residue of emigrants from earlier in-movements. At most, one immigrant in three leaves the United States. (The number of native-born Americans who emigrate is negligible.) Eventually, the number admitted would be extremely small if based on the number leaving. This would in effect end immigration. If 100,000 are accepted, for example, 30,000 may leave. Thus, it seems to us that zero net immigration is not a viable option. However, lower levels than 300,000 might be considered.

**The Census Bureau has prepared selected projections of U.S. population assuming net migration of zero. With low fertility (TFR=1.5) and life expectancy of 77.9 years, the population peaks at 255 million in 2010 and falls to 147 million by 2080. With moderate fertility (TFR=1.8) and life expectancy of 81.2 years, the population peaks at 270 million in 2020 and falls to 220 million by 2080.*

THE DEMOGRAPHIC QUANDARY

For those of us who would prefer that eventual zero growth be either at current population levels or lower, certain problems present themselves. First, while increases in life expectancy are favored by all, they contribute to additional numbers as well as aging the society. Second, the built-in momentum for growth inherited from the baby boom means that some increases will occur. It would take drastic and unrealistic reductions in fertility to end growth immediately. Third, immigration could be ended but most Americans, being either immigrants or descendants thereof, would undoubtedly disapprove of such governmental policies.

Together these problem areas limit the range of possibilities to a narrow band of fertility and immigration options. Recalling the open stable model, if fertility remains below replacement, that is, below 2.1, and if some constant level of immigration is maintained, an eventual stationary population will emerge. However, the lower the fertility, the greater and more rapid the ethnic shift in the composition of the population. As long as the resident American fertility is below replacement, the residents and their descendants will eventually be replaced by the immigrants and their descendants.

That is the quandary facing Americans who desire an end to population growth in the near future. The other alternative is cultural amalgation where widespread intermarriage occurs between groups. How long it will take before a 'nomajority' situation obtains depends on how low the fertility, how high the immigration, and the extent of intermarriage.

Demographic Behavior Reconsidered: The "population acts" of millions of Americans and immigrants to this nation have given us today's United States population. By population acts, we mean the fertility, mortality, and migration behavior of these millions of individuals. Today's and tomorrow's population acts will give us the population of 2000; of 2050; of 2080—not only the numbers of people but their age and ethnic composition. Advocating a specific ideal size necessarily means also considering the age and ethnic composition of that ideal. The "practical" scenario sees the population size reach 300 million before levelling off and then declining. The "hard" scenario sees population peaking at 278 million before falling.

Equally important is the fact that that population will be aging and be increasingly heterogenous. Aging and diversity are not problems to be avoided. Aging and diversity challenge the society to better adapt to these changing situations. **If the desire is to limit the size of the nation's population, then the demographic dynamics assure us both, increased age and diversity.** It is up to us to adapt to these shifts as we enter the twenty-first century.

CONCLUSION

There is little agreement as to what "optimal population" means and what numbers best reflect the optimum. We must be realistic in our efforts to determine what population size is achievable as opposed to optimal. Three, and only three, factors determine population size. One, mortality, is untouchable in that we all advocate increased longevity. A second, fertility, is in the hands of millions of American population actors. While fertility declines should be encouraged, nothing can be done in a democratic society to enforce those suggestions. That leaves immigration as the most maneuverable variable. Yet even here, there is doubt as to whether Americans would allow a total end to immigration. Thus, when trying to define what is an "optimal population," we are limited by these factors. We must also consider age and diversity almost as much as size. Finally, we should not get carried away with long-term models and projections. The next fifty to ninety years are sufficiently long-term, bearing in mind, of course, the potential for possible further exponential growth, to allow the development of specific demographic routes that will show us "how to get there from here."

Ending population growth and beginning population decline will be rough and it will be a slow process. If the problems described elsewhere in this series are as real and as serious as their authors believe, I suggest that we begin to concentrate on the demographic dimension of the problem. From the evidence described in this piece, it is clear that time is not on our side.

NOTES:

1. L.F. Bouvier, "The Census Bureau's-1989 Projections of Future U.S. Population: Which Scenario is Reasonable?" *Backgrounder*, Center for Immigration Studies, Washington, 1989.
2. L.F. Bouvier, *The Shape of the Future: Immigration and Population Change in the United States*, forthcoming.
3. L.I. Dublin and A.J. Lotka, "On the True Rate of Natural Increase," *Journal of the American Statistical Association* 20, (105), 1925, pp. 305–339.
4. T.J. Espenshade and L.R. Bouvier, "Fertility, Immigration and Isopops' " *Intercom*, 10 (3). 1982, pp. 8–10.
5. T.J. Espenshade, L.F. Bouvier, and W.B. Arthur, "Immigration and the Stable Population Model," *Demography*, 19, 1982, pp. 125–133.
6. J. Simon, "Getting the Immigrants We Need," *Washington Post*, August 3, 1988.
7. U.S. Bureau of Census, Current Population Reports, Series P25, No. 1018, *Projections of the Population of the United States, by Age, Sex and Race: 1988 to 2080*, by Gregory Spencer, Washington: USGPO, 1989.
8. B.J. Wattenberg, "The Case for More Immigrants," *U.S. News and World Report*, Feb. 13, 1989, p. 29.

LAND, ENERGY AND WATER: THE CONSTRAINTS GOVERNING IDEAL U.S. POPULATION SIZE

David and Marcia Pimentel

January 1995

INTRODUCTION

For most of this century, leading scientists, public officials, and various organizations have been calling attention to the rapidly growing human population and the deteriorating environment throughout the world (Ehrlich and Holdren, 1971; Meadows et al., 1972; CEQ, 1980; Keyfitz, 1984; Demeny, 1986; Hardin, 1986). Based on these assessments, genuine concerns about maintaining prosperity and quality of human life in the future have been expressed.

In the United States, humankind is already managing and using more than half of all the solar energy captured by photosynthesis. Yet even this is insufficient to our needs, and we are actually using nearly three times that much energy, or about 40 percent more energy than is captured by all plants in the United States. This rate is made possible only because we are temporarily drawing upon stored fossil energy. We are approaching the end of the petroleum era, and other fossil fuels are not inexhaustible. Moreover, the very use of these fossil fuels, plus erosion and other misuse of our natural resources, are reducing the carrying capacity of our ecosystem.

These are not sustainable conditions, and our natural resources cannot be expected indefinitely to maintain a population as large as the present one, without a remarkable decline in our living standards.

Thus far, our society appears unable to deal successfully with problems of the environment, resources, and population. It has a poor record of effectively managing and protecting essential environmental and natural resources from over-exploitation caused by ignorance, mismanagement, and the impact of growing human numbers. History suggests that these escalating problems exist because the United States has not developed a cohesive policy that recognizes a specific standard of living for its citizens, while clearly acknowledging that the attainment of such a standard depends on the interaction of environment, resources, as well as population density.

When decisions concerning the environment and natural resources are made in the United States, and indeed throughout the world, they are **ad hoc** in nature and are designed to protect or promote a particular or immediate aspect of human well-being and/or the environment. All too often solutions are sought only after a problem reaches a crisis status. As Benjamin Franklin wrote long ago in Poor Richard's Almanac, "it is not until the well runs dry, we know the worth of water." Based on experience, it will not be until the pressure of human population on the environment and resources becomes intolerable that some corrective action will be taken by individuals and governments. Then it may be too late to avert hunger and poverty.

In this essay, we examine the degradation of the environment, the consumption of non-renewable resources, population growth, and the possible decline in U.S. prosperity. We also suggest that **dramatically reduced U.S. population densities would insure individual prosperity and quality environment for future generations.** The goal is to have sufficient information and understanding of the problems so that sound policies are possible.

RESOURCES AND POPULATION DENSITY

Innate human behavior indicates a strong will to survive and to achieve some level of prosperity and quality lifestyle. Nations as well as individuals differ in their perception of what they consider a good life for themselves. A comparison of some aspects of life in the United States and China reveals startling extremes and clarifies what Americans can expect in the future if our population continues to grow at its present rate. Both birthrates and immigration function in the population equation.

The present population of the United States stands at 246.1 million and is growing at a rate of about 1 percent per year (depending on one's estimates of emigration and illegal immigration). If the number of immigrants coming into the United States increases, the rate of U.S. population growth will increase. China has a population of 1.1 billion, and despite the government's policy of one child per couple it is growing at a rate of 1.4 percent or 15 million per year (PRB, 1988).

Statistics suggest that in the United States **we produce and consume about forty-seven times more goods, and services, per capita, than China does** (PRB, 1986). Because achieving and maintaining such consumption levels depends upon the availability of resources and the health of the environment that sustains them, our position is very tenuous when projections of future resource availability are considered.

Currently, approximately 1,500 kg of agricultural products are produced annually to feed each American while the Chinese make do with only 594 kg/capita/year (Table 1). To produce food for each person in the United States, a total of 1.9 ha of cropland and pasture land is used, whereas in China only 0.4 ha/person is used (Table 2). The data in these tables confirm that each person in China is fed essentially a vegetarian diet and that they have nearly reached the carrying capacity of their agricultural system.

Since colonial times and especially after 1850, Americans have relied increasingly on energy sources other than human power for their food and forestry production. Relatively cheap and abundant supplies of fossil fuel have been substituted for human energy. Thus, man-made fertilizers and pesticides as well as machinery have helped our farmers and diminished the level of personal energy they must expend to farm. **The Chinese have not been as fortunate and still depend on about 1,200 hours/hectare (h/ha) of manual farm labor, compared with only 10 h/ha in the United States** (Wen and Pimentel, 1984).

Industry, transportation, heating homes, and producing food account for most of the fossil energy consumed in the United States (Pimentel and Hall, 1984, 1989). Most fossil energy in China is used by industry and a lesser amount for food production (Kinzelbach, 1983; Smil, 1984). Per capita use of fossil energy in the United States amounts to about 8,000 liters of oil equivalents per year or twenty times the level in China (Table 2).

China, with its population of 1.1 billion and a land area similar to ours, already is experiencing diminished per capita supplies of food and other essential resources, plus a deteriorating natural environment as evidenced by the loss of forests and intense soil erosion. The relative affluence presently enjoyed by Americans has been made possible by our abundant supplies of arable land, water, and fossil energy relative to our present population numbers. As our population escalates, our resources inevitably will experience pressures similar to those now experienced by China.

STATUS OF U.S. ENVIRONMENTAL RESOURCES

Basic to making decisions about our future is the need to assess both the quality and quantity of land, water, and energy, as well as biological resources we will have at our disposal in coming decades. At our present population level of 246 million we are affluent consumers of all these vital resources, many of which are being depleted, with no hope of renewal after the next 100 years. Although these components function inter-dependently, they can be manipulated to make up for a partial shortfall in one or more. For example, to bring desert land into production, water can be applied to the land, but only if groundwater or river water is available and if sufficient fossil energy is available to pump the water. This is the current practice in California and many other western states, enabling some of our western agricultural regions to be highly productive.

Table 1. Foods and feed grains consumed per capita (kilogram) per year in the United States and China (Pimentel et al., 1989).

Food/Feed	USA[a]	China
Food grain	69	269[b]
Vegetables	112	204[c]
Fruit	63	11[d]
Meat and fish	103	25[d]
Dairy products	265	3[d]
Eggs	15	6[d]
Fats and oils	28	6[d]
Sugar	66	6[d]
TOTAL	**721**	**530**
Feed grains	801	64[b]
GRAND TOTAL	**1,522**	**594**
Kilocalories/person/day	3,500	2,484[e]

[a] USDA, 1985.

[b] total grain production per capita in 1985 was 364kg (CDAAHF, 1986). It is estimated on the basis of some unpublished data that 8.5 percent of the total grain production was used for seeds and industrial materials, 17.5 percent for feed and 74 percent for food (Wen, personal communication, 1987).

[c] Estimated on the basis of total vegetable planting area (Wen, personal communication, 1987).

[d] CDAAHF, 1986.

[e] CAA, 1986.

Land, that vital natural resource, is all too often taken for granted; yet, it is essential for food production and the supply of other basic human needs, like fiber, fuel, and shelter. Currently, Americans use about 0.6 ha/capita of arable land to produce our food. Nearly all the arable land is in production, and in fact some marginal land is also in production (Pimentel and Hall, 1989). Thus, Americans do not have new arable land to open up to take care of a growing U.S. population.

At present the soil on U.S. cropland is eroding at rates that average eighteen t/ha/year (Lee, 1984). This is of particular concern because soil reformation is extremely slow; thus, **we are losing topsoil eighteen times faster than replacement** (Pimentel et al., 1987). Even now, in what used to be some of our most productive agricultural regions, soil

Table 2. Resources utilized per capita per year in the United States and China to supply basic needs (Pimentel et al., 1989).

Resources	USA	China
Land		
Cropland (ha)	0.6[a]	0.1[b,c]
Pasture (ha)	1.3[a]	0.3[b]
Forests (ha)	1.3[a]	0.1[b,d]
TOTAL	3.2	0.5
Water (liters x 101/yr)	2.5[e]	0.46[c]
Fossil Fuel		
Oil equivalents (liters)	8000[f]	413[g]
Forest Products (tonnes)	14[a]	0.03[c,d]

[a] USDA, 1985.

[b] Wu, 1981.

[c] Smil, 1984.

[d] Vermeer, 1984.

[e] USWRC, 1979.

[f] DOE, 1983.

[g] State Statistical Bureau PROC, 1985.

productivity has been reduced 50 percent, and in some areas it has been so severely degraded that it has been abandoned (Follett and Stewart, 1985).

All arable land that is currently in production, and especially marginal land, continues to be highly susceptible to degradation (OTA,1982; Follett and Stewart, 1985). Although some marginal land has been withdrawn under the new Conservation Reserve Program, all marginal land cannot be removed from production because it is essential to feed Americans. Certainly, efforts should be made to implement soil and water conservation practices on both arable and marginal land (OTA, 1982).

Despite serious soil erosion, U.S. crop yields have been maintained or increased because of the availability of cheap fossil **energy** for inputs like fertilizers, pesticides, and irrigation (Pimentel et al., 1987). Currently on U.S. farms, **about three kcal of fossil energy are being spent to produce just I kcal of food.** Our policy of supporting this three to one energy ratio has serious implications for the future. One cannot help but wonder how long such intensive agriculture can be maintained on U.S. croplands while our non-renewable, fossil energy resources are being rapidly depleted.

In addition to use in agricultural production and throughout our entire food system for processing, packaging, and transportation, fossil energy is used to fuel diverse human activities. Overall fossil energy inputs in different economic sectors have increased twenty- to 1,000-fold in the past three decades, attesting to our heavy reliance on this energy (Pimentel and Hall, 1984, 1989).

Projections of the availability of these energy resources are not encouraging. In fact a recent study published this year by the Department of the Interior reports that, based on the most current oil drilling data, the estimated amount of oil resources has plummeted. This means that instead of having about a thirty-five-year supply of oil we are now limited to a sixteen-year supply if use remains at about the current rate. Concurrently, natural gas, an important energy resource, is being rapidly depleted (Matar, 1989). Reliable estimates indicate that coal reserves are sufficient to last for more than a century (Schilling and Wiegand, 1987; USBC, 1988). Note that nuclear energy is also limited because uranium resources also are facing eventual depletion (Matar, 1989). A larger population can be expected to put additional stress on usage of all energy resources. Thus, considering population growth and the forecasts about our non-renewable energy supplies, all efforts need to be focused on conserving current supplies while intensifying research on developing new energy sources.

Along with land and energy supplies, we take **water** supplies for granted and often forget that all vegetation requires and transpires massive amounts of water. For example, a corn crop that produces about 7,000 kg/ha of grain will take up and transpire about 4.2 million liters/ha of water during just one growing season (Leyton, 1983). To supply this much water to the crop, not only must 10 million liters (1,000 mm) of rain fall per hectare, but it must be evenly distributed during the year and especially during the growing season.

Of the total water currently used in the United States, 81 percent is used in agriculture while the remainder is needed for industry and for public use (USWRC, 1979). In the future, the rate of U.S. water consumption is projected to rise both because of population growth and because of greater per capita use (USWRC, 1979; CEQ, 1983). The rapid increase in water use already is stressing both our surface and groundwater resources. **Currently, groundwater overdraft is 25 percent higher than its replenishment rate** (USWRC, 1979) with the result that our mammoth groundwater aquifers are being mined at an alarming rate. In addition, both surface and groundwater pollution have become a serious problem in the United States, and concern about the future availability of pure water is justified (CEQ, 1980).

THREATS TO THOSE RESOURCES

Pollution is pervasive throughout our environment and degrades the quality and availability of resources like water, land, air, and biota. For example, when salts are leached from the land during irrigation (up to eighteen tons of salts per hectare during the growing season) and deposited in rivers, the effectiveness of the river water for further irrigation is reduced (Pimentel et al., 1982).

Air pollution has a more pervasive impact than water pollution. In the United States, the estimated 21 million metric tons of sulfur dioxide from factories and cars that are released into the atmosphere annually cause serious environmental problems in both our natural and agricultural environments (EPA, 1986). For example, acid rain produced in part from sulfur dioxide is having major environmental impacts on aquatic life in streams and life in U.S. forests.

Further, a wide array of chemical pollutants are released to the air, water, and soil and already are adversely affecting the growth and survival of many of the 400,000 species of natural plants and animals that make up our natural environment. For example, each year about 500 million kg of toxic pesticides are applied to control pests, but all too often kill beneficial species as well. Some of these pesticides leach into groundwater and streams, damaging the valuable plants and animals that inhabit surface waters (Pimentel and Levitan, 1986; Pimentel et al., 1990).

In addition to toxic chemicals, the conversion of forests and other natural habitats to croplands, pastures, roads, and urban spread, in response to expanding population numbers is reducing biological diversity of plants and animals. These **natural biota are vital for the recycling of organic wastes, degrading chemical pollutants, and purifying water and soil** (Pimentel et al., 1980).

Further, **they are the essential reservoirs of genetic material for agriculture and forestry.**

TRANSITION FROM FOSSIL TO SOLAR ENERGY

Instead of relying on the finite supplies of fossil energy research must be focused on ways to convert solar energy into usable energy for society. Many solar energy technologies already exist, including solar thermal receivers, photovoltaics, solar ponds, hydropower, as well as burning biomass vegetation. Using some technologies, biomass can be converted into the liquid fuels, ethanol and methanol (ERAB, 1981, 1982).

As recently as 1850, the United States was 91 percent dependent on biomass wood or solar power for energy (Pimentel and Pimentel, 1979). Gradually that has changed until today we are 92 percent dependent on fossil energy while biomass energy makes up only 3 percent of the fuel we use (Pimentel et al., 1984).

Looking to the future, reliance on biomass energy use will grow and again become one of our dominant forms of solar energy (Pimentel et al., 1984). However, use of biomass has major limitations. Consider that the total amount of solar energy captured by vegetation each year in our country is about 13×10^{15} kcal (Pimentel et al.,1978). This includes all the solar energy captured by agricultural crops, forests, lawns, and natural plants. According to all estimates this yield cannot be increased to any great extent (ERAB, 1981).

Furthermore, the total solar energy captured by our agricultural crops and forest products is about 7×10^{15} kcal or slightly more than half the total solar energy captured (ERAB, 1981). Because this portion of biomass energy provides us with food, fiber, pulp, and lumber, it cannot be burned or converted into biomass energy.

Another factor to consider is that only 0.1 percent to 0.2 percent of the total solar energy per hectare can be harvested as biomass in the temperate region (Pimentel et al., 1984). This is because solar energy is captured by plants only during their brief growing season and for three-quarters of the year most plants are not growing (ERAB, 1981). To solve this problem will necessitate the use of relatively large land areas and large capital equipment investments for conversion of the energy into usable form.

This same biomass vegetation provides the food and shelter for a wide variety of important natural biota that help keep our natural environment healthy. Some species recycle wastes and nutrients, others help clean our air, soil, and water of pollutants. Without sufficient biomass these essential processes would stop.

Yet at our present population level, to sustain our lives and activities we are burning 40 percent more fossil energy than the total amount of solar energy captured by all plant biomass (ERAB, 1981). Clearly, our consumption of resources, especially non-renewable fossil fuels, is out of balance with our supplies. The plain fact is that we are depleting these resources at an alarming rate and we now need to find and develop other energy sources.
Because almost three-quarters of the land area in the United States is devoted to agriculture and commercial forestry (USDA, 1987), only a relatively small percentage of our land area is available for harvesting biomass and other solar energy technologies to support a solar energy-based U.S. economy.

The inevitable conclusion is that **the availability of land will be the major constraint to the expanded**

use of solar energy systems because land is needed for solar energy, and this need cannot encroach on that needed by agriculture, forestry, and natural biota in the ecosystem. Our expanding human population can be expected to put increasingly great pressure on land availability and use.

The amount of land required to provide solar-based electricity for a city of 100,000 people illustrates the land constraints. To provide the needed 1 billion kWh/year from wood biomass would require maintaining 330,000 hectares of permanent forest (Table 3). Even hydropower is, in part, land based, because on average it requires 13,000 hectares of land for an adequate size reservoir. Then too, the land used for the reservoir is often good, productive agricultural land (Pimentel et al., 1984). Thus, solar energy and hydropower have serious land and environmental limitations. Note that nuclear and coal-fired power plants, including mining, require relatively small areas of land compared to biomass and hydropower production.

Unfortunately, **the conversion of biomass like corn into energy such as liquid fuels requires enormous inputs of fossil energy.** For example, about 1.5 liters of oil equivalents are used to produce one liter of ethanol equivalents (ERAB, 1981; Pimentel et al., 1988). Thus, under optimal conditions only about one-third of the biomass can be converted into valuable liquid fuels (Pimentel et al., 1988). Even if we quadrupled the efficiency so that I kcal of fossil energy produced 2 kcal of ethanol, about ten acres of corn land would be required to fuel one U.S. automobile per year (Pimentel et al., 1988).

Table 3. Land resource requirements for construction of energy facilities that produce 1 billion kWh/yr of electricity for a city of 100,000 people (Pimentel et al., 1989).

Electrical Energy Technology	Land in hectares
Wind Power	2,700
Hydropower	13,000
Forest Biomass	330,000
Solar Ponds	9,000
Nuclear	68
Coal	90

If we make the optimistic assumption that the amount of solar energy used today could be increased about three- to ten-fold without adversely affecting agriculture, forestry, or the environment, then from 3 to 10 x 10^{15} kcal of solar energy would be available (Pimentel et al., 1984; Ogden and Williams, 1989). This is one-fifth to one-half the current level of energy consumption in the United States, which is about 20 x 10^{15} kcal and averages 8,000 liters of oil equivalents per capita per year (USBC, 1988). One possibility is that fusion energy will eventually be developed and make up the shortfall. The odds for this happening in time are about one in 1,000 (Mataré, 1989), and further, the intense heat its production generates would have to be overcome.

TOWARD A SUSTAINABLE AGRICULTURE

Analyzing the 1100 liters of oil we now use to produce food on one hectare of land suggests ways we might decrease that fossil-based energy expenditure. Both fertilizers and pesticides are lost or wasted in agricultural production. For instance, about $18 billion per year of fertilizer nutrients are lost as they are eroded along with soils (Pimentel, 1989). Further, livestock manures, which have five times the amount of fertilizer nutrients used each year, are underutilized, wasted, or allowed to erode along with soil. Much fossil energy could be saved if effective soil conservation methods were to be implemented and manures were used more extensively.

Another waste occurring in agriculture that affects energy use can be attributed to pesticides. **Since 1945 the use of synthetic pesticides in the United States has grown thirty-three-fold, yet our crop losses continue to increase** (Pimentel, et al., 1990). More pesticides have been used because agricultural technology has drastically changed. For example, crop rotations have been abandoned for many major crops. Now about 40 percent of our corn acreage is grown continuously as corn and this has resulted in an increased number of corn pests. Despite a 1,000-fold increase in use of pesticides on corn-on-corn, corn losses to insects have risen four-fold.

Improved agricultural technology and a return to crop rotations would stem soil erosion, conserve fertile land, reduce water requirements for irrigation, decrease pesticide and fertilizer use and thereby save both fossil fuels and water quality. **The use of more land to produce food reduces the total energy inputs needed in crop production and would make agriculture more solar energy dependent and sustainable.** For example, instead of raising a given crop on one hectare with an energy input of about 1100 liters of oil, the use of two hectares for the same crop would make possible a reduction in energy inputs from 50 percent to 66 percent (Pimentel et al., 1988).

This of course assumes the availability of sufficient land, and a halving of yields per hectare. Some estimates suggest that if losses, waste, and mismanagement were eliminated, we would be able to produce present yields of food on the same amounts of land with one-half the energy outputs, and still have a more sustainable system (Pimentel et al., 1989). This should probably be considered an upper boundary. Since arable land cannot be much expanded, and since we have already hypothesized the diversion of some land to solar energy uses, **prudence would suggest that in planning any such shift to sustainable practices we anticipate lower yields and lower total production.** This, in turn, forces a choice between a smaller population, or a less well fed one.

PROSPERITY AND POPULATION

If the United States were to move to a solar energy-based economy and become self-sustainable, what would be our options and levels of prosperity? With a self-sustaining solar energy system replacing our current dependence on fossil energy, the energy availability would be one-fifth to one-half the current level. Then if the U.S. population remained at its present level of 246 million, a significant reduction in our current standard of living would follow. This would occur even if all the energy conservation measures known today were adopted.

If, however, the U.S. population wishes to continue its current high level of energy use and standard of living and prosperity, then its ideal population should be targeted at 40–100 million people. With sound energy conservation practices and a drastic reduction of energy use per capita to less than one-half current usage, it might be possible to support the current population. One projection suggests a significantly lower population level and the other a dramatic reduction in the standard of living. On the positive side, however, we do have sufficient fossil energy, especially coal, to help us make the needed transition in energy resources and population numbers over the next century, if we can manage the environmental impacts.

CONCLUSION

At present levels of fertility and migration, the U.S. population will rise one-third by 2080; A modest increase in fertility could drive it past a half billion.

We could be heading eventually toward population densities like those in present-day China. Comparisons to China clearly emphasize why the United States will be unable to maintain its current level of prosperity and high standard of living, which is based on its available land, water, energy, and biological resources. We know that supplies of fossil energy, a non-renewable resource, are being rapidly depleted. In just a few years, most U.S. oil resources will be consumed. Fortunately, natural gas reserves will last for nearly fifty years while coal reserves will carry us beyond the next century.

Therefore, we must start now to make the slow transition from our dependence on fossil fuels to development of solar energy power as our major energy resource. For the United States to be self-sustaining in solar energy, given our land, water, and biological resources, our population should be less than 100 million—significantly less than the current level of 246 million. However, with a drastic reduction in standard of living, the current population level might be sustained. With planning and determination, the United States could gradually reduce its numbers to more manageable levels.

The available supply of fossil fuels, especially coal, will provide the time we need to make the necessary adjustments involving new solar energy technologies and agricultural practices. Coupled with this, Americans will have time to change their behavior and respect for natural resources and the environment.

With a population of 40 to 100 million, the United States could become self-sustaining on solar energy while maintaining a quality environment, provided that sound energy conservation and environmental policies were in effect to preserve soil, water, air, and biological resources that sustain life. With these far-reaching changes, we feel confident that future generations of Americans would be able to enjoy prosperity and have a high standard of living. Starting to deal with the future before it reaches crisis level is the only way we will be able to avert real tragedy for our children's children. By education, fair population control, sound resource policies, the support of scientific research, and all people working together, Americans will be able to face the future with optimism and pride.

NOTES:

1. CAA. 1986. Is it necessary to have 400 kg grains per capita in China? Chinese Agricultural Academy. *Chinese Agr. Sci.* (Zhonggue Nongye Kexue) 5:1–7 (in Chinese).
2. CDAAHF. 1986. The Statistics of Agriculture, Animal Husbandry and Fishery in China in 1985. China's Department of Agriculture, Animal Husbandry and Fishery. Agriculture Press, Beijing (in Chinese).
3. CEQ. 1980. The Global 2000 Report to the President. Technical Report, Vol. 2.
4. Council on Environmental Quality. U.S. Govt. Print. Off., Washington, D.C.
5. CEQ. 1983. Environmental Quality 1983. 14th Annual Report. Council on Environmental Quality. U.S. Govt. Print. Off., Washington, D.C.
6. Demeny, P.G. x1986. Population and the Invisible Hand. Working Paper No. 123. Center for Policy Studies, Population Council, New York.
7. DOE. 1983. Energy Projections to the Year 2010. DOE/DE-0029/2 Office of Policy, Planning and Analysis, U.S. Department of Energy, Washington, D.C.
8. Ehrlich, R.P. and J.P. Holdren. 1971. The Impact of Population growth. Science 171:1212–1217.
9. EPA. 1986. National Air Pollutant Emission Estimates, 1940–1984. Environmental

Protection Agency, EPA-450/4-85-015. Office of Air Quality Planning Standards, EPA, Research Triangle Park, N.C.

10. ERAB. 1981. Report on Biomass Energy. Prepared by the Biomass Panel, Energy Research Advisory Board, Department of Energy, Washington, D.C. ERAB. 1982. Solar Energy Research and Development: Federal and Private Sector Roles. Report of the Energy Research Advisory Board, Department of Energy, Washington, D.C.
11. Follett, R.F. and B.A. Stewart. 1985. Soil Erosion and Crop Productivity. Am. Soc. Agron., Crop Sci. Soc. Am., and Soil Sci. Soc. Am., Madison, Wisc.
12. Hardin, G. 1986. Cultural carrying capacity: a biological approach to human problems. BioScience 36:599–606.
13. Keyfitz, N. 1984. Impact of trends in resources, environment and development on demographic prospects. pp. 97–124 in Population, Resources, Environment and Development. United Nations, New York.
14. Kinzelbach, W.K. 1983. China: energy and environment. Environ. Manage. 7:303–310.
15. Lee, L.K. 1984. Land use and soil loss: a 1982 update. J. Soil Water Conserv. 39:226–228.
16. Leyton, L. 1983. Crop water use: principles and some considerations for agroforestry. pp. 379–400 in Plant Research and Agroforestry.
17. P.A. Huxley, ed. Intl. Counc. Res. Agrofor., Nairobi, Kenya.
18. Mataré, H.F. 1989. Energy: Facts and Future. CRC Press, Boca Raton, Fla. 229 pp.
19. Meadows, D.H., D.L. Meadows, J. Randers, and W.W. Behrens 111. 1972. The Limits to Growth. Universe Books, Washington, D.C.
20. NAS. 1989. Alternative Agriculture. National Academy Press, Washington, D.C. 448 pp.
21. Ogden, J.M. and R.H. Williams. 1989. Solar Hydrogen: Moving Beyond Fossil Fuels. World Resources Institute, Washington, D.C. 123 pp.
22. OTA. 1982. Impacts of Technology on Productivity of the Croplands and Rangelands of the United States. Office of Technology Assessment, Washington, D.C.
23. Pimentel, D. 1989. Waste in agriculture and food sectorsenvironmental and social costs. Manuscript.
24. Pimentel, D. and C.W. Hall, eds. 1984. Food and Energy Resources. Academic Press, New York.
25. Pimentel, D. and C.W. Hall, eds. 1989. Food and Natural Resources. Academic Press, San Diego.
26. Pimentel, D. and L. Levitan. 1986. Pesticides: amounts applied and amounts reaching pests. BioScience 36:86–91.
27. Pimentel, D. and M. Pimentel. 1979. Food, Energy and Society. Edward Arnold, London.
28. Pimentel, D., D. Nafus, W. Vergara, D. Papaj, L. Jaconetta, M. Wulfe, L. Olsvig, K. Frech, M. Loye, and E. Mendoza. 1978. Biological solar energy conversion and U.S. energy policy. BioScience 28:376–382.
29. Pimentel, D., E. Garnick, A. Berkowitz, S. Jacobson, S. Napolitano, P. Black, S. Valdes-Cogliano, B. Vinzant, E. Hudes, and S. Littman. 1980. Environmental quality and natural biota. BioScience 30:750–755.
30. Pimentel, D., S. Fast, W. L. Chao, E. Stuart, J. Dintzis, G. Einbender, W. Schlappi, D. Andow, and K. Broderick. 1982. Water resources in food and energy production. BioScience 32:861–867.
31. Pimentel, D., L. Levitan, J. Heinze, M. Loehr, W. Naegeli, J. Bakker, J. Eder, B. Modelski, and M. Morrow. 1984. Solar energy, land and biota. Sun World 8:70–73, 93–95.

32. Pimentel, D., J. Allen, A. Beers, L. Guinand, R. Linder, P. McLaughlin, B. Meer, D. Musonda, D. Peldue, S. Poisson, S. Siebert, K. Stoner, R. Salazar, and A. Hawkins. 1987. World agriculture and soil erosion. BioScience 37:277–283.

33. Pimentel, D., A.F. Warneke, W.S. Teel, K.A. Schwab, N.J. Simcox, D.M. Ebert, K.D. Baenisch, and M.R. Aaron. 1988. Food versus biomass fuel: socioeconomic and environmental impacts in the United States, Brazil, India, and Kenya. Adv. Food Res. 32:185–238.

34. Pimentel, D., L.M. Frederickson, D.B. Johnson, J.H. McShane, and H.-W. Yuan. 1989. Environment and population: crises and policies. pp. 363–389 in Food and Natural Resources. D. Pimentel and C.W. Hall, eds. Academic Press, San Diego.

35. Pimentel, D., L. McLaughlin, A. Zepp, B. Lakitan, T. Kraus, P. Kleinman, F. Vancini, W. J. Roach, E. Graap, W.S. Keeton, and G. Selig. 1990. Environmental and economic impacts of reducing U.S. agricultural pesticide use. Chapter in Handbook of Pest Management in Agriculture. 2nd ed. CRC Press, Boca Raton, Fla. In press.

36. PRB. 1986. World Population Data Sheet. Population Reference Bureau, Washington, D.C.

37. PRB. 1988. World Population Data Sheet. Population Reference Bureau, Washington, D.C.

38. Schilling, H.-D. and D. Wiegand. 1987. Coal resources. pp. 129–56 in Resources and World Development. D. J. McLaren and B. J. Skinner, eds. Wiley, New York.

39. Smil, V. 1984. The Bad Earth, Environmental Degradation in China. M. E. Sharpe, Inc., Armonk, New York.

40. State Statistical Bureau PROC. 1985. Statistical Yearbook of China 1985. Economic Information and Agency, Hong Kong.

41. USBC. 1988. Statistical Abstract of the United States: 1987. 108th Ed. U.S. Bureau of the Census, Washington, D.C.

42. USDA. 1985. Agricultural Statistics 1985. U.S. Govt. Print. Off., Washington, D.C.

43. USDA. 1987. Agricultural Statistics 1987. U.S. Govt. Print. Off., Washington, D.C.

44. USWRC. 1979. The Nation's Water Resources 1975–2000. Summary and Vol. 1. United States Water Resources Council. U.S. Govt. Print. Off., Washington, D.C.

45. Vermeer, E. B. 1984. Agriculture in China-a deteriorating situation. Ecologist 14(1):6–14.

46. Wen, D. and D. Pimentel. 1984. Energy flow through an organic agroecosystem in China. Agr. Ecosyst. Environ. II: 145–160.

47. Wu, C. 1981. The transformation of agricultural landscape in China. pp. 35–43 in The Environment: Chinese and American Views. L. J. C. Ma and A. G. Noble, eds. Methuen, New York.

POLITICAL CONFRONTATION WITH ECONOMIC REALITY: MASS IMMIGRATION IN THE POST-INDUSTRIAL AGE

Vernon M. Briggs, Jr.

February 1990

As the United States enters its post-industrial phase of economic development, its labor market is in a state of radical transformation. A marked break has occurred from the nation's evolutionary patterns of employment growth as well as in the composition of its labor force. The introduction of new and extensive technological advances now means that more output can be produced with fewer labor inputs. Major shifts in consumer tastes have altered the character of the demand for labor, by contributing to the meteoric growth of the service sector and the decline of the goods sector.

The co-existence of labor shortages and vacant jobs is becoming the operative policy challenge. In such an environment, labor force policies must focus on the qualitative aspects of the supply of labor rather than on its merc quantitative size. The nation does not need more workers per se; it does, however, desperately need specific types of labor to meet the emerging requirements of its post-industrial economy.

On the supply side, major changes have occurred in the expectations of minorities and women concerning their participation and their status in the labor force. If you combine these trends with greatly enhanced foreign competition, and rapidly changing population demographics, it is clear that unprecedented demands are being placed upon the U.S. economy and government to nurture and educate the nation's citizens and to help them find employment opportunities.

Because mass immigration has reemerged during this period of extreme flux, *it is essential that the nation's contemporary immigration policy be consonant with the pursuit of these economic and social goals. Presently, it is not.* Instead, it is perceived by policymakers as being essentially a political policy whose features are to be manipulated without any serious concern given as to its economic impact.

All other advanced industrial nations—to varying degrees—are experiencing similar quantum changes in their employment patterns. No other such country, however, is experiencing such major simultaneous alterations in its labor force as is the United States. Of the multiple influences on the size and composition of the U.S. labor force, it is the revival of mass immigration that is by far the most unique. Indeed, a recent comprehensive study of U.S. society that was conducted by an international team of social science scholars concluded that "America's biggest import is people." It added that "at a time when attention is directed to the general decline in American exceptionalism, American immigration continues to flow at a rate unknown elsewhere in the world."[1]

THE PHENOMENON OF MASS IMMIGRATION

The revival of mass immigration began in the mid-1960s when the nation's existing immigration laws were overhauled. The reform movement of that era sought to purge the system of the racism associated with the "national origins" admission system which had been in place since 1924. Modest increases in the level of immigration were envisioned. No one, however. anticipated what has subsequently occurred. The ensuing mass immigration flow has been the cumulative result of the tyranny of seemingly small politically motivated policy decisions as well as the product of a massive dose of political indifference to the ensuing policy outcomes.

Of all the factors that influence population and labor force growth, immigration is the one component that public policy should be able to control. To date, however, policymakers in the United States have been unwilling to view immigration policy in this light. Unguided in its design, immigration policy is dominated by the pursuit of purely political objectives. It has yet to be held responsible for its sizable economic consequences.[2]

Prevailing immigration policy primarily promotes the migration of relatives of recent migrants and provides little room for immigration to supply those persons who already possess needed skills and experience. Less than 8 percent of the immigrants and refugees who are legally admitted to the United States each year are admitted on the basis that the skills and education they possess are actually in demand by U.S. employers. The percentage is considerably less if illegal immigrants are included in the total immigrant flow.

Each successive immigration "reform" since the 1960s has increased the annual level of immigration. Furthermore, the failure to enforce the existing laws has permitted the largely unfettered influx of illegal migrants from less economically developed nations to compete with this country's poor and to aggravate their collective poverty. *Immigrants constitute a rising portion of the total growth of the labor force, and, at current U.S. fertility rates and immigration levels, they will lead within a century to a U.S. population one-half again as large as would occur with natural increase alone.*[3]

In all of its diverse forms, the immigrant flow has accounted for anywhere from one-quarter to one-third of the annual growth of the U.S. labor force during the decade of the 1980s. The presence of a considerable number of illegal immigrants complicates efforts to be precise. It is highly probable that, when the rising female labor force participation rate eventually stabilizes (as it soon must) and as the influences of the "baby boom generation" on the size of the work force ebbs (as it is beginning to do), immigration could, by the turn of the century, comprise all of the annual growth of the nation's labor force. *Immigration, therefore, is already a vital determinant of the nation's economic welfare; it can only be expected to become more so.*

PUBLIC UNAWARENESS OF POLICY CONSEQUENCES

Public recognition that immigration has once again assumed a prominent role in the U.S. economy has, unfortunately, been slow to develop. Immigration had significantly declined in importance from World War I through to the mid-1960s. As officially measured, the foreign born percentage of the population had steadily fallen from 13.2 percent in 1920 to 4.7 percent in 1970. The foreign born population in 1980, however, rose to 6.2 percent of the U.S. population (a 46 percent increase over the decade). Given immigration developments during the 1980s, the figure for 1990 should easily approach 9 percent (or about one of every eleven persons in the U.S. population). Even these percentages are widely suspected of being far too low due to the belief that there was a significant undercount of illegal immigrants by the 1980 Census and the anticipation of similar problems in the 1990 Census. Given policy obligations already built into existing immigration laws and prevailing Congressional tendencies to incrementally expand immigration without regard to overall policy consequences, the percentage should again approach or exceed the high level of 1920 by the year 2000.

The main reason that the effects of the resurgence of mass immigration have not aroused more public attention is that the impact is geographically concentrated. Six states—Califomia, New York, Florida, Texas, New Jersey, and Illinois—account for 38.4 percent of the U.S. population but 71.4 percent of all immigrants admitted to the U.S. in 1987. The additional flows of illegal immigrants, non-immigrants and refugees have followed similar settlement paths. Moreover, within these states, immigrants have overwhelmingly settled in urban areas.[4] In 1980, 92 percent of the foreign born population that was actually counted that year by the Census lived in metropolitan areas compared to only 72 percent of the native born population. Thus, the magnified effects of mass immigration are largely manifested in the urban areas of a handful of states. They are, however, the largest labor markets in the U.S. economy (e.g., New York, Los Angeles, Chicago, Houston, and Miami). Hence, there is still a pronounced national as well as a clear local significance to these developments.

In 1981, a presidential commission-the *Select Commission on Immigration and Refugee Policy-bluntly stated that U.S. immigration policy was "out of control" and it urged policymakers to confront "the reality of limitations."*[5] Subsequently, on two occasions Congress attempted to adopt legislation that would address the nation's immigration policy in a comprehensive manner. Both efforts failed. A new tactic was next pursued: piecemeal reform. The immediate consequence was the adoption of the Immigration Reform and Control Act of 1986 that was targeted largely to the issue of illegal immigration. But even this policy thrust was watered down. Its provisions fail to adequately address the issue of worker identification. Congress, in a period of fiscal constraint, has been unwilling in the years since its enactment to sufficiently fund the enforcement mechanisms required to make the law effective. Moreover, as Congress has turned its attention to the remaining areas of policy reform—those pertaining to legal immigrants, non-immigrant workers, and refugees, it has encountered well organized special interest groups who have placed selfish and short-sighted goals ahead of any consideration for the national welfare. These groups focus their power on each of the separate policy components that Congress takes up. *There is, apparently, no one interested in watching what is the cumulative outcome.* The consequence is that Congress is in the process of making a mockery of the Select Commission's informed plea for a policy of "limitations." Thus, if anything, immigration policy is now more "out of control" than it was when the reform process began almost a decade ago.

THE CHANGING NATURE OF THE LABOR MARKET

Paralleling the return of mass immigration, the years since the 1960s have also witnessed a dramatic restructuring of the nation's industrial and occupational patterns. The goods producing industries—which had been the country's dominant employment sector since the founding of the nation—have rapidly declined. As late as 1950, over half the labor force was employed in this sector; by the late 1980s, it accounted for only about 26 percent of all employed persons. It is projected to decline even further in the 1990s. Moreover, the largest employing industries in the goods producing sector have sustained the most significant contractions. Agricultural employment has declined annually since the late 1940s—accounting now for only about 3 percent of all employed workers. Manufacturing—which in the mid-1950s provided jobs for over one-third of the labor force now does so for less than one-fifth. Mining has also had a steady decline. Only the construction industry has shown moderate growth, but it is characterized by significant cyclical fluctuations in any given year.

The rapid fall-off in employment in the goods producing sector has been caused by the confluence of several broad economic forces. First, there has been a shift in consumer spending patterns that is the hallmark of the coming of the post-industrial economy. The maturing of the mass consumption society is symbolized by shifts in expenditures away from goods toward services. It is a truism in economics that where spending increases, employment increases (i.e., the service sector); where spending falls, employment declines (i.e., the goods sector). In addition to spending shifts, the advent of computer controlled technology has created self-regulating production systems that have reduced the demand for unskilled and semi-skilled workers in the goods producing section.[6] Lastly, of course, there have been the intrusive effects of international competition in the past two decades that have exceeded any such previous pressures in all of U.S. economic history. The manufacturing sector in particular has been hard hit by the tide of foreign imports (and the inability to export) associated with the largely unilateral pursuit of a free trade policy by the U.S. government.[7]

In the wake of the sharp declines in employment in the goods producing sector, there have been dramatic increases in the service producing industries. Responding to the shifts in consumer spending patterns, 70 percent of the U.S. labor force is now employed in services. The U.S. Department of Labor projects that 90 percent of the new jobs that will be created in the remainder of the twentieth century will be in the service industries and that the service sector will account for 75 percent of all employment by the year 2000. Thus, the demand for labor is being radically restructured.

The supply of labor is slowly adapting, but the adjustment process is not as easy nor as automatic as it was in earlier eras when the goods producing sectors dominated. The displaced workers from the agricultural sector in the early twentieth century had little difficulty qualifying for newly created jobs in the burgeoning manufacturing sector. They only had to relocate and, when immigration flows were sharply reduced between the 1920s through to the 1960s, they tended to do so. But the emergence of the service economy has imposed an entirely different set of job requirements on the actual and potential labor force. While the technology of earlier periods stressed physical and manual skills for job seekers, the service economy stresses mental, social, linguistic, and communication skills. As a consequence, the shift to services has meant declining job opportunities for those who lack quality educations and skills. As former Secretary of Labor William Brock succinctly said in 1987, "the days of disguising functional illiteracy with a high paying assembly line job that simply requires a manual skill are soon to be over. The world of work is changing right under our feet."[8] Tragically, a disproportionate number of those who are presently vulnerable to these adverse employment effects are racial minorities, women and youths.[9]

Directly associated with these dramatic industrial trends are the derivative changes in occupational patterns. Over onethird of the growth in employment since 1972 has occurred in the professional, technical and related workers classifications. Other broad occupational groups experiencing substantially faster-than-average growth over this period were managers, administrators, and service and sales workers. The greatest decline in employment was among operatives, farmers, farm laborers, and private household workers. The U.S. Department of Labor projects that the occupations expected to experience the most rapid growth over the next decade are those that require the most highly educated workers.[10] These include executives, administrators, and managers; professionals; and technicians and related support workers. Collectively, these three occupational categories accounted for 25 percent of total employment in 1986 but are expected to constitute 40 percent of the nation's employment growth for the remainder of the century.

THE CHANGING COMPOSITION OF THE LABOR FORCE

The composition of the U.S. labor force is also experiencing major changes. Since the mid-1960s, blacks, Hispanics, and Asians, as well as women from all racial and ethnic groups have dramatically increased their proportions of the total labor force. The Bureau of Labor Statistics projects that these trends will continue (see Table 1). Women will account for two-thirds of the annual growth in the labor force and blacks about 25 percent over the next decade. The Hispanic population grew in the 1980s at a rate five times faster than the population as a whole and Hispanics are projected to account for 15 percent of overall growth in the labor supply during the 1990s. The same general pattern also holds true for Asian Americans.

Presently, the incidence of unemployment, poverty, and adult illiteracy are much higher and the labor force participation rates and educational attainment levels are much lower for blacks and Hispanics than is the case for non-Hispanic whites (comparable data for Asians is unavailable). It is also the case that blacks and Hispanics are disproportionately employed in the industries and occupations that are already in sharpest decline (i.e., in the goods producing industries and in blue collar occupations).[11] Thus, those groups in the labor force that are most rapidly increasing are precisely those most adversely at risk by the changing employment requirements. Unless public policy measures are addressed to their human

Table 1. Selected labor force characteristics, 1986–2000

Millions of Persons

	Labor Force Total In:		Absolute Change	Percentage Change	Share of Total In:	
Group	1986	2000	1986-2000	1986-2000	1986	2000
TOTAL	117.8	138.8	20.9	17.80%	100%	100%
White	101.8	116.7	14.9	14.6	86.4	84.1
Black	12.7	16.3	3.7	28.8	10.8	11.8
Hispanic	8.1	14.1	6	74.4	6.9	10.2
Asian	3.4	5.7	2.4	71.2	2.8	4.1
Women	52.4	65.6	13.2	25.2	44.5	47.3
Men	65.4	73.1	7.7	11.8	55.5	52.7

NOTE: The race/origin subgroups overlap and therefore do not add to total. Hispanic figures are included in both the White and Black classifications.

SOURCE: U.S. Department of Labor

resource development needs, both these and other vulnerable groups have dim prospects in the emerging post-industrial economy.

If mass and unguided immigration continues, it is unlikely that there will be sufficient pressure to enact the long term human resource development policies needed to prepare and to incorporate these groups into the mainstream economy. Instead, it is likely that the heavy but unplanned influx of immigrant labor will serve—by providing both competition and alternatives—to maintain the social marginalization of many citizen blacks and citizen Hispanics. If so, *the chance to eliminate once and for all the underclass in the U.S. economy will be lost—probably forever.*

THE IMPACTS OF IMMIGRATION

Immigration policy, by definition, is capable of influencing not only the quantitative size of the labor force but also its qualitative composition. As matters now stand, *there is virtually no synchronization of the immigrant flows with the demonstrated needs of the labor market.* With widespread uncertainty as to the number of illegal immigrants, refugees, and non-immigrant workers who will enter, it is impossible to know in advance how many actual persons from foreign countries are actually entering the U.S. labor force each year.

Moreover, whatever skills, education, linguistic abilities, talents or locational settlement preferences most immigrants, refugees, and non-immigrants have is purely incidental to the reason that they are admitted or enter the country. The legal system reserves 80 percent of the 270,000 visas issued each year for various family reunification purposes. The immediate relatives (i.e., spouses, children, and parents) of each of these visa recipients—an additional 219,000 persons in 1988—are, of course, exempt from meeting any labor market standard. The same is true for the refugees admitted each year (e.g., about 125,000 at present levels) and for the estimated 200,000 to 500,000 illegal immigrants who continue to enter the United States each year. The vast preponderance of the illegal immigrants and refugees of the 1980s have had very few skills, little formal education, and limited (if any) literacy in English. An additional several hundred thousand non-immigrants are admitted each year to work in the United States for various lengths of time after only minimal checks as to whether citizen workers are available or could be trained to do the work.

As a consequence, the labor market effects of the current politically driven immigration system are twofold. Some of the immigrants do have human resource endowments that are quite congruent with the labor market conditions currently dictated by the economy's needs. In fact, they are desperately needed due to the appalling lack of sufficient attention given by the nation to the adequate preparation of many citizen members of its labor force. But most do not. Hence, they must seek employment in the declining sectors of the goods producing industries (e.g., agriculture and light manufacturing) or the low wage sectors of the expanding service sector (e.g., restaurants, lodging or retail enterprises). Unfortunately, it is also the case that *many of the nations citizens who are in the underclass are also in these same employment sectors.* A disproportionately high number of these citizens are minorities, women, and youth. As these citizen groups are growing in both absolute and percentage terms, it is they who the logic of national survival would say should have the first claim on the nation's available jobs. *The last thing they need is more competition from immigrants for the limited number of existing jobs as well as for the scarce opportunities for training and education that are available.*

The post-industrial economy of the United States is facing the real prospect of serious shortages of *qualified* labor. It does not have a shortage of actual or potential workers. No advanced industrial nation that has 23 million illiterate adults (some say the figure is now 27 million) and another 40 million adults who are marginally literate need have any fear about a shortage of unskilled workers in its foreseeable future.[12] Immigration is a contributing factor to the growth of adult illiteracy in this nation. As a consequence, immigration-by adding to the surplus of illiterate job seekers-is serving to diminish the limited chances that many poorly prepared citizens have to find jobs or to improve their employability. It is not surprising therefore, that the underground economy—with its culture of drugs, crime and gangs—is thriving in many of the nation's urban centers. The nature of the immigration flow is also contributing to the need to expand remedial education, training, and language programs at a time when such funds are desperately needed to upgrade the human resource capabilities of much of the citizen labor force.

The popular notion of the need for labor force growth for growth's sake is obsolete. It is doubtful that the idea was ever completely valid since it is, in essence, the deadly theory of the cancer cell. It is a general principle that can distort normal adjustment processes. *With respect to the labor market, shortages are a wonderful issue for society to confront.* Shortages force public policymakers to look first at how society is using and preparing its human resources. It is no accident that such issues as education, health, housing, transportation, training, rehabilitation, poverty prevention, and anti-discrimination measures have only recently come to the fore. Labor shortages should compel policymakers to resolve these domestic needs before they turn to the placebo of mass immigration. It is the quality of life that is the key to the achievement of a fully employed economy and an equitable society in the postindustrial era.

The prospect of shortages of *qualified* labor offers to this country a chance to improve the lot of the working poor and to rid itself of its large underclass. It can force public policy to focus on the necessity to incorporate into the mainstream economy many citizens who have been "left out" in the past. It was in this precise context that William Aramondy, the President of the United Way, recently said, "We have the biggest single opportunity in our history to address 200 years of unfairness to blacks. If we don't, God condemn us for blowing the chance."[13] The major threat to "the opportunity" he correctly identified is the perpetuation of the nation's politically dominated immigration policy. It is long past time for immigration policy to cease being a contributor to the problems of the U.S. labor force. Instead it must become accountable for its economic consequences so that it can be part of the answer to the nation's pressing needs in an increasingly competitive world economy.

LABOR FORCE AND POPULATION SIZE

The preceding discussion (and indeed my professional experience) is focused on the size, composition and change of the U.S. labor force. Other authors in this series have much greater professional expertise to address the question of optimum population, in the sense of an overall number. There are, however, close connections between the policies I have advocated above and the nation's demographic future.

As to immigration: I have argued that the current pattern of mass immigration of primarily unskilled people is a direct threat to the nation's well-being. We do require the immigration of certain skills and professional expertise, but not in such numbers as to discourage our national effort to produce professionals and skilled workers in those categories.

The nation's requirements could possibly change again in the future, and we should retain the flexibility to examine immigration policies in the light of changing realities. For the foreseeable future, however, *I have suggested immigration policies that would involve a movement far smaller than at present,* and from economic strata that tend in most countries to have fewer children than the poor and unskilled. This of course means that their contribution to U.S. population growth after their arrival would be smaller than for the average present immigrant.

As to the character of the indigenous labor force: I have argued that we need skilled labor, not mass labor, and that there is already a substantial population of functional illiterates who have great trouble entering the labor force.

Our national policies and social behavior have constituted a nearly total mismatch with these needs. We have let educational standards slide, and our graduates, by and large, are neither literate nor (in Garrett Hardin's phrase) numerate.

In the first paper in this NPG Forum series, Lindsey Grant pointed out that fertility among the affluent and the educated is far below replacement level. It is about twice as high among the poorest and least educated. This difference is geometric as the generations progress: four times as many grandchildren, eight times as many great-grandchildren, and so on. Those who can or will educate their children are having very few of them; the population growth is occurring among those who cannot educate theirs. Presently, the poor are in a vicious circle, with their poverty often perpetuated by their ignorance. Social policies that sought to reduce this discrepancy in fertility would lead to fewer of the poor children, and a better hope that society can find the means to educate those whose parents cannot.

In a society such as ours, one is on delicate ground even to suggest that there is a public interest in fertility levels. Our view of the role of government would certainly preclude any very large government role in any effort to change the national mindset about them. *One can, however, posit a happy situation wherein the poor have about the same number of children as the more educated and prosperous, and in which those children—precisely because their parents and society can better afford to rear and educate them—will escape the vicious cycle of poverty and, having escaped it, adopt the fertility habits of their new economic condition.*

In another of this series of NPG Forum articles, demographer Leon Bouvier has sketched out several demographic scenarios, drawn from Census Bureau projections. What I have said about immigration and fertility in this paper would lead me somewhere close to or below his "hard" path—i.e. a total fertility rate of 1.5 and net immigration of 300,000. *That scenario yields a slight rise in population from the present 248 million to 278 million in 2020, and then a gradual decline to 218 million in 2080.*

I find this prospect rather attractive.

Certainly, everything I have said here suggests that immigration and education and the size and composition of the labor force and population should be seen as interconnected, and with fundamental consequences for the national wellbeing. Our politicians must work themselves out of the illusion that immigration is simply a political issue, and a way of rewarding vociferous interest groups. It is an important determinant of our future.

NOTES:

1. Oxford Analytica, *America in Perspective*. (Boston: Houghton Mifflin, 1986), p. 20.
2. Vernon M. Briggs, Jr., *Immigration Policy and the American Labor Force* (Baltimore: The Johns Hopkins University Press, 1984).
3. U.S. Bureau of the Census Current Population Reports, Series 25, No. 1018, *Projections of the Population of the U.S., by Age, Sex, and Race: 1988 to 2080*, by Gregory Spencer (Washington: USGPO, 1989). Projections #14 and #29. This calculation assumes annual net immigration of 800,000, which is a reasonable estimate of the current level.
4. Elizabeth Bogen, *Immigration In New York*. (New York Praeger Publishers, 1987), p. 60.
5. Select Commission on Immigration and Refugee Policy, *U.S. Immigration Policy and the National Interest*. (Washington, D.C.: U.S. Government Printing Office, 1981), pp.2 and 5.
6. Richard M. Cyert and David C. Mowery (eds.), *Technology and Employment*, (Washington, D.C.: National Academy Press, 1987), Chapter 4.
7. John M. Culbertson, *The Trade Threat and U.S. Trade Policy*, (Madison: 21st Century Press, 1989).
8. William E. Brock, U.S. Secretary of Labor, "Address to the National Press Club," Washington, D.C. (March 5, 1987), p.
9. Cyert and Mowery, *op. cit.*, Chapter 5.
10. George T. Silverstri and John M. Lukasiewicz, "A Look at Occupational Employment Trends to the Year 2000," *Monthly Labor Review*, (September, 1987), pp. 46–63.
11. Cyert and Mowery, *op. cit.*, Chapter 5.
12. Jonathan Kozol, *Illiterate America*. (Garden City, N.Y.: Anchor Press, 1985). pp. 4 and 115.
13. Neal C. Peirce, "Unique Opportunities for the Nation's Blacks," syndicated column printed in *The Ithaca Journal*, (April 19, 1989), p. 8.

SUSTAINABLE IMMIGRATION: LEARNING TO SAY NO

David Simcox

March 1990

February 1990 was a dismayingly typical month in the uncertain course of American immigration policymaking, demonstrating the varied and intense pressures that are steadily working to drive up overall immigration. Here are just a few:

- Early in February Immigration Commissioner Gene McNary announced he was using his executive authority to grant what amounts to limited permanent resident status to illegal aliens who are spouses and minor children of legalized aliens, but who arrived too late to qualify for the 1986 amnesty. By the stroke of the pen, McNary added an estimated 800,000 to 1.5 million persons to the permanent legally resident population.
- Congressman Bruce Morrison, Chairman of the House of Representatives Immigration Subcommittee—in February introduced his legal immigration reform bill that would boost the flow of newcomers in the 1990s to about 1.5 million a year—almost twice the current number. Morrison's bill also provides for the admission of some 250,000 temporary resident workers and their families, most of whom would ultimately become permanent residents.
- Under pressure from Congress, the Immigration and Naturalization Service (INS) further liberalized the criteria for Soviet and Eastern European minorities to claim refugee status in the United States. Since the current authorized ceiling on refugees of 125,000 does not cover all the demand, many excess refugees join the 25,000 or so now entering the U.S. as "parolees," with the prospect of permanent resident status in a few years.
- Border Patrolmen were regrouping in south Texas to cope with a new surge of young Central American illegal immigrants in flight from that region's demographic eruption and widespread joblessness. But pro-immigrant forces in the Congress were predicting success in their six-year battle for a blanket admission of migrating Central Americans under the new concept of "temporary protected status." This measure would give quasi-permanent residence to half a million Central American settlers, and could attract more illegal immigration in the future.
- In this month, like all others, businessmen and hospital administrators continued to press Congress for the admission of more foreign clerks, orderlies and nurses, the universities for more foreign students and researchers, the churches for more refugees and church workers, the fruit and vegetable growers for more farm workers, the Asian-Americans for more Asians, and the Irish-Americans more Irishmen.

UNLIMITED IMMIGRATION DEMAND

Underlying the *ad hoc* concessions and steady upcreep is a profound imbalance between the numbers abroad who want to live in the United States and the limits and conditions imposed on their coming by U.S. law. As world population has swelled by more than 80 million yearly, proliferating family migration chains have lengthened the waiting list for U.S. visas from 1.0 million in 1980 to 2.4 million in 1990.

Congress responds distractedly to these pressures with special exceptions for relief measures to alleviate perceived refugee and asylee emergencies, putative labor shortages, or the clamor of powerful special ethnic interests. Cumulative concessions have pushed total immigration to nearly 900,000 a year in 1990. But regularly missing from this ongoing legislative bazaar is concern for the long range population effects of so many newcomers.

Even allowing for emigration, immigration under current law and practice directly accounts for 32 percent of national population growth, and the proportion is rising. The 1990 census is expected to show that the foreign born population has grown from 4.7 percent in 1970 to 8.5 percent in 1990. Fears of labor shortages—although the U.S. unemployment rate of 5.2 percent is twice that of Japan's—has warmed Congress to the idea of further expansions of immigration. If the House of Representatives' current version of legal immigration reform wins out, annual legal immigration would climb to about 1.4 million by 1995, or nearly 55 percent of population growth. Two to three million aliens amnestied under the 1986 law will convert to permanent status in the early '90s, further swelling the permanent population as they bring their families to this country.

Census data and immigration statistics understate the degree of population growth due to entries from abroad. The census count disregards such categories as foreign students, long staying temporary workers, and most illegal and commuter aliens-categories that add another million to the U.S. population on any given day. Many of these immigrants have children, and their children have children, swelling the population base.

Census Bureau projections of future population growth use 800,000 as the "high" assumption of net yearly immigration.[1] Demographer Leon Bouvier notes that Census' "high" assumption is now more reasonable as a medium projection. Bouvier warns that if American fertility rose only to the 2.2 replacement level, net immigration of 800,000 per year would push the U.S. population to 394 million in 2050 and 471 million by 2080. Even applying current fertility and medium mortality rates (TFR of 1.8 and life expectancy rising slowly to 81.2 years), immigration of 800,000, according to the Census Bureau, will lift the U.S. population to the 300 million mark by the year 2015, and to 333 million by 2080.[2] Positing a "low" net annual immigration of 300,000, Census projects the U.S. population would peak in 2030 at 288 million and then gradually decline to 265 million in 2080. Clearly, if the United States is to begin to reverse its population growth, net immigration of 300,000 or less is imperative. But as annual entries have crept up since the 1960s, we have come to see a net inflow of newcomers of at least twice that number as the norm.

THE PSYCHIC FUNCTION OF GENEROUS IMMIGRATION

Indeed, many Americans regard the accommodation of hundreds of thousands of immigrants and refugees as a peculiarly American mission in the world, one that is deeply intermingled with the nation's sense of self-worth and high moral values. For many others, immigration yields only positive benefits by reuniting families, bringing in needed labor or investors, or aiding our foreign policy. Underlying all these particular interests is the pervasive sense that our generous immigration policies are an ennobling American statement to the world. Thus basic immigration policy, as the Senate debates of immigration reform in the summer of 1989 demonstrated, is most often legislated on the basis of anecdotes, slogans and impressions, vague notions about the nation's immigrant past, and a desire to use immigration law to affirm standards of charity and generosity. These sentiments becloud the national interest, edging out practical concerns for the nation's population future.

Commonly, long term population concerns are dismissed with the argument that the ratio of immigrants to the general population is far lower now than in 1910. The implication is that as the U.S. population grows it should take in steadily more newcomers to maintain a historically ordained ratio.

IMMIGRATION AUSTERITY: CURBING ILLEGAL SETTLEMENT

Given the diversity and intensity of the current demands on our national immigration system and the powerful sentiments involved, which of the many claimants would receive priority if the nation were to decide to reduce immigration to a more sustainable 300,000 yearly or less? How could a democratic system fairly allocate the pain that would accompany a two-thirds reduction in immigration?

The first and most politically defensible step toward far lower immigration would be deep cuts in illegal immigration, now estimated by the Immigration and Naturalization Service (INS) to add some 200,000 a year to the settled population, though unofficial estimates go as high as 300,000. Firm commitment to enforcement of the immigration laws—so far never conscientiously attempted in the United States—could soon reduce this number by two-thirds. The task would demand a doubling of the money and manpower of the 13 thousand member, billion dollar a year INS. But much of the added cost could be recovered by vigorous application of fines, service fees and tax penalties on illegal aliens and their employers and sponsors in the United States.

But even an expanded INS could not successfully combat such a pervasive national problem unaided. The Federal Government must mobilize other agencies having regular contact with illegal immigrants and their employers, such as Internal Revenue, the Department of Labor, the Social Security Administration, the department of Housing and Urban Development, and national law enforcement agencies. Federal funding and federal leadership would be essential to animate state and local labor, revenue, welfare, and police agencies to act against illegal alien employment and settlement.

Two new weapons against illegal immigration emerged in the 1980s. Penalties or "sanctions" against employers of illegal aliens are intended to turn off the magnet of jobs. "Entitlements verification" known by the acronym "SAVE," uses computer matching and identity checks to deny welfare and public assistance to illegal aliens.

Not surprisingly, both devices are under fierce attack from immigrant advocacies and civil rights groups. But they need to be strengthened and additional deterrents brought to bear. Among those worth considering are:

- Proof of legal status or citizenship as a condition for:
  a. Entering into real estate contracts, such as home purchases or leases.
  b. obtaining drivers' licenses, motor vehicles registration or liability insurance.
  c. qualifying for professional and occupational licensing.
  d. enrolling in state or federally assisted colleges and universities.
  e. securing business and alcoholic beverages licenses.
- Internal Revenue Service audits of employers found hiring illegal aliens and disqualification of

wages paid to unauthorized aliens as deductible business expenses.

- Such internal controls to be matched by increased numbers of border patrolmen backed up by more expeditious procedures for deportation and summary exclusion of aliens entering illegally.
- Tightened strictures against illegal immigration, utilizing a tamper-proof system of identification and more rigorous controls over birth, death and other vital statistics documents.[3]

LIVING WITH LOWER LEGAL IMMIGRATION

While working to reduce illegal immigration to zero, federal policymakers would also need to reorder current priorities to reduce legal immigration and refugee flows from their present 600,000 to 700,000 a year to 300,000 a year. A sustainable annual immigration level of 300,000 could continue to be organized around the three general streams that now dominate the current immigration system: refugees, family reunification and independent immigrants. A reasonable and politically acceptable allocation among the three might be as follows:

Projected U.S. Population Growth 1988-2080

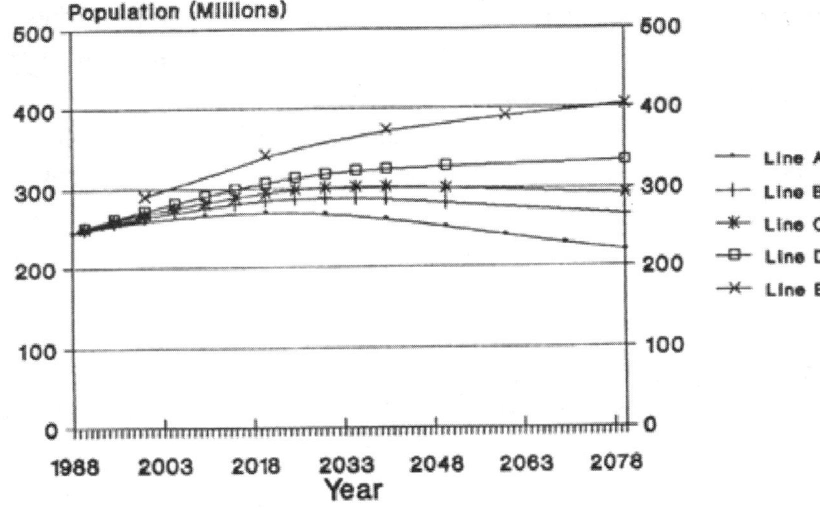

See below for explanations.

Line A: with immigration equal to emigration, the population of the United States would peak at 270 million in 2020, and would decline gradually to 220 million in 2080.

Line B: with a net annual immigration of 300,000, the population would be 288 million in 2030 and 266 million in 2080.

Line C: with a net annual immigration of 500,000, the population would peak at 302 million in 2040 and would decline slightly to 292 million by 2080.

Line D: with a net annual immigration of 800,000, the population would pass 333 million in 2080 and would still be rising. This line represents a reasonable, conservative estimate of today's net immigration levels.

Line E: a net annual immigration of 1.5 million—which could result from current proposals—would lead to a population passing 403 million in 2080.

Sources: Lines A through D: Gregory Spencer, *Projections of the Population of the United States, by Age, Sex and Race: 1988 to 2080* (U.S. Bureau of the Census, Series P-25, No. 1018, January 1989). Line E: Leon F. Bouvier and Cary B. Davis, *The Future Racial Composition of the United States* (Washington, D.C.: Population Reference Bureau, August 1982). The assumptions in the two studies are comparable, though not identical. The latter study assumes a total fertility rate 0.092 lower than the Census study and life expectancies converging in 2080 at a figure 0.5 years lower. Both assume fertility very slightly below current levels.

Figure 1.

1) *Refugees and asylees*, now entering at the rate of 125,000 yearly, could be reduced to 50,000 a year-the figure determined by Congress to be "normal flow" in the 1980 Refugee Act. The privilege of refuge would be awarded by rigorous case-by-case examination of applicants of special concern to the United States and given only to those who demonstrate the clear probability of life-threatening harm. Unsuccessful applicants would have the option of competing as candidates for independent immigration.

2) *Family reunification* in 1988 brought in 220,000 quota-free immediate relatives of U.S. citizens and nearly 200,000 other immigrants claiming family relationships to citizens or legal resident aliens. Immigration austerity would require limits on the privilege of U.S. citizens to bring in immediate family members, reducing the inflow in this category (now 220,000 yearly and growing) to 100,000 a year. Preferential immigration of spouses and minor children would be limited to those whose marriages were contracted before the immigration of the petitioning U.S. citizen occurred. Parents of U.S. citizens, children over eighteen and married children of any age would no longer qualify for family reunification visas but could compete as independent immigrants. Neither native born nor foreign born U.S. citizens would be entitled to bring in newly acquired spouses for residence under this category, though they could seek independent immigrant visas for them.

3) A pool of 150,000 numbers annually for *independent immigrants* would serve the nation's most pressing needs for the importation of highly skilled workers and professionals, family members of U.S. citizens and residents not otherwise covered, and persons of special foreign policy interest. Visas would be awarded through a point system which would assign variable values for criteria such as skills, investment potential, adaptability, family connections, hardship, importance to foreign policy, and number of children (with smaller families receiving extra points).

Table 1. Allocation of Immigration Spaces

Category	Current Law – 1988	Proposed Austerity Allocations
Family Immigration	430,000	100,000
Refugees & Asylees	111,000	50,000
Independent Immigrants	102,000	150,000
(Professionals & Skilled Workers, Special Immigrants)		
TOTALS	643,000	300,000

Since refugee emergencies could not be ruled out, unforeseen urgent, presidentially-certified refugee demands would be met by preempting numbers, first in the independent category, and then in the family category until both were exhausted. For such emergencies, the President could also borrow up to two-thirds of the succeeding year's immigration numbers, but never for more than two consecutive years. (The outcry from those Americans with an interest in the regular flow of immigrants would probably assure that no president would use this authority except in the most unusual circumstances.)

Heads of families authorized for independent immigration would receive the numbers needed to bring their spouse and minor children with them, thus avoiding the need for subsequent special arrangements for reunification.

Reduction of the supply of visas would have to be accompanied by measures to dampen demand. Applications of nonrefugee aliens should carry a sizable fee. Those successful in winning a visa should pay a front-end service charge of up to $5000 per family unit. Employers sponsoring aliens for jobs should pay a surtax of 15 percent on the alien's earnings during their first five years here.

THE TOUGH SCENARIO

If population pressures were determined to be unusually severe, could the United States manage even lower migration? Cutting inflow to 150,000 a year or less, thus off setting or falling below emigration, would significantly hasten population reduction if fertility stays low. But it would leave national policymakers with excruciating choices. At such a low volume of immigration, three distinct categories would have little purpose. More appropriate would be a single comprehensive point system with all types of applicants competing together for a single pool of visas.

Congress could periodically review and if necessary adjust the weightings given different migration criteria, such as persecution or political hardship, family connections, skills or investment potential.

The nation's economic and cultural interaction with the world will continue to demand a sizable flow of foreign sojourners. The current immigration laws provide a range of specialized temporary or "non-immigrant" visa categories to meet this need. But these provisions are frequently abused to arrange defacto permanent residence for many who are ineligible or unwilling to compete for regular immigration slots.

A MORE CAREFUL COUNT OF INFLOW

The Immigration Service logged 377 million entries into the United States in 1988, including returning American citizens and repeat visits by aliens with border-crossing cards, aircraft crews and the like. Sixty percent—225 million—were non-citizens. 14.6 million of those persons entered the United States with non-immigrant visas. Of that number, the Immigration Service estimates that 255,000 stayed beyond the period allowed by the terms of their admission.

If population benefits are to be gained, overall cuts in legal and illegal immigration would have to be matched by more comprehensive methods of counting the total permanent alien population in the United States and keeping it within an overall ceiling. Policymakers must make less of the fictional legal distinctions between "permanent resident aliens" and nominally "temporary" longstayers who can easily remain in the United States indefinitely. Notwithstanding the disparity of labels, the aggregate pressure of the foreign source population on the environment, demand for services, infrastructure, and consumption of resources is the same. Population planners should consider anyone who comes with the reasonable expectation of staying a year or more an addition to the population count, regardless of his personal intentions or temporary category.

Worth exploring is the concept of "full-time equivalence" as a measure of the total foreign impact on population and resources. The full-time equivalence system would, for example, be a convenient way of measuring the presence of the transient and sojourner portions of the population in person-years. Two hundred thousand persons in the United States for six months yields 100,000 person-years. This type of measurement provides a far more revealing assessment of the effects of foreign born persons on population and environment.

The 1990 census is expected to show 21 million of the nation's 250 million as foreign born. Under a full-time equivalence count, 21 million alien person-years would increase substantially with the addition of person-years for nearly one million foreign students, temporary workers and specialists, seasonal agricultural workers and some 2 to 3 million longstaying tourists.

THE PUBLIC AND IMMIGRATION LEVELS: WANTING IT BOTH WAYS

Obviously, such a disciplined approach to the management of immigration will not come easily for a beleaguered Congress. National polls in the past two decades have consistently shown that a heavy majority of Americans support freezing immigration levels or rolling them back. A 1965 Gallup Poll, for example, at a time when legal immigration was less than 300,000, showed 72 percent favored allowing it to go no higher. Almost half of those favored reductions. In 1985, when legal immigration had risen to 370,000, 77 percent of respondents to a Roper Poll favored curbs.

Congress's mild response to what seems like clear public opinion on the issue suggests a greater public ambivalence. The electorate's strong but unfocussed demand for lower immigration repeatedly yields to the highly focussed demands of segments of the public for ad hoc responses to the short term perceived needs for refugee admissions, farm workers, separated family members and the like. Often wanting to respond compassionately to urgent needs, the general public—and its congressional representatives—take the view that "a few more can't hurt." Overlooked in the process are the higher future immigration demands that often result because of new precedents, additional family reunification chains, or the opening of new migration streams through "onetime" refugee relief measures.

The public needs to become aware of the sizable long range, cumulative population consequences of isolated short-term concessions. Only the discipline of a tight, all inclusive immigration "budget" or ceiling can regularly force the tradeoffs and tough choices that true immigration austerity will demand.

Table 2. Longstaying Temporary Workers (Not Counted as Immigrants)

Category and Visa Symbol of Admission	1984	1986	1988	Period
Treaty Trader or Investor (E-1, E-2)	22,419	30,424	31,920	Indefinite
Student (F-1, M-1)	136,129	137,573	159,406	4 Year +
Temporary Worker of Distinguished Merit & Ability (H-1)	25,903	31,052	41,202	2-6 Years
Other Temporary Workers (H-2)	5,828	8,725	6,656	Up to 1 Yr
Industrial Trainees (H-3)	2,115	1,915	1,600	Up to 1 Yr
Exchange Visitor (J-1, J-2)	97,652	129,563	157,994	24 Years
Fiance or fiancee of U.S. Citizen (K-1, K-2)	7,645	8,291	7,082	Permanent
Multinational Companies (L-1)	13,621	114,174	12,707	Indefinite
TOTAL VISAS ISSUED	311,312	361,717	418,587	

Source: Report of the Visa Office 1988, Washington, D.C.: Department of State, 1989.

NOTES:

1. U.S. Bureau of Census, Current Population Reports, Series P25, No. 1018, *Projections of the Population of the United States, by Age, Sex and Race: 1988 to 2080*, by Gregory Spencer,
2. Leon Bouvier: "How to Get There from Here: the Demographic Route to Optimal Population Size," The *NPG Forum*, Fall 1989.
3. David Simcox: *Secure Identification: A National Need-A Must for Immigration Control*, Center for Immigration Studies. Washington: USGPO, 1989.Washington, DC, 1989.

MANNING THE AMERICAN MILITARY: DEMOGRAPHICS AND NATIONAL SECURITY

Martin Binkin

May 1990

It is said that Josef Stalin, once cautioned against offending the Vatican, asked his advisers how many divisions the Pope could field. Traditionally a nation's standing in the world has been determined by its military power and, for most of history, military power has been expressed in terms of division flags or the number of men under arms. By the middle decades of the twentieth century, however, mass armies had become an anachronism, first because of the introduction of thermonuclear weapons and later with the spawning of sophisticated military technologies that became substitutes for raw manpower. Even small nations, like Israel, were able to prevail in military confrontations with much more populated enemies. More recently, the Japanese have demonstrated that economic power may be at least as important as military power in contemporary global relationships. Despite these trends, however, much of the conventional wisdom still holds that large armed forces are the *sine qua non* of national power. Thus the prospect that the population of United States may not continue to grow into the twenty-first century and, depending on national policy choices, could decline markedly—has aroused some concern. These fears, however, are unwarranted.

This essay examines the question: "Is a rising United States population needed to meet our future military manpower requirements?"

In brief, I will argue that:

- U.S. military strength is not presently constrained by population size,
- in the future, a reduction in military manpower requirements is more likely than an increase,
- but, through efficient manpower management, even a substantially larger military requirement could be sustained by the smaller population envisioned in the Census Bureau's "lowest" projections through the middle of the twenty-first century.

DEMOGRAPHICS AND MILITARY RECRUITMENT: RECENT EXPERIENCE

Dwindling birthrates in the United States—a trend that started in the late 1950s and brought the baby boom to an end in the mid-1960s—raised a host of public policy issues. As the children of that period (dubbed the "birth-dearth" generation) have grown older, the effects have already been felt, most notably by the nation's primary and secondary educational institutions. As the first cohorts of that generation completed high school in the early 1980s, higher education institutions and the civilian labor force began to notice the effects, while the armed forces braced themselves for the challenges expected to accompany the decline in the size of the pool of prospective volunteers for military service.

The concern was somewhat similar to the alarm now expressed by some observers as they contemplate the prospect of an eventual turnaround in U.S. population growth.

At the turn of the decade, in fact, there was good reason to worry about the impact of demographic trends on the nation's ability to field a peacetime force of two million strong: during the latter half of the 1970s, when the number of Americans in the military-eligible population (eighteen-to twenty-two-year-olds) was at an all-time high, the armed forces compiled the poorest recruitment record in its history. In fiscal year 1979—the peak-year for "baby-boomers" turning eighteen years of age and entering the military's prime recruiting pool—about half of the Army's new recruits had standardized aptitude test scores in the lowest acceptable category (below the thirtieth percentile). Thus the prospect that the youth population would shrink by 25 percent over the next fifteen years and uncertainty about birth and fertility rates beyond that period set off alarms among defense manpower planners. If the armed forces were having trouble maintaining a force that comprised less than one percent of the American population, some feared, how would the nation ever hope to raise an Army large enough to win World War III, should that horrible prospect materialize? After all, at the peak of World War II the United States military establishment had under arms over eleven million men and women, or close to ten percent of the total population.

TOTAL POPULATION PROJECTIONS

Such concerns, however, can be readily discounted. First, even before recent events in the Soviet Union and Eastern Europe, a replay of World War II between NATO and the Warsaw Pact—that is, a protracted conventional conflict involving millions of troops—was considered an extremely long shot.

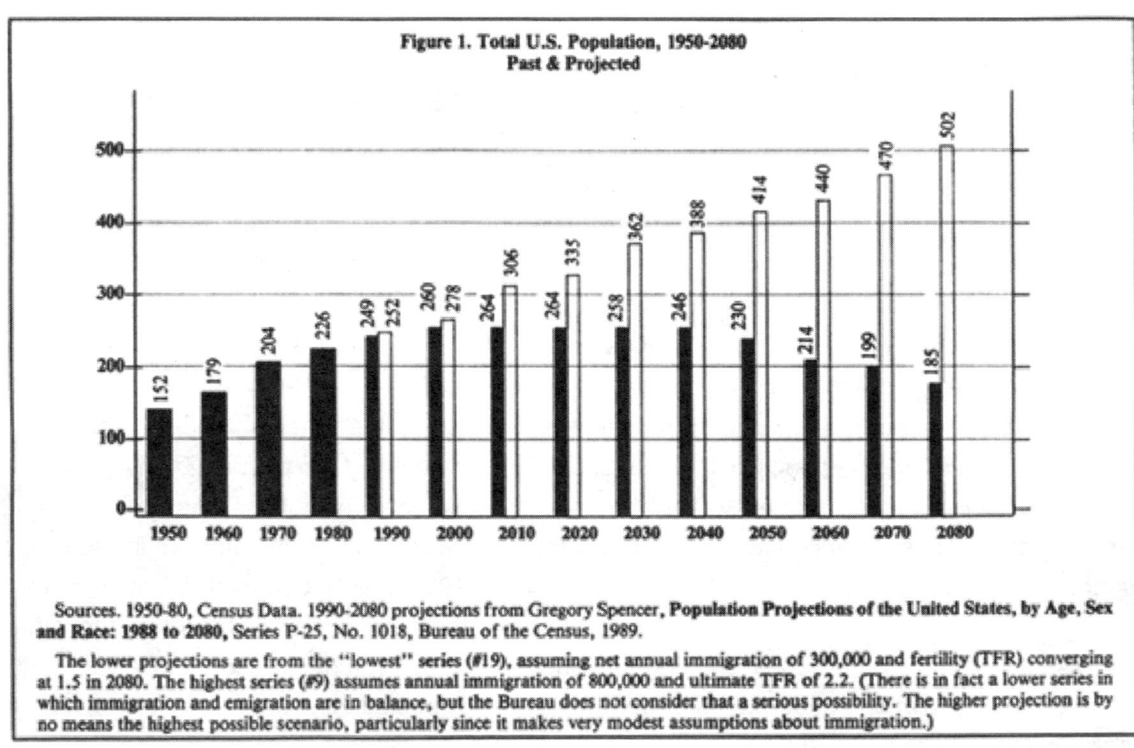

Figure 1.

The betting among serious analysts was that any conventional military confrontation between the two sides would be measured in terms of days or weeks, rather than months or years, ending early either in negotiations or in escalation to nuclear conflict. In any case, few envisaged any situation that would require tens of millions of Americans to serve in the armed forces.

But even if, against all odds, the nation was to get involved in a protracted war of attrition that would require a substantial expansion in the size of the armed forces, full mobilization would be ordered, conscription would be reinstituted and some 18 million American men in the eighteen through twenty-six year cohorts would provide the initial pool of draftees, followed as necessary by men in the older age groups and perhaps expanded opportunities for American women to serve or, indeed, be conscripted into military services. In the extreme, a U.S. military force equal to that of the second World War (11 million) would now constitute less than 5 percent of the total population compared with close to 10 percent in that conflict. In short, the current size of the American population is more than adequate to support "worst-case" scenarios, provided that the nation is willing to reinstitute conscription. And, as Figure 1 shows, even at the "lowest" projections by the Census Bureau, total population size would not be an issue in the foreseeable future. The population projected for 2080, for example, while substantially smaller than the current figure, would still be larger than the population that sustained our armed forces during the second World War.

THE "QUALIFIED AND AVAILABLE" POPULATION

The more relevant issue is the requisite population to sustain American military forces under voluntary peacetime conditions. The key consideration here is not so much the size of the total American population, but rather the size of the relevant-age youth cohorts that form the supply pool of prospective volunteers.

The magnitude of the challenge can be seen in Table 1, which calculates the proportion of "qualified and available" males who would have to volunteer for military service before reaching age twenty-three if the military services are to attain their projected active and reserve manpower needs.[1] This calculation follows one age group through time—excluding those who, because they are on a college track, are not likely to volunteer and those who, because they would be mentally, physically, or morally unqualified, cannot volunteer.[2]

As the table depicts, during 1984–88, an average of about 1.8 million males turned eighteen each year. Based on past experience, about 525,000 of them were considered to be "dedicated" college students (those who would remain in college at least into the third year) with a low propensity for enlisted military service. (This group, of course, provides the bulk of military officer candidates, but the military officer corps represents such a small fraction of the relevant age cohorts that the size of those cohorts is not an important consideration in staffing the officer corps.) Another 526,000 would fail to meet the minimum physical, moral, or aptitude standards for entry into the armed forces.

To maintain an active military force of about 2.1 million and a reserve force of roughly 1.0 million, about 376,000 males had to be recruited annually (278,000 active and 98,000 reserves), or about 50 percent of the "qualified and available" pool of eighteen-year-old males. Daunting though this task might appear, recruiting goals were met with relative ease, at relatively modest cost, and without compromising the quality of the forces. In fact, the armed forces faced

Table 1. Proportion of Qualified and Available Males Required Annually for Military Service, Fiscal Years 1984-88

Thousands unless otherwise indicated

Item	*1984-88*
Total nonistitutionalized 18-year-old males [a]	1,800
Minus: nonavailable college students (adjusted for dropouts) [b]	525
Minus: Unqualified males	526
Mental [c]	337
Physical or moral [d]	189
Equals: Qualified and available male pool	729
Total male recruit requirement	376
Active forces	278
Reserve forces	98
Percent of pool required	52

Sources: Total 18-year-old male population from Bureau of the Census, *Current Population Reports*, series P-25, no. 704, "Projections of the Population of the United States: 1977 to 2050" (GPO, 1977), pp. 4448, 51-55. Institutionalized population estimates based on preliminary data from the 1980 census provided by Bureau of the Census. First- and second-year dropouts based on estimates provided by National Center for Educational Statistics. Mentally unqualified derived from data contained in special tabulations provided by Office of the Assistant Secretary of Defense for Manpower, Reserve Affairs, and Logistics. Physically and morally unqualified derived from unpublished data provided by Office of the Assistant Secretary of Defense for Manpower, Reserve Affairs, and Logistics. Male recruitment requirements compiled from Department of Defense, *Manpower Requirements Report, FY 1984*, vol. 3: *Force Readiness Report* (DOD, 1983), pp. III-12, 111-20,111-21, IV-10, V-7, VI-6, VI-9, VI-10. Projections of Navy and Marine Corps reserve requirements based on fiscal 1983 recruitment data.

a. Assumes 1.5 percent of the male population aged 18 to 24 is institutionalized.

b. Estimates based on 1980 participation rates: in 1980, 74.4 percent of the youth cohort that had entered the ninth grade in 1972 completed high school and 46.3 percent of the initial group enrolled as full- or part-time students in programs creditable toward a bachelor's degree. Assumes that 25 percent of first-time enrollees leave during the first year and 12.5 percent during the second year.

c. Based on 1981 military aptitude requirements, 2 percent of males with one or more years of college would be expected to be unqualified, 10 percent of high school graduates without college experience would not meet minimum standards, and 60 percent of non-high school graduates would not qualify.

d. Assumes that 16.3 percent of the male youth population meeting minimum aptitude requirements would be disqualified on physical grounds and 3.9 percent would fail to meet moral standards.

the formidable task of meeting these recruitment goals over a period during which the youth population was in decline. As matters turned out, they not only survived a 15 percent dip in the youth population that occurred during the 1980s, but they literally thrived, attracting recruits with record-setting levels of education and aptitude test scores. By the close of the decade, close to 90 percent of all new military recruits had earned their high school diplomas, compared with just over 70 percent in the late 1970s. Likewise, fewer than 5 percent of the new recruits in 1989 scored in the lowest acceptable category (below the 30th percentile) on the standardized military aptitude test, compared with close to 30 percent a decade earlier.

A variety of factors contributed to this seeming paradox, including an economic recession that led to diminished employment prospects for American youth, substantial military pay increases, an improved educational benefits package, and a growing popularity of the military among America's young, attributed partly to the replacement of President Jimmy Carter's characterization of American "malaise" with President Ronald Reagan's "standing tall" jingoism.[3] In any event, the message should be reassuring for those concerned that a decline in the size of the American population over the long term might preclude the nation from fielding adequate military forces.

YOUTH POPULATION PROJECTIONS

For the near term, the size of the youth population will continue to shrink until the middle of the 1990s, when the effects of the "birth dearth" will run their course. While the size of the eighteen-to-twenty-one male population will dip to 6.66 million in 1994, the number of young American males will still be large relative to the pre-"Baby-Boom" era, making it unlikely that the armed forces will run into any difficulties in attracting a sufficient number of volunteers. Cohort sizes will begin to increase again after 1995, an upturn that can be expected to last at least until 2010[4], after which estimates are uncertain, depending on assumptions about immigration and fertility rates. As Figure 2 indicates, the differences between the U.S. Census Bureau's "highest" and "lowest" projections are substantial; by 2038, the size of the eighteen-to-twenty-two year-old cohort is expected to range from a low of about 7 million to a high of close to 13 million.

At the low end, the size of the cohort would be about 20 percent smaller than now exists, but it would still surpass the size of the similar-aged cohorts of the 1950s and early 1960s.

FUTURE PROSPECTS

What are the chances that the armed forces could continue to meet their manpower needs under the lower population projections? The answer depends on a variety of factors that become more uncertain the further in time that one projects, but the conclusion here is that the nation could field requisite military forces under the "lowest" population scenario, especially if current prospects for reducing the size of the military establishment do in fact materialize and especially if a variety of manpower policies—many legacies of the conscription era—were remodeled to meet the needs of the contemporary military establishment. It is convenient to separate these policies into those that affect the demand for "qualified and available" males and those that affect their supply.

DEMAND OPTIONS

On the demand side, the most important variable is the size of the armed forces. Obviously, the smaller the forces, the fewer personnel will be needed out of the youth cohort, all other things equal. Given the recent changes in the Soviet Union, Eastern Europe, and Central America, the prospects have brightened for sizable reductions in the United States armed forces. Indeed, it does not seem premature to speculate that the large standing forces maintained by the

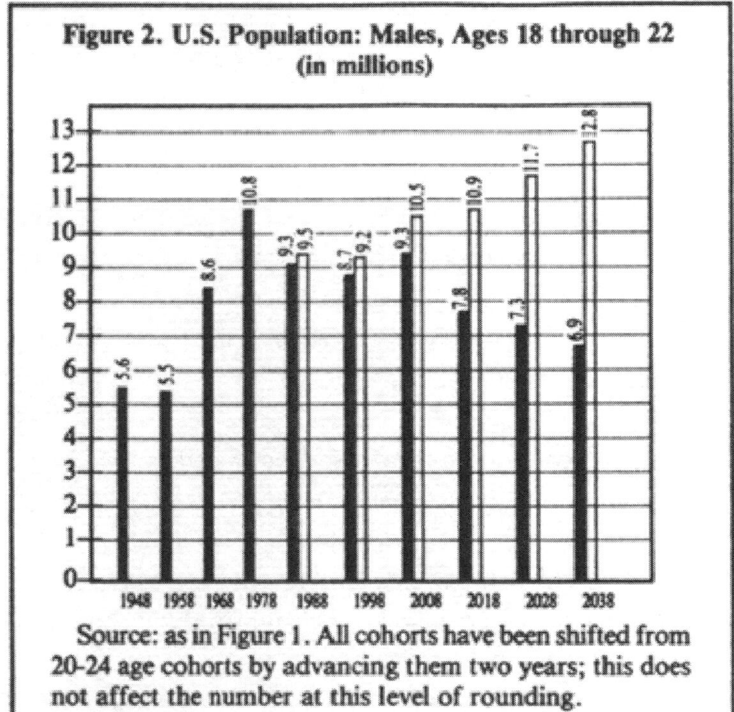

Figure 2. U.S. Population: Males, Ages 18 through 22 (in millions)

Source: as in Figure 1. All cohorts have been shifted from 20-24 age cohorts by advancing them two years; this does not affect the number at this level of rounding.

Figure 2.

world's superpowers during the years of the Cold War will become an anachronism. While the ultimate size of the U.S. armed forces, given present trends, is difficult to predict with precision, some knowledgeable observers believe that the military establishment could be cut in half by the end of the century.[5] Under those circumstances, it is reasonable to assume that the annual flow of personnel into the military could be cut from close to 400,000 to less than 200,000. Should that situation transpire, any remaining concerns about the adequacy of the population to support the armed forces, even under a low-growth population trajectory, would evaporate.

But even if the current trend toward greater superpower stability is reversed, and if cuts in the size of the armed forces do not occur, the demand for new male recruits can still be reduced substantially by substituting women or civilian personnel for uniformed males. Some steps have already been taken toward this end. In fact, the role of women in the military has been expanded appreciably over the past two decades: compared with 1972, when women constituted less than 2 percent of the force, today they account for close to 11 percent of the total. This expansion has leveled off in recent years, primarily because of laws and policies that prevent them from filling a range of "combat" positions. This expansion could be resumed if recent efforts to relax the combat exclusions are successful.[6]

The demand for young male Americans to perform military service could also be reduced by staffing more of the jobs now filled by uniformed personnel with civilians. The ground rules that govern the relative numbers of military and civilian employees in the armed forces are imprecise, and the rationale underlying the determination of the current composition is unclear. Whether combat forces—for example, Army or Marine Corps infantrymen, naval destroyer crews, and Air Force strategic bomber crews—should be military or civilian is obviously not at issue. And few would doubt that those who directly support the combat forces and are expected to operate in a combat zone should be uniformed personnel.

Even when agreement is reached on this obvious point that "combat forces" should be composed of military personnel—question remains: what constitutes "combat forces?" The distinctions are not as sharp as they appear. Must crews flying and servicing airlift aircraft similar in configuration to those used commercially, such as the C-5, be military? Must naval support ships, such as oilers and tenders, be manned by uniformed sailors? In fact, some civilian contractor employees routinely deploy with the combat fleet. And drawing the line between military and civilian personnel combat support functions becomes more difficult when it is recalled that U.S. combat forces currently deployed rely on foreign national civilians for certain forms of support.

The retention of a larger proportion of military personnel beyond one term of service would also reduce turnover and hence the annual requirement for new recruits. For example, to sustain a force, say, of 500,000 enlisted personnel of which 36 percent are careerists (i.e., serve beyond an initial tour of four years) would require an annual input of about 80,000, while the same size force with 44 percent careerists would need only 70,000 new recruits per year. Thus, to the extent that the military services retain a larger proportion of their personnel, they could substantially control the demand for new volunteers while continuing to meet total manpower needs. Arguably, this would be a prudent course to follow in any event, since modern military technology places a higher premium on an experienced workforce.[7]

SUPPLY OPTIONS

Turning to the supply side of the issue, the "qualified and available" male population, as defined above, excluded certain categories of individuals. Changes in recruitment policies and entry standards could bring some of these categories into the supply pool, thus increasing the number of potential volunteers.

Since college students have typically not shown an interest in serving in the enlisted ranks, the armed forces understandably dedicate few recruiting resources to the campus market. Although it is unreasonable to expect that the military services could attract large numbers of graduates of four-year colleges and universities into the enlisted force, it is appropriate to consider programs designed to attract graduates of two-year junior or community college programs. Just how many of the approximately 525,000 youths in each cohort that might be attracted is difficult to predict, but the success of the Army College Fund program during the 1980s, which offered extra educational benefits to certain classes of volunteers, suggests that incentive programs could be devised to increase the propensity among the college-bound to serve in the armed forces and thereby expand the supply of those who would be "qualified and available" for military service.

Another approach for expanding supply is to adjust educational and test score entry requirements. Actually, specifications concerning the quality mix of recruits are arbitrary since there are no hard-and-fast rules for judging how smart or how well-educated individuals must be to function effectively in the armed forces. As indicated in Table 1, about 29 percent of each eighteen-year-old cohort can be expected to fail to meet current standards for entrance into the armed forces. Relaxation of these standards, which has been done periodically in the past depending on supply and demand, would give the services access to a larger supply pool within cohorts of the same size. Furthermore, an adjustment in physical standards along the lines of those adopted during the second World War that allowed people who were not "combat fit" to fill limited duty billets, could enlarge the pool even more.

SUMMING UP

The United States has been able to field armed forces of sufficient size to support its national security strategy under challenging conditions—declining youth cohorts and an all volunteer recruitment system. The force of the evidence indicates that total population growth is neither a necessary or sufficient condition to ensure that the nation is able to protect its security interests.

At bottom, it is becoming increasingly apparent in the closing years of the twentieth century that military strength is not necessarily synonymous with national security. Other elements—the availability of energy and food at reasonable cost; the natural resource balance; the skill levels of the population; and the degree of popular identification with the system—also deeply influence a nation's security.

I do not profess to expertise in these areas. Elsewhere in this series of essays the Pimentels have argued that a smaller population is essential to the maintenance of living standards as the country moves into a solar-based energy system and changes its agricultural practices to save its resource base. Vernon Briggs has argued the importance of better education and less job competition at the unskilled level to avoid generating an alienated underclass over represented with ethnic minorities. If the lower Census projection would in fact contribute to the pursuit of these and other elements of national security, I am confident that future military manpower requirements would not stand in the way of a national decision to take that course.

NOTES:

1. The calculation here is confined to male youths since, under present policies, they will continue to constitute about 90 percent of all military personnel. Obviously, if the armed forces expanded the role of women beyond the current goals, a smaller proportion of the male population would have to be attracted. This possibility is discussed later.
2. For a description of this methodology, see Martin Binkin and John D. Johnston, *All Volunteer Armed Forces: Progress, Problems, and Prospects*, prepared for the Senate Committee on Armed Services, 93 Cong. 1 sess. (GPO, 1973), pp. 40–42, 59–60.
3. For a further discussion of these factors, see Martin Binkin, *America's Volunteer Military: Progress and Prospects* (The Brookings Institution, 1984, pp. 13–14.)
4. The annual number of births began to rise in 1975 not because of increases in fertility rates but rather because of the delayed 'echo effect': more women, born during the baby boom, reached their childbearing years. Once this generation passes beyond childbearing, starting in the 1990s, annual births will decline once again, barring larger-than-expected increases in fertility rates.
5. See, for example, William W. Kaufmann, *Glasnost, Perestroika, and U.S. Defense Spending* (Brookings Institution, 1990)
6. According to the conventional wisdom, the supply of women who are interested in military service is too small to support anything more than a modest expansion. Recent research indicates, however, that higher recruiting goals for women could probably be met if the same enlistment incentives, recruiting techniques, and advertising strategies that have been used for attracting male volunteers were applied to females. See James R. Hosek and Christine Peterson, *Serving Her Country: An Analysis of Women's Enlistment* (Rand Corporation, January 1990).
7. For a discussion of this issue, see Martin Binkin, *Military Technology and Defense Manpower* (Brookings Institution, 1986).

NEIGHBORS' PROBLEMS, OUR PROBLEMS: POPULATION GROWTH IN CENTRAL AMERICA

Robert W. Fox

June 1990

I was walking through the streets of Cartago, Costa Rica, some twenty years ago when the bells rang and the elementary schools let out. A thousand scrubbed and uniformed children flooded the streets. That Lilliputian world was a dramatic reminder that Costa Rica, like the rest of Central America, is a nation of children. Nearly half the population is under fifteen.

Central America's population explosion was captured for me in that incident. Today, ever larger numbers of children are pressing hard on small and shrinking economies. The 8 million Central American children (zero to fifteen) in 1970 represented a large increase from 4 million in 1950. There are 13 million now. If projections hold true, there will be 19 million by 2025.

In one lifetime, Central America's population is just not doubling or trebling. It is rising by a factor of seven—if the ecology can support it. And growth will not stop in 2025 (Table 1).

In the first half of that seventy-five-year period, just a third of the expected increase occurred. The much larger share, nearly two thirds, is projected between now and 2025. Past 2025, the projections call for still further increases of about one million annually. It is yesterday's, today's, and tomorrow's issue in Central America.

These amounts may seem modest next to the population size and growth in the United States, but by comparison they are actually massive. Applying Central America's pace of growth, it is as though the United States' population would be passing one billion in 2025.

The population explosion that began in the 1950s and continues today is arguably Central America's

Table 1. Central America: Population Estimates and Projections (in thousands)

	1950	1975	1990	2000	2025
Costa Rica	862	1,968	3,016	3,712	15,250
El Salvador	1,940	4,085	5,251	6,739	11,299
Guatemala	2,969	6,022	9,197	12,221	21,668
Honduras	1,401	3,081	5,138	6,846	11,510
Nicaragua	1,098	2,408	3,872	5,260	19,219
Panama	893	1,748	2,419	2,893	3,862
Central America	9,163	19,312	28,893	37,671	62,808

Source: United Nations, World Population Prospects, 1988. Population Studies No. 106, ST/ESA/SER.A/106, New York, 1989. Belize, with 180,000 population, is not included in this study.

most significant historical event, overriding in importance the Spanish Conquest and Independence Movement 270 years later. Never has the region experienced anything of this magnitude and force. Not only is the amount of growth of serious concern, but also the speed with which it is occurring.

It is wreaking havoc on the region's cultures, the economies, social systems and on the natural resource base. Forget the failure of political systems and civil wars as the leading issue. Likewise economic depression and unemployment, affecting as much as half the labor force. Forget old debates over land-holding systems where power is concentrated in the hands of a few export crop producers. Forget low levels of living and miserable urban slums that appear occasionally to be clusters of smoking cardboard and tin boxes strung along the arroyos. Forget the exodus of tens and hundreds of thousands headed north to cross the porous Mexican and U.S. borders in search of jobs.

Focus instead on the rise in population as the single basic issue. Redoubling every twenty to twenty-five years, it has put an incredible burden on attempts to resolve old problems and has, meanwhile, created new ones. In Central America today you truly must run faster and faster just to stay in the same place.

HOW DID ALL THIS HAPPEN AND WHY DO WE NOT READ MORE ABOUT IT?

Foreign writers on Central America seem genuinely unaware of the issue's strength and of the intertwining of demographic trends and political and economic issues. A glance through recently published books in English on the region turned up only a few references to the subject and they simply recite the facts of population size. Why the inattention? There are at least two reasons. Writers have little exposure or training in the basic principles of demography. It is a matter considered technical and best left to the experts. Secondly, the topic has been subjected to a concerted effort to narrow it down and find it a niche. Accordingly, it is invariably classified and bottled up in the health and family planning arena.

Largely ignoring it, writers instead focus on the visible results. They include rapid urbanization and growing slum settlements, crowded labor markets and high unemployment, declining purchasing power and falling levels of living and a rapidly deteriorating natural resource base. These major problems have been exacerbated in Central America during the "lost decade" of the 1980s. Now in the 1990s, the economies continue to lose ground while population growth relentlessly moves ahead.

WHY THE POPULATION EXPLOSION?

Central America's recent demographic history is typical of most Third World regions. Prior centuries of high fertility and high mortality and the resulting small gap between these levels allowed for very low growth—well under one percent annually. Population grew slowly during the 16th to nineteenth century Colonial era and in the first century of Independence as well. By 1920, numbers had increased to 5 million and as the pace of growth quickened, to 7 million twenty years later.

By the 1940s, major health improvements were underway. The ages-old era of pestilence and plague faded and the modern one emerged. Radical changes took place in the next quarter century. Field reports of the Pan American Health Organization from the 1940s discuss matters that seem current—the positive results from the installation of sewage and potable water systems, for example, rather than reports of plague or cholera outbreaks in port cities.

Following World War II, massive resources were invested in the region to improve general health conditions including medical treatment, food processing, sanitation, education, and to control communicable and transmissible diseases. As a result, the death rate—then high—dropped sharply in a very brief period of time.

The decline in deaths depended on imported technology such as medicines, pesticides and insecticides. The birth rate, meanwhile—which depended on slowly changing cultural norms—remained high. A growing gap developed between the two rates. This gap is the rate of natural increase, the basis of the population explosion.

While mortality levels plummeted, the birth rate—exceptionally high in 1950—stayed high. Compared to twenty-four births annually per 1,000 population in the United States (1950), the rate was forty in Panama, and in a higher range elsewhere from forty-seven to fifty-four. By the mid-1970s, while dropping substantially in Costa Rica, it fell just modestly elsewhere. Today, the birth rate is still moderately high—ranging from two-thirds to three-quarters its 1950 level. Women in Central America in 1950 averaged six to seven children. The range today is from three to six. These time period differences narrow, however, in terms of surviving children when the sharp drop in child mortality is applied.

Population growth represents the excess of births over deaths (absent migration). There were on average 290,000 more births than deaths annually in Central America during 1950–55, the difference is about 800,000 and by 2020–25 it is projected to increase to around 1 million annually.

The answer is tied to the vast increase in the number of women of reproductive age, associated in turn with Central America's very young age structure.

In Central America in 1950, there were 2.1 million women of reproductive age. By 1990, they numbered 6.7 million; by 2000, 9.2 million are projected; and by 2025 , 16.4 million. In essence, and although they are having fewer children apiece, this vastly greater number of women will produce many more children than before.

The population of Central America will continue to increase until these forces are played out and the number of births is equal to the number of deaths in any given interval (absent migration). The youthful age structure that has emerged, however, combined with its product—the rising numbers of females fifteen through forty-nine—as well as the fertility and mortality trends described, constitute the inertia that ensures this relationship will not be attained for decades in spite of a falling birth rate.

Out of this population well-spring flow enormous consequences for the deteriorating natural resource base particularly the forests—for urbanization and labor force growth, and eventually for the pressures that lead to flight to the United States.

THE TROPICAL FORESTS

To see the linkage to population growth, look at the destruction of Central America's tropical rainforest.

To accommodate the region's growing numbers, the pressures on natural resources are severe. With few mineral or petroleum reserves and limited amounts of good agricultural land—mostly tied up in large estates—the region is heavily dependent on its few remaining resources. Among them, the forests are prominent.

The forest resource has been increasingly drawn on to generate income in the "productive" economic sectors by supplying raw materials for manufacturing and processing industries. Precious woods are marketed abroad for making furniture, doors, beams and carved figures. Local demand for less desirable wood is high. Sawmills provide timbers and finished lumber for house construction to shelter the burgeoning urban population. Charcoal sellers ply the streets of the cities. The forests are being harvested but there is little new growth to assure the resource's regeneration.

Man's forest incursions have led to a process of continuous deterioration. To bring out prized timbers such as mahogany, primitive logging roads are built. These become waterways fed by tropical downpours. The local population exacerbates the situation by harvesting the readily available wood on the slopes next to the road. Heavy erosion results, soils in a widening radius are lost, and gullies develop.

Meanwhile, the roads permit penetration into the jungle by "forest farmers" who apply slash and burn techniques to clear small plots. This has gone on for centuries, but earlier involved far fewer people who farmed a plot for only a few years, moving on as erosion and mineral leaching depleted the land's fertility. Now, under conditions of rapid rural population growth, other farmers follow in their footsteps to try and coax one or two more crops out of the soil. Rather than resting the land for many years as required to rebuild its fertility, this increased population pressure has led to even further soil deterioration.

As patches of cleared jungle coalesce and the forest line retreats it is then valued only as pasture. From the early 1960s to 1987, the United Nation's Food and Agricultural Organization (FAO) reports that land in permanent pasture nearly doubled, increasing from 7 to 13 million hectares, while land in forests and woodlands dropped from 27 to 17 million hectares. The newly cleared land has supported a vastly expanded cattle industry. Much of the beef is exported, and thus the "hamburger connection" is forged between tropical forest destruction and the economic demands of industrialized nations.

Deforestation in particular areas threatens to produce devastating results. Panama Canal operations depend on the water in Lake Gatun. Ships are raised from the Atlantic ocean to the higher lake level through one set of locks. After crossing the Isthmus they are lowered to the Pacific ocean through other locks. Enormous amounts of lake water flush out to sea with these operations. Replenishing Lake Gatun's water supply is vital and that depends on the heavy rainfalls that regularly sweep the area.

Canal authorities now worry about the amount of forest clearance taking place in the immediately surrounding watershed basin. With reduced tree cover, the hydrological cycle is disturbed. Evapotranspiration is reduced, which diminishes local water vapor recycling in the atmosphere. In the absence of tree cover, the increased reflectivity heats the atmosphere, and this in turn counteracts cloud formation and rainfall. With the forest cover intact, the ground soaks up rainfall, releasing it slowly to the lake. Without cover, water runoff increases, eroding the land, carrying soils with it that threaten to silt up the lake.

Central America faces a dilemma. The remaining forest must be preserved for its intrinsic value along with the vast genetic diversity it contains that undoubtedly will lead to future medical and scientific discoveries. The tropics harbor many more times the number of species than exist in temperate climates. Tropical forests have taken millions of years to evolve into their extremely diversified biological states. Many species—plant, animal and insect—

survive symbiotically. They live in mutual interdependence. Thus the felling of one commercially desirable tree in the tropical rainforest may assure the destruction of an entire habitat and many of the distinct life forms it supports.

Yet the region's explosive population growth exerts enormous pressures on this natural resource. Given economic demands, short-term interests often prevail to the detriment of forest preservation. The Central American nations are caught up in cycles that require income for new investments and old debt repayment. Earnings are needed to maintain current investments and to satisfy basic needs of very young populations. The difficulties of meeting daily national expenses are presently compounded by economic stagnation and economic instability. Coping with these issues presses hard on the region's limited natural resource base, particularly its forests.

URBANIZATION

The growth of Central America's major cities since 1950 was an early sign of the population explosion. Shunning nearfeudal agricultural conditions, attracted by the city lights, and bussed on good road systems in these relatively small countries, tens of thousands migrated to the cities. Voting with their feet, it continues today.

Guatemala City, with 330,000 inhabitants in 1950 is the "megalopolis" of Central America. Along with the other capitals including Tegucigalpa and Managua it was then compact and retained a distinct colonial period feel to it. Quite suddenly, and along with Panama City, San Salvador and San Jose, they all faced growth onslaughts (Table 2). Each increased three to six-fold in population size between 1950 and 1980. What had until recently been the entire city became the old "colonial" part of town just a generation later.

Burgeoning urban populations pressed for expanded services. Dusty streets, torn up for months and years at a time to place water and sewer pipes, vied with overhead power line installations for general disruptiveness. In a very new development in the 1960s, expansive squatter settlements emerged on the outskirts, particularly around the capitals of Guatemala, Nicaragua and Honduras. Here, sharp conflicts with municipal authorities arose over two very basic issues of ownership of the ground and legal recognition of the settlements—whose resolution was prerequisite to home improvements and the extension into the communities of water, sewage and electrical lines. In San Salvador, squatters built makeshift dwellings in the ravines that radiated outward from the city core, threading their way through upper and middle class residential zones. Social class in San Salvador is literally tied to one's topographical position.

Yet, that massive urban growth was but a harbinger of the much greater increases to come. Practically all cities and towns continue to grow rapidly with no letup in sight. In roughly half the seventy-five year period, or from 1950 to 1990, the urban population of Central America increased from 2.8 to 13.7 million. This net gain of 11 million, however, is just over a quarter of the expected total increase during 1950–2025. The much larger proportion, 73 percent, or some 30 million additional urban dwellers, lies immediately ahead.

The major cities seem already to have reached saturation and face significant constraints to further growth. Guatemala City is crowded onto a small plateau; San Jose's and San Salvador's further physical expansion threaten to take scarce and fertile adjacent lands out of agricultural production; Tegucigalpa is wedged into a small valley; Panama City is bordered on three sides by the Pacific Ocean, the Canal, and hills to the north. Managua, its vacant downtown area converted to cow pasture after the 1972 earthquake, and now reeling from the effects of a destroyed economy, must determine how to reconstruct a city around a hollow core, should confidence in the economy be regained and funds become available.

Automobile and bus fumes, factory smoke and nearby fires burning in the fields contribute to a steady decline in the quality of the urban environment. The once clear sky over Guatemala City, for example, is often grey with smog. Generally crowded conditions are apparent, affecting the public transportation system in particular as old and overloaded busses, belching black smoke, slowly thread their way through narrow city streets. Most shocking of all is the contrast between clear upstream river and reservoir water before it passes through the cities and the black untreated sludge that pours into the stream beds at the other end—and from there is used in the agricultural fields. Unfortunately, resources to remedy these and many other deteriorating urban conditions are nowhere in sight.

The urban share of the total population in all the countries was about one-third in 1950. (Honduras was less than 18 percent urban.) It has now risen to about one-half. By 2025 it is expected to range from two-thirds to three-fourths. It will continue to increase as rural areas approach saturation in the amount of population they will absorb, and as the "redundant" rural numbers pour into the cities. In earlier times, rural "saturation" resulted from miserable rural socioeconomic conditions including inequitable land ownership and tenure systems, rigid systems of social stratification and the absence of social mobility, a lack of rural schools and medical facilities, and the absence of rural credit and financing institutions. While these conditions have little changed, they have been compounded by rising rural population densities and a rapidly increasing labor force.

Table 2. Central America: Population of Capital Cities, Estimated and Projected (in thousands)

	1950	1980	2010	2025
San Jose, Costa Rica	146	508	1,150	1,525
San Salvador, El Salvador	213	858	2,050	3,200
Guatemala City, Guatemala	337	1,430	4,550	7,200
Tegucipalpa, Honduras	72	406	1,430	2,200
Managua, Nicaragua	109	662	2,550	3,750
Panama City, Panama	217	794	1,870	2,425

Sources: see source note, Table I and, Robert W. Fox and Jerrold W. Huguet, Population and Urban Trends in Central America and Panama, Inter-American Development Bank, Washington, D.C., 1977.

GROWTH OF THE LABOR FORCE

A generation later, those children of Cartago, Costa Rica are now working or looking for work. Yet the region is in the second decade of a severe economic recession. The economies are in disarray as the value of the currencies and primary export commodities have fallen—coffee, bananas, timber, cattle, cotton and sugar. Investors, jittery over unsettled political and economic conditions, have transferred capital to safer haven abroad.

Disadvantaged by falling export commodity earnings, limited in natural resources, short on investment capital and supported by outmoded technology, few of Central America's new labor force entrants are finding meaningful employment. And those numbers are indeed large (Table 3).

Overall, this parallels the urbanization trend; that is, about three-quarters of the 1950–2025 labor force increase will occur between 1990 and 2025. But, with the agricultural labor force expected to increase by relatively small amounts, this will throw the largest burden on the cities.

As these massive urban labor force increases occur, and should the poor economic growth climate persist, unprecedented international labor force flows could result. This is already the case with El Salvador where it is estimated that up to 15–20 percent of the total population has fled to the United States. Affecting this potential, however, are other key issues, including the as yet unmeasured capacity of the informal employment sector to absorb labor increases in the cities, and the ability or desire of the United States to absorb the flow.

OTHER REALITIES

Central Americans have for decades sought to find a proper place for the population issue in their social and economic institutions. This has been a tough, uphill battle made more difficult by moral and ethical implications in predominantly Roman Catholic societies. It has been and continues to be a struggle.

Both as creed and operating mechanism, "economic development" has dominated Central America's view of its future since the 1960s. A fast pace of economic growth was expected to more than offset the demographic reality. All this was to be fostered through export earnings, "soft" loans and grants from the multilateral banking community (World Bank and Inter-American Development Bank), by loans from OECD nations and by commercial bank funds.

National policies focused on "development" in the context of an eventual fully integrated economic union—the Central American Common Market. This was to be supported by the Central American Bank for Economic Integration that was to attract the resources of the international lending community, then awash with petrodollars.

Policies and programs were aimed at clearing the forests, colonizing and "developing" the land and increasing export crops and livestock production levels. As the region's cities mushroomed in size, multiple urban industrialization options were advanced, some to deal with regional opportunities offered by the fledgling Central American Common Market, others to take advantage of the export market and the cheap and growing local labor force supply.

Such conscious policies for economic growth were not matched on the demographic front. Population growth was still considered a "given." The idea of slowing it down, of tampering with "natural" forces offended many and grated deeply on personal convictions. Beside, the notion of any "limitations" went completely against the grain of economic development and "growth," its corollary. Instead, commercial interests advanced the notion that growing markets would need more consumers. Rural interests stated that agricultural land remained to be developed. The military argued that more people were necessary to settle the fringes of national territory to prevent encroachments from the neighbors. Indigenous leaders railed at the thought that their groups would be targets of population "control" efforts.

Religious orders fought against the very notion of family planning and provision of contraceptives. Many politicians behaved likewise in the male-dominated societies. Uncomfortable with the subject, they were often painfully shy to discuss it. Outright hostility to family planning was not unknown.

It was always recognized that economic growth had to keep pace with population growth. If the

Table 3. Central America: The Economically Active Population (in thousands)

	1950	1975	1990	2000	2025
Costa Rica	295	637	1,050	1,338	2,016
El Salvador	685	1,349	1,743	2,295	4,277
Guatemala	961	1,767	2,630	3,666	8,234
Honduras	467	911	1,582	2,256	4,564
Nicaragua	367	722	1,204	1,776	3,674
Panama	315	588	873	1,111	1,597
Central America	3,125	5,974	9,0821	2,442	24,362

Sources: see source note, Table I and, Economically Active Population, 1950–2025, Volume III, Latin America, ISBN 92-2-005347-0, International Labour Office (ILO), Geneva, 1986.

economies faltered, the continuing population gains would slip right on by, producing lower and lower levels of living, and wiping out the forward momentum of the 1960s and 1970s. This is precisely what has happened. Living conditions in Central America have fallen back to 1960s levels.

The struggle to convey the demographic message in Central America in overwhelmingly “growth and development” oriented societies has been difficult. The principal actors have very divergent views and interests in mind.

It was initially confined to the resolve of private family planning organizations. Later, its base broadened with acceptance as a maternal and child health care issue in the Ministries of Public Health. During the 1970s, several countries went so far as to create demographic evaluation units at the national planning level. Elevating the topic to this level was both an attempt to raise awareness and yank control of it from economists, who more often than not considered population size and growth as a given, an “externality” to their analyzes.

Demographers have informed politicians they have a very major problem emerging for which there is no short term solution. Further, it is guaranteed to continue to intensify for the next half century and longer. To ameliorate it over the long term by implementing and supporting family planning programs will touch on and alter the deepest of cultural sensitivities. All this, they argue, will contribute to unrest and eventually bring about profound changes in individual and family value systems.

Slowly but surely the old attitudes are changing. The technical soundness of the population projections is recognized, and accompanied by common sense observations in the increasingly crowded streets outside, politicians realize that a serious and intractable problem has emerged. Their response has become, “I already know that (the population problem). Don’t bring me, problems, bring me solutions.”

Central America’s demographic future contains hard messages that are difficult to swallow and the subject is still viewed from many different perspectives. Generally speaking, this is where the matter rests today.

CONCLUSIONS

I have selected Central America for this brief examination since it is a typical case of the demographic forces working in the Third World. It has also been at the center of much foreign policy debate in the U.S. (including proposals recurrently made in Congress to make it possible for various Central

Americans, once here, to stay here), because the demographic future of Central America is linked with the U.S.'s population future through immigration, and because the demographic trends in Central America imperil the prosperity and political stability of a region of considerable importance to the U.S.

Much of what has been said about Central America could be said also of Mexico, which is three times as populous as all of Central America, and shares a long border with the U.S. High birth and rapidly falling death rates, a young age structure and vast increases in the number of women of reproductive age are similar themes there.

The strongest distinction between Mexico and Central America is the Mexican government's deliberate decision in the 1970s to bring down its very high rate of population growth and to act quickly on this decision. Programs were drawn up and implemented and have since been reinforced by each successive national administration. While the initial target of reaching a 100 million population size by year 2000 may be overshot by some 6–10 million, this nevertheless represents a major change from the 132 million Mexicans earlier projected for year 2000.

With shared features, Mexico has long realized that the demographic "passages" in store for Central America are also inevitable there. Appreciating that they have some control over the time required to work through these passages, Mexican authorities have made deliberate and concerted efforts to take advantage of this and speed up the process. Accordingly, while the age structure has changed very little (the Mexican median age was slightly over eighteen years in both 1950 and today), the total fertility rate has dropped precipitously, from 6.7 children during 1950–1970 to around 3.7 today. This represents enormous change in a very short period on the demographic scale of things. In Central America, only Costa Rica and Panama have had comparable fertility declines.

Nevertheless, with population momentum still driving their demography, neither Central America nor Mexico is likely to stabilize at a level and in time to take the pressures off their social, ecological and economic systems—or ours.

BALANCING HUMANS IN THE BIOSPHERE: ESCAPING THE OVERPOPULATION TRAP

Robert Costanza

July 1990

Cultural evolution has allowed humans to change their behaviors and adapt to new conditions much faster than biological evolution. It has also removed the inherently long run bias of biological evolution and made us susceptible to several social traps. The most critical of these is the overpopulation trap, caused by the imbalance between the short term incentives to have children and the long term social and ecological costs of having too many. But the severe and very real uncertainty about the long run costs of too many humans has hindered debate and action on this issue. We cannot wait for the uncertainty to be resolved, because by then it will be too late. What we must do is deal with the uncertainty in a more appropriate way. We should tentatively assume the worst and then allow ourselves to be pleasantly surprised if we are wrong, rather than assuming the best and facing disaster if we are wrong. A crude worst case estimate of optimal U.S. population based solely on renewable resources and current consumption levels yields about 85 million people. An average resource consumption level of one half current levels combined with a more equitable distribution of resources would yield a high quality lifestyle for 170 million.

Human beings, like all other animals, make decisions based on responses to local, immediate reinforcements. They follow their noses, with some mediation by *genetic* (and in the case of humans and some other species *cultural*) programming. To understand the human population problem, one needs to understand how this complex of local reinforcements and programmed responses interact over several different time scales with the ecosystem within which humans are embedded.

Biological evolution has a built-in bias towards the long run. Changing the genetic structure of a species requires that characteristics (phenotypes) be selected and accumulated by differential reproductive success. Characteristics learned or acquired during the lifetime of an individual cannot be passed on genetically. Biological evolution is therefore an inherently slow process requiring many many generations to significantly alter a species' physical characteristics or behavior.

Cultural evolution is much faster, and in recent years it has accelerated to hyperspeed. Learned behaviors that are successful can be almost immediately spread to other members of the culture and passed on in the oral, written, or video record. The increased speed of adaptation that this process allows has been largely responsible for *homo sapiens'* amazing success at controlling the resources of the planet[1]. But there is a significant downside. Like a car that has picked up speed, we are in much more danger of running off the road or over a cliff. We have lost the built-in long-run bias of biological evolution and are susceptible to being led by our hyper-efficient short run adaptability over a cliff into the abyss.

THE OVERPOPULATION TRAP

This process of short-run incentives getting out of sync with long-term goals has been well studied in the last decade under several rubrics,[2] but the one I like best is John Platt's notion of "social traps."[3] In all such cases the decision-maker may be said to be "trapped" by the local conditions into making what turns out to be a bad decision viewed from a longer or wider perspective. We go through life making decisions about which path to take based largely on "road signs," the short-run, local reinforcements that we perceive most directly. These shortrun reinforcements can include monetary incentives, social acceptance or admonishment, and physical pleasure or pain. In general, this strategy of following the road signs is quite effective, unless the road signs are inaccurate or misleading. In these cases we can be trapped into following a path that is ultimately detrimental because of our reliance on the road signs. For example, cigarette smoking has been a social trap because by following the short-run road signs of the pleasure and social status[4] associated with smoking, we embark on the road to an increased risk of earlier death from smoking-induced cancer. More important, once this road has been taken it is very difficult to change to another (as most people who have tried to quite smoking can attest).

The problem of overpopulation is a classic social trap, as has been pointed out by Garrett Hardin, Paul Ehrlich and many others[5]. The biological and cultural incentives to procreate that are incumbent on individuals in the short run, combined with rapid reductions in mortality that have changed the long run ecological cost structure, have led us into the jaws of this most serious of traps. Cultural evolution has so far changed only the short-run half of the equation (lower mortality) and has put us on the path to unsustainable population growth. It is time for cultural evolution to change the other half of the equation to bring us back into balance.

SHORT-TERM BENEFITS AND LONG-TERM COSTS OF HUMAN POPULATION GROWTH

What are the major costs and benefits of human population growth? We can divide them into three broad groups, individual, cultural, and ecological.

Individuals make decisions about family size, so ultimately it is the costs and benefits individuals *perceive* that will make a difference. Culture's role is to translate long-term ecological costs and benefits into individual behavior. The major benefits to parents of additional children are as (1) workers; (2) care givers in old age; and (3) genetic carriers. The major costs are rearing to a productive, independent age. In most of the world the benefits of children as workers and care-givers are still significant, and the costs to raise children to a productive age are low, since levels of education are low and children can start working productively at a very early age. In many countries children begin to "pay for themselves" by age ten or so. In the U.S. and other "developed" countries the situation is quite different. Children have little or no direct benefit to parents as workers and the prevalence of social security systems means they are not absolutely necessary as care givers in old age (although they are still desirable in this role). Meanwhile their costs to raise to "productive age" are enormous. In highly industrialized countries "productive age" means after at least four years of college and the costs to the parents are daunting. It is little wonder that family sizes in industrialized countries have fallen so dramatically.

But it is the long-term ecological costs of more humans that are now becoming critically important. These long-term costs are caused by our speeded up cultural evolution and must ultimately be solved by the next wave of cultural evolution.

Cultural evolution also has an interesting effect on human impacts on the environment. By changing the learned behavior of humans and incorporating tools and artifacts, it allows individual human resource requirements and their impacts on their resident ecosystems to vary over several orders of magnitude. Thus it does not make sense to talk about the "carrying capacity" of humans in the same way as the "carrying capacity" of other species since, in terms of their carrying capacity, humans are many subspecies. Each subspecies would have to be culturally defined to determine levels of resource use and carrying capacity. For example, the global carrying capacity for *homo americanus* would be much lower than the carrying capacity for *homo indus*, because each American consumes much more than each Indian does. And the speed of cultural adaptation makes thinking of species (which are inherently slow changing) misleading anyway. *Homo americanus* could change its resource consumption patterns drastically in only a few years, while *homo sapiens* remains relatively unchanged. I think it best to follow the lead of Herman Daly[6] in this and speak of the product of population and per capita resource use as the *total impact* of the human population. It is this total impact that the earth has a capacity to carry, and it is up to us to decide how to divide it between numbers of people and per capita resource use. This complicates population policy enormously, since one cannot simply state an optimal *population*, but rather must state an optimal number of *impact units*. How many impact units the earth can sustain and how to distribute these impact units over the population is a very dicey problem indeed, but one that must also be included in our next round of cultural evolution.

THE IMPORTANCE OF UNCERTAINTY AND HOW TO DEAL WITH IT

One key element that has frustrated population policy is the enormous degree of uncertainty about long-term human impacts on the biosphere. The argument can be summarized as differing opinions about the degree to which technological progress can eliminate resource constraints. Current economic world-views (capitalist, socialist, and the various mixtures) are all based on the underlying assumption of continuing and unlimited economic growth. This assumption allows a whole host of very sticky problems, including population growth, equity, and sustainability to be ignored (or at least postponed), since they re seen to be most easily solved by additional economic growth. Indeed, most conventional economists define "health" in an economy as a stable and high *rate of growth*. Energy and resource limits to growth, according to these world-views, will be eliminated as they arise by clever development and deployment of new technology. This line of thinking is often called "technological optimism."

An opposing line of thought (often called "technological pessimism") assumes that technology will *not* be able to circumvent fundamental energy and resource constraints and that eventually economic growth will stop. It has usually been ecologists or other life scientists that take this point of view[7] largely because they study natural systems that *invariably do* stop growing when they reach fundamental resource constraints. A healthy ecosystem is one that maintains a stable level. Unlimited growth is cancerous, not healthy, under this view.

The technological optimists argue that human systems are fundamentally different from other natural systems because of human intelligence. History has shown that resource constraints can be circumvented by new ideas. Technological optimists claim that Malthus' dire redactions about population pressures have not come to pass and the "energy crisis" of the late '70s is behind us.

The technological pessimists argue that many natural systems also have "intelligence" in that they can evolve new behaviors and organisms (including humans themselves). Humans are therefore a part of nature, not apart from it. Just because we have circumvented local and artificial resource constraints in the past does not mean we can circumvent the fundamental ones that we will eventually face. Malthus' predictions have not come to pass *yet* for the entire world, the pessimists would argue, but many parts of the world are in a Malthusian trap now, and other parts may well fall into it.

This debate has gone on for several decades now. It began with Barnett and Morse's "Scarcity and Growth" and really got into high gear with the publication of "The Limits to Growth" by Meadows et al. [8] and the Arab oil embargo in 1973. There have been thousands of studies over the last fifteen years on various aspects of our energy and resource future and different points of view have waxed and waned. But the bottom line is that there is still an enormous amount of uncertainty about the impacts of energy and resource constraints, and I doubt that the argument will ever be decided on scientific grounds.

In the next twenty to thirty years we may begin to hit *real* fossil fuel supply limits as well as constraints on production due to global warming. Will fusion energy or solar energy or conservation or some as yet unthought of energy source step in save the day and keep economies growing? The technological optimists say yes and the technological pessimists say no. Ultimately, no one knows. Both sides argue as if they were certain, but the worst form of ignorance misplaced certainty.

The optimists argue that unless we *believe* that the optimistic future is possible and behave accordingly it will never come to pass. The pessimists argue that the optimists will bring on the inevitable leveling and decline sooner by consuming resources faster and that to sustain our system we should begin to conserve resources immediately. How do we proceed in the face of this overwhelming uncertainty?

We can cast this optimist/pessimist choice in a classic (and admittedly oversimplified) game theoretic format using the "payoff matrix" shown in figure 1. Here the alternative policies that we can pursue today (technologically optimistic or pessimistic) are listed on the left and the real states of the world are listed on the top. The intersections are labeled with the results of the combinations of policies and states of the world. For example, if we pursue the optimistic policy and the world really does turn out to conform to the optimistic assumptions then the payoffs would be high. This high potential payoff is very tempting and this strategy has paid off in the past. It is not surprising that so many would like to believe that the world conforms to the optimist's assumptions. If, however, we pursue the optimistic policy and the world turns out to conform more closely to the pessimistic technological assumptions then the result would be "Disaster." The disaster would come because irreversible damage to ecosystems would have occurred and technological fixes would no longer be possible.

If we pursue the pessimistic policy and the optimists are right then the results are only "Moderate." But if the pessimists are right and we have pursued the pessimistic policy then the results are "Tolerable."

Within the framework of game theory, this simplified game has a fairly simple "optimal" strategy. If we *really* do not know the state of the world then we should choose the policy that is the maximum of the minimum outcomes (i.e. the Maxi Min strategy in game theory jargon). In other words, we analyze each policy in turn, look for the worst thing (minimum) that could happen if we pursue that policy,

Table 1. Payoff matrix for technological optimism vs. pessimism

Current Policy	**Real State of the World**	
	Optimists Right	Pessimists Right
Technological Optimist Policy	High	Disaster
Technological Pessimists Policy	Moderate	Tolerable

and pick the policy with the largest (maximum) minimum. in the case stated above we should pursue the pessimist policy because the worst possible result under that policy ("Tolerable") is a preferable outcome to the worst outcome under the optimist policy ("Disaster").

Given this analysis, what can one recommend for population policy? Because of the large uncertainty about the long term impacts of population growth on ecological sustainability, we should *at least provisionally assume the worst*. We must *assume* that the dire predictions of the Ehrlichs and Pimentels[9] are correct and plan accordingly. If they are right we will still survive. If they are wrong we will be pleasantly surprised. This is a much different scenario than the consequences of provisionally assuming the best about the impacts of population growth, as Julian Simon[10] would have us do. If we assume Simon is right and he is not, we will have irreversibly degraded the planet's capacity to support life. We cannot rationally take that risk.

ESCAPING THE OVERPOPULATION TRAP

How then do we communicate this conclusion to the people who make the decisions—the potential parents—and escape the overpopulation trap? The elimination of social traps requires intervention—the modification of the reinforcement system. Indeed, it can be argued that the proper role of a democratic government is to eliminate social traps (no more and no less) while maintaining as much individual freedom as possible. Cross and Guyer list four broad methods by which traps can be avoided or escaped from. These are education (about the long-term, distributed impacts); insurance; superordinate authority (i.e., legal systems, government, religion); and converting the trap to a trade-off , i.e. correcting the road signs.

Education can be used to warn people of long-term impacts that cannot be seen from the road. Examples are the warning labels now required on cigarette packages and the warnings of environmentalists about future hazardous waste problems. People can ignore warnings, however, particularly if the path seems otherwise enticing. For example, warning labels on cigarette packages have had little effect on the number of smokers.

The main problem with education as a general method of avoiding and escaping from traps is that it requires a significant time commitment on the part of individuals to learn the details of each situation. Our current society is so large and complex that we cannot expect even professionals, much less the general public, to know the details of all the extant traps. In addition, for education to be effective in avoiding traps involving many individuals, *all* the participants must be educated.

Governments can, of course, forbid or regulate certain actions that have been deemed socially inappropriate. The problem with this approach is that it must be rigidly monitored and enforced, and the strong short-term incentive for individuals to try to ignore or avoid the regulations remains. A police force and legal system are very expensive to maintain, and increasing their chances of catching violators increases their costs exponentially (both the costs of maintaining a larger, better-equipped force and the cost of the loss of individual privacy and freedom).

Religion and social customs can be seen as much less expensive ways to avoid certain social traps. If a moral code of action and belief in an ultimate payment for transgressions can be deeply instilled in a person, the probability of that person's failing into the "sins" (traps) covered by the code will be greatly reduced, and with very little enforcement cost. On the other hand, the problems with religion and social customs as means to avoid social traps are: the moral code must be relatively static to allow beliefs learned early in life to remain in force later, and it requires a relatively homogeneous community of like-minded individuals to be truly effective. This system works well in culturally homogeneous societies that are changing very slowly. In modern, heterogeneous, rapidly changing societies, religion and social customs cannot handle all the newly evolving situations, nor the conflict between radically different cultures and belief systems.

Many trap theorists believe that the most effective method for avoiding and escaping from social traps is to turn the trap into a trade-off. This method does not run counter to our normal tendency to follow the road signs; it merely corrects the signs' inaccuracies by adding compensatory positive or negative reinforcements. A simple example illustrates how effective this method can be. Playing slot machines is a social trap because the long-term costs and benefits are inconsistent with the short-term costs and benefits. People play the machines because they expect a large short-term jackpot, while the machines are in fact programmed to pay off, say, $0.80 on the dollar in the longterm. People may "win" hundreds of dollars playing the slots (in the short run), but if they play long enough they will certainly lose $0.20 for every dollar played. To change this trap to a trade-off, one could simply reprogram the machines so that every time a dollar was put in $0.80 would come out. This way the short-term reinforcements ($0.80 on the dollar) are made consistent with the long-term reinforcements ($0.80 on the dollar), and only the dedicated aficionados of spinning wheels with fruit painted on them would continue to play.

BALANCING THE HUMAN SPECIES IN THE ECOSYSTEM

Balancing the human species in the ecosystem is therefore *in principle* a simple problem. Simply make the long-run, distributed, whole-system, *worst case* costs and benefits of human population growth (and all other human activities) incumbent on all individuals in the short-run and locally, at least provisionally until the worst case impacts can be lowered. If your next child will be a net cost to the planet of x, you should be required to pay x, up front, for the right to have it, at least until it can be proven to have a lower impact. In a sense, this is an extension of the "polluter pays principle" to the polluter pays (at least provisionally) for uncertainty too. If and only if this whole system cost accounting (including uncertainty) is in place can we expect individual decisions about population growth to have any meaning for the planet as a whole.

Of course, *in principle* is very far from *in practice* in this particular case. The problems of devising cultural mechanisms to effectively communicate that cost to the individual parents are daunting. But no one said it was going to be easy. The next stage of our cultural evolution has got to be the development of just this capacity to put back in the long run constraints that the initial phase of cultural evolution appeared to release us from. We need to develop and use cultural "road maps" and "scouts" to counter our dependence on “road signs” in the tricky terrain we now find ourselves. I offer the following summary suggestions, and challenge the anthropologists and sociologists to put their research to practical use in devising cultural mechanisms to implement them

1. Establish a *hierarchy* of goals for national and global ecological economic planning and management. Sustainability should be the primary long-term goal, replacing the current GNP growth mania. Issues of justice, equity, and population are ultimately tied in with sustainability as preconditions. Only sustainable levels of human population are desirable. Economic growth in this hierarchy is a valid goal only when it is consistent with sustainability. The goals can be put into operation by having them accepted as part of the political debate, and implemented in the decision making structure of institutions that affect the global economy and ecology (like the World Bank).

2. Develop *better global ecological economic* modeling capabilities to allow us to see the range of possible outcomes of our current activities, especially the interrelated impacts of population, per capita resource use, and wealth distribution.

3. Adjust current incentives to reflect long run, global costs, *including uncertainty*. To paraphrase the popular slogan, we should: model globally, adjust local incentives accordingly. In addition to traditional education, regulation, and user fee approaches, a flexible assurance bonding system has been proposed to deal specifically with uncertainty.[11] Curbing population growth requires that long term worst case ecological costs be made apparent to potential parents in a culturally acceptable way.
4. Allow no further decline in the stock of *natural capital* by taxing natural capital consumption. This policy will encourage the technological innovation that optimists are counting on while conserving resources in case the optimists are wrong. Revenues can be used to mitigate problems (like counteracting the economic forces for unwise population growth) and easing up on income taxes especially for the lower end of the income scale.

OPTIMAL U.S. POPULATION UNDER PRUDENTLY PESSIMISTIC ASSUMPTIONS

Given all this, what can be said about the “optimal” size of the U.S. (or any other country’s) population? Obviously, it depends on the level of per capita resource consumption, the ability of technology to overcome resource constraints, and the long-term impacts of humans on the biosphere. These last two involve enormous uncertainties. But I have argued that in the face of this uncertainty we should be prudent until it can be proven otherwise. We should assume the worst. Then if cold fusion or some other technology comes in to save the day we can be pleasantly surprised. But we should not *bank on* cold fusion, hot fusion, or anything else since the costs of being wrong are disaster. “Don’t count your solutions before they hatch” applies to fusion technology, population policy, and all other uncertain endeavors.

So if we make some prudently pessimistic assumptions where do we end up? First we should assume that technology will be no more effective at removing resource constraints than it is now, and that per capita resource consumption will remain at current levels. Actually for a true “worst case” analysis we could assume consumption per capita would continue to rise, but we’ll leave a little optimism in the assumptions. Assuming the worst as regards the long-term impacts of humans on the biosphere leads us to conclude there are already far too many humans. Many authors have documented the potential adverse impacts of our current population on soil erosion, forest depletion, water and air pollution, and a host of other impacts. How many people could we sustain at current technology and consumption patterns if the worst of these impacts were true and unremediated? Certainly no more than we now have, but how many less?

I fall back on a rough energy calculation. In the worst case we must stop burning fossil fuels, both because we are running out and because the greenhouse effect is causing adverse climate changes. Assume also that in the worst-case nuclear energy is too unsafe to use. So the question comes down to how many people could we sustain at current technology and consumption patterns on renewable energy alone. This level is also consistent with the earlier recommendations to maintain the stock of natural capital at current levels to insure sustainability. Remember that the worst case means no significant improvements in energy efficiency as some technological optimists are predicting, but to balance this I will allow that all the renewable energy currently incumbent on the U.S. can ultimately be used.

The fossil and nuclear energy consumption in the U.S. in 1986 was $74x10^{15}$ BTU. The U.S. population in 1986 was about 240 million. This gives an annual per capita fossil and nuclear energy consumption of about 300 million BTU per capita per year, which I'll use to represent total current resource use.[12] The total solar energy captured by the U.S. environment (including nearshore waters) is about $100x\ 10^{18}$ BTU per year.[13] But solar energy is much more dispersed and lower quality than fossil fuel. It has been estimated to take about 2000 BTU of solar energy to do the equivalent amount of *useful* work as 1 BTU of fossil fuel.[14] So the solar energy captured is equivalent to about $5x10^{16}$ BTU of fossil fuel. Assume that no more than half of this is available to drive human society directly, with the rest necessary for the ecological life support system. Dividing this remainder of $2.5x10^{16}$ BTU by the $3x10^{8}$ BTU/person/year energy needs of current U.S. citizens yields about 85 million people, or about 35 percent of the current population. But current U.S. per capita resource consumption is arguably more than what is required for a high quality lifestyle, and is not distributed very equitably over the population. Let us assume that with a more equitable distribution and a more "European" level of consumption per capita we could support about twice the above estimate or 170 million at a high quality lifestyle on renewable energy alone. This is admittedly a very rough calculation, and it is not the most pessimistic one possible. But I think it's a good general benchmark. 170 million people might be supportable on a sustainable basis at something approaching our current quality of life, but 240 million probably cannot unless some major technical breakthroughs happen or we all reduce our standard of living significantly. Prudence requires that we target 170 million or less until the technical breakthroughs happen (if they happen). Otherwise our standard of living may go down to disastrous levels due to ecological deterioration from which we could never recover.

NOTES:

1. Vitusek, P., P. R. Ehrlich A. H. Ehrlich, and P. A. Matson. 1986. Human appropriation of the products of photosynthesis. *BioScience* 36:368–373. They estimate that humans now directly control from 25 to 40 percent of the total primary production of the planet's biosphere. Human activity is also beginning to have an effect on global climate and the planet's protective ozone shield.
2. Including, but not limited to, the "Tragedy of the Commons" (cf. Hardin, G. 1968. "The Tragedy of the Commons." *Science*. 162:1243–1248), and the "prisoner's dilemma" (cf. Axelrod, R.

1984. *The Evolution of Cooperation*. Basic Books, New York.)

3. Platt, J. 1973. "Social traps." *American Psychologist*. 28:642–651.; Cross, J.G., and M.J.Guyer. 1980. *Social Traps*. (University of Michigan Press, Ann Arbor); Teger, A. I. 1980. *Too Much Invested to Quit*. (Pergamon, New York); Brockner, J. and J. Z. Rubin. 1985. *Entrapment in Escalating Conflicts. A Social Psychological Analysis*. (Springer-Verlag, New York. 275 pp.); Costanza, R. 1987. "Social Traps and Environmental Policy." *BioScience*. 37:407–412.
4. This particular positive reinforcement has in the last few years begun to turn into a negative one. As smoking becomes less socially acceptable we should expect the number of new smokers to fall and many old smokers to escape the trap. But the process of escape is much more difficult than the process of avoidance.
5. Hardin,G. 1986. "Cultural Carrying Capacity: a Biological Approach." *BioScience* 36:599–606. Ehrlich, P. R. and J. P. Holdren. 1971. "The Impact of Population Growth." *Science* 171:1212–1217. Ehrlich, P. R. and A. H. Ehrlich. 1990. *The Population Explosion*. (Simon and Schuster, New York. 320 pp.)
6. Daly, H.E. 1977. *Steady State Economics*. (W.H. Freeman, San Francisco. 185 pp.)
7. Notable examples are Paul Ehrlich and Garrett Hardin. Herman Daly is a rare economist who shares this view.
8. Barnett, H.J.and C. Morse. 1963. *Scarcity and Growth:The Economics of Natural Resource Availability*. (Johns Hopkins, Baltimore.) Meadows, D. H., D. L. Meadows, J. Randers, and W.W.Behrens. 1972. *The Limits to Growth*. (Universe, New York.)
9. Pimentel, D. and M. Pimentel. 1990. "Land, Energy and Water: The Constraints Governing Ideal U. S. Population Size." The NPG Forum.
10. Simon, J.L. and H.Kahn (eds). 1984. *The Resourceful Earth: A Response to Global 2000*. (Basil Blackwell, New York.) 585 PP.
11. Costanza, R. and C.H. Perrings. 1990. "A Flexible Assurance Bonding System for Improved Environmental Management." *Ecological Economics*. 2:57–76.
12. Although this is still an underestimate because we are currently using at least 50 percent renewable fuels in the form of wood and hydropower, and solar energy runs the ecosystems that provide life support functions.
13. Costanza, R. 1980. "Embodied Energy and Economic Valuation." *Science*. 210:1219–1224.
14. All BTU's (British Thermal Units) are equal in their ability to raise the temperature of water. A BTU is defined as the amount of heat energy required to raise one pound of water one degree Fahrenheit. A BTU is equal to .252 kcal, 1054 J, or 0.0002929 kWh. But in terms of ability to do useful work, the concentration or quality of the energy is important. Because sunlight is very dispersed relative to fossil fuel, it takes about 2000 BTU of sunlight to grow enough trees to produce as much electricity as 1 BTU of oil (Odum, H. T. and E. C. Odum. 1976. *Energy Basis for Man and Nature*. McGraw Hill, NewYork. 296pp.)

ENERGY AND POPULATION: TRANSITIONAL ISSUES AND EVENTUAL LIMITS

Paul J. Werbos

1990

OVERVIEW

The editors of this series have asked me to address what appears to be a straightforward set of questions: what U .S. population size is compatible with the environmental consequences of energy use? What levels of population would lead to maximum efficiency in the energy sector, as a guesstimate, in long-term equilibrium?

Many energy analysts tend to ignore the population question, or to treat population as a minor background variable in forecasting twenty years into the future. A few analysts, following the first report to the Club of Rome, decry all forms of economic and population growth. Both sides—the pessimists and the defenders of the status quo—have built elaborate models and theories to defend their viewpoints, often based on questionable hidden assumptions. After years of working through this maze of theories and building a few models myself, I would make the following personal judgements[1] about energy and population:

1. *The present mix of fuels and energy technologies is not sustainable in the long-term,* even if population were dramatically reduced. In the long term, fossil fuels will run out. Even now, our present ways of using energy have led to unhealthy levels of ozone in almost every American city, to toxic pollution leaking into ground water and into natural bodies of water. In the next decade or two, oil imports may return to being a crisis-level problem, as demand increases and domestic supply decreases, almost inevitably. Sooner or later, we must also deal with the problem of greenhouse warming, which is associated with all realistic uses of fossil fuels.

   To meet all the present energy demands, worldwide, plus economic growth, with conventional nuclear power, would imply an *accumulating* problem with nuclear waste, nuclear proliferation, nuclear material available for terrorists, and nuclear safety orders of magnitude larger than what we face today.

2. *Once a complete transition to sustainable technologies is achieved,we could probably sustain a wide range of possible populations* at a reasonable level of efficiency. From an efficiency viewpoint, populations between 50 to 100 percent of the present population would probably be ideal, though environmental quality would probably be better at the lower end of the range. Populations as low as 25 million or so would probably be a problem, because it would be difficult to sustain a complex mix of technologies (even soft technologies) on such a small engineering base; however, we probably could not sustain a population much greater than that if we insisted on using only less expensive, less

risky soft technologies. With a high degree of optimism about the soft technologies, and allowances for peak load electricity supplied by solar power, one might hope to sustain a population as large as 60 million or so. For larger populations, we would probably have to rely mostly on direct solar technologies, including a certain mix of technologies as yet unproven. Populations much larger than the present would begin to present problems, because solar energy would become more expensive (due to higher land prices) and also because the concentration of water pollution tends to increase in proportion to population. If our income per capita were as low as that of China, we could support a similar population, but in an economy as rich as ours the pollution and land supply problems would become difficult.

3. *Regardless of long-term sustainability, the growth of population and the composition of this growth in the next two to three decades is possibly the most serious problem reducing our chance of a successful transition to sustainable technology.* At first glance, the connection may not be obvious, but it is really quite strong. Sustainable technologies will take a long time to bring onto the mass market, and the transition will cost billions upon billions of dollars. An important part of the cost will involve research and development which is highly profitable in the long-term; even so, finding the money in the next five years will clearly be a problem and the next twenty years may not be radically different from the next five.

In these circumstances, the nation will be well advised to do whatever it can to slow the present rate of population growth and the increased energy demand posed by a larger population. Perhaps more important, it needs to change its investment habits to accumulate the capital to make the transition away from petroleum. The biggest obstacle to finding the money—either in the public or private sector—is the general shortage of capital associated with a low national savings rate and the federal budget deficit. We need a skilled and productive labor force. Neither our immigration policies nor our national social policies are focused on this goal. We admit immigrants based on kinship rather than skills. We face rising teenage pregnancy and continuing differential pregnancy with the poorest who can least afford to raise them having the most children. We wrestle with the costs and results of these problems, rather than trying to avoid them. The costs are very high, and they divert resources from the challenges ahead. A national policy preparing us to cope with those challenges would probably result in immigration and fertility levels corresponding roughly to the "hard path," described by Leon Bouvier elsewhere in this series, and an immediate slowing of population growth.

Finally, it is not obvious that the United States will be able to make the transition to sustainable technologies in time to prevent severe, debilitating rises in energy prices and environmental problems worldwide. Rising energy prices and shifts in the composition of the labor force can slow down economic growth, making it ever more difficult to make such a huge transition, if we wait too long. The solutions and the problems will both take decades to develop, and no one knows which will happen first. If demographic problems over the next few decades result in too much of a delay here, the consequences for our civilization might well be permanent.

The remainder of this paper will elaborate on some of these points. First it will discuss the near-term problem of dependency on oil, and the difficulty of achieving a transportation system which frees us from that dependency. Then it will discuss the longer-term issues of how we fuel this transportation sector and other sectors of the economy.

OIL: ITS IMPORTANCE, ITS FUTURE AND HOW TO ESCAPE

Oil and gas currently account for 66 percent of the primary energy consumed in the U.S.[2] Oil and gas are both in highly finite supply, and there will be major difficulties in replacing them. Oil, in particular, tends to be used in applications where it is difficult to substitute other fuels. Unless there is gross mismanagement of the electric utility sector, shortages and high prices for oil are likely to be the next major "crisis" in the energy sector, just as they were in the 1970s.

The last great oil crises came in 1974 and 1979, when oil prices rose 119 percent and 42 percent, respectively[2]. These oil crises led immediately to slowdowns in economic activity. From 1973 to 1975, GNP was reduced by 10.6 percent compared to the previous growth path (1961 to 1973); this works out to a loss of $285 billion in 1982 dollars, just in 1975. From 1978 to 1980, the loss was more like 6 percent. Those who remember living during those days of gas lines and uncertainty may remember how this understates the actual pain involved. (For example, time lost in gas lines does not show up in the GNP.) Also, it does not really account for the loss to our balance of payments, which leads to a loss in our ownership of our own economy; if we produce a lot of goods but do not own what we produce, our own wellbeing may suffer.

Was this loss of GNP in 1974 and 1979 really due to the oil price rises? Some economic models predict that price rises of this sort should have little short-term impact; however, most of those models have a "potential GNP" equation which does not depend on energy, or assumes that it is easy to replace energy with capital or labor. In effect, they *assume* that we can easily produce goods without using energy (even in cases where energy is represented in great detail in *other* equations of the model). Naturally, they do not predict big impacts in the future either. One famous modeler, whose model could not explain the full impact of the 1974 price rises, came up with a very ingenious excuse, which he used in selling his model during the Reagan administration: he argued that it was the *government's* fault that the GNP fell so much, due to mismanagement by the Nixon-Ford Administration; however, his model assumed a very high price elasticity (i.e. easy replacement of energy), which is enough to explain the failure of its forecasts. However, the Wharton Annual Energy Model of the 1970s did contain a detailed account of how energy influences the economy, in the short-term, through a detailed representation of production; that model *was* able to explain[3] the economic downturn in 1973–75, and would also predict larger short-term effects in case of future price rises.

Does this loss of $285 billion in 1975 represent the full cost of the price rise of 1974? Many analysts simply calculate this kind of short-term loss, and assume that the economy bounced back thereafter to its previous growth path. However, if the previous growth path depended on tangible things like investment, this becomes a questionable assumption. The well-known economist Dale Jorgenson has shown very convincingly that one would expect a *long-term* effect, shifting both the level and the rate of growth of GNP. In fact, the year 1974 marks a sudden and very disturbing shift in the U.S. economy, from a sustained growth in the 4 percent range—based on large growth in productivity—to sustained growth in the 0–1 percent range. The growing percentage of women working for wages has helped to keep up the growth in average monetary income over the past fifteen years, along with tax cuts, but real wages *per person working* have not grown in this period. Real wages are probably a better measure of economic well-being than income per capita.

The evidence cited here suggests that the drop in productivity growth after 1974 might be due to higher energy prices; however, other explanations are possible. For example, one might argue that short-term efforts to keep up high standards of consumption, despite the rise of energy prices, led to short-sighted actions which lowered productivity growth—such as cuts in research and development. Some economists have argued that changes in the labor force—related to the population issues alluded to in the overview—were the major culprit. If *any* of these arguments are correct, then the problems cited in the overview would be the main culprit for this chronic loss in economic growth since 1974. Our hopes of returning to sustainable economic growth, and restoring that high spirit and morale which led us to the moon, may depend on solving our energy and population problems. Those who believe that lower oil prices have already begun to bring back some of the old high spirits in the last two to three years should be concerned about the danger of going *back* into malaise, if oil prices go back up again.

What are the dangers of new oil crises, leading to effects as large or larger than those of the 1970s? The basic situation, which allowed an oil crisis in 1974 was the growth in U.S. dependency on imported oil. By 1974, U.S. oil imports had grown to 35 percent of our oil consumption, and 20 percent of the total came from OPEC.[2] *Those* are the numbers, which made us vulnerable to unexpected events in the Middle East. By 1979, the situation was worse, with a 43 percent import dependency and a 30 percent OPEC dependency. In fact, the *steady* rise in oil prices from 1973 to 1981 was undoubtedly a factor in the lower economic growth in that period.

By the late 1970s, it seemed clear to many people that low or stable oil prices were a thing of the past. As a result, there were massive changes in energy use, including one-time improvements in efficiency, and conversion from oil to other fuels in markets where conversion was relatively easy. This, in turn, led to reduced oil demand, and downwards pressure on prices. By 1986, there was talk of an oil glut. However, even *before* prices bottomed out in 1986, oil imports began to rise again, as certain inexorable forces began to reassert themselves. From 1986 to January 1990, oil prices rose back to $20 per barrel, about half again as large as the 1986 price.[2] But from 1986 to 1989, our dependency on oil imports rose back from 33 percent to 41 percent (and is still rising); our dependency on OPEC rose from 17 percent to 24 percent, despite the rise in oil prices. We are now more vulnerable than we were in 1974, and we are moving rapidly back to the 1979 level. From 1988 to 2010, EIA now forecasts that U.S. oil imports will double[4], based on a relatively conservative analysis of these trends. All of this implies a relatively serious threat to the U.S. economy, growing steadily without an end in sight.

Looking beneath the surface, the dangers are even greater than the import numbers would suggest. For one thing, the situation in the MidEast appears more intractable than it did in 1974, particularly in the light of nuclear and chemical weapons proliferation. For another thing, there is less slack in our use of energy than there was in 1974. The easy things have already been done. From 1974 to 1989, the use of oil in the residential/commercial sector dropped by 30 percent, and the electric utility use of oil dropped by 50 percent. Most people who could convert easily to natural gas have done so.[5] (Many areas still lack sufficient gas pipeline capacity, however.) As a result, the transportation sector grew from 53 percent of oil use to 63 percent. The remaining oil use in the U.S. is overwhelmingly concentrated in vehicle use in industry (such as tractors and bulldozers), and in petrochemical feedstock use.[6]

In brief: further reductions in oil use—either in a crisis or before—will mainly have to come from cutbacks in motor vehicles, or cutbacks in our use of bulk plastics and petrochemicals.

How hard would it be to make such cutbacks in a crisis, if we did not have time to change our capital stock? In a future crisis, our main opportunity to cut back on oil use would be through reductions in driving. From historical data, it seems overwhelmingly clear[7] that a 1.0 percent increase in the real price of gasoline reduces driving by only 0.2 percent; in economists' jargon this is a price elasticity of .2/1.0 or –20 percent. To cut back driving by 10 percent without a direct reduction in personal income would thus require something like a 60 percent increase in prices. The loss of all U.S. oil imports from OPEC—which are far more than 10 percent—would therefore seem to imply a bigger impact than we observed in 1974 or 1979.

What would happen if we allowed for the possibility of conservation, so that cars get more efficient, but they still use gasoline in internal combustion engines? In actuality, the EIA forecasts have *already assumed* a very high level of conservation, rising to thirty-five miles per gallon for the *average* new car.[5] Higher mpg is possible, of course, in small or slower cars, but the research embedded in these assumptions was based on very extensive studies of what the public is or is not willing to buy under different price regimes—something which the private sector has been very sincere about wanting to know.[7] Phil Patterson, of the Conservation Office of DOE, published a critical review of the EIA efficiency assumptions in a recent World Energy Conference in Paris. Patterson argued very persuasively that the EIA assumptions were on the optimistic side. Patterson's review was especially persuasive, because it drew heavily on work by engineering research groups who had worked with people like Amory Lovins in the past, and comes from an office, which seriously tries to champion the cause of conservation. In summary, continued conservation is expected to have an important impact on oil use, but it is not enough by itself to prevent a worsening situation on imports.

There are laws in thermodynamics, discovered by Carnot, which limit the ultimate efficiency of internal combustion engines and other heat engines. Back when engines were highly inefficient, there was substantial waste and slack, which allowed a rapid improvement in mpg until 1982. Many econometric models show more potential for conservation, because they are based in large part on data from that period, and do not account for the diminishing returns, which are obvious in the engineering. (Also, they usually focus on "new car" mpg, without accounting for the shift of many car buyers towards pickup trucks and vans.) Nowadays, engines are pushing the limits of what is physically possible with this class of engine; already the complexity of new systems has begun to create problems involving cost and maintenance. Serious improvements in aerodynamics and lighter materials are certainly possible, but are already assumed in the forecasts. To do a whole lot *better* than the existing forecasts—and to avoid massive disruptions in the case of import cutbacks—one would have to go beyond the use of gasoline in heat engines.

Back in the era of Jimmy Carter, synthetic fuels were supposed to solve these problems. However, early cost estimates for synthetic fuels—like estimates for nuclear power and many other complex new technologies—were off by a factor of two or three. Ed Merrow of the RAND Corporation performed a more in-depth analysis of cost escalation, and predicted costs more like $3/gallon (in 1980 dollars) for gasoline based on synfuels technologies. This did not include the environmental costs, which would have been large as well. If the United States consumes 100 billion gallons of gasoline per year, now priced at under $1/gallon (in 1980 dollars), then the cost of switching entirely to synfuels would have been over $200 billion per year—not the kind of thing one likes to do a decade early for the sake of insurance.

The current president has chosen, for excellent reasons, to focus on methanol as the immediate way out of this dilemma. Economists from Ford have argued that one gets more miles per ton of coal if one converts the coal to methanol, and uses it as methanol, rather than making synthetic gasoline.[8] Furthermore, the use of methanol opens the door to a whole variety of other fuel supplies (such as wood alcohol), and makes it far easier (as I will discuss) to change over to fuels like hydrogen in the more distant future.

If we assume 60 cents per gallon to produce methanol using established technologies,[9] and 30 cents per gallon for distribution, and account for the lower heat content of methanol, we arrive at a price of$1.80 per gallon equivalent, in 1989 dollars and in conventional automobiles. This is far less than what synfuels would cost. Unfortunately, it is still not as cheap as gasoline, and it still requires an expensive transition. Also, it only helps a little bit in reducing those emissions which cause ozone buildup (about 20 percent , my judgement—less than the 50 percent claimed by some authoritative advocates but more than the 0 percent claimed by critics). Ozone buildup is now a major health hazard in most American cities. Dual-fueled methanol-gasoline vehicles would have only half the driving range using methanol that they would with gasoline. (Driving range would be a serious problem with other alternate fuels as well, except for ethanol.) In 1989, Congress rejected an Administration version of the Clean Air Bill, which would have mandated an initial effort to begin deploying this technology.

Finally, there are ways to move vehicles, which are *not* covered by the Carnot limitations. Los Alamos National Laboratories[10] have made substantial breakthroughs in the development of methanol-powered fuel cells for transportation, breakthroughs, which solve a wide variety of earlier problems. Such vehicles are expected to be twice as efficient as cars based on heat engines, *if* we use low-temperature technologies like the LANL technology (or others discussed by the National Hydrogen Association). These technologies now require the use of methanol or hydrogen as fuels. (Natural gas *might* become possible someday, with further research.) Ozone-related emissions are reduced by a factor of ten or twenty, conservatively. In this technology, a fuel cell provides electricity to an electric motor; therefore, if breakthroughs in battery technology should occur, the widespread use of the fuel-cell technology would make a further transition much easier.

Money has gone into this technology from both DOE and the private sector, and the most recent (unpublished) results are extremely promising. However, we are rapidly approaching a point where large investments will be required from the private sector, and it is uncertain whether the incentives now available are large enough. The House of Representatives recently added an amendment to the Clean Air Act of 1990 mandating an advanced vehicle program in Southern California, which might conceivably provide the required incentives. The bill is not yet law, there are special interests working very hard against it, and it is in any case just one step. There is room for much stronger incentives giving more positive (and profitable) encouragement to the automobile manufacturers. The most optimistic among us are hoping for thousands of fuel-cell vehicles per year by the year 2000, under a sustained push beyond what present circumstances point towards. Sober forecasters are expecting something more like 2010 to 2030—and many years more to achieve full penetration of the existing automotive fleet. Between the methanol suppliers and the auto manufacturers, the required investments will undoubtedly add up to hundreds of billions of dollars by the time we are through.

In summary, as stated in the overview, the solutions to oil dependency will take a long time and a lot of money, and may or may not actually happen (given our present political and budgetary climate). If we are lucky, they may come online before oil prices ratchet way up again, but no one knows which will happen first—the crisis or the cure. Anything which improves the budgetary climate could make a big difference here, and an early cessation of growth in the entitlements population would certainly help.

TRANSITION TO SUSTAINABLE ENERGY SUPPLIES

Billions of dollars and decades of work will be required just to complete the transition away from oil, as described above. This transition away from oil is justifiably our most immediate priority in the energy sector, because of the need to minimize the threat of a big new oil crisis and to eliminate unhealthy levels of ozone in American cities. However, this still does not solve the problem of where to get the methanol in the long-term, and it does not solve the problem of sustainability across all sectors of the economy. Additional, expensive transitions will be required to solve these longer-term problems.

Traditionally, there are four "sources" of energy, which could meet our long-term needs—conservation, renewables, nuclear and coal.

THE SOFT PATH

Advocates of the "soft" energy path argue that we might create a sustainable energy system by combining conservation along with reliance on "soft" renewables such as biomass, solar water heaters, wind, hydro, and geothermal energy. Some conservatives have strongly endorsed this idea, and argued that this kind of transition will ocur easily and naturally, simply by relying on free markets and eliminating government interference (such as R&D on conservation and renewables).

As I will discuss later, there *are* some renewable technologies—like advanced solar cells—which *could* produce a very large amont of energy; however, the "soft" renewables are usually not defined to include these. In the past, when EIA published very long-term forecasts and documentation explaining those forecasts, the projections of supply from renewables were mainly based on carefully worked out estimates of the *upper limit* of potential supply. Hydroelectric supply is limited by the energy in our rivers; wind supply is limited by our supply of exploitable wind sources; etc. (EIA now predicts[4] that renewable energy will *lose* market share from 1990 to 2010, because of a combination of limited potential and economic forces.) By and large, the *total* potential from these sources is something like one-tenth of present U.S. energy consumption.

Advocates for specific soft technologies often argue for somewhat greater potential. For example, one report on biomass from OTA[11] began with an executive summary stating that wood alcohol might contribute as much as 10 quadrillion Btu (quads) of additional energy to our economy—by itself about 12 percent of what we use. But later volumes of that report warned that this assumed the widespread use of fast-growing evergreen monocultures, so as to double production, and an avoidance of soil conservation rules which USDA has laid down for croplands (rules which many believe are still inadequate to prevent soil loss). A more objective estimate of the sustainable potential would be less than half of that 10 quads.

Most of these upper bounds are based on physical constants—like flows of wind and water—which are independent of population. However, if population were reduced substantially, there would be a major increase in the potential supply of biomass energy, because there would be less competition from the food industry and other users of biomass. It is hard to guess how large this increase would be, in the absence of truly comprehensive studies. For example, if *all* the corn and wheat in the United States were converted to alcohol fuels (based on 2.6 gallons per bushel[12]), and if the U.S. crop were reduced in half to achieve sustainability (as per the Pimentels' essay in this series), this would yield 10 billion gallons per year—only 1.5 quads of gross energy, and only 0.8 quads net. On the other hand, OTA[11] has estimated that an additional 5 quads might be available from grasses and the like *(with* a smaller population), and one might hope to achieve greater net efficiency by developing new conversion technologies and the like. Personally, I incline towards conservatism here, but the uncertainties are large; I can imagine the possibility of a case for *doubling* the potential from soft technologies, if population were cut very sharply. This would still only amount to about of 20 percent of present U.S. energy consumption, which (together with a low-risk scenario for solar energy) explains the 60 million population figure in the overview. Again, I would not be surprised if a smaller figure showed up after more extensive analysis.

Serious advocates of the soft path have generally recognized these limits of soft energy supply, and have argued that conservation can bridge the gap. But *80 percent* of the end-use fossil fuel used in the U.S. lies in two sectors—transportation and industry.[5] The preceding section described how conservation—important though it is—is far from enough to create a sustainable economy. Fuel-cell cars *would* allow a factor of two reduction in energy intensity, compared with the alternatives, but only at a price: the conversion losses in *making* methanol lead to only a marginal net improvement in efficiency.

The industrial sector is already going through a similar transition away from fossil fuel towards efficient electric technologies, without government intervention (aside from R&D). These technologies are relatively benign, environmentally, and they enhance industrial productivity; however, if one accounts for conversion losses in *generating* the electricity, they often lead to *greater* energy intensity in production. The energy used per *dollar* of product may decline, because the *quality* and *value* of products goes up (e.g., more effective drugs); however, this greater quality also leads to a greater total value of product (a *qualitative* growth in GNP), and the net effect on energy use is often positive.

Some economists have argued that higher energy prices should increase conservation in industry beyond the present trends; however, a recent comparison of the best in-depth models of industrial energy use shows that *all* of them report relatively low price elasticities.[13–15] This includes both econometric (or trend-based) models and engineering-based models. Earlier, more aggregate models showed larger elasticities because of *apriori* "consistency constraints," databases ending in 1974, and failure to account for the detailed *structure* of industrial demand as it varies from time to time and place to place.

If population should grow much beyond present levels in the U.S., there will probably be an *additional* source of energy demand for desalinization of water, which some cities in California already are getting into; with anything like a population doubling, desalinization could become a big part of where we get water, and the additional energy requirements would be enormous[21].

On balance, if one assumes some minimal level of growth in income per capita, it is hard to imagine a totally "soft" energy economy, without a drastic reduction of population. Given the difficulty of maintaining a complex economy on a small engineering base, I would question the feasibility of this. A dramatic improvement in international communications (requiring both advanced technology and cultural shifts) might increase our effective engineering base, but even so I find this scenario hard to visualize. If there *is* any hope for this scenario, it would require drastic reductions in population growth, not only in the U.S., but—for the sake of stability—worldwide.

COAL AND NUCLEAR

The conventional wisdom in energy forecasting says that we will shift, first, to a coal-based economy and then, as the coal grows more expensive, shift more to nuclear. Coal may be used more in the developed world and nuclear more in the developing world, for political reasons. Many long-range forecasting models simply assume that coal and nuclear are available in unlimited quantities.

The conventional wisdom may well be right. However, there are severe environmental problems with both fuels, which will make this transition less than automatic. There are national security issues on the nuclear side, which merit more serious action than we have seen as yet.

The environmental consequences of using coal have received a lot of attention. For example, many people associate coal with sulfur dioxide, which they associate with acid rain, which they associate with the massive recent dieback of trees in Germany—a true environmental disaster. Careful studies by the Germans[16–17] suggest that nitrogen oxides (NOx) may actually be the most important pollutant responsible for this damage (and for high ozone levels). About 40 percent of the NOx emitted in the U.S. comes from motor vehicles, and about *50 percent* from large boilers burning coal. Fuel-cells cars would eliminate the *40 percent*, but conventional, affordable pollution control technologies would have only a marginal impact on the *50 percent*. Fortunately, there has been great progress in clean coal research,[18] which could solve this problem, and probably even save money in the process, at least for new boilers. What to do about existing boilers is a harder problem. The government is already spending billions on clean coal technology, and it is clear that strenuous efforts on these lines must be continued or expanded if we really want to clean up ozone and make a safe, economical transition to coal. Likewise, it is clear that a lot of private capital would be required to build the new plants, and that the federal budget deficit—as described in the overview—will have a big effect on capital availability.

In the long-term, there are two other concerns about coal: (1) it contributes to greenhouse warming (more so than natural gas, but far less so than shale oil); (2) it is in finite supply. If the world relied *entirely* on coal, if we maintained economic growth, and if we avoided using environmentally questionable forms of coal (or depended on undiscovered coal speculated on by officials in Communist countries), then coal might last somewhere on the order of six to ten decades.[19–20] This may seem like forever to some people, but the development of safe alternatives might also take many decades; in any case, the sooner we stop the accumulation of greenhouse gases, the better. It is not too soon to think about the transition away from coal.

Nuclear power has often been advocated as a sustainable alternative to fossil fuels. However, a huge amount of research would be needed, at a minimum, to make this technology acceptable to the public. Furthermore, it is clear that existing controls on nuclear proliferation have not been effective enough to prevent major emerging problems in the Mideast (Iraq/Israel and India/Pakistan) and elsewhere. As recently as 1983, nuclear power accounted for only 3.3 percent of world energy supply.[5] Studies for the Second Report to the Club of Rome[21] showed graphically how huge an increase in that industry would be required to supply all the world's energy needs, especially if one allows for population and economic growth in developing nations and the eventual need for breeder reactors. The opportunity for nuclear weapons proliferation and terrorism is directly proportional to the availability of nuclear materials for diversion; a growth by orders of magnitude in civilian nuclear power would lead to a similar growth in the potential for diversion. If the number of political actors with access to nuclear weapons increases by orders of magnitude, and if the new political actors are more diverse in their motivations than the old ones (e.g., include crazies), then the probability of a first use of a nuclear weapon would increase by orders of magnitude as well. There are many scenarios for what could happen after such a first use, ranging all the way from global horror and authoritarian repression through to a greater willingness of other actors to use nuclear weapons. (Herman Kahn has pointed out how many other weapons went through similar cycles in the past, from religious revulsion through to widespread use and death.) It is not clear whether high civilization and vigorous economic growth would be sustainable under any of these scenarios.

Some analysts hope that a new form of nuclear energy—controlled fusion—would solve all this. But after decades of research, the future of fusion as an affordable source of energy now seems debatable, and major budget cuts have resulted from the debates. Known forms of fusion produce neutron radiation just as much as fission does, and the most economical form of fusion would probably be a hybrid fission-fusion reactor, leading to all the same national security problems. Breakthroughs in fundamental nuclear science, such as neutron-free "cold-fusion," may yet be possible, but should certainly not be counted on.

From a forecaster's point of view, the nuclear path may well be the most likely path (after a short recess), and the hazards of nuclear proliferation have already begun to yield serious consequences. This underlines the need for more conscious effort and heavy investment to open the doors to any real alternative, for the sake of national security.

HIGH-TECH RENEWABLES

Beyond coal and nuclear technologies, there is one family of technologies which does *not* face the tight upper limits which affect the soft technologies: high-tech renewables, such as direct solar. Simple physical calculations show that a modest fraction of the U.S. land area would be quite enough to sustain all of our energy needs. Many years ago, DOE published a program plan for solar cells in which they would achieve economic competitiveness at least for peak power (e.g., noon time in the summer) by the end of this century. For many years, the actual price reductions actually exceeded the DOE plan, as one might expect from a solid-state technology which is a cousin to microchips and PCs; however, after drastic cuts in the DOE budget for solar cells, and cuts in private research due to falling oil prices, the prices of solar cells flattened out. Progress is still going on, but is very slow. Work is also going on on more direct solar technologies to produce methanol or hydrogen, through new programs at the Solar Energy Research Institute in Colorado.

In addition, there still remains the problem of what to do about baseline electric power—the bulk of our electricity use. All of the possibilities involve risk and—if they look good on a first evaluation—would still require enormous investments. It is essential to develop technologies which can compete economically with nuclear power, in order to persuade other countries to resist the nuclear path and to avoid even domestic resistance base on price shock (which killed synfuels). There is a vague hope that ground-based solar might become cheap enough somehow to compete with nuclear; however, baseload power generally costs five to ten times less than peak power,[22] and it is questionable whether costs can be reduced that much beyond the present projections. Still, there are new technologies to produce methanol or hydrogen directly using sunlight whose costs are difficult to project. There is also some hope that radically new forms of geothermal energy might work out, with more research. Some people have even hoped for vast amounts of primordial gas deep in the earth's crust, though recent assessments of this are not encouraging. Finally, it is still quite possible that one could generate electricity from solar cells in space, and beam the energy down to earth, at a marginal cost competitive with nuclear power. (This would be better for the environment than ground-based solar, because the microwave receiving zones would require less land per kilowatt-hour than solar cells, in part because of twenty-four-hour operation; also, low-level microwaves have only a higher-order effect on plant life, at the most, while cutting off light simply kills them.) From a sheer engineering point of view, the last of these alternatives is easier to visualize,[23] but it would require the development of cheaper space transportation systems, such as a second-generation National Aerospace Plane, and automated lunar mining technology; such technologies are within the range of what we now know,[24] but would require an enormous amount of effort. It would require not just money, but an effort to avoid wasting the money on distractions. In any case, when no *one* technology is guaranteed of success, the safest path is to fully explore a *variety* of them, even if it does cost more money to do so.

Even if we successfully switch to these advanced technologies, there will still be limits on the population which we can sustain comfortably and efficiently in the United States, because of land costs and water pollution.

The cost of high-tech energy will depend critically on the cost of land. The cost of land *near people* is a critical issue, because of transmission and maintenance costs. Real estate costs in urban and suburban areas are already an economic burden to many people, and a doubling or tripling of population would make this phenomenon more pervasive across the country; this in turn would certainly raise the cost of land, and the cost of solar energy. Reductions in population from the present level would reduce land prices in some areas, but the effect would not be so pervasive. (Perhaps a population reduction would allow more people to move to areas which receive more sunlight.)

On the environmental side, high-tech renewables are much more benign that the status quo, but they are not problem-free. Even today, in California, there are major concerns about ground water contamination, much of which has been traced to gasoline stations, to chemical plants, and even to computer manufacturers. Replacing gasoline with methanol would not change the overall magnitude of the problem (though methanol is more biodegradable), and a big increase in population density would presumably increase the concentration of pollutants. Likewise, high-tech renewables would not prevent undesirable byproducts in most chemical plants or chip factories, and it would not prevent plastic bags from choking fish in lakes or oceans. Given that the problems today are already a concern, it would seem very worrisome to imagine increases in population which could double or triple the scale of the problems.

CONCLUSIONS

This essay has only touched the surface of some very difficult and complex issues.

The transition to sustainable sources of energy will require a whole series of major transformations in the economy, each costing billions of dollars, each entailing major risks, and requiring serious attention now. Failure to make a timely or benign transition would lead to serious problems for national security, the environment and longer-term economic growth. Successful transitions would require major government investment in accelerated R&D, stronger incentives to the private sector, and trillions of dollars in investments from the private sector; all three of these will be hard to come by in the coming years, if the present deficit environment persists. Any population policy which encourages investment and reduces the growth in the nonproductive population would have an *immediate* impact on the growth of the federal deficit, and help a great deal in increasing the probability of a successful transition away from oil. In the long term, the energy sector and the environment would probably be healthiest if the U.S. population were somewhere around 50 to 100 percent of the present level, in my view. If one were very optimistic about biomass and international cooperation, and pessimistic about high-tech renewables, then the optimum would be more like 60 million people.

If the issue of population growth is neglected, then, as the essay by Bouvier has shown, it may be difficult to avoid a doubling or even tripling of U .S. population, which would clearly pose problems for energy and the environment, due to higher land costs and water pollution.

NOTES:

1. The views expressed in this essay are personal judgements, and do not in any way reflect the official view of my employers, past or present.
2. EIA, *Monthly Energy Review: February 1990,* Washington, D.C.: National Energy Information Center (202-586-8800). p7, 13, 91.
3. Glickman, N., *Econometric Analysis of Regional Systems.* Academic Press, 1977.
4. EIA (1), *Annual Energy Outlook 1990*. p.41, 46.
5. EIA (1), *Annual Energy Review 1989*. p.245.
6. EIA (1), *State Energy Data Report,* national aggregation of public use computer tape.
7. Paul J. Werbos, *Documentation of the Transportation Demand (TED) Model.* DOE/EIA-M013. Washington, D.C.: NEIC (1), 1987. (Almost exactly the same equations were used in the subsequent "spreadsheet" model of transportation demand.)
8. Charles Gray and Jeffrey Alson, *Moving America to Methanol.* Ann Arbor, Michigan: U. of Michigan Press, 1985.
9. *Methanol Prices During Transition.* JACK FAU-86-322-8/11. Bethesda, Maryland: Jack Faucett Associates, April 1987.
10. Ross Lemons, "Fuel Cells for Transportation," *Journal of Power Sources*, Vol. 29, January, 1990, p.251–264.
11. OTA, *Energy from Biological Processes,* OTA-E-124 and –128 and Vol. III. Washington, D.C.: Office of Technology Assessment, 1980.
12. SERI, *Fuel From Farms,* SERI/SP-451–519. Washington, D.C.: National Technical Information Service, 1980. p.D-6.

13. J. Weyant and P. Werbos, "An Overview of EMF8 on Industrial Energy Demand, Conservation and Interfuel Substitution." In *Proceedings and Papers of the Eighth North American Conference of the International Association of Energy Economists,* David Wood (MIT) ed, 1987.
14. P. Werbos, "Econometric Techniques: Theory Versus Practice," in *Energy: The International Journal,* March/April 1990.
15. P. Werbos, "Industrial Structural Shift: Causes and Concequences for Electricity Demand." In Faruqui and Broehl, eds., *The Changing Structure of American Industry and Energy Use Patterns.* Battelle Press. 1987.
16. B. Prinz et al, *Forest Damage in the Federal Republic of Germany.* LIS Report number 28. Essen: Landesanstalt for Immissionsschutz des Landes Nordrheinwestfalen, 1982.
17. R.F. Huettl, "Research Methods and Preliminary Results in the Black Forest of Germany," in *Proceedings Of Mid-South Symposium on Acid Deposition*, available from Prof. Blackmon or Beasley (eds), Forest Resources Dept., U. of Arkansas, Monticello, Arkansas. (April 1986).
18. "Quickening the Pace of Clean Coal Technology," *EPRI Journal*, Jan/Feb 1989.
19. D.L. Meadows et al, *Dynamics of Growth in a Finite World.* Cambridge, Mass.: Wright-Allen Press, 1974.
20. OTA (11), *Global Models, World Futures and Public Policy: A Critique,* Appendix C. April 1982.
21. Mesarovic, M. and Pestel, *Mankind at the Turning Point: The Second Report to the Club of Rome.* New York: E.P. Dutton, 1974.
22. National Academy of Sciences, *Issues in Electric Energy Systems.* Washington, D.C.: National Academy Press, 1986.
23. P. Glaser, "A Solar Power Sattelite Built of Aluminum Materials," *Space Power*, Vol. 6, Num. 1, 1986.
24. P. Werbos, "Neurocontrol and Related Techniques," in A. Maren, ed., *Handbook of Neural Comp. Appl.* Academic Press, 1990.

HOW TO INFLUENCE FERTILITY: THE EXPERIENCE SO FAR

John R. Weeks

September 1990

INTRODUCTION

The population of the United States is currently growing at a rate of one percent per year—well below the world average rate of 1.8 percent. The average number of children born per woman is, as is well known, right at two—a level that is just below replacement. Less well understood is the fact that the number of births each year in the United States is considerably higher than the number of deaths, owing to the demographic momentum built into the age structure. In 1990 American women were giving birth to 3.8 million babies, while 2.1 million people of all ages were dying. Thus, we are increasing by 1.7 million people each year just from natural increase. Net legal migration is estimated to be 600,000 and an additional 200,000 undocumented immigrants are also augmenting the total population.[1] The population of the United States thus continues to grow by more 2.5 million people each year. In less than two years this country adds as many people as there are in Norway, and it would take only four years for the annual growth in the United States to equal the total population of Sweden. Some people react to such numbers with alarm because they think the rate of growth is too low—how can business expand when markets are not increasing at as rapid a pace as in the past? Others react to the numbers with a potentially xenophobic concern about the balance between natural increase and immigration—shouldn't the birth rate be higher so that the rate of growth would be composed of a higher fraction of native-born babies and fewer imported workers? Still others react to the U.S. growth rate by noting that the average American consumes a vastly disproportionate share of the world's resources and so the impact of population growth in this country is far greater in the long-run than is true of population growth in Asia, Africa, or Latin America.

This uncertainty about how to respond to our current demographic situation is both a cause and a consequence of the fact that the United States has never had a formal population policy—has never tried directly to influence the direction or size of the birth rate. On the other hand, we have sat back rather smugly with our relatively low levels of fertility and dispensed advice (often unsolicited) to other countries (mainly developing nations) about how *they* should proceed to lower their fertility. Could we do the same? If it became clear that our national interest would be better served by a lower fertility rate, would we know how to go about designing a set of policies to influence fertility?

Developed nations have very little experience in directly influencing fertility levels to drop, but a great many things that governments have done in the West have serendipitously helped to generate lower fertility, and there may be much to be learned from these "accidental" or indirect policies. Most governmental efforts to influence fertility in developed societies have been attempts to *raise* levels that are perceived to be too low, and there is also something to be learned in the general failure of these policies to have much impact. However, most of the direct fertility policy lessons come to us from the developing world and while the third world experience may not always be directly applicable to a country such as the United States, some of the successes and failures may be guideposts to effective policy.

DIRECT AND INDIRECT POLICIES DESIGNED TO INFLUENCE FERTILITY

Based on the detailed histories of fertility trends in Europe, Ansley Coale has argued that there are three preconditions for a sustained decline in fertility: (1) the acceptance of calculated choice as a valid element in fertility, (2) the perception of advantages from reduced fertility, and (3) knowledge and mastery of effective techniques of control.[2] Each of these components has implications for population policy, as can be seen in Table 1. Some policy initiatives are aimed *directly* at influencing demographic behavior, while others are oriented toward trying to change social behavior, which will then *indirectly* have an impact on population processes.

Rational Choice. The first example of policy initiatives confronts the awareness of population issues at both the private and public levels. The principal barrier to recognition of personal freedom in determining reproductive goals is *tradition*—in particular the attitude that reproduction is in the hands of God or those of a woman's husband. It is a world view that does not admit to self-determination of family size. Rather, the view could be summed up by the phrase "children happen."

This is an attitude that is often associated in the western world with third world nations, especially Islamic nations[3], but shades of it are evident in all human societies, because it is often associated with religious *fundamentalism*, regardless of the specific religious *preference*. In the United States, Christian fundamentalists (including both Catholics and Protestants) argue that certain aspects of reproduction (such as abortion or contraception for unmarried teenagers) should not be under the control of the woman herself.

In order to change such behavior, policies can aim directly to grant women more freedom to act in their own interest (in combination with family interest, rather than solely on the basis of what others wish). This would include providing full legal rights to women, including the right to obtain birth control devices, an abortion, or a sterilization without having to obtain permission from the husband or some other family member. In Bangladesh, for example, a young women wishing to use contraception will typically have to do so through the cooperation of her mother-in-law, with whom she lives. This will almost certainly be called to the attention of her husband, and may well lead to considerable family strife. Thus, it is often easier for a woman to get pregnant than to risk the social ire of others by seeking contraception.[4]

Other legislation that may directly influence a woman's ability to think and act for herself is a raising of the legal age at marriage, making it more difficult for a family to push daughters into an early marriage. These direct policy initiatives go hand-in-hand with indirect measures to raise the status of women and thereby increase the awareness that they, their husbands, and other family members have of the contributions that they can make to the family and to society besides simply being baby-machines. Articulating and attempting to alter the basic components of traditionalism (which is almost always pronatalist) would be one type of indirect population policy, albeit a vague and controversial one. Indeed, thus far, no one has explicitly promulgated such a policy, but mass secular education is the most successful antidote to the kind of

Table 1. Examples of Policies to Limit Fertility

Precondition For Which Intervention is Desired	Examples of Direct Policies	Examples of Indirect Policies
"Rational Choice"	• Provide full legal rights to women • Increase legal age at marriage for women	• Promote secular education • Promote communication between spouses
"Motivation for Smaller Families"	**Incentives** • Payments for not having children • Priorities in jobs, housing, education for small families • Community improvements for achievement of low birth rate	**Incentives** • Economic development • Increased educational opportunities for women • Increased labor force opportunities for women • Peer pressure campaigns • Lower infant and childmortality rates
	Disincentives • Higher taxes for each additional child • Higher maternity and educational costs for each additional child ("user fees")	**Disincentives** • Child labor laws • Compulsory education for children • Peer pressure campaigns • Community birth quotas
"Availability of Means of Limiting of Family Size"	• Legalize abortion • Legalize sterilization • Legalize all other forms of fertility control • Train family planning program workers • Manufacture or buy contraceptive supplies • Distribute birth control methods at all health clinics • Make birth control methods available through local vendors • Establish systems of community-based distribution	• Public campaigns to promote knowledge and use of birth control • Politicians speaking out in favor of birth control

See text for explanation of preconditions

traditional attitudes that prevent women (and couples) from exercising full control over their reproductive capacities. Associated with this is the need to promote communication between spouses on all matters, including reproduction. Without interpersonal communication, a spouse is more likely to assume that his or her partner holds the stereotypically traditional attitudes, and behavior will follow suit. Recent studies in rural Peru and in Burkina Faso have shown that, even in these geographically disparate societies, male men appear to have more accurate knowledge about female reproduction than women, and know nearly as much about contraception. However, cultural norms tend to maintain the traditional gender roles and limit the amount of such information that is passed between spouses.[5] Mass education helps to break down some of these walls by exposing both sexes to the same information in a context in which both men and women know that the other knows about reproduction and contraception, and thus the subject is easier to broach and discuss.

The importance of education as a factor in reducing fertility cannot, in fact, be overstressed. Virtually every study ever done on the topic has revealed that higher education is associated with lower fertility, no matter what the cultural setting, geographic region, or religious preference of the respondents. In a recent review of four Latin American countries, for example, researchers concluded that improvements in female education alone could account for 40 to 67 percent of the fertility decline, other things being held constant.[6] Education works directly to lower a woman's fertility by delaying her exposure to intercourse, and indirectly by showing her alternatives in life to early marriage and numerous children. More broadly and fundamentally, though, education changes the way all people think about their lives and the role that reproduction plays in life.

In a less developed society, as in some areas in the United States, a sixteen-year-old female may appear in every way to be a *woman*. She has been raised with the expectation that she will be a wife and mother and by age sixteen she is physically and socially ready to take on those roles which, when accepted, will hold her in virtual bondage for the rest of her life. Her family may be delighted at her marriage because, among other things, it relieves them of the worry that she will shame the family name by having an out-of-wedlock pregnancy.[7] By contrast, in a more developed nation, a sixteen-year-old female is still a *girl* with several years of schooling ahead of her and a job to start or career to establish before marriage and reproduction enter her social picture. Physically, of course, she is ready for parenthood and that is a dilemma that most developed countries outside of the United States have dealt with by providing access to contraception (which is discussed below) for young people who are literally bursting with hormones, but who are not yet ready to be shackled by premature parenthood. Parenthood at younger ages is only premature, however, because a more educated society redefines its terms and reorients its expectations.

Motivation for Smaller Families. Self-detrermination of reproduction does not necessarily mean fertility limitation. Thus, the second precondition suggests policies oriented toward motivating a person or a couple to limit family size. If societal leaders are convinced that reducing fertility levels is an important way to reach desired social goals, then these policies are designed to reduce the gap between public needs (lower fertility) and private wishes (the maintenance of high fertility in the face of pronatalist pressures). Such policies include direct and indirect initiatives, within which we find both incentives and disincentives (rewards for small families; punishments for large families).

Direct incentives include payments to women or couples for not having a pregnancy during a specified interval (as is practiced on several tea estates in India)[8], or payments to individuals to undergo voluntary surgical contraception (VSC), such as was instituted in the now-famous vasectomy programs in India. Non-cash incentives include priority for housing, or for educational placement of children for first or second children, but not for higher-order births. Even broader still are incentives practiced in some rural areas of China in which communities are rewarded with improved community infrastructure (a new school, paving of streets, etc.) if they meet targeted birth rate levels. Of course, the farther away from the individual is the reward for a small family, the more important is the indirect policy of social pressure to encourage compliance with a low fertility regimen.

In the now developed nations, the path to lower fertility was alongside the road to economic development and the classic statement of the demographic transition spotlights development as the major stimulus to fertility limitation. From that concept were born the maxims that "development is the best contraceptive" and "take care of the people and population will take care of itself."[9] The problem with development as a policy initiative is that it is a much slower process than imitation. But, we don't need to imitate our past. We simply must extract the appropriate lessons. One of the crucial elements of industrialization was that it reversed the flow of income between children and parents—children became economic liabilities rather than assets. Furthermore, it was built on the back of a better educated labor force which has increasingly moved toward maximizing human capital by bringing women into the paid labor force.

The lesson, then, is that economic development appears always to be associated with fertility declines because the process of development incorporates a complex set of direct and indirect incentives to limit family size along with direct and indirect disincentives to have large families. The task of the modern policy-planner is to sort through those factors that may be implemented independently of the process of development and which, through diffusion rather than innovation, may lead to lower fertility. For example, the motivation to have a small family can be enhanced by indirect incentives such as greater opportunities for women to become educated and to enter the paid labor force. As I have argued elsewhere[10], economic independence is the key to raising the status of women which, in turn, is a key element in the decline in fertility. Even direct public pressure may influence behavior by publicly changing norms in a manner not unlike the spread of fad and fashion in a society. Thus, governments that wish to lower fertility sometimes begin the process by "spreading the message" that small is beautiful when it comes to family size. There is evidence that fertility in Europe, for example, was subject to strong social influences independent of levels of socioeconomic development,[11] so the idea that family size preferences can be influenced at least to some extent by social pressure seems to be a reasonable one.

Since it is often argued that the development of high fertility norms in societies was an historically rational response to high death rates, it is reasonable to suggest that the lowering of infant and childhood mortality may help indirectly to lower fertility by reducing the pressure that couples feel to have several children so that a few will survive to adulthood. Of course, as I pointed out above, most societies are already devoting as many resources as they can to the lowering of mortality for purely humanitarian, if not social and economic, reasons, but the policy certainly can be explicitly incorporated into a population policy. Interestingly enough, there is some evidence emerging to suggest that lower levels of fertility themselves help to lower infant mortality (a reversal of the expected causal direction) by lengthening the interval between children and allowing a mother to concentrate her physical and social resources on her new-born child.

Disincentives may also be employed to limit fertility. Children may be taxed after the second one (in direct opposition to the pronatalist policy in the United States of permitting tax deductions for each child), and each successive child might result in higher "user fees" for maternity care, educational services, and other public resources. Indeed, subsequent children might result in a loss of specific benefits for a family, especially in a socialist state (such as China) where many resources are distributed through the government. Similarly, at the community level there may be punishments (such as less electricity or oil available, or higher community tax rates) if a community does not meet a preestablished birth quota. As was true with incentives, these disincentives are most effectively implemented when combined with measures of indirect pressure on couples to use contraception or to abort a birth if it might cause the community to exceed its quota. This latter situation, which has the elements of coercive abortion, has apparently existed within some rural Chinese communities[12] and is the root of the Reagan and now Bush administration's unfortunate and misguided policy of withholding money from the United Nations Fund for Population Activities because the latter organization supports family planning programs in China. The United States is in the incongruous situation of withholding funds from the United Nations Fund for Population Activities because that organization supports family planning efforts in China that may include abortion (which is legal in China), when abortion is also legal in the United States. Indeed, the abortion ratio in China (31 abortions per 100 pregnancies) is not significantly different from the level in the U.S. (thirty per 100).[13]

Draconian coercive measures may be implemented if quick results are required at the expense of individual freedom, but there is a variety of indirect disincentives that historically have had important long-term effects on the motivation for small families. Child-labor laws, if rigorously enforced, help to lower (or at least delay) the economic benefit of children to their parents and thus may cause parents to think again about the value of an additional child. Similarly, a societal mandate (again when enforced) that children must attend school not only takes children out of the labor force so that they can no longer contribute to the parents' income, but schooling may cost money—for appropriate clothes, books and supplies, meals, et cetera—either directly (cash spent on each child) or indirectly (through some system of taxation to pay for schooling).

Availability Of Means For Limiting Family Size. Even if a person is motivated to limit family size, implementing that desire is facilitated by the accessibility of effective means of fertility control. "Accessibility" includes knowledge of methods—what is available, where to get them, and how to use them, and the actual availability of methods—making it possible for them to use a method. Thus, policies oriented to a direct implementation of this precondition for a fertility decline will be focused on legalizing all those methods of fertility control (including abortion, voluntary surgical sterilization, and other means of contraception) that are culturally acceptable in that society. An ideal program of fertility control (and one that prevails in most Western nations) is to teach boys and girls about the reproductive processes of both sexes (often called "fertility awareness" classes), and then to have a wide range of highly effective chemical contraceptives (such as the pill and injectables) and barrier methods (such as the IUD, contraceptive sponges, and condom) available for those who wish to delay pregnancy while still engaging in sexual intercourse. Postpartum breast-feeding accompanied by barrier methods of birth control enhance maternal and infant health by maximizing infant nutrition and spacing the next pregnancy. Voluntary surgical contraception for those who wish to avoid further pregnancies reduces the risk of unwanted children at older ages and permits societal resources for the more expensive chemical and barrier methods to be spent on the younger members of society.

The success of a fertility control policy aiming to make methods available to the citizenry depends upon the way in which such a policy is implemented. This is of course true for any policy, but the private nature of reproduction seems to highlight the importance of program effort in achieving success. For example, legalization of methods is but a first step. This must be followed by the training of people who can teach others to use a method, accompanied by the mechanism for manufacturing or buying a supply of the method, along with an organized distribution system. The various ways by which contraceptives (especially the more popular ones such as the pill and condom) are distributed has been the subject of considerable evaluation over the past decade and, while the results suggest that there are many different ways successfully to organize a program, female contraceptives have the highest continuation rate when a consistent supply is available through a discreet mechanism of personal transfer (such as a community worker making a personal delivery). Condoms are also most widely accepted when they are routinely available at stores and other outlets such as street vendors. Vasectomy programs have proven successful even in strongly "macho" areas such as Brazil if they are performed in high quality, male-only clinics. Not surprisingly, vasectomy adopters are typically married men who have consulted with their wives and are concerned about the adverse health consequences for their wife of an additional pregnancy. Thus, we are reminded that these policies work best when we have gotten past the first two preconditions.

The idea that a motivation for a smaller family is perceived to drive the demand for effective contraception is a reasonable one, but it appears that it does not exhaust the possibilities. There also appears to be a "supply side" factor in fertility limitation. That is to say, the availability of an effective program of contraception may, in fact, create its own demand. Discussing their experience with the Matlab project in Bangladesh, Phillips and his associates have pointed out that "an intensive service program can compensate for weak or ambivalent reproductive motives and create demand for services, leading to contraceptive adoption where it might otherwise not occur."[14]

For a program to have that kind of impact, however, it must have a broad base of support, which is typically generated or least enhanced in two different ways: (1) by public campaigns that promote the knowledge and use of birth control, and (2) by important politicians and other community leaders speaking out in favor of birth control. The latter is particularly important because political support is often the leading edge of resources being made available to mount and maintain a successful family planning program.

The above paragraphs set out the range of possibilities for policies to limit fertility. Success with such a policy will depend partly on the mix of strategies employed, and partly on the effort expended to implement the policy. Let us now turn to an examination of some of these factors in the context of policies that have been put into place in various nations around the world.

POLICIES TO LIMIT FERTILITY: THE EVIDENCE

Out of 170 countries surveyed by the United Nations in 1989, sixty-eight (40 percent) perceived their rate of growth to be too high."[15] These countries included 64 percent of the population of the globe, but did not include a single industrialized nation. In 1974 (the year of the United Nation's first such survey) only 28 percent of countries (encompassing 59 percent of the total population) had perceived their growth to be too high. Most, although not all, of these countries had a government policy in 1989 designed to lower the fertility level. Thus, as of 1989, sixty-four countries, comprising 63 percent of the world's population had some kind of policy designed to lower fertility.

In the abstract, of course, it is impossible to evaluate the efficacy of those policies, but we can note that between 1974 and 1989, the crude birth rate for the world declined from thirty-five births per 1,000 population to twenty-eight per thousand,[16] representing a 20 percent decline. Objectively, then, the short-term past has not witnessed dramatic declines in fertility, but clearly the world-wide trend is in the direction of lower fertility. To assess these patterns, it is useful to examine the globe regionally and look at some representative instances of the implementation of policies designed to limit fertility.

East Asia. Eastern Asian nations have generally been the most successful in engineering short-term rapid declines in fertility. The decline in Japan, for example, seems to have been born of necessity. A population trying to rebuild a nation after war, but swamped with repatriated Japanese who had been living in occupied countries needed demographic relief and found it in abortion. Between 1947 and 1957 the birth rate was cut in half in Japan, almost exclusively through the use of abortion, which had been legalized as part of the "Eugenics Protection Act" of 1948 in Japan (which had been passed primarily to eliminate illegal abortions which had been on the rise). Only since the 1960s have other forms of contraceptives (especially the condom, and more recently the pill) increased in importance as a factor in keeping birth rates low. At present, fertility levels in Japan are below replacement level and the government has no fertility control policy.

Singapore's fertility decline has somewhat different roots. Singapore is a city-state that used to be part of Malaysia and more than three-fourths of its 2.5 million inhabitants are ethnic Chinese. Upon independence in 1965 there was governmental recognition that rapid population growth would deter the nation's ability to continue developing economically. The government first established a family planning program to make contraceptives available on the assumption that the demand for such services existed. The results were disappointing, however, and in 1969 the government adopted a "Two is Enough" slogan, while legalizing abortion and introducing some direct disincentives for large families, including steeply rising maternity costs for each additional child, low school enrollment priorities for third and higher-order children, withdrawal of paid two-month maternity leave for civil service and union women after the second child, low public housing priority for large families, and no income tax allowance for more than three children. The impact on fertility was dramatic, with the average number of children being born to women dropping from 4.5 in 1966 to 1.4 in 1988. So low did fertility drop that Singapore's prime minister began to worry that too many of the wealthier, better educated women were cutting back on births, while too few of the poorer, less educated women were, so in a plan that generated world-wide controversy, selective incentives were instituted to encourage "elite" women to increase their level of reproduction. Indeed, since 1986 the official government view is that fertility is too low and the policy is to try to raise it, and available evidence suggests that the birth rate is edging back up.

The People's Republic of China has instituted the most famous program of fertility control ever devised, although the one-child policy does not actually explain low fertility in that country. Fertility began to drop steeply in China as early as the mid-1960s, long before the one-child policy was established in 1979. Communism brought with it a significant restructuring of family and gender roles, particularly among younger people. Children became less of an economic asset and women had increased access to education and to the labor force and were no longer so likely to be dominated by elders in the family. Thus, the motivation for fertility limitation had been growing, especially within the Han majority, for some time before the government moved in the direction of more coercive measures. The current policy is, in essence, designed to keep fertility low among those groups who already have low fertility, and to extend the pattern of fertility limitation to rural areas and ethnic minority groups where high fertility norms still persist. Thus, the one-child policy, with its mix of direct incentives for small families, and direct disincentives for large families, enforced by the indirect mechanism of strong social pressure, has been viewed by the government as an interim measure to bring a halt to population growth—stabilizing the population size at a target of 1.2 billion—after which the controls can be eased just enough to maintain that numerical limit. Despite U.S. concern about abortion in China, the official statistics indicate that fertility is kept low by the use of the IUD until the family is completed, at which time voluntary surgical contraception is the norm. We should note in passing, that despite the one-child *policy*, China's fertility rate remains above the replacement level (at about 2.3 children per woman-virtually the same level as in 1980) because some groups such as rural ethnic minorities are exempted and some families do not comply.

Since one in five humans lives in China (although less than one in seven newborn *babies* is Chinese) world interest remains riveted on that part of the world. The government's policy continues to favor limitations on fertility and the success of that policy will influence world growth rates for the foreseeable future. On the other hand, the Chinese have a disproportionately small impact on world resources because it is one of the poorest countries in the world, with a per person income that is less than two percent of the average income in the United States.

Southern Asia. An additional one in five humans lives in the southern Asian Indian subcontinent, including India, Pakistan, and Bangladesh. High fertility remains more firmly entrenched in this part of the world, despite government policies designed to limit fertility. The average woman in India continues to bear more than four children, despite nearly forty years of official government effort to lower the birth rate, and despite the fact that per person income in India is virtually the same as in China. The major difference between the two countries is in the amount of effort and resources that the government has been able to mobilize to impact any of the three preconditions for a fertility decline. India's first family planning effort in 1952 relied heavily on the rhythm method, whose high failure rate is well known.[17] Indeed, the old joke asks: What do you call users of the rhythm method? and the answer is "parents." India's next major foray into family planning was with the vasectomy campaigns of the 1960s, but this program was hampered by the fact that many men who were sterilized had already fathered several children, and some had wives who were already past menopause. Furthermore, there were claims that men were being forced into sterilizations by recruiters who (like the person undergoing the vasectomy) were rewarded with a transistor radio or similar premium. The IUD has also been available in India since 1961 and abortion was legalized in 1971, but the pill is still not widely distributed. In various areas of India there have been experiments in paying women not to have babies by depositing money in a pension-type account for them for each month or year that they delay or avoid a pregnancy. Such schemes have been generally successful but they have had neither the funding nor the local government backing necessary to make them widespread.

The contrast between China and India reveals that in poor populous countries beset by a variety of problems including multiple ethnic groups and diverse linguistic and cultural practices, the birth rate can be dramatically lowered if the government insistently promotes a small-family norm, helps to generate a demand for fertility control by instituting social changes that undermine traditional pronatalist practices, make it worth a young person's while to delay marriage and within marriage to limit the number of children, and then backs up these motivations with widespread availability of the means by which fertility can be limited. At the same time, the case of China shows that a decline in fertility can be wrapped around a concomitant decline in mortality, as China's leaders clearly understood that "barefoot doctors were the indispensable allies of intrauterine devices."[18] Indeed, in the mid-1950s China and India had virtually the same mortality and fertility levels. In 1990, China has mortality and fertility levels nearly comparable to those in Europe, while Indians continue to die at rates well above the world average. Yet, during all of the this time, average income in the two countries has remained roughly the same.

Indonesia provides good evidence of the way in which government support for subtle social change and effective delivery of family planning services can impact fertility. Indonesia is the fifth most populous nation in the world, and the most populous Moslem nation. In a relatively short period of time women in Indonesia have brought their fertility down from 5.7 children per woman in 1960 to an average of 3.3 in 1990—higher than China, but clearly lower than anywhere on the Indian subcontinent. There is some evidence that oil-based development in Indonesia was beginning to build a latent demand for smaller families, but most analysts agree that the strong support of President Suharto and of Islamic religious leaders for the government's programs were crucial in its widespread adoption. A survey in 1971 suggested that only 3 percent of married couples of reproductive age were using contraception, whereas by 1987 the percentage had increased to 48 percent. "Of great importance in the country's achieving this shift was Suharto's support for the family planning program's budget even when, as in 1986, government revenues were falling."[19] The government accommodated Islamic religious beliefs by omitting abortion and sterilization from the family planning program, and from the beginning religious leaders were included in the policy-planning phases. They have thus been able to assist the program by assuring the community that family planning was in accordance with the Koran, by adding family planning messages into wedding ceremonies, and by actively telling individuals about the program. Educational levels are rising in Indonesia and that has accompanied delayed marriage among women, along with a later start and earlier stop to childbearing. As is true throughout the world, this pattern of childbearing also helps to reduce infant mortality which then circles back to reassure parents that they are safe in having a smaller family.

Latin America. Latin America (including the Caribbean) reveals considerable regional diversity in achieving low levels of fertility, ranging from a low in the tiny islands of Antigua and Barbuda of 1.7 lifetime births per woman to a high in Guatemala where woman are having children at the rate of 5.6 each. The Caribbean islands in general have achieved low fertility, but the case of Haiti (where the total fertility rate is 5.1 births per woman) shows that being an island is not necessarily a defense against high fertility. Several of the islands have been aided in achieving lower fertility by the out migration of young people (especially males), many of whom head to the U.S. mainland to search for jobs. Cuba has not recently had the U.S. as a major migration outlet, but did find some temporary relief in its military adventures in Angola and elsewhere, effectively removing young men from the island for substantial periods of time. In recent years this has facilitated a rise in the average age at marriage in Cuba which, in combination with legalized abortion and access to free contraceptives, has pushed Cuban fertility to below the replacement level.[20]

The government of Mexico has also become increasingly active in promoting small family norms and of providing family planning assistance through public and private outlets. For decades, if not centuries, women in Mexico had been bearing an average of seven to eight children, until the 1960s. In the middle of that decade it appears that the birth rate began to drop, perhaps as economic development began tentatively to take root. In 1974 the government rather dramatically reversed its previously pronatalist position and the General Law of Population was rewritten to encourage "responsible parenthood, " and to offer family planning services to Mexican couples. Less than fifteen years later, in 1987, a nation-wide fertility survey indicated that fertility had dropped to an average of 3.8 children per woman nationwide.

CONCLUSION: WHAT CAN THE U.S. LEARN?

Any policy oriented toward fertility limitation must keep in mind that population control is rarely an end in itself but rather an implementing strategy that helps to achieve other goals. Our eye is on the prize of a desired social order, and population policies must be kept in that perspective. Policies based on racism or elitism should be clearly unacceptable in American society. Instead, policies need to focus on groups whose fertility is above average and ask: (1) why do these groups have higher fertility? and (2) what policy lessons learned from elsewhere in the world can be applied to encourage lower levels of fertility within the context of a society in which the small-family norm is already well rooted?

In the United States, as in most areas of the world, fertility rates are highest among the least educated, among the poor, and among racial/ethnic minority groups. Using data from the U.S. Census Bureau's Current Population Survey in 1988 (the most recent data available as of this writing), we can see that, among women aged eighteen to twenty-nine (the ages in which most childbearing takes place), women who had less than a high school education were almost twice as likely to have had a baby during the previous year as were college graduates. Women in families with income under $10,000 per year were nearly three times as likely to have had a baby in the previous year as those women in families with $50,000 or more income. Hispanic women were 25 percent more likely to have a child than non-Hispanic women, and black women were 40 percent more likely to have had a child than a white woman. These categories are not mutually exclusive, of course, since racial/ethnic minority group members tend disproportionately to have lower levels of education and to have lower incomes. Indeed, these structural features explain much of the racial/ethnic differences in fertility in the United States. In Figure 1 it can be seen that in the United States in 1988, the differences between racial/ethnic groups in fertility were much less than were the differences in education.

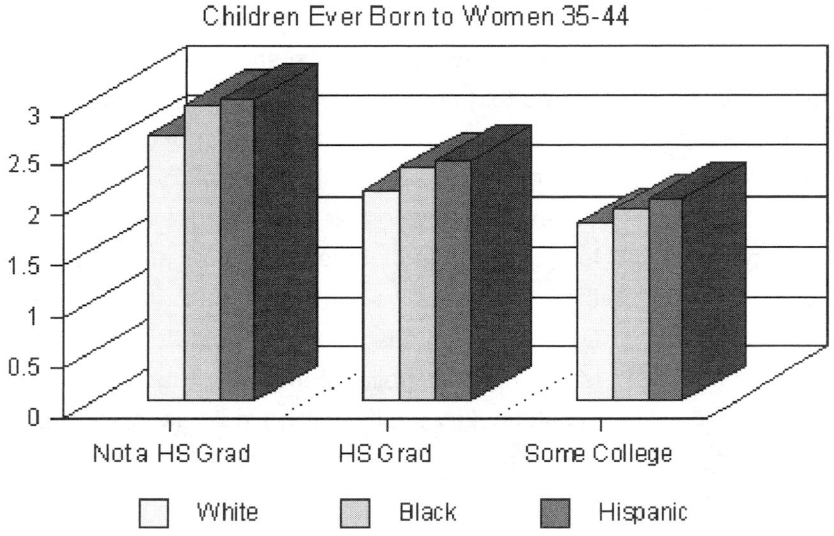

Figure 1. Fertility Levels Are Highest Among the Least Educated, Regardless of Race/Ethnicity, United States, 1980
Source: U.S. Bureau of the Census, Current Population Reports, Series P-20, No. 436, 1989

Given the previously discussed policy initiatives, one could imagine a two-pronged approach to fertility limitation in the United States. Fertility could be brought down by increasing educational and income levels within society, and it could be brought down by increasing the motivation of less educated and less well-off persons to have small families and increasing their access to effective means of fertility control. It must be recognized, though, that we are referring to a multi-cultural, multi-lingual group in American society and it is almost certain that no single approach will work best in all situations. In areas dominated by immigrant groups, some of the methods utilized in their own homelands may be effective when adapted to the U.S. environment. In other inner-city areas characterized by fractured families, high unemployment, and high crime, a system based on the Chinese "barefoot doctors" may be the model for the delivery of family planning, maternal, and infant health services. In Caroline County, Maryland, a page has been torn from the third world with an experimental program to pay high school girls not to get pregnant.[21] However, before running off and designing a program only for the least educated and poorest segments of the population, we should bear in mind that in the year prior to the 1988 survey referred to above, women with less than a high school education accounted for only 18 percent of all births in the United States, whereas those women who had graduated from high school, but had not attended college accounted for 43 percent of all births. If we concentrated on the least educated group and reduced their birth rate to the level of high school graduates, we would reduce the annual number of births by 3 percent. On the other hand, if we concentrated on lowering fertility of the high school graduates down to the level of women who have attended college, we could reduce the annual number of births by 7 percent. Clearly the latter is the more effective strategy in terms of a quantitative impact on the birth rate. It is probably also more effective in terms of cost-efficiency because this is a group more apt to be amenable to policy pressure. Governmental policies that affect motivation for small families through taxation, the housing market and the consumer credit market, and the availability of educational and labor force opportunities for women are more likely to find a response among the middle classes than among the group often labeled the underclass.

The experience of other nations suggests also that government policies influence family size decision-making partly through their economic impact, but partly also through the social message they carry.

Humans are inherently social creatures (not simply rational economic beings) and we are constantly looking about us for clues to social behavior. A consistent set of government initiatives aimed at lower fertility is almost certain to have the long-term effect of leading couples to think more consciously about their family size decisions. Such consciousness could be raised especially by the adoption of what has been called a Demographic Impact Report. Analogous to the Environmental Impact Reports (which initially contained the clear intent that demographic issues be addressed) the DIR would be required of all (or at least broad classes of) legislation to evaluate the proposed law's effect on either raising or lowering the fertility rate. The importance of the DIR lies in the fact that the demographic implications of most public policies are hidden to the untutored eye and only become apparent when it may be too late to overcome the consequences.[22] The DIR would have the effect both of actually promoting lower fertility (by rejecting legislative initiatives that would have the opposite effect) and of promoting low fertility values through the example set by legislative leadership.

Throughout the world the success of fertility limitation policies often depends upon the strength of leadership, and there is little reason to think that the U.S. would be an exception to this. The personal support of national leaders such as Suharto in Indonesia, Lee Kuan-yew in Singapore, and Bourguiba in Tunisia has seemed to have an unmistakable influence in the promotion of lower fertility in those countries. In this country, our complacency about low fertility has allowed national leaders to sidestep the population issue. Yet, every addition to the population in a country like the United States yanks a vastly disproportionate hunk out of the world's storehouse of known resources. For this reason, policies that affect population growth in the U.S. have a major long-term effect on all aspects of the world's ecosystem. We should assist globally in every way we can and we should lead by example. We do that now *implicitly* by having low fertility, but it is not always clear to the world that we, as a nation, actually *prefer* the level of fertility we have. We exhibit considerable ambivalence about national fertility levels, and pronatalist voices are often louder than antinatalist voices. A mechanism such as the Demographic Impact Report could be one part of a larger national policy condoning the concept of a small, healthy family which would generate a lower and more equitably distributed birth rate in the United States while adding clout to our international assistance efforts by reducing the perception that those efforts are patronizing or even genocidal in their intent. In the words of the President of the Swiss National Bank, the United States would be offering "a frank and unashamed word in favor of family planning."[23]

NOTES:

1. U.S. Bureau of the Census, "Estimates of the Population of the United States to March 1, 1990," *Current Population Reports*, Series P-25, No. 1056, 1990; and "Population Profile of the United States, 1989, " *Current Population Reports*, Special Studies, Series P-23, No. 159, 1989.
2. Ansley Coale, "The demographic transition." Proceedings of the International Population Conference, Liege. Volume I pp. 53–72.
3. I have discussed elsewhere the fact that the prevalence of these attitudes in Islamic nations appears to be more a matter of social structure, than it is religion *per se*. See John R. Weeks, "The Demography of Islamic Nations," Population Bulletin 43(4), 1988.
4. James Phillips, Ruth Simmons, Michael Koenig, and J. Chakraboty, "Determinants of reproduc-

tive change in a traditional society: evidence from Matlab, Bangladesh," *Studies in Family Planning* 19(6),Part 1:313–334, 1988.

5. Gisele Maynard-Tucker, "Knowledge of reproductive physiology and modern contraceptives in rural Peru," *Studies in Family Planning* 20(4):215–224, 1989; Therese McGinn, Azara Bamba and Moise Balma, "Male knowledge, use and attitudes regarding family planning in Burkina Faso," International Family Planning Perspectives 15(3):84–87, 1989.
6. Mary Booth Weinberger, Cynthia Lloyd, and Ann Klimas Blanc, "Women's education and fertility: a decade of change in four Latin American countries," *International FamilyPtanning Perspectives* 15(1):4-14, 1989.
7. Saad Gadalla, *Is There Hope? Fertility and Family Planning in a Rural Community in Egypt* (Chapel Hill: Carolina Population Center), 1978.
8. J. Satia and R. Maru, "Incentives and disincentives in the Indian Family Welfare Program," *Studies in Family Planning* 17(3):136–145, 1986.
9. Quoted by Michael Teitelbaum, "Relevance of the demographic transition for developing countries," *Science* 188:420–425, 1975.
10. John R. Weeks, *Population: An Introduction to Concepts and Issues, Fourth Edition* (Belmont: Wadsworth Publishing Co.), 1989
11. See, for example, Ronald Lesthaeghe, "On the social control of human reproduction," *Population and Development Review* 6(4):549–580, 1980.
12. John Aird, *Slaughter of the Innocents* (Washington, D.C.: American Enterprise Institute for Public Policy Research), 1990
13. Stanley Henshaw, "Induced abortion: a world review, 1990," *Family Planning Perspectives* 22(2):76–89, 1990.
14. Phillips, et al, op cit, p. 323.
15. United Nations, *Trends in Population Policy*, Population Studies, No. 114 (New York: United Nations).
16. Data for 1974 are from the "World Population Estimates" prepared by the Environmental Fund, while the 1989 are from the Population Reference Bureau's "World Population Data Sheets."
17. The rhythm method must be distinguished from more modern methods of periodic abstinence such as the symptothermal method, which have failure rates that are similar to the condom.
18. United Nations, *World Population at the Turn of the Century*, Population Studies, No. 111 (New York: United Nations), 1989, p. 122.
19. Donald Warwick, "The Indonesian family planning program: government influence and client choice," *Population and Development Review*, 12(3):, 1986, p.455.
20. See, for example, Paula Hollerbach, Sergio Diaz-Briquets and Kenneth Hill, "Fertility Determinants in Cuba," *International Family Planning Perspectives* 10(1): 12–20, 1984.
21. "Pregnancy Propositions-Dollars for Those Who Don't," *New York Times*, May 29, 1990.
22. This is example of "foresight" in public policy-making, and I am indebted to Lindsey Grant for suggesting this line of thought.
23. Quoted in *Popline* 6(4):I,1984.

OPTIMAL CITY SIZE AND POPULATION DENSITY FOR THE TWENTY-FIRST CENTURY

Alden Speare, Jr. and Michael J. White

October 1990

INTRODUCTION

Within the United States, as in many other parts of the world, there are several large cities, which seem to be constantly beset with problems of crime, congestion, pollution, and mismanagement. At times the mere population size of these areas seems to make them unmanageable. The City of New York, for example, had a population of about 7.3 million in 1988 within 302 square miles. Los Angeles had over 3 million within 465 square miles and Chicago had 3 million within 228 square miles. Each of these cities is surrounded by smaller cities and densely settled suburban area which bring the total in these metropolitan areas to 18.1 million for New York, 13.8 million for Los Angeles, and 8.2 million for Chicago.[1] Are such cities the combined product of outdated agglomeration economies and continued population growth, or is their current size justifiable in terms of greater efficiencies in the production of goods and services and the amenities offered to their inhabitants?

In this essay, we will reexamine the old arguments that larger scale leads to greater efficiency, reduced costs, and a better quality of life. We shall look at the environmental and social costs associated with different scales of settlement. We will also look at how people's perception of the desirability of a particular place and the perceived problems of that place vary with size. Finally, we will question the common view that population decline has negative consequences for cities.

There is much disagreement on the subject of optimal city size and we do not expect to arrive at a single type of urban settlement, which is optimal or ideal for all persons. In a recent Gallup Poll, New York City received the largest number of votes for both the best city and the worst city in the U.S. [2] Its supporters pointed to the number of job opportunities, the shopping, and the cultural activities, while New York's detractors mentioned the high cost of living, crime and pollution. Which of these advantages and disadvantages are likely to continue into the next century and how is technology changing the relative advantages of large vs small cities? Before addressing this question, we will briefly summarize the history of city growth.

CURRENT POPULATION DISTRIBUTION AS A RESULT OF HISTORY

The current distribution of population in the United States reflects the history of settlement of the nation. The vast variations in population density are largely the result of the location of past economic opportunities and the establishment of self perpetuating migration streams. If the United States were being settled today, the distribution would probably be quite different.

Eight of the ten largest metropolitan areas in the United States have central cities, which developed in the nineteenth century.[3] These cities were primarily dependent upon water transportation and were located at major ports for sea transportation (such as New York, Boston and San Francisco) or at the junction of major rivers or lakes (such as Detroit and Chicago). These cities were all settled before automobiles and buses were available, and businesses and houses had to be close together to permit most people to travel on foot between them. The rivers along which they are located often divide the land and create barriers to land transportation.

Newer cities such as Dallas, Los Angeles and Phoenix were designed for automobile transportation and have fewer water barriers, although they can still have traffic jams due to population growth beyond what was anticipated in the design of highway systems. With the development of land transportation, fewer people need live near sea ports and high residential densities are not needed. Metropolitan areas developed in the past decade, such as Bradenton, Florida and Naples, Florida have much lower densities and are almost entirely suburban in character, lacking a dense core.

While the earlier history of the nation was one of growing population concentrations, the trends of the 1970s were in the direction of population deconcentration. John Long shows that population growth was greatest in the lowest density states and in the smallest places.[4] What caught people's attention were two observations. First, that nonmetropolitan growth exceeded metropolitan growth during the decade and second, that the largest metropolitan areas, those with over 1 million people, experienced absolute population decline during the decade. While central city decline had been observed in some cities since the 1930s, this was the first time that both cities and suburbs lost population in several areas. Since 1980, growth has been more even across size categories, while still favoring states with lower population densities.

One reason for the continued growth of some of the larger and older cities during the 1980s was the flow of immigrants from abroad to these cities. The recent upsurge in immigration, both legal and undocumented, has found its way disproportionately to larger urban areas. For example, in the 1980 census 94 percent of the foreign born population lived in metropolitan areas of one million or more, whereas only 75 percent of the general population did.[5]

During the 1970s, immigration accounted for one-third of the growth of all metropolitan areas, and a larger fraction in some of the largest areas.[6] Los Angeles, which grew 14 percent from immigration in the 1970s, would have lost population had there been no immigration and internal migration had remained the same. Immigration also kept population growth from declining or significantly reduced the decline in Boston, Chicago, New York and San Francisco. In the Washington, D.C. area, immigration accounted for almost all of the net growth.

In the 1980s, this urban concentration has continued. For the approximately 600,000 immigrants legally admitted to the United States in Fiscal Year 1987, the three largest metropolitan areas (New York, Chicago, and Los Angeles) accounted for about thirty percent of intended destinations (places of residence), whereas only about 10 percent of the general population lives in these places.[7] Non-metropolitan destinations accounted for seven percent compared to 24 percent of residences for the population as a whole. Illegal immigration is also concentrated in urban areas (New York, Los Angeles, Houston, Miami), although there is substantial movement to rural agricultural areas, too. In sum, the admission of immigrants to the United States (as well as their unauthorized arrival) has served to make the distribution of population more concentrated than it would otherwise be.

AGGLOMERATION ECONOMIES—DO THE OLD ARGUMENTS HOLD?

One argument for the existence and development of cities rests on the notion of agglomeration economies. These economies are advantages in production that derive from the spatial proximity of producers of goods and services in an interrelated economy. By agglomerating, producers reduce the transportation costs of moving goods from one firm or stage of the production process to another.

Invocation of the agglomeration economy argument seemed to work well in explaining the development of the great industrial urban centers in the U.S. and elsewhere during the late nineteenth and early twentieth century. In the production of durable goods (automobiles, appliances, and the like) it was advantageous for producers to congregate, and indeed, the growth of Chicago, Detroit, and Pittsburgh seem to bear this out.

Such agglomeration economies were also viewed to be operating in the service sector, where again, face-to-face contact through physical propinquity served to cut costs and foster the more rapid spread of ideas. The archetype here is the very dense clustering of financial services in the Wall Street area of lower Manhattan.

Throughout the twentieth century technological advances have chipped away at agglomeration economies. Improvement in roads and the shift toward truck from railroad car, and most recently, the development of high speed electronic communication have worked in this direction, promoting suburbanization and then enabling movement to even lower density settings, including smaller metropolitan areas and rural communities. Now an organization far from a major metropolis can have access instantly through telephone lines to the financial markets and other sources of news and information, just as it can deliver that information quickly and electronically. For this reason we have observed many of the so-called back offices of major financial institutions move out of the high rent downtown areas to suburban or exurban locations.

In addition to economies of agglomeration, there also exist diseconomies of agglomeration, increased costs or disadvantages associated with higher density and proximity. Congestion costs are the most frequently mentioned of these. (Pollution is another, discussed in the next section.) Proximity should reduce the cost of delivering goods and services by decreasing the length of transport needed, but traffic, the bane of the urbanite's daily travel routine, is perhaps the most obvious congestion cost. Indeed, data from U.S. censuses indicate that workers in larger metropolitan areas spend a longer time getting to work than in smaller metropolitan areas. Much of this difference is due to congestion; the remainder is due, ironically, to the greater physical distance to be covered in a larger, more agglomerated urban area.

These are the ideas, but what is the evidence? Is there an optimal city size? There appears to be no consensus on an exact optimum value for city population, but social scientists have tried to estimate the magnitudes and effects of agglomeration economies and diseconomies. As one might imagine, it is very difficult to disentangle the "true" effects of agglomeration on industrial productivity, congestion and pollution.

One attempt to estimate recent changes in agglomeration economies focussed on those industries which have provided one third of employment in production industries.[8] It found that the productivity advantages of large cities have declined. In a study using industrial data from the United States and Brazil, Vernon Henderson found that economies of scale in manufacturing were more due to localization (being near related activity) rather than to urbanization (size of place), per se.[9] Productivity improvement rose with size of place, but then declined. If technological change continues along the same line as it has in recent years, then any productivity advantage of large urban areas will continue to dissipate.

Still, one recent review of a number of empirical studies concluded that "despite these shortcomings and potential biases, the message from the empirical literature is clear: economies of proximity exist and exhibit considerable quantitative strength."[10]

We can see, then, that both economies and diseconomies of agglomeration are operating, and an accurate assessment of their overall effect requires the difficult task of estimating each. The question to ask for policy is whether or not the markets for goods and labor as currently constituted are adequate to maximize well-being, balancing the positive and negative aspects of urbanization. It is probably accurate to say that the market does much to promote an optimal location of firms and households, with each weighing individually the costs and benefits of agglomeration. If so the movement of the most mobile—large corporations and prosperous families—from the cities to their suburbs in recent decades would seem a judgement against high density.

It is also probably the case that the market does not capture all of these influences. Many people do not have a wide range of choice in the type of place where they live. They are restricted by the need to be within commuting range of an acceptable job based on their skills and interests and they must be able to afford housing.

THE ENVIRONMENTAL COSTS OF LARGE POPULATION CONCENTRATIONS.

Pollution of the environment results both from the concentration of population and from the way in which individuals and businesses act towards controlling potential sources of pollution. Even in low density rural areas, certain processes of mining and manufacturing can result in serious environmental problems. While the growth of population and incorporation of territory into townships or other political units can sometimes facilitate action to control pollution, as population growth continues, it more often increases the environmental problems.

Large population concentration usually requires higher costs per person for the maintenance of clean water and the safe removal of garbage. Air quality, in particular, may be difficult to maintain at high population densities if there is not a natural flow of air through the area. Some cities, such as Los Angeles, have particularly difficult problems dealing with air quality because air is often trapped.

It is somewhat difficult to measure the quality of the environment in different metropolitan areas because of the lack of sufficient monitoring sites or the lack of common means of measurement from one area to another. Air quality, for example, is often measured at only one site and the location of that site affects the level of the measurement. If measures from that site indicate poor air quality, there is no way of telling whether all persons in the metropolitan area breathe poor air or only those close to the monitoring site. According to one study, single site measures appeared to be adequate for small particle pollution, but not for larger particles, which varied more across metropolitan areas.[11]

The staff at Zero Population Growth have constructed an index of environmental pollution which combined measures of air quality, water quality, sewage treatment and hazardous waste.[12] This index showed that the environment in larger cities was poorer than that in smaller cities. There was a significant dividing line between central cities of 250,000 or more and smaller ones.

Smaller cities have two advantages in dealing with the environment. First, because of smaller size and typically lower density, they have less concentration of pollutants to deal with, other things being equal. Second, because they have a smaller and often more homogeneous population, they may have an easier time mobilizing support for programs to regulate and reduce pollution.

THE SOCIAL EFFECTS OF URBAN SCALE

Much of the attention in the scholarly literature on the costs and benefits of urbanization has focused on economic criteria, as the discussion above does. Other important aspects of the costs and benefits of cities may be viewed from the social side. These include the relative distribution of income (or more generally resources) for urban areas, crime, antisocial behavior, and racial and ethnic conflict. In some sense these are also externalities or agglomeration diseconomies, just seen through a sociological or psychological lens. Although many ad hoc theories exist, solid empirical evidence linking city size to these social disamenities is hard to come by.

Are the rich richer and the poor poorer in large cities compared to smaller ones? The statistical evidence is weak and mixed. Using data on income distribution for the 79 largest U.S. metropolitan areas,[13] we found that a ten percent increase in metropolitan population was associated with a .2 percent increase in income inequality. This is quite a modest relationship, but it does suggest that the distribution of income is more unequal in larger metropolitan areas. Up to about 1980 income inequality in the United States declined, despite increasing urbanization over much of this period.[14] It has risen since then. In 1980 the mean income deficit, the average amount of additional income needed for poor households to move out of poverty, was $3,075 in the United States as a whole and $3,014 for rural areas. New York, Los Angeles, and Chicago, the three largest metropolitan areas, recorded mean income deficits higher than the national average, but the deficit was lower than the national average in Boston, Cincinnati, Buffalo and Detroit.[15]

Whether the poor are worse off in large urban areas than in other places is more difficult to ascertain. Costs of living are higher, and so an equivalent amount of money may provide less in terms of goods and services compared to a rural area. For the individual poor person to be better off in the large city, there must be some factors which compensate, such as the chance of getting a better paying job (and moving out of poverty), other social services provided "in kind," lower transportation costs (no need to own a car) and the like. It is very difficult to get an accurate estimate of the net balance of these factors, because so many components are unmeasured.

Casual observation of the news media would suggest that large cities are the sites of more crime, personal danger, and other deviant behavior. The statistics bear this out. The rates of robbery and property crimes show the sharpest rise with urban size.[16] Certainly the recent wave of drug-related violence has been heavily concentrated in large cities. Historically, however, urban areas have not been appreciably disadvantaged with regard to murder rates, with rural areas having higher rates than small metropolises.

Crime is one indication of social alienation. There are several others, including school dropout rates, suicide, and teenage pregnancy. These problems are often worse in urban areas, particularly central cities. Among younger never married women (eighteen to twenty-four years of age), for instance, the rate of childbearing of central city residents was nearly 45 percent above the national rate, although it was still lower than the rate for corresponding women living in non-metropolitan areas.[17] We also find that persons aged twenty to twenty-four residing in central cities are much more likely not to be high school graduates than their suburban counterparts, and the incidence of dropping out is slightly higher than for non-metropolitan residents.[18] While in both of these cases some of the apparent central city-suburb non-metropolitan difference could be due to compositional influences (and movement out of the cities after the change in behavior), it is consistent with the notion that cities, particularly inner cities, do not foster mainstream behavior.

Another place to look for social differences is in the infant mortality rate, a statistic often quoted (and lamentably so for the United States) as an indication of level of development. While infant mortality rates do not tell us directly about behavior they do provide a window on how adequate the social service delivery system is. They also reflect some differences in social behavior. Maternal drug use, teenage parenthood, etc. all put infants at higher risk. In 1987 the United States had an infant mortality rate (IMR) of 10.1 deaths in the first year of life per 1000 live births. Most but not all of the top ten metropolitan areas show higher IMR in 1987. For the New York metropolitan area the figure was 11.7 (Brooklyn 13.9); Los Angeles 9.8; Chicago 12.5 (Cook County 13.8); San Francisco 7.6; Philadelphia 11.7 (City of Philadelphia 17.3); Detroit 12.1; Boston 7.2 (Suffolk County 11.9); Dallas 9.4; Houston 9.3; Washington, DC 11.0 (DC 19.3).[19] Clearly central city (county) areas show higher rates than their suburbs. Children born in more urban areas are disadvantaged for survival through childhood.

Racial and ethnic conflict is pronounced in cities, for urbanization brings into close proximity those of disparate backgrounds. We also observe that larger metropolises exhibit higher rates of segregations[20]. Certainly ethnic antagonism becomes manifest in big-city politics, where the race of the candidate matters greatly. It is important to note that urban areas also provide advantages to minorities. One school even argues that immigrant ethnic groups in particular form enclave economies, garnering local resources that tend to bolster the well-being of the group in the long run. In less diverse, less urbanized areas, a majority group may exert virtual hegemony over the minority in politics and economic life. As the history of race relations in the U.S. South reminds us, ethnic conflict and violence are not limited to large urban areas.

Despite the evidence of an association between city size and crime, income disparity, and ethnic conflict, one must ask the question, "Would changes in the scale of living produce changes in these outcomes?" In other words, we must determine whether these outcomes are simply the result of the composition of cities, or whether urbanization itself generates these phenomena. A subcultural theory of urbanism developed by Claude Fischer argues that there is an urban effect, which builds upon differences in composition. Because urban areas are large, they contain a critical mass of individuals who share a common disposition. Organized crime is one example; the arts provide another. Urban residence also allows one to achieve a greater degree of anonymity, facilitating socially deviant behavior.

Would decreases in urbanization reduce some of these negative social externalities? Probably yes, but only insofar as the differences were due to agglomeration per se. Compositional differences between urban and rural areas, and among cities of different sizes, are not likely to be removed merely by changes in the scale of living.

WHERE WOULD PEOPLE LIVE IF THEY HAD A CHOICE?

The widescale population deconcentration of the 1970s touched off a lively debate on whether or not people were giving up the higher incomes and other benefits of large cities for the higher perceived quality of life in small towns and rural areas. Studies of residential preferences over the past forty years have consistently shown that many people who live in large cities would prefer to live in smaller cities, towns or rural areas. However, most of those wishing to live in rural areas preferred them to be within thirty miles of a city over 50,000.[21] What seems to be preferred is a relatively small scale for one's immediate residential surroundings, but, at the same time, the availability of shopping, services, cultural and recreational opportunities associated with a metropolitan area.

The preference for smaller urban settlements can also be seen in the degree to which people in different size places are satisfied with the neighborhoods in which they live. The 1985 American Housing Survey asked a representative sample of Americans about their satisfaction with their neighborhood and perceived neighborhood problems. The results, which are shown in Table 1, indicate that satisfaction is greater in smaller and more suburban places and that residents of these places perceive fewer problems than those in cities. The differences are particularly strong for the perception of crime as a problem. While cities are often thought to offer better services in exchange for putting up with other problems, few people in any areas noted services

Table 1. Satisfaction and Problems by Type of Place (American Housing Survey 1985)

Type of Place	Neighborhood Satisfaction*	% Citing Any Problem	% Citing Crime	% Citing Noise	% Citing Traffic	% Citing Litter	% Citing Poor Service
City, Large MSA	7.5	47.5	25.1	22.9	17.6	16.1	5.4
City, Small MSA	7.8	41.1	11.6	21.2	19.1	14.1	1.1
Suburb, Large MSA	8.2	39.1	9.3	20.4	23.6	11.5	4.8
Suburb, Small MSA	8.4	35.7	6.7	16.8	17.8	11.5	5.7
Other Urban Place	8.2	34.7	5.3	20.9	17.4	13.5	3.5
Rural	8.7	28.3	4.2	14.4	14.3	10.8	4.5

Note: Large MSA's are Metropolitan Statistical Areas or Consolidated Metropolitan Statistical Areas with populations of 1 million or more.
*Scale of 1 to 10

as a problem and there was little difference by type of area.

While race is often discussed in relation to city/suburb differences, blacks shared the same relative evaluation of satisfaction and problems as whites. With the exception of rural areas, which they did not rate better than small urban areas, blacks were also more satisfied in smaller and more suburban places than they were in larger places and central cities. While there is some tendency to associate the problems of large cities with the racial or ethnic composition of these cities, members of minority racial or ethnic groups appear to suffer at least as much from the problems in these areas as others do. It would appear that all races would be better off with smaller scale settlements.

Although data on preferences for different size communities would seem to suggest that we should be involved in a continuing process of population deconcentration, this has not been the case since around 1980. While the process of suburbanization continues within most metropolitan areas, there is no longer a net flow from metropolitan to nonmetropolitan areas.

To some extent the nonmetropolitan movement of the 1970s was self defeating. It redistributed people to counties adjacent to metropolitan areas, which then got redefined as metropolitan due to their movement; or it resulted in sufficient growth in and around small cities that they grew to metropolitan status.

CONSEQUENCES OF CITY DECLINE

In the past, the decline of population in cities and metropolitan areas has often been judged negatively. Bradbury, Downs, and Small, for example, list a host of problems associated with urban decline.[22] Frey and Speare show that metropolitan areas which declined between 1970 and 1980 had increasing proportions who were poor, increasing unemployment and declining house values.[23] They also found less satisfaction among residents of declining areas. However, not all consequences of past decline have been negative. The Pittsburgh Metropolitan Area, which has experienced population decline over the past four decades, was rated as the top city in the Places Rated Almanac in 1985 and in third place out of 333 metropolitan areas in 1989.[24] This rating was based on a combined set of ratings of jobs, housing, living costs, health, environment, education, arts, recreation and climate. In contrast, Houston which has been touted as a success in free enterprise induced growth, had a score of 66. Fagen, who did a careful case study of Houston's growth, concludes that while growth may have satisfied business interests, the city now has serious problems of air, water and hazardous waste pollution, an inadequate education system and other serious problems.[25]

The perception that urban shrinkage leads to negative consequences is due to two facts which are usually associated with such declines. First, declining cities have usually experienced the loss of jobs and relatively high unemployment rates. Second, those who leave for better opportunities elsewhere are often younger workers with above average education and skills. While unemployed persons are somewhat more likely to move than those who are employed, they comprise only a small part of the migration stream from declining places and in general these cities end up with a population which has lower average education, a lower proportion of skilled workers, and a lower per capita income. This makes it harder for the city to compete for new jobs or to find tax revenues to pay for services for a population which has increased needs.

The cause of the problem is not population decline per se, but the loss of jobs and the selective out-migration of younger, more educated and better skilled persons. In the past, the natural increase rate has always been greater than zero, and population decline has occurred only where there has been substantial out-migration. We have not been able to observe what would happen if the decline occurred due to a negative rate of natural increase, that is a birth rate lower than the death rate. This would be a very different type of decline, one which would not change population composition, except in terms of average age. Since incomes tend to rise with age, the effects on the tax base ought to be positive and the demand for some of the most expensive urban services, schools and police to deal with teenage offenders, would be reduced.

CONCLUSION

There are considerable advantages to smaller scale and lower density settlements. We believe that past economies which no longer hold, continued growth from natural increase, and immigration have acted to slow the deconcentration process. Nevertheless, deconcentration is likely to continue in the future because of lower costs in low density areas and preferences for living in lower density areas.

Natural increase, while low by international standards, continues to contribute to urban growth. Since 1950, natural increase has accounted for about two-thirds of the growth of metropolitan areas within constant boundaries.[26] In 1989, natural increase for the United States increased to 7.5 per 1000, the highest level since 1971. Rates of natural increase tend to be somewhat greater in large metropolitan areas because these areas have younger age distributions than nonmetropolitan areas and because of the concentration of immigrants and minority groups with higher than average birth rates in these cities. Thus, to the extent that population growth in large cities and metropolitan areas is associated with a lower quality of life, these problems would be reduced if overall population growth were lower.

Lower rates of fertility and immigration would make it easier to achieve lower population densities and would help to alleviate the congestion, air pollution and some other problems of large cities. If the reduction of population in large cities takes place gradually and through declines in natural increase and immigration, the negative consequences of decline ought to be avoided. In the long run, the poorer quality housing and other buildings can be removed and replaced with more open space and the quality of life for all should improve.

However, society should ensure that cities continue to attract all classes of people and that the opportunities which are offered in smaller scale areas are equally available to members of all groups, so that movement from the larger cities to smaller ones is not selective of certain classes of people as it has been in the past. If large city decline can be accomplished without a change in the composition of population and jobs, then the consequences of such a decline ought to be positive in the long run.

NOTES:

1. U.S. Bureau of the Census, "Population Estimates for Metropolitan Areas, 1988," *Current Population Reports*, P-26.
2. Gallup Reports, October 1989.
3. William Frey and Alden Speare, Jr. *Regional and Metropolitan Growth and Decline in the United States*. New York, Russell Sage Foundation, 1988.
4. John Long, *Population Deconcentration in the United States*, U.S. Bureau of the Census, 1981.

5. William Frey and Alden Speare, *Regional and metropolitan Growth and Decline in the United States* (New York: Russell Sage, 1988), p40, p 69)
6. Alden Speare, Jr. "The Role of Immigration in U.S. Population Redistribution," Paper presented at the Annual Meeting of the Population Association of America, Chicago, 1987.
7. U. S. Immigration and Naturalization Service, 1987 *Statistical Yearbook* (Washington, DC: U.S. Government Printing Office, 1988) U.S. Bureau of the Census, *Statistical Abstract of the United States* (Washington, DC: U.S. Government Printing Office, 1986)
8. Ronald L. Moomaw, "Firm Location and City Size: Reduced Productivity Advantages as a Factor in the Decline of Manufacturing in Urban Areas." *Journal of Urban Economics* 17(1985): 73–89.
9. J. Vernon Henderson, "Efficiency of Resource Usage and City Size." *Journal of Urban Economics* 19 (1986): 47–70.
10. Mark R. Montgomery, "The Effects of Urban Population Growth on Urban Service Delivery." Paper presented to the meetings of the American Academy for the Advancement of Science, February, 1990.
11. D. Kotchman, T. McMullen and V. Hasselblad, "Adequacy of a Single Monitoring Site for Defining Mean Outdoor Concentrations of Fine Particles in Demarcated Residential Communities," *International Journal of Air Pollution Control and Waste Management* 37:4 (April 1987): 377–381.
12. Zero Population Growth, "Urban Stress Test," 1988. Air Quality was measured by the number of EPA long term and twenty-four-hour standards for seven possible pollutants; Water was assessed for both abundance and lack of pollutants; Sewage was judged by the extent of wastewater treatment and hazardous waste by EPA reported hazardous waste sites within city limits.
13. We were provided these data on metropolitan area income inequality by Hilary Silver, Department of Sociology, Brown University.
14. Frank Levy, *Dollars and Dreams* (New York, Russell Sage, 1986). I
15. U.S. Bureau of the Census, *Census of Population and Housing 1980*, Detailed Characteristics (Washington, U.S. Government Printing Office, 1984).
16. Claude Fischer, *The Urban Experience* (New York: Harcourt Brace, Jovanovich, 1980), p 104.
17. Current Population Reports, *Fertility of American Women*, 1988, Table 2.
18. U.S. Bureau of the Census, *Current Population Reports* P-20 429, School Enrollment.
19. U.S. Office of Vital Statistics, *Vital Statistics 1987. Mortality* Table 2-10.
20. Michael J. White, *American Neighborhoods and Residential Differentiation* (New York, Russell Sage, 1987).
21. G. V. Fuguitt and J. J. Zuiches, "Residential Preferences and Population Distribution," *Demography* 12 (1975): 491–504.
22. Bradbury, Katherine L., Anthony Downs, and Kenneth A. Small, Urban Decline and the Future of American Cities, Washington, D.C.: Brookings Institution, 1982.
23. Frey and Speare, op. cit. pp. 108–144.
24. Richard Boyer and David Savageau, *Places Rated Almanac*, New York: Prentice Hall, 1985 and 1989.
25. Joe R. Feagin, *Free Enterprise City: Houston in Political—Economic Perspective*, New Brunswick: Rutgers University Press, 1988.
26. Frey and Speare, op. cit. p. 51.

YOU CAN'T GO WEST: STRESS IN THE HIGH COUNTRY

Dennis Brownridge

November 1990

The West has long been the fastest growing part of the country. In 1900 it held 4 million people—5 percent of a nation of 75 million. Now, a lifetime later, it has 50 million, 20 percent of a nation of 250 million.[1] It has the most populous state, California, and several of the biggest and fastest growing metropolises. Nevertheless, much of the West remains thinly populated—the "wide open spaces" of lore. The phrase "rural West" is almost an oxymoron. The dense networks of rural farmsteads and villages typical of the East or Europe are rare in the west. The great majority of Westerners have always lived in cities and towns. So, to a New Yorker or Midwesterner, the nonmetropolitan interior West must seem empty indeed.

But sheer living space doesn't limit population. All the cities and towns of America would fit into Utah with room to spare, but there would be nothing for people to do—no way to make a living. Most of the West is thinly populated for good reason: it has little or no economic use.

GEOGRAPHIC CONSTRAINTS

There are three things, other than funny hats and pointy-toed boots, that distinguish the West from the rest of the country:

(1) Mountains. The shifting crustal plates have rippled it with range upon range of rugged mountains. From the Rocky Mountain front to the Pacific Coast, mountains are almost always in sight. There is lots of flat land between the mountains, of course—the land you see from the highways. But most of it is high plateau, averaging 1500 meters above sea level. High altitude means cold winters and short growing seasons.

(2) Aridity. Thanks in part to the rainshadow effect of the mountains, most of the West is also dry. It is either steppe (a semiarid climate that can support short grass) or full-fledged desert. With minor exceptions, it is too dry to farm without irrigation. A good many homesteaders discovered that the hard way. You can still see their decaying cabins dotting the landscape. Only a narrow coastal strip of the Pacific Northwest is both wet and warm enough to support Eastern style farming. It is no coincidence that Oregon was the original destination of settlers trekking west in the 1840s.

In short, nine-tenths of the West is too dry, too cold, too steep, or too rocky for crop farming. And it is farming that sustains large rural populations.

(3) Public Land. Mainly because it is useless for farming, half the West was never claimed under the various nineteenth century land grant laws. Since the nation is now full, the land giveaway laws have been repealed (except for the controversial 1872 Mining Law). The land that no one wanted remains in public ownership, freely accessible to all, the last vestige of a public domain that once stretched from the Appalachians to the Pacific. The public lands include:

Table 1.	
BLM land (Bureau of Land Management)	23.% of the West
National Forests	18.%
National Parks and Monuments	1.50%
National Wildlife Refuges	0.70%
National Recreation Areas (mainly reservoirs)	0.40%

Another 2 percent of the West is government land, used for bombing, war games, and weapons development. The military says it needs much more and is currently trying to appropriate another half percent (14000 km^2) from the public lands. Several additional percent is owned by the states and might be considered public. Since the public lands have no permanent inhabitants, they appear empty on a population map. But they are by no means unused. Their resources are open to private commercial exploitation and they serve tens of millions of recreational visitors a year.

The Great Plains are sometimes included in the West, dividing the country in two at the 100th meridian. While the Plains lack the mountains and public land of the "real West," they satisfy the high-and-dry test. Figures in this essay are for the 11 western states, the West of the statisticians, which roughly splits the differences between these two geographic definitions.

FORESTS

The West has—or did have—the finest coniferous (softwood) forests in the world. They include the tallest trees (Redwoods), the most massive trees (Sequoias), and the oldest trees (Bristlecone pines) found anywhere on Earth. The Pacific Northwest (coastal Washington, Oregon, and northern California) supports magnificent rainforests rivaled in lushness and beauty only by the hardwood rainforests of the tropics.

But some perspective is in order. Seventy percent of the West is unforested. And half the nominal forest land is so dry or cold that is supports only brushy, stunted, or slow-growing trees with no commercial use—trees valuable only as watershed and wildlife habitat. Only 15 percent of the West is commercial forest land, capable of growing timber.[3]

Nevertheless, Western forests supply 50 percent of the nation's softwood (construction) lumber. Half of that comes from the great Douglas-fir, cedar, and Redwood forests of the Pacific states. Ponderosa pine, a large and beautiful tree of the drier interior, supplies another fifth. The trees of the high Rockies—lodgepole pine, spruces, true firs, and aspen—are relatively unimportant. The South produces three times as much lumber as all eight Rocky Mountain states put together.

For three centuries the U.S. was self-sufficient in wood. But since the 1940s we have been a net importer and the gap is widening rapidly. We export a large volume of irreplaceable old-growth timber, mostly to Japan, but we import much more. The U.S. cuts more wood than any other nation—half a cubic kilometer per year, a literal mountain of wood. We are cutting more than ever before. Yet we now consume 13 percent more wood—and 30 percent more lumber—than we produce.

Can we blame this on increasingly profligate consumption? Not at all. We use only half as much wood and lumber, per person, as Americans did in 1900. There has been an explosion in pulp products (paper and cardboard) but it has been offset by a corresponding decline in barrels and boxes and countless other products once made of wood. Many have been replaced by petroleum-based plastics, metals, and other non-renewable materials. Lumber consumption has dropped, per capita, because we build smaller and plainer houses; because we use more stucco, concrete, and aluminum; because we use trees more efficiently; and because we get along with inferior products like particle board (a miserable, ersatz wood made of glued sawdust).

But if we use much less wood per person and are cutting more from our forests, then how did we go from being a net exporter to the world's biggest importer? The answer is simple: U.S. population has more than tripled since 1900. In a single lifetime, we have added 175 million people.

Almost all of our wood shortfall is imported from Canada. Canada's forests aren't as fine as our own. She has a vast taiga forest in her subarctic North, but it is a stunted, slow growing spruce/fir forest with little value other than for pulp. Canada cuts only 40 percent as much wood as we do. Canadians use wood the same way we do. Yet Canada is the world's greatest *exporter* (44 percent of world lumber exports) while we are the biggest *importer*. How is this possible? Again the answer is simple: the U.S. has ten times more people than Canada.

Much western timber is still cut from virgin forest. The trees are often hundreds and sometimes thousands of years old. In little more than a lifetime, 90 percent of the virgin, old growth forest in the Pacific Northwest has been destroyed.[4] Only small patches remain and they are currently being logged at 250 square kilometers a year. At that rate all that is not protected in parks or Wilderness Areas will be gone in a decade or so. In the interior, the great stands of old-growth Ponderosa pine are also virtually gone. Somewhat more virgin forest survives in the Rockies, but it contains only small pockets of old-growth, since most Rocky Mountain species are small and short-lived.

Of course trees grow back. In fact we are growing wood at a faster rate than in the past, simply because small, immature trees grow faster than big old ones. However, while we may appear to be getting more "interest" out of the forest, the wood is of much lower quality and our "capital" is rapidly being eroded. Since 1952 the net volume of softwood saw timber standing in Western forests has declined 17 percent. This represents a per capita decline of 48 percent (since U.S. population has mushroomed during the same time). For each American, there is only half as much saw timber standing in the Western forests as there was a generation and a half ago. The decline is obvious to anyone who drives the backroads of the Pacific Northwest. Clearcuts—large, completely deforested patches—are everywhere to be seen. Huge stumps remind you of the forest that once was, like the ruins of a great civilization.

Large virgin trees bring high prices because the wood is superior and because more of the tree is useable as lumber. When a tree matures, its lower limbs drop off and growth slows, producing a stronger, finer-grained, straighter grained, and knot free "clear" wood. The deep, rich colors that give Redwood and yellow (Ponderosa) pine their names also develop only in old trees.

Aesthetically, there is no comparison between diverse old-growth forests and the dreary tree farms that replace them. Old-growth forests are verdant, multi-canopied, cathedral-like places with huge trees and an astonishing complexity of life. Managed forests are monotonous, even-aged monocultures of uniform small trees, their interiors tangled with dead lower branches. There is no match for old-growth timber, alive or dead. But once these ancient forests are gone, they and whatever organisms depend on them are gone forever.

But haven't we saved a lot of old-growth in national parks and wilderness areas? Unfortunately not. Reserves where logging is prohibited are mostly rock, ice, desert, or noncommercial forest. Productive timberlands were usually excluded when boundaries were set. National parks are often confused with the much larger national forests that surround them. National forests did function as preserves for half a century, but when private timberlands were exhausted in the 1940s the national forests were attacked with vigor. Today they are managed primarily for timber production. However, the Forest Service is very good at public relations (witness Smokey the Bear). Since the 1960s, the agency has left thin screens of trees along major highways-like stage sets or Potemkin villages—to give motorists the illusion of driving through primeval forest. But step off the road for a stroll in the woods and you're surrounded by stumps and rusting logging cables.

As I write this, environmental groups are engaged in a last-ditch battle to save as much of the remaining old-growth as possible. Daring activists are dangling from ropes high in the treetops or chaining themselves to trunks in a desperate attempt to forestall the loggers and convince Congress to protect what little is left. There are no really big chunks; it is all bits and pieces.

It is clear that Western forests will supply a declining fraction of our wood. In 1970, they held almost 90 percent of the country's standing softwood saw timber. Now only 75 percent is in the West, partly because old-growth is disappearing and partly because the pine forests of the South have come back after generations of abuse. It is also clear that the annual cut from Western forests will have to be reduced. It will have to be reduced substantially if we want to save what little virgin forest remains and if we want to manage the rest in a genuinely sustainable way that doesn't diminish fish, wildlife, water quality, biodiversity, or other resources.

What about conservation? We do consume an astounding amount of wood: 2.2 cubic meters per person, per year—a ton and a half for every American. Half of that is lumber, the most critical use because it requires quality wood and mature trees (you can't make twelve-inch boards out of ten-inch trees). Most lumber goes for housing. We could use more substitute materials, but they have many drawbacks (expensive, not renewable, take a lot of energy to manufacture, hard to work, poor insulators, unsafe in earthquakes, toxic, ugly, etc.). A much simpler way to reduce per capita lumber consumption is to have a stable population. Lumber is not "consumed" in the usual sense, since buildings don't wear out. A well maintained wooden house can last for centuries. But a growing population means that new housing is constantly needed just to maintain the status quo. More subtly, it means that many buildings are razed unnecessarily, long before their time. In a growing city, rising land values mandate that buildings be replaced with higher density structures. The condition of the buildings doesn't matter; even the finest structures are destroyed. But in a city with a stable population, buildings last much longer and there is much less waste. Indeed, one can usually reconstruct the population history of a place just by looking at its architecture. Curiously, Western cities and towns that were stable or lost population in the past are among the most prosperous and desirable today, because they have retained the ambience of fine old buildings (Portland, San Francisco, Santa Fe, Aspen, and Telluride, to name some well known examples).

More than a quarter of our wood is pulped for paper and cardboard. Much of that is undeniably wasted, since paper makes up 40 percent of the mass in our landfills.[5] Newspapers and magazines are two-thirds advertisements. If we could finance them some other way, we might reduce paper consumption significantly (but how can we do that without making reading matter prohibitively expensive?). An easier target is over packaging, especially the absurd American habit of giving out paper bags with every purchase. Recycling should also be stepped up, of course. But even if we slashed paper consumption in half, we couldn't be self sufficient and maintain healthy forests, given our present population. Nor would paper conservation necessarily help the lumber shortage.

A fifth of our wood is burned as fuel, for heat and some electricity. A generation ago, use of fuelwood was almost negligible, but since the oil crises of the 1970s it has jumped six-fold. We now burn almost as much wood as we did at the turn of the century, when wood and coal supplied nearly all of our energy. Per person, we burn only a quarter as much, but the population is so much bigger that total consumption is back at historical levels. Even so, wood supplies only a tiny fraction of the nation's energy.

Most fuelwood comes from logging culls, mill waste, thinning projects, and non-commercial forest. Supply is not yet a problem, although firewood cutting has decimated rare mesquite bosques and some ancient juniper/pinyon stands in the Southwest. But commercial energy projects using forest biomass would run into supply problems and conflicts with other uses. Today the limiting factor on wood fuel seems to be air pollution. Many Western towns have had to restrict wood stoves because of severe winter pollution problems.

Wood is one of our few genuinely renewable raw materials. As petroleum runs out, wood could supply more of our needs, as it did in the past But it certainly can't do so with our present population, much less an expanding one. Nor can we expect Canada to supply us with unlimited wood, since the Canadians are increasingly concerned about the destruction of their own forests.

WATER

Humans use far more water than all other resources combined. Water is the life blood of the West—the limiting factor for almost every activity. Land without access to water is virtually worthless. Western history is filled with political and legal battles, and even shooting wars, over water.

Since the turn of the century, the federal government has been subsidizing massive water projects in the West with the express purpose of increasing population—agricultural population at first, later urban populations as well. Water development has followed a familiar pattern: First, population grows where there is a good natural supply. Eventually population growth outstrips the supply, but by then the place has enough political and economic clout to import water from afar. The infusion of new water stimulates rapid new growth as worthless land becomes valuable overnight. In two or three decades, population growth again precipitates a crisis and another heroic project is conceived to bring water from still more distant sources. In some areas this vicious circle has repeated itself several times. Many Western politicians have built their entire careers around water.

Modern water engineering was invented in the West, where the world's first big dams were built. Aqueducts hundreds of kilometers long carry water across deserts and mountains. Vast quantities of energy are consumed to pump water out of the ground and over mountains. But the limits are being reached. Virtually every river has been dammed. Some are little more than a chain of reservoirs, stretching for hundreds of kilometers (like the Columbia and lower Colorado). Others have been literally sucked dry (like the Owens in California, the Gila and Santa Cruz in Arizona, and the Arkansas). The once mighty Colorado which carved the Grand Canyon and drains a quarter of the West no longer reaches the sea. On a typical day, every drop is diverted for human use before it reaches the Gulf of California. Indeed the Colorado is oversubscribed. Because hydrologists overestimated its flow, more water was allocated in law than exists in the river.

A quarter of the West's supply is groundwater, much of which is non-renewable or "fossil" water stored during the Ice Age when the climate was wetter. In many places, groundwater is being "mined"—pumped much faster than nature can recharge it. In southern Arizona, for example, water tables are dropping one to two meters a year.[6]

The combination of diverted rivers and falling water tables is drying up the wetlands even where they are not being deliberately drained for agriculture. This was prime waterfowl and wildlife habitat, and their populations are crashing.

In recent years, water quality has proved to be as serious a problem as water quantity. Western surface and ground waters are being polluted by a variety of non-point sources: heavy metals leached from old mine tunnels and tailings; logging sediments; sediments and nutrients from livestock grazing; nutrients and pesticides from agriculture; and oils, metals, and solvents in the cities. But paradoxically, the most widespread cause of water pollution seems to be water development itself. Salts are concentrated when water evaporates from reservoirs, canals, and irrigated fields and can reach toxic levels. Irrigation also leaches salts from the ground. Most irrigated land in the West is underlain by sediments with high concentrations of toxic salts, left there when ancient seas and Ice Age lakes dried up. Long term irrigation dissolves out these salts, which either percolate down and contaminate the groundwater or are carried off by field drains and end up in a river or in the sump lakes and marshes that occupy many of the closed basins in the West. Most of these lakes and marshes are wildlife refuges—critical habitat for migratory birds and endangered fish—but they are rapidly becoming cesspools of poison. Of greatest concern is selenium, which deforms and kills fish and waterfowl at very low concentrations, and may be passed up the food chain to humans as well. In California's Kesterson National Wildlife Refuge, selenium poisoning has caused the greatest incidence of wildlife deformity ever recorded. Similar disasters are occurring in at least three other refuges and high levels of selenium have been discovered in dozens of other refuges throughout the West—all associated with large irrigation projects.

A related problem is salinity in irrigation water, which can stunt or even kill crops if concentrations are high enough. salinity is an acute problem in the Colorado River and in California's rich San Joaquin Valley.

Ninety percent of the West's developed water is used for irrigation. Western farms tend to be very large and productive. They also tend to be very profitable, thanks to numerous subsidies—cheap water, cheap power to pump the water, and price supports. Yet only ll percent of the West is farmed since there is far too little water to irrigate it all. In many areas, further population growth can only occur at the expense of farming. "Water ranching"—buying up distant farms and abandoning them for the water rights—is increasingly popular. Since the 1930s, thousands of square kilometers of productive farm land have been abandoned to tumbleweed and sagebrush as the water has been carried off to distant cities. Owens Lake, one of the largest and most picturesque lakes in California, has been reduced to a salt flat—the victim of population growth in Los Angeles. Mono Lake, equally large and beautiful, is now meeting the same fate. Current efforts by Phoenix, Denver, and Las Vegas to secure distant water rights are precipitating bitter struggles between urban and rural communities. Cities don't waste water; they use much less, per hectare, than farming. And cities as well as farms in the and West are making strenuous efforts to conserve water and recycle sewage effluent. In Tucson, Arizona, per capita use has declined sharply as lawns and shade trees have given way to cactus and rock gardens. But population growth inevitably wipes out any conservation gains.

Many Western dams were built for hydroelectric power, not water supply. In fact, excessive damming reduces water yield because so much is evaporated from the surface of the reservoirs. For example, Utah's Lake Powell wastes enough water by evaporation to supply a million people. Yet the reservoir supplies no water; its only function is to generate power to finance other water projects. And in the process, it has destroyed Glen Canyon, one of the world's most beautiful canyons.

Dams produce half the West's electricity—almost an exajoule per year—although they pale in comparison to the total U.S. energy consumption of 90 EJ.[7] If the West had 20 million people (as it did in 1950) it could presumably generate all of its electricity with existing dams. Hydropower is clean and renewable, at least until the reservoirs silt up, which can take centuries. Theoretically, we could double Western hydropower but it would mean the utter destruction of remaining rivers and would further reduce the water supply because of evaporation. The best sites have long since been dammed. There were plans at one time to dam the Grand Canyon at both ends and divert the rest of the river through a tunnel, but an outraged public quashed the idea. A battle is now raging to reduce generation at Glen Canyon Dam (at the head of the Grand Canyon) because the fluctuating flows are devastating the park's beaches and fish. Fish, incidentally, are the most endangered class of native animals in the West, thanks to massive water engineering.

Proposals have been made to transport water from the Columbia River (the only drainage with a significant surplus) or even from the Yukon in Canada. While technically possible, these projects would be astronomically expensive and would require equally astronomical amounts of energy to pump the water over mountains. They would also be enormously destructive of the natural environment. And to get the Yukon water we would probably have to conquer Canada. Desalinization of seawater is another possibility, but again expense and energy are limiting factors.

GRAZING

Almost all of the land in the West that can possibly support a cow or sheep and is not otherwise developed is used for commercial grazing. Even wilderness areas, wildlife refuges, military reservations, and some national parks are open to commercial grazing. Yet western rangelands produce an almost insignificant fraction of our meat. The public lands (the bulk of the range) grow less than 2 percent of the nation's beef. Their main function is producing calves, although only a tenth-of the country's cattle are born there.[8]

Most of our beef is grown in the East, on irrigated pasture, or in feedlots. Although beef consumption per capita has declined, we are no longer self sufficient, consuming 3 percent more than we produce. In fact, the U.S. is the world's largest net importer of beef. Again, it is instructive to compare Canada, which has the same beef eating habits we do and much less pasture land. Canada is a net exporter, simply because it has a tenth as many mouths to feed.

Despite the cowboy mythology ingrained in our culture, the Western range is not a very good place to raise livestock. Forage is produced at a slow rate. Animals can only be grazed part of the year. In drier regions it may take a square kilometer to support a single cow (compared to 500 cows per square kilometer in Missouri). All of the public lands—half the West—support only 30,000 ranchers. For most of them ranching is a part-time occupation, pursued more as a lifestyle than as a livelihood. Although public lands ranchers are heavily subsidized, paying grazing fees far below market value, it is not a lucrative business for most of them.

A century of commercial grazing has taken a heavy toll on the land. Large cattle-like animals are not native to most of the West, so the vegetation is not adapted to them. Bison (buffalo) were mainly a plains animal and generally didn't range west of the Rockies. The Bureau of Land Management (BLM) estimates that 68 percent of its rangeland is in "unsatisfactory" condition ("poor" or "fair"). Only 2 percent is rated in "excellent" condition.[9] The virgin steppes of a century ago supported far more livestock than they do today. In an effort to increase grass and water for livestock, thousands of square kilometers of juniper/pinyon woodland have also been deforested.

Commercial grazing competes directly with wildlife. At the behest of ranchers, the government spends millions of dollars a year to poison and trap wildlife deemed a threat to livestock. Grizzly bears, wolves, and jaguars have been all but eliminated. Ranchers generally oppose attempts to reintroduce native carnivores or build up herds of native herbivores. In my own county, for example, a rancher was recently convicted of slaughtering a large number of elk, out of fear that his grazing allotment would be reduced if elk numbers grew. Drinking water, not forage, is often the limiting factor for livestock as well as wildlife. While wells and catchment basins developed for livestock can benefit wildlife, livestock have a serious impact on riparian (streamside) environments. In the arid West, riparian habitat is of critical importance, harboring most of the rare and endangered species of plants, fish, and wildlife.

One might argue that grazing is the best use for land with no other commercial value. Growing cattle feed is certainly an inefficient use of prime Eastern farmland, which might better be employed growing human food for a hungry world. With careful management, Western rangelands could probably support some commercial grazing without diminishing other resources. But current livestock numbers will certainly have to be reduced and the rangelands—the least productive lands in the West—will never support significant numbers of people.

AMENITIES

For many people, the West's most valuable resources are open space, natural beauty, wildlife, and the physical freedom offered by the public lands. This is not just a value judgement; tourism is the biggest industry in many Western states. Chambers of commerce invariably list the natural environment as a major asset. But amenities and freedoms diminish in direct relation to the number of people trying to enjoy them. It is clear, for example, that most national park visitors today are cheated of the natural experience they presumably came to find. They spend most of their time jostled by crowds, fighting traffic, or struggling to find a place to stay. It has become fashionable to blame the problem on cars, but shuttlebuses, bicycle paths, raftable rivers, and foot trails are often crowded too. It is hard to escape the conclusion (though managers try) that there are just too many people in the parks. Nor is the problem much better in national forest campgrounds. Even the open desert is becoming crowded. In the winter months, tens of thousands of sunseeking retirees from colder states camp on the public lands of the Southwest. Whole cities of trailers and motor homes spring up, stretching as far as the eye can see across the fragile desert plains. It is still easy to car-camp in solitude, at least if you don't mind cowburnt rangeland or cutover forest. But overuse—too many people—is certainly the number one problem threatening the natural areas of the West.

Earlier in this century, human activity had decimated most large native animals. Several were on the verge of extinction. Since then wildlife agencies have brought many of them back, at great expense and with much artificial manipulation. But would-be hunters and fishermen outnumber the game and fish, so increasingly complex restrictions are necessary. On many streams, fish must be released after they are caught. Hunting permits are often rationed, using lotteries and auctions. In my own state of Arizona, a hunter recently paid $60,000 for a permit to shoot a bighorn. He missed.

The greatest freedom of all is found in wilderness—a place to experience the world without being manipulated by other humans. The idea of preserving land in its natural state is an American invention which author Wallace Stegner has rightly called "the best idea we ever had." It is an idea which has been admired and copied by more than 120 nations around the world. The modern wilderness movement, which culminated in the landmark 1964 Wilderness Act, began in the 1920s after the national parks had been opened to automobiles and the national forests were earmarked for logging. Its aim was to keep small parts of the country free of the sights and sounds of man and his machines-places big enough to assure solitude and absorb a two week trip on horse or foot. But wilderness is rapidly disappearing as logging, grazing, mining, oil and gas development, off-highway vehicles, resort development and urbanization saturate the land with roads. Only 4 percent of the West is protected as designated Wilderness.[10] At this writing, another 9 percent or so survives as *de facto* wilderness. Environmental organizations are engaged in prolonged political battles to save as much of it as they can. They won't be able to save it all, since competition for other uses is intense.

Few wilderness areas remain that are big enough for a two week trip. There are so many people and so little wilderness that visits are often rationed with computerized permits. It is ironic that wilderness—which survives mainly because no one wanted it in the past—is the only place where the government has tried to determine an optimum population and enforce it with fines. In some areas you must reserve space months in advance. To raft some rivers you must apply years in advance. Because of overuse, onerous restrictions have become necessary. Campfires are often prohibited. Lakes and streams are often polluted. Solitude is difficult to find. And it is almost impossible to escape the noise of aircraft. Many wilderness areas, national parks, and wildlife refuges have been designated Military Operating Areas (MOAs), used for aerial war games. Others are deluged by tourist planes, helicopters, and commercial jets. It might be honest to say that there is no real wilderness left in the West, as the authors of the Wilderness Act envisioned the concept.

It is important to distinguish sustainable population from optimum population. Optimum population is reached when adding more people does not improve the quality of life. Of course, what you regard as optimum population density depends on your background, age, and many other personal factors. Residents of Wyoming, our least populous state save Alaska, like to say that "Wyoming has more antelope than people and that's the way it should be." But many people are content to spend their entire lives in teeming cities. So I suggest that an optimum population would offer the greatest freedom of choice—the greatest diversity of experiences. It is clear that the West has long since passed that point. There is no shortage of high-density experiences, but low-density experiences are increasingly at a premium. The Rural Renaissance which began in the late 1960s is hard evidence that we have passed what people regard as the optimum population. For the first time in history, the flow of people from rural to metropolitan areas has reversed. Western cities are still growing rapidly, partly by natural increase and partly by immigration from other regions or countries. But at the same time, waves of urban refugees are filling up the hinterlands.

I should point out that the energy schemes discussed in other essays in this series—coal, natural gas, oil shale, nuclear, direct solar, wind, and biomass—would all have devastating effects on the natural environment of the West. Vast expanses of land would have to be sacrificed. We saw a small example of this devastation during the Rocky Mountain energy boom of the late 1970s and early '80s. Other areas will be affected as well. For example, tapping our uranium reserves will wreak havoc on the scenic Colorado Plateau. Grand Canyon National Park is already ringed by tens of thousands of uranium claims, waiting for the price to rise. In the fragile Western environment where the tracks of a single vehicle can last a generation, the scars left by mining usually last forever. And renewable energy sources can destroy even more land than mining because the energy density is so low. For example, the wind farms in California's San Gorgonio Pass have blighted San Jacinto Peak, one of the most dramatic mountainscapes in the nation, while generating only a minuscule fraction of our energy.

CONCLUSION

In the American West, the limiting factors for sustainable population are water (both quantity and quality), altitude and topography, and energy. The 50 million people now in the West certainly exceed these limits. But sustainable population is not the same as optimum population. Optimum population allows the highest quality of life, provides the greatest diversity of experiences, and permits the greatest freedom of living styles. Optimum population for the West has also long since been exceeded, perhaps by a factor of two or three. Forests, rivers, grasslands, wildlife, scenic beauty, quiet, solitude, and freedom have been drastically diminished by the impact of too many people.

NOTES:

1. Unless otherwise noted figures in this essay are from the following sources: *Statistical Abstract of the United States, 1989*. (U.S. Bureau of the Census, Washington, DC);*Historical Statistics of the United States, Colonial Times to 1970*. (U.S. Bureau of the Census, Washington, DC); *Goode's World Atlas*, 1990 edition. (Rand McNally, Chicago)
2. *High Country News* (Paonia, CO). February 12, 1990. p. 1
3. Commercial forest is defined as capable of growing at least 1.4 M3/ha per year of commercially useful species.
4. Old growth forest is defined, in part, as containing at least twenty 200-year-old trees per hectare. See *National Geographic* 178:3 (September 1990) pp. 106–136.
5. U.S. Environmental Protection Agency. *The Solid Waste Dilemma: An Agenda for Action.* Draft Report, September 1988.
6. Arizona Republic (Phoenix, AZ). October 14, 1990. p. 1

7. exa = 10^{10}. The joule is the international unit of energy, defined as a newton meter of work.
8. *High Country News* (Paonia, CO). March 12, 1990. pp.6–8
9. National Wildfife Federation. *Our Ailing Public Lands. Condition Report 1989*. (Washington, DC)
10. The Wildemess Society. *1989 National Wilderness Preservation System* (map). (Washington, DC). Defacto Wilderness is defined as roadless areas of 20 km2 or larger.

THE PLIGHT OF THE CHESAPEAKE

Stephen Tennenbaum & Robert Costanza

December 1990

SUMMARY

The Chesapeake Bay is the largest estuary in North America, and it has been the subject of more scientific study and political wrangling than any other body of coastal water in the world. It has become clear that what happens in the Bay is in large part a function of activities in the drainage basin, but the focus of most past studies has been rather narrow. We are only now beginning to develop a comprehensive picture of the Bay and its connections to its drainage basin.

Population increases in the Chesapeake Bay watershed have led to changes in land use and agricultural practices resulting in increasing volumes of wastes which impact natural terrestrial and aquatic systems, and ultimately lead to the deterioration of the Bay itself. Regulation of human activities may slow these effects but the only long term cure is a stable or declining population ensconced in a healthy and likewise stable economy.

We develop an historical and spatial perspective of human activities in the Chesapeake Bay drainage basin. Fundamental in gaining this perspective is conceptualizing the Chesapeake Bay system as the combination of the drainage basin and the Bay itself. We have assembled and mapped past and present human activities in the Chesapeake Bay drainage basin in order to gain this perspective.

BACKGROUND

The Chesapeake Bay is an ecological system whose beauty and vitality have led to high human population growth rates. These high population growth rates have directly and indirectly caused its infirmity, including declining fisheries, receding wetlands, vanishing sea grasses and a devastated oyster industry. The larger scale terrestrial trends within the entire Chesapeake Bay watershed which have produced these impacts are the subject of this essay. These trends have also led to a decline in the quality of human life. Traffic congestion, disappearing natural and agricultural areas, swelling landfills, and overtaxed water treatment facllltles are some of the effects.

The Chesapeake Bay is a mosaic of estuaries which taken together comprise the largest single estuary in the United States. It was formed from Atlantic waters eroding and drowning the mouths of the rivers which feed it. It is 193 miles long, 3 to twenty-five miles wide, and with its tidal tributaries covers an area of 4,400 square miles and has 8,100 miles of shoreline.[1] The drainage basins which feed it comprise 64,000 square miles in six states, and three major cities lie on the banks of its tidal system (Figure 1).

There are complex factors affecting the Bay which have manifested themselves as substantial changes in water quality and structure of the biological communities. Many of these changes have been observed for some time due to the importance of the Chesapeake Bay as a commercial fishery. The Chesapeake Bay Program has documented some of these trends.[2,3] For example, increased levels of nutrients in the upper reaches of the Bay and its tributaries have contributed to eutrophication and increasing blue-green algae and dinoflagellate blooms. Concentrations have increased as much as 250 times in the past thirty years. Areas of the Bay that have experienced oxygen depletion have increased fifteen-fold times in the same period. There are high concentrations of toxic organic compounds and metals in the water column and sediments near industrial facilities and river mouths such as the Patapsco and Elizabeth rivers. Submerged aquatic vegetation (SAV) is rapidly disappearing in all but a few areas. Commercially important fish such as alewife and shad which spawn in freshwater and whose young use SAV for refuge and as feeding areas have decreased substantially as well, replaced in part by marine breeding species such as bluefish and menhaden. Oyster harvests have declined from over 100 million pounds annually in the late 1800s to only around 20 million pounds in the latter part of this century. And there are increasing worries about the sustainability of the blue crab population because of these problems along with the ever increasing crabbing pressures. In spite of all this, the Chesapeake fishery has for over thirty years provided an average of 10 percent of the total U.S. fishery catch and employment for 14 percent of the nation's fishermen.[4]

Figure 1 — Location of Watershed and some Major Cities within 100 Miles

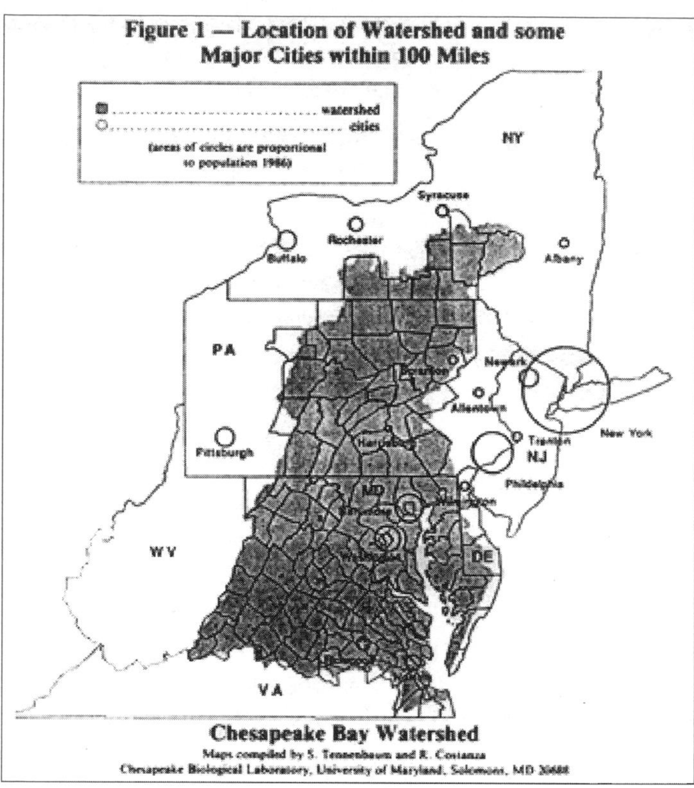

Chesapeake Bay Watershed

Maps compiled by S. Tennenbaum and R. Costanza
Chesapeake Biological Laboratory, University of Maryland, Solomons, MD 20688

WATERSHED DEMOGRAPHICS

Population changes in the watershed are shown in Figures 2a–b. The number of dots is proportional to population in each county and distributed randomly within each county. Between 1940 and 1986 the population of the watershed increased 87 percent. About 20 percent of this increase was due to net migration into the watershed, the majority of it to the areas surrounding Baltimore and Washington in Maryland and Virginia. The population of the watershed grew at an average annual rate of 1.6 percent between 1952 and 1972, almost the same as the U.S. average of 1.5 percent for the same period. But the growth was concentrated in the Maryland and Virginia portions of the watershed, which averaged 2.6 percent growth compared to the remainder of the watershed which grew more slowly at only 0.4 percent.

The most striking changes were in three areas: Richmond, the Norfolk-Virginia Beach area, and the Baltimore-Washington corridor. Growth can, in part, be attributed to increases in industry related directly and indirectly to the expanding U.S. Government as well as the increasing fashionableness of the Chesapeake Bay as a recreation area. The latter forces are amplified by the high immigration rates to the area.

Figure 2a. — Population 1940

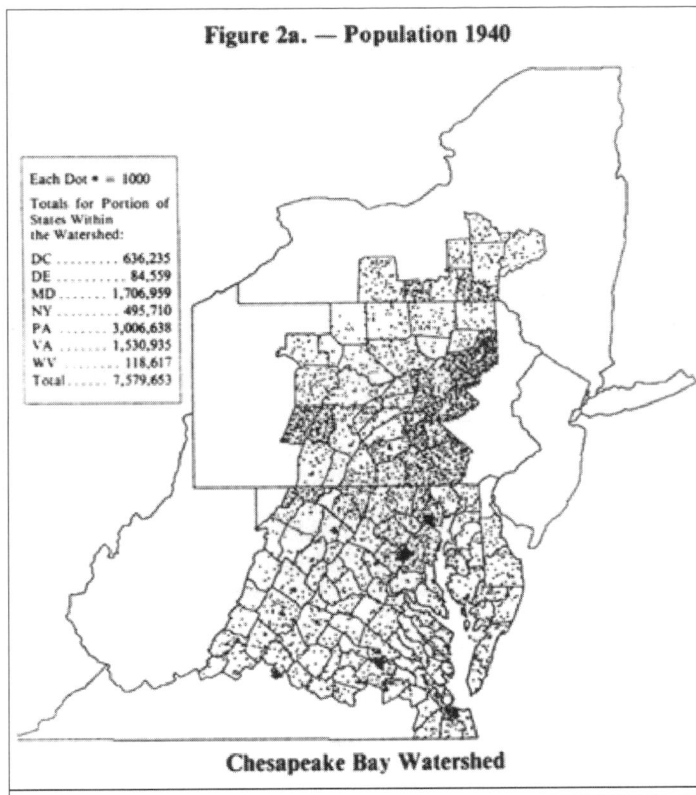

These areas also illustrate the 'urban flight-suburban sprawl' phenomena that has at once undermined the more natural and rural atmosphere that many originally left the city for, while at the same time removing businesses and middle and upper income residents which served as a revenue base for the cities. The resulting deterioration of services and infrastructure worsens as people move further and further out. Increasing travel times required to reach work with the concurrent degeneration of traffic conditions, and soaring property values are some of the resistive forces that quell the further spread of suburban development.

It appears that these forces may be approaching an equilibrium at least for the time being. Between 1972 and 1986 the growth rate of the Maryland watershed population slowed to an annual rate of 0.9 percent, and in Virginia to 1.8 percent, and emigration rates from the cities have slowed. For example, Washington D.C.'s emigration rate decreased from an annual average of 1.3 percent in the 1960s to less than 0.8 percent in the early 1980s. In addition, the spatial extent of the sprawl appears to be presently limited to the counties immediately surrounding the cities in question (Figure2b). However, the information contained in these maps is only suggestive. Demographic trends can be the result of any number of factors. Variation in birth rates, cultural heritage, local versus long distance moves, political climate, and zoning laws all muddy the waters. In addition, as sprawl and growth occur simultaneously, secondary economic centers inevitably spring up, initiating their own cycles.

Patterns of settlement and resettlement broadly affect land use in other ways as well. For example, there has recently been a slight but noticeable increase in woodland in the New York portion of the watershed. The fact that there was a concurrent loss of cropland and pasture only indicates that there were net changes from one type to another but no indication as to why. In fact, the marked differences in changes in agricultural and forested acreage from one state to another strongly suggest these are due to differences in state agricultural policies and tax laws. On the other hand, the pattern of urbanization is more straightforward in light of the population changes discussed above (Figure 3).

Increases in evidence of human activity accompany the increases in population in both magnitude and distribution. Maps of manufacturers, energy consumption, housing units, water use, solid waste production, and air pollutants all closely resemble the maps of population. However, changes in lifestyle have caused accelerated increases in consumption and waste production. From 1952 to 1986 we have seen the following increases in the watershed: per capita energy consumption has gone from 567,000 BTU/day to 744,000 BTU/day; NO_X emissions by vehicles have gone from 1.0 lb/week per person to 1.7 lb/week per person; and per capita solid waste production has risen from 2.2 lb/day to 3.7 lbs/day. In contrast, public and industrial per capita water use has decreased in the same period for the watershed as a whole from 334 gal/day to 278 gal/ day. This is due in large part to the decline in total use in Pennsylvania during this period from 1.46 billion gallons per day in 1952 to only 1.18 billion gallons per day in 1986. In the Maryland and Virginia portions of the watershed, the per capita use rate held nearly constant at about 237 gal/day. This suggests that the former change may be due to changes in heavy industry in Pennsylvania while the latter lack of change may be due to a relatively constant per capita public demand for water in a region which is primarily residential and light industry.

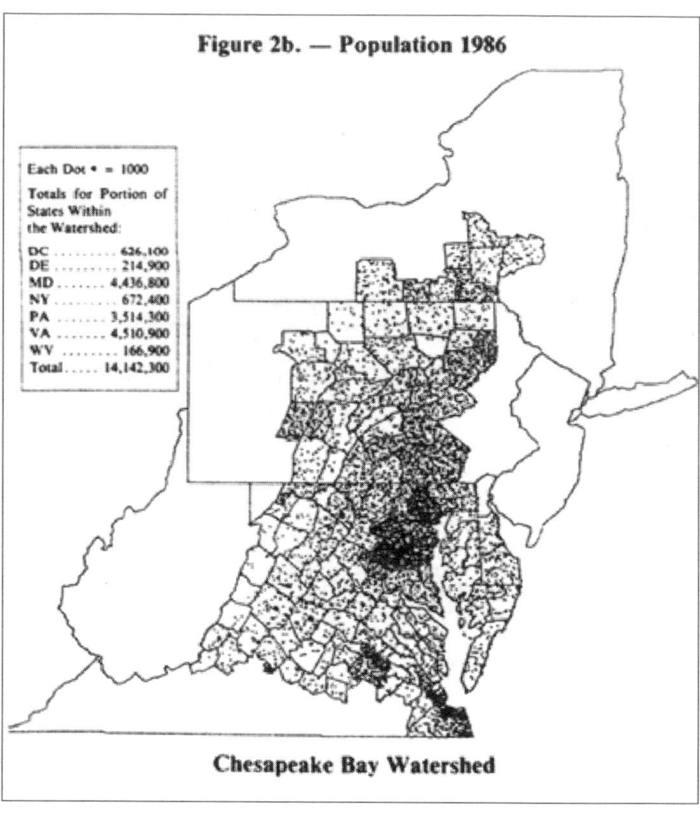

Figure 2b. — Population 1986

Chesapeake Bay Watershed

AGRICULTURE

Changes associated with agriculture are tied to increases in population in their overall magnitude, and to cultural and historical practices in their distribution and local magnitude. Heavily populated areas necessarily exclude agriculture. Some of the best agricultural land in the country, which was the basis for the initial local growth, is rapidly being converted to residential developments, industrial parks, and shopping malls as rising property values make farming unprofitable. It is not clear, however, whether agriculture itself is more benign to an ecosystem such as the Chesapeake Bay than urban and suburban development. Both load the system with wastes and nutrients while consuming "natural" areas that could have absorbed some of that load.

While total farm acreage has decreased from 23.2 million acres in 1954 to 14.4 million acres in 1987 in the watershed, cropland has only decreased from 10.5 million acres to 9.0 million. Meanwhile from 1954 to 1987 the average farm size increased from 126 acres to 190 acres. This means larger percentages of farms are devoted to crops (64 percent versus 45 percent) while less lies fallow, pastured, and wooded. Operations are larger and more intensive. Irrigation has increased from 40 thousand acres to 180 thousand acres. Fertilization rates have increased from about 210 lbs per cultivated acre to 250 lbs per cultivated acre, and the nitrogen content has more than doubled. Figures 4a-b show that pesticide use, which was almost non-existent in the early 1950s, peaked in the 1970s, and subsequently decreased from 15 thousand tons in 1974 to l3 thousand tons in 1986. This reflects the greater specificity of the pesticides used in 1986.

If we examine the application of fertilizer nitrogen (Figures 5a-b) we see a pattern which follows the

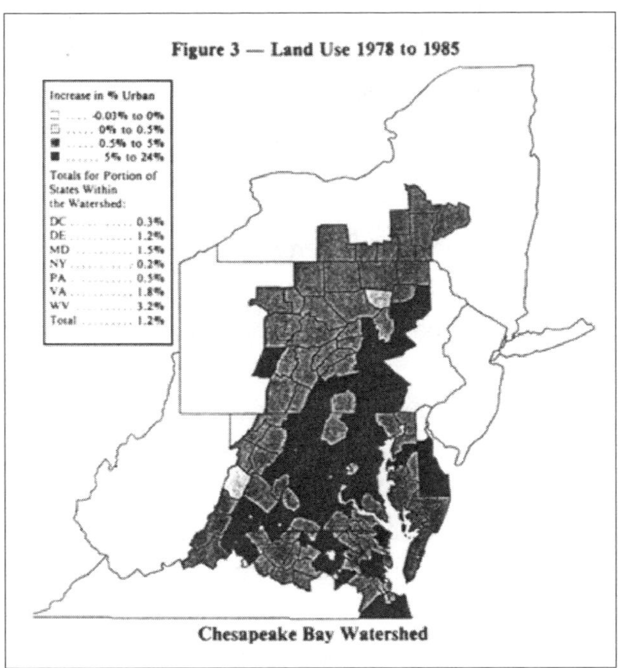

Figure 3 — Land Use 1978 to 1985

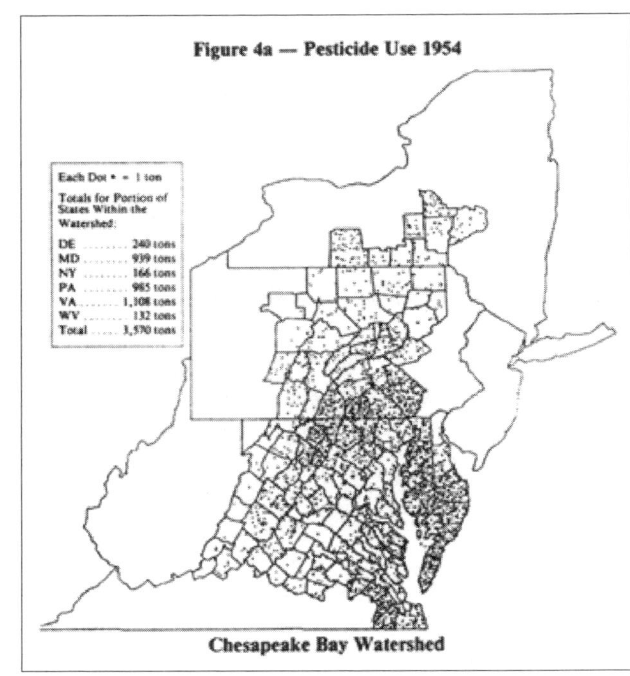

Figure 4a — Pesticide Use 1954

general distribution of farmland, but with an overall increase in the intensity of use. The nutrient loading rates for the mainstream Chesapeake Bay are 78.7 thousand tons per year nitrogen and 3.6 thousand tons per year phosphorus[5]. If one assumes that the loading rate is proportional to the amount of nutrients applied within the watershed, then this implies that phosphorus loading has increased around 4 to 10 percent and nitrogen loading has in-creased somewhere between 34 to 125 percent since 1954 (depending an one's estimate of the run off from manure). This would not only be a great change in amount of nutrients but (and this may be even more crucial) a great change in the relative proportion of nutrients. The increased concentrations of nutrients in specific localities such as Lancaster County, Pennsylvania may intensity this problem.

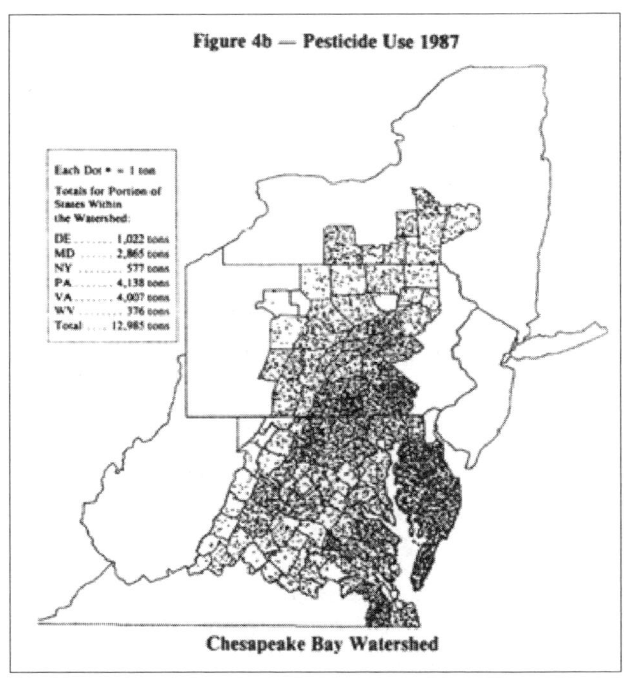

Figure 4b — Pesticide Use 1987

CONCLUSIONS

The Chesapeake Bay has undergone very rapid population growth with its associated environmental impacts. We have mapped some of these changes as they are reflected in the characteristics of the Bay's watershed. The impacts of these activities in the watershed on the Bay itself are known to be large, but their specific interconnections are only now being investigated. The Chesapeake Bay has 200,000 people living in its drainage basin for every km^3, of water in the Bay (the Baltic sea has 4000 people/km^3, and the Mediterranean has 85 people/km3 by way of comparison). Even if all of

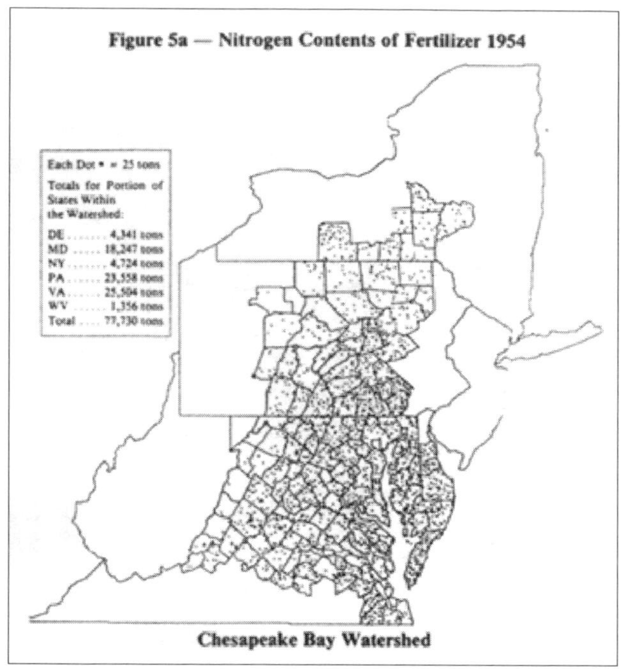

Figure 5a — Nitrogen Contents of Fertilizer 1954

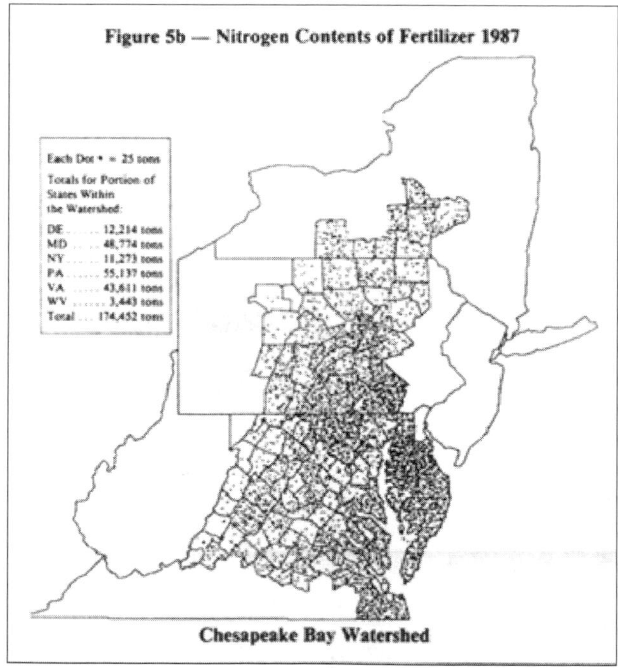

Figure 5b — Nitrogen Contents of Fertilizer 1987

these people were minimizing their environmental impacts (which they are not) their sheer numbers are daunting to a system as sensitive as the Chesapeake. If these numbers continue to increase as they have been in the past, the prospects for America's largest estuary seem bleak.

NOTES:

1. V.K. Tippie, 1984. "An environmental characterization of Chesapeake Bay and a framework for action." In: *The Estuary as a Filter*. pg. 467–488. V. S. Kennedy editor. Academic Press. Orlando, Florida.
2. *Chesapeake Bay Program*. 1983. *Chesapeake Bay Program: Findings and Recommendations.* Environmental Protection Agency, Washington, D.C.
3. Chesapeake Bay Program. 1989. *The State of the Chesapeake Bay: Third Biennial Monitoring Report* -1989. Environmental Protection Agency, Washington, D.C.
4. U.S. Department of Commerce. *U.S. Statistical Abstract 1977 and 1986*. U.S. Government Printing Office, Washington, D.C.
5. W. Boynton, J. Garber, and M. Kemp. 1990. "Patterns of Nitrogen and Phosphorus input, storage, recycling, and fate in the Chesapeake Bay and selected tributary rivers." In preparation.

REFERENCES:

1. Bureau of the Census. *County and City Data Book 1952, 1972 and 1988*. U.S. Government Printing Office, Washington, D.C. U.S.
2. Department of Commerce. *U.S. Statistical Abstract* [various years]. U.S. Government Printing Office, Washington, D.C.
3. U.S.D.A. *1954 Census of Agriculture* U.S. Government Printing Office, Washington, D.C.
4. U.S.D.A. *1974 Census of Agriculture* U.S. Government Printing Office, Washington, D.C.
5. U.S.D.A. *1987 Census of Agriculture* U.S. Government Printing Office, Washington, D.C.
6. D. VanDyne and C. Gilbertson. 1978. *Estimating U.S. Livestock and Poultry Manure and nutrient Production*. U.S.D.A., Washington, D.C.

THE MOST OVERPOPULATED NATION

Paul R.Ehrlich and Anne H. Ehrlich

January 1991

Those of us who deal with population issues all the time are frequently confronted by people who believe the population problem belongs to someone else. It traces, in their view, to poor Indians who do not understand how to use condoms, or to Mexican peasants who invade our country to steal our jobs, or to the Catholic hierarchy which persists in its irrational opposition to the use of effective birth control methods. But Indian peasants mostly want the children they have—they know how to use condoms. And at the moment Mexican immigration is probably a net benefit for the United States—although in the middle term it could become a disaster. And crazy as the Vatican's position is, relatively few Catholics pay any attention to it. After all, Italy has the smallest family size in the world!

But it just does not wash. Yes, poor nations have serious population problems, but in many respects rich nations have worse ones. Nothing recently has made the degree of overpopulation in the United States more obvious than George Bush's confrontation with Iraq. If the United States had stabilized its population in 1943, when it was in the process of winning the largest land war in history, today it would just have 135 million people. Assume that per-capita energy consumption nevertheless had grown to today's level—that is, our smaller population was still using sloppy technologies: gas guzzling automobiles, inefficient light bulbs and pumps, poorly insulated buildings, and so on. Even if its citizens were just as profligate users of energy as we are, the 135 million United States citizens could satisfy their energy appetite without burning one drop of imported oil or one ounce of coal.[2]

Of course, if we had been smart, we also would have become energy efficient and would have made a transition to some form of solar-hydrogen economy. It has been estimated that an energy efficient America could have the goods now supplied by energy use at an expenditure of about one-third the energy now employed. And it is crystal clear that for the environmental health of the globe as a whole, and the United States itself, a drastic reduction in the use of energy technologies that place greenhouse-enhancing carbon dioxide into the atmosphere is mandatory.

I = P A T

The impact of a population on the environment can be roughly viewed as the product of three factors: the size of the population (P), the level of per-capita consumption or affluence (A), and the measure of the impact of the technology (T) used to supply each unit of consumption. This provides the short-hand equation I=PxAxT which, although oversimplified (because the three factors P, A, and T are not independent), provides a basis for comparing the responsibility of different nations or groups for environmental deterioration.

Using the I = P A T equation, one can see that the population problem in the United States is the most serious in the world. First of all, the P factor is huge—with 250 million people, the United States is the fourth largest nation in the world. And compared with other large nations, the A and T factors (which when multiplied together yield per capita environmental impact) is also huge—on the order of twice that of Britain, Sweden, France, or Australia, fourteen times that of China, forty times that of India, and almost 300 times that of a Laotian or Ugandan. In per-capita energy use, only a few oil producing nations in the Middle East such as Qatar and Bahrain, plus Luxembourg and Canada, are in our league, and those nations have comparatively tiny populations. When the population multiplier is considered, the total impact of the United States becomes gigantic, several hundred times that of Bangladesh.

Those multipliers are based on per-capita commercial energy consumption, which is the best surrogate for A x T that is readily found in government statistics. The contributions of very poor countries to environmental deterioration are underestimated by these statistics, since they don't include the impacts of use of "traditional" energy sources (fuelwood, dung, crop wastes) that comprise 12 percent of energy use globally, but a much larger component in poor countries. Considering them would not change the U.S. position as the planet's primary environmental destroyer, though.

That preeminence makes sense intuitively, too. Few Laotians drive air-conditioned cars, read newspapers that transform large tracts of forest into overflowing landfills, fly in jet aircraft, eat fast-food hamburgers, or own refrigerators, several TV's, a VCR, or piles of plastic junk. But millions upon millions of Americans do. And in the process they burn roughly a quarter of the world's fossil fuels, contributing carbon dioxide and many other undesirable combustion products to the atmosphere, and are major users of chlorofluorocarbons, chemicals that also add to the greenhouse effect and attack Earth's vital ozone shield.

We have destroyed most of America's forest cover (replacing a small fraction of it with biologically impoverished tree farms) and are busily struggling to log the last of the old growth forests in the Northwest, threatening the long-term prosperity of the timber industry, in part to service the junk bonds of rich easterners. The western United States is one of the largest desertified areas on the planet from overgrazing by cattle and sheep—not because we need the meat (only a small portion of our beef comes from the arid West), but because of the political power of ranchers in the western states and a nostalgic view of western history. And Americans have contributed mightily to the destruction of tropical forests by purchasing products ranging from beef to tropical hardwoods derived from forests.

Furthermore, each additional American adds disproportionately to the nation's environmental impact. The metals used to support his or her life must be smelted from poorer ores at higher energy cost, or transported from further away. The petroleum and water he or she consumes, on average, must come from more distant sources or from wells driven deeper. The wastes he or she produces must be carried further away, and so on. Activities that created little or no environmental burden when the United States had a small population—such as putting CO_2 into the atmosphere by burning fossil fuels—increase that burden with every additional individual when the population is large.

CONSUMING OUR CAPITAL

Basically, like most of the rest of the world, the United States has been consuming environmental capital—especially its deep, fertile soils, ice-age ground water, and biodiversity– and calling it "growth." Furthermore, directly and by example, it has been helping other nations to do the same. It would not be remotely possible for Earth to support today's 5.4 billion people on humanity's "income" (which consists largely of solar energy) with present technologies and lifestyles—even though for billions their life-style is living in misery, lacking adequate diets, shelter, health care, education, and so on. And in the last decade, America has retarded the world-wide movement towards population control because of the brain dead policies of the Reagan and Bush administration.

The key to civilization's survival is reduction of the scale of the human enterprise and thus of the impact of human society on our vital life support systems. This can be achieved most rapidly by reducing all of the P, A, and T factors. In rich nations, this means immediate and rapid conversion to much more efficient use of energy and an immediate press towards population shrinkage. Fortunately, rich nations have the kind of age composition that makes the transition towards negative population growth (NPG) a relatively simple matter (a few European countries have already achieved it).

THE HOLDREN SCENARIO

The best overall strategy would be based on the Holdren scenario.[3] That scenario deals with a combination of population size and per-capita energy use. As you can see in the chart below, total annual worldwide energy use today is almost 14 terrawatts, produced by the combination of a relatively small population of rich people each using a great deal of energy, and a huge population of poor people each using relatively little energy. The essence of Holdren's scenario is that rich countries would become much more energy efficient, reducing their per-capita use from almost 8 kilowatts to 3 kilowatts (this means a reduction in the United States to less than one third of current use, but this clearly is technically feasible with no loss in quality of life). In poor countries, per-capita use would increase from 1.2 to 3 kilowatts, so that at the end of a century everyone would basically have the same standard of living (at least as measured by access to energy).

If population shrinkage in rich countries and population control in poor countries could limit the peak size of the human population to 10 billion, the Holdren scenario would result in a total global energy use of about 30 terrawatts. Whether or not that would be sustainable for even a short time

Table 1.

		POPULATION [billions = 10^9 people]	X	ENERGY/PERSON [kilowatts =kW = 103 watts]	=	TOTAL ENERGY USE [terawatts = TW = 1012 watts]
1990	RICH	1.2		7.7		9.2
	POOR	4.1		1.1		4.5
		5.3				13.7
2025	RICH	1.4		3.9		5.4
	POOR	6.8		2.2		15
		8.2				20.4
2100		10		3		30 (>2X now)

would depend, among other things, on whether or not the poor countries repeat the previous mistakes of the rich countries in development or concentrated on using more environmentally benign energy technologies—in particular, some form of solar power and the use of hydrogen as a portable fuel. Our guess is that it might be possible to run a world temporarily on 30 terrawatts, but to prevent long-term deterioration it will be necessary to reduce the population size substantially below 10 billion. Indeed, the population eventually should be reduced to the vicinity of 1 or 2 billion with an aggregate energy use of, say 5–7 terrawatts, if the health of ecosystems is to be restored and a substantial safety margin provided.

THE AMERICAN ROLE

A large part of the responsibility for solving the human dilemma rests on the rich countries, and especially on the United States. We are the archetype of a gigantic, overpopulated, overconsuming rich nation, one that many illinformed decision makers in poor nations would like to emulate. Unless we demonstrate by example that we understand the horrible mistakes made on our way to overdevelopment, and that we are intent on reversing them, we see little hope for the persistence of civilization.

The first step, of course, is for the United States to adopt a population policy designed to halt population growth and begin a gradual population decline. Such steps can be taken without immediately targeting an eventual optimum population size, since that optimum is far below 250 million. With a little leadership at the top—say a president who kept pointing out that patriotic Americans stopped at two children maximum—we could probably achieve NPG in the United States within a couple of decades.

IMMIGRATION AND POPULATION

Americans would also, of course, have to recognize that for every immigrant that arrives in the United States who is not balanced by an emigrant, a birth must be forgone. We can never have a sane immigration policy until we have a sane population policy. What the mix of births and immigrants should be is a difficult question which must be solved by public debate. Our own view is that immigration adds important variety to our population and permits America to give refuge to people who really need it. So our preference would be to maintain a reasonable level of immigration and compensate for it with fewer births. But many others would consider the small family sizes that required would be too high a price to pay, or they simply do not like 'foreigners' (or are outright racists) and would prefer much stricter limits on immigration. Throughout this debate, it must be kept in mind that from a global environmental perspective, immigration into the United States is not neutral. Immigrants from poor nations, often among the brightest and most ambitious members of their societies, are frequently very successful financially and even the less well-off quickly acquire American superconsuming habits. They tend to bring with them the reproductive habits of their societies, so that they also produce larger families of superconsumers than those of us whose families immigrated earlier. So even though immigration to the U.S. does not produce a net increment to the global population,[4] it does produce a net increment in total environmental impact.

The immigration issue is extremely complex and ethically difficult,[5] but it must be faced. Equally daunting, after a decision on levels of immigration is made, is monitoring the flow and enforcing the quotas. Badly needed now is a wide-ranging discussion first of population policy and then of immigration within the context of that policy.

OPTIMUM POPULATION

Which brings us finally to the question of an optimum population for the United States. What can be said about it in light of the foregoing discussion? About the only thing that is certain is that the optimum will depend upon the scale of the A and T factors. And with a quality of life that more or less resembles today's or a superior quality, and present or foreseeable technologies, the optimum would be far below the present population.

Calculating an optimum size for any human population today is no easy task. First of all, the optimum will depend on the standard of living of the average individual. A population of vegetarian Gandhis can be much larger than one made up of superconsuming Trumps. Then it depends on the environmental impacts of the technologies used to support the life-style. An optimum population that uses light, highly fuel-efficient vehicles for personal transportation can be larger than one that drives Detroit gas guzzlers. And one that uses commuter trains, buses, carpool vans, or even redesigns its cities to eliminate most commuting can be even bigger. The optimum size also depends, on this interdependent globe, on population sizes, technologies, and life-styles adopted by other populations. And, of course, the optimum population size depends upon the answer to the question: 'For how long will it be sustained?' With a Reaganesque program of consuming all natural resources for the exclusive benefit of people now alive, the optimum will certainly be much higher than one that gives importance to the long-term maintenance of society.

Finally, optimum population depends upon the aggregate of life-style choices of individual citizens. An America where nearly every family wanted to live on at least a five-acre parcel of land would have a much lower optimum population size than an America populated with people who loved crowded living in action-filled cities.

With all of these caveats, let us give some personal opinions on optimum population for the United States. No sensible reason has ever been given for having more than 135 million people. The putative reason for choosing that number is that America fought and won (with lots of help from others) the greatest war in history with that number of people. But there is no sign today, indeed there wasn't during the World War II, that brute numbers led to victory. The Germans and Japanese, with tiny populations compared to the allies, almost won the war—with a combination of, on average, better military leadership, better weapons, interior lines of communication, and, often, superior troops. The struggles of Germany with the Soviet Union and Japan with China highlighted these factors—clearly if the other allies hadn't been involved, David would have mopped up Goliath in both cases. And, of course, Israel today puts permanently to rest the notion that a large population is essential for military power.

Our personal preference would be to design a nation with a maximum of life-style options, so if we were forced to make an estimate of the optimum population size of the United States, we'd guess around 75 million people. That was about the population size at the turn of the century—a time when the United States had enough people for big, industrial cities and enough wilderness and open space that people who wanted it could still find real solitude. At about that number we believe a permanently sustainable nation with a high quality of life could be designed—if it were embedded in a world that was similarly designed.

The critical point, though, is that views of an optimum are going to change as society and technology change and as we learn more about the environmental constraints within which society must operate. It is fun to make guesses now, but those guesses may be far from the consensus view of our society a century hence (when, for example, the concept of solitude may be well-nigh forgotten). Unless there is a disaster, it will probably take a century or more even to approach an optimum—plenty of time for research and discussions. It suffices today to say that for our huge, overpopulated, superconsuming, technologically sloppy nation, the optimum was passed long ago. And because of decades of destruction of natural capital, the optimum will surely be lower the second time we approach it, and lower still for every year we postpone the turnaround. For our own sakes, and that of humanity as a whole, a rapid move to NPG is essential.

NOTES:

1. Documentation for many of the statements found in this article can be found in P.R. Ehrlich and A.H. Ehrlich, 1990 *The Population Explosion* (Simon and Schuster, New York) and in P.R. Ehrlich and A.H. Ehrlich, 1991, *Healing the Earth* (Addison Wesley, New York) *in press*. We thank Gretchen C. Daily for helpful comments on the manuscript.
2. Technically, the economic system would not have worked quite that way as demand varied, but the point is valid nonetheless.
3. John P. Holdren, 1990, "Energy in Transition," *Scientific American,* September 1990.
4. Most likely it produces a net decrement, since the high TFRs of the immigrants tend to fade in a generation or so, but presumably would have remained higher in the country of origin.
5. See P.R. Ehrlich, D.L. Bilderback, and A.H. Ehrlich, 1979 *The Golden Door* (Ballantine Books, New York).

THE KINGDOM OF THE DEAF

Lindsey Grant

February 1991

IT CAN HAPPEN HERE

To be more precise: it is happening here.

Even as this study was being written, American women's fertility has moved back up from 1.8 to 2.0 children, making most of the population projections we have used look very conservative. Moreover, new legislation (see below) will sharply increase immigration for the foreseeable future. Taken together, these rates would lead to a population in 2080 between 409 and 558 million.[1] The rates will change again, of course (and not necessarily downward), but the projection shows the direction in which we are presently heading.

There is a sardonic irony in current policies. The enthusiasm of the Reagan and Bush administration for consumerism, taken together with their indifference or outright hostility to population limitation, is hastening the end of the era when their "Texas" view of consumption is supportable for any but a tiny fraction of the population. They are, in effect, encouraging the unrestrained growth of two of the three variables that determine the size of environmental and resource problem—population and per capita consumption—leaving technology as the only tool with which to address those problems.

In the process, the nation is limiting its options for the future and foreclosing the pursuit of what—if we stopped to think—would be the optimum.

Let me get personal, to illustrate the point. I am in favor of policies that would discourage the use of private cars (by making their users pay their real social and environmental costs) and would promote the use of public transportation. This is not because I like to ride buses. Anybody who has waited in the snow for a homebound bus that never came, or caught a winter cold from a fellow passenger sneezing in his face, is not likely to idealize buses. On the other hand, I love my car. An automobile, more than a horse or a sailboat, is a ticket to freedom, and I have spent a lot of happy time on the back roads of America. Not necessarily a big car. My puritan streak rebels, and besides, I like little cars.

If I were to select the optimum transportation—in isolation from other considerations such as the environment or the energy transition, or the real world of snarling traffic jams I would unhesitatingly choose an automobile.

I advocate buses because I recognize that we are past the population level that will tolerate my optimum mode.

We are being forced to make more and more of those less than optimum choices. We may not even recognize them as compromises. Necessity conditions us so deeply to think of the *possible* that we seldom distance ourselves sufficiently to ask "What is *desirable*?" If we would recognize that society already makes the demographic bed in which it must lie, and that we have the option of making the choice consciously rather than inadvertently, then perhaps we can begin to pursue the ideal, rather than choosing among unsatisfactory alternatives.

There are demographic consequences from most of the decisions that we take, and the population change engendered by a decision on—say, immigration or welfare policy—may imperil the pursuit of policies in some entirely different area, such as the integration of Blacks into mainstream American society (Briggs), or the protection of the environment (Ehrlichs), or the preservation of the cities as good places to live (Speare and White), or the productivity of the Chesapeake Bay (Tennenbaum and Costanza), or the preservation of the Western high country from continued savaging (Brownridge).

HOW MANY AMERICANS?

The two most visible and perhaps the controlling restraints on population are energy and food. Environmental problems set a limit to the scale of economic activities, but it is not easy to say exactly where that line lies. Some very crowded places can prosper, particularly if they are surrounded by water or less developed countryside to absorb their effluents. Witness the success of South Korea, Taiwan, Hong Kong, Singapore and Japan.

These places all depend on a benign and open world economy to enable them to exchange their products for energy and food. In a sense, in a world trading system, they are the world cities, trading with the "world countryside."

However, the assured availability of cheap energy is running out for all of us. In the present energy transition, because of the scale of its economy, the United States will be a major determinant as to how abrupt the worldwide transition will be, or how smooth. Moreover, unlike those island economies, the United States does not have the luxury of simply assuming that food will always be there. We are the world's residual food supplier, and neither we nor the food importers have anywhere to turn if that source is imperiled.

Energy. It is no wonder, then, that four of the authors in this study, quite independently, identified energy as a key factor determining optimum U.S. population. They employed different reasoning but came to somewhat similar conclusions. The Pimentels come up with the range from 40 to 100 million. Costanza reaches a "prudently pessimistic" estimate of about 85 million at current per capita consumption levels, or twice that with a more energy conserving "European" style of consumption. Similarly, the Ehrlichs propose a range from 70 million, if we choose to remain profligate, to 135 million if we do not. Werbos, in the most detailed energy analysis, offers a wider possible range, depending upon the progress of technology. He starts with a "pessimistic" figure of 60 million—which is the point at which direct solar energy would be needed for baseline electric power, driving the cost substantially upward—and puts the upper limit at 125–250 million, depending upon the performance of new technologies, but with the cautionary note that environmental problems could be mounting at the upper end of that range.

Werbos also underlines the immense capital cost of adjusting in coming decades to the energy transition, beginning with oil. For that reason, he advocates population policies that would hold down the growth of demand, plus national policies that would contribute to the rate of capital formation and enhance the productivity of labor. He believes that, as a nation, we are paying for the luxury of supporting the present pattern of differential fertility, in which the poorest and the least educated are the most fertile, and their children generate disproportionate social costs and transfer payments. He believes that wiser policies concerning immigration and fertility would lead toward something like the Bouvier "hard" scenario and an immediate slowing of population growth.

Notice that all four writers assume that "optimum" means renewables, conservation, the end of the fossil fuel era and no nuclear power. The view of fossil fuels is driven by environmental constraints and by the fact that they are exhaustible and, therefore, transitional. If we face a mounting energy crisis, we also face an opportunity, since the ways we produce and use energy lie at the heart of many of our environmental problems.

Some readers may interpose that nuclear power can fill the gap. This would be to confuse the *possible* with the *desirable.* Given the dangers of nuclear energy that Werbos has so eloquently stated, would the world not be a better place without it, even if—because of a failure of population policy—we wind up without that option?

One might add that power from nuclear fission is also transitional because of the limits of uranium deposits, unless we go to the breeder reactor, which raises all the problems of safety and control in a much more concentrated form.

Agriculture. The Pimentels also point to the agricultural limits on optimum population. We are mining our soils, drawing down the nation's groundwater supplies, and damaging the environment through concentrated use of fertilizers and pesticides. They recommend a 50 to 60 percent reduction of inputs, in order to address those problems.

Farmland is limited. Some of it is too erosive for sustained cropping. Given the energy future already described, there will be competition with biomass for energy. Improved strains may possibly lead to yields comparable to the present, even with less intensive inputs. Prudence would set this as an upper limit, however. The optimum population resulting from these calculations may be as low as half the present population.

Humans and the Biosphere. By definition, the nation is past the point of sustainability—and therefore overpopulated—at the existing levels of population, per capita consumption, and the uses of technology. The proof lies in the documented deterioration of our environment: water, soils, air, wetlands. Beyond that, however, in these essays we have not come up with calculations as to exactly *how* overpopulated.

Proponents of conservation believe they have the cure. The problem with their "solution" lies in the trade-offs I mentioned in the introductory essay. Indeed, we could live an environmentally benign life with a lot more people, if we cut consumption to Chinese levels (and, incidentally, managed our environment better than the Chinese are doing.) The question, of course, is: "Is that optimal? If not, where on the consumption scale is the optimum?"

The technology buffs propose more technology, but—even when the investment costs are known—one needs to answer the question: "Which would be the better way? to meet a particular problem with a given technology, at such and such a cost? and with the "solution" itself generating certain by-products? or should we reduce the demand side through population policy, with the prospect of addressing multiple problems with one solution?"

There are different combinations of population, consumption and technology that could, for instance, bring us back to desirable limits on ozone, acid precipitation sources, and greenhouse gases. Various scientific explorations underway, such as the acid rain study now moving toward completion,[2] will perhaps lead to a better understanding of the variables and may help a future effort to put a number on optimum population, but it is beyond the reach of this exploratory study.

We have put together some of the parts. Tennenbaum and Costanza have demonstrated why the Chesapeake would benefit—and so would we—if there were fewer people pressing on it. Brownridge has made a similar case concerning the high country of the West.

The Ehrlichs have dramatized the United States' obligations to a shared planet. We are introducing a disproportionate share of the pollutants that threaten the Earth, and so—for our own good and that of others—we are under particular pressure to reduce the perturbation that we generate.

Labor Force and Population Size. Vernon Briggs is concerned about the well-being and productivity of the labor force. He does not make an estimate of optimum population, but his views as to present immigration and U.S. fertility would, if continued, lead to something like Bouvier's "hard" scenario, and an eventual turnaround in U.S. population growth.

Labor productivity is perhaps the most difficult area in which to attempt to calculate a theoretical optimum population, and Briggs was wise to avoid it. There are too many variables and value judgements. In principle, the optimum productivity (and, theoretically, earnings) might perhaps be one of those famous Japanese factories, with robots and three or four supervisors, where they operate at night without even leaving the lights on. But what happens to the displaced workers? and who would buy all the goods produced? and are maximum production and consumption optimal? We are in danger here of circling back to the fallacy for which we criticize GNP as a measure of well-being: the belief that bigger is necessarily better.

Those of us who try to define optimum populations will probably need to rely on some vague and intuitive feeling that optimal is the point at which workers earn a "decent" reward for their labor, and at which there is little or no involuntary unemployment.

National Security. Binkins does not try to derive an optimum figure from the security standpoint. He does, however, make the case that the Census "lowest" projection (which leads to a U.S. population plateau for the next half century and then an accelerating decline) is compatible with U.S. security interests through 2040, which is as far ahead as he thinks one can look. He observes that manpower considerations do not stand in the way if a population turnaround would enhance the national security broadly defined: a successful energy transition; a healthy agriculture; a skilled and contented labor force.

Given the expense of modern arms, one wonders if the nation could afford to keep many more of its people under arms, as we did in World War II. A P-51 Mustang fighter cost less than $52,000 in 1944, complete. An F-15E costs about $24 million, without the weaponry. Even in the narrowest military sense, national security in the modern world may depend upon capital, technology, skilled labor, and energy resources more than on manpower.

This brings us back to the question of energy, and it dramatizes the importance, in the real world, of an exercise such as this one. If a present or future Saddam Hussein succeeds in the old dream of uniting the Arab world, we will soon need his permission to embark on a military or peace keeping mission, not just in the Persian Gulf, but anywhere, or even to assure the flow of energy for our own economy.

Our ships and airplanes and equipment operate on oil, and oil is increasingly becoming a monopoly of the Arab world. If you are interested in national security, managing the energy transition is a more important issue than manpower.

If we and the other industrial nations had had the foresight and the political nerve to begin to address the energy transition a decade or more ago, when it became apparent that oil was a dwindling natural resource, we would not be so vulnerable now to the ambitions of a Middle Eastern dictator, and we might now be able to save billions of dollars and an unpredictable number of human lives.

Moreover, by slowing down the rate at which remaining world petroleum resources are drawn down, we would have been in a better position to make a more orderly and less crisis-laden transition from reliance upon petroleum as an input for agriculture, transportation, power and industry.

A population policy will not save us the pain of the energy transition. The oil is being depleted faster than demographics can keep up. It would, however, help.

One Nation, Indivisible. American public opinion seems to be, right now, at the rather primitive stage of feeling that it is too crowded where one happens to be, but people could of course go somewhere else. I hope that the essays on the cities, the Chesapeake, and the high country will demonstrate that the big cities are indeed too big, and it is a myth to believe that the extra people could somehow be transported to the countryside or the "wide open West."

Population is not a local affair. It is a national issue, fed in large part by national policies and attitudes.

In all these essays, we have not really come to grips with the intangibles and the things that make up the "quality of life." Some of the them were touched upon in the first essay. These will perforce be left to some later study, and perhaps the best way to approach them is to identify them, and then to consider what population densities would help achieve them, as Speare and White have suggested.

What we *have* done is to identify some of the more tangible limits that will define optimum population. At the very least, what comes clear is that a smaller population, and the lower levels of immigration and fertility required for its achievement, would benefit us in some of the critical areas of national policy.

I will try to avoid making impossible claims for population policy. The population of the United States in 1900 was just passing 75 million—less than one-third of the present population—and yet we had already stripped most of the forest cover east of the Mississippi. We had inflicted damage on our settled farmlands from which they have yet to fully recover. Our urban population was tiny by today's measure, and yet they already suffered from poor water quality, waste disposal problems and air pollution. And, for all this damage, we were a poorer nation than we are today.

Population policy is not the only issue, but it may be the condition precedent to achieving the better world that most of us seek.

Having said all this, let me try my hand at a figure for optimum population: about half the present level, or 125–150 million, achieved over the next century.

This target lies within the population range of most of the estimates in this study. It is ambitious, but not completely impossible. By allowing a century, the target becomes achievable (if unlikely). As I will explain, a shorter time frame would generate severe transitional problems.

It reflects optimism that we will learn to make better use of multiple energy technologies, including the wind, and that we will continue to find ways of diminishing energy inputs without serious deprivation. The timing is consistent with the transitional availability of coal, which will almost certainly be needed to accommodate the time lag involved in a shift to renewables. There are combustion techniques, such as coal gasification, that would substantially mitigate the environmental impacts of using the coal.

My target also reflects the hope that we can sequester more of the land from direct human exploitation, both for our own future good and for the preservation of a biosphere not totally dependent upon human goodwill and prudence.

I am quite prepared to raise my target if technology justifies more optimism, or downward if—as we learn more about the web of connections in which we live—it becomes clear that even fewer is better.

As a nation, we are not likely to get there. Not, at the least, for a long, long time. (Barring a catastrophe, even Leon Bouvier's "hard scenario" would leave us still with 87 percent of the present population in 2080.) We may decide, along the way, that we don't want to go there, because we have learned to accommodate more people in a benign environment, because we decide that other goals such as accommodating persecuted or hungry foreigners are more important than optimizing well-being in the United States, because we are simply unwilling to pay the price in social engineering that might be necessary to achieve optimum population, or—most likely—because of inertia.

However, if for any of these reasons we do not try to head in that direction, we have been warned.

TRANSITIONAL BENEFITS

The reader may have noticed a curious harmony. Some writers in this series have addressed a future optimum population. Others have focused on current issues. In both approaches, however, the prescription is the same: sharply limited immigration aimed at acquiring skills in short supply; and a leveling of fertility to bring the poor and less educated on a par with the educated and more affluent.

Take, for instance, the example of labor. Briggs has argued for these remedies as a way of stopping the pauperization of the poor and helping more Blacks enter the economic mainstream. I have argued for them as a way of enabling society to concentrate on the better education and integration of smaller cohorts. Speare and White argue for them as a way of addressing the problems of the cities. Binkins says that the military needs skills, not raw labor, to man modern weapons. Werbos argues the need for highly productive labor, with high savings, coupled with a reduction in the costs to society of an unemployed underclass, as a way of accumulating the capital needed to finance the forthcoming energy transition.

All of these are transitional arguments, but the effects would be to slow and eventually reverse population growth.

Moreover, there is another reinforcement. Education and jobs for women rank at the top of Dr. Weeks' ways of achieving lower fertility.

I do not know whether this is fortuitous or whether it reflects a larger underlying unity that I do not understand. It does serve, however, to widen the support for a population turnaround. You do not need to select an optimum population to play this game. If you are concerned about any of the issues that have been raised in this study, you have reason to advocate the policies that point us in the direction of the optimum.

EXCRUCIATING CHOICES

The transitional and the long term optimum might part company if a serious effort were launched to reach an optimum population much below 150 million in the next century. As I have noted, Bouvicr's "hard" scenario would lead to a population still larger than 200 million in 2080. The Census "low" projection uses the same fertility (1.5) and net immigration (300,000 per year). It is less optimistic about improvements in life expectancy, yet it is still nearly 200 million in 2080.

The only Census Bureau projection that would take population below 150 million in the next century is the low "zero immigration" scenario (Series 28 in the 1988 study cited by Bouvier). With fertility at 1.5, it would lead to a population of 147 million in 2080, declining by about one percent a year. The name is misleading. Because of emigration,there could still be immigration in these assumptions, but it would gradually decline as emigration declined.

To translate these mathematics into policy terms: immigration would not contribute significantly to U.S. population growth if we limited gross annual immigration to 200,000 at first, gradually declining to about 100,000. These figures are generous by most world standards, but they are stringent indeed in terms of recent American experience.

I have elsewhere rebutted the argument that the United States needs more immigrants or higher fertility to take care of the old (themselves the legacy of the "baby boom") a generation hence.[3] Throughout these essays, we have reiterated the importance of persuading the poor and the less educated to bring their fertility down to the level that presently prevails among the educated and the middle class, or about 1.5 children. Nevertheless, a fertility drop below 1.5, particularly if it is sudden, would skew the population structure toward old age so dramatically as to cause some severe transitional problems. The "one child family" is indeed a desperate remedy.

This leaves the tightening of immigration, below Bouvier's "hard scenario" and the Census Bureau's "low" projection of 300,000, as a necessary element in moving the population much below 200 million in anything but a remote future.

Simcox has observed that this would leave national policy makers with some excruciating choices. Indeed it would, and as a nation we seem to have a hard time making tough choices. It is not simply that the cumulative voice of many interest groups tends to drive immigration up rather than down. There is a genuine moral dilemma as to whether, rich in a world that is largely poor, we can justify restrictive immigration policies. I have resolved that dilemma to my own satisfaction[4]. In a world of nation states, we have neither the authority nor the ability to save the rest of the world. The Ehrlichs have pointed out that we could make matters much worse by increasing our population to reduce theirs. I would do more to help other countries address their population problems, but we have a responsibility to our own people, and to our descendants.

As we watch environmental and social problems unfold, and as the energy transition comes to the crunch, our society may come to realize that choices must be made. If so, this study helps to understand the choices.

WHAT CAN BE DONE?

We have seen that population momentum is a mighty force, and that any change in direction will take most of a century to become apparent. We have also learned, however, that demographic change is not simply in the hands of fate or the Gods, but that conscious social policy can affect it.

John Weeks has described ways in which fertility can be influenced. Many of them center on raising the educational levels, the dignity and sense of self-respect, and job opportunities for women. If more direct motivation is needed, it can be provided through incentives and disincentives such as priorities in jobs, educational opportunities and education for small families, taxation policies that discourage large families, and even direct payments for not having children. The means to limit child-bearing must be available, and women must know about them. Leadership is essential, and it must come from role models and those in authority.

These are some of the means, but they alone are not sufficient. We are unlikely, as a society, to devote such efforts to population limitation until we become aware of the ways that population growth will hinder the pursuit of other goals, and we need to become aware that we may be influencing fertility when we undertake policies that are superficially unrelated.

Enter "foresight" and the processes for handling complicated and interconnected issues.

THE USES OF FORESIGHT

How do we get a better fix on causes and connection in complex systems?

As a nation, we have come to resemble a pugnacious collection of single interest groups. Our political discourse sounds like deaf men in a pit, shouting insults at each other.

Perhaps, and oddly enough, we have come to this point from an excess of self-righteousness. It is very easy and satisfying to promote a social objective into an absolute moral principle. Environmentalists oppose the development of power plants (particularly if they are nuclear). Few of them consider the connection between population and demand, or the need for sufficient power to run the economy. Civil rights activists call others "racist" if they disagree with a particular formula to bring minorities into the mainstream. Right-to-lifers dismiss as "murderers" those who disagree with their proposals.

However, in human affairs few if any principles are absolute. Even the First Amendment has its limits. Good and reasonable objectives collide. When they do, "white hats" are pitted against each other, each absolutely certain of his total moral superiority.

I would like to persuade those antagonists to see the connections between their objectives and other social desiderata, e.g.

- to encourage those environmentalists to recognize that their proposals may cause the poor to freeze until we can develop energy alternatives, and to broaden their advocacy to include a population policy to address the fundamental source of demand.
- to persuade the civil rights activists that there are also other goals to protect. "Affirmative action" and "equal opportunity" for all (including the majority) are a see-saw balanced on a moral knife edge. There may be ways of achieving the first objective while limiting damage to the second. For example, if we could revamp the educational system and the children's attitude toward it, we might help them become more competitive in the modern world. A new look at immigration might ease the competition for entry-level jobs, and the activitists might also take a new look at fertility among the poor, to give a smaller cohort a better chance.

- to bring the right-to-lifers into the population debate. Some or all of the arguments for a turn-around in U.S. population growth might strike them as reasonable. If they also understood that, historically, abortion has been—but is not necessarily—a principal method whereby population growth had been controlled, then perhaps they could be enlisted in the search for policies to influence fertility. Opposition to abortion implies either a commitment to other methods of birth control or an indifference to the well-being of the children who are born unwanted or in desperate circumstances. One can hardly take refuge in the advice to"just say no." For individuals, it is good advice, but it is folly to think that it will significantly affect the pregnancy rate of poor young girls, unless a lot of education and social training and other opportunities go with it.

The enemy is one-track thinking. The effort to address population change has been particularly vulnerable to it. Any proposals to intervene deliberately in human fertility have long been in conflict with the Biblical injunction to "be fruitful and multiply," and now they have become ensnared in that most explosive of current U.S. moral and political issues: abortion.

In this embittered environment, the process of "foresight" used in this study offers some hope of a return to moderation and good sense, by requiring that issues be addressed in terms of their consequences rather than of preconceived moral absolutes.

If the debate were re-cast in these terms rather than in moral absolutes, perhaps the Bush Administration would find heart to address the population issue.

The Environmental Protection Agency's Science Advisory Board has discovered that policies in one area generate consequences in other areas. It has found that "Changing Federal policies in sectors not traditionally linked with environmental protection could provide cost-effective environment benefits that equal or exceed those that can be achieved through more traditonal means. Environmental considerations should be an integral part of national policies that affect energy use, agriculture, taxation, transportation, housing, and foreign relations."[5]

The same thing could be said about population considerations. I wish they had said it.

On occasion, the U.S. Government has tried to engage in that kind of thinking: the Rockefeller Commission report of 1972; the *Global 2000 Report to the President* of 1980. Neither had identifiable effects upon national policy, because their conclusions were not connected with other current policy issues.

There have been a few stalwart proponents of better ways of making the connections. In Congress, Senator Albert Gore, Jr. has been a tireless advocate. With various cosponsors, he has introduced his Critical Trends Assessment Act into successive sessions. The most recent version is S1345, introduced in 1989. Like its predecessors, it has died in committee.

If our governmental processes are ever to catch up with a fast changing world, public advocacy groups and the citizenry would do well to learn about and advocate such reforms. Dull as these "process bills" may sound in competition with our daily TV fare, they are more important.

There is one process already available, but it has never been used for the big decisions, and it has fallen into disuse even for the smaller ones. The Environmental Policy Act of 1969 specifically made the connections that we have been talking about in this study, and it required the preparation of environmental impact statements (EIS) to examine those connections before decisions are made.

That Act included population, but the bureaucracy left it out in preparing the implementing regulations, so the population impacts of proposed actions have seldom been considered.[6]

We would have a process for bringing demography into our national thinking if that Act.

- were vigorously enforced, and
- if the regulations were amended to require that population be considered among the impacts, and
- if the Act were extended to include Congress rather than only the Executive Branch.

The process of examination would force our society, case by case, to ask the question: What is optimum population? if the participants in this present study are right, it would lead to a wide acceptance of the concept that population has gone too far already. I can hardly imagine, for instance, that in a debate over energy policy there would be much support for the idea that we need more people. If I am wrong, then it will come out in such debates.

The Kuwait crisis and the energy issue provide a dramatic example of why we need some way to put the issues together. In the midst of that crisis, and with the budget impasse staring at them, Congress took time out in October 1990 to pass the Immigration Act of 1990 (S358), and the President signed it. Census projections suggest that, even without that law, the country's population will rise by about 25 million during this decade. The new law will add perhaps 5–10 million more, by increasing immigration quotas and promoting future chain immigration.[7] The bill also generates immediate new budgetary costs for the federal and local governments. The question did not arise as to whether it is a good idea to bring in more oil consumers precisely when we are coming to recognize the fragility of the petroleum supply, nor did the connection between increased immigration and the effort to reduce government expenditures.

Another example, if one is needed, is the new Department of Transportation (DOT) "national transportation policy."[8] This "plan" was produced, after months of labor, in February 1990.

There are environmental constraints on the ever increasing use of fossil fuels. We must prepare for the transition away from petroleum, in any case; the Geological Survey warns that the country's remaining petroleum resources total just sixteen years' at present consumption rates. Our dependence on the Persian Gulf is increasing very fast, which has fundamental foreign policy and national security implications. DOT should have been asking itself, "How does transportation policy relate to these issues? what should we be planning? can we simply go on building highways forever? if transportation is the principal driving force in generating the energy demand that causes these problems, should we not be looking at how to control that demand? and if population size is a major element in the total demand for transportation, does DOT not have an interest in policy proposals that affect the two demographic variables of immigration and fertility?

Did DOT address these questions? Hardly. The report touched on the environment only with a promise to minimize the destruction of wetlands. None of the other connections was addressed, and there was no indication that DOT had thought ever to be in touch with the Departments of State of Defense, the Geological Survey, or anybody else.

This is indeed the kingdom of the deaf.

The interdependence of issues requires that these acts be put together, but the connections are not always so glaringly obvious. Let me take the rather mundane example of the Washington METRO.

Few people relate transportation to demography, but it can affect, not just where we live and work, but the level of fertility itself.

If the population impact had been addressed when the METRO subway was being planned, some population sociologist would perhaps have had the chance to point out (as Dr. Weeks has done) that fertility declines when women have jobs and the dignity that goes with self-support. There is a circular connection between poverty and high fertility. Anybody who is interested in ameliorating the isolation and alienation of the Blacks in the inner city should have had an interest in where the subway went.

What has happened? The Metro is nearly complete, but the last part of it—still with no completion date—is the "Green line" into Anacostia, the part of the city where it is most needed. If jobs have fled the inner city, we have yet to help connect the inner city residents with the jobs. Different priorities would have helped to address, not just the poverty and fertility, but—as a result—the violence and drug traffic that bedevil the inner city. Because we have not yet learned to think across issues, the planners did not weigh these implications in their choice of construction priorities.

The process of foresight is not all-seeing. It cannot pretend to draw a map of the future. Nobody has been very good at prediction, yet, and the outlook for improvement is not very good, given the growing complexity of mankind's manipulation of the environment.

The object, rather, is to get away from the single minded pursuit of sometimes conflicting goals. Better foresight would help our society to see the connections, to weigh the effects of demography on the pursuit of other objectives, and to understand how other policies might influence demography.

It can help us apply what vision we have to the issues before U.S.

CODA

The skeptic, comfortable in his affluence, seeks to put off remedial action with the argument that more study is needed.

Humans seldom have the luxury of knowing all about a problem before they must do something about it. The nation is hardly likely to agree on a fixed number for optimum population, if even a group of rather like-minded specialists have not, but I think that we have made a pretty strong case that, whatever it is, it is smaller than the present population and much smaller than the population levels toward which they are presently heading. And the policies that would lead to an eventual turnaround in population growth are the same ones that would help us to address major social and economic issues now confronting us.

Change has accelerated, and vast forces are set in motion that cannot be easily directed. With population, it may take half a century or more to turn growth around. If there is good evidence that we are already too big, even immediate action may not be fast enough to achieve the optimum for generations to come, and delay compounds the problems and worsens the choices.

As the Pimentels have described with respect to energy, human impacts on the environment have grown to the point where they may even exceed natural processes. This awesome power imposes corresponding responsibilities. As a tribe, the human race needs to learn an "unnatural" way of thinking. We are genetically conditioned to perceive and respond to sudden and fast-moving emergencies (such as a charging carnivore.) We need to become sensitive to vaster but much slower changes, such as those in our environment. We need to establish baselines from which to measure change, and to condition our behavior to deal in a much longer time frame.

The professional optimists reassure us that the human mind can solve any problem. Robert Costanza warns us, more prudently, that we had better use our minds to avoid problems before they become traps, and we are already at least part way into the population trap.

The time is long past when, with Mr. Micawber and various economists, we can afford simply to hope that something will turn up.

I wonder if anybody is listening, out there in the kingdom of the deaf.

NOTES:

1. Leon F. Bouvier, *The Impact of Immigration on U.S Population Size* (Washington: Population Reference Bureau, 1981). The two figures are based upon annual net immigration of one and two million, respectively.
2. National Acid Precipitation Assessment Program (NAPAP), 722 Jackson Place NW, Washington DC 20503. Review draft September 1990; final report scheduled 1991.
3. Lindsey Grant, "Too Many Old People or Too Many Americans?" NPG FORUM series (Teaneck, NJ: NPG, Inc., 1988).
4. See my concluding chapter, "How Many Americans?," in David E. Simcox et al, *U.S. Immigration in the 1980s: Reappraisal and Reform* (Boulder: Westview Press, 1988).
5. Environment Protection Agency Science Advisory Board, "Reducing Risk: Setting Priorities and Strategies for Environmental Protection" (Washington: EPA, September 1990). Recommendation 8, p.23.
6. For a detailed discussion of the methods and history of foresight, see Lindsey Grant, *Foresight and National Decisions: the Horseman and the Bureaucrat* (Lanham, MD: University Press of America, 1988).
7. See "Updated Estimates of Immigration Under Current Legislative Options, 1991–1995" (Center for Immigration Studies, 1424 16th Street NW—Suite 603, Washington DC 20036; March 1990) for projections of the five-year impacts of different legislative proposals then before Congress.
8. *Moving America. New Directions, New Opportunities: A Statement of National Transportation Policy Strategies for Action* (Washington: U.S. Department of Transportation, February 1990).

FREE TRADE AND CHEAP LABOR: THE PRESIDENT'S DILEMMA

Lindsey Grant

October 1991

Foresight is the art of recognizing how changes in one sector may affect policies in another.[1] Lacking a systematic foresight process, our government is apt to be astonished by results it did not anticipate. The President's pursuit of hempispheric free trade is a dramatic and potentially tragic case in point. The demographics of Central and South America threaten to make a disaster of a policy that was envisaged as simply an economic and trade issue. This paper is an effort, by a writer on foresight and erstwhile Deputy Assistant Secretary of State for Environment and Population Affairs, to make those missing connections.

The President has embarked upon a project to create a hemispheric free trade area, with Canada already aboard and negotiations with Mexico next on the agenda. Congress has tentatively acquiesced. It has given the President authority to negotiate an agreement with Mexico, reserving only the right to say yes or no to the entire package.

Organized labor has tried unsuccessfully to focus attention on the implications for American wages and employment, but nobody has really looked at the numbers, and the environmental movement has yet to address the demographic implications and what they mean for our future.

Congress and the President would do well to scrutinize the proposal more closely. There are theoretical and even real arguments for free trade, but there are land mines in the present project.

THE DILEMMA DEFINED

With the collapse of socialism as a means of organizing economies, the proponents of laissez-faire have been riding high. It is now very unpopular to argue with Adam Smith and the "invisible hand" of the unfettered market, or with the idea of "comparative advantage." However, the classical economists never promised a good deal for the worker; that came later, with increased worker bargaining power. As John Cobb and Herman Daly have pointed out, "comparative advantage" was premised on the assumption that capital and technology would stay put and would not depart for the "backward regions" of the period.[2] It was a comfortable doctrine for Englishmen when England was on top of the heap.

Free trade, despite the textbook arguments in its favor, creates a basic problem: In a situation with free movement of goods and technology and capital—but not of labor—what happens? Employers tend either (a) to move toward the cheaper labor, or (b) to press for removal of impediments to importing cheap labor.

Choice (a) leads to the loss of jobs in the United States—as industries produce goods in Mexico for sale in the U.S.—and falling wages as a result. Choice (b) leads to similar, but not identical, results

FIG. 1

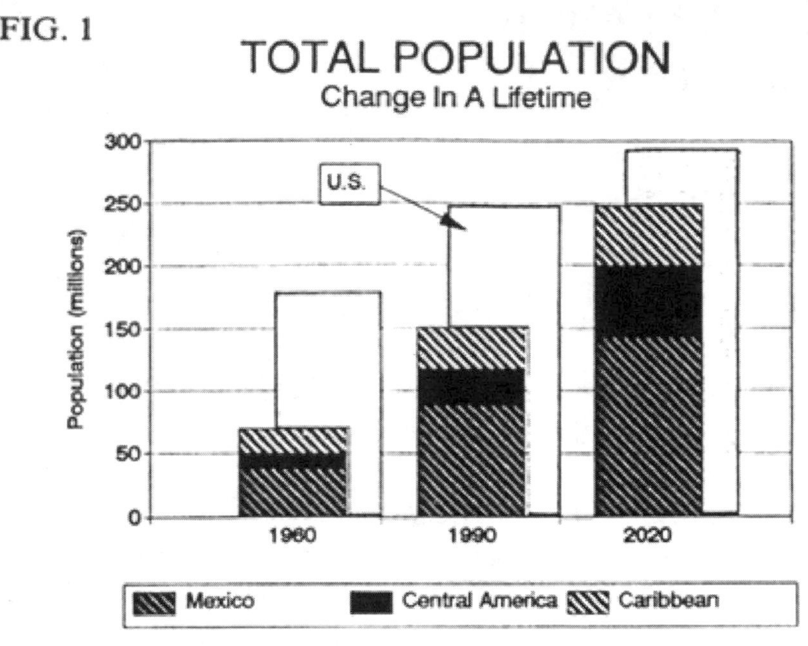

Figure 1.

The Immigration Reform & Control Act of 1986 (IRCA) provides a good example of strategy (b). Commercial farm interests, as their price for passage of the act, put in a provision making it very easy for farm laborers (or people who claimed to be farm laborers) to legalize their residence in the U.S. When the dust settled, 1. 3 million people had applied including 1.1 million Hispanics, one million of them Mexican. The problem is that the Bureau of Labor Statistics believes there were only 234,000 real Hispanic farm workers in the country, including U.S. citizens and those here legally.[4] The *New York Times* headlined it "Fraud On A Massive Scale," but almost all these "farmers" have been admitted.

as the importation of cheaper labor drives the price of labor down.

The *maquiladora* factories along the U.S.-Mexican border, taking advantage of a limited free trade arrangement, are an existing example of strategy (a). Major U.S. companies such as AT&T, Chrysler, Ford, General Motors, General Electric, Electrolux and Zenith have moved in, and employment has risen to nearly 400,000—at wages less than one-tenth of those in the U.S. Those jobs disappeared from the U.S.[3] Apologists argue that the U.S. would have lost the jobs, anyway, to cheap foreign labor; but this is not necessarily an argument for facilitating the process.

The process is far from instantaneous. There are reasons for hesitation: entrepreneurs' concern as to the prospects for economic and political stability; the lack of infrastructure such as good roads, reliable power, urban services, and banks; inertia. However, those factories demonstrate that the process does move.

This rather sordid example dramatizes the pressures from would-be immigrants and from employers willing to facilitate the flow of cheap labor, whatever the by-products.

The Mexican Government in its submission at the Uruguay Round of GATT (the General Agreement on Trade & Tariffs) said that "The expansion of the service exports of developing countries and their increased participation in world trade in services depends on the liberalization of cross-border movement of personnel, covering unskilled, semiskilled and skilled labor, . . ."[5] Take good note of that statement. They are forewarning us that we will not necessarily have free trade on our terms; they need to unload people as well as goods, and they want legal access to the market for services in the U.S., not just more manufacturing jobs in Mexico.

The alternative of accelerated immigration is more threatening than the loss of manufacturing jobs. Only part of the manufacturing sector is mobile and can pick up and leave. If, as part of a free trade agreement, we accede to the Mexican demand for "liberalization of cross-border movement," we invite low-wage competition into services, transportation, construction, agriculture—i.e. into the entire economy. More broadly, we accelerate U.S. population growth.

FIG. 2

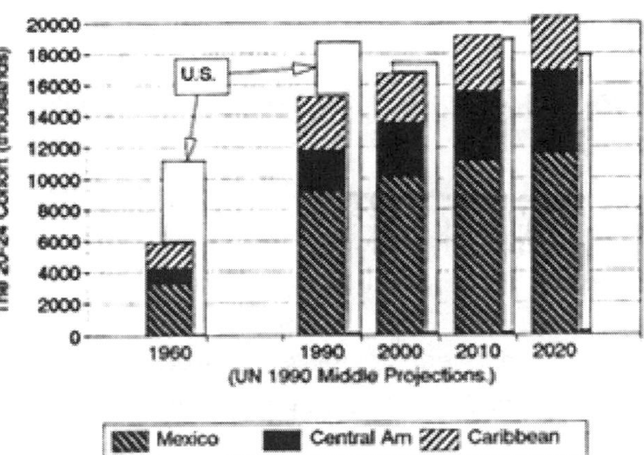

Figure 2.

Why, in the face of the potential impacts, does the President seek a free trade agreement (FTA)? There are reasons. Cheap labor means cheaper consumer goods. A wider trading area offers economies of scale and benefits American business.[5] The prospect of investment, more employment and greater exports will help Mexico, and we have a stake in the well-being of our neighbor. Indeed, an impoverished Mexico generating streams of illegal migrants could generate massive problems for the U.S. and American labor.

With Europe moving toward economic union and the possibility of higher walls against U.S. trade, the U.S. may feel the need for a trading area of its "own." This may be necessary if the world continues its drift toward regional trading arrangements. However, the comparison with the European Community is strained. The European Community does not incorporate the vast wage and fertility differentials that would characterize a Mexico U.S. free trade zone. Moreover, there is no indication that Mexico expects to offer the U.S. a preferential status in investments. Without such a preference, a free trade agreement would facilitate European investment in Mexico, selling the products to the U.S. market.

The President's dilemma, of course, is the conflict between the advantages offered by free trade and the potential impact upon U.S. wages, employment and population growth. It raises a fundamental question: Do we want to try to preserve our wage differential in a world four-fifths of which is less developed? In the third world, the engine of population growth generates so many potential workers that Ricardo's Iron Law drives wages down toward subsistence levels. Are we willing to let it happen here?

THE DILEMMA IGNORED

If the administration sees the dilemma as an impediment to its free trade proposals, it has not admitted it, and U.S. Trade Representative Carla Hills has called the proposed Mexican agreement "the first step toward President Bush's longer term goal of hemispheric free trade." An early target, presumably, will be the moribund Central American Free Trade Area.

Ms. Hills, questioned in Congress about the impact upon U.S. labor, said "Our studies show . . . businesses will not migrate to Mexico because of the poor infrastructure and because U.S. workers are more skilled and productive than Mexican workers."[6] An MIT professor, supporting the proposed free trade agreement, says "American workers lack skills, not jobs."[7] A journalist argues that " . . . every job lost by an American will go to a Mexican who is poorer and more desperate. . . . Piously denying Mexicans such jobs does nothing to improve the alternatives (sic)."[8]

Those three proponents dismiss the issue in mutually contradictory ways, but they have one thing in common: none of them, apparently, gives a damn about U.S. labor. They share a ruthless and frightening vision of the nature of society. If it's good for business and promises to lower prices, it makes no difference what effect a policy may have on the poor.

Workers and the unemployed are people, too. Policy should not be a zero-sum game. The image of the nation as a chance collection of hostile interests is finally self-destructive. It offers little promise of preserving a society capable of acting for the common good, in economic policy, environmental protection or anything else. Eventually, we are all hurt if we destroy the purchasing power of the working class.

There is, perhaps, a real conflict of moral goals involved in this blindness to one's fellow citizens. A generation raised on the idea of a shared planet, for whom the only "aliens" are from outer space, may find it hard to value a U.S. worker's prosperity higher than a foreigner's.

A firm moral position, tightly held, is a good way to blind oneself to the consequences of what one advocates. Those who take this position are generally not from the economic classes that are hurt, and they play into the hands of employers who are unconcerned about the well-being of either American or foreign labor.

There are limits as to how much we can do for the world. As Americans, we have obligations to each other, and to our descendants.

The U.S. International Trade Commission (USITC) studied the probable impacts of a free trade agreement on the U.S. economy. It devoted just over one page (out of seventy-four) to potential labor effects.

It concluded that there would probably be "little effect" on overall U.S. employment in times of full employment but more effect in times of less than full employment. This is a common sense proposition. It should, I believe, be sending us a signal. Formal unemployment has risen to 6.8 percent. Beyond that, discouraged workers are dropping out of the labor force and are no longer counted. For a better measure of the problem, look at the percentage of young (twenty to twenty-four year old) people who are out of school but have not found full time jobs; they are the ones who bear the brunt of mass immigration. The proportion in 1990 was 50 percent for Blacks (up from 48 percent in 1989), 38 percent for Hispanics (not all immigrants or their children find jobs, but the "safety net" is better here than in Mexico), and 30 percent for Whites.[9]

The USITC report said that the wage gap between the two countries would narrow, and that unskilled U.S. workers would suffer, but it saw skilled U.S. labor as profiting from the growth of exports. It noted that differences in population growth rates might sustain migratory pressures into the U.S., affecting U.S. wages, but said that "this possibility was not examined separately."[10]

The USITC, like the nation, seems unwilling to come to grips with demographic change and the labor implications. This may result in part from a failure to recognize the size of the problem. During the entire debate, nobody has undertaken to bring this simple issue of scale into focus, and that is what I propose to do here.

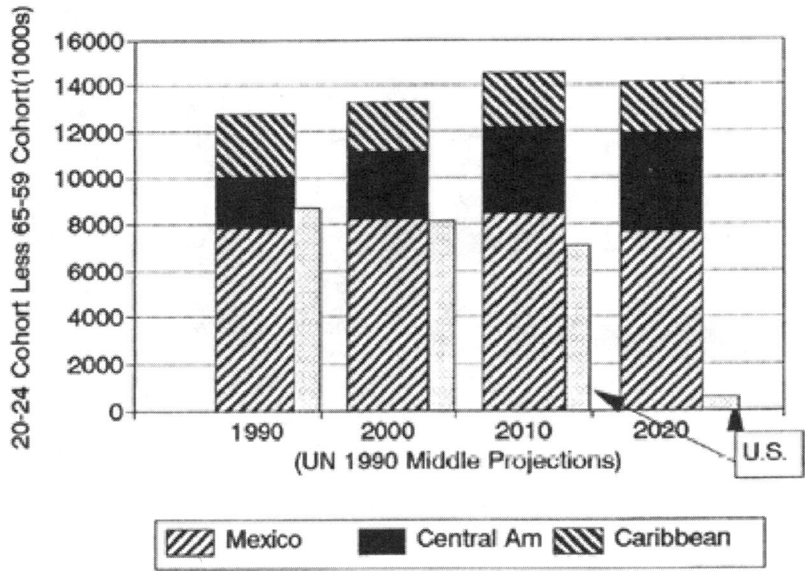

Figure 3.

We may perhaps still tend to think of Mexico, Central America and the Caribbean (or, for brevity, "meso America") as "little countries to the south of us." In 1930, they were only one-fourth as populous as the U.S. Now look at Figure 1. The population of those countries has doubled since 1960 and will be approaching that of the United States by 2020.

This is just the tip of the issue. Because of the dynamics of population growth, the growth is even faster in the age groups that are just entering the labor market. Figure 2 shows the twenty to twenty-four age cohorts at successive ten year periods. In 2010, among our southern neighbors, that group will be as large as in the U.S. In 2020, it will be larger. One is entitled to be skeptical of most demographic projections, but not these. Those cohorts through 2010 are already born.

Finally. Figure 3 is perhaps the most frightening of all. It gives the net change in the working age population in five-year periods, by deducting the numbers leaving their working years from those entering them. This is the real measure of the problem.

Not all those young people will be seeking jobs, but most of them will, particularly if there are jobs available. In a happier world, they should be able to find them. We would all profit if the young women could find jobs, since this would be a powerful incentive to reduce fertility, and reduced fertility in turn is the only long-term escape from the population trap they are in.[11]

In the real world, their numbers limit their opportunities and keep wages down, and the young people try to escape.

The common wisdom (more a guess than an estimate) is that half the labor force in the region is already unemployed or under-employed. Just to keep things from getting worse, those societies must create jobs faster than the United States did in the 1970s and 1980s, in economies that, altogether, are about 1/17th as large as the U. S. economy.[12]

It would require an investment of perhaps $50 to $200 billion per year (at a very rough guess) to enable those meso American cohorts to find jobs.[13] That is a substantial share of their entire GNP. Are

FIG. 4

The U.S. Job Seeking Cohort
Both Sexes, Ages 20-24 incl.

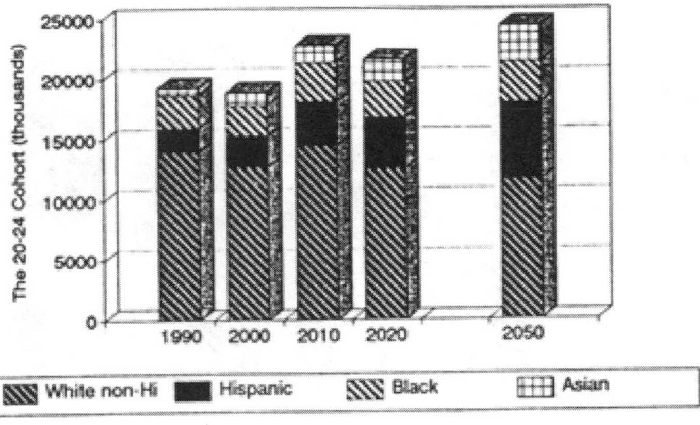

Figure 4.

Mexico and its neighbors likely to accomplish their Herculean task? With the best will in the world—or a level of foreign investment that would pauperize the sending country—one must conclude: "almost certainly not." As a result, the pressures will mount to migrate to the only accessible place where there are jobs: the United States. I can sympathize. If I were courageous, and young, and in their shoes, I would do the same.

By contrast, the United States during the next generation may *hope* to see its job market come into better balance, with a slowdown in the rate of growth and, potentially, a reduction in the present oversupply of unskilled labor. (I underscore the word "hope." We will shortly see why.)

This raises again the question: Where do our responsibilities lie? And the President's? The Constitution obligates him to "promote the general welfare" of the U.S., not of foreigners who may be victims of a demographic imbalance that got out of control, even though they may be deserving, and in need of work.

Let us turn (Figure 4) to a closer look at the demographics of the U.S. labor force. The numbers here are somewhat larger than they are for the same cohorts in Figure 2. That is because the projection is more recent and more realistic.[14] The UN projections reflect assumptions about migration that have already been overtaken. The future, in other words, is already happening.

This graph makes clear that the U.S. is not simply a White (or Black and White) country facing infiltration by other cultures. We are already well on the way to being a mixed society. I have taken the projection out to 2050 because, although projections so far ahead are necessarily conjectural, it shows the direction of present movement. That graph suggests that the moral choice I mentioned above is blurred in an unexpected way. Because of their higher fertility, minorities—and particularly U.S. Hispanics—are most heavily represented in the younger working age cohort, and most exposed to competition from immigration or the effects of free trade and cheap labor. They are the ones who will be hurt.

Elsewhere in the NPG Forum series, Vernon Briggs has made an impassioned case for less rather than more immigration, and for efforts to persuade the less educated to bring their fertility down toward that of the educated, as steps toward helping them escape the cycle of poverty.[15] The U.S. labor market needs skills, not numbers. It cannot absorb the current supply of unskilled people. The last thing we need is an increase in mass migration.

To sum it up: The demographic problems of our southern neighbors are so huge that they are already spilling over into the United States, and they threaten to do so on a much larger scale in the next few decades. This will happen whatever we do about free trade, but a free trade agreement—particularly one negotiated by an administration that seems to be unaware of the demographic realities—will worsen the impact upon U.S. labor.

RATIONALIZING THE PROBLEM AWAY

Several lines of argument are used to dismiss concerns about the labor impact of free trade.

One argument is that, since average tariffs into the U.S. are only about 4 percent and into Mexico 11 percent, a free trade agreement will not really have all that much impact.

One's initial response is: 'then why bother?' In fact, however, Carla Hills has told Congress that improving the investment climate is on our list of things to negotiate. That will make a difference, because it will encourage capital to go there and thus to transfer job opportunities out of the U.S.

Another free trade argument is that the best way of controlling migration is to make Mexico so prosperous that Mexicans will feel no need to migrate. The numbers I have cited should dispose of that argument.

Another argument, from a respected economist, is that prosperity in Mexico will generate demand for imports from the U.S., there by generating enough jobs to makeup for those lost in the initial transaction.[16] Sort of "pay now; play later." This kind of generalization is easy to make, but U.S. experience in the past twenty years suggests that it should be recognized for what it is: an unproven and uncertain hypothesis.

The same economist, in the same article, made two other arguments: first, investment will go somewhere else if it does not go to Mexico, and we have an interest in seeing it go to Mexico. Second, "There is no practical way for us to close our border. " In other words, we have to make the best of it and try to help Mexico's economy grow faster than its labor force. He did not get into the numbers, and the statistics I have already cited would suggest that this is simply wishful thinking.

I am not sure I would go to an economist for advice as to whether we can effectively patrol our border, but one commonly hears that it is "impossible"—a convenient way of dismissing any proposal to try it. I wonder if our economist sought the advice of experts. Starting perhaps with the Immigration & Naturalization Service, which has views on the matter.

If no effort is made to control the anticipated movement—which is not necessarily the same thing as "closing our border"—we will, in effect, be making the decision to go with the tide and give up any effort to preserve the wage structure the U.S. has enjoyed.

FORECLOSING THE FUTURE

At this dispiriting thought, readers may wonder whether we should not indeed let it happen and accept the prospect of sharing the wage levels of an increasingly crowded world.

The costs go much beyond the wage and employment issue. Let me identify the other issues, even if space does not permit a fuller treatment of them.

Population. I said earlier that the consequences of exporting jobs are similar but not identical to those of importing labor. One difference of course is population growth. At current fertility and immigration levels, the country will pass the 400 million mark some time around 2050.[17] (It is now about 250 million.) A change of a half million in annual net immigration would represent a change of about 50 million in the 2050 population, and more, of course, in subsequent years.

Environment. Paul and Anne Ehrlich have pointed out that the U.S. is the world's leading source of pollution, because of the combination of large population and high consumption.[18] Any policy that serves to increase immigration worsens that problem. The Ehrlichs argue that our policies should be leading to a falling rather than a rising population.

The same potential migrants, if they stay in meso America, will intensify the rapid forest destruction and soil erosion that now characterize the area. They will probably not contribute so much to acid precipitation and the greenhouse effect, but that is a very tentative "probably." It depends on the rate of industrialization in the area, success or failure in imposing environmental controls on the new factories, and how the closure of emigration options affects fertility.

This suggests, tentatively, that option "a" (exporting jobs) is less damaging to the U.S. than importing workers (option "b").

Resources. Similar reasoning applies to resources. David and Marcia Pimentel argue that the present pattern of U.S. agriculture—high energy inputs and monocultures—is unsustainable not just because of prospective rising energy costs, but because it is vulnerable, increasingly subject to loss from pests, and leading to impoverishment of our soil, ground water and wetland resources.[19] Like the Ehrlichs, they advocate a smaller U.S. population. Particularly if population growth drives up domestic demand, we face a daunting prospect: that the United States may eventually stop being a grain exporter. Grain importing nations would suffer immediately. U.S. consumers would eventually feel the pinch, since there are no potential residual grain exporters to replace us.

Something of the same calculus applies to forests. Our per capita supply of standing timber has been declining for decades. We have been able to maintain production through timber farms and the destruction of old growth, but the environmental benefits of timber plantations do not begin to compare with natural stands.

A turn-around in population growth would help deal with these issues; growth through immigration would intensify them.

Option "a" is the lesser evil. If it leads to Mexican prosperity, it may intensify the pressure on U.S. resources in a free trade situation, but it does not directly contribute to U.S. population growth.

Energy. This is a special sub-case of the resource issue. Population growth, particularly in the high-consumption U.S., intensifies the problem as we approach the end of the oil era. With U.S. resources equivalent to about fifteen years' consumption,[20] conservation and the limitation of demand become critically important. We already import half our petroleum, and we cannot afford the foreign exchange to import more. Perhaps the central strategic issue before the country is managing the transition from oil dependence. A smaller population—or slower growth—makes the problem easier. (The Ehrlichs have pointed out that we could do without coal and imported oil, if our population were what it was two generations ago.[21]) There is also a capital crunch coming as we try to pay for the transition to renewable and environmentally benign energy sources. We may need that capital at home rather than trying, as Carla Hills promises, to facilitate its movement to Mexico.

The Government and Congress have not made the population connection. With U.S. population already heading toward a growth this decade of about ten percent, they passed the Immigration Act of 1990, which will raise immigration rates by perhaps one-half, which generates more consumption. It is this kind of tunnel vision that justifies an observer's skepticism as they approach a free trade negotiation.

One argument for the free trade agreement is, in fact, the need to assure access to Mexican oil. This is legitimate, but it is a Band-Aid rather than a solution. Mexican oil resources are thought to be only two-thirds of the United States',[22] which would add about a decade of U. S. consumption—even if they obligingly sold it all to us, which they have made clear they are not about ready to do. They want to support an indigenous petrochemicals industry. The President has yet to learn that he cannot solve fundamental issues with temporization. Let us hope that he does not trade off a permanent demographic liability for that much oil.

Cities and the Quality of Life. The second alternative allowing more migration—is clearly the worse one from the cities' point of view. Faced with deteriorating infrastructures, economies that cannot provide employment for the growing ranks of semiliterate and unskilled youth, with problems of urban violence, drugs and crime, the major cities do not need in-migration of unassimilated poor Hispanics. They need the respite of slower growth of the troubled twenty to twenty-four cohort, which Figure 4 suggests may happen in a generation. Yet those cities are precisely where the immigrants go.[23]

Alternative "a" is less destructive, but hardly desirable. We need the capital at home, if we can find ways of making it productive here.

As to the nation at large: though the amenities provided by uncrowded space are hard to quantify, we are ill served by a trade policy that promotes or accedes to higher immigration rates.

Trade policy should be linked with a national vision of where we want to be heading, in terms of wages, employment, social problems, the environment, resources and a sustainable society. The government has not made those connections, and it resists the suggestion that it begin to do so through an environmental impact statement. Ms. Hills, in response to a question, told a Congressional subcommittee the Government does not plan to do an environmental impact statement (EIS) on the proposed trade negotiations, though they may do some less formal environmental analysis. This is precisely the kind of governmental action that, by law, requires an EIS. Environmental groups have started a lawsuit to require that she go through the EIS process.[24] That would at least be a beginning at cross-sectoral foresight.

TOWARD COMPROMISE

From the demographic aspect, the conclusion seems clear: the proposed free trade agreement threatens a tradeoff of long-term structural change in the U.S. economy and society in exchange for immediate benefits that have been oversold.

We have been a high-wage economy for a long time, and it has fostered technological change and "the American dream" of prosperity in exchange for hard work. It is not a change we should make lightly.

We have every reason to talk with the Mexicans about trade arrangements that will benefit us both, but perhaps we had better look at our own interests, broadly defined, and at our bargaining position. Is an FTA really in the U.S. interest?

The proposal is one-sided. It is justified by "access to a larger market," yet I have pointed out that the meso-American economies together are only six percent as large as ours. On the other hand, the increase in the labor force, which Mexico wants us to help absorb, is much larger than ours, and the disparity is growing.

Mexico needs capital more than American capital needs Mexico.

The putative Mexican energy bonus is evanescent; the U.S. uses a quarter of world production of fossil fuels, and we are going to have to face the energy transition with solutions much more fundamental than a deal with Mexico. The U.S. will need a lot of capital to finance that transition, and a more foresighted president might be less eager to facilitate the export of U.S. capital.

The administration's free-traders are pushing regionalism with excessive zeal. After all, to the free trade faithful, regionalism is a poor second to worldwide free trade. Despite the problems of GATT, is there not still room for a worldwide approach? If we seek to protect U.S. wages, a "wage differential tariff" (analogous to developing countries" "infant industry" tariffs) would provide some protection. It could be set at a level that would enable third world countries to sell us goods with a high labor component, in which they would be most competitive. It might even be a vehicle to enable the U.S. to phase out some objectionable practices such as "voluntary" trade quotas. Tariff policy is a complex area, and I hesitate to tread further, but we seem to be on the way to dismantling the post-World War II trade system in return for a very dubious alternative.

If the Bush administration is determined to push ahead with the proposed regional approach, certain approaches would mitigate the damage:

First, we should not allow "free trade" to be a cover for increased migration. If anything, we should call for closer cooperation to stop illegal immigration. The President of Mexico has been telling American audiences that, if there is no free trade agreement, we will be swamped by illegal Mexican migration.[25] This is very close to blackmail. We do not need to accede to the threat.

We can do much more than we have done to control the border.[26] We could even consider using the Army. It has been used to help control drug smuggling along the border. It could be used for the intimately related problem of illicit movement of people. Border security is one of the most ancient functions of armies.

It is not a prospect that we would gladly embrace. We would be happier if we could preserve relative freedom of movement into and out of the country. If we can find and deport the illegal residents within the country, it becomes much less important to stop would-be illegal entrants at the borders. To achieve that condition, we would need improved ways of identifying people (perhaps by moving to fraud-proof social security cards and a nationally integrated system of birth and death certificates), and we would have to enforce employer sanctions and the rest of our existing immigration laws.[27] All of this, hard-nosed as it may seem, is part of the trade-off we may need to make in an increasingly crowded world, unless we simply decide to go with the flow.

The Mexican President uses the threat of illegal migration only because he is well aware that there are subtle and powerful resistances within the U.S. to any serious effort to stop it. The INS was quietly dissuaded when it proposed the simple expedient of putting up a better fence in the worst smuggling area at Tijuana. Perhaps President Salinas would pull back a bit if he thought we were serious about stopping the traffic.

Second, Mexico already has huge pollution problems, and new uncontrolled factories would add to regional and worldwide pollution. If Mexico is to get more U.S. investment, everybody but the miscreant entrepreneur would gain if we insisted that some way be found to improve and enforce Mexico's pollution laws. We should perhaps call for some form of joint or international factory inspection, with a provision banning exports to the U.S. from non-complying factories.

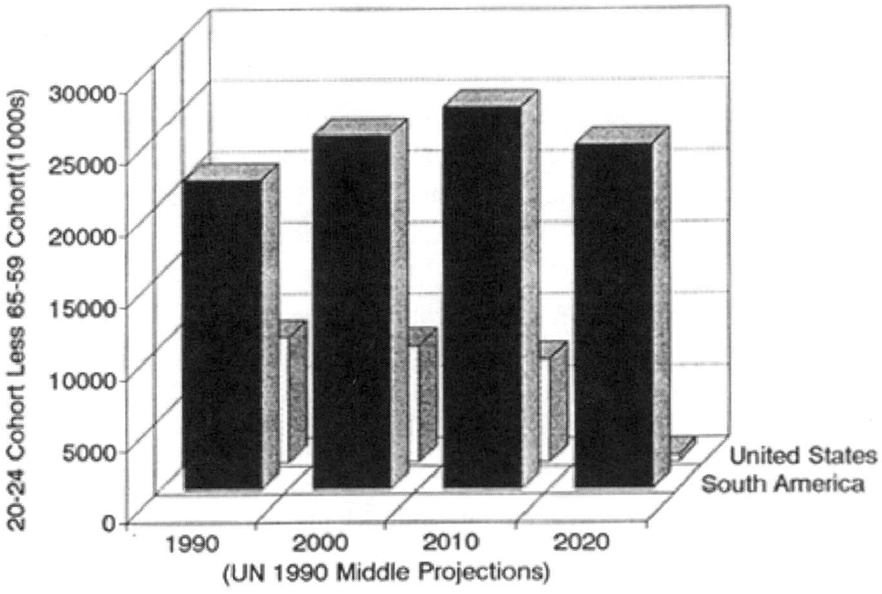

Figure 5.

Finally, the problem is a demographic one, and it should be approached on its own terms. The objections to a free trade zone that I have described would diminish or vanish if our neighbors could control the problems of meso-American population growth and if the United States could reduce the vulnerability that results from its surplus of unemployed, unskilled (and presently untrainable) young people. Population aid is a niggardly 2 percent of our foreign aid budget. It should have top priority and be available to any country that needs and wants and can use it.[28] Domestically, it is hard to envisage a priority higher than bringing our alienated or undisciplined young people into productive roles in society. As part of that effort, we need to turn from the endless battles about abortion to the real task of helping the young control their pregnancies. An unwed, unemployed, untrained young mother does not have much of a future, nor do her children.

CODA

If the advocates of hemispheric free trade believe the demographic problems will be less serious once we start negotiating with the countries south of the Isthmus, let me close with a graph depicting the coming growth of the working age population in South America.

NOTES:

1. See Lindsey Grant, Foresight and National Decisions: *The Horseman and the Bureaucrat*, University Press of America, Lanham, MD, 1988.)
2. John B. Cobb, Jr. and Herman E. Daly, "Free Trade vs. Community: Social and Environmental Consequences of Free Trade in a World with Capital Mobility and Overpopulated Regions," *Population & Environment*, Vol. 11, No. 3, Spring 1990. Aside from Adam Smith and Ricardo, they quote an interesting passage from

John M. Keynes: " . . . let goods be homespun whenever it is reasonably and conveniently possible; and, above all, let finance be primarily national."

3. The *Wall Street Journal* (9-22-89) gave the total as 389,245 in 1988, and the average wage as the equivalent of USSO.8 1. The General Accounting Office (GAO) gives the figure as $1.39 in 1989 (GAO/NSIAS-91-220 U.S. Mexico Trade).
4. Data from Immigration & Naturalization Service Public Affairs Office, Jerry Ficklin, February 2-33-90, *U.S. Statistical abstract 1989*, Table 642, and *New York Times* 11-12-89.
5. Quoted by Thomas R. Donahue, Secretary-Treasurer, AFL-CIO, in testimony 2-6-91 before the Committee on Finance, U.S. Senate.
6. Testimony before the Subcommittee on Trade, House Committee on Ways and Means, 2-20-91.
7. Prof. Rudiger Dombusch, quoted in the *Wall Street Journal*, 4-11-91.
8. Michael Kingsley in the *Washington Post*, 3-14-91.
9. Bureau of Labor Statistics, *Employment & Earnings* January 199 1, p. 170. The data are for civilians not enrolled in school.
10. "The Likely Impact on the United States of a Free Trade Agreement with Mexico." U.S. International Trade Commission, Washington, February 1991, p. 2–5.
11. See John R. Weeks, *How to Influence Fertility: The Experience So Far* (NPG Forum paper, Negative Population Growth, Inc., Teaneck NJ, 1990.)
12. In the U.S., employment arose about 2.3 million/year in the 1970S and 2.0 million/year in the 1980s (Bureau of Labor Statistics, *Employment & Earnings*, January 1990.) As Table 3 shows, the meso-America working age population, most of whom are assumed to need jobs, will rise 2.6 to 2.8 million annually for the next three decades.
13. Estimates have been attempted of the total investment, including infrastructure, nec to generate one job, but they are notoriously difficult. The $200 billion figure assumes a cost of $80,000 per job and employment for everybody twenty to sixty-four. At one quarter of that figure, $50 billion is a very conservative guess indeed.
14. Figure 4 data are from personal communication from Dr. Leon F. Bouvier. They are drawn from projections made for his forthcoming book *Peaceful Invasions* (University Press of America, Lanham, MD; forthcoming late 1991.) Unlike available UN and U.S. Census Bureau projections, they reflect current fertility and migration levels.
15. See NPG Forum paper by Vernon M. Briggs, Jr., *Political Confrontation with Economic Reality: Mass Immigration in the Post-Industrial Age* (Negative Population Growth, Inc., Teaneck NJ, 1990.) See also Lindsey Grant, *The Kingdom of the Deaf* from the same publisher, 1991.
16. Robert J. Samuelson, "Mexico's Initiative," in the *Washington Post*, June 20, 1991.
17. For alternative projections of the demographic results of fertility levels at 1.8, 2.0 and 2.2, and of net immigration levels from zero to 2 million, see Leon F. Bouvier, *The Impact of Immigration on U.S. Population Size*, Population Reference Bureau, Washington DC, 1981. NPG Forum essay *Sustainable Immigration: Learning to Say No* by David M. Simcox, discusses immigration and population, though the fertility assumptions have been overtaken.
18. NPG Forum article *The Most Overpopulated Nation*. January 1991.
19. NPG Forum paper *Land, Energy and Water. The Constraints Governing Ideal U.S. Population Size*, 1989.

20. U.S. Geological Survey, *Estimates of Undiscovered Conventional Oil and Gas Resource in the United States—A Part of the Nation's Energy Endowment*, U.S. Government Printing Office, 1989.
21. See NPG Forum paper *The Most Overpopulated Nation*. Extensive discussions of the implications of the energy transition are contained in NPG Forum papers *Land, Energy and Water* (op cit), *Balancing Humans in the Biosphere: Escaping the Overpopulation Trap*, by Robert Costanza, and *Energy and Population: Transitional Issues and Eventual Limits*, by Paul J. Werbos.
22. For authoritative recent estimates of worldwide petroleum and gas reserves and resources, see C.D. Masters, D.H. Root and E.D. Attanasi, "Resource Constraints in Petroleum Production Potential." Science 7-12-91.
23. For a discussion of the merits and disadvantages of megalopolis, see NPG Forum paper *Optimal City Size and population Density for the 21st Century*, by Alden Speare, Jr., and Michael J. White. 1990.
24. The groups are Friends of the Earth (FOE), Public Citizen and the Sierra Club. FOE news release 8-1-91.
25. *Los Angeles Times*, April 13 and 22, 1991.
26. The Federation for American Immigration Reform (FAIR), for instance, published a study as to how to achieve better enforcement, advised by retired Border Patrol officers. See *Ten Steps to Securing America's Borders*, FAIR, Washington DC, January 1989.
27. For a discussion of techniques to control illegal immigration, see the NPG Forum article *Sustainable Immigration: Learning to say No*, by David Simcox, 1991.
28. See NPG Forum Paper *A Population Focus for U.S. Aid* by Lindsey Grant, 1987.

OIL, EGYPT AND ISRAEL: THE VIEW IN 1995

Lindsey Grant

April 1991

SCENARIO

I recently had reason to construct the following grim and hypothetical scenario for a naval strategic studies group. The scenario, ostensibly, is written in February 1995. Under the group's ground rules, Saddam Hussein has been eliminated but little progress has been made on the Israel-Palestine issue, and peace in the Gulf region is still "fragile." Here goes.

> *1. Egypt's population has risen from 37 to 63 million in just twenty years. The stagnation in domestic food output that became apparent in the 1980s has intensified. Aside from making Cairo virtually unlivable, urban growth has continued to encroach on farmlands. Arable acreage is being reduced by erosion, and farm productivity by the loss of nutrients. Both are consequences of the construction of the Aswan Dam, which blocked the annual flooding of the Nile. Egypt depends on imports, including PL 480, for most of its foodgrains. Even in the mid-1980s, Egypt's total exports covered less than half its imports, and 70 percent of those exports were petroleum products. As anticipated, Egypt's limited petroleum resources declined quickly, and since 1992 Egypt has been a net importer of petroleum. Remittances from Egyptians working in the Persian Gulf states have never returned to their pre-1990 level. Egypt has in effect no way to compete in the commercial market to import food for its rising population.*
>
> *2. Worldwide grain stocks began to decline to dangerously low levels between 1987and 1989. There was a temporary reprieve, resulting principally from bumper North American grain harvests. In 1994, however, the U.S. crop was less than the bad year of 1988, and for the second time in history (the first was in 1988) the U. S. consumed more grain than it produced. A dry winter has generated concerns that even U.S. reserves may become dangerously low in 1995.*
>
> *3. The U.S. balance of payments has worsened, primarily as a result of increasing petroleum imports. Imports reached 5O percent of U.S. consumption in 1991 and have risen as domestic production has declined. The U.S. Geological Survey estimated in 1989 that the U.S. then had only sixteen years' current consumption levels of reserves and exploitable resources, and the projection has proven regrettably prophetic. Annual crude oil production in the United States has been declining about 10 percent per year since 1990, and imports now account for about two-thirds of total consumption.*

4. European import requirements have also been rising with the decline of the North Sea oil fields and the East European search for suppliers to replace the Soviet Union, whose production decline started in the late 1980s and has been worsened by the continued political turmoil in that country.

5. Rising petroleum prices are leading U.S. consumers to economize on petroleum and to shift to other fuels, but the Government as of February 1995 had not taken steps to encourage the trend. Population growth in the United States has tended to increase the demand for energy. Because of the rise in women's fertility since 1989 and the increased rate of immigration that resulted from the Immigration Act of 1990, the U. S. population is growing at a rate of about 12 percent in this decade, which makes the problem of petroleum supplies that much harder.

6. A mounting crisis of confidence is generated by the triple problems of declining grain reserves, an uncertain and higher cost energy supply, and the foreign trade deficit. Foreign investors begin to move their liquid capital out of the country. The U.S. Government announces a reduction in foreign aid, a suspension of PL 480, and a policy of licensing grain exports to assure domestic grain stocks.

7. In Cairo, the government is forced to reduce the subsidized bread sales. Food riots topple the government, which is replaced by a fiery, Khomeini-style Moslem fundamentalist demagogue named Abdallah. Unlike Khomeini, however, Abdallah is a Sunni and an Arab, and he rapidly becomes the charismatic rallying point for fundamentalists and mullahs throughout the Arab world. In the disorders that ensue, terrorists succeed in cutting Saudi oil exporting capability by one-third. The leaders in Iraq, Syria and most other Moslem countries feel compelled to express their support for Abdallah, in order to save their skins. He declares a holy war against Israel.

8. These changes generate an unexpected reverberation in the United States. It had already become clear that Blacks were increasingly separating into two very distinct streams: those who were making it in the general society and tended to identify with it; and the poor ghetto Blacks who were increasingly isolated and hostile. The problems were reflected in the statistics: in 1989 less than 62 percent of young black males twenty to twenty-four years of age were in school or had full-time jobs. The figure for their white counterparts was 76 percent. About half the U.S. prison population was Black, though Blacks constituted only 12 percent of the general population. The situation has been worsening since then as rising immigration has crowded poor Blacks out of the entry-level jobs to which they might aspire, and as their population has grown much faster than the country as a whole. (The poor and uneducated tend to be about twice as fertile as the prosperous and educated. This is a matter of class, not race. Black and white fertility are roughly the same if adjusted for income or education. It is simply that more blacks are poor and uneducated.)

Out of this ferment has emerged considerable support for the Black Moslem movement. The influence extends into the ranks of black enlisted men, though it is counteracted in some degree in the military services by a sense of belonging and of purpose. The upshot, however, is that, when Abdallah announces his crusade, about one-third of the black members of one crack U. S. Army division sign a pledge that they will not go to war against fellow Moslems on behalf of Israel. The army faces the difficult question of how to handle this massive, spontaneous outpouring of feeling.

I did not attend that futures game run by the Navy strategic planning group. I don't know whether they took on my scenario, or how they handled it. In any event, let me congratulate them. They are asking the right questions, and that is not a common habit.

WHY THE SCENARIO?

This scenario sounds like the vision of a man who enjoys inventing nightmares. Is it likely to happen? Almost certainly not—at least not in just that way. But all the data for 1990 and earlier are taken from published sources, mostly from U.S. Government statistics. The trend projections for the 1990s are reasonable extrapolations from those data, though of course the confluence of the trends into the "events" of 1995 is hypothetical.

I could have made it worse. I could have created a revolt in Mexico against the political stranglehold of the PRI, and sent a million refugees across the border to add to our problems and our population and, particularly, to intensify the job competition for the urban Blacks.

The scenario was meant to be scary. It was designed to make the point that the circumstances that created Saddam Hussein have not gone away. There will be other Saddam Husseins.

The scenario was meant to dramatize the interplay of demographic and environmental forces with the more conventional elements of "national security." Security does not consist simply of troop numbers, weapons inventories or dazzling military technology. It rests upon things as disparate as a stable agricultural base, a sustainable environment, skilled and contented populaces both here and abroad, and a reasonable world balance between population and resources. These are the foundations on which the superstructures of prosperity, such as an orderly world trading system, are laid. When men make inadvertent changes in their environment, such as the consequences generated by the Aswan Dam, it is not simply a matter of concern to environmentalists.

And the principal destabilizing force that has upset those balances has been the unparalleled population growth of the past few decades, accompanied by technical transformation and sustained by levels of energy use unimaginable in earlier generations.

EGYPT

Why is this important? Because, judged in these terms, Egypt is very badly out of balance, and so is the United States. As the man said, where there is no vision the people perish. The growing desperation of the Egyptian situation has been apparent for years—for decades. The United States, committed to Egypt because of Egypt's toleration of Israel, tried to put off the day of reckoning by adopting a very American makeshift: throw money at it. U.S. bilateral aid to Egypt was only about $34 million annually in the 1950s, was terminated and resumed, and rose to over $2 billion annually following the Camp David accords.

The aid helps Egypt cover its food and foreign exchange deficits, but the deficits keep going up because of population growth, and the aid does not. It has been flat for a decade—and declining in real terms—because of U.S. budget problems.

Egypt is in a bind. Acreage in cereals peaked in 1954. Present acreage is substantially what it was before World War II. Yields are very good indeed—more than twice those before World War 11. But there were 16 million Egyptians then. Egypt produced 246 kilograms of grain per capita then; it produced only 170 kilograms in 1987 (the latest official figures.) After getting almost back to the pre-War level in 1970, the trend since then has been irregularly but ineluctably downward. Who will feed them?

Egypt, which was a net exporter of cereals before World War II, imported more than 5 million tons in 1980 and 9 million by 1987. That year, they imported more than half the cereals they ate. There was a slight drop in 1988—preliminary data show that 1988 and 1989 were good years; but the noose has been tightening. And yet on this shaky base we have built our Middle Eastern policy.

Presidents Sadat and Mubarak have both recognized the need for population limitation but, judging by Egypt's fertility rate, nothing has been achieved. We could have helped Egypt more if we had done more to help them control the demographic engine that has driven their worsening situation. This would not be easy, given the bureaucratic and social resistances, but the alternative is to run a race that we are certain to lose.

In fact, in the past fifteen years, far less than one percent of our bilateral aid to Egypt has gone to family planning. The Reagan administration, bogged down in ideology, once tried to zero out all assistance for foreign family planning programs. If such assistance still exists in our foreign aid program, it is because of Congress.

THE UNITED STATES

To shift back from 1995 to 1991, and from Egypt's problems to ours: Make no mistake. The Kuwait crisis has been about oil. It is not altruism that leads the United States to mount its expensive white horse and charge off to save distant feudal principalities from neighboring dictators. We embarked upon that risky and uncertain adventure because two-thirds of remaining world petroleum reserves are in the Persian Gulf area, and because the U.S. administration viscerally perceives the danger if all those reserves are brought under the control of one unfriendly despot.

As I said, there will probably be other Saddam Husseins. The stakes are too large, and the region too unstable, for us to face an increasing dependency with any confidence in the reliability of the supply. And even Arab oil is not forever. With respect to oil, we are in much the position that the Egyptians are with food—except that, fortunately, there are substitutes for oil.

The question is: why didn't we think ahead? Our Middle Eastern and our energy policies, and what passes for an immigration policy, are misbegotten monuments to a perhaps fatal penchant for ad hoc improvisation.

In 1956, a geologist named M. King Hubbert projected that U.S. domestic oil production would peak about 1970. He was widely considered a crank, of course, but sometime in the mid-1970s, after the first "oil shock" and when Hubbert's projections were proving scarily prophetic, a responsible U.S. administration should have waked up to the point: more than Vietnam, or Panama, or Grenada, or UNCTAD, or the emergence of Eastern Europe, or a hundred other passing issues which absorb us from time to time, the management of the transition away from reliance upon petroleum is arguably one of the three (or perhaps two) principal strategic issues of our time. (The second is the avoidance of ecological catastrophe; the third was or perhaps is the nuclear weapons issue.)

President Carter tried to address the energy problem with his ill-fated synfuels proposal. He probably chose the wrong vehicle, and we now recognize that arriving at a reliable energy supply during the petroleum transition will require a much more complex balancing of demand (population and per capita consumption), new sources and technologies and environmental considerations. At least he tried. Do you remember "MEOW," the Moral Equivalent of War?

Are we even trying, now? No. The prevailing wisdom apparently is "business as usual; the American people don't want to hear tough news." Perhaps the politicians are right, and we should not put all the blame on them. Nevertheless, there should come a time when even the most political of leaders recognizes that leaders sometimes should lead.

For years, President Reagan stalled the timetable for increasing automobile efficiency. I do not believe any politician has suggested that we induce energy conservation and the development of new energy sources by incrementally multiplying petroleum (or perhaps "pollution") taxes, to bring them into line with the rest of the industrial world (other than Canada). Instead, our Department of Transportation labored for months and in early 1990 proposed a "transportation plan" that gave no sign that the Department had ever heard of EPA or the Geological Survey, of atmospheric pollution or the "greenhouse" or the increasingly chancy petroleum future. At DOT, it is business as usual and more highways, apparently, forever.

The Department of Energy has developed an energy plan, reportedly under very close White House tutelage. Since the draft was written after the Kuwait crisis, it recognized—as the DOT plan did not—that we have a problem of oil supply. The draft is remarkably unimaginative. The proposals: more of the same. Open up the Arctic National Wildlife Refuge to oil drilling. More deregulation for oil and gas, and tighter rules to make it harder for citizen groups to derail nuclear power plants. No new gas tax. No new mileage standards. Very little on efficiency. Very little about new and benign energy; and of course nothing about population, which is the fundamental determinant of how big the problem is. Clearly, the President still believes that the supply is infinite, and it is just a matter of getting it out. The experts, including the oil industry, know better. The head of the Petroleum Industry Research Foundation remarked to the press that increased imports are inevitable; the proposals might just slow it slightly.

With this sort of governmental thinking, my scenario is looking better and better.

THINKING AHEAD

The "business as usual approach" not only promises failure in addressing the immediate problem of diminishing oil supplies. It misses the opportunity to address a whole series of problems together: air pollution and "greenhouse" effect; the foreign trade and budget deficits. The nation could have tackled all these problems with a broad approach focussed on conservation, benign energy technologies, and the control of the problem by controlling the demand side: population growth.

If we dared to bring that population aspect into our planning, we would also be addressing two other major issues of our time: the breakdown of the cities; and the state of U.S. education. With a sterner view of immigration, we could slow urban growth and reduce the competition for jobs that is leading young Blacks to drop out of the labor force. With a "two child" policy on fertility, we could begin to slow down the increase in the size of the problem. With smaller cohorts, perhaps we would be in a better position to educate the young and bring them into the mainstream.

As a society, we are still a long way from the state of mind that would encourage the government to advocate a conscious fertility policy—even though from time to time we urge such social engineering on third world countries.

Even so, did we have to exacerbate the problem by increasing immigration rates in the Immigration Act of 1990?

If we do not learn to tie such issues together, we will worsen the problems in one area of the society as we make decisions in other areas.

The problem is a lack of foresight—an inability or unwillingness to make the connections between the issues we face. I have discussed the problem in the previous issue of the Forum and elsewhere (see Notes.) I will not belabor it here.

I do not pretend that by recognizing the issues we will make the irresolution easy. What I propose is simply that we can do a lot better than we are doing if we take cognizance of the connections and bring population, resource and environmental issues systematically into planning about national security and the other issues that we now address piecemeal.

Whatever the machinery, the government's leaders must find a way of connecting national security with the underlying forces that affect it, or they may find, belatedly and after much expense and anguish, that they cannot go where they thought they wanted to go. If they do not put it together and find a way to escape from ad hoc and catch-up decision making, the Kuwait exercise is only a foretaste of the price we will pay for the failure to look ahead.

I wish us luck.

NOTES:

1. For a detailed discussion of the methods and history of foresight, and proposals for foresight machinery in the U.S. Government, see Lindsey Grant *Foresight and National Decisions: The Horseman and the Bureaucrat* (Lanham, MD: University Press of America, 1988.) A brief discussion of the failure of foresight in dealing with current issues, and of the foresight machinery in the White House, is in "The Kingdom of the Deaf," the concluding essay in the NPG Forum series on optimum population.
2. Sources used in this paper include the United Nations Food & Agriculture Organization (FAO), *1948–85 World Crop & Livestock Statistics* (Rome: FAO 1987), and various FAO *Production Annuals* and *Trade Annuals* from 1950–1989. Plus the World Resources Institute *World Resources 1990–1991* (New York: Oxford University Press, 1991); U.S. Department of Labor *Employment & Earnings, January 1990.* (Washington: USGPO, 1990); U.S. Agency for International Development (AID) *U.S. Overseas Loans and Grants*, and Assistance from International Organizations: Obligations and Loan Authorizations, July 1, 1945—September 30,1985; Duff Gillespie et al *Egypt Population Assessment: A Report for USAID/Cairo* (Report No. 89-040-082, March 17, 1989, Dual and Associates, Inc., and International Science and Technology Institute, Inc., 1601 North Kent Street, Arlington VA 22209); *Countries of the World 1986* (Gale Research Company, Book Tower, Detroit MI 48226); *New York Times*, February 9 and 10, 1991; and personal communications from the U.S. Department of State, U.S. AID, and the Petroleum Information Corporation, Houston, TX.

POPULATION AND THE "EIS"

Joseph J. Brecher

May 1991

Population was the first issue to be mentioned in the "Declaration of National Environmental Policy" (Title I of NEPA, the National Environmental Policy Act of 1969.) And yet, when it came time to draft the regulations to enforce that law, population was inexplicably demoted to an indirect or "secondary" impact. Because of that change of focus, population has seldom figured in the environmental impact statements (or EIS) that were mandated by NEPA.

The population aspect of a decision is frequently the aspect with the most profound implications, even when that impact was not an intended result. The interstate highway system provides an example. Because of NEPA, EIS have regularly been prepared for construction of those highways. They have dealt usually with such issues as the filling of a wetland. The completion of each section has, however, usually had much vaster ramifications. It changes the economy of its area—not just because of the cluster of motels and service stations at the interchanges—but because industries and populations come with the Interstate, like Brazilian peasants following a new logging road. That effect is more or less predictable, and it is just such effects that the EIS should examine.

The environmental community is coming to understand the fundamental connection between population change and ecological impacts. As a rough rule of thumb, it is fair to say that—at any given level of consumption and technology—the environmental impact of any activity is roughly proportional to the population being served.

Recognizing the connection, eighteen of the principal environmental groups in the country, in a concerted "Blueprint for the Environment" delivered in late 1988 to President-elect Bush, called for the Council on Environmental Quality to amend its regulations to provide "for the consideration of population growth and other socio-economic impacts of federal programs and actions." (Recommendation EOP-18)

It is time to get on with that proposal. It is hard to imagine any other single change in U.S.Government regulations that would do so much to force the nation to look at the population implications of what it is doing, and to consider how induced population change might affect the quality of life in specific places and times. Armed with such analysis, the "NIMBYs" of the nation—the local groups fighting uncontrolled growth in their own backyards—would have a powerful new tool to require policy makers to look at the implications of what they are doing.

With this thought in mind, we asked Joseph Brecher to provide us with a brief as to the legal justification for another concerted effort at persuading the government to change its regulations so as to do what the law told it to do, in the first place. Mr. Brecher is an attorney in private practice in Oakland CA, specializing in environmental law. Before establishing his practice in 1975, he worked for the Native American Rights Fund.

We hope that organizations trying to deal with the chaotic by-products of population-associated growth will find the brief of use and will consider acting upon it.

—Lindsey Grant, Editor

INTRODUCTION

Almost any kind of development usually induces population growth. Construction of a relatively small infrastructure project in an undeveloped area may cause limited environmental impact, in and of itself, but it often serves as the opening wedge for a tidal wave of development that surges in behind it. This results in profound changes in an area extending far beyond the scope and boundaries of the original project.

Although the law recognizes this problem, the existing legal mechanisms do not adequately deal with this important question. Instead, it is shunted off to second-class status under the rubric of "indirect" or "secondary" impacts. Until the applicable agencies develop procedures to analyze induced population growth, the public and the decision-makers will be approving projects blindly, unaware of the true costs that will inevitably have to be paid down the road. This paper examines the current state of the law in this area and suggests a course of action for remedying the situation.

THE ROLE OF NEPA

The National Environmental Policy Act (NEPA) is the nation's most important environmental statute, creating a duty for all federal agencies to give serious consideration to the environmental impacts of projects they approve or carry out. NEPA recognizes the importance of the issue of population and growth. Forty-two U.S.C. [8]331(a) notes "the profound influences of population growth [and] high-density urbanization . . ." All federal agencies are required to "use all practicable means . . . to . . . achieve a balance between population and resource use which will permit high standards of living and a wide sharing of life's amenities . . ." Forty-two U.S.C. [8]4331(b)(5).

Despite this strong statutory language on the need to control population growth and new urbanization, the issue is rarely broached under NEPA. When population growth is made an issue, with a few exceptions, the courts have ruled that the subject need not be given serious attention. This unfortunate situation can be attributed to the inadequacy of the Council on Environmental Quality's regulation in this area. The following sections discuss the regulation and its interpretation in the courts, and recommends a course of action to rectify the situation.

THE CEQ REGULATION

The Council on Environmental Quality (CEQ) is authorized to issue binding guidelines for the implementation of NEPA. See Executive Order No. 11514, May 24, 1977, Section 3(h); *National Indian Youth Council v. Watt* (10th Cir. 1981) 664 F.2d 220.

The CEQ Guidelines deal with the population issue in an unfortunate manner. The definition of the term "effects" is divided into two parts at forty C.F.R. [8]1508.8. "Direct" effects "are caused by the action and occur at the same time and place." "Indirect effects" include

> growth inducing effects and other effects related to induced changes in the pattern of land use, population density or growth rate, and related effects on air and water and other natural systems, including ecosystems.

This arbitrary division into "primary" and "secondary" impacts, which is not sanctioned by the statutory language, is probably the main reason the courts have been reluctant to take the issue of induced population growth seriously.

NEPA IN THE COURTS

There have been approximately one dozen cases which put major emphasis on the population issue in the context of NEPA. They present a very mixed bag. The following sections describe the various approaches the courts have adopted.

A. *Favorable cases.* The strongest and most often cited case favoring a serious analysis of population growth impacts is *City of Davis v. Coleman* (9th Cir. 1975) 521 F.2d 661. In that case, federal and state highway authorities proposed to build a freeway interchange near Davis, California without filing an Environmental Impact Statement (EIS) or a California Environmental Impact Report (EIR). Instead, they issued a Negative Declaration, claiming that there would be no significant environmental impacts. The court noted that the purpose of the interchange was "to stimulate and service future industrial development in the Kidwell area . . ." Environmentalists argued that, aside from failing to prepare an EIS, the highway authorities had also erred by refusing to consider the growth-inducing impacts of the interchange.

The proceedings were governed by 23 U.S.C. [8]128, which requires highway authorities to hold a hearing and consider "the total impact of the project as a whole . . ." See *Lathan v. Brinegar,* 506 F.2d 677, 690. The implementing regulations for [8]128 provided that the highway departments are to consider direct "and indirect benefits or losses to the community and to highway users," including regional and community growth, conservation and preservation including general ecology, public facilities and utilities, "community cohesion including residential and neighborhood character and stability, and displacement of people, businesses and farms."

The court noted that the Negative Declaration discussed only the "primary" environmental impacts of the interchange but not the "secondary" or "indirect" impacts, such as population effects. The court noted these effects were dismissed as "speculative" and "uncertain." The court responded sternly: "This will not do." It continued:

> The purposes of [8]128, as amplified by NEPA, are ill-served by rigid bifurcation of potential social, economic and environmental effects into those which are "primary" or "direct" and those which are "secondary" or "indirect." 521 F.2d at 680.

The court criticized the Negative Declaration for leaving a large number of questions unanswered: it did not discuss "probable impact on growth, land use or the planning process." In addition, there was no estimate of the increased demand for city services which would be occasioned by increased population and no discussion of the possible impacts on community cohesion and the tax base. All these matters should have been considered, the court ruled. 521 F.2d at 680–81.

In *Coalition for Canyon Preservation v. Bowers* (9th Cir. 1980) 632 F.2d 774, the plan was to widen a narrow highway into a major four-lane facility, including parking lanes, in a number of small tourist towns near Glacier National Park in Montana. The court ruled that the EIS on the project should have analyzed "secondary impacts such as growth, land-use development, and social and economic activities." 632 F.2d at 782.

The court noted: "Although treatment of secondary impacts is not a specific requirement of an impact statement, the central focus is on those impacts, both primary and secondary, that have a 'significant impact' on the environment." 632 F.2d at 783. Speaking of the small towns that would be connected by the upgraded highway, the court noted that "tourism is their main source of income and roadside businesses are common. It is likely that this project will have major effects on the character of these towns. This case requires analysis of these secondary effects. The subject was not addressed in the EIS." 632 F.2d at 774.

Another case which endorses the study of population impacts in an EIS is *McDowell v. Schlesinger* (W.D. Mo. 1975) 404 F.Supp. 221. In that case, the court ruled that the Department of Defense would have to prepare an Environmental Impact Statement on a plan to move and close certain military facilities. The court acknowledged that the major impacts asserted by the plaintiffs were "secondary" social and economic impacts, "as contrasted to direct impacts on the ecology." 404 F.Supp. at 244. However, the court noted, concerns such as impact on population are specifically set forth in NEPA, forty-two U.S.C. [8]4331(a) and the Guidelines' definition of secondary impacts. 404 F.Supp. at 244–45.

In addition, the court relied on Department of Defense regulations which specified that the Department give close environmental scrutiny to mission changes and troop developments "which precipitate long-term population increases or decreases in any area, with special attention to the secondary impacts which may cause indirect environmental impact." 32 C.F.R. [8]214.7(d)(7). See 404 F.Supp. at 246.

On the basis of these authorities, the court concluded that "NEPA's ambit extends to the effects of proposed action on neighborhood cohesiveness and character, population density, crime control, and aesthetic considerations." 404 F.Supp. at 246.

B. *Unfavorable cases.* Despite the few beacons of light described above, most courts have concluded that an EIS need not discuss population impacts of development. The courts have offered two principal reasons to support these holdings. First, some cases have held that if there is no direct, primary effect on the environment, secondary impacts need not even be considered. This was the ruling in *Image of Greater San Antonio v. Brown* (5th Cir. 1978) 570 F.2d 517, 522. There, the issue was the effect of moving 1,200 civilian employees away from an Air Force base. The court noted that the plaintiffs alleged no physical effects on the environment. In its view, "the primary concern [of NEPA] was with the physical environmental resources of the nation." It continued as follows:

> *We do not mean to say that socio-economic effects can never be considered under NEPA. When an action will have a primary impact on the natural environment, secondary socio-economic effects may also be considered. [Citations.] But when the threshold requirement of a primary impact on the physical environment is missing, socio-economic effects are insufficient to trigger an agency's obligation to prepare an EIS. 570 F.2d at 522.*

This holding was followed in *Monarch Chemical Works, Inc. v. Exon* (D. Neb. 1979) 466 F.Supp. 639. There, the chemical company claimed an EIS should have been prepared when the City decided to condemn vacant land for a correctional facility. The company was trying to acquire the same land to expand its own facilities. The company said the City should have considered "induced changes in patterns of land usage, the population density . . . and the socio-economic consequences of the construction of a prison upon industrial and commercial growth." 466 F.Supp. at 655.

As in *Greater San Antonio, supra,* the court found that, absent a primary environmental impact, no EIS need be prepared. It distinguished the McDowell case on the ground that a primary impact might have existed there. (Alternatively, the court found that the plaintiffs had failed to show that any of the predicted secondary impacts would, in fact, occur.) 466 F.Supp. at 656–57.

Another reason the courts use for rejecting analysis of population effects is that those impacts are too "speculative" or "remote." For example, in *Trout Unlimited v. Morton* (9th Cir. 1974) 509 F.2d 1276, environmentalists claimed that an EIS on a proposed reservoir should include an analysis of possible second home development at the new lake. The court acknowledged that the failure to discuss that possibility "gives us pause. We agree that the statement could have been improved by a discussion of these issues." 509 F.2d at 1283. But the court concluded that second home development and its consequences "are only remote possibilities." The court accepted the Bureau of Reclamation's conclusion that because the area was now highly developed for agriculture with only a few small towns, "no significant change could be expected either in population or land use patterns." Because there was no specific plan to build second homes, the court could not assume that they would come into being. 509 F.2d at 1284.

Even more discouraging, the *Trout Unlimited* opinion states in a footnote that there might not be *any* requirement to study population impacts at all: "While agreeing that under a given factual situation, failure to include a discussion of secondary impacts might render an EIS fatally defective, we cannot say that a specific treatment of secondary impacts is a substantive requirement of the impact statement. The central focus should not be on a primary/secondary impact analysis but upon those impacts (either primary or secondary) which have a 'significant impact' upon the environment." 509 F.2d at 1283 note 9.

Some unfortunate cases go even further than *Trout Unlimited* in deeming future growth too "speculative" to require analysis. In *Trout Unlimited,* there was no evidence of any specific plan for second homes, at all. But in *Pennsylvania Protect Our Water v. Appalachian Reg. Com'n.,* 574 F.Supp. 1203 (E.D. Pa. 1982), the induced growth effects of a proposed project appeared far more certain. There, the plan was to develop a motel, civic arena, and ski area. Environmentalists sought to require a study of the growth impacts of the development, pointing to an early feasibility study prepared by the landowner for a massive residential development adjacent to the recreation area.

However, the landowner had never proceeded with the residential project, so the court accepted the conclusion in the EIS that future development is "too remote and speculative to discuss in detail." The court found the discussion in the EIS "of secondary growth was minimally acceptable under all the circumstances." 574 F.Sup. at 1236. It distinguished *Coalition for Canyon Preservation* and *Davis v. Coleman* on the ground that "increased and foreseeable development was one of the immediate goals of the projects, which thus required more detailed FEIS consideration." 574 F.Supp. at 1236.

SUMMARY OF THE STATE OF THE LAW

Under the present state of the law, there is only a minimal chance that agencies will give serious consideration to the growth and population impacts of new development. The CEQ regulations are drawn in such a way that they do not clearly require such analysis. By placing population and growth issues in the category of "secondary" impacts, they relegate those issues to a subordinate status, to be discussed only if there exists some other, "primary" impact from a proposed growth-inducing action. Furthermore, growth and population issues need not be analyzed unless the developer or the agency concedes that specific plans for secondary development already exist.

The few cases which *have* required growth and population analysis rely heavily on specific agency policies for implementing NEPA, rather than the weak CEQ Guidelines. It is obvious that the Guidelines, themselves, do not effectively require federal agencies to focus on these crucial issues.

PROPOSAL FOR ACTION

Individuals or groups who are interested in this issue should file a petition with the Council on Environmental Quality, requesting the adoption of a revised Guideline that specifically requires analysis of the growth and population impacts of any development. The specific language of the proposed rule would, of course, have to be crafted with very special attention to detail, so as to avoid loopholes. The petition would be filed under the authority of the Administrative Procedure Act, 5 U.S.C. [8]553(e), which states: "each agency shall give an interested person the right to petition for the issuance, amendment, or repeal of a rule."

Perhaps CEQ would accept the proposal or an acceptable variant. If that agency rejected the petition, the next step would be a petition for review in federal district court for the District of Columbia. As with all efforts to make new law, trying to assess the chances for success in such litigation is difficult. The petitioners could make a convincing showing that Congress meant for population and growth to be studied and that the present Guidelines have not, in fact, resulted in any effective consideration of those issues. On the other hand, the government would point out that CEQ *has* a regulation on the subject already and, although it might not be entirely to our liking, it fulfills the statutory mandate to deal with the issue. This argument, too, has some credibility. Which argument the judge chooses is, in part, the luck of the draw.

In the final analysis, it might be well to proceed as outlined here despite the obvious problems. The petitioners would have two chances to win—before CEQ and in court. The goal of getting meaningful studies of growth and population as part of the NEPA process is important enough to warrant bucking the odds. And even if the petitioners were not victorious, the litigation would publicize and promote discussion of a complex and important issue.

NPG COMMENT

Another point deserves mention. The EIS process simply requires that we look at the implications of what we are doing. It does not mandate a given policy. Others may very well hold different views from NPG's as to desirable population size and yet agree that the question needs to be looked at, in the context of specific projects and programs.

On the matter of "programs": since NEPA began, the government has been much better about doing EIS on limited and concrete projects like highway bridges than on the broader programs that drive them. There are EIS on individual timber concessions from National Forests, but none on the broader decision to accelerate cutting, including much of the remaining old growth in the Northwest. There are EIS on specific oil leases, but not on energy policy. If, at the same time that we try to bring the government to open its eyes to the population connection, we could persuade it to do EIS on the really big decisions, we would have a better governmental decision process.

NPG believes that the proposal in this paper should be pursued and hopes to cooperate with others to bring it about.

WHAT WE CAN LEARN FROM THE MISSING AIRLINE PASSENGERS

Lindsey Grant

November 1992

The passenger manifests of airplanes flying into and out of the United States provide disturbing indications that immigration may be running at a substantially higher level than is generally supposed. If it is, the present estimate of U.S. population and the Census projections for the future are all brought into question. If our population in fact, is bigger than the statistics show, the discrepancy may point to an unrecognized source of problems like urban unrest and fallen wages. If the data from the manifests are faulty, the country is failing to use one of the few potentially solid sources of information concerning the scale of illegal migration.

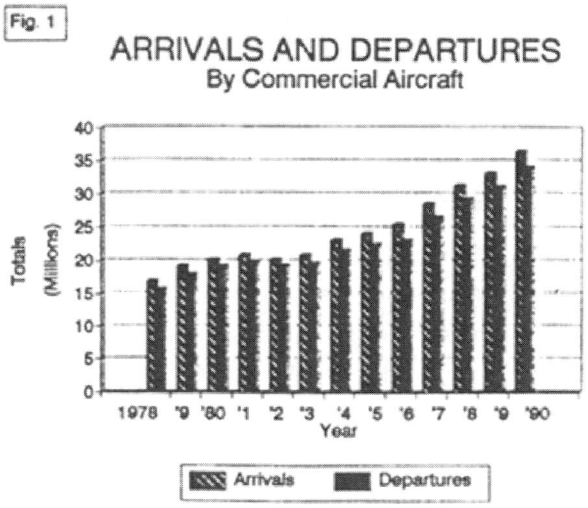

THE EVIDENCE IN THE MANIFESTS

Last year, two very wise commentators discussed the idea that anomalies—the things that don't fit comfortable into our view of the nature of reality—may point the way to the next stage of understanding.[1] They took their examples from astronomy, geology and biology. One might well start with the more mundane example of the aircraft manifests.

To begin with the facts—

All commercial and private aircraft entering or leaving the country are required to submit summaries of their passenger manifests (Form I-92), along with the individual arrival/departure forms (I-94) that are required of arriving and departing aliens. These are collected by the Immigration and Naturalization Service (INS), and the summaries are processed by a contractor for the Department of Transportation (DOT). The data are not published, but they are available.[2] The traffic now exceeds 30 million annually in each direction. The totals since 1978 are showed in Figure 1 and the net excess of arrivals over departures is highlighted in Figure 2.

Figure 1.

Cutting through the confusion about immigrant vs. non-immigrant vs. American, the second graph shows that about one to two million more people fly into the U.S. each year than fly out—and the number has been rising. Remember, this is just commercial and private air traffic; it says nothing about land arrivals and clandestine movements by land or air or sea. The popular image of illegal immigration is of Mexicans or

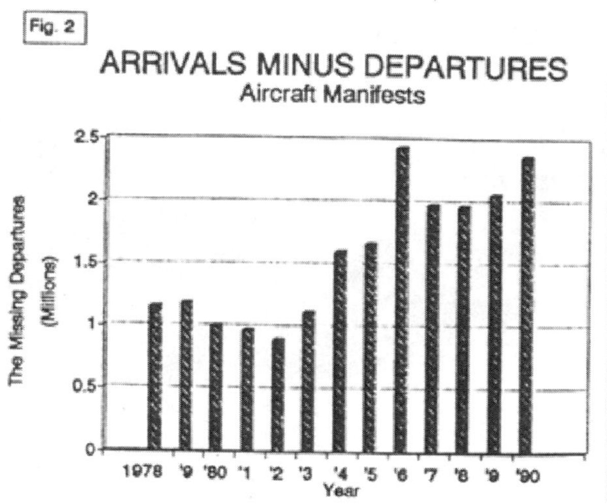

Figure 2.

Central Americans running across our land border, or of Cubans and Haitans in tiny boats. Even Census Bureau efforts to estimate the total numbers of "undocumented aliens" (as the delicately call them) has focused on Mexian migration by land. Here is another ball game, and a less dramatic one, that has been largely ignored.

We can run the series back for thirty years (Figure 3).[3]

The gap between arrivals and departures has widened from less than four million in the '60s to nearly 16 million in the '80s.

HOW THE EVIDENCE IS GATHERED

The total should be pretty solid for arrivals. Incoming alien passengers are required to fill out Form I-94, and the carriers must complete Form I-92 summary reports. INS itself, collects the I-94 forms.

The data are broken down by region and country, and by "Alien" vs. (U.S.) "Citizens" (resident "aliens" are included in citizens). These breakdowns are of dubious validity, for reasons that will become clear.

Since INS is little interested in departures, it simply asks the carriers to collect the forms in their behalf on outgoing flights, which the carrier may or may not do. The carriers have very compelling operational, legal and financial reasons not to falsify their total payloads, which should therefore be fairly solid. Not so the country-by-country and citizen/alien breakdowns. The carriers are supposed to report them on Form I-92, but in practice they frequently simply submit the total number. The local INS office then tries to reconstruct the breakdowns using the I-94 forms collected from passengers on the flight. Every departing alien whose I-94 form is not turned in is automatically counted as an American. This, says INS, gives "the false impression that many more visitors overstay their period of admission than actually do."[4]

The common wisdom thus is that the failure to collect all the I-94 forms leads to an undercount of departing aliens and an overcount of departing Americans. This would be a convenient way of explaining all those disappearing "visitors," except for one problem: it doesn't explain the overall gap. Even with the alleged overstatement, the statistics show fewer U.S. citizens leaving than arriving, in every decade from the '20s through the '70s, by a

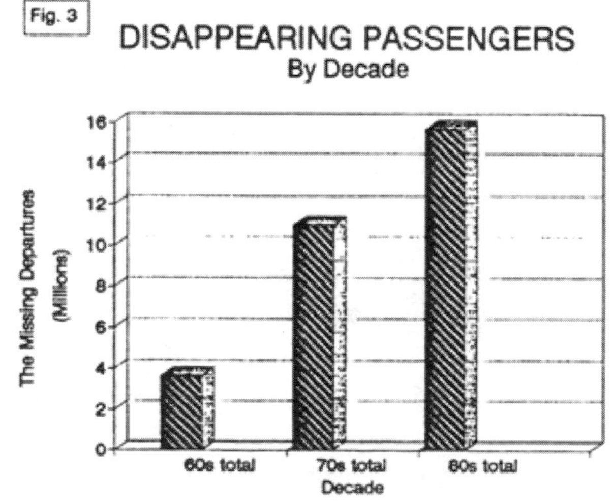

Figure 3.

grand total of over two million.[5] The discrepancy has mounted. In 1990, it was 351 thousand. Over time, this comes close to a mathematical immpossibility. Where do all the incoming "Americans" come from? There aren't that many American citizen babies born overseas. Is the passport fraud business that large?

THE STATISTICAL CONFUSION

By contrast, with the annual gap of over two million in the data from the manifests, the Bureau of the Census uses a figure of 200,000 per year for illegal immigration, most of it by land from Mexico. They started using that figure in 1986. Before that, they had made no allowance for illegal immigration, because they had no good data. Perhaps they changed because they were stung by the charge that they had been "using the only figure that was sure to be wrong." Census statisticians have put the likely total of illegal immigrants in the U.S. between two and four million, while admitting that any estimate of this figure is particularly conjectural. (One key Census report on illegal immigration was described as an effort to "count the uncountable.")[6]

The 1980s debate about the number of illegal immigrants was a response to some very high estimates by government officials, including an INS Commisioner, and I wonder if perhaps the subsequent estimates may have reflected a human impulse to debunk the high guesses and reassert their own statisitcal authority.

The problem is not with the Census Bureau, which is a highly professional organization. It is the lack of basic data. Since illegal immigrants are unlikely to check in unless they are caught, the estimates are neccesarily based on statistical inference rather than direct evidence, and the calculations are based on estimates of residuals, which tend to magnify any inherent errors.

Aside from clandestine border crossers, those who overstay non-immigrant visas are presumably the principal source of unrecorded immigration. INS stopped trying to count emigrants in 1957. In 1980, they stopped collecting the data needed even for an estimate of total emigration.[7] At the same time, they stopped publishing estimates of the rate at which non-immigrant visitors departed the country. Without departure statistics for migrants or non-migrants, the government has little direct evidence on which to calculate net legal migration or clandestine immigration through the second loophole.

During the 1970s, before it stopped reporting them, the INS figures for departing aliens ran far below arrivals, suggesting that a lot of them were simply staying here. (In FY1976, the gap was nearly 2.7 million; in FY1977 it was over 3.2 million.[8]) This was, naturally enough, a source of embarrassment to the INS, and it probably helps to explain the decision to stop publishing the figures.

There are, in short, large and growing holes in the data needed for any estimate of net immigration, legal or illegal.

Quite a mess. Our immigration statistics are bad and getting worse.

In this murk, it would seem prudent to make use of whatever direct information is available, and the figures from passenger manifests should be a principal source.

In the case of movement between the U.S. and Puerto Rico, the Census Bureau in fact has been using the data from air passenger manifests as their principal source—though with considerable misgivings.

CAN THE GAP BE EXPLAINED?

There is a ready explanation for part of the gap between arrivals and departures. Many legal immigrants arrive by air, and are expected to stay. INS compiles unpublished statistics for the ports of entry of each year's immigrants.[9] The data are no longer explicitly broken down between air and land arrivals (legal arrivals by sea are negligible); but one can arrive at an approximate figure for arrivals of immigrants by air, by breaking out the traditional airports of entry. In FY1990, the figure was 365 thousand. The figure will rise as the immigration act of 1990 increases the flow.

In 1990 (Figure 2), the overall gap from the manifests was about 2.4 million. This calculation reduces the unexplained gap to about two million.[10]

There is another, somewhat more obscure, explanation for part of the discrepancy. The official statistics for gross legal immigration were fairly steady, rising from 531 thousand in FY1980 to 643 thousand in FY1988. These figures aren't what they seem. About 1/3 of those "arrivals" are actually "adjustments." In other words, there are people who arrived illegally or stayed illegally in earlier years, and who have managed to get their status legalized. Whether or not they were supposed to be immigrants, they have immigrated, and upon "adjustment" they enter the statistical system. This phenomenon is particularly dramatic right now. The official figure for immigration jumped to 1.09 million in FY1989 and 1.54 million in FY1990, but about half of each of those figures represented legalizations of illegal resident aliens under the 1986 amnesty.

With the data available, there is no way to match the adjustments with their year of arrival, but be it noted that some part of the gap—perhaps something like 100 to 200 thousand per year on a long term basis—is eventually regularized in the immigration statistics.

That is some help, but not much. We must still face an apparent gap approaching nearly two million each year, and growing.

HOW SOLID ARE THE FIGURES FROM THE MANIFESTS?

Some private planes may carry unmanifested passengers from—or more likely to—the U.S. (Anybody who has seen the lineup of executive jets at the airport at Eagle Pass, Texas, a poor little border town, must suspect that there is considerable activity going on that doesn't get into the statistics. Sample radar searches in connection with drug control activities have suggested that there are hundreds of unrecorded flights across U.S. borders daily.) Compared to the scale of the recorded movements, however this movement is unlikely to be statistically important—and, if anything, it probably adds to the net inflow.

Military flights are not covered. They will introduce some element of error, in a period when we had about a half million military personnel and their civilian support staff overseas. Most of those who leave by military aircraft return the same way, but there are exceptions, plus some wives acquired and babies born overseas. Again, however, they are more likely to increase than to decrease the true net inflow.

For the bulk of the traffic—airlines, charters, private planes not breaking the law—I have suggested that the regional and citizen/alien breakdowns are very shaky, but that the overall numbers should be pretty solid. There are probably some transciption errors in typing up the summaries, but it is hard to believe this is an important source of error.[11] I can identify only two significant sources of error:

- Perhaps there is an assymetrical triangular traffic. With many people arriving by direct flights from overseas and then departing by land via Mexico or Canada, and with fewer people running the triangle in the opposite direction. This is an ingenious hypotheses, but not a very convincing one. It could be checked out. However, the U.S. Government does not maintain sufficient records to prove or disprove this hypothesis, and it would be diffficult to sort out such movement from the background noise (there are literally hundreds of millions of land border crossings per year.) There is another variant: the "gap people" may have been leaving by air via Canada since the collect manifests do not cover airtraffic with Canada. Daniel Vining (see Note 3) looked at Canadian airtraffic records and found little support for that hypothesis.

- Departing aircraft (charters, in particular) may perhaps sometimes fail to submit I-92s. This could be an important source of error. Departing aircraft are required by statute to submit passenger manifests, but INS considers the requirement to be met by the submission of any I-94 forms collected. Apparently, neither INS nor DOT has any procedures for checking airport departure logs to assure that the requirement has been met, nor is submission of the I-92 required in order to get airport clearance for departure. They do check Airline Guide to see if a flight was missed. When they find one, they make an estimate (based on samples a decade old), of the number and characteristics of the passengers. This is said to happen in about 15 percent of departures.

We have here another annoying residual. If 3 percent of departing aircraft in 1990 fail to report, it could have lead to a 40 percent error in the apparent gap. It wouldn't take many such failures to explain the gap. This is an important potential source of error and an easily corrected one.

Because of tight budgets, the tabulation of data from the manifests is already nearly two years behind. There apparently is some current dicussion in DOT of doing away entirely with that process, and relying on periodic reports directly to DOT from the airlines. One such system, using the "T-100" form, was instituted in 1990. No data have yet been published. A report on 1990–1991 is in process but I am told it will give only gross traffic totals, not arrivals and departures. DOT considers more detailed information to be confidental. Airline-by-airline data may indeed be privledged information, but the totals in the regional patterens should not, and it may be another useful check.

The question would still arise: how complete are the data? If prior experience is any indicator, a shift to reliance upon the periodic reports would be a backward step. IATA (the International Air Transport Association) collects such data on a voluntary basis, and their own evaluation is that it is not complete enough to be a useful guide to total net flows.[12]

I have suggested that there is a possibility that incomplete reporting of departures could explain some or even all the apparent gap. This is, however, no excuse for ignoring the data from the manifests, as is presently the case. It is one of the few sources of hard data available. If there are errors, they could easily be corrected. There is no substitute for enforcing the law and making the submission of manifests or I-92 summaries a condition for airports' departure clearance.

THE INTRACTABLE GAP

How do the government's statisticians explain the gap? In short: they don't. In a number of conversations with the hands-on technicians, I found most of them puzzled and somewhat embarrassed by it. Since it flies in the face of conventional wisdom, some of them attempt to minimize it, but the explanations do not go beyond the discussion of potential sources of error above.

I myself am overwhelmed at the apparent size of the gap. The experts in Census have the same problem. They point out that so large an influx should turn up in other statistics. Specifically, they argue that there is no sign in the 1990 decennial census count of something like 10–15 million unexpected residents. (They do admit to a probable undercount of about 5 million, some of whom presumably are illegal entrants.) The census numbers, they say, are broadly consistent with what was known about the earlier population, plus recorded births and estimated net immigration, and minus known deaths.

This is all very well, but the argument encounters two serious problems.

The first one, again, is that problem of residuals. Birth and death records in the U.S. are thought to be very good, but no effort is made to match individual births and deaths. Even if there is indeed a large illegal population that does not want to be found, births and deaths among that group would not change the overall data in a way that would make it possible to count them with any precision. (In fact, a larger population base would help to explain the circumstance that our urban birth and death rates seem unusually high, compared with other industrial countries.)

The second problem is related to the first one. The specialists argue that those people must live somewhere, and that the Census Bureau knows where the housing is and would find the inhabitants. This reasoning is questionable for two reasons. For one thing, Census may not know where all the housing is. The traditional definitions are changing. Some years back, the authorities suddenly discovered that many garages in Los Angeles had been covertly converted into rental housing; the people who lived there would be unlikely to volunteer to be counted. Warehouses in New York City are being converted to dormitories, sometimes occupied on the "hot bed" system, where people may occupy a bed in shifts. This practice was long known in—for instance—Hong Kong. Developed in a time of less desperate population pressures, our census system may be behind the curve in recognizing what now constitutes a place to live. The 1990 effort to find the homeless may be the tip of the iceberg. Our cities certainly look a lot more crowded, and with a remarkable variety of racial types and accents, than the Census Bureau's modest 200,000 figure would suggest.

More important is the assumption fundamental to our census system: that people are willing to be counted. In 1990, one-fourth of those people in indentified housing units didn't send in their forms. There is provision for personal follow-up, and there are post-enumeration surveys to test the undercount. There are ingeniously devised, and they succeed in finding some of the people. Still, a person who didn't want to be counted the first time probably doesn't want to be counted the second time. If people are unwilling to open the door, the census counters use "imputation." They assume that the occupants of that unit are identical in number and characteristics to those enumerated in a comparable unit nearby. If the person who responded in that other unit was less than candid, the undercount is simply doubled.

Undercount, apparently, is most serious among Black males. Why? Laws make mores. Our principal welfare program (AFDC) has a "man in the house rule." If there is a male breadwinner, the women and children are not entitled to welfare. This makes it prudent to conceal any evidence of a man's presence, and certainly to avoid telling an official enumerator of any sort that a man lives there. Who is likely to open doors during the daytime in poor neighborhoods? Single welfare mothers, who are not away at work.

If that syndrome works among citizens, how much more powerful it must be for those who live in fear of being sent back to, say, Haiti, or Somalia.

The census is designed by the middle class. I wonder whether many of us understand the visceral urge to stay away from government, except perhaps to apply for welfare, that motivates people who have long been in an uneasy relationship with the law. During the 1990 census, posters blossomed in the poor neighborhoods of Washington D.C., warning people to avoid being counted or they would be drafted. This doesn't make it easy.

Until we are prepared to cordon off sample areas to conduct surprise counts—and I hope that time is far away—this problem will be with us. The present approach will not tell us much about that gap in the manifests.

There remarks are not meant as criticism of the beleaguered Census Bureau. It is forced to work with limited and questionable data. They do very sophisticated demographic analyses, but the analyses are built on a pyramid of assumptions and judgements, and on data sources that are themselves questionable. The cumulative error can become formidable. I hope that the professionals would leap at the chance to spend more time developing hard data, even at the expense of time spent on the theoretical models. In the particular case of the manifests, they haven't leapt yet.

IS IT ALL REALLY THAT IMPORTANT?

In modern societies, relying as they do on statistics, bad data almost insure bad policies. Governments are surprised by urban riots that may be generated in part by worse crowding and more desperate conditions than the official figures—fed by bad immigration data—suggested. Infrastructure investment, the planning for schools, the allocation of funds among the states and cities, all can go awry if they are based on bad data. Our expectations concerning per capita resource use, income, environmental impacts, are all skewed by bad demographic data.

Most important, from my perspective, is the connection between immigration and population. We stand already at 250 million, and current fertility and assumed immigration levels could take us past 500 million within the next century. Immigration constitutes something like half of present growth (depending on how one counts it), and the proportion is rising. This is one of the few issues truly central to our national future, and it is fundamentally important to know whether we really do understand what is happening.

This essay cannot begin to go again over the grounds for believing that such growth is thoroughly bad for us. The arguments have been set forth elsewhere in the NPG Forum series.[13] Perhaps I can summarize it in a well-worn formula:

$$I=PCT$$

The impacts that a society inflicts upon its environment and its resource base (I) are determined by the size of the population (P) times the consumption levels (C), times the technology coefficient (T). (The equation is really a rule of thumb. It does not account for thresholds and non-linearities, but they usually make the problem worse rather than better, and it is a useful rule.)

Of those three variables, population is perhaps the most fundamental and difficult one to address. Small wonder, then, that is becomes a matter of deep concern if we cannot correctly estimate the size of a principal determinant of population change.

This is not to say that, if we can find unadmitted immigrants, the source should be closed. For example, about 300,000 of the annual "nonimmigrant" arrivals are students. Many students, notoriously, do not go home. However, those alien students constitute a large proportion—more than half, in some scientific fields—of our current crop of graduate students. It may be a sad commentary on the state of American education, but we need those skills. Perhaps, with better counting, we would have a better fix on just who makes up the immigrant stream, and adjust our quota system according to a clearer vision of who is migrating, and who we want.

We need the best information we can get, not simply to limit immigration, but to fit it to our national needs and priorities.

WHAT CAN BE DONE ABOUT IT?

If the nation thinks it important to know how large it is or how fast it is growing, the time perhaps has come for a serious look at the way it collects information—before the 2000 census leads to an even larger proportion of statistical dropouts.

At the simplest level, a serious effort should be made to check out the validity of the gap in the manifests. Let me offer a caveat: the study should involve but not be controlled by the Census Bureau. The Bureau has staked out its position. Specialists tend to circle the wagons when they are challenged, particularly by an outsider. I know. I used to be a specialist. This is too important to be brushed off.

If the gap proves real, it will change our fundamental thinking about a component of immigration that has been almost ignored and perhaps it will lead to a new look at the even more complicated statistical problem of judging illegal immigration by land.

If the gap proves illusory, the data should be improved. Here, afterall, is one of the few potential sources of solid data about one major element of U.S. demography.

The information in the manifests would be less important if we made better use of available technology in logging people in and out of the country. We should perhaps take a hard look at the way INS collects data on international movement of people. From the outside, the system seems thoroughly antiquated. It is, after all, a question of inventory management, and there are sophisticated systems throughout the private sector that can do that job remarkably well. One can visualize an integrated, computerized system keeping track of movements, starting with the issuance of visas, continuing through arrival in the U.S., and completed with the logging out of departures, and capable of summarizing the results in a way that can be used by Census. It would probably be cheaper and require less hours of hard work than the present process. In 1992, should we still be manually logging I-94s, in and out?

For anybody still professing faith in the present system, consider the total breakdown when President Carter asked INS to locate the Iranian students, or the frenzied effors last spring to find the passengers who had disembarked in Los Angeles from an airplane that turned out to be carrying passengers from Latin America with active cholera.

If the "manifest gap" or some part of it is real, as I suspect it is, we come to an even more fundamental question: what price do we pay for the peculiarly American aversion to asking people to identify themselves?

There are 30 million annual arrivals by air and hundreds of millions by land. Keeping track of them, and persuading the visitors to leave eventually, would be a formidable task even with better information systems. The solution is not to try to halt the flow and retreat into a sort of Fortress America. We gain too much from the flow of people and ideas. On the other hand—as I have suggested—we have powerful reasons not to surrender our national right to decide who—and how many—shall aquire the right to live here.

If as a nation we should really decide to control the traffic rather than simply counting it, there is an elegant and straightforward solution: better identification, coupled with laws that permit only those admitted to reside here to hold jobs, obtain professional licenses, or do the other things that only residents should be doing. The required identification presumably would be a Social Security card or a call-in system comparable to those used by credit card companies, but using Social Security numbers.

The "right to anonymity" is not enshrined in the Constitution. In that simpler time, anonymity was hardly a realistic possibility. In practice, we expect to be identified. We voluntarily forego anonymity in all sorts of transactions every day, and we rely on documentation—usually Social Security cards or drivers licenses—to prove who we are.

The civil rights advocate warns that Big Brother will be watching you, and indeed there is a tradeoff, but it is only one of many tradeoffs required as our society becomes bigger and more complex. In fact, the Social Security number is already mandatory, and it is widely used as an identifier. The proposed new use is hardly revolutionary.

Big Brother is watching you, anyway, and the person most likely to profit from the ability to manipulate false identities is unlikely to be doing much good for society. Like million-dollar transactions paid in cash, it is usually an adjunct to some sort of anti-social activity, from the trucker obtaining a new driver's license in another state when he has been convicted of DWI in his own state, to the drug trafficker.

History does not suggest any particular correlation between mandatory identification systems and personal freedom. Despotism has flourished with and without identity cards. On the other hand, most other modern industrial societies have some identity system without infringing on individual rights.

This proposal has been treated at greater length in other NPG Forum papers, and we may return to it.[14] For the purposes of this essay, the point is that, with better identification, the flow into and out of the U.S. could continue unimpeded, but the restrictions on employment and perhaps other activities would prevent most would-be back door immigrants from converting an ostensible visit into permanent residence. The information from the aircraft manifests would then be simply a useful check against the computerized log-in log-out process, and perhaps a warning signal when a gap re-emerged.

Until we reach that happy stage, we would be well advised to make better use of the information that lies, unused, at hand.

NOTES:

1. Alan Lightman & Owen Gingerich, "When Do Anomalies Begin?," *Science*, Vol.255, February 7, 1991, pp.690–695.
2. Unpublished data through CY 1990 are available through the Center for Transportation Information, DTS-44, Volpe National Transportation Systems Center, Kendall Square, Cambridge, MA 02142, Phone 617/494-2450. Traffic to and from Canada and Puerto Rico is not included.
3. Professor Daniel R. Vining, Jr., University of Pennsylvania, in 1982 published a study of net migration suggested by INS/DOT and International Air Transport Association (IATA) passenger manifest data: "Net Migration by Commercial Air: A Lower Bound on Total Net

Migration to the United States," published with a rebuttal and counter-rebuttal in *Research in Population Economics,* Vol.4, pp. 333–360. The pre-1978 data in Figure 1 are drawn from his work. I should, however, note that he went on to the formidable task of attempting an estimate of net migration by air; my purpose is the simpler one of calling attention to data that are dramatically at variance with the current wisdom concerning immigration levels.

4. *1989 Statistical Yearbook of the INS,* September 1990, p.xxxvi.
5. *INS 1977 Annual Report*, Table 11, p.58. The figures do not include traffic with Canada.
6. The Bureau at the same time raised the estimate of annual emigration from 36,000 to 160,000, thus cushioning the arithmetical impact of recognizing the fact of illegal immigration. The judgement process that led to the selection of the 200,000 figure is detailed in Robert Warren & Jeffrey S. Passel, "A Count of the Uncountable: Estimates of Undocumented Aliens Counted in the 1980 United States Census," *Demography,* Vol.24, No.3, August 1987, pp. 375–393. See also Jeffrey S. Passel and J. Gregory Robinson, "Methodology for Developing Estimates of Coverage in the 1980 Census Based on Demographic Analysis: Net Undocumented Immigration," Preliminary Evaluation Results Memorandum No. 114, Bureau of the Census, September 1988.
7. INS Bulletin #5, April 1990.
8. *INS 1977 Annual Report,* Table 2, p.34 and Table 11, p.58. Internal evidence suggests that the gap was created in part by incomparable series, with "aliens admitted" including certain aliens entering by land and "aliens departed" limited to form I-94 holders leaving by international common carrier, but the documentation is unclear and INS cannot clarify it.
9. INS, "Detail Run 422. Immigrants Admitted by Port of Entry," assembled annually by fiscal year.
10. Note that the manifest data are for calendar years; the INS figures are by fiscal years.
11. I have noticed that least one internal inconsistency. It is negligible in the gross data but (because of the problem of residuals mentioned above) it amounted to about 5 percent of the net gap. This is not sufficient to alter the basic proposition that there is a massive and unexplained gap, and I assume that any errors are more or less random.
12. Telephone conversations 4-9-92 with Terry Denny, IATA Montreal and Peter Morris, IATA London.
13. A list of NPG Forum papers is available from Negative Population Growth, Inc. The papers bearing on environment and population are included in Lindsey Grant, *Elephants in the Volkswagen* (New York: W.H. Freeman & Co., 1992).
14. David Simcox, *Secure Identification: the Weak Link in Immigration Control* and *Sustainable Immigration: Learning to Say No* (NPG Forum papers dated 1988 and 1990, Negative Population Growth, Inc.)

HURRICANE ANDREW: THE POPULATION FACTOR

Robert W. Fox

September 1992

The scale of destruction caused by Hurricane Andrew in south Florida is shocking. Numbing pictures appeared on television showing flattened homes and businesses and boats piled on top of one another. A million people lost their electricity. Roughly 250,000 still-dazed people in south Dade county have no place to live and no place to go, little food or water or other basics.

But this is just the latest of the hurricanes that regularly sweep across the peninsula. The entire state is vulnerable, with no portion more that seventy-five miles from the open sea. All counties in Florida are designated as "coastal counties" by the National Oceanic and Atmospheric Administration (NOAA). A major hurricane has been fully expected and long overdue.

The last big one, also of a near "Category 5" status, to hit this region was in 1947. It was said to have wiped out "hundreds" of buildings—not Andrew's 60,000—and to have damaged the citrus crop, but

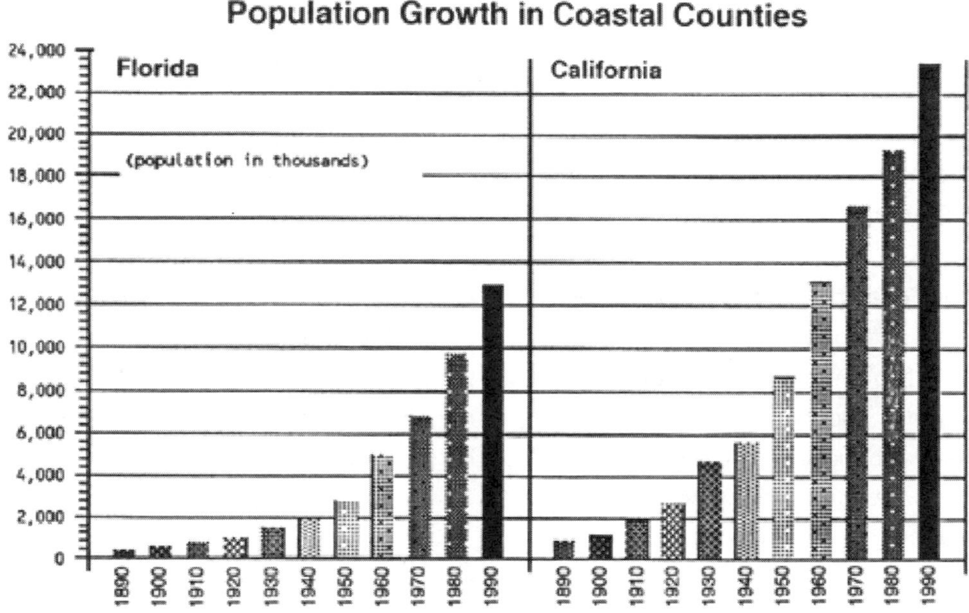

This chart shows population size and growth from 1890 to 1990 for Florida and for California's twenty two coastal counties.

Figure 1

that damage was not evident in the total U.S. citrus output that year.

Contrast that with Hurricane Andrew and the initial estimate of over $20 billion damage to south Florida. That easily makes it the most costly natural disaster in U.S. history. The destruction would be far greater had the center hit just twenty miles to the north in the more densely populated cities of Miami and Coral Gables.

The difference is Florida's population size. There were fewer than 2 million people in the entire state a half-century ago. There are more than 13 million today. For every 100 people in Florida, there were just fifteen a half-century ago and three a century ago. In the seven southernmost counties, there were just nine residents in 1940 for every 100 today and the Everglades, that "river of grass," readily absorbed strong winds and high water. Florida's year round warmth, clear water and beaches continue to attract immigrants, seasonally transplanted northern "snowbirds," and retirees by the thousands. Florida's population grew by three million in the 1980s alone.

Hurricane Andrew dramatically reminds us of what is likely to happen eventually when great numbers settle in environmentally unsound territory.

Florida is one vivid example, yet California represents a threat of a different sort. Its coast is the contact zone where two great geological plates are moving past each other, and the residents await "the big one"—another earthquake like the major ones that have hit before. And California is heavily populated and fast growing.

Other coastal zones are vulnerable, and hurricanes have come ashore from Texas to Maine. Yet the U.S. population is flocking to the coasts, and nobody asks whether this is wise. The 426 coastal counties have just 11 percent of the territory in the continental U.S., but hold 110 million people—45 percent of the population. In 1940, the population of these counties was 50 million.

Without a national population policy or even an ongoing debate on what is a desirable U.S. population size and its geographic distribution—and one in balance with the environment—this nation will continue to grow more rapidly than any other industrialized country. If we are to learn from disasters such as Hurricane Andrew, we must look at the size and growth of the U.S. population. That involves a new look at natural increase and at immigration levels, which increasingly are the source of national population growth as our own fertility settles close to replacement levels. We must also ask ourselves whether the recent pattern of growth is healthy, and whether the nation should continue to encourage or support movement of people—Americans and immigrants—into the most vulnerable parts of the country.

Hurricane Andrew is a stunning reminder that nature is still in charge. Other incompatibilities and environmental problems are generated by population growth and changing land use patterns, if not with this speed and ferocity. For example: barrier island beach erosion and loss of wetlands, and overtaxed water supplies. These are all part of the same question. We must ask, what is the appropriate population size suitable to conditions in various regions of the country if we are to respect and live in harmony with nature?

THE BIOLOGIST AND THE ECONOMIST: IS DIALOGUE POSSIBLE?

Nathan Keyfitz

June 1992

Resumption of the nineteenth century dialogue between economists and biologists could resolve ambiguities in current policymaking. Beyond that, however, we need a sustained effort to educate the country and eventually the politicians if demography is to be brought into policymaking.

Leaders who seek to protect the environment ask advice from biologists; leaders uninterested in environment ask advice from economists who share their indifference. That applies in particular to population; biologists on the whole see the current multiplication of our species as a potential disaster for the planet; economists say that population increase may hamper development, but not much, and with sound economic policies little or not at all.

I recently attended a meeting called by Brandeis faculty to reconcile the thinking of biologists and economists on population. It included prominent scholars on both sides, all courteous, even amiable. Each waited in silence until the other had finished, then expounded the perspective of his or her own discipline, neither contradicting nor agreeing with anything the other had said, in fact taking no notice of it at all. In three days of pleasant talk and good fellowship no one made the leap required to understand enough of the other discipline to say why it seemed wrong.

Biologists gave concrete expositions of species destruction, desertification, etc. while economists did not speak to such points but expounded the elementary principles of market economics. They insisted that those principles are universally applicable; they could be applied without any need to be modified to recognize the limited capacity of the ecosphere to stand what 5 billion people and something like 20 trillion dollars worth of economic production are doing to it.

We need some device for lifting the interdisciplinary dialogue off dead-center, where it was stuck in our meeting and in other forums. Before suggesting such a device, which is my purpose here, it may be worthwhile to see how this apparent deafness to ideas from another discipline has arisen and is maintained.

Such a difference did not always exist. Running parallel to the economic theory of development, from Adam Smith to the present century, has been expression of concern by biologists, what may be called an ecological preoccupation, about the capacity of the planet to support the increasing human population and to withstand the operations humans were carrying out on it. For Malthus this focussed especially on limits to food supplies, for his successors on limits of other raw materials, then about the middle of this century on the limited capital available for development.

At the start there was no problem of communication between the economic and the ecological side; the same scholars wrote on both and they could be consistent with themselves. Alfred Marshall, the leading economist of the late nineteenth century, said that biology was the natural science that had most to teach economics. But in the past two or three decades the two sides have diverged. It would be too much to say that a debate is going on, for a debate requires that each side answer the points raised by the other. How can the conditions for debate be established, and the public understanding and democratic decision making advantages of a debate be secured—that is another way of putting the question of this article.

The non-communication with which we are concerned arises because of the organization of academic life.

> Disciplines are practiced in separate departments, with separate budgets, separate national societies, separate journals. Each has its own criteria for selection of students, its isolation of practitioners starting with the beginning of graduate study, its distinct vocabulary. Students are selected and ultimately given degrees; they are hired as assistant professors and elevated to tenure or not, their researches are funded or not, all according to the judgment of practitioners in one single field. That does not make a discipline a mutual admiration society. Work within any discipline is subject to the harshest of criticism, but always by other practitioners of the same discipline, with both the critic and the criticized animated by the same loyalty to a certain body of thought. (Nathan Keyfitz, 1992. Interdisciplinary analysis in four fields. *Bulletin of the American Academy of Arts and Sciences,* Vol.XLV, No.5, p.6.)

Yet this separation of the disciplines still does not explain how economists could arrive at the conclusion (that seems so strange to biologists) that population and its growth do not make much difference to development and hence to human welfare. One way of understanding the logic of that is in terms of the limits to population and its welfare, as these have come to be seen by economists, especially in the last two or three decades.

THE CHANGING MEANING OF LIMITS

For Malthus the limit on population numbers was food, and he saw availability of food as in all times and ages drawing a line beyond which mankind could not numerically expand. At their own choice, in deciding the number of their children, people could press against that line, or they could stay well inside it. Before the food limit was reached Malthus foresaw misery, as though within the boundary that surrounds us is a ring of increasing trouble. Like other economists of his time, Malthus did not foresee the technical changes of the nineteenth and twentieth centuries.

Yet now we are all aware that limits to the numbers and prosperity of mankind depend on technology, and a limit that crowds mankind in one epoch can suddenly widen with some innovation. The Green Revolution is to be interpreted as a moving outward of the food limit to population. Of course localities must be differentiated, for some countries and parts of countries have little access to world supplies. We had better think of each area having its set of concentric circles, representing the various limits to which it is subject, and for some the food limit is already very close.

As the nineteenth century advanced it came to be thought that minerals (for Jevons it was coal), at least from the viewpoint of economic progress set a closer limit than food. But now economists believe that with the advance of technology and observation of the possibilities of substitution the minerals limit has moved far out, so far that it can be disregarded for all minerals except oil. However, water is essential, and in particular fresh water is one resource that cannot be substituted, whose lack is in some parts of the world already making life miserable. On the whole the neglect of all natural inputs to the productive process represents a degree of technological optimism that is hard to accept.

When all these limits of natural resources are pushed far out there remains shortage of capital, the tools and equipment that would enable people to be productive. That was the limit to be found in the work of economists Arthur Lewis, Coale and Hoover, and others writing in the 1950s and 1960s, and universally applauded. Yet that has since been increasingly dismissed by economists; capital is seen more as the result of development than its cause. Labor, they say, can make the tools with which its work will be productive. The difficulty that unequipped workers would have in creating modern agricultural and factory equipment is dismissed. Yet to one not an economist the current shortage of capital in the world makes it hardly possible that population can grow without reducing the share of each of us, and so reducing welfare by making our work less productive.

But overlooking all limits of food, other materials, and capital, there remains the strongest argument of all for holding down population numbers. That is the stability of planetary support systems, everything from species diversity to the ozone layer to global climate. Especially because of our ignorance of these there are many advantages in not pressing against the world population carrying capacity, whatever that may be. In terms of the limits concept, this translates into having mankind's numbers stay well within the boundaries set by the concentric circles of the various kinds of life sustaining resources. I have to stress our ignorance of just what we are doing to the terrestrial support systems on which we press; in our ignorance we may unwittingly be bringing some other limiting circle uncomfortably close to us; more than that we may be preparing a sudden disaster.

To establish the boundaries set by various essentials for human life that are finite in quantity is a complex matter, as many of those that write about carrying capacity do not sufficiently recognize. The circles that bound us are constantly in motion, with the advances of technology and changes in natural conditions, many of them initiated by human action. The global warming of the next century will extend deserts, and so probably bring closer the food limit for the world, and will without question bring it closer for many already dry localities. In the face of complexities and uncertainties, and without any deeper knowledge than we now possess, it is fortunate that some actions can be clearly specified, some sequences of behavior initiated, that unambiguously make the human population more secure and prosperous, irrespective of what the ultimate total solution of the overall environment problem may turn out to be. Of these reducing the population by having fewer births than deaths is the easiest and surest.

Economists have insisted that no one yet knows enough about those limitations for economic policy to take the environmental constraints into account. Much of the discussion has been on points of fact: what will global warming do to agricultural productivity in various regions, is the ozone hole really going to spread, will we not be able to get along without those species that are being lost, can we really not find places to dispose of toxic waste?

Indeed uncertainties abound on these and other matters. Yet few seem to have noticed that every economic question from whether or not to buy a dozen eggs in the town market to national policy on money supply has to cope with uncertainties. It is not explained why uncertainties have become such an obstacle to serious thought and action just on one matter of supreme importance—the environment. And on what is central to that, the role of population in damaging it.

Notice how uncertainty is for some of us a strong argument for holding down population, for not pressing against the limits we know, for there may be other limits that will do bad things to mankind long before the limits we can clearly discern are reached. On the other hand some economists (and President Bush at one point) say, in effect that the scientists yet do not know exactly what is happening, so let us continue business as usual until they can make up their minds. This is not the first time that the same fact (here uncertainty) is used to justify contrary attitudes.

BRINGING THE TWO SIDES INTO CONTACT, AND SO INITIATING A REAL DEBATE

The device I propose for getting the debate off dead center is to ask each side to accept, just for the sake of the argument, the facts and conclusions presented by the other side. To ask, that is, IF the biologists' worst horror stories are true, what WOULD BE the right economic policies? And IF the economists' characterization of the merits of markets and the incompetence of governments are correct, what action would biologists recommend to avert catastrophe?

I am not the best student to go on from here, but can offer some suggestions. Making the extreme assumption that the present course of economic growth and population increase would turn much of the planet into desert within the next century or two, what change in economic policies should be initiated now? Simply checking economic progress, stopping the clock, freezing haves and havenots where they are now, will not do. What are the minimum and most likely-to-be-accepted changes in the direction of progress, what limits on the trajectory of the economy and of the population, would deflect spaceship Earth from the disaster (of warming, of desertification, etc.) towards which we will assume it is heading?

Asking economists to forego debate on the findings of the alien discipline, and to accept them for the argument, has as its dual asking the biologists to accept the economists' view that the market is the best decider on all issues, infinitely wiser and more farseeing than government. Of course there are cases of market failure, through externalities, or increasing returns to scale that lead to monopoly, or gross inequities where some individuals are disadvantaged through initial poverty, or commercial rates of discount too high to protect later generations. But attempts of governments to correct these failures can often go wrong. Let us suppose that biologists accept the market, notwithstanding the many instances of market failures, that can after all be corrected.

Then what lines of biological research would develop new technologies—say in agriculture—that could make the tread of humans fall more lightly on the earth. No one, least of all demographers, would want to go so far as to prescribe how many people can be sustained on the earth and its separate regions, that being intertwined with unforeseeable technical and social changes. But IF those deserts are truly spreading, warming accelerating, etc. THEN one would have to accept the conclusion that the number of increase from the present ought to be as small as can be secured with the widest distribution of family planning instruments and the most vigorous presentation of information on why they ought to be used.

This was exactly U.S. policy until the last decade and it was beginning to work, when we officially reversed ourselves. Many in the social science community went along with the official change, and found reasons (reasons are always to be found) why the reversal was justified, why population increase did not make all that much difference to development, and why conditions of sustainability no longer had to be taken seriously. Man's inventiveness, human capital, they said, would overcome all difficulties, and the more people the more geniuses who will provide the necessary inventions.

The conclusion of economics that biologists on their side would be asked to accept is the shortsightedness of governments. The myopia of the market cannot be corrected by official agencies that are more myopic than businessmen. If business is only concerned with the profits of the next few years, governments are only concerned with the next election. That is if they are democracies; if they are dictatorships they do have the power to protect the environment without asking approval of an electorate, but I know of no case where they have seized the opportunity to protect the environment so presented.

The conditional acceptance on the part of each discipline of the conclusions of the other could even become a habit. Economists and biologists would each find that they can live with the results of the other, a mutual acceptance not to be found today. Neither side could argue for the kind of facile solution that one now hears. Economists would accept the facts and estimates made by biologists, who on their side would give up the hope that governments would act against the wishes of their constituents, however noble the purpose. Recognizing that the limits are severe and permanent—that they are going to be with us for all of the remaining tenure of man on Earth—would become part of the basic assumption of all disciplines.

SCIENCE, EDUCATION, AND THE POLITICAL PROCESS

But if the disaster is truly facing us within the next century, and there are means to avoid it but we cannot push legislators out ahead of their least informed constituents—that way leads to electoral failure—then what is to be done by the union of economists and biologists here postulated? The answer can only be in more knowledge—creating that is what scholars are expected to do anyhow—AND its diffusion to the public.

Effectively getting knowledge into the minds of the public is frustrating for scholars. We have seen in Europe that a steady 10–12 percent of electorates vote for green candidates, and the prospect of increase in this percentage is not imminent. In the attempt to increase their following the greens widen their platform to include matters unrelated to environment, but this dilutes their appeal. Nothing is going to change this quickly, but that need not make us despair.

The results of science do in fact get to be disseminated. The extraordinary change in health practices shown by current statistics of meat consumption, smoking habits, exercise, have all been occurring within a very few decades of the first announcement of the Framingham study results, the Surgeon-General's Report, and other analyses. Similarly it must be with environment questions: a result comes out of the laboratory or the field, it works its way through undergraduate courses, and from there it penetrates downwards via the Sunday Supplements to the literate population, and it penetrates upwards to the legislators.

In short the process of change can only be as fast as the creation of knowledge and its diffusion through conventional paths in societies with free flow of information. Our public sensitivity to environmental problems may not be instant and complete, but compare it with the total lack of sensitivity under totalitarian regimes! And in any country the environment can only take its place within a scheme of priorities. It lost its place on the front page with the opening of hostilities in the Persian Gulf, nor has it entirely regained that place now that hostilities have died down. The process of scholarship and its diffusion goes at its own pace, and sooner or later gets its results accepted even among the most fickle of publics.

Thus the process of communication in which the relevant new knowledge emerges into the public domain includes a first stage (after initial discovery) in the college classroom, a second stage in the media, a third by word of mouth for those who are neither students nor readers. It can well be that politicians are among the last to be reached, or at least the last to be convinced to the point where they take action.

A democracy requires independence and leadership on the part of its legislators, at the same time as it requires them to do what constituents want. No one has shown how these two contradictory requirements can be reconciled, and in our age of opinion polling followership on the part of democratic rulers has become more prominent than leadership.

Thus the necessary knowledge to understand the condition of the ecosphere spreads through the schooled part of the public, and then to the less schooled, and more informed publics can then move the politicians in various desired directions. We have gone through these stages in respect of personal health consciousness, and in respect of family planning in the developed countries, so let no one say that the sequence described is impossible.

What must come sooner or later are such changes as moving from an income tax to an expenditure tax, with differential rates according to the impact on the environment of various kinds of expenditure. Critics will be quick to say that an expenditure tax is regressive, but progressiveness can be restored by services to those of lower income, even a demogrant or negative income tax. And once this becomes general in the MDCs it will be noted and taken up by the LDCs just as surely as they have taken up our refrigeration, our supermarkets, and our motor cars. That will complete the worldwide change. But it will not happen this year or this decade.

I emphasize that in the initial stages of its diffusion the discovery proceeds by instruction and precept. Some countries will apply it and show how it works, and others will follow their example. Such a path of change, going by example from rich countries to poorer countries, is exactly what took place in the field of birth control. It is hard to imagine any other route of transfer. Imagine what the response would have been if we had continued to have 8 children and urged the LDCs to stop at 2!

Natural science tells us that with growth of population and of the world economy on its present consumption path the environmental condition is bound to become more critical year by year. Some of the problems will be resolved by individuals acting in free markets, while many others require collective action. When the condition becomes severe enough the action to be taken will be obvious to all, so that policy makers will act vigorously, but it may then be too late to reverse the worst effects. In that sense we have a race between deterioration of the planet on the one side, and the fostering and spread of knowledge on the other.

Thus I am saying that we should assume that biologists and economists are both right, each in their own field. A debate carried out with that assumption should then reveal what feasible path of discovery and diffusion of knowledge will deal with the most pressing problem of our times, and actuate publics and the politicians representing them to deal effectively with it: the destruction of the physical habitat within which mankind and its civilization will have to sit for all foreseeable time.

IMMIGRATION AND JOBS: THE PROCESS OF DISPLACEMENT

Donald L. Huddle

May 1992

In this paper, I attempt to measure the displacement of American labor by illegal aliens. As a first step I analyze a 1982 experiment by the Immigration and Naturalization Service, which tried to provide jobs for American citizens and legal residents by deporting illegal aliens who held relatively high paying jobs in nine major U.S. cities. Second, I describe my own practical on-the-ground measurement, correcting for false "displacement" of Americans and legal residents not actually looking for work.

In this second project, we completed three separate field surveys during different phases of the business cycle in the 1980s, each of which gave a more serious picture of the displacement problem than did the econometric models in my earlier NPG Forum article. Moreover, the field surveys showed the process whereby illegal immigrants undercut the legitimate job market and create an underground economy serving unscrupulous employers.

It is particularly important during this technological era in which unskilled jobs at livable wages are drying up to understand how the process of displacement squeezes the poor and the minorities—who are the beneficiaries of massive government spending programs—out of the opportunity to join the economic mainstream.

PROJECT JOBS AND WHAT IT SHOWED ABOUT LABOR DISPLACEMENT

In the spring of 1982, during the depths of a recession when the U.S. unemployment rate was nearly 10 percent, the Immigration and Naturalization Service decided to remove "undocumented" workers from job sites in nine major cities, including Los Angeles, San Francisco, Denver, Chicago, Detroit, New York City, Newark, Dallas and Houston. During a five-day period, April 26–30, special forces of some 400 immigration investigators and border patrolmen, under the operation called "Project Jobs," raided employers who commonly hired illegal aliens.

The two-fold purpose of the operation was: first, to prove that illegal aliens were holding jobs that paid much better than the minimum wage of $3.35 per hour and second, to make such jobs available to unemployed Americans and legal-resident aliens.

In total the INS picked up 5,440 employed aliens at 460 job sites, plus 195 others who were hanging around the job sites. About 78 percent of the undocumented workers were in industry, 13 percent in services, and 8 percent in construction. Of the total apprehended, 87 percent were of Mexican origin.

What did my follow-up study of Project Jobs show? First, an average of seven U.S. workers applied for each job vacated by an alien and second, about 80 percent of the job openings were filled—at least for a short time—by citizens or legal-alien workers.

The primary reason for the strong response was the relatively high wage rates reported for these jobs. According to INS statistics, only 2 percent of the apprehended aliens made less than the federal minimum wage of $3.35 per hour. Six percent made more than $7.85 per hour. In the nine cities we studied, the hourly pay on vacated jobs ranged from $4.37 up to $9.00 per hour while the average wage was $4.87 per hour—more than 45 percent above the minimum wage.

Follow up work by reporters of the *Wall Street Journal* and the *Los Angeles Herald Examiner* found that at least 40 to 50 percent of the illegal aliens had returned to their former jobs by July in Los Angeles and in Houston.[1] The *Journal* reporter quoted migrant labor expert Wayne Cornelius who suggested that U.S. workers may have quit for any of three reasons: A declining belief in hard work as a means of improving ones economic position; higher educational levels of U.S. workers; and expectations of a better job. Moreover, according to Cornelius, jobs opened by the raids were mostly seen as "Mexican jobs" or "Haitian jobs" that "people born, brought up and educated in the U.S. shouldn't have to do."[2]

We did our own careful and extensive analysis of the evidence from the nine U.S. cities where aliens had been rounded up during Project Jobs. We reached two conclusions: first, that U.S. workers really wanted many of the vacated jobs—but not the most exploitative ones; and second, that the explanations of the *Journal* and Professor Cornelius were misleading simplifications based on superficial evidence.

Shortly after the raids, we interviewed jobless workers at the office of the Texas Employment Commission. Eighty-two percent of the job applicants were minorities, mostly Blacks, but also Hispanics and others. As an experiment to determine whether such unemployed U.S. workers were really displaced, we tried to place the job applicants with the seventeen Houston employers who had been raided by the Immigration Service task forces, and who had complained that U.S. workers could not be found for such work. But we were too late. The employers had already refilled most of the vacancies, usually less than one week after the raids. The significant fact is that 60 percent of these jobs were filled with U.S. workers who had learned about the INS raids and the job openings not from state employment agencies, but from the local newspaper, and then rushed directly to the employer. The other 40 percent were filled by undocumented workers who had returned after their apprehension, in many cases, to jobs that had been held open for them by employers who preferred illegal workers.[3]

THE CONCEPT OF DISPLACEMENT AND WHAT FIELD STUDIES OF DISPLACEMENT IN THE SOUTHWEST HAVE SHOWN

The displacement rate is defined here as the number of American and legal immigrant workers who are not able to work per 100 undocumented workers who have jobs. Displacement will vary with the wage and employment rate, the safety and pleasantness of the job, the potential for raises and promotions, and other factors. For example, few Americans would be displaced in dirty, unsafe minimum-wage jobs with no prospect for promotion. The displacement rate would be much higher for clean, safe jobs at $5 per hour. Our own studies have arrived at a rate of displacement for a large number of jobs. However, it is useful to also look at the array of recent wage rates and jobs held by illegals to see actual examples of individual displacement.

As a prelude to discussing the three field surveys done on the ground to determine labor displacement, we can compare two other sets of data shown in Table 1. The first shows the wage structure of a sample of 431 Houston illegals who worked in services, light manufacturing and construction and were apprehended by the INS during the year 1985. Only 5.8 percent earned less than $3.35 per hour—the then minimum wage—while more than 20 percent earned more than $5.25 per hour. The second set of data shows what pay rates 250 Houston citizen and legal residents said they would require to take unskilled jobs similar to those held by illegals in the very same industries. Almost 13 percent of the legal unemployed claimed they would work at or less than the then minimum wage of $3.35 per hour; 51 percent at $5.25 or less; and fully 82 percent would work full time at $7.00 or less. If we compared the two wage structures of legals and illegals, we find that at least 80 percent of the sample unemployed legal Houstonians could have been employed at or above the wage rate they said they would need.

We recognize that this displacement rate (80 percent) will likely be too high. First, the unemployed legal worker may not reveal his true intentions and preferences. Despite assurances to the contrary, he may suspect that the field researcher is somehow connected to the Texas Employment Commission and that he could possibly lose access to unemployment insurance if he answered that he would not be willing to take an unskilled job at $7 an hour or less. This was a criticism leveled at a survey by the *Los Angeles Times* which showed that a sizable majority of unemployed native workers would take jobs vacated by apprehended illegal aliens.[4]

We wanted to go beyond prior surveys in determining whether U.S. workers would in fact take jobs similar in kind and wage rate to those held by undocumented workers. To test the true intentions of the U.S. unemployed, we set up an elaborate job bank and distributed a number of unskilled job openings on a weekly basis to a sample of unemployed Houstonians at wage rates less than $7 per hour. We then tracked the actual job search efforts of the sample unemployed over a period of two to three-months. The results are shown in Table 2. Under part 1 are set out the number of unemployed originally surveyed, their ages, race, education, the number of dependents, and gender. In section 2, we adjust the number for those unemployed who were overqualified for unskilled employment by virtue of past experience and education by removing them from the sample. In section 3, is indicated the percent of those remaining who said they would take illegal alien type unskilled jobs at $7 or less per hour. Then in section 4 we subtract the percent who failed the job search requirements in order to arrive at the measure of gross job displacement. Finally, we have computed a more conservative figure defined as the net displacement rate—it is the gross displacement rate minus that percent of the legal unemployed who actually obtained jobs either through our job bank or by

TABLE 1. Comparison of Illegal Wages and Wage Rates at Which Unemployed Houston Workers Would Work

U.S. Worker Wage Rate Required	Cumulative Percent	Illegal Worker Actual Wage Rate	Cumulative Percent
$3.35 or Less	12.9	Under $3.35	5.8
$3.36 to $4.25	26.7	$3.35 - $4.25	59.9
$4.26 to $5.25	50.8	$4.25 - $5.25	77.6
$5.26 to $7.00	80.0	Over $5.25	100.0
Above $7.00	100.0		

Source: Field Surveys, Donald L. Huddle, Houston Metropolitan Area, 1985.

some other means during the period of the survey. Thus, our measures not only indicate the rate of job displacement at the point in time at which the survey was initiated—gross displacement—but displacement after a period of months in which we actively sought to place the unemployed legal workers.

The three field surveys on displacement were completed in the years 1983, 1985 and in 1990. The most important finding of the field surveys is that—while 85 to 100 percent of the 463 Houston unemployed said they would do unskilled labor at $7 per hour or less—after adjustments for job-search failure, between 63 and 91 percent were displaced in the different surveys by the definition of gross job displacement and 23 to 53 percent were displaced by the definition of net labor displacement. After months of effort to find them jobs, between 9 and 22 percent of the unemployed failed the job search tests. One-third to two-fifths of the samples actually found jobs.

As can be seen in Table 2, both the gross and net

Table 2. Three Micro Studies of Job Displacement in the Houston Metroplex: 1982,1985, and 1990

Category	Statistical Results		
	1982-83 Study I	1985 Study II	1989-1990 Study III
1. Number Surveyed of Unemployed Natives	130	252	81
Average Age	31	31.2	31.4
Race: Black	52.30%	62.70%	53.00%
Hispanic	16.20%	12.30%	23.50%
White	23.10%	20.60%	19.80%
Other*	8.40%	4.40%	3.70%
Average Education in Years	12	12.1	12.1
Average No. Dependents	2.6	2.5	2.4
2. Number Surveyed Adjusted for Those Who Were Overqualified:	87	215	76
3. Percent of Qualified Who Agreed to Take Labor Jobs @ $7/hr. or Less:	100%	94%	85.30%
4. Percent of Qualified Who Failed Job Seach Requirements	9.40%	11.10%	22.40%
5. Gross Job Displacement:	90.60%	82.90%	62.90%
6. Minus Actual % of Qualified Who Got Jobs During Study:	37.50%	33.30%	39.80%
7. Net Displacement Rate:	53.10%	49.60%	23.10%

*Other consisted of Oriental, Indian and Mideastern.

** The major factors for failure in job search were: transportation, failure to follow up on job leads by telephone or in person where appropriate, dislike physical labor with no physical handicap, pay too low despite no college or special training, poor attitude, and lack of any job search skills and failed to return calls. Some participants had failures in several areas.

Source: Field studies of Houston Metroplex in 1982-83 for Study I; 1985 for Study 11; and Study III in 1989-90 at Rice University under Professor Huddle's direction

displacement rates varied over time. This variation is explained primarily by the deepening Houston recession between 1982 and 1985, followed by economic recovery by 1989–90. Both the net and gross displacement were fairly constant between 1982 and 1985, during a time of rising overall unemployment in the city (from 8 percent in 1982 to 8.3 percent in 1985).

By 1989–90 gross displacement had fallen dramatically to 63 percent and net displacement to 23 percent as the city's unemployment rate fell (from 10.2 percent in 1986 to 5.2 percent by 1990). In short, by 1989–90 the unemployed had higher expectations and became more choosy about jobs, and greater numbers failed the job search tests (from 11.1 percent in 1985 to 22.4 percent in 1989–90).

What does it mean to measure net displacement rates varying from 53 to 23 percent between 1982 and 1990? First, it means that the rate of displacement is variable and partly dependent upon the business cycle. Second, it means that even in recessionary times there are some jobs which the native unemployed do not want due to low pay, poor working conditions, and lack of upward job mobility. Labor economists and immigration specialists agree that few native workers want to work as domestic servants, or as migrants in agriculture. For one thing, in the Southwest, according to Professor Stoddard, these jobs and job standards have become "Mexicanized" and so has the recruiting and contracting system for such labor; American workers do not compete—or want to compete—for jobs created by immigrants for immigrants.[5] For many of these jobs, there are no fixed labor or wage standards, no paper receipts, no social security tax receipts. These jobs involve the employment of undocumented aliens, often through relatives, compadres, or friends of the same ethnicity working in family grocery stores, restaurants, boarding houses, retail shops, food preparation and processing, garment work in the home, and so on. This is part of America's half trillion dollar underground economy. Obviously, the more immigrant colonies expand, the more job opportunities there are for immigrant workers, legal and illegal. But again this market is not for U.S. workers.

Some of the urban jobs not currently desired by U.S. workers would be attractive to them, however, if wages and working conditions were not depressed by large numbers of illegals. The econometric literature suggests that wage depression caused by illegals can be sizable. For instance, more American workers would be interested in jobs in farming, textiles, general labor, cooks, and food preparation (now among the lowest paying jobs) if wages were higher due to a smaller labor supply. The argument that there are in fact "jobs Americans won't take"—at least at the going wages—is often made as if these jobs should be filled. This argument does an injustice to American labor. Only the cynical can believe that the nation benefits if low-end wages are systematically pushed down toward subsistence levels. It should be the object of policy to help assure that, even at the low-wage end, an honest day's work brings a decent living. Immigration policies that deliberately drive wages down toward desperate levels for the temporary benefit of employers and consumers are in fact class behavior with ominous long-term implications for American society. (Vernon Briggs has addressed this point with eloquence in an earlier NPG Forum essay.[6])

THE ADVANTAGES OF HIRING ILLEGAL ALIENS

Why is it that so many unemployed U.S. workers who want to work at a wage comparable to that paid to illegal aliens in metropolitan areas have difficulty finding jobs in the same labor market?

During the severe economic recessions of 1983 and 1985, our field studies followed unemployed American workers in their frustrating search for jobs in the Houston job market where, all the while, undocumented workers were continuously hired at above the minimum wage. We concluded that employers find it advantageous to hire illegal aliens in common labor and some semi-skilled jobs. First, illegal aliens will often work harder under more difficult conditions than will U.S. workers. Second, entry-level illegal workers are often paid less than the prevailing wage in an industry, and always less than the union wage. Third, and most significant, according to our research findings, the employer has a "net advantage" in hiring an illegal even if he pays them the equivalent of the prevailing wage. How so?

As surveys have shown, between one quarter to half of the employers, contractors, and subcontractors who employ illegals do not deduct any taxes from the workers' gross pay. A Texas survey done for Governor William Clements in 1982 showed that an estimated forty to fifty percent of the illegals interviewed did not have income tax and FICA taxes withheld from their pay. This survey was done in several Texas cities including Houston, Dallas, and San Antonio. A total of 1,526 aliens were interviewed. Nearly all were apprehended aliens.[7]

Our own three Houston metroplex surveys support. the findings of the statewide survey and yield additional corroboration because we had in-depth interviews with over four hundred undocumented workers, only one hundred of whom had been apprehended by the Immigration Service.

Significantly, we found that illegal aliens commonly receive a tax-free wage that is around twenty to thirty percent less than the going wage in a given occupation. Yet this wage, with no tax deductions, is roughly equal to the net after-tax wage paid U.S. workers for the same job. What matters to the illegal worker is his take-home pay, not his gross pay. So to an employer the illegal will be "cheaper to hire." Moreover, we have found that employers gain further excess profits from this arrangement. In the same instances that illegals pay no withholding or FICA, neither does the employer pay any FICA and payroll taxes. So the employer saves another seventeen percent of the illegals' wage.

Aside from the under-the-table cash payments, employers and undocumented workers, in collusion with one another, use at least three cover-ups for dodging tax payments. First, and most commonly, the illegal is paid as a casual laborer. Under IRS rules one may work temporarily for up to thirty days with no withholding or income or FICA taxes. Many illegals in Texas work continuously for the same employer under this rule.

Second, there is the independent contractor ruse. By treating illegals as independent contractors, who are themselves responsible for payment of all taxes, the employer avoids payment of FICA and Workmen's Compensation. In Houston, and in other metropolitan areas such as Los Angeles, Denver, and Miami, this ruse is much used in subcontracting construction jobs, cable TV installation, landscaping, and the service trades.

Third, an undocumented worker who has taxes deducted from his wages may, and commonly does, declare a large number of dependents so as to minimize withholding taxes, often with the assistance of the employer. The family of the "undocumented taxpayer" may be fictitious or it may reside abroad, and it often includes extended-family members. Our 1985 field study indicated that illegal workers in the Houston metroplex paid only about three percent of their gross wages into withholding taxes, as compared to a legally required amount of about 12 percent. Since we found that only ten percent of the illegals ever filed their income tax returns at the end of the year, those owing the federal government never paid their bills.

Many of the Third World immigrants find entry-level jobs in the underground economy. A work week for illegals in outdoor jobs, service jobs, and in common-labor assembly plants is frequently between fifty and sixty hours per week at straight-time wages. Moreover, not even half of the illegals injured on the job in this sector are covered by medical insurance or Workmen's Compensation. If injured, they are immediately replaced by reserves of illegal aliens on call locally and in the home country. They are tractable because employees may turn them into the INS, often without paying them for their last week's work.

It needs to be emphasized that businessmen who are trying to gain a competitive advantage from hiring and exploiting illegal aliens have a constant thirst for newly arriving illegals rather than the older, more experienced illegals who have gained job experience after living in the U.S. for some years. This is because more experienced illegals have learned the ropes and have left the poorer jobs for better ones paying higher wages which often also include social security payments and other fringe benefits. We found this to be the pattern in our 1985 and 1989–90 field surveys.

NETWORK RECRUITING

New infusions of illegals are facilitated by the network recruitment which links "coyotes," U.S. jobs, and Mexican villages. Professor Phillip Martin was able to show that the Southern California lemon industry not only brought in new illegals via the network, but that the network also systematically excluded American workers.[8] We verified this phenomenon in our 1985 survey when we attempted to place Houston unemployed with employers who depended upon the network to supply new workers. We also found, as did Martin, that although some networks continue to link villages with farm jobs, the transition time can be quite rapid from entry-level, low-paying jobs to higher paying semi-skilled jobs. The illegals in the survey averaged just over twenty-seven years of age and had seven years of schooling. They had progressed from an initial average wage of $3.79 per hour to $5.13 per hour in an average of just 4.3 years despite the onset in 1982 of a severe recession in Houston. Comparatively, the average wage of the U.S. worker rose by only half as much and the Houston legal alien worker by one quarter as much.

THE SHAPE OF THE FUTURE

The growth of the working age population in Mexico, Central and South America in the next three decades will dwarf that of the United States, as Lindsey Grant documented in a recent NPG Forum essay.[9] There is no prospect that all of these people will find jobs at home. Many of them will seek to come to the United States, as a matter of survival, and the problems of competition with unskilled American and legal resident labor will intensify rather than fading away.

As we have seen, the process of job displacement and wage depression is more intense when studied on the ground than the econometricians' models would suggest. Econometric models have consistently underestimated job displacement and wage depression for reasons pointed out in my earlier NPG Forum essay.[9] In actuality, after a lull in illegal immigration brought about by the 1986 Immigration Reform and Control Act, both illegal and legal imnigration are on the rise. More legal immigration due to the 1990 Immigration Reform Act means higher displacement and wage depression for America's unskilled workers. Perhaps more ominously, the rising tide of illegal aliens means that the underground economy will thrive and also threaten to bring about fundamental changes in the character of the U.S. labor market. California, the immigrant state, where the term Third World is increasingly used to describe the population, labor and cities, may be a harbinger of what is to come unless immigration is brought under control and then articulated to U.S. labor needs.

NOTES:

1. Wolin, "Dirty Work," the *Wall Street Journal*, Dec. 6,1982, p. I and 16. My Houston survey results were reported by Don Browning, "Revolving Door Border: 40 percent Deported After Raids Are Back at Old Jobs," Los Angeles Herald Examiner, (July 11, 1982) pp. IA, 6A.
2. Wayne Comelius, Cablegram to Immigration and Naturalization Service, Project Job File, (Washington, D.C. May 1982) 3 pp.
3. For details see Huddle: "Illegal Immigrant Workers: Benefits and Costs to the Host Country in the Context of the INS Raids . . . Projected Jobs." American Economics and Social Science Meetings, (New York City, Dec. 27, 1982), 25 pp.
4. Harry Bernstein, "The Times Poll' 75 percent of Jobless Would Accept Menial Work," *Los Angeles Times*, (April 6,1981), pp. 1, 10.
5. Ellwyn Stoddard, "Illegal Mexican Labor in the Borderland: Institutionalized Support for an Unlawful Practice," Pacific Sociological Review (19:2, April 1976) 203.
6. Vernon Briggs, Jr., "Political Confrontation With Economic Reality: Mass Immigration in the Post Industrial Era," The NPG Forum, (Feb. I 990).
7. Tarrance and Associates, A Study of Undocumented Workers in the State of Texas. (Presented to the Govemor's Budget and Planning Office, Austin, March-July 1982) 7–13.
8. Philip Martin, Illegal Immigration and the Colonization of the American Labor Market, (Center for immigration Studies, Washington, D.C., January 1986) 1–52.
9. Lindsey Grant, "Free Trade and Cheap Labor," the NPG Forum 1991.

THE L.A. RIOTS AND U.S. POPULATION NON-POLICY

Lindsey Grant

May 1992

The riots in Los Angeles have generated a new wave of self examination in the White establishment. It should perhaps be tempered with realism as to the underlying forces involved, if not the triggering incident. The effort to bring minorities (and particularly Blacks) into unfettered participation in U.S. society takes good will on all sides and a sustained effort by the minority poor to master the economic skills of modern society. It cannot simply be done for them.

However, even if the country's leadership cannot undertake to guarantee everybody the job of their choice, it should try to create an environment in which those who are willing and able to work can find work to do. In this respect, over the past three or four decades, the nation could not have botched the job more thoroughly if it had deliberately set out to start riots. Unemployment, the sense of frustration and hopelessness, and the competition for jobs from people coming from desperate lives in other countries—these were the tinder on which the LA riots fed.

THE HISTORY

In the 'fifties and 'sixties, the nation set out on perhaps its greatest moral crusade: to bring Blacks into the economic and social main stream. There were problems to begin with, and we made them worse.

- The crusade began at a tough time, when the country faced the prospect of finding jobs for particularly large cohorts of young people, as a result of the baby boom.
- Jobs had to be created, initially at the unskilled level, just as the technological revolution—which continues today—was drying up the demand for unskilled labor.
- The social revolution that has led most young women into the paid labor force had been unleashed by World War II and was gathering momentum. It increased the competition for jobs.

How did the nation respond?

- Just as the crusade began, the country embarked upon an immense engineering project: the Interstate highway program. One result was to facilitate White flight (and bourgeois flight generally) to the suburbs as poor Blacks continued their historic migration from farms to the cities. The cities were effectively resegregated, the poor Blacks were isolated, the cities' tax base eroded, and there went both the social contact and the financial resources to help educate poor young Blacks to join the rest of the society. "Busing" was hardly a solution when the middle class lived in different educational jurisdictions and was fighting to preserve its own schools.
- Even more important, we increased the competition for unskilled jobs, rather than trying to limit it.

IMMIGRATION

Every immigration "reform" of the past two decades has increased legal immigration, and our policies have encouraged the immigration of the unskilled, to compete with our own minorities and with earlier immigrants. Because of some employers' demands for cheap labor, we have failed to enforce the immigration laws we have, and this has encouraged illegal immigration. The *New York Times* called it the "policy of the wink." The Census Bureau counts a net movement of 2.3 million foreign immigrants into California in the 'eighties, and this does not include the illegal immigrants who chose not to be counted. They intensified the already intense competition for jobs and housing.

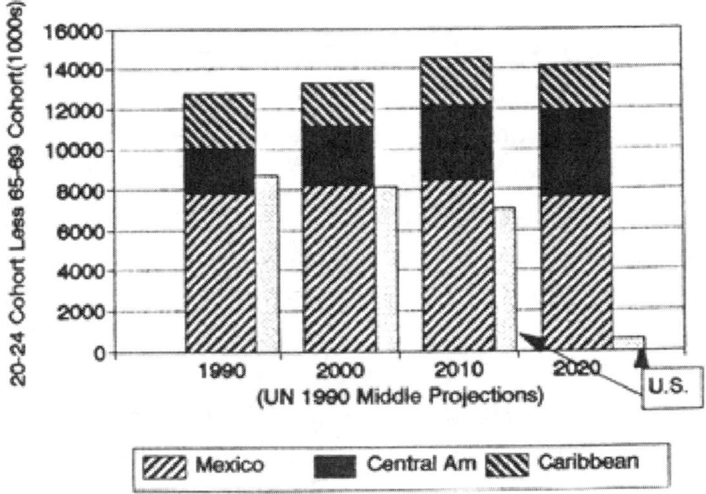

Figure 1

FERTILITY

Public and private efforts to provide help in reducing unwanted pregnancies among the poor have been undermined by the abortion debate and the attacks on family planning centers which Presidents Reagan and Bush have at least tacitly supported. The higher pregnancy rate among the poor (of all races; this is not a racial issue) has multiplied the size of the national problem of nurturing and educating poor children to escape the cycle of poverty.

In pursuit of an ideological debate about Chinese population policy, the President cut off U.S. support for the U.N. Population Fund and the International Planned Parenthood Foundation. We thus did what we could to postpone third world efforts to address the population problems they themselves recognize, and to assure that third world population pressures—and the pressures to migrate to the U.S.—will continue to rise, offering the prospect of more and bigger "LA riots."

THE PROSPECT

This is not something that has happened. It is happening, and it will get worse. At the risk of repetition, let us reprint a key graph from a recent NPG Forum (*Free Trade and Cheap Labor: the President's Dilemma.* 1991).

This is not just a guess. The young adults of twenty years hence are already born. The countries of meso-America, already bedeviled by high unemployment rates, will have to absorb an expansion of the working age population comparable to ours during the 'seventies and 'eighties when we absorbed the baby boomers—and those economies in total are 1/17th as large as ours. In this country, during that process, the poor got poorer and the rich got richer. The problems just south of us are likely to be infinitely more intense.

If one looks beyond, to South America and the rest of the world, the numbers are of course enormously larger.

The problem is not going away. It is growing, and it will intensify the competition for jobs and housing among our own young and unskilled.

. . . AND SOME THOUGHTS ABOUT PUBLIC POLICY

Issues like this won't be solved by a presidential commission looking at the L.A. Police Department. They require that—for the first time—our government begin to make the connections between huge forces such as population change and urban unrest.

For starters:

- Reject Congressional proposals (S.1734 and H.R.3366) to undo the 1986 law that imposed penalties on employers who hire illegal aliens. That provision was the one bright spot in recent legislation on immigration, and it was passed at the cost of a compromise that legalized over 3 million illegal immigrants (including hundreds of thousands of fraudulent "farm workers.") We don't need more competition for jobs. S.1734 is cosponsored by Senators Kennedy, Hatch, Specter, DeConcini. H.R.3366 is sponsored by Representatives Richardson and Roybal. They should all be told that the nation needs a tougher "employer sanctions" law, not an emasculated one that benefits some employers but harms poor Americans.
- Revise the Immigration Act of 1990 so as to protect vulnerable Americans rather than simply facilitating the immigration of favored ethnic groups. Begin a serious effort to stop illegal immigration.
- Watch the government's negotiations for a free trade agreement with Mexico and, later, the rest of the hemisphere. We should not be exporting more unskilled jobs or importing more unskilled labor.
- Presently, about 2 percent of our foreign aid goes to population assistance. Most of the rest goes to special interests and the pursuit of foreign policy objectives that are rendered obsolete by the end of the Cold War. Population growth is the single overwhelming issue that spreads across the third world, and we have our aid priorities precisely wrong. A reversal of priorities would help them to manage a problem that is both theirs and ours.
- Put aside the ideological battles and restore family planning services to young women who want and need them. Get on with the job, and encourage those who would limit their fertility to do so. Help them to understand that limiting the numbers means that their own children will have a better shot at the help they need. Offer them hope. Fewer young people offers each of them a better chance. Is that a bad idea?

WHY WE NEED A SMALLER U.S. POPULATION AND HOW WE CAN ACHIEVE IT

Donald Mann, President,

Negative Population Growth, Inc.

July 1992

We need a smaller U.S. population in order to halt the destruction of our environment, and to make possible the creation of an economy that will be *sustainable* indefinitely.

All efforts to save the environment will ultimately prove futile unless we not only halt, but eventually reverse, our population growth so that our population—after an interim period of decrease—can be stabilized at a sustainable level, far below what it is today.

We are trying to address our steadily worsening environmental problems with purely technological solutions, while refusing to come to grips with their root cause—overpopulation. Population size—not just population growth—is important because it multiplies and intensifies our overwhelming environmental problems. Sheer numbers of people can prevent the achievement of such vital national goals as a healthy environment and sustainable economy.

At any given level of technology and conservation, our impact on the environment is proportional to the size of our population. There is an indisputable correlation between population size and environmental degradation. Regardless of new technologies and heroic conservation efforts, we must recognize that population size is the central, core issue and address it as such.

By any measure, the United States is already vastly overpopulated. We have long since exceeded the long range carrying capacity of our resources and environment, yet we continue to grow rapidly, by about 25 million each decade.

If present rates of immigration and fertility continue, our population, now in excess of 256 [as of April 1998, 269 million], will pass 400 million by the year 2055, with no end to growth in sight!

Could any rational person believe that U.S. population growth on such a scale could be anything other than catastrophic for our environment, and our standard of living? Already, with our present numbers, we are poisoning our air and water, destroying croplands and forests, and triggering fundamental climate changes.

Asking ourselves the right questions is supremely important, because failure to do so can prove fatal. As a nation we have failed to ask ourselves the essential question regarding a national population policy: *At what size should we seek to stabilize U.S. population?* Surely that is the central issue.

As a direct result of our failure to ask that question—and find an answer to it—we are doing absolutely nothing to first halt, and then reverse, our explosive population growth.

The question of an optimum population size for the U.S. is a public policy issue of crucial importance. It is, however, an issue that is completely ignored not only by our policy makers in all branches of the Federal government, but also by the mass media who could, and should, bring it forcefully to the attention of the American public.

We at NPG believe that the optimum size for U.S. population lies in the range of 125 to 150 million, or about the size it was in the 1940s. With a slow and gradual decrease in our numbers, that size could be reached in about a century (see Figure 2 below).

To progress toward a smaller population we would need to lower substantially our present rates of immigration and fertility. Those two factors, together with increases in life expectancy, are responsible for our population growth. Our detailed recommendations will be presented later in this paper.

For the moment, however, let us examine the concept of optimum population size.

OPTIMUM POPULATION SIZE

Some years ago, when world population was perhaps half its present size, famed British scientist Sir Julian Huxley wrote:

> "The recognition of an optimum population size (of course relative to technological and social conditions) is an indispensable first step towards that planned control of population which is necessary if man's blind reproductive urges are not to wreck his ideals, and his plans for material and spiritual betterment."

Optimum population size should not, of course be confused with *maximum* population size or the number of people our country could possibly be made to feed, with a low standard of living for everyone, accompanied by the rapid destruction of our ecosystem.

If bare levels of subsistence, and the perhaps irreversible destruction of our environment were acceptable, then *maximum* U.S. population size might exceed *optimum* size by a factor of five, ten, or even more.

Various experts are forever trying to estimate how many people in our nation, and the world, could possibly be made to support. Their focus, for some odd reason, seems to be on the possible rather than the desirable.

Critics often claim that the concept of optimum population size is so value-laden that it will be forever impossible to develop a broad consensus on a specific number, or range. We need not be deterred by such objections.

Judgments on public policy issues can never be completely value free, nor need they be. For example, is there some magic number for the size of our defense budget, foreign aid, or the Federal discount rate? Of course not. *The essential point is that, after all the evidence is carefully weighed, a final figure must be determined as a matter of policy so that the process of government can proceed.*

The same holds true for optimum population size. We must decide on a figure, or range, for optimum size, or at least decide whether it is smaller or larger than present numbers. Failure to do so condemns us to continued inaction, and makes it virtually impossible to progress beyond vague calls to stabilize population at some unspecified level, at some indefinite date.

What someone has said about the greenhouse effect is fully applicable to optimum population size: "In the face of threats of irreversible environment damage, lack of full scientific certainty is no excuse for postponing action."

What we must try to define are the criteria that will guide our search for answers to the question: What is the optimum size at which we should seek to stabilize U.S. population?

PROPOSED CRITERIA

We submit that the concept of optimum population size should be based on the following criteria:

1. The primacy of environmental considerations, because our economy, and our very lives, depend on the proper functioning of the earth's natural ecosystems.
2. The idea of time, duration, and sustainability. An optimum population size would allow the creation of a society, and an economy, that would be sustainable indefinitely.
3. The idea of an adequate standard of living for everyone.
4. Ample room for open space and wilderness, and for other creatures and forms of life.
5. Prudence. Given our incomplete knowledge of the world's natural ecosystems, and given that the damage we inflict on the ecosystem may be irreversible before we are even aware of it, a large margin of safety should be built into the goal, just as engineers build large margins of safety into the design of a bridge.

If, for example, it appeared that the optimum U.S. population could reasonably be set at 200 million, prudence would dictate reducing the goal by at least 25 percent, in order to ensure an adequate margin of safety.

If the above criteria are accepted, would anyone maintain that our present population of over 256 million is optimal, given the impact of those numbers on our environment and resources?

Could anyone possibly believe that a U.S. population of 400 or 500 million—numbers we seem determined to reach—would be optimal?

Any goal set for a smaller U.S. population should, of course, allow for mid-course corrections based on increased knowledge with the passage of time. Since any substantial decrease in numbers would be difficult to achieve in much less than a century, there would be ample time for periodic revisions of the initial goal, either up or down.

Finally, we must recognize that to determine an optimum population size with scientific precision down to the last person, or down to the last ten million persons, will be forever beyond our grasp. The goal eventually decided upon will be a "best estimate" based on our present knowledge. This will always be the case.

NPG STUDY

Over the last two years Negative Population Growth, Inc. has conducted the most significant study ever made of optimum population size. Under the able leadership of editor Lindsey Grant, NPG published a series of fifteen papers on optimum population size, written by experts in various fields.

Many of these experts believe that optimum U.S. population size is far below present numbers.

For example, David and Marcia Pimentel, of Cornell University, believe that, "With a population of 40 to 100 million, the United States could become self-sustaining on solar energy while maintaining a quality environment, provided that sound energy conservation and environment policies were in effect to preserve soil, water, air and biological resources that sustain life."

Dr. Robert Costanza, Associate Professor at the University of Maryland's Chesapeake Biological Laboratory places optimal U.S. population between 85 and 175 million, depending on the level of per capita consumption.

In their paper, Paul and Anne Ehrlich estimate the optimum U.S. population to be around 75 million—about the size it was in 1900. They believe that "for our own sakes, and that of humanity as a whole, a rapid move to NPG is essential."

Editor Lindsey Grant, a retired Foreign Services Officer, and a former Deputy Assistant Secretary of State for Environment and Population Affairs, estimates that optimum U.S. population size is between 125 and 150 million, a goal that NPG, Inc. has adopted as its own.

This series of fifteen papers was published in the spring of 1992 by W.H. Freeman and Co. The book, *Elephants in a Volkswagen,* by Lindsey Grant, is available at book stores or from the W.H. Freeman Order Dept. at (800) 877-5351 ($13.95 paperback, $22.95 hard cover).

A final thought about defining a specific number or range for the optimum population size of the United States. We might try and proceed by a process of elimination, rejecting those numbers that clearly exceed an optimum population.

Thus, we might ask not what optimum population size is, but what it is not. It is certainly not the 400 to 500 million we will reach in the next century if present rates of immigration and fertility continue.

A COMPROMISE POSITION

A specific goal, or range, for optimal U.S. population size is desirable. If, however, this were finally deemed to be impossible to define, there is an alternate goal that could still set us on the path to a smaller U.S. population.

A substantial body of opinion, while agreeing that a negative rate of population growth is necessary, holds that we simply do not know enough at present to set a precise goal. It believes that the essential question we must ask is not the exact size at which our population should be stabilized, but simply: Should we be striving to achieve a smaller or larger population?

If smaller, as we believe, then it follows that we should take immediate measure to achieve a *negative rate of population growth* as soon as possible.

HOW TO GET THERE

We could start now on the path toward a smaller U.S. population by substantially reducing the present rates of immigration and fertility, the two factors chiefly responsible for our population growth.

Our immigration policy should be an integral part of a national population policy aimed at reducing our numbers. *If immigration remains at or near current levels it would be virtually impossible to lower our fertility sufficiently to achieve a negative rate of population growth.*

We need to reduce annual immigration to an overall ceiling of about 200,000 (including all relatives and refugees) so that it roughly balances with emigration (out-migration). Then, immigration will no longer contribute significantly to our population growth, as it does now.

At present, immigration accounts for 40 to 50 percent of our annual population increase.

In addition to reducing immigration, we must also lower our total fertility rate (the average number of children per woman) to about 1.5 and stabilize it there for roughly 50 years. Our fertility rate hovered around 1.8 from 1973 to 1987, but has risen steeply since then to 2.1 in 1991.

If almost all women had no more than two children, the U.S. fertility rate would drop to 1.5, since many women remain childless by choice, and many others choose to have only one child. We promote the ideal of the two-child maximum family as the social norm, because that is the key to lowering fertility.

We must recognize that, in an already overpopulated nation, no parent has the "right" to have more than two children.

At the heart of the problem is how to help the poor and less educated of all races lower their fertility rate to the level that now prevails among the educated and more prosperous sectors of all races.

To do so, society must make an all-out effort to improve the status of women, with vastly improved opportunities for higher education and good jobs. But this fundamental and long-term effort must be complemented by specific non-coercive incentives that act directly to lower fertility.

INCENTIVES TO LOWER FERTILITY

NPG proposes these incentives to motivate parents to have no more than two children:

- Eliminate the present Federal income tax exemption for dependent children born after a specified date.
- Give a Federal income tax credit only to those parents who have no more than two children. Those with three or more would lose the credit entirely.
- Give an annual cash grant to parents who pay little or no income tax, and who have no more than two children. Those with three or more would lose the cash grant entirely.

Incentives to encourage parents to stop at two will be necessary because a substantial number of births at present are what demographers term third order births, or higher, meaning births to women who already have two or more children.

For example, of the roughly four million births in 1989, slightly over 1 million (27 percent) were third order or higher.

It would help to achieve a fertility rate of 1.5 if all unwanted pregnancies could be prevented by family planning. But even if they were, incentives would still be necessary, however, because a substantial number of women expect to have more than two children, by design rather than by accident.

According to a recent report by the Census Bureau, 29.9 percent of women interviewed, married or single, ages eighteen to thirty-four, expect to have three or more children during their lifetimes. An even larger percentage—34.4 percent—of women in that age group who are currently married expect to have three of more children.

Regarding our proposal to limit a tax credit only to parents with one or two children, we are often asked why we do not propose that the credit be given as well to individuals and couples with no children.

The reason is that we are not trying to promote the no-child family, because the goal of a smaller U.S. population could be reached if maximum family size were limited to two children.

The fundamental purpose of a tax exemption or credit for dependent children is to benefit the children and help compensate the parent or parents for the expense of raising them. In our view, that purpose should now be broadened in order to encourage the two-child maximum family.

But a tax credit extended to non-parents would be tremendously costly, and an added burden to the American taxpayer. How could a financial subsidy to non-parents be justified?

THE PATH TO A SMALLER POPULATION

NPG calls for the U.S. total fertility rate to be reduced to 1.5 and maintained at that level for fifty years, before rising gradually to the long term replacement rate of 2.1 (Line A in Figure 1 below. Line B is a projection of U.S. fertility in 1991.)

Together with zero net migration, this reduction in fertility would result in a slow and gradual decrease in our numbers over a period of about 100 to 125 years, at which time we could reach a stationary population size of 140 million, with a stable age structure.

Our recommended path to a smaller population (Line A) is shown in Figure 2 below. It is contrasted with the course we are now following (Line B.)

The assumptions for Line A are: zero net migration, and a total fertility rate reduced from 2.1 to 1.5 and maintained at that level for fifty years before rising to the long term replacement rate of 2.1.

The assumptions for Line B are: net annual immigration of one million (about the current level), and our 1991 fertility rate of 2.1.

The difference between the two paths is enormous. It would be 100 million by 2030, less than forty years from now (351 million minus 251 million). At that time, the population size of Line B would be 40 percent larger than that of Line A. These things being equal, our impact on the environment and resources would be 40 percent greater as well.

In another twenty-five years, by the year 2055, (only 63 years away), the difference between the two paths would be almost 200 million. The population of Line B (401 million) would be almost double that of Line A (205 million), or about U.S. population size in 1970.

Line A shows a U.S. population size of 157 million by the year 2090. That would mean a reduction of nearly 100 million from our present numbers in about a century, or roughly 10 million per decade.

This would represent a relatively gradual change in population size. For example, for the last several decades we have been growing by about 25 million per decade.

For projections in Figures 1–5, life expectancy was assumed to climb gradually, as follows:

- Female: From 78.4 to 82.3 by the year 2100.
- Male: From 71.2 to 76.6 by the year 2100.

All projections in this section were made for NPG by Decisions Demographics, a division of the Population Reference Bureau in Washington, D.C.

AGE STRUCTURE

In Figures 3–5 below, we see the age structure that would result from the above projections.

Age of immigrants was based in data from the U.S. Immigration and Naturalization Service, *Statistical Yearbook of the Immigration and Naturalization Service*, 1989.

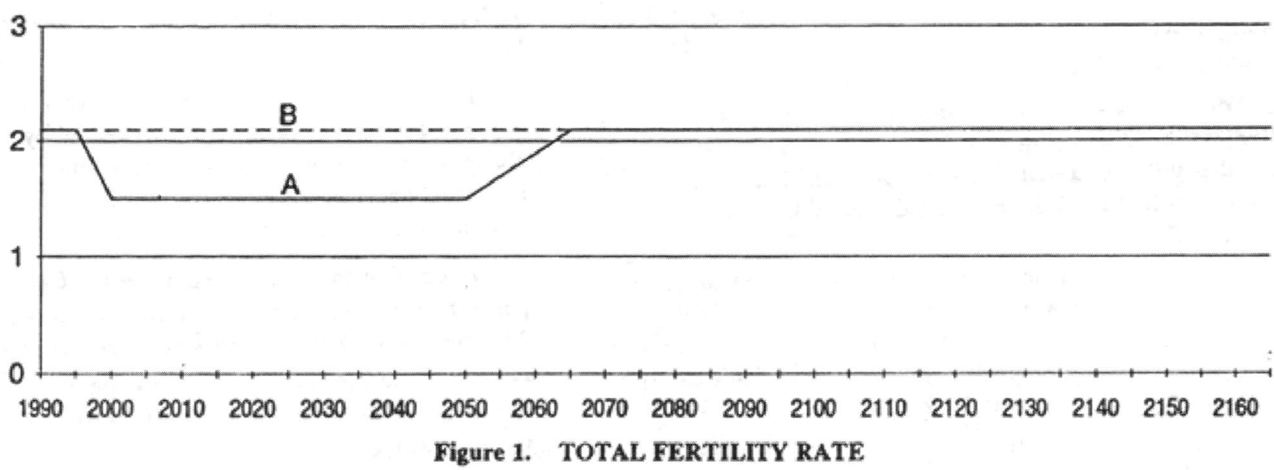

Figure 1. TOTAL FERTILITY RATE

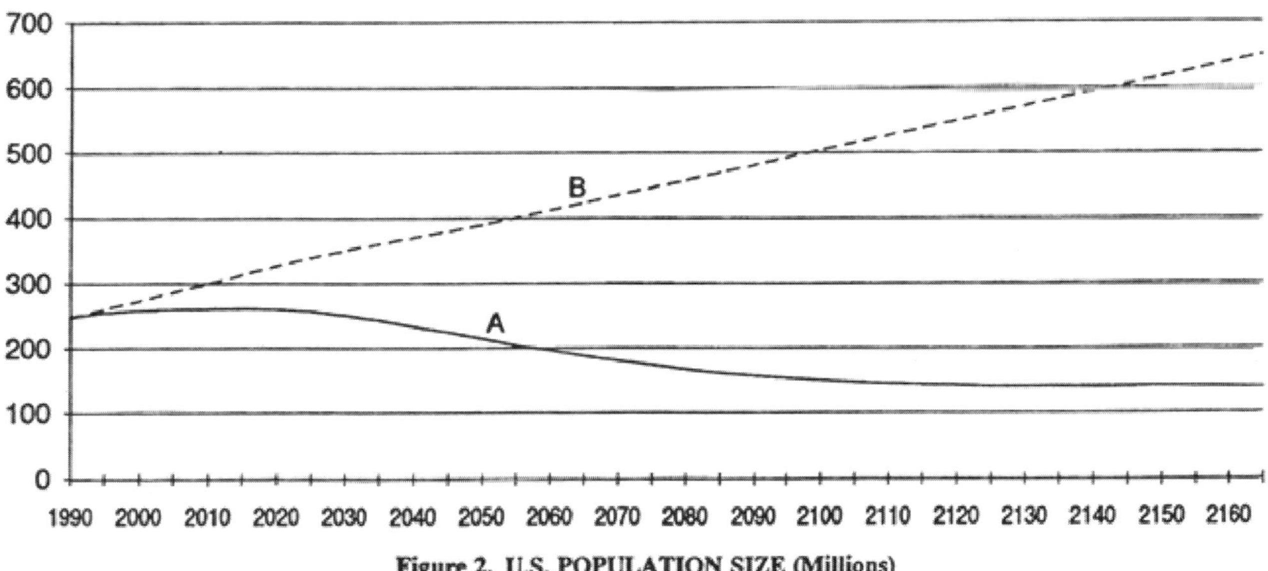

Figure 2. U.S. POPULATION SIZE (Millions)

Some have expressed fears that either reversing or merely halting our population growth would result in an unacceptable ratio of the elderly (sixty-five and older) to the working age population, commonly defined as those fifteen to sixty-four.

While the age structure of a decreasing population would be different from that of our present growing population, the differences would not be great enough to cause any severe problems during the transition period to a smaller, stationary, non-growing population.

For example, there would be no significant difference in the size of the working age population, as a percent of the total population. For most of the transition period to a smaller population, however, the older segment would represent a greater proportion of the total population than it does now.

This increase in the older segment would be roughly balanced by a decrease in the younger (zero to fourteen) segment of the population. The young, of course, are dependents just as are the old (plus the unemployed of all ages), and the cost to society to

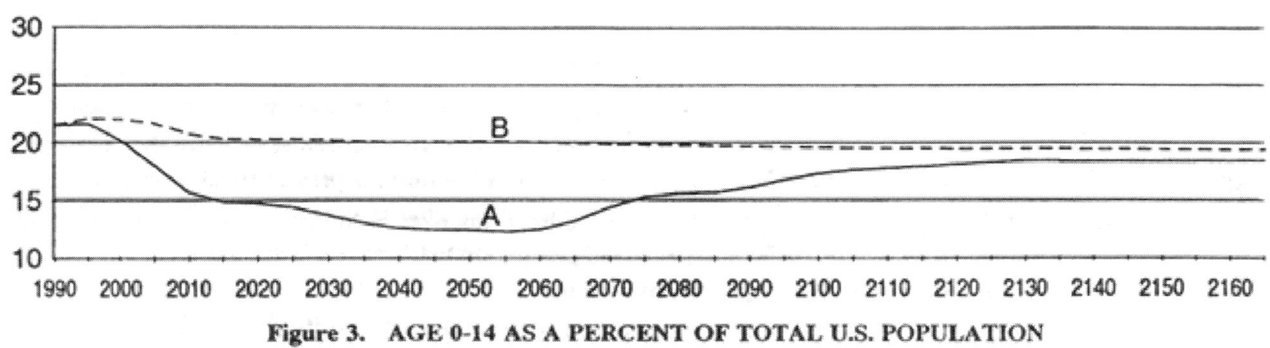

Figure 3. AGE 0-14 AS A PERCENT OF TOTAL U.S. POPULATION

Figure 4. AGE 15-64 AS A PERCENT OF TOTAL U.S. POPULATION

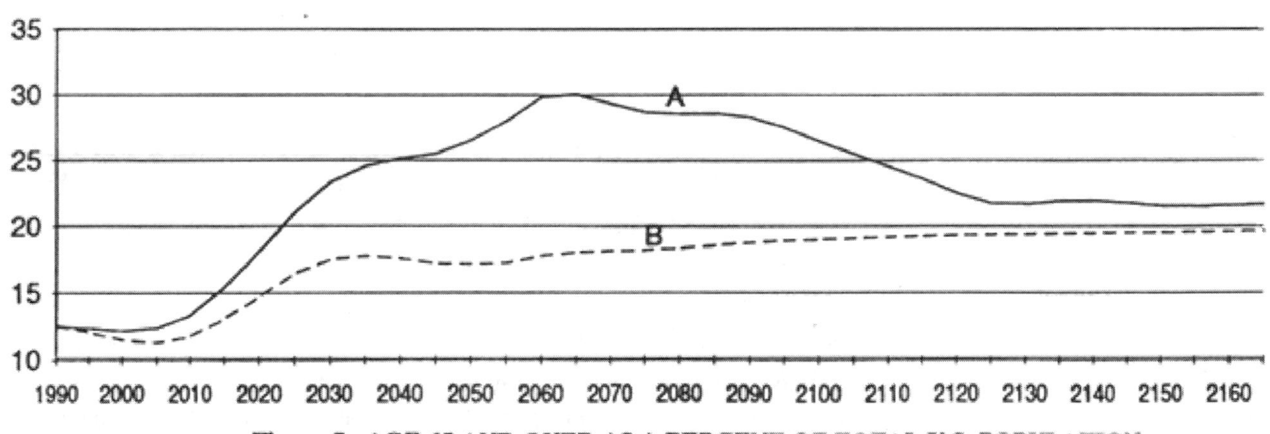

Figure 5. AGE 65 AND OVER AS A PERCENT OF TOTAL U.S. POPULATION

support them may be as great, or greater, than the cost to support the old.

In any event, since we cannot grow forever in a finite world, we must accept the fact that sooner or later our age structure will be that of a non-growing population. Whatever the eventual size, whether 140 or 150 million, the age structure of any stationary, non-growing population with replacement level fertility, low mortality, and no net immigration would be identical.

This would be true whether or not the population was stabilized following a period of increase or decrease.

Further, we must recognize that, because of the impact of sheer numbers of people on our resources and the environment, the size at which our population is eventually stabilized will have far greater social and economic consequences than any that could conceivably result from changes in the age structure itself.

TWO VASTLY DIFFERENT PATHS LIE BEFORE US

We have tried to make the case for an optimum U.S. population size of 125 to 150 million. Since merely setting a goal is not sufficient, we have also tried to present a coherent, reasonable plan to reach that goal.

The hallmark of our recommended program is moderation. The rates of immigration and fertility we advocate are not far from those that actually existed in the fairly recent past.

We would not be alone if we succeed in reducing our fertility to 1.5. A number of countries already have a fertility rate of 1.5 or below. These include Austria, Italy, Germany, Greece, Portugal, Spain , and Japan.

As for immigration, our proposed overall ceiling of 200,000 annually would still be generous compared to that allowed by any other country. Of the over 160 nations comprising the United Nations only two, besides the United States, allow any sizable immigration: Canada and Australia.

Small differences in immigration and fertility rates can, if maintained over a considerable length of time, mean the difference of hundreds of millions in the size at which U.S. population is eventually stabilized.

With the reduction in immigration and fertility we advocate, our nation could start now on the path toward a sustainable, and prosperous, population of 125 to 150 million.

Without such a program, we are almost certain to continue our mindless, headlong rush down our current path. That path is leading us straight toward catastrophic population levels that can only devastate our environment, and produce universal poverty in a crowded, polluted nation.

Can there be any doubt which of the two directions would best serve the broad public interest, and the welfare of present and future generations of Americans?

ADDENDUM

NPG is just as concerned about world population size and growth as it is about U.S. population. We believe that world population, now about 5.5 billion, should eventually be stabilized at no more than two billion, rather than the 12 to 14 billion predicted for the next century, if present trends continue.

Our present world population is not sustainable over the long run, even with the impoverished living standards of much of the Third World. A far smaller world population than today's is the *sine qua non* for sustainable development, and for a healthy global environment.

For the benefit of both the Third World nations and ourselves, the first priority for our aid to them should be to help them develop their own programs of real population control. The goal of those programs should not be merely to slow down "rapid" or "excessive" population growth, but to achieve a sub-replacement level of fertility that would eventually result in a negative rate of population growth.

The focus of population control programs must be on non-coercive incentives to motivate parents to have not more than one or two children. They must aim at family limitation, not just family planning.

While family planning is an essential element of any population control program, it is not sufficient by itself to halt population growth in Third World countries, and must be complemented by incentives.

In Third World countries, couples typically want three to six children. Even with the complete prevention of all unwanted pregnancies, the populations of those countries would still escalate quickly to catastrophic levels. What is needed, therefore, is to change desired family size. A program of non-coercive incentives is the key to achieving this.

IMMIGRATION, JOBS & WAGES: THE MISUSES OF ECONOMICS

Donald L. Huddle

February 1992

THE NEW ORTHODOXY: IMMIGRATION IS GOOD FOR U.S. LABOR

There is a new orthodoxy that immigrants, legal and illegal, create jobs and improve wages. In this paper, I will challenge that orthodoxy.

Open-border advocates such as Julian Simon and Karl Zinsmeister of the Heritage Foundation and the American Enterprise Institute[1] assert that immigrants do not threaten even vulnerable, minority unskilled workers. They believe that immigrants complement rather than compete with native workers by filling minimum wage jobs which domestic workers will not take, by attracting industries which otherwise would move offshore to find cheap labor, and by expanding the macro economy through spending wages earned in the United States. Simon and Zinsmeister also believe that the U.S. is entering an era of long-term labor shortage in which more and more immigrants are needed to reach national goals of robust economic growth, rising labor productivity, and stable prices.

More recently, University of California Professor George J. Borjas has published a book which has been highly praised by Senator Alan K. Simpson (Ranking Republican, Senate Subcommittee on Immigration and Refugee Affairs). Borjas concludes as follows:[2]

> *"Remarkably, economists have quickly reached a consensus on the direction and magnitude of the labor market impacts of immigration. The conclusion suggested by the empirical evidence is likely to be controversial: the methodological arsenal of modern econometrics cannot detect a single shred of evidence that immigrants have a sizable adverse impact on the earnings and employment opportunities of natives in the United States."*

Indeed, Professor Borjas claimed evidence that immigrants not only do not cause harm, but are beneficial in many instances by creating jobs and raising the wages of natives.

This rosy view may already have affected immigration policy. In November 1990, the U.S. Congress passed, and President Bush signed, new immigration legislation (P.L. 101–649). In the parade of witnesses before Congress, the view was often expressed that the U.S. has too few immigrants and that their numbers ought to be increased.

As a result of this legislation, legal immigration was increased by 40 percent from the old limit of 500,000 to a new limit of 700,000 per year, not counting refugees, family members and others outside the quotas. Although the legislation was characterized as a move away from immigration based on family connections to immigration based on skills, in fact both were increased proportionately.

At the same time that legal immigration limits are being raised, levels of illegal immigration are increasing. Border apprehensions of illegal aliens climbed dramatically to over 1 million per year in 1990 for the first time in three years as the residual effects of the Immigration Control and Reform Act of 1986 began to dissipate.

Do Americans really gain from the new higher legal immigration quotas and rising illegal immigration? Undoubtedly there are individual gains due to cheaper labor costs to businesses, lower costs of goods and services to consumers and to more demand for skilled labor as the costs of unskilled labor decline [due to skilled/unskilled labor demand complementarity]. Unfortunately such gains may not be generalized across the economy. What is worse, highly vulnerable unskilled minority groups may often be harmed. Even Professor Borjas, who admits to being pro immigrant, finds the quality of U.S. immigrants has declined dramatically since the 1970s due to an emphasis on family reunification in U.S. immigration policy. The worsening quality of immigrants has led to a precipitous decline in immigrant productivity and increased welfare dependency which Borjas would offset by shifting U.S. quotas toward more highly educated and capitalized immigrants.

There are serious flaws in the analyses of both Simon and Zinsmeister as well as in Professor Borjas' typification of the econometric evidence on job displacement and wage depression. As is explained below, the average immigrant, especially the illegal, most probably constitutes a drain and not a gain for the unskilled native worker in the economy.

In the remainder of this paper, I shall look at the econometric studies that have been cited as justification for the policies and developments I have described. By no means do all the studies justify those policies. We will look first at the studies of immigration and its impact on wages, and then turn to the question of displacement of American and resident alien workers by immigrants. I will devote a separate section to the particular issues raised by illegal migration, which poses very different problems from legal immigration (although the distinction is typically blurred by open border advocates.)

Finally, as an interesting if imperfectly determinate exercise, I will construct a "Misery Index" drawing upon the best of the econometric exercises.

DOES CURRENT ECONOMETRIC RESEARCH SUPPORT THE ASSERTION THAT IMMIGRATION DOES NOT DEPRESS WAGES?

Most current scholarly research does not, in fact, support the open-border advocates. Let us examine that research.

The Borjas Study. Borjas found that for each 10 percent increase in immigrant numbers, there is only a slight, if any, negative impact on natives. For instance, for all natives, a 10 percent rise in the number of immigrants decreases native wages by only .2 percent. Thus, a doubling of immigrants, would decrease all natives' wages by only 2 percent, hardly worth a quibble by those concerned with wage-depression.

For native minority subsets of the population, he reaches the same conclusion: neither Black men, young or old, nor Hispanics are harmed. Women actually gain and even the White male is only minimally harmed.

Unfortunately for Borjas, the econometric evidence he cites is not so good. The methodology itself is somewhat weak. The data do not fit the model very well (as evidenced by low regression coefficients). And perhaps most important, Borjas himself has ignored the counter results by citing selectively from the literature.

The conceptual approach in Borjas' model looks simple and straightforward. Native earnings are compared across SMSA's (Standard Metropolitan Statistical Areas) in which there are varying numbers of immigrants to determine if SMSA's with large proportions of immigrants have lower or higher wages than SMSA's with smaller proportions of immigrants.

Here is where we come to that problem of assumptions and simplifications mentioned in the introduction. They can seriously affect the validity of the model. Naturally, native wages among different SMSA's will vary not only because of the different number of immigrants in each SMSA, but because of many other factors. The model used by Borjas and other econometricians attempts to correct for those other important factors such as skill differences, differences in the amount of capital per worker, and whether an SMSA is in a recession or a period of economic growth. Attempts to correct for these other economic factors are imperfect, however, and this in turn affects the validity of the model.

More seriously, the models have oversimplified reality by assuming that the factors they have corrected for have included all of the important factors. But they have not. For instance, economic conditions in a labor market depend upon its history of economic growth and development, the quality of its educational system, and on myriad other variables. That these factors were not explicitly accounted for in the models means that the findings will likely be distorted and yield misleading results.

Borjas turns to other comparative models to attempt to validate his assumptions and results. But when he does so by analyzing the data of SMSA wages between 1970 and 1980, he runs into other serious problems. The foremost of these is that the explanatory power of the models falls from fifty percent to only ten percent. Econometricians would agree that a model which explains only ten percent of the difference in wages between SMSA's is not very useful.

Bean, Lowell and Taylor. Borjas cites three other recent econometric studies as providing support for the near zero displacement and wage depression hypothesis. The first of these by Professor Bean, Lowell, and Taylor, which seeks to determine displacement brought about by illegal aliens, has virtually the same limitations and small explanatory power as does the study by Borjas above.[3] The assumptions needed to create the model itself were incredibly heroic. To mention merely one example, the authors assume a perfectly competitive market in which all firms maximize profits and employ each factor of production until the wage is equal to its marginal productivity. They also assume that they have been able to completely separate all capital and labor inputs in the model, although this is doubtful at best. Finally, they have no direct independent measurement of the numbers of illegal aliens in each SMSA, but depend upon unconfirmable estimates.

Despite this large number of empirically unsupportable assumptions, the final results of the Bean et al study also shows little explanatory power. Fewer than half of the findings were acceptable in terms of normal statistical significance, yet they formed the basis for the conclusion that Mexican illegal aliens do not displace native labor.

LaLonde and Topel. The second study cited is by LaLonde and Topel. It also reaches very strong conclusions such as . . . "the effect of immigration on natives appears to be minor."[4] As in the previous works cited, it has very weak explanatory power. For instance, in their several cross-section models of immigrants' and natives' earnings as between various cities, the mathematical range of error ("standard error") of their statistical estimate is actually larger than the size of the impact they derive on wages and earnings in six of eight cases for Blacks and Hispanics in one model and in eleven of twenty-four cases in another model. Moreover, in all other instances their standard errors are well over half of the coefficient values on which they base their conclusions.[5]

The Altonji-Card Model. A much more puzzling aspect of Borjas' summary of the evidence is that he completely ignored some of the best and most robust econometric results. A study by Professors Altonji and Card was cited by Borjas, but he selected out only one result of one model, the 1980 cross section model for women; he ignored their results showing more definite wage depression for Blacks, Hispanics, Whites, and earlier immigrants.[6]

Altonji and Card have progressed from a model similar to Borjas', to a more sophisticated one. Interestingly, the results varied widely. Their 1970–1980 "cross-sectional" model results were similar to Borjas'. They suggested that immigrants positively affect native unskilled earnings. They then developed an "instrumented first differences model" for the same period. It showed negative impacts. The question is: which results are "better," i.e. based upon a more sound methodology and lower standard errors?

For Altonji and Card, the answer is clear. As they state in technical language:[7]

> *"the instrumented first-differences results indicate a significantly negative effect of immigration on wages. The coefficient is -1.2 with a standard error of .242. The more negative effect associated with the instrumental variables scheme is consistent with the hypothesis that the least squares estimate is positively biased by endogenous immigration inflows."*

In other words, the better model showed a decline of more than 12 percent in the earnings of low-skilled natives for each 10 percent increase in immigrants in a SMSA. The standard error for that model, incidentally, was the lowest of the models discussed.

These are powerful results. A 10 percentage point increase in the number of immigrants in an SMSA results in almost a 20 percent fall in Black males' earnings, and 14 percent for Black females. Since the percentage of immigrants has been rising dramatically in many SMSA's in the U.S.—by more than 10 percent per decade in cities such as Los Angeles, Long Beach, Miami, Atlanta, Albuquerque, and Jersey City, the issue is of more than academic interest.

According to Altonji and Card, the newer model is econometrically much better than those on which Borjas based his summary. Unlike the models by Borjas, Bean, LaLonde and Topel, Altonji and Card focussed on low-skilled native workers—Black males and Black and White females with not more than 12 years of education, White males with less than 12 years of education, and male immigrants with less than average wages. Aside from that shift of focus, they believe the new model eliminates any bias introduced by city-specific effects. Their "instrumental variables" approach takes account of the possibility that immigrant inflows are influenced by local economic conditions. Finally, their "first difference" approach captures the short-run effects of immigration, when the capital stock and the industry skill composition of labor demand have not had time to adjust fully.

For Borjas to have ignored such powerful negative results which the authors believe to be derived from superior statistical techniques has greatly distorted the debate regarding wage depression. Even if Borjas disagrees, the Altonji-Card results cannot be ignored—that less educated Blacks, Whites, and prior immigrants have all experienced wage depression to a substantial degree in SMSA's where there have been numerous and growing immigrant populations.

WHAT DO THE ECONOMETRIC STUDIES SHOW ABOUT JOB DISPLACEMENT?

Do larger number of immigrants cause native workers to work fewer weeks per year or lose their jobs altogether? Does increased labor market competition cause natives to have greater difficulty in finding jobs, leading to higher unemployment rates?

The Borjas Study. According to Borjas' econometric summary, job displacement caused by immigration is minuscule at best. Following the same SMSA methodology as for wages, a 10 percent rise in the number of immigrants has virtually no negative impacts on Black or White male labor force participation rates or number of weeks worked. And the impact on the unemployment rate of natives is 0.

Altonji and Card. Borjas cites Altonji and Card as the data source for the impact of immigrants on both labor force participation rates and weeks worked. Once again, Borjas focuses only on their "cross-section" results. His figures, however, are an inaccurate representation even of the results of those studies. For example, Altonji and Card in the 1980 "cross-section" study find that an increase of 10 percentage points in the proportion of immigrants in a SMSA causes a 1.4 percent decline in Black male labor force participation, whereas Borjas quotes it as being from -0.1 percent to +0.4 percent points. Similarly, Altonji and Card state the impact on White males to be -0.8 percent per 10 percent whereas Borjas quotes them as stating it to be -0.1 percent. Similar differences appear in his citations for weeks worked for both White and Black males. And Borjas entirely ignores Altonji and Card's findings for both White and Black females and prior immigrants.

What Borjas does not report is as important as those differences. For example, in the 1980 study Altonji and Card show results for five categories of labor force data. Borjas reported only two. Of those not reported, many results were negative. The most flagrant example is from the category "fraction of last year worked." This category showed large negative coefficients for both unskilled Black and White males (-2 percent per 10 percentage point increase in immigrants) and Black females (-1.3 percent per 10 percentage points).

In short, Borjas understated the degree of labor displacement found by Altonji and Card even in their earlier, less sophisticated studies.[8]

The Altonji-Card coefficients in the "first differences" model show even larger negativity than did the other model for "fraction of last year worked" for both Black and White males as well as for labor force participation for Black males and Black females. The other categories were mixed—some positive and some negative, not showing a clear pattern.

THE ILLEGAL ALIEN PROBLEM

Up to this point no distinction has been made between legal and illegal alien immigrants. The econometric studies, excepting that by Bean et al, focus on all immigrants, most of whom are legal. Since the 1980 Census data included up to 2 million illegal aliens, they are included, though as a minor fraction, in the comparisons between cities.

This section will focus almost solely upon illegal aliens. Illegals hurt low-skilled U.S. workers more than do legal immigrants for the following reasons: First, illegals work cheaper, often below minimum wage, and off the books. Second, they have little legal protection from employers who may exploit them. Such employers pay substandard wages, no overtime, and seldom contribute to medical insurance and workers compensation. Third, employers of illegals seldom pay even the legally required social security and federal income withholding taxes on illegal employees' wages. As a result, the employer pays a lower gross wage and gains a cost advantage over his market competitors largely at the expense of the U.S. taxpayer and the competing legal immigrant worker.

Public recognition of the tremendous social and private cost of illegal immigration finally forced Congress to take action and pass the Immigration Reform and Control Act of 1986 (IRCA). In fact, IRCA has been a deeply flawed reform, but it temporarily reduced illegal immigration and it took pressure off Congress and the President to do anything about the rupturing U.S.- Mexican border, at least for the time being.

Aside from the econometric studies above, which were cited by Borjas, there is an extensive literature, based on field studies and other approaches, that addresses the problems of labor displacement and wage depression.[9] On balance, it supports the wage depression and job displacement hypothesis.

Unfortunately, given the paucity of data on illegals and the difficulty of separating their impact from that of legal aliens, the evidence about the specific impact of the illegal migrants is blurred, but here are the highlights of those studies.

Cornelius. Professor Wayne Cornelius, a political scientist who heads the Center for Latin American Studies at the University of California, San Diego, is a noted advocate scholar who has propagated the windfall thesis with respect to Mexican migrant labor. Dr. Cornelius has done extensive field studies on Mexican transborder migrants. His thesis, based on 1960s and 1970s data, was that Mexican villagers, who worked in the U.S. seasonally for over three generations on agri-related businesses, have not displaced U.S. labor.

Cornelius believed this migrant cycle to have been advantageous to both Mexico and the U.S. Should U.S. immigration policy attempt to cut off the flow of Mexican seasonal labor, he argued that American laborers would lose out because U.S. businesses would seek out cheap labor overseas, not only in agribusiness, but also in the garment, shoe, and electronics industries as well.

One long standing empirical controversy began when Wayne Cornelius claimed proof that Mexican illegals did not cause the displacement of U.S. workers.[10] His premise was that for displacement to be occurring, unemployment rates in areas with many illegal alien workers should be higher than the national average. Cornelius found the rates were not higher. There seemed to be virtually no correlation between number of illegals and levels of unemployment in the eight labor areas he examined, four of which—Dallas, Fort Worth, Houston, and San Antonio—were in Texas. Contrary to expectations, Cornelius found that unemployment rates in the high-impact areas were even less than the U.S. average. He concluded, therefore, that there had been no labor displacement.

Yet even Cornelius realized that his thesis about migrants had become partly outdated by the early 1980s. As Mexico's population surged, bringing one million new entrants into the labor force yearly, along with the deep recession of the 1980s, there were too few jobs to be had in Mexico. Millions were pushed out of Mexico to the U.S. for economic survival. Although many intended to eventually return to Mexico, most have not because the employment situation has not improved. By now many will not return to Mexico because several million have received amnesty to remain legally in the U.S.

Though not fully admitting that his old model was no longer operational, Cornelius indicates as much indirectly in his summary of current knowledge on Mexican migrants in Southern California. He sums up the evidence as follows:[11]

> *"In some labor markets, especially those where labor contractors and sub-contract shops have become prevalent, downward pressure on wages and working conditions may be more severe, and some U.S.-born workers (and even legal immigrants) may be discouraged from seeking jobs in those sectors. . . . There is undoubtedly some level of direct displacement of U.S. born workers and legal immigrants by Mexican illegals, in certain job categories, certain industries, and certain geographical areas . . ." The new conclusion was that illegal immigrants brought both benefits and costs rather than all windfall benefits as in his prior model. Interestingly, the incontrovertible evidence for the new model was gathered mostly by field researchers and scholars working out of Cornelius' own Center for Mexican—U.S. Studies.*

North. David North, himself a pioneer immigration researcher, found that Cornelius had used simple averages of regional unemployment rates. North then took the analysis a step further by comparing unemployment rates of U.S. cities with different ratios of legal Mexican immigrants to the total population. He found that cities which had relatively large number of immigrants, such as El Paso, Santa Ana, Stockton, Los Angeles, and San Antonio, had more unemployment (7.6 percent) compared to intermediate levels (6.2 percent) for medium impact cities, and low levels (5.7 percent) for low-impact cities.[12] Thus, North's results strikingly reversed Cornelius'. North's approach was more convincing than Cornelius', but his basic assumption that illegal aliens were distributed in proportion to the distribution of legal aliens cannot be verified, along with other unverified assumptions, so even his results remain less than completely convincing.

Cross and Sandos. In a later survey, Cross and Sandos concluded that North's results were the more persuasive and support the displacement hypothesis.[13]

Cross and Sandos concluded that both economic theory and wage data suggest that citizen workers are directly displaced by illegals from Mexico. However, they could not determine conclusively the real extent of displacement. To them the most difficult question is not "whether" displacement occurs but to "what extent" it occurs. Their best estimate was that three million illegal workers would displace between 300,000 and 600,000 American workers. Thus, direct displacement would be between ten and twenty percent.

Briggs. Vernon Briggs showed a similar connection within the state of Texas: correlations between the number of undocumented Mexicans and unemployment and between lower wages and poorer working and social conditions in south Texas as compared to non-border areas.[14]

Smith and Newman. Later on, Smith and Newman carried out a fairly sophisticated check of the Briggs hypothesis when they compared labor market conditions in three border areas—Brownsville, Corpus Christi, and Laredo—to those in Houston.[15] The study presumed that any "unexplained" variance between wage scales in Houston and those in the border areas would be a result of the (assumed) lesser presence of illegal migrants in Houston. In fact, they did find an eight percent real wage differential in Houston's favor, their conclusion being that forces along the border did depress wages and earnings.

Smith and Newman's approach, while it was a step forward, understates the amount of displacement simply because Houston is proximate to the border and has the largest illegal population in Texas. Illegals regularly come to Houston and, if they are apprehended by the INS, they rapidly return in a short time. Since Houston is so close to the border areas and since its economy was expanding rapidly during this period, its attractiveness to illegals seeking work held down its wage differential. Otherwise the eight percent differential found by Smith and Newman would have been larger, implying much greater displacement. Moreover, wage differences and measured displacement were held down in the border cities themselves as both Mexican Americans and non-Mexicans emigrated in search of higher real wages elsewhere in the U.S. If not for this movement, observed displacement would have been higher.

Van Arsdol. Quite aside from wage rate and unemployment differences between areas and cities, other researchers have analyzed wage scales of legal workers and compared them to those of illegal workers of similar skill. If illegals are working at wages as high as or higher than the minimum at which legals are willing to work, displacement may be occurring.

The Van Arsdol team data for Los Angeles indicated that of 1,956 workers interviewed between 1972 and 1975, the majority of whom were Mexicans, the upper quartile earned between $17,000 and $18,000 per year in 1986 prices.[16] In Texas, annual earnings levels for the top forty percent of illegal workers apprehended by the INS have been lower than in Los Angeles, but are still higher than commonly believed—ranging from $14,000 to $15,000 per year.

Papademetriou and Muller. A joint study of New York City by these authors asserts a thesis closer to Cornelius. Although Papademetriou and Muller admit there were some negative effects of immigrants on New York natives, they believe these were much more than counterbalanced by the positive impacts of greater competition, more jobs, wage growth, keeping industries at home, and the positive macroeconomic impacts of greater immigrant spending.[17]

Unfortunately, the authors upbeat conclusions regarding immigrants, particularly illegal aliens, are not persuasive. First, their study apparently excluded micro-economic labor markets—labor displacement is studied only at the macro level. Second, their study offers little detail and is limited almost exclusively to the legal immigrant population. Third, the study takes little notice of other economic factors which influence displacement.

Marshall. One study by Adrianna Marshall, which did take account of the influence of these other economic factors, arrived at very different conclusions. When comparing New York's high immigrant population with other cities, such as Philadelphia, with a low immigrant population, she found that wage growth was actually much slower in New York than in low immigrant cities after controlling for important factors such as industrial structure, unionization, productivity, inflation, and unemployment rates.[18]

Other Studies. Council of Economic Advisers Chairman Beryl Sprinkel in 1987 claimed that labor displacement was near zero.[19] He later drew back from that claim. In fact, neither Sprinkel nor the Council itself had conducted any studies, but merely seemed to be reciting Simon, Muller, and a Rand Corporation study selectively.[20]

The only official study, by the U.S. Government Accounting Office, which synthesized information from more than 51 studies, in 1986 very cautiously concluded the following:[21]

> *". . . illegal workers were found in all major categories of industry and occupation. Their presence in agriculture decreased and in other sectors of the economy increased as they became more settled. This suggests the possibility of widespread displacement . . .data from both types of study are consistent with the findings that illegal alien workers probably displace native workers."*

THE "MISERY INDEX": THE IMPACT OF IMMIGRATION GROWTH ON THE UNSKILLED NATIVE WORKER

To measure just how the unskilled are affected by the growth of immigration, the concept of the "immigration misery index" is developed here, drawing upon the Altonji-Card "first differences" model. The misery index is defined as the measured negative changes in three labor force categories—the wage rate, the ratio of labor force participation to population, and the fraction of the past year worked. Obviously, declines in these measures mean less work and lower earnings and hence more misery for the unskilled native work force.

The data and the derivation of the "immigration misery index" for 1970–1980 are shown in the table. The index is derived for all unskilled natives—in all SMSAs the overall misery index increased by over 15 percent for each 10 percentage point increase in immigrants—and for each category of the unskilled. The greatest negative impact was on Black males, for whom the index increased by almost 25 percent. Black female and White male earnings and jobs declined by about 18 percent. White females were least impacted at 12 percent.

Real wages were already declining during the 1970–80 decade by more than 8 percent, so immigration-induced misery was added to an already deteriorating real standard of earnings.[22]

Admittedly, the immigration misery index is based upon an econometric study and therefore it is not definitive due to potential biases and sources of error. It is, however, based upon Altonji and Card's "instrumented first differences" model—considered by some to be the most definitive study to date of the impact of immigrants upon unskilled natives.

Nor does the immigration misery index pretend to measure all impacts of immigration. For instance, the index excludes overcrowding, environmental deterioration, and crime, all of which would tend to increase misery.

Quite aside from these excluded factors, however, the index probably understates negative impacts on wages and employment of unskilled workers because it is diluted. The employment data that Altonji and Card (and Borjas) use are for Standard Metropolitan Statistical Areas (SMSAs). As Vernon Briggs pointed out:[23]

> *"An SMSA contains a large central city and, usually, its several adjacent counties . . . If foreign born workers are disproportionately concentrated in the central cities of SMSA's (which they are), the inclusion of the data for*

adjacent counties will dilute the measurement of their impact in the labor markets of the central cities."

Moreover, the misery index does not reflect the facts as seen on the ground. Net labor displacement was shown to vary over time from 27 to 50 percent in the Houston SMSA according to our field experiments (to be reported in a subsequent FORUM article). Yet, according to the econometrically derived "misery index," displacement in Houston was only 2.8 percent and wage depression 9.6 percent.

The misery indexes for the native unskilled in the central cities could be substantially higher (perhaps by a factor of 3 or more times) than the totals shown in the table. But there is no definitive way of accounting for the large differences at this juncture.

CONCLUSIONS AND FINAL OBSERVATIONS

Contrary to statements made by Borjas, Cornelius, Papademetriou and Muller, the most sophisticated and perhaps methodologically sound econometric studies strongly support the wage depression-labor displacement hypothesis for unskilled citizen workers. I have pointed out that the Altonji-Card study suggests that increasing numbers of immigrants caused an average 12 percent decline in the wage rates of unskilled legal U.S. workers in samples covering 91 to 121 SMSA's across the U.S. between 1970 and 1980. Labor displacement occurred, and labor force participation rates were also negatively affected across the nation, though less than the wage depression.

Notwithstanding the apparent improvement in methodology reflected in the newer Altonji-Card model, we cannot be confident that their estimates are definitive. The current state of econometrics in this area is in some disarray. Estimates vary widely, as do the models.

Despite this state of confusion, there seems to be emerging some consensus that there are real negative impacts on low-skilled natives. Professor Borjas himself, in a recent working paper, substantially revises his earlier conclusion that immigrants do not depress wages of unskilled natives. To quote:

> *By 1988, trade and immigration increased the effective supply of high school dropouts by 28 percent for men and 31 percent for women. We estimate that from thirty to fifty percent of the approximately 10 percentage point decline in the relative weekly wage of high school dropouts between 1980 and 1988 can be attributed to the trade and immigration flows.*[24]

Numerous non-econometric studies (including ours in the Houston SMSA) have also concluded that immigration has substantial negative wage and employment effects.

The plight of the unskilled worker will likely become more rather than less serious. The Immigration Act of 1990 will increase legal immigration by 200,000 or more per year. Although some of the new immigrants will be skilled and educated workers who will presumably not compete with unskilled workers, the great majority of the new immigrants will compete with them. In an earlier NPG FORUM paper Vernon Briggs pointed to our failure to synchronize immigration flows with the demonstrated needs of the U.S. labor market.[25] U.S. immigration policy has penalized U.S. minorities and unskilled workers.

Efforts are now under way in Congress to repeal the employer sanctions portion of the Immigration Reform and Control Act of 1986. Imperfect as they have been, employer sanctions have at least partially slowed potentially massive flows of illegal aliens from Mexico and Central America. Employer sanctions have been found to be discriminatory by the GAO, but hiring practices are probably no more discriminatory now than they were prior to employer sanctions. Their repeal, in any event, will primarily hurt those who compete most directly with illegal aliens—the unskilled, minority worker. If anything, employer sanctions should be strengthened.

The Bush administration is also pushing hard for a Free Trade Agreement (FTA) with Mexico. An FTA will mean an exportation of U.S. jobs as our capital flows to Mexico. It may also result in increased immigration.[26]

As more U.S. jobs and capital go south, and as larger numbers of immigrants, legal and illegal, enter the U.S. job market seeking a shrinking number of unskilled jobs, we must wonder when we as Americans will begin to weigh the plight of our own unemployed and low-wage underemployed more heavily in our policy decisions. With more than 32 million Americans in poverty and more than 10 percent of the potential labor force unemployed and underemployed, a well conceived and implemented shift in policy is needed now.

NOTES:

1. Julian L. Simon, *The Economic Consequences of Immigration*, (Basil Blackwell Ltd. and The Cato Institute, 1989) especially pp. 194–253. Simon has many other articles devoted to questions of labor displacement and wage depression which are quoted in the above chapters. Karl Zinsmeister, "Does the United States Need Immigration Generated Growth?" presented at the conference: The Purpose of Legal Immigration in the 1990s and Beyond. The Federation for American Immigration Reform, Washington, D.C. June 10, 1988. Zinsmeister was basically attacking Governor of Colorado 0Richard Lamm's position on the negative impacts of both legal and illegal immigration.
2. George J. Borjas, *Friends or Strangers: The Impact of Immigrants on the U.S. Economy.* (Basic Books Inc., New York, 1990) 80–81.
3. Frank D. Bean, B. Lindsey Lowell, and Lowell J. Taylor, "Undocumented Mexican Immigrants and the Earnings of Other Workers in the United States," *Demography*, (Vol. 25, No. 1, Feb. 1988), 35–52.
4. Robert J. LaLonde and Robert H. Topel, "Labor Market Adjustments to Increased Immigration": in John M. Aboud and Richard B. Freeman (eds.), op. cit. (Table I (5)), 167–200.
5. Ibid, Table 6.10, p.186.
6. Borjas, *Friends or Strangers*, op. cit. p. 87. Borjas does not explain how he derived average values in his table. He explained to me in a telephone conversation on January 24, 1992 that he did not fully understand the instrumented variables model of Altonji and Card and therefore he did not use it.
7. Joseph G. Altonji and David Card "The Effects of Immigration on the Labor Market Outcomes of Less-skilled Natives," in Aboud and Freeman, op. cit., p. 221.
8. This may have been partly unintentional. Professor Borjas stated in a 1/24/92 telephone conversation with me that he was working with an early draft of the Altonji-Card paper.
9. David North and Marion Houstoun, *The Characteristics of Illegal Aliens in the U.S. Labor Market: An Exploratory Study* (Washington, D.C. Linton and Company and New Transcentury Foundation. March 1976.)
10. For this controversy see Harry E. Cross and James A. Sandos, *Across the Border: Rural Development in Mexico and Recent Migration to the United States* (Institute of Government Studies, University of California, Berkeley, 1981), pp.85–89.
11. Wayne A. Cornelius, Leo R. Chavez, Jorge G. Castro, *Mexican Immigrants and Southern California: A Summary of Current Knowledge*

(Center for U.S.-Mexican Studies, University of California, La Jolla, California, 1982), p. 46.

12. David North in U.S. Congressional Record, Senate, (S 19523-S 19525, December 20, 1979.)
13. Op. cit. Cross and Sandos, p. 85.
14. Vernon M. Briggs, Jr. *Mexican Migration and the U.S. Labor Market* (Center for the Study of Human Resources and the Bureau of Business Research, The University of Texas, Austin, 1975), pp.25–30.
15. Barton Smith and Robert Newman, "Depressed Wages Along the U.S.—Mexico Border: An Empirical Analysis," *Economic Inquiry*, (15 January 1977), pp.51–66.
16. Maurice Van Arsdol, Joan W. Moore, David M. Heer, and Susan Paulivir Haynie, "Non-Apprehended and Apprehended Undocumented Residents in the Los Angeles Labor Market," (Report prepared for the Employment and Training Administration, U.S. Department of Labor. Los Angeles, 1979.)
17. Demetrios G. Papademetriou and Thomas Muller, "Recent Immigration to New York: Labor Market and Social Policy Issues." A Report Prepared for the National Commission for Employment Policy (Washington, D.C. February 1987), p.166.
18. Adrianna Marshall, "Immigration in a Surplus Worker Labor Market: The Case of New York." (New York University, Research Program in Inter-American Affairs. 1983.) Gregory De Freitah and Adrianna Marshall, "Immigration and Wage Growth in U.S. Manufacturing in the 1970s." (Annual Meeting of the Industrial Relations Research Assoc., San Francisco, CA, Proceedings 1984.)
19. The original statement by Sprinkel was in *The Economic Report of the President* (Washington, D.C., February 1987).
20. Kevin McCarthy and R. Burciago Valdez, *Current and Future Effects of Mexican Immigration in California*, (the Rand Corporation, R-3365-CR, Santa Monica, May 1986, pp.1–103.
21. United States General Accounting Office, *Illegal Aliens: Limited Research Suggests Illegal Aliens May Displace Native Workers*. (Washington, D.C. April 1986), p. 35.
22. *Economic Report of the President* (U.S. GPO,Washington DC, 1990). Table C-44, p.344. Private average weekly earnings fell from $187 in 1970 to $173 in 1980; 1977 dollars.
23. Vernon M. Briggs, Jr., "The Declining Competitiveness of Immigrants—Review: George J. Borjas Book," Friends or Strangers: The Impact of Immigrants on the U.S. Economy." (The Center For Immigration Studies, Scope, No. 5, Summer 1990),p.4. Note that the employment effects in industry are likewise understated by the econometric studies by using the broad classifications such as manufacturing rather than specific sub-classifications such as apparel manufacturing. Since immigrant workers tend to be crowded into a few sub-classifications, the adverse effects of immigrant workers on wages and employment opportunities for all workers in the broad industrial classification are minimized.
24. George J. Borjas, Richard B. Freeman and Laurence F. Katz, "On the Labor Market Effects of Immigration and Trade," National Bureau of Economic Research Working Paper No. 3761, June 1991, p.33.
25. Vernon M. Briggs, Jr., "Political Confrontation with Economic Reality: Mass Immigration in the Post-Industrial Age," the NPG FORUM (February 1990).
26. Lindsey Grant, "Free Trade and Cheap Labor: The President's Dilemma," the NPG FORUM (October 1991.)

REFUGEE AND ASYLUM POLICY: NATIONAL PASSION VERSUS NATIONAL INTEREST

David Simcox and Rosemary Jenks

February 1992

For most of its history, the United States considered itself a haven for refugees but did not do much about it. With increasing third world population growth and turmoil in many countries, however, provisions for refugee admissions have become increasingly generous. Part of this has reflected conscious policy; more of it has been more or less accidental, resulting from an accretion of specific concessions won by interest groups through Congress or the courts.

The flow of refugees and other humanitarian admissions now approximates 1.6 million each decade, or some 15.6 percent of total immigration. Immigration, in turn, constitutes a major element in U.S. population growth. At current fertility levels, with immigration at the level set by present law and continued illegal immigration, the United States population will pass 400 million around 2050.

If this prospect daunts the reader, as it does the authors, there are humane ways to bring some degree of order to refugee and humanitarian admissions, which presently are not numerically limited by statute.

THE AMERICAN "MISSION"

Few public concerns have engaged America's sense of humanitarianism, generosity, and openness to the world more than the needs of refugees. In 1783 George Washington called America a land whose "bosom is open to receive the persecuted and oppressed of all nations." Washington was one of the first of many national leaders to proclaim acceptance of refugees as a redemptive national mission in which the best instincts of American society are manifest. Immigration historian John Higham notes that early in America's history ". . . the idea of America's mission to provide a home for the oppressed became a cliche, an incantation."[1]

Republican presidential candidate Ronald Reagan repeated the incantation 200 years later in his acceptance speech at the 1980 Republican Party Convention:

> *Can we doubt that only a Divine Providence placed this land, this island of freedom, here as a refuge for all those people who yearn to breathe free? Jews and Christians enduring persecution behind the Iron Curtain; the boat people of Southeast Asia, Cuba, and of Haiti; the victims of drought and famine in Africa; the freedom fighters in Afghanistan . . .* [2]

When George Washington welcomed the world's persecuted and oppressed, the newly independent United States was home to fewer than four million people. The planet Earth's population was estimated at about 800 million, one seventh of its present total. Three quarters of the world's people were in Europe and Asia, then separated from the United States by forbidding oceans. Latin America, now the major source of migrants to this country, had fewer than 20 million people, most of whom had no awareness of George Washington's offer or the means to act on it in any event.

The numbers of those perceived as "persecuted and oppressed" have grown even more rapidly than world population since Washington's time. The United Nations High Commission for Refugees (UNHCR) estimates there are now 15 million persons who could be classified as refugees in the world—uprooted Afghans in Pakistan, fugitives from conflicts in a wide swath of East African states, displaced Central Americans and Middle Eastern minorities, those fleeing Southeast Asia's interminable wars, and those reeling from the social and economic upheaval in the former Eastern Bloc nations.

But the UNHCR far understates the rising pressures for resettlement of restless people in the United States and other stable western industrial countries. As population growth has spiraled in the third world, and the mass media have presented migration as an option, demand for immigration to the United States by whatever means and in whatever categories has intensified. Cheap and easily available transportation makes large scale transfers of population a practical option. In the scramble for admission, distinctions between refugees and ordinary immigrants have blurred.

THE WIDENING GATE

As demand for entry has risen—and in part because it has risen—lawmakers and jurists in United States have responded by expanding the pool of potential humanitarian entrants by easing the criteria for refugee and asylum status and by creating new humanitarian admission categories. In 1989, for example, the Bush Administration created a new class of "reproductive refugees" by ordering "enhanced consideration" for the asylum claims of pregnant Chinese women and their spouses claiming to flee mandatory abortion or sterilization in the Peoples Republic of China.[3] 1990 immigration legislation provides a new "temporary protected status" for aliens in the U.S. either illegally or temporarily, whose countries are experiencing generalized violence or environmental disaster (PL 101–649, Sec.302).

Even though harboring the oppressed has become virtually a secular religion, for many years U.S. immigration laws made no special concessions for persons fleeing oppression. They came as ordinary immigrants, were admitted under the same conditions, and received no government resettlement assistance. Since the U.S. had no quota limits on immigration until 1921, those claiming to flee turmoil or oppression had no need for priority admission. But with the adoption of quotas, refugees began competing with ordinary immigrants for a finite pool of visas.

Beginning in the post-World War II period, the government devised a series of special measures to speed the admission of a variety of troubled groups such as holocaust survivors, displaced Europeans, Hungarian freedom fighters, anti-communist Cubans, and war-scarred Indochinese. Since 1945 the United States has admitted over 2.8 million people for humanitarian reasons outside the normal immigration stream.

The 1980 Refugee Act: Seeking an Elusive Discipline. Congress passed the 1980 Refugee Act to consolidate the profusion of special and ad hoc arrangements, to bring U.S. criteria and procedures for granting refugee status into line with international law, and to grant resettlement assistance. The Act (8 USC 1101 (a)(42)) defines refugees as persons who are persecuted or who have

". . . a well founded fear of persecution on account of race, religion, nationality, membership in a particular social group, or political opinion."

The Act anticipated a "normal flow" of refugees into the United States of 50,000 a year. One of its goals was to establish political and geographic neutrality in judging refugee status, ending the then-existing presumption that all those leaving communist lands were refugees.

After a decade of rising demands for refugee admissions, how successful has the Refugee Act been in imposing restraint, consistency, discipline and political neutrality in granting refugee status?

The record for the decade since the Act is unpromising. It highlights the unrelenting pressures on Congress and the Executive to bend the existing rules or devise new ones when admission of those backed by powerful constituencies would otherwise be delayed or denied. The political pliability displayed by Congress and the Executive Branch, and the insensitivity of the Courts on questions of asylum law to the broader public interest in immigration control, don't augur well for discipline in the years ahead. The uneven record of the recent past points to the problems of management likely in the near future:

"Ad Hocracy" over Consistency. Scarcely a month after the Refugee Act was passed in March 1980, the Carter Administration faced a major mass asylum situation when 125,000 Cuban boat people and several thousand Haitians landed in South Florida over several months. Washington declined to use the refugee machinery or apply the criteria and adjudications procedures in the Act, but instead created a new, ad hoc blanket immigration category for the Cubans: "entrant, status pending." (Since then Cuban and Haitian entrants have been awarded permanent resident status.) There was no effort to make a case by case determination of the extent of individual persecution of the boat people or to return those found not at risk.

The Refugee Act also aimed at curbing the Attorney General's use of his sweeping "parole" authority, which had been used in the 1970s for emergency admissions of hundreds of thousands of Southeast Asian Refugees. But "paroles" continue to be handed out, exceeding 18,000 in 1989, mostly for high priority refugee applicants, such as Eastern Europeans and Soviet minorities, who did not fit within the numerical limits or failed to meet the definition of refugees.

Congress itself has legislated special exceptions when application of the criteria in the Refugee Act would have turned away too many. Political liberalization in the Soviet Union in 1989 opened wider the gates for the emigration of thousands of Soviet Jews, but at the same time made it more difficult to prove a well founded fear of persecution. In the 1989 Morrison-Lautenberg Act, Congress legislated a "presumption of eligibility for Soviet Jews." Certain other groups at risk were also granted the presumption in the legislative logrolling: Soviet Pentacostals, Ukrainian Christians, and certain Southeast Asians.[4] (Congress began feeling similar pressures in early 1991 to legislate a special humanitarian admission program for some of the nearly half-million non-minority Soviets expected to take advantage of free emigration from the former-USSR in the coming years. Mostly ethnic Russians, the Soviets will not qualify as refugees and lack the family connections in the United States for regular immigration.)

In creating a presumption of persecution, Congress was just following a precedent set by the Executive. After the Refugee Act came into force in 1980, Immigration and Naturalization Service (INS) interviewers in Southeast Asia began rejecting large numbers of applicants under the new and tighter criteria. Led by the State Department, a displeased Washington changed the INS leadership in the area and issued a directive that INS presume any alien

MIGRATION TO THE U.S. BY DECADES

	1951-1960	1961-1970	1971-1980	1981-1990
Humanitarian Immigration	492,371	212,843	539,447	1,608,389
Total Immigration*	4,515,479	5,321,677	6,993,314	9,871,059
Humanitarian as a % of Total Immigration	10.9%	4.0%	7.7%	16.3%

SOURCE: Immigration and Naturalization Service

* Total Immigration for 1951-1970 includes an estimated 200,000 illegal entrants each year, while Total Immigration for 1971-1990 includes an estimated 250,000 illegal entrants each year (except 1981 and 1982 since illegal entrants from that period were later legalized by IRCA and counted in total immigration figures for 1989 and 1990).

Figure 1.

who left an Indo-Chinese country to be a refugee, without further inquiry.[5]

Creation of favorable "presumptions" for preferred groups abroad has had costs. One of those costs has been the undermining of the Executive's position in trying to hold the line against special preferential arrangements for other applicants for refugee or asylum status.

The Loophole Created by Political Bias. Before the 1980 Act U.S. refugee policy was designed largely to benefit fugitives from communism. But a decade after the Act established the principle of ideological neutrality in determining refugee status, refugees continue to come overwhelmingly from communist or communist-influenced states unfriendly to the U.S. 1990 was a typical year. Refugees were admitted predominantly from the former-USSR, Vietnam, Laos, Cambodia, Poland, Romania, Afghanistan and Cuba, all now—or until recently—communist or communist-controlled. Asylum seekers from those same countries also were approved at rates significantly above the worldwide average. Non-Communist countries with repressive governments, but which are friendly to the United States, such as those of Central America, have asylum approval rates markedly below the worldwide average. Soviet asylum seekers were approved at a rate of 82.4 percent in 1990, while only 2.6 percent of those from El Salvador were approved. This seeming lack of evenhandedness has made the U.S. government vulnerable in litigation. Refugee advocates successfully used this revealing data on asylum approvals to prove government bias against Central Americans in a negotiated settlement in 1990 of *American Baptist Churches v. Thornburgh.*[6]

The Law's Delay: Asylum as a Mass Immigration Channel. Although they are like refugees in many respects and are judged under the same criteria, asylum seekers differ under the 1980 Act because they are persons already in the U.S., or at a port of entry, who seek to remain here by proving a well founded fear of persecution.

The right of aliens to apply for asylum, which was strengthened in the 1980 Act, has become a powerful magnet for illegal immigration and a major obstacle to quick and consistent removal of illegal entrants. Aliens applying for asylum can pursue a chain of tedious and time-consuming hearings and appeals through the INS adjudication machinery, the Department of Justice's immigration courts, and the Federal court system—a process that can easily take several years. Deportation of the alien claimant must await resolution of this process, which provides time for the alien affected to marry an American, have U.S. citizen children or gain other "equities" in the U.S. that will make him deportation-proof. Decisions in Federal court have steadily increased the procedural safeguards for alien claimants or eased their burden of proof. INS, as a deterrent to frivolous asylum claims, has denied work authorization to some asylum claimants. This practice is now also under attack in the courts, in addition to its not being fully implemented because of INS's lack of staff.

The 1990 court settlement in *American Baptist Churches v. Thornburgh* required the U.S. government to grant rehearings or new hearings under more lenient ground rules to more than three hundred thousand illegal aliens from El Salvador and Guatemala who have applied for asylum. The decision will grant work authorization to those aliens and in most cases provide an additional three years in the United States, whatever the outcome.

Most of those claimants denied formal asylum remain here underground or in some temporary status. In fact, an estimated 80 percent of all asylum claimants will remain in the U.S., even though the current (1990) approval rate is less than 20 percent. Ultimately, those who stay illegally or in temporary status are likely to be the beneficiaries of special legalization arrangements. Awareness abroad of the asylum system's lenience and ease of manipulation is a powerful incentive to thousands of other hopeful migrants abroad to try their luck.

Temporary Protected Status: How Temporary? Until 1990, the Department of Justice had used a special administrative authority of the Attorney General, "Extended Voluntary Departure," to stay temporarily the deportation of aliens from troubled countries who did not qualify as refugees. Since the 1960s some sixteen countries had been designated for this status. While this form of protection was considered temporary, many of its beneficiaries have eventually become permanent residents through amnesty, marriage or special legislative arrangements.

In the Immigration Act of 1990 Congress refined and expanded the concept of "Extended Voluntary Departure" into "Temporary Protected Status (TPS)," an arrangement for ostensibly temporary refuge for aliens from troubled countries. The legislation significantly expands the coverage of American refugee policy, extending potential eligibility for safe haven in the United States to hundreds of millions of those threatened in their home countries by generalized violence or environmental disasters such as famines, earthquakes and floods.

The law specifically designated migrants from El Salvador, in the U.S. by September 1990, as eligible for Temporary Protected Status for at least eighteen months, requiring no test of individual risk. Estimates of eligible Salvadoran illegal aliens run as high as 350,000. Subsequently, the Attorney General has used his authority under the statute to give similar safe haven to aliens from Liberia, Lebanon, Kuwait and Somalia. As of December 1991, 196,335 migrants had been granted TPS, of whom almost 95 percent were Salvadoran.

Immigrant advocates have been pressing for similar status for Guatemalans and for more than 50,000 Nicaraguans in irregular status who can no longer hope for asylum because of the restoration of democratic government in Managua in 1990. The chronic poverty and instability of most of the Third World ensures a continuing abundance of candidate nations for designation for temporary protected status.

THE RISING NUMBERS

All indicators point to a migrant intake system near overload. Net legal and illegal immigration to the United States has surpassed one million annually.

Some 2.5 million are on waiting lists abroad for visas. A recent study by the Census Bureau found that there are 20 million immediate relatives of American citizens and resident aliens living abroad potentially eligible for entry with an immigration preference. A 1989 *Los Angeles Times* poll in Mexico found that 4.7 million Mexicans—about 7 percent of the total population of 67 million—intended to immigrate to the United States. More than 100 thousand persons applied for asylum in 1989 and 75,000 in 1990—twenty-five times the numbers of the yearly applications in the 1970s. And after some decline between 1987 and 1989, arrests of illegal entrants by immigration officials have since risen sharply, breaking one million in 1990.

Just under one million refugees were admitted during the decade of the 1980s, and 1.5 million since 1975. Parole, grants of asylum, and extended voluntary departure ("EVD"—an administrative measure used to delay the deportation of persons from troubled countries) added more than 700,000 to those settling under humanitarian categories during the decade. Refugee admissions peaked in 1980, the first year of the Act, at 207,000, but by 1986 had declined to 62,000 a year because of budget pressures (in the 1980s, refugees received Federal and State cash grants or services that cost about $7000 per person per year during their initial period of settlement) and concern in Congress that the outflow of Southeast Asians was evolving into a permanent migration stream. But in no year since the Act was passed have refugee admissions fallen to the 50,000 level "normal flow" envisioned by Congress.

Indeed, refugee admissions began climbing again in 1988 because of the Soviet government's looser emigration rules for minorities such as Jews and Armenians. By 1990 admissions of refugees and parolees were up to 143,000, 80 percent Soviets and Southeast Asians, and still climbing.

Worldwide demand for settlement in the United States is expected to continue surging in the 1990s: the growth of the working age population of the Third World will accelerate; the expanded numbers of earlier immigrants now in the U. S. will strive to bring in family and friends by any available admissions channel; and political and social unrest will most likely continue to trouble much of Africa, Latin America, the Middle East, Eastern Europe and the former-Soviet Union. Admissions under refugee and other humanitarian provisions, which are unlimited by law, could become a much more important source of new settlers during the present decade, adding as many as two and a half million to three million newcomers.

Powerful humanitarian impulses within Congress, the prevalence of ethnic politics on Capitol Hill, overloaded machinery for intake of regular immigrants, and the magnetic pull of asylum could make humanitarian admissions the largest and most rapidly growing form of migration in the 1990s.

CONTROLLING THE GROWTH OF HUMANITARIAN ADMISSIONS

What are the options for better control and management of this swelling flow?

A Comprehensive Ceiling. Basic to the return of discipline to an overtaxed immigration system is a comprehensive ceiling on all admissions, including refugees, that takes into account broader population and labor force considerations. This concept has surfaced occasionally in Congress and, in emasculated form, appears in the 1990 Immigration Act, though it exempts refugees. In a truly effective ceiling, refugee and mass asylum emergencies requiring higher admissions would be offset by lower admissions of other categories of entrants in that year, such as immediate family members and professionals and skilled workers. To cope with extraordinarily large and urgent refugee flows that could pre-empt all other immigration, the ceiling could provide for "borrowing" ceiling slots from subsequent years, to be fully repaid in the form of reduced admission in no less than three years. Those admitted in temporary protected status would be charged to the ceiling, but the ceiling numbers would be restored if they were to leave the United States within three years.

Curbing Abuse of Asylum Claims. Prolonged delays in making decisions on asylum claims are an opportunity for the determined illegal settler and a magnet for hopeful migrants abroad. Both the number of asylum claims accepted for adjudication and the time used to decide them need to be reduced. Just as the U.S. Government determines in advance the countries from which it will accept refugees, it should maintain a specific limited list, subject to periodic revisions, of countries whose residents would not be eligible to claim asylum. Included on this list would be a sizable number of the world's countries where human rights standards are adequate, where evidence of persecution is weak, or where sufficient alternative remedies for those problems are available to the aggrieved citizen at home. Asylum seekers from countries not listed as ineligible for asylum consideration would receive prompt and rigorous screening to determine their suitability for full asylum adjudication. Those found in screening to have no arguable basis for pursuing asylum would be promptly repatriated to their home countries. The prospect of a rapid decision and quick repatriation would deter others seeking to immigrate through the asylum channel. All persons approved for asylum each year would be charged to the overall immigration ceiling.

Even with these prudent limitations, the United States would maintain a generous and flexible policy of humanitarian admissions by world standards. Failure to move now toward discipline and rational management of this emotion-laden immigration category means open-ended growth of admissions and continued decline in the integrity and efficacy of U.S. refugee and asylum programs.

NOTES:

1. John Higham, *Strangers in the Land: Patterns of American Nativism*, 1860–1926 (New Brunswick, NJ: Rutgers University Press, 1965).
2. Reagan, *Acceptance Speech*, Detroit, Michigan, July 17, 1980.
3. Presidential Memorandum of Disapproval, November 30, 1989.
4. Foreign Operations Appropriations Act for FY1990, P.L. 101–167.
5. Barnaby Zall, "The U.S. Refugee Industry: Doing Well by Doing Good," in David Simcox (ed.): *U.S. Immigration in the 1980s: Reappraisal and Reform* (Boulder, Co.: Westview Press, 1988).
6. Civ. No. C-85-3225 RFP (N.D. cal., Dec. 19, 1990).
7. David A. Martin, "Alternative Futures for International Refugee Processing," *In Defense of the Alien—Vol. XIII,* (New York: Center for Migration Studies, 1991).

ALICE IN WONDERLAND: U.S. IMMIGRATION POLICY

Lindsey Grant

June 1993

Lewis Carroll would be proud. Present U.S. asylum and immigration policies bear the distinctive mark of the Mad Hatter.

THE SEQUENCE OF EVENTS

As a starter, we have laws concerning the permissible levels of immigration—not very rigorous laws, perhaps—but then we create an asylum policy whereunder any person who can get here and claim political asylum is given a work permit and allowed into the country. (They could be held for a hearing, but INS—the Immigration and Naturalization Service—does not have the funds to detain any but a tiny fraction. There is a huge backlog, and detention regularly leads to legal appeals. Years later, INS will send an invitation—frequently to a fictitious name at a fictitious address—to have his or her case heard. Half the invitees do not show up, at which point the INS marks the case "closed" and the person presumably lives happily ever after.)

To make sure the invitation is understood, the Attorney General in the Bush administration issued an order that there would be a presumption of refugee status for Chinese who object to the Chinese government's "one child family" policy. Acting on these instructions, immigration judges have been granting 85 percent of the asylum applications to Chinese who do show up for their hearing. Moreover, after the 1989 Tiananmen massacre, the U.S. Government invited all Chinese here at the time to stay. These invitations are still in effect, overseen by a Republican General Counsel of IRS (Grover Reese) whom the Clinton administration has not gotten around to replacing.

Then we are astonished when ships begin arriving along both coasts, run by smuggling gangs and bearing poor Chinese looking for work, who have been instructed to tear up their identity documents and say the magic words "political asylum." Concurrently, and acting perhaps on tips, the INS discovers apartments and a warehouse full of Chinese workers who are being held as slaves while they work off their $30,000 passage fee in gang-affiliated sweatshops. One said he had been working for 70 cents an hour.

What does the government do? It announces rather huffily that it is seeking international action to curb the smuggling of illegal aliens (Reuters, June 7.) The Chinese government says it will cooperate. It arrests a few alleged smugglers and (Chinese justice being swifter than ours, if not necessarily just) it hands out some light sentences. At the same time, the Foreign Ministry spokesman makes the not unreasonable point that U.S. asylum policy has encouraged the human smuggling operations.

As if to underline the extent to which U.S. immigration laws have become a mockery, consider the odyssey of the Chinese gang leader who managed the arrival this month of one group of nearly 300, six of whom drowned coming ashore. As the INS reconstructs it *(New York Times* June 10), he came to the U.S. as a teenager (illegally) in 1980, was convicted of attempted grand larceny in 1986, served time and was deported, returned across the Mexican border the next year, was soon arrested for gang activity, was convicted of illegal entry but beat the deportation proceedings by claiming political asylum. During those years, he apparently travelled to and from the U.S. at will on false papers.

THE WONDROUS CONTRADICTIONS

In short, the asylum procedures, seen by their more idealistic proponents as a lifeboat for those who are in danger because they have stood up to tyrants, become the means for the enslavement of some desperate Chinese and the enrichment of street gangs, and a source of cheap and obedient labor for employers in our cities' Chinatowns. The nation has minimum wage laws and a law against importing people for indentured servitude, and the asylum process is making a travesty of both.

This is the labor that, apologists say, fills the "jobs that Americans won't take." Do those apologists really believe that Americans should work for as little as 70 cents an hour and be locked up every night in a crowded and windowless room? As with other commerce, the lowest bid tends to set the price of labor, and this indentured labor drives down wages and takes jobs from the other unskilled people in the cities. At a time when only 45 percent of young Blacks and 58 percent of young Hispanics have regular jobs, nationwide,[1] we are frightened by the periodic eruptions in our cities, but the government does not make the connection between immigration and those tensions.

To continue this weird tale: the Bush administration extended the invitation to placate zealots who sought to punish the Chinese for using abortion as a population growth control. Granted, the Chinese have used measures that most of us would decry. On the other hand, we don't have 1.2 billion people. Not yet. The time may come, for us too, when desperation overcomes squeamishness. In effect, President Bush was attacking the Chinese for trying to deal with the population problem that generates the flow of desperate migrants that we are trying to stop. Whatever its faults, and despite the efforts of the Bush administration, the Chinese policy succeeded last year in bringing fertility below replacement level (and lower than ours.) Despite us, they may eventually work their way out of their problem, and thus spare us the problem of illegal Chinese migration.

The Clinton administration has disavowed the Bush population policies but has not yet reversed them in this instance.

The odyssey of the gang leader dramatizes another twist in our immigration law. The Immigration Reform and Control Act of 1986 (IRCA) was intended to forbid the hiring of illegal aliens (unless of course they uttered those magic words "political asylum.") However, it provided no way of identifying who is entitled to work here. This in turn led to a massive traffic in false identity documents, with the result that an entire class of people can now move in and out of the country with one or more false identities, and it makes it very easy to elude the law, whether your purpose is terrorism, drug smuggling, the trade in indentured servants, tax evasion, or simply getting a job.

THE TURN OF OPINION

After years of political torpor, this tragicomedy of the Chinese boat people has spurred a sudden frenzy of reform proposals. There are more than twenty new bills before Congress. The National Security Council is said to be chairing an inter Departmental group developing ways of dealing with illegal immigration, including tougher laws and the use of sophisticated surveillance procedures heretofore unavailable to the INS. If this is a fruit of the change of administration, congratulations.

For the first time in decades, genuine reform of our immigration procedures may be a possibility. Congressman Romano Mazzoli (D-KY), chairman of the House Subcommittee on Immigration, Refugees and International Law, has introduced legislation (HR 1679) to give the INS more power to judge asylum applicants speedily and send the unqualified applicants home. Members of his committee have introduced even tougher legislation, including Bill McCollum (R-FL; HR 1355) and Elton Gallegly (R-CA), whose HR 1078 would increase Border Patrol personnel; his HR 1079 would create a tamper proof identity card for aliens entitled to work in the U.S., HR 1080 would ban direct federal financial benefits and unemployment benefits to aliens not lawfully permanent residents, and HR 1083 would ban federal assistance to localities that do not cooperate in apprehending illegal aliens (there are jurisdictions that refuse to cooperate.) Rep. Anthony Beilenson (D-CA) has introduced bills (HR 1029 and 1031) that would enlarge the Border Patrol and provide a fraud-proof Social Security card.

In the Senate, the key player is Senator Edward Kennedy (D-MA), chairman of the Subcommittee on Immigration and Refugee Affairs. Long an obstacle to effective immigration controls, he is singing a new tune. He says the asylum problem "has been festering for years, but these Chinese slave ships have made inaction indefensible." *(Washington Post,* June 12.) He plans to introduce a bill to toughen asylum procedures. His Republican counterpart, Alan Simpson of Wyoming, has already done so (S 667).

Out of all these proposals, there may emerge some serious legislation. Readers who are concerned about the role of immigration in population growth are urged to take note of those names, perhaps to commend the two chairmen for their initiatives, and to urge their own congressperson and senators to sign on.

DON'T STOP THERE

In part, this FOOTNOTE is intended to alert readers to the window of opportunity. Beyond that, however, it is intended to warn that Chinese are not the only illegal immigrants, and asylum fraud is not the only way they come. Illegal immigration is a major if unmeasurable element of U.S. population growth, an important component of the disintegration of the cities, and one source of the impoverishment of the nation's urban poor, who are themselves disproportionately minorities.

The dramatic arrivals by boat are probably a small part of the problem. These people have all been from Fujyan (Fukien) Province, which has not heretofore been a major source of migration to the U.S. We may assume that similar rings are operating, more effectively, in Toisha and Chungshan districts, the traditional "Chinese connection," and indeed in various other countries.

In earlier papers, NPG has addressed the questions of how to control illegal immigration,[2] and another study of asylum policy is in the works.

Meanwhile, the Bureau of Census clings to the belief that net annual illegal immigration is only 200,000, most of it from Mexico. The INS puts the figure at 250,000–500,000 per year, about 100,000 of them Chinese.[3] Nobody in government really addresses the government's own statistics suggesting that overstaying "non-immigrants" arriving by air may add hundreds of thousands or even more to our population annually.[4] With all those people in the inner cities eluding identification, part of our problem may be that the cities are simply bigger than we think. Perhaps it is time for a real hard look both at the evidence and at the arguments for an improved identification system that will make it possible for the INS and the police to keep a better watch on these elusive customers.

NOTES:

1. Bureau of Labor Statistics *Employment and Earnings*, January 1993, p. 22. The figure are for the non-institutional (i.e. not in jail) population twenty to twenty-four years of age not enrolled in schools who have full time employment.
2. See David E. Simcox *Sustainable Immigration: Learning to Say No* (NPG FORUM March 1990), reprinted as Chapter 14 of Lindsey Grant et al *Elephants in the Volkswagen* (New York: W.H. Freeman & Co., 1992), or David Simcox & Rosemary Jenks *Refugee and Asylum Policy: National Passion versus National Interest* (NPG FORUM February 1992).
3. Associated Press, 6-7-93, 22:08.
4. Lindsey Grant *What We Can Learn from the Missing Airline Passengers* (NPG FORUM November 1992)

A CONGENIAL JOB FOR THE VICE-PRESIDENT

Lindsey Grant

March 1993

Although it has escaped general notice, Vice President Gore, President Nixon, John D. Rockefeller 3rd and the Commission on Population and the American Future, Ambassador George Kennan and the U.S. Department of State all have something in common. They all have expressed the belief that the United States' population should stop growing, and some of them have stated the proposition in eloquent language.

President Nixon:

> *"In 1917 the total number of Americans passed 100 million, after three full centuries of steady growth. In 1967—just half a century later—the 200 million mark was passed. If the present rate of growth continues, the third hundred million persons will be added in roughly a thirty-year period. This means that by the year 2000, or shortly thereafter, there will be more than 300 million Americans.*
>
> *"The growth will produce serious challenges for our society. I believe that many of our present social problems may be related to the fact that we have had only fifty years in which to accommodate the second hundred million Americans. . . .*
>
> *"Where, for example, will the next hundred million Americans live? . . .*
>
> *"Other questions confront us. How, for example, will we house the next hundred million Americans? . . .*
>
> *"How will we educate and employ such a large number of people? Will our transportation systems move them about as quickly and economically as necessary? How will we provide adequate health care when our population reaches 300 million? Will our political structures have to be reordered, too, when our society grows to such proportions? . . .*
>
> *". . . we should establish as a national goal the provision of adequate family planning services within the next five years to all those who want them but cannot afford them."*[1]

John D. Rockefeller, 3rd:

> *"After two years of concentrated effort, we have concluded that, in the long run, no substantial benefits will result from the further growth of the Nation's population, rather that the gradual stabilization of our population would contribute significantly to the Nation's ability to solve its problems."*[2]

Ambassador George Kennan:

> *" . . . then there is the optimal balance, depending on the manner of man's life,*

between the density of human population and the tolerances of nature. This balance, in the case of the United States, would seem to me to have been surpassed when the American population reached, at a very maximum, two hundred million people, and perhaps a good deal less . . . . And there is a real question as to whether "bigness" in a body politic is not an evil in itself, quite aside from the policies pursued in its name . . ."[3]

The **U.S. Department of State** and the **Council on Environmental Quality** called for *"a national population policy which addresses the issues of: population stabilization; Availability of family planning programs; . . . Just, consistent, and workable immigration laws;"* . . . and five other specific proposals.[4]

This congruence of opinions is not just of historical interest. A number of very perceptive observers have seen the need to stop or reverse population growth, but there has been a decade of slumber, during which the nation's population grew by 23 million people and we passed three major laws promoting immigration and further U.S. population growth. As to poverty in the third world, the U.S. delegate to the U.N. Population Conference in Mexico City in 1984, argued that poverty was a result of "governmental control of economies" rather than population growth. President Bush reiterated that "population growth, in and of itself, is a neutral phenomenon" in dealing with economic development and environmental degradation.[5]

We now have a new administration likely to be more concerned about the environment and the things that affect it, and we are heading toward the third decennial UN population conference, this one scheduled for September 1994 in Cairo.

Vice President Gore should have views on this. He has written at length on the population issue and concluded that

"The United States should restore full funding of its share of the costs of international population stabilization programs and increase the effort to make birth control available throughout the world— . . . Clearly, it is time for a global effort to create everywhere on earth the conditions conducive to stabilizing population."[6]

The U.S. Government must prepare a position for the 1994 conference, and the occasion offers a superb opportunity for this country to rejoin the rest of the world community and to develop and announce a U.S. population policy—concerning its own population as well as its population aid to other countries. In world conferences addressing environmental issues such as acid precipitation and climate warming, the United States has been in the unpopular position of arguing for "more study." Because of our size and high consumption patterns, the U.S. is by far the largest single contributor to such problems. In our own interest and that of the Earth's other inhabitants, we would be in a much stronger position to advocate world cooperation in meeting those problems if we could announce, not only that we were prepared to cooperate to reduce emissions, but that we were undertaking to put a brake on our own population growth, which drives our consumption levels.

The conference is not really the reason for undertaking the task; it is an occasion for doing something we must do in our own national interest. Presently, we are making U.S. population by accident, and with present fertility and immigration patterns, we are headed past 396 million by 2050—another 140 million in fifty-seven years.[7]

Vice President Gore while in Congress was unique for his combination of vision and a practical understanding of how it could be pursued. He proposed a Critical Trends Assessment Act to successive congresses. Washington is distinguished for tunnel vision; it regularly passes laws and sets policies in motion without considering the consequences. As an example, in 1990 it passed a law increasing immigration without seriously considering how it would impact on the jobless and restless in the cities. And then we wonder why we have riots in Los Angeles. The Gore proposal would have forced Congress and the executive to look at the lateral and long term implications before it passed legislation. It was not a partisan bill; in one of its incarnations it was co-sponsored by (of all people) Congressman Newt Gingrich.[8]

Can anybody nominate a person better qualified and better situated than the Vice President to lead the governmental process of preparing the U.S. position for the forthcoming conference on population?

For that matter, isn't there somebody in Congress ready to pick up where Senator Gore left it, and reintroduce the Critical Trends Assessment bill in the new Congress? "It is morning in America" is a great pitch but not much policy guidance. Having learned that, Congress and the nation may be ready to give a more serious hearing to a proposal that we learn to look before we leap.

NOTES:

1. U.S. President Richard M. Nixon, "Special Message to the U.S. Congress on Problems of Population Growth, July 18, 1969," in Public Papers of Presidents of the United States (Washington: Office of the Federal Register, 1969, p.521.)
2. Letter of transmittal from Chairman John D. Rockefeller 3rd of the Report of the Commission on Population Growth and the American Future, to President Nixon, the Senate and the House, March 27, 1972.
3. George F. Kennan, Around the Cragged Hill (New York: W.W. Norton, 1993), pp.142–144.
4. U.S. Council on Environmental Quality and Department of state, Global Future: Time to Act (USGPO, January 1981), p.11.
5. White House press release October 25, 1991, Presidential Proclamation of World Population Awareness Week, 1991.
6. Al Gore, Earth in the Balance, Ecology and the Human Spirit (New York: Penguin Books USA, 1992, 1993) p.317.
7. New projection by Leon F. Bouvier, publication pending. The middle figure for 2050 in the Census Bureau's latest projections is 383 million.
8. For a discussion of the proposed Act, and indeed of the whole issue of "foresight," which is a term of art for the broadened decision process described here, see Lindsey Grant, Foresight and National Decisions: the Horseman and the Bureaucrat (Lanham, MD: University Press of America, 1988.)

EPA'S POPULATION NON-POLICY

Roy Beck

June 1993

The Environmental Protection Agency heretofore has shown no interest in population growth as a cause of environmental problems, and recent remarks by its new administrator suggest that the situation has not improved.

EPA Chief Carol Browner may be at the head of her class in technical knowledge and administrative skill, but an exchange with environmental journalists indicates she is in urgent need of education on the importance of population growth in the nation's ability to achieve environmental goals.

This is a serious gap. Not only is demography a major source of the problems that EPA itself must address but, since President Clinton is abolishing the Council on Environmental Quality, EPA is in line to be the agency primarily responsible for seeing that other government agencies prepare environmental impact statements (EIS) on their activities, under the National Environmental Policy Act (NEPA). That act attached great importance to the population issue. The record has been spotty in translating this importance into environmental impact statements, but efforts to beef up the population aspects had begun to show promise of bearing fruit under the Bush administration last year.

Browner's inarticulateness on population themes is surprising in view of her job history. She has worked for years with and around environmental advocates, including then-Sen. Al Gore. Recently, as Florida's top environmental officer, she had to deal with problems resulting in large part from that state's six-fold population increase since World War II.

Yet, when asked if the EPA needs a person or department that specializes in population issues, Browner said she couldn't imagine why.

Browner met with a few dozen members of the Society of Environmental Journalists and the D.C. Science Writers' Association on the evening of May 18. She was impressive fielding highly technical questions and in articulating her goals for the next four years. She said the nation was ending the first phase of its quest for environmental quality. During that phase, thirteen major acts have set "end-of-stream" standards, she said.

"The huge gains (from end-of-the-pollution-stream enforcement) have been realized now," said Browner. Although EPA will need to see that those gains are maintained, "we need to move upstream to prevent pollution from taking place in the first place."

That seemed to be a perfect opening for talking about population growth which may be the most important "upstream" contributor to negative environmental impact.

I noted to the EPA chief that concern about multiplying the agents of pollution was a key part of the National Environmental Protection Act of 1969. Dealing with population growth was integral to the landmark act, as it was to mainstream environmental thinking at the time. Reflecting that, NEPA's opening "Declaration" began:

> *"The Congress, recognizing the profound impact of man's activity on the interrelations of all components of the natural environment, particularly the profound influences of population growth, high-density urbanization, industrial expansion, resource exploitation . . . declares that it is the continuing policy of the Federal government . . . to create and maintain conditions under which man and nature can exist in productive harmony . . . (emphasis added)."*

NEPA set up the Council on Environmental Quality which was to establish rules for environmental impact statements and help the President with an annual report that, among other things, would assess the "adequacy of available natural resources for fulfilling human and economic requirements of the Nation *in the light of expected population pressures* (emphasis added)."

But the Council on Environmental Quality never formulated strong rules forcing the federal government to assess how any project or policy might increase population and what environmental impact that growth would cause.

Last year as U.S. population was soaring more than 50 million higher than the level at passage of the 1969 NEPA, three environmentalists lobbied the general counsel of Bush's Council on Environmental Quality to start paying attention to population growth, said Dale Didion, executive director of Renew America.[1] The CEQ counsel was quite receptive and mapped out a sequence of events through which the change could occur, but the fall election halted all progress, Didion said.

Now, with the disappearance of the CEQ, EPA's Office of Federal Activities is in the process of inheriting the overall responsibility for the EIS process.

When asked if she will take the opportunity to require population impact assessments, Browner seemed confused, indicating no knowledge of the issue and finally stating, "I don't feel qualified to answer that."

Probing further for a sign of commitment or understanding of the population issue, I told her a personal story from a year ago. I had called EPA's public affairs office to be directed to an official or researcher who could talk about how population growth has affected efforts to achieve environmental goals. I was bounced from phone to phone, office to office and city to city over a couple of weeks. An official in the "mobile source air pollution" area told me: "We don't talk much about growth. We do talk about the number of cars. I think it generally is true that the (Bush) administration doesn't like to talk about population growth. You'll never get anybody in government suggesting communities meet air standards by limiting their population growth." When I asked incredulously if there wasn't at least somebody stuck away in a basement cranny who remembered the earlier ideas of controlling pollution through population stabilization, the official huffed that she certainly remembered "ZPG and all of that two-child family talk" but the idea of controlling population "just doesn't fly in a democratic country. Americans don't want you messing with their freedom. . . You seem really keen on pressing the population issues, but our agency does not deal in those issues. You need to talk to some environmental group, although I'm not sure they'd want to talk about it either." Feeling like Diogenes in his search for one honest man, I eventually gave up my quest for an EPA population expert.

Recounting that spirit of the Bush EPA, I asked Browner what changes she would make, especially in light of calls by some groups that EPA have a population department or at least a desk.

"I can't imagine what a population desk would do," Browner said. She allowed that air pollution officials, for example, certainly compute projected population in their calculations, but she had no thoughts to offer about how EPA might treat population growth as a variable that could be influenced rather than an inevitable factor to which EPA can only react.

I would offer the vision of a population desk that could have played a major role in 1990 by giving expert testimony to Congress about the population and environmental effects of passing the Immigration Act that year. As it was, Congress never discussed how much the Immigration Act's encouragement of large scale population growth might undercut the Clean Air Act passed the very same week. And Browner—if she is responsible to the nation's children, including her five-year-old son—must come up with a plan for how the nation will protect its environmental resources from the impact of the 383 million Americans projected by the Census Bureau for the year 2050. Much of that 130 million increase (from today) is the result of federal immigration policies since the 1969 NEPA was enacted. But neither the EPA nor the Council on Environmental Quality ever raised a word about it.

Population consciousness is not totally absent in the Clinton administration. Browner might do well to talk with Bruce Babbitt, Secretary of the Interior. In April, he addressed journalists at the National Press Club. Suggesting that much of Interior's task is rationing the natural resources on federal lands, I asked Babbitt how much more difficult it will be to ration among 383 million Americans than the 203 million at the time of the first Earth Day.

"That's just it," Babbitt immediately replied. "That (population growth) is at the root of all of our problems."

If population growth is so important, why had Babbitt failed to say a single word about it in his prepared text? Perhaps even officials who understand population growth implications eventually stop talking publicly about them because there is no formal process that calls upon them to address the population factor.

And perhaps in that line of thinking, EPA's Browner could begin to imagine a rationale for a population desk—and a policy requiring a population impact assessment of all other federal policies.

NOTE:

1. *For details concerning the inadequacy of the EIS procedures in dealing with population, see Joseph J. Brecher "Population and the EIS" (NPG Forum, May 1991). The three groups that approached CEQ in behalf of a larger coalition were Carrying Capacity Network, Negative Population Growth, and the Sierra Club Legal Defense Fund.*

A BELEAGURED PRESIDENT, A FIZZLED "ECONOMIC STIMULUS PACKAGE," AND A NAFTA TIME BOMB

Lindsey Grant

May 1993

For President Clinton, it has been a short, rough honeymoon: the early reversal when he faced the prospect of a mass migration of Haitian boat people; the fracas over gays in the military; Congress' rejection of his proposal to allow AIDS sufferers to migrate to the U.S.; the backdown over grazing fees and mining rights; the withdrawal of his first nominee for Attorney General, who showed a remarkably cavalier attitude toward the immigration laws that an Attorney General is pledged to uphold. The Senate deadlocked over his $16.3 billion "economic stimulus" package. Coming up: Senate debate of his predecessor's North American Free Trade Agreement (NAFTA), and Hillary's proposals for national health care.

In most of these issues, we seem to see a man who is predisposed to be generous to everybody, suddenly facing unexpected and rising resistance. A certain realism seems to have invaded Congress, and perhaps an awareness of limits; even America is not omnipotent.

THE "ECONOMIC STIMULUS" PACKAGE

In the recent battle over the budgetary "economic stimulus" proposal, the President allowed Minority Leader Robert Dole to choose the battlefield. Even several Democrat senators were restless. Congress, apparently, has gotten the message that the voters right now want fiscal discipline more than pork. The President has not. The so-called stimulus program was a mixed bag of projects: job training, summer jobs, sewers, roads and mass transit, a $4 billion extension of unemployment benefits, an ice skaters' warming hut in Manchester CT.[1] Many of them would be nice if we can afford them, but they are hardly the stuff that justifies undercutting the concurrent effort to balance the budget. In the hyperbole of politics, it was claimed ("based on standard macroeconomic modeling"[2]) that the package would generate 500,000 jobs, 219,000 of them in the first year, but there was no detailed justification of the numbers. Remember that 219,000. We will come back to it.

EMPLOYMENT AND WAGES

The new administration shows a refreshing interest in the problems of working people, and it is disconcerted by the failure of the current recovery to generate enough jobs. If the concern is genuine, the President should stop trying to bull his way through problems in the old American way, and attempt instead to identify and correct the causes. The proposed "stimulus" was negligible in a five trillion dollar economy, and the dislocation in the labor market is going to require changes much more fundamental than BandAids.

The root problem is population growth, not the number of jobs. In a functioning economy, jobs should reflect the number of people willing and able to work, but ours has been a dysfunctional economy for years, because of technological and social changes.

For fifteen years, real hourly wages have gone down and the gap has widened between the rich and the poor. Part time and minimum wage service jobs have replaced better and more skilled jobs. The movement of women into the paid labor force, now nearly completed, has increased the supply of labor in an era of diminishing demand for it. The economy has had to absorb the baby boom. More fundamental, the technological revolution that has raised productivity has also diminished the numbers of employees needed. Nobel Laureate Wassily Leontief years ago identified the problem: if fewer people can produce the goods and services the economy needs, what happens to the other people?

As a result of these changes, the national effort to help poor Blacks and other minorities get into the economy has been taking place in a hostile environment, as the jobs that they could start with have been evaporating.

The President's advisers worry about the persistence of an unemployment rate of about 7 percent. That figure far understates the problem. It does not count those who have simply dropped out. The problem is worst among the young and the vulnerable. Last December, of young Blacks twenty to twenty-four years old not enrolled in school, only 45 percent had full time jobs.[3] Combine that with the competition for jobs, housing and services generated by current third world immigration to the cities, and perhaps it will help us understand why the cities are erupting.

The growing desperation is reflected in the rising unemployment rolls. Even the Senate Republicans went along with the $4 billion addition to unemployment benefits. The number of people on food stamps reached a record 26.8 million this winter. The new 1994 budget, in a reversal of the usual optimism of budget projections, anticipates that it will go higher.[4]

The Labor Department estimates that 700,000 defense-related jobs have disappeared since 1987 and that another 1.3 million will disappear between now and 1997.[5]

The personnel cuts announced by Boeing and IBM have brought the problem to the middle class, which is likely to be much more vocal about its pain than the poor and the minorities who have been the principal victims. The *Wall Street Journal* quotes an estimate that "re-engineering" of production may wipe out 25 million of the 90 million jobs in the private sector. One observer says that "This may be the biggest social issue of the next twenty years."[6]

NAFTA AS A WILD CARD

Suddenly the press is singing a new song. Added to the dislocations generated by technological change and the shift away from defense production, there is a wild card: the growing integration of the world trading economy, and the impact that it is having upon employment and wages in the older industrial economies. The problem is dramatized by the NAFTA proposal, which will be extended to the entire hemisphere if its proponents have their way.

Eighteen months ago, I felt very lonely arguing with respect to NAFTA that "in a situation with free movement of goods and technology and capital—but not of labor—what happens? Employers tend either (a) to move toward the cheaper labor, or (b) to press for removal of impediments to importing cheap labor."[7] I am getting company. Two recent *New York Times* articles were titled **"America's Newest Industrial Belt"** (northern Mexico) and **"Those High-Tech Jobs Can Cross the Border, Too".**[8] The second article exposed a critical and false assumption: that we can expect to keep the good jobs, ship the high value stuff to Mexico, and let them do the low skilled work. Haven't Taiwan and Korea and Hong Kong yet taught us the folly of that patronizing assumption?

Resistance to NAFTA is rising. A few months ago, its passage seemed assured. Now, although President Clinton endorses it with certain reservations, his own Budget Director believes it could not pass in Congress.[9] There may be a growing awareness of the implications for labor.

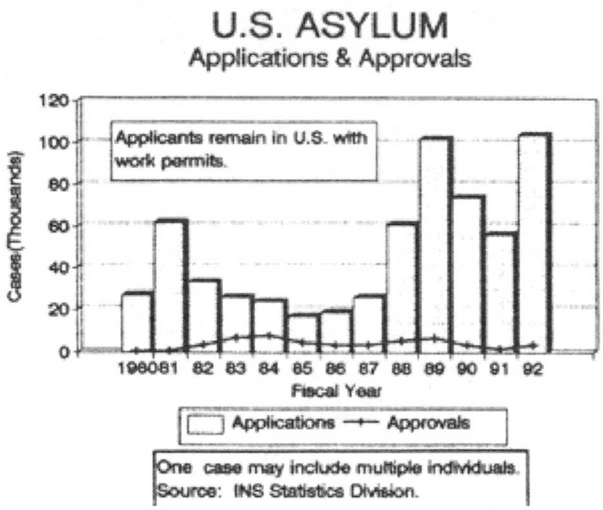

Figure 1.

A LOOK AT THE SUPPLY SIDE

If for all those reasons the private sector cannot absorb the workers, a policy based only on job creation—as distinct from efforts to make American labor more competitive—is nugatory. If we don't yet really know how to handle the side effects of technological change and the evolution of a world market, shouldn't we at least avoid making the problem worse? A sane policy maker would ask the question: "what can we do about the **supply** of labor?"

For years our national policies have been making it worse.

Immigration and fertility are the two significant determinants of the size of the U.S. labor force. Fertility presently plays a secondary role in driving labor force growth. That leaves immigration.

In 1980, the Refugee Act eliminated the quota on refugees, substituted a loose, non-binding "ceiling" of 50,000 per year, which has been substantially exceeded every year since. It regularized the category of "asylum" for those who could reach our shores. For the U.S. as well as European nations, this is becoming the preferred avenue for migrants who can't pretend to be "non-immigrants" and who face interminable waiting lists. Get here, and claim asylum. You will automatically be given a work permit until your case is adjudicated, and almost nobody is penalized for failing to turn up for his hearing, which may be years away, because of the backlog.

The graph shows the number of cases, each of which may involve one or more individuals. The total of 631 thousand cases may involve 800–850 thousand people.[10] The trend is upward, and will probably continue upward as more people learn that this is the way to come.

In 1986 there was the Immigration Reform & Control Act (IRCA). It forbade the hiring of illegal aliens, in exchange for an amnesty of those here for five years or more and for resident farm workers, which turned into an especially inviting loophole. Some 3.1 million aliens applied, among them 1.3 million "farm workers," almost all of them Hispanic. Never mind that the Bureau of Labor Statistics believed there were only 234,000 real Hispanic farm workers in the U.S. at the time, including American Hispanics and legally resident aliens.[11] The *New York Times* ran a page one headline ". . . Fraud on a Huge Scale," but

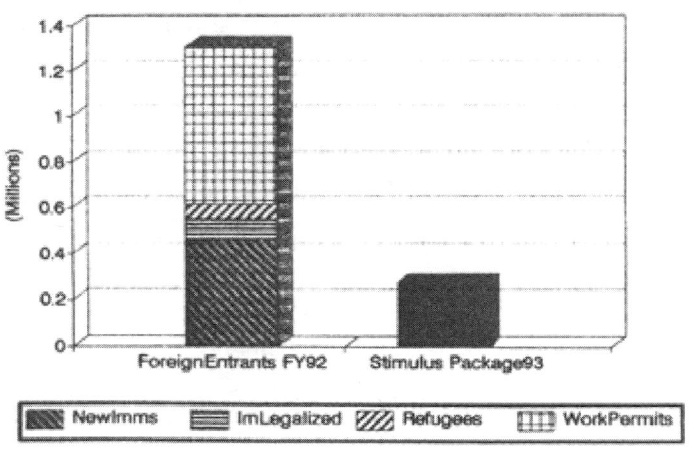

Figure 2.

nothing else happened. The Immigration and Naturalization Service (INS) was totally unequipped to handle the problem, and the courts made sure that the burden of proof was on the INS. Few of the applicants were successfully challenged, and perhaps a million fraudulent "farm workers" scattered into our unprepared cities. It is not a one-shot affair. As they qualify for citizenship, they will be able to bring in their family members legally.

Legal immigration was around 600,000 each year during the '80s. This doesn't include the 800–850 thousand asylum applicants since 1980, or Cuban and Haitian boat people or non-immigrant visa overstayers or illegal border crossers, unless and until they are formally admitted as immigrants. (The "immigrant" count for 1989 and 1990 rose by 1.36 million over the normal flow because of legalizations under the 1986 IRCA.)

Whatever "normal" was, the Immigration Act of 1990—Senator Kennedy's "Irish relief act"—raised the rate to over one million. Friends and family will follow them, legally or illegally. Again, consider the irrelevance of the recent political deadlock over an effort to create 219,000 somewhat dubious jobs, in the face of that sort of immigration, year after year . . .

As a result of this generosity, our economy is called upon to absorb a lot more job-seekers than it would if it needed to absorb only young Americans coming of age. From INS data and estimates, one can calculate that about 1.3 million aliens came on the U.S. labor market in FY 1992.[12] (There are data gaps, and there are no good figures for illegal immigration. The government probably underestimates it and has not been anxious to improve its data.[13] The case of the ill fated Attorney General-designate who was employing cheap illegal labor suggests a reason: there are a lot of influential people who don't want to inquire too closely.) Nevertheless, 1.3 million is a starter. Alone, it would overwhelm a 219,000 job package, even if that package were solid.

WHAT IS TO BE DONE?

If the President is serious about unemployment, the place to start is with the supply of labor, and that means

- *a hard look at our 1980 Refugee Act and at the flood of asylum applications it has generated;*
- *a review of our other immigration laws, the way they are enforced or not enforced, with the question placed uppermost: "How do they affect the national welfare, and particularly the U.S. labor market?"*
- *the repair of a failed statistical support system that makes it impossible even to know what is going on.*[14]
- *a very close look at NAFTA.*

The question about NAFTA is not just whether big industries like it—the list of U.S. companies already moving to Mexico for the docile and cheap labor looks like a subset of The Forbes 500—but whether it serves the U.S. economy, and particularly what it does to our mounting unemployment problem and the related tensions between those who are in the system and those who are out of it.

The President would also find that a more restrictive immigration policy and better data would generate benefits beyond the scope of this paper, in saving resources and protecting the environment, putting our agriculture on a sustainable basis, extending our energy reserves, reducing our balance of payments problem, addressing the problems of the cities and even helping to control terrorism. (The "CIA gunman" was an asylum applicant. At least one of the World Trade Center suspects and his spiritual leader were here illegally, and nobody knows quite how.)

It is not often given to Presidents to achieve so much with one policy—and it is a great deal cheaper to limit immigration than it is to try to create jobs in an economy that cannot use them.

TAKING THE PLUNGE

However, presidents have regularly found it very difficult to take on this issue. There is enormous emotional freight riding on it. We see ourselves as a nation of immigrants. Generosity seems to demand liberality. Dare a President risk the charge of "racism" or "intolerance"?

There is a choice between helping our own people and helping others, and it would be a painful one for any decent human being. I believe the right choice is clear, however, once President Clinton comes to recognize the limits of U.S. power to redress all the world's ills. World population is growing more than 90 million each year, and the biggest surge of numbers in the working ages is yet to come. There is only so much we can do, and we risk doing it at the cost of our poor, our cities, and the future our children inherit. Seen thus as a choice among alternatives where we cannot do everything we want, it may be an easier choice to make. The President is, after all, committed by his oath to promote the general welfare of the people of this country and our posterity, not of the whole world.

The President will find, as he has in his early brushes over Haitian boat people and the feckless would-be Attorney General, that opinion is well ahead of him. Over the years, polls by organizations such as Gallup and Roper have regularly shown majorities in the 60 to 70 plus percent range believing that immigration is too high. Most people—as distinct from their "leaders" and special interest groups—understand what is being done to them. The view is shared by those most affected. A recently released poll found that 66 to 79 percent of different Hispanic ethnic subgroups thought immigration was too high, compared with 74 percent for "Anglos" (non-Hispanic Whites).[15]

In a way, the choice resembles—on a much larger scale—the agonizing process of facing a world of limits as we try to balance the budget and to provide equitable health protection for all. We cannot always do everything for everybody. And on this point, the people may be ahead of the President.

NOTES:

1. *Associated Press* (AP), 4-11-93, 15:15 EDT, and 4-12-93, 15:14 EDT.
2. OMB Director Leon Panetta et al, budget press briefing 4-9-93. The package was reduced from $30 billion in the President's February 17th State of the Union message. What the budgeteers missed is that the "standard macroeconomic models" have failed to explain why recent economic growth itself has not created more jobs. Structural change is not the province of such models.

3. U.S. Department of Labor, Bureau of Labor Statistics *Employment Earnings,* January 1993, Table A-7.
4. AP 02:10 EDT 4-9-93.
5. Testimony by Ronald E. Kutscher, Associate Commissioner, Bureau of Labor Statistics. AP, 4-12-93, 18:08 EDT.
6. "Price of Progress. "Re-engineering" Gives Firms New Efficiency, Workers the Pink Slip," *Wall Street Journal* March 16, 1993, p.1.
7. See Lindsey Grant *Free Trade and Cheap Labor: The President's Dilemma,* in the NPG Forum series (Teaneck, NJ: Negative Population Growth, October 1991) for an elaboration of the argument that the proposed agreement largely ignores the potential impact on U.S. labor.
8. Both articles were by Louis Uchitelle, 3-21-93 Business Section p.1. and 3-28-93 p.E4, respectively.
9. United Press International (UPI) 4-27-93, 10:12 EDT. Interestingly, the President may have more support from Republicans than Democrats on this one. 27 GOP senators sent him a letter pledging support for NAFTA as negotiated.
10. The proportion of "persons" to cases for asylum approvals 1982–91 was 1.294. Applying that ratio to applications would yield a figure of 817,000. The database does not offer a summary total of denials and deportations, but the magnitudes involved and the length of the appeals process do not suggest they would much affect the total. In FY1992, there were 3919 approvals, 6506 denials, and 11571 cases closed, mostly because the applicant failed to appear.
11. U.S. Statistical Abstract, 1989, Table 642.
12. Personal communications, INS Statistics Division, 4-13 & 4-14-93. The actual estimate works out to 1.315 million. Using Bureau of Labor Statistics estimates, they assume that 57 percent of the 810,635 immigrants and 115,330 newly admitted refugees entered the labor market, as did 57 percent of the 163,342 earlier illegal immigrants legalized in FY1992 under the act of 1986, and that all the 693,393 recipients of work permits (issued to asylum seekers and "non-immigrants" such as foreign students) entered the labor market. The figure is necessarily imprecise. Some of the legalized aliens had already been working. Not all of the work permits represent new jobs. On the other hand, more than 15 million people arrive each year on non-immigrant visas. Some of them stay and work without permits, but they are not in these figures, nor are the illegal entrants, numbering somewhere in the hundreds of thousands, who came and sought work in the fiscal year.
13. See Lindsey Grant, *What We Can Learn from the Missing Airline Passengers* (Teaneck, NJ: NPG, NPG Forum article November 1992.) There is an unexplained annual gap of over one million between passengers arriving and departing on civil aircraft flights. Census estimates of illegal immigration almost ignore this potential source. In so far as it is real, the gap demonstrates that illegal immigration through visa overstays is far larger than the official estimates. If the gap is partly illusory, the Census Bureau and INS are missing a chance to tighten up aircraft manifest reporting procedures and acquire some hard data.
14. For evidence of the state of statistics, see *Immigration Statistics, A Story of Neglect* (Washington: National Academy of Sciences, 1985.)
15. Summary report released 12-19-92 of findings by Rodolfo O. de la Garza et al, *Latino Voices: Mexican, Puerto Rican and Cuban Perspectives on American Politics* (Boulder: Westview Press, publication planned 1993), Table 7.24. Interestingly, the survey was financed in part by the Ford Foundation, which has been a major supporter of ethnic immigration advocacy groups.

DEMOGRAPHY AND HEALTH CARE REFORM

Lindsey Grant

October 1993

Joseph Califano (who was there when it happened) has recently given a vivid description of the way in which President Johnson and Wilbur Mills created Medicaid and Medicare and of their failure to address either the demographics of an aging and changing society or the costs of the proposed programs.[1] He was not being critical. We have something of a national habit of understating the difficulties when we want to do something, and national health care is an idea whose time seems to have come.

Perhaps this time, when people are coming to sense that perpetual growth is not necessarily the natural order of things, we should take a serious look at some of the constraints on the proposed program.[2]

Two key points emerge: first, Congress should be very cautious about any proposal to create further **entitlements.** The costs of the proposed program could escalate beyond the nation's ability to pay. While keeping the principle of universal coverage, the government should preserve room to draw limits as to how much can be spent on each individual. Second, the issuance of National Health Cards could become riddled with fraud unless the country finally faces up to the need for a **secure system of identification**—i.e. the ability to tell who a person is. The development of such a system would help to control illegal immigration, drug smuggling and terrorism, aside from making it possible to know who is entitled to health care.

MULTIPLICATION OF THE ELDERLY

The chart shows the anticipated growth of the elderly. Count on it. Only a plague will keep people from getting older.

A rise in the elderly population is natural and indeed inevitable for any nation as it gets off the population growth treadmill. It is not necessarily a problem.[3] However, we must anticipate a particularly sharp rise from 2010–2030. It represents the last hurrah of the post-World War II baby boom. (Any enthusiast for population growth should consider that poor generation: from crowded schools to trouble finding jobs in the '80s, to the layoffs and deteriorating job structure of the '90s, finally to become an unappreciated burden a few years hence.)

Look at the graph. That is quite a curve. Moreover, the numbers of the "old old"—those eighty and over—will grow even more sharply and will peak a decade or so later. They are the ones who will require the most care.

This trend is unsettling partly because care of the elderly is now borne in large measure by government, as a result of the societal shift away from support by the old folks' children (accentuated perhaps by Medicaid and Medicare, which made an alternative care supplier available). This means, one way or another, that the support comes out of taxes. Moreover, this charge will probably fall largely in the

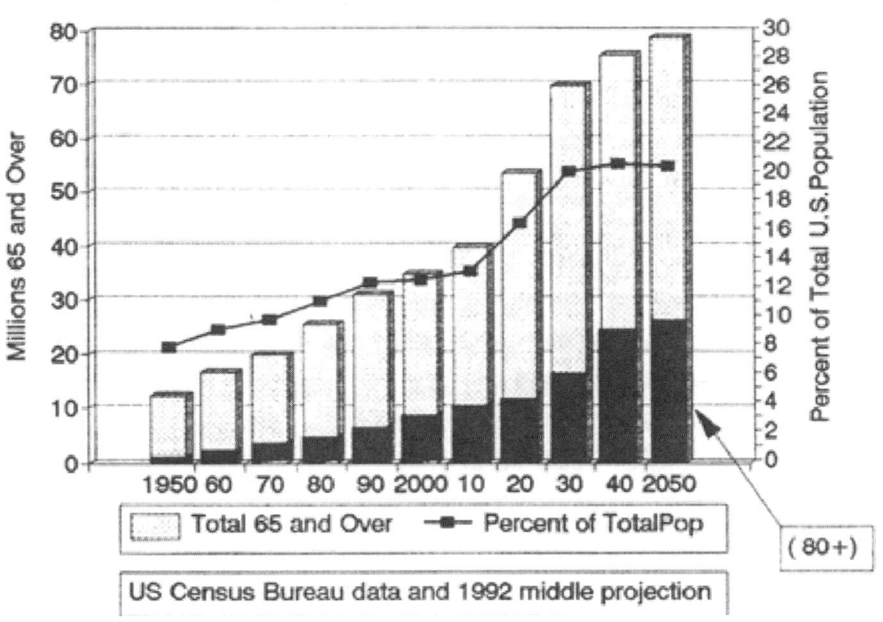

Figure 1.

AIDS AND PLAGUES

The politicians are going to hate to have to face this one.

Reported AIDS cases rose from 4442 to 43,672 from 1984 to 1991, and an additional 89,804 cases have been reported since then, with 180,000 cumulative deaths reported. The number of HIV-infected persons is unknown, but estimated at one million. Infection rates seem to be declining among gay white men twenty-five to forty-four years old, but rising among younger gays, drug users and—particularly—women.[4]

public sector of the health plan rather than in the component that is to be hidden in the proposed increase in charges to employers. It will add to other forces tending to expand the publicly supported portion of the program.

The cost of the program will escalate rapidly in decades to come, particularly since it is planned to include prescriptions, long term care, and treatment for the diseases of the aged, which can be very expensive. The plan's proponents say that long term care will "emphasize home—and community-based care." A laudable goal, but it bucks the recent trend in behavior. At least, we may hope that the planners are aware that they have a problem.

The issue should not be swept under the rug, as happens so regularly when advocates of particular legislation understate the out-year costs.

In 1992, AIDS cases rose 2.5 percent among men, and 9.8 percent among women.[5] That is an ominous shift. It suggests that AIDS is moving from gays and intravenous drug users into the larger general heterosexual population.[6] Perhaps we are more like Africa than we thought. There, the incidence has always been heterosexual, and in four countries it exceeds 5 percent of the total population. At that rate, the U.S. would have more than 12 million AIDS patients.

Perhaps even more ominous, the epidemic in the U.S. is growing fastest among the young. One expert reported that AIDS cases among adolescents had risen 77 percent in the last two years.[7]

AIDS is a particularly insidious epidemic, partly because of the ten year average incubation period. Barring a cure that is not yet in sight, we may anticipate an explosive growth of a very expensive class of potential health care recipients. Like care for the elderly, this expense will probably tend to fall in the public sector of the health program; employers will do everything they can to avoid it.

AIDS is not the only problem on the horizon. The popular press seems largely to have missed the story, but there has been a fundamental erosion of confidence within the scientific community as to whether we can handle other infectious diseases. Humankind is being subjected, in a sense, to a counterattack in a war that we thought we had won. The U.S Surgeon General in 1969 told Congress that the war against infectious diseases was effectively finished. Now we are watching the resurgence of a number of treatment-resistant disease strains: cholera, tuberculosis, hantavirus. The pathogens are learning to handle the poisons and antibiotics that our race launched against them a generation ago. A *Science* magazine editorial called it a "subterranean war" and said that

> *"Those who believed a plague could not happen in this century have already seen the beginning of one in the AIDS crisis, but the drug-resistant strains in this issue [of the magazine], which can be transmitted by casual contacts in movie theaters, hospitals and shopping centers, are likely to be even more terrifying . . ."*[8]

This raises a question whether Congress should be passing an entitlement program to cover a future that is very far from clear. Other entitlement programs have been a potent force driving our budget deficit in the past two decades because their size is dictated by demand (as defined in the legislation), rather than by the budgetary process. The nation may find that it cannot do all it would like for everybody, whether the old or the plague patient, and it may need the flexibility to address the questions: "What are the priorities? If forced to it, how can we best use each medical insurance dollar? Should we, for instance, try to underwrite extremely expensive operations for the elderly, or when the odds against full recovery are not very good?" Oregon has led the way in addressing these questions, and to its credit the Clinton administration (unlike its predecessor) has allowed it to proceed with the experiment.

THE MAGNET EFFECT

The AIDS epidemic, with the possibility of others to come, raises some important questions about immigration policy.

AIDS cases worldwide are projected to quintuple to about 10 million by 2000.[9] In Haiti, 7 to 10 percent of adults have HIV, the forerunner of AIDS. Haitians with HIV have been brought into the U.S. by court order. Congress has now voted resoundingly to forbid the immigration of HIV-infected persons, and the President signed the bill despite his campaign statements in favor of admission. It is far from certain that the decision will stop the movement. The availability of free hospital coverage for AIDS in the U.S. will attract HIV sufferers in less generous lands and, given the casual way we enforce our immigration laws, many of them will probably be able to get here.

Perhaps it sounds heartless. One would like to be able to help everybody, everywhere. There is, however, a conflict between moral obligations, and it is driven by the reality that resources are not infinite. We may well have trouble in doing what we would like for our own people in the years ahead.

There is a widespread misapprehension that third world population growth, the chief engine of migration to the U.S., is waning. On the contrary, it is intense and growing. The second graph shows the ongoing growth of the working age population in the so-called third world. Most of the third world suffers already from massive unemployment. Witness the desperate efforts by Chinese to get to the U.S. even in the midst of a touted economic boom, or the approval of a governmental "overseas employment agency" to help Chinese to emigrate.[10] Migration is the only hope for a decent living for many or most of the people represented in that graph. Only in eastern Asia and some Caribbean islands has fertility fallen enough to offer some confidence that the pressure will disappear some day, and even for most of those areas the relief is a long way off, because the labor market entrants of two decades hence are already born.

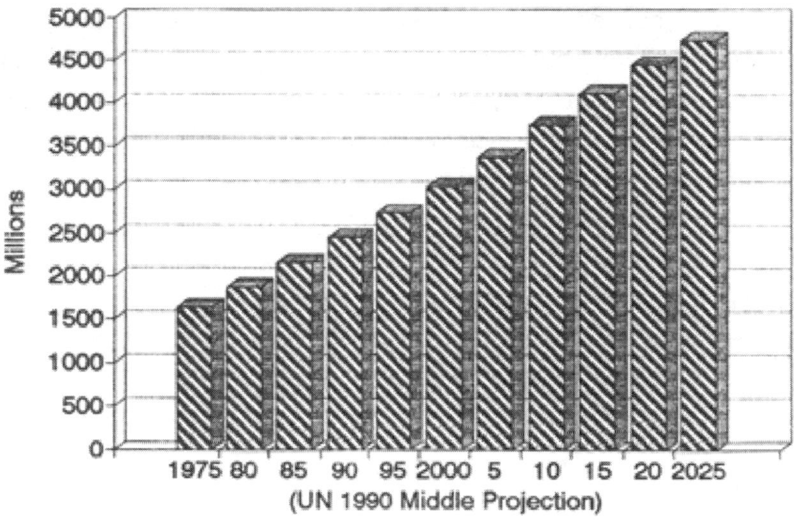

Figure 2.

I do not mean to suggest that those billions of people will all suddenly decamp for the United States. If one-tenth of them did—a proportion much smaller than the exodus from Europe to the New World in the nineteenth century—it would double our population. That presumably would make the U.S. about as attractive to job seekers as India, thus discouraging the rest.

In a world that is approaching intolerable crowding, the United States is not immune. We are already heading toward 400 million around 2050—140 million more people in about 60 years.[11] Most of this growth will result from immigration, because the pull of our relative prosperity is very strong for the poor elsewhere.

Post-1900 immigrants and their descendants have contributed 43 percent of the trebling of U.S. population so far in this century. Post-2000 immigrants and their descendants are projected to contribute 73 percent of the population growth during the first half of the next century. This assumes, conservatively, that annual net immigration is about one million and will stay there. If it continues to increase, our population is headed well past 400 million by 2050.

The connection with health reform is not simply about whether to take in very expensive immigrants such as those with HIV. It involves the question whether the health care package may encourage immigration and thus population growth. The administration has decided to limit the benefits to citizens and legal residents. HUD Secretary Henry Cisneros, a strong figure in the Cabinet and leading Hispanic, says we should deny health and welfare benefits to illegal aliens.[12] Presumably, the benefits would not be available to non-immigrants, of whom there are about 20 million every year. (Although it has not been said, one assumes that both groups will continue to get treatment for contagious illness and emergency care, for humanitarian reasons and the protection of others.)

The question is whether the nation can make that decision stick. No one can seriously pretend to predict the effect of improved medical services in promoting immigration, legal and illegal. However, we must assume that, added to food stamps and other sources of welfare, health care will constitute another strong inducement to come here or, once arrived, to stay. Already, the practice of crossing the border for treatment in welfare hospitals is well established. The proposed government program will cover the jobless and those in the sorts of jobs that tend to be filled by illegal immigrants. Many may agree with the illegal alien who had just lost his job but told a reporter "it's still better than where I came from."

The point here is that the health care package may generate another strong inducement to illegal immigration, and in the process it will drive up the cost of the health care itself.

A QUESTION OF IDENTITY

We may find ourselves receiving more illegal migration even if we do not welcome it. There is a major flaw in the Immigration Reform and Control Act of 1986 (IRCA). Various groups, including Congressional commissions, had urged that there be a better process of identifying U.S. citizens and aliens with a right to work here, in order to avoid widespread fraud. As part of the final compromise, that proposal was weakened to nullity, and subsequently there has been a proliferation of fraudulent documentation. If the health program is not to be offered to the whole world, we will need to know who is entitled, and that will require a much better system of identification than now exists, based perhaps on one's Social Security number and a call-in system such as has been perfected by the credit card companies.

Help seems to be on the way from an unexpected quarter: California. The state is the immigrants' primary destination, and it is foundering. Governor Wilson (who as a senator sponsored the biggest loophole in the 1986 act and later voted for the 1990 act increasing legal immigration) has seen the light. He has called for a series of measures to bring illegal immigration under control. With considerable fanfare—he appeared at one news conference surrounded by stacks of forged identity cards—he has asked President Clinton to "use California as a testing ground for a tamper-proof identification card to combat illegal immigration."[13]

In response, President Clinton has said the unutterable: that his administration is studying the feasibility of such a card, and he linked it specifically to the health care proposal, even while remarking that a national identity card "sort of smacks of Big Brotherism."[14]

The argument I would make, and that the President apparently understands, is that a better national system of identifying individuals is a necessity if we are to institute a national health program that the nation can afford. There are already powerful arguments for better identification, such as the protection of wage and labor standards, the identification of terrorists and criminals, and the imperative need to control illegal immigration if we are to regain some degree of control over the nation's demographic future.

The argument against a "a national ID card" is somewhat spurious. We already have a national identity card, the Social Security card, which is used as an identifier for tax purposes, drivers' licenses, and other purposes. We do not control it very well or use it very effectively. The health insurance aspect seems to clinch the argument. We should get on with an improved system.

THE IMPACT ON FERTILITY

A true national health program would constitute a fundamental change of direction, akin to the New Deal. It deserves, not just a close examination of the budgetary implications, but a policy debate integrating it with other broad national questions. Where, for instance, do we want to go, demographically, and how does health care relate to that question?

Migration and fertility are (along with mortality) the two determinants of our demographic future. A priori, one assumes that the completeness of insurance coverage of child-bearing will have some effect on women's decisions whether to have babies. There is very little systematic evidence on the matter. We have made our national policies affecting fertility—tax policy, welfare and health policies, etc.—without considering the demographic impact, just as we have made immigration laws without any thought of the demographic results.

If the nation cares where it is heading, it should look to the connection between our population future and the environmental, social and unemployment problems we face. The debate on the health care package provides an opportunity to consider whether we wish to encourage lower fertility, and to get some expert testimony as to how the two might be connected. We might, for instance, look to the Singapore example and offer maternity benefits only for the first two children.

Lest the reader think I have gone mad, I hasten to admit that opinion in the U.S. is presently very far from any such decision.

It would probably be seen as intolerable governmental interference in private behavior, and by the religious Right as morally intolerable. I would counter that behavior is no longer private when it is publicly financed and results in major and probably undesirable demographic results. If we see ourselves as a modern nation capable of exerting some conscious influence on our future, we should perhaps compare our timidity in this area to Iran, which U.S. opinion would probably select as an excellent example of a backward theocracy. Iran has recently passed legislation to withhold insurance benefits and maternity leave for children after the third.[15]

THE CHANGING NATURE OF EMPLOYMENT

The high costs of health and retirement benefit packages—which now total 25 percent or more of labor costs—have forced employers in the past year to scramble to meet new legal requirements to fund those packages. To minimize the long term costs of hiring full time employees, employers are turning increasingly to part time and temporary help. The trend has been underway for some time but it seems to have accelerated in the current shaky economic recovery.

The President hopes to finance the new health care program in large part from mandatory employer contributions. If he does so, employers will have further reason to turn increasingly to temps and part time help not covered by the benefit package—or they will seek to substitute technology for labor, or plan to move their operations to lower wage countries.

The more that business shifts to temporary and part time help, the larger the portion of the health program that must be funded from the government program—financed presumably by general taxes—intended as a safety net for people without a health program at work. An attempt to force business to absorb the costs will make the alternatives—automation and departure—more attractive. As if it were fated to propose policies with synergistic ill effects, the administration is concurrently pressing for passage of NAFTA (the North American Free

Trade Agreement), one purpose of which is to make it easier for American business to move its operations to Mexico.

The nation is headed for an expensive surprise if it estimates the public costs of the proposed health program on past experience rather than current trends.

CONCLUSION

The health care decision is going to shape the society, fundamentally, in future years. Because it is so important and has the sort of ramifications described above, it offers both a danger and an opportunity. The danger is that, if we take the decisions without looking at those ramifications, the nation's health bill may put us in even deeper financial trouble, and one by-product—further encouraging population growth—may turn out to be even more important than the health bill itself. The opportunity is the chance to get out of the tunnel in which the nation's important decisions are usually made and to look before we leap to decisions in this fundamental area.

NOTES:

1. Joseph Califano, "The Last Time We Reinvented Health Care," *Washington Post*, OpEd page a23, 4-1–93.
2. It is perhaps instructive that other industrial nations with national health plans find themselves moving in the opposite direction from the United States, toward cost containment driven by unemployment and stagnant economies. France, Germany, the United Kingdom, Spain and Italy have been debating or instituting cost control measures. Reuters, Paris, 6-29-93, 10:37am.
3. See Lindsey Grant et al, *Elephants in the Volkswagen* (New York: W.H. Freeman & Co., 1992), Chapter 12 "Too Many Old People?."
4. Annual figures from *Statistical Abstract of the U.S., 1992*, Table 192. An unknown part of the growth resulted from improved reporting. Other data through March 31, 1993, by telephone May 28, 1993 from HHS Centers for Disease Control, Atlanta.
5. Centers for Disease Control (CDC), Atlanta, quoted in Boyce Rensburger, "AIDS Spreads Fastest Among Young Women . . . ," *Washington Post*, 7-28-93.
6. United Nations, *World Population Prospects: the 1992 Revision*, Chapter III. The countries are Malawi, Rwanda, Uganda and Zambia. One cannot even draw from this catastrophe the bitter hope that AIDS may slow Africa's population growth rate. Not yet. The UN projects that, as a result of the epidemic, the annual population growth of the fifteen most affected nations (all in Africa), from 1995–2000 will be 2.96 percent rather than 3.26 percent. At 2.96 percent, it still takes just twenty-four years for populations to double. Expect more trouble.
7. Karen Hein, director of the adolescent AIDS program, Montefiore Medical Center, to the Ninth International Conference on AIDS, quoted by Cynthia Johnson, "Teenagers Seen Leading Next Wave of AIDS Epidemic," Reuters, Berlin, 6-5-93.
8. Daniel E. Koshland, Jr., "The Microbial Wars," Editorial, *Science*, 8-21-92, p.1021.
9. U.S. Department of State, *The Global AIDS Disaster: Implications for the 1990s* (Department of State Publication 9955, July 1992.) In sub-Saharan Africa, the incidence of HIV infection is expected to quadruple to 48 million by 2000.
10. The proposal came from Shenyang, in the Northeast, and was cited approvingly by the official New China News Agency. Reuters, Beijing, 7-31-93, 07:41.
11. The Census Bureau 1993 middle projection for

2050 is 392 million. A new projection by demographer Leon Bouvier yields 397 million by 2050. (Leon Bouvier & Lindsey Grant, *How Many Americans? Immigration, Population and the Environment*. San Francisco: Sierra Club Books, publication scheduled August 1994.) Both are based on current fertility and immigration patterns.

12. Associated Press, Washington, 8-23-93, 10:52.
13. Reuters, Los Angeles, 8-9-93, 18:55 and United Press (UP), 9-3-93, 16:40.
14. Reuters, Los Angeles, 8-13-93, 14:21.
15. Reuters, Nicosia, 6-3-93, 10:48 am.

THE TIGHTENING CONFLICT: POPULATION, ENERGY USE, AND THE ECOLOGY OF AGRICULTURE

Mario Giampietro and David Pimentel

October 1993

In the last half century the technological development of agriculture has dramatically changed the performance of farming. The changes have been both positive and negative: on the positive side a more stable and abundant food supply has resulted; on the negative side more environmental degradation, more dependence on fossil energy, and a lower energy efficiency. Understanding the reason for these changes requires exploring the relationship between technological development, population, natural resources and environmental sustainability for development. For this reason, in this paper we will discuss the use of energy in agriculture and its relation to the performance of the economy (in part I), and the issues of future development, standards of living and a sustainable envirortment related to population pressure (in part II).

ENERGY, AGRICULTURE AND DEVELOPMENT

The dual nature of agriculture. Agriculture must be compatible with both society's needs and the natural ecosystem. Rapid population growth and the technical development of society have led to difficulties for farmers worldwide to maintain this dual compatibility. In fact, today farmers face demands for a high productivity as well as environmentally sound, sustainable farming practices.

In rural, developing societies, local environmental constraints historically shaped techniques of production and socioeconomic structures. Agricultural strategies and social activities favored long-term ecosystem sustainability. However, the quality of life reached by traditional farming systems is low compared with that of modern western agricultural systems—short life span, low level of education, and absence of social services, etc. In other words, "subsistence farming systems" are *economically not sustainable* when these societies interact with more developed socioeconomic systems.

The dramatic transformations that have occurred in the economy of developed countries have radically changed their farming strategies. Farmers operating in developed countries abandoned traditional techniques of production to keep their income competitive with that in other sectors of society. This required the adoption of techniques that provide high returns per hour of labor. Therefore, large monocultures which rely heavily on technical inputs resulted. For example, in the United States, the amount of corn produced per hour of labor is today 350 times higher than the Cherokees could raise with their traditional agriculture.

This enormous jump in farmer productivity would not have been possible without large injections of fossil energy and machine power. In fact, the flow of energy input in modern U.S. agriculture is fifty times higher than in traditional agricultural.[1] However, the higher income of modern farmers has a price: high-technology agricultural techniques depend on non-renewable stocks of oil and have negative environmental impacts which lower the sustainability of the agroecosystem. These impacts include soil erosion, reduced biodiversity, chemical contamination of the environment by fertilizers and pesticides, and mining of groundwater. Hence, current intensive agriculture based on heavy technological subsidies of fossil energy is *ecologically not sustainable.*

Energy and Society. Humans transform energy inputs found in their environment into a flow of useful energy used to sustain their social and economic needs. This conversion can be obtained in two ways. First, by transforming food energy into muscular power within the human body; this is called *endosomatic or metabolic energy.* Second, by transforming energy outside the human body, such as burning gasoline in a tractor; this is called *exosomatic energy.* In order to have either endosomatic or exosomatic energy conversions, society must have access to adequate energy inputs.

The two major sources of energy used by humans are solar energy and fossil energy resources. Solar driven or renewable energy sources represent almost 100 percent of the endosomatic and exosomatic energy flows in preindustrial societies; they sustained human development for more than 99 percent of human existence. Fossil or non-renewable energy represents more than 90 percent of the exosomatic energy used in the United States and other developed countries; however, this growing reliance of modern societies on fossil energy started only 150 years ago, or much less than 1 percent of human existence.

Solar and fossil energy sources have different characters. The solar energy captured by photosynthesis is renewable or unlimited in its time dimension, but its exploitation is limited in its rate of flow. This means that if we want to double the quantity of biomass harvested (such as crops for food or cornstalks, fast growing trees, etc. for energy), at a fixed technological level, we need to double the land exploited. To double animal power we need more animals and double the land devoted to fodder. On the other hand, fossil energy is a stock-type resource, that is limited in its time dimension—sooner or later it will be exhausted—but, while the stock lasts, it can be exploited at a virtually unlimited rate.

The access to fossil energy removed the limitation on the density at which exosomatic energy can be utilized, and societies experienced a dramatic increase in the rate of energy consumption. The exo/endo energy ratio has jumped from about four to one, a value typical of solar powered societies, to more than forty to one in developed countries (in the U.S. it is more than ninety to one). Clearly, this brought about a dramatic change in the role of the endosomatic energy flow. Endosomatic energy, that is food and human labor, no longer delivers power for direct economic processes. Humans generate the flow of information needed to direct huge flows of exosomatic power produced by machines and powered primarily by fossil energy. To provide an example of the advantage achieved: a small gasoline engine will convert 20 percent of the energy input of one gallon of fuel into power. That is, the 38,000 kcal in one gallon of gasoline can be transformed into 8.8 KWh, which is about three weeks of human work equivalent. (Human work output in agriculture = 0.1 HP, or 0.074 KW, times 120 hours.)

Fossil energy and the food system. More than ten kcalories (kilogram-calories or "large calories") of exosomatic energy are spent in the U.S. food system per kcalorie of food eaten by the consumer. Put another way, the food system consumes ten times more energy than it provides to society in food energy. However, since in the U.S. the exo/endo energy ratio is 90/1, each endosomatic kcalorie (each kcalorie of food metabolized to sustain human activity) induces the circulation of 90 kcalorie of exosomatic energy, basically fossil. This explains why the energy cost of food of ten exosomatic kcalories per endosomatic kcalorie is not perceived as high when measured in economic terms. Actually, despite a net increase in the energy and monetary cost per kcalorie of food in the U.S. over the last decades, the percentage of disposable income spent by U.S. citizens on food has steadily decreased and is now only about 15 percent of disposable income.[2]

Based on a 10/1 ratio, the total direct cost of the daily diet in the U.S. is approximately 35,000 kcalories of exosomatic energy per capita (assuming 3,500 kcal/capita of food available per day for consumption).[3] However, since the average return of one hour of labor in the U.S. is about 100,000 kcalories of exosomatic energy,[4] the flow of exosomatic energy required to supply the daily diet is made accessible by about twenty minutes of labor.

In subsistence societies, about 4 kcalories of exosomatic energy (basically in the form of biomass) are required per kcalorie of food consumed. Thus, the total direct cost of the daily diet is much lower in absolute terms, approximately 10,000 kcalories of exosomatic energy per capita (assuming a food supply of 2,500 kcal/day per capita).[5] On the other hand, because of the limited access to fossil energy, the average return of human labor in subsistence societies is low. In such a system up to five hours of labor are required to supply the daily diet. In terms of human labor, in subsistence societies the daily diet costs sixteen times more than in the U.S. food system.

In countries with a high exo/endo energy ratio, food production no longer provides a direct energy or power supply to society. Food production, however, is still essential to the economy of all nations. Because of the high opportunity cost of human time, there is a strong incentive to lower the human time allocated to the management of the food system. Therefore, technological development in food systems of developed societies is principally aimed at (i) reducing the requirement of labor in food production, (ii) increasing the safety of food, and (iii) reducing the time required for food preparation. Although this strategy of technological development causes an increase in the direct costs of food security, both in production and processing of food, it allows humans to switch a large fraction of their time to other, more productive economic sectors.

For example, in West Europe the percentage of the active population employed in agriculture fell from 75 percent before the industrial revolution (around the year 1750) to less than 10 percent today; in the U.S. this figure fell from 80 percent around the year 1800 to only 2 percent today.[6] The percentage of the total U.S. female population active in the money economy rose from 9.7 percent in the year 1870 to 44.7 percent today.[7] Thanks to energetically expensive, but time-saving food products women no longer have to spend long hours in food-related activities, but can participate in paid economic activities.

Fossil energy and agriculture in developed and developing countries. Modern techniques for farming in developed countries are based on massive infection of fossil energy. This results in lowering the energy efficiency (output-input ratios), and a rapid depletion of non-renewable oil stocks. The two forcers driving this development are (i) the increasing productivity per hour of labor of farmers (=increasing the income and standard of living of farmers, and making available more labor for other ecomomic sectors), and (ii) the increasing productivity per unit of land area (=increasing the total food supply).

Although there are numerous negative effects in terms of environmental sustainability and energy efficiency with modern farming techniques, farmers in developing countries are adopting some of them, especially high yielding varieties, fertilizers, irrigation and pesticides. This adoption, along with more cash crop production, has resulted in some disruption of structures and functions of traditional socio-economic systems. Fossil energy is used to overcome the ecological constraints limiting food output. This has contributed to the widespread relaxation of cultural control on human fertility. Between the end of World War II and 1970, fertility rates rose virtually everywhere in the third world.[9] The rapid growth in the world population is associated with the maximum expansion of fossil energy use.

The increase in birth rates plus the reduction in mortality rates by control of disease resulted in an explosive growth in world population. This resulted in a dramatic shrinkage in the quantity of natural resources available per capita. Under this demographic pressure, developing countries were forced to increase their use of fossil energy in agriculture.

In developing countries, the use of fossil energy has been to prevent starvation rather than to increase the standard of living of farmers and others. Concluding his analysis of the link between population growth and the supply of nitrogen fertilizer Smil[10] makes this point beautifully: "The image is counter-intuitive but true: survival of the peasants in the ricefields of Hunan or Guangdong—with their timeless clod-breaking hoes, docile buffaloes, and rice-cutting sickles—is now much more dependent on fossil fuels and modern chemical synthesis than the physical well-being of the American city dwellers sustained by Iowa and Nebraska farmers cultivating

Table I. Current pattern of energy use in different agricultural systems producing cereals (1988/89)

	World	U.S.A.	E.C.	China	Africa
OUTPUT (cereal yield/year)					
kilogram/hectare (ha)	2,660	4,470	4,880	4,030	1,230
kilogram/worker	1,700	95,600	1,840	800	600
Cereal (106 kcal/haa)	8.8	14.7	16.1	13.3	4
Cereal (106 kcal/workera)	5.6	315.5	60.7	2.6	2
INPUT (energy subsidies/year)					
Exosomatic (106 kcal/ha)	3.2	5.4	10.9	5.7	0.8
Exosomatic (106 kcal/worker)	4.4	342.9	96.9	1.2	1
Nitrogen (kg/ha)	50	48	112	140	13
Exosomatic input (kcal/kg cereal)	1,220	1,200	2,240	1,420	670
CEREAL OUTPUT/EXO INPUT	2.7/1	2.7/1	1.5/1	2.3/1	5.0/1

(a) assuming 3,300 kcal/kg cereal; Data on yield, workers, fertilizer use, hectares in production from: WRI (1991) and FAO (1991).

Estimates on exosomatic energy from Faidley (1992); Fluck (1992); Smil (1990); Stout (1990).8 Note: Calculations are for on-farm energy costs only.

Table 2. Population density, standards of living and work force in agriculture (1988/89)

	World	U.S.A.	E.C.	China	Africa
Arable land per capita [a] (ha)	0.28	0.76	0.24	0.09	0.29
Arable land per agricultural worker [a] (ha)	1.3	63.8	8.9	0.2	1.2
EXO/ENDO energy ratio [b]	20/1	90/1	40/1	1-Aug	1-May
GNP p.capita (1988 US$) [c]	3,010	17,500	9,130	300	620
Life Expectancy at Birth (years) [c]	63	75	75	66	52
Fraction of economically active population in agriculture (%) [d]	47	2	6	67	64
Productivity of agricultural labor [e] (kcal of cereal produced/hour labor)	3,300	175,230	33,600	1,650	990

(a) WRI (1991) and FAO (1991); (b) Exo data from UN (1992), Endo is assumed, average population: 2,100 kcal/day p.c. for China and Africa; 2,400 kcal/day p.c. for USA and EEC; 2,200 kcal/day p.c. world; (c) PRB 1988; (d) FAO, 1989; (e) from Table I assuming an average 1,800 hours/year for agricultural workers.11

sprawling grainfields with giant tractors. These farmers inject ammonia into soil to maximize operating profits and to grow enough feed for extraordinarily meaty diets; but half of all peasants in Southern China are alive because of the urea cast or ladled onto tiny fields—and very few of their children could be born and survive without spreading more of it in the years and decades ahead."

Strategies of energy use in world agriculture. Different strategies in energy use in agriculture can be found in the U.S.A., Western Europe, Africa and China. Data are presented in Table 1. These differences can be explained in terms of availability of natural resources, population density and standard of living (Table 2).

For example, farming systems in Western Europe use heavy energy subsidies in order to keep labor productivity high and also to make maximum use of the limited land. In the U.S., fossil energy is mainly used to boost farmers' productivity (income), and productivity per hectare is not as much a concern as in Europe.

In China, large quantities of fossil energy are used to boost the productivity of the land, because there is little land arable per capita. Agriculture provides the major source of employment in China (67 percent of the economically active population). Therefore, the standard of living of that society is low.

In Africa, little fossil energy is used in agriculture. Thus, the productivity both per farmer and per hectare is low. If the situation remains unchanged, shortage of food will continue to grow as the population increases.

This comparison shows that energy can be used in agriculture to boost the productivity of labor and/or land.

For example, the food energy yield per hour of labor in *Western Europe* is more than twenty times higher than in China, but less than a fifth of that in the U.S. Even though Western European agriculture uses almost twice as much energy as U.S. agriculture per kilogram of cereal produced, the productivity of cereal per hour of European farm labor is lower than in the U.S. For this reason, European farmers require more government subsidies than U.S. farmers to have comparable incomes. The lower agricultural performance in Europe despite higher energy use is due to the limited availability of land (the land area available per farmer in Europe is about 1/7th of that available in the USA).

The effect of demographic pressure can also be seen by comparing the performances of Chinese and U.S. agriculture. *China* has a fossil energy consumption per hectare higher than the U.S. However, this high fossil energy use has the goal of boosting the yield per hectare (increase the food supply) and does not generate an increase in farmers' income (as indicated by the low productivity per hour of labor). To get approximately the same yield, U.S. farmers work only ten hours/year per hectare in grain production compared with more than 1,000 hours/hectare for Chinese agriculture.[12] The U.S. economy manages in this way to sustain its farmers at an income level that is almost comparable to that of workers in other U.S. economic sectors, but that is almost a hundred times higher than the income of Chinese farmers.

In this example, again, we can assess the importance of the land constraints: the average area cropped per farm worker in the U.S. is about 64 hectares (ha), compared with only 0.2 ha/worker in China. Where the population density is high, as in China, fossil energy-based inputs are required in large quantities not so much to increase the standard of living, but to increase food yield per hectare. The U.S. enjoyed in the past a fairly low demographic pressure and this resulted in the possibility of using fossil energy mainly to increase the productivity of labor (guaranteeing an acceptable income for farmers). At low population density, fossil energy can be used to guarantee a high income to farmers, and to make workers available for the rest of the economy.

Put another way, if China tried to modemize its society reaching levels of exo/endo energy typical of western standards, it would have to (i) absorb an enormous number of farmers in other economic sectors (hundreds of millions!!), and (ii) further boost the energy consumption in the agricultural sector, since due to the limitation of land (0.09 ha per capita of arable land) Chinese agriculture would face a situation even worse than in Western Europe. A "modernized" Chinese agriculture would be required to provide food for the population, while absorbing only a little fraction of human time, and providing a high income to farmers.

Moreover, it should be noted that when farmers comprise only a small fraction of the population, and society undergoes a massive process of urbanization, the real energy cost of supplying food is shifted from agriculture to the post-harvest section of the food system. In general, three to five kcal are spent in processing, distribution, packaging and home preparation for each kcal spent in producing food at the farm level.

Such a development would imply not only a formidable flow of energy required to build and run the technological plant required to absorb at least 80 percent of the current Chinese farmers into the industrial/services sector, but also a further increase of energy use in the agricultural sector (well above the western European levels). They might theoretically be able to get such an energy input for a while, by using their coal resources, but they would probably choke themselves on the pollution and induce an environmental impact of enormous dimensions. Furthermore, in case of continued demographic growth, it is also doubtful that it would be possible to further boost the productivity of land (output per ha) to accommodate the increased population. It is well known that, after a certain threshold, energy subsidies (fertilizers, pesticides, irrigation, etc.) have a declining return. "Available long-term comparisons show that in China's Zhejiang and Shandong provinces the typical rice response to additional units of nitrogen application during the 1980s was only 50 to 60 percent of that of the 1960s, in the Suzhou area of Jiangsu province it was only around one-third, and around Wuxi (also in Jiangsu) there have been no returns at all."[13]

The excessive demographic pressure in China seems to mean that food security, a high standard of living, and respect for the environment are goals almost impossible to achieve at the same time.

Finally, a look at the current performance of *Africa's* agriculture is another source of serious concern. From the low level of fossil energy consumption, it can be inferred that many farmers are still using traditional techniques of production (fallow rotation, a use of land which requires a low population density). Because of the demographic explosion experienced in the last decades, the African situation will get even worse: (i) declining food supplies, because there is too little land per capita and little fossil energy and technology for food production; (ii) increasing poverty, because the limited natural resource, fossil energy and technology available are mostly diverted to their own uses by the few elites; (iii) increasing environmental degradation, because traditional methods of agriculture performed at too high population density shorten crop rotations and further stress the environment.

Actually, all three of these effects are already taking place, and current demographic trends do not leave much hope for positive changes in the near future. Africa has the highest rate of population growth in the world at 3 percent per year, a doubling time of 23 years! In the future the trends appear to be increasing dependence on fossil energy for agricultural production, increasing poverty, increasing deficits in food supply, and increasing ecological destruction.

From the above, it is clear that ecological and human perspectives collide when it comes to technological performance in agriculture. For example, an increase in the output/input ratio can be seen as a positive event on the ecological side. However, this is not always beneficial at the societal level, as illustrated by African agriculture, which has the highest energy output/input ratio but the lowest exo/endo energy ratio and life span. For developed societies, the output/input energy ratios in agriculture are lower than those in Africa, but this allows the labor force to move to other economic sectors. When a society has an exo/endo ratio so low that it is convenient to use labor intensive techniques to save capital and fossil energy, the standard of living is much lower than those considered acceptable in the western world.

THE FUTURE: ENERGY, POPULATION AND SUSTAINABILITY

Limits to the Intensification of Agriculture. The prime resources of agriculture—land, water, energy, and biological resources—function interdependently, and each can be utilized to a degree to make up for a partial shortage in one or more of the others. For example, to bring desert land into agricultural production, it can be irrigated.

However, this can occur only if groundwater or surface water is available, if sufficient fossil energy is available to pump and move the water, if monetary resources are available to buy the required technology, and if the soil is suitable for irrigation and fertile to support crop growth.

Moreover, intensive farming techniques have an impact on the pattern of energy flows in ecosystems. In general, they reduce the capability of an ecosystem to use solar energy for evapotranspiration, gross primary production, and recycling nutrients. This "ecological cost" of agriculture has been overlooked by most economic analyses.

The long-term productivity of agroecosystems depends on the sustainability of natural resources including biological, soil, and water resources. Therefore, an environmentally sound agriculture has limits in its use of these renewable resources. For example, an upper limit exists to the productivity of an agroecosystem.[14] Currently, with most intensive agriculture there is serious land degradation, loss of top soil, chemical pollution, and groundwater mining.

Fossil energy inputs and sustainability. About 330 quads (1 quad = 10^{15} BTU) of all forms of energy per year are used worldwide by humans. A large fraction of this energy, about 81 percent, is provided by fossil energy worldwide each year.[15] Moreover, about 50 percent of all solar energy captured by photosynthesis worldwide is already used by humans, but most of it is captured as food and other agricultural products, which are not included in the 330 quads. That agricultural output is already inadequate to meet human needs for food and forest products.[16] We would be in grim trouble if we had to derive our energy needs from current basic photosynthetic production, as our ancestors did. Given the anticipated decline in fossil fuel use, and the continued growth of human populations, that problem is ahead of us rather than behind us.

The total consumption in the U.S. is 77 quads of energy. This is almost three times the 28 quads of solar energy harvested as crop and forest products, and about 40 percent more energy than the total amount of solar energy captured each year by all U.S. plant biomass.[17] Per capita use of fossil energy in North America (expressed as conventional fossil fuel equivalent) is about 7,000 liters of oil per year or five times the world average level!

As noted earlier, large quantities of fossil energy based fertilizers are major sources of nutrient enhancement of agricultural soils throughout the world. Pesticides are also fossil based and their production and use imply a significant consumption of fossil energy.[18] Annual world pesticide use has been estimated at 2.5 million metric tons, of which 0.6 million metric tons are used in North America.[19]

Projections of the availability of fossil energy resources are discouraging. A recent report published by the U.S. Department of Energy based on current oildrilling data indicates that the estimated amount of U.S. oil reserves has plummeted. This means that instead of the thirty-five-year supply of U.S. oil resources, that was projected about ten years ago, the current known reserves and potential discoverable oil resources are now limited to less than fifteen years' consumption at present levels.[20] Since the United States is now importing more than half its oil, a serious problem already exists.[21] It should be noted that an increased demand of the U.S. economy for oil on the international market could lead to higher prices. This would dramatically affect U.S. agriculture as well as the agriculture of many developing countries already heavily dependent on fossil energy based inputs (mainly fertilizers).

Clearly, there is a room for substitutability among fossil energy sources, and natural gas and coal are expected to increase their share as soon as oil supply will decrease. However, gas supplies are not at all that much better off. Coal is not infinite and it exacts a high environmental cost or a high price to clean it up.

Increased standard of living and population pressure. The large increases in fertilizers and pesticides used in developed countries are due to the abandonment of traditional agricultural technologies. For some major crops like corn, crop rotations have been abandoned. Now nearly 50 percent of U.S. corn land is grown continuously as a monoculture. This has caused an increase in the number of corn pests and the need for more pesticides to protect the crop. Since 1945 the use of synthetic pesticides in the U.S. has grown thirty-three-fold, yet crop losses to pests continue to increase.[22]

In developing countries, it is population pressure and poverty that push the abandonment of sound techniques of agricultural production, such as fallows and crop rotations. Population growth means shrinking environmental resources per capita (land, soil, water and biological resources), a need for increasing yields per hectare and sooner or later a dependence on fossil energy. When the development of a country at a low exo/endo ratio is prevented by its demographic trap, negative ecological side effects are generated by the increased use of energy in agriculture. Environmental degradation tends to drive down the income of farmers and the available food supply per capita.

Overall, demographic pressure and the search for a high standard of living are forcing increased use of fossil energy while oil and gas stocks are rapidly disappearing.

The population-resource equation and the law of decreasing returns. The population-resource equation can be written as follows:

Natural resources use x Technology = Population x per capita Consumption.

However, the ability of technology to make up for the shortage of natural resources is limited. It is not possible to achieve an unlimited increase in both the population and the per capita consumption by simply adding more technology to the limited endowment of natural resources. The efficiency of a technological process can never be higher than 1, meaning that technological capital should be considered a complement to natural capital rather than a substitute.[23] Technology cannot make accessible more natural resources, such as land and water, than are available; it can only improve the limited efficiency of resource use.

A decreasing return per unit of effort takes place when an intensification of exploitation of natural resources occurs.[24] Moreover, after a certain threshold there is no substitution of technology for natural services. For example, the world fish catch is already close to 100 million tons, and that is thought to be the maximum possible catch from the sea.[25] Improving fishing vessel technologies, as has been done, reduces the fishery stock and leads to decreasing fishery yields. "Maintaining even 80 million tons sustainability will depend upon careful fisheries management, protection and restoration of coastal wetlands, and abatement of ocean pollution-none of which seems in prospect at the moment."[26] Aquaculture is supplying today about 12 million tons but the expansion of this supply is limited by environmental risks and operation costs. A further large increase in human population numbers simply lowers the availability of fish per capita.

Future changes and the potential transition toward sustainability. Currently worldwide there is serious degradation of land, water, and biological resources generated by the increasing use of fossil energy by the world's population.[27] Already, more fossil energy is used than is available in the form of a sustainable supply of biomass, more nitrogen fertilizer is used per year than could be obtained by natural supply, water is pumped out of underground reservoirs at a higher rate than it is recharged, and more minerals are taken out of mines than are formed by biogeochemical cycles. Fossil energy and technology enabled humans to (temporarily) sustain excesses. At present and projected world population levels, the current pattern of human development is not ecologically sustainable. The world economic system is built on depleting, as fast as possible, the very natural resources on which human survival depends.

Clearly, this is a flaw in human logic. Humans must learn how to manage natural resources in a sustainable manner and determine the number of humans compatible with an acceptable standard of living.

A sustainable use of renewable resources is possible only if (i) known environmentally sound agricultural technologies are implemented, (ii) various known renewable energy technologies are put in place, (iii) major increases in energy efficiency are achieved to reduce the exosomatic energy consumption per capita, and (iv) population size and the consequent level of withdrawal of natural resources are compatible with maintaining the stability of environmental processes.

Assuming (optimistically) that the first three points will be achieved in the U.S. in the next decades (with a reduction to less than half of the exosomatic energy consumption per capita), still the "sustainable U.S. economy" mentioned would be possible only with a smaller population than the current 256 million (e.g., about 200 million.)[28] In general, the lower the population density the higher the ratio of natural resources of land, water, clean air, biota, and solar energy per capita, and the lower the cost humans have to pay for these vital services. Agriculture would have more natural nutrients, water, and biological resources. Chemical pollutants would be reduced. With more abundant natural resources per capita, the standard of living for everyone would be improved.

Unfortunately, the actual trend of demographic growth both in the U.S. and world is not toward sustainability (=a population size within the ecosystem's carrying capacity) or optimum population size (=a population size lower than the maximum possible, thus permitting a higher standard of living). U.S. population is projected to rise to 400 million in just sixty years and world population is projected to double to over 10 billion.

Approximately one-third of the world's arable land and forests were lost during the past forty years due to mismanagement and degradation. Currently, there is only 0.28 ha of arable land per capita with a world population of 5.5 billion people. It is estimated that about 0.5 ha per capita is needed for a diverse and varied diet. With the world population to double to 11 billion people, there will be less than 0.15 ha per capita in just forty years (very close to a "Chinese situation"). At the same time, evidence suggests that arable land degradation is increasing as poor farmers burn more crop residues and dung as fuel for cooking and other purposes, instead of returning them to the land.

The threat to food and environmental security created by population growth is clear today. (i) Most of the 183 countries in the world are now dependent in some degree on food imports. Cereal exports that supply most of those imports now come from the surpluses produced in a few countries with relatively low population densities and intensive agriculture (in 1989 the United States, Canada, Australia, Oceania and Argentina provided more than 81 percent of net cereal exports on world markets.[29]) (ii) Some developing countries, like China, already use more fertilizer per hectare than the U.S. This intensive use of fossil based fertilizers is just to help meet food needs in these developing countries. What will a future slowdown of fossil energy consumption (either because of a decline of oil supply or because of growing restrictions on fossil fuel use to limit its environmental impact) mean to both developed and developing countries?

CONCLUSION

To use a Dutch expression:

> *"A development policy without a population program is like mopping the floor with the water turned on."*
>
> (-P. Bukman).

At this stage of human development, any serious policy concerned with energy saving, environmental sustainability, increasing jobs, and improving the standard of living has to be based on reducing population pressure. This applies to both developed countries (as the U.S.) and developing countries. The U.S. has a privileged situation in that it can afford to escape the demographic trap in which many developing countries are already struggling. However, it must set the goal of an adequate quantity of arable, pasture and forest land available per capita. This will provide the margin to make agriculture enviromnentally sound. It will offer the option of using some biomass production for energy, and it will reduce the pressure on land, water, air, energy, and biological resources. Such a program is vital if we want to maintain a decent standard of living for future generations.

The level of energy consumption that will be enjoyed by a future "sustainable society" will lie below the one reached today by developed countries (based on the rentless exploitation of fossil fuels) and above the one typical of pre-industrial societies which rely completely on photosynthesis. Renewable energies have to play a major role to substitute for the role currently played by fossil energy. The lower the population density, the lower will be the demand of energy for food production, the lower the environmental impact of agriculture, the larger the choice of possible alternative energy sources and in the last analysis, the higher the probability of achieving an acceptable standard of living and eco-compatibility.

NOTES:

1. Pimentel, D. and Pimentel, M. *Food, Energy and Society*. London, UK: Edward Arnold, 1979.
2. Manchester, A., Food spending. *Food Review*, 14 (3), 1991: 24–27.
3. FAO. *Food Balance Sheets*. FAO, Rome, 1991.
4. Giampietro, M., Bukkens, S.G.F. and Pimentel, D. Labor Productivitiy: A Biophysical Definition and Assessment. *Human Ecology* 3: 1–36 (in press, 1993).
5. See note 3.
6. Cipolla, C.M., *The Economic History of the World Population*. Bames and Noble Books, New York, 1978, pp. 30–31. FAO, *Comprehensive Demographic Estimates and Projections* 1950–2025. FAO, Rome, 1989.
7. Bairoch, P., Deldycke, T., Gelders, H. and Limbor, J.-M., The Working Population and its Structure. *International Historical Statistics*, Vol. 1. Editions de l'Institut de Sociologie de l'Universitk Libre debruxelles, Bruxelles, 1968. International Labour Office (ILO), *1989–1990 Year Book of Labour Statistics*. ILO, Geneva, 1990.
8. World Resources Institute (WRI), *World Resources 1990–91*. New York: Oxford University Press, 1991. FAO, *Production Yearbook 1990* (Vol. 44). Rome: Food and Agriculture Organization of the United Nations, 1991. Faidley, L.W., Energy and agriculture. In R.C. Fluck (Ed.), *Energy in Farm Production* (Energy in World Agriculture, Vol. 6), pp. 1–12. Amsterdam: Elsevier, 1992. Fluck, R.C., Energy of human labor. In Energy in Farm Production, op cit, pp. 31–37. Smit, V., Energy cost of Chinese crop farming. In T.C. Tso (Ed.),

Agricultural Reform and Development in China. Beltsville, MD: Ideals, Inc., 1990. pp. 260267. Stout, B.A., *Handbook of Energyfor World Agriculture*. New York: Elsevier, 1991.

9. Abernethy, V. 1993. The demographic transition revisited: Lessons for foreign aid and U.S. immigration policy. *Ecological Economics*, in press, 1993.
10. Smil, V., Population growth and nitrogen: An exploration of a critical existential link. *Population and Development Review*, 17 (4), 1991: 569–601. p. 593.
11. WRI, *World Resources*, 1990–99 1, op cit. FAO, *Production Yearbook*, 1991, op cit. UN, *1990 Energy Statistics Yearbook*. New York: United Nations, 1992. PRB, *World Population Data Sheet*. Washington D.C.: Population Reference Bureau, Inc., 1988. FAO, *Comprehensive Demographic Estimates and Projections*, 1950–2025. Rome: Food and Agriculture Organization, 1989.
12. Dazhong, W. and Pimentel, D., Energy use in crop systems in Northeastern China. In: D. Pimentel and C.W. Hall (Eds.), *Food and Energy Resources*, Academic Press, New York, 1984.
13. Smil, op cit, p. 586.
14. A review of these limits for the U.S. has been provided in a previous *NPG Forum* article (Pimentel, D. and Pimentel, M., Land, energy and water: The constraints governing optimum U.S. population size. NPG Forum, January, 1990. Teaneck, NJ: Negative Population Growth, Inc.) A more general analysis at world level is provided in Kendall and Pimentel (Kendall, H. and Pimentel, D., Constraints on the expansion of the global food supply. *Ambio*, in press, 1993) and Erhlich et al (Ehrlich, P.R. Ehrlich, A.H. and Daily, G.C. 1993. Food security, population, and environment. *Population and Development Review*, 19 (1), 1993: 1–32.)
15. United Nations, 1988 and 1990 *Energy Statistics Yearbook*. New York: United Nations 1990 & 1992.
16. Pimentel & Pimentel, Land Energy and Water: The Constraints Governing Optimum U.S. population size. *NPG Forum*, op cit.
17. ERAB, *Biomass Energy*. Washington, DC: Energy Research Advisory Board, U.S. Department of Energy, 198 1.
18. Pimentel, D., Dazhong, W., and Giampietro, M., Technological changes in energy use in U.S. agricultural production. In: S.R. Gliessman (Ed.), *Agroecology*, pp. 305–32 1. New York: Springer Verlag, 1990.
19. CGIAR, *Facts and Figures-International Agricultural Research*. New York: The Rockefeller Foundation/Washington, DC: EFPRI, 1990.
20. DOE, *Annual Energy Outlook*. Washington, DC: U.S. Department of Energy, 1990. DOE, *Annual Energy Outlook with Projections to 2010*. Washington, DC: U.S. Department of Energy, 1991. Lawson, R.L., The U.S. should increase its use of coal. In: C.P. Cozic and M. Polesetsky (Eds.), Energy Alternatives (pp. 41–45). San Diego: Greenhaven Press, 1991.
21. Gibbons, J.H. and Blair, P.D., U.S. Energy transition: On getting from here to there. Am. Inst. of Physics, July, 1991: 21–30.
22. Pimentel, D., McLaughlin, L., Zepp, A., Lakitan, B., Kraus, T., Kleinman, P., Vancini, F., Roach, W.J., Graap, E., Keeton, W.S. and Selig, G., Environmental and economic impacts of reducing U.S. agricultural pesticide use. In: D. Pimentel (Ed.), *Handbook of Pest Management in Agriculture*, pp. 679–718. Boca Raton, FL: CRC Press, 1991.
23. Daly, H.E., From Empty-world Economics to Full-world Economics: Recognizing an Historical Turning Point in Economic Development. In: R. Goodland, H.E. Daly, S. El

Serafy (Eds.) *Population, Technology and Lifestyle*, p. 23–27. Washington D.C.: Island Press, 1992.

24. Hall et al. present a detailed analysis for agriculture, fisheries, range—land and all forms of mining. (Hall, C.A.S., Cleveland, C.J. and Kaufman, R., *Energy and Resource Quality*. New York: John Wiley & Sons, 1986.)
25. World Resources Institute (WRI), *World Resources 1992–93*. New York: Oxford University Press, 1992.
26. Ehrlich, Ehrlich et al, op cit note 12, pp. 6–7.
27. Kendall, H. and Pimentel, D., Constraints on the expansion of the global food supply. *Ambio* op cit, in press 1993.
28. Pimentel, D., Giampietro, M. and Bukkens, S.G.F., An optimum population for North and Latin America. Paper presented at the First World Optimum Population Congress, Cambridge University, U.K., 9l lth August 1993.
29. FAO, *Trade Yearbook 1989* (Vol. 43). Rome: Food and Agriculture Organization of the United Nations, 1990.

THE COSTS OF OVERPOPULATION

Don Mann

September 1994

We at NPG believe our members should know about this book. NPG played no role in its production, but both authors have written articles in the NPG Forum series. We think it is so important we have ordered copies to distribute to major libraries.

Too much of American population writing is about other countries, particularly those in the third world. This one is about our own country, and the authors state their message at the beginning: "First, the human race is a part of the natural ecosystem of Earth, not a privileged superspecies given the earth as its inheritance. Second, the disturbances caused by human activities have accelerated so dramatically in this half-century, driven by population growth and the technological explosion, that they threaten not only the continuation of a way of life that we have come to take for granted, but perhaps even the continuation of life systems as we understand them. Third, the United States, because of its size and consumption habits, is the most destabilizing unit of the vast ecosystem we call Earth . . . And fourth, the means for controlling and reversing these terrible forces lie within our hands, if only as a society we can be wise enough to understand and employ them."

The authors point out that the nation grew from 76 million in 1900 to 249 million in 1990, and 43 percent of that growth consisted of post-1900 immigrants and their descendants. Present immigration and fertility patterns would lead to a population of 397 million in 2050 and 492 million in 2100, and 91 percent of that growth would be post-2000 immigrants and their descendants.

In other words, American fertility and particularly American immigration policies place us in a league with the ruinous population growth patterns of India and Bangladesh. Moreover, our growth is far more destructive because of our style of living. Continued high levels of consumption combined with third world-like population growth is a prescription for disaster.

The book catalogues the present problems, and it shows how population increase will make things worse. Urban problems and unemployment, the energy transition away from petroleum, nuclear waste and sewage sludge (most city dwellers will be drinking water from sewage plants). Biodiversity, and the rising resistance of agricultural pests and diseases to pesticides and medicines. Acid rain, climate change, water resource depletion and the poisoning of our supplies, topsoil and agriculture, forests, wetlands and fishery (which is already in a state of collapse.) They don't leave much out.

Nevertheless, their message is not simply one of gloom. In detailed projections, they show a way out. They point out that we could bring population growth to a halt in the next century and even, if we wish, turn it around. Fertility would have to come gradually down to an average of 1½ children—this would result if we would "stop at two"—and annual net immigration would have to be limited to 200,000 (somewhat lower than the level that prevailed for much of this century). I find this an encouraging thought. Population planning alone will not solve all our problems, but the problems won't be solved if we do not bring the engine of population growth to a halt.

A population policy will not materialize by itself. We must persuade our national political leaders to face their obligations to their own people and to their descendants. They need to pass new legislation, and to enforce the laws we have.

The authors are concerned about the third world, caught in a population explosion, and they would make family planning assistance the first priority in our foreign aid, but they argue that our primary responsibility lies at home. They believe the national goal should be first to avoid adding to the annual load of pollution and environmental damage, and then to reduce it.

Dr. Bouvier is a noted demographer, and Mr. Grant is a former State Department and National Security Council official. I commend the book to you. So does Congressman Tony Beilenson, co-chair of the Congressional Coalition on Population and Development. He says "Bouvier and Grant are absolutely right: population is the big issue . . . No one with hope for the future can afford to ignore this book."

THE CAIRO CONFERENCE: FEMINISTS VS. THE POPE

Lindsey Grant

July 1994

DONNYBROOK IN NEW YORK

The final preparatory conference for the Cairo meeting ("PrepCom III") was held in New York City in April. A *New York Times* headline characterized the lineup as "Vatican Fights Plan to Bolster Role of Women," and that pretty well summarizes what happened at the conference.[1] Many delegations (including the U.S.) sought a sweeping declaration of the rights and needs of women, coupling it only very loosely to the issue of world population growth. The Vatican, mobilizing a few responsive governments, fought back in an unusually blunt effort to weaken the language concerning women's rights and to delete references to family planning, "reproductive health" and, above all, abortion. It succeeded only in getting such references "bracketed" (marked for final decision in the September conference.)

In the process, very little was heard about the population issue.

The population community has learned not to expect help from the Vatican. On the other hand, there is reason to believe that improvements in the status of women will help to bring human fertility down. To some considerable degree, the interests of the population community should parallel those of the feminists.

Things are, however, seldom what they seem, and a close reading of the draft Programme raises two fundamental issues:

First, the militant feminists' position rests on the unproven and dubious propositions (a) that, given unimpeded freedom of choice, the women of the world will choose the socially desirable fertility level, and (b) therefore that money spent on women's advancement is the most effective way to pursue population goals.

Second, having made (but not tried to prove) those assumptions, the militant feminists would divert some of what little money there is for direct population programs into feminist causes, some of which may be a long time coming. This is not a distant threat, it is proposed in the Programme and occurs in the U.S. AID program.

Most modern Americans endorse the principle of women's equality and the importance of assuring that they are not discriminated against, but that does not necessarily translate into support for the document that has come out of PrepCom 111. The Department of State has been going along with the extreme feminists' agenda; it would do well to back off and look where it is being taken.

CRISIS DENIED

No Crisis? The more severe the population crisis is in the third world, the more justification there is for effective measures to bring fertility down, rather than simply stating that women (and couples) have the unqualified "right to decide freely and responsibly the number and spacing of their children . . ." (draft Cairo Programme, Chap.11, Principle 7).

Ergo, there must be no crisis.

Several U.S. NGOs (nongovernmental organizations) held a series of town meetings preparatory to the Cairo Conference. One organizer, in a statement that comes across as a remarkable combination of arrogance and error, wrote: " . . . the opinions expressed largely echoed the crisis formulation heard two decades ago, rather than the tempered position developed over the past twenty years by U.N. and U.S. officials . . . Instead of measured language about population change, many people attending the town meetings stridently evoke 'the population problem.'"[2]

Wait a minute. The "tempered position" is brand new, not a twenty-year development; it is the product of a small and determined group of militant feminists, worldwide, rather than a response to third world pressures. The local speakers were right. There is not only a "problem"; there is a crisis.

The Continuing Crisis. Wishing does not dispose of it. The problem in most of the third world is overwhelming and immediate. It is asserted (without elaboration) that the Programme "would result in world population growth during this period (1995–2015) and beyond at levels close to" the UN 1992 low projection (section 1.4) and that it would lead to world population stabilization in the next century (section 6.1). The Programme is more optimistic than its technical advisers.[3]

Let us look at the low projection. To take Africa, because it is the most desperate continent: it would require that average fertility (TFR) decline from 5.9 children now (and 6.4 in sub-Saharan Africa) to 2.31 in 2015–2020 and stabilize at 1.7 in forty-five years—a 70 percent reduction in a region that has achieved only a 10 percent reduction since 1950. For India, the required decline is from 3.6 now to 1.5 before 2030. The low projection is a tough and unlikely scenario even with massive efforts on all feasible measures to reduce fertility.[4]

Let us look at another UN projection (see figure). It shows what will happen to population growth if fertility stays where it is now. For comparison, I have included the UN's conventional high, medium and low fertility projections.

What that "constant fertility" curve dramatizes is that the third world is less than half way to manageable fertility levels. The same constant fertility projection made a generation ago would have looked even worse, but the war is far from won. Excluding China (which has had remarkable success in reducing fertility, partly through the very means the feminists decry), overall third world fertility has declined less than one-third since the 1950s, to 4.2. It must still be cut in half again, to about 2.1, if population is ever to stabilize. (That is, barring a disastrous rise in mortality, which is quite possible.) That's a crisis.

All other long term world population projections (UN, World Bank, Census Bureau) are optimistic. They all assume declines in third world fertility. They simply posit different timetables.

Arithmetically, growth is faster right now than it has ever been, about 90 million each year.

The UN demographers remark that the "constant fertility" projection is unrealistic. Of course it is; it's absurd. The projection for 2150 would mean about 2000 square feet (that is forty-five by forty-five feet) of ice-free land per human, including deserts, mountains, forests, plains, farms, cities, and highways. Famine and disease will arrest that curve before it goes very far. The point the "constant fertility" curve makes is that human population growth must stop, and very soon, and the central question before any population conference should be "How do we continue the progress and get to replacement fertility or below? Now."

For that matter, the "high" and "medium" projections may be nearly as unrealistic. There is no assurance that a world of deteriorating environment and resources can support 28 or even 12 billion people, particularly if the more prosperous countries in the third world insist (quite understandably) on trying to live like the first world does.

We are living through a tragedy. World population was about 2.5 billion in the 1950s. With the new technologies available, such a population could reasonably have aspired to a world in which all could live at a decent level. Instead, the technology was used to reduce mortality long before we addressed fertility, thus generating the population explosion that now makes a mockery of the hopes. There was a "baby boom" of sorts in much of the world, adding to population growth. Belated efforts to reduce fertility, flawed as they may be, have at least begun to correct the demographic imbalance without leaving it to famine and pestilence to do the job. Now we are being told to abandon that approach and trust the militant feminists that investment in their issues alone will do the job. The world doesn't have that kind of money, that kind of time, or probably that faith.

Not a crisis? The 1994 UN Human Development Report says that Afghanistan, Angola, Haiti, Iraq, Mozambique, Burma, the Sudan and Zaire are facing "collapse," with Algeria, Burundi, Rwanda (the report was prepared before the current civil war), the Cote d'Ivoire, Egypt, Liberia, Nigeria and Sierra Leone close behind. It did not list Bangladesh, where six million people have applied for perhaps 5000 U.S. visas that will come available under the brutal "visa lottery" created by the Immigration Act of 1990.[5] Right now there are famines brewing in Africa that have put about 20 million people at risk of starvation this year.[6]

Scientists—the National Academy of Sciences and the Royal Academy; a joint statement by some 1670 scientists (including most living Nobel laureates in science); fifty-seven of the academies of science at a recent meeting in New Delhi—tell us in different ways of the urgency of stopping population growth. A Nobel laureate says that "The human race now appears to be getting close to the limits of global food productive capacity based on present technologies . . . (Many agricultural experts) are desperately worried about the food problem."[7] Scientists were not included in the U.S. PrepCom III delegation.

To Demolish a Myth . . . The proposal to let women and couples "freely and responsibly" decide about child-bearing is taken intact from a tortured compromise between those who wanted to set goals and those who opposed them at the Bucharest population conference twenty years ago. There is no rationale for assuming that "responsible" free choice will, unguided, lead to the socially desirable level of fertility, and U.S. experience suggests otherwise. It is myth masquerading as truth.

Of the hundreds of millions of people who will be making love tonight, how many will be thinking about a socially responsible population policy?

This is the first century in which human population growth has been fast enough, and the numbers large enough, to threaten our own future, and that is what makes this century different from any earlier one. A difference of 10 percent in world fertility—between 2.0 and 2.2—makes the difference between eventual stabilization and continued growth toward the mathematically absurd. A difference of one child—between average fertility of 1.7 and 2.7, for instance is literally a matter of billions of people within the next century and fertility surveys indicate that most third world women presently want more than three children. If no effort is made to steer this vector, beyond offering homilies about free choice, then the Cairo conference has nothing to offer to the governments that must face the population problem or perish.

THE PLAYERS AND THEIR AGENDAS

The Vatican. The women's movement and the Vatican have been at odds at least since the issue first arose of ordaining women priests. Perhaps, in retrospect, the lasting importance of the ICPD will be that it is bringing that conflict to a head. The Vatican has of course opposed all birth control other than the "rhythm method" for years. Under Pope John Paul II, the position on all population issues has toughened, and in response, feminist criticism of the Pope has become sharper and more explicit.

The Pope in March convened all the ambassadors to the Holy See, in a most unusual step, and top Vatican officials lectured them on the evils of birth control. He has privately lectured President Clinton and publicly chastised Nafis Sadik (Executive Director of the UN Population Fund [UNFPA] and Secretary-General of the ICPD) calling contraception "immoral," abortion a "heinous evil" and sterilization "a grave threat to human dignity and liberty when promoted as part of a population policy." He has condemned "propaganda and misinformation directed at persuading couples that they must limit their families to one or two children." He is writing an encyclical on abortion. Following his lead, the U.S. Conference of Catholic Bishops wrote President Clinton, saying his administration was acting as an "agent of coercion" by promoting birth control and abortion.[8] In a unanimous message, 114 cardinals called the promotion of "artificial" population control "cultural imperialism."

The Pope has thus taken on both the radical feminists, who seek more subsidized family planning including abortions, and the population movement, which is trying to persuade the world that people must indeed limit their families.

The Pope has increasingly couched the issue in terms of family values. In an encyclical in October 1993 and subsequent speeches, he has asserted that the traditional family is not just a Christian ideal but a "natural right" and that his position is an "absolute truth." He denounced the draft Programme for creating "models for hedonism and permissiveness."

The Vatican observer at PrepCom III lectured it for lacking "a coherent moral vision."[9] The conference organizers retaliated. Conference Chairman Fred Sai chided the representative for his language, and several women's groups—including Catholic groups—called a press conference the next day that was highly critical of the church. The battle is indeed joined.

One can only speculate as to how much the Vatican position hinders the advance of family planning. On one hand, Italy and Spain, both ostensibly Catholic countries, have among the world's lowest fertility rates; they apparently have become used to drawing their own conclusions. The progress of contraceptive use in many third world Catholic countries also suggests that the Vatican's position is not seen as necessarily compelling. On the other hand, the Vatican can hinder the creation of family planning programs in Catholic countries where it is politically unwise to take on the church. Moreover, the Vatican's position must inhibit family planning in Latin America and parts of Africa, where the population problem is worst and where the advice of the parish priest is taken very seriously.

The Vatican guards its decision processes very well, but there are some rumblings suggesting that movement is afoot. The church has, after all, learned to adjust over time to other inconvenient realities, such as the heliocentric solar system. Change, clearly, will not come in the tenure of the present Pope, who has made this his personal issue. He is old, however, and maneuvering may be under way.

A peculiar thing happened in June. The Italian Bishops' Conference released a study by the Papal Academy of Science, entitled "Too Many Births?" It argued that birth control is necessary "to prevent the emergence of insoluble problems. . . . To deny responsibility towards future generations" would have devastating consequences, especially in the third world. It suggested that the birth rate must not "notably exceed the level of two children per couple."[10] The release of the paper, and the timing, can hardly have been accidental.

The Vatican reacted in fury. It released two successive statements denying that the Academy was entitled to "be an expression of church teachings or the pastoral strategies of the Holy See." The second statement went on to suggest an effort on the part of "some commentators" to "weaken the position of the Holy See in the international arena by means of self-serving and misleading information."[11] The Pope himself reiterated that his position is unchanged, and a conference of 114 cardinals unanimously endorsed a reaffirmation of church doctrine drafted by Cardinal O'Connor of New York.

Perhaps those inside know something we do not. A reporter asked about the Pope's health, and was given a "no comment" by a Vatican spokesman, who added that "every pope is in good health until he dies." A succession may well be accompanied by a power struggle over the extent to which the church adapts to modern problems and to feelings that are widely held even within the church. Certainly, many in the church must be aware that the Vatican multiplies its problems by confounding its support for the traditional family—where it might find considerable support among people who dislike the permissiveness promoted by the radical feminists—with its position on the population issue.

Militant Feminists. The President of the Planned Parenthood Federation of America (PPFA) told a press conference at PrepCom III that "there can be no advancement in the world if the status of women is not improved." That was the tone of the meeting.[12]

The intensity of feminist opposition to any outside interference in women's right to "control their own bodies" can be measured by a U.S. domestic development quite separate from the Cairo preparations. The State of New Jersey refuses additional welfare payments for children conceived by women after they go on welfare. That rule has been challenged by a remarkable coalition of some 85 organizations that are traditionally at each other's throat, ranging from conservative religious and antiabortion groups to pro-choice groups, spearheaded by NOW and the ACLU. The NOW argument is that it "violates women's constitutional rights to privately make decisions about conception and childbirth without governmental intrusion"—and with a governmental subsidy, apparently.[13]

Some of the activists at the PrepCom attacked even the idea of giving priority to unmet needs for contraception. The U.S. Women of Color (USWOC) position paper for PrepCom III said "industrialized countries should reduce poverty by tackling social and economic imbalances, not just by pushing contraceptives.

We don't want to wait until the 'umnet need' for contraceptives has been satisfied before realizing that we have utterly neglected to boost social and economic progress and failed to alleviate poverty."[14] This is a strong reminder of the disinterest or hostility many Blacks feel toward population planning. They won't be appeased; they must, like the feminists, come to believe that stopping population growth is to their own benefit.

The agenda of the militant feminists can perhaps best be seen by looking in detail at the product of PrepCom III.

THE DRAFT "PROGRAMME OF ACTION"

The Programme is not really a program. A program states a specific target and specific steps to achieve it. The Programme is a wish list, and a very long one.

Population. It is not really about population and development. The words appear periodically, usually together, but there is no real discussion of the connections.

It is certainly not about population growth. In a draft 118 pages long, four perfunctory paragraphs describe world population growth. By very rough count (the format permits no precision), there are about 1,170 individual action proposals in the Programme (including much duplication and overlap.) I find only a dozen proposals that directly address population growth; several will be quoted here. Meeting umnet needs for contraception is treated as an aspect, not of slowing population growth, but of assuring "reproductive rights and sexual health," avoiding AIDS or minimizing the need for abortion.

Of sixteen chapters, one is labeled "Population Growth and Structure," and most of it is given over to the protection of children, elderly people, minorities, indigenous peoples, and persons with disabilities. All are valid objects of social policy, but the proposals have very little to do with what happens to world population in the next few decades.

It is asserted from time to time (e.g. section 3.5) that "population policies should be integrated into . . ." the development of other programs." In one place (section 3.9), it is said that "To achieve sustainable development and a higher quality of life for all people, Governments should reduce and eliminate unsustainable patterns of production and consumption and promote appropriate demographic policies." Whatever that means.

The nearest thing to a recommendation on population policy (section 6.4) is that "Countries that have not completed their demographic transition should take effective steps in this regard within the context of their social and economic development and with full respect of human rights. Countries that have concluded the demographic transition should take necessary steps to optimize their demographic trends (sic) within the context of their social and economic development." (It turns out that "necessary steps" means economic development, alleviating poverty, improving women's status, education including sex education, and health care including "reproductive health and family planning services" . . . This is a call to arms?

Nowhere is it said that population growth **should** stop. Nowhere are growing countries urged to give a high priority to stopping (or even slowing) population growth.

Targets and goals for population and fertility are explicitly avoided (though section 7.10 admits that they are legitimate tools for governments if they do not set targets or quotas for family planning providers.) Early in the ICPD process, Nafis Sadik proposed targets for population and fertility in 2015. In the face of the overwhelming opposition to "coercion," the targets quietly disappeared. At the start of PrepCom III she said that "'There is now an international consensus that we should invest in people, especially in women, and let them make the choices about family size . . ."[15] The Programme says that "Governments and the international community should use the full means at their disposal to support the principle of voluntary choice in family planning." (section 7.13)

The Programme is negative about any stronger action. It repeatedly warns against "coercion" and "intimidation," and "Governments are encouraged to focus most of their efforts toward meeting their population and development objectives through education and voluntary measures rather than schemes involving incentives and disincentives." (section 7.20)

Above all, the brief treatment of population is notable for its placidity. On the environmental connection: "Demographic factors, combined with poverty and lack of access to resources in some areas, and excessive consumption and wasteful production in others, cause or exacerbate problems of environmental degradation and resource depletion and thus inhibit sustainable development." (section 3.25) There are no specifics. Nothing is said about the connections between population growth and land degradation, intensive agriculture, desertification, water supplies, soil acidification, climate change or species extinction that the scientists are warning us about.

Elsewhere, the Programme treats population growth, if it is mentioned, as a hindrance to improving the "quality of life" or "sustained economic growth." The authors have yet to discover that "sustained growth" is a mathematical impossibility on a finite Earth. That is why reducing fertility becomes so critically important.

In short, no serious guidance is offered on population issues; the draft Programme instead seeks to discourage any effort to deal with them directly.

Women, and Other Agendas. The Programme is reticent about population, but it is full of explicit recommendations on a multitude of topics, from female genital mutilation (which comes up repeatedly) to old folks' homes. Fundamentally, it is a plea for women's emancipation and an exhaustive list of the things that should be done for (and occasionally by) women to achieve it. Most of four chapters is given over to women's issues, and proposals for specific assistance to women are scattered through the other chapters.

Of the 1170 or so action proposals, maybe half are endless administrative proposals about cooperation, research, funding, NGO participation and the like. Of the others, 285 are directed to improving women's status. They go pretty far. A proposal to "eliminate stereotypes" (section 4.19) sounds like a veiled demand for censorship to enforce the politically correct view of the relationship between sexes. Reverse discrimination is called for in educating young girls. (section 4.20)

A UN Conference on Women is scheduled for 1995, in Beijing. I wonder what new they will find to say, other than criticizing their hosts for China's family planning practices.

The proposals concerning the status of women at least have a presumptive connection with population dynamics. Many of the remaining 250 or so proposals don't. They are about the population issue only in the sense that people are population.

They deal largely with the protection of children, the right to education and health services, the search for a cure for AIDS and the support of AIDs sufferers, the rights of migrants, minorities, the aged, and the needs of the "underserved" components of the population—so broadly defined as to include everybody but adult, nonelderly, non-minority, non-migrant, non-indigenous male suburbanites. (section 12.20)

The Family. The Programme calls for an end to coercion and discrimination related to the "plurality of forms" of the family and "other unions." It avoids explicit reference to homosexual families but calls for governments and employers to assist single parent families. (sections 5.2–5.4)

It is highly permissive about sexual morality. The sections on "reproductive health" are a paean to happy sex. "Reproductive health is a state of complete physical, mental and social well-being . . . in all matters relating to the reproductive system and to its functions and processes. . . . Sexual health is the integration of somatic, emotional, intellectual and social aspects of sexual being, in ways that are positively enriching and that enhance personality, communication and love, and thus the notion of sexual health implies a positive approach to human sexuality . . ." (section 7. 1)

Times change. Two generations ago, that sort of message would have been mailed in a plain brown envelope.

Adolescent fecundity is an important source of population growth, but the drafters try to accommodate to it rather than influence it. Nafis Sadik said at a press conference that "I told him (the Pope) that I can't preach to young people about their behavior."[16] The Programme says "Sexually active adolescents will require special family planning information, counseling and services, including contraceptive services, and those who become pregnant will require special support from their families and community during pregnancy and early child care. Adolescents must be fully involved in the planning, implementation and evaluation of such information and services . . ." (section 7.45)

There is nothing about discouraging the pregnancies. Section 8.24 on women's nutrition includes counselling to delay pregnancy, but only for the physically immature. Voluntary abstinence is encouraged (section 8.35) only as a way to avoid AIDS.

Most of these proposals would if anything promote population growth. There is one suggestion that might work the other way: "The equal participation of women and men in all areas of family and household responsibilities, including [family planning], childbearing and housework, should be promoted and encouraged by Governments." (section 4.26) By extension, the drafters are calling for governments to promote the two-earner family. In conservative societies, this is not likely to happen very fast, which in turn means that—if the drafters even thought of it as a way of promoting lower fertility—its effect may be far in the future.

Other agendas turn up. The UN promotes its role, including a proposal that it compile data on indigenous people "in full collaboration with indigenous people[s] and their organizations" (section 6.26), but without mentioning the governments involved. This would raise hackles in a number of countries, including ours. Advocacy groups got a whole chapter urging that they be included in official policy formulation. In the chapter on international migration, somebody slipped in a reference (still bracketed) to "the right to family reunification" (section 10.12), which would raise hob with many countries' immigration laws if they paid attention to it. The document is full of these little excursions.

For a conference on population, they have wandered pretty far afield.

"Breadth" and Illusions. Most of the action proposals would require funding, and the total is incalculable. There is an Arabian Nights quality to all this. For one example, to improve the quality of life in cities, "Governments should increase the capacity and competence of city and municipal authorities to manage urban development, to safeguard the environment, to respond to the needs of all citizens, including urban squatters, for personal safety, basic infrastructure and services, to eliminate health and social problems, including problems of drugs and criminality, and problems resulting from overcrowding and disasters, and to provide people with alternatives to living in areas prone to natural and man-made disasters. . . . to promote the integration of migrants from rural areas into urban areas and to develop and improve their income-earning capability by facilitating their access to employment, credit, vocational training and transportation, with special attention to the situation of women workers and women heads of households. Child-care centers should be established, and special protection and rehabilitation Programs should be established for street children." (sections 9.14 & 9.15) A lovely dream.

On international immigration: the best way to deal with immigration is for "recipient" countries to help the "sending" countries to make life at home "viable" so people will not want to leave. (sections 10.1 and 10.3) This is to be achieved by "ensuring a better economic balance between developed (and) developing countries . . . by "defusing international and national tensions before they escalate," by promoting good governance and democracy and ensuring that the human rights of minorities and indigenous peoples are respected, by improving education, nutrition and health, by ensuring environmental protection, reviewing tariffs and increasing access to world markets, creating more jobs (and, incidentally, supporting "population relevant programs" that are never described.) Poof! just like that. The irreverent thought arises: am I supposed to take this seriously? In this brave new world, people might well decide to stay home, but apparently nobody looked into either the price tag or the realism of the proposals. Similar flights of imagination appear throughout the Programme (see for instance sections 5.9 to 5.13 on the family.)

Funding. Specific funding targets are set for a few programs. They are all still "bracketed." The annual costs in 2000 are estimated as follows: (a) family planning, $10.2 billion; (b) "reproductive health," $5 billion, not including expenditures in the "overall health budgets"; (c) preventing AIDS and STDs (sexually transmitted diseases), $1.3 billion; and (d) research and analysis, $500 million. These numbers rise through 2015, but not as fast as current third world population growth. "Up to two-thirds" would be met by the countries themselves.

There is a hooker in there. The "delivery costs" for the other items are hidden in the "family planning" account. Those costs represent 65 percent of the total. If they are distributed by project, reproductive health changes to $8 billion, family planning to $6 billion, and AIDS/STDs to $2.2 billion.

The cynical and wise have learned to read the fine print when population or family planning targets are announced. There is an old habit of robbing family planning accounts for other activities, particularly for other public health uses when the programs are commingled. It has been a problem for the U.S. AID population program for years. Even now, as the Clinton administration points with pride to its budget proposal to raise the population assistance appropriation to $585 million, AID has said it plans to set aside some of the funds for reproductive health, female education and "women's empowerment" projects.[17]

There is no effort to cost out the rest of the action proposals, except to say they will require "substantially increased investments" and to propose that 20 percent of public sector expenditures and of official development assistance go to "the social sectors," especially to poverty eradication. (Section 13.23; this is the UN "20:20" formula.) Section 14.11 reiterates the UNCED (Rio de Janeiro) target of doubling donors' development assistance to 0.7 percent of GNP.

WHAT TO EXPECT FROM CAIRO

In Cairo, the militant feminists will almost certainly win the battle with the Vatican. The draft Programme will probably not be much changed. With some 180 governments represented, with about 1000 NGOs on the sidelines, there isn't that much time. There is much bureaucratic momentum and much "face" committed to this draft. Some references to reproductive health, family planning and abortion may be softened to meet the objections of governments responsive to the Vatican. Some of those Governments and some conservative Arab countries may refuse to endorse the Programme, or sign on with written reservations. The expenditure targets will probably be rephrased in more general terms. Otherwise, the tone of the document is pretty well cast in concrete.

The Descent to Irrelevancy. If that is so, the document will leave little imprint. It offers no real advice about demographic policy, except to back off. As to all those other recommendations: governments are in no position to mobilize new resources in response to an impossibly long wish list from Cairo. Donors are not undertaking new commitments, as the recent UN conferences on Sustainable Development and on Small Island Developing States have demonstrated. Societies will change and women's status will probably improve, but not because the UN told them to.

National delegations (including ours) tend to accept rather casually the generalizations that emerge from such UN conferences. They are achieved by a loose consensus process, are not formally signed or ratified, and the U.S. Government does not consider them legally binding. Some of it gets pretty unreal. Would the U.S. Government really consider endorsing the two-wage-earner family? would it commit itself to "promote and encourage" men sharing housework?

The Feminists. It is hard to say how important these international circuses are. This one certainly has served to focus press attention briefly on population—or on the players' agendas. The Programme will seldom be read—it is terribly repetitious and almost unreadable—but it will be cited by interest groups to legitimize future demands for governments to act on the proposals that interest them. And therein perhaps lies the importance of the ICPD.

The Cairo conference, even more than the Rio conference on the environment that preceded it, generated a massive mobilization of militant feminists and feminist groups. They have strongly influenced the evolution of the U.S. position. They have largely shaped the Programme. At home, their advocacy has resulted in the proposal mentioned above, to shift U.S. AID funds from family planning to feminist programs. They have become a force. They probably like it, and governments can expect to hear more from them.

THE U.S. ROLE

For a change, the U.S. administration is promoting international population assistance. It has raised budgetary appropriations and restored the U.S. support for UNFPA and private third world population assistance programs. It has been willing to tough it out with the Vatican and endorse language on abortion, which, in a felicitous new turn of phrase, it says should be "legal, safe and rare." (It would face a firestorm in its domestic constituency if it caved in on that one.)

The administration has not addressed U.S. population growth, and the draft Programme offers little help, but that is a topic for another FORUM paper.

Population and Politics. In the Cairo conference process, the U.S. voice has changed. The Vice President and Department of State Counselor Tim Wirth probably understand the dangers of population growth as well as any U.S. political leaders, but the Vice President has been silent—he will be at Cairo and may recover his voice then—and Wirth has shifted his rhetoric to accommodate his new constituency. (In a March 30th speech on the ICPD, he said "I would suggest that the empowerment, employment and involvement of women must be the overriding catalyst for common purpose in the journey to and from Cairo. At the end of this century, the extent to which we fostered the transition to sustainable development will be measured in part by our success in refocusing scarce resources and redirecting national priorities on behalf of women . . ." He described 7 objectives, all of which were directed toward women's issues; only one of them, "reproductive health services," included a reference to "voluntary family planning.")

There may be good political reasons for handing the topic over to the militant feminists. They are a constituency that can cause trouble if thwarted. Generalizations at Cairo about "free choice" and support for feminist causes avoid the tough and controversial issues—migration and governmental involvement in human fertility that would arise if the conference got serious about population. The President may feel he hardly needs any more problems right now. Why not pay off the ladies and stay away from the tough issues?

Tim Wirth remarked that "women's groups pretty much drove this."[18] Not all women. Women do not speak with one voice. I am willing to bet that Phyllis Shlaffly was not invited, or any of the women who agree with her. If the full range of women's voices had been invited to participate, there would have been cacophony. The U.S. official delegation to PrepCom III included ten private sector advisers, nine of them women, several of whom represented women's groups. This sort of presence in an official delegation may well be unique, and Wirth has remarked that cooperation with the NGO interest groups at PrepCom was also very close.

I suspect that the Department of State stumbled into this relationship rather than thinking it through. Undeniably, it has allowed voices to be heard that were ignored before. On the other hand, it bypasses the traditional ways of reconciling different interests in our diverse society.

In leaning heavily on feminist advocacy groups, the government fails to hear the range of views on their issues, and this may narrow the administration's support base rather than widening it.

There is something in the Programme for many other interest groups: minorities; immigrant advocates; refugees; the education lobby; the elderly; people with disabilities, etc. The danger is backlash. There is no way that even a modest fraction of the Programme proposals can be delivered in most third world countries, and it may create false expectations even in the U.S.

Whether or not it is good politics, the government's approach leads to bad population policy, because it is not listening to the voices of bioscientists, demographers and others who might have tempered the advocacy approach reflected in the Programme. Princeton demographer Charles Westoff says: "So much potential common ground exists in the goals of the family planning movement and in women's concerns for their reproductive health and rights—as well as for improving their status—that it would be perverse if extremist feminist groups managed to deflect a worldwide effort to address the population question head-on."[19] Joseph Speidel remarked that "they never face the issue of what to do if resources are scarce, and they are."[20] Three population analysts argue that " . . . although development and social change create conditions that encourage smaller family size, contraceptives are the best contraceptive . . . . independently of the effect of social and economic changes—family-planning programs played a significant role in reducing fertility in developing countries between 1975 and 1990. . . . changes in contraceptive use and in fertility depend as much on the strength of a country's family planning movement as on its economic development."[21] This is a far cry from what the administration has been hearing from the women's groups.

WHERE NOW?

The New Agenda. One hears a constant refrain: this is a new and broader approach to population policy. It isn't really new. Improvements in the educational and economic status for women contribute to fertility decline, and the correlation has long been recognized. Population advocates have an interest in women's status, and in investments to achieve it. What is new is the fixity with which militant feminist groups are attempting (a) to subvert the existing "narrow" population programs, and (b) to divert resources and attention from population programs to women's issues.

The question is: how far should U.S. policy commit itself to the proposition that the way to stop world population growth is to put our money and effort into women's rights and women's programs?

If It Ain't Broke . . . Running a population program without population goals is about like trying to build a road without deciding where it should go.

Human fertility has been declining, and some of that decline is legitimately attributable to the single-minded effort by AID and other population organizations to make family planning broadly available, to get out the message about population, and to recruit governmental and opinion leaders. It is possible to achieve something without achieving everything at once—the PPFA speaker not withstanding—and a focused program may be better than spurious "breadth."

The draft Programme, by trying to be "broad," has lost all focus. Modernization, eventually, results in lower fertility. High fertility and resultant population growth throughout much of the third world are delaying that modernization and perhaps making it impossible. The issue is how to get birth rates down without waiting for the traditional "demographic transition," which may never happen in much of the third world.

The drafters of the Programme have a certain vision of the new world they want, and they want it all at once. Prescriptions for the drastic social changes proposed in the Programme not only encounter immense traditionalist opposition and inertia; they presuppose the availability of enormous funds. They may bear fruit over time, but it will take time. Do the militant feminists themselves really believe that, in the next two decades, their exhortations will be heeded by governments and societies everywhere, that discrimination against women will end, that funding for the Programme's endless list of causes will somehow materialize, and that fertility will obediently drop so far, so fast?

On the other hand, the traditional "narrow" approach offers investments with tangible and immediate results—and it helps the women by easing the burdens of motherhood and by improving women's status as they escape the treadmill of constant pregnancy.

Pursuing the Possible. The Programme has gotten it backwards. At one point, it says "Eradication of poverty will contribute to slowing population growth and to achieving early population stabilization." (section 3.15) The problem is that you can't get there from here. With the working age population growing some 60 million per year, and rising, and the ILO reporting that one-third of those in the labor force do not earn a minimal subsistence wage, this "solution" simply ducks the issue. A better bet is that a successful population policy would help reduce poverty.

The Programme calls for universal health care, universal primary education, jobs, and leadership roles for women, in a time when unemployment is rising, national budgets are caught in the increasing costs of dealing with pollution and unemployment and their consequences, living standards are declining, and many governments are impotent in the face of overwhelming immediate problems. You cannot spend enough to achieve those goals when you don't have enough even now. You must identify those things that will do most to match the reality with the dream.

Direct population programs have the advantage of simplicity. If necessary, they can still be pursued even in pretty chaotic conditions. They are easier to control; one can audit a contraceptive delivery program more easily than an effort to assist third world governments (which may well be in the hands of self-enriching dictators) to promote women's rights, improve their educational systems and provide jobs for the poor. And it is much, much cheaper.

Priorities. I would urge that at Cairo the U.S. Government ignore most of the rhetoric to which it has contributed, and that it look before it leaps to change the way the international population issue is approached. I propose a shorter "wish list":

1. Meet unmet needs for contraception, i.e. make it available to those who want it but cannot obtain or afford it. (To his credit, Tim Wirth has regularly listed this as the first priority. The ICPD Secretariat obviously thinks it is central.) Make this the top priority in our entire foreign development assistance program, even if we must contribute more than our "share." Keep "population" as a budgetary line item so the funds don't get siphoned off. (The administration's new foreign assistance bill would remove that protection.)

2. Support the expansion of third world family planning facilities and services wherever possible, including unconventional approaches such as commercial distribution of contraceptives, until there are no significant populations uncovered. Don't wait to create full-fledged health clinics, but use them where they exist. (Taiwan began its successful family planning program in the 1950s simply by making contraceptives available and making sure people knew where. Fertility dropped quickly, not only in the first test neighborhoods, but in nearby areas, because the word spread.)

3. Back it up by continuing the efforts to convince third world leaders that the population issue is important, and they should lead. Say the things that will not be said at Cairo.

4. Endeavor to reinstate *goals* in the international population dialogue. Numerical targets are for each country to decide individually, but the *two child family*—stop at two—is worth considering as a simple and comprehensible way of phrasing a worldwide target. It is a good target even if it isn't reached, and nations that come close would achieve a period of below-replacement fertility to stop population momentum. "Stop at two" means fertility somewhere around 1.5, because some women have no children, or one.[22]

5. Give the next priority in our developmental assistance to women's and children's health, coordinated with family planning services. (Don't integrate them completely, or the family planning funds will disappear.) Discreetly encourage proposals to promote the status of women, and point to the demographic consequence—lower fertility—as one practical argument for doing so. Beyond that, support for education and jobs for women are legitimate areas and would promote lower fertility, but there are fiscal limits to how much the U.S. can do.

6. On the issue of incentives and disincentives: encourage third world countries to learn from the experience of countries such as Singapore that have used them effectively, recognizing that it is their decision. People are unlikely to buy onto the "two child family" without leadership and self-interest pushing them.

The militant feminists are going to press their advantage. One can understand why, given their long memories of being the "second sex." The problem is that they see this as a zero-sum game, when it is not. Women, men and children all suffer from the population crisis, and all gain if can be controlled. The feminists have compiled a list of recommendations that are unattainable under present world conditions, are related tangentially if at all to the population issue, and divert attention and funding from that issue. In their own interest—and that of women generally—they should look again at their priorities.

Sound Advice Forgotten. In 1991, the Population Crisis Committee analyzed the U.S. performance in international population efforts and concluded: "The U.S. population assistance program . . . has been a bold and pioneering effort for much of its history. In less than a generation, the program has significantly expanded the availability and use of modern contraceptive technology and lowered family size in many developing countries. By helping to slow the pace of world population growth, the U.S. foreign aid program has made an enormous contribution of global importance to the future of the world."

The report went on to say that "AID's programs have generally had more measurable impact than those supported by other donors. To a far greater degree, AID has focused resources on increasing the availability of family planning services . . ." It praised AID's "unique partnership with private institutions working in the population field."

The report went on, however, to say that "In AID's other development programs there has been little systematic focus on activities, such as female education, which could potentially reinforce population and family planning investments. AID should far more aggressively seek to exploit potential synergies between its population and other development activities, especially female education and child survival programs."[23]

There, I believe, is the sensible amalgam between programs directed explicitly at population stabilization (or reduction) and programs, legitimate in themselves, directed toward women's well-being and the nurture of children.

NOTES:

1. *New York Times* 6-15-94, p. 1.
2. Martha F. Riche, "How Far Is It to Cairo?" (Washington: Population Reference Bureau, *Population Today*, April 1994, p.3.)
3. Two ICPD Secretariat papers (*Background Note on Goals for the International Conference on Population and Development, 1994, 6-2-94; and Background Note on the Resource Requirements for Population Programs in the Years 2000–2015*, 6-23-94) suggest that "satisfying existing uninet need for contraceptive and reproductive health services and additional needs likely to be generated over the next two decades could lead to a contraceptive prevalence level in the developing world of at least 69 percent." This would be consistent with a fertility level somewhat closer to the UN medium projection than to the low projection. The statement is based on sample surveys of umnet needs and historical trends in the use of family planning, raised by a factor reflecting the hope that better reproductive health care will increase the demand for family planning.
4. The Programme uses two somewhat different 1992 UN projections: The intermediate range *Current Population Prospects, the 1992 Revision and the Long-range World Population Projections, 1950–2150*. In this discussion and the following graph, I have used the latter (p. 12 and Table 4).
5. Reuter, Dhaka, 6-20-94, 03:43.
6. Estimate by U.S. AID Administrator Brian Attwood after a fact finding tour of East Africa. He cited population growth as a principal cause. Reuter, Nairobi, 5-31-94, 13:05:00.
7. Henry W. Kendall and David Pimentel, "Constraints on the Expansion of the Global Food Supply," *Ambio* Vol.23, May 1994, pp.198–205. See also interview with Dr. Kendall by Nick Ludington, AP, Washington, 5-26-94, 18:00:00.
8. Philip Pullella, "Vatican Summons Envoys over Population Issues," Reuter, Vatican City, 3-25-94, 06:56:00. AP, Vatican City, 4-17-94, 09:35. AP, Washington, 5-31-94, 16:24.
9. Susan Chira, "Women Campaign for New Plan to Curb the World's Population," *New York Times*, 4-13-94, pp.AI, AI 2.
10. *Washington Times*, 6-11-94, p.11. DPA Rome, 6-11, 0720. *New York Times* 6-16-94, p.A4. The Academy is a body of lay scientists, not necessarily Catholic. In December 1993, the German Bishops' Conference released a document, *Population Policy and Development*, that said the church "has to respect responsible (family planning) decisions made by couples."
11. AP Vatican City, 6-18-94, 16:34 EDT.
12. ICPD Newsletter No. 14, April 1994, p.7.
13. William Claiboume, "New Jersey Effort . . . *Washington Post* 3-3-94.
14. UNFPA *Populi*, May 1994, p.10.
15. ICPD Newsletter No. 14, April 1994, p.5.
16. Greg Burke, "Pope Warns U.N. Not to Limit Family Size," Reuter, Vatican City, 3-18-94.
17. Private communication from Population Action International, 7-5-94.
18. See Susan Chita article cited note 9.
19. Charles F. Westoff, "Finally, Population Control," *New York Times Magazine*, 2-6-94, p.32.
20. See Susan Chita article note 9.
21. Bryant Robey, Shea 0. Rutstein and Leo Morris, "The Fertility Decline in Developing Countries," *Scientific American*, December 1993, p.65.
22. See Lindsey Grant, *The Two Child Family* (NPG FORUM, May 1994.)
23. Shanti R. Conly, J.Joseph Speidel and Sharon Camp, *U.S. Population Assistance: Issues for the 1990s* (Washington: PCC, now Population Action International, 1991.)

INTO THE WIND . . .
UNEMPLOYMENT AND WELFARE REFORM

Lindsey Grant

March 1994

THE STACKED DECK

The President hopes to submit proposals for welfare reform to Congress in early April. The general philosophy has been discussed by the administration, but the details have not been released. The reform will encompass the Food Stamp program and AFDC (Aid to Families with Dependent Children). It may perforce include SSI (Supplemental Security Income) payments, since the Senate has just discovered that, unsurprisingly, SSI cash benefits are being used by recipients to support their drug habit.

Separately, the President on March 9th proposed a Re-Employment Act, intended to regularize unemployment compensation and consolidate some 150 governmental retraining programs. The welfare reform is priced (optimistically) at $6 billion per year when it gets running, and the Re-Employment Act at about $3 billion.

A Mouse by Any Other Name . . . There may be less here than meets the eye. Food Stamps and AFDC represent only the beginning of welfare and income support: about 15 percent of the total. There are literally hundreds of welfare and income transfer programs and vast bureaucratic structures to support them. The federal, state and local governments spend more than $250 billion annually on those programs, by a very conservative estimate.[1] Social Security disability pensions. The Child Nutrition Act and National School Lunch program, Surplus Food for the Needy, and other nutrition programs for children, the elderly, pregnant women and mothers. The Comprehensive Employment and Training Act and other vocational rehabilitation programs. Community Services Administration programs. Subsidized housing programs of all sorts. Various Federal and state unemployment compensation programs. Job Training & Partnership Act programs and the Job Corps. Summer youth employment programs. The work incentive program. Assistance with heating bills. The College Work Study Program. The new National Service Act for students. Not least, the IRS' Earned Income Tax Credit for poor working families, which quintupled to $6 billion from 1985–1990 and has just been dramatically increased again. The agricultural price support programs started as a sort of welfare program and have gone awry, at a cost of some $7 to $17 billion annually. And so on. It would take a sweeping reform indeed to make a coherent program out of these pieces; it would cut across bureaucratic and Congressional fiefdoms and stir opposition at every turn.

Welfare and Unemployment. In its health care proposals, the Clinton administration is seeking to expand the coverage. In its proposals for welfare reform, it will be seeking to shrink the program by motivating or training people to get off welfare. It sounds easier.

It isn't. The financier Felix Rohatyn (best known for his role in rescuing New York City from bankruptcy in the '70s) recently asked what is the purpose of retraining and education if there are no jobs.[2] A very good point.

Our enthusiastic young President came along at a bad time. *He cannot deal with welfare in isolation from unemployment,* and unemployment in turn is linked to a synergistic set of fundamental changes that is driving unemployment upwards, worldwide. Those changes are

- a third world population explosion that has driven their working age population up by nearly 1.7 billion since 1950 and will add another 2 plus billion by 2025. It is causing a new Age of Migrations from farm to city, across national boundaries, and spilling over into the United States and Europe.
- a restructuring of world commerce that very nearly assures that wages in the high-wage countries will decline and unemployment will increase.
- a technological transformation of work that demands fewer and fewer people just as there are more people competing for work.
- a social transformation that has expanded the work force as women seek employment and, with it, a sense of dignity and independence.

Let us take a closer look at each of those forces.

The Migration of the Hungry. World population growth accelerated around 1950. The peasants soon ran out of land and in desperation began to move to the cities or abroad. Central America provides a good example. By 1975, total arable acreage had stagnated, but population growth did not. The population is crowding into the cities, and the economically active population is increasing at a rising arithmetic rate: from 3 million in 1950 to 6 million in 1975, to 12 million on the way by 2000, with 24 million projected for 2025.[3]

The working age population of the so-called third world is rising more than 60 million each year and will continue to do so. The International Labor Office estimates that 30 percent of those in the worldwide labor force are not earning a minimal subsistence wage; most of them are in the third world.[4] These are the forces that drive migration, and anybody who plans to address welfare without factoring in the migratory pressures is bound to fail.

The third world's problem becomes ours. U.S. population has risen by more than 100 million since 1950, 31 percent of the rise attributable to post-1950 immigration.[5] The Census Bureau projects a population of 392 million by 2050, 50 percent larger than the present population. By that time, 86 percent of the growth will result from post-1992 immigration. The working age population (sixteen to sixty-four years old) is projected to rise 24 percent by 2025 and 40 percent by 2050. (These projections are optimistic; they assume an immigration probably lower than at present—nobody really knows the present level—while third world growth argues that immigration pressures will rise.) President Nixon a generation ago worried whether we could accommodate 300 million Americans. President Clinton needs to worry about employment and welfare for a population heading past 400 million.

Trade, Jobs and the Multinationals. Somebody remarked that the generals are always fighting the last war. The economists are still fighting the Great Depression. I came through that era, and I believed what was taught me: to hate the Smoot-Hawley tariff act, which helped to precipitate the Depression, and to believe that free trade is sacred.

Some economists are now questioning that faith, but they may be shooting at the wrong target. Japan's balance of payments surplus, associated with its unwillingness to play by open trading rules, has led some to suggest the possibility of managed trade. Japan is certainly a problem, but another much deeper structural problem—at least for those who are interested in the well-being of American labor—has arisen almost unnoticed: the role of the open world market itself, and of the multinational corporations (MNCs). They have fundamentally altered the world trading system, yet U.S. conventional wisdom is unchanged, and we are trying to play by the old rules.

The question is this: How do we live in a world with free movement of capital, technology, organizational and marketing systems, and goods—but not of labor? The multinationals can move to where the labor is cooperative, trainable—and cheap. Do we reconcile ourselves to meeting the competition and letting third world labor prices dictate wages here? We know the world labor force will rise; the work force entrants of a generation hence are already born. With that sort of supply entering an already glutted labor market, we may be pretty confident that the downward pressure on wages already apparent in the U.S. and Europe will continue, and it in turn will magnify the need for welfare assistance. Food stamp recipients have risen to 27 million; they will continue to rise.

There is a standard answer to that. Look, they say, our balance of payments problems are with higher labor cost countries, not the poor ones. Look at the way our exports to Mexico have risen!

Look again. We generally ran a merchandise trade surplus with Hong Kong and Japan until the early 1960s, with Taiwan through the late '60s, with South Korea until the mid-70s, with Singapore until the early '80s, and with China through the mid-80s. NAFTA was justified in part on the grounds it will help Mexico modernize. If it works, be prepared for the competition.

The U.S. International Trade Commission (USITC) study that justified NAFTA, insofar as it dealt with U.S. labor impacts at all, assumed that the U.S. would keep the skilled jobs and Mexico the unskilled ones. Our experience should teach us the falsity of that patronizing assumption. The U.S. may well keep a leading role in cutting edge technology (if our universities don't go the way of our primary and secondary schools), but except for aerospace, the big net foreign exchange earnings are not in high tech products. To make automobiles or clothes or appliances, all the big corporations need is a place with a fair prospect of political tranquillity, a degree of protection against corruption, some infrastructure such as roads and harbors, and that cheap and trainable labor. And what does that portend for American wages and unemployment, and for welfare?

Technological Change. Technological displacement of labor has been around at least since the invention of the wheel, and it is a transitional price that humankind has paid for higher productivity and a better life. The problem right now is that it is happening very fast and it is paired with unprecedented population growth.

The problem has come home to the U.S. with a bang: computerization, new managerial techniques, automation, the movement of some industry overseas, and now the efforts of corporate America to control the costs of the President's health reform proposal, most of which he expects business to carry. They are downsizing to limit their vulnerability and contracting for temporary help when necessary. A private survey indicates that downsizing resulted in the loss of perhaps 740,000 jobs in 1993, with the prospect of more in 1994.[6] The second biggest employer in the U.S., after General Motors, is Manpower, Inc., a firm that supplies "temps" to businesses. In this environment, even high-salaried people may come to need help.

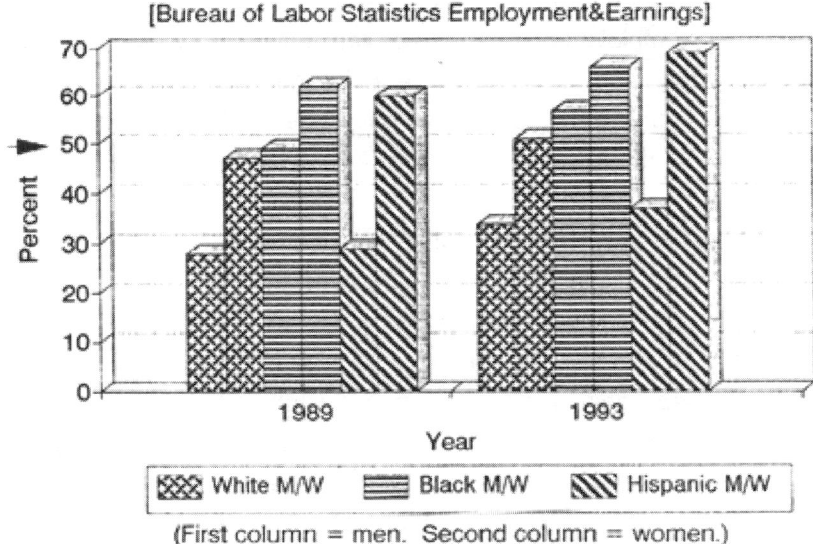

Figure 1.

Vassily Leontief years ago predicted the effects of the technological revolution. He observed that, with very high productivity, there are limits as to how many goods and services a society (I would add "or the environment") can absorb. The result is a small technological elite and a vast number of marginal service workers and jobless. He suggested that modern societies will either have to limit work hours or arrange for massive income transfers to those not in the system. The first proposal would be circumvented as workers moonlight to occupy their idle time. The second requires an expansion rather than contraction of welfare.

The Role of Women. Throughout the world—including the U.S.—the non-agricultural labor force has grown as more women seek paid work. One can hardly begrudge them the opportunity, since with it come self respect and a sense of independence. Experience suggests that the process leads to lower fertility, and this in turn may eventually slow down or stop the third world population juggernaut. The dilemma for the third world is that that process makes the immediate unemployment problem worse, even as it offers hope for its eventual solution. And the worse the unemployment, the greater the pressures to emigrate.

In the U.S., the biggest change has been in the proportion of young married women (twenty to forty-four years old) who are in the work force. Since 1960, it has grown from about 33 percent to about 70 percent. Some of that other 30 percent may still seek to enter, as declining real wages cause them to seek work to maintain family income.

The President's campaign promise to put welfare recipients to work is politically popular. Welfare is resented by both the donors and the recipients. The problem is that those four synergistic forces—population growth, the internationalization of production, technological change and the entry of women into the work force—are driving the nation in the opposite direction.

. . . AND WHAT HAPPENS?

The First Post-World War II Crisis of the Industrial World. Unemployment is approaching crisis levels through most of the industrial world. The rate for the European Union is 10.9 percent, over 20 percent in Spain and nearly that in Ireland. (No wonder Senator Kennedy tries to facilitate Irish immigration.) Unemployment has passed four million in Germany. The unemployment is not transitory; nearly half the unemployed have been out of work for a year or more.

The Italian Minister of the Interior warned last summer of the danger of urban riots if the unemployment crisis continues. The U.S. Undersecretary of the Treasury has warned of a "huge increase in global unemployment" and said that "administration's top economic priority (is) restoring job creation in industrial countries."[7] The Managing Director of the International Monetary Fund warned that high and rising unemployment is a "devastating trend," but had nothing to offer but trade liberalization (which I have suggested is part of the problem), lower interest rates (which raise the specter of re-igniting inflation) and lower budget deficits.[8]

The Europeans' problem is much like ours. They do not see Europe as a region of immigration, but a new study suggests that immigration into European countries, adjusted for population size, has generally been higher than ours.[9] As with the U.S., the glut of labor exacerbates a difficult technological and social transition. The response has been swifter. Germany amended its constitution to slow the rate of immigrants. France, Switzerland and others have passed tough new immigration laws. Even traditionally receptive Sweden has stiffened its procedures as boat people from Asia via Russia have been landing on its shores.

Japan has the least immigration and the lowest unemployment in the industrial world. It is not immune as lower wage countries out-bid its now-expensive labor, but Japan is not squeamish about finding ways to limit imports.

The Crisis in the U.S. We console ourselves with the official statistic: the unemployment rate here is only 6.7 percent. Nonsense. That figure helps us ignore the scale of the problem. It counts only active job applicants, not "discouraged workers" no longer beating the streets for jobs. For a more realistic look at what is happening, look at the proportion of those of working age who do not have jobs. Even worse, look at the young. People who cannot find a job by the time they are twenty-four are probably going to wind up defeated, resentful, alienated, and perhaps violent.

The first graph is about the young people who are not in school, not in the military, and not already in prison. The proportion who do not have regular jobs ranges from 34 percent for young White men to 69 percent for young Hispanic women. Granted, some small proportion, particularly of the women, may be home makers or voluntarily living with their parents and not working, but by and large, these people have been excluded by the system, or have simply not tried to join it. They are getting by on crime and whatever scraps they can earn in the "informal economy." As the comparison with 1989 shows, the problem is not just bad; it is rapidly getting worse. Don't just think of the social costs. Think of the wrecked lives.

With statistics like that, we are not going to reform welfare by simply getting deadbeats off the rolls.

THE AD HOC RESPONSES

The "Group of Seven" industrial nations (G-7) met in Detroit in March and offered old nostrums for a new problem: economic growth, more trade, and the admonition (expressed by Secretary Bentsen in behalf of the group) to "workers everywhere to recognize the benefits, and not just the pain, from rapidly advancing technology."

President Clinton's March 14th address to the G-7 was particularly revealing of his mindset: "There is no rich country on Earth that can expand its own job base and its incomes unless there is global economic growth. In the absence of that growth, poorer countries doing the same thing we do for wages our people can't live on will chip away at our position. When there is a lot of growth you can be developing new technologies, new activities and new markets. That is our only option." Somebody should tell the President that perpetual growth is impossible on a finite planet. We must find other solutions.

Others in Europe have proposed a deliberate erosion of Europe's high wages, benefits and health care, and a shorter work week to spread the work. The President has taken up the last idea, and one part of the Reemployment Act would encourage employers to shorten working hours rather than discharging workers (which is precisely contrary to employers' present policy.)

One or two leaders have suggested the unthinkable. A senior official of the OECD, refusing to be identified, said that protectionism, "silly" as it is, may be better than a "social explosion" in the industrial world.[10] The French President, picking up a theme never very far from many French minds, has called for higher European trade barriers against competition from low wage countries.[11] The OECD Trade Union Advisory Committee has called upon governments to slow or cushion the internationalization of trade and capital flows.[12]

None of these people suggested that population growth, the resultant migration and job competition have any bearing on the problem—this despite the fact that in almost all of the industrial world immigration has become an intense political issue.

In a patchwork way, the U.S. Government is beginning to address some of the issues, but it has yet to put it all together.

Education as a Solution. The President and his welfare task force put their faith in education and training.[13] The U.S. has sunk to a miserable condition. A recent Department of Education survey indicated that one-quarter of adult Americans could hardly read and could not add. (Among them, 25 percent were immigrants still unfamiliar with English.) Another quarter could do basic addition but little more.[14] There is good reason for the new emphasis is on education and (one hopes) on finding ways to motivate the young. We would not be competitive with societies where the young are still motivated to learn, even if there were no wage differential. The wage differentials are there. They are enormous in many third world countries, and they beckon manufacturers abroad.

The President should heed Felix Rohatyn's question (which even Secretary Bentsen mentioned at the G-7 conference). Education and job training are essential in the modern world labor market, but they are not a sufficient solution. Even the skilled are losing jobs.

Trade and Investment. Mr. Clinton, Meet Mr. Clinton. The ad hoc nature of our policies is strikingly evident in our trade policy. In his 1994 State of the Union Address, the President said "We can't renew the country when our businesses eagerly look for new investments and new customers abroad, but ignore those people right here at home who would give anything to have their jobs and would gladly buy their products if they had the money to do it." (He was applauded.) Why didn't he think of that when he was twisting arms to pass the

NAFTA treaty, much of which is devoted to facilitating the movement of U.S. investment capital into Mexico?

My concern is not for the multinationals. They may well profit from moving to Mexico, at least in the short run. I am worried about whether the government of all the people should be investing its effort in facilitating that capital movement.

Whether or not the nation takes action on the problem of immigration, the downward pressure on wages will continue with free trade until U.S. wages are so bad they are competitive, or until some distant millennium when third world population growth is under control and wages have risen to decent levels.

Trade is a particularly tough nut, conceptually. A sharp rise in U.S. tariffs would plunge many exporting countries in turmoil. It would also raise prices in the U.S. and exacerbate unemployment in our exporting industries. Whether or not we would like to address it, however, our hand may be forced by European and Japanese actions. We need a new look at the human effects of our trade policy, unencumbered by shibboleths about free trade. If we try to survive as the last bastion of free trade in the industrial world, the pressures on our jobs will rise, unemployment will go up, and welfare reform will go a'glimmering.

Perhaps we need some sort of managed trade policy, much as it will offend the orthodox. Perhaps a solution lies in some sort of agreed "wage differential tariffs" keyed to the labor content of the product. In any event, the government must take a new look at trade policy before it has much hope of containing unemployment or the expense of welfare.

The Third World Population Bomb. We should help the exploding nations bring population growth under control. We would help ourselves as we helped others to reduce fertility and the pressures to migrate. Eventually, we would mitigate the competitive pressures in the U.S. for jobs. But that is a long process.

The government has begun, finally, to take the international population issue seriously. State Department Counselor Tim Wirth says that "If we can't stabilize the world's population, we're not going to be able to control any other problems." Population assistance has doubled in this administration, and the 1995 budget will include nearly $600 million for population programs. A good start, but still only about 4 percent of all foreign aid.[15]

The "New Look" Foreign Assistance Policy. The administration has sent Congress a proposed new policy on foreign assistance, based on the catchwords "promoting sustainable development," "promoting democracy," "promoting peace," "providing humanitarian assistance" and "advancing diplomacy." Population is prominently featured under the first rubric.[16] It remains to be seen how much of this will eventuate in real programs. The real priorities are seen in the numbers, and for years about half of the money has gone to Israel, and to Egypt for making peace with Israel.

I am not optimistic that domestic political realities will allow those priorities to be shifted very much. Nonetheless I believe we need to take Counselor Wirth's proposal another step: make family planning and family health and the status of women the top priority for foreign aid. Money does not come cheap to the U.S. Government nowadays, and foreign aid has long been under pressure. This is a focus that would justify itself in terms of the recipients' long term good and ours. We are no longer in a position to fill investment gaps abroad. World Bank and other studies suggest that meeting the unmet demand for family planning would cost far less than the U.S. spends now on foreign assistance.

We need revised priorities in foreign aid.

The Immigration Problem. As a nation, we will need to make a very tough decision: do we want to try to preserve American jobs and wages, if that means a tougher view of immigration and the willingness to be a relatively prosperous island in a world of intensifying poverty? It is not an easy choice, but it must be made, and acted on.

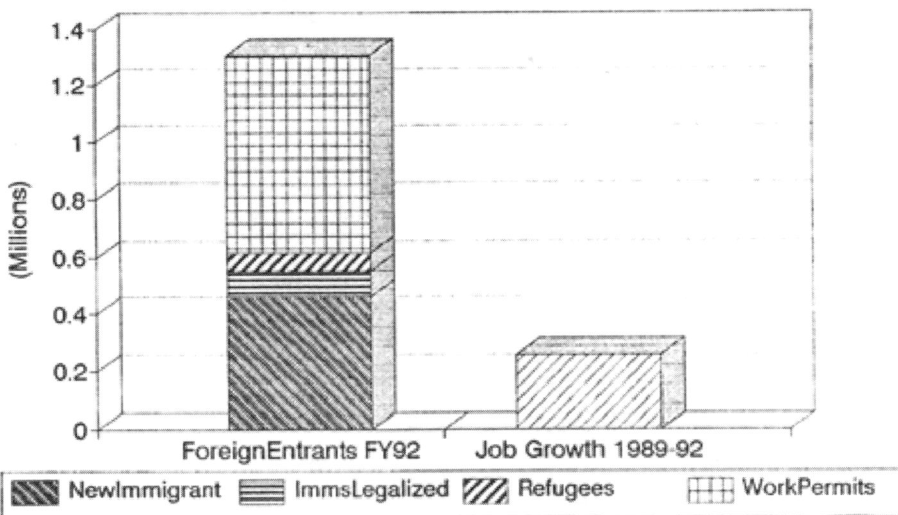

Figure 2.

There is a tremendous inertia in our decision processes. The graph below gives one dramatic example. With job growth stagnant and the U.S. working age population growing by 1.5 million per year, wouldn't a rational society avoid intensifying the competition for those jobs? Yes, but decisions in this country are not made rationally. They are made in different cubbyholes in Congress and the executive branch, and such questions don't get asked.

As the second graph shows, our immigration policy introduced many more job applicants into the economy in one year (FY1992) than the 256,000 jobs created by the economy in three years of stagnation.[17]

These disconnected decisions pervade our immigration policy.

The administration is equivocating. Attorney General Reno has responded to rising criticism by making some administrative changes and proposing a 22 percent increase in the Immigration & Naturalization Service (INS) budget for FY 1995, but at the same time she says that "the administration is committed to maintaining the U.S. tradition of liberal immigration policies . . . ' we will not permit this cherished tradition to be jeopardized by weakness in enforcing our immigration laws.'"[18]

It is curious that the Attorney General is so committed to a "tradition" that has existed fitfully, and is partly fanciful. During some periods (e.g. the '20s through the '50s) immigration laws were rather restrictive. They have been growing increasingly liberal since the '60s, but not because of popular demand, which for years has been consistently in favor of greater restrictions. The enthusiasm for liberal immigration is perhaps a reaction to a curious combination: special interests, and an academic climate in which immigration is politically correct.

Several scholars and think tanks (notably the Urban Institute) have for years tried to prove that immigrants do not displace unskilled U.S. labor (a counterintuitive proposition to begin with, and one on which there is plenty of contrary evidence[19]) and that they contribute more in taxation than they take out in welfare. This latter debate is especially silly, because it is irrelevant. Taxes do not simply pay for welfare. They pay for environmental protection, roads, the administration of justice, national defense, public land management, education, public libraries, police protection, public hospitals, street cleaning, and all the other services that government provides. Taxpayers who do not cover their share of those burdens, aside from any welfare they may draw, are not carrying their part of the load. Nobody has argued that recent immigrants carry that burden, but this is hardly a cause for blame. The poor, by and large, do not pay their "share" of taxes, and most immigrants are poor; that is why they had to leave home.

The governors of California, Florida, New York and Texas, who must meet the bills, have pretty well ended the argument that current immigrants are on balance net contributors to state and local government. (The governors are demanding federal help, since it is the federal government that is responsible for controlling immigration.) But the same academics now argue that yes, immigrants are a net cost to the states, but that on balance they contribute to the federal budget. When the facts are obscure, one tends to "prove" one's preconceptions.

Perhaps we need to say again that the argument is not against immigrants; it is about numbers. Immigrants (who include all our ancestors) have made great contributions to America. Uncontrolled immigration exacerbates the unemployment and social problems we presently face. The two statements are compatible.

The President is not going to get very far with unemployment or with welfare reform until he faces the issue. Immigration will not long be hindered by the tragi-comic game of Border Patrol agents chasing desperate would-be immigrants. The Refugee Act of 1980 needs a thorough new look. The Immigration Reform and Control Act of 1986 (IRCA) was effectively gutted by making it almost impossible to know who is here illegally, and it is riddled with fraud. It needs to be revisited. There is no effective control over immigration by those who overstay their nonimmigrant visas. The Immigration Act of 1990 led to at least a 40 percent increase in annual immigration. It should be undone.

There is legislation before Congress that would do much to bring immigration under control. Senator Harry Reid (D/NV) has introduced a bill (S1351) which would lower legal immigration to about one-third its present level, create better identification procedures, and make the immigration laws enforceable. A companion bill (HR3320) has been introduced into the House by Congressmen Bilbray (D/NV), Hunter (R/CA), Lehman (D/CA), Goodlatte (R/VA) and Traficant (D/OH).

The administration should consider endorsing that legislation, rather than dancing around the immigration issue to the tune of the interest groups that like it as it is.

Perhaps there is hope. Bruce Reed, co-chairman of the welfare task force, was pressed by reporters as to why it is planned to give better treatment to the U.S. citizen children of illegal alien parents than to U.S. citizen parents. He finally said: "The most important thing we can do to prevent such cases is to strengthen our border patrol efforts . . . . It's a tough issue and the best way to deal with it is to keep people from coming here illegally in the first place."[20]

Jobs, Self Respect, Fertility—and Competition. There are now about 5 million people on Aid to Families with Dependent Children (AFDC)—almost all of them single mothers—plus about 10 million babies and children.[21] Welfare reform is supposed to get these mothers off the roles, but from the women's perspective there are a lot of reasons to have a baby and become entitled: a monthly paycheck; entitlement to Medicaid; help with other welfare programs such as housing. In that world, there is not much incentive to go out on the economy—despite the President's exhortations—and very little they can do. The young women on AFDC are probably largely unemployable in this technological society. One estimate is that only one-fourth of them could pass the IQ test for the U.S. armed forces.[22]

An internal government study, quickly squelched, estimated that 2.3 million new jobs would be needed to accommodate welfare recipients pushed off the rolls after two years.[23] (Subsequently, the welfare task force has decided to introduce the work requirement gradually, starting only in 1999, and only for those born since 1972.) Whatever the figure, much of it will be make-work jobs, and this raises some social questions. Are the young mothers really better off with such an arrangement? Are their children, if they must be put in creches so their mother can work?

If the young women do get real work, they are probably competing with somebody. As with the comparable problem in the third world, this is something we must simply factor into our calculations, but it doesn't make welfare reform any easier.

I would argue that the best solution is a slow one, and it requires restructuring welfare so that lower fertility is rewarded. As a beginning, the Surgeon General has pointed out in sulphurous language that the welfare problem would be smaller if Medicaid funded family planning to avoid unwanted children.[24]

Perhaps we are in for a pleasant surprise. An unidentified source in the welfare task force has said that one of the ways to shrink the AFDC rolls will be to mount "a campaign against teenage pregnancy."[25]

The government speaks bravely of educational reform; it will become a lot more practicable if the numbers of children decline and the per capita effort can be increased, and it will be much more successful if gradually the competition for jobs is reduced by a decline in fertility.

Any policy of discouraging high fertility must be across the board. It cannot be targeted simply at the poor. Perhaps the time has come for encouragement of "the two child family." If so, we are backing slowly into.

A U.S. Population Policy. U.S. population growth affects most of the social and environmental goals we espouse, not just welfare. The advantage of an overall population policy is that it would provide a broader and more appealing rationale than simply cutting welfare costs.

A population policy doesn't just mean platitudes about "slower growth." It means a policy that integrates immigration policy with a systematic process to assure that our national policies encourage lower fertility.

The U.S. Government has views about other countries' population policy but has never had a policy for the United States. It is probably too much to expect the President to adopt an explicit population policy, although the Vice President would see the need for it.

A Question of Identity. We must think about practical measures to create a better system of identifying people. There is no constitutional right to be unidentifiable, and it is an expensive luxury. Necessity is slowly driving the government to do piecemeal what it should do as good policy. Already, the President has rather reluctantly agreed that his health care program will not work without a way of identifying those eligible. Otherwise, we will find ourselves undertaking to treat a lot of people who will come here for the purpose. The Food Stamp program is looking toward tamper proof identity cards as a way of reducing fraud, and Texas is prepared to experiment with a plastic "credit card" for that purpose. The Attorney General proposes to make legal residents' "green cards" less easily falsifiable.

A tamper-proof system of identification, perhaps combined with a call-in verification system such as credit card issuers have perfected, would be a significant welfare reform in itself, since it would help to identify those ineligible. More important, it would make possible for the first time the effective application of the Immigration Control and Reform Act of 1986, which forbids the hiring of illegal aliens; this would reduce the rate of growth of the labor force and the pressures on existing jobs. It would have side benefits such as the better identification of criminals and tax evaders and a new Census enumeration process that might really tell us how many people there are in the U.S. The time has come for the government to bite the bullet on this one, rather than nibbling at the edges. The government is going to need all the savings it can find, and we cannot squander the job opportunities that exist.

THE CONUNDRUM OF THE WHIRLPOOL

Our social system is coming apart in complex and interrelated ways that our decision processes are simply not prepared to deal with. The budget deficit. Our growing indebtedness to the rest of the world and our own rich. The cities. The decline of wages. Job uncertainty even among groups that had felt themselves secure. The breakdown of law. The rise of crime. The wanton destructiveness by wasted youth. The loss of the family and the destruction of traditional anchoring values.

We are in a whirlpool, and those elements of decomposition are synergistic. We cannot, as we have done before, undertake to deal with them in isolation. The Government is trying to shore up one crumbling structure after another when it needs an overarching vision of what the nation must do and what we can afford to do.

The solutions themselves may be compromises that, as a nation, we did not expect to have to make. The illusion of omnipotence and unlimited possibilities began to crumble sometime in the '70s, and it will not come back.

My beat is population, not welfare. As I look at the connections, however, the rough outline of a workable welfare/unemployment policy emerges, and I will try it out on the reader who has accompanied me this far:

1. Universality. Competition may be eroding traditional American generosity, but as a civilized society, we cannot let our fellows starve or freeze on the streets.

2. Modest expectations. The industrial world has experimented in the past several decades with the height of the "safety net." Some, like Sweden, have almost obliterated the differential in living standards between those who work and those who don't, and they are finding they cannot support the net at that level. We may need to experiment with simpler solutions than the law now provides, such as soup kitchens and the simplest of accommodations. Hong Kong in the 1950s helped to accommodate a flood of

refugees from China in the simplest and least destructible of buildings, with a central plumbing core and cubicles to live in.

3. Realism. The pressures will continue. Welfare and unemployment are not temporary conditions. They need to be treated together as aspects of the same worsening problem. Narrow solutions will not work. Even education is not the answer if there are no jobs. The street kids are not irrational; they play the cards as they see them, and their estimate of their prospects in the main stream is not far from right. The young mothers are not competitive in this society, and they probably know it and hang on to what they can get. In short, let us face the expectation that the market is not going to produce enough jobs, and that this society is going to need a massive and continuing program of "make work jobs"—some sort of National Service Corps.

4. Dignity. Dependency degrades people. There is much that needs to be done in this country, even if doing it cannot command a competitive wage. Look at our cities; or remember what the Civilian Conservation Corps (CCC) did in planting trees and improving our forests in the 1930s. Our parks, public lands and national forests could use help. Everybody who is not completely disabled should have a job if they want it, and participation should be the key to remuneration. Responsibility begets responsibility. Young people would be less likely to trash urban parks if they had helped build them.

   Above all, consider our children. One of the primary functions of our social species is the social rearing of the young. That responsibility has been neglected as women have moved into the job market, and "latchkey children" are a major national problem. The young mothers (and indeed fathers) could serve in supervised creches, learning to take care of their children and those of the people who go off to work. The administration plans to spend billions more on child care, anyway; it should be part of a larger plan.

   The supervisors should be members of the Service Corps, not members of a separate bureaucracy. This would get rid of the handout mentality, and trainees who showed promise could work their way up. In the same way, education and training opportunities should be offered through the corps. Bringing in the upwardly mobile would remove the stigma, and the corps would be seen as a stage of life through which many successful people pass—and perhaps even as a period of real national service.

5. Simplicity. We need to rationalize the present Rube Goldberg contrivance of programs into something more equitable and understandable, and one which does not put the recipient at the mercy of the administrator. As a starter: if we made the public food and lodging arrangements simple enough, those who could afford to would stay out of them, and they could be offered without a means test. All those welfare workers chasing around trying to enforce the rule against a "man in the house" could be put to better uses. One demeaning aspect of AFDC would be eliminated, there would be fewer single mother families, and kids would have a father—which would generally be good for the fathers, the children, the mothers and probably society itself.

6. Toughness. This may sound a bit too much like an idyll. The Chinese did not trash those Hong Kong housing units I described—but the Chinese had more social self-discipline than is

presently evident in our society. I can hardly forget the vivid newsreel of the demolition of the Pruitt-Igoe project in St.Louis, which had been made uninhabitable by its inhabitants. Street sleepers stay out of shelters for fear of what goes on inside. To make anything work in our demoralized society, we will need to become much less tolerant of anti-social behavior. There are laws; we will need to enforce them, even if this requires the segregation of the incorrigible.

7. —and Generosity. Some but probably not all the cost could come from the $250 billion or more spent on the existing hodgepodge of welfare and unemployment compensation programs. We may need to look beyond it to Leontief's proposed social transfers. We may need to transfer resources from those in the system to those who have fallen out of it. With a labor glut, skills are not rewarded. U.S. labor productivity has been rising even as wages have been falling. If indeed the nation decides to provide some protection against low wage imports, it is entitled to expect business to return some of the windfall. The rich have been getting richer as the poor have gotten desperate. This has got to stop.

Those who know welfare better than I are urged to put together their own outlines. I offer one caveat: that any proposal must address the fateful synergy as a whole.

Successful welfare reform is rooted in dealing with unemployment, and unemployment in turn is generated by the forces that I described at the beginning. We have only limited flexibility to adjust foreign trade and investment policies without jeopardizing the benefits of world economic arrangements. We would be ill-advised to attempt the Luddite maneuver of trying to stop technological advance. We would not want to hinder the progress of women into the job market, because training will work only if there are jobs available at the end of the process.

And that means we must take on the least discussed of the causes: population growth, and its two sources, migration and fertility. With the will, we could rewrite our foreign assistance priorities and revitalize foreign aid by a shift in resource use rather than new expenditures. Similarly, we could address immigration and domestic fertility; it is a matter of will and policy rather than another drain on resources.

We must look squarely at the impacts of immigration, of unwanted children and indeed of fertility. Without a policy on these issues, there is no way that the government can simply get people off welfare without tremendous human costs.

NOTES:

1. *U.S. Statistical Abstract, 1993,* Tables 579 and 583 give the totals of federal, state and local benefits for persons with limited income plus certain unemployment and non-medical workers' compensation programs under "Social Welfare Expenditures" as $255 billion in 1990. (The total does not include medical or retirement plans, veterans' and military dependents' assistance programs, or subsidies such as agricultural price supports, or [for the most part], the administrative expenses of running the programs.) Of that, $37.5 billion went to Food Stamps and AFDC.
2. Herbert Rowen "How to Create a Million New Jobs," *Washington Post,* 11-15-93. Rohatyn advocated a huge public works program to be financed with a gasoline tax.
3. Robert W. Fox, "Neighbors' Problems, Our Problems," Chapter 18 in Lindsey Grant et al *Elephants in the Volkswagen* (New York: W.H. Freeman, 1992.)

4. Rich Miller, "World Economy Faces Jobs Crisis, UN Agency Says," Reuter, Washington, 2-2-94, 11:07:00, quoting a new ILO report titled "Defending Values, Promoting Change."
5. Leon Bouvier and Lindsey Grant, *How Many Americans?* (San Francisco: Sierra Club Books, publication scheduled July 1994), Table 2.1
6. The consulting firm Challenger, Gray & Christmas runs periodic surverys and counted 615,186 jobs lost in 1993 and 108,946 in January 1994 alone. They estimate that they missed 20 percent more. Quoted by Frank Swoboda, "U.S. Companies Speed Pace of Downsizing" (*Washington Post,* 2-8-94.)
7. AP, Washington, 9-24-93, 17:57 EDT.
8. Reuter, Washington, 9-24-93, 20:30.
9. David E. Bloom & Adi Brender, *Labor in the Emerging World Economy* (Washington: Population Reference Bureau, Population Bulletin Vol.48, No.2, October 1993), Table 9. Part of the discrepancy probably results from better European data, and part of it is a matter of definition of "immigration," but it is a surprising compilation nevertheless.
10. Alan Wheatley, "OECD Fears Social Explosion from Unemployment," Reuter, Paris, 6-1–93, 11:24:00.
11. Reuter, Paris, 6-18-93, 10:25:00.
12. Alan Wheatley, "Unions Say 'Yes, but' to OECD's Jobless Cure," Reuter, Paris, 6-3-93, 07:03:00.
13. AP, Washington, 2-5-94, 09:05:00.
14. Reuter, Washington, 9-8-93, 11:37:00.
15. AP, Washington, 2-5-94, 09:14:00.
16. John M. Goshko and Thomas W. Lippman, "Foreign Aid Shift Sought by Clinton," *Washington Post* 11-26-93.
17. For the derivation of the "Foreign Entrants" column, see my NPG Forum article *A Beleagured President, A Fizzled "Economic Stimulus Package," and a NAFTA Time Bomb,* May 1993, note 12. The Bureau of Labor Statistics estimates that 57 percent of new immigrants, refugees and legalized alien residents are in the work force, plus all of the non-immigrants who apply for temporary work permits. The estimate is necessarily imprecise. Some of those legalized or given work permits were probably already holding jobs. On the other hand, the figure does not include FY1992 illegal border crossers and those on non-immigrant visas working illegally. Job creation data from *U.S. Statistical Abstract, 1993.*
18. William Claiborne, "Administration Unveils Plans to Beef Up Border Control," *Washington Post,* 2-3-94.
19. For a survey of studies on displacement and wage impacts, see Donald L. Huddle, *Immigration, Jobs & Wages: the Misuses of Econometrics* (NPG Forum paper April 1992.) For studies of the displacement process itself, see Huddle's *Immigration & Jobs: the Process of Displacement* (NPG Forum May 1992) or various studies of the process in California lemon groves by Philip L. Martin, Univ. of California, Davis.
20. AP, Washington, 3-11-94, 10:55:00.
21. AP, Washington, 6-1-93, 20:31 EDT.
22. "Fixing the Welfare Mess," *U.S. News & World Report,* 12-13-93, quoting "a recent study by LaDonna Pavetti."
23. AP, Washington, 1-30-94 15:50 EST.
24. Surgeon General Jocelyn Elders, herself Black, said that Medicaid must have been "developed by a white male slave owner," because nobody else would want to encourage the proliferation of healthy, pregnant and unemployed young women. AP, Washington, 2-25-94, 22:16 EST.
25. AP, Washington, 1-30-94, 15:50 EST.

THE TIMID CRUSADE

Lindsey Grant

January 1994

U.S. population, at present rates, will approach 400 million, and perhaps even pass 500 million, by 2050.[1] *The only two variables available to influence that growth are fertility and migration.* That proposition seems self-evident, but it poses an apparently insuperable stumbling block to the big environmental organizations that advocate an end to U.S. population growth.

THE HEROIC AGE

In 1969, the President Nixon raised the issue of U.S. population growth. Let me quote him at some length, even though readers may have seen this quotation before. His was a prophetic vision from, perhaps, a surprising source.

"In 1917 the total number of Americans passed 100 million , after three full centuries of steady growth. In 1967—just half a century later—the 200 million mark was passed. If the present rate of growth continues, the third hundred million persons will be added in roughly a thirty-year period. This means that by the year 2000, or shortly thereafter, there will be more than 300 million Americans.

"The growth will produce serious challenges for our society. I believe that many of out present social problems may be related to the fact that we have had only fifty years in which to accommodate the second hundred million Americans. . . .

"Where, for example, will the next hundred million Americans live? . . .

"Other questions confront us. How, for example, will we house the next hundred million Americans? . . .

"How will we educate and employ such a large number of people? Will our transportation systems move them about as quickly and economically as necessary? How will we provide adequate health care when our population reaches 300 million? Will our political structures have to be reordered, too, when our society grows to such proportions? . . .

" . . . we should establish as a national goal the provision of adequate family planning services within the next five years to all those who want them but cannot afford them."[2]

President Clinton might well be urged to repeat that final recommendation, as the first plank in any program to address welfare reform and the exploding problem of pregnancy among unmarried teenage girls.

The President proposed and Congress later created a distinguished National Commission on Population

Growth and the American Future, chaired by John D. Rockefeller, 3rd. In 1972, the Commission concluded that the country would benefit if population growth stopped. It made many explicit recommendations. Among them:

- that the government establish a permanent long term strategic planning capability to monitor demographic, resource and environmental trends, to serve as a "lobby for the future" and recommend policies to deal with looming problems.
- that preparations be made to deal with the anticipated growth of metropolitan areas by reforming governmental arrangements it characterized as "archaic."
- that there be a national, publicly funded "voluntary program to reduce unwanted fertility, to improve the outcome of pregnancy, and to improve the health of children." This was to include education, contraceptive information and—delicate as the subject was even then—abortion.
- that immigration levels not be increased, that those levels be periodically reviewed to see if they are too high, that there be civil and criminal penalties for employers of illegal aliens, and that the enforcement program be strengthened.[3]

Although the Rockefeller Commission recommendations were quickly swept under the rug—they were controversial and it was an election year—the Commission took on the issues squarely. The recommendations would be a good starting place even now for organizations seeking to make realistic proposals as to how to address U.S. population policy.

Eight years later, the "Global 2000 Report" to President Carter described some of the connections between U.S. population growth and resource and environmental problems. It offered no recommendations, but it was followed up by a booklet of action proposals from the U.S. Department of State and the Council on Environmental Quality which included eight broad recommendations concerning U.S. population growth. *"The United States should develop a national population policy which addresses the issues of:*

- *Population stabilization*
- *Availability of family planning programs*
- *Rural and urban migration issues*
- *Public education on population concerns*
- *Just, consistent, and workable immigration laws*
- *The role of the private sector—nonprofit, academic and business*
- *Improved information needs and capacity to analyze impacts of population growth within the United States*
- *Institutional arrangements to ensure continued federal attention to domestic population issues."*[4]

These proposals were less specific than those of 1972, but they offered the basis on which to begin to think about population.

THE ENVIRONMENTALISTS' SLOW START

Initiatives on U.S. population growth during the '70s came principally from government, with the distinguished exception of the role of the Rockefellers. The Sierra Club recognized the population-environment connection very early and created its Population Committee in 1968, but most private environmental organizations stayed away from the U.S. population issue out of concern that it would be controversial and lose support for their programs.

There was a widespread tendency—it was still the age of affluence and unlimited expectations—to regard population growth as a third world problem. The population groups of the period such as the Population Crisis Committee (now Population Action International) and the Population Institute helped to mobilize public and Congressional support for population aid abroad, but did not (and still do not) lobby on U.S. population growth. The Environmental Fund (now Population Environment Balance), NPG (Negative Population Growth, Inc.), and ZPG (Zero Population Growth, Inc.) pretty much had that field to themselves, and ZPG has always found it difficult to address immigration.

TO INTRODUCE THE CRUSADERS . . .

In the late '70s and '80s the big environmental groups came slowly to realize that one cannot address U.S. environmental issues without addressing population growth. During the 1988 presidential campaign, a coalition of eighteen environmental organizations prepared an environmental "Blueprint for the Environment" for the guidance of the incoming U.S. administration. The Blueprint made the point that "U.S. population pressures threaten the environmental all across our nation," and gave some examples. It said that family planning and the availability of contraceptives must be expanded worldwide (presumably including the U.S.). It recommended "an official population policy for the United States . . ." and said that "We must assure that federal policies and programs promote a balance between population, resources, and environmental quality."[5]

Among the eighteen organizations sponsoring that statement were eight of the major environmental groups: Defenders of Wildlife, Friends of the Earth, the National Audubon Society, the National Parks and Conservation Association (NPCA), the National Wildlife Federation, the Natural Resources Defense Council (NRDC), the Sierra Club, and The Wilderness Society; plus a major population group, Zero Population Growth (ZPG, Inc.)

That is about as far as it has gotten. Subsequent statements have been more general. On May 22, 1991 there was a "Priority Statement on Population" signed by just about everybody involved with population and the environment, and some others. It urged simply that "The United States and all nations of the world must make an effective response to the issue of population growth a leading priority for this decade." Other generalized declarations as to the importance of stopping population growth have emerged from Arden House and Carnegie Endowment deliberations, from the National Academy of Sciences and from an ad hoc coalition of scientists that included most living U.S. Nobel laureates.

HOW DO THEY PLAN TO GET THERE?

The question of course is "How do you do it?"

The following description applies to the organizations' views on **U.S.** population. They generally advocate more U.S. support for other countries' population efforts.

Five of the eight environmental organizations listed do not address U.S. population beyond signing general statements such as those described. Defenders of Wildlife, the NRDC and The Wilderness Society, for example, presently have no specific policy concerning U.S. immigration, population or fertility.

Friends of the Earth apparently finds the issues of U.S. population too hot to handle. The staff said that only the President could speak on the record on the topic, and he did not return `phone calls.

The NPCA believes that active lobbying on population issues does not fall within its mandate. (That argument seems to overlook the fact that NPCA has already recognized that U.S. population change impinges on its mandate. In other situations, organizations have formed coalitions led by the most knowledgeable to address major issues of current concern. *The Blueprint for the Environment* itself was such a coalition effort. With the will, organizations can make themselves heard without diverting resources from their principal mandate.)

The caution is not limited to the *Blueprint* signatories. Greenpeace, which had its origins in a highly activist brand be addressed . . . (but) has made no public statements on U.S. population, immigration or fertility"[6] The Population Institute, like Friends of the Earth, simply avoids questions on the topic, even though the question apparently has been raised within its Board as to whether it shouldn't begin to look at U.S. population growth. The World Wildlife Fund believes U.S. population lies outside its area of expertise. Its Chairman did, however, testify before Congress in 1993 on U.S. over-consumption and energy use, and one wonders how those issues can be disentangled from population size.[7]

The generalize as to what the others (Audubon, NWF, the Sierra Club) and ZPG advocate concerning U.S. population policy:

They —-

- describe the population-environment connections, sometimes very eloquently. Audubon and ZPG have developed extensive materials for school use to teach the connections.
- urge that family planning be made universally available in the United States, subsidized as necessary.
- argue for greater attention to women's rights as a way of influencing fertility.
- continue to call for a national population policy

None of them ——

- advocates deliberate governmental policies to influence fertility through incentives and disincentives.
- makes its views known when national policies are being considered that will influence the direction U.S. demographic change.
- has a policy on immigration.

ZPG "believes that the United States should adopt an overall goal for immigration as part of its national population policy" but does not suggest a figure or propose how to enforce it.[8]

Positions have not necessarily been constant over the years. There has in fact been something of a pendulum effect, with the pendulums oscillating on different schedules. NPCA in the late '70s under the late Anthony Wayne Smith was a pioneer in population policy advocacy; it subsequently pulled back.

The National Wildlife Federation in 1980 said all the right things. In its Resolution No 49 of March 1980, it

> *"expresses its policy that world population should be stabilized at replacement levels through national and global programs of family planning and population limitation; and BE IT FURTHER RESOLVED that in furtherance of this goal, the U.S. provide tax incentives for family planning of an optimal two in size, make birth control education and resources and sterilization operations widely available at low cost, accelerate medical research into new, safer and more effective contraception and undertake a vigorous effort to stop illegal immigration into this country, while, at the same time, offering necessary help to the countries affected to lessen their population pressures; and*

BE IT FURTHER RESOLVED that a full range of alternatives should be pursued to effectuate this policy through administrative, legislative and judicial avenues as well as educational means; and

BE IT FURTHER RESOLVED that NWF public statements, magazines and educational materials will accurately reflect the policy of this resolution."

There you have it all. NWF is the largest environmental organization in the country, with a membership of over 5 million. They could have had an enormous impact if they had simply followed that resolution. Instead, NWF has been generally silent on U.S. population and in 1992, without formally revoking Resolution 49, it resiled to a much weaker Resolution 14 on "Population and Environment" which did not mention U.S. population, called only for the NWF to "proceed with international programs" in the population field, and urged the government to increase and improve its assistance to foreign health programs that include voluntary family planning. The 1980 call to arms is apparently a dead letter.

Defenders of Wildlife has not recently been active on the population issue.

SIGNS OF AWAKENING

For several of the organizations, the pendulum may be swinging in the other direction. Audubon—which had a very strong population role years ago under the presidency of Russell Peterson—backed away from it but now seems to be prepared to approach the immigration issue again. In 1992 it was unwilling even to carry an NPG ad in its magazine that said one cannot deal with U.S. population growth without addressing both fertility and immigration. Apparently, it is beginning to rethink its position. It has yet to state a policy on immigration, but its President in a letter of April 16, 1993 to President Clinton urged a national "conference on population and natural resources," and listed immigration as one of six examples of "critical issues" it should address. Eight months later, the *Audubon Activist* carried a pro and con discussion entitled "Should Environmentalists Adopt an Immigration Policy?," and invited comments.

NRDC has just created a new Population, Consumption and Environment Initiative and may well begin to take a more active population role.

The Wilderness Society is presently developing a "Population Project" linked to the concept of sustainability. A November 1993 brochure says the Society will promote Congressional oversight hearings on the impact of population growth; the rest of the planned program is more generally educational. Ex Senator Gaylord Nelson is involved, and we may hope that he will help move the Society toward an active role in population. As a starter, the Fall 1993 *Wilderness* magazine gave its members a general introduction to the population question.

ZPG seems to be going through a phase of internal turmoil. When I inquired, they gave a spirited defense of their policy of gradualism. They did not mention an October 16th memorandum from their Board of Directors that called for ZPG to change policy, but I have a copy of such a memorandum. It is a strong document. In language much like the 1980 NWF resolution, it says "The time has come . . . to focus more energies and attention on domestic concerns. We recommend that ZPG call for and work toward policies aimed at stabilizing U.S. population as soon as feasible . . . ZPG policy should call for the United States to address the causes of high fertility and examine immigration laws and policies." It called for advocacy of energy efficiency, conservation of natural resources, sustainable environmental practices, control over illegal immigration, and a revamping of foreign aid to emphasize social programs, education, sustainable development and "the root causes of international migration." It called for the U.S. Government to develop a population policy and instructed the ZPG staff to draft a policy statement based on the memorandum.

Quite a memorandum. The Board was telling the ZPG staff to do what it is supposed to have been doing for a generation.

The new policy statement has not yet materialized but, perhaps as a result of the instruction, ZPG is actively examining its positions. It is considering whether to return to sponsoring population legislation in Congress, as it did a decade ago with a series of bills introduced by Senator Hatfield and Congressmen Ottinger and MacKay. It is also examining the President's health insurance proposal to see whether it is consistent with the goal of universal access to family planning.

The Sierra Club is a special case, and its problems in developing a policy on U.S. population underline the difficulty of the issue. The Club came to the population issue early. It has a small but dedicated professional population staff. Since 1990, international population growth has been one of the Club's seven major issues. Its Population Committee, with multiple regional chapters, is probably the strongest cadre of enthusiastic and well informed volunteers in the field. The Club still has no policy on immigration, or on fertility, but in December 1992 the Population Committee invited its chapters to begin to develop a Club position on U.S. population issues. The process has been a rocky one. More than most big environmental groups, the Club involves its membership in decisions and attempts to move by consensus. The Club leadership is sensitive to the danger of alienating substantial numbers of the membership or of being considered racist. The Population Committee, in cooperation with other parts of the Club's massive policy-making structure, is still in the process of developing a position which will win the trust of the organization, including its minority members.

That position, it now appears, will state the need to solve the problems of U.S. over-consumption and population growth together, as one part of a unified approach to environmental preservation. One member described it as an emerging "social contract." If the draft language survives in the final compromise, it will call for consumption to be brought down to environmentally sustainable levels, for an effort to bring population down to an optimal size to be determined, and for immigration and fertility levels consistent with those goals. Perhaps in 1994 the Club will find a formula that will enable it to take on those delicate issues and thus become a major activist concerning the country's demographic future.

These are signs of spring, and they are being encouraged by several big foundations that contribute to environmental groups but have made clear they want to see more attention given to U.S. population issues.

The movement needs to get on with those changes. Other organizations such as Worldwatch, the World Resources Institute, the Global Tomorrow Coalition, and the Population Council consider their mission to be educational and do not engage in advocacy on specific issues. Advocacy on the real issues—fertility and migration—has thus been left pretty much to the few organizations listed earlier, to regional groups such as Californians for Population Stabilization (CAPS), and to the Federation for American Immigration Reform (FAIR), formed in 1979 for the sole purpose of addressing immigration.

WHAT IS MISSING?

I have said that there are only two variables at hand to influence U.S. demographic change. One of them is fertility. The other is net migration. (I assume that nobody proposes to raise mortality.)

Some of the germinating ideas described above are aimed at generating new studies or Congressional hearings on the impacts of population growth. Such educational efforts are certainly desirable as a way of predisposing public and Congressional opinion toward effective measures to deal with population. They are not, however, enough. Immigration and fertility policy are made in a series of incremental steps, and not in study committees. One can only influence the direction by weighing in when those decisions are being taken; and that process itself is perhaps the best way to educate the nation about the demographic implications of what it is doing.

The nation presently makes its demographic policies by accident. Welfare, health, or housing policies may make it easier for young women to have children and thereby raise fertility, but those policies are usually framed in terms of *needs* without considering *consequences.* We had better look at the consequences. Do we make it attractive to have fewer children, or more?

Immigration directly determines future population size, both because of the immigration itself, and because the immigrants' descendants add to the total. However, immigration laws are the product not of such demographic thinking but of humanitarian concerns or employers' pressures to get cheap labor, or the desire to please ethnic groups. (The Immigration Act of 1990 was the direct product of Senator Kennedy's wish to please his Irish American constituents, and as Chairman of the Senate Subcommittee on Immigration and Refugee Affairs, he was in a position to do something about it.)

If advocacy organizations are to do anything about population growth, they must go beyond generalized statements. When the real issues arise that decide our demographic future—things like immigration or refugee or welfare legislation—the environmental movement needs to be heard, pointing out the demographic consequences. Declarations are fine, in principle, but declarations to the ambient air do not have much effect in the real world. Population growth will not stop simply because environmentalists say it should.

Migration is theoretically a less important variable than fertility in determining our demographic future. That is to say, a 10 percent change in immigration changes the demographic projections less than a 10 percent change in fertility. But migration is presently the more explosive variable. Post-1900 immigration has contributed 43 percent of U.S. population growth in this century, and it will contribute nearly 90 percent in the next century, if present patterns hold.[9] A position in favor of halting population growth without a policy on immigration is simply a nullity.

The organizations' views on **fertility** contain more that is useful. Certainly we need universal access to family planning. One can hardly argue with the importance of measures that promote education, jobs and self-respect among women. However, the silence on immigration can vitiate the recommendations about fertility. Young American women's access to jobs, for instance, is impeded by immigrant competition.

Above all, the organizations are caught in a monumental non-sequitur. The assertion of women's right to decide the number of their children offers no assurance that population growth will stop, if women want more than two children or if immigration is left open. The fluctuation of fertility between the great depression, the baby boom and the baby bust is dramatic evidence that women do not automatically seek a fertility level bases on societal needs.

In other words, the policies advocated—and the silence on immigration—do not reasonably lead to the results the organizations endorse.

We face the likelihood that two desirable goals are in conflict: freedom of choice, and the nation's demographic destiny. One must, individually, decide which goal is more important. It is self-delusion to try to escape the choice by pretending that they are necessarily compatible.

If one is serious in advocating a halt to population growth, the corollary is that—while preserving intact the principle of voluntarism—it may be necessary to move toward governmental and societal policies that encourage people to choose to have fewer children. In other words: change the context in which that choice is made. For the present, a halt to population growth requires a lower fertility level. How do we achieve it without the trauma of a depression? U.S. experience in this area (as compared with the experience that some third world countries have accumulated) is so limited that one cannot afford to be dogmatic as to what policies, incentives and disincentives would work, but the exploration must begin.[10]

The environmentalists need to lobby on population, if they are serious about it. One thing is clear: the failure to relate immigration policy to its demographic consequences, and the national unwillingness to enforce even the laws we have, helps to insure that population growth will not stop. Add to that the fertility level arising from the present unintended mix of incentives and disincentives, and we have an explosive mixture.

WHAT THEY COULD DO

The environmental organizations are not shy about lobbying. Watch them lobby for wilderness areas or against the destruction of old forests. They know that their opponents don't sleep, and they are quite willing to take them on. Here are a few examples of situations in which the environmentalists could have weighed in if they were serious about population.

Immigration. Where were the big environmental groups in 1986 when the Immigration Control and Reform Act was being gutted with loopholes that led to what the *New York Times* called "fraud on a massive scale"?[11]

Where were they as the Immigration Act of 1990 was being debated? The official estimate is that it raised immigration by 40 percent, and this estimate makes very little allowance for "chain migration." That Act led the Census Bureau to raise its middle projection of U.S. population in 2050 by 100 million. So far as I know, only FAIR and Population Environment Balance testified against it.

These questions could be extended almost indefinitely. Did the environmentalists say anything when President Bush created a presumption of eligibility for all Chinese women who claim asylum because they oppose their government's policy on abortions? There are over 300 million Chinese women in their child-bearing years. Plus their husbands, and their children . . . Have the organizations looked at the needs of the Border Patrol? Have they made any proposals as to how immigration might better be enforced? Have they looked at the issue of identification? (It is not all that contentious; even President Clinton agrees that better identification is needed.) The answer of course is that they have simply not entered this whole era.

As to Fertility . . . Where were those environmental organizations during the 1992 presidential campaign, when most of the principal aspirants made proposals for liberalized allowances or deductions for children, thus sending a clear pro-natalist signal? Even Senator Gore, who knows better.

Where are they now, for that matter, when a health reform is being debated that will probably influence U.S. demographic patterns for generalizations?[12]

Where will they be later this year as the nation begins to debate welfare reform?

To avoid those debates is to admit impotency in addressing a problem the organizations themselves profess to recognize. Given their pugnacity in other areas, the silence on real population issues suggests a continuing, or in some cases, rising ambivalence.

WHY THE CAUTION?

It is not easy, particularly for organizations that rely on their membership for their political clout, to take on immigration and fertility. Politically, those are perhaps the toughest questions that one could ask them to address.

For the purpose of this paper, let us accept that population growth hinders the pursuit of environmental goals—the argument is made elsewhere[13]—and that the major environment organizations know it.

We are here discussing the role of serious environmental organizations, not the attitudes of employees seeking cheap labor, or the Zoe Bairds of the country looking for docile and cheap household help. We assume from their own statements that the organizations recognize that the nation cannot hide behind cliches; we cannot solve the issues facing us simply by changing our national consumption habits, or by technological fixes. We need all three: a population policy, a less consumption-driven society and technical solutions.

If simply proclaiming the population connection has very little effect on population growth, why are the organizations reluctant to take on the real determinants of population growth? I hope I do the organizations no injustice in the following effort to describe their concerns and to sketch out (in italics) the rebuttals that are available if the organizations choose to take on the issues.

Immigration. We take seriously our self-image as "a nation of immigrants," and the sense of obligation to give others the chance our ancestors had is probably strongest among idealists, who are the soul of the environmental movement.

There is a new generation that takes seriously the idea that we live on a shared planet and that we are all brothers (and sisters). To many people under thirty, it would seem, an "alien" comes from outer space, not from Mexico. To that generation, and those of their elders who are tuned in, any proposal to limit immigration conjures up images of nativists, racists and skinheads. The debate is thus plunged into a region of moral absolutes, where to compromise is to sin. This is a powerful deterrent to organizations that rely in great degree on the enthusiasm of youth and the righteous.

There is a critical point to be made here. These are good people, but they must realize that the population issue, like many others, is not a battle of unalloyed good against unalloyed evil. It is a choice forced upon us by the reality that resources and the environment are not infinite. It is, to use the cowboy movie image, a battle between "white hats." To put it bluntly, the choice is between an obligation to the stranger and the obligation to our own disenfranchised and to the environment our children inherit.

Though the choice is between desirable objectives, it is far from symmetrical, a point usually ignored. We cannot save the world. We have a fighting chance of dealing successfully with our own problems.

A recent piece in the Letters to the Editors of *Sierra* pretty well summarizes the state of mind that gives pause to environmental leaders. The writer argued: "What victimizes black workers today is not the influx of immigrants . . . but the flight of industry to other countries where labor is cheaper. (I) do not suggest support for endless growth in the United States . . . (But) to treat the symptoms by closing national borders to keep out `the disease' rather than commit ourselves to eliminating the cause of the illness, is both futile and irresponsible."[14]

Those brief sentences are driven more by passion than analysis. They call for an exegesis.

1. *Both immigration and the departure of capital hurt the American labor competing with immigrant or cheaper foreign labor. Technological change has been drying up entry level jobs in American industry. The letter writer is arguing that increasing the supply of a factor of production (labor) in a situation of glut does not lower the price of the labor. He thus denies the principle of supply and demand. Polemically, of course, the denial makes it possible to blame bad guys (industrialists) and to absolve oneself of any obligation to limit immigration or worry about American labor.*[15]
2. *Projections cited earlier in this paper make it clear that to be for unlimited immigration is in fact to espouse "endless growth in the U.S."*
3. *There is a certain, probably unconscious, arrogance in the assumption that the U.S. can "eliminate the causes of the illness." The illness, presumably, is third world poverty and population growth. The U.S. can and should do what it can to help the afflicted countries. The assume that we can somehow save them requires a remarkably inflated view of our power.*
4. *The reader is offered an unjustifiable either/or choice. There is no reason to accept the letter writer's assertion that we cannot simultaneously limit immigration and provide support to family planning and self-help efforts in other countries. In fact, we may be better able to help others if we are not overwhelmed by our own labor, urban and environmental problems.*

   To refuse to address the problems at home in the belief that we should instead solve those in the rest of the world is a very questionable bit of reasoning. One might remind the letter writer of another rule of thumb beloved of environmentalists: "Think globally; act locally."

The writer to *Sierra* is hardly alone in the thought that "I don't want to focus on numbers and quotas, but to solve the problem at the sources." For another example: in 1991, in answering the question "Is immigration the major cause of U.S. population problems?," an Audubon/Population Crisis Committee booklet suggested that pressures to migrate to the U.S. can be relieved by "investments in economic development and family planning in migrant sending countries . . ."[16]

Well enough, but they did not calculate how much that might cost or suggest what we should do for the next twenty years; most of those migrants are already born. This is more a crutch than a policy proposal; nobody looks seriously at the question "Is it really possible?" The third world working age population is rising about 61 million per year, and will continue to do so for the indefinite future. For Meso-America alone, the increase is 2.7 million, nearly twice the comparable figure for the U.S. this year; they must find the resources to absorb more new working age people *than we tried (less than successfully) to do as the baby boomers came on the job market—and they must do it in economies that, in total, are, 1/17th as large as ours. A rough calculation suggests that a total annual investment of perhaps $50 to 200 billion is needed to provide the additional employment in that one region; even this does not provide for any progress in employing the presently unemployed, and the end result would be to face the same problems in more crowded societies.*[17] *That investment is a substantial portion of their entire GNP. How much of that capital are we likely to provide, and what happens to our own unemployed as the capital goes abroad to employ foreigners?*

The population problem must be addressed where it exists, in the third world and here. We should do what we can for others, both for their own good and our long term benefit. However, that is no answer to our present immigration problem. Immigration and demography are matters of numbers; to take refuge in cliches about solving the problem at its source—meanwhile refusing to challenge the immigration quotas other propose for the U.S.—is to accept the consequences. Environmentalists are not shy about talking numbers where other environmental concerns are at stake; the timidity about immigration is another sign of ambivalence rather than a principle.

People who are solicitous of the foreign are strangely impervious to the problems of Americans. It may be easier to sympathize with the stranger, who is an abstraction, than with our own poor, who are a sometimes troublesome presence.

The poor and the urban minorities do not have the luxury of distance. Among those most affected—but who might be expected to welcome more immigration for reasons of ethnic solidarity—are the U.S. Hispanics. An in-depth survey co-sponsored by the Ford Foundation (which itself funds pro-immigration groups) confirmed the result of many other poles and showed majorities of 66 percent (Cuban) to 79 percent (Puerto Rican) among different Hispanic groups favoring reduced immigration.[18] *Those who are being hurt have made their choice in the moral dilemma I have posed.*

When faced with an unwelcome dilemma, there is a natural human tendency to deny it exists. The argument is regularly heard that immigrants "take jobs Americans won't take."

The rebuttal to that one is pretty straightforward: it is not the jobs; it's the conditions. In 1993, the nation watched the arrival of ships full of Chinese who even Senator Kennedy called "slave labor." This is the labor that, apologists say, fills the "jobs that Americans won't take." Do any environmentalists really believe that Americans should work for as little as 70 cents and hour and be locked up every night in a crowded and windowless room? As with other commerce, the lowest bid tends to set the price of labor, and this indentured labor drives down wages and takes jobs from the other unskilled people in the cities. At a time when only 45 percent of young Blacks and 58 percent of young Hispanics have regular jobs, nationwide,[19] *we should begin to think of our own people.*

The largest environmental group also have a practical problem. They look toward cooperation with counterparts in other countries to save the shared planet, and they fear that advocacy of immigration limitations may threaten that cooperation, particularly if their counterparts are wedded to the idea that the U.S. has an obligation to accept those who want to come here.

The fear is misplaced. Other countries (including Mexico) do not propose that their borders be opened. They recognize their limits, if not ours.

Fertility. For the largest organizations, with substantial conservative membership, the largest obstacle in the way of addressing fertility is probably the visceral fear of being drawn into the abortion issue. Most of the big organizations, including NWF and Audubon, take no position on abortion.

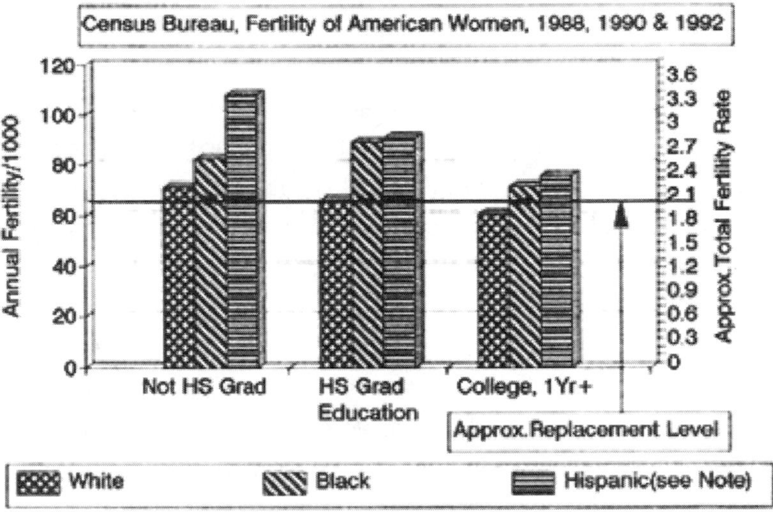

Figure 1.

So far as I know, there are no survey data to guide them in deciding whether anti-abortionist belong to environmental organizations in any numbers. I rather suspect they do not. There is no necessary connection between abortion and fertility levels. Better family planning should actually help to reduce the number of abortions; it would certainly reduce the number of unwanted children. It is quite possible for an organization to favor policies to discourage fertility without advocating abortion. Abortion does, however, provide an escape for those who didn't think about family planning at the right time.

This is one of those issues that the organization will have to face. Is it more important to keep the marginal members, or to address the fertility issue?

From another quarter, there is the dread charge of "racism," to which environmentalists are particularly sensitive. The movement in fact is very close to being "lilly white," and it is trying to reach out to people of color.

Fertility is at least as much a function of education as of race. (A graph of fertility plotted against race and income would show a similar pattern.[20]) The more educated women are about at replacement level fertility, which would eventually stop population growth if there were no immigration, but they are above the fertility level needed if population growth is to be turned around. It is not an insult to the uneducated to urge the adoption throughout the society of an approach to fertility that will improve the condition of all, and perhaps of the uneducated particularly. Nor is it racist; in total numbers, more whites than others would be asked to reduce their fertility.

The environmentalists have different views about population here and abroad. What is sauce for the goose is sauce for the gander. U.S. AID for years has had a program (Plato and its successors) to show third world leaders why they must bring population growth down, plus a program to show them how to organize to do it. The environmental movement generally encourages the effort, but it finds itself unwilling to advocate comparable leadership at home.

Divided Feminists. Environmental groups face a serious problem within their own ranks. There is an element of the feminist movement that takes the position that "nobody is going to tell women what they will do with their own bodies." Such feminists, who may be quite willing to espouse government intervention in other issues such as pollution, find themselves in this instance lined up with the Libertarians.

This viewpoint reflects a long standing fault line within the family planning movement between those who promote family planning to give women absolute control over themselves, and those who are interested in family planning as a way to bring down fertility.

The resolution of the conflict within feminism, I have suggested, is to preserve the principle of voluntarism but to press political leaders to shape an environment in which people make the decisions that lead to lower fertility. This might not win over the most extreme, but the alternative is to allow the extremists to control the direction of population advocacy.

Sensitivity to this division has tended to muzzle the groups actually providing family planning services and guidance in the U.S. The Family Planning Association of America cautiously makes the connection between fertility and population. It advocates education on the connection, but as to society's role in influencing fertility, it copies the guarded Bucharest Convention Formula of 1974 (" . . . the fundamental right of every individual to decide freely *and responsibly* when and whether to have a child" -emphasis added). The Alan Guttmacher Institute avoids taking any position on U.S. population size.

The tensions are reflected in a draft document sponsored by NWF and presently being circulated for signatures.[21] It is intended to develop a common ground. The non-governmental organizations' (NGOs) role in the 1992 Rio de Janeiro UNCED conference was marked by factional struggles among feminists.[22] They hope to avoid a repetition in the September 1994 UN International Conference on Population and Development (ICPD) at Cairo.

The recommendations start: "Women's empowerment/ability to control their own lives is the foundation for action linking population, environment and development." They continue with many proposals for improving the status of women, including a call for "increased targeting of development projects towards a better quality of life for women and **their** children." (emphasis added) Other proposals cover international population assistance, family planning, comprehensive health care, honesty in packaging, energy efficiency, overconsumption, poverty, local participation in decision making, CO_2, greenhouse gases, "fair trade, land redistribution, debt all alleviation, equitable tax systems, regulation of transnational corporations, an end to structural adjustment policies" (sic), and much more. There is a recommendation that nations develop the ability to "assess the implications of population growth and distribution."

Many of the proposals are good. Some are tangential to population. Taken together, they would overwhelm any government; they are a compendium of the authors' vision of a world made anew. Unwilling to take on the central issue of governmental leadership to lower fertility, they have compiled a wish list of attractive policy directions, some of which would help to lower fertility. What is missing is a clarion call to government, and to find ways to encourage people to have fewer children—even if they cannot in all other respects promise to bring about Utopia. It can be done. It has been done, in places like Singapore, Hong Kong, Taiwan and South Korea.

There are three references to migration in the draft document, of which the most specific is that "All governments, especially in the North, should adopt natural resource and population policies that take into consideration population growth, demographic patterns (such as migration), access to and availability of resources."

I am not quite sure what that means, but at least it suggests that the drafters are aware that migration plays a role in demographic change.

The paper reflects the non-sequitur I described earlier: the ademption that women's rights and population objectives are identical. In considerable degree, particularly in countries where women are still legally and socially disadvantaged, they do indeed overlap. Women's rights and education, a sympathetic understanding of the way they view the world, and the availability of family planning guidance and service are important elements in any population program. By assuming an identity of interests, however, the more extreme feminists are able to coopt the population issue. This can be a disaster. In much of the world, it is apparent that women, by and large, do not want replacement level fertility or less.

One can understand why the drafters of a multinational consensus document have taken refuge in generalities on the contentious issues. There is a vast difference, however, between generalization and falling into the error described above. The ICPD will be a frail instrument indeed if it cannot take a stronger position on population than-by present indications-the "offical" NGOs will be urging on it.

When criticized for timidity, the population spokespersons for those NGOs say that the population problem is "compiled—more than just a matter of numbers."

Indeed, it is complex. It is also urgent, and demography is, finally, a matter of numbers. (One wishes that all environmental advocates were—in Garrett Hardin's phrase—as "numerate" as they are literate.)

Because of population growth, and particularly in light of the power of population momentum, the world and this country are in grave trouble. Population and environmental groups should be telling political leaders that they must lead, and this means supporting those leaders in the effort to find ways to encourage people to seek lower fertility. Pursuit of consensus within the tiny and contentious elites that write the positon papers for most NGOs is a sad diversion if it focuses attention away from the big issue.

The more extreme feminists, one may surmise, are not themselves likely to be driving birth rates up, but they constitute a considerable element within the environmental movement, and their influence hinders the adoption of platforms favoring more active government action to influence population growth. Insofar as the organizations are limited by this influence, they can claim—legitimately—that they are sensitive to the concerns of their constituency. They can claim that they are promoting a moral good. What they cannot claim is that they are doing much about population growth.

Women's rights have very little to do with immigration policy, at least until that most unlikely day when somebody proposes to allow only male immigrants because they can't have children. In dealing with the immigration variable, organizations need not be constrained by the feminist issue.

Alliance Building. One group's public affairs officer defended its caution in staking out stronger positions on the grounds that the first priority is to enlist other groups—women's organizations, labor, ethic and minority groups in the population cause. She said those groups are suspicious of a strong position on immigration or fertility.

The concern is understandable, but her organization may in the process lose its own purpose. A priori, it would seem better advised, not to weaken the message, but to identify the issues that are important to the other groups, and which lead to shared positions on immigration and fertility. With labor or minority organizations, for instance, the "hot button" is likely to be unemployment and urban problems. With some 55 percent of young Black adults neither employed full time nor in school, it is understandable if Black organizations find it hard to identify with environmentalists who talk about trees and sustainability and endangered species those young people have never seen. If the environmental group would call the Black groups' attention to the impact of immigration on the wasted young, they might find new allies, but I have seen nothing to suggest that the big environmental groups make that connection.

In Short . . . Courage! friends. If the environmental organizations come to see that they must take positions on immigration and fertility, and want to convince the doubters, the arguments are there.

THE DEMOGRAPHICS OF MODERATION

The population debate—when people think about population at all—is usually conducted in caricatures. It degenerates into horror stories about abortion and forced sterilization and "Chinese example."

The statistics do not support that apocalyptic vision.

Let me draw a happier picture of what is needed. The "two child family" is the goal to which most U.S. women aspire, and by that point about 75 percent of American mothers stop having children. If it could be promoted as a national standard, and if it were combined with an immigration level of 200,000 per year—about the level that prevailed for much of this century—it would lead to the end of U.S. population growth within a generation and to a gradual decline thereafter. By the middle of the twenty-first century our society would have the luxury of deciding what population size is desirable and encouraging a return to the fertility levels of the '80s or higher, depending on what consensus emerged.

The projections to back up this generalization will be the topic of a forthcoming NPG Forum article.[23]

THE VISION OF A BETTER FUTURE

If the environmental organizations could bring themselves to lobby for more reasonable levels of immigration and for national policies that encourage lower fertility until population growth is stopped, they would be making a major contribution to addressing the nation's problems.

Presently, it seems more likely that if the nation indeed faces up to the population issue, the decision will be a product of unemployment and the costs of welfare. If so, it will be addressed in terms of immigration and fertility rather than population per se. The problems of the cities and the desperate situation of the uneducated young, particularly among minorities, are exacerbated by population growth just as are the environmental problems we face. Environmental degradation tends to move at a glacial pace, and our action-oriented society loses interest. The problems of the poor and of the cities are immediate and explosive, and reactions are visceral. From California, Governor Wilson is demanding action on immigration, and the state's two new Democratic senators are hurrying to catch up. Those three have probably done more in the past year to focus national attention on that source of population growth than have all of us who toil away at out computers. It is a wonderful thing to see how direct responsibility clarifies the mind: As senator, Pete Wilson was a sponsor of the principal loophole in the Immigration Reform and Control Act of 1986, and he supported the 1990 legislation increasing immigration.

Health reform is already on the table. Welfare reform is on President Clinton's 1994 list of issues to address. Immigration and fertility are intimately connected with both those issues. The President has said that we cannot provide health services for illegal aliens and that we must consider a national system of identification to find who is entitled.[24] It is the beginning of wisdom.

The people who respond to opinion polls see the connections between population growth and their well-being. The politicians on the front line in California, Florida and New York, and even the administration in Washington are coming to see it. The environmental organizations have a perspectives that should be heard. It is the perspective of hope rather than the politics of fear, the vision of a society living on a sustainable basis with its environment rather than the specter of exploding cities. They can help to formulate a national change of direction that, while recognizing that we live on a spatially limited Earth, points us to a better future. They have a lot to contribute.

Population growth must stop. I know it, and so do the environmental organizations. The only real question is when—before or after we have destroyed the things we seek to protect. The environmental movement should not be bringing up the tail on an issue that is so important to it.

NOTES:

1. Bureau of the Census *Population Projections of the United States, by Age, Sex, Race, and Hispanic origin: 1993 to 2050*, Current Population Report P25-1104, 9-29-93.
2. U.S. President Richard M. Nixon, "Special Message to the U.S. Congress on Problems of Population Growth, July 18, 1969," in *Public Papers of Presidents of the United States* (Washington: Office of the Federal Register, 1969. p.521.) This passage was quoted in NPG FOOTNOTE *A Congenial Job for the Vice President* (NPG, Inc., March 1993).
3. *Population and the American Future. The Report of the Commission on Population Growth and the American Future* Summary volume. (New York: Signet Books, 1972), pp. 76, 184–190 and 204–206. For a summary of the recommendations and a follow-up report on what has happened, see David Simcox "The Commission on Population Growth and the American Future. Twenty Years later: A Lost Opportunity" (*The Social Contract*, Summer 1992, pp. 197–202.)
4. U.S. Council on Environmental Quality and Department of state, *Global Future: Time to Act* (USGPO, January 1981), p.11.
5. Kennedy P. Maize, Editor, *Blueprint for the Environment* (Salt Lake City: Hope Brothers, 1989), pp. 6, 28-29.
6. Greenpeace Press Officer Blair Paleze, telephone conversation 6-25-93. The sources for subsequent quotations will not be individually footnoted but are on file.
7. WWF Chairman Russel Train's March 3, 1993, testimony before the House Foreign Affairs Committee on world environmental issues. He listed "helping people voluntarily limit their family size" among four "broad points," but in the context of help to other countries.
8. ZPG Statement of Policy May 4, 1991, p. 5.
9. Leon Bouvier and Lindsey Grant *How Many Americans?* (San Francisco: Sierra Club Books, publications scheduled for August 1994), Tables

2.1, 2.2 and 2.6. The 43 percent estimate is for the period 1900; it includes post-1900 immigrants and their descendants.

10. For an examination of ways to influence fertility, see John R. Weeks "How to Influence Fertility," Chapter 15 in Lindsey Grant et al *Elephants in the Volkswagen* (New York: W.H. Freeman, 1992.)
11. Some 1.3 million "farm workers" illegally in the U.S. almost all of them Hispanic, applied for permanent residence, and almost all were accepted, at a time when the Bureau of Labor statistics estimated that there were only 234,000 Hispanic farm workers in the U.S., including citizens and legal residents. (*Statistical Abstract of the U.S. 1989*, Table 642.)
12. See Lindsey Grant *Demography and Health Care Reform*, NPG FORUM series, October 1993.
13. The connections between environmentalresource issues and population growth are treated at length in Leon Bouvier & Lindsey Grant *How Many Americans?* (op cit), Chapter 1.
14 Mark Mardon in *Sierra*, January/February 1994, pp. 12,14. He was responding to criticisms of his review of a book by Garrett Hardin.
15. For a refutation of the common argument that "immigrants do not supplant U.S. labor," see Donald L. Huddle, *Immigration, Jobs & Wages: The Misuses of Econometrics* (NPG FORUM, April 1992). For a report of an effort to measure the displacement in one city, see his NPG FORUM paper *Immigration and Jobs: the Process of Displacement* (NPG FORUM, May, 1992).
16. National Audubon Society and Population Crisis Committee *Why Population Matters. A handbook for the Environmental Activists*, 1991, p.5.
17. See Lindsey Grant *Free Trade and Cheap Labor: the President's Dilemma* (NPG FORUM paper, October 1991.)
18. Latino National Political Survey report "Latinos Speaking in Their own Voices," released 12-15-92, Table 7.24. Multiuniversity research project jointly funded by the Ford Foundation and a consortium of the Rockefeller. Spencer and Tinker foundations.
19. Bureau of labor Statistics *Employment and Earnings*, January 1993, p.22. The figures are for the non-institutional (e.g. not in jail) population twenty to twenty-four years of age not enrolled in school who have full time employment.
20. The 1982–92 fertility surveys are averaged, and all women with some college education are grouped together, to provide a meaningful sample size. Hispanics may consider themselves either black or White, and thus are included in the first two columns and separately reported in the third.
21. See "Population, Development and Environment. An NGO Position Paper for the 1994 International Conference on Population and Development" being circulated by the NWF. The 10-28-93 draft was co-signed by over eighty environmental, population, family planning and women's groups, worldwide.
22. For an excellent discussion of relations among the feminist, environmental and population movements, and of the Rio conference in particular, see Susan A. Cohen, "The Road from Rio to Cairo: Toward a Common Agenda" (*International Family Planning Perspectives*, 6-2-93), pp.61–66.
23. Tentatively to be titled *The Two Child Family*. A set of more gradual—and therefore more likely—but still optimistic projections of how population growth could be turned around in contained in the forthcoming How Many Americans?, op cit.
24. Reuters, Los Angeles, 8-13-93, 14:21.

THE TWO CHILD FAMILY

Lindsey Grant

May 1994

In the NPG FORUM series, we have detailed the benefits that a reversal of U.S. population growth would have on the pursuit of environmental, energy and resource policies, in the rescue of our collapsing cities, and in addressing the horrendous problems of a society moving toward a two-tiered stratification of a few "ins" and more "outs." In recent issues, we have argued that two present national projects—health reform and welfare reform—cannot be achieved without addressing population growth. We have made the point, repeatedly, that—unlike the proposals before the nation—a demographic policy would begin immediately to reap budgetary savings.

If the proposal finds few takers, it is perhaps because it conjures up fears of families limited to one child, of fertility controlled by forced sterilization and mandatory abortions, and of a "Fortress America" with all migration barred. The reality is much simpler and gentler. Let us show what could be achieved with the "two child family" and with immigration returned to the levels that prevailed for much of this century.

"STOP AT TWO"

The idea seems so transparently simple. Now that child mortality is under control, parents should have two children to carry on the family. The alternative—having many children so that some might survive to maturity—may once have been necessary but it is no longer relevant. To behave as if we still lived in that unhappy condition is to invite population growth that goes, within a very few generations, from intolerable to unimaginable to mathematically absurd.

The two child family is a rather attractive idea, for those who would avoid the loneliness of the only child or the prospect of old age with few descendants or none. On the other hand, if there are no more than two, parents and society can hope to provide them with a decent upbringing and—even at today's educational costs—an education to start them off in life. With no more than two, fewer families would fall below the poverty line.

THE AMERICAN FAMILY

When one is introduced to the mother of a dozen children, the traditional response used to be to offer congratulations. By now, it is as likely to be incredulity or embarrassment. "Stopping at two" is already the norm for most Americans. Of mothers completing their child bearing years, 70 percent have had only one or two children—thus in effect "stopping at two." Married women's expectations have dropped sharply in the past generation, from three or more children to an average of just over two.[1]

If parents indeed "stop at two," it would lead to a total fertility rate (TFR) of about 1.5 children because not all women have children, and some have only one.[2] In all the debate about population growth, I have yet to see anybody other than NPG call attention to this simple proposition. As we shall see, a national TFR of 1.5 would make possible a gradual turnaround in the population growth that presently drives our social and environmental problems.

IMMIGRATION IN MODERATION

The two child family alone will not get us there.

In 1900 we were a nation of less than 76 million. About 43 percent of the population increase since then has been post-1900 immigrants and their descendants. U.S. population right now, as best the government can tell, is passing 260 million.

The Census Bureau's middle projection for 2050 is 392 million, a rise of 50 percent. (They raised that estimate by 100 million after Congress passed the Immigration Act of 1990.) The high estimate reaches 522 million, a doubling. Of the population growth anticipated in the twenty-first century, nearly 90 percent will be post-2000 immigrants and their descendants.[3] In other words, immigration is the driving force in a continuing and remarkable surge of population growth.

That kind of growth will not just lead to a much more crowded nation. It will have profound impacts upon the environment, on renewable resources like farmland, forests and water, and on our society itself. Our cities are being pulled apart by tensions we do not yet fully really understand, as job competition among Americans and immigrants tightens, and the opportunities are dried up by technological change. There are direct money costs as immigrants require services or displace U.S. labor, but even more poignant is the waste of human beings and, over the long term, the damage to the land that our children will inherit.

We are on a treadmill as we try to keep up with the expanding population, and it is a race that mathematically we cannot win.

THE WAY OFF THE TREADMILL

The average annual level of recorded immigration from the passage of the Immigration Act of 1924 through the 1960s was 198,000. Immigration is now over a million (nobody knows the real figure, because we cannot measure illegal immigration or total emigration.) If we were willing to make the choice, and to bring net immigration back to 200,000, our demographic future would change dramatically. Net immigration of 200,000, by the way, would permit a somewhat higher level of total immigration, because some people emigrate.

If we moved instantly to the "two child family" and concurrently brought immigration under control at a level of 200,000, it would lead in the next century to the population projection shown in the graph.

In that graph, the black bars labeled "planned" represent the population curve that would result if net annual immigration were to drop instantly to 200,000 and the total fertility rate were to drop to an average of 1.5 children. The "unplanned" bars are for comparison and show where our population appears to be headed with current levels of fertility and immigration.[4]

The "planned" bars make the point that population could be brought down to 150 million in the next century, and stabilized there, with the relatively humane assumptions of the two child family and 200,000 annual net immigration. Perhaps even more dramatic is the "TFR" line (right scale). By the middle of the next century, families could be encouraged to have more children (for a TFR of 1.9), if as a society we decide that the 150 million range is a good size for the nation.

Singapore has actually gone through a comparable experience. It was so successful in using inducements and disincentives to bring fertility down that it has changed course and encouraged somewhat larger families.

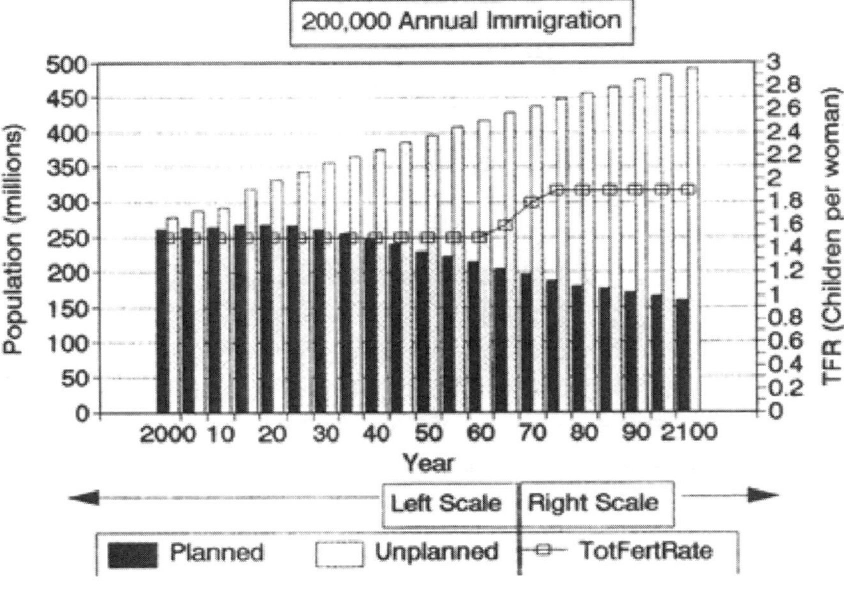

Figure 1.

The graph shows one way of achieving a desired demographic result. One could make another graph with fertility held low and an increase in immigration, and arrive at the same population size.

All demographic projections are just that: projections, not predictions. Fertility rates and migration change constantly, and these projections simply illustrate what trends would result from certain behavior patterns and immigration policies. Having said that, the "planned" curve is perhaps too dramatic. It would be more realistic to assume that it will take time to bring fertility down to 1.5. If we assume a gradual decline to that level by 2050, and annual immigration of 200,000, the population in 2100 will be 193 million and still declining.[5] The difference between the two projections is one of timing; the more gradual projection simply defers the day when the nation has the luxury of deciding what mix of fertility and migration would stabilize population at a desirable level.

GETTING THERE

To achieve a population turnaround, the two child family must be accepted as the place to stop. If third and fourth children are more than an exception, the demographic prospects grow dimmer. In pursuing the various ways of encouraging lower fertility,[6] this requires an explicit effort, both by leaders and role models and through the manipulation of incentives and disincentives, to make it clear that going beyond two is socially undesirable.

If this sounds like too much management for the American taste, I would suggest that the reader look again at the "unplanned" alternative in the graph and consider whether it is worth avoiding. The human tribe, including this nation, has learned how to manage mortality—at least for the time being—without a corresponding willingness to manage fertility. The result has been a profound worldwide demographic imbalance that lies at the heart of our own environmental and social problems and that generates the painful necessity for choosing between limiting immigration and continuing the demographic explosion here in the United States.

The combination of the two child family and a moderate immigration level of 200,000—which was sufficient to absorb many legitimate refugees from

World War II—offers the prospect of addressing our own future without slamming the door.

We need the courage to take on our demographic future. If we can so confidently urge African nations to bite the bullet and face their demographic problems, what about doing it ourselves?

NOTES:

1. U.S. Bureau of the Census, *Fertility of American Women: June 1992*, Publication P20-47O, June 1993, Tables 1 and 10. The propor-tion of one and two child families among Blacks and Hispanics is somewhat lower: 62 and 50 percent, respectively. This probably is a reflection of economic status and education more than of race, but data are not available to check that assumption. Expected number of children is almost identical for Blacks and Whites, still somewhat higher among Hispanics.
2. The TFRwould actually be 1.495. One can make the calculation from Table 1 of *Fertility of American Women* (note 1). The oldest cohort (forty to forty-five years old) has a (substantially) completed TFR of 1.999, of which 0.504 represents third order children and above. The residual is 1.495.
3. See Leon Bouvier and Lindsey Grant, *How Many Americans?* (San Francisco: Sierra Club Books, publication scheduled August 1994). Chapter 2.
4. The "unplanned" projection is from Bouvier and Grant, op cit. Chapter 2. The "planned" projection was run by Decision Demographics, a branch of the Population Reference Bureau, at the request of Negative Population Growth, Inc. in 1992 and is the basis for the calculations in NPG Position Paper *Why We Need a Smaller Population and How We Can Achieve It*, July 1992.
5. Bouvier and Grant, op cit. Table 4.4.
6. See John R. Weeks, *How to Influence Fertility: the Experience So Far*, in the NPG FORUM series, 1990, or in Lindsey Grant et al, *Elephants in the Volkswagen* (New York, W.H. Freeman & Co., 1992) Chapter 15.

PERSPECTIVES ON IMMIGRATION: THE ISSUE IS OVERPOPULATION

Lindsey Grant and Leon F. Bouvier

August 1994

This Op-Ed piece was originally published in the August 10, 1994 edition of the Los Angeles Times.

Given recent budgetary problems, it may be difficult to convince Californians that the drain on public services is not the principal issue in determining how much immigration we can afford. In the long run, however, the impact on population growth will be the most lasting legacy of our current immigration policies.

Largely as a result of immigration, the United States now has the fastest-growing population in the developed world, while immigration-driven population growth in California rivals that of some Third World countries. Population growth comes at great cost that cannot always be measured in dollars and cents.

First, we must realize that the human race is a part of the natural ecosystem of the Earth, not a privileged super-species that can transcend the laws of nature. The United States, because of its size and consumption habits, is most destabilizing entity within Earth's fragile ecosystem. Population growth here has a far more profound impact on that ecosystem than growth elsewhere.

The disturbances caused by human activities have accelerated dramatically in the past half a century. Driven by population growth and the technological explosion, these disturbances threaten not only the perpetuation of a way of life we have come to take for granted, but even the continuation of life systems as we understand them.

The good news is that the means for controlling and reversing these terrible forces are within our power. What we require, as a society, is the wisdom and understanding to employ them.

The United States grew from a nation of 76 million in 1900 to 249 million in 1990 (and to an estimated 260 million in 1994). Forty-three percent of that growth consisted of post-1900 immigrants and their descendants. Present immigration and fertility patterns place us on the path to a population of 397 million by 2050 and 492 million in 2100. More than 90 percent of that growth will be a direct result of post-2000 immigration.

In other words, our immigration policies place us in a league with the ruinous population growth patterns of countries like India and Bangladesh. Moreover, our growth is far more destructive because of our style of living. Continued high levels of consumption combined with the Third World-like population growth is a prescription for disaster.

We find the idea of another doubling of U.S. population thoroughly frightening. Consider the impact on many of the nation's current problems; urban decay and unemployment; energy dependence, nuclear waste and sewage disposal; loss of biodiversity and resistance of agricultural pests and diseases to pesticides and medicines; acid rain, climate change, depletion of water resources, topsoil erosion, loss of agricultural lands and destruction of forests, wetlands and fisheries, to name just some.

Nevertheless, there is the possibility of light at the end of the tunnel. We could bring population growth to a halt in the next century and even turn it around. First, fertility would have to fall gradually from current levels of two children per woman to and average of 1.5. But even that would not be enough to achieve population stablization in the United States. Without substantial reductions in immigration, to perhaps 200,000 annually, our population still would reach 337 million by 2050.

A return of immigration to the levels that prevailed through the middle of this century will not happen by itself. We must persuade our national leaders that, while the problems of Haitian boat people and other would-be immigrants are heart-rending and real, they cannot be solved by sacrificing our own future. The United States has an obligation to its own people and descendants, one that cannot be served by allowing the population to swell to half a billion.

A commitment to our own future does not mean ignoring the problems of the rest of the world. Many developing countries are caught in a population explosion, and the United States should make family-planning assistance the first priority in foreign aid. No amount of aid will have much significance unless population growth is curbed as well.

Our primary obligation is to our own future and our primary responsibility is to control our own consumption and population growth. Our national policy goal should be to avoid adding to the annual load of pollution and environmental damage, and then to reduce it. That can happen only if we lower our fertility rate and our immigration level.

THE CAIRO CONFERENCE ON POPULATION AND DEVELOPMENT

Donald Mann, President

Negative Population Growth, Inc.

August 1994

The preparations for the International Conference on Population and Development (ICPD) to be held in Cairo, September 5–13, 1994, leave me convinced that the Conference will offer a totally inadequate response to the crisis confronting humanity as a result of the relentless growth of world population.

If the international community cannot propose better ways to stop world population growth than those recommended in the Draft Final Document for the Conference, then we must reconcile ourselves to living in a world, a few decades from now, with 12 to 14 billion people, or more. There is the disturbing possibility, of course, that world population growth will be halted long before those numbers are reached by higher mortality rates brought on by famine and pestilence, at an incalculable cost in human suffering.

Part of the problem is that some refuse to see any crisis. But it looms nonetheless. With a present population of nearly six billion, already far beyond a sustainable level, and still growing by almost 100 million each year, the world faces a cataclysmic threat.

The Draft Final Document and the twenty-year Program of Action, which set the agenda for the Conference, offer us only business as usual, as is evident from its grave flaws and omissions:

LACK OF POPULATION AND FERTILITY GOALS

Setting specific goals for world population size, and for fertility, then recommending policies to achieve them, should be the central concern and primary focus of the Conference. Sadly, that is not what the Preparatory Documents offer. As Lindsey Grant, a former State Department population expert recently noted, "Running a population program without population goals is about like trying to build a road without deciding where it should go."[1]

For the Conference to produce action for change, the following should have been its essential goals:

1. Halting population growth before world population reaches eight billion (the awesome momentum imparted by past population growth makes it virtually impossible to stop it before that).
2. Gaining acceptance of the two-child maximum family as essential to achieve sub-replacement fertility.

Setting such goals, which are designed to halt population growth as soon as it is humanely possible to do so, then to reverse it, would reveal a massive problem, one that both our own government, and the international community, have been simply unwilling to grapple with. The problem is that to achieve those goals measures would be required that go beyond family planning programs.

Specifically, family planning would have to be supplemented by non-coercive incentives to encourage couples not to have more than two children.

The Draft, however, frowns on just such "schemes," noting in Chapter 7.20:

> "In support of fully responsible, informed, (legally permissible) reproductive choices, Governments are encouraged to focus most of their efforts towards meeting their population and development objectives through education and voluntary measures rather than schemes involving incentives and disincentives."

But what if the measures recommended offer little hope of halting population growth before world population doubles or triples? What then? Do we just go quietly to our doom, or do we consider measures that offer the hope of halting and reversing population growth soon, such as non-coercive incentives to reduce desired family size?"

AN UNFOUNDED CLAIM

The twenty-year Program of Action proffers many goals and objectives, but inducements to reduce desired family size are missing. If the action program's proposals were adopted, what would be their impact on world population growth?

The Preamble of the Draft claims that, "Implementation of the goals and objectives contained in the present twenty-year Program of Action . . . would result in world population growth during this period and beyond at levels close to the United Nations' low variant." That is an astonishing and baseless claim. According to the United Nations' low variant (for projected population growth) world population would peak at 7.813 billion in 2050, and then gradually decline.

For that to happen, major and unprecedented declines in fertility would have to occur in a very short time. Specifically, by 2025–2030, fertility would have to decline by the following percentages: in Africa by 61 percent; in Latin America by 34 percent; in China by 25 percent; in India by 57 percent; and for the world as a whole by 44 percent.

This means that in just thirty to thirty-five years the total fertility rate would have to fall:[2]

> In Africa, from 5.9 now to 2.31
> In Latin America from 3.2 now to 2.11
> In China from 2.0 now to 1.50
> In India from 3.6 now to 2.04
> In the entire world from 3.2 now to 1.79

The actions recommended in the Draft Final Document rely chiefly on family planning to achieve fertility reduction. They also emphasize gender equity, and the empowerment of women and improvement of their status. Not only are these goals extremely important and laudable in their own right, but they would also help to reduce fertility. As Lindsey Grant has pointed out in a recent NPG Forum paper, "Improvements in the educational and economic status for women contribute to fertility decline, and the correlation has long been recognized."

Significant progress toward those commendable goals, however, will require the virtual remaking of the entire societies and cultures of many nations. Overcoming sheer inertia and centuries-old customs will require time, measured in decades if not centuries, while the planet's population crisis is now. We must improve the education and status of women, but with no illusions that it will markedly reduce fertility within the short space of a few decades.

In sum, it is unrealistic to think that the measures recommended in the Draft Final Document, even if fully implemented, could result, in only thirty to thirty-five years, in the dramatic declines in fertility noted above. The drafters of the Preamble, and those who approved it, must re-examine their data. If the review shows Conference officials that the statement in question is in fact wrong, then the Conference leaders should delete it from the Final Document.

NEEDED: RESPONSIBILITIES TO BALANCE RIGHTS

The Draft asserts an array of rights of various sorts. But it says little about reproductive responsibilities, either of individuals or of nations. Such a vitally important subject deserves an entire chapter in the Draft. It should state explicitly that individuals, nations, and international organizations have the responsibility to make their actions and policies consistent with halting world population growth as quickly as is humanely possible.

A right of nations that is not mentioned in the Draft, but one that deserves emphasis, is the right and responsibility of all nations to make their immigration policies conform with the objective of population stability or reduction.

A troubling omission is the Draft's silence about the responsibility of each nation to stabilize its population size at a sustainable level, well within the carrying capacity of its resources and environment.

For most countries in the world, and certainly for the United States, that would mean a substantial reduction in present population size. That fact should be explicitly affirmed.

The devastation of the planet's resources and environment by overpopulation threatens all nations. But in a world of sovereign states overpopulation can only be solved by the actions and commitment of each individual nation.

CAN ANY "RIGHT" BE ABSOLUTE?

With regard to individual rights, the Draft Final Document states that, "All couples and individuals have the basic right to decide freely and responsibly the number and spacing of their children and to have the information, education and means to do so." That is, of course, a prescription for further population growth, since 90 percent of future world population growth is projected to occur in the developing countries where couples desire, on average, three or more children.

If that statement could be deleted, and the following statement substituted for it, it might prove to be, if heeded, the salvation of the world: "Because world population growth cannot otherwise be halted, in nations that have not yet achieved a sub-replacement fertility, no couple or individual should have the right to have more than two children." The argument for that statement of rights is both simple and irrefutable. Population growth can never be halted unless almost all couples and individuals around the world have two or fewer children. Yet, many people and organizations, including our own government, have great difficulty acknowledging that simple, indisputable fact!

A recent report by the Pontifical Academy of Sciences, a lay panel of the Vatican, stated the obvious. It noted that increases in life-span and advances in medical care "have made it unthinkable to sustain indefinitely a birth rate that notably exceeds the level of two children per couple—in other words the requirement to guarantee the future of humanity."

All nations must make the two-child maximum family, and a sub-replacement level of fertility their fundamental planning goals. Those should have been a central theme of the Cairo Conference.

Blind adherence to an impractical idea (such as the unqualified right of parents to have as many children as they wish), regardless of consequences, can prove fatal. One is reminded of the sad tale of the king and queen that Thorstein Veblen recounted in his book, *The Theory of the Leisure Class.* The royal couple was obliged by long tradition never to walk, but to be carried about on their thrones by servants. One day the palace caught fire, the courtiers fled, and the king and queen, unable to escape by walking away, were obliged to remain on their thrones and were burned to death.

FAMILY PLANNING IS ESSENTIAL, BUT NOT ENOUGH

Why does the international community (and our own government) persist in espousing family planning as the means to halting world population growth, even though it is obvious that family planning programs alone are insufficient to achieve that goal?

Family planning is a necessary, but not sufficient, measure for halting population growth in most of the world's nations. The provision of contraceptive information and services, together with safe, legalized abortion are essential parts of any national population policy. But in countries where the desired family size is three or more children, family planning must be supplemented by non-coercive incentives to encourage couples, and individuals, to have no more than two children.

In an article in the March 1994 issue of Population and Development Review, Dr. Lant H. Pritchett, Senior Economist at the World Bank, argues convincingly that high fertility primarily reflects desired births, and that couples are roughly able to achieve their fertility targets. According to Dr. Pritchett, " 'Excess' or 'unwanted' fertility plays a minor role in explaining fertility differences. Moreover, the level of contraceptive use, measures of contraceptive availability (such as 'unmet need'), and family planning effort have little impact on fertility after controlling for fertility desires."[3]

Dr. Pritchett concludes that, "Our analysis indicates that the challenge of reducing fertility is the challenge of reducing people's fertility desires, not reducing 'unwanted' fertility."

Findings of Dr. Pritchett and others bear out what we at NPG have contended for nearly a quarter of a century: the present focus of population assistance programs on family planning alone should yield to a twin focus on family planning and on non-coercive incentives to encourage couples everywhere to desire two children at most. Their view, and NPG's as well, is that, "fertility desires are largely determined by socioeconomic forces other than family planning and that fertility desires determine fertility."

But even if the opposite were true, and contraceptive prevalence did significantly reduce fertility, as family planning advocates mistakenly believe, our main contention would still be valid: Incentives are necessary to reduce fertility sufficiently to achieve the United Nations' low variant, which requires a total fertility rate of 1.7 by 2025–2030.

In support of that assertion, consider the following example. According to Steven Sinding of the Rockefeller Foundation, if all the demand for family planning were met, the use of contraceptives in developing countries would rise from 51 percent to more than 60 percent.[4] Such an increase would cause fertility to fall from the current average of four children per woman to about three, Sinding believes. If that estimate is accurate, such a decline in fertility would, of course, be a major step in the right direction, but it would still fall far short of the 1.7 total fertility required in order to achieve the United Nations' low variant.

SUSTAINABLE DEVELOPMENT, AN OXYMORON?

The Draft Final Document is replete with calls for sustained economic growth, and sustainable development, ignoring the fact that the inevitable by-products of economic and industrial activity are resource depletion and environmental pollution. United Nations documents often cite the complex relations among population, resources and the environment. Yet, in reality, the relationship is simple and direct. Our impact on the environment is the product of numbers of people times per capita consumption.

Per capita consumption can be reduced in some measure by changing life-styles, and by using energy and materials more efficiently. But those measures alone would not be sufficient for the creation of a truly sustainable economy in a world with our present population of nearly six billion people.

The evidence is overwhelming that sustainable development is impossible in a world with a population of that size. If impossibility admits of degrees, how much more impossible would it be in a world of 10, or 12, or 14 billion people? Can the world provide a higher standard of living for ever increasing numbers? The question answers itself. Attempts to achieve that impossible dream of unending growth with sustainability are doomed to fail.

NPG'S PROPOSAL: PROMPT REDUCTION OF WORLD FERTILITY

NPG's conviction is that the world must expect disaster if population growth is not stopped short of eight billion, and then reversed. After all, eight billion is larger by a factor of at least four than the two billion or less we consider to be the optimum size for world population.[5]

The world community must set adequate goals, and stop population growth rather than try to accommodate to it. An interim goal must be to stop population growth short of eight billion, with the long term goal of reducing it to an optimum size. We propose measures that would result in achieving the United Nations' low variant, i.e., stopping population growth when world population peaks at 7.8 billion by the middle of the next century, after which it would start a gradual decline.

Mere attainment of a replacement level of fertility (roughly, an average of 2.1 children per woman) would not stop growth short of eight billion. A sub-replacement level of fertility is essential—specifically, the 1.7 rate projected by the United Nations by 2025–2030 to reach the low variant population projection. That means that fertility of women around the world would have to fall rapidly by nearly half, from the 3.2 they average now. Such a drastic reduction of fertility would, beyond any doubt, require measures that go beyond family planning.

THE URGENCY OF CHANGING DESIRED FAMILY SIZE

Unless we can succeed in reducing desired family size in almost all nations to not more than two children, there is no hope of achieving sub-replacement fertility, and, therefore, no hope of halting population growth before world population reaches eight billion. Lowering desired family size in all nations (including the United States) that have not yet achieved a sub-replacement level of fertility, is the critical key to halting growth short of eight billion.

There is a good deal of controversy about how best to go about reducing fertility. As we have seen above, increased contraceptive prevalence by itself is not the answer. Couples use contraception to achieve their desired family size, which is independent of contraceptive supply. The correlation between contraceptive prevalence and fertility is clear. But, as Dr. Pritchett points out above, association does not prove causation. Rather than contraception prevalence resulting in lower fertility, it is the other way around. Lower desired family size results in increased contraceptive prevalence. In brief, it seems clear that we cannot look to increased supply of contraceptives alone to reduce fertility, but rather we must increase demand for contraceptives by reducing desired family size.

Achieving population stabilization will take more than universal access to family planning, Judith Bruce, senior associate at the Population Council, told the House Foreign Affairs Committee last September. The Population Council estimates that if today's level of unwanted childbearing fertility were entirely eliminated, the developing world would still move only one-third of the way towards population stabilization.[6]

That is because people in many societies want more than two children (the average desired family size in sub-Saharan Africa remains between five and six) and the built-in momentum of population growth would keep world population rising for decades after replacement fertility was achieved.

CAN THE WORLD WAIT FOR "MODERNIZATION"?

How about modernization to reduce fertility? As Lindsey Grant writes in his recent NPG Forum paper on the Cairo Conference:

> "Modernization, eventually, results in lower fertility. High fertility and resultant population growth throughout much of the third world are delaying that modernization and perhaps making it impossible. The issue is how to get birth rates down without waiting for the traditional 'demographic transition,' which may never happen in much of the third world."[1]

Assertions that eradicating poverty is a prerequisite for halting population growth have the process backwards. Only by halting their population growth can the developing nations begin to bring their standard of living up to an adequate level.

Improving the education and status of women holds a great deal of promise for the long term, and is essential for its own sake. Like modernization, however, it cannot realistically be expected to markedly lower desired family size in the near term.

There is almost no chance that better education and higher status of women will come fast enough, and in enough countries, to lower fertility sufficiently to achieve the goal we propose: halting the growth of world population at 7.8 billion by 2050, and then reversing it.

Certainly we must move ahead with family planning, modernization, and improving the education and status of women. The point is, however, that even taken all together, they would be clearly incapable of achieving the United Nations' low variant. Those programs must be supplemented by non-coercive incentives to reduce desired family size in almost all nations to not more than two children.

There is simply no other way. Incentives do not, of course, guarantee the attainment of our population goal. But they do offer a reasonable expectation of success.

NON-COERCIVE INCENTIVES

The purpose of incentives is to reduce desired family size in a non-coercive manner. There can be incentives for individuals and couples, as well as community incentives for villages or even entire regions. Possible

incentives vary widely, and include tax and financial incentives, and those for schooling, housing, jobs, pensions and late marriages, among others.
They also include cash bonuses for voluntary sterilization for individuals of fertile age who have already had no more than one or two children, and desire to have no more. Such bonuses should not be paid to health care providers, since that invites coercion.

For example, NPG has long recommended that a tax credit be given to couples in the United States with not more than two children, but that this credit be taken away completely if that number is exceeded.

China and Singapore are examples of countries where incentives have resulted in unprecedented and rapid declines in fertility. In China, from 1965–1970 to 1975–1980, fertility fell by more than three births per woman, largely due to its national program of incentives and disincentives.

There were undoubtedly elements of coercion in the Chinese program, and those elements have been widely, and rightly, denounced. Without either condoning or defending those coercive practices, we should, however, endeavor to understand the magnitude of the problem China faces. Chinese authorities point out that they are struggling to feed 22 percent of the world's population on just seven percent of its arable land. They maintain that the staggering pressure of China's huge and still growing population on a land of scarce resources made tough controls unavoidable.

The point here is that a program of incentives need not be coercive, and is not, as some might argue, inherently so. Because China's program was in some respects flawed, does not mean that the entire concept should be abandoned. No less an authority than the late Bernard Berelson, formerly President of The Population Council, had this to say about incentives:

> " . . . by definition incentives are rewards or penalties, tangible or intangible, given to a couple or group in order to induce some specific fertility behavior. As such, they are expressly designed to alter parental choice; their use would otherwise be unnecessary.
>
> " . . . positive incentives serve to enlarge options, not diminish them, and hence can serve both freedom and (interclass) justice. The individual is presented with a choice he did not have in the absence of the incentive, since he can decline the incentive, he has lost nothing from his previous state but has gained an option—the incentive rather than his normal fertility behavior."[7]

TO SUMMARIZE

The Draft Final Document for the Cairo Conference simply reflects the conventional wisdom with regard to population size and growth. It does not come to grips sufficiently with the problem of world overpopulation. In discussing it in this paper, I have tried to comment on these aspects of it:

1. **A goal for stopping world population growth.** The Draft does not mention one. I have argued that the only adequate goal is to follow the United Nations' low variant, and to stop world population growth at 7.8 billion by 2050, then reverse it. Even that goal, the best we could possibly hope for, would result in an increase of 2.2 billion people in world population in a little more than a half century! That would increase our present world population of 5.6 billion by 39 percent. It is sobering to realize that because of the tremendous momentum of past population

growth, and the resulting age structure of world population, we cannot possibly halt population growth before the number of people added to world population (2.2 billion) exceeds the total world population of 1.65 billion at the beginning of the century.

2. **What measures would be necessary to achieve the United Nations' low variant?** Incentives are essential. Family planning, modernization, and better status and education for women alone are incapable of achieving that goal. As I have tried to show, reaching the low variant would require tremendous reductions in fertility in a very short time.
3. **Sustainable development.** According to the conventional wisdom, sustainable development is possible in a world of 10 billion people, or even more. I have argued that we cannot possibly create a sustainable economy in a world with our present population, much less in one with double that number.

A far smaller world population than today's is the *sine qua non* for sustainability.

THE OPTIMUM RATE OF GROWTH IS NEGATIVE

World population should have been stabilized long ago at one to two billion (it was 1.65 billion at the beginning of this century). Our urgent task now is to halt world population growth as soon as humanely possible, then to reduce world population gradually, so that it can eventually be stabilized at a sustainable level of two billion or less.

To some, that goal might appear utopian. But it is not nearly as unrealistic as the expectation that we can create a sustainable economy in a world of six billion people, or more, with an adequate standard of living for all.

In any event, there is no need to decide now on an exact number, or range, for optimum population size. At this point a precise numerical target is relatively unimportant. For purposes of setting population policy, the central fact to be taken into account is that optimum size is substantially below our present numbers.

It follows, therefore, that what is needed is a gradual decline in population size, and that can only be achieved by a negative rate of growth. Once it is agreed that we need a smaller population, it should be obvious that the optimum rate of growth is negative, not positive.

At best, it will take a half century or more to halt population growth, and then reach a negative rate of growth. A substantial reduction in numbers will take much longer. We will have ample time, therefore, to do research and decide at what level world population should eventually be stabilized.

The world is now vastly overpopulated. Population must be rolled back to a state of balance with our resources and environment. That can only be achieved with a negative rate of growth. That must be our top priority goal.

WHITHER HUMANITY?

Erich Fromm, the psychologist, once said, "The history of man is a graveyard of great cultures that came to catastrophic ends because of their incapacity for planned, rational, voluntary reaction to challenge."

It is more than likely that the entire human race will meet with catastrophe if our present unwillingness to face up to the crisis caused by world population growth continues for just a few more years. As Eugene Linden wrote in a recent essay in Time magazine, "If governments continue to fiddle while human numbers explode, it becomes ever more likely the horsemen of famine, disease and anarchy will have their day."[8]

I am convinced that if we do not take steps now to halt, and then reverse, world population growth, humankind's ancient dream of a good life for all, free from material want, will be destroyed, perhaps forever.

NOTES:

1. Lindsey Grant, *"The Cairo Conference: Feminists vs. the Pope,"* NPG Forum paper, July 1994.
2. Current fertility from the Population Reference Bureau, *1994 World Population Data Sheet*. Target fertility from the United Nations publication, *Long-Range World Population Projections, Two Centuries of Population Growth*, 1950–2150, published in 1992.
3. Lant H. Pritchett, *Desired Fertility and the Impact of Population Policies*, Population and Development Review, Volume 20, Number 1, March 1994.
4. *Scientific American*, December 1993, p. 67.
5. See Gretchen C. Daily, Anne H. Ehrlich, and Paul R. Ehrlich, *Optimum Human Population Size*, Population and Environment, Volume 15, Number 6, July 1994. The authors conclude that, "To us it seems reasonable to assume that, until cultures and technologies change radically, the optimum number of people to exist simultaneously lies in the vicinity of 1.5 to 2 billion people."
6. *See Global Stewardship*, May/June 1994, published monthly by the Population Reference Bureau, Inc., Washington, D.C.
7. Bernard Berelson and Jonathan Lieberson, *Government Efforts to Influence Fertility: The Ethical Issues*, Population and Development Review, Volume 5, Number 4, December 1979.
8. *Time* magazine, July 1994, Volume VIII, Number 4.

THE CASE FOR REDUCING IMMIGRATION FROM OVER ONE MILLION TO 100,000 A YEAR

Donald Mann, President

Negative Population Growth, Inc.

February 1995

The evidence is overwhelming that with its present population of over 260 million, the U.S. is already vastly overpopulated in terms of the long range carrying capacity of its resources and environment. Yet we continue to grow rapidly, by 25 to 30 million each decade.

Contrary to our own national interest, we now permit over a million immigrants to settle here each year. Because it contributes to the growth of our population, immigration is basically, and most importantly, an environmental issue. Indeed it is the driving force behind the population growth that is propelling our nation rapidly down the road to environmental ruin. Projections show that if present trends continue, 89 percent of our population growth in the next century will come from post-2000 immigrants and their descendants.

If we are to have any hope of achieving a smaller, more sustainable population size, we must halt illegal immigration and sharply reduce legal immigration.

THE IMPLICATIONS OF CURRENT TRENDS

If our fertility remains at its present rate of 2.0 (an average of two children per woman) and if immigration at the present level continues, we will grow to nearly 500 million before the end of the next century, almost twice our present size.

It could be even worse. According to demographers Dennis S. Ahlburg and James W. Vaupel we could easily have a population of 811 million (near the present population of India) by 2080. They write:

> A U.S. population of 800 million may seem incredible, but the annual average growth rate that produces it runs at only 1.3 percent per year. This is the same as the average annual growth rate that has prevailed in the United States over the last half-century, and not too much above the one percent average growth rate of the last decade.

And even worse scenarios are possible. Demographer Leon Bouvier has asked the question: But what if American women had an “extra” child from now on (that is, three births as advocated by some) and what if immigration doubled to two million (as advocated by some)? What would that mean demographically?

Dr. Bouvier’s answer: By 2050, the U.S. population would surpass 677 million; by 2075 it would have reached one billion and still be growing rapidly!

We simply cannot allow any of those scenarios to happen. Such growth would destroy our environment, our standard of living and the quality of our lives. *We at NPG believe that our goal must be to stabilize our population at not more than150 million,*

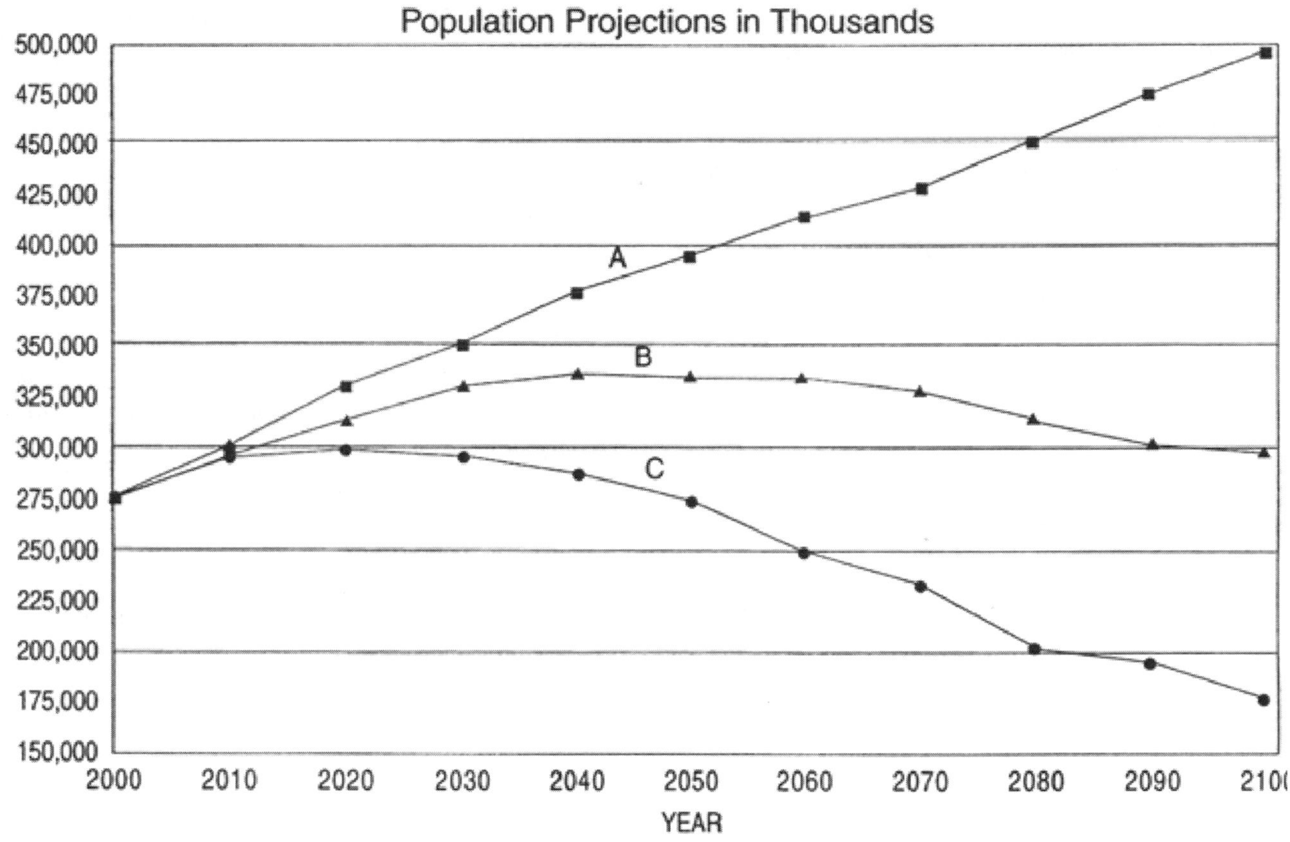

Projected Population of the United States: 2000-2100

Figure 1.

our nation's size in 1950. We consider that to be the optimum size for sustainable use of our resources.

There is no need, however, for agreement now on the exact size of the smaller population we need. Even small reduction in today's numbers, as we shall see, will at best take many decades to achieve. For now we need only agree on the urgent need to halt, and then reverse, U.S. population growth.

STEPS TO PUT THE UNITED STATES ON THE PATH TOWARD A SMALLER POPULATION

To halt as quickly as possible, and then reverse, the disastrous growth of our population, we need to do three things:

1) *We need to reduce legal immigration from the present level of 900,000 a year to a maximum of 100,000 a year,* which would include all relatives, refugees, asylees, and skilled workers.
2) *We need to halt illegal immigration.* Over 300,000 illegal immigrants now settle here each

year, joining the estimated four to five million illegal aliens already residing here permanently. Those numbers must be reduced to near zero.

3) *We need to make every effort to reduce our fertility from the present 2.0 to 1.5,* a goal NPG has long recommended. If most women had no more than two children, our fertility would fall to 1.5 because many women choose to have no children, or only one.

The first goal would be the easiest to achieve. It would only require Federal legislation. The second and third goals would be more difficult, but, given the political will, can be achieved.

THREE SCENARIOS

The graph above projects three different paths that our population growth might follow, depending on different levels of fertility and immigration.

For all three of these projections it is assumed that both illegal immigration (entering) and emigration of citizens (leaving) are gradually reduced to roughly the same very low level so that their net effect on population is neutral.

The particular assumptions for each projection are as follows:

Line A—That present rates of fertility (2.0) and net immigration (legal and illegal) or one million a year will continue.

Line B—That our fertility rate, now 2.0, is gradually reduced to 1.5 by the year 2050, while net immigration remains at its present level of one million a year.

Line C—That our fertility rate, now 2.0, is gradually reduced to 1.5 by the year 2050 (the same as Line B), and that, starting in 1996, legal immigration is capped at 100,000 per year, including all relatives, refugees, asylees, and skilled workers, and remains at that level thereafter.

ANALYSIS OF THE THREE PROJECTIONS

Projection A—The only comment possible is a simple one: this line leads straight to disaster.

Projection B—Under these assumptions (reduced fertility, but immigration at the current level) our population would continue to grow for another 55 years, not peaking until 2050 at 337 million, *some 75 million greater than our population today.*

U.S. population would then begin a slow decline, reaching 298 million by the end of the next century. Population then would still be some 36 million larger than our present 262 million, *and 121 million greater than in Projection C (low fertility and low immigration).*

The conclusion to be drawn is obvious: *If massive immigration is allowed to continue, it will be well over a century before our population gets back to its present unsustainable level*, even if fertility is drastically reduced.

Projection C—This scenario (lower fertility and drastically reduced immigration) demonstrates the gravity of our predicament. Even with drastic reductions in both fertility and immigration our population *would still grow for twenty-five more years*. It would not peak until 2020 at 300 million, and then begin a very slow and gradual decline.

It would then take another thirty-five years after 2020 for our population to return to its present size of around 260 million. Under the best case scenario, therefore, with low fertility and with immigration reduced to 100,000 a year, *it would still take at least sixty years for our population to get back to its present size.* That is an astonishing, and even frightening, fact that says much about the awesome momentum of population growth.

Reducing our population to a smaller, sustainable level would, of course, take much longer. Only by the end of the next century would our population decline to around 180 million, still a considerable distance from the optimum of 150 million, but far less burdensome to the environment than our present numbers.

In a few more years, however, our population would decline to the level we consider optimum—150 million—and could then be stabilized at that level, even allowing a slight increase in fertility and/or immigration.

THE PROBLEM WITH COUNTING ON DECLINES IN FERTILITY

The projections represented by Lines B and C were based on the assumption that our fertility rate would gradually decline from its present 2.0 to 1.5 by 2050.

Is that being overly optimistic? Probably it is. Dr. Bouvier has pointed out that no country has ever exhibited for so long a time the low rate of fertility that we have assumed for Projections B and C.

Fertility rates are unpredictable: even with tax and other incentives to encourage lower fertility (long recommended by NPG) there is no guarantee that fertility rates will not increase rather than decrease. Over the last nineteen years, for example, the trend has been upward, from a low of 1.7 in 1976 to 2.0 in the last few years.

And, in any case, lowering our fertility to the rate assumed for Projections B and C would be virtually impossible if high immigration continued (as in Projection B) since the fertility of most current immigrants typically remains high in the early generations.

That is all the more reason why we must reduce immigration to a level consistent with our long-term national interest. Reducing immigration is a much faster and more certain way to get results than counting on fertility decline.

Apportioning the 100,000 Slots for Legal Immigration

If legal immigration were capped at 100,000 per year as we propose, how might those numbers best be allocated to meet the country's essential needs? Recognizing that the political process must decide, NPG believes that the following allocation would be reasonable:

75,000 —	Spouses and minor children of American citizens
5,000 —	Persons with extraordinary skills.
20,000 —	Refugees and asylees.
100,000	

Immediate relatives of citizens now enter without limit, outside of quota. The 75,000 yearly quota on this category of immigrants would include only spouses and unmarried children under eighteen, and not parents, as is now the case.

For the first few years, the number of immediate relatives seeking to immigrate might exceed the yearly quota; some waiting might therefore be required. After an initial period, however, a quota of 75,000 for immediate relatives should be adequate.

To discourage chain migration, immigrants entering under the "skilled" and "refugee" categories would only be allowed to immigrate as family units, with spouses and any minor, unmarried children charged against the ceiling at that time.

The Attorney General should have the authority to shift numbers among the categories according to need, but under no circumstances should the total number exceed 100,000 per year.

CAN ILLEGAL IMMIGRATION BE STOPPED?

Yes, it can and must be stopped. Any reduction in legal immigration would be futile if illegal immigration were allowed to continue. If legal immigration were reduced, continuing our present lax controls at the border and ports of entry would invite even higher illegal entries.

What can be done? The means for stopping illegal immigration and reducing to near zero the number of illegal immigrants living here permanently will be the subject of an NPG Policy Paper to be published soon. We will include here only a brief summary.

1. **First and foremost we must have a secure national system of identification.** This is a fundamental requirement without which there is simply no hope of controlling illegal immigration.

   A secure system of identification must include an upgraded, tamper-proof Social Security card with personal identifiers such as a photograph and fingerprints. Manufacture or possession of false identification documents should be made a felony punishable by long prison terms, and, in the case of aliens, deportation.

   Closely linked to the secure ID system should be a national computer registry, as proposed by Barbara Jordan, Chair of the U.S. commission on Immigration Reform. A centralized registry would permit telephone verification by employers that a job applicant was either a citizen or a legal resident, and therefore eligible to work.

   A registry would also allow local officials to easily determine the eligibility of applicants for a driver's license, school enrollment, or public assistance. The telephone verification procedure would place verification responsibility where it should be, and should always have been, on the shoulders of Federal authorities.

2. **We must stop rewarding illegal aliens with jobs and benefits** and start penalizing them severely for breaking U.S. laws. Illegal aliens who have been deported once should forfeit forever their right to seek legal entry. If they return here, they should be penalized by a mandatory prison term, and a fine or confiscation of property.

3. **We must reduce to near zero the population of illegal aliens now living here**, now estimated at four to five million. Their presence is a magnet for millions of others who perceive, correctly, that there is little risk in entering our country illegally, and, once here, remaining indefinitely.

Congress must increase the budget for the Immigration and Naturalization Service so that it can identify and deport large numbers of illegal aliens. The INS should set as its goal at least 400,000 deportations a year, but it does not now have the resources for such a program. In 1992 it deported only 38,000 illegal aliens.

Congress must also simplify the rules on deportation, and Federal, state and local investigative agencies must be required to cooperate fully with federal immigration officials.

Some of our proposals may seem harsh, especially when compared with our Federal government's present ineffective measures. We must bear in mind, however, that as poverty and social unrest increase in most third world countries (the direct result of overpopulation and continued population growth) the number of poor and desperate people seeking to enter our country illegally is bound to increase greatly.

Strong measures to halt illegal immigration are the only realistic response to the fact that tens of millions of people are absolutely determined to flout our laws by entering our country illegally.

REASONS FOR NOT HALTING LEGAL IMMIGRATION COMPLETELY

An NPG member wrote me recently and asked, "Since our country is already overpopulated, and needs above all to halt and then reverse its population growth, why does NPG advocate any legal immigration at all, since immigration adds to our population growth?"

That is a difficult question. In an already seriously overpopulated country such as the United States how can any immigration be justified?

Demographically speaking, there is no question that our nation would be far better off with zero immigration. But given our history and long traditions, it would be virtually impossible to stop all immigration, and NPG does not advocate doing so.

The United States cannot, and should not, turn its back on all legitimate refugees, even though we can only hope to take in a tiny fraction of all the hundreds of millions who have a well-founded fear of persecution, or who live under oppressive regimes, or who suffer from economic or environmental distress.

In addition, our country will benefit from admitting a small number of scientists and other exceptionally skilled persons. A limit of 5,000 a year, including spouses and minor children, should not cause a serious brain-drain from other nations.

Finally, it would be difficult indeed to sustain an immigration policy that denied American citizens the right to bring their spouses and minor children here.

A maximum immigration ceiling of 100,000 yearly would allow us to meet our core domestic and international obligations. However, if illegal immigration is not halted with the next few years, then ALL legal immigration should be suspended until illegal immigration has been stopped.

IS NPG ANTI-IMMIGRANT?

No, it is not. We believe that those who have already settled here legally deserve our respect and the full protection of our laws. Nor does it follow that we harbor negative feelings toward would-be immigrants because we advocate restricting immigration to a level consistent with our own national interest.

IS NPG ANTI-MASS IMMIGRATION?

Yes, unequivocally, for all the reasons we have discussed.

Could our recommendations be accurately and fairly characterized as being xenophobic, nativism, racist, isolationist or any other label that proponents of massive immigration commonly apply to those who advocate reasonable levels of immigration?

Certainly not. Immigration of 100,000 a year is, by world standards, a generous number. It appears small only in comparison with today's astronomical numbers. Curiously, well-intentioned advocates of massive immigration never reckon with the likely impact of their recommendations on our population and environment.

OUR RESPONSIBILITY TO THE WORLD COMMUNITY

Our primary responsibility is to present and future generations of Americans, not to the entire world. As responsible stewards we have, first and foremost, a moral obligation to preserve for future generations of Americans the magnificent land we have inherited.

We cannot fulfill that obligation unless we succeed in stabilizing our population at a lower, more sustainable level. If we fail to do that, we will be unable to maintain a viable society and economy, and will become powerless to help either our own people or the community of nations.

At the same time we sympathize with the plight of less fortunate people in other countries who want to come here. We should do all we can to help their nations improve their standards of living in a sustainable way. That would mean, above all, helping them (if, of course, they want our help) to halt and then reverse their catastrophic population growth.

But while overpopulation is a global problem, in a world of sovereign nations the solutions must ultimately be worked out at the local level, that is, by each nation. The problems of already overpopulated, and still rapidly growing, developing countries are beyond solution by emigration: the numbers are too vast.

The population of the developing countries is growing by some 80 million a year. Their population increase over the next fifteen years or so will by itself exceed the present population of all the developed countries, roughly 1.2 billion.

Developing countries can never relieve their poverty and permanently improve their standard of living until they stabilize their numbers at a sustainable level. In most cases that level is only a small fraction of their present numbers. The time required to achieve this goal will have to be measured in centuries.

Perhaps the greatest contribution our country could make toward eliminating world poverty would be to serve as an example of a nation that is committed to working toward a population size that is in balance with its resources and environment, and sustainable indefinitely.

SUMMING UP

Because we have allowed our nation to become seriously overpopulated, we are in deep trouble. A quick and painless solution does not exist.

As the projections have shown, it will be virtually impossible for the United States to achieve a sustainable level of population in less than a century. We must waste no more time in taking the actions that will get us on the path toward that goal.

Changes in fertility rates are difficult, slow, and unpredictable. We must, therefore, quickly reduce immigration to a level consistent with our long-term national interest. Reducing immigration, while at the same time trying to lower fertility, offers the best hope of getting results.

Our critical task at NPG is to persuade our government to act decisively now to halt illegal immigration and reduce legal immigration from 900,000 to 100,000 a year. If we succeed, our nation will have taken the first vital step on the path toward a smaller, more sustainable population.

THE CARIBBEAN IMMIGRATION CENTRIFUGE

David Simcox

February 1995

Washington's agreement with Castro last fall to increase Cuban immigration to at least 20,000 a year once again sacrifices much needed immigration restraint for foreign policy quick fixes. The administration's bending of the immigration law's eligibility rules is a reckless precedent that will encourage future circumventions.

Moreover, Washington's policies toward both Cuba and Haiti betray its tendency to see only the short-term political and economic factors in the outflow of Caribbean peoples, ignoring the long-term social and demographic forces driving mass migration from the Caribbean's twenty-two island nations, whether rich or poor, democratic or dictatorial.

In the past decade, Caribbean island nations, with a population of 35 million, have sent more than one million legal and illegal immigrants to the United States—one-sixth of the region's population increase over the decade.

The islands, with a population density five times that of the United States, now grow by 1.8 percent yearly and have a total fertility rate of 3.1 children per woman. Population density in Barbados, Jamaica, Haiti and smaller islands matches or exceeds India's. Since 1983, the region's ratio of north-bound migrants to population has been 35 percent higher than in Mexico, the world's single largest exporter of migrants to the United States. The table below shows nearly one-sixth of the region's annual population growth moves to the United States each year, and about one-third of the annual growth of the Caribbean labor force. Nearly ten percent of all yearly immigration to the United States thus comes from a region containing six-one thousandths of Earth's population. These figures would be even higher in the absence of tight travel controls of the

Table 1.

Country	Population 1992 (Millions)	Annual Population Growth %	Immigrants to U.S. Yearly 1983-92 (Avg.)	Immigrants as % of Population Increase
Cuba	10.8	1.1	16,230	13.7
Barbados	0.3	0.07	1,570	74.7
Dominican Republic	7.5	2.3	29,950	17.4
Haiti	6.4	2.9	18,320	9.9
Jamaica	2.5	2	21,430	42.9
Trinidad & Tobago	1.3	1.4	4,680	25.7
Caribbean (All)	35	1.8	98,960	15.7

Cuban government and the U.S. interdiction at sea of Haitian illegal migrants.

What must be confronted is that immigration from the Caribbean is likely to continue growing whatever the outcomes of local political and economic conflicts. The islands' population is projected to increase by 50 million by 2025, while the labor force of that region grows by 300,000 restless, would-be workers each year.

Years of heavy migration from the islands and a pervasive U.S. cultural presence in the region have created both wide-spread expectations of settlement in the U.S. and the extensive kinship, ethnic and employer networks needed to make it happen. For millions, the United States is now an alternate homeland and a virtual entitlement.

High emigration dependency on the United States has had a serious brain-draining effect on the islands' thin professional ranks. Haiti, which lost much of its small, educated elite during decades of instability and economic stagnation, has more than 12,000 of its professionals residing in the United States. Most prone to migrate are the professionals of English-speaking states, such as Jamaica, Trinidad, and Tobago. With populations totaling only 3.8 million, those two countries now have 38,000 of their professionals here. A comparable migration from the United States would mean outflow of 2.6 million professionals. Inexplicably, in awarding 55,000 extra "diversity" visas this year to states presumably lacking opportunities to send people here, the U.S. government gave extra slots to all but two Caribbean states, despite their ownership of the highest per capita immigration rates in the world. The "diversity visa" program will open new immigration channels to other heavily populated third world nations, who have until now lacked the number of "anchor" immigrants here to start prolific migration chains.

Improved political conditions will not make a decisive difference in migration from the Caribbean. The democratization of Cuba, by ending current travel controls, will open the valves for release of intense pent-up emigration demand. Immigration into the U.S. from the Dominican Republic, now the region's largest single immigrant-sender, has grown relentlessly since constitutional government replaced decades of dictatorship in 1966. Jamaica, with a consistently admirable record of democracy and human rights since independence, now sends 43 percent of its annual population growth to the United States.

Neither does economic progress necessarily dampen immigration demand. Trinidad and Tobago and Barbados, among the third world's richest nations, together send a third of their annual population growth to the United States. Economic growth in Haiti would further increase outmigration by giving tens of thousands the means to pay travel and resettlement costs.

The emigration culture that has mushroomed in the Caribbean is a warning. It shows how years of generous family reunification and refugee policies and tolerance of illegal immigration can acquire the momentum of a mass population transfer. Similar migration momentum is growing in the Andean nations of South America and the Philippines, and is looming in China and India, a troubling portent for U.S. population growth. Migration from China at just one-third the Caribbean rate of 15.7 percent of population growth would bring 750,000 immigrants yearly.

If the United States is to bring its own population into balance with its resources and environmental limits, immigration must be neutralized as a population accelerant. The route to environmentally permissible immigration numbers is through elimination of all illegal immigration and an airtight ceiling of not more than 300,000 yearly on legal migrants and refugees.

It cannot be in the country's interest to admit the nearly four million relatives of U.S. residents now on waiting lists abroad. The extravagant and unrealistic family reunification features of current immigration law that create such overblown expectations for millions and that feed Caribbean-type mass population transfers must end. Finally, Washington policymakers must recognize immigration control as a major national interest in itself, not a bargaining counter for ephemeral diplomatic advantages.

A CHECKLIST FOR CIR

Lindsey Grant

March 1995

I participated recently in a round table organized by the Commission on Immigration Reform* and was asked to make a brief list of suggestions for its attention. Here is that list.

You have solicited round table members' ideas as to topics and proposals the commission should consider. I have looked at your interim report and offer my congratulations for your courage in taking on many of the key problems. My comments will touch only briefly on what you have already done. I will focus instead on what I see as the toughest issues ahead.

LEGAL IMMIGRATION

How Many Americans? The critical issue in immigration policy is not how many immigrants there are, but how many Americans there will be. Immigration is the primary driver as population growth threatens to drive the nation to about a half billion people in the next century. The relationship of immigration to population growth—not secondary questions such as the costs to welfare programs—should guide national policy on immigration levels. **I urge that you address the problems of jobs, education, housing, urban deterioration, energy, agriculture and the environment, that you weigh the impact that population growth will have on those problems, and that you undertake to describe what immigration levels would best contribute to the solution of the problems we face.**

What Categories of Immigrants? My own belief (as you will see in the briefing books before you) is that the nation's future well-being depends on stopping population growth, and that would require immigration far lower than at present—probably something like the 200,000 annual flow that prevailed between the immigration acts of 1924 and 1965. Present law is largely based on "family reunification," and its importance is reasserted in your mandate. It is a beguiling phrase, but dangerous because it leads to chain immigration. This policy in turn squeezes out valuable potential immigrants such as scientists, artists, writers and technicians. Coupled with our refugee and asylum policy, and with the categories of immigrant already outside the quota, it means that total de facto migration levels are only very loosely constrained by the ostensible numerical limits. Something has to give. Although I recognize you must respond to the mandate, I suggest that the CIR consider recommending that immigrants' families remain unified by bringing their nuclear families with them, within the quota, and that most quota numbers be reserved for "enrichment" migrants.

Refugee and Asylum Policy.

The U.S. is formally committed to the principle of "non-refoulement"—i.e. that it will not repatriate anybody who has a credible reason to fear coercion. This is an open-ended commitment. With millions of would-be migrants, and many governments anxious to see them leave, it gives any dictator the power to decide that asylees will stay in the U.S. simply by saying he would persecute those who tried to come back. Should the CIR suggest that the government clarify and limit that provision?

Nonimmigrant Refugees. Most countries assume that real political refugees will not stay forever, but will return when the danger in their home country subsides. The U.S. treats them as immigrants. Shouldn't refugees be admitted as non-immigrants and their status periodically be reviewed?

The Cuban Refugee Adjustment Act of 1966. This law is a relic of the Cold War. It has been used to provide almost automatic residence to any Cuban who can get here. It is an invitation to try, and it is widely seen as racial discrimination in favor of White Cubans vs. Black Haitians and others. Shouldn't the CIR consider proposing its repeal?

Quasi-legal Migration. The government has used ad hoc decisions and the Attorney General's parole power in ways the law never intended: making a deal with Castro guaranteeing the admission of 20,000 Cubans a year, granting "humanitarian parole" to Chinese, inventing "extended voluntary departure" and other devices to defer the departure of various groups. Should the CIR propose that these practices be restricted?

ILLEGAL IMMIGRATION

Better Identification. You have proposed an improved way of establishing people's identity. That addresses a fundamental need. I hope that you will pursue it despite the administration's lukewarm response. I am sorry that two of the commission members were so hesitant in their endorsement. Would they have had similar reservations about an effort to help the IRS to identify who should pay taxes? The "right" to be unidentifiable is not enshrined in U.S. law. Some means of identifying people is central to the orderly administration of complex societies. Should you make the point that better identification would contribute to national objectives such as the control of drug traffic, tax evasion and other crime?

Other Internal Controls. The best way to discourage illegal immigration is to persuade prospective migrants that it won't work. Your proposal on identification is a start. There are many other points at which the illegal migrant could be identified and deported, given the will: a law against continued employment, not just hiring, of those not entitled to work here; laws against issuance of drivers' and occupational licenses to illegal residents; voter and school registration; forfeiture of property for submission of false documentation; and so on. I urge that you summarize the techniques available to identify illegal residents, to discourage them from seeking to migrate and their potential employers from luring them.

Control of the Border. In its unsuccessful effort to persuade Congress to approve $40 billion in loan guarantees for Mexico, the administration made the (dubious) claim that otherwise there might be a flood of half a million illegal immigrants. Are we so helpless? Whatever the merits of the loan guarantees, there is another lesson there: instability is endemic in much of the third world, and probably rising. We may expect more waves of "boat people" and more desperate border crossers. The inability of the INS to control present movements is very nearly a guarantee that it could not handle a massive wave. Border control is a traditional and legitimate function of the military (perhaps of the National Guard.) A case might well be made that some such augmentation is already necessary, as in the use of the Coast Guard last autumn, or of the National Guard against drug smuggling. I hope that the Commission will be prepared to offer some untraditionally blunt contingency planning on a subject long taboo: how would we handle massive waves of illegal would-be immigrants?

Learning the Facts. You have described (a) the need for an integrated system of birth and death records to stop the assumption of false identities (p.180) and (b) the appalling state of our national database on visitors and migrants. Both deficiencies degrade our ability to administer the immigration laws and affect other matters such as population and unemployment data and welfare needs. Supermarkets engage in far more complex merchandise inventory management than the government is presently capable of, with people. Unified vital statistics and a computerized process of logging entrants' movements to, within and from the U.S.—from visa issuance to departure—would go far to control the problems of false identity and visa overstayers and would give the nation a much better handle on issues such as the cost of immigrants to certain states. I hope that you will underline the need for comprehensive reform of our national vital statistics and IRS records, not just patchwork computerization.

GENERAL

Dealing with the Problem at the Source. One regularly hears the argument that we wouldn't have the problem if sending nations could be helped to prosper. You have been commendably cautious as to how much can be done. The third world working age population is growing by record numbers, and the children are already born who will migrate twenty years hence. The pretense that the U.S. can solve the problem by investment or trade ignores the vast size of the problem, and it raises some disturbing questions as to what would happen to our own poor and dispossessed. I urge you to underline that migration must be addressed directly; it cannot be wished away by indirect measures.

Developing a National Consensus. Presently, even many law enforcement agencies do not cooperate with the INS. There is no prospect that immigration laws will be made sensible, or the current ones enforced, unless there is a national consensus as to why it is necessary. Abstractly, public opinion is far ahead of the politicians on the need to limit immigration. However, we are a generous nation, strongly inclined at the individual level to help those who come here from desperation. There will be real immigration reform only when most people understand the limits of our national capabilities to absorb more people, the penalties that our generosity imposes on our own poor and on future generations, and the necessity for determined action to manage immigration. I urge the Commission to emphasize that immigration reform will require national will, and that that in turn will require leadership by political leaders and opinion makers.

THE COWERING GIANT

Lindsey Grant

October 1995

I think I have found a job for the U.S. Army.

Last December, the Mexican peso collapsed, losing 40 percent of its value against the dollar. The Clinton administration reacted by calling upon Congress to authorize $40 billion in loan guarantees to prop up the peso. The President said that it "would help us better protect our borders." The Treasury Department put out a projection showing a potential influx of some 460,000 illegal immigrants if the Mexican Government should default on its international obligations.

A $40 billion commitment to stop 460,000 refugees works out to $87,000 per potential entrant deterred. A pretty costly bill. In fact, the number was largely mythological, an unwarranted projection from a speculative study of past correlations between Mexican economic conditions and migration, which itself had concluded that most of the influx would be temporary.[1] (In defense of the Mexicans, no Mexican is on record as making the threat.)

Mythological or not, is that the way to make policy? Are our frontiers so indefensible, our laws so unworkable, that we must resort to such pleas? What happens with the next economic crisis in immigrant-sending countries?

The most immediate losers from the collapse of the peso were those international bankers holding peso loans. Moreover, the administration was heavily committed to avoiding another major depression in Mexico, since it had put its credibility on the line in the battle over NAFTA and assured its opponents that NAFTA would prevent such economic crises. So, when Congress refused to take action, the President in January took the dubious step of bypassing Congress by guaranteeing $20 billion of loans from a fund set up to protect the U.S. dollar. And, except for Senator d'Amato (Chairman of the Senate Banking, Housing and Urban Affairs Committee), the House and Senate leadership on both sides of the aisle praised the action or remained silent.[2] International bankers have their little ways.

A rather sordid transaction. $20 billion here, $20 billion there . . . Perhaps, however, we can learn something about the immigration issue from that incident.

There is one lesson that we should have learned, but apparently didn't. Stability in Mexico, or in Central America to the south, is hardly guaranteed. The working age population of our southern neighbors is growing far faster than ours. Unemployment is endemic, and there are rising numbers of desperate people. The pressures to get into the United States will intensify, not diminish. A worse economic crisis, political warfare or a larger version of the Chiapas revolt could send millions of people trying to cross the border.

If the argument about immigration was more than a convenient smoke screen, a more courageous government would be seeking ways to enforce the laws in such a contingency. Earlier *NPG Forums* have spelled out the impact of illegal immigration on population growth, on unemployment and our wasted youth, and on future generations. The question is not whether to enforce the law, but "how?" (I will encounter disagreement from those who believe our obligation to admit illegal immigrants outweighs our obligations to our own poor and our descendants. That is, however, not the position of the U.S. Government. Not officially, at least.)

Do we try to deal with those pressures by continuing indefinitely to increase the budget for the Immigration & Naturalization Service (INS)? This is a very tight time for budgets. Or do we use the resources we have?

Primary among those resources is the Army. The traditional role of armies—other than conquest—has been to defend the borders. The Italians are doing it right now, in Calabria, to cope with an influx of migration coming mostly by way of Albania. We have used the Navy and the Coast Guard to fend off illegal arrivals by sea.[3] We have used the National Guard to help fight drug smuggling, but there seems to be a taboo against even suggesting the use of the Army. It arises in part from images of the Iron Curtain.

The taboo may possibly be weakening. The Departments of Defense and Justice are cooperating in developing contingency plans for housing massive numbers of border crossers if they overwhelm the civilian agencies.[4] That is a beginning, but only a beginning. The real task is to deter or catch the border crossers.

The Army should be told to make plans as to how they would discourage entry, with minimal bloodshed. The most effective and least destructive way is deterrence: set up the patrols and controls before the crisis, so that would-be entrants would know that it would not be easy.

The role of the military should be to supplement, not supplant, the work of the Border Patrol. The routine manning of checkpoints and dealings with the would-be immigrants should remain the province of the Border Patrol, who know how to do it. The military should be used to narrow the avenues of entry, to funnel the movement to keep it more controllable. It would turn over any persons apprehended in designated zones to the Border Patrol.

Some years ago, I arrived in the little border town of Eagle Pass, Texas just after the Texas National Guard had been conducting training exercises in the area. The local Border Patrol people told me that efforts at surreptitious entry virtually stopped for a time, until the would-be entrants discovered the maneuvers were not directed at them. The Army has the personnel and the equipment to make the long stretches of open, arid borderland very hard to cross unseen.

There is another reason for using the Army. From my own Navy experience long ago, and in casual contacts since then, I am regularly impressed by the bearing and self confidence of the young people, many of them Black and Hispanic, who have been through the military training process. They have jobs and they know how to do them. They have developed self respect. They have, at least for a time, job security. When they go back to civilian life, they will be changed men and women. Right now, there is intense pressure to reduce the deficit. The rest of the government is being squeezed, but the Republicans so far have protected the military budget. Here is a use for that money. Our civilian efforts to reach and help those young people have failed pretty dismally. Until the civilian world can provide as good an educational process and as valuable an experience, I doubt that we should create new machinery when we have an institution that is working. And I think they could do their job on the border with discipline and self-control.

Improved border surveillance is of course only part of the solution to the illegal migration problem. Even more important is the development of better identification of people who are here, so that legal immigrants can be protected and illegal immigrants deported. The Jordan Commission has made some excellent bipartisan recommendations as to how to do it, and one hopes that Congress will act on them.

The two questions of controlling the border and enforcing our laws internally should be considered together.

Congress is considering immigration legislation, and this may be a good time to take a hard look at the possibility of using the Army. Now, with the administration at odds on so many fronts with the Republican majority in Congress, is a propitious time to offer a proposal that might find widespread Republican support.

NOTES:

1. *Migration News*, University of California at Davis, January 1995.
2. AP Washington 1-31-95. Messrs. Dole and Gingrich were quoted as praising the action.
3. AP Miami 3-29-93.
4. "U.S. Drafts Plan for Influx of Illegal Immigrants. Pentagon, Justice Department Discuss Holding Camps for Larger Flow From Mexico," by Pierre Thomas; Bradley Graham, *Washington Post*, quoting Department of Justice spokesman Carl Stem, following up on a revelation earlier made by the *Journal of Commerce*. An unnamed (and apparently nervous) military spokesman was quoted as emphasizing that the planning reflected a task earlier given to the military and that it did not reflect a change of policy. Stern said that so far as he knew it did not reflect orders from the White House or National Security Council. CompuServe Executive News Service, 4-26-95.

DOWN WITH GROWTHISM

Leon F. Bouvier

February 1995

Acceptance of Proposition 187 by California voters will undoubtedly lead to an acceleration of name calling by advocates of continued high levels of immigration. Racists, xenophobics, nativists, and worse are typical epithets aimed at those of us who favor reductions in immigration, legal and illegal.

Let me be candid about this. Sadly, a few Americans do favor immigration reduction for the wrong reasons. The "browning of America" bothers them. I totally reject the arguments of people like Pat Buchanan. Whether immigrants speak Swahili or Cockney is no matter to me, their numbers are my concern.

U.S. population should be reduced if the quality of life of all Americans is to remain high. The evidence is overwhelming that 260 million is far above the carrying capacity of the nation. Our resources are being depleted; our environment is worsening; our infrastructure cannot keep pace with growth. Now is the time to say enough. Let's get started on the road to an eventual population of 150 million, or about the same as it was in 1950.

That number is not carved in stone. For example, the eminent statesman, George Kennan, has written: "This (optimal) balance, in the case of the United States, would seem to me to have been surpassed when the American population reached, at a very maximum two hundred million people, and perhaps a good deal less." We should begin now to work at reducing our numbers until such time as we are more comfortable.

The population can be reduced in three ways: lower fertility, higher mortality, and/or lower migration. Although increased longevity would contribute to raising the population, any measures that would allow all Americans to live longer and healthier lives should be favored by all of us. That leaves births and migration.

If population size could be reduced solely through lower fertility, I wouldn't even be talking about immigration. However, that is not feasible. Even if fertility fell from its present rate of 2.0 births per woman to 1.7 in 2000 and down to 1.5 by 2050, (no country has ever exhibited such a low rate for so long a period) the nation's population would grow to 337 million in 2050 and still be just under 300 million in 2100, if current net immigration levels (of about 1 million per year) remained constant.

If our population problems are to be taken seriously and reductions in size is our goal we must consider lowering immigration—not for racist or nativist reasons—but for sheer numbers. With the same extremely low assumptions about future fertility, and with net immigration (legal and illegal) limited to 200,000 annually, the population would still grow to 290 million in 2040 before falling to just under 200 million in 2100. To attain the preferred goal of 150 million would require even lower immigration (perhaps 100,000 per year) or fertility even lower than 1.5 births per woman.

Those advocating more immigration and, in some cases, higher fertility never tell us what the impact of such policies would be. We do know, from Census Bureau projections, that a population of 382 million Americans is highly likely by the middle of next century; their high scenario suggests that population could be as high as 507 million. But what if American women had an "extra" child from now on (that is, 3 births as advocated by some) and what if immigration doubled to 2 million (as advocated by some)? What would that mean demographically? By 2050, the U.S. population would surpass 677 million; by 2075 it would have reached 1 billion and be still growing rapidly! Those are the sort of numbers that are in store if we listen to pro-growth advocates. Surely, that is not in the best interests of the nation.

Whether the labelling is racism, nativism or whatever, these clearly do not apply to my position. But isn't it about time to turn the table and begin labelling those who would give the nation permanent unlimited growth?

I propose the term "growthism." Let those in favor of continued massive immigration and (in some cases) higher fertility be called population growthists. There is precedence for this negative labelling. Already in many cities and counties in fast growing states, pro-growth mayors and commissioners (usually financed by realtors and developers) are being voted out of office and the expression "pro-growth" is taking on a negative connotation.

When Americans look at the alternatives: 1 billion people or 200 million people, I am confident that they will agree with my position. Now is the time to get to work on reducing population size as soon as possible. Down with "growthism!"

A NEW LOOK AT THE IMMIGRATION DEBATE

Leon F. Bouvier

July 1995

Environmental journalist Roy Beck has produced a truly worthwhile gem of a book for anyone wishing to learn more about population growth and immigration or for anyone planning to debate the issues. As is stated on the cover, his are "responses to arguments against stabilizing U.S. population and limiting immigration." Thus, Beck makes it clear that he is aligned with those Americans who favor a limit to both population growth and immigration.

But the author is eminently fair. It would have been relatively easy for him to set up "straw men" and thereby easily destroy opposing arguments. Rather, Beck states these opposing positions in an objective manner. He then proceeds to calmly point out how incorrect they are and, in the process, often citing important sources to bolster his position.

The author tackles a variety of controversial topics such as the politics of religion and population growth and family planning as well as politics that lie behind the failure of some in the environmental movement to confront population growth and immigration as contributors to environmental degradation. This is especially relevant today as the anti-environmental movement grows since the November elections.

For anyone wanting to learn more about the problems associated with population growth and immigration, *Re-Charting America's Future* is must reading. The book looks at all the relevant aspects of these problems and explains in plain English exactly what the problems are. The book truly answers "everything anyone ever wanted to know" about population growth and immigration.

For anyone anxious to debate these issues, again this book is a must. In each of the seventeen chapters, Beck first lays out the basic opposing arguments in an extremely fair manner. He then argues against the basic premise of that argument before proceeding to more detailed opposing views. These are followed by relatively brief replies and then by more detailed arguments, richly footnoted, opposing the generally cornucopian adversary positions.

His chapter on religion serves as an excellent example of the Beck approach. He begins by citing the often repeated statement that "Population issues are too sensitive to handle because *Faith groups are offended*." But Beck points out that most religious groups recognize that the task of taking care of God's natural creation "is undermined by population growth." He then goes into more detail looking first at the claim that "the Catholic church opposes family planning and population stabilization." In his, reply, Beck quotes the U.S. Bishops who in 1991, "spoke glowingly of education, good nutrition and health care for women and children that promise to improve family welfare and contribute to stabilizing population." In this chapter and others, Beck then addresses other so-called claims and shows convincingly that they are incorrect.

He provides answers to the hackneyed arguments that we've all heard many times: "Population can grow forever with no effects" or "the demographic transition means worldwide population growth will level off naturally."

Full chapters are devoted to answering each of the following arguments:

1) We don't need to stabilize U.S. population because . . .

- There is plenty of room
- We can cut consumption
- Technology and the free market will save us
- Stabilization equals stagnation
- What matters is world population

2) We shouldn't limit immigration because . . .

- We depend on foreign workers
- We need diversity
- We have international obligations to the poor
- We must honor our traditon

Beck does an especially admirable job of linking immigration with population growth whenever appropriate. He correctly points out that as long as immigration remains at current levels, reductions in fertility would never suffice to put an end to population growth in the United States. Likewise, of course, even massive reductions in immigration would not result in an end to population growth if fertility remained at current levels.

It is important to bear in mind that this is not a whitewash job absolving all restrictionists, whether of population growth or of immigration. Chapter 13 is entitled Fear of Name Calling. The general claim cited by Beck is that "It is frightening to agree to limit immigration because **some limitationists are bigoted**. Beck clearly admits that "there are self-service people with ugly motives on both sides of the immigration issue, as there are highly-principled people; like other issues, this one needs to be decided on its merits, not by name-calling." He continues: "There are undoubtedly bigots who want immigration stopped for racial reasons . . . But opposition to racial bigotry should not blind us to the facts. There are limits to population size, in a theater or in a state, in a phone booth or on the planet." It is critically important that people realize that one does not have to be a bigot to be a restrictionist.

Beck then proceeds to examine in some detail five separate claims noting, among other things, that racial minorities in the United States are as opposed to massive immigration as is the majority.

Roy Beck has done all Americans (as well as others) a tremendous favor in preparing this book. Now, for the first time, it is possible for a layperson, concerned with the issues of population growth and immigration, to turn to an honest analysis of these all-important topics and find clear, lucid, and fair-minded answers. As a tool for anyone engaged in speaking, writing, or debating, Beck has made an indispensable contribution—a fine set of rebuttal arguments all presented honestly, fairly, and usefully in well under 200 pages.

THE POPE'S VISIT: IS MASS IMMIGRATION A MORAL IMPERATIVE?

David Simcox

October 1995

Pope John Paul II's visit to the United States in October was a critical stage in the lobbying campaign for high immigration that the U.S. Catholic hierarchy has waged for three decades. The U.S. Catholic bishops have been on a special offensive since 1994 in the face of California voters' support for Proposition 187's curbs on illegal aliens and rising public and Congressional support for lower legal immigration.

TOP LOBBYIST FROM ROME

The Pope's visit capped this campaign, coming during Congress's consideration of bills cutting legal immigration, combatting illegal entry and abuse of political asylum, and barring immigrant's from welfare. John Paul II made the presumed moral obligation of Americans to accept more immigration a key theme of his homilies in New York, New Jersey and Baltimore, and in his meeting with President Clinton. He voiced the hope that "America would persevere in its own best traditions" as a "haven for generation after generation of new arrivals."

The House of Representatives' proposed reductions (H.R. 2202) of about 25 percent in legal immigration are modest at best, falling far short of the deep cuts needed to end immigration's accelerating effect on U.S. population growth. The cuts would roll back part of the 40 percent increase in legal immigration rushed through Congress in 1990 by a coalition of immigration advocates in which the American Bishops played a central lobbying role. The current bills in both chambers would also provide new tools to stop the annual growth of more than 300,000 in the number of illegal aliens living here.

John Paul is not a neophyte in using his visits here to step into the politics of immigration. In Texas in 1987 he publicly endorsed the "sanctuary movement." Sanctuary activists, many sponsored by churches, were then smuggling and harboring illegal aliens from conflicted Central American countries as a condemnation of allegedly unresponsive U.S. refugee law.

IMMIGRATION NOT A LIFE ISSUE

In a more troubling turn for Catholics and for other Christians concerned about population growth, Papal pronouncements here and in Rome, such as the Papal Letter on the "Gospel of Life" early in 1995, increasingly imply a morel equivalence between immigration restrictions and practices of what the Pontiff calls the "Culture of Death;" abortion, contraception, capital punishment, euthanasia and assisted suicide.[1]

Immigration has thus assumed a prominent place in the Church's consistent ethic of life." This ethic enjoins the Christian to stand in "solidarity with society's weakest members—the "elderly, the infirm, the unborn"—and now the immigrant. In this view, setting appropriate immigration levels becomes a critical ethical decision that cannot legitimately be based on national interest, but on an overarching "common good" of all humanity.[2]

The U.S. hierarchy's creeping radicalization of church teaching on immigration blurs the distinction between the state's first obligation to the welfare of its own members and the obligations it may have to all humankind. Rejected is the primacy of the contractual obligations among members that has been at the heart of the democratic nation-state. National interest as a basis for immigration and population policies is deeply suspect in the hierarchy's view. In its place the Church offers a high-minded but amorphous sentiment of a global "common good," but without a global social contract or a global entity to define or implement it.

Both Rome and the U.S. Bishops have radicalized Catholic social teaching on immigration in other ways since the Vatican councils of the 1960s. The Church in the post-World War II era for the first time proclaimed a "right" of immigration. But it balanced that new-found right with acknowledgement of the right of governments to regulate immigration. Church pronouncements now confirm immigration as a virtually absolute right, while they have qualified the regulatory rights of states to the point where persons to emigrate and to immigrate are held up as a universal norm binding Catholics:

> "Catholic citizens are required to work to see that as far as possible the laws of their countries adhere to this universal norm."[3]

OVERPOPULATION: MYTH OR REALITY IN ROME'S WORLD VIEW?

Most disconcerting is the absence in current Church positions of any concern with numbers or limits. If immigration itself is held to be a spiritually regenerating process, the inference from recent church statements is inescapable: just as there can never be too many people, there can never be too many immigrants. In Rome's and the bishops' prevailing cornucopian view, overpopulation is a non-issue. A 1994 report of scientists of the Papal Academy of Sciences warned that the birth rate "must not notably exceed two children per couple," concluding that birth control on a global scale was "absolutely necessary . . . to prevent the emergence of insoluble problems." The Vatican strongly denied that the Academy's finding represented church teaching.[4] Since then Cardinal Lopez Trujillo, Chair of the Papal Council on the Family, has dismissed overpopulation as a "myth."

Pope Pius XII acknowledged in 1952 that overpopulation and scarcity of jobs were conditions in sending countries that justified emigration.[5] In that light, the hierarchy's current reasoning is curious: overpopulation and scarcities of jobs exist and emigration is a legitimate way of relieving them: but limits on immigration are not a morally legitimate response of states to overpopulation or job scarcities.

AMERICAN CATHOLICS AND THE POPE: SPIRITUAL ASSENT, PRACTICAL DISSENT

Americans of all faiths are right to be edified by the Pope's and the bishop's eloquent promotion of human rights. But such generalized exhortations on immigration make a fragile basis for workable public policies in the temporal world. The otherworldly tone of papal teaching on immigration and population issues helps explain the increasing tendency of American Catholics to respect the holy Father and the Bishops as spiritual leaders while rejecting their specific guidance.

A *Time*-CNN poll shortly before the Pope's arrival showed that 83 percent of U.S. Catholics had a favorable opinion of John Paul II. But 69 percent of Catholics believed that abortion is not morally wrong in every case; and 93 percent felt that artificial birth control was morally acceptable for Catholics.[6]

On immigration, 54 percent of Americans contacted in a recent *New York Times*-CBS News poll wanted immigration reduced. The results for the Catholic respondents were statistically undistinguishable from the country as a whole.[7] Archbishop Roger Mahony of Los Angeles, the most outspoken Catholic hierarch on immigration, blamed strong Catholic support for Proposition 187 (49 percent of all California Catholics supported it and 59 percent of non-Hispanic Catholics) on the "low formational level" of many Catholics.

Mahony affirmed the Church's intent to "re-evangelize" Catholics on such issues.[8] But even "re-evangelization" is not likely to make the majority of Catholic voters accept the proposition that the nation's right to control its borders must take second place to the rights of immigrants to enter and remain.

AN ETHIC OF SUSTAINABILITY

The unconditional pro-natalist, immigration expansionist doctrines of the church hierarchy overlook other equally compelling moral and ethical issues of population and immigration and their consequences for the common good. The dignity of human life is ultimately related to its quantity. And the survival of human life is fatally tied to the viability of its support systems.

The hierarchy's obsession with maximizing human life on earth now may well negate the planet's ability to support human life in future centuries. A sustainable population now will help ensure the world's and America's ability to support human life indefinitely.

The United States has historically been generous in receiving immigrants. But its bounty is not limitless. Contrary to the hierarchy's cornucopian view, the nation's ability to provide for its own needy is diminished by today's mass immigration. Remarkably the U.S. bishops, even as they press for more immigration, have spoken out strongly against the deteriorating real wages and conditions of American workers, the lack of low-income housing, and Congressional proposals to cut welfare benefits, as if high immigration were unrelated to those conditions.

To lump immigration in with searing life issues such as abortion, euthanasia, and capital punishment, misrepresents them all and further polarizes debate. Declining to admit immigrants when clear national interests so demand is hardly a denial of life. An environmentally sound and sustainable United States can make a far greater contribution to the quality and permanence of human life on earth than can a nation that is overcrowded, resource-depleted, and seriously polluting to both itself and the world.

NOTES:

1. Richard A. McCormick. "The Gospel of Life," America, April 29, 1995
2. U.S. Catholic Conference. One Family Under God, July 4, 1995
3. Alfonso Figueroa Deck, S.J. New Directions in the Catholic Understanding of Immigration Rights. Migration World, VOL. XXII, No4
4. Lindsey Grant. "The Cairo Conference: Feminists vs. the Pope." The NPG Forum. July 1994.
5. New Catholic Encyclopedia—Volume IX. "International Migration." New York: McGraw-Hill, 1967
6. "Love the Messenger, Not His Message." *Washington Post* National Weekly Edition, October 9–15, 1995
7. *New York Times*, October 4, 1995
8. "An Interview with Cardinal Mahony." *America,* January 28,1995.

IN PRAISE OF PATRIOTISM

Lindsey Grant

August 1995

On the old road between Albuquerque and Santa Fe, at a crossing called Budaghers, there is an abandoned roadhouse and gas station, bypassed by the new Interstate. Whoever owned it retreated in good order. Plywood was put over the windows to protect the place. On one of those sheets of plywood, now partly obscured by an ailanthus, somebody took a paint brush and wrote "U.S.A.#1!" in big, bold letters.

There is a lot of courage reflected in that little scene. I don't know who owns the place, and I don't know who wrote the graffiti. I suspect it was an Hispanic. It was probably somebody who had had his share of lumps, culminating in a distant decision to cut off his roadhouse with a new highway. He was undaunted nonetheless. He believed in the system, and he believed in an abstraction called country.

In a fractioning age and society, we could use more of that spirit. In fact, we desperately need it. There is not much to rally the spirit in the cry "I'm all right, Jack"—i.e., I've got mine—that animates the era. Humans are at least in part a social species. In the absence of a larger group with which to identify, we tend to fall back to identifying ourselves with subgroups, whether they be urban street gangs, ethnic groups, or economic class.

It is less divisive to invest a sense of identity and altruism in one's country, to be proud of it and concerned about its well being. At the local level, the parallel is civic pride. We need a global system to perform the same role for societies that those concepts do for individuals, but it will be a long time coming. Meanwhile, we need the nation. We have a better chance of making it work than of reforming everybody, everywhere.

Patriotism is not presently a popular idea. Driven too far, it can indeed become jingoism. Its savage cousin, ethnic bloodshed, is riding high in much of the world. We don't need more of that. Patriotism is, however, a different concept and a powerful emotion. It has been prematurely counted out. Before Marx changed our perceptions and redivided humankind by economic class, Western historians wrote in terms of nations as the natural social unit. Marx overstated his case. At the advent of World War I, many German Socialists could not believe that workers from different nations could be herded into armies to shoot at each other. They were wrong. The writer Thomas Mann at about that time observed that different occupational groups have more in common even across national lines—a German and French banker, for instance—than they have with their fellow countrymen from other classes. Perhaps so, but it is an alliance of self interest more than a visceral identity.

My interest in patriotism is partly emotional. (On Census forms, I perversely insist in writing in

"American" where it asks about race, thus assuring, I imagine, that my data will be recorded with American Indians or "other.") My present purpose, however, is intellectual.

In the debate about population and immigration, the adversaries tend to talk past each other, because the concept of the national good is simply absent from the thinking particularly of immigration advocates. They dismiss the argument as racism or xenophobia.

Immediate personal self-interest often argues for immigration; witness the recent stories of politicians who were found to have illegal alien servants. Most of the arguments for stopping population growth rest upon societal considerations—the plight of the poor, the preservation of the land for our descendants—and not upon immediate individual or sectarian benefit. Individually (unless you yourself are being displaced), the costs of massive immigration and population growth are gradually imposed, while the benefits are immediate: cheap labor and lower prices. Only if you believe that the social good is important and worth the sacrifice of some immediate individual benefits does the argument even reach you. In a society where the social good is seldom invoked except as a cover for parochial interest, it simply sounds irrelevant.

Individual interest is concentrated. The social interest is dilute. At every turn, when one argues the disadvantages of population growth, one encounters a phalanx of those for whom the growth is immediately profitable: realtors, landowners, businessmen seeking cheap labor, politicians seeking a larger constituency.

Moreover, there is a conflict of moral values involved here. The two World Wars resulted in part from the excesses of nationalism, and the word has become pejorative in many minds. Add to that the dawning recognition that we share one world and that "all men are brothers." The result is that arguments based on the national good are suspect.

It is easy to associate that state of mind with liberals, who tend to be Democrats. I want to be fair, however, so I intend to blame both political parties.

The Democrats (with some Republican help) inadvertently promoted the divisions within our society by using ethnic identity to categorize who should benefit from President Johnson's Great Society program and the other efforts of the past three decades to achieve racial justice. The discrimination was real, and I can think of no other way to propel people from those minorities into the middle class, into corporate boards and senior governmental jobs, and into a position to be heard. Nevertheless, reverse discrimination, like subsidies, creates its own vested interests. Our government created a powerful inducement for people to think of themselves as members of a particular minority. The need to know who was there and how they were faring led to other self-perpetuating divisions such as racial questions on job applications and the Census questions about race (a thoroughly unscientific concept) and ethnicity.

Perhaps we should have written sunset provisions into those laws to terminate them when they had served their purpose. It is hardly rational for the child of a Black PhD to have a hiring advantage over a White manual laborer's child. Reverse discrimination in the name of ending discrimination has a certain Alice in Wonderland quality, and there may be hope in recent proposals—voicing the unthinkable—to gear the legislation more closely to individual wrongs.

As to the Republicans: The Republican majority elected to the House of Representatives in

November 1994, with its demolition derby approach to government, seems intent on validating Karl Marx's class view of society. Their proposal for a "capital gains cut and indexation" is a rich man's dream. In the name of a balanced budget, they have embarked upon two thoroughly incompatible projects: wiping out the deficit; and cutting taxes for the prosperous. They propose a massive income transfer from the poor to the prosperous and a removal of social controls on the latter, as if to emphasize that America consists of those two classes and to show which one is in control.

That, apparently, is what the people want. The Republicans won.

The rich get richer and the poor get bitter. The rich don't need a tax break. A recent article in the *Wall Street Journal*—not usually considered a radical rag—pointed out that in the past two decades the real earnings of the bottom fifth of Americans have dropped 24 percent, while those of the top fifth have risen 10 percent. A company CEO then typically earned thirty-five times as much as the average worker; the ratio has risen to 150, the highest in the industrial world. The proportion of our country's wealth held by the rich has been growing.

If Congress seeks to address the deficit, and to share the burden fairly, is this the way?

We are destroying the sense of community. There is no automatic rule as to what income disparity should be tolerable in a society, but we are widening the gap. Those at the bottom suffer first, but our society is being torn apart, and not only the poor will suffer. The new Republican House majority seems to see the nation simply as a space in which the ground rules are dog eat dog. Witness its eagerness to dismantle the environmental protections and the national parks and forests built up over the years, as they seek to cut expenses, make room for a tax cut, and get rid of impediments to business as usual.

In the past, Americans have responded to appeals to the social good. Franklin Roosevelt's second inaugural speech in 1937 is still stirring: "I see one-third of a nation ill-housed, ill-clad and ill-nourished." Many Republicans of his time were convinced he was a Communist, but his message was rooted in precisely the opposite view of society: that we all had a stake in that one-third of the nation, and that we would not prosper if they remained excluded.

We need to bring back that state of mind. I think that, as we do, it will become much clearer why some of us argue that the social good calls for a smaller population.

WE'RE ALREADY BAILING OUT MEXICO

B. Meredith Burke

July 1995

Like the NAFTA debate, that on the proposed $40 billion financial bailout of Mexico is silent on the demographic gulf separating the two countries. Yet the situation of a major industrialized country whose native-born population has replacement fertility or below sharing a long border with a higher-fertility country just emerging from third-world status is unique.

Demographically unschooled Americans are unaccustomed to factoring concerns about fertility and population growth rates into our international policy considerations. Even Doris Meissner, commissioner of the Immigration and Naturalization Service, persists in confusing a symptom—illegal immigrants seeking jobs—with its root cause: high population growth rates in the sending nations.

The sharp post-1980 surge in Mexico migration roughly coincided with the labor force entrance of the first few Mexican birth cohorts benefiting from the decreasing mortality rates beginning in the late 1950s. The just-released 1992 Mexican Demographic Survey recorded 3.9 million Mexicans age forty to forty-four; 5.8 million age twenty to twenty-four; and 10.7 million age ten to fourteen.

The United Nations estimated Mexico's 1989 population at 86.7 million with two million additions annually. The 1992 Mexican survey found 85.6 million residents; a short-fall of seven million persons. It also found up to ten percent more women than men in the young adult age groups twenty to thirty-nine. Where have these people, particularly the men, vanished?

Certainly some have slipped across the border. IRCA, the Immigration and Reform Act of 1986, legalized the status of three million illegal aliens who had entered the country before 1983; about 80 percent were Mexicans. Since IRCA the INS estimates four million new illegals, 1.5 million of whom are Mexicans, have arrived (other estimates go up to 5.1 million). This compares with 100,000 or fewer legal Mexican admissions annually.

But a substantial part of the shortfall is represented by births current and projected which Mexico has de facto exported. In 1992 Mexican-born women in the U.S. bore 275,000 or 6.8 percent of 4.05 million U.S. births. This compares to about two million births in Mexico. Mexico has effectively exported about 12 percent of births to its nationals while securing them an educational far above the less-than-grade-school education it gave their parents. Mexico has thus obtained a terrific capital transfer.

California has provided most of this capital. In 1992 Mexican-born women bore 161,000 (double the 1985 number) or 26.8 percent of the state's 601,000 births. Medical data indicate at least 70 percent of these mothers had entered the U.S. illegally. Using prior years' birth data to estimate school enrollment I calculated that in 1993 980,000 of California's K–12 enrollment were citizen children of Mexican-born mothers; I will round this to one million. Of course, there are also Mexican-born students legally here plus, according to the GFAO, 336,000 illegal entrant children—presumably a majority Mexican born—enrolled in K–12 in California in 1994–95.

At $5,000 per student California spends about $5 billion annually per million students. But English as a Second Language (ESL) students from poor families with a grade-school-educated family head and requiring various forms of compensatory education cost nearer $8,000 per student. On education alone California is financing an $8 billion aid program to Mexican nationals. (The vast majority are in households with below $20,000 income who pay on average $81 in taxes to the state General Fund which finances education.) If immigration and immigrant fertility continue apace and we do not enact the Beilenson-Gallegly bill restricting citizenship at birth to only those infants whose parents are legally here, by 2005 California will be educating 1.5 million citizen children of Mexican nationals. Proposition 187 adherents had it wrong: it is the services to citizen children of illegal entrants, all of whom are entitled at the very least to K–12 years of schooling and AFDC, which will bankrupt the state.

Small wonder that Senator Dianne Feinstein (D-CA) told both the Treasury Secretary and Secretary of State that she knew "no one in (her) constituency who is for it (the bail-out)."

Mexican fertility declined since the Mexican government belatedly approved a national family planning program in late 1973. Rural women age fifteen to forty-nine have a projected lifetime fertility of 4.9 (down from 6.8 for women age forty-five to forty-nine); urban women, three children (down from 4.7); and all women 3.5 children (1.75 times the long-term replacement number of two).

But because of past high fertility, women age fifteen to nineteen are nearly three times more numerous than women age forty-five to forty-nine. If they bear 3.5 children on average, their descendants will be 3 x 1.75 or over five times more numerous than the grandparent population. If fertility declined 40 percent overnight to replacement level, these young women will still bear 3 x 1.00 or three times more descendants than the grandparent generation.

This continued growth after replacement fertility is reached (population growth momentum) is an artifact of an age structure skewed towards the young. Stabilizing population today requires that these three daughters bear a total of one granddaughter, or only 1/3 of a daughter (or 2/3s of a child counting sons) per woman. Present fertility is over five times that level.

No country can generate sufficient modern-sector jobs at that rate. Options include state-financed labor-intensive jobs, soaring unemployment rates, and where possible high levels of out-migration. Vanderbilt University professor Virginia Abernethy has compiled data suggesting that where physical resources are demonstrably limited and out-migration infeasible, sharp fertility declines ensue. China is one example; islands such as Taiwan, Singapore, and later Mauritius set records for the sharpness of their fertility declines. Jamaica, which has exported 10 percent of its nationals, and Haiti have displayed slower declines or none at all.

In Mexico, the large number of emigrants and their high remittances, especially to rural areas, have mitigated demographic distress and muted the fertility response. Meanwhile the fertility of recent Mexican immigrants to the U.S. reflecting their largely rural origins and far-brighter prospects for their U.S. citizen children than their home villages could offer, is over four children per woman. (The Hispanic fertility rate in California has risen from 2.75 children in 1980 to 3.5 in 1992; the contribution of Mexican-born women has risen from 54.9 percent to 60.9 percent.)

The U.S., which just twenty years ago was projecting a stable population of 200 million, now confronts forecasts of 400, 500, and even 600 million by the year 2050; all due to post-1970 immigrants and their offspring, disproportionately from Mexico. California's population has increased at least 60 percent since 1970, while the U.S.'s has grown 30 percent.

The taxes, social investments, and physical infrastructure required to support such a population are less daunting than the spectre of environmental collapse which ecologists are foretelling.

Viable futures for both the United States AND Mexico required a speedy end to ALL population growth in both countries. All bilateral agreements must be crafted to that end. If Mexico dissents, we must try the tough love solution of ending our current subsidization of a fertility level its own resources cannot support. A further bailout permitting demographic business to continue as usual will doom us both.

CONFRONTING THE TWENTY-FIRST CENTURY'S HIDDEN CRISIS: REDUCING HUMAN NUMBERS BY 80 PERCENT

J. Kenneth Smail

May 1995

My position is simply stated. Within the next half-century, it will be essential for the human species to have fully operational a flexibly designed, broadly equitable and internationally coordinated set of initiatives focussed on reducing the then-current world population by at least 80 percent. Given that even with the best of intentions it will take considerable time and exceptional diplomatic skill to develop and implement such an undertaking, perhaps on the order of twenty-five to fifty years, it is important that the process of consensus building—local, national and global—begin now. The mathematical inevitability that human numbers will continue their dramatic increase over the next two generations, to perhaps 10 billion by the year 2040, and the high probability that this numerical increase will exacerbate still further the systemic problems that already plague humanity (economic, political, environmental, social, moral, etc.), only reinforces this sense of urgency. There are, however, hopeful signs. In recent years, we have finally begun to come to terms with the fact that the consequences of the twentieth century's rapid and seemingly uncontrolled population growth will soon place us—if it hasn't already done so—in the midst of the greatest crisis our species has yet encountered.

SOME REALITIES

In order better to appreciate the scope and ramifications of this still partly hidden crisis, I shall briefly call attention to eight essential, incontrovertible and inescapable realities that must not only be fully understood but soon confronted.

First, during the present century world population will have grown from somewhere around 1.6 billion in 1900 to slightly more than six billion in the year 2000, an almost four-fold increase in but 100 years. This is an unprecedented numerical expansion. Throughout human history, world population growth measured over similar 100-year intervals has been virtually non-existent or at most modestly incremental; it has only become markedly exponential within the last few hundred years. To illustrate this on a more easily comprehensible scale, based on the present rate of increase of some 90 to 95 million per year, human population growth during the 1990s alone will amount to nearly one billion, an astonishing 20 percent increase in but ten years. Just by itself, this ten year increase is equivalent to the total global population in the year 1800 (barely 200 years ago) and is approximately triple the estimated world population at the height of the Roman Empire (ca. 300 million). It is a chastening thought that even moderate to conservative demographic projections suggest that this billion-per-decade rate of increase will continue well into the next century, and that the current global total of 5.7 billion (1995 estimate) could easily reach 10 to 11 billion by the year 2050.

Second, even if a fully effective program of zero population growth were to be implemented immediately, by limiting human fertility to what demographers term the replacement rate (roughly 2.1 children per female), human population would nevertheless continue its rapid rate of expansion. In fact, demographers estimate that it would take at least two to three generations (fifty to seventy-five years) at ZPG fertility levels just to reach a point of population stability, unfortunately at numbers considerably higher than at present. This powerful population momentum results from the fact that an unusually high proportion (nearly 1/3) of the current world population is under the age of fifteen and has not yet reproduced. Even more broad-based population profiles are to be found throughout the developing world, where the under-fifteen age cohort often exceeds 40 percent and where birth rates have remained high even as mortality rates have fallen. While there are some recent indications that fertility rates are beginning to decline, the global composite (ca. 3.8) is still nearly double that needed for ZPG.

Third, in addition to fertility levels, it is essential to understand that population growth is also significantly affected by changes in mortality rates. In fact, demographic transition theory predicts that the earlier stages of rapid population expansion are typically fueled more by significant reductions in death rates than by changes in birth rates. Nor does recent empirical data suggest that average human life expectancy has reached anywhere near its theoretical upper limit, in either the developing or developed worlds. Consequently, unless there appears a deadly pandemic, a devastating world war or a massive breakdown in public health (or a combination of all three), it is inevitable that ongoing global gains in human longevity will continue to make a major contribution to population expansion over the next half-century, regardless of whatever progress might be made in reducing fertility. A further consequence is the fact that populations will inevitably get "older," with mean ages in the forty to forty-five range and perhaps as many as one-third of their members over age sixty, as both mortality and fertility rates decline and human numbers (hopefully) reach stable levels. Not surprisingly, these aging populations will develop their own unique set of problems to resolve, not the least of which might be understandable but misguided efforts to increase the size (and economic productivity) of younger age cohorts by encouraging higher fertility.

Fourth, it is important to recognize that the quantitative scale, geographic scope, escalating pace and functional interconnectedness of these impending demographic changes are of such a magnitude that there are few if any historical precedents to guide us. For example, at the current rate of increase of 250,000 people per day (more than 10,000 per hour), it is ludicrous to speak of there being any significant empty spaces left on earth to colonize, certainly when compared with but a century ago. And it is even more ridiculous to suggest that "off earth" (extraterrestrial) migration will somehow be sufficient to siphon away excess human population, in either the near or more distant future.

Fifth, given the data and observations presented thus far, it becomes increasingly apparent that the time span available for implementing an effective program of population control may be quite limited, with a window of opportunity that may not extend much beyond the middle of the next century. While future population trends are notoriously difficult to predict with precision, dependent as they are on a broad range of factors, most middle-of-the-road demographic projections for the year 2040—less than two generations from now—are in the 9 to 11 billion range, nearly double our present numbers (see point #1 above). Several observations might help to bring this "limited" time span into somewhat better perspective: 1) the year 2040 is as close to the present as the year 1950; 2) an infant born in 1995 will be but forty-five years old in the year 2040;

and 3) a young person entering the job market in the mid-1990s will just be reaching retirement age in the year 2040. By any reasonable standard of comparison, this is hardly the remote future.

Sixth, it is extremely important to come to terms with the fact that the earth's long term carrying capacity, in terms of resources broadly defined, is indeed finite, despite the continuing use of economic models predicated on seemingly unlimited growth and notwithstanding the high probability of continued scientific/technological progress. Some further terminological clarification may be useful. "Long-term" is most appropriately defined on the order of several hundred years at least; it emphatically does not mean the five to ten year horizon typical of much economic forecasting or political prognostication. Over this much longer time span, it then becomes much more reasonable—perhaps even essential to human survival—to define a sustainable human population size in terms of optimums rather than maximums. *In other words, what "could" be supported in the short term is not necessarily what "should" be humanity's goal over the longer term.* As far as resources are concerned, whether these be characterized as renewable or non-renewable, it is clear that the era of inexpensive energy (derived from fossil fuels), adequate food supplies (whether plant or animal), readily available or easily extractable raw materials (from wood to minerals), plentiful fresh water and readily accessible "open space" is rapidly coming to a close, almost certainly within the next half-century. And finally, the consequences of future scientific/technological advances—whether in terms of energy production, technological efficiency, agricultural productivity or creation of alternative materials—are much more likely to be incremental than revolutionary, notwithstanding frequent and grandiose claims for the latter.

Seventh, it is becoming increasingly apparent that rhetoric about "sustainable growth" is at best a continuing exercise in economic self-deception and at worst a politically pernicious oxymoron. Almost certainly, working toward a "steady-state" sustainability is much more realistic scientifically, more attainable economically and (perhaps) more prudent politically. Assertions that the earth "might" be able to support a population of 10, 15 or even 20 billion for an "indefinite" period of time at a standard of living "superior" to the present are not only demonstrably false but also cruelly misleading. Rather, ongoing analysis by ecologists, demographers and numerous others suggests that it is quite likely that the earth's true carrying capacity—defined here (simply) as humans in long-term adaptive balance with their ecological setting and resource base—has already been exceeded by a factor of two or more. To the best of my knowledge, there is no clear-cut or well-documented evidence that effectively contradicts this sober—even frightening—assessment. Consequently, since at some point in the not-too-distant future the negative consequences and ecological damage stemming from continued and uncontrolled human reproductive profligacy could well become irreversible, and because there is only one earth with which to experiment, it is undoubtedly better for our species to err on the side of prudence, exercising wherever possible a cautious and careful stewardship.

Eighth and finally, only about 20 percent of the current world population (ca. 1.2 billion people) could be said to have a "generally adequate" standard of living, defined here as something approximating that of industrialized Western Europe, Japan or North America, the so-called developed world. The other 80 percent (ca. 4.5 billion), incorporating most of the inhabitants of what have been termed the developing nations, live in conditions ranging from mild deprivation to severe deficiency. Despite well-intentioned efforts to the contrary, there is little evidence that this imbalance is going to decrease in any significant way, and a strong likelihood that it may get worse, particularly in view of the fact that more than 90 percent of all future population growth is projected to occur in these less-developed regions of the world. In fact, there is growing concern that when this burgeoning population growth in the developing world is combined with "excessive" per capita energy and resource consumption in much of the developed world, the potential for wide-spread environmental deterioration (systemic breakdown?) in a number of the earth's more heavily-stressed ecosystems becomes increasingly likely. This is particularly worrisome in regions already beset by short-sighted or counterproductive economic policies, chronic political instability and growing social unrest.

If the above "inescapable realities" are indeed valid, it is obvious that rational, equitable and attainable population goals will have to be established in the very near future. It is also obvious that these goals will have to address and in some fashion resolve a powerful internal conflict: how to create and sustain an adequate standard of living for all the world's peoples (minimizing the growing distance between rich and poor) while simultaneously not over-stressing (or exceeding) the earth's longer-term carrying capacity. *I submit that these goals cannot be reached, or this conflict resolved, unless and until world population is dramatically reduced—to no more than two billion people—over the next two or three centuries.*

THE CENTRAL ARGUMENT RESTATED

On the assumption that the foregoing observations are indeed close to the mark, the logic underlying the above recommendation—and the statement that began this essay—seems both inexorable and clear. It deserves a brief reiteration.

Over the next several generations, and beginning as soon as possible, humanity must not only take significant steps to arrest the rapid growth of human population but also begin to reduce it dramatically. However, it will be very difficult if not impossible to stop current growth short of 9 to 10 billion. This is due not only to the momentum effect but also to the great difficulties, both diplomatic and temporal, in developing and implementing the necessary political, economic, scientific and moral consensus about both ends and means.

Because there is no clear-cut evidence to support assertions to the contrary, and precious little margin for error, it is only prudent to work from the increasingly legitimate assumption that the earth's long-term carrying capacity is no greater than two billion people. It is therefore necessary to confront the inescapable fact that human numbers will have to be reduced by 80 percent or more, from the all-but-inevitable 9 to 11 billion in the mid-twenty-first century to something approaching 2 billion by the end of the twenty-second century, some 200 years from now. Obviously, a numerical dislocation of this magnitude will require a massive reorientation of human thought, expectations and values.

Just as obvious, time is short, with an implementation window that will last no more than the next fifty to seventy-five years, and perhaps less. This process of population stabilization and reduction should have begun a generation or more ago—say in 1960 when human numbers were "only" three billion and demographic momentum more easily arrested—and certainly cannot be delayed much longer. For it is abundantly clear that if we do not choose to address and resolve this problem ourselves, "nature" will almost certainly solve it for us, with consequences that would be at best unpredictable and at worst unimaginable.

The problem of establishing rational and defensible population "optimums" deserves further comment. Perhaps most surprising is how unusual it is to find individuals—or organizations—who are willing to state publicly and emphatically that just reaching a point of "population stability" during the next century will not be enough, either to solve our near-term demographic difficulties or to stave off a future demographic catastrophe. For the latter scenario will almost surely come to pass if humanity naively and/or unquestioningly accepts global population levels that are set so high—in the 10 to 15 billion range—that they are clearly unsustainable over the longer term. One only has to consider the stresses already evident at the current level of nearly six billion to recognize that any sort of long-term stability at figures double that number will be impossible to accomplish. Put most simply, *there seems to be no credible alternative to the premise that a very significant population reduction must necessarily follow population stabilization.*

Admittedly, the above-mentioned global goal—a sustainable optimum of approximately 2 billion people by the beginning of the twenty-third century—has a substantial inferential component. This "subjectivity" is undoubtedly due to a number of factors, among which might be included: 1) the fact that as yet only a modest amount of empirical scientific research has been directed toward establishing quantifiable (and testable) parameters for what the earth's long-term carrying capacity might actually be; 2) the strong likelihood that the sheer complexity, multidisciplinary nature and sociopolitical "sensitivities" surrounding analysis of the population problem have not only inhibited scientific research and funding but have also elicited (in some) a sort of "scale paralysis"; 3) the obvious fact that the process involved in initially establishing—and subsequently implementing—future population goals will involve complex "qualitative considerations" that significantly transcend a strictly scientific (quantitative) analysis; 4) the presence of a persistent (and probably deep-seated) human "reticence" to give serious consideration to a demographic future that seems quite remote from one's daily life and activities, not to mention a future for which there is little historical precedent; and 5) the distinct possibility that, even with the best of political intentions and unprecedented cooperation at all relevant levels, it may take considerably longer than 200 years to reach the desired demographic goals.

Notwithstanding these and other uncertainties, the two billion "global optimum" utilized here is quite consistent with estimates to be found in several of the sources listed at the end of this essay (see particularly the articles in the volume edited by Grant, the books by Hardin and the Ehrlichs, and various publications and position papers prepared by NPG). Actually, this two billion estimate may be somewhat on the generous side, particularly in light of the fact that some recent projections for the earth's long-term carrying capacity have been set much lower, in the one-half to one billion range (David Pimentel: pers.com.).

On the other hand, even if future research shows that this global carrying capacity figure has been underestimated by at least half—that is, if further analysis demonstrates that an optimum population estimate of two billion is "off-target" by a factor of two or more—the argument put forth here loses little if any of its validity or persuasive power. For example, if it is indeed inevitable that global population size is destined to reach 10 to 12 billion within the next half-century, even efforts to reach a somewhat "larger" optimum population—one (say) in the four to five billion range-would still require a very significant decrease in human numbers, roughly on the order of 60 percent. From a practical standpoint, this figure differs little from the 80 percent reduction postulated earlier; certainly, either of these "projections" is more than adequate to dramatize the need for a profound—and immediate—response to this looming demographic crisis.

FUTURE PROSPECTS

I am cautiously optimistic that this crisis can be averted, if only because all humans—despite our many differences—share a deep-rooted "investment in immortality," an individual and collective concern for posterity. This powerful commitment to the future manifests itself biologically (through the children we beget), socioculturally (through our relationships with others) and morally (through our religious and/or ethical systems). As an essential first step, our species will soon have to establish a difficult but very necessary balance between individual reproductive rights and collective reproductive responsibilities. That is, all of the world's peoples must come fully to terms with the fact that a person's (biological) right to have children must be mediated by his or her (social) responsibility not to have too many. Certainly, any hope for success in this massive reorientation of basic biological propensities and strongly-held sociocultural expectations will require attention not only to quantitative but also to qualitative issues and concerns. In fact, it will likely be easier to elicit broad-scale agreement on the pressing need for a significant reduction in human numbers—the "quantitative dimension"—than it will be to foster a broad scale consensus on the "qualitative" restructuring of individual, political, economic, social and ethical perceptions that will also be necessary.

In pragmatic terms, the initial stabilization and subsequent 80 percent reduction in human numbers suggested earlier could be brought about with relative ease by establishing a worldwide average fertility rate of approximately 1.5 to 1.7 over the next several generations (lasting throughout the twenty-first century at least). Essentially, all that would be necessary is for couples to "stop at two"; because some women have no children, and others only one, this would rather quickly result in an overall (sub-replacement) fertility rate in the desired range. It is important to note that rates approaching this 1.5 to 1.7 level have already been reached in a number of nation-states (including the U.S.), at least for limited periods of time, and further that these fertility levels have in most instances been attained voluntarily (without external coercion).

Certainly an important early step in this process of population reduction would be to promote appropriate (i.e. culturally acceptable) local incentives to significantly postpone age at marriage and/or age at first pregnancy, from (say) the mid/late teens until at least the mid-twenties. If these same incentives also encouraged increased intervals between births, the almost certain consequence would be markedly smaller family sizes coupled with a significant decrease in the number of generations per unit time (from nearly six generations per century to fewer than four). Once an optimum population size is within reach—perhaps toward the end of the twenty-second century when global numbers begin to come into balance with carrying capacity as then understood—fertility rates could then be increased to the previously mentioned ZPG replacement level (ca. 2.1).

However, it is also abundantly clear, to judge by the agenda and controversies emanating from the recent (September 1994) United Nations-sponsored International Conference on Population and Development, that implementation of these greatly reduced fertility rates is inextricably intertwined with a number of very sensitive political and ideological concerns. Chief among these are matters pertaining to: the enhancement of gender equity; the educational and economic empowerment of women; ongoing controversies surrounding family planning, birth control and abortion; problems of development and modernization; differential access to resources and/or inequities in their distribution; various forms of pollution and environmental degradation; endemic poverty and implementation of effective public health measures; the growth of nationalism and ethnic/religious tensions; human migration and political/ecological refugees; etc.; etc. These are all very important issues, and there is little doubt that they are frequently interconnected in complex cause-and-effect relationships with population growth.

However, it is even more important not to confuse short-term means with longer-term ends. More specifically, it is essential that humanity does not lose sight of the over-arching and exploding demographic "forest" in the midst of legitimate and deeply-felt concerns about particular political/ideological "trees."

For the stark reality is this. Population regulation is the primary issue facing humanity; all other matters are subordinate. Proponents of the above-mentioned agenda items, at the United Nations and elsewhere, must become fully cognizant of the fact that solutions to the problems that deeply concern them will be far more likely (and lasting) in a world that is moving rapidly and effectively toward population stabilization and eventual population reduction. For it must be obvious that the alternative—a world inexorably expanding toward 12 to 15 billion people by the end of the next century—offers much less hope for successful resolution of these matters.

Quite simply, hard-won gains would almost certainly be overwhelmed by continuing and uncontrolled numerical growth, similar to what can be observed even now in those regions of the world where populational doubling times of twenty-five to thirty-five years are the norm.

In fact, to judge by the available evidence, it is entirely possible that the conventional wisdom of the past fifty years—particularly to the extent that this "wisdom" has been characterized by large-scale economic aid (transfers of wealth) and liberal immigration policies (transfers of people)—has done more to stimulate rapid population growth than inhibit it. It's almost as if a demographic Parkinson's Law were in effect, to wit: "Births tend to expand to fill the perceived socioeconomic space." In other words, when the true limits of this "perceived space" are obscured at the local level by overly generous international aid and relatively easy opportunities for emigration, the unfortunate demographic result has all too often been "counterproductive" incentive structures, creating reproductive contexts in which local fertility rates have generally tended to increase rather than diminish.

This leads to a crucial final point, the ineluctable fact that in our multi-national world solutions cannot be imposed from without. Ultimately, the people of each sovereign state must come to terms with, and subsequently resolve, their own local and unique demographic problems (hopefully motivated by a full awareness of global realities). In this regard, given the limited time available and the excruciatingly difficult decisions that must be made, it is daunting to realize that population problems are often the most pronounced in areas of the world where national sovereignty—and the requisite political, economic and social stability—is most tenuous.

Because of these difficulties, it remains to be seen whether humanity will be capable of mounting a unified and lasting effort toward population control. For surely this is an undertaking that has no quantitative nor qualitative precedent, an effort that must be conducted on a species-wide scale, and an endeavor that by its very nature must be sustained for a century or more. While posterity demands that we be successful, I am only cautiously optimistic that such success can be achieved by rational human forethought, or by means compatible with contemporary social, political and ethical norms.

NOTES ABOUT SOURCES:

This hortatory essay—written and revised during the period November 1994 to May 1995—hopefully captures the essence of a demographic perspective I have been developing over the past two decades in my introductory biological anthropology course here at Kenyon College. My primary goal was to provide a clearly-stated and reasonably jargon-free "position paper" for my undergraduate students to think about, react to, and perhaps improve upon. For my part, I have gathered ideas and utilized data from a number of sources. The following are the most important:

1. Abernethy, Virginia. 1993. *Population Politics: The Choices That Shape Our Future*. New York: Plenum.
2. Brown, Lester R. and Hal Kane. 1994. *Full House: Reassessing the Earth's Population Carrying Capacity*. New York: W.W. Norton.
3. Connelly, Matthew and Paul Kennedy. 1994. "Must It Be The West Against the Rest?," *The Atlantic Monthly*, vol. 274, no. 6, pp. 61–84, December.
4. Ehrlich, Paul R. and Anne H. 1990. *The Population Explosion*. New York: Simon and Schuster.
5. Grant, Lindsey. 1992. *Elephants in the Volkswagen: Facing the Tough Questions About Our Overcrowded Country*. New York: W.H. Freeman.
6. Hardin, Garrett J. 1992. *Living Within Limits: Ecology, Economics, and Population Taboos*. New York: Oxford University Press.
7. Hornby, William F. & Melvyn Jones. 1993. *An Introduction to Population Geography* (2nd edition). Cambridge: Cambridge University Press.
8. Kaplan, Robert D. 1994. "The Coming Anarchy," *The Atlantic Monthly*, vol. 273, no. 2, pp. 44–76, February.
9. Lutz, Wolfgang. 1994. "The Future of World Population," *Population Bulletin*, vol. 49, no. 1, June (Population Reference Bureau).
10. Moffett, George D. 1994. *Critical Masses: The Global Population Challenge*. New York: Viking Penguin.
11. Negative Population Growth, Inc. 210 The Plaza, P.O. Box 1206, Teaneck, New Jersey, 07666. (various publications)
12. The Population Reference Bureau, Inc. 1875 Connecticut Avenue, N.W., Suite 250, Washington, D.C., 20009. (various publications)
13. Quick, Horace F. 1974. *Population Ecology*. Indianapolis: Bobbs-Merrill (Pegasus).
14. Westoff, Charles. 1995. "International Population Policy," *Society*, vol. 32, no. 4, pp. 11–15, May/June.
15. Worldwatch Institute. 1776 Massachusetts Avenue, N.W., Washington, D.C., 20036. (various publications)

POLITICAL ASYLUM: THE ACHILLES HEEL OF IMMIGRATION REFORM

David Simcox

January 1995

Immigration of 1.1 million persons a year perpetuates population growth and dims prospects for a smaller, environmentally sustainable U.S. population. Since the 1970s the vast majority of Americans have voted by their fertility rates to stabilize population. But immigration has nullified their choice. Humanitarian immigration—refugees, asylees and temporarily protected persons—has swollen to more than one-quarter of all immigration. Often driven by emotional impulse and perceived national obligations, and unlimited by law, humanitarian intake has escaped rational management.

Political asylum is the most idealistic, most uncontrollable, and most poorly managed of all features of the country's convoluted immigration rules. As envisioned in the 1980 Refugee Act, asylum offers safe haven to persons already in the United States or at a port of entry who can show a well-founded fear of persecution in their countries for reasons of race, ethnicity, religion, political opinion or associations.

The criterion of persecution is the same for asylum seekers here and refugees abroad. But a key practical distinction between refugees and asylees under present arrangements is that the United States chooses from abroad the refugees it will resettle; with political asylum, the United States passively allows itself to be chosen by hundreds of thousands of international migrants, many driven by motives other than refuge.

A WORLD-WIDE LURE

As now applied, U.S. asylum laws proclaim to the globe's 5.5 billion non-Americans that if they can somehow enter the United States and claim persecution within their homelands, they will be able to live and work here for many months, if not years, during the slow paced adjudication of their claims. A greater attraction not lost on millions abroad is that even among those ultimately denied asylum, few have been removed from the United States.

Compassion Gone Awry—In 1992, 45 percent of asylum claimants failed to appear for their initial hearing; they simply took the work authorization card granted by the Immigration Service (INS) and disappeared into U.S. society. Others go through the hearings process, but drop out of sight if asylum is denied. The government now has neither the means nor will to track them down. Other applicants acquire U.S. spouses and citizen children during the lengthy process, making their removal harder. Small wonder then that the system has become an enormous magnet for hundreds of thousands of would-be settlers who cannot qualify under regular immigration rules or are unwilling to wait in line for a visa.

The asylum system is subverted by interest groups' skillful manipulation, by often uninformed compassion among Americans, and by the extreme and unworkable definition of "due process" that asylum's advocates have fastened upon it. An article of faith among immigration advocates is that there can never be too much due process. Allied to this is the assumption that it is better that thousands of marginal claimants receive asylum than one bona fide claimant be denied it.

Thus the system sets itself up to be manipulated by hundreds of thousands. The asylum applicant enjoys far more due process than is required by international obligations or by the U.S. constitution. Prospective refugees abroad have far fewer rights. Court decisions, unchallenged by the executive branch, have expanded the definition of persecution and further reduced the evidentiary burden on the asylum claimant.[1] A history of inconsistent policies, capitulations to interest group demands, and unfounded presumptions have created grounds for expansive rulings in the federal courts.

The scope of asylum's protection has been extended to new allegedly persecuted classes: homosexuals; women in male-dominated societies, or who are victims of spousal abuse, or who are from societies where female circumcision is practiced; and persons claiming to flee China's family limitation laws. Efforts to protect more and more victim classes are as often driven by domestic political wrangling over issues such as women's and gay rights, or right to life, as they are humanitarian reactions to events abroad. **An underlying fallacy that makes asylum open-ended is the assumption of its defenders that the Western yardstick on human rights must be applied to the entire crowded and impoverished world.**

ASYLEES AND ASYLUM ABUSERS: SUBSTANTIAL POPULATION FACTOR

Political asylum, as now legislated, is truly an "Achilles' Heel"—an inherently unpredictable and unmanageable feature of U.S. immigration policy that is the antithesis of the discipline and rationality needed to manage immigration in accord with sound population goals.

A Half-Million Asylum Immigrants, and Growing—The current law's 10,000 ceiling on the number of asylees granted legal permanent residence each year far understates the program's much larger impact on population. Most asylum claimants manage to stay, with or without the blessing of the "green card," the talisman of legal permanent residents. Though the number actually granted asylum is far lower, nearly 500,000 aliens outside the legal immigration process now have gained legal or de facto permanent residence with the help of their access to the asylum channel. In 1993 and 1994 the pool of those admitted for asylum claims grew by nearly 100,000 each year. Uncounted others now living illegally in the United States, but who have not yet claimed asylum, were emboldened to come here and to remain by the availability of the asylum defense if needed to ward off deportation.

The backlog of more than 500,000 asylum claims expected by the end of 1995 is unlikely to be cleaned up under present sluggish procedures. Meanwhile, the long waiting list and the numbers of rejected applicants who stay on are a standing invitation to another quick-fix government amnesty. Indeed, the Justice Department's reluctance so far to remove unsuccessful claimants or cancel their work authorizations amounts to a tacit amnesty.

PUBLIC OUTRAGE OVER ASYLUM ABUSE SPURS SOME GOVERNMENT ACTION

The Clinton administration introduced legislation in 1993 providing for prompt removal of asylum seekers whose claims were clearly frivolous. But it languished in the 103rd Congress. Using existing authority, the administration late in 1994 made changes it contends will reduce decision time on claims by 75 percent while withholding work authorizations for up to six months.[2]

The INS claims this speedier, no-frills treatment of claimants is sending a warning to prospective emulators, reducing new applications 15 to 50 percent from 1994 (depending on the INS source). It is too early to judge the administration's claims of progress.

But even a reduction of 33 percent (the mid-point of the INS estimates) would still mean nearly 100,000 new applications a year. Unless deportations increase—and the current trend is toward fewer non-criminal deportations—most of those applicants will remain in the country. **At best, these remedies will palliate but not cure a flawed premise of asylum—namely that the United States is able and willing to provide full due process to all the millions that could now reach here and make a claim.**

THE WORLD'S PERSECUTED—A CLASS WITHOUT BOUNDS

The prudent assumption must be that the asylum system, without radical reforms, will become an even larger conduit for extra-legal immigration in the future. Rapid world population growth will worsen social and environmental conditions in overpopulated regions and produce millions of new candidates abroad for entry by any means.

The Trap of Definitions—The current expansive definition of persecution opens up the prospect of vast new categories of claimants in a world increasingly given to ethnic and religious divisions. Some legislators would by law make China's mandatory abortion and sterilization policies a legal basis for asylum, opening the door to millions of Chinese of reproductive age and their children. Sponsors of the legislation deny that the number of potential claimants would be that high (reminiscent of Congress's disingenuously low projections of the increase in immigration likely to result from the 1965 immigration law). But the bill's authors themselves admit that a "few million men, women and children" now suffer from China's policy.[3]

The spread of an intolerant Islamic fundamentalism bodes vast new asylum claims from liberal Muslems, non-believers, Christians and other religious minorities in the Muslem world. At the same time, the rise of militant fundamentalist Hinduism in overcrowded India carries the potential to convert that nation's 100 million Muslems into a persecuted class. Current unrest in Africa's largest nation, Nigeria, already an increasing source of illegal immigrants, could revive the ethnic programs of the 1960s, stimulating new waves of asylum seekers. The emphasis on human rights for women has the potential to make countless women in the third world eligible for asylum claims, since their home countries have gender-based customs that they—and western societies—find increasingly difficult to accept.

Current efforts in Congress to reduce legal immigration and end illegal immigration, even if partly successful, will heighten the attractiveness of the asylum gateway for desperate would-be settlers. The recent experience of Germany, where asylum was a constitutional right, dramatizes the explosive growth potential of a lax system. There, asylum claims surged from about 50,000 a year in 1987 to over 400,000 a year in 1992 before the German government applied tough restrictions.

The abuse of the current asylum system mocks the good faith applicants for immigration who wait to enter the United States by the rules. Public support for the needs of genuine refugees suffers in the process. **This uncontrollable immigration valve confounds rational immigration planning, saps the credibility of U.S. immigration controls, and invites greater mass influxes in the future.**

THREE STEPS TO DEMAGNETIZE ASYLUM

If asylum is to cease being the wild card of immigration control, it must be reformed in three general aspects.

First, asylum's value as an alternative route to permanent settlement must be ended by making all grants of asylum temporary only. This would "demagnetize" asylum as an easy way to circumvent legal immigration limits while still helping those truly at risk.

Second, the flow of claimants through the asylum pipeline, now potentially unlimited, must be restricted by far more judicious selection of cases to be considered. While Congress is now considering major increases in the number of asylum officers,[4] huge backlogs, with the attendant danger of "rubber stamping," are likely as long as we pretend that everyone capable of reaching U.S. shores is entitled to his day(s) in court.

Third, the United States must show the world that it will no longer allow its laws to be "gamed." **Those applications for asylum that are accepted for adjudication must be decided quickly, followed by the prompt removal from the country of those rejected.** The administration now talks as if it accepts this principle. But the President was vague about when action would begin on the plan he announced in May, 1995, to triple deportations from the present 40,000 a year.

Sustained deportations of 120,000 a year, once the priority target of criminal aliens has been removed, would greatly reduce the pool of overstays and no-shows by either timely removal or by the credible threat of it[5], thus discouraging potential abusers abroad. The administration must follow through on it.

Here are some specific actions for consideration by policy makers that would support the three general objectives outlined above. Most are drawn from proposals already made in Congress or the executive branch or developed by other industrial nations or presented by other immigration specialists:

Grant asylum for a temporary stay only, ending it when conditions are satisfactory in a country where the asylee has a right to reside. The present practice of granting successful asylum claimants "green cards" is a powerful attraction to economic migrants. Conflict and instability in such countries as Lebanon, Central America, Ethiopia, Poland, and the former Soviet Union brought new waves of political asylees to the United States in the 1970s and 1980s. Most have remained as permanent residents, often joined by relatives from abroad, even though peace and stability have returned to their home countries.

The purpose of asylum should be to protect the truly persecuted rather than to resettle them. The United States should follow a practice of some other western democratic countries in making grants of asylum only for the duration of the conditions abroad that motivated flight. Decisions of U.S. officials to extend or terminate asylum would be based on yearly reviews of asylees' cases and the conditions in countries in which the asylee could legally reside. Important here also would be continuing U.S. diplomatic efforts to persuade sending countries to accept returnees, foreswear persecution of them, and even accept international monitoring if necessary.

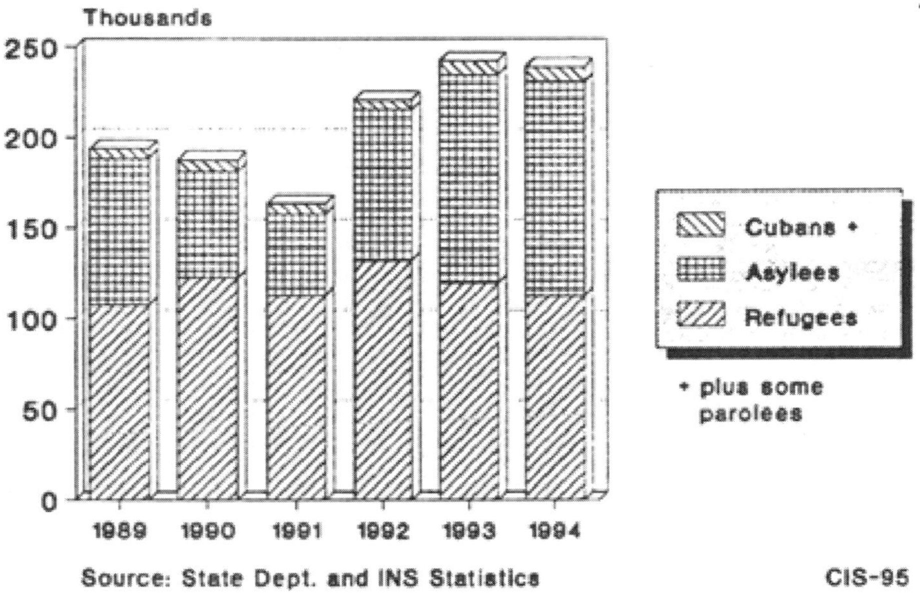

Figure 1.

Family members would be admitted to live with asylees in the United States only if they independently established a well-founded fear of persecution in their own right. Marriage to a U.S. citizen or having U.S. citizen children would no longer be a basis for automatic permanent residence, nor would that status bar removal from the country. Although considered temporary admissions, asylee numbers should still be subject to an overall annual ceiling on allforms of immigration. Those granted asylum should be charged to the ceiling when their stay exceeds two years. That deduction could be restored to the ceiling upon confirmation of the permanent departure of the asylees.

Reject outright all applications for asylum from persons with the rights of residence or sojourn in a country classified by the U.S. government as having adequate human rights protections. The Justice Department now wastes immense resources in processing cases of persons from countries that have satisfactory human rights standards. Often these claimants are "asylum shoppers" seeking the best deal, economic migrants, or persons who have not exhausted their legal remedies in their home countries.

A list of countries with adequate human rights standards should be developed by the Justice and State Departments and updated periodically. Asylum claims from persons eligible to reside or sojourn in those countries would no longer be entertained. The absence of any country from the list, however, would in no way be considered a presumption that asylum is warranted. Strict standards of proof of individual persecution would continue to apply.

Many countries now grant passports without the stringent requirements of nationality applied by the United States. Aliens in possession of a valid passport from a country other than the one they allege to be fleeing would be presumed to have accepted the protection of the issuing country and would be repatriated there.

These examples from asylum adjudication of the past ten years illustrate how such an approach would prevent unjustified claims from tying up the system:

1) The case of an asylum applicant from Northern Ireland claiming to fear IRA violence was under adjudication for several years. Under the proposed approach, her asylum claim would have been summarily rejected because she had the right to reside in the United Kingdom or the Republic of Ireland, both of which have adequate human rights protections.
2) A Somalian and his family claimed asylum at the airport during transit through New York after passing through at least two safe countries, the United Kingdom and Italy. To justify transiting the United States, the family had obtained a valid visas to enter Brazil. Under the proposal, the claimants would have been sent on to Brazil, a country with satisfactory human rights that they had permission to enter.
3) A migrant from apartheid-ruled South Africa flew to New York from Spain, where he had been granted political asylum. He applied for asylum in the U.S., was detained and entered the adjudication system. Under the proposed approach, after appropriate interviews he would have been returned immediately to Spain, a satisfactory human rights country.
4) Afghan asylum seekers in the 1980s often traveled on Pakistani passports to the United States to claim asylum. Under these proposals, no claims for asylum would have been accepted and the travelers would have been returned to Pakistan, whose protection they had accepted.

The prompt rejection of applicants from countries known to be safe would curb "asylum shopping," deter frivolous requests, and spare Justice Department resources for higher enforcement priorities.

Stop illegal aliens and prospective visa overstayers before they can get to the United States and enter the asylum system.

Tighter border and visa controls are needed for a range of good reasons. This is one of them. Specific measures to curb illegal immigration and abuse of visitors' visas will be detailed in a separate NPG position paper. Worth special mention here is INS "pre-clearance" of U.S.-bound passengers at top international airports abroad. Overseas screening of suspect U.S.-bound travelers spares INS the legal and political complications that immediately come into play on U.S. soil.

Quickly remove applicants who have used false documents or otherwise entered illegally.

Congress and the administration are now considering several variants of a process of immediate removal of claimants who have entered surreptitiously or are document abusers and who are determined in an interview with asylum officers not to have a "credible fear" of persecution. These proposals are now variously termed summary exclusion, expedited exclusion, and expedited removal. **The test of "credible fear" would be more stringent than in the past, requiring the asylum officer's finding that "persecution would be more probable than not" if the claimant were sent home.**

Persons entering the United States illegally often do not claim political asylum until detected and threatened with removal. Limiting applications for asylum to a short period after entry or after the presumably threatening political event in the home country would discourage use of the process as a stall. Article 31 of the Geneva Convention on Refugees states that aliens entering a country to claim refugee status must "present themselves without delay to the authorities and show good cause for their illegal entry or presence."

Deserving support is a congressional proposal that an alien must state his intent to seek asylum within thirty days after coming to the United States. Aliens who fail to appear for hearings without good cause—a common occurrence—should have their applications summarily dismissed and be subject to immediate removal.

Make the system credible: adopt effective procedures for finding and removing ineligible aliens. All other proposed changes would be useless in the absence of such procedures. Success here would demand elimination of open-ended deportation processes, such as provisions for multiple appeals provisions. Also essential would be the commitment of more time and money by Justice and other U.S. law enforcement agencies, and improved systems for identifying aliens and determining their whereabouts.

Another element required for success is better cooperation with the receiving countries of deportees to bring about prompt issuance of travel documents and admission of those removed from the United States. One congressional proposal calls for denying visas to those countries that will not take back their citizens. **Credible deportation machinery will strengthen not just asylum processing but the entire system of immigration controls.**

Charge a fee for asylum applications. The sure way to bring about overuse of a product is to give it away. INS was on the right track in 1994 in proposing, unsuccessfully, a fee of $130 per person to apply for political asylum. The fees would have recovered some of the cost of processing and equated the cost of entering through asylum to that of legal immigration. Even temporary asylum in the United States greatly increases the earnings of most of those who gain it. It is only reasonable that the cost of the asylum system be borne by its users and beneficiaries. A non-refundable application fee of $300 per person would be reasonable, with an additional fee of $600 payable on the approval of an application. In cases of proven indigence, deferred payment would be considered. In the same vein, attorneys who file clearly frivolous asylum claims should be required to pay court costs.

MASS FLIGHT TO THE UNITED STATES

So called "mass asylum" situations, such as the arrival of 140,000 Cuban and Haitian boat people in Florida in 1980, can overwhelm the most rational methods for screening would-be asylees and lead to rubber-stamping approvals. The most troubling, but least discussed scenario of mass asylum involves grave political turmoil in Mexico that could send millions of Mexicans to the U.S. border in search of safety.

In its handling of more recent Cuban and Haitian immigration emergencies, and in its multilateral responses to mass asylum situations elsewhere

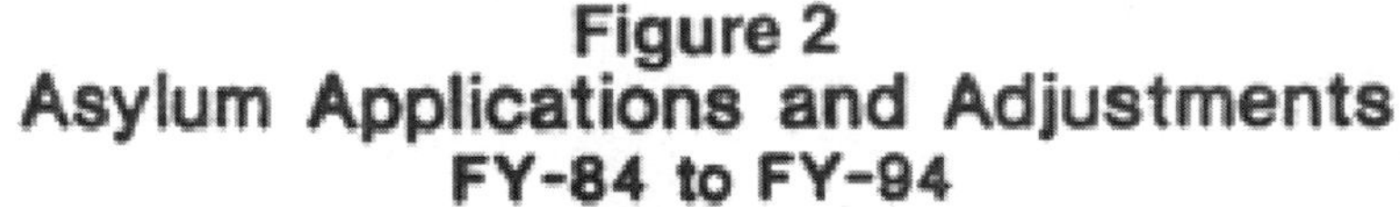

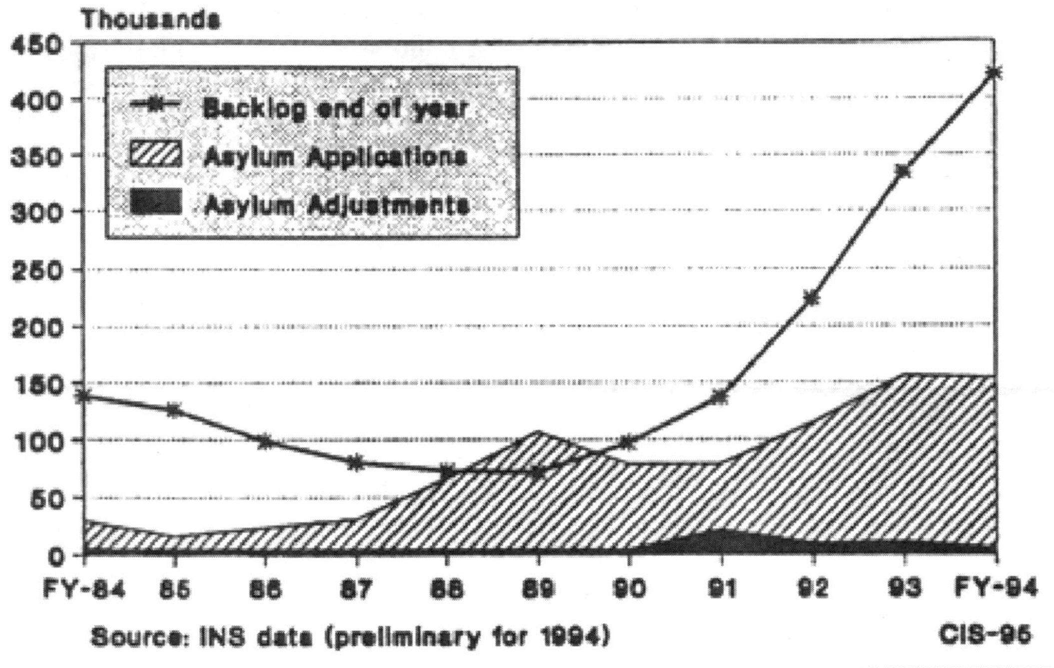

Figure 2.

(Iraq, Rwanda, Southeast Asia and Hong Kong), the United States has gained valuable experience and learned that there are alternatives to passive acceptance of Mariel-type mass population transfers. Interdiction of U.S.-bound migrants, their return to the source country or to a safe haven outsjde the United States, and diplomatic pressure on the sending countries have been shown to be effective.

The Mexican Apocalypse—The United States, in preparing for possible future mass humanitarian migration from Mexico or elsewhere, must further examine the options for developing internationally protected areas within those countries that generate mass flight or in nearby areas. The zones created within Iraq to protect Kurdish and Shiite minorities are good models, as is France's protected enclave within Rwanda.

In the case of mass flight from Cuba and Haiti, The United States effectively used Guantanamo in Cuba and areas in Panama to house asylum seekers and had successfully negotiated similar access to Turks and Caicos islands in the British West Indies. Additional sites, controlled either by third countries or international organizations, or by the United States, should be identified as internationally protected safe havens where unworkable U.S. asylum procedures would not apply.

WARNING: U.S. RHETORIC ANIMATES MILLIONS ABROAD

Since George Washington's time, U.S. political leaders' rhetoric has regularly proclaimed the United States as a haven for the world's downtrodden. It is high time to realize that in a world of instant media coverage and cheap mass travel, these self-congratulatory incantations are taken very seriously abroad. A related complication has been the notion in the cold war years that outflows of people from an adversary nation somehow represent a diplomatic victory.

President Jimmy Carter greeted the initial waves of Mariel boat people in the 1980 with the words, "We'll continue to provide an open heart and open arms to refugees seeking freedom from communist domination," even as U.S. agencies were struggling to slow the flow of boat people.[6] The statement was subsequently used successfully as a defense in court by Cuban-Americans charged with immigration violations. The 1966 Cuban Adjustment Act had helped create a magnet, offering blanket refugee status to Cubans reaching the United States. That cold war measure remains on the books: it stands as a threat to rational control of the Cuban influx that must be expected when travel controls end on the island, and as an incentive to other emigre groups to seek similar preferential treatment.

Congress in the 1970s and 1980s applied pressure on the Soviet Union through such devices as the 1974 Jackson-Vanek trade sanctions act to allow freer emigration of its people. The collapse in 1990 of the Soviet Union and its travel restrictions set the stage for mass Russian immigration to the United States. The Clinton administration even now continues to press China to allow more emigration[7], echoing an appeal of President Carter during Chinese Vice Premier Deng Xiaoping's 1979 visit to the United States. (Hearing this, Deng was reported to have commented: "Are you prepared to accept ten million?")

Even faint and confused signals about immigration from U.S. leaders spur movement abroad. In June 1995, a House of Representatives bill to deter the UN-planned voluntary repatriation of 40,000 refugees in Southeast Asian camps set off riots in the camps, caused thousands of the refugees to reverse their decisions to return voluntarily, and risked stimulating a new exodus from Vietnam.[8] Similarly, presidential candidate Bill Clinton's 1991 pledge to end the Bush administration's interdiction of Haitian boat people sparked a major surge of boat building within Haiti.

The National Interest in Less Immigration—Taming the familiar political rituals of more than two centuries must come as part of a new American appreciation of the limits of U.S. society and resources and the dangers of leaving migration choices to the migrants themselves in a world surging toward ten billion inhabitants. Immigration control is itself a vital national interest, not a diplomatic bargaining chip. Every question of whom to admit and how many is at heart a question about how many Americans there will be in the not distant future.

An America already overpopulated in relation to its resources must make these choices within the limits set by an overall population policy—a careful balancing of fertility, mortality and immigration that will rapidly stabilize the U.S. population and permit it to recede toward a sustainable level in the next century.

The message America must now send abroad is not an open invitation to scores of millions more, but an affirmation of its commitment to bring its own population size down to the limits of the nation's and the planet's life supports. Control and limitation of political asylum are important parts of that message.

NOTES:

1. Testimony of Dan Stein, Executive Director, Federation for American Immigration Reform On Senate Bill S.269, *The Immigration Control and Financial Responsibility Act*. U.S. Senate Subcommittee on immigration. March 14, 1995.
2. "Immigration Agency Revises Rules on Political Asylum." *New York Times*, December 3, 1994
3. Chris Smith and Henry Hyde. "The Mortal Dangers of Parenthood in China." *Washington Times*, June 7, 1995.
4. Report of the House of Representatives Task Force on Illegal Immigration, 104th Congress, June, 1995. P. 41.
5. President's Press Conference of May 6, 1995.
6. Gil Loescher and John Scanlan. *Calculated Kindness*. New York: The Free Press, 1986. p. 184–185.
7. Report to the Congress on Most Favored Nation Trade Status for China, May 28, 1993. *Weekly Compilation of Presidential Documents*. May 31, 1993. p. 987.
8. Doug Bereuter. "Trouble in the Camps of Hong Kong." *New York Times*. June 19,1995.

CLINTON ON POPULATION, PART 1
SOBERING NEWS FROM THE REAL WORLD

Lindsey Grant

February 1995

As the story goes, the optimist said "this is the best of all possible worlds," and the pessimist agreed. What they meant depends on what they expected.

The Clinton administration's performance on population issues would probably satisfy the pessimist and disappoint the optimist. On international population assistance, and measured against the preceding two administrations, it has done well. Measured against third world needs, it has not done nearly so well. As to U.S. population growth—and despite the presence in the administration of people like the Vice President and Under Secretary of State Tim Wirth—it has done almost nothing and may not recognize there is a problem.

The possibilities for the rest of the term must now be judged against the Republican victories last November and the adjustments the Democrats will make as they attempt to regain lost ground.

To put the policies in the context of the problem, let us look first at what is happening to population and to the country.

THE PROBLEM

The nation more than tripled from 76 million in 1900 to 262 million now, and about 43 percent of that growth consisted of post-1900 immigrants and their descendants. A conservative projection with some decline in immigrants' fertility leads to a population of 397 million in 2050 and 492 million in 2100. About 91 percent of that growth would be post-2000 immigrants and their descendants. If fertility and immigration stay where they are, the figure goes up to 440 million by 2050 and passes a half billion long before the end of the century. Growth will be even faster if fertility rises to reflect the higher average fertility of immigrants, compared to the native born.

That begins to put us in a league with China and India, and we would be far more destructive because of our style of living. We are already suffering the environmental pressures generated by population growth; our cities are disintegrating and a generation of youth being wasted. And there is more to come. We are assaulted by urban problems and unemployment, the energy transition, nuclear waste and sewage sludge. More city dwellers will be drinking water from sewage plants. We are threatened by the loss of biodiversity, even as we watch the rising resistance of agricultural pests and human pathogens to pesticides and medicines. Acid rain, climate change, water resource depletion, topsoil loss and stagnating agricultural yields, more pressure on our forests, wetlands and fishery (which is already in a state of collapse.)[1]

The purpose of this paper is not to repeat the evidence but rather to make a point that should be self-evident: U.S. population growth and its driving engine, immigration, should be central issues in governmental policy making.

Population is not even treated as a peripheral issue.

POPULATION ASSISTANCE: THE GOOD FIRST ACT

This section, regrettably, will be brief.

One of President Clinton's first actions was to reverse the Reagan/Bush position that population growth is irrelevant to third world economic success.

Following up on that change, the Clinton budgets have more than doubled U.S. population assistance abroad, to nearly $600 million, in the face of a declining overall foreign aid program. Population assistance is still only about 5 percent of total U.S. foreign aid, and it is much less than the U.S. Government itself recognizes would be necessary to play our part in meeting unmet contraception needs in the third world. There is nevertheless real progress, in the face of political realities such as the domestic unpopularity of foreign aid and the Israeli-Egyptian stranglehold on about half of that aid. A decade earlier, President Reagan proposed to zero out all U.S. population assistance. The U.S. Government has come a long way back toward its traditional leadership in population aid.

THE NEW TOWER OF BABEL

Something ominous has taken place as the participants in the political dialogue have multiplied in recent years. Attention to the dangers of population growth has been submerged by dozens of different voices pressing parochial agendas. The agendas in themselves are sometimes worthy, but we head for disaster as the support for a population policy fragments and the role of population growth in the human future is forgotten.

Representatives of American Indian groups assert that non-indigenous populations are the source of their problem and that "overpopulation is not an issue for indigenous peoples"[2]—even though American Indian fertility is the highest in the nation.

U.S. Women of Color (USWOC) takes the position that poverty should be attacked "by tackling social and economic imbalances, not just by pushing contraceptives. We don't want to wait until the "unmet need" for contraceptives has been satisfied before realizing that we have utterly neglected to boost social and economic progress and failed to alleviate poverty."[3] Those people have yet to consider that a population policy might help achieve their aims, and consequently they bitterly oppose the idea.

The *Earth Island Journal* carries a "declaration" that population and immigration are the "least" of causes of environmental damage, that illegal immigration is the fault of the industrialized countries, that immigrants help rather than harm the economy, etc. etc.[4] Faced with this sort of advocacy, and concerned to retain their own constituency, the main line environmental groups address population only in anodyne generalities and avoid positions on immigration.[5]

Even more significant is the role of militant feminist groups. The Women's Global Network for Reproductive Rights demands that the Population Council stop research on antifertility or contraceptive vaccines. The President of the Planned Parenthood Federation of America (PPFA) told a press conference that "there can be no advancement in the world if the status of women is not improved."[6]

The new stridency and the polarization of our politics have rendered the traditional politics of compromise inoperable. It does no good to say to the true believer: "I agree that your cause is reasonable, and I will support it, but give me the same support for population control. It will help you." The answer is likely to be: "My cause is the only cause!"

CAIRO: THE COMMANDEERED CONFERENCE.

Faced with this sort of militancy, the administration decided to join them rather than fighting them. Department of State Undersecretary Tim Wirth remarked of the U.S. role at the UN International Conference on Population and Development (ICPD) that "women's groups pretty much drove this."[7]

The Programme produced in Cairo at the ICPD last September contains hundreds of recommendations about women's rights and other issues, but almost literally none about population. The assumption is that, given unimpeded freedom of choice, the women of the world will choose the socially desirable fertility level. Therefore, money spent on women's advancement is the most effective way to pursue population goals.

These assumptions are simply speculation. There is no justification for the assumption that free choice will, unguided, lead to the socially desirable level of fertility, and U.S. experience suggests otherwise. It is myth masquerading as truth.

Nowhere does the Programme say that population growth should stop. Nowhere are growing countries urged to give a high priority to stopping (or even slowing) population growth. Governments are urged to "support the principle of voluntary choice in family planning." (section 7.15) The Programme is negative about any stronger action, including "schemes involving incentives and disincentives." (section 7.22) [8]

The Programme has gotten it backwards. At one point, it says "Eradication of poverty will contribute to slowing population growth and to achieving early population stabilization." (section 3.15) The problem is that you can't get there from here. With the third world working age population growing some 60 million per year, and the ILO reporting that one-third of those in the labor force do not earn a minimal subsistence wage, this "solution" simply ducks the issue. A better bet would be to turn it around: a successful population policy would help reduce poverty.

The Programme calls for universal health care, universal primary education, jobs and leadership roles for women, in an era when unemployment is rising, national budgets are caught in the increasing costs of dealing with pollution and unemployment and their consequences, living standards are declining, and many governments are impotent in the face of overwhelming immediate problems. You cannot spend enough to achieve those goals when you don't have enough even now. You must identify those things that will do most to match the reality with the dream.

As William Catton has remarked, "to exalt goals that unalterable circumstances make unattainable is to play with dynamite."

Longtime Sierra Club population activist Judith Kunovsky has given perhaps the most telling response to the argument that population will take care of itself if we take care of women's needs and social inequity. At a Sierra Club round table, it was proposed that in order to deal with population growth "We need to relearn how we treat each other, how whites treat blacks, how men treat women, how rich treat poor, how educated treat uneducated . . . The patterns of dominating the oppressed . . ." Judy responded: "The problems you are describing have been around for thousands of years, and we don't even have a hundred in which to make this stupendous change . . . Resource shortages and population-driven problems are already causing violence throughout the world as people retreat into their own ethnic/religious/national groups for some measure of security. The earth's ecological system, on which we depend for survival, is already threatened . . . We really have very little time to make very dramatic transitions."[9]

Most modern Americans endorse the principle of women's equality, and population advocates have an interest in bettering women's status. Apart from its intrinsic merit, it would probably eventually contribute to a reduction in fertility. The problem is that the third world is not within sight of achieving all the good things that Cairo advocates, and the resources of the richer countries cannot do it for them. If—as I believe—stopping population growth is a condition precedent for the eventual achievement of those goals, and if funds are not unlimited, the issue for a population conference should be "what uses of limited funds would achieve the biggest bang for a buck in lowering fertility." At Cairo, they undertook instead to subvert existing population programs and to divert resources and attention from population programs to women's issues.

The Cairo conference explicitly disavowed the "narrow" population programs, including those developed by the U.S. Agency for International Development, that have had some success in lowering third world fertility. Heretofore, the focus has been on assuring the availability of contraceptives and knowledge about them, promoting awareness of the threat that population growth poses for the pursuit of national goals, and rallying indigenous leaders to promote the population movement. (The connection between women's fertility and their status has been recognized, but it is true that because of bureaucratic resistances and inertia, not enough has been done to make use of that connection.)

At the practical level, there is not enough money for direct population programs, and the Cairo Programme would divert some of it into other causes. The administrative costs for "reproductive health" and AIDS prevention—two-thirds of their cost—are taken from "family planning." (sec. 13.15)

If the administration shifts to the Cairo Programme for its policy guidance, U.S. policy on third world population growth will consist of rhetoric more than practical advice, and the hard-won funds for family planning assistance will now be fair game for anything that can be construed as "women's and reproductive health" or even for the more general Cairo objectives such as helping minorities, children, the aged, or indigenous peoples, or "eliminating poverty."

Unfortunately, the U.S. Government played an active role in creating the Programme, now endorses it, and has modified its statements accordingly. Tim Wirth probably understands the dangers of population growth as well as any U.S. political leader, but he sometimes shifts his rhetoric to accommodate his new constituency. In a March 30, 1994, speech on the Cairo Conference, he said that "the empowerment, employment and involvement of women must be the overriding catalyst for common purpose in . . . Cairo . . . . At the end of this century, the extent to which we fostered the transition to sustainable development will be measured in part by our success in refocusing scarce resources and redirecting national priorities on behalf of women . . ." He listed seven objectives, all of which were directed toward women's issues; none touched on population growth and only one of them included a reference to "voluntary family planning." A good speech on women's rights but not on population.

The Programme says very little about migration, perhaps the most politically explosive demographic issue in the world today, other than to call for the good treatment of migrants. After a brief skirmish, a third world proposal to make family reunification across borders into a "right" was somewhat fudged to call upon receiving countries to "recognize the vital importance of family reunification" and adjust their laws accordingly. (sec. 10.12) The point is far from minor, and the U.S. Government accepted the language, even though Tim Wirth in April 1994 had called for more attention to migration at Cairo. U.S. immigration policy particularly since 1965 has centered on family reunification. This has been a primary reason for the growth of immigration. Any effort to control immigration must address family "chain migration," and the Government's acquiescence in this formula suggests its lack of interest in the subject.

U.S. POPULATION GROWTH: THE MISSING ISSUE

As often happens, the most important thing about the U.S. position at Cairo was what wasn't there. The Cairo Programme was meant to apply to all nations—including the United States. Clearly, the government was thinking about the third world. Indeed, Tim Wirth's March 30th speech would sound ludicrous if it were read as applying to the U.S., where most of the women's rights he advocated already exist.

Wirth apparently believes that population growth is just a third world problem.

The Vice President makes that explicit. In his impassioned and moving book *Earth in the Balance* (1992), he said that "No goal is more crucial to healing the global environment than stabilizing human population." But he was thinking of the third world. As to the United States, he simply listed it among the countries "with relatively stable populations."

Pretty clearly, neither Wirth nor Gore considered recent projections of U.S. population growth. Nor have they made the connection between immigration and population growth. Underlying their statements is the assumption—perhaps unconscious—that third world population growth will simply stay in the third world. In fact, immigration has become the major demographic driving force here and in western Europe. If the administration's two best thinkers on population issues are still at that stage, one may be pretty sure that U.S. population is a non-issue for the rest.

THE AMBIVALENT ADVOCATE

President Clinton's June 29, 1994 population speech to the National Academy of Sciences summarizes the state of his thinking. The President emphasized the need to invest in women. He added that "reducing population growth without providing economic opportunities won't work," and that the population problem would be pursued "as part of the larger issue of sustainable development." He said that "Our population policy is rooted in the idea that the family should be at the center of all our objectives," but he did not elaborate how that relates to population growth. In short, to be unkind: bromides a la Cairo.

Perhaps more fundamental, the President suffers from an internal dichotomy. The speech reflected a mind set that has not yet absorbed the lessons of a finite Earth under environmental onslaught. He would solve every problem by growth. "We're going to talk about what we can do within the G-7 to promote not just growth, but more jobs—because a lot of the wealthy countries are finding they can't create jobs even when they grow their economy."

On world population, he said variously that "you must reduce the rate of population growth" or (ambiguously) "stabilize population growth."

Few people in the population movement would consider that a sufficient goal. If the rate were halved, third world population would still double every three generations. The Earth could not sustain it. The President himself, in a different context (Earth Day 1993) observed that there may be nine billion people on the planet in the future, and that "its capacity to support and sustain our lives will be very much diminished." Unfortunately, he also spoke of "keep(ing) faith with those who left the Earth to us." The first step toward ecological wisdom is that the Earth does not belong to us.

Even the Vice President, for all his eloquence, has dared go no farther than to decry "rapid (world) population growth" and call for its "slowing" (address to the United Nations Commission on Sustainable Development, 1993). It is very difficult for a politician to come right out and state a difficult and perhaps unpopular truth, even if he knows it is true.

The President or his apologists might argue that "of course growth cannot go on forever, but we badly need it right now, to create jobs and eliminate injustice, and to permit the third world to achieve the living standards that the first world enjoys."

The answer to that is that the immediate grows into the long term. Whatever happened to the idea of "sustainability"—so honored in the abstract, so ignored in practice? It is wise to focus on jobs. Indeed, technological change has led to the situation the President described; economic growth in industrial countries does not necessarily translate into more jobs. However, the dream of social justice and prosperity for all cannot be achieved for an expanding population, and the effort would fundamentally alter the Earth's ecosystem. It can only be achieved if we attack the twin evils of population growth and destructive consumption. Starting now.

The dream of perpetual growth is past. We cannot grow our way out of our problems.

THE SILENT CENTER

Perhaps the President should not be blamed. He is a politician, and there is very little political pressure on him to take a more forthright position on population growth.

At a personal level, I encounter everywhere—among friends, at lectures, on radio talk shows—the recognition that the twin problems of population growth and wasteful consumption are, along perhaps with social disintegration, the principal threats to America's future. If others believe that, they are silent. When did the reader last see an editorial, or hear a politician or TV pundit, call upon the President to address population growth?

They say we get the politicians we deserve. If this is the best we can do now, when will we do better? Meanwhile, one hears the ticking of the population clocks.

PCSD: THE TINY WHITE KNIGHT

In Washington, if you have a problem but don't want to address it, create a committee.

On June 14, 1993, the President created the Presidential Council on Sustainable Development (PCSD). He charged it with helping to "set policies to grow the economy and preserve the environment . . ." Five times, in uncharacteristically brief remarks, he returned to that theme, saying "That is what we mean by sustainable development." He said that energy-efficient and less polluting light bulbs, computers, refrigerators and automobiles would sell around the world and make America prosperous. In effect, he equated sustainability with environmentally benign technologies. He did not mention population growth.

He said nothing about depletion of renewable resources or destructive levels of consumption.

The Council consists of a mix of cabinet members, industrialists, environmental organization leaders, and one labor union officer, with a judicious mix by gender and ethnicity. The co-chairs are an industrialist and an environmentalist. It does not include academicians or scientists, but there are some on the various working groups created to help carry out the mandate. It initially had seven Task Forces, covering some appropriate areas such as Energy and Transportation, Natural Resources, and Sustainable Agriculture. Others such as "Sustainable Communities" are almost certain to get mired in debate among proponents of different visions of Utopia. Inexplicably, the Population and Consumption Task Force was created only belatedly and over some opposition, after Tim Wirth made a very strong pitch that "the United States must adopt a process to address the impact of overpopulation/consumption."

The Council in April 1994 adopted a fifteen-point "Vision Statement." It was the sort of thing that one might expect such a group of well-intentioned people to adopt. Nevertheless, when put out for public comment, it was criticized from both sides: for being too "pro-growth" and for being both "anti-growth" and incompatible with "basic American values." So much for national consensus.

On population, the Vision called for stabilization "at a level consistent with the capacity of the earth to support its inhabitants." It was very general and did not address the U.S. specifically. It failed to address the question: " . . . at what consumption level, and with what margin of safety? Bangladesh? the United States?" I wish that it had gone beyond "sustainability" to the search for "optimum." Nevertheless, it did say "stabilize" rather than hiding behind vague language about "rapid population growth."

The Council's report is presently scheduled for next October, after which it will presumably dissolve, though its mandate can be extended to 1997. It would be premature to guess in detail as to what will emerge. By current indications, it will probably be a good general primer on modern social and economic issues, and it may have some good ideas for resolving conflicts between environmental and industrial policy. However, if experience is a guide, it faces the following limitations:

- **Irrelevancy.** There has been a succession of such reports for nearly fifty years. None of them has had a perceptible effect on policy.[10] To affect policy as it is made, any group trying to address the broad issue of "sustainability" must be in the action line, as the National Security Council is. It must be able to bring its concerns to bear as any new policy or development is discussed—welfare, health, the Haitian/Cuban boat people or whatever—before the policies are decided. Perhaps the best that can be said of the Council process is that some Cabinet members may read the things that are being written in their names, and that this may affect their own thinking—about the time they leave. One Secretary of Agriculture has already left.

- **Lack of specific recommendations.** If a press conference by the co-chairmen last October 21st is any indication, the Council will place a very high premium on unanimity or consensus, and this forces it to generalize. Only very specific recommendations—e.g. "There should be a federal carbon tax, rising to $xx by 2000."—are likely to receive much attention or create specific issues on which the administration will feel it must take a position. However, such recommendations would stir up opposition everywhere. (Look what happened to the President's modest proposal for a fuel tax increase.) The new Republican Congress would react to an encroachment on their turf, and the President's advisers would be pressing the Council to cool it for political reasons.

- **Impermanence.** When the Council dissolves, there is no indication that there will be any continuing mechanism to incorporate its recommendations into policy.

- **Bureaucracy.** The Council will report to the President through the Director of the White House Office of Environmental Policy, which is now being folded into the Council on Environmental Quality. CEQ has been around for a generation and has never been able to carve out much of a place for itself in the decision process.

It pays to be cynical. One is not disappointed. The best bet is that the report will reach the President's desk, he will say "thank you," and that will be that.

The time would have been better spent within the system, hammering out specific proposals to deal with the real issues raised by "sustainability." On population policy, the Council activity permits the administration to say it is doing something. If it really wanted to do something, it should be seeking a "process," as Wirth said, to bring population issues into the policy process. (I will come back to this in the next NPG FORUM.)

THE REPUBLICAN CHALLENGE

Prospects for continued support for U.S. assistance to international population programs have dimmed with the November elections.

Senator Jesse Helms (R/NC), long-time scourge of "liberals" and opponent of foreign aid, is to take over the Senate Foreign Relations Committee. Senator Mitch McConnell (R/KY) will become chair of the Senate Appropriations Foreign Operations Subcommittee. He has already said he wants to zero out all population assistance and all aid to Africa.[11] A tight budget will reinforce these negative signals about population assistance. The brief period of a rejuvenated U.S. role in international population aid is in for heavy going.

The effects of the elections on U.S. population growth are much less predictable.

The now famous "Contract with America" originated in the House Republican Conference and was endorsed by more than 300 Republican candidates for the House and by candidates for state and local positions. Three of the proposals in the Contract relate to population, undoubtedly by accident.

1. In reforming welfare, the Contract would prohibit welfare to minor mothers, limit AFDC (Aid to Families with Dependent Children) to five years, and deny increases for children born to mothers while on welfare. If carried out, these measures would make raising children much more unattractive for young unwed mothers. (The counter argument that AFDC does not encourage pregnancy is less than convincing.) It would also raise some horrendous questions about the well-being of the children who are born, anyway.
2. The Contract promised "a $500 per child tax credit." One can only speculate how much a credit of this size would influence child-bearing. If anything, however, it is certainly pro-natalist.
3. The Contract would limit welfare benefits to citizens. That provision might discourage some people from bringing elderly "dependents" to the

U.S., but the impact on population growth would be negligible. Perhaps more important, the anti-immigrant message might dissuade some would-be immigrants.

The tax credit idea is not new. The $500 credit was in the Republicans' March 1994 budget proposal. In 1992, most of the presidential candidates—even Al Gore—offered some sort of proposal for exemptions or tax credits for children. The principal effect of the Contract proposal—aside from its fiscal irresponsibility was to encourage President Clinton to make a counter-offer only slightly less "generous." He would give the credit for children below age thirteen. Both parties are thus inadvertently in favor of a pro-natalist proposal. Other recent laws and proposals will affect fertility and thus population growth. The Democrats' Family Leave Act is probably pro-natalist; on the other hand, they raised tax benefits in the Earned Income Credit but limited the benefits to two children, and thus could be seen as promoting the two child family. Both parties are calling for efforts to limit teenage pregnancies, which would depress fertility.

These demographic effects are accidental and conjectural. Immigration is the real current population issue.

A columnist remarked that there is a battle going on for the soul of the Republican Party. The center has shifted on immigration policy, from advocacy of liberal immigration to opposition. Messrs. Kemp and Bennett opposed California's Proposition 187 (which calls for an end to most educational and welfare assistance to illegal aliens) and argued for a permissive view on immigration. They were roundly excoriated within the party.

The battle is far from over. The business interests that like more immigration because it provides cheap labor are hardly defeated, yet. In fact, Congressman Gingrich has already backed away from his "Contract" on the question of welfare payments to non-citizens. The Social Security Administration reported that the proposal would cause over 400,000 of them to lose Social Security SSI (Supplemental Security Income) benefits. Shortly thereafter, he told the National Restaurant Association that the Republicans would "revisit" that proposal. He went on to say: "I am very pro legal immigration. I think legal immigration has given America many of its most dynamic and creative citizens, and I think that we would be a very, very self-destructive country if we sent negative signals on legal immigration."[12]

On the other hand, the November elections brought advocates of more restrictive immigration policies into new and powerful roles. Two restrictionist Texans move into powerful House committee assignments: Archer into the Chairmanship of the Ways and Means Committee, Lamar Smith to chair the Immigration Subcommittee. A critical shift occurs in the Senate, where Senator Kennedy, arch foe of immigration control, is replaced by Senator Simpson, who advocates lower legal immigration, a better system of personal identification to control illegal immigration, and repeal of the 1966 Cuban Refugee Adjustment Act (which practically assures Cubans of legal residency if they can get to the United States). Simpson is seen as a moderate conservative on immigration; he differed with the House Republicans' "Contract" on the treatment of legal aliens and their children, and California's Proposition 187 on illegal aliens. He will probably carry considerable weight on both sides of the aisle.

Some sorting of priorities needs to be undertaken. Simpson would like to move on legal immigration levels; Smith counters that the first priority is illegal immigration. Rep. Elton Gallegly (R/CA) has been charged with putting together a special task force on immigration reform. The chances look pretty good that a proposal on immigration will emerge in Congress.

President Clinton is trying to govern a lion's den. In this era of polarized politics, he is unlikely to get very far with his international population policy, but political strategy may force him to address immigration. If so, it hasn't happened yet.

IMMIGRATION: POLICY BY ACCIDENT

Representative Tony Beilenson says that "population is the big issue." Those of us who agree with him can draw little comfort from his assessment. The depressing fact is that the powers in Washington are not thinking about population.

Population policy is being made quite incidentally as a byproduct of immigration policy. Immigration is a very hot issue indeed, right now—because of the budgetary costs and the competition for jobs, not because of its impact on population growth. And the issue has reached Washington, not because of those effects, but because of the struggle for political advantage. (Perhaps the politicians are beginning to hear what public opinion polls have been reporting for years.)

Nevertheless, to a large degree immigration policy is population policy, even if it is accidental. If immigration is reduced, the country's growth rate will slow. If it is sharply reduced, the country will stop growing, barring a rise in fertility. If, by accident or design, immigration policy drives population, how does the administration stack up by that pragmatic test?

Very badly. To be charitable, it is rudderless. Each of us has our own version of "politically correct," and Democrats find it very hard to seem to be "against immigration." The Governors of California and Florida, and the belated Republican embrace of better control, have dragged the Democratic administration into addressing illegal immigration, but it has not gone willingly.

The Jordan Commission. The President after considerable delay appointed ex-Congresswoman Barbara Jordan to head the Commission on Immigration Reform, a temporary body created under the Immigration Act of 1990 to examine U.S. immigration policy. Jordan briefed Congress last August and the Commission submitted its first report in September.

The report came out in favor of restricting illegal aliens' access to all but emergency public health and welfare services. It also proposed the phased introduction of a system of identification that would permit the government to know who is and who is not legally in the U.S. A better system of identification would help to control crime and drugs and to assure that the tax burden is equitably shared. It is essential if the Immigration Reform and Control Act of 1986 (IRCA), is to work. IRCA makes it illegal to hire illegal aliens, thus in theory diminishing the appeal of the United States to prospective immigrants. Official study groups for years have underlined the need for better identity documents, but that provision was gutted as the price of passage for the 1986 act. Since then, the principal effect of the act has been to generate a huge business in false documentation.

Barbara Jordan was the ideal person to reintroduce the issue of identity. A Black woman with excellent liberal credentials and considerable personal stature, she could make the proposal without providing a target for those who see the ability to remain anonymous as a natural right.

The White House reaction has all the earmarks of an internal struggle. Leon Panetta said that the

Justice Department would make recommendations in the fall (it didn't), and that the Jordan proposal would be "one of the ideas we need to look at," but he warned about violating "individual rights." An unidentified spokesman dismissed the Jordan proposal. There things sat until January.

The President himself has admitted that his health reform proposal would not work without means of identifying who is entitled. This is another of those "politically correct" hot buttons. On the eve of an election the administration did not dare touch the proposal, whatever its merits and despite the fact that the United States is probably alone among modern nations in having no reliable way of ascertaining who a person is. Somebody in the White House is hung up over symbols and myths and is thereby resisting an opportunity to do something real about illegal immigration.

"Accepting the Immigration Challenge." The administration in November 1994 published a triennial report, as required by the immigration act of 1986. (This is separate from the "Jordan commission" report.) It has good news, bad news, and—most ominously—no news at all for those concerned by mass immigration's propulsion of already high U.S. population growth.

The good news is that the report professes a commitment of the Clinton Administration to curb illegal immigration and to halt the abuses of political asylum that have swelled the backlog of applications to more than 400,000 in 1994, and increasing by some 150,000 a year. The administration has begun to build up the numbers, equipment and technology of the U.S. Border Patrol, concentrating on major points of illegal entry, such as San Diego and El Paso. The early numbers from the border give reason for hope.

As a deterrent to fraudulent claims of asylum, the administration has begun to deny work authorization permits to pending claimants for six months and is working to speed up both the decisions on claims and the deportation of those rejected. Washington hopes that shortening the waiting period for a ruling on claims from twenty-four months to six months will end a key disincentive to frivolous claims.

Other promised measures to combat illegal immigration and the accompanying abuse of asylum involve a crackdown on alien smugglers, more diplomatic pressure on sending countries, such as Taiwan and China, more cooperation with major air carriers, and better identification and swifter expulsion of criminal aliens. (The promise of "better identification," be it noted, is in conflict with what the White House was saying about the Jordan commission proposal.)

INS (Immigration and Naturalization Service) expenditures have been rising about 10 percent per year since 1990. They are scheduled for a 20 percent rise in FY1995. Personnel strength, not counting short-term hires for the 1987–90 amnesty program, has remained essentially flat since 1985. Positions are projected to increase 7 percent this fiscal year.

For these efforts, however, the Clinton administration deserves limited credit at best. The Administration has professed its determination to manage the border and the asylum process while sending contrary signals by rhetoric and actions that promote illegal entry and asylum claims. As we will see later, the government has been lamentably indecisive in handling Haitian, Cuban, Chinese and Salvadoran asylum seekers and illegal residents.

In its rhetoric, the administration continues to hold out the United States as the willing recipient of all the world's oppressed, with no limits. The language of the report commits the country to an asylum policy that is breathtaking in its expansiveness and ultimately unrealizable:

> *"Under these reforms, anyone, from any place, at any time, despite entry or immigration status, may still apply for asylum in the United States, and not be returned to any place where he or she fears persecution due to race, religion, membership in particular social group, or political opinion."*

The really bad news in the President's report is the news that is missing. The report fails to even acknowledge or discuss problems with legal immigration, now at nearly one million a year, and its consequences for the country's population and environmental future. Despite the role in immigration policy of environmentalist Al Gore, this report says not a word about the long-term soundness of the nation's population-resource balance. The report is short on analysis and long on frothy verbiage. Gore himself is prominently quoted as saying . . . "our approach to immigration must not be on closing borders, but on opening our hearts."

Rhetorical references to the country's immigration "traditions" and its need to maintain "generous" policies suggest an Administration committed basically to more of the same for legal immigration. Indeed, the report affirms that Washington feels compelled to deal with illegal immigration and asylum abuse largely because public anger could threaten our "generous" legal immigration.

Equally troubling is the President's quickness to affirm as national doctrine presumed benefits of legal immigration which are still in dispute in academia and within his own bureaucracy, such as job creation, "needed workers" for employers, and establishment of businesses. Whatever the outcome of the Jordan commission studies of immigration's costs and benefits, it sounds as if the President's mind is already made up.

Major immigration reform advocacies are demanding a moratorium on immigration so that the nation can decide how many immigrants should come and from where, and how should we enforce the rules. A moratorium is indeed needed, first of all a moratorium on the use of Ellis Island rhetoric in weighing the troubling demographic, environmental and resource implications of continuing mass immigration.[13]

Controlling the Border. Politics may have helped to drive the steps that have been taken. IRS personnel were transferred to San Ysidro just before the election, in an unsuccessful effort to placate California voters. At El Paso, the INS achieved some success in slowing the cross-border movement by transferring all available personnel to the border itself. Apparently, this was a local idea, and the first reaction from INS Washington was to worry about the political fallout.

INS has announced that work permits will henceforth be issued at the regional level rather than by local offices, to control the supply and restrict their illegal issuance (they are said to be worth about $500 each.)[14]

Haiti and Cuba. The tragicomedy of the "boat people" from Haiti and Cuba is a dramatic example of the troubles that result from a vacillating policy.

Part of the problem is the Cuban Refugee Adjustment Act of 1966, previously mentioned. It was passed in the enthusiasm of the Cold War, to score propaganda points, and it has assured Cubans of almost automatic permanent residence—if they can get to the United States. Over the years,

Haitians (whose economic situation is far more desperate) have, like the Cubans, been making their way to Florida, and they have learned that the charge of racism embarrasses the United States Government when it gives them less favorable treatment. They watch U.S. policy very closely for any signs of softness.

President Bush in May 1992 ordered the repatriation of Haitian boat people intercepted at sea, to forestall their landing and claiming asylum. Presidential candidate Clinton denounced the policy. When elected, however, he did not change it. Then, in April 1994, facing criticism from human rights groups, he allowed several hundred Haitians ashore in the United States for interviewing. Other Haitians got the word and started moving. On May 8, the White House announced that thenceforth they would not be allowed ashore, but would be interviewed aboard ships or at "safe havens" elsewhere.

For both Cubans and Haitians, the prospect of getting picked up for an interview, usually just off their own coast, seemed like a great idea, and they came in waves. The White House tried in July to reverse the May 8 announcement, but too late. We stuffed boat people into our Guantanamo base and negotiated with governments around the Caribbean to let us store them there.

In early January, having put Haiti's elected president back in office, we forcibly returned the Haitians from Guantanamo to Haiti.

The Cubans have given us more trouble. The 24,000 or so in Guantanamo are hanging tough. To stop further movement, we negotiated a deal with Castro. He stopped the boat people, and we promised to take at least 20,000 legal immigrants a year from Cuba—an unparalleled deal, and an end run around U.S. immigration laws, using the Attorney General's "parole" power. We insisted that those at Guantanamo would be processed under that agreement, and that we would not allow the Cubans to come from Guantanamo to the United States. Then, in November we took some old and ailing Cubans to the U.S. In December, the INS announced that we would move one-third of the others—children and their parents—to the United States. Cubans in Florida have a lot of political clout. Cubans we had stored in Panama rioted because they weren't getting the same treatment.

The Haitians and their allies, of course, screamed "racism." Parole was given to only 23 Haitians, all relatives of strongman Cedra, apparently as part of the deal to persuade him to leave.

The whole mess presented the country with an example—perhaps unique in our history—of immigration issues driving foreign policy. Our intervention in Haiti resulted, not from some sudden urge to "restore democracy" in that beleaguered country, but from the visceral recognition, at the last minute, that Florida and the United States cannot accommodate the flood of boat people.

Perhaps there is progress, of a sort. The last time there was one of these surges (the "Mariel" boatlift of 1980), President Carter initially welcomed them "with open arms and open hearts." As we have seen, the Vice President still goes in for "open hearts," but not when faced with an immediate test of the rhetoric.

The administration's visceral response was right, if belated, but only partly relevant to the problem. The boat people were not fleeing dictatorship; they have never had a functioning democracy. They were escaping a land that has been devastated by its population growth. Population has almost doubled since 1960; the forested area has declined to less than 2 percent of the land area, and the remnant forests are still being cut. The soil has washed away, and the people are desperate. The surge of boat people occurred because the Haitians saw opportunity in a vacillating U.S. policy and hoped that they might be treated like Cubans.

Assisting Haiti's first elected president to return to his country was well enough, once we had gotten mired in Haitian politics, but Haitians are not going to stay obediently in Haiti even if democracy establishes a tentative foothold there. They will try to get to the United States and the possibility of a better life, and they will stop trying only if they are convinced that they will not be allowed to stay.

There are other potential "Haitis" around the world. If we are to avoid driving United States population toward the desperate conditions that prevail now in Haiti, we will need to reform our immigration policies and procedures so as to avoid drawing the desperate from elsewhere. We must convince Haitians and others that they will not be allowed to stay illegally in the United States.

Beyond that, if we are to help Haiti or anybody, we must recognize that there is little hope of success unless population growth is stopped and reversed. We should help them in that epochal task, but a military occupation itself doesn't tackle the job. By restoring some degree of order, it may in fact accelerate Haitian population growth.

Byzantium on the Potomac. The floundering was not limited to Cubans and Haitians. The government has been unable to develop a clear and consistent idea of what constitutes a refugee or asylee.

Since the Bush administration, the government and the courts have been wavering as to whether opposition to the Chinese government birth control program was grounds for granting Chinese asylum. In 1993 the Board of Immigration Appeals ruled it out. In 1994, when Chinese began wading ashore on both coasts, the INS started out firm. It put them in detention while their asylum applications were heard.

That lasted until August. Then the White House decided that if they really faced persecution for resisting Chinese birth control policies, Chinese should be allowed to stay in the U.S. Granting them refugee status was a bit embarrassing, however, so a new category was created (without benefit of law): "humanitarian relief." Now, they can stay, but in an indefinite legal limbo.

Another ambiguous message was the Clinton Administration's announcement in December 1994 that it would no longer extend the "temporary" protected status granted to Salvadoran migrants in 1990, because El Salvador is now peaceful. But at the same time an administration spokesmen acknowledged that the nearly 200,000 Salvadorans affected would not necessarily have to go home. They can apply for political asylum (guaranteeing months or years of judicial process), or seek permanent residence status if they have an American spouse or have been in the U.S. for seven years. Those with work permits were promised nine months' stay of deportation.

Communist rule has ended, but we are accepting about five times more "refugees" from the erstwhile Soviet Union than we did in 1989. Twenty years after the end of the Vietnam war, we still taking in Vietnamese war refugees, despite any evidence of continuing persecution, and even as we move toward formal recognition of Vietnam.

We send a message of weakness with the vague and sometimes bizarre rules as to what constitutes grounds for asylum. A judge in 1990 allowed a Mexican gay's claim that his sexual preference would lead to harassment in Mexico. The Attorney General promoted the decision to a general principle in 1994. (Last August, the original Mexican asylee died in California of AIDS.) Another applicant has successfully resisted deportation on the grounds that her daughters would be exposed to female circumcision if they went home to Nigeria. We have stretched the definitions beyond rational limits, and a good share of the world's population, if it could get here, could find a basis to claim asylum.

In a forthcoming NPG FORUM paper, we shall outline what the government might do to control illegal immigration, if it wished. The problem is that the government really doesn't really know what it wants to do about illegal immigration. As a result, it veers with every criticism and multiplies its problems. As to rising legal immigration, the administration quite clearly would rather just avoid the issue.

The 1995 State of the Union address. The President said very little about immigration. Buried deep in the speech was the statement that "All Americans . . . are rightly disturbed by the large numbers of illegal aliens entering our country. The jobs they hold might otherwise be held by citizens or legal immigrants; the public services they use impose burdens on our taxpayers." This was followed by a (much overstated) description of what the administration has done, a promise to speed the deportation of illegal aliens arrested for crimes, and a final almost throw-away promise to do more to "identify illegals in the workplace as recommended by the commission headed by . . . Barbara Jordan." After every evidence of a pitched struggle in the White House, he thus seems to have come down, albeit unenthusiastically, on the side of better identification. We shall wait to see if anything happens.

Sometimes, presidents have to recognize where the buck stops, politically painful though it may be. Vacillation is not always good for a president, and the time has come for the Democratic Party to re-examine its traditional pro-immigration mind set. It could turn out to be good politics as well as good policy.

THE PROSPECT

After two years in office, an administration that seemed to offer the prospect of a real U.S. population policy has shown that the hope was false. Population policy has become an accidental offshoot of immigration policy. Both parties are offering rhetorical praise of legal immigration, and both are equivocal about handling illegal immigration. And both parties are divided on both issues.

Nonetheless, the Republicans seem to be moving around the Democrats' flank. Governor Pete Wilson of California is a born again hero in the immigration wars. While Senator, he fought in 1986 for the "agricultural labor" loophole and in 1990 for increased legal immigration. Now, reversing course, he seems to have legitimized immigration control as a Republican issue.

The Republicans may be getting tougher on immigration, but they are likely to oppose spending money to help third world nations to deal with the problem at the source. The Democrats are somewhat better on that question, but abysmal on U.S. population issues.

It isn't clear-cut. In Congress, Democrats (e.g. Senator Reid and Rep. Bilbray) have sponsored or cosponsored bills to limit immigration. At the state level, Democratic Governor Graham in Florida based his successful reelection effort on the demand for a more responsible Federal role in immigration policy. In this and other areas such as welfare and health policy, political lines seem to be shifting: the states and their governors vs. the center, instead of Democrat vs. Republican. And the states are on the offensive. This probably means continuing pressure for better control of immigration, since the pain occurs at the state and local level.

What we are seeing is complex: the possibility of practical action on part of the population problem in the absence of any general national resolve to address it. What does this mean for those of us who believe that population growth must stop? I will offer some thoughts on that conundrum in the following NPG FORUM.

NOTES:

1. The projections, and the environmental consequences, are available in Leon Bouvier & Lindsey Grant *How Many Americans?* (San Francisco: Sierra Club Books, 1994) Recent Census Bureau projections are roughly comparable and also make the point that immigration will become the principal source of growth in the next century. The "constant fertility" projection was done for this paper.
2. National Audubon Society *Population Newsletter*, Summer '94 p.5.
3. UNFPA *Populi*, May 1994, p. 10.
4. *Earth Island Journal*, Spring (Northern Hemisphere), Fall (Southern Hemisphere) (sic), 1994.
5. See NPG FORUM paper *The Timid Crusade*, January 1994.
6. ICPD Newsletter No. 14, April 1994, p.7.
7. Susan Chira, "Women Campaign for New Plan to Curb the World's Population," *New York Times*, 4-13-94, pp A 1, A 12.
8. For a detailed discussion of the Cairo Conference, see NPG FORUM paper *The Cairo Conference: Feminists vs. the Pope*, July 1994. That paper analyzed the draft Programme, but the final version is substantially unchanged except for the use of compromise language on abortion.
9. *Sierra* September/October 1994, p.52.
10. For a history of "foresight" efforts such as this, and a summary of proposals that have been made for their improvement, see Lindsey Grant *Foresight and National Decisions: the Horseman and the Bureaucrat* (Lanham, MD: University Press of America, 1988; still in print but available more inexpensively from The World Future Society, Bethesda MD. 301-656-8274.)
11. AP 12-29-94.
12. AP, Washington, January 9, 1995.
13. I am largely indebted to David Simcox for this section.
14. AP 1-1-95.

CLINTON ON POPULATION, PART 2
WAITING FOR AL

Lindsey Grant

February 1995

Tom Lehrer used to sing a song about Vice President Hubert Humphrey: "Whatever became of Hubert? . . . Are you sad? Are you cross? Are you gathering moss? . . . Oh, Hubert what happened to you?" (My memory of the lyrics may be inexact, but that was the idea.) Vice Presidents are not supposed to be heard, and Al Gore has disappeared into the traditional obscurity. He is doing some useful but unsung work—"reinventing government"; cleaning up the bureaucracy—which may well be swept away by the sledgehammer proposals for cutting government now being voiced.

There are a few people in government who have made the connection between population growth and environmental decline. Among them is the Vice President. More than any other national U.S. political leader, he has grasped the reality that growth cannot continue forever in a finite space. He has not yet applied that wisdom to his own country, but the United States has reached a level of population and consumption that brings "forever" into sight. He might yet play a role in bringing population into policy, and one of his ideas—for better foresight machinery—could be employed in a deliberate effort to build a consensus for a population policy.

This in itself is good reason for trying to enlist the Vice President.

SOURCES OF OPPOSITION

Earlier Forum articles have mentioned some of the resistances that make population a particularly difficult and unpopular topic to take on. To list several of them:

- Immigration and fertility. These are the only two variables available to influence population change. To limit immigration is to break the faith for many people who are imbued with the "one world" dream. To address population growth through fertility stirs up hornets on both sides: doctrinaire feminists who fight any proposal to meddle with women's decisions about child-bearing; and right-to-lifers who equate family planning with abortion.
- Multiple agendas. There has been an explosion of groups seeking social justice of one sort or another. Very few of them have made the connection with population growth. The political landscape is full of lobbies working at cross purposes or competing for resources. They do not see the ways in which population growth and intensified competition block their own agendas, and consequently they look upon the population movement as a competitor.
- Innumeracy (in Garrett Hardin's memorable neologism). How often I have heard people resist the idea of a population policy because "it's not just a matter of numbers," when they don't know the numbers. In fact, demography is supremely a matter of numbers, and those numbers affect the

pursuit of most personal and social goals. Comparative national math proficiency tests repeatedly demonstrate that Americans by and large are less able to deal with numerical concepts than other nations' students. The deficiency makes it difficult to reach people with numerical arguments.

- Relativism. Any proposal to address population growth encounters the response: "but you must take cultural differences into account." True, but that applies to the way in which the population argument is presented, and to the approach that different cultures might take to limiting fertility. It does not somehow vitiate the impact of population growth on a society. (Interestingly, this "cultural difference" argument disappears when advocates are pressing their own agenda. At the Cairo population conference last September, the feminist agenda was hardly muted in deference to Vatican and conservative Arab views.)

Other attitudes play a role. Many young people, in particular, ferociously criticize their own society and idealize others, defer to the immigrant and ignore their own less fortunate compatriots. I am hesitant to get into psycho-history, but there does seem to be an element there of hatred and rejection of their own society.

Whatever the source of opposition, the response is denial. Deny there is a population problem, and you do not face a challenge to your own mindset.

- Passivity. At the other end of the line, at various levels of government, population growth is taken as a given—an "independent variable"—that must be accommodated but cannot be changed. This attitude can be seen in Washington and among the professional planners in my county of Santa Fe, even while the voters have elected City and County councils on "no-growth" tickets.

Beyond these attitudes, there is a fundamental block to an effective population policy. It is the mindset that growth is the natural and necessary solution to immediate problems.

GROWTH AS A "SOLUTION"

We pointed out in the preceding NPG Forum that even those politicians who abstractly recognize the population problem instinctively revert to growth as a solution to the problems facing them. President Clinton has said some of the right words about population growth, but when faced with a real problem such as unemployment, he reverts to the thoroughly American and Romantic idea of growing out of them.

Clinton is not alone. Our society is emerging from an era that William Catton has called "the Age of Exuberance."[1] Endowed by a seemingly limitless abundance of fossil energy, first the United States and then Europe and Japan have been swept up in a remarkable spurt of growth. Growth has seemed to work before, and the natural response to challenges is to go back to that solution. If we are running out of oil, create incentives so the industry will find more. If people are hungry in the third world, they need a "green revolution."

For a time, success succeeds, but eventually it may generate its own destruction. Since petroleum resources are finite, incentives simply hasten their exhaustion. The green revolution was only a temporary fix, to provide a little time while the third world tries to stop population growth from eating up the increase, as Norman Borlaug, the leading figure in that "revolution," has pointed out.

Most of the world thought that growth was the divine order of things and a permanent condition, when in fact its continuation is both a danger and, eventually, a mathematical impossibility.

FAILURE OF THE DECISION PROCESS

Let me take energy as one important example of the ways in which the U.S. Government is digging us into a hole because it has no mechanism—no "process" in Tim Wirth's words—to weigh the impacts of our population growth on the pursuit of policy.

Overall, we depend on imports for 22 percent of our national energy needs, compared with 6 percent in 1970. For petroleum, we crossed the 50 percent line last year, relying on imports for more than half our consumption.[2] The figure will keep rising. The big oil companies have pretty much given up on the United States other than Alaska. They are shifting their exploration energies elsewhere.

Meanwhile, Sen. Murkowski (R/Alaska) is the new Chairman of the Senate Energy Committee, and he has announced that he plans to press to open the Arctic National Wildlife Refuge to exploration. With luck, we may gain a year or two of consumption, at the expense of the kind of mess typified by the Exxon Valdez disaster.

Our dependence on Middle Eastern petroleum grows. The Gulf states have lived very high on oil revenues, creating lollipop economies where most of the citizens' needs are supplied free or at reduced prices. Saudi Arabia has run out of money and has had to raise taxes and cut expenditures some $7 billion, which has not made it popular. From another quarter, the kingdom has begun to face open criticism from some of its intellectuals for the lack of democracy. It has worried the king enough so that he leaned on Britain not to give political asylum to the critics.

Arab fundamentalism has been on the rise in the Middle East; unrest, assassinations and security problems have dogged the region. It is not a stable area. Does the U.S. Government look with equanimity on our increasing dependence? It moved very quickly when Iraq threatened to destabilize the Arab peninsula. At least we had allies in the region. There is a specter of widespread chaos threatening our fossil energy-built economy, along with those of Western Europe and Japan. We would be under immense pressure to mount a "peacekeeping force"—very possibly against Arab opposition—to try to keep the wells pumping and the pipelines open. Not a pleasant prospect.

There are even more compelling long-term reasons not to be dependent on fossil fuels. It took millions of years for plants to store all that carbon in the ground and create a carbon/oxygen balance in the atmosphere that made possible the advent of animals. For a century, our thoughtless species has been putting it back into the atmosphere. We are attacking the very balance that supports us, and promoting global warming in the process. The proportion of carbon in the atmosphere creeps relentlessly up. It has risen 6 percent since 1980. That is a very short time.

The country has responded to the oil crises of the '70s by using 60 percent more coal, the dirtiest of fossil fuels, than in 1970. We pledged following the 1992 UN Rio de Janeiro Conference on Environment and Development to reduce our carbon dioxide emissions to 1990 levels by 2000. Not an ambitious target, but the reversion to coal makes it more difficult to meet.

Nationally, we look in every direction but population growth to address our energy problems. We are trying to become more efficient in our use of energy. We have made progress. We use only 60 percent as much energy per dollar of GNP (in constant dollars) as we did in 1970. Part of the gain has been because of the growth in services, which don't generally use much energy. Very good, but you can only carry that process so far. You cannot eat services, or wear them, or live in them.

Our energy use has risen 27 percent since 1970—right in step with our population growth—despite the increased efficiency. And efficiency gains become progressively more difficult to achieve as the easier gains are used up. Right now, population growth makes solutions ten percent more difficult with every passing decade. We don't need that hurdle.

Japan is often cited as the model of efficiency. It is, but it is not so far ahead of the United States as some comparisons suggest. On its tight little archipelago, living in tiny houses and flats, with a population dense enough to support public transport, distances too short for aircraft, and not much room to drive or park automobiles, Japanese use just over half as much energy as Americans do, adjusting for the difference in GNP per capita.[3] We can move in that direction—theoretically if not in the real political world—but it would take some fundamental changes in living habits, and it would take time. Having gotten people out of their energy intensive cars and into smaller houses, the question would arise: what do we do next?

Japan has answered that question for itself. It is approaching zero population growth. Our Government should also be looking at population growth as part of the issue.

The pursuit of benign and reliable energy technologies should be near the head of our national priorities. It will be an expensive change, involving high capital costs and more expensive energy. A deliberate effort to reverse the growth of the demand side—population—is much less expensive. It would lead to rising efficiencies, as the pressure on our resources diminishes, rather than raising costs as we try to squeeze every ounce of energy out of nature, and it would contribute to the solution of many issues aside from the energy problem.

One could run the same sort of analysis of social and urban problems, agriculture, forestry, fisheries, and most other areas of economic and social activity, but this paper is about decision making, not about the problems themselves.

DEMOGRAPHICS AND DECISION MAKING

How do we bring demography into national thinking as the government goes about making decisions? There is no ground swell of support for a population policy. There is no reason to hope that politicians will get out in front of public opinion, or to expect that they will automatically think of population when they are addressing seemingly unrelated policy decisions.

Moving a Reluctant Government. The administration's performance so far (as summarized in Part I of this two part series) would suggest that politicians do not yet dare take on the issue frontally and say "growth must stop." If that is so, they can more safely approach it by asking, in one context after another: "what are the impacts if we don't stop?"

As a nation, we need mechanisms to bring the practical consequences of population growth into focus on a case by case basis—a conscious national process of self-education, if you will. The process would improve governmental decision making. At the same time, if the decision process can be made more open so as to reach the public, it would help to move population up the scale of people's awareness. Once people have seriously thought of the connections between immigration and population growth, they will probably never look at immigration in quite the same way again.

A Cure for Tunnel Vision. Let me start with the immigration example and propose a straightforward mechanism to avoid ad hoc decision making such as happened when the Haitian and Cuban boat people set out to sea.

One may be pretty sure that immigration policy, when it has reached the White House at all, has been dominated by the usual "big players": the National Security Council, State, Defense, Justice, Treasury. Simply because of the problem of coordinating diverse views, most of the consequences are not addressed when decisions are made on "foreign policy" or "Justice Department" issues.

I suggest that the White House take the lead in creating a permanent inter-agency policy group on population and immigration. It would provide individual agencies such as the Department of Labor or HUD with an opportunity to consider the role of immigration in the pursuit of their goals. Out of the interagency group would come an improved sense of what U.S. immigration policy should be, which in turn would inform the decision process when issues arise such as the surge in boat people from Cuba and Haiti. It might even influence the thinking when Congress undertakes one of its periodic "reforms" to increase immigration in behalf of one or another interest group.

Immigration impinges on almost every area of government, both directly and because of its effect on U.S. population growth. Because of that demographic impact, every department of government is (or should be) interested in immigration policy. For some examples:

- The Department of Labor needs to bring in its perspective about the impacts on jobs and wages.
- The Department of Agriculture should be heard on the connections between U.S. population growth and our continued ability to export food over the coming decades, or even to supply the projected U.S. population.
- HUD should be asked how the additional population input, most of it at economic levels that will need subsidized housing, will affect current housing availability and future housing budgets.
- HEW could bring several interesting perspectives into the debate: tuberculosis and AIDS control; public health costs; welfare budgets; local, state and national expenditures to provide schooling.

There are antecedents for such a policy group. In the '80s, following the creation of the Domestic and Economic Policy Councils, inter-agency groups were created to address cross-cutting issues such as acid precipitation. In the Carter administration, there was an NSC-chartered Interagency Task Force on Population and a less formal Interagency Committee on International Environmental Affairs, both of them chaired by the Department of State and both (unfortunately) dealing only with international aspects of population and environmental policy.

The White House held ad hoc interagency consultations when making the decisions about policy toward the boat people. My proposal is that the machinery be made inclusive and permanent, that it be at a policy level, and that it be charged with addressing the long-term issues such as the connections between immigration, population growth and agriculture. Or wages. Or housing.

That shouldn't be too difficult. It would begin the process of seeing the implications when national decisions are being made.

The Critical Trends Assessment Act. One reason for singling the Vice President out for this perhaps unwanted attention is that he has addressed the population issue so forthrightly in the past and he has described processes to bring it into governmental decision making. The immigration/population consultative machinery described above could be folded into this broader proposal if it ever got off the ground.

The Vice President during his time as congressman and senator repeatedly introduced a bill called the Critical Trends Assessment Act. The proposed Act was the best of several proposals to create "foresight" machinery in government to address cross-cutting issues such as population growth and its effects. He submitted the bill because the **Global 2000 Report to the President** in 1980 made it very clear that the nation lacks the capability to get out of its tunnel and see the side effects of what it is doing.

The heart of the proposal was to create a process in the White House to insure that new and unfolding national and international trends are identified and their policy implications assessed. It was not a perfect bill. For one thing, it did not contain a provision for the automatic scanning of proposals reaching the White House, to consider the side effects. Nevertheless, it was a good start.[4]

Sponsorship by the White House of a bill to create a broader and better thinking process might just catch the public eye. It would certainly fit in with the Vice President's recent work on "reinventing government." It might even be endorsed by the Republicans. Several years ago it was cosponsored in the House by Newt Gingrich, of all people. This might be one of the few imaginable bills that could get top level bipartisan sponsorship in the present political standoff in Washington.

TO BE OPTIMISTIC . . .

Friends ask why I press for policies that seem so unachievable. Perhaps they are right. This article is fueled by hope more than by expectation.

Nevertheless, a break may be coming. The "foresight" concept is not just a personal brainstorm. The Vice President pushed for it for years until he became Vice President and was muzzled by discretion.

The proposal for a national foresight process is still the only specific policy proposal in which most of the environmental and population community is formally united.[5]

Immigration problems may begin to force the nation to look at the population issue, if governments can be brought to see the connection. In California, Florida, Texas, New York and Arizona, immigration has become a very serious political issue, and they are likely to keep it on the political stage.

The Clinton administration realized that it had to say "enough" when the Haitian and Cuban boatlift started.

Perhaps this and the Proposition 187 firestorm in California have sufficed to bring the real effects of immigration into the open and permit a national debate a step above the present level of shouting "racist" at those who would raise the issue.

It would be an act of statesmanship to create the machinery to make us hold that debate. It is, as I have said before[6], a good job for the Vice President.

THE ROLE OF ADVOCACY

What, if anything, can be done by non-governmental advocacy groups to help move the population issue?

A Little Genteel Hardball. The circumstances argue for pragmatism. In the land of the possible, go for immigration control. The ground has shifted beneath us. Traditional allies are of little help. The environmental movement has feet of clay. Planned Parenthood is led by a militant feminist and has no position on population growth.

Population advocates should consider supporting those who would do something about immigration. I do not argue that we abandon environmentalism or vote automatically for anybody who would limit immigration. There is too much single-issue voting already. We should, however, praise any politician for a "good" position on immigration and warn the others that they may lose support if they are too wary or too timid to embrace the issue.

We are entitled to tell the family planners that they may narrow their support base by failing to make the social argument for their activity. By way of example, my local Rio Grande chapter of Planned Parenthood solicits contributions with an envelope bearing an ancient quote from Margaret Sanger asserting women's absolute right to control their own bodies and denying that government has any role. (That was when governments encouraged higher fertility.) The Planned Parenthood group should be reminded that their pledge envelope may turn off those supporters who believe that society has a stake in how many children women have.

We should perhaps be telling our environmentalist friends "whether or not you pay attention, population growth is a central issue in the deterioration of our country." The local Sierra Club chapter is ahead of the national organization on population. However, it supported Bill Richardson for Congress. Richardson gets high ratings from local environmental groups because his voting record on the usual environmental issues is pretty good. On population, however, he has regularly supported bills that would increase immigration. He even voted against a proposal to require the federal government to reimburse the states for the costs of illegal immigration. When I was asked by the Club to support Richardson, I asked whether they had included his population and immigration positions in their rating. They said no, but perhaps they should. We'll see.

Environmental groups, even if they avoid immigration and fertility as too "hot," should be willing to press for the creation of real foresight machinery in government. They are already on record as favoring the process. It might help to educate them in the importance of population as a national issue, as it educates the government. There is no harm in reminding them.

Reaching the Public. Active popular advocacy would be the most solid base for a national population policy. The problem is in getting there. One way perhaps would be to emulate the environmental movement, which has enlisted public idols such as movie stars in its cause. Promoting grass-roots advocacy is not my long suit. I can simply point to the lack of it.

Similarly, children get a great deal of environmental education in school nowadays, but population policy apparently is a topic too hot for inclusion. My grandchildren come home from school with all sorts of materials and ideas about the environment but none about population. Zero Population Growth and the National Audubon Society have developed teaching materials on population growth and its ramifications. It is a first step. The need is enormous.

The population movement tends to preach to the choir. We do not reach the poor and the uneducated who are, by and large, the ones having the babies. We should perhaps look at one intriguing idea from the third world. With the support of American groups such as Population Communication International "soap operas" have been developed for TV audiences in several third world countries, and apparently they are effective in getting out the message about population (at least at the family level) and family planning. Are Americans too cynical? Too hardened to respond to such messages? How would the messages be developed and aired? Is there any hope that public television, beleaguered as it is, could touch such programs? What other channels exist?

It would be much easier to move the politicians if they were being pushed.

Finding Allies. Above all, the population movement needs to find ways to reach other advocacy groups to persuade them that a population policy could help them in the pursuit of their goals.

How do we make contact?

At the risk of boring those readers who read for information and are not themselves involved in advocacy, let me try out an idea: There is by now a group of writers and advocates who share many of the same broad concerns about the impact of population growth. The most severe limiting factor in their effectiveness (other than their advanced average age) is probably the lack of an organizational base to promote the wider dissemination of their ideas.

There is need for an institution that identifies target audiences and undertakes to bring the existing literature to their attention. It would not itself publish or promote the publication of articles and books. However, such an organization would-

- maintain up-to-date target lists of opinion formers in different areas, such as minority organizations, labor unions, farmers' organizations, urban welfare advocates, national social policy groups, the League of Women Voters, and so on.
- make these lists available to organizations wishing to reach them with a specific publication, or perhaps even itself mail relevant publications to the leaders of such target groups.
- maintain a clipping service of individuals writing or speaking on radio or television about population issues, and encourage non-population advocacy groups to listen to them.
- place materials with libraries, or supply lists of major libraries to advocacy organizations for placement of appropriate materials.
- maintain a Congress watch, and alert advocacy groups coming legislative proposals that relate to the groups' interests, identifying the specific individuals involved.
- establish and maintain contact with talk show hosts and programmers to remind them of the connections between demography and currently newsworthy issues and to suggest names of potential talk show participants.

On particular issues, there may be an opportunity for networking. For example: a coalition with labor groups on an impending immigration bill.

Some of this is being done, but sporadically and piecemeal. The effort is beyond the systematic reach of small organizations. Population advocacy needs something like the capability of the big political advocacy groups.

I submit the idea to any foundation executives who may be reading this paper and who are bold enough not to retreat before the dread word "advocacy."

In this fractioned society, one generation's literary allusion is Greek to another generation. Perhaps I should clarify the allusion in the title. There was a play in the 1930s by Clifford Odets named *Waiting for Lefty,* and another in the '50s by Samuel Beckett titled *Waiting for Godot.* Neither Lefty nor Godot ever showed up.

NOTES:

1. *Overshoot. The Ecological Basis of Revolutionary Change* (Urbana: Univ. of Illinois Press, 1980.)
2. AP Washington 1-18-95
3. The comparisons in this section are taken from the *U.S. Statistical Abstract*, 1994, Tables 920, 1366, 1370, 1393 and earlier issues. GNP is in constant dollars per capita, energy use per capita, and the comparison is adjusted (Table 1370) to reflect the somewhat lower real GNP per capita in Japan, in terms of purchasing-power.
4. Lindsey Grant.*Foresight and National Decisions*. The Horseman and the Bitreaucrat (Lanham, MD: University Press of America, 1988.)
5. In December 1981, the Global Tomorrow Coalition, a broad coalition of most major U.S. environmental and population organizations and many futures study groups and interested individuals, unanimously adopted at its first annual meeting a position statement entitled,*The Need to Improve National Foresight*. It called for the government to "establish in the Executive Office of the President an improved capacity to coordinate and analyze data . . . on the long-term interactions of trends in population, resources, and environment—and their relationship to social and economic development—and to provide information relevant to current policy decisions . . ."
6. *A Congenial Job for the Vice President*, NPG FOOTNOTE 1993.

POPULATION AND THE PCSD

Lindsey Grant

April 1996

The PCSD has completed its report on sustainability in America, to almost total press and public silence, and so quietly that it took multiple phone calls to the White House to find anybody who knew what it was.

The PCSD came into being on June 14, 1993, by Vice Presidential order. The council's path was not easy. The President's message charged it with helping to "grow the economy and preserve the environment . . . ," objectives that are likely to conflict. The twenty-nine council members were balanced to include industrialists, labor, environmentalists, cabinet members and critics, and a mix by sex, race and ethnicity; and it undertook to proceed by consensus, which usually leads to harmless generalities. It had no real authority or role in decision making, and such impermanent bodies have neither time nor authority to carry their ideas through. At first, population and consumption—key issues in sustainability—were not even in its scope. They were introduced, over opposition, at the insistance of council member and Undersecretary of State Timothy Wirth.

Nevertheless, the PCSD's report deserves a footnote in the history of U.S. Government population policy. It, and the President's acceptance of it, were the nearest thing on record to an official U.S. endorsement of the proposition that U.S. population should stop growing. President Nixon raised the issue in 1969, but in 1972 did not endorse the Rockefeller Commission report that explicitly stated the case for stabilization. The CEQ/State Department *Global Future: Time to Act* of January 1981 said the country should "develop a national population policy which addresses the issues of . . . population stabilization . . ." but did not say flatly that we must stabilize, and President Carter, in his last days of office, probably did not see it.

The PCSD report contains seven chapters, sixteen principles, and ten goals, each of which in turn is identified by several "Indicators of Progress." Moreover, six of the chapters each have several of their own "Policy Recommendations" and/or "Actions." It is a bit confusing.

There are chapters on Building a New Framework, Information and Education, Strengthening Communities, Natural Resources Stewardship, U.S. Population and Sustainability, and International Leadership. I will focus on the population section, noting only that there are many good if generalized homilies in the other sections about cooperating for the common good and promoting environmentally benign policies.

As to population: principle 12 said that "The United States should have policies and programs that contribute to stabilizing global human population. . . ." On the other hand, principle 1 said that "some things must grow—jobs, productivity, wages, capital and savings, profits . . . ," and principle 14 called for a growing economy. More workers with higher productivity are likely to stress the environment even more—even with efforts at amelioration—and growth itself is at some point unsustainable. Not surprisingly, the report did not explore in depth what sustainability really is.

Goal 8 was specific: "Move towards stabilization of U.S. population." Chapter 6 took the steam out of this resolution. There were good if cautious suggestions for making family planning available to all—and a sharp reminder that Title X family planning services have declined 70 percent since 1980 in real dollars. There were the obligatory proposals to promote the status of women. On the gritty issues, however, the council punted. It adopted the compromise formula from the 1972 UN Bucharest population conference that parents should "decide freely and responsibly the number and spacing of their children. . . ." Neither Bucharest nor the council offered guidance as to what is "responsible" or how that would lead to a stable population. (Incidentally, it avoided the abortion issue.)

On immigration, the council simply emphasized the delicacy of the issue and the need for fairness to everybody. It called attention to the work of the Commission on Immigration Reform (the "Jordan Commission") but did not endorse its proposals. It made the familiar proposal that the U.S. should "address the factors that encourage people to leave their home countries," but did not try to show how the United States somehow can end world poverty or political oppression.

The report was submitted to the President on March 7th, and he "was pleased . . . to accept it. . . ." He asked the council to continue its work until December. He assigned followup to the Vice President, who in turn delegated to the Chair of the Council on Environmental Quality (CEQ) the task of exploring what recommendations can be put into effect, and he proposed a joint federal/city/county (but not state) Joint Center on Sustainable Communities.

A much reduced staff will carry on "phase two," and the council is expected to meet twice, perhaps once in May to approve the followup and again in October to review progress. CEQ's thinking is still in flux, but it apparently is under instructions to create an Interagency Working Group on Sustainable Development reporting to the Vice President.

The Susquehanna River, they say, is "a mile wide and an inch deep." That seems to be true of the council's enthusiasm for the population position it endorsed. The council included the Secretaries of Agriculture, Commerce, Energy, Interior, the Deputy Secretaries of Agriculture and Education, Under Secretaries from State and Commerce, and the Administrator of EPA (all participating "as individuals"). The council published its report just as both houses of Congress were debating legislation on immigration, which is the critical determinant of whether U.S. population growth will stop. The Clinton administration, after much vacillation, undercut the effort to reduce legal immigration. If that impressive collection of administration leaders was really interested in the population issue, they could perhaps have influenced the administration's position or at least called public attention to the connection between their report and what was going on in Congress.

The CEQ has since its inception been peripheral to the Washington decision process, and it is hard to be sanguine as to what will result from this little known effort. Let me say in its behalf, however, that the PCSD showed that even such a diverse group can recognize the need to stop population growth. They were not alone in their inability to face the tough decisions that would be needed to do it.

CHINA AS AN "EMERGING" NATION WHAT IT MEANS FOR THE REST OF US

Lindsey Grant

April 1996

China is not just an example of an industrializing nation. Alone, it is one fifth of the human race, and every nation has a stake in its future. The Chinese are cursed if they try to master their problems, damned if they don't, in trouble if they succeed and in worse trouble if they fail. And what is happening to China is happening, in varying degree, in other nations just now in the process of modernizing. Let me explain.

THE RACE AGAINST HUNGER

The Chinese have a massive population program underway, epitomized in the slogan "the one child family." Unlike most poor countries, they are financing most of it themselves. The program involves very intense social pressures not to become pregnant after the first child, and to abort if they do. There are various exceptions involving minorities, twins, peasant families with labor shortages. The program—like most campaigns in China—is not so totally effective as propaganda would suggest. (UN figures give total fertility—the average number of children a woman may be expected to have in her lifetime—in China right now as 1.95 children.) The program has been bitterly criticized abroad, particularly in the U.S., for coercion. It has in fact had its excesses, as have many of the campaigns launched in China.[1] Yet they cannot afford to give it up.

Let's look at their problem.

China's population is 1.22 *billion*, growing just over one percent per year. The rate of growth is about like the U.S., but in China that works out to more than 12 million people. Every year.

Traditional agriculture in China could achieve food yields sufficient to support as many as seven persons per hectare of arable land, on a simple vegetable diet, but that was in only a few favored areas, under ideal conditions, and with massive human labor, legume rotations and the recycling of manure and nightsoil.

Now, the population per hectare is thirteen persons, and rising.[2] And those people have gotten used to having a little meat, rather than living at or below the margin, as they used to, on a grain diet supplemented by a few vegetables and some vegetable oil. How did they do it?

THE NITROGEN FIX

A Canadian professor named Vaclav Smil asks a fascinating question: What was the most important invention in the twentieth century? His unlikely answer: the Haber-Bosch process of synthesizing ammonia and therefore nitrogen, introduced in 1913.

Nitrogen, Smil pointed out, is essential to chlorophyll, DNA, RNA, proteins and enzymes—in short, to life itself. There are only three natural atmospheric processes for converting atmospheric nitrogen, which is locked up in N_2 molecules, into a form usable by plants and animals: falling meteors, ozonization and ionization by lightning. The only biotic process is the creation of ammonia by various bacteria, most notably by the rhizobium bacteria that live symbiotically on the roots of legumes (such as peas and beans).

Nitrogen and water are the two most important limiting factors in plant growth. Until the Haber-Bosch process, humankind could obtain nitrogen only by green manuring with legumes and recycling nitrogen by spreading animal manure, guano from seabird rookeries, and nightsoil.

Yields per hectare are the critical issue in China. By and large, the land that can be farmed is being farmed, as is some that should not be farmed. Arable land is shrinking because of urban sprawl, industrialization, salination of fields, and desertification. The official figures show a decline of six percent in arable land from 1970–1991 and a loss in 1992 to urbanization alone at the rate of nearly 5 percent per decade.[3] Those losses are particularly significant, since the land closest to cities gets the most nightsoil and is highly productive. Moreover, the amount of land *per capita* declines with population growth. Food yields must more than match population growth just to stay in place.

That is where synthetic ammonia comes in. Its invention permitted agriculture to support an unprecedented population. By Smil's calculations, synthetic fertilizers now provide the nitrogen for about half the annual global crop harvest. To phrase the point more starkly: perhaps one-third of the people in the more crowded and land-poor third world countries would starve, were it not for synthetic fertilizer. Moreover, "virtually all protein needed for the growth of more than 400 million babies to be added in the eight populous but land scarce countries during the 1990s will have to come from synthetic nitrogen."[4] (China, of course, is one of the eight countries.) China escaped from subsistence agriculture by building fertilizer plants, starting in the mid-1950s. It has about reached the end of that road. China uses nearly three times as much fertilizer per hectare as the United States, but grain yields are only 87 percent as high, probably because they must farm poorer land in drier areas, and they have less experience with modern high yield hybrids and crop varieties. In some areas of heaviest application, the response to further fertilization in China is zero.

Those are the limits that every nation encounters when it goes in for massive use of artificial fertilizer. China's situation is particularly tight, because it has so little arable land. It cannot go back to organic agriculture, with its much lower average yields. Smil points out that synthetic fertilizer furnishes roughly half the nitrogen in Chinese food production, and even if China reverted to subsistence consumption levels it would furnish 40 percent of the essential nitrogen. Despite its harmful environmental effects, it is essential. Without it, China would face mass starvation. Moreover, since China has long farmed substantially all its arable land and is using the available sources of organic nitrogen, any future increase in Chinese population will depend largely upon synthetic nitrogen, at a stage when the additional nitrogen produces very little food.

To add to its woes, China is losing topsoil to erosion. A Chinese official told an environmental meeting in Hong Kong that one-third of arable acreage is seriously affected.

Irrigation is pushing its limits. For one example: some 622 km. of the Yellow River went dry for nearly four months in the summer of 1995. It was a dry year, but the phenomenon was blamed in part on a nine-fold increase in irrigation from the river since

1950.[5] Around Beijing, irrigation is being reduced to meet urban water needs.

Every growing population is on an agricultural treadmill, but China is the ultimate example. It is in a race against time; they know they must solve their own problems. No supplier on Earth could feed them if they fail. Their birth control program must succeed, or they face a descent into starvation.

Those who criticize Chinese family planning policies should perhaps consider their problem. As the Chinese Premier bluntly told ex-President Bush: "If China's population goes on increasing uncontrolled . . . China will land in a backward state and even head for self-destruction."[6]

CHINA AS IMPORTER

China is entering the world grain market on a massive scale just at the time when stagnating yields and competition from other emerging countries are making that market very tight.

In the bad old days, China could not afford imported grain. If the crops failed, people starved. Then, as commercial fertilizers became available and food output rose, China briefly became a food exporter. That has changed again, and China now runs a net annual grain deficit around fifteen million tons, second only to Japan. As a result of their relaxation of controls and their economic boom, they can afford to buy grain. They need to for domestic reasons. The price of grain rose 60 percent in 1994. That is the kind of thing that leads to food riots.

There has been something of an international intellectual skirmish as to how much grain China will need a generation hence, and where it will get it. The Worldwatch Institute projects a requirement for 479 million tons by 2030, of which 207 million tons would have to be imported, even if improvements in the Chinese diet should stop now. If the diet continues to improve to something like the level in Taiwan, Worldwatch projects the need at 641 million tons, 369 million tons of which would have to be imported.[7] That is nearly twice the present level of total world grain exports.

China's Agriculture Minister responded with an ambitious goal of avoiding imports by raising grain production to 500 million tons in 2000 and 625–675 million tons in 2020—about 45 percent above current production. As the cynical would say: lots of luck.

Other specialists, Chinese and foreign, offer a wide range of production projections and estimates of import requirements early in the next century, ranging from zero to 136 million tons per year.[8] Nobody really knows, but nobody is claiming they will again be exporters.

One does not need to take the astonishing Worldwatch Institute projections literally in order to agree with the thrust. They assumed a decline of 20 percent in Chinese grain production as a result mostly of declining acreage and irrigation and stagnating yields. That may be pessimistic, but the Minister of Agriculture is extremely optimistic.

Chinese imports will depend on how much they can afford—how much foreign exchange they can muster and what the price will be. I read the Worldwatch message as saying, not that they will buy that much, but that they will not be able to, because the world's importers will be competing bitterly for a limited supply.

If they cannot raise the grain or import it, the Chinese government will have to tell the Chinese to tighten their belts. A lot of peasants may be reluctant to part with their grain and insistent on sharing in the benefits of a rising market for what they do sell. A very tough spot for government, and one that leads me to repeat the refrain: China's problems should not be worsened by rising population driven demand.

If China had succeeded by now in its hope of reversing population growth, the specter raised by the Worldwatch projections would disappear. Population growth is the problem on both sides of the calculation. It raises demand, while it competes for farmland and demands more and more water from limited resources for irrigation, more housing, larger cities, and expanding industries.

A less desperate parallel arises in connection with petroleum. One expert predicts that China's petroleum imports will rise fourfold to 1.4 million barrels per day by 2005.[9] Imports at that scale would absorb about 5 percent of current world exports and would be competing with rising demand from other emerging countries. It would hasten the energy transition for the whole world. On the other hand, if it cannot buy the petroleum, China will intensify its use of coal—the "dirtiest" fuel—and nuclear power, the most dangerous. These both have profound environmental consequences for China and the world. Damned if they do, damned if they don't.

INDUSTRY AND THE PEASANTS

There are at least two Chinas. Not just the familiar China vs. Taiwan division, but the far more fundamental fission line between the prospering southern coastal cities and the peasantry, particularly in China's vast interior. Only a small part of China is participating in the present economic boom. The peasants know that some Chinese are getting rich, while they have financed the cities through grain levies and taxes. There have been riots and attacks on local government offices. It is not comfortable out there in the countryside.

That division has far reaching implications. A restless and growing peasantry is in danger of losing the gains of the past thirty years, and the loss of expectations is a dangerous mood indeed. They are running out of farmland and crowding into overloaded cities, encountering a small business plutocracy, some prospering entrepreneurs and a small group of skilled workers who are "in the system."

The Ninth Five Year Plan (1996–2000) addresses the problem with considerable candor. Rural and urban unemployment and the "polarization of rich and poor" are identified as critical problems. One drafter, in presenting the draft plan, said "Unemployment was the deciding factor in setting the growth rate . . . the only way to keep unrest from boiling over . . . is to create a certain number of jobs."[10]

The official figures on unemployment are indeed hair-raising. Aside from the cities, there are reported to be 450 million people in the rural work force, of whom 120 million are employed in rural industrial enterprises. Agriculture can use 200 million at most, leaving 100–200 million already surplus workers in rural areas by various officials' estimates. By 2000, the number is expected to be somewhere between 180 to 300 million.[11] Look at those figures again. The rural unemployed alone may equal the total population of any other country in the world, other than India.

To cap that, the government hopes to modernize farming along Western lines and proposes over time to shift 80 percent of farm labor into other work.

The total labor force grows about 10 million every year. The cities also generate substantial unemployment as the government tries to reduce the padded rolls of state enterprises.

This nightmare drives wages toward minimal subsistence levels. Quite reasonably, the poor want out.

Witness the desperate efforts by Chinese to get to the U.S. even in the midst of a touted economic boom—and most of those boat people come from a coastal province that is supposed to be prospering. There is even a governmental "overseas employment agency" in one depressed Northeastern city to help Chinese to emigrate.[12]

Because China's family planning program has succeeded pretty well, there is hope down the road. The number of young people entering their working years is already below the 1985 figure. It will fluctuate downward if China can hold its fertility down,[13] thus ameliorating the unemployment problem.

INDUSTRY AND THE ENVIRONMENT

Like most other people, the Chinese do not simply want to stay alive. They want to succeed, and the economic liberalization that Deng Xiaoping launched has created a class of people for whom that dream has become possible.

China epitomizes some uncomfortable realities. The poor want to be rich; poor nations want to live like us.

China is one of the world's fastest growing economies. GNP grew from 1991–1994 at an average annual rate of 11.7 percent. They plan a "more balanced" growth of 9.3 percent through 2000, and 8 percent from 2001–2010. That would mean a seven-fold increase in twenty-five years. They hope to reach the per capita GNP level of a "middle income developed country" by mid-century.[14] They are talking of the median of OECD countries. Allowing for projected Chinese population growth (UN 1994 medium projection), they are aiming at a total GNP more than seventy times as large as in 1990—even assuming the OECD level stands still.

They are not likely to get there, but in the process of trying they will generate some profound disturbances to themselves and the world. Their problem is that, having abandoned the Communist model (in fact if not in word), they have adopted the capitalistic model—conspicuous consumption and all—just as it begins to run against the realities of a small Earth. China produced 10,000 automobiles in 1985 and 1.4 million in 1994. It hopes to treble that rate by 2010. By then, they expect to have 40 to 50 million private automobiles.[15] They could hardly have selected a worse way to go. Automobiles eat up land for roads and parking and the urban layouts they promote, and much of that land will come out of China's dwindling farmland. Their pollution may harm farm production. It will contribute carbon to global warming, which would be a disaster for low-lying coastal areas and would imperil food production if it leads to less rainfall in a hinterland already suffering from lack of water. Their demand for gasoline will eat up foreign exchange that the Chinese will need, to import food.

In retrospect, it may seem a tragedy that the Chinese leaders, given the chance, did not set out to define a more benign course of modernization when they abandoned the Maoist rigidities. One could envisage a China built upon freer enterprise and the price mechanism, but organized around the countryside and smaller cities, emphasizing labor intensive occupations and avoiding the energy intensive Western industrial models. Apparently, the leaders did not see the vision or did not feel they had the choice. Chinese want the things they see on television, and TV now reaches most villages. If their government fails in its ambitious plans, it will face a restive populace. If it succeeds, they may well choke themselves, and us.

> *There is a lesson here for other third world countries. That sudden tuck in the bottom of the Chinese pyramid, compared with the flaring African pyramid, means fewer chil-*

dren to support now, an eventual reduction in the huge number of unemployed, fewer mothers having babies in the next generation, and the hope for stopping runaway population growth. The comparison with Africa's plight is a dramatic argument for population programs. (UN 1994 Medium Projections)

As with other nations that have been poor, China's leadership does not yet appreciate the penalties that growth will bring. Already, 86 percent of rivers in urban areas are regarded as heavily polluted. Shanghai alone dumps five million cubic meters of raw sewage into its rivers daily.[16] Unwashed coal provides most of China's energy. The air is foul. Entrepreneurs are even setting up "oxygen kiosks" in some cities, where people can stop for a whiff of pure oxygen. Despite some help from the World Bank and the Asian Development Bank, Chinese environmental leaders themselves say that they cannot afford to do all that needs to be done.

China alone will not suffer. Already, acid precipitation from China is affecting western Japan. China has every intention of using its coal, and coal is the dirtiest fuel in terms of acid precipitation and the greenhouse effect. There are technologies that could help to lessen the damage. In the United States, we demand that power plants use limestone slurry scrubbers to lessen the pollution. We have developed coal gasification processes that would be competitive if oil were not so cheap. They capture most of the pollutants other than CO_2.

The world has a stake in helping China avoid inflicting irreparable damage on the atmosphere. It could make those technologies available on concessional terms, if China could be persuaded to use them. There are limits, however. In China most coal is used in small home stoves that are particularly dirty.

Population of China, 1995
Estimated total 1,221 million
Population by Age Group and Gender

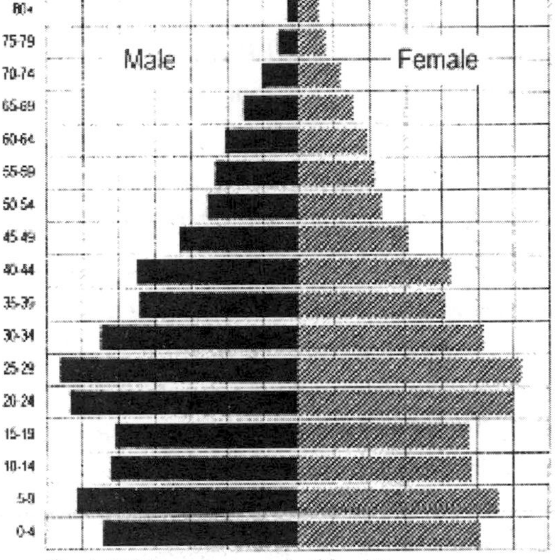

Each full box represents 10 million

Population of Sub-Sahara Africa, 1995
Estimated total 596 million
Population by Age Group and Gender

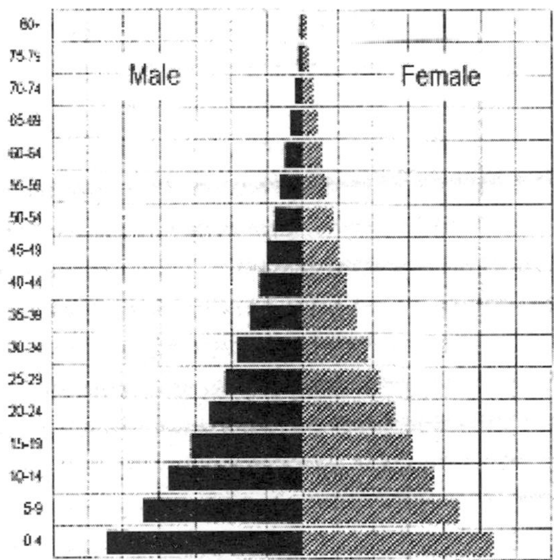

Each full box represents 10 million

Figure 1 snd 2.

They can be improved, perhaps by adding limestone to the coal briquettes they burn, but they will remain a dirty source of energy.[17]

CHINA AS EXPORTER

The immense and under-utilized pool of cheap and trainable labor will keep Chinese wages low. If Chinese labor is organized, whether by Chinese entrepreneurs or multinational corporations, and if they can get their goods into foreign markets, they will drive wages down in labor-intensive industries wherever they have unrestricted entry. If they are closed out, the Chinese government will be sitting on that immense powder keg of people with nothing to do.

The United States has been providing that market, which has grown from $1 billion in 1980 to $39 billion in 1994. The U.S. China trade deficit is second only to that with Japan. The U.S. will probably begin to recover the deficit as China's grain needs rise, but as the imports soar there may be rising pressure to limit that access to the American market.

The Chinese need us much more than we need them, as a market and a source of food. As the proud heirs of "The Central Kingdom," they undoubtedly resent it. This makes our politicians' moralizing to them about personal freedoms and their population policy particularly galling. They pretty much have to take it, but our politicians are building a tremendous tension of suppressed resentment. It is remarkable how insensitive nations can be to each other's needs.

However that may be, the central trade issue is that China needs trade opportunities that the rest of the world, in attempting to save its own economies, may not be able to provide. Again, as with so many other things, population plays a central role. The Chinese are trying to work their way out of the box created by a growing labor force, and the graph suggests they have a chance. Let us not make it more difficult.

THE NERVOUS GIANT

China may seem huge and invulnerable from the outside, but it is a nation trying to survive on very treacherous ground. The question is regularly asked: "what will China do with Hong Kong when it takes over in 1997." Perhaps a more important question is what Hong Kong will do to China. The Chinese leaders don't trust democracy. For a century, they have tried to accommodate their ways of managing a huge nation to the needs of modernism. Confucianism was their traditional political framework, and it didn't work. The experience of the Soviet Union and Eastern Europe has made clear to them that statism doesn't work. Communism as a belief and unifying force has eroded in China just as it did in the rest of the Communist world.

China traditionally has broken apart when strong central government failed. Its leaders are intensely aware of that tradition. With the gradual passage of Deng Xiaoping from the scene, the succession issue is at the forefront of Chinese politics. Communism does not provide a reliable way to manage successions. This is a critical time for China, and today's policies are not perpetual. One issue may become crucial: the one child policy was not introduced because the Chinese like it. The leaders knew they had to stop population growth, even at considerable political risk, to avoid future catastrophe. In the present power struggle, will they be able to stick to that policy, or will one or another leader, courting popularity, propose to revoke it? Or will it simply become unenforceable if central authority weakens? Population policy has shifted before in the political seesaw since the idea of family planning was first introduced in the mid-1950s. There are ominous reports of rising resistance in the countryside to the population program.

We should perhaps consider that context when we evaluate the violent Chinese reaction when Hong Kong Governor Patten began to introduce direct elections into Hong Kong, just two years before its 1997 reversion to China. The Chinese were not just throwing their weight around. Patten was introducing a democratic precedent that the incorporation of Hong Kong into China will inject into the body politic, and the Chinese leaders are probably terrified at the injection.

China faces an uncertain future. Some people perhaps would like to see it fail. I disagree. Aside from the human aspect—which is important—one can hardly be comfortable with the prospect of chaos and hunger in that much of the human race, in a major military power quite capable of producing modern armaments including atomic weaponry.

On the other hand, if China succeeds, it will tighten an already tight world grain supply, hasten the end of the petroleum era and multiply the insults the human race is already inflicting on the environment. Environmentalism has been low among China's priorities, and it will take some tolerance and understanding to bring them to agree that they share our interest in protecting the environment.

MIGRATION

Fail or succeed, China will probably generate migration. If they fail, there will again be hunger in China, and that raises the prospect of hungry Chinese pushing into any area where they can find land and food—not on a scale that would make much difference to China, but it would affect the neighbors. The Chinese have not traditionally been thought of as a nation of migrants, but that is a simplification. They have been pushing and drifting southward for over two thousand years. With a very few exceptions, they have not mounted invasions when they encountered a sufficiently organized non-Chinese society, such as the Thai or Vietnamese, but the informal flow of migrants into Southeast Asia continued. There are something like 30 million "overseas Chinese" in that region now. One may assume that chaos in China would revive that flow. There is a similar flow across the border into Siberia, even though the Chinese and Russian governments have an agreement to control it. The Russian Defense Minister has told the Russian Cabinet that "Chinese citizens are peacefully conquering Russia's Far East." The Cabinet concluded that some of the ethnic Russians coming back to Russia from the erstwhile Soviet empire should be resettled in the border region as a buffer.[18]

On the other hand, economic success will provide the funds to finance boat people to more distant lands. The movement has quite a tradition, starting with the movement of Chinese from China's south coast near Canton to America in the nineteenth century. The boat people recently apprehended in the United States said they paid $10,000 or more for the trip. One needs relatives with enough money to bankroll that sort of movement, and candidates to undertake it. The combination of economic growth with widespread unemployment is precisely the matrix to support such a flow.

WHAT IS AT STAKE?

What does that all mean for the rest of us? We may see China becoming several things at once:

- a new and aggressive exporter of low tech, high labor content goods, utilizing a vast pool of disciplined and trainable labor, and by their competition depressing world wages,
- a major new bidder on world food and energy markets,
- a desperately polluted coastal zone, adding substantially to the world's atmospheric pollution and contributing to global warming,

- an impoverished, hungry and unemployed peasantry,
- a rising source of migration, and
- a region of instability comprising about one-fifth of humankind.

Where does the logic of these trends force us? The only single solution that cuts across all those problems is the one the Chinese are already trying: an end to population growth. We have every reason to applaud and support China's desperate efforts to bring its population under control, rather than engaging in the constant warfare against it that has marked American, and particularly Republican, policy for more than a decade. Our criticism reflects domestic politics. We pay a high price for our fixation with the abortion issue. There are few if any moral principles as absolute and over-riding as their more fervent adherents believe.

We have an investment in their population program, and an interest in helping them to find the most benign possible ways of modernizing. If they fail, they may add less stress to the world's ecosystem, but the government will answer to a billion very unhappy people, and China could become a dangerous loose cannon on the world scene.

If only from the standpoint of diminishing the flow of illegal immigrants, the United States has an interest in Chinese success in stopping their population growth.

THOSE "OTHER CHINAS"

Add Brazil, India, Indonesia, Mexico, perhaps Pakistan, the Philippines and Thailand, plus the smaller "emerging market economies," to China. Their economies are growing, their needs are multiplied by population growth, and they will be low wage competitors on world markets.

Although the most successful emerging countries are also generally the ones with lower fertility, they will continue to grow. Those eight countries alone will have three times the population by 2020 that the developed world has today. Development pollutes. Their development will almost certainly precipitate the huge resource and environmental problems that are just now surfacing.

The UN "Brundtland Commission" in 1987 concluded that, in equity, we must anticipate a five or ten-fold growth in world industrial output to accommodate the modernization of the less developed countries.[19] I believe that statement epitomizes the problem of trying to relieve poverty for a growing world population. It is inconceivable to me that, even with best efforts at pollution control and conservation strategies, such a growth would be environmentally tolerable, and there is yet no sign that the emerging countries will make those efforts. To take the greenhouse effect as an example: the developed countries are trying unsuccessfully to hold CO_2 emissions at the 1990 level, the developing countries won't commit themselves, and a five or ten-fold increase in such emissions would blow apart the present calculations as to the rate of global warming.

The newly prosperous countries will be competing for food, in a world market that cannot accommodate them. The established industrial regions, other than Japan, are net exporters of grain, but the newly emerging nations are major and growing importers. Asia, Africa and Latin America were roughly self-sufficient in 1950. They have now passed an annual grain deficit of more than 100 million tons. The Worldwatch Institute examined ten of the major food importers aside from China and concluded that their grain import needs will rise from 32 million tons in 1990 to 190 million tons in 2030. The world's exporters, led by the United States, are most unlikely to be able to double or treble exports to meet the prospective demand from the developing countries that can afford it. The poorest countries such as most of sub-Saharan Africa and Bangladesh will be frozen out of the market. They have been getting food aid from the United States and Western Europe. Grain surpluses are declining; the FAO expects the 1996 carryover of stocks to be the smallest, in terms of days' supply, since it has kept records. Experts warn that a crop failure in a major nation would be catastrophic. Grain prices are rising. In those circumstances, food aid is drying up despite pleas from the FAO. Even without a production crisis, the poor countries face their own threats of starvation.

Food is connected with population in a particularly inelastic way. Most countries have a stake in stopping population growth, to enable them to avoid or work their way out of the looming food crisis.

American grain traders are celebrating the tightening market, and so perhaps are those who watch our balance of payments, but as a nation we will not gain from the prospect of a world grain shortage. At some point, not very far away, the emerging industrial nations particularly in Asia will not be able to afford the growth pattern on which they have embarked, or they will be increasingly divided, like China, between the rich and the hungry. Desperation in the poor countries will rise. One can hardly predict how those conflicts will play out, but the prospect is for a less and less stable world until it is brought into a better balance. And that balance begins with the end of population growth and the accompanying explosion of demand.

What should the United States be doing? Our support for population programs in the developing world has been less than 5 percent of our foreign aid, and even that figure represents a doubling of foreign population aid in the current administration. The present Congress is determined to shrink foreign aid or—if Senator Helms had his way—eliminate it, and population aid gets a reduced share of the 1996 aid budget. We are heading exactly the wrong way. Assistance to foreign governments in addressing their population problems should be the first priority for American aid and a major element of our foreign policy.

NOTES:

1. The worst excess apparently is that of overzealous local officials forcing late-term abortions on women in order to stay within quotas. The recent report by Human Rights Watch (AP, Beijing, 1-6-96) of orphanages starving the children probably reflects official loss of control over expanding corruption. Pilfering from food budgets has a long history in penal institutions and orphanages, worldwide. China probably has not deliberately extended its demographic policies to raise mortality. There is a suspiciously high proportion of males in the official birth statistics, suggesting some female infanticide and/or parents' failure to report the birth of girl children in order to try again for a boy. However, child mortality is extremely low in China by comparison with other countries with similar per capita income.
2. Official Chinese statistics are frequently in conflict, underlying the danger of too close a reliance upon detailed data. The official Xinhua News Agency quotes the State Land Administration: "China has 120 million hectares of cropland, not just 100 million hectares as long reported." The Ministry of Agriculture refused to comment. (Reuter, Beijing, 3-10-95). The larger figure is credible, since peasants, local and provincial governments all have reason to understate to avoid forced deliveries of grain to the center. A 25 percent discrepancy suggests that inferred fertilizer use and crop yields per hectare are substantially less than the official

figures. Perhaps China has a bit more room for improvement than official data suggest.

3. USDA data and Reuter, Beijing, 8-29-94, quoting the Director General of the State Land Administration.
4. Most of the discussion in this section is drawn from Vaclav Smil, "Population Growth and Nitrogen: An Exploration of a Critical Existential Link," *Population and Development Review*, December 5. Reuter, Beijing, 7-19-95.
6. AP, Beijing, 9-11-95, quoting the Xinhua News Agency.
7. Data, including 1994 price change, and projections are from Lester R. Brown, *Who Will Feed China?* (New York: W.W. Norton, 1995) pp.96–97.
8. Reuter, Beijing, 3-5-95 and 8-3-95, quoting Xinhua News Agency and experts from the Chinese Academy of Social Sciences and Academy of Agricultural Sciences, who estimated the shortfall at 50 million tons. A group of Chinese and Japanese economists arrived at a shortfall of 136 million tons in 2010. Reuter, Bangkok, 9-29-95.
9. The energy program director at the East West Institute, Honolulu, quoted Reuter, Singapore, 9-16-94.
10. Reuter, Beijing, 10-4-95 report on the draft Plan. The employment figures below are drawn from this release and from a Reuter, Beijing, 5-29-95 summary of a report by a Central Committee researcher quoted in the *Economic Daily*.
11. Reuter, Beijing, 1-5-94, quoting from the Minister of Agriculture and a provincial labor official, respectively.
12. The proposal came from Shenyang, in the Northeast, and was cited approvingly by the official New China News Agency. Reuter, Beijing, 7-31-93, 07:41.
13. The World Bank, U.S. Bureau of the Census and United Nations projections involve different assumptions as to what China's fertility has been and will be, leading to different conclusions as to the pace of decline.
14. Premier Li Peng to the World Bank President. Reuter, Beijing, 9-20-95.
15. *Beijing Review*, 11-6/12-95.
16. AP, Beijing, via Compuserve Executive News Service, 9-30-95. The figure cited was 6.5 million cubic yards. The figure presumably includes industrial sewage.
17. Masayoshi Sadakata of Tokyo University, quoted in *Science* July 21, 1995, p.296.
18. Open Media Research Institute, Prague, "Cabinet Ministers Express Concerns Over Illegal Chinese Immigration," August 25, 1995.
19. UN World Commission on Environment and Development (or "Brundtland Commission" for its Chair, Gro Harlem Brundtland, Prime Minister of Norway), *Our Common Future* (Oxford; Oxford University Press, 1987), p.213.

IT'S TIME TO STOP AT TWO

Leon Bouvier

April 1996

FERTILITY IS THE OTHER FACTOR

Such changes will go a long way in reducing population pressure in the United States in the future. But the other most significant contributor to population growth—fertility—is sadly missing from the debate.

Population growth is not exclusively an immigration issue. It is my belief that the optimum rate of population growth for the United States should be negative until such time as the scale of economic activity, and its environmental effects, is reduced to a level that would be sustainable indefinitely. Then, and only then, should we, as a nation, consider a return to zero population growth.

If present rates of population and economic growth are allowed to continue, the end result, within the lifetimes of many of us, would inevitably be near universal poverty in a hopelessly polluted world. Somehow, we must find a way—or ways—to eventually reduce population size if our quality of life is to be maintained and improved. A substantial decline in immigration is a start toward that goal—a much smaller population than today's 265 million—be it 150 million or 200 million as the eminent senior statesman, George Kennan, recommends.

Yet, according to the most recent projections from the Census Bureau, if fertility remained at its current level, even a reduction to net immigration of 200,000 per year would still lead to a population of some 350 million in 2050. Even if immigration came to an end immediately, our numbers would still increase for many years. That is a startling statement and strongly suggests that we do something about our fertility and do it now.

U.S. FERTILITY IS INCREASING

For about a decade during the peak years of the baby bust era (roughly 1975–1985), women averaged between 1.7 and 1.8 births (what demographers call the total fertility rate). But by 1988 fertility again began to rise. Now women are averaging approximately 2.0 to 2.1 births. Furthermore, the number of births has climbed and is now around four million annually for the first time since the baby boom years which ended in 1964.

A number of reasons have been given for this sudden and unexpected recent rise in fertility. Older women, still childless or perhaps with one offspring, have decided to have another baby before menopause. The increase in the share of the population that is foreign-born contributes to raising the fertility rate, since the foreign-born generally have higher birth rates than do the native-born and their share of the total population is growing. As the foreign-born share of the population grows, that could contribute to further increases in fertility. Both arguments have some validity, but in actuality the fertility rate has gone up at all ages. Simply stated, American women have decided to have more children.

THE IMPACT OF SMALL CHANGES

To the uninitiated, it may seem odd to refer to changes from 1.8 to 2.1 births as being worthy of mention. After all, we are talking about less than 1/3 of a birth! But such an increase is monumental when talking about a population the size of the United States. A recent Census Bureau publication illustrates the tremendous power of a slight change in fertility.

By 2050, the difference between averaging 1.5 and 1.8 births (0.3 births) would mean a difference of 42 million people! If the fertility were 2.2, the difference between 1.8 and 2.2 (0.4 births) would result in 63 million more people. While major reductions in immigration are vital to lowering our population size, such reductions alone cannot get the job done. Together with limiting immigration to 200,000, fertility should be gradually reduced to no more than 1.5 births per woman, on average. That is just barely lower than the rate attained during the birth dearth period, so it is a reasonable goal. Even then, it would take sixty years before the nation's population was back to its current size and it would be eighty before it fell to below 200 million.

HOW TO REDUCE FERTILITY

Is it reasonable to expect fertility to fall to 1.5 births and stay in that vicinity? As we have already noted, fertility remained around 1.7 and 1.8 for over a decade during the late 1970s and early 1980s.

Fertility rates vary considerably among sub-groups of American women. Rates are highest among the least educated and the poor. According to the most recent Census Bureau survey, minority women have higher fertility than White women. Then again, minority women are far more likely to be poor and undereducated than Whites.

It should be clearly understood that any fertility reduction based on race must be totally rejected. Rather, we should examine the reasons for high fertility among certain subgroups of American women and then propose appropriate solutions. For example, the relationship between education and fertility is far more significant than that between race and fertility. White women, regardless of years of school completed, have higher fertility than Black women with a college education.

The same is true of income. Among the higher earning families, Blacks have lower fertility than Whites, but Hispanic fertility remains fairly high. There is evidence, however, that Hispanic fertility falls in the second generation particularly where some assimilation has occurred. As immigrants and their descendants become more proficient in English—a good indicator of acculturation as well as increased education—fertility falls. Thus, one way to reduce fertility is to raise the educational levels for all and improve the economic status of women. If the fertility of all subgroups can be brought down to that exhibited by the better educated and the wealthier, irrespective of race, a good start will have been made toward the goal of 1.5 births per woman, on average.

Today, in predominantly Catholic countries like Italy and Spain, women are averaging 1.2 births! These are undoubtedly temporary aberrations in their fertility behavior. Nevertheless, no less than twenty-six nations, including Japan, Netherlands, Germany, Switzerland, etc., have fertility rates below 1.6. If all American families, rich and poor, accepted the motto "Stop at Two," an overall rate of 1.5 would be well within the realm of possibility since many women remain childless and some have only one child.

The contraceptive methods are available to ensure that families limit their families to no more than two offspring, if they so desire. Admittedly, pharmaceutical firms have been reluctant to proceed with more advanced research in this field, in large part to avoid offending religious conservatives, but present methods, if available to all, can do the job. Equally important are the new developments in abortion research. While I do not recommend abortion as a population control measure, it is a regrettably necessary backup when contraception fails. As Vice President Al Gore has said so well: "If abortion becomes necessary, it should be safe, legal, and rare." Our prime target is unwanted conceptions and not unwanted pregnancies. Whether through the use of contraceptives or new abortion techniques as a backup, the tools are available for all American couples to stop at two.

What would it take to convince young American couples to take that vital step? Certainly, we could follow the examples set by other countries like Mexico and Thailand where advertising, even through soap opera themes, has paid off in lowering rates. In Thailand, fertility is now lower than it is in the United States. In Mexico, while it remains too high, it has fallen considerably over the past decades.

Perhaps more successful would be government policies that would encourage lower fertility. Tax deductions after two offspring should be discontinued; the outrageous attempt by a majority in Congress to hand out subsidies of $500 for each child should be rejected outright through a presidential veto if necessary. Rather, women should be monetarily rewarded for remaining childless until reaching at least age twenty.

We must also try to reduce out-of-wedlock pregnancies at all ages. Demographer Kristin Moore has pointed out that there has been an eightfold jump nationwide since 1940 in the number of babies born to single mothers. Moore states that this "is not a teen problem, not a minority problem and not a poverty problem. We are looking at something society-wide." Moore also noted that 72 percent of all teenagers having babies are not married.

Together, a massive advertising campaign, governmental regulations, a re-examination of our family values and a sincere concern for the common good could result in our reaching the goal of 1.5 children in a relatively short period of time.

BENEFITS TO THE NATION

The benefits for the society of low fertility and low immigration and the resulting reduced population size are too numerous to mention. Consider the benefits for our resources such as water and air; currently these are being increasingly polluted through the use of more automobiles and growing numbers of people using up a dwindling water supply. As a result, our aquifers, so important to plant life, are suffocating. Consider the benefits for our infrastructure such as schools and highways and national parks. Our schools are deteriorating. Our highways are being increasingly crammed with vehicles as the number of cars rises along with population growth. It is next to impossible to visit our National Parks without making reservations years ahead and then waiting in long lines to simply enter. Our once beautiful beaches are now overcrowded and becoming more and more polluted—all because of population growth. The list goes on and on.

We need to instill in all Americans a sense of responsibility for the common good. While some families may be financially and emotionally able to have five or even ten children, they should resist this temptation for the good of all Americans.

BENEFITS FOR THE INDIVIDUAL

I am not only concerned with numbers. There is no magic involved in advocating 150 million or 200 million Americans. My concern is with improving the well-being of each individual and I am convinced that a smaller population would contribute greatly toward achieving such a goal. But population change can only come from alterations in the three demographic variables: fertility, mortality, and immigration. I wholly favor increased life expectancy and long healthy lives even if the result is a larger population. With longer life expectancy, fertility and immigration would have to fall even more to allow us to reach our population goals, but improving the longevity and health of Americans is more important.

Fertility differs substantially from the other two demographic variables. When we discuss immigration, we are thinking of a person who leaves one country and moves to another. When we talk about mortality, we think of the one person who has passed away. But when we talk about fertility, three persons are involved: the mother, the father, and the baby. The quality of life of all three is dependent to a great extent on the number of offspring the parents have.

The first rule should be this: Every child should be wanted, planned, and loved. If all couples (whether married or not) first arrived at a decision that they wanted (or didn't want) a child, if they agreed that a child was desired, they would then plan (and take the necessary precautions) on when to have that child (in a year, two years, five years), then that child when born would be truly loved. I do not deny that unplanned children can be loved by their parents. Further, love may be infinite, and that love, itself, can be given to more than two children. But our capacity to give children tangible expressions of that love is limited.

For most couples, the pie of love is only so large and cannot be divided into an unlimited number of pieces. Social and economic conditions almost mandate that both parents work. The few hours, usually in the evening, when the parents can give their undivided attention to their offspring are limited and with more than two children, can sometimes result in at least one child being neglected, albeit unintentionally.

LOVE IS THE MAGIC WORD HERE

Nothing is sadder than the sight of an unwanted, unplanned, and unloved child who often ends up being abused, whether physically or psychologically. On the other hand, is there anything more beautiful than the sight of all children being wanted, planned, and cared for—loved—by their parents?

When I urge all American families to stop at two, my primary goal is to improve the quality of life and standard of living of all Americans in this and future generations. But I am convinced that this goal can only be achieved if U.S. population is eventually stabilized at a level substantially smaller than it is today. Just imagine our country sometime in the next century where the population had stopped increasing and was even beginning to fall and where no families had more than two children and these children were loved because they were wanted and planned. Consider the differences it would make throughout the lives of all of us. Fewer abused children, physically and emotionally, massive reductions in juvenile delinquency, better schools and more success in those schools—in a word—more happiness for all American families.

If Americans can do both—reduce immigration and limit fertility to no more than two children, the twenty-first century could indeed become the Age of Aquarius—an era of peace and prosperity for all Americans.

THE CASE AGAINST IMMIGRATION

Reviewed by David Simcox

October 1996

Journalist, immigration scholar and active protestant layman, Roy Beck is pro-immigrant but anti-immigration—at least immigration at its present level of one million-plus yearly. His book is a powerful case against today's mass immigration that is compassionate, racially-sensitive but not racist, and profoundly moral.

Steering clear of concerns about the nation's culture or racial composition, Beck sees the issue as not who the immigrants are, but how many. Numbers of newcomers, not their race or national origins, are burdening the environment, resources, and public services, disrupting labor markets, and diluting community cohesion.

Today's rigid, mechanistic immigration policy has tripled intake in three decades, something its legislative backers neigher wanted nor expected. The 1965 act's enshrinement of principle of family reunification made it an engine of ever rising intake, while ignoring the budding problem of illegal immigration.

America's ossifield immigration regime permits no adjustments to changing conditions and serves no recognizable national interest. Instead, Beck argues, a careless policy has made immigration a pernicious spoiler of efforts to realize four great goals of American society:

GOAL 1: PRESERVING THE MIDDLE CLASS

Immigration is worsening income inequality, in the process helping diminish the once expansive American middle-class that has been central to high quality of civic, social and work life. Wage depression nurtured by cheap foreign workers now costs U.S. workers $133 billion a year. This "perverse Robin Hood scheme" robs from the middle class and gives it to the affluent. Established immigrants themselves are no less victimized by this process.

GOAL 2: ENSURING EQUAL OPPOUTUNITY FOR AFRICAN-AMERICANS

The admission of armies of complaint low-wage workers and their needy dependents through legal and tolerated illegal immigration has high moral and social costs. It undercuts the nation's unfulfilled moral obligation to provide equal opportunity, the descendants of slavery.

African-Americans are triply disadvantaged by imported job completion. Immigrants bring their lower wage expectations just as those of African-Americans have been justifiably rising. Blacks, who have long been pushed to the end of the nation's hiring queue, must now face mounting employer preference for foreign workers.

Inexplicably, a perverted concept of affirmative action allows employers and ethnic networks to hire minorities while shunning Black Americans. African-Americans also face tougher competition for quality housing, public education, and social services in areas of major immigrant settlement.

GOAL 3: ENHANCING THE QUALITY OF COMMUNITY LIFE

Harmonious and safe community life retreats under the pressure of hyper urbanization, population growth, churning displacement, transience, and alienation nourished in part by mass influxes of immigrants.

GOAL 4: ENDING POPULATION GROWTH

New immigrants and births to the foreign-born now are the main accelerant of U.S. population growth—a growth that complicates the solution to every environmental ill. Beck reminds us again that we must curb immigration, not because the immigrants are bad people, but because . . .

Anything that adds to the number of Americans flushing toilets, riding in vehicles and consuming electricty is anti-environment.

Immigration since 1965 has been "Congress's forced population growth program:" under present trends, post-2000 immigrants and their descendants will account for 90 percent of the nation's projected growth of 210 million in the twenty-first century. Without any net immigration since 1970, the country would have reached zero growth in 2030 at 245 million and begun receding by mid-century toward a more environmentally sustainable level.

Beck doesn't argue that immigration is the sole culprit in these complex ills, but sees their solution as immensely more difficult as long as immigration-driven population growth persists.

Polls consistently show the American people badly want lower immigration. For Beck the answer is a break with the myths and selective memories of our immigrant past for an excercise of political will to cut back immigration to its "average historical levels" between 175,000 and 300,000 a year.

Specifically, Beck proposes a ceiling of 250,000 and an end to all illegal entries. Two hundred thousand slots would be exclusively for admission of spouses and children of U.S. citizens, a long-established privilege he finds too entrenched to end. The remaining 50,000 would be for bona fide refugees (maximum 30,000) and for commercial needs and intake of high skills unproduceable here.

Beck's 75 percent reduction is politically feasible. His 250,000 ceiling in close to the 300,000 upper limit an NPG-sponsored Roper Poll in 1996 found was backed by 70 percent of Americans (54 percent wanted fewer than 100,000 immigrants a year). He notes that an end to the self-expanding intake of extended family members would eventually bring down demand for entry of spouses and children and lower overall admission well below 200,000 approximately zero net immigration.

Zero net immigration is absolutely critical to early attainment of a stationary population that can then progress toward what should be the vital national goal of a population below 200 million, a number environmentally sustainable indefinitely.

Persisting in our present immigration habits will heighten the social and environmental evils that Beck so eloquently decries, while bequeathing to our descendants a tragically congested and environmentally devastated land.

ENDING THE EXPLOSION: POPULATION POLICIES AND ETHICS FOR A HUMANE FUTURE

Reviewed by David Simcox

October 1996

Two years ago the world badly needed William Hollingsworth's tough-minded but humane prescription for urgent reduction of human fertility.

His book offers what the 1994 UN Conference in Cairo on Population and Development (UNCPD) should have produced but studiously avoided: a strategy and a moral and political justification for a global effort to reduce world fertility to replacement level in the next fifteen to twenty years. Just such an urgent endeavor, he warns, is the world's best chance to stabilize its population at less than 10 billion by the end of the next century. A central argument of this book is that humankind's ability to limit its own fertility is now the most critical determinant of finding or losing a humane future.

Where the UNCPD uttered only exhortations, the author prescribes fertility and population goals and timetables. While the UNCPD soft-pedaled money talk, Hollingsworth suggests the sums needed and their sources. Most crucially, he makes the case that incentives and disincentives, a concept scorned at Cairo, can reduce fertility while enhancing human freedom and dignity.

It is folly, says Hollingsworth, to wait for glacial social trends such as the improved status of women or economic development to slow fertility in time to prevent a population disaster. Women's rights are a moral imperative in themselves, but not a cure-all for exploding population. Waiting for a demographic transition, which is unpredictable and at best gradual, is more temporizing the world can't afford.

Two tough tasks must be begun. First, family planning services must be provided to those who now want lower fertility but lack the means—about one in five of the world's women of childbearing age. The second task is far harder. Effective contraception can only lower fertility enough if most couples want no more than two children. Individual and community incentives are vital in lowering desired family size.

THE GREATEST IMMORALITY: MASSIVELY TRAGIC OVERPOPULATION

For ethicist Hollingsworth, an ordained minister and Professor of Law at Tulsa University, the greatest violation of human dignity will not be democratically-chosen antinatalist incentives, but a global population between 12 billion and 17 billion by 2100—a terrifyingly likely outcome with today's global population momentum if attainment of replacement fertility is delayed.

Massively tragic overpopulation will not redeem, liberate or dignify anyone. Rather, it will imprison the human spirit, heighten economic inequality and kindle unending strife and despair.

Where is the human dignity, Hollingsworth asks, in a trend that will yield rising child mortality and morbidity, extinction of species, and apocalyptic [illegible] sees overpopulation as intrinsically at war with the preciousness of every person. The self-perceived and socially perceived value of each human suffers in a world of too many people.

INCENTIVES AND DISINCENTIVES: ANTIDOTE TO COERCION

Incentives can expand freedom and dignity. They can signal the larger society's support for the childbearing couple against extended family and traditional pressures for high fertility. Planners must weigh whatever coercion that may come from incentives against the coercion inherent in the status quo. The author examines the subtle and shifting line between coercive and humane incentives with realism and sensitivity.

The author anticipates and rebuts the long-held moral objections to incentives—they encourage abortion; bear unduly on the poor; deny freedom of choice; "monetize" childbearing; or impose Western cultural norms. He responds:

- *Sound family planning will reduce abortions, along with maternal and infant mortality.*
- The poor are already those most burdened by their societies' pressures for large families. But any program of incentives and disincentives can and must apply equally to all.
- Freedom of choice is essential in a humane, non-coercive program. Disincentives must never be life-threatening. But freedom to choose can never mean that the individual's choices themselves are cost-free.
- The seeming economic advantage of children has long been a factor in high fertility. State and community incentives can bring solutions other than more childbearing to the search for economic security.
- The plummeting world death rate that has sustained the population explosion itself reflects the penetration of such Western cultural norms as public health and antibiotics. The West has a moral obligation to help deal with the effects it helped bring about.

Incentives envisioned by Hollingsworth might even involve priority access for smaller families to some jobs, advanced education, housing, or fertility taxes. If it sounds draconian, Hollingsworth reminds us that scarcity is the draconian reality—one that overpopulation would tragically intensify.

FROM A CONSCIENTIOUS EFFORT, QUICK RESULTS

Hopeful of generous Western aid, Hollingsworth optimistically estimates rapid dramatic results from a combination of endeavors in family planning, health, education and direct incentives. Fertility in developing nations would likely fall by about one child per woman every three to four years, reaching replacement level before 2015.

His scenario may sound too optimistic. The third world lacks the participatory institutions to build a democratic consensus for prompt fertility reduction. The process of creating goals and incentives democratically would, for many societies, be an unnatural and, accordingly, a time-consuming act.

Yet what is a better alternative? Certainly not the dilatory, "something will turn-up" approach of the UN's population conferences. Less palatable authoritarian measures are likely if the problem is allowed to grow. Hollingsworth points to a way out of a disastrous population trap that is within the world's means and morally defensible.

The book's good advice is valid for growing developed countries such as our own. The remaining pronatalist biases in American society must be offset with education and incentives if U.S. population growth is to be halted quickly and begin to recede to a size that is sustainable indefinitely.

HUDDLED EXCESSES

Michael Lind

April 1996

Sooner or later America must face reality. It is going to be painful. . . . What America is fighting is a piece of poetry. . . . The poetry is thrilling. It is on the Statue of Liberty: "Give me your tired, your poor, your huddled masses yearning to breathe free. . . ."

The trouble is that huddled masses need jobs.

PATRICK BUCHANAN?

No, Richard Strout, the eminent liberal journalist who wrote this column for several decades. Since Strout wrote those words in 1980, more than 10 million people have immigrated to the United States legally. The number of new immigrants and their higher-than-average birthrate recently forced the Census Bureau to revise its 1989 estimate of U.S. population in 2080 [sic: should be 2050] upward, by an additional 100 *million*—to 400 million.

But it is not numbers alone that should convert liberal immigration defenders. As Strout observed, the "huddled masses need jobs." According to a 1995 Bureau of Labor Statistics study, competition with immigrants has accounted for roughly half the recent decline in wages among unskilled American workers. According to University of Michigan demographer William Frey, competition for jobs with poorly paid Latin American and Asian immigrants is driving low-income whites and blacks out of high-immigration states like California and high-immigration cities like New York. No wonder Steve Forbes and Dick Armey favor high levels of immigration, and *The Wall Street Journal* has proposed a five-word amendment to the U.S. Constitution—"There shall be open borders." It's great for business.

But not so great for poor Americans. And they're not the only ones under threat. U.S. companies can legally hire 140,000 *skilled* foreign workers each year. Business lobbyists have claimed that the U.S. computer industry needs a never-ending supply of East Asian and Indian scientists because there are not enough Americans able to do the work. Really?

Why can't American industry train native and naturalized citizens for high-tech jobs? Some companies do the reverse. In 1994, the American International Group Insurance Company fired more than 250 American computer programmers and replaced them with Indian workers brought in under the H-1B visa program (which allows firms to pay only the foreign prevailing wage plus a living allowance). To add insult to injury, the laid-off workers, on pain of losing their severance pay, were forced to train their foreign replacements for sixty days.

The greatest gain in income by the American middle and working classes, both white and black, took place during the era of immigration restriction, from the 1920s to the 1960s. Not coincidentally, this was also the heyday of union membership, which is inevitably hampered when mass immigration produces a workforce divided by ethnicity. And, of course, it was the golden age of public support for universal entitlements and anti-poverty efforts. Coincidence? Not likely. The most generous and egalitarian countries in modern times have been culturally homogeneous nation-states admitting few or no poor immigrants, like those of northern Europe and Japan (where corporate paternalism substitutes for social democracy). The equation of social justice and national solidarity seems much less compelling in the modern U.S., where immigrants overall are much more likely than native-born Americans to receive welfare benefits. (In Chinese-speaking Asia, one widely distributed book tells potential immigrants how to obtain SSI and other benefits of the American welfare state.)

There is, then, a liberal case for immigration restriction that has nothing to do with the absurd and offensive claims of some conservatives that growing numbers of nonwhites threaten our civilization (Patrick Buchanan) or our gene pool (Charles Murray). What's more, the obsession with illegal immigration on the part of politicians like Pete Wilson evades the main issue. Each year, 300,000 to 400,000 illegal immigrants arrive in the U.S. to stay, a fraction of the roughly 1 million legal immigrants who take up permanent residence each year. We can and should crack down on illegal immigration—with a stronger border patrol, fences and a computerized national employment verification system—but legal immigration represents the greater threat to American wages and unions.

Reducing legal immigration is a perfectly legitimate liberal cause—if "liberal" means protecting the interests of ordinary wage-earning Americans. Unfortunately, for thirty years the Democratic Party has not acted like a liberal or social-democratic party. It has acted as a coalition of ethnic patronage machines (each seeking to enlarge the number of its group eligible for affirmative action) and affluent white social liberals (whose lifestyle in many cases depend on a supporting cast of low-wage Latin American maids and nannies). Unlike free-market conservatives, who can at least invoke a principled libertarian viewpoint, pro-immigration liberals have no theory, merely the "piece of poetry" of which Strout wrote—and the N-word (nativist). But now that majorities of black Americans and even a slight majority of Hispanics, according to a Roper poll commissioned by Negative Population Growth Institute [sic], support reducing immigration to less than 300,000 a year, it will no longer do to accuse all supporters of immigration reform of racism and xenophobia.

As Strout concluded in a critique of immigration policy back in 1981, "people must face facts, whether they like them or not." A brave minority of liberal Democrats, including Wisconsin Congressman David Obey, have done so, signing on as cosponsors of the immigration reform bills introduced by Alan Simpson in the Senate and Lamar Smith in the House. Though the bill wisely cut back on extended-family reunification—a Ponzi scheme that has resulted in escalating immigrant numbers—they would reduce legal immigration by only a third, to about 700,000 a year.

That's still much too high. The numerical cap envisioned by the original Kennedy-Johnson reform in 1965—290,000 a year—would do more to bring U.S. population growth in line with other developed countries and to raise U.S. wages, particularly at the bottom of the income scale. Yet there would still be room for plenty of humanitarian refugees, spouses and children of Mexican-American citizens, Taiwanese grad students and English journalists. Though the U.S. would no longer take half the world's legal immigrants, we would still have the world's most generous immigration policy.

TRB was right. Genuine liberals should unite with populist conservatives to reform an immigration policy that benefits few Americans other than exploitative employers. It is easy to talk in poetry. But it is necessary to govern in prose.

OFFICIAL OPTIMISM, JOURNALISTIC HYPE: THE UN 1996 POPULATION PROJECTIONS

Lindsey Grant

December 1997

The United Nations a year ago distributed its periodic population projection World Population Prospects. The 1996 Revision. The media have belatedly discovered it and distorted it almost beyond recognition. What was a moderate and mildly optimistic adjustment of the 1994 projection has been read as a revolutionary portent of a new population era, to the joy of some but the dismay of other commentators, who display an irrational addiction to continued growth and a visceral fear of its end. A less panicky look is needed at what the UN said, what it may mean, and how much credence can be given to the numbers.

Last April, a Hollywood reporter began a UPI story with these breathless sentences:

> *"What might be the most significant news story of the century will be unveiled April 18 in a PBS documentary. The story . . . reveals that the planet-threatening human population boom is at an end. It suggests over-population, leading to food shortages, ozone holes, unemployment, acid rain, war, environmental poisoning, ominous climatic changes and other catastrophic assaults on Mother Earth, is in abeyance."*[1]

Wonderful news, indeed, if it were true. The problem is that the reporter promoted a mildly optimistic UN forecast [2] into a glorious new dawn.

The *Wall Street Journal* and *New York Times* have been similarly misled but hardly ecstatic. A February *Journal* article (built upon a factual error) predicted that much of the world will soon be in a "demographic free fall" and used the occasion to castigate the "population-control crowd."[3] It "adjusted" the UN tables to predict a peak world population of about 7 billion in 2030—170 years sooner and 3.7 billion people less than the UN's own projection.

The hype seems to be originating primarily with the American Enterprise Institute (AEI), which is funded heavily by business interests, and publicized by the *Journal* and the *Times*. A *Journal* article in October avoided the errors and "adjustments" but had much the same message: that world population growth is about to turn around, and that a turnaround will be catastrophic.[4]

A *New York Times* article in November was distinguished primarily by the tenor of the headlines: "How to Fix a Crowded World: Add More People," "Problem for a Crowded World: Not Enough People" and (in a California paper running the article) "Now the Crisis is Underpopulation."[5] Ben Wattenberg, another AEI associate, reappeared (see note 1) in another *Times* article titled "The Population Explosion is Over" on November 23rd. This was a bit less hyperbolic than the others, even recognizing some advantages. Like the others, however, he treated a recognized trend as a dramatic discovery.

(The UN statisticians, as we shall see, have been very consistent in their projections over the years.) And presumably to sell the article, he pretended that environmentalists have been saying that population will grow forever, when their point in fact has been that it cannot.

It sounds like an orchestrated effort by business, following up on its opposition to immigration reform in 1996, to downplay the population issue and thereby reduce potential opposition to large scale immigration. Am I being too suspicious?

Several themes were more or less constant in these articles:

- They treated the projection as though it were a major change, which it was not.
- They used (or misused) the UN "low" projection as if it were indeed the UN projection. Most of them ignored the others. In fact, the UN statisticians regard the "low" series as a probable lower bound for anticipated future population change and the "medium" projection as the most likely one.
- They were mesmerized by the fear that there will be too few working age people to support the old.
- They justified that concern by focusing on Western Europe and Japan—which together constitute less than 10 percent of the world's population—and almost ignored trends among the other 90 percent.
- Except for Wattenberg, they treated the slowdown in fertility as a natural phenomenon. I will make the case later that some credit is due to deliberate efforts to bring it about. This leads to very different conclusions as to what the world should be doing now.
- Except for the Hollywood reporter, they paid little or no attention to the benefits of stopping population growth for environmental sustainability, for living standards and for wages and employment, which should be the central issues in any discussion of population policy.
- Most important, they displayed a visceral attachment to continued growth and a fear of its cessation, despite the mathematical fact that physical growth must end on a finite planet. More people, it is argued, are needed to promote economic growth. Why is more economic growth needed? To provide jobs. For whom? For more people. It is a circularity from which conventional minds apparently cannot escape.

We are confronted with the remarkable scene of a journalistic panic at the prospect that some nations may be on the way to stopping or reversing population growth—although stopping it has been an objective of the United Nations for decades, of most third world leaders [6], and of all the world's major national and international multidisciplinary scientific societies, including the U.S. National Academy of Sciences.[7]

Perhaps we should see just what the UN statisticians really said and what the implications are.

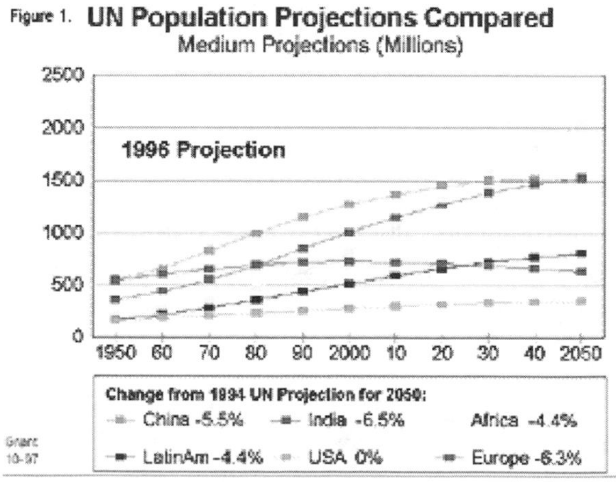

Figure 1. **UN Population Projections Compared**
Medium Projections (Millions)

1996 Projection

Change from 1994 UN Projection for 2050:
China -5.5% India -6.5% Africa -4.4%
LatinAm -4.4% USA 0% Europe -6.3%

Grant 10-97

Figure 1.

WHAT THE UN STATISTICAL DIVISION SAID

In fact, the 1996 UN projection was a sober and rather modest modification of the 1994 projection. Growth in the third world (the UN's "less developed countries") is slowing somewhat more quickly than was expected two years before. World population is now about 5.9 billion. The medium projection for 2050 is 9.4 billion, or 64 percent more than the present population. This is hardly a "demographic free fall." It is 4.7 percent below the 1994 projection (a difference that Wattenberg overstated)—but close to a projection made fifteen years ago.[8] Contrary to the media stories, world population growth is not projected to stop soon. The medium projection, carried forward by the UN, shows growth to a figure of 10.7 billion just after 2200, followed by a slow decline.

A graph may be a useful way to compare the most recent projections for key regions.

Much of the change from the 1994 projection reflects Chinese and Indian success in bringing fertility down—in China's case despite excoriation from the United States. The changed projection for Europe reflects a reassessment of Russia and Eastern Europe; the projection for Western Europe declined only 1.8 percent.

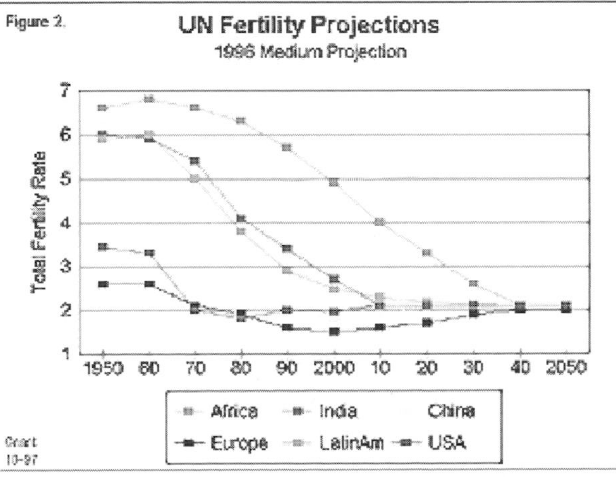

Figure 2.

The signs that led to the optimism can be read in Figure 2, which shows selected historical and projected fertility trends.

The projections necessarily reflect the mindset of the UN statisticians. They project trends as they understand them, anticipating fertility and mortality changes that have not yet happened. By way of comparison, they also run a "constant fertility" projection. If fertility and mortality should stay where they are now, world population would pass 14.9 billion in 2050—if the ecosystem could support such a staggering number.

DIVERGING FUTURES

The central worldwide demographic reality right now is divergence between the industrial countries and the poorest, complicated by the emergence of some third world countries as industrialized societies.

The Industrial World. Fertility is below replacement level in almost the entire industrial world. Left to itself, present fertility (the "constant fertility" projection cited above) would lead to a population decline of 15 percent in Europe [9] by 2050, bringing it back down almost to the 1960 level. For Japan, the decline would be 21 percent, to a level it passed in 1965. However, the medium variant shows declines of just 12 percent for both, because the authors expect fertility in those regions to rise again.

The Blurring Middle. Low fertility is spreading to the newly industrializing countries, particularly in East and Southeast Asia. Total fertility (TFR; or the number of children expected per woman over a lifetime) is now below the U.S. rate of 1.96 and below replacement level in ten third world nations, including a key one, China.

The Poor Countries. In the poorer parts of the third world and in the Middle East, population growth is terrifying. Among the UN's forty-eight "least developed countries," with a present population of 600 million, fertility still averages 5.25 children, and population is growing at the rate of 30 percent per decade. Figure 1 shows the population curve for Africa. The medium projection for Africa in 2050 is over two billion, almost triple the present population. That projection is optimistic. It assumes that fertility decline will accelerate to 60 percent between now and 2040, in a continent that has experienced a decline of only 20 percent since the 1950s. Lots of luck. If it could be brought off, it would offer the hope for eventual stabilization late in the twenty-second century—at a population somewhere around three billion.

I would challenge anybody to make the case that Africa can support two or three billion people, or even the 1.7 billion of the low projection. If it cannot, population growth will slow and stop, indeed, but for the wrong reason: rising mortality.

EUROPE AND THE "DEPENDENCY RATIO"

I have mentioned the journalists' fears about the projected dependency ratios. That ratio is a crude measure of the number of people each worker must support. Mathematically, it is the total population of the old and young expressed as a percentage of the "working age" (fifteen to sixty-four) population. In theory, the lower the ratio, the higher the standard of living, because a worker's earnings do not have to be shared by so many people. I think that its importance has been exaggerated, but it needs examination.

The changes for Europe are less dramatic than the more lurid press accounts because the journalists ignored the tradeoff: more old dependents but fewer young dependents. Moreover, prosperity and dependency ratios are not closely correlated. Look at the United States in the sixties and seventies, a period of ebullient economic growth—when our dependency ratio was at a peak because of the baby boom.

A drop in fertility first lowers the dependency ratio, because there are fewer children, and then raises it as their parents move out of their working years. (This phenomenon is dramatically illustrated by the projection for Africa, which shows a very good ratio by 2050—Figure 3—but the plunge in African fertility—Figure 2—would lead eventually to crushing dependency levels in the following two generations as smaller cohorts of children enter the labor force and the larger cohorts grow old.)

The speed at which fertility declines, and to what level, determine how far the dependency ratio rises. Figure 3 gives a graphic comparison. Sweden dropped to a TFR of 1.65 in the 1970s (then considered remarkably low) but is now back to about 1.8. Its dependency ratio is expected to stay much more favorable than Italy's, where fertility has dropped suddenly to 1.19. Italy, indeed, is something of a special case. Worldwide, only Italy, Spain, Greece and Japan are expected to have dependency ratios higher than 80 percent in 2050. Overall, the curve for Europe in Figure 3 is hardly a cause for concern; it will turn around.

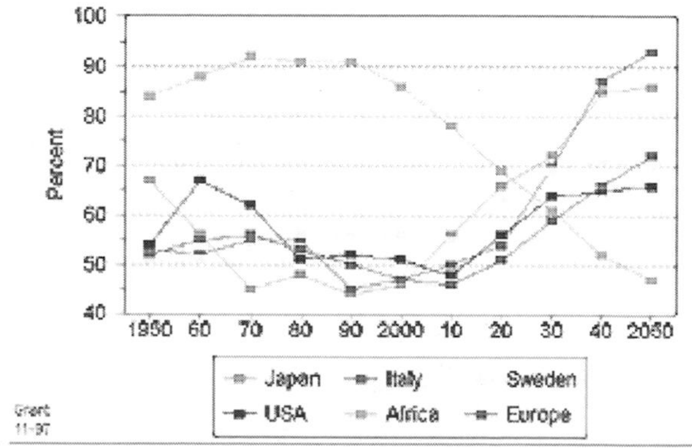

Figure 3.

Right now, when the principal economic problem in Europe is unemployment, fears of labor shortages seem a bit unreal. Nevertheless, the increased proportions of old people in the low fertility countries will require adjustments. Europe and Japan may need to reconsider their retirement and medical aid programs. People can find ways of retiring in their forties in some European countries without a substantial loss of income. Modern societies tend to write a blank check for medical care, in an extremely expensive effort to extend human life if not its pleasures. A more balanced approach, making it more attractive to stay in the labor force and recognizing that death at some point is inevitable, may preserve some social support systems that are already heavily stressed.

To leave the mathematical for the speculative, there will indeed be social and political adjustments as the population grows older. Less risk-taking, perhaps, and a more conservative electorate. Nevertheless, Florida has a very old population and Utah a very young one, and both seem to function in their fashion.

Most of the other consequences of population decline would be positive:

- fewer young people to train, and consequently the chance to train them better for more skilled work;
- less abundant labor, with the consequent incentive to substitute capital for labor, leading in turn to higher productivity and higher wages;
- reduced infrastructure needs, freeing capital for productive investment; Europe will be able to save the best houses, factories, schools and office buildings rather than building for population growth as they have had to do in recent decades.

Most important, a smaller population would make it easier to correct the environmental problems that now trouble Europe, to manage the transition away from fossil fuels, and to participate in the global effort to control global warming. At any level of conservation and pollution-control technology, the level of damage is proportional to the number of people being served.[10] Perhaps Europeans and Japanese are groping toward a population level that will lead to a more benign style of industrial and agricultural activity and a less crowded environment.

A transitory rise in the dependency ratio is inevitable, unless population growth is to continue forever, simply as part of the process of ending growth. The phenomenon is temporary. When population stabilizes at a new level, the dependency ratio tends to settle in the 60 percent range. Even in the extreme case of Italy, the medium projection, extended, suggests a decline in the ratio from 93 percent in 2050 to 80 percent in 2100 and 60 percent in 2150. The higher transitional levels are manageable, given the productivity of labor that has resulted from the technological revolution and the mobility of labor in the European Union; a move to a somewhat less drastic fertility level would of course lower the peak.

The European projection, which assumes a gradual trend back up to replacement level, offers a rather attractive prospect, if they have the resolve and the luck to pursue it. Population would stabilize at about 78 percent of the present level in 2150—a level it passed forty years ago—and the dependency ratio would settle at 61 percent. (I should note, however, that this sanguine sketch of the future depends on their ability to control immigration.)

Sub-replacement fertility leads eventually to zero. At some point, Europe will have to bring fertility back to replacement level or tolerate mass immigration, but they have time to consider a question that is now almost never asked: what would be the optimum?

They may well be better off with the population levels they left behind two or three generations ago than they are now, or smaller.

Italy, again, represents the extreme case. China talks about the "one child family" but averages about two children; Italy is down almost to one child. Only six other countries, all of them in Europe, have fertilities below 1.4. Because of population momentum, Italy's population would drift downward to 22 million by 2150 and stabilize there even if Italy returned to replacement level fertility in 2050. That takes it back to the nineteenth century. Perhaps not a bad idea—Italy created the Renaissance with a lot fewer people -but they and the six other countries should be holding national debates now about where they want their population to go, and how to get there.

So should we, but for a very different reason: continuing growth.

IS THE UN PROJECTION RIGHT?

Can the diverging futures between the poor and the rich continue to diverge? The UN statisticians expect not. They project a third world getting more like the industrial world, with all converging to a "modern" model of low fertility and low mortality, with less disease and hunger, an end to large scale international migration, and no nasty "surprises."

An optimistic vision.

Not so fast. A convergence of sorts will indeed occur, in the sense that the third world must stop growing, but that limited convergence could well conceal vast differences in fertility and mortality, or a worldwide deterioration of living conditions.

Fertility. The key to the UN projection is the assumption that third world fertility will continue and indeed accelerate its decline. Figure 2 should take some of the mystery, and perhaps the magic, out of demographic projections. In brief, the demographers have simply assumed that all regions will converge to an average total fertility rate (TFR) at or near 2.1 children per woman before 2050. The 2.1 figure is of course that magic figure, beloved of demographers, which would lead eventually to a static population at low levels of mortality.[11]

This mechanical assumption of a stable replacement level fertility rate can be justified by the impossibility of predicting what will actually happen to fertility and mortality, but it is almost certain to be wrong. Reality isn't that tidy. Fertility may hang up in some countries, fluctuate in others, and plunge far below 2.1 in others, as it has in Europe and Japan.

Mortality. The middle projection calls for life expectancy, worldwide, to rise from sixty-six years now to seventy-seven years in 2045–2050, with the most dramatic gains occurring in the least developed countries.

Statistics do not always track reality. In some regions, particularly Africa, the reality has probably left the official statistics behind. There has been widespread economic retrogression; the International Labor organization says that the modern sector in Kenya has "collapsed" and that real wages have fallen 50 percent since 1975 in Kenya and 80 percent in Tanzania. Food availability per capita in sub-Saharan Africa has declined for decades. Nevertheless, the UN believes that African life expectancy has risen throughout that period and it projects a rise from fifty-three years now to seventy-two years by 2045–2050. It recognizes that AIDS presently raises mortality in some African countries, but it assumes that AIDS will be brought under control in the next decade and begin to taper off.

There are reasons to question the UN statisticians' optimism.[12] The two improvements that generated the population explosion are in jeopardy:

- **Health.** If improved medicine and public hygiene started the population explosion, population growth may stop it. Urban slums can generate terrifying epidemics. The urban population of the third world has increased sixfold since 1950, adding 1.4 billion people. It is expected to add another two billion people by 2025. These figures are incomprehensible. The equivalent of two Chinas, nearly 40 percent of the world's present population, will be piled upon cities that are already in or approaching breakdown. The highest rates of urban growth are expected in the poorest countries that are least prepared to accommodate it.

City services such as water and sewage cannot handle the influx. Diseases of filth and poverty such as cholera have reappeared. The World Health Organization has pointed out that the conditions that made low mortality possible are being wiped out by population growth.

Into this cauldron, add the increasing resistance of pathogens to medicines. The assumption of a continuing decline in mortality becomes tenuous indeed.

Disease will not stay in the third world. It crosses borders. The industrial countries are better equipped to handle epidemics, but there is no assurance that third world problems will not affect mortality in the industrial world.

- **Nutrition.** Trade in food is already a paradox: the industrial world, by and large, provides the food exports to the third world. In the industrial countries, yields have reached a plateau in basic foodstuffs, and there is no "miracle" yet in sight to maintain the growth in yields that was, for about four decades, unprecedented in world history. Even present production levels are under threat from diversion of farmlands and water to other uses, pesticide-resistant pests, erosion and salinization. The ability of exporters to meet rising food demand is in deep question, as is the ability of the importers to pay for rising imports.

Those are the looming costs of past failure to adjust fertility when we changed the demographic imbalance by lowering mortality.

- **Migration.** As disease crosses borders, so do migrants, if there is no food and no work at home. There is a lag of about fifteen to twenty-five years between changes in birth rates and changes in the number of those seeking employment. The third world working age population is projected to grow by 64 percent between now and 2025, fueling migratory pressures.

The UN demographers recognize that the poor and rich worlds are mingling, but they don't expect it to continue. The projections phase out most international migration by 2005 and all of it by 2025. They are betting that the industrial nations (and the more prosperous developing countries that are now drawing migrants from their poorer neighbors) are going to be willing and able to stop immigration. Indeed, immigration is a very hot issue right now, throughout much of the world, but there is little reason to believe that it will stop. In fact, most of the debate has been about whether to enforce controls on illegal immigration, not whether to lower legal immigration. Many third world countries have enforced draconian deportations apparently to the satisfaction of their citizens, but there is no indication they are succeeding in stopping the migration. One wonders whether recipient countries will be ready or indeed able to stop it.

The UN assumes that immigration into the United States will stop in 2025 and projects our population at 348 million in 2050. The U.S. Bureau of the Census, which does not make that assumption, expects that it will be passing 394 million. Quite a difference for twenty-five years' migration, and a measure of the importance of immigration to our national future.

Worldwide, if the UN assumptions about migration turn out wrong—and I think there is overwhelming reason to believe that they will—the error will throw out all the projections. It will, particularly, raise the population figures for the industrial countries, since migration is a much more important demographic variable for them than for the developing world as a whole.

- **The Interactions.** These uncertainties can affect the projections in different ways. If the fertility assumptions turn out to have been too low, population growth will outstrip the projection. If the mortality assumptions turn out too optimistic, the population will be lower. If migration does not in fact stop, the industrial nations will be much larger. And nobody can predict exactly how such changes will interact.

Rather than the benign convergence suggested by the projections, there may be a different kind of convergence: population growth slowing and perhaps reversing, everywhere, but under vastly different conditions: rising mortality especially in the third world; a continuing gap in fertility between rich and poor nations, as there is between rich and poor individuals.

TESTING THE LIMITS

The *Hollywood Reporter* on page 1 had it partly right. The end of population growth would be good news if it were true. Over the long term, the alternative is unimaginable. We face an intolerable combination: growing populations in the poorest countries, rising consumption levels in industrializing countries, and immigration-induced population growth in the United States. Together, they lead to a rising curve of economic activity that would dwarf the present worldwide pressures on the environment. The "Brundtland Commission" in 1987 concluded that, in fairness, we must anticipate a five- or ten-fold growth in world industrial output to accommodate the modernization of the less developed countries. The International Panel on Climate Change forecasts a seven-fold rise in world gross domestic product (GDP) by 2050 and twenty-five-fold by 2100. The Chinese target is a seventy-fold increase by 2050. Those expectations epitomize the problem of trying to relieve poverty for a growing world population. It is inconceivable to me that, even with the best efforts at pollution control and conservation strategies, such growth would be environmentally tolerable, and there is yet no sign that the emerging countries will make their best efforts. Where are the limits?

I have argued elsewhere (note 12) that the Earth's ecology and the climate issue suggest that a world population of perhaps two or three billion might be sustainable. The world was at that level fifty years ago. The 1993 long term "low" projection would lead to a world population of 4.3 billion in 2150, which is about where we were in 1980. On the right track, but probably still well above the optimum.

Misquoted as it was, the UN Statistical Division's 1996 message was simply that the world is making some progress toward solving the population issue in a comparatively humane way, by lowering fertility rather than allowing mortality to rise to close the gap.

Statisticians are supposed to be value-free, but perhaps they will forgive me if I charge them with compassion. The medium projection is in a sense an artifact: the demographers use it to draw a picture of a tolerable future. They recognize, if businessmen and politicians and some journalists do not, that perpetual growth would lead to chaos and collapse. The medium projection can be fitted—with a bit of hope—to present trends.

The problem is that others who don't want to think about the consequences of growth then pick up the "low" series and interpret it as an assurance that the population problem has gone away. They should listen to the principal architect of the projections, who has said that "unless couples have access to safe contraceptives compatible with their cultural and religious beliefs, they are limited in how they can fulfill their hopes of smaller families, and population declines are much slower."[13] In other words, "keep up the population programs if you want to see that demographic future."

Don't just wait for it. If fertility in many developing countries is moving in the right direction, perhaps the governmental population programs have been doing something right. Not all declines in fertility are simply attributable to modernization. In the U.S. Congress, the endless debates about whether to continue population assistance should give way to a recognition of what those programs have accomplished, in our own direct interest. The question should be changed to "how much more is needed?"

NOTES:

1. Vernon Scott, "Scott's World," UPI Hollywood, 4-17-97. Scott was promoting a Public Broadcasting Service (PBS) documentary put together by Ben Wattenberg and scheduled for release the following day.
2. *World Population Prospects. The 1996 Revision* (New York: the United Nations Statistical Division). Projections circulated November 1996. Text to be published in 1998; date uncertain because of editing delays. This Forum is drawn from the tables and press release, in light of the continuing and often erroneous press citations of the report.
3. Article by Steven W. Mosher titled "Too Many People? Not by a Long Shot," 2-20-97. He claimed that seventy-nine countries are already below replacement level fertility—the actual UN figure is forty-nine—and he arrived at his numbers by "adjusting" the UN "low" series downward by assuming that the developing countries' fertility will drop to the present fertility level of Europe—which he understated. Even the UN "low" projection assumes no such convergence.
4. Nicholas Eberstadt, "The Population Implosion," 10-16-97.
5. Barbara Crossette, *New York Times and Orange County Register* 11-2-97. To its credit, the *Christian Science Monitor* on October 22, 1997, carried an article by David R. Francis, "Global Crowd Control Starts to Take Effect," which interviewed several specialists and presented the benefits of halting population growth.
6. See, for instance, the "Statement on Population Stabilization by World Leaders," signed by seventy-five heads of state or government and presented by Indonesian President Soeharto to the UN Secretary General in October 1995.
7. The U.S. National Academy of Sciences and the British Royal Society of London issued a warning of the dangers of population growth in 1992, which was followed up in 1994 by a declaration signed by 58 national scientific federations, worldwide. The International Council of Scientific Unions issued a comparable warning in 1992, as did 1600 scientists mobilized by the Union of Concerned Scientists in 1992.
8. UN projections have fluctuated slightly over the years. The new "medium" projection for 2050 is 8 percent below the 1993 long-term projection but very close to the 1982 projection. The 1996

"high" and "low" variants are 6.3 percent and 3.3 percent lower, respectively, than in 1994.

9. "Europe" as defined by the UN includes Russia and Siberia, carrying it to our Alaskan border. When I use the common term "western Europe," it includes the UN's Northern, Southern and Western Europe—the European Union plus a few small countries.
10. For a fuller discussion, see Lindsey Grant, "Europe in the Energy Transition: the Case for a Smaller Population," NPG Forum, 1987.
11. The high projections terminate at TFRs of 2.36 to 2.6 for different countries, implying population growth for the indefinite future. The low projections terminate at TFRs of 1.14 to 1.6 for different countries and would lead to world population of 7.75 billion in 2040 and a subsequent decline.
12. The data for this section are taken from my book *Juggernaut. Growth on a Finite Planet* (Santa Ana, Seven Locks Press: 1996), drawn mostly from earlier UN reports.
13. Joseph Chamie, Chief of the UN Population Division, interviewed by Barbara Crossette, reported in "World is Less Crowded than Expected, the U.N. Reports," *New York Times*, 11-17-96.

IN SUPPORT OF A REVOLUTION

Lindsey Grant

December 1997

In 1995, Dr. J. Kenneth Smail wrote an NPG Forum essay entitled "Confronting the 21st Century's Hidden Crisis: Reducing Human Numbers by 80%." *The article was picked up by other journals, and an expanded version was published in the September 1997 issue of the journal Politics and the Life Sciences under the title "Beyond Population Stabilization: The Case for Dramatically Reducing Global Human Numbers." Concurrently, the editors of the journal asked me to comment on the article. That commentary—which is in reality a presentation of concrete examples supporting Dr. Smail's thesis—is the basis for this Forum.*

Very few writers seem to recognize that growth cannot continue forever in a limited space, and that mathematical truism applies to the real world, today. Dr. Smail is one of those few who do. Moreover, he suggests that human numbers have already passed the long term capacity of the Earth to sustain us and that an optimum world population lies perhaps in the range of 2–3 billion. So short is memory that the proposal sounds revolutionary—almost blasphemous—to most ears. Humans' ability to accommodate to change is both our strength and our peril. People have learned to consider six billion "normal," and presumably they will try to adjust to 10 or 12 billion, desperate as their situation may be by that time. More public concern is being expressed at the prospect that Europe and Japan (two of the most crowded regions on Earth) may experience a population decline than that most other regions on Earth are drawing us into a nightmare born of population growth. Yet Dr. Smail's target is a population that was "normal" in 1950.

I agree with Dr. Smail and have no problem with his argument or with most of his assumptions. Rather than doing an exegesis on them, let me offer some brief examples of specific ways in which the interactions of demography and the environment are presently driving the human condition in precisely the wrong direction. They will, I believe, corroborate his thesis that a population turnaround is necessary.

DIVERGENCE AND CONVERGENCE

We live in a world riven by a deepening dichotomy. For most of the "third world," the issue is sheer numbers. The present population explosion resulted from a terrible failure of foresight. Starting particularly in the 1950s, the application of basic hygiene generated a sudden decline in mortality. In the subsequent decades, the revolution in agricultural productivity made it possible to feed those expanding populations—at a very high environmental price. A fundamental instability occurs when one side of a natural balance (mortality) is lowered without lowering the other side (fertility). The price of that failure, in much of the world, was the loss of a dream that was momentarily possible: the hope of creating a world in which there is enough for all.

The old industrial countries, on the other hand—and now some "newly industrializing countries" that are joining them—have benefitted from the technological explosion that started with the industrial revolution. In one vital respect, success fails. The distinguishing feature of modern human economic activity has been the accelerating rate at which we have altered the environment in the pursuit of economic production. This unintentional by-product must at some point limit economic activity, simply so we can preserve the ecosystems that support us. Although we do not have the knowledge to identify the precise point, it is clear that in some vital respects human activity is beyond a supportable level. Keynesian economics takes no account of such "externalities," and they go largely unrecognized.

Those two human conditions, contradictory as they may appear, are synergistic in their effect on the planet.

The biosphere lies about us and seems to extend forever. That perspective is a result of our own eye level. We are part of it. Consider it from a more distant vantage point, and one sees it as hardly more than a molecular film on the Earth's surface. On land, it lies almost entirely within the tiny thickness stretching from the plant roots to the treetops. It is much thinner than that in the treeless areas covering most of the Earth's land surface. On the oceans, it is somewhat thicker but much more diffuse.

Into that very limited space, the industrial revolution and human proliferation have been pouring carbon, nitrates, phosphates and sulfur at a rate comparable to the natural input. The industrial emissions of lead into the atmosphere in 1990 were twelve times the natural releases. For copper, the ratio was nearly six to one, for cadmium five to one, for arsenic 1.6 to one, and we have introduced literally millions of chemicals unknown in nature—with little or no understanding of the consequences.

We need a period of consolidation, not driven by rising demand, to learn more about the consequences of our own activity.

I will offer three brief case studies of the impact of demography on human well being.

CHEMICAL FERTILIZER AND FOOD PRODUCTION

My first example is the agricultural trap into which we have fallen in the effort to drive yields up to feed growing populations.

A Canadian professor named Vaclav Smil asks a fascinating question: What was the most important invention in the twentieth century? His unlikely answer: the Haber-Bosch process of synthesizing ammonia, and therefore nitrogen, introduced in 1913.

Nitrogen, Smil pointed out, is essential to chlorophyll, DNA (deoxyribonucleic acid), RNA (ribonucleic acid), proteins and enzymes—in short, to life itself. There are only three natural atmospheric processes for converting atmospheric nitrogen, which is locked up in N_2 molecules, into a form usable by plants and animals: falling meteors, ozonization and ionization by lightning. The only biotic process is the creation of ammonia by various bacteria, most notably by the rhizobium bacteria that live symbiotically on the roots of legumes (such as peas and beans).

Nitrogen and water are the two most important limiting factors in plant growth. Until the Haber-Bosch process, humankind could obtain nitrogen only by recycling it or green manuring with legumes.

Yields per hectare are the critical issue. By and large, the land that can be farmed is being farmed. Worldwide, arable acreage is headed downward. Food yields must more than match population growth just to maintain a constant level of nutrition.

That is where synthetic ammonia comes in. Its invention permitted agriculture to support an unprecedented population. By Smil's calculations, synthetic fertilizers now provide the nitrogen for about half the annual global crop harvest. Put more starkly: Were it not for synthetic fertilizer, the richest nations could probably get by with a change of diet, substituting cereals for meat, but perhaps one-third of the people in the more crowded and land-poor third world countries would starve. This dependence is absolute. If more nitrogen cannot sustain the growth of yields, our only choice is to constrain the demand for food—voluntarily or otherwise.

This brings us to a critical problem. We are in the era of the declining response curve. Adding progressively more fertilizer produces diminishing increases in food output. Eventually, it produces a zero increase. Corn yields in the United States are now flat. The only escape is to keep finding new technologies, and one of the great unanswered questions of our time is "can we keep it up?" An FAO official listed "the plateauing of yields of high-yield varieties" as the principal food supply problem right now, along with land degradation. The only dramatic new technology in sight is genetic engineering. At best, its contribution is a long way off; at worst, it may be very limited. Population growth is with us now, and to argue the hope of salvation by technology is an imprudent policy indeed.

The absolute limit to fertilizer use is reached, of course, well before the response reaches zero. When the added output doesn't pay for the fertilizer, food production hits a wall.

The developed world is very close to that wall. U.S. fertilizer use per hectare is only one-fourth of that in Japan, because Japan maintains rice prices five times the world level. Our average cereal yields are 85 percent of those in Japan, even though we grow cereals in generally drier regions. The Japanese didn't get much for that extra fertilizer. Both we and they know that. Fertilizer use in both countries has been declining for years.

The reliance on chemical fertilizers has even more serious consequences.

It tends to lower quality of the soil.

The pursuit of high yields leads to reliance on a very few high-yield crop strains and to continuous planting rather than crop rotation. Limiting the number of plant varieties and continuous cropping are both invitations to the proliferation of crop pests. This leads to the intensive use of pesticides. The fertilizer and pesticides in turn cause water pollution and threaten fisheries and other species. We still cannot measure the impacts on forest and water resources of that activity.

Pests mutate and become resistant to known pesticides. The very process of fighting insects and other pests has a frightening side effect: it promotes the evolution of resistant strains and species. The mechanism is fairly straightforward: create conditions that are ideal in all respects except one—for example, a field full of corn, replanted annually, as seen by a corn borer—and there is a tremendous reward to the organism that learns to handle that one negative factor, the pesticide. That is what leads to successful mutations. Successful, that is, from the standpoint of the pest. The more intensive the agriculture, the more likely the consequence. If farmers have no effective defense, a blight can lead to the loss of an important fraction of food supplies. The United States narrowly averted such a corn blight in 1980. The fungus that led to the Irish potato famine is endemic in the United States. Aggressive and resistant forms appeared in Europe in the 1980s and the United States in 1990. Either the corn or potato blight, or something else, could surface in a more virulent form.

Losses to pests have risen despite massive increases in pesticide use in the past two generations. U.S. crop losses from insects, by one estimate, doubled between 1945 and 1989 to 13 percent despite a tenfold increase in the use of insecticides. Losses from all pests, including plant pathogens and weeds, are estimated at 37 percent of total potential food and fiber crops. The pesticides, aside from promoting resistant pests, destroy the natural predators that could control pest outbreaks, and they kill bees that are important to crop pollination.

Despite the penalties, farmers are dependent on pesticides and herbicides. The farmers are on a treadmill because they would lose part or all of their crops if they stopped spraying, given the decline of natural predators.

Some 20 to 40 million tons of nitrogen escape annually from the world's croplands into the atmosphere as nitrous oxide (N_2O). Commercial fertilizers account for perhaps 40 percent of that release, depleting stratospheric ozone and contributing to the greenhouse effect. This consequence intensifies as intensive agriculture spreads, and it gets progressively worse because a flattening response curve demands more and more fertilizer, until one reaches the wall.

In sum, population imbalance requires a pursuit of high yields that in turn demands reliance upon "solutions" of diminishing effectiveness and rising cost, which in turn generate a ripple of disturbances.

This is a picture of agriculture out of balance. It can be put in balance only if potential productivity is enough higher than demand so that farmers will move back to more benign but less intensive agricultural practices. And that shift gets harder and harder as population grows.

That is the synthetic fertilizer trap. With six billion people on Earth, we cannot go back to techniques that supported two billion.

CLIMATE CHANGE

My second example involves climate alteration, primarily the result of carbon releases from fossil fuel use and the destruction of forests by rising demand for logs and by rising populations seeking land to cultivate.

Amid a welter of scientific controversy, the Intergovernmental Panel on Climate Change represents the nearest thing to a world scientific consensus on the human effect on climate. The IPCC in December 1995 produced its "Second Assessment" of climate change and its probable results.

Their key finding was that "The balance of evidence . . . suggests a discernible human influence on climate." Global mean surface temperature and global sea level have risen in the past century. If the trend is not reversed, the scientists expect that temperature will rise 1° to 3.5°C by 2100—faster than any warming trend in the past 10,000 years. They warn that climate is a complex and nonlinear system and that "surprises" may happen, such as "rapid circulation changes in the North Atlantic," with profound consequences for European and world weather.

They project a rise of fifteen to ninety-five centimeters (cm) in average sea level by 2100, with a best guess of fifty cm (twenty inches).

Even if the immediate stabilization of greenhouse gases were achieved, the present level of climate forcing would continue, and "global mean surface temperature would continue to rise for some centuries and sea level for many centuries." Scientific caution has limited their projection, but hidden in that sentence is the possibility that, uncontrolled, human activities could take us back to the climate of the Cretaceous, when shallow seas covered much of what is now densely populated land. With 6 or 10 billion people, or more, there would be nowhere on Earth for those displaced to go.

What would it take to stop the engine? It would require *"an immediate 50 to 70 percent reduction in CO_2 emissions and further reductions later on to stabilize atmospheric carbon dioxide at current levels."* (my emphasis) This would be needed—not to end the human impact on the climate—but simply to keep the trends from accelerating.

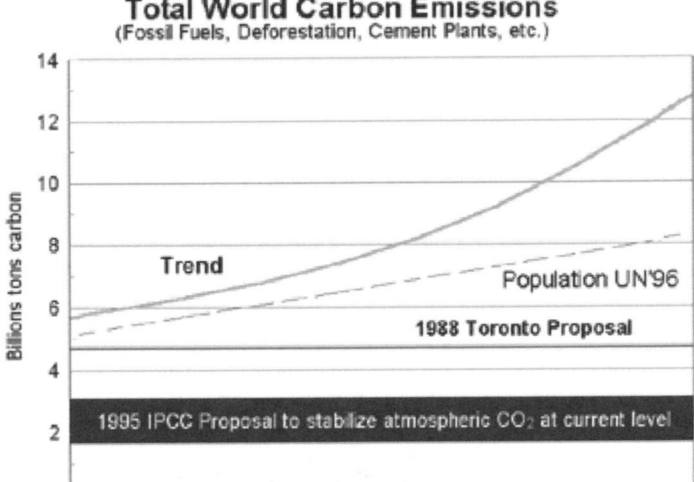

Figure 1.

Let us see how humanity is succeeding in that awesome task. The graph below may help.

Far from approaching that level, or even the more modest goal of the Toronto convention, real world emissions are rising rather than falling. I have drawn the UN median population projection (in billions) into the graph. Carbon emissions are rising even faster than population, because of forest cutting and accelerated industrial activity.

This graph brings us face to face with the problem most people would like to ignore: What level of human population can the Earth sustainably support? Climate may be a limiting factor if food production is not. The data are not available to draw a tight logical conclusion, but I would ask the reader to consider how much better our prospect would be if the "Population" line on the graph were a flat line somewhere between two and three billion. It would put us within sight of the goal by the IPCC scientists. A smaller population would not need to cut forests at the present rate, and the forests could perhaps even become a sink for atmospheric carbon rather than a source. Coupled with reasonable energy efficiencies, we could be on the way to solving the problem of human forcing of the climate.

BIOLOGICAL DIVERSITY

My third example may be the nearest of all to a doomsday scenario. Human activities are sequestering something like 40 percent of terrestrial productivity for human use, and we are changing the atmosphere and the climate everywhere. The combination is causing the loss of species at a rate we cannot measure but which certainly is unparalleled since the Cretaceous extinctions.

Biological diversity is probably associated in the public mind with a fondness for pandas or elephants or our relatives, the great apes. In Africa, we are watching a dramatic change as human populations displace other large mammals. But biodiversity is much more than that. We are just beginning to recognize our interdependence with microorganisms, but we still know very little about the effects we are having upon them. In 1983 the President's Acid Rain Review Committee pointed out that soil microorganisms are particularly susceptible to a change in acidity and warned that:

> *"it is just this bottom part of the biological cycle that is responsible for the recycling of nitrogen and carbon in the food chain. The proper functioning of the denitrifying microbes is a fundamental requirement upon which the entire biosphere depends. The evidence that increased acidity is perturbing populations of microorganisms is scanty, but the prospect of such an occurrence is grave."*

The early successes of the Clean Air Act Amendments momentarily alleviated the acid precipitation problem in the United States, but it and the related issues of ozone and nitrogen leaching are driven by the levels of our economic activity, and our knowledge of soil bacteria and their limits of tolerance has not much improved. Prudence suggests that we must reduce those harmful emissions—by better control of fossil fuel burning in the short term and its reduction or elimination as soon as possible—and by limiting the demand that makes the heavy use of chemicals and fossil fuel necessary.

We must control air pollution and climate change, and we must reserve some space for other creatures. How much? There is no certain answer, but some substantial fraction of the Earth must be left. This can be achieved only with a smaller population, not with the sort of growth that rapidly displaces other species.

OPTIMUM POPULATION

Discussions of the Earth's carrying capacity are usually founded on an unstated premise: that the objective is to see how many people can be crammed on a finite Earth. That is the wrong question. For one thing, it is usually based on a one-time calculation. Slowly, we are learning that a wiser question is "would that level be sustainable?"

Dr. Smail has pointed out that there is yet another and better question: "how many people would constitute a desirable level?" Consumption is not an environmental sin, though one might infer from much current writing that it is. For poor individuals and nations, it is a highly desirable objective. The moral issue arises from an impossible combination: large and rising populations, and the hope of achieving a decent standard of living for all. A smaller population could live better, and still preserve the environment.

Conservation and technology can help to mitigate environmental problems without a loss in real living standards, but they are no substitute for a wiser demographic policy. Dr. Smail cites the possibility of reducing energy and resource wastage by half or two-thirds through such measures. An optimistic estimate. Moreover, energy is not a legitimate surrogate for all environmentally damaging activities. I have pointed out that large and rising populations require rising food yields, which in turn require massive and rising chemical fertilizer inputs. This is not "wastage" in the usual sense, but most of it could be avoided with a population half the present size, requiring half the yields. That could be achieved with benign farming using organic inputs. The decline in chemical fertilizer use would be more than proportional, and world agriculture would escape the nitrogen trap I described.

For the poor, a better living is a dream realizable only with a smaller population; for the prosperous, the preservation of decent living standards depends on the same change. Two or three billion is not a bad target. We must not bog down in scholastic debate as to the exact number. The issue is the direction. And that must be down, and as soon as possible.

There is not much time for a revolutionary change in human behavior. Barring a catastrophe, momentum will carry human population upwards to 9.4 billion in the next half century even if average fertility in the poorest countries (the UN's forty-eight "least developed") should plunge by 60 percent. That would be a remarkable achievement indeed; it has declined only 15 percent since the 1950s (UN 1996 data and medium projection). To turn growth around, humanely, and bring population down to two billion would take centuries—unless we suffer the consequences of our present behavior, and population growth is reversed through the brutal mechanism of rising mortality.

NOTE:

1. *This paper is based upon my book* **Juggernaut: Growth on a Finite Planet** *(Santa Ana: Seven Locks Press, 1996). Except as noted, data taken from that source.*

STORMY SEAS AND HEAD IN THE SAND

Lindsey Grant

July 1997

The *Wall Street Journal* on April 1st ran a page one lead story about the promise of the new Hibernia oil field off Newfoundland ("Politics, Money and Nature Had Kept Vast Deposit on Ice," by Staff Reporter Allanna Sullivan). The lead sentence set the tone:

> *"Just as the ice-filled seas near here hid the secrets of the Titanic for decades, so too has the stormy North Atlantic concealed vast reserves of oil buried deep beneath its seabed."*

Then the article rhapsodized:

> *" . . . one of the largest oil discoveries in North America in decades should deliver its first oil by year end. At least twenty more fields may follow, offering over one billion barrels of high-quality crude and promising that a steady flow of oil will be just a quick tanker-run away from the energy-thirsty East Coast. At a time when most of the U.S.'s oil comes from politically risky nations, the security of a nearby oil reserve largely owned by U.S. companies and in a friendly country is hard to overestimate."*

The energy transition will not be so easily resolved. What the author left out is that a billion barrels of oil is just fifty-six days' U.S. consumption at current levels, or fourteen days' world consumption. Even that "billion or more" figure may be hyperbole. It is supported by only one citation: an estimate of "a minimum of 615 million barrels of oil, and likely more" by Mobil, the principal partner in the Hibernia field. That lowers its contribution to thirty-four days and nine days, respectively.

The chicken has not yet hatched, and none of that oil has yet started pumping. And, barring massive discoveries yet to come, bringing the field on line will not significantly affect estimates of potential economically recoverable oil resources, given the size of the claim (about 1/2500th of present world estimates) and the field's location in an area where discoveries have been expected.

The price of Mobil's stock must benefit from such stories. The *Wall Street Journal* presumably likes them, too. They suggest that warnings about the coming transition away from oil are alarmist, that we do not need to change our economic behavior or consumption patterns, and that we can continue with business as usual.

For one specific example: the *Journal* has long been a proponent of high immigration. It holds labor prices down. What the editors miss is that high immigration drives high population growth. Using conservative assumptions, U.S. population is headed past a half billion around 2100, and more than 90 percent of that growth will result from post-

2000 immigrants and their descendants. And population growth, along with our consumption style, drives U.S. dependency on "those politically risky nations" and hastens the end of the oil era.

There is only a certain amount of time. With the present growth in consumption worldwide, the experts' estimates of the world's economically recoverable petroleum resources are the equivalent of forty-two to forty-eight years' consumption. The U.S. cannot continue to rely more and more on others' oil. We must begin to move to benign—and expensive—energy sources. More than that, we must reverse the growth in demand. For twenty-five years, NPG has been asking the question that others consider taboo: *Why not address population growth, which determines the number of consumers and drives the demand?*

The Journal is grasping at straws. It would do much better to grow out of its fixation with growth as usual. It should listen to what scientists are saying about the impacts of such growth on resources, the environment, world climate and the American future —and it should reexamine its narrowly based advocacy of high levels of immigration.

THEY ASKED THE WRONG PEOPLE

NATIONAL RESEARCH COUNCIL (NRC) THE NEW AMERICANS: ECONOMIC, DEMOGRAPHIC AND FISCAL EFFECTS OF IMMIGRATION

Reviewed by Lindsey Grant

Executive summary released May 17, 1997

The NRC has released the executive summary of a report on the economic, demographic and fiscal effects of immigration. It had been requested by the Congressionally-mandated U.S. Commission on Immigration Reform (CIR). The *New York Times* headline was "Report Says Immigration is Beneficial to U.S." The media picked up that interpretation, and the net impression on the public probably has been to underline the one idea: "beneficial."

That was not an accurate characterization. In fact, the report confined itself to the three specific issues cited in its title, which were the questions put to the NRC by the CIR. Moreover, its conclusions were by no means so uniformly favorable as the press suggested.

DEMOGRAPHY

The central—and usually forgotten—issue raised by mass immigration is "how many Americans does it lead to?" The panel performed the calculations and came out with projections similar to the Census Bureau projections. Their middle projection shows annual immigration "at current levels" (which I believe they understate at 840,000) leading to a population of 387 million by 2050, two-thirds of that increase being the result of post-1995 immigration. The projection, they point out, leads toward an increasingly multiethnic society, unless ethnic lines become blurred.

The panel reported their projections but drew no conclusions from them. The key sentence in the executive summary—the smoking gun—is this: " . . . we assume that the U.S. economy is characterized by constant returns to scale—that is, growth in the size and scale of the economy neither reduces nor increases the productivity of labor and capital." In other words, so far as they are aware, a growth of 124 million people in our population (with more to come) has no economic significance. The panelists were clearly uncomfortable about that conclusion, but used it.

Their problem lay in the narrowness of their approach. If agricultural response curves are plateauing (as they are) and soil erosion continues (which it does), the pursuit of higher agricultural production means lower returns to labor and capital, and poorer workers. If the CPUE (catch per unit of effort) in fishery continues to decline, the marginal cost of maintaining fish production will continue to rise, and with it the cost of fish. Already, as we cut down the old growth timber and come to rely on timber plantations, the cost of lumber and wood products has risen. If, because of immigration, there is an almost unlimited supply of cheap, unskilled labor, the incentive to substitute capital for labor declines, and with it the productivity and wages of workers. Economic activity pollutes. As its scale goes up, so do the costs of trying to control that pollution, and that must come out of investment.

They said there was no evidence one way or the other. They should have said "we don't know about the evidence." The executive summary does not mention the environment or the natural world. A different panel would have explored the limits of the natural support system in which we live: the realities of food supply and "renewable" natural resources, the effects of different levels of economic activity—GNP—on the atmosphere and climate and the biosphere, on land and water resources, on crowding and health. They could have learned a great deal about their "constant productivity" assumption.

They might even have explored the less easily quantified aspects of crowding. If the panel had been chaired by a philosopher (if indeed there are any left) and included a biologist, an agronomist, a forestry expert, a fisheries specialist, a climatologist, a couple of leading ecologists, and a labor proponent, it would have been a very different report.

The CIR posed the wrong questions. It should have asked "what are the impacts of different levels of immigration on the well-being of America?" and allowed the panel to explore the question of sustainability. It went to the wrong people. The panel was chaired by an economist and consisted of 8 economists, three sociologists and a demographer. Keynesian and post-Keynesian economics, which are still the dominant element in current conventional economics, contain no methodology for dealing with the environment or with resources, or with scale or limits, or indeed with qualitative change. So the problems are ignored by the creation of convenient fictions: "infinite substitutability"; the Earth as an infinite source of resources and sink for pollution. Thus the panel of economists simply adopted the "constant productivity" assumption, not knowing how to question it.

ECONOMIC IMPACT

Having thereby avoided drawing any conclusions whatever from the prospect of an ongoing rise in U.S. population, the panel addressed the economic effects of immigration mostly in terms of labor, prices and economic growth. The report did admit that the least skilled Americans have suffered from the competition and that African-Americans have been harmed, but it dismissed that as a problem because less than a majority are affected. It left unsaid that these tend to be the most vulnerable sector of our population. Otherwise, the panel saw mostly benefits: a net gain from lower prices; no effect on most wages; and a gain for some. This pleasant view created a dilemma. Lower prices require the assumption of generally lower wages, which they had just denied would happen, or of higher investment levels in industry—which is precisely what immigration discourages. They escaped, if that is the word, by resorting to the familiar argument that immigrants fill "jobs American won't take." They ignored the fact that, nationwide, all the job categories (even farm workers, food preparation and service, and cleaning and building services) are still filled largely by Americans. The shortage of labor to fill some of them—and the reason that hourly U.S. real wages have been falling almost every year since 1975—is that desperate immigrants will work for wages that Americans don't want to work for—and they are right.

That is not my idea of a prospect " . . . Beneficial to U.S."

The economists' mindset appears most dramatically in their other criterion of economic success: the unstated assumption that GNP growth is the highest objective. That seems to be the national myth, so we must forgive them. They projected an annual addition of $1 to $10 billion to the nation's GNP as a result of current immigration, and applauded it, even though one wonders whether such a tiny gain, accompanied by such a range of error, is statistically significant. (By the way, they apparently did not realize it, but their own calculations indicate that immigration slightly lowers GNP per capita.[2] This panel is not the first to applaud overall GNP growth without remembering that GNP says nothing about individual consumption unless converted to per capita income.)

Keynesian economics abets the fixation on growth. Born of the trauma of the Great Depression, it is entirely focused on how to make the economy grow. Keynes himself recognized the limits of that goal, but his successors tend to be more Keynesian than Keynes.

After nearly seventy years, the time should have come to raise the more fundamental question: "can we avoid the treadmill of perpetual economic growth by learning to control the demand—driven by population growth—that makes it necessary?" This may be the most important question of our time. Scientists keep telling us of the environmental dangers of economic growth, while the conventional non-scientific wisdom is that growth is necessary to provide jobs. Lower the demand for jobs that drives the need for economic growth, and the dilemma resolves itself. And that should be the first question asked of immigration policy: does it drive the demand for growth?

FISCAL

The panel plunged into the endless debate as to whether immigrants take out more in welfare and direct services than they contribute in taxes. They concluded that immigrant households imposed a net fiscal burden of $1,178 on each native-headed California household in 1994–5. For the country as a whole, however, they estimated the burden at far less: "on the order of $166 to $226." So far, the immigrants' impact thus is mildly negative. The panel then built a model of the future. From it, they predicted, with many reservations, that "the net fiscal impact of immigration is positive under most scenarios," but that "the impact of an increase in the annual flow of immigrants would initially be negative overall for a couple of decades before turning positive." In other words: pie in the sky. Later.

There are two fatal internal flaws in the whole welfare debate: first, the statistics are not adequate to justify a solid conclusion. A projection drawn from weak data, incorporating a series of speculations about future events and their effects, resembles those shaky towers of chairs balanced one on the other that acrobats sometimes erect. It may show more about the inclinations of the participants than it predicts about the future. The Study Director for the report came to the NRC from the Urban Institute, which has been the most ardent defender of the argument that immigrants put more into taxes than they take out in benefits. From the outside, it is impossible to tell whether that background influenced this report.

Second and even more important: the comparison between taxes and welfare is meaningless, because taxes must pay for all the services an individual receives beyond welfare and direct benefits, from sewers and roads and justice to police protection to national defense. To be valid, the comparison would have to include all those costs.

Moreover, the comparison is unfair—to the immigrants. The poor generally pay less in taxes than they receive in services, and most immigrants are poor. That is why they came here. The whole welfare argument is tertiary at best. If mass immigration were otherwise good for us, we should be willing to accept its fiscal costs. But it isn't good for us, because of its effect in forcing demographic and economic growth.

ASKING THE RIGHT QUESTIONS

We must begin to listen to the scientists and send the economists back to monetary and fiscal policy. (All, that is, except for the few who are beginning to realize that the economy exists within the environment, not vice versa.)

CIR has paid very little attention to the broadest issues raised by high immigration levels. Of some 47 roundtables, consultations and site visits listed on its web site, only one (the Phoenix roundtable in March, 1995[3]) dealt with population and the environment, and that was a cursory three-hour potpourri of about twenty diverse individuals from population specialists to a real estate developer. Only one solicited research paper dealt with the environment, and the only major research effort commissioned by the CIR is the NRC study described in this Booknote. I hope that the CIR will take another look—before we dismiss the need for immigration reform—at the real questions posed by growth rather than authorizing more hypothetical models based on a static model and the flawed presumption of "constant returns to scale."

NOTES:

1. The news release can be accessed by going to the NRC website http://www.nas.edu/new/, which leads to the executive summary and tells how to get an advance copy of the draft report. Formal publication was in September. Or call (800) 624–6242.
2. The summary (p.4) says that immigration "does not change the rate of growth of income per capita," which is an odd statement in light of the fact that the immigrants' income is less than the U.S. average. Their own figures contradict their statement. Their estimated figures of a $1 to $10 billion increase in GNP work out to $3.75 to $37.45 per capita of the initial population, which translates to a new income of 1.00014 to 1.0014 of current per capita GNP ($27,000)—hardly an impressive gain—but there are now roughly 840,000 more residents as a result of one year's immigration, raising total population by 0.3 percent (to 1.003). Dividing the increased income (1.00014 to 1.0014) by the increased population (1.003) leads to a *decline* in per capita GNP of $77 or $54, depending on which gross figure ($1 billion or $10 billion) one chooses.
3. See NPG Footnote "A Checklist for CIR," March 1995, for my presentation to that meeting.

UNCOUPLING GROWTH FROM PROSPERITY: THE U.S. VERSUS JAPAN

B. Meredith Burke

July 1997

Who faces the brightest quality-of-life prospects for the year 2100: Japan with a population projected to decline by nearly 60 percent, or the United States, whose 1997 population of 267 million will nearly triple to 750 million (en route to a billion) if present levels of migration and fertility continue? [1]

Demographically-unschooled politicians in both countries' recent elections tipped their hats towards America. Since 1990 Japanese politicians have alternately wooed and criticized their childbearing-age women who at current rates will have fewer than 1.5 births each. Immigration is minuscule, so death rates and personal childbearing choices solely determine population size. Assuming constant fertility and mortality, the population will peak around the year 2005 at 130 million, then slowly diminish by the year 2100 to 55 million (its 1920 population level). At this level will Japan still be a world power?

THE U.S. HAS EXCEEDED ITS OPTIMUM POPULATION

Most politicians have uncritically accepted the business leadership message that we need ever more workers to support the bloated Baby Boom generation in its retirement years. They tune out the ecological community's message that the U.S. has exceeded its optimum population (one maximizing environmental protection and the lifestyle values held by Americans) of 150 million (or fewer) ever since 1950. Both politicians and business leaders espouse that "a growing America is a healthy America."

For a population with a bulge in the childbearing age group to stabilize, let alone decline, requires that there be fewer births than deaths. If there is net immigration, births have to be very much fewer. Since 1920 the U.S. and Japan have both experienced sharp fluctuations in births. Bloated past cohorts must be balanced by subsequent smaller ones. This inevitably results in a short-term drop in the ratio of prime-age group workers to retirees—and nervousness among pro-growth interest groups.

Traditionalists, seeing a smaller work force supporting an enlarged retirement population, identify the problem as how to augment the former. They tend to have inflexible attitudes towards work and family organization, wage determination, and pension plan financing. Hence traditionalists endorse importing workers from elsewhere. But this proposal implicitly endorses a demographic perpetual motion machine: more childbearing-age adults result in more births (barring a very sharp fertility reduction) and an ever-growing population.

Confronting the same rise in elders, sustainability advocates look to lighten the dependency burden two ways. The first is to encourage increased worker productivity and lengthened work life. They endorse more flexible work and pension arrangements permitting a gradual and later tapering-off by older workers. The second is to reduce the other part of the dependency burden: the proportion of children. If an industrial-country baby boom mimics a stomach swollen by a Thanksgiving feast, the appropriate response is to cut back on food intake until the stomach shrinks back to a size consonant with healthy body weight.

Japan has had two postwar birth peaks—2.7 million in 1947 and 2.1 million in 1975—and two birth valleys—1.5 million in 1995 and 1.2–1.3 million in the 1990s. The twenty to twenty-four age group—the main labor force entrant category—accordingly peaked in both the early 1970s and the early 1990s at just over and just under 10 million persons respectively. With the 1990s' sluggish economy Japan has confronted rising unemployment. Fortunately, the demand for new entrant slots has crested and will soon plummet. In 1993 the age group twenty to twenty-four numbered 9.8 million; that fifteen to nineteen, 9.3 million; that ten to fourteen, 7.8 million; and that five to nine, 7 million.

Japan's educational burden is simultaneously growing lighter. Primary school enrollment has declined steadily since 1980, from 11.8 million to 9.4 million in 1990 and 8.8 million in 1993. The country is well-placed to devote more individual parental attention to as well as greater societal investment in each child.

THE CONCEPT OF AN ECOLOGICAL FOOTPRINT

Responsible politicians should welcome a return to a 1920s population level—or even below. They might educate themselves about the concept "ecological footprint," a term invented by University of British Columbia regional planner William Rees. This represents the land area necessary to sustain current levels of resource consumption and waste discharge by a given population. Rees and his students, notably Mathis Wackernagel, have calculated that Japan, with one-quarter hectare of productive land per capita, has an "ecological footprint" of at least two hectares. That is, it consumes at least eight times more than its own renewable resource production. This makes it (along with other industrialized countries) a "resource predator" in the international market. Third world nations have already served notice they will not forever appease this appetite.

In particular, despite the most intensive agriculture in the world Japan is the world's largest food importer. As its population has grown 20 percent since 1970 its dependency upon imported cereals has risen from 55 to 75 percent while its rice prices are five times the world level. With a population of 55 million Japan could return land to agriculture, aim for food self-sufficiency, and see a reduction in its food bill.

The U.S., whose per capita ecological footprint is twice that of the Japanese while its land endowment is eleven times, is currently just barely ecologically self-sufficient. Our wetlands have all but vanished, our fishing banks are plundered, and our native flora and fauna are threatened even as we are assured that our "wealth" has increased. Provisioning, educating, employing, and housing the Baby Boom of the 1950s was very expensive.

Much has been made of the fact that the Baby Boomers themselves have had below-replacement fertility. Yet the absolute number of births rose steadily from the mid-1970s' nadir of 3.1 million until hitting 4 million in 1989, the same level we experienced during the peak "Baby Boom" years of the late 1950s. Even though the "baby bust" generation is well into its twenties, births have not receded as expected. Instead, they have been buoyed by the increasing contribution of foreign-born women: over 700,000 births in 1994 or nearly 18 percent of total births.

THE FIRST EARTH DAY MESSAGE ABANDONED

Our "leaders" readily abandoned the first Earth Day message that the United States was overdue for a demographic diet. Dieting is not fun: it generally requires renunciation of a short-term pleasure in favor of long term benefits. Because of our age structure, total population would have grown through the 1990s even in the absence of immigration. Evading demographic accountability, politicians generously courted the greatest influx of immigrants in the nation's history. This denied us the "demographic valley" Japan entered in the 1980s.

The result is here now in growing rather than decreasing primary school enrollments; after the year 2005, in increasing numbers of young adults seeking jobs and bearing children. According to the Census Bureau's "high" estimates (its most realistic) there will be 519 million Americans in 2050. More liberal assumptions yield 600 million or more. The prospect of a sustainable population has receded from view while we will battle the rest of the world for the resources demanded by our growing ecological footprint.

In 2100, Japan will be approaching greater ecological balance while its citizens will be disbelieving of the two and three-hour commutes and tiny dwellings of their great-grandparents. Conversely, Americans will routinely live in cities of 25 million, prize their few passes a year to crowded beaches and parks, and accept housing, diets, and physical movements unimaginably constricted by mid-twentieth century American standards. This country will have been permanently removed from the tiny group of net food exporters.

Because Japanese politicians cannot avert a desirable shrinkage of the Japanese population, Japan has a bright future. In contrast, American politicians are solely responsible for demographically irresponsible immigration and reproductive health policies. These have already tarnished the well-being of today's average family. By the year 2100, Americans will apply the words "bright and shining" to their past, not their present—and certainly not their future.

NOTES:

1. Extrapolated from *Alternate Projections of the U.S. Population*, by Dennis A. Ahlburg and James W. Vaupel, *Demography*, Vol. 27, No. 4, November 1990, pp. 639–652.

"U.S. POPULATION POLICY"—LET'S TALK

John R. Bermingham

August 1997

Proposals relating to a "U.S. population policy" are circulated from time to time and several have been circulated in 1997. All seem to have been prepared by persons who—like myself—wish the U.S. population were smaller than it now is and who would very much like to see our growth slowed, stopped, and then reversed.

None of the proposals contain specifics on how a national population policy might achieve such a goal, and this vagueness is bothersome even though I am sympathetic to the goal. The time has come to ask questions.

I am prompted to take this approach by a recent newspaper column praising Fred Friendly's instruction to participants in his PBS discussion series—a series that brought together Supreme Court justices, senators, columnists, nationally known law enforcement officials, and other prominent Americans. His instruction was this: "Our job is not to make up anyone's mind, but to open minds—to make the agony of decision making so intense that you can only escape by thinking."

So, what follows is a collection of questions and for many of them—probably most—I do not claim to have answers. Instead, this is a plea for help with my own agonizing.

A POPULATION POLICY MUST CONTAIN BOTH AN IMMIGRATION POLICY AND A FERTILITY POLICY

I am sure that all will agree with this basic equation:

GROWTH equals **BIRTHS** plus **IMMIGRATION** minus **DEATHS** and **EMIGRATION**

Since I am also sure that increases in deaths and emigration must be ruled out as elements of a politically acceptable population policy (other than deportation of illegal immigrants), the only means to slow, stop, or reverse U.S. population growth are through reductions in immigration and fertility. Is there any escape from the basic equation? In other words, whenever we open a discussion of a policy to slow, stop, or reverse population growth doesn't the reality of the equation immediately force us into discussions of immigration policies and fertility policies? (I would include tax incentives as a portion of a fertility policy).

ANY WORTHWHILE POLICY REQUIRES MECHANISMS FOR IMPLEMENTATION

Implementation of any policy is necessary or the policy is a nullity. I am reminded that prior to Fidel Castro, the Batista government decreed that all Cubans had a right to two weeks vacation with pay. The hitch was this—there was no policy or procedure to implement this right. At the other extreme, our Fifth Amendment right that no person shall be deprived of liberty "without due process of law" only has meaning thanks to the Constitution's guarantee of the Writ of Habeas Corpus.

So, to declare a U.S. population policy that growth should be slowed, stopped, or reversed without simultaneously getting bloodied in debates over some very specific immigration and fertility reduction recommendations seems totally unrealistic.

In short, can any population policy proposal have any practical value unless it (1) makes explicit policy proposals for reductions in fertility, and (2) also states explicitly the means and mechanisms by which immigration and fertility reduction policies are to be implemented?

SHOULD EFFORTS TO REDUCE IMMIGRATION AND FERTILITY BE KEPT SEPARATE?

If it is true that a population policy must consist of an immigration policy and a fertility reduction policy, then—rather than first making an effort to persuade America that there are "too many people"—would not the desired policy result be achieved most expeditiously and efficiently by working directly and immediately, but separately, on fertility and immigration?

Congress is the ultimate arbiter of U.S. policy—certainly for immigration and probably for fertility. How does one get a majority in Congress? Is it better to put all eggs in one basket or work separately on the different parts? Consider the experience of the splitting of last year's immigration bill.

HOW SHOULD EFFORTS BE ALLOCATED BETWEEN IMMIGRATION AND FERTILITY?

If the goal is slowing, stopping or reversing growth, then how should our limited resources be focused? Can agreement be reached on the focus of efforts without agreement first being reached on the contribution of immigration as a share of total U.S. population growth? For the year 1994 the three recognized calculation methods have produced answers of 23.2 percent, 45.1 percent and 60.1 percent.[1]

If immigration produces less than one-fourth of our growth then shouldn't most efforts be focused on the fertility component, but if immigration produces 60 percent of our growth then shouldn't that component receive the most attention?

Perhaps the calculation issue will never be resolved—what then? Doesn't this possibility suggest that our best bet is to encourage friends and allies to work on whatever interests them the most—some giving help to those who already are focused on the immigration issue and others helping those who are already focused on the fertility issue?

IMMIGRATION ISSUES

To implement a population policy is there any escape from the necessity to become involved in Congressional debates over both legal and illegal immigration? How can the immigration issues be resolved other than in Congress?

If immigration issues must be resolved by Congress, then population policy advocates need to put themselves in the shoes of members of Congress. To what extent should legal immigration levels be changed and in what manner? Should more emphasis be placed on education levels or relatives, etc.?

Similarly with respect to illegal immigration. This is not the time or place for a laundry list of the issues—it is sufficient to note that the array of issues that advocates of a population policy must sooner or later take positions on is very broad: Border enforcement issues; Budget for INS; Workplace enforcement and employer sanctions; Expulsion of illegals; Minimum wages for farm workers; NAFTA; Financial assistance to Mexico; etc.

How can any collection of population activists be held in the same harness on these many issues? Isn't it best to separate them now?

FERTILITY ISSUES

The problems relating to fertility issues are also many in number and very divisive. Should a fertility reduction policy address only "unwanted pregnancies" or should it target Mexicans, Indians and other specific high fertility groups? If policy is to focus on unwanted pregnancies only, should policy proposals produce alternatives or supplements to improve upon what Planned Parenthood is doing already? How can these issues be avoided?

Everything is hitched to everything else. Should a fertility reduction policy get into: Sex education in schools; Dollars appropriated by Congress for abstinence programs; Sex ratings for TV shows; Abortion; etc.? What about the proposed Constitutional Amendment that would bar citizenship to children of illegal aliens?

CAN THE "CULTURAL ISSUE" BE EXCLUDED FROM DISCUSSION?

The extremely provocative "cultural issue" is like a cancer creeping into both the immigration and fertility domains. Is cultural concern the same as racism? Of course not, but all too often that is exactly what it is called. Doesn't the cultural issue exist whether we like it or not? Can we arbitrarily rule it out of order in all discussions?

Is every minority group to be locked into its present proportion of the total? Can or should any effort be made to affect the now projected changes in the ethnic and racial mix of America fifty years from now? What will a Population Policy do about American Indians who want their populations to increase? Should they be exempted from any reduction policy?

If 60 percent of growth is due to immigration, won't lowering the fertility of white America bring on an "Alien Nation" reaction with a vengeance? How will this be handled? Teaching two languages in schools rather than just English means teaching less of something else. While this may be acceptable for a small proportion of students, doesn't society have a problem if a large number of students require courses in two languages and have only reduced time for science, the arts, history, etc.? Can this debate be ignored?

OVERCONSUMPTION

People recognize that land use and congestion problems are exacerbated by population growth, but will any significant number respond to overconsumption as a trigger for action on population? I doubt it. Consumption is responsive to economic forces and environmental pressures on manufacturers, etc., but how much have consumption patterns actually changed due to talk about overconsumption during the past few years? Very little, I suspect.

Nevertheless, one overconsumption argument is sure to arise: A farm worker in Mexico adds little or nothing to the CO2 buildup, but upon becoming an American he will sooner or later have an automobile. Isn't this another argument that will be given the "racism" tag? How will this be handled?

CARRYING CAPACITY

The overconsumption arguments are often bolstered by studies that show that the United States is already living beyond its carrying capacity, that we are already in an overshoot mode, and that our much touted American lifestyle cannot be sustained.

They make their arguments with great persuasion and they cite the I = P x A x T equation to show that to bring Impacts down to a reasonable level not only must our Population be reduced but we must also reduce our Affluence (i.e., consumption patterns) and Technological harms.

It is at this point that an extremely sensitive issue arises. Is there anyone in the "we must lower consumption" school who does not believe that to achieve this goal some major shifts must be made in our economic system? Realistically, how many in the "we must lower consumption" school will argue that our economic system need not be changed? And, if the "we must lower our population" advocates go to the public arm in arm with the "we must lower our consumption" advocates, who cannot hear Rush Limbaugh and his talk-show buddies pounding the airwaves with, "Don't you realize these anti-population people are trying to tear down our cherished free enterprise system?"

Just as "free choice" became baggage for the population movement following Roe v. Wade in 1973, will not joining force with advocates for lower consumption only make work on immigration and fertility more difficult?

GETTING PEOPLE TO TALK

Immigration, unplanned pregnancies, teen pregnancies, welfare pregnancies—these are hot topics today and efforts to work on them will resonate with broad sections of the American public. People will come to meetings and give of their time to discuss these topics. However, will individuals interested in immigration be willing to invest their time sitting through discussions on how to reduce fertility and vice versa?

Let's face it—population is not a "hot" topic and overconsumption even less so. Broad swaths of the public will not come to meetings or give of their time to work on this topic. Is there any need to bring together focus groups to tell us this fact? Is it not best that we recognize at the outset that the environment and carrying capacity issues will not energize any significant number of Americans on the population issue?

There are certain to be opponents to proposals to reduce population. Some will refuse to listen or engage in any discourse of any sort, some will listen politely but refuse to engage in true discourse, and some (probably a very small percentage) will actually exchange ideas. So, discourse with population policy opponents, such as Wattenberg, Simon, and their followers cannot be expected. Instead, will they not simply counter attack? What organized steps should be taken now to develop the most compelling rebuttals to their arguments?

USE OF WORDS SUCH AS "FAIR," OPTIMUM, MAXIMUM, ETC.

It is always good public relations to finish one's own proposal by wrapping it with words such as: "fair"—"equitable"—"comprehensive"—"ethical"—"coherent" etc. However, whether these words accurately apply to the substance of what is proposed depends upon the eye of beholder. There will always be those on the fringes who disagree with the majority's idea of what is fair and equitable, etc. Optimum population, maximum population, and carrying capacity are concepts that cannot be quantified without value assumptions with respect to quality. How can these words be used or quantified without generating charges of elitism or being narrow-minded? How fruitful will it be to spend time and energy attempting to obtain broad public agreement on these concepts?

OTHER QUESTIONS NEEDING ANSWERS BEFORE PROCEEDING

Business and labor and their lobbyists as well as countless economists in academia have been debating the pros and cons of population growth for generations. The Cato Institute advocates an increase in legal immigration. Is it the purpose of those pushing in favor of a U.S. Population Policy to persuade all those with existing positions to join together in a consensus or is it to create a pressure group strong enough to vanquish the opposition? Which is the better strategy for success to carefully focus on getting majority votes in Congress on specific issues or to make an attempt at persuading the whole world?

Is there any escape from the conclusion that those who push for a U.S. population policy have an underlying agenda of wanting fewer people? Can this perception be avoided? Will anyone who promotes the idea of a U.S. Population Policy be satisfied by any policy statement that calls for anything other than a slowing, stopping or reversing of population growth? Who will be surprised if those who want a population policy reject any other outcome?

Are the population policy pushers at a point at which they should obtain a number of "devil's advocate" reactions to their proposals before trying to obtain foundation funding for their projects?

Before making an effort to produce consensus, shouldn't advocates of a national population policy have in hand a sampling of population policies of other countries? How can they be obtained? What can Americans learn from England, France, Germany and other European nations that are struggling with immigration issues?

How have successful "movements" of any kind been organized in the past? Should not an answer to this question be obtained before moving further towards adoption of a process or procedure for developing or changing America's positions on population, immigration and fertility?

CONCLUSION

Do population policy pushers want a free "trust me" blank check in answering these many and varied questions? If the more important of these questions are not answered in advance, isn't it likely that a number of groups that have unthinkingly signed on will then fall away once the discussions start? Is it not best to address the issues early on?

If not now, when? Questions such as these are certain to be raised almost immediately once population policy discussion groups are assembled. Is it not best for those pushing for a national population policy be in agreement on how these questions are to be handled before precipitating discussions with the public at large?

NOTE:

1. See *Immigration's Share of U.S. Population Growth*, **Focus,** Vol. 7, No. 1, pp. 68–72.

SUSTAINABILITY, PART I
ON THE EDGE OF AN OXYMORON

Lindsey Grant

March 1997

The term "sustainable development" has become fashionable, but it is regularly used in the sense of "sustainable growth," a self-contradictory concept beloved by those who want to continue at the same old stand—growth as a solution to all problems—and yet couch it in terms that will not offend environmentalists. The United Nations has a Commission on Sustainable Development (supported by an elaborate bureaucracy), which will meet in April to prepare for a UN General Assembly Special Session on "Agenda 21," scheduled for late June. We may anticipate torrents of words in praise of an oxymoron.

"Sustainability" contains no such internal contradiction and is perhaps the single best word to express environmentalists' goals. It is a word under which they could unite with population policy proponents, if somehow they could come to see that material growth is mathematically unsustainable.

On the face of it, one can hardly take exception to the definition popularized by the Brundtland commission (the World Commission on Environment and Development):

> *Sustainable development is development that meets the needs of the present without compromising the ability of future generations to meet their own needs.*[1]

An excellent characterization, but it got off to a wobbly start. The WCED itself, because of its diverse international membership, could not agree on the need for policies to deal with population growth; moreover, it foresaw a five to tenfold growth in world GNP in fifty years, to meet the minimal needs of the world's poor. It even concluded that "the international economy must speed up world growth while respecting the environmental constraints." Others have pointed out that it never really addressed how those antithetical goals could be achieved. Note that the WCED report spoke of "sustainable development" rather than "sustainability." Growth is deeply ingrained, and the WCED view of "sustainable development" comes perilously close to being an intellectual inanity.

The WCED led to the "Rio Conference" in 1992 (the UN Conference on the Environment and Development), which in turn passed a set of environmental proposals ("Agenda 21")and spawned the groups described above. "Sustainable development," with its fuzziness about growth, is firmly enshrined in the language of the world bureaucracy.

Very few people seem to have grasped the simple fact: growth—demographic or economic—is unsustainable. This century is unique. Worldwide growth has never before lasted for so long at such levels. Any math teacher will tell you that perpetual growth is mathematically impossible in a finite space such as the Earth. Give them a starting figure and a growth rate—the rate is more important than the starting level—and they can show just when the assumption of continued growth becomes absurd, by any standard you may choose. This is not a theoretical exercise. Current growth rates would reach the absurd very fast. As the United Nations Statistical Office pointed out in 1992, world population would reach the absurdity of 694 billion people in 2150 if current fertility and mortality rates were maintained.

Growth will stop. Will it stop in benign or catastrophic ways? That depends largely on whether or not we recognize what is happening and take steps to deal with it.

President Clinton fell into the trap. Even as he created the President's Council on Sustainable Development (see NPG Forum paper "Sustainability, Part II"), he charged it with helping to "grow the economy and preserve the environment . . . ," objectives that are bound to conflict in any but the shortest time frame. The council itself was caught in the same conflict. It called for stabilizing U.S. population and helping other countries to stabilize theirs, but it also called for a growing economy and growth in "jobs, productivity, wages, capital and savings, profits. . . ." It did not really explore what sustainable development means. It was not prepared to advocate early population stabilization to escape the treadmill of economic growth.

An acceleration of GNP growth is hailed; a slowdown generates jitters. Politicians regularly reach for economic growth as a panacea, because it offers a vision of perpetually rising consumption. That is a swifter way to disaster than population growth itself, because it is our activity, not simply our presence, that does the damage. Growth is necessary, but why? To provide jobs and goods for an expanding population. Bring one form of growth under control, and the need for the other subsides.

An oxymoron is a great cover for ambivalence. Precisely because of its popularity in the environmental community, the phrase "sustainable development" is in danger of being coopted by people who want to give the appearance of environmental commitment while avoiding the harsher decisions that a true commitment would require. Beware of those who profess an enthusiasm for sustainable development if by "development" they mean "growth." Another tricky phrase is "managed growth." Granted, one may mitigate the immediate impacts of growth by restricting the ways in which it develops, and thus perhaps defer the day of reckoning. However, such compromises should be seen for what they are: temporizations.

THE CONFLICT OVER GROWTH

The industrial revolution, with its apparently unlimited prospects, created the myth of perpetual growth. At the same time, some thinkers began to recognize that such growth contains its own eventual destruction. John Stuart Mill in 1848 proposed the concept of a *"stationary state of capital and wealth"* and said that despite the *"unaffected aversion so generally manifested towards it by political economists of the old school . . . I am inclined to believe that it would be, on the whole, a very considerable improvement on our present condition."*

He went on to point out that the lack of growth does not mean the end of improvement of the human condition; it would more likely lead to the improvement of *"mental culture and moral and social progress . . ."* At that early date, he thus challenged the stereotype that growth and progress are synonymous.

It has been a hard lesson to learn, especially in America.

The environmental and population communities have historically had a hard time recognizing how deeply their goals are interlinked. Thomas Malthus and his successors have long argued that population growth becomes unsustainable at some point. On the other hand, some of the great environmental writers—John Muir, Aldo Leopold, and Rachel Carson—led the American environmental awakening but paid little or no attention to the population connection.

The Dust Bowl of the 1930s dramatized the damage we were inflicting on our resources. It led to President Roosevelt's conservation policies such as creation of the Civilian Conservation Corps and the Soil Conservation Service. At that stage, population was hardly seen as a factor in the destruction. U.S. fertility was momentarily below replacement level, and net migration was around zero. The population issue came later.

The post-World War II surge in U.S. population forced us to look at the connections. By 1969, President Nixon was asking whether projected population growth would lead to a deterioration of American living standards. He and Congress created the Commission on Population Growth and the American Future and asked John D. Rockefeller III to head it. In 1972 the Commission reported that *"we have concluded that . . . no substantial benefits will result from the further growth of the Nation's population, rather that the gradual stabilization of our population would contribute significantly to the Nation's ability to solve its problems."*

That message did not reverberate in America. The faith in growth is deeply rooted. Growth is invoked as a solution to current problems by both political parties and by most pundits.

The WCED was not alone in equivocating about "sustainable development." Others, even while claiming the mantle of sustainability, have tried to straddle the contradiction and argue that, somehow, "good" growth is possible. Dennis Pirage's introduction to *The Sustainable Society. Implications for Limited Growth* is a good example. He called the introduction "A Social Design for Sustainable Growth." He admitted that "sustainable growth is a difficult concept," but nevertheless he chose it as "the best guide to the future" by a bit of sophistry: " . . . even steady state advocates have foreseen significant growth in the quality of life taking place within the constraints of limited resource consumption."[2] He thus did an injustice to Herman Daly and "steady state" advocates; and in pretending that quality and quantity are synonyms he fell into an error that John Stuart Mill had avoided more than a century earlier.

That argument is regularly heard: growth is somehow desirable if it can be described as an improvement in "quality." It is never spelled out in detail, and it is a fallacy. "Quality" in the popular modern idiom means monster trucks and all-terrain vehicles, thirty-foot trailers, yachts and bass boats, trophy homes, vacation houses, and ski trips to distant places. As we are defining it, "quality" eats up many more resources and does more damage than the simple life.

There is a better definition for quality, but a string quartet generates much less GNP than a pro football team. A hill to climb, a clean breeze, a walk down a quiet country lane, silence and solitude, a glimpse of a lonely sea; these are all aspects of quality, but they do not generate much GNP. In fact, population growth makes them less accessible. A quality house costs less over its life cycle than a shoddy one, and thus creates less GNP. Quality thus defined is more likely to be at war with growth than a justification for it.

The real issue is this: can physical growth continue? for how long? and at what cost? Quality is a legitimate and desirable pursuit, but one cannot simply wave the word in the belief that it will dispel those questions.

Writers have wasted a lot of misspent effort trying to cling to the faith in growth in face of the evidence of the damage it leads to. We owe thanks to writers such as Herman Daly, the Ehrlichs, Donella and Dennis Meadows, E.F. Schumacher and William Catton for taking the lead in recognizing the contradiction between growth and sustainability and addressing it, in different ways.

As the connection between growth and environmental damage became apparent, the conflict became intense. The proponents of growth recognized that the new awareness threatened their fundamental mindset. Conventional Keynesian economists, practicing a discipline that contains no conceptual process for studying limits, regularly attempt to avoid the philosophical issue of growth by assuring us that pollution is declining and that no resource scarcities stand in the way of continued growth because of "the infinite substitutability of resources." This is dogma rather than a proven proposition. They have yet to name good substitutes for food and water—to name two critical resources. A former President of the Royal Society of Canada stated their problem briefly and elegantly:

> *The economists largely ignore population growth and consumption because they ignore the ecosystem. They think in terms of an infinite world. Because of population growth, however, most inhabited regions tend to be overpopulated in terms of stress on local ecosystems, and far beyond sustainability. Standard economic theory depends on a closed system with a circular flow of exchange values, to which the environment and the reservoir of resources are externalities. The future looks bright because no heed is paid to uncosted materials such as water, air, forests, animals, plants and soils, without which the ecosystem would cease to exist and so inevitably would we. Economics as a science must become concerned about the ecosystem because we are part of it, cannot manage it, and cannot live outside it.*[3]

Nevertheless, economists are heeded, in a world that worships GNP growth, and thus growth is accepted as the solution to our problems.

The argument is regularly made that growth is acceptable "up to a point." In most respects, we are already beyond that point. I hardly need remind *Forum* readers that the country—far from being in a sustainable state—is on a course that will be catastrophic if long continued. Farmlands are losing soil at a net rate of about 12 tons per hectare annually and the best ones have lost half or more of their topsoil in little more than a century. We are losing better farmland to urbanization and industrialization than we can recover from wasteland. Agricultural yields are stagnating while the demand for food grows.

Our per capita timber resources are declining, and old growth forests and their genetic resources are being destroyed. The forests are under attack by a man-made combination of "ozone, acidic deposition, sulfur dioxide, and nitrogen oxides." These in turn affect "plant physiological processes that provide resistance to insects, pathogens and climactic stress."[4] We know that there is a complex synergy leading to forest decline, but we do not yet understand it or its potential consequences.

We are still losing wetlands, and pollution accelerates the collapse of fisheries. We are drawing down groundwater tables where the water is most needed. We are altering biological systems and playing a sort of Russian roulette with the natural systems that support us. We cannot stop the growth in our emissions of carbon dioxide, and we are thereby affecting global climate. I could go on.

It is sometimes argued that economic growth is needed to make environmental reforms affordable. This is the ultimate squirrel cage. The growth of population and consumption generates problems that must be solved by further growth. Even economic activity directed toward benign ends is itself polluting. Building an interceptor sewer may cost billions of dollars; it will relieve some of the water pollution—though it will not eliminate the nitrates and phosphates that are a byproduct of population growth—but in the process it contributes to air pollution, carbon dioxide releases and climate change.

There are other environmental problems that cannot be solved by investment, no matter how intense. Preservation of our farmlands is a case in point; it needs reversion to good conservation practices—even if they yield less food—more than it needs massive investment.

Briefly, this sums up the case. Economic growth is the problem, not the solution, and population policy is a central element of environmental sustainability.

In Europe, population growth is on the verge of turning around, unless immigration stops the trend. Those who know of the European experience may argue that population growth is a fading issue in the industrial world, and hardly a matter for concern.

Were it not for immigration, one could perhaps make that case for the United States. At present fertility levels, we would peak at something over 300 million if natural increase alone were the driver. The problem, of course, is that immigration drives population growth in this country. Some 43 percent of growth in this century has been post-1900 immigrants and their descendants. The comparable projection for the next century—when we are headed for a half billion Americans—is about 91 percent. (This estimate is conservative. It assumes a lower level of immigration than we are now experiencing, and it assumes that immigrants' fertility will move down, whereas in fact it is driving the average fertility upward.) Starkly put, this means that the issue of growth is the immigration issue in the United States right now. What does this mean? Immigration policy becomes population policy, which becomes environmental policy. Many environmentalists don't want to hear that. Somehow, we must bring them around.

ON TO SUSTAINABILITY

Socrates complained that classical Athens in its glory was destroying the forests and farmlands of Attica, but he offered no thoughts as to how to stop the process. Sustainability states the goal of avoiding that degradation. The WCED definition at the start of this paper fits the goal of "sustainability" better than it does the ambiguous term "sustainable development."

"Sustainability" has a lot going for it. It has broader connotations of human well being than "environmentalism," and it is less easily lampooned as an excessive concern for whales and wolves at the expense of other humans.

It is popular with environmentalists. It is particularly felicitous because, mathematically, it embodies the recognition that true environmentalism demands an end to growth. This should commend the word to population policy advocates, which in turn suggests that we might well adopt it as a shorthand for the population movement, which has never really had a satisfactory title.[5] Adoption of "sustainability" by population policy advocates might help to bridge the rift that exists between them and environmentalists. Although some environmentalists are reluctant to face up to the mathematical truism described above, it is hard to imagine that even the most insular of them would dare to stand up and claim that perpetual growth is sustainable.

Sustainability demands a redefinition of consumption goals and a search for the least damaging ways of providing for them. Above all, however, a smaller population would make the pursuit of sustainability less difficult and the conflict between it and other goals less intense. A smaller population, or even slower growth, makes it less necessary to reduce consumption (e.g. for the poor) or to restrict freedom than does a large and growing population. It would be less damaging to the environment, at any given level of conservation or technological solutions. A successful policy to stop population growth makes sustainability less painful to achieve. This should be welcomed by those who are pursuing other goals such as social justice or urban revitalization or human rights.

A CAUTIONARY NOTE

There is a delicate line at which "sustainability" itself can degenerate into a burlesque.

How broad is its meaning? The term requires clarification. Some proponents apply it simply to humans. Others point out that human well-being depends on preservation of the ecosystem in which our species evolved.

Among national and social objectives, what priority does sustainability have? Does it have an absolute priority over individual freedom (e.g. in forest management or wetlands preservation)? If not, where are the compromises drawn?

One can argue that preservation of the nation is essential to the "ability of future generations to meet their own needs." Is national defense therefore a prerequisite for sustainability—and at what level—even though defense expenditures may divert funds from resource preservation or environmental protection?

Is sustainability more important than the maintenance or—for the poor—the improvement of living standards? What are the specific measures of sustainability, and how are they to be achieved? What degree of certainty is needed to persuade the nation to forego current consumption in pursuit of a better future?

What claim does sustainability have on the budget, and what costs can be borne in its pursuit? Conversely, is a balanced budget a goal of sustainability, since growth of public debt cannot be sustained forever?

Writers have defined "sustainability" to include everything from justice, social equity, women's rights and budgetary reform to decentralization of economic power. Such wide definitions can cause any campaign for sustainability to degenerate into generalizations. It would seem wise, for the purposes of this paper, to accept Prof. Herman Daly's restrictive elaboration of the WCED definition of a sustainable economy:

- Its rates of use of renewable resources do not exceed their rates of regeneration.
- Its rates of use of non-renewable resources do not exceed the rate at which sustainable renewable substitutes are developed.
- Its rates of pollution emission do not exceed the assimilative capacity of the environment.

How far do we carry it? This is a beginning, but even here we encounter problems. Zero soil loss is not really compatible with any agriculture. Some soil, even if it is replaced, descends into streams, accelerating siltation and change. Humans do not control all the elements of sustainability. Change and degradation can occur without human involvement; the Mississippi delta was being formed out of prairie topsoil long before humans arrived (though much more slowly). Aluminum constitutes 8 percent of the Earth's crust. One can contemplate running down the resource with equanimity; the argument for recycling, aside from aesthetics, is the high energy cost of extracting the aluminum from the ore. A similar and even more compelling argument can be made concerning the use of silicon to make glass.

Advocates of sustainability should define their goal in clear and limited terms. Otherwise, they may be dismissed as flower children for demanding the impossible, or on the other hand they may become encumbered with "allies" who demand that they advocate other social goals that—while they may be desirable enough in themselves—are irrelevant to the central task of sustainability. That task is to confine human activity so that it can be pursued without peril to the natural systems that support us.

Sustainability too rigidly defined does not admit of much compromise. No goal, even sustainability, is absolute. We must develop guidelines for its application. Perhaps as a start we should pose the issue in these terms: For every contemplated policy or action, how serious is the threat to sustainability? are the anticipated gains so overwhelming that they would justify bending the absolute?

ALL TOGETHER, NOW: "SUSTAINABILITY!"

These are cautionary notes only. My real message is that "sustainability," properly defined, is a great rallying cry for both environmental and population policy advocates. By its nature, it forces them to recognize that they share the same goals. Continued growth is not just a failed "solution" but indeed an eventual impossibility. And "eventual" may be closer than we think.

NOTES:

1. *Our Common Future*, report of the World Commission on Environment and Development (WCED or "Brundtland commission"), 1987.
2. *The Sustainable Society. Implications for Limited Growth* (New York: Praeger, 1977), p.10.
3. Digby J. McLaren, past Director General of the Geological Survey of Canada, "Population and the Utopian Myth," in *Ecodecision*, June 1993, pp.59–63. In fairness, be it said that a large and growing number of economists recognize the frailty of the Keynesian assumptions and are beginning to recognize the limits to growth.
4. National Acid Precipitation Assessment Program (NAPAP), 1992 Report to Congress (U.S. Government Printing Office, June 1993), p.3.
5. I am indebted to Alan Weeden of the Weeden Foundation for the genesis of this idea.

SUSTAINABILITY, PART II
A PROPOSAL TO FOUNDATIONS

Lindsey Grant

March 1997

The nation grows, but public and political interest in the consequences is close to negligible. That inattention makes the issue more, not less, important. What is here proposed is the use of a systematic foresight process—a "Sustainability Project"—to bring population growth back into the national debate by publicizing the consequences of ignoring it.

Football heroes and TV stars have little trouble getting their opinions heard, but serious discussion of serious issues is usually not self-supporting in this distracted and media-hyped society. For better or worse, it is subsidized by universities, corporations or the government. At least two of those three sources are not usually inclined to take adventurous positions on public issues.

The non-profit sector is a key player in promoting perspectives that may not accord with the conventional wisdom. Private foundations dispense millions of dollars annually. Several of them, through their assistance to non-governmental study or advocacy groups, have been critically important in getting a hearing for major issues such as the role of demography in shaping our future. Without that support, those who are not otherwise subsidized could not have afforded to spend their time on those issues.

Without sustained pressure from advocacy groups, our lawmakers' attention turns to other, more immediate and perhaps less difficult matters. The issue of population growth, worldwide and in the United States, became a matter of widespread public concern in the late 'sixties but soon became "stale news."

That decline was hastened, in the case of U.S. population growth, by the dawning recognition that there are only two accessible variables driving our demographic future: fertility, and migration. U.S. fertility dropped dramatically in the 'seventies, remaining above replacement level only for the poor, the uneducated and particularly the minorities. To suggest the need for further decline thus came to be seen by many idealists as veiled elitism or racism. At the same time, immigration was growing rapidly and has become the driving force in U.S. population growth, but many of those same people see any proposal to limit immigration as xenophobia.

Population restraint is central to achieving long term environmental sustainability, but those charges frightened away people who should be proponents of a population policy. In the face of those fears, demographic arguments are rejected by many environmentalists, valid as the arguments may be. The politicians follow suit. Witness the complete silence about population in the recent election campaigns and the almost total silence about the demographic consequences when Congress debated and gutted the immigration reforms proposed in early 1996.

The population community is preaching to the choir, without enlisting the sort of coalition that will be needed if the country is to change its present demographic behavior. Polls show that the public is concerned about U.S. population growth, but that concern is not being focused and brought to bear on the politicians.

We are not getting to those who are most fertile or—more important—to those who make policy. If we cannot reach them by simply reiterating the population arguments, perhaps it is time to take another tack: persuade them that there will be disastrous consequences for the things they hold important, if they don't address population growth. Make the appeal, not as an abstraction, but by showing what will happen to their interests. Enlist the rich in the preservation (or restoration) of social tranquillity, the urbanite in the avoidance of urban disintegration, the middle class in the preservation of a decent standard of living, the poor in the hope of finding a job and a role in society, and the environmentalist in the pursuit of sustainability.

Enter foresight.

FORESIGHT

One can hardly expect the politicians to get much ahead of political realities, as they see them. If we cannot convert them immediately into advocates of demographic restraint, perhaps we can eventually convert them by asking, in the context of one policy decision after another: "What are the consequences of the proposed policy?"

This process is usually referred to as "foresight." It is not simply a concept. It requires institutional machinery to provide a systematic multidisciplinary evaluation of the probable consequences of trends or of anticipated actions. It needs

- an organizational structure to bring disciplines together,
- an ongoing review of environmental, social and demographic trends and their probable consequences, and
- perhaps most important, a means of bringing those conclusions to bear in the decision process.

It is, in other words, a dedicated "think tank" located at the key intersection of decision making in government. If government will not create such a mechanism (which so far it has not), perhaps the non-profit sector can. I will come back to that point.

THE STALLED DECISION PROCESS

These ideas are far from new. Various governmental and private initiatives have been directed toward identifying the issues that confront us. There have even been ephemeral efforts to create a systematic foresight process to inform national decisions, but they have foundered on bureaucratic resistance to change, the lack of a public consensus on the need for action, and simple inertia.

Let me briefly survey recent government foresight projects.

The National Environmental Policy Act of 1969 (NEPA). Anybody interested in sustainability should reread NEPA. It begins with these eloquent words:

> *The purposes of this Act are: To declare a national policy which will encourage a productive and enjoyable harmony between man and his environment; to promote efforts which will prevent or eliminate damage to the environment and biosphere and stimulate the health and welfare of man; to enrich the understanding of the ecological systems and natural resources important to the Nation; . . . .*

> *The Congress, recognizing the profound impact of man's activity on the . . . natural environment, particularly the profound influences of population growth, high density urbanization, industrial expansion, resource exploitation, and new and expanding technological advances . . . declares that it is the continuing policy of the Federal Government . . . to create and maintain conditions under which man and nature can exist in productive harmony, and fulfill the social, economic and other requirements of present and future generations of Americans.*

—a beautiful statement of the idea of sustainability, before the word itself came into use.

The Act then goes on to spell out a process—the Environmental Impact Statement (EIS)—to enable the government to examine proposed governmental actions to see whether they meet those goals.

The Act does not tell the government what it can or cannot do. It was conceived as a "process bill." It tells the government that it must consider the potential environmental consequences of proposed actions, and it provides for public participation. The problem is that the law has been used for limited projects such as interstate highway intersections but never really applied to major national decisions.

Anybody who wishes to bring long term goals back into the national dialogue could hardly find a better place to start than demanding that NEPA be followed. Ignored though it is, it is still the law of the land.

The Rockefeller Commission (the Commission on Population Growth and the American Future, chaired by John D. Rockefeller III) was created at about the same time by President Nixon and Congress. (see NPG Forum paper "Sustainability, Part I"). It concluded in 1972 that further population growth would do more harm than good, and it offered suggestions as to how to stop that growth. It was too controversial for the time. The President did not accept it, and it is largely forgotten. It deserves better. The recommendations would be a good starting place even now for organizations seeking to make realistic proposals as to how to address the U.S. future.

Back in 1972, the Rockefeller Commission concluded that further population growth would do more harm than good, and it offered suggestions as to how to stop that growth.

The Global 2000 Report to President Carter in 1980 had two broad purposes:

1. to present an integrated description of major world trends in resources and the environment and to relate them to population growth; and
2. to evaluate the capability of the U.S. Government to conduct such integrated foresight on an ongoing basis. In a three-volume report, it warned of the dangers posed by current trends. It stated flatly that the government does not have the capability to make integrated cross-sectoral analyses. That was 1980, and it is still true.

Global Future: Time to Act. The Global 2000 Report offered no recommendations, but it was followed up in January 1981 at the very close of the Carter administration by a booklet of action proposals from the U.S. Department of State and the Council on Environmental Quality which included eight broad recommendations concerning U.S. population growth: *"The United States should develop a national population policy which addresses the issues of:*

- *Population stabilization*
- *Availability of family planning programs*
- *Rural and urban migration issues*
- *Public education on population concerns*
- *Just, consistent, and workable immigration laws*
- *The role of the private sector—nonprofit, academic and business*
- *Improved information needs and capacity to analyze impacts of population growth within the United States*
- *Institutional arrangements to ensure continued federal attention to domestic population issues."*

Those last two proposals were expanded into extensive recommendations for foresight machinery, including a proposal for a "Global Population, Resources and Environmental Analysis Institute, a hybrid public-private institution . . . ."

The proposal for foresight machinery was unanimously endorsed in December 1981 by the non-governmental Global Tomorrow Coalition (GTC), which included all the major environmental and population groups. (GTC itself was never able to make such a clear recommendation again, and it was dissolved in 1995; this is a warning that large coalitions tend to lose focus.)

The Global Issues Working Group (GIWG). The Global 2000 Report generated widespread public interest. The Reagan administration responded by instructing Chairman Alan Hill of the Council on Environmental Quality (CEQ) to create an interagency group to "identify global environmental and resource issues of national concern, and recommend appropriate government action. . . . and to improve the U.S. national capability to gather information and to forecast future trends."

The GIWG had a short and dispiriting history. Chairman Hill seemed genuinely enthusiastic, but he was reined in by more powerful players in the White House Cabinet Council. The GIWG lost its all-important bureaucratic "clout"; it was ignored by the powerful and it became mired in inter-agency disagreements over proposed papers. Launched in 1982, it generated one harmless statement of "Global Environmental Principles" and two position papers for minor international conferences before it simply went dormant about 1985.

The moral is that the pursuit of foresight is doomed unless there are powerful advocates at the top. The CEQ, technically part of the White House, has never had that sort of power. Somehow, the President and his top advisers need to become convinced that this is a process they cannot ignore.

The House Committee on Energy and Commerce Oversight Subcommittee in May 1982 held hearings on various foresight proposals. They were summarized in a Congressional Research Service report, but nothing else happened.

The Critical Trends Assessment Act. During the '80s, Representative and then Senator Gore repeatedly introduced variants of a bill to create a foresight process within the White House. He did not press it, and the bill got as far as committee hearings only once. Three Senate committees on April 30, 1985, held a Joint Hearing on the whole issue of foresight. Senator Gore presented his bill, but the committees took no further action. (That bill could still be used as the basis for foresight legislation, perhaps as a way of giving force to NEPA. See below.)

Blueprint for the Environment. During the 1988 presidential campaign, a coalition of eighteen major environmental organizations prepared a "Blueprint for the Environment" for the guidance of the incoming U.S. administration. Among dozens of recommendations on environmental issues, the

Blueprint said that "U.S. population pressures threaten the environment all across our nation," and gave some examples. It said that family planning and the availability of contraceptives must be expanded worldwide. It recommended "an official population policy for the United States" and said that "We must assure that federal policies and programs promote a balance between population, resources, and environmental quality." It went on to propose better decision machinery in the government and a government-wide foresight process reporting directly to the White House Chief of Staff.

Nothing happened. What is perhaps worse, the environmental organizations that sponsored the Blueprint have, with one exception, subsequently avoided addressing the two things that drive population growth: immigration and fertility. One did not expect a strong environmental position from President Bush, but the timidity of the environmental organizations themselves is a shocking reminder how far the nation is from a population policy.[1]

The President's Council on Sustainable Development (PCSD). Like President Reagan and the GIWG (above), President Clinton saw that "sustainability" had a constituency; on June 14, 1993, he created the PCSD. Its mandate was equivocal from the start. The President charged it with helping to "grow the economy and preserve the environment . . . ," objectives that may be expected to conflict. It was a mixed body with members from the Cabinet, environmentalists, labor leaders, industrialists and a mix by sex, race and ethnicity. Population and consumption—two of the critical elements of sustainability—were initially not even in its scope. They were introduced, over opposition, at the instance of council member and Undersecretary of State Timothy Wirth.

To its credit, the council, in its report presented in March 1996, called for a "Move toward stabilization of U.S. population" (Goal 8) and said that "The United States should have policies and programs that contribute to stabilizing global human population . . ." (Principle 12). It remained equivocal, however, as to the broader issue of growth itself. " . . . some things must grow—jobs, productivity, wages, capital and savings, profits . . ." It did not address the likelihood that more workers with higher productivity are likely to increase environmental stress, even with efforts at amelioration, and that growth itself is at some point unsustainable. It did not, in other words, explore what sustainability really is. It avoided the problem of how to stabilize population, by leaving fertility up to "responsible" individual decisions and avoiding positions on abortion or on immigration levels.

The President was "pleased . . . to accept" the report.[2] This is a small footnote to history. The report and the President's acceptance of it, casual as it was, constitute the first explicit acceptance by a President of the proposition that U.S. population should stop growing. Let it be said in its behalf that the council showed that even such a diverse group can recognize the need to stop population growth. They were not alone in their inability to face the tough decisions that would be needed to do it. (The PCSD, in truncated form, has been extended through 1998, with a mandate to collaborate with the Environmental Protection Agency (EPA) in sketching out a "new environmental management system for the twenty-first century," to address the climate issue, work on developing "sustainable metropolitan communities" and participate in "relevant" U.S. international delegations—but not to work further on the population issue.)

Presidents, one might conclude, prefer the appearance of action on sustainability to the substance—unless, perhaps, they are forced by sustained pressure and an aroused public.

The Science Advisory Board of EPA in January 1995 issued a set of recommendations titled Beyond the Horizon: Using Foresight to Protect the Environmental Future (EPA-SAB-EC-95-007). It started with the recommendations that:

> *As much attention should be given to avoiding future environmental problems as to controlling current ones. . . . EPA should establish an early-warning system to identify potential future environmental risks.*

First among the "forces of change" they listed was *"The continuing growth in human populations, and the concentration of growing populations in large urban areas . . .".*

Nothing, so far, has come of the Advisory Board's recommendation.

A principal lesson to be learned from this gloomy recital is that temporary groups or projects cannot move the nation on issues so vast and complicated as these. Moreover, none of the projects had a specific "peg"—a current issue or pending decision to which they were relevant and which forced their conclusions into policy making.[3] A report published in a vacuum tends to disappear, particularly if it calls for difficult actions.

MOBILIZING FOR ACTION

Those initiatives have come and gone without perceptibly affecting national decisions. Let us ask whether some other approach might fare better.

Several private foundations have been attempting with limited success to make population growth into a national issue. I would propose a new and central focus for their approach: that they consider creating and supporting a long-term, systematic foresight process outside of government. It would call attention to the demographic consequences of proposed actions and warn of the effects of population growth on those proposed policies. It would, in effect, be a "think tank" that would inform national decision-making on a continuing basis. Most of its effort would be given to the analysis of current governmental policies and legislative proposals.

The project should probably hook into the environmental community's current enthusiasm for "sustainability." It is a popular idea (see Forum paper "Sustainability, Part I"). It is a good one-word summary of the goals of environmentalism. It permits a somewhat broader focus and is probably a better slogan for mobilizing people than the words "population policy."

As a convenient shorthand, I will refer to my proposal as the "Sustainability Project."

Why a Private Initiative Is Needed. In the face of governmental inaction, the situation cries out for such a project: a permanent, small, like-minded group of people with sufficient funding to call upon experts and assemble them to exercise the foresight function.

It would be, in effect, a continuing private foresight institute to hold the government's feet to the fire, to point out the consequences for sustainability of

- current trends,
- proposed governmental initiatives, or
- legislative proposals,
- and to point the way toward sustainable policies.

Praise for "sustainability" is worthless unless it is translated into policy when new initiatives are afoot.

Speeches aside, Congress and the Administration do not address "sustainability" directly. Rather, it is advanced or set back by policies or legislation that are ostensibly directed toward quite different ends: welfare; health; employment; trade; land use; agricultural price supports and the Conservation Reserve Program; immigration regulation; budgetary decisions. Decisions in those areas are likely to affect the rate of resource use, the environment, or immigration, fertility and U.S. population growth. Most of those issues, and many others, will come up for decisions in the next several years. There must be a way of showing how each of them affects our future.

Such a project should be focused on the United States. One issue might indeed be the level of U.S. support for third world population or environmental programs—in their interest and ours—but anodyne generalizations about other people's problems are a popular way to avoid our own. Sustainability is unachievable unless we focus on our own future.

There are of course other think tanks addressing one aspect or another of sustainability, but

- they almost never address the population aspects;
- they tend to be focused on one issue (e.g. energy, or mineral resources, or forests) rather than on the cross-disciplinary character of what we are doing to our society and the environment; and
- they tend to have their own schedules and priorities, rather than engaging in true foresight—identifying the cross-sectoral implications of decisions currently contemplated.

What the Project Would Be. It would consist of an ongoing secretariat directed by a small governing group. It could be a new organization or perhaps be attached to an existing environmental or resource group if one can be found sufficiently courageous to sponsor a project that might be highly controversial. If so, the project would still take its directions from its own governing board, not from the larger organization.

It should not be a broad membership organization, because servicing a national membership can be a distraction from the pursuit of focused policies. It would be an action group dedicated to the proposition of sustainability, not a debating club. There is no shortage of debates, elsewhere. It will need to hammer away at its agenda: how does a proposed action affect demographic growth? with what consequences? how does population growth affect the prospects of success for a particular policy? Simply stating the need for sustainability is not enough.

It would enlist academics from various disciplines, either in-house or on a cooperative basis with universities and research centers. They would be organized to interact and thus provide the interdisciplinary input that is the soul of foresight. Cooperatively, they would produce papers targeted to specific issues and longer periodic analyses.

This arrangement would have valuable byproducts. Those academics would themselves become familiar with interdisciplinary research and might indeed promote it. If they passed that knowledge and enthusiasm on to their students, it might help to build a new generation of leadership that is less afflicted than the present one with tunnel vision. Academics concerned about present cross-sectoral trends would be introduced to the press and the general public and would get a better hearing for their views.

What It Would Do. One can envisage several productive areas of activity.

- **Briefing Papers.** The most immediate product would be targeted papers discussing the likely consequences of specific trends and proposed policies. The Project would need to promote and market those analyses, bringing them particularly to the attention of the media and to the congressional or executive offices involved.
- **Polls.** The public is in many respects ahead of its "leaders"—who may be responding to money or power more than to public opinion. This is certainly true of the immigration issue, where the public sees the impact of high immigration levels on its own well-being, but Congress does not respond. If that public feeling is identified and mobilized, Congress cannot ignore it so easily.
- **News Conferences** are a natural vehicle to mobilize the media, to call attention to the Project's studies and polls, or to publicize more ambitious projects such as those below.
- **Periodic "State of the Nation Reports."** Perhaps in time, as the experts develop their interactive capabilities, there could be periodic private "Global 2000 Reports" (briefer than the original, and centered on the demographic connections) assessing where the nation is heading and showing the interaction of trends and how they influence the pursuit of national goals. In this as in its other work, the Project would presumably couch its conclusions in the language of education, not of advocacy.
- **The National Environmental Policy Act of 1969 (NEPA).** The law is not being enforced, because it gets in the way of decision makers. Congress from the beginning exempted its own activities from NEPA. While the strict application of the EIS process, as it has evolved, would have to be modified to deal with Presidential decision making, a determined private group might be able to force the application of NEPA to national decisions. That in itself would be a long step toward institutionalizing the pursuit of sustainability. Environmental organizations have used NEPA and the courts to force their viewpoint into more limited decisions; it is high time to make more ambitious use of the Act.
- **Governmental Foresight.** There may be a singular opportunity in the next few years to promote better foresight and more sustainable policies within the government. I have described the Critical Trends Assessment Act which Representative/Senator Al Gore proposed to Congress from time to time but never pressed. As Vice President he has been silent on it. However, he understands the need for foresight and has educated himself in the issue. To be of real use in influencing policy, the office he proposed should be placed more directly in the line of authority than it is in his bill, but that flaw can be remedied. The remarkable thing about that bill—and the reason that the opportunity exists—is that Newt Gingrich sponsored it in the House when Gore sponsored it in the Senate. Here is a wonderful chance for productive bipartisan statesmanship. The Sustainability Project could urge that that bill be revived and passed.
- **"The Coalition for Sustainability."** It might be useful for the Project to organize the most diverse possible coalition to popularize the concept of sustainability, as coalitions have done for the environment. It should go beyond statements about the social interest. Most people must be convinced of the importance of sustainability in advancing their own interests. Otherwise, immediate individual interest overrides long term social interest, and sustainability remains a platitude while the nation undermines it.

Such a coalition could support demands for improved foresight capability in government. It might take positions on specific legislation. It could support a general educational campaign on sustainability.

What to Avoid. The Project should not lose its identity in any such coalition. Indeed, there might be different coalitions, most of them transient, on specific issues. The history of environmental coalitions (including the Global Tomorrow Coalition cited above) suggests that coalitions function best when they are pulled together more or less briefly to achieve specific legislative or policy goals.

If the Project does not keep its own identity, it runs the danger of being coopted by those with other agendas such as feminist goals or social justice. Such agendas may be valid in themselves and potentially they could make a contribution to sustainability, but those advocates have already shown themselves capable of co-opting the population movement. Sustainability will not get very far if the Project is diverted from its central issue.

There is another reason for my advice to create coalitions but not lose oneself in them: the demonstrated reluctance of U.S. environmental groups to take on the causes of population growth. High immigration and differential fertility are two of the most controversial topics in the United States, but they are precisely the ones that must be addressed if our future population size is to be the product of the national will rather than accident. It would be a calamity for the population cause if the Sustainability Project were held hostage by its "allies" and reduced to silence on the most important decisions.

This does not exhaust the possibilities. I have emphasized that a population policy is central to the achievement of sustainability, but the "Sustainability Project" might well trade its support for other projects in exchange for support on population issues. For a few examples: it could endorse environmentally sound building techniques, or benign industrial processes, or better waste handling (the nation produces far more tons of waste each year than economic goods), or more stringent rules on recycling

There might be room for cooperating with groups at the state and local levels of decision-making, but I have yet to figure this possibility out.

"Sustainability," properly used, is an exciting idea. It can be the vehicle for moving the United States away from unthinking reliance on laissez-faire—which presently is driving the country in dangerous directions—toward a systematic way of recognizing our obligations to future generations, establishing our social goals, understanding how they relate to each other, and successfully pursuing them.

NOTES:

1. For a full description of this failure, see my *NPG Forum* paper "The Timid Crusade" (Washington, DC: Negative Population Growth, Inc., 1994.) Since then (in 1996), the Sierra Club has moved farther from a population policy by passing a formal Board resolution that it will not address immigration. The Wilderness Society, on the other hand, has adopted a resolution taking note of the adverse impact of Immigration on its goals.
2. Summaries of the council's work are available at http://www.whitehouse.gov/PCSD. Full texts of its reports and those of its task forces are available at http://www.sustainable.doe.gov. See also *NPG Booknote* "Population and the PCSD" (Washington, DC: Negative Population Growth, Inc., April 1996). *NPG Forum* articles, *Footnotes and Booknotes* are available from NPG, and full texts are carried on its Internet site: http://www.npg.org.
3. A detailed look at foresight proposals through 1987 is available in my *Foresight and National Decisions: the Horseman and the Bureaucrat* (University Press of America, 1988; available at the World Future Society bookstore, Bethesda, MD; 800-989-8274.)

SUSTAINABILITY, PART III
CLIMATE, POPULATION AND UNCED+5

Lindsey Grant

October 1997

Most major world environmental and social problems can be solved only if population policy is an integral part of the solution, but population growth is only occasionally identified as part of the problem and population policies are almost never proposed as part of the solution. I have given a private nickname to the phenomenon: "zip re pop"—nothing about population. In June, the United Nations again demonstrated this blundered approach. If it were only bureaucrats' nattering, perhaps it wouldn't matter, but it was a UN meeting in 1992 that led governments to pledge action on climate warming, and the UN remains sponsor of the effort. If it will not recognize the connection with population policy, hopes of doing anything about climate warming are remote indeed, and so are any hopes for successful action on the other environmental issues on the table.

The United Nations is a good place to observe the "zip re pop" phenomenon. Last June, the UN General Assembly held a Special Session on Agenda 21, or "UNCED+5"—i.e. "UNCED plus five years." (UNCED was the UN Conference on Environment and Development, held in Rio de Janeiro in 1992. It passed "Agenda 21," which is a list of environmental action proposals, most notably an agreement that industrial nations should cut their carbon emissions by 10 percent from 1990 to 2000 to help forestall further human impact on the climate.)

The June meeting was to be the triumph of "sustainable development." A special UN Commission on Sustainable Development (CSD) spent years preparing for the meeting, which was intended to summarize progress on "Agenda 21" and to initiate further action. What it did, rather, was to underline the problem of compartmentalized thinking. There were reports—separate little boxes—covering most of the world's environmental and resource issues. There was even a box about population growth. That growth is an overarching issue and driver of the other issues. The connection was recognized in some of the other reports, but none of them suggested that population policy can be part of the solution.

POPULATION AND CLIMATE

Climate warming was the big story, and even the president of the meeting (the Malaysian prime minister) described it as a failure because it waffled on climate. News stories echoed that assessment and blamed it on U.S. and Japanese unwillingness to state a target for reduction of greenhouse gas emissions. This silence contrasted with a European Union proposal to pledge a reduction of 15 percent between 1990 and 2010 (which itself was a revision of the 1992 commitment, necessary because nobody is going to reach the 2000 target.) I would call that a secondary failure. The real failure was the unwillingness to make the population connection. If that connection is not made, stopping the human effect on climate is, like many other environmental objectives, almost certainly an impossible task.

Population was mentioned only once in the Secretary General's background report on climate change "Protection of the atmosphere (Chapter 9 of Agenda 21).[1]" It was a casual reference to "low population densities" in North America. In contrast, the report dwelt at length on consumption habits and technology, both of which influence climate change, but both of which are arguably secondary to population size as the fundamental driver.

The General Assembly at its close agreed to a Programme for the Further Implementation of Agenda 21. It recognized *"climate change as one of the biggest challenges facing the world in the next century,"* but didn't make the population connection.

In discussing energy, population growth was mentioned only once—and in the wrong context: *"In developing countries sharp increases in energy services are required to improve the standard of living of their growing populations."* (paragraph 43) It did not comment on what that will do to the climate. When it did discuss energy and climate, the Programme reflected the different pressures from industrialists protecting their parochial interests, from developing countries that plan to use more energy, from oil producing countries protecting their market, and from low-lying countries that fear inundation if climate warming cannot be stopped. The Programme was consequently very cautious. It offered some generalized suggestions about things such as the need for further study, for cleaner fuels, for alternative fuels, and the phaseout of fossil fuel subsidies—but not about population growth.

On the other hand, the Programme was forthright in calling for a re-examination of present transportation policies. *"Current patterns of transportation with their dominant patterns of energy use are not sustainable and present trends may compound the environmental problems the world is facing . . ."*

On greenhouse emissions themselves, the Special Session simply chided unnamed industrial nations for failure to do more and then passed the ball to the Kyoto Conference scheduled for December, which is supposed to finalize the industrial countries' 1992 pledge at UNCED to reduce their greenhouse gas emissions.

The U.S. unwillingness to state a target for carbon dioxide emissions was the result of intense domestic pressures. The Business Roundtable lobbied hard against any commitments, arguing that the science was problematical, that the economic effects had not been studied, and that the developing countries weren't doing their share. The Roundtable met with the President and with Congress. The Senate passed by 95 to 0 a resolution urging the President not to sign a treaty that would harm the U.S. economy, or one in which developing nations did not undertake "comparable" commitments.

President Clinton, when he addressed the Special Session, offered eloquence but no concrete commitments. He graphically described the effects of climate change. He applauded the Europeans' push for a 15 percent reduction, but he said only that the "U.S. must do better, and we will . . . in order to do our part, we must first convince the American people and the Congress that the climate change problem is real and imminent. We will work with our people—and we will bring to the Kyoto conference in December a strong American commitment to realistic and binding limits that will significantly reduce our emissions of greenhouse gases." He has subsequently scheduled a series of scientific meetings, culminating in a White House meeting on October 7th, to build political support for such a commitment, and he has begun to send signals to the third world via Under Secretary of State Tim Wirth that they will have to make some commitments, too.

In fact, emissions are going the wrong way. Far from meeting the target set at Rio, U.S. carbon dioxide emissions are expected to be 11 percent higher in 2000 than they were in 1990. European Union emissions will be about 6 percent higher. (Per capita, we emit twice as much.)

The United States' problem is partly demographic. It is easier for the Europeans, whose population is essentially static, to contemplate a 15 percent reduction than it is for the United States. Our population is expected to grow by 20 percent between 1990 and 2010. The proposal would be twice as difficult for us, because it would require a reduction, per capita, of 30 percent from 1990 to 2010. That is quite a stretch, and we have yet to begin.

The Europeans' proposal is far from enough to stop the engine that drives climate change. Worldwide, it would require **"an immediate 50 to 70 percent reduction in CO_2 emissions and further reductions later on to stabilize atmospheric carbon dioxide at current levels."** (Quoted from the International Panel on Climate Change [IPCC] 1996 report, on which all this activity is based.) This would be needed—not to end the human impact on the climate—but simply to keep it from accelerating. One can imagine such a reduction if somehow population could be brought down to something like half the present level. Without some such reduction, even the most optimistic brainstorming offers little hope of finding ways in which it can be achieved.

The third world compounds the problem. It is there that population growth is occurring, and—although their energy use and carbon emissions are small on a per capita basis—the developing nations' carbon emissions are big overall, and rising fast. In this decade, they are rising 48 percent. China alone is rising 60 percent. Third world emissions are expected to pass total industrial world emissions around 2015.[2] (If forest destruction, which is largely a third world phenomenon, were included in the calculation, third world impact on climate would already be close to industrial nations' impact.) Developing country spokesmen insist they will not be bound to any meaningful measures to stop or reverse that growth until the industrial nations have taken steps to restore "equity" in emissions per capita.

Here is an issue that finally brings us face to face with the question: How many is too many? What is the trade-off between population and consumption?

- Would the Europeans and Japanese—living in two of the most crowded regions on Earth—not be well advised to welcome the prospect that their populations will decline? With a much smaller population, they could look forward to a standard of living comparable to the present one, without the climate damage they are inflicting.
- The United States would be on the way to population stabilization if it were not for mass immigration. Our present demographic policies (or lack of them) are in stark conflict with the extraordinary change in living styles we face if we are to stop driving climate change. Even with our present population, we would face a fundamental reordering of our energy, industrial, transportation and urban policies. But we are heading toward a population doubling in the next century. The possibility is about nil that we would willingly cut back to levels of economic activity that would permit such a population to live in harmony with the climate. On the other hand, with a population of 150 million (about half the present one, and the level we passed in 1950), we could just meet the IPCC's 50 percent to 70 percent target (above) with present per capita emissions, and we would have room to offer further reductions in light of our role as the source of one-quarter of the carbon emission problem.

- The desperation of the Chinese effort to stop and reverse population growth (which is severely criticized in the United States) suddenly comes into focus as a policy that will benefit us all, when seen in the context of climate change. The third world is four times as populous as the old industrial countries and it is still growing fast. The combination of population growth and industrialization for even a fraction of that number would be an environmental disaster for all the world.

There is no way that the climate problem can be resolved at Kyoto. A beginning could be made if the nations of the world were to commit themselves to tough policies on transportation, on energy prices, and on the shift of subsidies away from fossil and nuclear power and toward benign energy sources. It would be a more auspicious beginning if third world countries would announce changes in their ambitions for industrialization on traditional lines. Beyond some token measures, none of those steps are likely. As to the central problem of population growth: some third world countries may taunt us with the fact that they are trying to stop it and we are not, but new and binding commitments to population policies at Kyoto are unimaginable, particularly by the United States. Since we cause so much of the problem, meaningful action on climate change is not possible without them.

Even if the world's nations come eventually to face the population issue, it will take more than a century to bring populations down to a level that would permit us to pursue a decent living in harmony with the climate. During the interim, we face the daunting prospect of rising third world and U.S. populations dependent upon a resource base diminished and made more unpredictable by climate changes that are already under way.

We had better get at it.

OTHER WORLDWIDE ENVIRONMENTAL ISSUES

I ran an electronic search for the words "population" and "demographic" in the principal conference papers on environmental and resource issues. Let me summarize what I found. I have underlined the references to population. This is all there was about population growth.

"Integrated approach to the planning and management of land resources (Chapter 10 of Agenda 21)."

> *"3. . . . the development and evolution of human institutions—for information-gathering and assimilation, for negotiation and decision-making, for provision of services and implementation—has seriously lagged behind the growth of populations, technology, and social and economic needs . . ."*

> *"23. Increased population levels and unsustainable resource use have produced social and environmental problems which are among the most serious that society now faces. While global population growth rates seem to have stabilized in recent years, these pressures are still increasing, particularly in many parts of Africa and Asia, regions where food production requirements will likely be greatest over the coming half century. They argue for the need to devise and apply more efficient systems of resource management as the greatest emerging priority facing the world."*

> *"26. Continuing rapid urbanization in developing countries is resulting in substantial land-use changes in the urban, peri-urban and even rural areas. The inability of planning functions and provision of services to keep ahead of urban population growth is*

manifested in the development of squatter settlements and slums; problems of pollution, water supply and waste disposal; and a host of social and economic problems. There is a growing need to . . . prepare strategies to meet the concentrated demands for food, energy and various material goods . . ."

The problem is recognized, but the authors have fallen each time into the fatal flaw of attempting to accommodate to the mounting pressures without seeking to mitigate or end them.

"Promoting sustainable agriculture and rural development (Chapter 14 of Agenda 21)" Paragraph 30, in addressing the need for intensified cultivation of the better lands, particularly in Africa, contained an incidental remark that *"Such development may be facilitated by increasing population densities that allow the higher labor inputs that intensification demands and the access to markets and inputs that are often required."*

I find the remark astonishing, applied to a continent that has gone from 250 million to more than 700 million since 1950, and is headed toward two billion by 2050—if starvation does not intervene—with the attendant decline of arable land per capita, the swiftest in the world. Lack of labor is hardly the problem in Africa, but that is peripheral to this paper. My present point is that the paper said nothing about the basic human dilemma of trying to keep agricultural yields rising as fast as population growth.

On the other hand, the final Programme said that *"The greatest challenge for humanity is to protect and sustainably manage the natural resource base on which food and fibre production depend, while feeding and housing a population that is still growing. The international community has recognized the need for an integrated approach to the protection and sustainable management of land and soil resources . . ."* (paragraph 62) Unfortunately, "integrated" or not, there was nothing about population.

"Conservation of biological diversity (Chapter 15 of Agenda 21)" said nothing about human population growth, even though the growth of human populations, the destruction of other species' habitat, and the pollution caused by human growth and development are the critical causes of the loss of diversity.

"Combating deforestation" (chapter 11 of Agenda 21) in paragraph 32 noted that

" . . . the Commission on Sustainable Development called for further attention to the cross-sectoral factors that were the underlying causes of deforestation and degradation of forests such as production and consumption patterns, poverty, population growth, insufficient environmental education and knowledge, terms of trade, discriminatory trade practices . . ."

"33. Although some corrective actions have been attempted to alleviate pressures exerted on forest resources, rapidly growing populations, poverty, unsuitable land use, adverse incentives, and the impact of human activities associated with production and consumption patterns have continued to damage forests."

Population growth was thus briefly mentioned late in the document, but there was no mention of population policy in the dozens of recommendations on ways to save the forests. (An Ad Hoc Intergovernmental Panel on Forests has been created, by the way, which submitted its own detailed recommendations; they touched upon population only with one delicate reference to "demographic pressure.")

"Comprehensive Assessment of the Freshwater Resources of the World," to its credit, stands alone among the reports in its detailed and ominous discussion of the role of population growth, along with industrialization and urbanization, in generating a worsening prospect for water supplies. It noted that *"already a number of regions are chronically water short"* and remarked on the *"increasing demands from a growing population and human activities. By 2025, as much as 2/3 of the world population would be under stress conditions."*

In proposing solutions, however, the Assessment backed away. It began with a dramatic statement that *"The holistic management of fresh water as a finite and vulnerable resource, and the integration of sectoral water plans and programs within the framework of national economic and social policy, are of paramount importance for actions in the 1990s and beyond."* It did not, however, get specific about population policies other than calling for better *demographic data.* Paragraph 78, in discussing certain arid and semi-arid countries, noted that *"In cases where there is high population growth or economic development, there is likely to be an increase in water demand. If that demand is not well managed, it could drive the country into a high vulnerability situation."* Perhaps they were hinting at a population policy, but elsewhere they retreated: *"To avert such problems countries, particularly water scarce countries, need to look at projections in such sectors as population, urbanization, economic and agricultural development, and establish water strategies and policies"*—not, I would note, population policies.

This assessment was drafted by the Stockholm Environmental Institute. It was used simply as a source document for the official Secretary General report **"Protection of the quality and supply of freshwater resources: application of integrated approaches to the development, management and use of water resources (Chapter 18 of Agenda 21),"** which avoided all reference, even indirect, to a population policy.

"Managing Fragile Ecosystems: Combating desertification and drought (Chapter 12 of Agenda 21)" did not touch upon the relationship between population growth and desertification in fragile regions.

"Protection of the oceans . . . (Chapter 17 of Agenda 21)" said in paragraph 19: " . . . *Governments are facing interacting problems resulting from global climate change, growing populations (in the developing world), demand for and pressure on living marine resources, and increasing pollution from urbanization and industrialization in the coastal zone."* There was no mention of population policies among the proposed remedies.

"Integrating environment and development in decision-making (Chapter 8 of Agenda 21)" made no reference to demographic issues.

"Assessment of activities that pose a major threat to the environment" was the response to specific instructions from the General Assembly to report on the "environmental impact of activities that are gravely hazardous to the environment." In a saner world, having too many children—and the resultant population growth—would fit precisely into that definition. The report, however, limited itself to hazardous wastes, chemicals and nuclear activities.

THE MISSING CONNECTION

There was, indeed, in its own compartment, a report titled **"Demographics and Sustainability (Chapter 5 of Agenda 21),"** prepared by the UN Population Fund. Unlike the mislabeled "Programme of Action" that came out of the 1994 UN Conference on

Population and Development at Cairo, this report mentioned the impact of population growth on urban degradation, land and ocean resources, resource use, forestry, water availability, agriculture, migration, and on investments in the social sector. As to what to do about it, however, the document adopted the cautious circumlocutions of the UN bureaucracy. It dared go no further than to call population growth one of many "significant factors" in undermining sustainable development. It noted that the Economic Commission for Africa "identified . . . managing demographic change" as one "strategic area" but did not explicitly endorse the idea. It spoke vaguely of providing technical assistance to officials *"responsible for implementing population and environmental policies and Programs,"* but like the ill-fated Cairo "Programme" it did not advocate an end to population growth.

Redundancy is the soul of UN meetings, and population was also addressed in a summary document titled **"Global Change and Sustainable Development: Critical Trends."** Amid the general inattention to population, it contained a very good summary of recent thinking about population growth.

There is a good deal of vitalistic thinking in most population projections—i.e. making the projection on the assumption that demographic change has a trend of its own, independent of what people do about it. This report seemed to come close to that fallacy, but avoided it. It is indeed true that, over time and very roughly, the "demographic transition" does happen as economies modernize and the roles of women and children change. In that degree, one may hope that, with luck and successful development, the problem of continuing growth will end in other countries, as it may have in Europe. That is not enough. The arguments for an active population policy are these:

- The process can be hastened and encouraged by education and leadership, as it was in many of the countries which are now cited as examples of falling fertility. Active population policies, as the report noted, are in place in many third world countries, some of them for decades. If things are now happening, in some places, that were intended by those programs and their sponsors, perhaps the policies deserve some credit for the result.
- Population growth itself may prevent the very development that leads to the demographic transition. Active sponsorship may lead to falling fertility in the absence of general modernization, thus freeing resources for that modernization process. This has happened in a number of countries, and it has brightened their prospects. It can be of immense importance in countries such as China, where modernization is under way, but very unevenly, and where the bulk of the population does not participate in the changing conditions that lead to the transition. Given the remarkable conclusion of the IPCC (above) as to how much must be done to forestall further human impact on climate, and given the desperate conditions in parts of the third world sketched out in the various sectoral reports, we cannot afford to miss any ways of stopping and reversing third world population growth as soon as possible.

The "Critical Trends" summary emphasized the long-term importance of economic and social improvement, particularly for women, in lowering fertility, but it also said that *"In the short term, providing contraceptives to close the 'fertility gap' between the number of children born and the number of children desired remains a powerful and logical policy priority."* (paragraph 39) Good advice. Unfortunately, it did not make an important corollary point: leadership, incentives and disincentives can strongly influence "the number of children desired." Nevertheless, this was the one explicit, substantive suggestion for a definable program of action on population to come out of the June meeting.

The Special Session's final declaration almost came to grips with the population issue, but it missed those critical ideas.

> *"There is a need to recognize the critical linkages between demographic trends and factors and sustainable development. The current decline in population growth rates must be further promoted through national and international policies that promote economic development, social development, environmental protection, poverty eradication, particularly the further expansion of basic education, with full and equal access for girls and women, and health care, including reproductive health care, including both family planning and sexual health, consistent with the report of the International Conference on Population and Development."* (paragraph 30)

Close, but very far. The recognition is encouraging, but the paragraph calls only for slower growth, not an end to growth, and the proposed "policies," drawn from the Cairo Programme, are a wish list rather than a population policy. *(See Note 3.)*

The Special Session's final document contained a "Programme of Work for the Commission on Sustainable Development 1998–2002." It did not mention population.

That is hardly a call to action. Only when population policies are seen as a necessary component of avoiding a water crisis or a food shortage, or rising sea levels, or political chaos, is something likely to be done about it. Population policies should be among the recommendations on each of the specific environmental/resource problems addressed. And we have seen that they were not.

If this be "sustainable development," it will not take us very far toward true sustainability. To repeat a point that I have belabored in other papers: perpetual growth in a finite world is a mathematical absurdity. The very identification of population growth as a problem in some of the Special Session background papers should remind us that the world has reached the point at which that truism is presently relevant.

I am sure that the drafters of all those documents would defend themselves on the grounds that population policy is the UN Population Fund's responsibility, not theirs. It is "not within their mandate." And yet they were willing to call for other actions outside their mandate: consumption policies, fiscal policies and taxation, new industrial, transportation and urban policies, and all sorts of specific cross-sectoral reforms not within their own areas. Only with population did this reticence about crossing jurisdictional lines arise.

How can we be so dense? If the solution to a problem lies outside the traditional confines of the issue itself, we had better learn to escape jurisdictional confines and say "If we do not solve population growth, we cannot solve the problem." The beginning of foresight is the willingness to make that connection.

NOTES:

1. The reports were prepared under the supervision of the UN Commission on sustainable Development (UNCSD) under the general title "Overall progress achieved since the United

Nations Conference on Environment and Development: Report of the Secretary-General." Most of them were prepared by the UN Food and Agriculture Organization (FAO), the Department for Policy Coordination and Sustainable Development (DPCSD), the UN Environmental Programme (which prepared the climate backgrounder), the UN Population Program (UNFPA)and other UN agencies and submitted to the General Assembly by the Secretary-General. Support papers were prepared by non-UN research groups. All were coordinated by the Inter-Agency Committee on Sustainable Development (IACSD). I will simple give the titles of the documents quoted. They are all available on the Web at http://www.un.org/dpcsd/earthsummit/ga97rep.htm.

2. The population data in this section are drawn from the U.S. Bureau of the Census' 1996 population projections for the U.S. (P-25-1130, 2-96) and from the UN 1996 World Population Prospects, Annex I, 10-24-96. The carbon emission projections are from the U.S. Energy Administration, International Energy Outlook 1996. For a detailed treatment of the IPCC report, see pages 61–77 of my book *Juggernaut, Growth on a Finite Planet* (Santa Ana, Seven Locks Press, 1996.)
3. For a critique of that conference, see my NPG Forum paper "The Cairo Conference: Feminists vs. The Pope," July 1994.

AMERICANS HAVE SPOKEN: NO FURTHER POPULATION GROWTH

Leon Bouvier

September 1997

INTRODUCTION

The [optimal] balance, in the case of the United States, would seem to me to have been surpassed when the American population reached, at very maximum, two hundred million people, and perhaps a good deal less.[1]

These words written recently by one of the nation's eminent statesmen are undoubtedly echoed, perhaps in less lucid terms, by millions of us. "The highways are too crowded. You can't hardly use them anymore." "Have you tried driving on the LA freeways lately? It's next to impossible." "Just going to the market is becoming an ordeal." "I remember when we could go to the beach and enjoy ourselves. Now they're too crowded." "How about our national parks? Have you tried to even get into one of them?" "There's just too many people nowadays."

These are all irritants, but are tolerable. Granted that quality of life has deteriorated as our population soars, we simply have to adjust to more people, or so we're told. When I was a child in the 1930s, it was such a pleasure to go to the beach. But then the nation's population was less than 150 million. Today, we are approaching 270 million. (See Figure 1.) You can't build more beaches, or public parks. Perhaps you can build more and more roads, or more and more lanes on those roads, but that simply aggravates an already critical traffic problem.

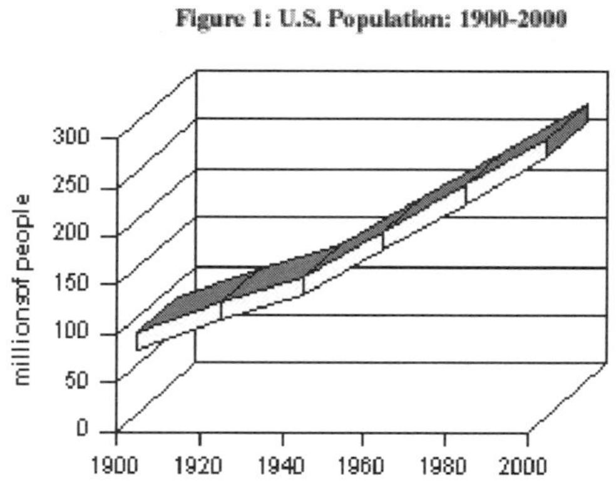

Figure 1: U.S. Population: 1900-2000

Figure 1.

Yet, while such growth is causing us major difficulties, some economists and quasi-economists tell us that it's good for the country to have more and more people. They insist that not only can we adjust to these problems, they actually reflect an improvement in our lifestyle!

But these "experts" don't tell us that each year we draw 25 percent more water from groundwater resources than are replaced by nature. They don't tell us that, as a result, our aquifers are rapidly drying up. It is predicted by knowledgeable scientists that many large aquifers may be entirely depleted within twenty-five years.[2] Can we accept the fact that the Everglades has already been reduced by half its original size? What about our waste deposits? We, as a nation, generate over 13 billion tons of waste each year. Of that, about 2 percent is identified as hazardous waste. That means each one of us generates about fifty tons of waste each year. Where will we put all that waste after we have added another 100 or 150 million more people?

What about our schools? Quality—from kindergarten through college—is down and, to a great extent, that is due to larger classes especially in the lower grades, and in many areas in part because so many students do not speak English. Furthermore, while we desperately need more and more schools to take care of our growing population, a recent General Accounting Office study estimated that we must invest $112 billion to bring the infrastructure of schools back to acceptable levels.[3] How much will it take to keep up with the soaring school-age population projected for the next few decades?

All these important problems are, at least in part, attributable to population growth. Yet, our policy makers seem convinced that nothing can be done about such growth, or perhaps many of them still don't see it as a problem. Rather, we are supposed to accept that growth and adjust everything else to it. Build more roads (or add lanes); build more schools (or make classes larger and go to twelve-month schedules), add more police and build more jails (without increasing taxes, of course). The list is endless.

Now, I must admit that growth is seductive. More people mean more stores and restaurants; more people mean more medical specialists; more people mean more jobs, though not always good ones. More people simply mean more, more, more.

But there are two sides to that argument. For a while, particularly in an underpopulated area, some growth is good. Every new resident contributes to lowering the cost of providing basic services to all—be they electricity, police protection, roads, schools, or libraries. These are economies of scale and reflect average costs, which are simply the result of dividing the total costs of the service by the total number of users.

In that sense, growth is good. But there is a limit to that growth. Sooner or later, the increased consumption means that much of the area's infrastructure bumps up against its carrying capacity. More police must be hired; roads and schools no longer satisfy the needs of a growing population, and on and on. The result is diseconomies of scale. Growth, instead of lowering the average cost of services, eventually raises it. As Philip Longman writes: "once population growth becomes sufficient to cause diseconomies of scale, marginal cost, which is the cost of providing for one extra person or unit of consumption, begins to rise faster than average cost."[4] Today, in the United States we have reached the point where we must live with the problems of "marginal costs" attributable to runaway population growth.

No small wonder then that we hear such expressions as cited above. "Too many people," "Let's stop growth," "Enough, already," etc. But are these the words of a small minority of malcontents, or is there a real concern among Americans that we, as a nation, have reached the point where marginal costs exceed average costs and, in a less pecuniary sense, where, very simply, quality of life just isn't what it used to be? Is the American way of life, of which we were so proud at one time, a thing of the past?

THE 1995 POLL

A new poll sponsored by Negative Population Growth, Inc. (NPG), conducted in December of 1995, provides answers to these and many other questions. A total of 1,978 randomly selected adults were questioned face-to-face by professional interviewers. The replies to the questions are illuminating and should be required reading for our policy makers and the media.

POPULATION GROWTH: FOR OR AGAINST

One of the questions in the poll deals directly with the issue of population size. Respondents were read the following statement and then asked the question: "The U.S. population was around 150 million in 1950. It is now 265 million. Do you think there are far too many people, somewhat too many people, somewhat too few people, far too few people, or about the right number of people?"

After subtracting the 9 percent who did not reply, 35 percent of the remaining respondents felt the nation had about the right number of people. Another 58 percent felt that the nation's population was already too big. Thus, while one-third of the respondents were content with the present size of our population, no less than 93 percent of those who responded to this question did not want any further growth, and many favored population reduction. One-quarter of respondents felt that there were already "far too many people."

Table 1. Percent of Respondents Who Feel U.S. Population Is Too Large, by Selected Characteristics

Characteristic	%	Characteristic	%
Gender		**Education**	
Male	53	< 12 Years	51
Female	53	HS Graduate	57
Age		Some College	53
18–29	56	College Graduate	48
30–44	55	**Occupation**	
45–59	51	Exec/Prof	54
60+	50	White Collar	54
Household Income		Blue Collar	55
Under $15,000	53	**Area**	
$15,000–29,999	54	Northeast	55
$30,000–49,999	55	Midwest	51
$50,000–74,999	56	South	46
$75,000+	55	West	67
Political Affiliation		**Marital Status**	
Democrat	54	Total Married	52
Republican	52	Both Work	55
Conservative	54	Single < 45	56
Middle of the Road	53	Children 0–7	52
Liberal	53	Children 8–17	53
Size of Household		**Race**	
1–2	51	White	53
3–4	55	African American	52
5+	57	Asian & Other*	51
Religion		Hispanic	64
Catholic	50		
Protestant	55		
Jewish*	50		
Other	48		

* The number of cases in the sample was less than 100. Because of lack of sampling reliability, these will not be considered in our separate analyses but will be included in the overall study.

What was particularly remarkable about the replies to this all-important question was their consistency. Ten widely different variables were included: gender, age, household income, education, occupation, geographic area, political affiliation and outlook, marital status, race, and religion. With rare exceptions, there was general agreement that "we've got enough, if not too many, people already." Table 1 summarizes the findings, listing the percentage who feel that the population is already too large. (The calculation includes those who had no opinion on the issue.)

The consistency of replies is amazing. In two subgroups more than 60 percent of the respondents favored a smaller population. Among Hispanics, 64 percent held such a view and among people living in the western region, two-thirds favored a smaller population.

Concern about overpopulation may be stronger in the west because the current rate of growth is more rapid there and the negative effects of rapid growth are most keenly felt. Moreover, people who choose to live in the west are drawn to it by their preference for an open, low-density, low-pressure environment.

On the other hand, only among people living in the south (46 percent), and those with college degrees (48 percent) did less than half favor reductions in numbers. On forty-three different indicators used to measure the ten variables, thirty-eight fell between 50 percent and 59 percent.

The proportions replying "About the right number of people" also varied slightly among groups. Exceptions were the Hispanics (19 percent) and college graduates (41 percent). Hispanics are the most crowded group in the country, and this is reflected in their response to this question. Furthermore, many live in the west, which may also explain in part the high rate in that region.

The picture is abundantly clear. A significant majority of Americans oppose additional population growth. The overall proportion who want no more growth (or a smaller number) is worth repeating: 86 percent of all respondents and 93 percent of those who actually replied to the specific question. No more than 4 percent of any group felt the country was vastly underpopulated. How much more of a mandate is needed to wake up our legislators in Washington?

Furthermore these attitudes on the part of Americans are not new. According to the 1996 Task Force Report of the President's Council on Sustainable Development (p.17):

> For decades, Americans have not had a desire for an ever larger population. In 1974, 87 percent of respondents to a Roper poll said they did not wish the country had more people. A 1972 poll by the U.S. Commission on Population Growth and the American Future found that 22 percent felt the U.S. population should be smaller than it was then, which was close to 200 million. As long ago as 1947, when the U.S. population was 140 million, Gallup found that 55 percent of Americans believed the country would be "worse" off with more people.

Now, it must be admitted that a fairly large minority of certain Americans favor population growth. While they are relatively small in number, they comprise a group, be they contractors, manufacturers, or just people who wish there were more fast-food restaurants within walking distance of their homes, who remain convinced that growth is a good thing. Their views cannot be ignored.

POPULATION SIZE IN HOME AREAS

It could be argued that while there is agreement that the U.S. population is too large (or large enough), such is not the case "in my home town." Perhaps the problem exists only in large cities, or in some cases, in exactly those cities where people are moving away from them because of overcrowdedness. NPG asked: "Thinking about conditions around here where you live and the number of people who live in this area, we'd like to know what you would like to see happen to the population here in the next ten years. Would you regard this as a better place if there were a lot fewer people living here, somewhat fewer, somewhat more people living here, or a lot more people living here, or would you like it to stay about the same as it is now?"

Overall, 48 percent of all the respondents did not want any further growth (i.e., "Stay about the same as it is now"), 17 percent preferred more growth, and 28 percent wished the population would fall over the next ten years. (Six percent didn't know.) Looking at all variables, generally only about half of the respondents were satisfied with the current size of their home area. Many more preferred fewer people than wanted more. Again, religion, political affiliation, income, etc. did not really matter. The pattern remained consistent. Roughly half of all respondents favored the current population size of their home towns.

A few exceptions are worth mentioning. In the west region, only 32 percent were satisfied with the present population size, while 43 percent preferred fewer neighbors. As one Seattle resident commented on a recent Newsweek article lauding the city: "Seattle's overcrowded, 'too damn many people,' griped a local."[5] Hispanic respondents also exhibited similar feelings—too many people around here. African Americans were not far behind. We suspect that this reflects big-city living. Hispanics and African Americans most directly experience the negative effects of crowded schools and housing, and the dilution of public services.

While the west includes such sparsely settled states as New Mexico, Idaho, and Montana, most of its population is concentrated in California and Arizona. Even in those other states, the population is highly urbanized. Indeed, Nevada, despite its small population, has a strong anti-population-growth sentiment, in part because of the explosive growth of Las Vegas. People living in those states are more likely to react negatively to additional growth in their home areas, which increasingly are merely suburbs in large metropolitan areas.

Only in the south did respondents favor more rather than fewer residents in their home areas—23 percent compared to 18 percent. Just over half were satisfied with present conditions. Despite the growth in states like Florida, where it is becoming a serious concern, the south remains relatively rural and thus may not see growth as an important problem.

Generally, those households earning higher incomes were more favorable to smaller "home town" populations than those with lower incomes. (See Figure 2.)

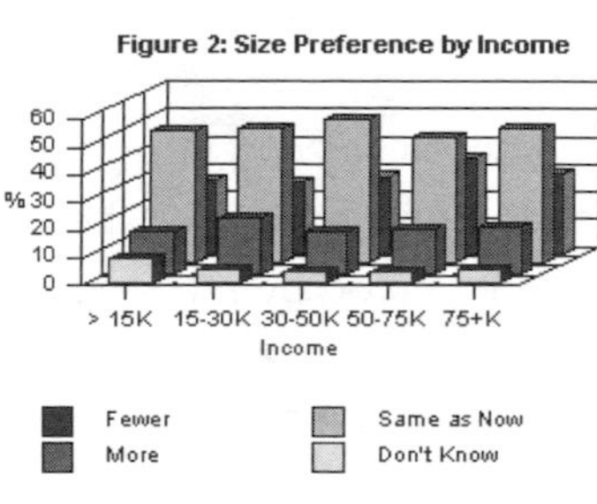

Figure 2.

Overall, about half of all Americans would like to keep their home towns or cities at about their current size—no more growth. With but one exception, the south, of all the other respondents, many more would prefer fewer rather than more neighbors over the next ten years.

Again, the evidence is clear. Not only do a majority of Americans perceive the nation to be somewhat overcrowded, they generally feel the same way about the areas where they live. Yet, cities and states throughout the nation are constantly trying to lure more and more people to their jurisdictions. When will they learn that many people disagree with this flawed economic policy? On the other hand, of course, in a few areas people favor more growth.

IS OVERPOPULATION A MAJOR PROBLEM?

As we approach the twenty-first century, the nation is faced with numerous problems: the economy, crime, the environment, etc. How does overpopulation rate? Do Americans consider it to be a major problem or is it merely something bothersome that we can live with, at least for the foreseeable future? We did grow from a nation of 75 million people at the turn of this century to 265 million today; why can't we live with 275 million at the turn of the coming century? And if we added 200 million people over the twentieth century, why can't we add another 200 million in the twenty-first century? In other words, while it may be a problem to some people, as we have seen, others might feel that population growth is something that we can adjust to as we have in the past.

We have been successful living in a rapidly growing country. How can continued growth be a problem? That's the argument offered by proponents of continued growth. But how do the people of this country feel about such continued growth?

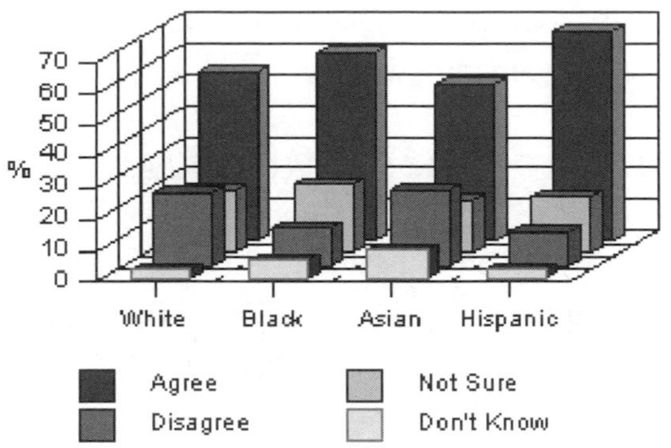

Figure 3: Population Problem Opinion

Figure 3.

When asked for opinions on the statement: "Overpopulation is a major national problem that needs to be addressed now," 55 percent were in agreement (24 percent strongly agreed). Another 20 percent weren't certain. That is, they neither agreed nor disagreed. Only 21 percent felt that overpopulation was not a major problem. Perhaps even those who are not certain will change their minds over the next few years as growth continues unabated and suburbs are extended further and further away from the central cities and more and more lanes are added to our congested highways. At any rate, a majority of Americans do consider population growth to be a major problem, one that should be addressed now. (See Figure 3.)

Consistency was noted here as in other responses in the survey with but one notable exception. Just under half (48 percent) of those earning at least $75,000 feel that overpopulation is a major problem. Otherwise, a majority of all respondents in all categories agreed with this statement. This was especially marked among residents of the west (66 percent), Hispanics (67 percent), and African Americans (60 percent). Thus some consistency exists within groups—especially regionally and ethnically.

The difference in attitude between Democrats and Republicans is minor. Whereas 58 percent of

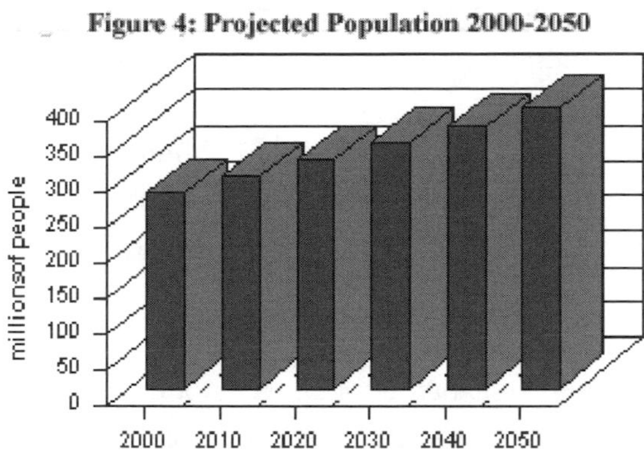

Figure 4.

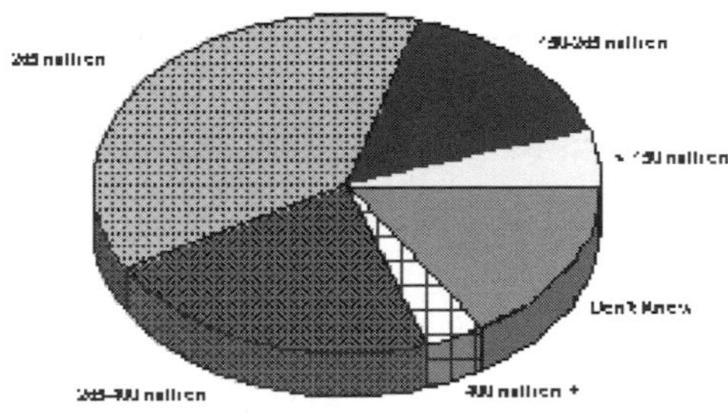

Figure 5.

Democrats (including 28 percent who strongly agreed) feel that overpopulation is a major problem, the share among Republicans was 52 percent. At the other extreme, 17 percent of Democrats disagreed compared to 26 percent among Republicans. Most important is the fact that irrespective of political affiliation, there was agreement that population growth was a major problem.

Not only do Americans think we are overpopulated, whether nationwide or in one's own area, Americans consider this a major national problem that needs to be addressed at this time. Yet not one word about population growth was mentioned during the ubiquitous Republican debates, and population growth was not discussed by either President Clinton or Senator Dole in their debates in the fall of 1996.

WHAT ABOUT THE FUTURE?

Recent Census Bureau and other projections foresee a population of close to 400 million Americans by 2050. (See Figure 4.) Some demographers criticize these projections as being too low. Indeed, a population of one billion Americans before the end of the next century is a definite possibility! Already, we are dangerously close to destroying our environment and exhausting our resources. Already, our schools are deteriorating, our wetlands are disappearing, we have no more room for waste disposal, and our parks and beaches are overcrowded. How will it be with 130 million more people living on the same amount of land? How will it be with a population double or even triple our current numbers? Will we simply keep building more schools (if we can find enough teachers), add more lanes to our highways, build new subdivisions and shopping malls? If we do, we must bear in mind that all this construction makes it more difficult for water to reach the aquifers. Instead, water simply contributes to more flooding. Asphalt and concrete cannot replace ground.

Respondents to the NPG poll were asked this question: "The current size of the U.S. population is 265 million. If present rates of fertility and immigration continue, our population will grow to around 400 million by the year 2050. . . . In your judgment, which of the following population sizes would be best for our country to have in the long run, say by 2050 and beyond?" Almost 60 percent answered 265 million or less—that is to say, our current population. About 38 percent were satisfied with our present size and another 22 percent preferred population decline. In other words, six out of ten Americans are satisfied with current levels of .population but quite a few would prefer a smaller number. (See Figure 5.)

At the risk of boring diffuseness, I must repeat that word once again: consistency. The highest proportions preferring current or smaller population are found among those earning $50,000 or more (63 percent). At the other extreme, African Americans have the lowest shares (46 percent). The proportion opting for over 400 million, a size that has been advocated by certain economists, is minuscule: 4 percent overall. However, among African Americans it rises to 8 percent. One can't help wondering if this is a wish to see their share of the U.S. population increase, particularly in light of the fact that it has been highly publicized that Hispanics may surpass African Americans in numbers within two decades. Ironically, Hispanics may feel crowded but have the highest fertility!

It should also be pointed out that 5 percent of the respondents felt that less than 150 million was the ideal population size for the nation. Interestingly, only Hispanics had a much higher share in that category. There, one in ten favored such a smaller population. Thus, the perceived "wish" of African Americans to see their population increase its portion of the total is not shared by the other large minority—Hispanics.[6] However, over one in five of all respondents preferred a smaller population for 2050 than we have today. Thus, a clear majority of Americans (almost 60 percent) indicated that they prefer a U.S. population either smaller than, or not greater than, our present size of 265 million. However, the concept of reducing population size was not well received by most respondents.

Many other population-related questions were included in the survey. The replies are quite similar to those noted above and are summarized in Table 2.

The results are abundantly clear—a majority of Americans feel that enough is enough. We have seen our numbers rise almost fourfold in this century. Since 1950 alone, our numbers have almost doubled. It is time to re-examine our demographic situation and begin thinking of a population policy for the next century. Are we really prepared for 500 million inhabitants? The people have spoken; now it is up to the media to make this known, and especially for policy makers to act accordingly.

ENDING POPULATION GROWTH

Although a majority of Americans favor an end to growth (indeed, many prefer a smaller population), the next question is more difficult. How does a nation put an end to population growth, much less

Table 2. Attitudes Toward Population Size and Growth
(% strongly/mostly agree)

Statement	%
Although the issue of population growth does not require immediate attention, we should start thinking of ways to control it now.	59%
Continued population growth is a threat to America's resource base.	50%
The United States is a huge country with plenty of space for more population growth.	36%
To maintain a sound economy and environment for the long term, the United States needs to reduce its population size.	33%
This country needs population growth in order to have economic growth.	30%
We need continued population growth to avoid a labor shortage.	21%
Unless the U.S. population continues growing we will cease being a world power.	20%

reduce its size? For years there was one answer and, in the 1960s, it was very popular: "Stop having so many children." Zero population growth (ZPG) became a well-known expression. And indeed, this is an excellent way to reduce population growth. "Stop at Two" should become our motto in the twenty-first century.

Unfortunately, even if we did "stop at two" and there was no immigration, population would still grow for some time because of what demographers call a "momentum for growth." As long as there is a sufficient number of women in their childbearing years, the number of births will increase simply because so many potential mothers are available to have those "two" births. Thus, while limiting ourselves to two offspring would slow down population growth, it isn't the complete answer.[7]

Populations change numerically in only three ways: births, deaths, and migration. No one advocates that we start dying younger to reduce the population. But reducing the level of immigration is a quick and relatively simple way to put an end to rapid population growth. More and more in recent years, "stop at two" has been accompanied by "lower immigration"

Table 3. Percent of Respondents Who Feel the United States should Accept Fewer than 300,000 Immigrants per Year, by Selected Characteristics

Characteristic	%	Characteristic	%
Gender		**Education**	
Male	70	< 12 Years	69
Female	71	HS Graduate	73
Age		Some College	69
18–29	67	College Graduate	66
30–44	72	**Occupation**	
45–59	73	Exec/Prof	69
60+	71	White Collar	70
Household Income		Blue Collar	76
Under $15,000	71	**Area**	
$15,000–29,999	72	Northeast	64
$30,000–49,999	69	Midwest	73
$50,000–74,999	73	South	75
$75,000+	70	West	66
Political Affiliation		**Marital Status**	
Democrat	70	Total Married	72
Republican	70	Both Work	76
Conservative	72	Single < 45	68
Middle of the Road	71	Children 0–7	72
Liberal	66	Children 8–17	70
Size of Household		**Race**	
1–2	71	White	71
3–4	70	African American	73
5+	68	Asian & Other*	64
Religion		Hispanic	52
Catholic	68		
Protestant	72		
Jewish*	61		
Other	73		

* The number of cases in the sample was less than 100. Because of lack of sampling reliability, these will not be considered in our separate analyses but will be included in the overall study.

as yet another way to reduce and eventually end population growth.

ATTITUDES TOWARD IMMIGRATION

Americans have long believed that immigration should be reduced and that illegal immigration should be ended. Poll after poll has documented these sentiments. Yet, as recently as 1990 the U.S. Congress increased legal immigration and in 1996 overwhelmingly turned down an attempt to reduce legal immigration by about 20 percent. All this despite massive majorities of Americans favoring reductions!

With the passage of the 1965 immigration legislation, immigration levels began to increase from around 300,000 to over 800,000 per year in the 1980s. Although the number fell slightly in 1995, it did increase dramatically in 1996 to 915,900.[8] When we add to that refugees and illegal immigrants, it is safe to say that well over one million people permanently enter the United States every year. This number is even greater than that recorded in the early part of the twentieth century when so many people came to the United States from eastern and southern Europe. Small wonder then that so many Americans say "enough is enough," or, as former Senator Alan Simpson has put it: "We are suffering from compassion fatigue."

Furthermore, lowering immigration levels as soon as possible is the quickest way to end, or at least reduce, population growth. Immigration advocates have been discussing the wrong issues. The issue is not cultural or racial as at least one former presidential candidate claims; the issue is not primarily whether immigrants take or don't take jobs from Americans—they do. Very simply, and paraphrasing James Carville in the 1992 presidential election campaign, "It's the numbers, stupid!"

ATTITUDES ABOUT IMMIGRATION

Respondents to the NPG poll were asked the following question: "Legal and illegal immigration combined has exceeded one million people a year in recent years. What do you think would be the most desirable number of all types of immigrants to allow into the United States each year?" Seven out of ten respondents replied that they would prefer total immigration to be under 300,000 annually.[9] One in five would allow no immigrants whatsoever. Some 54 percent preferred fewer than 100,000 or none at all. When one takes into consideration the fact that 15 percent of the respondents didn't reply, this means that over 83 percent of all those who answered the question felt that less than 300,000 immigrants per year was sufficient. An infinitesimally small proportion (2 percent) felt that immigration should be increased—that is, over one million per year.

As with the first question on population views, the various categories by percent favoring less than 300,000 immigrants per year are listed in Table 3. These numbers illustrate once again the amazing consistency that was found in most of this survey. Some variations are noted in views on immigration levels. In almost all instances, between 65 and 75 percent of respondents agreed that fewer than 300,000 immigrants should be accepted in any given year. However, a few exceptions were noted. Especially noteworthy was the smaller proportion of Hispanics who favored lower levels of immigration. While over half of Hispanics (52 percent) still thought 300,000 was a maximum number, this was far lower than the average of 70 percent. Nevertheless, a majority of Hispanics still want less immigration than now. Otherwise, only residents in the northeast had such a low proportion. One can't help wondering if ethnicity is a factor in the low proportion for Hispanics. Recall that Hispanics favor reduced population size, yet some may wish to be reunited with their compatriots in the United States.

Of all the polls taken in recent years, this is the most convincing. The American people want to drastically reduce immigration. Yet the U.S. Senate, even after these data were announced, voted eighty to twenty against any minor reductions in legal movements.

Thus far, I have concentrated on legal immigration. But undocumented movements have increased dramatically in recent decades despite a 1986 law making it illegal to hire nonlegal immigrants. How many enter the country and stay remains a guess. The INS estimates that perhaps 300,000 illegal residents move permanently to the United States every year. Others have argued that this is a conservative estimate. There is little doubt that the actual number residing here surpasses five million.

The NPG poll listed a number of statements related to population growth and asked the respondents if they agreed or disagreed with them. One of those statements read: "We should have strict laws to identify and deport illegal aliens already in this country." Just under three-quarters of all respondents agreed (12 percent neither agreed nor disagreed). However, the level of agreement among groups was not as consistent as in earlier questions. In eight groups, less than 70 percent agreed with the statement: these included those earning under $15,000 (68 percent) as well as those earning over $75,000 (69 percent), those living in the northeast (63 percent), African Americans and Hispanics (68 percent and 60 percent respectively), and Catholics (69 percent). Quite possibly some of the respondents earning under $15,000 are illegal themselves; while some of those earning over $75,000 benefit from the hiring of illegals. College graduates were also less likely to advocate deportation than their less educated counterparts.

At the other extreme, 82 percent of Protestants favored the statement, as did 84 percent of people living in the midwest. Otherwise, most other groups hovered around 75 percent. Here, then, we see one of the few instances where Catholics and Protestants differ rather significantly on one of these issues. Only 69 percent of Catholic respondents agreed with this statement. Recall that Pope Paul visited the United States in 1996 and urged the admission of more immigrants. He did not distinguish between legals and illegals. His views may have had some impact on a few Catholics.

Looking at both immigration-related questions, it is clear that an overwhelming majority of Americans favor dramatic reductions—whether of legal or illegal movements. However, minorities are not as strongly convinced of the need for such reduction as others. This may reflect their desire to have more of their countrymen and countrywomen join them in the United States. However, it is important to add that despite these variations, even these groups favor immigration reductions.

ATTITUDES TOWARD REDUCED FERTILITY

In the long run, reductions in fertility are more important than reductions in immigration if the goal is to level off and eventually reduce population size. However, because of the momentum for growth mentioned earlier, any reductions in fertility are slow in showing results. When the impact is finally felt, however, it is enormous. Consider this example from the 1992 Census Bureau projections. Holding constant both immigration and mortality, if fertility remained at 2.1 births per woman the 2050 population was projected to reach 383 million. Maintaining the same levels of immigration and mortality, if fertility fell gradually to 1.8 births per woman, the 2050 population would be 340 million—a difference of 43 million people in less than 60 years! Not only does this illustrate the importance of a small difference in family size, it should warn us of the need to reduce

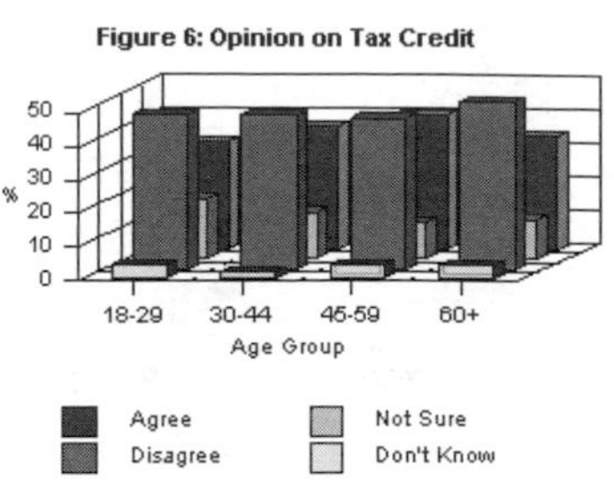

Figure 6.

our fertility if we are to assure ourselves that the nation's population does not increase much more, and perhaps, begins to decline in the future.

Currently U.S. fertility is around 2.1 births per woman, which is among the highest of any industrial nation. In Spain and Italy, for example, it is down to 1.2, and is 1.3 in Germany. Our current fertility, combined with our high level of immigration, almost guarantees that we will reach, if not surpass, 400 million by mid-twenty-first century and possibly come close to 1 billion by the end of the next century. Most Americans would agree that such an eventuality cannot be allowed to transpire. Given the momentum for growth, now is the time to act to stop this population juggernaut.

NPG did not inquire about ideal family size or such related matters. Numerous polls have been done in the past and the Census Bureau annually asks a large sample of American women their fertility plans. For some time now, the answer has been around 2.0 or 2.1. According to the latest Census Bureau projections using 1995 data, the total fertility rate for non-Hispanic white women is 1.8, for blacks 2.4, Asians 1.9, Native Americans 2.1, and Hispanics 3.0.[10]

The current poll emphasized policy-related questions dealing with how fertility could be reduced. The following statement was read to all respondents and they were asked to agree or disagree: "To encourage couples not to have more than two children, the federal government should give an income tax credit to people who have two or fewer children. If they have more than two children they would lose the credit." Only 36 percent of the respondents agreed with this statement while 47 percent disagreed. About 14 percent couldn't make up their minds; that is, they neither agreed nor disagreed. Overall, then, a plurality of respondents disagreed with the statement, which admittedly is a radical departure from current tax policies. For example, both parties and the President recently agreed to reward families for having additional births with a $500 tax credit from their actual income tax for each additional child. (See Figure 6.)

Variations from the overall average were rare. The highest percent agreeing with the statement were Hispanic respondents (49 percent). This is quite surprising and may reflect a desire on their part to begin limiting their high fertility. Other groups where the agreement share surpassed 40 percent were the executive/professionals (43 percent), and westerners (42 percent). Interestingly, agreement generally rose with the age of respondent.

On the other hand, low (i.e., under 30 percent) proportions in agreement with the statement were found only among African Americans (28 percent). In sum, while a plurality disagreed with this statement, so many were not sure that it could almost be called a "wash." In fact, only among those families with children between eight and seventeen did over half disagree with the statement.

The U.S. adolescent pregnancy rate is among the highest in the industrialized world and is climbing. Many of these pregnancies are to single women. Sex education in schools has become a controversial issue in many areas as the religious right attempts to take over school boards in an effort to bar any discussion of sexual activities. With that in mind the following statement was included in the poll: "To try to reduce teen-age pregnancies, the federal government should pay all women between the ages of fourteen and nineteen a monthly cash stipend as long as they remain childless."

Although 30 percent agreed with the statement, 57 percent disagreed. Another 10 percent weren't sure either way and 3 percent just didn't know. This, of course, is another fairly radical solution to our soaring teenage pregnancy rate and such an approach has been suggested in other countries. The only groups where less than half of the respondents disagreed with the statement were African Americans (42 percent) and Hispanics (36 percent), suggesting a possible desire to limit family size among these groups. As for the others, perhaps financial concerns played a role in the decision-making process. No mention was made of how the money for these young women would be raised.

Americans have long had an aversion to increased taxes, even when it helps preserve

Table 4. Percent of Respondents Who Feel the United States should Provide Free Sterilization, by Selected Characteristics

Characteristic	%	Characteristic	%
Gender		**Education**	
Male	59	< 12 Years	58
Female	57	HS Graduate	54
Age		Some College	62
18–29	62	College Graduate	57
30–44	61	**Occupation**	
45–59	57	Exec/Prof	58
60+	49	White Collar	61
Household Income		Blue Collar	63
Under $15,000	59	**Area**	
$15,000–29,999	57	Northeast	44
$30,000–49,999	56	Midwest	64
$50,000–74,999	59	South	59
$75,000+	50	West	61
Political Affiliation		**Marital Status**	
Democrat	59	Total Married	57
Republican	53	Both Work	61
Conservative	61	Single < 45	62
Middle of the Road	54	Children 0–7	61
Liberal	61	Children 8–17	61
Size of Household		**Race**	
1–2	56	White	58
3–4	60	African American	51
5+	57	Asian & Other*	50
Religion		Hispanic	61
Catholic	54		
Protestant	62		
Jewish*	46		
Other	55		

* The number of cases in the sample was less than 100. Because of lack of sampling reliability, these will not be considered in our separate analyses but will be included in the overall study.

our environment (witness the political squabble over a mere 4.3 cent tax on gasoline!). In addition, welfare has become a major issue in current policy discussions. Although it is a wild exaggeration, many middle-class Americans have visions of these huge poor families living on welfare and having more and more children just to get additional funds from the government. While studies have proven this not to be the case, it has become an accepted myth by many Americans.

Poorer families do have more children than their more affluent counterparts although the difference is not enormous. To get at the thinking of Americans on this subject the following statement was made and respondents were asked to agree or disagree: "The federal government should provide free sterilization for any low-income men and women of childbearing age who voluntarily choose it." More than twice as many respondents agreed with the statement as disagreed (58 percent to 28 percent). Another 11 percent were uncertain and 3 percent didn't know. (See Table 4.)

In only one instance did less than 50 percent agree: northeasterners (44 percent). Many simply couldn't come to a conclusion. In numerous cases, the proportion agreeing with the statement easily surpassed 60 percent. When we consider that those who couldn't decide one way or another are included in these percentages, it seems quite clear that a substantial majority of the American people (including those earning under $30,000 annually) favor this suggestion. Interesting was the fact that 54 percent of Catholics agreed with the statement on sterilization. However, the percent of Protestants agreeing was substantially higher (62 percent).

WHAT ABOUT A NATIONAL POLICY?

In 1969, President Nixon spoke out forcefully, and as it turned out, prophetically, about population growth. His words are worth repeating:

> In 1917 the total number of Americans passed 100 million, after three full centuries of steady growth. In 1967—just half a century later—the 200 million mark was passed. If the present rate of growth continues, the third hundred million persons will be added in roughly a thirty-year period. This means that by the year 2000, or shortly thereafter, there will be more than 300 million Americans.
>
> The growth will produce serious challenges for our society. I believe that many of our present social problems may be related to the fact that we have had only fifty years in which to accommodate the second hundred million Americans . . .
>
> Where, for example, will the next hundred million Americans live? . . .
>
> Other questions confront us. How, for example, will we house the next hundred million Americans? . . .
>
> How will we educate and employ such a large number of people? Will our transportation systems move them about as quickly and economically as necessary? How will we provide adequate health care when our population reaches 300 million? Will our political structures have to be reordered, too, when our society grows to such proportions? . . .
>
> . . . we should establish as a national goal the provision of adequate family planning services within the next five years to all those who want them but cannot afford them.[11]

These words are as appropriate today as they were in 1969. Nixon went on to propose, and Congress formed, a National Commission on Population

Growth and the American Future. It was chaired by John D. Rockefeller, III. Its recommendations, published just twenty-five years ago, should be must reading for all Americans concerned with how we will handle yet another 100 million or more people in another fifty years. The Commission concluded: "After two years of concentrated effort, we have concluded that, in the long run, no substantial benefits will result from further growth of the Nation's population, rather that the gradual stabilization of our population would contribute significantly to the Nation's ability to solve its problems."[12] At that time, the U.S. population was a little over 200 million.

Apparently, the American people have been more likely to listen to the Commission's views than their leaders. Indeed, Nixon himself disavowed the Commission's report because of its family-planning recommendations. Since then, except for some brief activities during the Carter administration, population growth has ceased being an issue that our national leaders are willing to consider.

Yet, the people have spoken in no uncertain terms and their thinking is summarized below:

- A large majority of Americans want no further growth of the nation's population and many would like to see its size reduced.
- A plurality consider their own home areas to be large enough and would prefer fewer rather than more neighbors.
- Most Americans consider overpopulation to be a problem that should be addressed immediately.
- An overwhelming majority of Americans think that immigration levels are far too high and should be reduced to less than 300,000 per year.
- Most Americans want to see illegal immigrants identified and deported from this country.
- While there is opposition to paying women fourteen to nineteen not to have children, those opposed only constitute a plurality of all respondents. A significant minority agree with the concept.
- A majority of Americans think the government should provide free sterilization for any low-income men and women of childbearing age who voluntarily choose it.
- Finally, almost 60 percent of Americans don't want their population to grow beyond current levels by the year 2050.

The message is clear. The American people have spoken: no further growth.

Not all the results from this survey are encouraging to advocates of a smaller optimum population. NPG has long favored an eventual U.S. population of about 150 million.[13] Recall the words of George Kennan on this subject. Nevertheless, we were encouraged by the backing shown for a national population policy which would have as its goal a smaller U.S. population. Support for such a policy was substantial (29 percent or almost one in three), even though it is not yet the view of the majority.

When asked if the U.S. Congress "should legislate a national policy to keep the population at a fixed level. That policy would set a specific numerical goal for a smaller U.S. population with a target date to reach that goal," 41 percent of the respondents opposed such an approach while 29 percent favored it. Another 20 percent were not sure.

Opinions were quite consistent across the board with the exception of region. As Figure 7 shows, 40 percent of the people residing in the west favored such a proposition compared to only 22 percent among northeasterners. This, of course, reflects the pattern noticed throughout this study. Westerners are the most adamant foes of overpopulation.

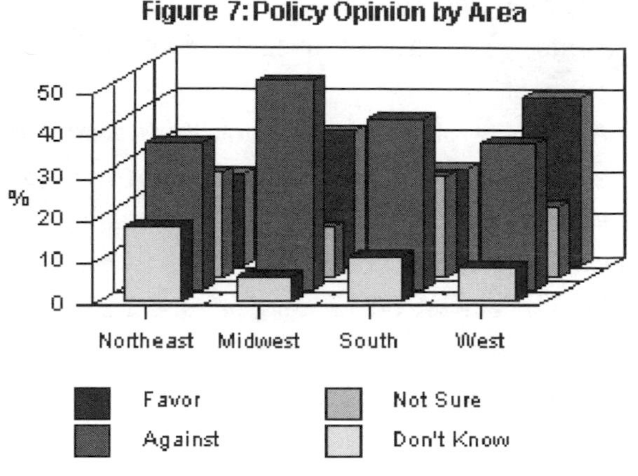

Figure 7.

No question about it: a majority of the American people oppose further growth and they would like to see immigration drastically reduced. But, when it comes to fertility and official national policy, there is some hesitation. Part of that hesitation may come from the implication of governmental intervention. There is a growing dissatisfaction with governmental activities that affect the lives of individual Americans.[14]

However, Americans should realize that population growth, in and of itself, contributes tremendously to limiting individual freedoms. Small, underpopulated areas need far fewer regulations than overcrowded metropolises. As numbers grow, new rules become mandatory. Laws must be passed to determine speed limits; zoning regulations become necessary; environmental regulations are imperative. This is a basic aspect of population growth—the more people in any given space, the more regulations are needed to regulate social behavior. This is a prime reason why I, for one, would favor a decline in numbers. Fewer people means more freedom for all of us.

Based on the results of our poll, a majority of Americans don't want any further population growth, but they are hesitant about the government becoming involved, except insofar as immigration is concerned. There is also some concern about the word "negative." Most Americans agree that the government should not become involved in determining family size, as it does in China. However, it should be noted that the U.S. government has historically taken pronatalist positions. The Comstock Laws of the nineteenth century, which banned even the mailing of family-planning literature and the prohibition of abortions, were forms of government interference in family size (favoring larger, not smaller, as in China).

Despite hesitancy about government involvement in fertility, the government does have the right to study how population growth is affecting every phase of American life. It has the right to encourage people to stop at two—a motto that we strongly urge be accepted by all Americans from this moment on.

Given the results of this poll, the government should be responsive to the wishes of its constituents by reducing immigration substantially and by seeking acceptable ways to encourage lower fertility and discourage population growth. Because of the momentum built into population growth, the time to act is now.

NOTES:

1. George Kennan, *Around the Cragged Hill: A Political and Personal Philosophy* (New York: W.W. Norton, 1993), 100. Concern about the population size of the United States is not new. For example, see the following quotation from Ralph Waldo Emerson: "If government knew how, I should like to see it check, not multiply, the population. When it reaches its true law of action, every man that is born will be hailed as essential." ("The Conduct of Life, Considerations by the Way," 1860).
2. Malin Falkenmark and Carl Widstrand, "Population and Water Resources: A Delicate Balance," *Population Bulletin* 47, no. 3 (November 1992): 13.

3. Cited in Peter Peterson, "Social Insecurity," *Atlantic Monthly* (May 1996): 64.
4. Phillip Longman, "We're in the Tax Revolt Zone," *Florida Trend* (October 1992): 18.
5. *Newsweek*, "Settling on Seattle," 10 June 1996, 15.
6. It should be pointed out that only English-speaking Hispanics were included in the survey, which was conducted solely in English. Thus, this may reflect the thinking of second-generation Hispanics more than newcomers to the United States.
7. "Stop at Two" if observed by all would actually mean that the fertility rate would be around 1.5 since a number of women have one child and quite a few remain childless.
8. Compiled from wire reports. "Immigration Surges to Four-Year High," *Orlando Sentinel*, 5 May 1997.
9. The proposed legislation offered in the Congress in 1996 would have reduced it by a mere 20 percent, to still well over 500,000!
10. Jennifer Cheeseman Day, *Population Projections of the United States by Age, Sex, Race, and Hispanic Origin: 1995 to 2050*, U.S. Bureau of the Census, Current Population Reports, P25-1130 (Washington, D.C.: U.S. Government Printing Office, 1996), 2. It should be added that much of the variation in fertility between racial groups can be explained by differences in income and education. For example, college-educated black women have the lowest rate of all groups.
11. President Richard Nixon, "Special Message to the U.S. Congress on Problems of Population Growth, July 18, 1969," in *Public Papers of Presidents of the United States* (Washington, D.C.: Office of the Federal Register, 1969), 521.
12. Cited in David Simcox, "The Commission on Population Growth and the American Future: Twenty Years Later: A Lost Opportunity," in *Social Contract* (Summer 1992): 197.
13. It should be emphasized that Negative Population Growth does not advocate a *permanent* negative rate of population growth. That would eventually result in zero population! It advocates a negative rate of growth only for an interim period until U.S. population can be stabilized at a sustainable level, which we judge to be not over 150 million.
14. On that point, it is interesting to note that such intervention doesn't seem to bother the so-called "right to life" movement advocating an anti-abortion Constitutional amendment. I can't think of any more personal intervention by government than in a family's bedroom!

THE IMPACT OF IMMIGRATION ON UNITED STATES' POPULATION SIZE: 1950 TO 2050

Leon F. Bouvier

November 1998

INTRODUCTION

Much has been written about the growing level of immigration into the United States over the past two decades. Since the mid-1950s, both the absolute and net numbers of such in-migration have equaled and surpassed those noted at the turn of this century. Far too little attention, however, has been paid to quantifying the importance of immigration as an engine of U.S. population growth. Due to the uncertainties in the data on illegal immigration and on emigration (out-migration) as well as the difficulties in ascertaining information on immigrant fertility, there has been disagreement on immigration's full impact on our population growth. Some previous efforts to assess its demographic impact have tended to focus only on direct immigration and have thus underestimated its affect. We know that currently nearly one million immigrants enter the country every year—legally or illegally—and stay here permanently. But of our total population growth, how much can be attributed to immigration?

First, growth can only come from natural increase (that is, births minus deaths) and/or through net migration (that is immigration minus emigration). The fact that two variables are involved must be considered when trying to determine the impact of immigration. For example, if fertility is so low that deaths equal births, then 100 percent of population growth could be attributable to immigration. Today, fertility, which just went through a so-called "baby bust" period, is now back to replacement level—women are averaging just over two births and life expectancy keeps climbing. Taken together, natural increase (or decrease, for that matter) and net migration are the two components fundamental to any discussion of the impact that immigration has on population size and growth.

Second, the effect of immigration is not limited solely to those who move here, an especially important consideration in the case of the United States. Since many of the immigrants are young adults, they often have children after arriving in the United States. These offspring are not considered immigrants; they are simply added to the native-born births in any given year. Yet, they are the result of immigration. By 2000, almost one in five U.S. births will be to foreign-born parents. As these children themselves reach child-bearing age, many will go on to reproduce and thus further contribute to U.S. population growth.

But here too, we must be careful with how the indirect impact of immigration is calculated. In one sense, aren't all residents of the United States "indirect" immigrants, including those who are descended from Native Americans who, historians tell us, came across the Bering Strait from Asia many centuries ago? Noted Census Bureau demographer Campbell Gibson has calculated the share of the U.S. population that is attributable (directly and indirectly) to the various waves of immigrants who have entered the U.S. since 1790.[1] For instance, Gibson finds that of the 248,710,000 Americans enumerated in the 1990 census, 127 million are attributable to the net 47,698,000 immigrants who have arrived since 1790. The remainder of the population is thus attributable to the 3,929,000 U.S. residents in 1790. Gibson's methodology in these calculations reflects not only net immigration but also the natural increase component attributable to immigration, by comparing population growth both with and without immigration under given fertility and mortality patterns. This report uses a methodology similar to that developed by Gibson.[2]

Calculating the indirect impact of immigration can become meaningless if it is carried to extremes or done without the appropriate parameters. Given this "caveat," and the variety of potential variables available, a number of estimates on the impact of immigration have been developed with the results often exhibiting considerable difference. In what year does the calculation begin? What rates of fertility, mortality and migration are used, and for whom: the native-born and/or the foreign born? How many generations are included? As a result, there has been a significant amount of disagreement over the impact that immigration has had on U.S. population size and growth.

This is not that surprising. Not only are the factors just mentioned likely to yield different answers; migration data are the least reliable of all demographic variables. We don't know for certain exactly how many people enter the country illegally; we only have indirect estimates of how many leave (emigration). Furthermore, the age-sex composition of these two groups are seldom totally accurate. So, while most demographers do their best to arrive at reasonable results, such estimates unavoidably have some margin of error. This applies to this study as well. While we use the most reasonable measurements available, we are aware of the fact that migration statistics are not as reliable as are those for fertility and mortality.

PARAMETERS

In this study, we are concerned solely with immigrants and their offspring. The question therefore is simply: what is the impact, direct and indirect, of immigration on the population size of the United States? To almost assure that generation upon generation are not included, we limit our analysis to two fifty year periods: 1950–2000 and, for the future 2000–2050. The question is asked: of our total population growth between 1950 and 2000, how much is attributable to immigration—direct and indirect? Then the same question is asked for the period 2000–2050 according to given assumptions about fertility, mortality, and migration.

For the first period, we rely on the demographic rates published by the Census Bureau in their series of projections. Thus, fertility and mortality rates from 1950 to 2000 are similar in both sets of projections (with adjustments made for the impact of immigration to be discussed later): those with immigration and those without immigration. The difference between the two projections (once differences in the fertility of immigrants is accounted for) is thus attributable to immigration.

For the second period (2000–2050) we emphasize that these are projections and not predictions. In one sense, if the mathematics are correct, a projection can never be wrong. When some people insist that projections are "always wrong," they are confusing projections with predictions and it is really the assumptions that they disagree with. In this analysis' projections, we make clear exactly what assumptions are being used and it is up to the reader to judge their soundness.

According to the Census Bureau, the United States currently has about 26 million foreign-born inhabitants, accounting for about 10 percent of its population. This is the largest number ever and the largest as a proportion of the total population since 1930. Furthermore, the number of foreign-born has tripled just in the last thirty years. According to the Federation for American Immigration Reform's *Immigration Report*, "In a new and dramatic testimony to immigration's impact on the nation's population growth and composition, the Census study suggests that, if current patterns hold, almost one-third of the nation's population increase this decade will come from immigration. Counting the U.S.-born offspring of immigrants brings the total closer to fifty percent."[3]

METHODOLOGY

Our approach is straightforward. First, we look at the actual Census Bureau total population counts for the years 1950–60–70–80–90 and their projected median population for 2000. These, of course, include immigration and its direct and indirect impacts. We then use the same levels of fertility and mortality (adjusted for no immigration) as does the Census Bureau but with no migration to calculate the hypothetical population in the same years. The difference is attributable to immigration, both direct and indirect.

For the 2000–2050 period, we rely on the latest projections prepared by the Census Bureau.[4] From this excellent and carefully thought out demographic monograph, we selected two series of projections that seem to be the most reasonable. One projection is without immigration and one with immigration. In both models, fertility and mortality are the same. The fertility rates rise from 2.055 in 1995 to 2.245 in 2050 reflecting the growing immigrant population and its higher fertility. Life expectancy is expected to rise from 75.9 in 1995 to 82.0 in 2050. Net immigration is assumed to be 820,000 annually. This results from immigration of 1.042 million immigrants minus 222,000 emigrants. Thus, any difference in population size between the two models would be the result of immigration, direct and indirect.

It should be noted that the Census Bureau projections do not lower fertility in their no immigration scenario. Since higher immigrant fertility is a significant and growing contributor to total births, the immigration impact from 2000 to 2050 is thus conservatively represented. That is, without immigration the U.S. fertility rate could be expected to drop rather than rise as in the Census Bureau projections. Thus, in relying on the Census Bureau projections for 2000 to 2050 we are presenting the minimum impact that continuing current immigration policies would have on U.S. population growth.

An analysis of the impact of immigration going back fifty years, and then going forward fifty years (1950 to 2050) gives us a broader idea of how important this demographic variable actually is.

IMMIGRATION AND U.S. POPULATION GROWTH: 1950–2000

According to the Census Bureau, between 1950 and 1990 the United States population increased from 152,271,000 to 249,910,000. By 2000, that population is projected to increase to 274,634,000 based on the middle series of projections from the Census Bureau for the period, 1995–2050.[5]

Our question then is: what would the population have been in 1990 and will be in 2000 if there had been no immigration since 1950? That seems like a relatively simple question to answer—simply take out immigration from the Census Bureau projection. As mentioned earlier, however, immigrants generally have higher fertility than the native-born. This is especially true of the first generation, and for some groups the second generation as well. Unfortunately, data are not published for fertility rates by place of birth (i.e. native born and foreign born). Thus we must make as reasonable an effort as possible to estimate the fertility rate for the 1950–2000 period assuming no immigration. Over the period, the number of immigrants, and their proportion of our population, expand and thus have an increasing effect on the overall fertility rate.

For this exercise, we feel that it is better to err on the low side rather than on the high side. In other words, we don't want to overemphasize the effect of immigration on overall fertility. Nevertheless there is an impact. In the no immigration projection, the overall total fertility rate was kept at its actual level through 1980. After 1980 total fertility was reduced from one percent to four percent to account for the fact that no immigration was included. For example, for the 1980-84 period, the actual overall total fertility rate was 1.82 and we assumed that it would have been 1.80 without any immigration. We repeated the same process for all five-year periods, assuming that the actual rise in U.S. fertility during the later two decades of this century would have slowed if there had been no immigration. We feel that this is a fair and conservative assessment of the impact of immigration on the fertility rate of the nation during this period.

For life expectancy, we made similar assumptions about the effect of immigration.[6] However, differences are quite minimal. For example, in 1980 the life expectancy for the nation was 73.7 years at birth. Without immigration, we raised it slightly to 75.5 years at birth. A similar pattern is followed throughout the assumptions. Given these assumptions about fertility and mortality, we then proceeded to calculate what would have been the population of the United States in the period 1950–2000. The results are presented in Table 1 below.

Table 1. Population of the U.S. 1950–2000, With and Without Immigration (in 000s)

Year	Actual Population	Actual Growth	With No Immigration	Growth with No Immigration	Immigration's Share of Growth	(% of growth)
1950	151,690		151,690		--	--
1955	165,980	14,290	164,770	13,080	1,210	(8.5%)
1960	180,671	14,691	176,340	11,570	3,121	(21.2%)
1965	194,303	13,632	186,480	10,140	3,492	(25.6%)
1970	205,052	10,749	193,380	6,900	3,849	(35.8%)
1975	215,973	10,921	199,590	6,210	4,711	(43.1%)
1980	227,726	11,753	205,620	6,030	5,723	(48.7%)
1985	238,466	10,740	212,610	6,990	3,750	(34.9%)
1990	248,911	10,445	219,350	6,740	3,705	(35.5%)
1995	262,820*	13,909	225,890	6,540	7,369	(53.0%)
2000	274,634*	11,814	231,621	5,730	6,084	(51.5%)
Total		122,944		79,930	43,014	-35.00%

* Based on Census Bureau "middle series" projections

As can be expected, the proportion of the U.S. population attributable to post-1950 immigrants and their descendants increases over time as more people enter the country every year. By 1990, it was 13.9 percent of the population. That is to say, of the population in 1990, 13.9 percent were post-1950 immigrants and their descendants. Likewise, of the 93,221,000 people added to the U.S. population between 1950 and 1990, 30,561,000 or 32.8 percent were post-1950 immigrants and their descendants. By 2000, the direct and indirect impact of post-1950 immigration will amount to an additional 43 million people added to the U.S. population (15.6 percent of the our total population). Of the some 122,944,000 people to be added to the U.S. population between 1950 and 2000, about 35 percent will be due to post-1950 immigrants and their descendants, a percentage that is steadily increasing due to our continued high immigration. Recall that the Census Bureau projected that over the decade of the 1990s, about half of the population growth would be accounted for by immigrants and their offspring.

Thus, over one-third of the growth in the nation's population in the period 1950–2000 is explained by post-1950 immigration—both direct and indirect. This is particularly remarkable given that part of that period included the baby boom era (1950–1964) when fertility was quite high among all groups. As we conclude this fifty-year period, it is evident that immigration has played a major role in our rapid population growth. Indeed, it is the prime reason that this country is the fastest growing industrial nation in the world. Without any immigration since 1950, the population as we approach the millennium would be 232 million rather than the expected 275 million—a truly substantial difference of 43 million in the year 2000.

Without immigration, the U.S. population would have a slightly older age structure. For example, without immigration, the elderly age group (sixty-five and over) would have increased its share of the population from 8.1 percent in 1950 to 14.0 percent in 2000. In actuality, that is with immigration, that group will increase from 8.2 to 12.6 percent of the total population. However, the total number of elderly, many of whom are beneficiaries of Social Security, would be slightly lower without immigration since 1950—32.5 million compared to almost 34.7 million with immigration. Thus, while the population may age slightly without immigration, the total number of elderly would be greater.

A similar situation holds true for the other dependent age group, children. For example, without immigration, young children under age five would make up 6.5 percent of the population in the year 2000. With immigration their share will rise to just 6.9 percent. Their numbers, however, will increase from under 15.1 million to almost 19 million. That amounts to a considerable difference in the number of future school-age children with or without immigration.

In sum, the impact of post-1950 immigration in the second half of the twentieth century has been enormous. When we consider that some 43 million persons will have been added to the 2000 population because of immigration since 1950, it becomes clear how significant immigration has been as a contributor to population growth. If immigration had stopped in 1950, today's population would be much more manageable and far less of a threat to our environment and to our quality of life in general.

IMMIGRATION AND U.S. POPULATION GROWTH: 2000–2050

Turning now to the future, our question becomes: what will be the impact of immigration for the fifty year period between 2000 and 2050? The Current

Population Report of the Bureau of the Census (prepared by a staff headed by Gregory Spencer) provides us with sophisticated and detailed projections of the United States' population beginning in 1995 and ending in 2050. (The slight difference in total population in 2000 between the two projections is attributable to the fact that the projection process actually began five years earlier.)

First, we examine the assumptions used to produce the results. As noted earlier, the total fertility rate (TFR) is assumed to be 2.055 per 1,000 women in 1995. It is expected to rise to 2.245 by 2050. Interestingly, the Bureau foresees no change in the TFR of each ethnic group, whether native-born or foreign-born. Contrary to previous projections from the Census Bureau, this study does not foresee any convergence of minority fertility toward the majority rate over the next half-century. For Non-Hispanic Whites the TFR is set at 1.826; for Blacks 2.398; for Native Americans and Others 2.114; for Asian and Pacific Islanders 1.919; for Hispanics 2.977. One might question why the rate is the same for native and foreign born, irrespective of racial background. The fact that the convergence is not assumed, however, would account for that fact, although it is not stated as such in the text.

Another question that may confuse the reader concerns the fact that although the fertility rates for each group do not change over the fifty-year period, the overall rate is expected to rise by almost 10 percent (from 2.055 to 2.245). This rise reflects what can be called "shifting shares" of the population.[7] Even if the rate remains constant for all groups, as the share of those with the higher rate (Hispanics, in this case) rises through immigration, the overall rate will be affected. Thus the almost 10 percent increase in the projected TFR is attributed solely to immigration—yet another confirmation of immigration's impact on population growth.

Life expectancy is projected to increase from 75.9 years at birth in 1995 to 82.0 in 2050. This improvement replicates that noted during the 1980s with the impact of AIDS taken into account. Again, no race-origin/sex convergence is assumed. Slight differences are noted among the racial/ethnic groups however and, again, this affects the final life expectancy in 2050. Non-Hispanic White male life expectancy in 1995 is assumed to be 73.6; for Blacks 64.5; Native American and Other 71.5; Asian and Pacific Islanders 79.6; Hispanics 74.9. These are all assumed to rise somewhat over the next fifty years. It is noteworthy that both Hispanics and Asians and Pacific Islanders have slightly higher life expectancy than do Non-Hispanic Whites.

It might be noted here that these mortality projections (as well as those from other government sources) have been criticized in some quarters as being too conservative. Clearly, there is room for improvement especially among African-Americans and improvement should be a goal of the government. However, some critics are also concerned that AIDS and increased assaults on the environment could result in lowered life expectancy. Significant changes in life expectancy can contribute to major changes in population size.

As mentioned earlier, the middle series of the Census projections assumes net immigration of 820,000 annually. Of these, 186,000 are Non-Hispanic Whites; 57,000 are Black; 350,000 are Hispanic; 226,000 are Asian; and 1,000 are Other. These proportions remain constant over the projection period. The age-sex composition of the immigrant component of population growth is consistent with the most recent information gathered by the Immigration and Naturalization Service (INS). It too remains constant.

CENSUS BUREAU ALTERNATIVE PROJECTIONS OF U.S. POPULATION 2000–2050

The Census Bureau projections also include a high-immigration model assuming that annual net immigration is 1,370,000. This has the same ethnic distribution as the middle-series assumptions. While we are convinced that 820,000 is on the low side, we will rely on that model for our analysis. However, we will also include the projected population that would result for the higher level of immigration, since that too has the same assumptions regarding fertility and mortality. Furthermore, such high levels of immigration are not impossible given the present mood of Congress and the intent of proposed legislation such as a bill currently before Congress that would afford asylee status to certain people based on a presumption of religious persecution. Thus, the three projections (no migration, and annual net levels of 820,000 and 1,370,000) all rely on the same levels of fertility and mortality and are thus comparable.

We are completely satisfied with these assumptions and feel that the future population of the United States will fall within these boundaries. Table 2 below specifies what the actual U.S. population from 2000 to 2050 would be according to these assumptions. Again, note that the Census Bureau "no immigration" projection does not lower the overall fertility rate to compensate for the absence of higher immigrant fertility and thus probably overestimates total growth from 2000 to 2050.

As we have seen, immigration has already accounted for a substantial portion of the growth of the nation's population since 1950. That is in the past and nothing can be done about it. However, there is still time to take control of our demographic future. As we approach the millennium, we must decide whether our nation can support any more people at a decent quality of life. We must determine if our environment and resources can support any more inhabitants at all.

Table 2. Census Bureau Alternative Projections, U.S. Population 1995 to 2050 (in 000s)

Year	Population with no immigration	Growth (from previous date)	Population with 820,000 Immigration[1]	Growth (from previous date)	Imm. Share of Growth[2]	(% growth)	Population with 1,370,000 Immigration[1]	Growth (from previous date)	Imm. Share of Growth[2]	(% growth)
1995	262,820	--	262,820	--	--	--	262,820	--	7,503	--
2000	269,299	6,479	274,634	11,814	5,335	-45%	276,802	13,982	8,303	-54%
2005	275,481	6,182	285,981	11,347	5,165	-46%	291,287	14,485	9,139	-57%
2010	281,499	6,018	297,716	11,735	5,717	-49%	306,444	15,157	9,817	-60%
2015	287,746	6,247	310,134	12,418	6,171	-50%	322,508	16,064	10,449	-61%
2020	293,744	5,998	322,742	12,608	6,610	-52%	338,955	16,447	11,172	-64%
2025	298,935	5,191	335,050	12,308	7,117	-58%	355,318	16,363	11,991	-68%
2030	303,106	4,171	346,899	11,849	7,678	-65%	371,480	16,162	12,825	-74%
2035	306,424	3,318	358,457	11,558	8,240	-71%	387,623	16,143	13,606	-79%
2040	309,181	2,757	369,980	11,523	8,766	-76%	403,966	16,363	14,339	-83%
2045	311,645	2,464	381,713	11,733	9,269	-79%	420,789	16,803	15,070	-85%
2050	314,085	2,440	393,391	12,218	9,778	-80%	438,299	17,510	124,214	-86%
Total	--	51,265	--	131,111	79,846	-61%		175,479		-71%

[1] Total population with annual net immigration of 820,000/1,370,000.

[2] Share of population growth attributable to direct immigration and descendants of post-1995 immigrants (and as a percentage of total growth).

We expect that the nation's population in 2000 will be approximately 275 million. By 2050, based on reasonable assumptions about fertility and mortality, it would approach 315 million—an increase of close to 45 million people over that half-century—without immigration. Although, many experts have concluded that we are already overpopulated,8 population momentum from our past growth dictates that we will be adding some 45 million more people in the near future even if we immediately put an end to immigration.

Now, let's examine the added impact if immigration continues beyond 2000. If immigration remains at current levels, the nation's population would approach 394 million by 2050—that's close to 75 million more than if immigration came to a halt around the turn of the century. Thus, of the total growth between 2000 and 2050, 62.5 percent would be accounted for by post-2000 net immigration of 820,000 annually. By 2050, over one in five inhabitants of the United States would be post-2000 immigrants or their descendants.

If we look at the higher series from the Census Bureau, the numbers become even more startling. Should immigration rise to 1.37 million per year (a possible scenario), the nation would grow by more than 175 million between 2000 and 2050. By the end of that period, our population would reach 438 million and still be growing rapidly. Post-2000 immigration would account for 71 percent of this enormous growth. In actuality, the immigration total (direct and indirect) would be somewhat higher since a certain number are included in 2000 that would still be alive in 2050.

The Census Bureau also prepared a low-immigration series assuming net immigration of 300 thousand per year (with the same levels of fertility and mortality as in the other models). Even under such a low assumption about future net immigration, the population would soar from 274 million in 2000 to 326 million in 2025 and 368 million in 2050. When we stop and consider the difference between 315 million (without immigration) in 2050 and either 394 million or 438 million (with different levels of immigration), it becomes clear that it is time to put severe limits on immigration, if not declare a moratorium.

CONCLUSION

To summarize briefly, during the fifty years between 1950 and 2000, over one-third of our population growth will come from net immigration; between 2000 and 2050, we anticipate, very conservatively, that close to two-thirds of our population growth will be attributable to immigration (direct and indirect) even if levels are limited to 800,000 per year (below current levels). The conclusion is obvious: immigration is far and away the chief contributor to population growth in the United States.

NOTES:

1. Gibson Campbell. 1992. "The Contribution of Immigration to the Growth and Ethnic Diversity of the American Population," (Revised version of a paper presented at the Autumn General Meeting of the American Philosophical Society, Philadelphia, Pennsylvania, Nov. 7–8,1991), *Proceedings of the American Philosophical Society*, Vol. 136, No. 2, pp.157–175.
2. Gibson, Campbell. 1975. "The Contribution of Immigration to United States Population Growth: 1790–1970," *International Migration Review*, Vol. 9, No. 2 (Summer), pp. 157–177.
3. Federation for American Immigration Reform. 1998. "Census Bureau Spotlights Explosive Growth of Immigrant Population," *Immigration Report*, Vol. 18, No. 4, May 1998.
4. Day, Jennifer Cheeseman. 1996. "Population Projections of the United States by Age, Sex, Race, and Hispanic Origin: 1995 to 2050," U.S.

Bureau of the Census, *Current Population Reports*, P25-1130, U.S. Government Printing Office, Washington, DC.

5. Day.
6. Improvements in life expectancy can also seriously affect future population size. For example, demographers Samuel Preston and Kevin White recently calculated what the population of the United States would have been in 1995 if the mortality rates at the turn of the twentieth century had not changed. They concluded that there would be about half as many Americans as in today's population, 139 million instead of 276 million. Half of the missing people would not have been born because their parents would not have survived to reproductive age. And the other half would have been born but would have died young. Kevin M. White and Samuel H. Preston, "How many Americans are alive because of twentieth-century improvements in mortality?," *Population and Development Review*, Vol. 22, No. 3, September 1996.
7. For a detailed explanation of this concept, see L. Bouvier, "Shifting Shares and Increasing Fertility," *Population and Environment*, Summer 1991.
8. For a detailed discussion, see Lindsey Grant, *Juggernaut*, Seven Locks Press, 1998.

SOCIAL SECURITY: THE PONZI PATH TO DYSTOPIA

David Simcox

October 1998

"Life is a ponzi scheme," according to pronatalist author and commentator Ben Wattenberg. Rarely has an aphorism so aptly expressed the American faith that growth is the solution to all problems, including problems brought on by growth itself.[1] Wattenberg is one of a number of influential Americans who believe that as the baby boomers retire after 2010 the solvency of the Social Security system requires another round of robust population growth. However, since today's Americans are having smaller families, vast numbers of immigrant workers and their dependents would be needed to join America's labor force between now and 2050 in order to pay for the retirement of the one in six Americans who will be sixty-five or older by 2020, reaching one in five by 2040.

PONZI'S REVENGE: THE POPULATION GROWTH TREADMILL

Population growth only postpones the day of reckoning. According to the Census Bureau's 1992 most likely "medium" projection, there is the troubling prospect of nearly 400 million Americans by mid-century. By even the most conservative projections, trying to populate our way out of Social Security's present actuarial[2] dilemma would further darken the nation's already problematic environmental and demographic future.

There is no denying that Social Security's viability requires some tough decisions well before 2012, when outlays are expected to begin exceeding cash revenues. Without remedies, the trust fund will be depleted by as early as 2032, and revenues will fund only 70 to 77 percent of benefits paid.[3]

But adding scores of millions of new workers would at best postpone—but not solve—Social Security's problem of too few wage earners supporting too many retirees. Such an expansion, even just enough to maintain a barely favorable actuarial balance of workers and retirees, would have to add at least 200 million more U.S. residents by 2050 to the nearly 400 million now projected. Consider the projections of the U.S. population's age distribution to 2050, based on Census data in Table 1 on the next page.

The graying of America is striking in these projections. The numbers sixty-five and over rise steadily from one in eight in 2000 to more than one in five by 2040, before beginning to recede. The ratio of working age residents to those sixty-five and over falls from 4.8 to one in 2000 to 2.7 to one in 2040.

The sixty-five and over population balloons after 2010 as the baby boomers born between 1946 and 1968 reach sixty-five between 2011 and 2033 and the life expectancy of the post-sixty-five population steadily advances. An additional drain on Social Security has been the thirty-four-fold increase since 1956 in those sixty-two to sixty-five who opt for early retirement.

Table 1. U.S. population projections by age, in millions, 2000–2050

YEAR	Total Population	Under 18	18–64	% 18–64	65+	% 65	Ratio 18–64 to 65+
2000	276.24	71.79	169.13	61.20%	35.32	12.80%	4.8 to 1
2010	300.43	73.62	186.71	62.10%	40.11	13.30%	4.6 to 1
2020	325.94	77.78	194.8	59.80%	53.35	16.40%	3.6 to 1
2030	350	83.04	196.78	56.20%	70.17	20.00%	2.8 to 1
2040	371.5	86.8	207.69	55.90%	77.01	20.70%	2.7 to 1
2050	392.03	91.75	220.17	56.20%	80.11	20.4%	2.7 to 1

Source: U.S. Bureau of the Census, 1992 Projections

A basic lesson here for examining our options is that rapid population growth—such as the birth of some 88 million baby boomers between 1946 and 1968—can furnish workers whose payroll taxes bolster retirement systems; but those same workers inevitably age and ultimately have massive claims of their own on those same systems, with expectations of returns that often exceed actuarial realities. One generation's boon for retirement resources is a later generation's drain on those resources—and more.

Immigrants are no exception. In 1994, 11.7 percent of immigrants were sixty-five or over (virtually the same as the native-born population), and they will supply a relatively larger cohort of persons reaching sixty-five over the next nineteen years than will the native population: 22.2 percent to 19.1 percent.

Trading ephemeral actuarial gains for lasting population liabilities. Since U.S. fertility has been under replacement level for the last twenty-five years, the kind of population growth necessary to infuse the Social Security system with more tax paying workers can realistically only come from radically increasing already high immigration. Under existing projections, post-1992 immigrants and their progeny will account for 74 million, or 64 percent, of the nation's projected population gain of 115.8 million between 2000 and 2050.[4] What if the country decided to follow the advice of the high immigration advocates? What would happen if the United States chose to admit enough immigrants who, with their U.S.-born progeny, would prevent the impending 43 percent drop in the ratio between working age persons (eighteen to sixty-four) and those sixty-five and over by 2040? The effects on population size in the next century would be catastrophic.

The following projection in Table 2 takes as a more conservative premise the maintenance of a minimum ratio of four working age persons (eighteen to sixty-five) to each person sixty-five and up. In this scenario, the age progression over time of the added immigrant population becomes a population growth factor. Rising numbers of added post-2000 immigrants will reach sixty-five in the ensuing four decades, requiring the infusion of four times their numbers of additional working-age persons to maintain the four to one ratio. Instead of reaching 2050 with 80.11 million persons sixty-five and over (the 1992 projection), the U.S. under this projection would have nearly 86 million seniors.

To maintain the four to one ratio of working-age to retirement-age persons in 2050, an additional 122 million persons age eighteen to sixty-four would

Table 2. Projections to 2050 of additional immigrants and descendants needed to maintain the 2000 ratio of working age to 65+ populations, (Figures in millions, except years and percents)

YEAR	65+ Population Projected	Added 18-64 Pop. Needed to Keep 4:1 Ratio	Dependants of Added Population	Added Pop. 65+ (Percentage)	Total US Pop. Projected for 4-1 ratio
2000	35.32	None	None	None	276.24
2010	40.11	None	None	None (3.2%)	300.43
2020	53.35	18.6	12.5	1.28 (4.1%)	357.03
2030	70.96	68.46	53.12	6.45 (5.3%)	502.66
2040	81.17	29.93	23.28	3.20 (6.0%)	577.38
2050	85.77	5.19	4.04	.0581 (6.3%)	607.14
2000-2050	--	122.18	92.94	--	--

Source: (1) 65+ population projections from Census Bureau P25-1092 of October 1992: Population projections of the U.S. by age, sex, race and Hispanic origin; (2) Projections of added 65+ population based on Census projections of age distribution under high-immigration, high-fertility scenario, adjusted decennially by the weighted averages of the projected growth rate of Hispanic and Asian populations 65 and up between 2000 to 2050 in P25-1092. (3) "Added Pop. 65+ (Percentage)" refers to the number of 65+ immigrants as a percentage of the entire cohort of added 18-64 workers and dependents added in the particular decade.

have been required by mid-century from either immigration or higher fertility. They would have been accompanied by another 93 million individuals who would have spent at least some period here in dependency status, based on age distribution rates of immigrants in the Census's 1992 high-fertility, high-immigration projection.

While a smaller percentage of the projected dependent population would be sixty-five or more than in the currently projected population, after 2050 the growth of the sixty-five and over population would accelerate rapidly as huge added cohorts of 2030 and 2040 began to reach retirement age, requiring another round of expansion of the working-age population to maintain the actuarially-desirable ratio. Moreover the presumed advantage of a smaller sixty-five and over cohort in the rapid growth scenario would be negated by the higher percentage that would be in the seven and below segment. The percentage of dependents in 2050 in the 1992 projections and the four to one growth projections would be the same.

The United States as "India West." A truly frightening prospect is that the United States would have boosted its population to well over 600 million in just five decades. Growth at that pace would produce severe social strains. The U.S. population would have to grow by almost 270 million—88 percent—in the three decades beginning in 2010. The four to one projection would require average annual growth of 3.0 percent between 2010 and 2040.

This growth, achieved mainly through high immigration and to a much lesser extent natural increase, would match Africa's current confounding growth rate. Immigration gateway cities, already coping with high population growth rates, such as greater Los Angeles, Phoenix, Houston, South Florida, Las

Vegas, Seattle, New York's New Jersey suburbs, and Texas border cities could expect unmanageable growth.

The nature and quality of life in the United States, and the country's ability to provide for the material, service and infrastructural needs of its residents, not to mention their retirement benefits, would be sharply curtailed. Well before reaching 600 million the country would begin to suffer the strictures imposed by diminished arable land and fresh water per capita, pollution and energy shortages, and social and political tensions mounting under the sheer weight of numbers and dizzying demographic change.

ADDITIONAL WORKERS NEGATED BY LOW PRODUCTIVITY AND OTHER NET COSTS

Most immigrants lack sufficient education or job skills to really boost the Social Security trust fund. Population growth advocates tend to visualize sheer numbers of workers as the solution rather than their ability to contribute. Proposals for populating our way to solvent retirement systems generally rest on the assumption that the additional foreign workers will be productive enough to make a net contribution, after taking into account the offsetting public service costs. The high poverty and unemployment rates and low educational attainment among a significant share of immigrants over the past two decades makes such assumptions a risky premise for policy.

One in three immigrants over twenty-five arriving since 1990 is a high school drop-out, compared to one in six natives. Yearly median income of all immigrants in 1996 was 17 percent lower than natives' median and 39 percent lower for immigrants who arrived after 1989. Their 1996 unemployment rate, at 7.7 percent, was nearly 35 percent higher (more than double for recent immigrants), while the poverty rate for recent immigrants was 33 percent higher and cash welfare assistance rates were 35 percent higher.[5] The Rand Corporation found in a 1996 study of the economic progress of immigrants that:

> . . . a significant number of immigrants in California and the United States currently have very low wages, and the evidence suggests that these wages will not improve substantially throughout their working lives. This evidence, combined with the fact that more recent immigrants have had lower (age-adjusted) wages relative to earlier immigrants, has substantial ramifications for public-service usage and tax revenues into the future.[6]

Increasing today's immigration of 1.3 million yearly by a factor of five or six over three decades—itself a migration of cataclysmic dimensions—would require the unselective recruitment of masses of unskilled foreign workers, whose drain on the general public treasury would exceed their contribution to the Social Security system.[7] Indeed, a doubling of the immigrant labor force by 2040 would require an additional capital investment of over $21 trillion (in 1994 dollars) for the equipment and training necessary to insure adequate productivity.[8]

"Instant adults" still come with costs. Immigration expansionists argue that the United States profits from immigrants because they are "instant adults," arriving already productive, with the costs of raising and training them through childhood borne elsewhere. Too good to be true? Yes, if you consider the stiff costs of all the training necessary to boost the productivity of the less-skilled new arrivals and the heavy cost of public education for the masses of U.S.-born children of high-fertility immigrants.

Table 3. Comparison of total population and numbers and percentages of population 65 and up under current projections and with population increase sufficient to maintain a 4 to 1 ratio between the sub-populations 18–64 and 65 and up. (Numbers except percentages are in millions.)

	Current				With 4 to 1 Ratio		
YEAR	Total US Pop	Number 65+	Percent 65+		Total US Pop	Number 65+	Percent 65+
2000	276.24	35.32	12.80%		276.24	35.32	12.80%
2010	300.43	40.11	13.30%		300.43	40.11	13.20%
2020	325.94	53.35	16.40%		325.94	53.35	15.00%
2030	350	70.17	20.00%		350	70.96	14.10%
2040	371.5	77.01	20.70%		371.5	81.17	14.10%
2050	392.03	80.11	20.40%		392.03	85.77	14.10%

Source: Tables 1 and 2

Even the most-skilled immigrants incur significant education costs to the United States. Foreign graduate students are 23 percent more likely than their U.S. citizen counterparts to get federal or university assistance. Three-quarters of the cost of training a foreign-born engineer from kindergarten to a doctorate is paid by the United States.[9] Some 85 to 90 percent of the funding used to finance doctoral degrees of foreign students comes from U.S. sources. In addition, partial overseas funding in the first year of study is often replaced with full U.S. funding in subsequent years.[10]

Also often overlooked in the calculation is the progressive nature of Social Security: those whose incomes have been in the lowest 20 percent receive benefits at 2.7 times the return on wages received by the highest earners. If the payout remains progressive, future payout to many immigrant workers will remain steeply disproportionate to their actual contributions.

Another myth of cost-free immigration. As current experience shows, a sizable fraction of immigrant workers will enter the U.S. labor market too late in their careers, or be unemployed or absent from the United States too often to earn enough Social Security credits. Some economists and actuaries have argued that this is a gain for the system, since the fund gains contributions with no corresponding liabilities.

At least two considerations cast doubt on that presumed gain. One, the major segment of the immigrant population that has low skills are far more likely to be in jobs in the informal economy where evasion of Social Security taxes is up to four times more likely than in the general economy.[11] Second, whatever gains from the added Social Security contributions paid are often more than offset by social assistance to those immigrants and their dependents. Under increasingly liberal legal interpretations, aging immigrants with insufficient work years to get benefits receive federal Supplemental Security Income (SSI) benefits, triggering in turn their eligibility for Medicaid and other social assistance programs.

Supplemental Security Income (SSI) as an immigrant retirement program. The drain on SSI has also been increased by the preferential immigration of aging parents of foreign-born U.S. citizens—now at about 600,000 per decade. The influx of parents of citizens should rise sharply in the next five years in the wake of a tripling of the number of new naturalizations since 1995. Arguments that immigrants can enrich aging Americans contrast glaringly with clear indications that immigrants now are increasingly unable or unwilling to provide for their own elderly here.[12]

Immigrants sixty-five and up are five times more likely to receive SSI than the native-born, and the average amount of aid per recipient is 50 percent higher. The percentage of immigrants sixty-five and up receiving food stamps and Medicaid in 1996 was, respectively, 65 percent and 160 percent higher than for the comparable native-born population. The total 1996 federal and state costs for SSI payments, food stamps and Medicaid for immigrants sixty-five and over was $4.68 billion. That amount is equivalent to the total 1996 Social Security contributions of the 3.13 million covered workers.[13]

While Congress in 1996 legislated restrictions on SSI and other benefits for elderly immigrants, the trend since then has been for Congress and state governments to restore the cuts or replace them with alternative aid programs (with a few exceptions), thus significantly weakening their effect and reducing any savings to taxpayers. Legislation passed in 1996 to ensure the financial responsibility of sponsors of elderly immigrants, has a means test so weak—an annual family income of less than $21,000—that even some public assistance clients can pass it.

1992 GOODMAN ROBBINS STUDY

Another study of the long-term feasibility of expanding immigration to keep Social Security solvent reveals even bleaker demographic and actuarial outcomes than this assessment.

John Goodman and Aldona Robbins of the National Center for Policy Analysis in a 1992 study projecting Social Security's financial condition to 2070 found the following under their assumptions:

- Some 57 million new immigrant workers would be needed by 2070 to pay retirement benefits (excluding Medicare) without increasing payroll tax rates. (Under their pessimistic assumption, 120 million immigrant workers would be needed.)
- If immigrant workers were allowed to bring their families, and if they had children at the current rate, immigrants and their children would outnumber the native born by 2050.
- If the productivity of the immigrant workers is assumed to be only half that of native workers, the United States would need to have taken in about 700 million immigrant workers by 2070, about six immigrants for each native entering the labor force in that period.
- Such a huge expansion of the labor force would require two to four times as much capital as the U.S. would otherwise have during that period to keep overall productivity from falling.

In its final report in 1997, the U.S. Commission on Immigration Reform recommended that the 1996 restrictions on welfare for legal immigrants be reversed. The courts, which have refused to uphold earlier obligations on sponsors, cannot be counted on to support the new requirements. Furthermore, Congress and the administration opened the year 1998 with new proposals to rescind the ban on food stamps for immigrants.

AN AGING POPULATION—GATEWAY TO A SUSTAINABLE POPULATION

The reality of an aging America is difficult to accept in a youth-worshiping society steeped in a creed of boundless growth. Yet the nation must accept that reality and capitalize on its many strengths if it is to attain zero population growth followed by a gradual retreat of the U.S. population toward a level sustainable over the long term.

Demographic quick fixes can postpone confronting this problem, not solve it, and only at an exorbitant cost in overpopulation, resource depletion and environmental destruction. Apparently the public itself suspects this seductive but risky solution. None of the past study commissions on Social Security or proposed congressional reforms have seriously entertained massive immigration or pronatalist efforts as a way out.

Aging America an opportunity to begin the transition to sustainability. All is not bleak for Social Security if we reconcile ourselves to the fact that the aging of America is in the long-term interest of a smaller American population. Until now our projections have dealt with two unpromising scenarios. The first, growth as now projected with high immigration, will bring the national population to nearly 400 million at mid-century. The second, super-growth fueled by hyper-immigration and high fertility (in order to have a presumably favorable balance between working age and elderly), would result in a total U.S. population of over 600 million by 2050.

A third scenario, low fertility and zero-net immigration, has the advantage of mirroring what the American people in the real world have been voting for with three decades of low fertility and solid, consistent public-opinion support for lower immigration. A realistic low-fertility option prepared by population specialist Lindsey Grant would have U.S. fertility, now at replacement level, decline to 1.7 by 2025 and to 1.5 by 2050, roughly the fertility of Europe in 1996. Immigration would be reduced to 200,000 a year by 2000.[14] Under this scenario, the sixty-five and up age group would constitute 24.9 percent of the population in 2050, a higher share than in either the current or high-growth scenarios, but considerably lower than either alternative in absolute numbers of those sixty-five and over with their share headed steadily downward.

Most important from the stand-point of future sustainability, the U.S. population in 2050 would be more than 40 percent lower than where our present demographic behavior is taking us, and 140 percent less than the scenario maintaining a four to one ratio between working age and retirement age residents. The United States would be on the way to a smaller and more environmentally sound population.

SOLVENCY AND SUSTAINABILITY: HOW TO GET THERE

Making Social Security solvent will demand some combination of measures to increase contributions to the fund, reduce benefits, or lower the number of prospective claimants. The last reforms in 1983 featured all but the third of these approaches: they accelerated increases in payroll tax rates, prospectively raised the retirement age from sixty-five to sixty-seven, and taxed the benefits of high income retirees.

Similar steps must be considered in framing the urgently needed reforms including lower cost-of-living adjustments, more taxes on benefits, means testing, delay of full retirement until seventy or later, investment of some of the trust fund in the stock market, and outside sources of revenue to help the Social Security trust fund through the transition to a smaller population.

Reforming Social Security and ending pronatalist incentives. Most favorable would be actuarially sound reforms to Social Security that would have the added effect of discouraging population growth. They would involve capturing for elderly Americans some of the savings from public assistance costs foregone or additional taxes collected that would come with lower immigration and fertility. Examples of reforms with the dual effect of raising revenues and reducing claims while discouraging population growth would include:

- New incentives to encourage more frequent and longer labor force participation of women. This would have both positive actuarial and antinatalist effects.
- Elimination of pronatalist features from the tax code and other legislation. Examples would be repeal of the recently enacted tax credits for children, dropping increases in the Earned Income Tax Credits for the second child, phasing out the Earned Income Tax Credit for immigrants, limiting the benefits of the Family Leave Act for maternity to one birth only.
- Immediate reduction of immigration to less than 200,000 a year as a way of reducing claims on the Social Security fund between 2030 and 2050, its period of greatest stress. Prospective immigrants born between 1965 and 1985 will reach sixty-five in that period. Many of them have not yet settled here.
- More scrupulous selection of the immigrants we do permit in to ensure those admitted are self-sufficient and productive.
- Further restrict immigration of persons fifty or over by adding special conditions for their sponsors such as bonding, special pre-paid insurance or annuities, or special immigration fees.
- An end to evasion of Social Security and other payroll and income taxes in the informal economy: this would increase revenues, eliminate the wage-depressing effects of informal firms on firms in compliance, and neutralize a major magnet for immigration.
- Charge a user fee to employers who sponsor and employ foreign workers, with the proceeds used to retrain and relocate U.S. citizen workers over 55.
- Denial of retirement credits for Social Security contributions of persons ineligible to work in the United States.

Above all, whatever course is taken, the nation's growing elderly population must be recognized as a resource in the transition to a smaller population—not a liability. The changing nature of both work and how the sixty-five and over population sees itself argue for new incentives for the aging to shun early retirement, to maintain and enhance their skills and to continue as earners and contributors beyond presumed biological and workplace limits that are long outdated.

No compulsion is needed; American seniors want to work, with 40 percent of those in retirement telling pollsters they would rather be working. The nation will gain from a workforce that is no less productive, but more stable and reliable and less prone to accidents, absenteeism and drug use.[15]

Rather than a threat to the Social Security system, the aging of the baby-boom generation offers the opportunity to begin the necessary transition to negative population growth and a smaller—and more sustainable—U.S. population. For the Social Security trust fund there is the crucial opportunity to restore its long-term financial viability by avoiding the temporary population growth quick-fix achieved by boosting the number of new workers.

The choice is ours. Continue on the treadmill of high immigration and population growth—with all the costs and perils that entails—while once again postponing real solutions for the next generation. Or, take advantage of the assets presented by the aging of America, adopt the structural reforms necessary to restore the long-term viability of the Social Security system, and begin the transition to a smaller, more sustainable America.

NOTES:

1. Ben J. Wattenberg. "The Easy Solution to the Social Security Crisis." *New York Times Magazine*, June 27, 1997.
2. Actuarial: the use of mathematical probabilities, statistical data, and accompanying assumptions to define, analyze, and project the financial sustainability, viability or risk of complex business or social obligations such as insurance or pension programs.
3. General Accounting Office: *Retirement Income: Implications of Demographic Trends for Social Security and Pension Reform*—GAO/HEHS-97-81, Washington, July, 1997.
4. The U.S. Bureau of the Census: *Population Profile of the United States*, 1995 (CPR P23-189). Washington, July 1995. pp. 9.
5. Bureau of the Census. *The Foreign Born Population: 1996*, CPR P20-494; Washington, DC. 1997.
6. Robert F. Schoeni, Kevin McCarthy and George Vernez. *The Mixed Economic Progress of Immigrants.* RAND: Center for Research on Immigration Policy, Santa Monica, 1996. pp. 67.
7. For example, Rice University economist Dr. Donald Huddle calculates that under the current Old-Age and Survivors Insurance (OASI) system immigrants caused a present value OASI deficit of $23.16 billion per year in 1994 ("Immigration and the Solvency of the Social Security System," American Immigration Control, January 1998). Likewise, Huddle in "The Net Costs of Immigration: The Facts, The Trends, and The Critics" (Carrying Capacity Network, 1996), lists the national net-deficit cost of immigration at over $65 billion in 1995.
8. Estimate is based on private and government investment per worker per year in 1994 (about $10,000) multiplied by the number of additional worker/years accumulated in the added eighteen to sixty-four population to 2050. A flat labor-force participation rate of 60 percent in the eighteen to sixty-four population is assumed.
9. David North. *Soothing the Establishment: The Impact of Foreign Born Scientists and Engineers on America.* Landover, MD: University Press of America, 1996.
10. David North. "The U.S. Pays: A Study of the Funding of Foreign-Born PhD Candidates in Science and Engineering."
11. U.S. Department of Labor. *Characteristics and Behavior of the Legalized Population Five Years Following Legalization.* May, 1996. pp. 46–48.
12. Roy Beck. *Recharting America's Future.* Petoskey, MI: Social Contract Press, 1994. p.89
13. Ways and Means Committee, House of Representatives: *1996 Green Book*, Washington: GPO, Nov. 4, 1996; General Accounting Office: *Supplemental Security Income: Growth and Changes in Recipient Population Call for Reexamining Program* (GAO/HEHS-95-137). Washington, 1995; San Francisco Chronicle, February 12, 1997.
14. Leon Bouvier and Lindsey Grant. *How Many Americans? Population, Immigration and the Environment.* San Francisco: Sierra Club Books, 1994. pp.115–122.
15. Ken Dychtwald. *Age Wave: The Challenges and Opportunities of an Aging America.* Los Angeles: Jeremy P. Tarcher, Inc., 1992. pp. 40–43,174–183.

MALTHUS: MORE RELEVANT THAN EVER

William R. Catton, Jr.

August 1998

MALTHUS, DARWIN, AND POPULATION COMPETITION

In 1798, Thomas Robert Malthus tried to inform people that a human population, like a population of any other species, had the potential to increase exponentially were it not limited by finite support from its resource base. He warned us that growth of the number of human consumers and their demands will always threaten to outrun the growth of sustenance. When Charles Darwin read Malthus, he recognized more fully than most other readers that the Malthusian principle applied to all species. And Darwin saw how reproduction beyond replacement can foster a universal competitive relationship among a population's members, as well as how expansion by a population of one species may be at the expense of populations of other species.

Others were not so perceptive. When I was in high school, the textbook used in my biology class listed "Over-production of individuals" first among "the chief factors assigned by Darwin to account for the development of new species from common ancestry through natural selection" (Moon and Man, 1933:457), but it did not cite Malthus nor discuss his concerns about population pressure. That neglect was typical because, for a while, "it was argued widely that developments had disproved Malthus, that the problem was no longer man's propensity to reproduce more rapidly than his sustenance, but his unwillingness to reproduce adequately in an industrial and urban setting" (Taeuber, 1964:120).

MALTHUS IN THE AGE OF EXUBERANCE

Most of us can remember learning in school to dismiss Malthus as "too pessimistic." Technological progress and the economic growth resulting therefrom, we learned to assume, can always provide the essential consumables (or substitutes) that have permitted exuberant population growth. One of my college textbooks put it this way: "For conditions as they existed in 1798, Malthus was reasonably sound in his doctrines; but scientific and technological changes in the interval since his day have made Malthusian principles, in large part, an intellectual curiosity in our era" (Barnes, 1948:51).

In graduate school one of my textbooks acknowledged that "Man's tendency to multiply up to the maximum carrying capacity of the land is superficially evident in many parts of the world" (Hawley, 1950:150–151). Its eminent author, who has been called the "dean" of American human ecologists, conceded the likelihood that most lands at most historic times "have been populated to capacity in view of the particular modes of life of their occupants" but insisted (pp. 160ff) changes in such modes of life had made "the Malthusian interpretation of population problems decreasingly useful." The article about

Malthus in the International Encyclopedia of the Social Sciences called his theory of population "a perfect example of metaphysics masquerading as science" (Blaug, 1968:551).

REASSESSING MALTHUS INAPPROPRIATELY

When co-authoring an introductory sociology text my colleagues and I began to dissent from these disparaging evaluations of Malthus, but for not quite the right reasons (Lundberg et al., 1968:682): "Despite his inadequate data," we said Malthus "was nevertheless correct in arguing that the food supply fixes an upper limit beyond which the population cannot go at any given time." And we gave him credit for having taken into account "certain social and psychological factors, such as celibacy and moral restraint, which might keep population below that theoretical limit, and in doing this he focused attention," we supposed, "on factors which were frequently overlooked at the time."

Looking back, I now see both of those sentences of ours as inaccurate or misleading. His essay did not fully succeed in directing most people's attention to all the relevant factors, i.e., those checks that would prevent a human population from expanding to its full potential. Further, and more importantly, Malthus's confidence that no population could overshoot carrying capacity, but would only press miserably against the limit, precluded foreseeing the prodigality-based affluence we achieved by running up carrying capacity deficits that would be disastrous later on.

OVERSHOOTING CARRYING CAPACITY DRAWING DOWN RESOURCES FROM THE FUTURE

Contrary to our partial endorsement, (1) Food is not the only component of "sustenance" for modern human living; industrialized human societies rely on continuing flows of many other resources, and a cessation of supply of any essential commodity can be devastating. (2) By drawing down "savings accounts" (i.e., using resources faster than their rates of renewal), populations can (and do) temporarily exceed carrying capacity. When the stockpile runs out, the once-thriving population finds itself in dire straits.

MISUNDERSTANDING CHECKS AND BALANCES

With respect to our second appraisal sentence, although Malthus meant to focus attention on factors that check population growth, the effort didn't always succeed. Readers' attention seems to have persistently strayed back to the notion that Malthus believed populations would inevitably doom themselves to starvation by growing exponentially, so populations that burgeoned and prospered have been seen as supposed refutations of Malthus.

What most of us just didn't see was that a relatively short feedback loop was assumed by Malthus because of his eighteenth century perspective on technology. He was not mistaken in attributing exponential growth potential to all populations, nor was he mistaken in recognizing the unlikelihood that required resource supplies would grow apace. He did err in supposing population could never grow significantly beyond a key resource limit. Populations can, and often do exceed carrying capacity—and come to grief only after a delay. Malthus was writing not only before there was a developed science of ecology but also before there were full-blown industrial societies making prodigal use of fossil energy and other non-renewable resources.

DELAYED FEEDBACK FROM THE ENVIRONMENT

Human over-reproduction may be curbed by its ultimate adverse consequences much less promptly than Malthus assumed, unlike what happens to animals with much shorter maturation times and without technology. Two facts make the feedback loop dangerously longer for us than for most nonhuman species. First, humans have an unusually long period of maturation compared to other species. The lag between birth and the age of maximum resource consumption hardly mattered in 1798. Then as now, people's offspring made small resource demands as infants, and in 1798 their adult demands exceeded those of their infancy by a ratio not much greater than the adult-to-infant resource demand ratio for other animal species (which grow to maturity in only a year or so). Second, a mere eight human generations after Malthus, today's technology and our colossal reliance as adults on exosomatic energy sources (Cottrell, 1955; Catton, 1980; Price, 1995) have enormously magnified that ratio, putting it too far out of adjustment with ecosystem processes that supplied the modest demands of our ancestors.

So continuing to suppose the world can afford all the precious progeny we may produce leads now to serious problems. Babies grow up. In an industrial society, as adults they expect to live lifestyles that involve taking from the environment enormous per capita resource withdrawals and dumping into it vast amounts of life's toxic by-products.

It was no fault of Malthus that in 1798 he did not foresee this magnification. Even today, parents seldom if ever base their decisions about sexual activity on calculations of the lifetime resource demands and environmental impacts of each prospective child that may result. Our affluence, technology, and extraordinary period of maturation combine to obscure and delay but do not avert negative feedback from the environment.

CRITICISM IGNORES HUMAN CAPACITY FOR OVERSHOOT

Malthus was not wrong in the ways commonly supposed. From his eighteenth century perspective he simply had no basis for seeing the human ability to "overshoot" carrying capacity. It was inconceivable to Malthus that human societies could, by taking advantage of favorable conditions (new technology, abundant fossil fuels), temporarily increase human numbers and appetites above the long-term capacity of environments to provide needed resources and services. But it is inexcusable today not to recognize the way populations can sometimes overshoot sustainable carrying capacity and what happens to them after they have done it.

Human economic growth and technology have only created the appearance that Malthus was wrong (in the way we used to learn in school). What our technological advances have actually done was to allow human loads to grow precariously beyond the earth's long-term carrying capacity by drawing down the planet's stocks of key resources accumulated over 4 billion years of evolution.

COMPETITION AND OVERSHOOT

HUMAN POPULATION GROWTH AND INTER-SPECIES COMPETITION

Nearly everyone (but not Darwin) ignored crucial parts of the Malthus message. Darwin (1859:63) stands out for understanding Malthus correctly. Just after those two famous sentences about geometric increase of population versus arithmetic increase of food, Malthus ([1798] 1976:20) had said, "Necessity, that imperious all pervading law of nature, restrains them [all species] within the prescribed bounds. The race of plants and the race of animals shrink under this great restrictive law. And the race of man cannot, by any efforts of reason, escape from it. Among plants and animals its effects are waste of seed, sickness, and premature death. Among mankind, misery and vice."

In the third chapter of On the Origin of Species, Darwin (1859:60–79) spelled out how checks on the growth of any one species population are exerted by populations of other species associated with it in the web of life. Because every population is part of what we have since learned to call an ecosystem, when a particular species is "fortunate" enough to expand its numbers phenomenally, catastrophic reduction of other species populations must result. "We suck our sustenance from the rest of nature . . . reducing its bounty as ours grows" (Leakey and Lewin, 1995:233). But the "prosperity" of an irrupting population is fatefully precarious, as its own future is imperiled by nature's disrupted balance.

ENVIRONMENTAL FEEDBACK: MASS EXTINCTION POSES A MAJOR THREAT

We have trebled the human load upon this planet in my lifetime by using the planet unsustainably and this has caused a new era of extinction. According to a recent survey, a majority of American biologists regard the mass extinction of plant and animal species now resulting from human domination of the earth as a grave threat to humans in the next century (Warrick, 1998). We live in a world losing biodiversity at an unprecedented rate (Koopowitz and Kaye, 1983; Wilson, 1992:215ff; Tuxill, 1998). It is high time to see that this consequence was implicit in the 1798 essay by Malthus.

Mankind is not only depleting essential mineral stocks. We are also diminishing the plant and animal resources available to future human generations, and destroying biological buffers against the effects of global climate change (Suplee, 1998). We are stealing from the human future. Had the "moral restraint" of our parents and grandparents been enhanced by understanding Malthus as cogently as Darwin did, a less ominous future might have been their legacy to us (and ours to our descendants).

NOTES:

1. Barnes, Harry Elmer. 1948. "Social Thought in Early Modern Times." pp. 29–78 in Harry Elmer Barnes (ed.), *An Introduction to the History of Sociology*. Chicago: University of Chicago Press.
2. Blaug, Mark. 1968. "Malthus, Thomas Robert." pp. 549–552 in vol. 9, David L. Sills (ed.), *International Encyclopedia of the Social Sciences*. New York: The Macmillan Co. & The Free Press.
3. Catton, William R., Jr. 1980. *Overshoot: The Ecological Basis of Revolutionary Change*. Urbana: University of Illinois Press.
4. Cottrell, Fred. 1955. *Energy and Society*. New York: McGraw-Hill.
5. Darwin, Charles. 1859. *On the Origin of Species By Means of Natural Selection*. London: John Murray.
6. Hawley, Amos H. 1950. *Human Ecology: A Theory of Community Structure*. New York: The Ronald Press Company.
7. Koopowitz, Harold, and Hilary Kaye. 1983. *Plant Extinction: A Global Crisis*. Washington, DC: Stone Wall Press, Inc.
8. Leakey, Richard, and Roger Lewin. 1995. *The Sixth Extinction: Patterns of Life and the Future of Humankind*. New York: Anchor Books Doubleday.
9. Lundberg, George A., Clarence C. Schrag, Otto N. Larsen, and William R. Catton, Jr. 1968. *Sociology* (Fourth edition). New York: Harper & Row, Publishers.
10. Malthus, Thomas Robert. 1798. *An Essay on the Principle of Population*. pp. 15–130 in Philip Appleman (ed.), *An Essay on the Principle of Population: Text Sources and Background Criticism*. New York: W. W. Norton & Company, Inc. 1976.

11. Moon, Truman J., and Paul B. Mann. 1933. *Biology for Beginners*. New York: Henry Holt and Company Price, David. 1995. "Energy and Human Evolution." *Population and Environment: A Journal of Interdisciplinary Studies*. 16 (March):301–319.
12. Suplee, Curt. 1998. "1 in 8 Plants in Global Study Threatened: 20-Year Project Warns of Major Diversity Loss." The *Washington Post*, April 8, p.A01.
13. Taeuber, Irene B. 1964. "Population and Society." pp.83–126 in Robert E. L. Faris (ed.), *Handbook of Modern Sociology*. Chicago: Rand McNally & Company.
14. Tuxill, John. 1998. *Losing Strands in the Web of Life: Vertebrate Declines and the Conservation of Biological Diversity*.
15. Worldwatch Paper 141. Washington, DC: Worldwatch Institute.
16. Warrick, Joby. 1998. "Mass Extinction Underway, Majority of Biologists Say." The *Washington Post*, April 21, p. A04.
17. Wilson, Edward O. 1992. *The Diversity of Life*. Cambridge, MA: The Belknap Press of Harvard University Press.

FORGOTTEN FUNDAMENTALS OF THE ENERGY CRISIS

Albert A. Bartlett

April 1998

REFLECTIONS IN 1998 ON THE TWENTIETH ANNIVERYSARY OF THE PUBLICATION OF THE PAPER: "FORGOTTEN FUNDAMENTALS OF THE ENERGY CRISIS"

BACKGROUND

Around 1969, college and university students developed a major interest in the environment and, stimulated by this, I began to realize that neither I nor the students had a good understanding of the implications of steady growth, and in particular, of the enormous numbers that could be produced by steady growth in modest periods of time. On September 19, 1969 I spoke to the students of the pre-medical honor society on "The Arithmetic of Population Growth." Fortunately I kept my notes for the talk, because I was invited to speak to other groups, and I gave the same talk, appropriately revised and enlarged. By the end of 1975 I had given the talk thirty times using different titles, and I was becoming more interested in the exponential arithmetic of steady growth. I started writing short numbered pieces, "The Exponential Function," which were published in *The Physics Teacher*. Then the first energy crisis gave a new sense of urgency to the need to help people to gain a better understanding of the arithmetic of steady growth, and in particular of the shortening of the life expectancy of a non-renewable resource if one had steady growth in the rate of consumption of such a resource until the last of the resource was used.

When I first calculated the Exponential Expiration Time (EET) of U.S. coal for a particular rate of growth of consumption, using Eq. 6, I used my new hand-held electronic calculator, and the result was forty-four years. This was so short that I suspected I had made an error in entering the problem. I repeated the calculation a couple of more times, and got the same forty-four years. This convinced me that my new calculator was flawed, so I got out tables of logarithms and used pencil and paper to calculate the result, which was forty-four years. Only then did I begin to realize the degree to which the lifetime of a non-renewable resource was shortened by having steady growth in the rate of consumption of the resource, and how misleading it is for leaders in business and industry to be advocating growth of rates of consumption and telling people how long the resource will last "at present rates of consumption."

This led to the first version of this paper which was presented at an energy conference at the University of Missouri at Rolla in October 1976, where it appears in the *Proceedings* of the Conference. In reading other papers in the *Proceedings* I came to realize that prominent people in the energy business would sometimes make statements that struck me as being unrealistic and even outrageous. Many of these statements were quoted in the version of the paper that is reprinted here, and this alerted me to the need to watch the public press for more such statements. Fortunately (or unfortunately) the press and prominent people have [illegible] a steady stream of statements that are illuminating because they reflect an inability to do arithmetic and/or to understand the energy situation.

As this is written, I have given my talk on "Arithmetic, Population, and Energy" over 1260 times in forty-eight of the fifty States in the twenty-eight years since 1969. I wish to acknowledge many constructive and helpful conversations on these topics I have had throughout the twenty years with my colleagues in the Department of Physics, and in particular with Professors Robert Ristinen and Jack Kraushaar, who have written a successful textbook on energy. (*Energy and Problems of a Technical Society*, John Wiley & Sons, New York City, 2nd Ed. 1993)

REFLECTIONS ON THE "FUNDAMENTALS" PAPER TWENTY YEARS LATER

As I read the 1978 paper in 1998, I am pleased to note that the arithmetic that is the core of the paper remains unchanged, and I feel that there are only a few points that need correction or updating.

1) When I derived my Eq. 6 in the Appendix, I was unaware that this equation for the Exponential Expiration Time (EET) had been published earlier by R. T. Robiscoe (his Eq. 4) in an article, "The Effect of Growth Rate on Conservation of a Resource." *American Journal of Physics,* Vol. 41, May 1973, p. 719–720. I apologize for not having been aware of this earlier derivation and presentation of this equation.
2) III. The world population was reported in 1975 to be 4 billion people growing at approximately 1.9 percent per year. In 1998 it is now a little under 6 billion people and the growth rate is reported to be around 1.5 percent per year. The decline in the rate of growth is certainly good news, but the population growth won't stop until the growth rate has dropped to zero.
3) VI. In 1978 I reported that "We are currently importing one-half of the petroleum we use." The data now indicate that, except for brief periods, this could not have been true in 1978. The basis for my statement was a newspaper clipping that said that the U.S. had experienced, in 1976, the first *month* in its history in which more oil was imported than was produced domestically. However, the imported fraction of the oil consumed in the U.S. has risen, and in early 1995 the news said that the calendar year 1994 was the first year in our nation's history when we had to import more oil than we were able to get from our ground ourselves. (*Colorado Daily*, February 24, 1995)
4) IX. The paper reported that by 1973 nuclear reactors (fission) supplied approximately 4.6 percent of our national electrical power. By 1998 this had climbed to approximately 20 percent of our electrical power, but no new nuclear power plants have been installed in the U.S. since the 1970s.
5) A table that I wish I had included in the original paper is one that would give answers to questions such as, "If a non-renewable resource would last, say fifty years at present rates of consumption, how long would it last if consumption were to grow say 4 percent per year?" This involves using the formula for the EET in which the quotient (R/r_0) is the number of years the quantity R of the resource would last at the present rate of consumption, r_0. The results of this simple calculation are shown in Table I.

   Example 1. If a resource would last 300 years at present rates of consumption, then it would last forty-nine years if the rate of consumption grew 6 percent per year.

   Example 2. If a resource would last eighteen years at 5 percent annual growth in the rate of consumption, then it would last thirty years at present rates of consumption. (0 percent growth)

TABLE I. Lifetimes of non-renewable resources for different rates of growth of consumption. Except for the left column, all numbers are lifetimes in years.

0 %	10	30	100	300	1000	3000	10,000
1 %	9.5	26	69	139	240	343	462
2 %	9.1	24	55	97	152	206	265
3 %	8.7	21	46	77	115	150	190
4 %	8.4	20	40	64	93	120	150
5 %	8.1	18	36	56	79	100	124
6 %	7.8	17	32	49	69	87	107
7 %	7.6	16	30	44	61	77	94
8 %	7.3	15	28	40	55	69	84
9 %	7.1	15	26	37	50	62	76
10 %	6.9	14	24	34	46	57	69

Example 3. If a resource would last fifty-five years at 8 percent annual growth in the rate of consumption, then it would last 115 years at 3 percent annual growth rate.

6) In the end of Section VIII of the 1978 paper I quoted Hubbert as writing in 1956 that "the peak of production of petroleum" in the U.S. would be reached between 1966 and 1971. The peak occurred in 1970. Hubbert predicted that "On a world scale [oil production] will probably pass its climax within the order of half a century . . . [2006]" My more recent analysis suggests the year 2004, while Campbell and Laherrere predict that the world peak will be reached before 2010, (*Scientific American*, March 1998, pp. 78–83) Studies by other geologists predict the peak within the first decade of the next century. Hubbert's analysis appears thus far to be remarkably good.

7) The "Fundamentals" paper was followed by a paper titled, "Sustained Availability: A Management Program for Non-Renewable Resources." *American Journal of Physics*, Vol. 54, May 1986, pp. 398–402. This paper makes use of the fact that the integral from zero to infinity of a declining exponential curve is finite. Thus, if one puts production of a non-renewable resource on a declining exponential curve, one can always find a rate of decline such that *the resource will last forever.* This is called "Sustained Availability," which is somewhat analogous to "sustained yield" in agriculture. This paper explores the mathematics of the options that this plan of action can give to a resource-rich nation that wants to divide its production of a resource between domestic use and exports.

8) Many economists reject this sort of analysis which is based on the assumption that resources are finite. A colleague in economics read the paper and later told me that "It is all wrong." When I asked him to point out the specific errors in the paper, he shook his head, saying, "It is all wrong."

9) The original paper dealt more with resources than with population. I feel that it is now clear that population growth is the world's most serious problem, and that the world's most serious population problem is right here in the U.S. The reason for this is that the average American has something like thirty to fifty times the impact on world resources as does a person in an underdeveloped country. (A.A. Bartlett, *Wild Earth*, Vol. 7, Fall 1997, pp. 88–90)

We have the jurisdiction and the responsibility needed to permit us to address our U.S. population problem, yet many prefer to focus their attention on the population problems in other countries. Before we can tell people in other countries that they must stop their population growth, we must accept the responsibility for working to stop population growth in the United States, where about half of our population growth is the excess of births over deaths and the other half is immigration, legal plus illegal. This leads me to offer the following challenge:

> *Can you think of any problem, on any scale, From microscopic to global, whose long-term solution is in any demonstrable way, Aided, assisted, or advanced by having larger populations At the local level, the state level, the national level, or globally?*

HORROR STORIES

Here are more recent horror stories to add to those that were recounted in the original paper.

1) The *Rocky Mountain News* of October 6, 1993 reported that: Shell Oil Co. said " . . . it planned to spend $1.2 billion to develop the largest oil discovery in the Gulf of Mexico in the past twenty years. The discovery . . . has an estimated ultimate recovery in excess of 700 million barrels of oil and gas." The 700 million barrels of oil sounds like a lot—until you note that at that time the U.S. consumption was 16.6 million barrels/day, so that this "largest oil discovery in the Gulf of Mexico in the past twenty years" would supply the needs of the U.S. for only forty-two days!
2) The headline in the *Wall Street Journal* for July 18, 1986 proclaimed that "U.S. Oil Output Tumbled in First Half as Alaska's Production Fell Nearly 8 percent." In the body of the story we read that the chief economist for Chevron Corporation observes that, "The question we can't answer yet is whether this is a new trend or a quirk." The answer to his question is that it is neither; it is an old trend! It is exactly what one expects as one goes down the right side of the Hubbert Curve.
3) Another headline on the front page of the *Wall Street Journal* (April 1, 1997) said: "Four Decades Later, Oil Field Off Canada is Ready to Produce. Politics, Money and Nature Put Vast Deposit on Ice; Now It Will Last Fifty Years: Shot in the Arm for U.S." In the body of the story we read that:

> *The Hibernia field, one of the largest oil discoveries in North American in decades, should deliver its first oil by year end. At least twenty more fields may follow, offering well over one billion barrels of high-quality crude and promising that a steady flow of oil will be just a quick tanker-run away from the energy-thirsty East Coast.*

Total U.S. oil consumption in 1996 was about 18 million barrels a day. Do the long division and one sees that the estimated "one billion barrels of high-quality crude" will supply the needs of the U.S. for just fifty-six days! This should be compared with the "50 Years" in the headline.

4) In the *Prime Time Monthly Magazine* (San Francisco, September 1995) we find an article, "Horses Need Corn" by the famous radio news broadcaster Paul Harvey. He emphasizes the opportunity we have to make ethanol from corn grown in the U.S. and then to use the ethanol as a fuel for our cars and trucks: "Today, ethanol production displaces over 43.5 million barrels of imported oil annually, reducing the U.S. trade balance by $645 million. . . For as far ahead as we can see, the only inexhaustible feed for our high horsepower vehicles is corn."

There are two problems with this:

A) The 43.5 million barrels must be compared with the annual consumption of motor gasoline in the U.S. In 1994 we consumed 4.17 billion barrels of motor vehicle gasoline. (Annual Energy Review, 1994, DOE/EIA 0384(94), p. 159) The ethanol production is seen to be approximately 1 percent of the annual consumption of gasoline by vehicles in the U.S. So one would have to multiply corn production by a factor of about 100 just to make the numbers match. An increase of this magnitude in the farm acreage devoted to the production of corn for ethanol would have profound negative dietary consequences.

B) It takes energy (generally diesel fuel) to plow the ground, to fertilize the ground, to plant the corn, to take care of the corn, to harvest the corn, and then more energy is needed to distill the corn to get ethanol. So it turns out that in the conventional production of ethanol, the finished gallon of ethanol contains less energy than was used to produce it ! It's an energy loser! The net energy of this "energy source" is negative!

5) The Clinton administration, in a "Draft Comprehensive National Energy Strategy" (February 1998) talks about America's oil as being "abundant," (pg. 4) and it advocates "promoting increased domestic oil . . . production" (pg. 2) to reverse this downward trend in U.S. oil production. The peak of the Hubbert Curve of oil production in the U.S. was reached in 1970 and we are now well down the right side of the Curve. The Draft Strategy calls for "stabilization of domestic oil production" (pg. 12) which is explained in "Strategy 1" (pg. 12) "By 2005, first stop and then reverse the decline in domestic oil production." The Hubbert Curve rises and falls in a manner like that of a Gaussian Error Curve, and once one is over the peak, one can put bumps on the downhill side, but except for such "noise," the trend after the peak is always downhill. A large national effort might reverse the decline in U.S. oil production for a year or two, but it hardly plausible to propose to "stabilize" domestic oil production for any extended period of time. It almost seems as though the U.S. Department of Energy has not studied the works of Hubbert, Campbell & Laherrere, Ivanhoe, Edwards, Masters and other prominent petroleum geologists.

"FORGOTTEN FUNDAMENTALS OF THE ENERGY CRISIS" (As originally published in 1978)

"Facts do not cease to exist because they are ignored," Aldous Huxley.

I. INTRODUCTION[1]

The energy crisis has been brought into focus by President Carter's message to the American people on April 18 and by his message to the Congress on April 20, 1977. Although the President spoke of the gravity of the energy situation when he said that it was "unprecedented in our history," his messages have triggered an avalanche of critical responses from national political and business leaders. A very common criticism of the President's message is that he failed to give sufficient emphasis to increased fuel production as a way of easing the crisis. The President proposed an escalating tax on gasoline and a tax on the large gas guzzling cars in order to reduce gasoline consumption. These taxes have been attacked by politicians, by labor leaders, and by the manufacturers of the "gas guzzlers" who convey the impression that one of the options that is open to us is to go ahead using gasoline as we have used it in the past.

We have the vague feeling that Arctic oil from Alaska will greatly reduce our dependence on foreign oil. We have recently heard political leaders speaking of energy self-sufficiency for the U.S. and of "Project Independence." The divergent discussion of the energy problem creates confusion rather than clarity, and from the confusion many Americans draw the conclusion that the energy shortage is mainly a matter of manipulation or of interpretation. It then

follows in the minds of many that the shortage can be "solved" by congressional action in the manner in which we "solve" social and political problems.
Many people seem comfortably confident that the problem is being dealt with by experts who understand it. However, when one sees the great hardships that people suffered in the Northeastern U.S. in January 1977 because of the shortage of fossil fuels, one may begin to wonder about the long-range wisdom of the way that our society has developed.

What are the fundamentals of the energy crisis?

Rather than travel into the sticky abyss of statistics it is better to rely on a few data and on the pristine simplicity of elementary mathematics. With these it is possible to gain a clear understanding of the origins, scope, and implications of the energy crisis.

II. BACKGROUND

When a quantity such as the rate of consumption of a resource (measured in tons per year or in barrels per year) is growing at a fixed percent per year, the growth is said to be exponential. The important property of the growth is that the time required for the growing quantity to increase its size by a fixed fraction is constant. For example, a growth of 5 percent (a fixed fraction) per year (a constant time interval) is exponential. It follows that a constant time will be required for the growing quantity to double its size (increase by 100 percent). This time is called the doubling time T_2, and it is related to P, the percent growth per unit time by a very simple relation that should be a central part of the educational repertoire of every American.

$$T_2 = 70/P$$

As an example, a growth rate of 5 percent/year will result in the doubling of the size of the growing quantity in a time $T_2 = 70/5 =$ fourteen year. In two doubling times (twenty-eight years) the growing quantity will double twice (quadruple) in size. In three doubling times its size will increase eightfold ($2^3 = 8$); in four doubling times it will increase sixteenfold ($2^4 = 16$); etc. It is natural then to talk of growth in terms of powers of two.

III. THE POWER OF POWERS OF TWO

Legend has it that the game of chess was invented by a mathematician who worked for an ancient king. As a reward for the invention the mathematician asked for the amount of wheat that would be determined by the following process: He asked the king to place one grain of wheat on the first square of the chess board, double this and put two grains on the second square, and continue this way, putting on each square twice the number of grains that were on the preceding square. The filling of the chessboard is shown in Table 1I. We see that on the last square one will place 2^{63} grains and the total number of grains on the board will then be one grain less than 2^{64}.

How much wheat is 2^{64} grains? Simple arithmetic shows that it is approximately 500 times the 1976 annual worldwide harvest of wheat? This amount is probably larger than all the wheat that has been harvested by humans in the history of the earth! How did we get to this enormous number? It is simple; we started with one grain of wheat and we doubled it a mere sixty-three times!

Exponential growth is characterized by doubling, and a few doublings can lead quickly to enormous numbers.

The example of the chessboard (Table 1) shows us another important aspect of exponential growth; *the increase in any doubling is approximately equal to the sum of all the preceding growth!* Note that when eight grains are placed on the fourth square, the eight is

Table 1. Filling the squares on the chessboard.

Square Numbers	Grains on Square	Total Grains Thus Far
1	1	1
2	2	3
3	4	7
4	8	15
5	16	31
6	32	63
7	64	127
64	2^{63}	2^{64} - 1

greater than the total of seven grains that were already on the board. The thirty-two grains placed on the sixth square are more than the total of thirty-one grains that were already on the board. Covering any square requires one grain more than the total number of grains that are already on the board.

On April 18, 1977 President Carter told the American people, "And in each of these decades (the 1950s and 1960s), more oil was consumed than in all of man's previous history combined."

We can now see that this astounding observation is a simple consequence of a growth rate whose doubling time is T_2 = ten year (one decade). The growth rate which has this doubling time is P=70/10=7 percent/year.

When we read that the demand for electrical power in the U.S. is expected to double in the next ten to twelve years we should recognize that this means that the quantity of electrical energy that will be used in these ten to twelve years will be approximately equal to the total of all of the electrical energy that has been used in the entire history of the electrical industry in this country! *Many people find it hard to believe that when the rate of consumption is growing a mere 7 percent/year, the consumption in one decade exceeds the total of all of the previous consumption.*

Populations tend to grow exponentially. The world population in 1975 was estimated to be 4 billion people and it was growing at the rate of 1.9 percent/year. It is easy to calculate that at this low rate of growth the world population would double in thirty-six years, the population would grow to a density of one person/m2 on the dry land surface of the earth (excluding Antarctica) in 550 years, and the mass of people would equal the mass of the earth in a mere 1,620 years! Tiny growth rates can yield incredible numbers in modest periods of time! Since it is obvious that people could never live at the density of 1 person/m^2 over the land area of the earth, it is obvious that the earth will experience zero population growth. The present high birth rate and/or the present low death rate will change until they have the same numerical value, and this will probably happen in a time much shorter than 550 years.

A recent report suggested that the rate of growth of world population had dropped from 1.9 percent/year to 1.64 percent/year.[2] Such a drop would certainly qualify as the best news the human race has ever had! The report seemed to suggest that the drop in this growth rate was evidence that the population crisis had passed, but it is easy to see that this is not the case. The arithmetic shows that an annual growth rate of 1.64 percent will do anything that an annual rate of 1.9 percent will do; it just takes a little longer. For example, the world population would increase by one billion people in 13.6 years instead of in 11.7 years.

Compound interest on an account in the savings bank causes the account balance to grow exponentially. One dollar at an interest rate of 5 percent/year compounded continuously will grow in 500 years to 72 billion dollars and the interest at the end of the 500th year would be coming in at the magnificent rate of $114/s. If left untouched for another doubling time of fourteen year, the account balance would be 144 billion dollars and the interest would be accumulating at the rate of $228/s.

It is very useful to remember that steady exponential growth of n percent/year for a period of seventy years (100 ln2) will produce growth by an overall factor of 2^n. Thus where the city of Boulder, Colorado, today has one overloaded sewer treatment plant, a steady population growth at the rate of 5 percent/year would make it necessary in seventy years (one human lifetime) to have $2^5 = 32$ overloaded sewer treatment plants!

Steady inflation causes prices to rise exponentially. An inflation rate of 6 percent/year will, in seventy years, cause prices to increase by a factor of sixty-four! If the inflation continues at this rate, the $0.40 loaf of bread we feed our toddlers today will cost $25.60 when the toddlers are retired and living on their pensions!

It has even been proven that the number of miles of highway in the country tends to grow exponentially.[1(e),3]

The reader can suspect that the world's most important arithmetic is the arithmetic of the exponential function. One can see that our long national history of population growth and of growth in our per-capita consumption of resources lie at the heart of our energy problem.

IV. EXPONENTIAL GROWTH IN A FINITE ENVIRONMENT

Bacteria grow by division so that one bacterium becomes two, the two divide to give four, the four divide to give eight, etc. Consider a hypothetical strain of bacteria for which this division time is one minute. The number of bacteria thus grows exponentially with a doubling time of one minute. One bacterium is put in a bottle at 11:00 A.M. and it is observed that the bottle is full of bacteria at 12:00 NOON. Here is a simple example of exponential growth in a finite environment. This is mathematically identical to the case of the exponentially growing consumption of our finite resources of fossil fuels. Keep this in mind as you ponder three questions about the bacteria:

(1) When was the bottle half-full? Answer: 11:59 A.M.!

(2) If you were an average bacterium in the bottle, at what time would you first realize that you were running out of space? Answer: There is no unique answer to this question, so let's ask, "At 11:55 a.m., when the bottle is only 3 percent filled (1/32) and is 97 percent open space (just yearning for development) would you perceive that there was a problem?" Some years ago someone wrote a letter to a Boulder newspaper to say that there was no problem with population growth in Boulder Valley. The reason given was that there was fifteen times as much open space as had already been developed. When one thinks of the bacteria in the bottle one sees that the time in Boulder Valley was four minutes before noon! See Table 2.

Suppose that at 11:58 A.M. some farsighted bacteria

Table 2. The last minutes in the bottle.

11:54 a.m.	1/64 full	(1.5%)	63/64	empty
11:55 a.m.	1/32 full	(3%)	31/32	empty
11:56 a.m.	1/16 full	(6%)	15/16	empty
11:57 a.m.	1/8 full	(12%)	7/8	empty
11:58 a.m.	1/4 full	(25%)	3/4	empty
11:59 a.m.	1/2 full	(50%)	1/2	empty
12:00 noon	full	(100%)		empty

Table 3. The effect of the discovery of three new bottles.	
11:58 a.m.	Bottle No. 1 is one quarter full.
11:59 a.m.	Bottle No. 1 is half-full.
12:00 noon	Bottle No. 1 is full.
12:01 p.m.	Bottles No. 1 and 2 are both full.
12:02 p.m.	Bottles No. 1, 2, 3, 4 are all full.
Quadrupling the resource extends the life of the resource by only two doubling times! When consumption grows exponentially, enormous increases in resources are consumed in a very short time!	

realize that they are running out of space and consequently, with a great expenditure of effort and funds, they launch a search for new bottles. They look offshore on the outer continental shelf and in the Arctic, and at 11:59 A.M. they discover three new empty bottles. Great sighs of relief come from all the worried bacteria, because this magnificent discovery is three times the number of bottles that had hitherto been known. The discovery quadruples the total space resource known to the bacteria. Surely this will solve the problem so that the bacteria can be self-sufficient in space. The bacterial "Project Independence" must now have achieved its goal.

(3) How long can the bacterial growth continue if the total space resources are quadrupled?

Answer: Two more doubling times (minutes)! See Table 3.

James Schlesinger, Secretary of Energy in President Carter's Cabinet recently noted that in the energy crisis "we have a classic case of exponential growth against a finite source."[4]

V. LENGTH OF LIFE OF A FINITE RESOURCE WHEN THE RATE OF CONSUMPTION IS GROWING EXPONENTIALLY

Physicists would tend to agree that the world's mineral resources are finite. The extent of the resources is only incompletely known, although knowledge about the extent of the remaining resources is growing very rapidly. The consumption of resources is generally growing exponentially, and we would like to have an idea of how long resources will last. Let us plot a graph of the rate of consumption r(t) of a resource (in units such as tons/year) as a function of time measured in years. The area under the curve in the interval between times t = 0 (the present, where the rate of consumption is r_0) and t = T will be a measure of the total consumption C in tons of the resource in the time interval. We can find the time T_e at which the total consumption C is equal to the size R of the resource and this time will be an estimate of the expiration time of the resource.

Imagine that the rate of consumption of a resource grows at a constant rate until the last of the resource is consumed, whereupon the rate of consumption falls abruptly to zero. It is appropriate to examine this model because this constant exponential growth is an accurate reflection of the goals and aspirations of our economic system. Unending growth of our rates of production and consumption and of our Gross National Product is the central theme of our economy and it is regarded as disastrous when actual rates of growth fall below the planned rates. Thus it is relevant to calculate the life expectancy of a resource under conditions of constant rates of growth. Under these conditions the period of time necessary to consume the known reserves of a resource may be called the exponential expiration time (EET) of the resource. The EET is a function of the known size R of the resource, of the current rate of use r_0 of the resource, and of the fractional growth per unit time k of the rate of consumption of the resource. The expression for the EET is derived in the Appendix where it appears as Eq. (6). This equation is known to scholars who deal in resource problems[5] but there is little evidence that it is known or understood by the political, industrial, business, or labor leaders who deal in energy resources, who speak and write on the energy crisis and who take pains to emphasize how essential it is to our society to have continued uninterrupted growth in all parts of our economy. The equation for the EET has been called the best-kept scientific secret of the century.[6]

VI. HOW LONG WILL OUR FOSSIL FUELS LAST?

The question of how long our resources will last is perhaps the most important question that can be asked in a modern industrial society. Dr. M. King Hubbert, a geophysicist now retired from the United States Geological Survey, is a world authority on the estimation of energy resources and on the prediction of their patterns of discovery and depletion. Many of the data used here come from Hubbert's papers.[7–10] Several of the figures in this paper are redrawn from figures in his papers. These papers are required reading for anyone who wishes to understand the fundamentals and many of the details of the problem.

Let us examine the situation in regard to production of domestic crude oil in the U.S. Table 4 gives the relevant data. *Note that since one-half of our domestic petroleum has already been consumed, the "petroleum time" in the U.S. is 1 minute before noon!* Figure 1 shows the historical trend in domestic production (consumption) of crude oil. Note that from 1870 to about 1930 the rate of production of domestic crude oil increased exponentially at a rate of 8.27 percent/year with a doubling time of 8.4 years. If the growth in the rate of production stopped and the rate of production was held constant at the 1970 rate, the remaining U.S. oil would last only (190—96.6) / 3.29 = 28 years! We are currently importing one-half of the petroleum we use. If these imports were completely cut off and if there was no growth in the rate of domestic consumption above the 1970 rate, our domestic petroleum reserves would last only fourteen years! The vast shale oil deposits of Colorado and Wyoming represent an enormous resource. Hubbert reports that the oil recoverable under 1965 techniques is 80 x 10^9 barrels, and he quotes other higher estimates. In the preparation of Table 5, the figure 103.4 x 10^9 barrels was used as the estimate of U.S. shale oil so that the reserves used in the calculation of column 4 would be twice those that were used in the calculation of column 3. This table makes it clear that when consumption is rising exponentially, a doubling of the remaining resource results in only a small increase in the life expectancy of the resource.

Table 4. United States crude oil (lower 48 states).

Ultimate total production (Ref. 7)	190
Produced to 1972	96.6
Percent of ultimate total production produced to 1972 (Ref.7)	50.8%
Annual production rate 1970	3.29
Units are 109 barrels	
(1 barrel = 42 U.S. gal. = 158.98 L).	

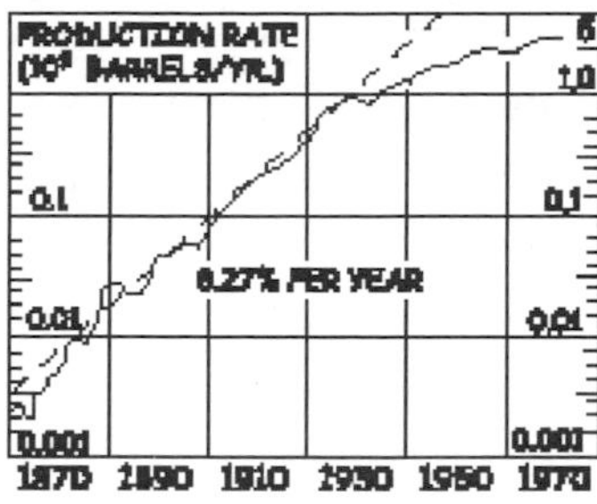

Figure 1. History of U.S. crude oil production (semilogarithmic scale). Redrawn from Hubbert's Figure 12, Reference 7.

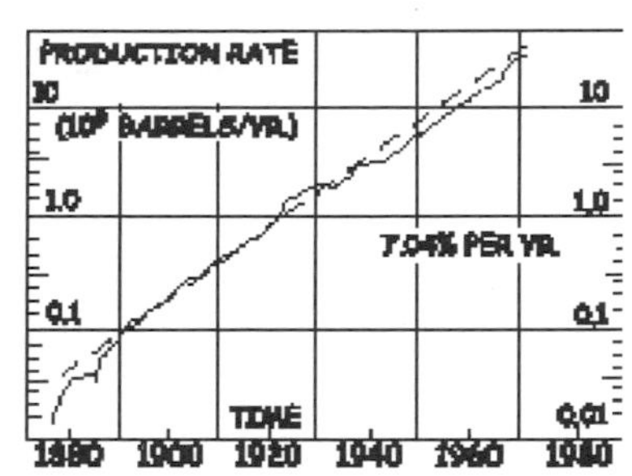

Figure 2. History of world crude oil production (semilogarithmic scale). Redrawn from Hubbert's Figure 6, Reference 7.

A reporter from CBS News, speaking about oil shale on a three-hour television special feature on energy (August 31, 1977) said, "Most experts estimate that oil shale deposits like these near Rifle, Colorado, could provide more than a 100-year supply." This statement should be compared with the figures given in column 4 of Table 5. This comparison will serve to introduce the reader to the disturbing divergence between reassuring statements by authoritative sources and the results of simple calculations.

Anyone who wishes to talk about energy self-sufficiency for the United States (Project Independence) must understand Table 5 and the simple exponential calculations upon which it is based.

Table 6 gives statistics on world production of crude oil. Figure 2 shows the historical trend in world crude oil production. Note that from 1890 to 1970 the production grew at a rate of 7.04 percent/year, with a doubling time of 9.8 year. It is easy to calculate that the world reserves of crude oil would last 101 year if the growth in annual production was halted and production in the future was held constant at the 1970 level. Table 7 shows the life expectancy (EET) of world crude oil reserves for various rates of growth of production and shows the amount by which the life expectancy is extended if one adds world deposits

Table 5. Exponential expiration time (EET) in years of various estimates of U.S. oil reserves for different rates of growth of annual production. Units are 109 barrels. This table is prepared by using Eq. (6) with r0 = 3.29 X 109 barrels/yr. Note that this is domestic production which is only about one half of domestic consumption! Column 1 is the percent annual growth rate. Column 2 is the lifetime (EET) of the resource which is calculated using R = 190 - 96.6 = 93.4 as the estimated oil remaining in the lower 48 states. Column 3 is the lifetime (EET) calculated R = 93.4 + 10 to include the Alaskan oil. Column 4 is the lifetime (EET) calculated using R = 93.4 + 10 + 103.4 = 206.8 to include Alaskan oil and a hypothetical estimate of U.S. oil shale.

Col.1(%)	Col.2(yr)	Col.3(yr)	Col.4(yr)
Zero	28.4	31.4	62.8
1%	25.0	27.3	48.8
2%	22.5	24.4	40.7
3%	20.5	22.1	35.3
4%	19.0	20.4	31.4
5%	17.7	18.9	28.4
6%	16.6	17.7	26.0
7%	15.6	16.6	24.1
8%	14.8	15.7	22.4
9%	14.1	14.9	21.1
10%	13.4	14.2	19.9

Table 6. World crude oil data. Units are 10^9 barrels.	
Ultimate total production (Ref.7)	1952
Produced to 1972	261
Percent of total production produced to 1972 (Ref. 7)	13.4%
Annual Production rate 1970	16.7
Note that a little more than 1/8 of the world's oil has been consumed. The "world petroleum time" is between 2 and 3 min before noon, i.e. we are between 2 and 3 doubling times from the expiration of the resource.	

of oil shale. Column 4 is based on the assumption that the available shale oil is four times as large as the value reported by Hubbert. Note again that the effect of this very large hypothetical increase in the resource is very small. Figure 3 shows a dramatic graphical model from Mario Iona that can be used to represent this growth.[11] When consumption grows 7 percent/year the consumption in any decade is approximately equal to the sum of all previous consumption as can be seen by the areas representing consumption in successive decades. The rectangle ABDC represents all the known oil, including all that has been used in the past, and the rectangle *CDFE represents the new discoveries that must be made if we wish the* 7 percent/*year growth to continue one decade, from the year 2000 to 2010!*

From these calculations we can draw a general conclusion of great importance. *When we are dealing with exponential growth we do not need to have an accurate estimate of the size of a resource in order to make a reliable estimate of how long the resource will last.*

A friend recently tried to reassure me by asserting that there remained undiscovered under our country at least as much oil as all we have ever used. Since it has been about 120 years since the first discovery of oil in this country, he was sure that the undiscovered oil would be sufficient for another 120 years. I had no success in convincing him that if such oil was found it would be sufficient only for one doubling time or about a decade.

As the reader ponders the seriousness of the situation and asks, "What will life be like without petroleum?" the thought arises of heating homes electrically or with solar power and of traveling in electric cars. A far more fundamental problem becomes apparent when one recognizes that modern agriculture is based on petroleum-powered machinery and on petroleum-based fertilizers.

Table 7. Life expectancy in years of various estimates of world oil reserves for different rates of growth of annual production. Units are 109 barrels. This table is prepared by using Eq. (6) with r0 = 16.7 X 109 barrels / yr. Column 1 is the percent annual growth rate of production. Column 2 is the EET of the resource calculated using r = 1691 as the estimate of the amount of the remaining oil. Column 3 is the EET calculated using R = 1691 + 190 = 1881 representing crude oil plus oil shale. Column 4 is the EET calculated using R = 1691 + 4 (190) = 2451 which assumes that the amount of shale oil is four times the amount which is known now.

Col. 1(yr)	Col. 2(yr)	Col. 3(yr)	Col. 4(yr)
Zero	101	113	147
1%	69.9	75.4	90.3
2%	55.3	59.0	68.5
3%	46.5	49.2	56.2
4%	40.5	42.6	48.2
5%	36.0	37.8	42.4
6%	32.6	34.1	38.0
7%	29.8	31.2	34.6
8%	27.6	28.8	31.8
9%	25.7	26.8	29.5
10%	24.1	25.1	27.5

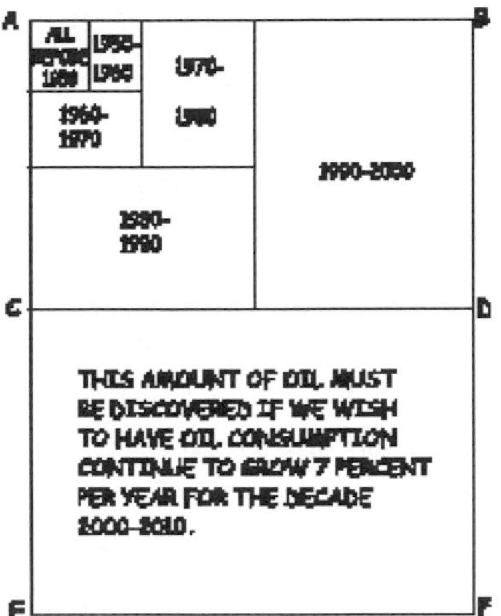

Figure 3.

This is reflected in a definition of modern agriculture: "Modern agriculture is the use of land to convert petroleum into food."

Item: We have now reached the point in U.S. agriculture where we use eighty gallons of gasoline or its equivalent to raise an acre of corn, but only nine hours of human labor per crop acre for the average of all types of produce.[12]

Think for a moment of the effect of petroleum on American life. Petroleum has made it possible for American farms to be operated by only a tiny fraction of our population; only one American in twenty-six lived on a farm in 1976. The people thus displaced from our farms by petroleum-based mechanization have migrated to the cities where our ways of life are critically dependent on petroleum. The farms without the large number of people to do the work are also critically dependent on petroleum-based mechanization. The approaching exhaustion of the domestic reserves of petroleum and the rapid depletion of world reserves will have a profound effect on Americans in the cities and on the farms. It is clear that agriculture as we know it will experience major changes within the life expectancy of most of us, and with these changes could come a major further deterioration of world-wide levels of nutrition. The doubling time (thirty-six to forty-two year) of world population (depending on whether the annual growth rate is 1.9 percent or 1.64 percent) means that we have this period of time in which we must double world food production if we wish to do no better than hold constant the fraction of the world population that is starving. This would mean that the number starving at the end of the doubling time would be twice the number that are starving today. This was put into bold relief by David Pimentel of Cornell University in an invited paper at the 1977 annual meeting of AAPT-APS (Chicago, 1977):

> As a result of overpopulation and resource limitations, the world is fast losing its capacity to feed itself . . . More alarming is the fact that while the world population doubled its numbers in about thirty years the world doubled its energy consumption within the past decade. Moreover, the use of energy in food production has been increasing faster than its use in many other sectors of the economy.

It is possible to calculate an absolute upper limit to the amount of crude oil the earth could contain. We simply assert that the volume of petroleum in the earth cannot be larger than the volume of the earth. The volume of the earth is 6.81×10^{21} barrels, which would last for 4.1×10^{11} year if the 1970 rate of consumption of oil held constant with no growth. The use of Eq. (6) shows that if the rate of consumption of petroleum continued on the growth curve of 7.04 percent/year of Figure 2, this earth full of oil will last only 342 year!

It has frequently been suggested that coal will answer the U.S. and world energy needs for a long period in the future. What are the facts?

Table 8. United States coal resource.	
Ultimate total production (Ref. 7)	
High estimate	1486
Low estimate	390
Produced through 1972 (My estimate from Hubbert's Fig. 22)	50
Percent of ultimate production produced through 1972	
Percent of high estimate	3%
Percent of low estimate	13%
Coal resource remaining	
High estimate	1436
Low estimate	340
Annual production rate, 1972	0.5
Rate of export of coal, 1974	0.06
Annual production rate, 1974	0.6
Annual production rate, 1976	0.665
Units are 10^9 metric tons.	

Table 8 shows data on U.S. coal production that are taken from several sources. Figure 4 shows the history of coal production in the U.S. Note that from 1860 to 1910, U.S. coal production grew exponentially at 6.69 percent/year (T_2 = 10.4 year). The production then leveled off at 0.5 x 10^9 tons/year which held approximately constant until 1972 whereupon the rate started to rise steadily. Coal consumption remained level for sixty years because our growing energy demands were met by petroleum and natural gas. In early 1976 the annual coal production goals of the U.S. government were 1.3 billion tons for 1980 and 2.1 billion tons for 1985. The 1976 production is now reported to have been 0.665 billion tons and the current goal is to raise annual production to a billion tons by 1985.[13] From these data we can see that the Ford administration's goals called for coal production to increase on the order of 10 percent/year while the Carter administration is speaking of growth of production of approximately 5 percent/year.

Table 9 shows the expiration times (EET) of the high and the low estimates of U.S. coal reserves for various rates of increase of the rate of production as calculated from the equation for the EET [Eq. (6)]. If we use the conservative smaller estimate of U.S. coal reserves we see that the growth of the rate of consumption will have to be held below 3 percent/year if we want coal to last until our nation's tricentennial. If we want coal to last 200 years, the rate of growth of annual consumption will have to be held below 1 percent/year!

One obtains an interesting insight into the problem if one asks how long beyond the year 1910 could coal production have continued on the curve of exponential growth at the historic rate of 6.69 percent/year of Figure 4. The smaller estimate of U.S. coal would have been consumed around the

Figure 4. History of U.S. coal production (semilogarithmic scale). Redrawn from Hubbert's Figure 10, Ref. 7. In the upper right, the crosses in the steep dashed curve show the coal production goals of the Ford Administration, and the circles in the lower dashed curve show the production goals of the Carter Administration. From the close of the American Civil War to about the year 1910, coal production grew at a steady rate of 6.69 percent/year. If this growth rate had continued undiminished after 1910, the small estimate of the size of U.S. coal reserves would have been consumed by about 1967 and the larger estimate of the size of the reserves would have been consumed by about the year 1990!

year 1967 and the large estimate would have expired around the year 1990. Thus it is clear that the use of coal as an energy source in 1978 and in the years to come is possible only because the growth in the annual production of coal was zero from 1910 to about 1972!

VII. WHAT DO THE EXPERTS SAY?

Now that we have seen the facts let us compare them with statements from authoritative sources. Let us look first at a report to the Congress.

> It is clear, particularly in the case of coal, that we have ample reserves . . . . We have an abundance of coal in the ground. Simply stated, the crux of the problem is how to get it out of the ground and use it in environmentally acceptable ways and on an economically competitive basis . . . At current levels of output and recovery these reserves can be expected to last more than 500 years.[14]

Here is one of the most dangerous statements in the literature. It is dangerous because news media and the energy companies pick up the idea that "United States coal will last 500 years" while the media and the energy companies forget or ignore the important caveat with which the sentence began, "At current levels of output . . ." The right-hand column of Table 9 shows that at zero rate of growth of consumption even the low estimate of the U.S. coal resource "will last over 500 years." However, it is absolutely clear that the government does not plan to hold coal production constant "at current levels of output."

> Coal reserves far exceed supplies of oil and gas, and yet coal supplies only 18 percent of our total energy. To maintain even this contribution we will need to increase coal production by 70 percent by 1985, but the real goal, to increase coal's share of the energy market will require a staggering growth rate.[15]

While the government is telling us that we must achieve enormous increases in the rate of coal production, other governmental officials are telling us that we can increase the rate of production of coal *and* have the resource last for a very long time.

> The trillions of tons of coal lying under the United States will have to carry a large part of the nation's increased energy consumption, says (the) Director of the Energy Division of the Oak Ridge National Laboratories. "He estimated America's coal

Table 9. Lifetime in years of United States coal (EET). The lifetime (EET) in years of U.S. coal reserves (both the high and low estimate of the U.S.G.S.) are shown for several rates of growth of production from the 1972 level of 0.5 (x10^9) metric tons per year.

	High Estimate (yr)	Low Estimate (yr)
Zero	2872	680
1%	339	205
2%	203	134
3%	149	102
4%	119	83
5%	99	71
6%	86	62
7%	76	55
8%	68	50
9%	62	46
10%	57	42
11%	52	39
12%	49	37
13%	46	35

> reserves are so huge, they could last 'a minimum of 300 years and probably a maximum of 1000 years."[16]

Compare the above statement of the life expectancy of U.S. coal reserves with the results of very simple calculations given in Table 9.

In the three-hour CBS television special on energy (August 31, 1977) a reporter stressed the great efforts that are being made to increase the rate of production of U.S. coal, and he summarized the situation in these words, "By the lowest estimate, we have enough (coal) for 200 years. By the highest, enough for more than a thousand years."

Again, compare the above statement with the results of simple calculations shown in Table 9.

While we read these news stories we are bombarded by advertisements by the energy companies which say that coal will last a long time at present rates of consumption and which say at the same time that we must dramatically increase our rate of production of coal.

> At the rate the United States uses coal today, these reserves could help keep us in energy for the next two hundred years . . . Most coal used in America today is burned by electric power plants–(which)–consumed about 400 million tons of coal last year. By 1985 this figure could jump to nearly 700 million tons.[17]

Other advertisements stress just the 500 years (no caveat): "We are sitting on half the world's known supply of coal–enough for over 500 years."[18] Some ads stress the idea of self-sufficiency without stating for how long a period we might be self-sufficient. "Coal, the only fuel in which America is totally self-sufficient."[19] Other ads suggest a deep lack of understanding of the fundamentals of the exponential function.

> Yet today there are still those who shrill (sic) for less energy and no growth . . . Now America is obligated to generate more energy—not less—merely to provide for its increasing population . . . With oil and gas in short supply, where will that energy come from? Predominately from coal. The U.S. Department of the Interior estimates America has 23 percent more coal than we dreamed of, 4,000,000,000,000 (trillion!) tons of it. Enough for over 500 years. (The non-sentences are in the original.)[20]

A simple calculation of the EET based on a current production rate of 0.6×10^9 tons/year shows that the growth in the rate of production of coal can't exceed 0.8 percent/year if the ad's 4×10^{12} tons of coal is to last for the ad's 500 year. However, it should be noted that the 4×10^{12} tons cited in the ad is 2.8 times the size of the large estimate of U.S. coal reserves and is 12 times the size of the small estimate of U.S. coal reserves as cited by Hubbert.

When we view the range of creative information that is offered to the public we cannot wonder that people are confused. We may *wish* that we could have rapid growth of the rate of consumption and have the reserves of U.S. coal last for a large number of years, but very simple calculations are all that is needed to prove that these two goals are incompatible. At this critical time in our nation's history we need to shift our faith to calculations (arithmetic) based on factual data and give up our belief in Walt Disney's First Law: "Wishing will make it so."[21]

On the broad aspects of the energy problem we note that the top executive of one of our great corporations is probably one of the world's authorities on the exponential growth of investments and compound interest. However, he observes that "the energy crisis was made in Washington." He ridicules "the modern-day occult prediction" of "computer print-outs" and warns against extrapolating past trends to estimate what may happen in the future. He then points out how American free-enterprise solved the great "Whale Oil Crisis" of the 1850s. With this single example as his data base he boldly extrapolates into the future to assure us that American ingenuity will solve the current energy crisis if the bureaucrats in Washington will only quit interfering.[22] It is encouraging to note that the person who made these statements in 1974, suggesting that the energy crisis was contrived rather than real, has now signed his name on an advertisement in *Newsweek Magazine* (Sept. 12, 1977) saying that, "Energy is not a political issue. It's an issue of survival. Time is running out." However, the same issue of Newsweek Magazine carried two advertisements for coal which said: "We've limited our use of coal while a supply that will last for centuries sits under our noses . . . Coal can provide our energy needs for centuries to come."

Carefully read this ad by the Edison Electric Institute for the Electric Companies telling us that: "There is an increasing scarcity of certain *fuels*. But there is no scarcity of *energy*. There never *has* been. There never *will* be. There never *could* be. Energy is inexhaustible." (Emphasis is in the original.)[23] We can read that a professor in a school of mining technology offers "proof" of the proposition: "Mankind has the right to use the world's resources as it wishes, to the limits of its abilities . . ."[24]

We have the opening sentence of a major scientific study of the energy problem: "The United States has an abundance of energy resources; fossil fuels (mostly coal and oil shale) adequate for centuries, fissionable nuclear fuels adequate for millennia and solar energy that will last indefinitely."[25] We can read the words of an educated authority who asserts that there is no problem of shortages of resources: "It is *not* true that we are running out of resources that can be easily and cheaply exploited without regard for future operations." His next sentence denies that growth is a serious component of the energy problem, "It is not true that we must turn our back on economic growth"(emphasis is in the original). Three sentences later he says that there may be a problem: "We must face the fact that the well of non-renewable natural resources is not bottomless."[26] He does suggest that lack of "leadership" is part of the problem.

We have a statement by Ralph Nader, "The supply of oil, gas, and coal in this country is enormous and enough for hundreds of years. It is not a question of supply but a question of price and profits, of monopolies and undue political influence."[27]

Expert analysis of the problem can yield unusual recommendations. We have the opening paper in an energy conference in which a speaker from a major energy company makes no mention of the contribution of growth to the energy crisis when he asserts that: "The core of the energy problem both U.S. and worldwide [is] our excessive dependence on our two scarcest energy resources—oil and natural gas." For him continued growth is not part of the problem, it is part of the solution! "*More* energy must be made available at a higher rate of growth than normal—in the neighborhood of 6 percent per year compared to a recent historical growth rate of 4 percent per year."[28]

The patient is suffering from cancer, and after a careful study, the doctor prescribes the remedy; give the patient more cancer. Here is a second case where cancer is prescribed as the cure for cancer. The National Petroleum Council in its report to the energy industry on the energy crisis: observed that "Restrictions on energy demand growth could prove (to be) expensive and undesirable. . . The council 'flatly rejected' any conservation-type measures proposing instead the production of more energy sources domestically and the easing of environmental controls."[29]

Study this statement carefully: "Energy industries agree that to achieve some form of energy self-sufficiency the U.S. must mine all the coal that it can."[30] The plausibility of this statement disappears and its real meaning becomes apparent when we paraphrase it: "The more rapidly we consume our resources, the more self-sufficient we will be." David Brower has referred to this as the policy of "*Strength through Exhaustion*." [31] This policy has many powerful adherents. For example, on the three-hour CBS television special on energy (Aug. 31, 1977) William Simon, energy adviser to President Ford said: "We should be "trying to get as many holes drilled as possible to get the proven (oil) reserve . . ."

Is it in the national interest to get and use these reserves as rapidly as possible? We certainly get no sense of urgency from the remarks of the Board Chairman of a major multinational energy corporation who concludes the discussion "Let's Talk Frankly About Energy" with his mild assessment of what we must do. "Getting on top of the energy problem won't be easy. It will be an expensive and time-consuming task. It will require courage, creativeness and discipline . . ."[32]

If one searches beyond the work of Hubbert for an indication of others who understand the fundamental arithmetic of the problem one finds occasional encouraging evidence.[33] However, when one compares the results of the simple exponential calculations with news stories, with statements from public officials, and with assertions in advertisements of the energy companies it is hard to imagine that this arithmetic is widely understood.

The arithmetic of growth is the forgotten fundamental of the energy crisis.

VIII. A WORD OF CAUTION

We must note that these calculations of the EET of fossil fuels are not predictions of the future. They simply give us first-order estimates of the life expectancies of known quantities of several fuels under the conditions of steady growth which our society and our government hold sacred. These estimates are emphasized as aids to understanding the consequences of any particular growth scenario that the reader may want to consider or to evaluate.

The rate of production of our mineral resources will not rise exponentially until the EET is reached and then plunge abruptly to zero, as modeled in these calculations and as shown in curve A of Figure 5 even though our national goals are predicated on uninterrupted growth. The rate of production of our non-renewable mineral resources will not follow the classical S-shaped transition from an early period of exponential growth to a horizontal curve representing a constant rate of production, curve B. Such a curve can be achieved in the production of renewable resources such as food, forest products, or the production of solar energy, provided the rate of production of the renewable resource is not dependent on fossil fuels. Reference has already been made to the dependence of modern agriculture on petroleum, and as long as this dependence continues, the curve of agricultural production would be expected to follow curve C, (the curve for non-renewable petroleum) rather than curve B.

Although the rate of production of mineral resources has been growing exponentially, one knows that at some time in the future the resource will be exhausted and the rate of production will return to zero. The past history, this one future datum and a careful study of

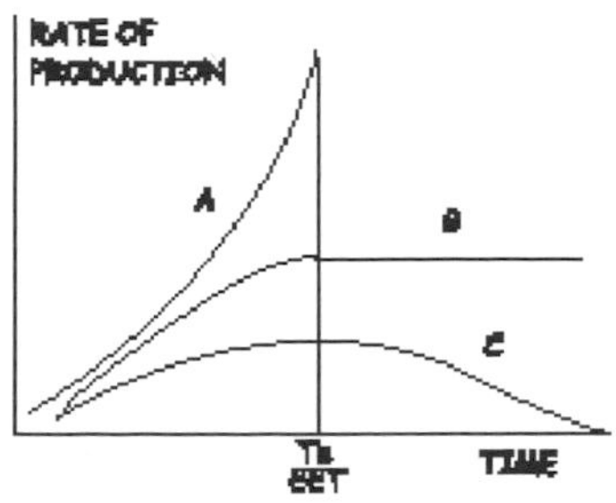

Figure 5. Three patterns of growth. Curve A represents steady exponential growth in the rate of production of a non-renewable resource until the resource is exhausted at Te, the exponential expiration time (EET). The area under the curve from the present (t = 0) to t = Te is equal to the known size of the resource. Curve C represents Hubbert's model of the way in which the rate of production of a non-renewable resource rises and falls. This model is based on studies of the rate of use of resources which have been nearly completely consumed. The area under the curve from the present to t = infinity is equal to the size of the resource. Curve B represents the rate of production of a renewable resource such as agricultural or forest products, where a constant steady-state production can be maintained for long periods of time provided this production is not dependent on the use of a non-renewable resource (such as petroleum) whose production is following a curve such as C.

---

the rate versus time of production of resources that have expired has led Dr. M. King Hubbert to the conclusion that the rate of production of a non-renewable resource will rise and fall in the symmetrical manner of a Gaussian error curve as shown in curve C of Figure 5. When he fits the data for U.S. oil production in the lower forty-eight states to a curve such as C, Hubbert finds that we are now just to the right of the peak. We have used one-half of the recoverable petroleum that was ever in the ground in the U.S. and in the future the rate of production can only go downhill. However, our national demand for petroleum has continued to grow exponentially and the difference between our demands and our production has been made up by imports. Bold initiatives by the Congress could temporarily reverse the trend and could put a small bump on the downhill side of the curve. Alaskan oil can put a little bump on the downhill side of the curve. The downhill trend on the right side of the curve was noted clearly by Deputy Energy Secretary John O'Leary under the headline, "U.S. Energy 'Disaster' Inevitable by 1985,"[34]

> Although U.S. oil and gas production hit their peak several years ago and are declining by about 8 percent per year, O'Leary said, the nation has avoided serious problems by using more foreign oil . . . We are walking into a disaster in the next three or four years with our eyes wide open.

The most dramatic conclusion that Hubbert draws from his curve for the complete cycle of U.S. oil production is that the consumption of the central 80 percent of the resource will take place in only sixty-seven years!

It is very sobering to face the downhill side of the curve and to note that in the past the rise in our annual per capita consumption of energy has gone hand-in-hand with the increase of our standard of living. It is more sobering to note the close coupling between our production of food and our use of petroleum. It is even more sobering to note that on March 7, 1956 (over twenty-two years ago) Dr. Hubbert, addressing the conference in San Antonio, Texas, of a large group of petroleum engineers and geologists said:

> According to the best currently available information, the production of petroleum and natural gas on a world scale will probably pass its climax within the order of half a century, while for both the United States and for Texas, the peaks of production can be expected to occur within the next ten or fifteen years. (i.e., between 1966 and 1971)

Pazik tells[33] of the shock this statement and the related analysis caused in oil industry circles and he tells about the efforts that were made by the "experts" to ignore this and the other results of the analysis made by Hubbert.

IX. WHAT DO WE DO NOW?

The problems are such that we have rather few options. All of the following points are vital:

(i) We must educate all of our people to an understanding of the arithmetic and consequences of growth, especially in terms of the earth's finite resources. David Brower has observed that, "The promotion of growth is simply a sophisticated way to steal from our children."

(ii) We must educate people to the critical urgency of abandoning our religious belief in the disastrous dogma that "growth is good," that "bigger is better," that "we must grow or we will stagnate," etc., etc. We must realize that growth is but an adolescent phase of life which stops when physical maturity is reached. If growth continues in the period of maturity it is called obesity or cancer. Prescribing growth as the cure for the energy crisis[28, 29] has all the logic of prescribing increasing quantities of food as a remedy for obesity. *The recent occasion of our nation's 200th anniversary would be an appropriate time to make the transition from national adolescence to national maturity.*

(iii) We must conserve in the use and consumption of everything. We must outlaw planned obsolescence. We must recognize that, as important as it is to conserve, the arithmetic shows clearly that large savings from conservation will be wiped out in short times by even modest rates of growth. For example, in one or two dozen years a massive federal program might result in one-half of the heat for the buildings where we live and work being supplied by solar energy instead of by fossil fuels. This would save 10 percent of our national use of fossil fuels, but this enormous saving could be completely wiped out by two years of 5 percent growth. Conservation alone cannot do the job! The most effective way to conserve is to stop the growth in consumption.

As we consider the absolute urgency of conservation we must recognize that some powerful people are hostile to the concept of conservation. One of our great multinational oil companies has advertised that conservation is: "Good for you–but not if there's too much." And in the same ad they noted that: "Conservation does no harm."[35]

In his message to the American people President Carter proposed a tax on large "gas guzzling" cars. General Motors Chairman Thomas Murphy had the following reaction to this proposal to conserve energy: Murphy calls the excise tax on big cars, coupled with rebates on small cars "one of the most simplistic irresponsible and short-sighted ideas ever conceived by the hip-shooting marketeers of the Potomac."[36]

Big labor is hostile to this same conservation measure. Leonard Woodcock, President of the United Auto Workers said of the tax: "I respectfully suggest that the proposal is wrong. It is not properly thought through and should be withdrawn."[37]

Congress is not enthusiastic about conservation: "Look for Senate leaders on both sides of the aisle–including Chairman Russell Long of the Finance Committee and Minority Leader Howard Baker–to gang up on Carter's energy package. The two influential lawmakers want more stress on the production of oil, not so much on conservation."[38]

Closer to home we can note that our governors don't show much enthusiasm for conservation: "The nation's governors told President Carter that the federal government is placing too much emphasis on conservation and not enough on developing new resources."[39]

With all this influential opposition one can see how difficult it will be to launch major national programs of energy conservation.

(iv) We must recycle almost everything. Except for the continuous input of sunlight the human race must finish the trip with the supplies that were aboard when the "spaceship earth" was launched.

(v) We must invest great sums in research (a) to develop the use of solar, geothermal, wind, tidal, biomass, and alternative energy sources; (b) to reduce the problems of nuclear fission power plants; (c) to explore the possibility that we may be able to harness nuclear fusion. These investments must not be made with the idea that if these research programs are successful the new energy sources could sustain growth for a few more doubling times. The investments must be made with the goal that the new energy sources could take over the energy load in a mature and stable society in which fossil fuels are used on a declining exponential curve as chemical raw materials and are not used as fuel for combustion. One great area of responsibility of our community of scientists and engineers is vigorous pursuit of research and development in all these areas. These areas offer great opportunity to creative young people.

Perhaps the most critical things that we must do is to decentralize, and consequently humanize, the scale and scope of our national industrial and utility enterprises.[40]

(iv) We must recognize that it is exceedingly unscientific to promote ever-increasing rates of consumption of our fuel resources based on complete confidence that science, technology, and the economics of the marketplace will combine to produce vast new energy resources as they are needed. Note the certainty that characterizes this confidence.

Coal could help fight a rear-guard action to provide time for scientific breakthroughs which will move the world from the fossil fuel era of wood, gas, oil, and coal to the perpetual energy era of infinitely renewable energy resources.[41] The supply (of coal) is adequate to carry the U.S. well past the transition from the end of the oil and gas era to new, possibly not discovered sources of energy in the 2000s.[42]

There seems to be an almost complete absence of the caution that would counsel us to stop the growth of our national energy appetite until these "unlimited energy resources" are proven to be capable of carrying the national energy load. We must recognize that it is not acceptable to base our national future on the motto "When in doubt, gamble."

Fusion is most commonly mentioned as being an unlimited energy source. The optimism that leads some people to believe that fusion power will be ready whenever it is needed should be balanced against this opening statement in a report on fusion from MIT. "Designing a fusion reactor in 1977 is a little like planning to reach heaven: theories abound on how to do it, and many people are trying, but no one alive has ever succeeded."[43]

If the generation of electric power from fusion was achieved today, we could ask how long would it then be before fusion could play a significant role in our national energy picture. The time-constant for the replacement of one major energy source by another can be estimated from the fact that the first nuclear fission reactor was operated in December 1942.

Even though the recent growth of nuclear energy in the U.S. has been spectacular, it was not until around 1972 that annual energy consumption equaled our annual energy consumption from firewood! By 1973 nuclear energy had climbed to the point where it supplied 1.3 percent of our U.S. total annual energy consumption and 4.6 percent of our electrical power.[44] Thus in thirty-one years nuclear energy has grown to provide only a small fraction of our energy needs. Had there been no growth of our national electrical needs since 1942, today's nuclear plants would be supplying 41 percent of our national electrical power.

(vii) We can no longer sit back and deplore the lack of "leadership" and the lack of response of our political system. In the immortal words of Pogo "We have met the enemy, and they's us." We are the leaders, we are vital parts of the political system and we have an enormous responsibility.

The arithmetic makes clear what will happen if we hope that we can continue to increase our rate of consumption of fossil fuels. Some experts suggest that the system will take care of itself and that growth will stop naturally, even though they know that cancer, if left to run its natural course, always stops when the host is consumed. My seven suggestions are offered in the spirit of *preventive* medicine.

X. CONCLUSION

The preceding calculations are offered as guideposts which must be understood by those who would deal constructively with the energy crisis. The role and limitations of science in analyzing and in solving our problems was beautifully expressed by Gustav Lebon (1841–1931).

> "Science has promised us truth; an understanding of such relationships as our minds can grasp. It has never promised us either peace or happiness."

Perhaps the most succinct conclusion that is indicated by the analysis above is taken from the immortal words of Pogo, "The future ain't what it used to be!" The American system of free enterprise has flourished for 200 years with spectacular achievements. Until recently it flourished in a world whose energy resources were essentially infinite. Whenever one fossil fuel came into short supply, another could always be found to take its place. We are now close enough that we can see the end of the world's total supply of fossil fuels. The challenge that we must meet is set forth clearly in the question, "Can free enterprise survive in a finite world?" President Carter observed (April 18, 1977) that: "If we fail to act soon we will face an economic, social, and political crisis that will threaten our free institutions." (See Figure 6)

XI. A POSTSCRIPT FOR SCIENCE TEACHERS

For decades physics teachers throughout the world have discussed the RC circuit and the decay of radioactive atoms and have thus introduced the simple differential equation that gives rise to exponential decay of the charge on the capacitor or of the number of remaining radioactive nuclei. These provide a wonderful opportunity for us to digress and to point out that exponential arithmetic has great value outside of these two special examples in physics and to show our students that exponential arithmetic is probably the most important mathematics they will ever see. It is especially important for students to see how the change in the sign of the exponent can make an enormous difference in the behavior of the function. But we will need to do more. We must integrate the study of energy and of the exponential arithmetic into our courses as has been done, for example, in one new text.[44] In

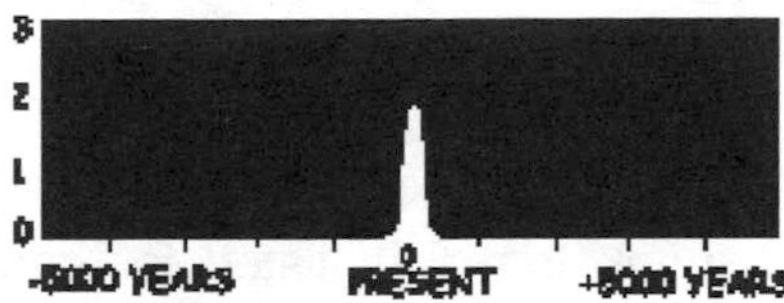

Figure 6. The delta function in the darkness. Redrawn from Hubbert's Figure 69, Ref. 7. The epoch of the world's use of its fossil fuels is shown on a time scale of human history from 5000 year ago to 5000 year in the future. The vertical axis is the rate of consumption of fossil fuels measured in units of 1014 kW h/year. The vertical scale is a linear scale.

addition, we have an even larger task. As science teachers we have the great responsibility of participating constructively in the debates on growth and energy. We must be prepared to recognize opinions such as the following, which was expressed in a letter to me that was written by an ardent advocate of "controlled growth" in our local community: "I take no exception to your arguments regarding exponential growth. I don't think the exponential argument is valid on the local level."

We must bring to these debates the realism of arithmetic and the new concept of precision in the use of language. We must convey to our students the urgency of analyzing all that they read for realism and precision. We must convey to our students the importance of making this analysis even though they are reading the works of an eminent national figure who is writing in one of the world's most widely circulated magazines. (The emphasis in the following quotations is in the original.

> The simple truth is that America has an abundance of energy resources . . . An estimated 920 *trillion* cubic feet of natural gas still lies beneath the United States. Even at present consumption rates, this should last at least forty-five years . . . About 160 *billion* barrels of oil still lie below native ground or offshore. That's enough to last us into the next century at present rates of consumption.[45]

When students analyze these statements they can see that the first statement is false if "abundance" means "sufficient to continue currently accepted patterns of growth of rates consumption for as long as one or two human lifetimes." An evaluation of the second and third statements show that they are falsely reassuring because they suggest the length of time our resources will last under the special condition of no growth of the rates of use of these resources. The condition of no growth in these rates is absolutely contrary to the precepts of our national worship of growth. It is completely misleading to introduce the results of "no growth:" unless one is advocating "no growth."

If it is true that our natural gas reserves will last forty-five years at present rates of consumption (R/r_0 = forty-five year), then Eq. (6) shows that this amount of gas would last only 23.6 years at an annual growth rate of 5 percent/year, and only seventeen years at an annual growth rate of 10 percent/year. When the third statement is analyzed one sees that the given figure of 160 x 10^9 barrels of reserves is roughly 60 percent larger than Hubbert's estimate. This amount would last forty-nine years if oil was produced at the 1970 rate of 3.3 x 10^9 barrels/year, held constant with no growth. However, our domestic consumption is now roughly twice the rate of domestic production, *so this amount of oil would satisfy domestic needs for only about twenty-five year if there was no growth in these domestic needs.* If R/r_0 = 25 year, then Eq. (6) shows that this amount of oil would last only 16.2 year if production grew 5 percent/year and only 12.5 year if it grew 10 percent/year.

We can conclude that the author is probably advocating growth in the rate at which we use fossil fuels from the following imprecise statement, "The fact is that we must produce more energy." Therefore the author's statements about the life expectancy of resources at current rates of use are irrelevant. When they are offered as reassurance of the lack of severity of our energy problem they are dangerously and irresponsibly misleading.

Students should be able to evaluate the same author's statement about coal, "At least 220 *billion* tons of immediately recoverable coal awaits mining in the United States." This "could supply our energy needs for several centuries." Students can see that the size of the coal reserves given by the author is significantly smaller than either of the two estimates given by Hubbert. They can see that it is imprecise and meaningless to suggest how long a resource will last if one says nothing about the rate of growth of production. In addition to encouraging our students to carry out their responsibility to analyze what they read, we must encourage them to recognize the callous (and probably careless) inhumanity of a prominent person who is perhaps in his fifties,[45] offering reassurance to younger readers to the effect, "don't worry, we have enough petroleum to last into the next century," The writer is saying that "There is no need for you to worry, for there is enough petroleum for the rest of my life." Can we accept the urgings of those who advocate unending expansion and growth in the rates of consumption of our fossil fuel resources and who say "Why worry, we have enough to last into the next century."

We must give our students an appreciation of the critical urgency of evaluating the vague, imprecise, and meaningless statements that characterize so much of the public debate on the energy problem. The great benefits of the free press place on each individual the awesome responsibility of evaluating the things that he or she reads. Students of science and engineering have special responsibilities in the energy debate because the problems are quantitative and therefore many of the questions can be evaluated by simple analysis.

Students must be alert not only to the writings in the popular press but to the writings in college textbooks. In the bookstore of a school of engineering I purchased a book that was listed for one of the courses, possibly in political science. Here are a few interesting statements from the book:[46]

> Our population is not growing too rapidly, but much too slowly . . . To approach the problem ("the population scare") from the standpoint of numbers per se is to get the whole thing hopelessly backward . . . Our coal supply alone, for example, is sufficient to power our economy for anywhere for 300 to 900 years–depending on the uses to which it is put–while gas and oil and coal together are obviously good for many centuries . . . So whatever the long-term outlook for these energy sources, it is obvious (that) natural shortage cannot account for the present energy crunch.

Dr. Hubbert, speaking recently, noted that we do not have an energy crisis, we have an energy shortage. He then observed that *the energy shortage has produced a cultural crisis.* (See Figure 7.)

We must emphasize to our students that they have a very special role in our society, a role that follows directly from their analytical abilities. It is their responsibility (and ours) to become the great humanists.

NOTE ADDED IN PROOF:

Two incredible misrepresentations of the life expectancy of U.S. coal reserves have been called to my attention recently. *Time* (April 17, 1978, p.74) said:

> Beneath the pit heads of Appalachia and the Ohio Valley, and under the sprawling strip mines of the West, lie coal seams rich enough to meet the country's power needs for centuries, *no matter how much energy consumption may grow*." (emphasis added)

In reply to my letter correcting this, *Time* justified their statement by saying that they were using the Citibank estimate of U.S. coal reserves which is larger than the estimate used by Hubbert.

A beautiful booklet, "Energy and Economic Independence" (Energy Fuels Corporation of Denver, Denver, 1976) said: "As reported by *Forbes* magazine, the United States holds 437 billion tons of known (coal) reserves. That is equivalent to 1.8 trillion barrels of oil in British Thermal units, *or enough energy to keep 100 million large electric generating plants going for the next 800 years or so.*" (emphasis added) This is an accurate quotation from *Forbes*, the respected business magazine (December 15, 1975, p.28). Long division is all that is needed to show that 437×10^9 tons of coal would supply our 1976 production of 0.665×10^9 tons per year for only 657 years, and we probably have fewer than 500 large electric generating plants in the U.S. today. This booklet concluded, "Your understanding of the facts about "energy and economic independence' issue is of great importance."

A very thoughtful comment on fusion was made to me recently by a person who observed that it might prove to be the worst thing that ever happened to us if we succeed in using nuclear fusion to generate electrical energy because this success would lead us to conclude that we could continue the unrestrained growth in our annual energy consumption to the point (in a relatively few doubling times) where our energy production from the unlimited fusion resource was an appreciable fraction of the solar power input to the earth. This could have catastrophic consequences.

Richard Stout, columnist for the *New Republic*, noted (*Time*, March 27, 1978, p. 83) that in America, "We consume one third of all the energy, one third of the food and enjoy one half of the world's income. Can a disparity like this last? I think that much of the news in the next fifty years is going to turn on whether we yield to the inevitable graciously or vindictively."

APPENDIX

When a quantity such as the rate $r(t)$ of consumption of a resource grows a fixed percent per year, the growth is exponential:

$$r(t) = r_0 e^{kt} = r_0 2^{t/T_2} \quad (1)$$

where r_0 is the current rate of consumption at $t = 0$, e is the base of natural logarithms, k is the fractional growth per year, and t is the time in years. The growing quantity will increase to twice its initial size in the doubling time T_2 where: T_2 (year) = (ln 2) / k » $70/P$ (2) and where P, the percent growth per year, is $100k$. The total consumption of a resource between the present ($t = 0$) and a future time T is:

$$C = \{T \text{ to } 0\} \quad r(t)\, dt \quad (3)$$

The consumption in a steady period of growth is:

$$C = r_0 \{T \text{ to } 0\} \quad e^{kt}\, dt = (r_0/k)(e^{kt} - 1) \quad (4)$$

If the known size of the resource is R tons, then we can determine the exponential expiration time (EET) by finding the time T_e at which the total consumption C is equal to R:

$$R = (r_0/k)(e^{kT_e} - 1) \quad (5)$$

We may solve this for the exponential expiration time T_e where:

$$\text{EET} = T_e = (1/k) \ln (k R/r_0 + 1) \quad (6)$$

This equation is valid for all positive values of k and for those negative values of k for which the argument of the logarithm is positive.

NOTES:

1. This paper is based on a series of articles, "The Exponential Function" which is appearing in *The Physics Teacher:*
   (a) Vol. 14, p. 393 (Oct. 1976); (b) Vol. 14, p. 485 (Nov. 1976); (c) Vol. 15, p. 37 (Jan. 1977); (d) Vol. 15, p. 98 (Mar. 1977); (e) Vol. 15, p. 225 (Apr. 1977); (f) Vol. 16, p. 23 (Jan. 1978); (g) Vol. 16, p. 92 (Feb. 1978); (h) Vol. 16, p. 158 (Mar. 1978).

   An early version of this paper was presented at the Third Annual UMR-MEC Conference on Energy, held at the University of Missouri at Rolla, Oct. 12–14, 1976, and appears in the volume of the *Proceedings of the Conference*. The early version, or minor revisions of it have been published in *Not Man Apart* published by Friends of the Earth: July/Aug. 1977, Vol. 7, No. 14 pp. 12–13; *The Vermillion Flycatcher* (Tucson, Arizona Audubon Society, December 1977); *The Colorado Business Review* (Grad. Sch. of Business Admin. of the University of Colorado, Jan/Feb 1978).
2. *Newsweek*, Dec. 6, 1976.
3. A. A. Bartlett; *Civil Engineering*, Dec. 1969, p. 71.
4. *Time*, April 25, 1977, p. 27.
5. W. Von Engelhardt, J. Goguel, M. King Hubbert, J. E. Prentice, R.A. Price, and R. Trumpy; *Environmental Geology*, Vol. 1, 193–206 (1976).
6. A. A. Bartlett, *Proceedings of the Third Annual UMR-MEC Conference on Energy*, University of Missouri at Rolla, Missouri, October 12–14, 1976, p. 10.
7. *U.S. Energy Resources, a Review as of 1972*, a background paper prepared at the request of the Hon. Henry M. Jackson, Chairman of the Committee on Interior and Insular Affairs of the United States Senate, pursuant to Senate Resolution 45: M. King Hubbert, *A National Fuels and Energy Policy Study*, Serial 93-40 (92–75) Part 1 (U.S. GPO, Washington, D.C., 1973), $2.35, 267 pages. This document is an invaluable source of data on consumption rates and trends in consumption, for both the U.S.A. and the world. In it Hubbert also sets forth the simple calculus of his methods of analysis. He does not confine his attention solely to exponential growth. He predicts that the rate of rise and subsequent fall of consumption of a resource will follow a symmetrical curve that looks like the normal error curve. Several figures in this paper are redrawn from Hubbert's paper.
8. L. Ruedisili and M. Firebaugh, *Perspectives on Energy*, (Oxford University Press, New York, 1975).
9. M. King Hubbert, *Resources and Man*, National Academy of Sciences and National Research Council, (Freeman, San Francisco, 1969), Chapter 8.
10. M. King Hubbert, "Energy Resources of the Earth," *Scientific American*, Sept. 1971, p. 60. Reprinted as a book (Freeman, San Francisco, 1971).
11. M. Iona, *Physics Teacher*, Vol. 15, p. 324 (1977).
12. Emile Benoit, "The Coming Age of Shortages," *Bulletin of Atomic Scientists*, January 1976, p. 7. Benoit attributes his information to David Pimintel *et* al., "Food Production and the Energy Crisis," *Science*, Vol. 182, p. 448 (Nov. 2, 1973). This article is the first of three by Benoit (*Bulletin of Atomic Scientists*, Jan., Feb., Mar., 1976,). These are one of the best presentations I have read of coming problems of food, fuels, and resources.
13. *Newsweek*, Jan. 31, 1977.

14. "Factors Affecting the Use of Coal in Present and Future Energy Markets" a background paper prepared by The Congressional Research Service at the request of Sen. Henry M. Jackson, Chairman of the Committee on Interior and Insular Affairs of the United States Senate pursuant to Senate Resolution 45, a *National Fuels and Energy Policy Study Serial No. 93-9 (92–44)* (U.S. GPO, Washington, D.C., 1973) pp. 41, 42, 15.
15. "The Energy Crisis" a booklet by the U.S. Energy Research and Development Agency (ERDA) Oak Ridge, Tennessee, no date, p. 3. (1975 or 1976).
16. Associated Press story "Energy Head Stresses Coal Reserves," in the *Boulder Daily Camera*, July 5, 1975.
17. "America's Coal: A Gold Mine of Energy," Exxon Corporation two-page full-color ad in *Newsweek,* 1975.
18. "They're trying to tell us something. We're foolish not to listen," American Electric Power Company, Inc. Two-page ad in *Newsweek*, 1975.
19. "The call to greater energy independence" American Electric Power Company, Inc., ad in *Newsweek*, Nov. 3, 1975.
20. "An open letter on energy to those who are still employed." American Electric Power Company, Inc., ad in *Newsweek*, Jan. 12, 1976.
21. W. H. Miernyk, *Journal of Energy and Development*, Vol. 1, No. 2, p. 223 (1976).
22. "The Whale Oil, Chicken, and Energy Syndrome," an address before the Economic Club of Detroit by Walter B. Wriston, Chairman, First National City Corporation, Feb. 25, 1974.
23. "The Transitional Storm, Part I, An Explanation," by the Edison Electric Institute for the Electric Companies, in *Broadcasting*, July 26, 1976.
24. Charles O. Frush, "Moral Basis for Mineral Resource Use and Development Policy" The Mines Magazine, Colorado School of Mines, March 1973, p. 20.
25. J. C. Fisher, "Physics and the Energy Problem," *Physics Today*, American Institute of Physics, New York, 1974.
26. "Opening Remarks, UMR-MEC Conference on Energy," R. L. Bisplinghoff, *Proceedings of the Conference*, Oct. 7–9, 1975, University of Missouri at Rolla.
27. *Washington Star*, Feb. 12, 1977.
28. L. G. Hauser, "Creating the Electric Energy Economy," *Proceedings of the Second Annual UMR-MEC Conference on Energy*, October 7–9, 1975, p. 3., University of Missouri at Rolla.
29. Gil Bailey, "Conservation–Development Proposed As Solution," Washington Bureau of the *Boulder Daily Camera*, March 13, 1973.
30. *Time*, May 19, 1975, p. 55.
31. D. Brower, *Not Man Alone*, Vol. 6, No. 20, Nov. 1976; Friends of the Earth, 529 Commercial, San Francisco.
32. C. C. Garvin, Jr., Chairman of the Exxon Corporation; Full page ad in the *Rocky Mountain News*, July 23, 1976.
33. G. Pazik, in a special editorial feature, "Our Petroleum Predicament," in *Fishing Facts* ("The magazine for today's freshwater fisherman"), Northwoods Publishing Co., P.O. Box 609, Menomonee Falls, WI 53051. Nov. 1976. Reprints are available at $0.30 each from the publisher. This is an excellent summary of the present situation and of the way we got into our petroleum predicament.
34. *The Arizona Republic*, Feb. 8, 1978.
35. "Conservation is like Cholesterol" an ad copyrighted 1976 by the Mobil Oil Corporation.
36. *Boulder Daily Camera*, April 4, 1977.
37. *Boulder Daily Camera*, May 16, 1977.
38. *U.S. News & World Report*, July 25, 1977, P. 8.
39. *Boulder Daily Camera*, July 10, 1977.

40. Amory Lovins, "Energy Strategy, the Road Not Taken," *Foreign Affairs*, Oct. 1976. This material is now available as a book, *Soft Energy Paths; Toward a Durable Peace* Ballinger, Cambridge, MA, 1977). It is said that this book "could very well be the most important book on energy policy of this decade."
41. W. L. Rogers, Special Assistant to the Secretary of the Interior, quoted in the *Denver Post*, Nov. 19, 1976.
42. *Time*, April 4, 1977, p. 63.
43. *Technology Review,* Dec. 1976, p. 21, reprinted in the second edition of Ref. 8.
44. Robert H. Romer, *Energy–An Introduction to Physics* (Freeman, San Francisco, 1976), pp. 594–597. In addition to making energy the central theme of an introductory text, this book has eighteen appendices (sixty-one pages) of data ranging from "Units and conversion factors" to the "History of energy production and consumption in the world and in the United States" to "Exponential growth" to "Consumer prices of common sources of energy." The book is at once a text and a valuable source of reference data.
45. Melvin Laird, "The Energy Crisis: Made in U.S.A." *Reader's Digest*, Sept. 1977, P. 56.
46. M. Stanton Evans, *Clear and Present Dangers*, (Harcourt Brace Jovanovich, New York, 1975).

NIXON AND AMERICAN POPULATION POLICY: ANNIVERSARY OF A MISSED OPPORTUNITY

David Simcox

March 1998

The post-mortems marking the twenty-fifth anniversary of Watergate earlier in 1997 overshadowed another quarter-century milestone of the Richard Nixon era—one of even greater long-term consequence for the nation's future.

In 1972 President Nixon rejected the report of John Rockefeller's Commission on Population and the American Future—the nation's sole consideration of an explicit population policy. While the idea of a national commission took form under Lyndon Johnson, President Nixon made population growth a major concern, calling it in 1969 "one of the most serious challenges to human destiny in the last third of this century." He backed legislation creating the commission and appointed most of its members. Senator Daniel Patrick Moynihan, then a Nixon White House advisor, was a driving force.

There was good reason then for Nixon's sense of urgency. The post-war baby boom had added fifty million Americans in just two decades. If that high birth rate had persisted there would have been 400 million Americans by 2013.

In its two years of study, the Rockefeller Commission produced recommendations that were bold, visionary and often counter-cultural. With the United States then at about 206 million, the Commission called for an early end to further population growth, appealing to Americans to abandon their "ideological addiction to growth" and the outdated pronatalist biases rooted in their social institutions. For the Commission, the critical corrective was for American couples to move from the prevailing three-child family to no more than two children.

Even business representatives on the Commission supported the central, near heretical finding: "the health of our country does not depend on population growth, nor does the vitality of business, nor the welfare of the average person."

The recommendation boldly confronted explosive issues:

- Abortion—decriminalize it;
- Contraceptives—remove the remaining legal bars to their availability;
- Sex education—make it available to all through schools and community institutions;
- Immigration—freeze legal immigration at 400,000 a year and stop illegal immigration;
- Equal Rights Amendment—support it and other efforts to ban all discrimination based on sex.

The Commission rejected charges that it would have the government tell citizens how many children they could have. Its proclaimed goal was freedom of choice under which . . . "it would be equally honorable to marry or not, to be childless or not, to have one child or two, or more. Our goal is less regimentation of reproductive behavior, not more."

Faced with splenetic opposition from major churches and conservative groups, and aware that America's fertility was finally dropping, the once enthusiastic Nixon rejected the report. He stressed that abortion was an unacceptable means of birth control and that contraceptives for youth would weaken families.

Rockefeller's report was shelved, but the issues it dealt with were not. A year later *Roe v. Wade* decriminalized abortion. Most state governments dismantled the remains of the Comstock laws restricting contraceptives, and expanded sex education. Fertility fell below replacement: the American public in the last quarter century has opted for the two-child family favored by the Commission.

Even so, the nation's population future remains troubling. Mass immigration, now three times the 400,000 annual limit the Commission wanted, accounts for almost 40 percent of current population growth, negating the population savings from lowered domestic fertility. And pro-natalist biases persist in our laws and official attitudes.

The United States has added 60 million people since the Commission spoke. The Census Bureau conservatively projects 125 million more in the next fifty-five years. Since the Commission convened in 1970, nearly 90 percent of that growth will be attributable to immigrants settling in the United States and their descendants. In the last quarter century the Rockefeller Commission's spurned goal of a stationary American population has become a receding prospect.

AN ESSAY ON A SUSTAINABLE ECONOMY

Donald Mann, President

Negative Population Growth, Inc.

1999

FOREWORD

Since NPG was founded over a quarter century ago it has argued that the most important task facing the human race is to create an economy that would be sustainable indefinitely, and afford an adequate standard of living for all the world's people. But to create such a sustainable economy would be impossible without a smaller world population than the 3.8 billion existing in 1972 when NPG was founded.

Until now we have never attempted to define what size global economy would be sustainable, but we feel that an attempt to do so, despite the obvious difficulties of such an undertaking, is long overdue.

The central purpose of this paper is to try and address the following two questions:

1. What is the optimal size of a global economy that would be sustainable indefinitely, and afford an adequate standard of living for all?
2. What size world population would be necessary in order to create such a sustainable global economy?

SUMMARY

A short definition of sustainability is the management of environmental and resource systems so that their ability to support future generations is not diminished. The term "sustainable development" is more difficult to define, and has given rise to widely different and at times conflicting interpretations. For environmentalists and conservationists it has come to mean the process of development toward a truly sustainable economy that respects environmental and resource limits. But too often others use the term sustainable development as a synonym for sustainable economic growth.

In contrast to that view, many scientists believe, as do we at NPG, that sustainable economic growth is an oxymoron and self-contradictory. Adherents of this view point out that, since the economy is a subset of our non-growing ecosystem, development, in order to be sustainable, can only mean qualitative change without material growth.

Given the damage to our environment and resources resulting from the present scale of human economic activity, the argument against further material economic growth appears to be unassailable. The need now is to go beyond the debate on growth vs. non-growth and address the fundamental question: what scale or size of global economic activity would be sustainable indefinitely? The preponderance of evidence clearly indicates that the global economy, to be sustainable, must be far smaller than it is today.

Population size is the crucial variable in achieving a sustainable economy. Only with a sufficient reduction in population would it be possible to envisage a decent standard of living for all, within the constraints of the world ecosystem.

What size world population would allow the creation of a sustainable economy? We at NPG believe that it is in the range of 1.5 to 2 billion, based on the assessments of the major population and resource scientists most concerned with the limits of economic growth. That was the level of world population as recently as the first decade of the twentieth century, before the pressure of numbers had generated the environmental damage now visible.

We recognize that a specific target can never be more than a rough approximation, given the uncertainties, value judgments, and changing human preferences involved. Nevertheless we are convinced that a specific population target is the essential prerequisite for action. The only alternative is to take refuge in vague warnings and exhortations, as almost all population and environmental organizations do, and consequently accept aimless drift. If we wait for absolute and likely unattainable precision before taking action on population, we will be forever locked into inaction on the most critical issue that will shape the human future.

But far from the 1.5 to 2 billion we believe would be sustainable, if present trends continue our present world population of six billion is projected to nearly double in the twenty-first century, with most of the growth in the developing countries. But a massive reduction in the size of world population will require a massive reduction in the population of every country in the world, developed and developing alike. That in turn will require the achievement of fertility rates well below the replacement level of roughly 2.1 children per woman. Such levels have already been reached by most countries in Europe, some of which are already experiencing population decline.

If almost no women had more than two children, the world's fertility rate would drop well below the replacement level because some women choose to have only one child, or remain childless. For at least the next two generations the two-child maximum family must become the world's norm.

Almost everyone concurs that sustainable development is desirable, but its meaning remains somewhat vague, and subject to widely divergent interpretations. As Professor Herman Daly has pointed out (Daly, 1996), it is a term that everyone likes, but nobody is sure of what it means. The latest trendy term, "smart growth" has the same appealing ambiguity.

The term "Sustainable Development" first came into prominence with the publication of The Brundtland Report Our Common Future (World Commission on Environment and Development, 1987). The report was tremendously influential in popularizing the concept. Regrettably, the report did not distinguish between growth in physical consumption and investment and qualitative development without growth, and never faced up to the inherent contradiction between sustainability and unlimited material growth.

Indeed the report begins with a clear call for economic growth: "What is needed now is a new era of economic growth—growth that is forceful and at the same time socially and environmentally sustainable." The Report even foresaw a five to tenfold growth in world GNP (about $30 trillion in 1996) in fifty years to meet the minimal needs of the world's poor, without ever explaining how such enormous growth could possibly be sustainable.

Perhaps the essence of the Report's message is captured in the following sentence: "The Commission's overall assessment is that the international economy must speed up world growth while respecting the environmental constraints." Prudently, the Commission refrained from attempting to explain how the two conflicting goals could possibly be reconciled.

The apostles of unlimited economic growth have endeavored to cloak their views in an aura of respectability by treating "sustainable development" and "economic growth" as being synonymous. The following quotation from the President's Council on Sustainable Development (1995) is a good example:

> "A sustainable United States will have a growing economy (underscoring added) that provides equitable opportunities for satisfying livelihoods and a safe, healthy, high quality of life for current and future generations. Our nation will protect its environment, its natural resources base and the functions and viability of natural systems on which all life depends."

It seems clear, therefore, that to the President's Council "Sustainable Development" means "Sustainable Economic Growth." The problem with the latter term, of course, is that it is an oxymoron, a contradiction in terms, since no material growth on a finite earth can possibly be sustainable indefinitely (Grant, 1997).

AN OPPOSING (AND REALISTIC) VIEW

There is a completely opposite view of the meaning of "sustainable development" that guides NPG. Economist Herman Daly, an originator of this view, has defined sustainable development as development without growth beyond environmental carrying capacity, where development means qualitative improvement and growth means quantitative increase (Daly, 1996).

Professor Daly writes, "The power of the concept of sustainable development is that it both reflects and evokes a latent shift in our vision of how the economic activities of human beings are related to the natural world—an ecosystem which is finite, non-growing, and materially closed. The demands of these activities on the containing ecosystem for regeneration of raw material "inputs" and absorption of waste "outputs" must, I will argue, be kept at ecologically sustainable levels as a condition of sustainable development. This change in vision involves replacing the economic norm of quantitative expansion (growth) with that of qualitative improvement (development) as the path of future progress" (Daly, 1996, p.1).

Professor Daly goes on to say that the principal property of sustainable development is that the scale of the economic subsystem is within the carrying capacity of the ecosystem. We fully agree with that statement.

A SUSTAINABLE ECONOMY

A great deal of confusion might have been avoided if The Brundtland Report had chosen as its theme "a sustainable economy," rather than "sustainable development."

The goal of a sustainable economy would have focused the debate about sustainability on the crux of the problem confronting us: how to create a global economy that can be sustained by the earth's resource base indefinitely, with an adequate standard of living for all.

We propose that the unattainable goal of sustainable economic growth be abandoned and replaced with a specific and unambiguous goal: a sustainable economy. A necessary condition of a sustainable economy is sustainable resource use (Lachenbruch, 1997).

A STEADY-STATE ECONOMY

Since growth in the annual throughput of energy and materials cannot be sustained in our finite world, a sustainable economy must, of necessity, be a steady-state economy, characterized by a zero rate of material growth. Once it becomes generally accepted that material growth in a finite world cannot be sustained, then the goal of a steady-state economy should become widely recognized as our only viable option.

Attainment of a non-growing, steady-state economy, however, is only part of the solution. We also need to recognize that the present size of our global economy (which is a subset of our global ecosystem) burdens our ecosystem far too much to be sustainable indefinitely. Therefore, merely halting economic growth at the present level of economic activity would, at best, be only a necessary first step. We would need thereafter to reduce the size of the global economy to a sustainable level and then stabilize it there.

As a first step in that direction we need to decide on two critical parameters:

1. The level at which a global economy (defined as the annual throughput of energy and materials) would be sustainable, and set that as our goal.

2. The conditions that would enable us to reach that goal, which would include first, and most importantly, defining what size global population would be required. Population size is crucial. All other considerations such as levels of technology and per capita consumption being equal, our impact on our environment is a function of numbers.

To be sustainable indefinitely, a steady-state global economy would have to meet the following criteria, as set forth by Daly (1990):

Output rule: Waste outputs are within the natural absorptive capacities of the environment (i.e. nondepletion of the sink services of natural capital).

Input rules: (a) For renewable inputs, harvest rates should not exceed regeneration rates (nondepletion of the source services of natural capital). (b) For non-renewable inputs the rate of depletion should not exceed the rate at which renewable substitutes can be developed.

Those are indeed rigorous criteria, but it would be difficult to argue that sustainability could be achieved with anything less demanding. Clearly, our present global economy does not meet those criteria. The evidence is overwhelming that the present level of world economic activity cannot long be sustained without causing permanent and irreparable damage to the earth's natural systems that make economic activity possible.

Global warming, the thinning of the ozone layer, acid rain, soil erosion, the loss of wetlands, deforestation, desertification, the disappearance of millions of plant and animal species, the problems with the disposal of solid, toxic and nuclear wastes, the depletion and pollution of underground aquifers, the impending exhaustion of world oil supplies; all these and more support that assertion.

There is already a scientific consensus that our present path will lead to disaster. In February 1992 the National Academy of Sciences and the Royal Society of London issued a joint statement warning that: "If current predictions of population growth prove accurate and patterns of human activity on the planet remain unchanged, science and technology may not be able to prevent either irreversible degradation of the environment or continued poverty for much of the world."

If the present size of the global economy (the annual throughput of energy and materials) is not sustainable, then what size would be? The preponderance of evidence indicates that it would be substantially smaller than its present size. The direction we need to move in, therefore, is clear, even if at the present time a specific target cannot be defined with scientific precision.

What is needed is a negative rate of physical economic growth (i.e. throughput of materials and energy and output of waste and pollution) until such time as the global economy has been reduced to a size that can meet Daly's criteria.

THE NATURE OF PROOF

A scientifically precise calculation that would pinpoint with absolute certainty a sustainable size for either the economy or for population may well be unattainable. In an infinitely complex and evolving world and society there are simply too many interlocked and frequently unquantifiable variables.

Moreover, the current accounting systems for measuring national and global gross product obscure rather than encourage the needed precision, failing to account for the ongoing depletion of natural capital. Adoption of environmentally aware accounting systems is essential to measuring progress toward true sustainability.

Fortunately, we do not need scientific precision before acting. If we wait for absolute proof before adjusting the economy and population to the earth's limits, we will be forever locked into inaction on the major issues that will shape the human future. In most social and political areas we must make every day decisions based on imperfect knowledge, while applying the rule of prudence. The same holds true for economics and population.

POPULATION—THE KEY VARIABLE

Without a gradual but drastic reduction in the size of world population a major reduction in the size of the global economy would be impossible. Our present world population of six billion is still growing rapidly by about 80 million each year. It is projected to reach 10 to 11 billion before the end of the twenty-first century, although rising mortality rates may well prevent growth of that magnitude from being realized. We at NPG have long believed that a sustainable world population size is in the range of 1.5 to 2 billion, and that we should look to scientists, in particular to biologists and ecologists, for the most reliable estimates of the optimum size of world population.

Cornell University Professor David Pimentel, and his collaborators, have argued convincingly that an optimal and sustainable world population would be no greater than 1.5 to 2.0 billion (Pimentel, Giampetro, and Bukkens, 1998).

Their arguments can be briefly summarized as follows: The natural resources needed to sustain human life—ample fertile land, water, energy, forests and diverse natural biota—are finite. Population growth is reducing their per capita availability, and forcing greater reliance on diminishing fossil fuels. Trade and technology have masked these natural limits, but cannot compensate for the shrinkage of natural resources per capita.

Overexploitation of the earth's natural capital is causing what Pimentel terms a "hypercycle:" rising fossil energy inputs yield progressively fewer resources. Top soil is lost thirty times faster than it is replaced. Fresh water sources are overdrawn and degraded. The myriad species which serve human life are disappearing at the rate of 150 a day. The planet's inability to process the waste products of mass consumption of fossil fuels results in acid rain and global warming.

Our unsustainable culture of growth, Pimentel states, requires recognition of harsh limits. Population size must be consistent with environmental constraints. The higher the standard of living the smaller the population size that can be safely maintained. Technology may ameliorate, but it cannot prevent, environmental collapse. The human population, already excessive, is rapidly damaging the life prospects of future generations. Pimentel, backed by other scientists, sets the optimum population for a sustainable earth, with existing technology and an adequate standard of living, at no greater than 1.5 to 2.0 billion.

The crux of the matter is this: in order to know what policies need to be put into place we need to know not only the direction in which we should be heading, but we also need to have as precise an idea as possible of the approximate extent of the changes needed, a notion of the order of magnitude.

In any event, at best it would require more than a century to reduce world population to within a range of 1.5 to 2 billion, (by reducing fertility, temporarily, to well below the replacement level). There would be, therefore, ample time to do further research with regard to optimum population size, to take into account advances in technology, and to make any midcourse corrections believed to be desirable.

Unless, however, we can develop a consensus now on a specific numerical target or goal for an optimum world population we will continue our rapid growth toward a world population size that will almost surely bring on an economic and ecological disaster. If we are unable to stabilize world population at a level far lower than today's, the result will be human misery and suffering on a massive scale.

Only by achieving a far smaller world population can we have any hope of eliminating forever hunger and poverty, and of creating a society that will be sustainable indefinitely in a sound and healthy environment, with a base of material prosperity that will minimize human suffering and allow civilization to flourish.

We also need, of course, to find more efficient ways to produce goods and services so that the input of materials and energy and the output of pollution per unit of production is reduced as much as possible. But no combination of efficiencies now in sight would obviate the need for a drastic reduction in the size of world population. That is the indispensable condition, the sine qua non, of a sustainable economy.

HOW TO GET THERE FROM HERE

How could we possibly go about the daunting task of halting and then reversing the growth of world population so that it could eventually be stabilized within a range of 1.5 to 2 billion? Barring a disastrous rise in mortality, a reversal of population growth would require a level of fertility substantially below replacement level (an average of 2.1 children per woman).

If our goal is to halt and reverse world population growth until world population can, after an interim period of population decline, eventually be stabilized at a sustainable level, then a below replacement level of fertility would be required for both the developing and developed countries of the world (including, of course, the United States).

We need a specific goal or target for fertility just as we need a specific target for world population size. I suggest that a fertility of 1.5 is needed for at least several decades in order to halt and reverse world population growth. As already mentioned, that level of fertility could be reached if almost no women had more than two children, since many women voluntarily have only one child, or no children at all.

In a few European countries today the level of fertility is below 1.5 and in those countries fertility needs to be increased to that level. Extremely low fertility (below 1.5) should be avoided because of its disruptive effects on age structure, and because population decline should be a slow and orderly process.

In many developing countries couples desire three children or more. Therefore, even with perfect contraception and no unwanted pregnancies, the population of those countries would continue growing unless desired family size is reduced. If that is not done there can be no hope of achieving what is needed: a level of fertility substantially below the replacement level.

Family planning, the provision of contraceptives, is essential. Other vitally important measures include improving the status of women, and their education and job opportunities. But all such measures need to be supplemented by non-coercive incentives and disincentives to reduce desired family size by encouraging couples to have not more than two children. Examples of non-coercive incentives and disincentives would include tax and financial incentives, and preferences for employment and housing for couples with not more than two children. Family limitation, not just family planning, must become the order of the day. The two-child maximum family must become the norm (Grant, 1996).

THE GLOBAL ECONOMY VERSUS PER CAPITA INCOME

We are faced with the following dilemma: On the one hand is the need to reduce the size of the global economy. On the other hand is the need to raise per capita income to an adequate level for most of the billions of people in the developing nations, and for tens of millions of poor people in the developed nations. There is also the need, of course, to maintain an adequate income for those whose income is already satisfactory.

There is only one way that this conflict can possibly be resolved, and that is by reducing the number of people. There is no other way that per capita income for many can continue to increase while, at the same time, the global economy is being reduced to, and then maintained at, a size that would be sustainable.

The conventional wisdom seems to be that economic growth must continue if what really counts, per capita income, is to continue to grow. If persisted in, however, global, or aggregate economic growth will diminish per capita income. That is because at some point, if we do not halt it voluntarily, economic growth will be brought to a halt by environmental constraints (either from resource shortages, or because the absorptive capacity of our environment for pollution has been exceeded).

Thus, over the long term, aggregate economic growth and per capita income growth are not compatible, but are in direct conflict.

ECONOMIC GROWTH—A TWO-EDGED SWORD

The industrial revolution, which has been responsible for our amazing economic growth over the last two centuries, has brought a better life and a higher standard of living to many of the world's people. Economic growth, in many ways, has been a blessing, but hardly an unqualified one.

At the same time it has created tremendous problems because of its unavoidable by-products: pollution and resource depletion. Among the terrible costs of economic growth have been rapid depletion of our fossil fuel deposits which took nature hundreds of millions of years to create, but which, if consumption continues at present rates, face imminent exhaustion.

Even more serious, because the pollution and waste products generated by human economic activity have overwhelmed the absorptive capacity of our ecosystem, continued economic activity at the present level, or at even higher levels, threatens to destroy the earth's natural systems, upon which all economic activity, and life itself, depend.

Cornucopians mistakenly believe that technology and human ingenuity can solve any problems associated with population and economic growth. They argue that both population growth and economic growth have historically gone hand in hand, and can continue to do so indefinitely. They point out that, in many countries, such indicators of human welfare as diet, life expectancy and per capita income have improved along with population growth.

But they fail to realize that the human economic activity that has made possible such improvements in welfare is not sustainable. Almost any size population at almost any standard of living can be maintained, but only for short periods of time. Their perception is akin to that of the man who jumped off a twenty-story building and was convinced that all was for the best in the best of all possible worlds until he arrived at the bottom.

The fact is that there is no technological solution to the problem confronting us—how to create an economy that will be sustainable indefinitely, with an adequate standard of living for all. It is true that science and technology can ameliorate the impact of a given level of economic activity on our environment by discovering new ways to use energy and materials more efficiently, in order to reduce the throughput of energy and materials and the output of waste and pollution per unit of production. But such measures are no substitute for reducing our impact on the environment by a reduction in population to a sustainable level.

EXPONENTIAL GROWTH AND DOUBLING TIME

An understanding of exponential growth and the concept of doubling time is essential to understanding that no material growth can long continue on a finite planet. Exponential growth can be described as the result of a constant annual growth rate applied to a constantly increasing base. Interest on a savings account is a good example.

One of the characteristics of exponential growth is that, at a given rate of growth, the time it would take anything (e.g. money, the economy, or population size, etc.) growing at that rate to double in size can be fairly accurately calculated by dividing the constant annual growth rate into seventy. For example, money invested at an interest rate of 7 percent would double in ten years. A population growing at a 2 percent annual rate would double in thirty-five years.

It is puzzling that those who advocate continued economic growth seem not to understand the basic concept of doubling time. For the United States and other developed countries, economists consider that an annual economic growth rate in the range of two to four percent is normal and achievable. The doubling time for economic growth at the rate of three percent a year, for example, is roughly twenty-three years (seventy divided by three). It would take, therefore, slightly more than 100 years for an economy growing at that rate to have doubled five times and be (if the world's resources could possibly allow such growth) a staggering thirty-two times larger than it is today. Another five doublings would result in an economy over 1,000 times larger than today's.

The absurdity of the belief that economic growth can long continue is apparent. No resource, regardless of how large, can possibly withstand more than a very few doublings (Bartlett, 1978).

PRETENDING WON'T MAKE IT SO

We must stop pretending that a global economy with a world population of 10–12 billion could possibly be sustainable. Our already overstressed ecosystem cannot provide, for the long term, an adequate standard of living for our present huge world population of six billion, much less for the even vaster numbers awaiting us unless we take action now.

Our nation's leaders, and world leaders, must face up to the reality that a global economy and world population that greatly exceed an optimum size are not sustainable, and will eventually result in an economic and ecological catastrophe.

Our present goal seems to be to provide an ever rising standard of living for ever increasing numbers, but that must be seen for what it is: an impossible dream. The great lesson of the industrial revolution is that vast numbers of people are simply incompatible with an industrial society.

Further population growth on the gigantic scale now projected is not inevitable. With the will, we could start now on the path toward a sustainable global economy by first reducing, then stabilizing world population in the range of 1.5 to 2 billion. The negative rate of population growth we need in order to do so depends on our achieving levels of fertility substantially below replacement level in all the countries in the world. Almost all the developed countries have already reached that level.

More than 90 percent of future world population growth is projected to occur in the developing countries. To achieve a below replacement level fertility in those countries, there must be put in place rigorous population programs geared to family limitation (no more than two children) rather than to family planning alone. Family planning must be supplemented by non-coercive incentives and disincentives to encourage the two-child limit per woman.

MANKIND AT THE CROSSROADS

Earth is truly in the balance as the third millennium opens. The United States has the opportunity to lead the world by its example and its support for family limitation toward a smaller, ecologically sustainable population and economy in the twenty-first century. The task before us, because of its size and complexity, is an awesome one. But the alternative to our goal of a sustainable world economy is unthinkable—widespread poverty and misery in a dreary and depleted environment inhospitable to human life.

If we continue to ignore the constraints to growth imposed by a finite world, technological and industrial man may well turn out to be a strictly temporary phenomenon in the long history of life on this planet. We are living at a momentous time in history. We still have the power—if we can only develop the will—to halt and reverse population growth. That power, if not exercised, may no longer exist even a few years from now.

Mankind today stands at a crossroads. One road, that of further population growth, leads inevitably to starvation, poverty, social chaos and war. It leads to the certain destruction of all that we hold dear, including personal freedom and political liberty, peace and security, a decent standard of living, and a healthy environment.

The other road leads to population stabilization at a sustainable level after a transition period of population decrease. That is the road humanity must start down now. It leads to a world population in balance with its environment and resources, thus creating the condition that will allow the human race to live in peace and prosperity for as long as spaceship earth shall continue to exist.

NOTES:

1. Bartlett, Albert A. (1978). Forgotten Fundamentals of the Energy Crisis. *American Journal of Physics, Volume 46, September 1978, pages 876 to 888.*
2. Daly, Herman E. (1990). Toward Some Operational Principles of Sustainable Development, *Ecological Economics*, 2, 1–6.
3. Daly, Herman E. (1996). *Beyond Growth*. Boston, MA: Beacon Press.
4. Grant, Lindsey (1997). On the Edge of an Oxymoron. *NPG Forum*, March 1997. Washington, DC, Negative Population Growth, Inc.
5. Grant, Lindsey (1996). *Juggernaut: Growth on a Finite Planet*. Santa Ana, CA: Seven Locks Press.
6. Lachenbruch, Arthur H. (1997). Buzzwords and Debate About the Human Future. *GSA Today, volume 7, no. 5*, May 1997, 12–14. (*GSA Today* is a monthly publication of the Geological Society of America.)
7. Pimentel, David, M. Giampietro, and S.G.F. Bukkens (1998). An Optimum Population for North and Latin America.
8. *Population and Development: a Journal of Interdisciplinary Studies.* 29(2).p.125. See also Pimentel, D., Bailey,O., Kim, P.,
9. Mullaney, E., Calabrese, J., Walman, F., Nelson, F., & Yao, X. (1999). *Will Limits of the Earth's Resources Control Human Numbers?* Environment, Development and Sustainability, in press.
10. President's Council on Sustainable Development, Final Report (1995). Washington, DC. (text at http://www.whitehouse.gov/PCSD).

. United Nations World Commission on Environment and Development (1987). *Our Common Future (The Brundtland Report).* New York, Oxford University Press.

THE WRONG APOCALYPSE

Reviewed by Lindsey Grant

1999

Peterson and his staff have assembled an impressive array of evidence about one consequence of population change. As population growth stops or reverses in the modern world, the population ages. This generates fundamental social and economic changes, which he explores in depth. The cost of taking care of the elderly may lead to fiscal collapse in the major industrial nations. He talks of an iceberg, a great hazard . . . that will likely dwarf the other challenges." I think he has mistaken a secondary population issue for the fundamental one, but—particularly after one gets past the hyperbole of the first two chapters—he has effectively focused attention on issues which developed nations must face.

THE DEPENDENCY RATIO

Peterson calls it "global aging," but he is really talking about the developed world,* particularly western Europe and Japan. (The problem is less serious in the United States, Britain and Australia.) In Europe, women may be expected to bear 1.42 children on average—down from 2.57 fifty years ago. For Italy and Spain, the number (i.e. the total fertility rate) is 1.2 or less. This is just above the "one child family" that China proclaims but does not approach. (Replacement level fertility is about 2.05 children at European mortality levels.) UN statisticians expect the population of Western Europe to decline by 10 percent to 376 million in 2050—and Italy by 28 percent to 41 million, even with a rise in fertility.

The "dependency ratio" measures the numbers of the old and young as a percentage of the working age population. The book's central point is that falling fertility raises the ratio, and shrinking working age populations cannot support the rising numbers of the old—at least in the way they have become accustomed to. He documents the point well. In much of Europe, one can live almost as well on unemployment insurance as by working, and retire very young on liberal disability pensions. Let me add that it works right now because when a population stops growing, the first consequence is to lower the dependency ratio. There are fewer children, and most people are in their working years. It is a temporary phase. As time passes, those people get old, there are fewer new workers, and the dependency ratio soars. Right now, Europe can just barely afford its welfare net. Soon, it won't be able to. The dependency ratio in Germany, for example, is now remarkably favorable. It went down from 59 percent in the early '70s to 44 percent in the late eighties—and unemployment became the major economic problem—but it has started rising and it may reach 71 percent in 2050.

Peterson argues that if modern societies try to continue present retirement and health programs they will bankrupt the fiscal system, with worldwide consequences. He offers some possible solutions:

- encourage people to work to age seventy or so, partly by changing retirement systems;

- encourage more working age people to get employed;
- increase immigration (judiciously);
- encourage women to have more children;
- restore the family system, emphasizing both better child rearing and filial responsibility for aged parents rather than turning the task over to the state; and
- convene a global summit to create an international Agency on Global Aging.

Most of the proposals are not new, but it is a useful checklist. His beat is fiscal policy, and the solutions he proposes are ways to get the burden off government's back and on to somebody else's, and to keep growth going. As he acknowledges, political resistance to losing benefits is the sticking point, not an unawareness of the problem.

THE PRIMARY ISSUE

Western Europe and Japan comprise less than 10 percent of the world's population. The traumatic problems of hunger, disease, deepening water shortages, resource depletion, and urban collapse lie elsewhere.

A few developing countries like China are attempting to expand governmental welfare programs at the same time they are lowering fertility, a combination that will in two generations put them in Europe's situation, but with poorer economies. They should heed the lessons Europe is learning. For China, however, the central demographic problem remains what it has been: growth to levels utterly unlike anything in the human experience, with the certainty that demographic momentum will carry that growth even higher and with uncertain but overwhelming consequences for the inhabitants and for the ecosystems that support them.

Fertility is declining in many developing countries, but it is down to replacement level (which would eventually bring growth to an end, but not right away) in only a few of them—fortunately including the major player, China. The UN middle projection assumes that fertility and mortality will continue to decline, but it still foresees developing world population rising by 73 percent to 7.75 billion in 2050. In the most desperate countries (the UN's "least developed"), fertility has hardly started to decline; it remains above five children, and their total population is expected to almost treble by 2050. I think rising mortality will intervene to interrupt that incredible growth curve.

In the United States, our central problem is not the dependency ratio, which is 52 percent now and is likely to be just under 70 percent in 2050—just a little above the level in 1960. Our problem is population growth and the environmental burden our consumption habits impose on the entire world. We are passing 275 million now and seem likely to pass a half billion around 2050. Because of the higher fertility of most immigrants, our fertility is rising, not stable; the Census Bureau medium projection (1996) shows a rise from 2.07 now to 2.24 in 2050, which is a prescription for endless growth.

Lopsided welfare programs in Europe and Japan—or the United States—can be adjusted. People can work longer if necessary. The problem may be ameliorated by continued technological growth of productivity, which Peterson downplays. The developed world faces a problem, not a catastrophe. With the will, the solution is at hand. The same cannot be said about hunger, urban collapse and disease in most of the world.

THE INFINITE EARTH FALLACY

Peterson admits to a fondness for growth. He describes economies as "stagnant" if they do not grow. He regards a declining GDP (gross domestic product) as "unthinkable," even if GDP per capita is rising (pp.183–184). Yet perpetual material growth in a finite world is an absurdity. He has not reconciled his contradictions; he recognizes that a "steady state" economy is an ultimate goal, but his proposals would have the effect of pushing it into an infinitely remote future.

Growth is beguiling to economists and politicians because it seems to solve a problem that concerns them: making a bigger pie, right away. And it offers the businessmen who finance politicians the prospect of slicing that pie. The side effects are those that concern biologists, resource managers, ecologists, philosophers and environmentalists. Unfortunately, the two camps are seldom in touch.

Peterson is a conservative financier, and his emphasis can be understood, but his is a provincial view. Along with most economists, he simply ignores issues of scale and limits. He dismisses the population issue thus: "overpopulation anxieties of the early post-war era . . . led, by the 1960s, to newspaper headlines about the population bomb and anti-birth movements. . . ." He thinks (wrongly) that the world problem was the result of the baby boom, "an historical anomaly" (pp.11–12). I find it remarkable that he can make such a statement about a world that has doubled in population since 1960 and is on the way to adding another three billion by 2050—if life support systems permit it.

He does not list population growth as an issue now or for the coming century, while he calls "global aging" the "transcendent" issue. He is dubious about the reality of climate warming and puts aside environmental issues with the remark that single nations cannot do much about them because other nations may not cooperate. He regards population growth in the developing world as a threat to us (pp.50–52, 197), but not as a problem for them. He talks about their age distribution, not about the intolerable conditions they face or the growth that generates the conditions.

Because of recent population growth, the world is facing, not simply a threatening future, but a dangerous present. Given the damage that that growth is already doing, one should ask whether present population levels are tolerable, to say nothing about the future. Peterson's dismissal of population growth is a bit premature. I would urge that he take a holiday from fiscal data and spend some time listening to the biologists.

Peterson has dismissed the greater issue to ring the alarm about a smaller one. Europe knows about its fiscal problem, and so do we in the United States. By downplaying the larger issue, he diverts Americans from two fundamental decisions: What are we doing to help the developing world in its desperate efforts to bring a halt to population growth? And, in this Age of Migrations, what are we doing to control the growth of U.S. population, which is driven primarily by immigration?

Are we willing to restrain consumption? Rising numbers and rising consumption are the twin forces that drive the destabilization of the world environment today. A smaller population can live better within a sound environment, but we cannot afford—or realistically expect—to have more people living better.

THE EUROPEAN FUTURE

When population has been growing, an end to growth forces any country through a period of high dependency ratios. It is a transient but mathematically inescapable phase. The swifter the change, the higher the dependency ratio. Eventually, it will peak, then drift downward and stabilize. Granted, that population will be older. Aging is the price we pay for low mortality. Unless he believes that growth can go on forever, Peterson must accept that transitional high dependency levels are inescapable. Unless he wants to see mortality rise, he must recognize that future populations will be older.

As Peterson points out, countries with fertility below replacement level will need to bring fertility back up, or invite immigration, if they are not to wither away. The issue is "just when?"

The go-go growth syndrome of our era has been built on a temporary foundation of cheap fossil energy. The remarkable economic growth of Western Europe and Japan in recent decades has been achieved mostly with imported energy, and both are particularly vulnerable to price shocks and supply uncertainties as world oil resources decline in the next generation. Both Europe and Japan are poorly placed to benefit from the most promising renewable sources—wind and direct solar energy—and potential tidal energy sources are localized along the Atlantic coast. The energy transition will involve some major economic shifts, and it will be expensive. It will be easier with a smaller population, even if it is an older one.

Recent world economic growth has put very heavy pressure on the environment. It has generated huge increases in the nitrogen budget, in water pollution and atmospheric acidification, and it drives the worldwide problem of atmospheric carbon loading and climate change. Moreover, Europe and Japan are two of the most crowded regions on Earth. Western Europe has grown by 27 percent since 1950, Japan by 50 percent. With populations more like those of 1950, or even earlier, they could enjoy the benefits of prosperity without the environmental costs that have come to characterize it.

They should be moving toward a smaller population but not quite so fast. A higher fertility rate would still lead to a smaller population, but it would slow down the aging process and ameliorate the problems that concern Peterson. But those problems can be addressed.

THE CASE OF ITALY

Perhaps, since this is a very hot topic, we should explore the question: just where do different assumptions about fertility and migration lead?

I will take Italy, as the extreme example of low fertility. In the two graphs, I plot Italy's population and dependency ratios through the coming century, making three different sets of assumptions:

- Current Fertility of 1.2, with current mortality (on the assumption that decreased budgets for medical care—especially for the old—will counterbalance medical improvements leading to greater longevity), and zero net migration.
- Rising Fertility to replacement level (2.05) in 2020, and staying constant thereafter.
- The Immigration Scenario, with annual net immigration of 200,000 men and women (in equal numbers), added to the preceding scenario.

Any scenario short of a fairly swift return to replacement level fertility is indeed frightening once fertility has gone so low as 1.2 children. A rise to 1.6, for instance, would only lead to a population in 2100 of 15 million rather than 8 million, and still declining. Given the intense migratory pressures generated by third world population growth, by political turmoil, and by the demands of employers in Italy for labor, it is hard to believe that extreme low-fertility scenarios would not be simply overwhelmed by migration.

I find the Rising Fertility option beguiling. With population numbers stable at the level of the 1920s, Italy will have more space, and the opportunity to move away from its present dependence upon intensive (and destructive) agriculture, chemicals and fossil energy.

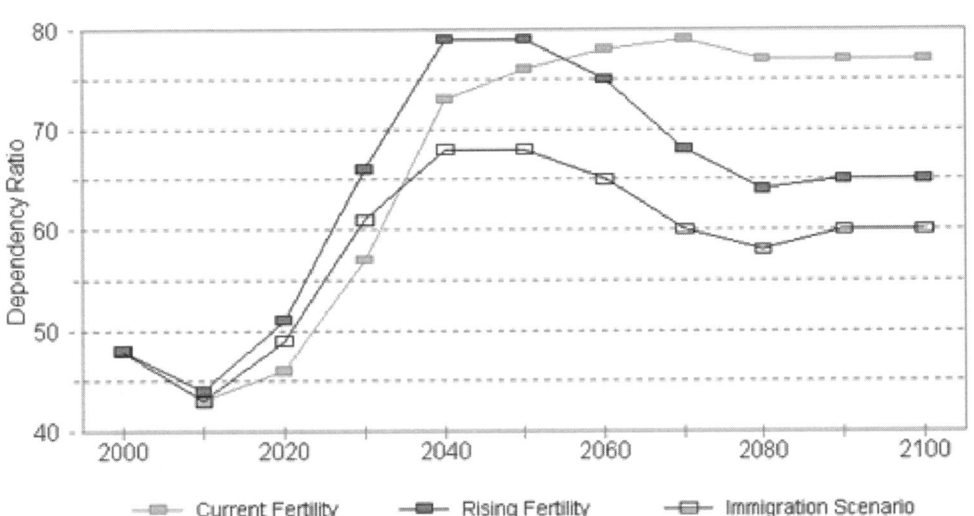

Figure 1.

However, it still results in a peak in the dependency ratio because there will be more children.

The Immigration Scenario holds the dependency ratio down. It preserves a larger population, if that is what they want, but it would transform Italy as post-2000 immigrants and their descendants become about half the total population. It is not unthinkable. Italy has gone through such changes before; Roman Emperor Trajan was a Negro. But that scenario would lead again to growth unless immigration or fertility decline.

These are just three of an infinite number of possible scenarios. It is by no means certain that demographic change can be engineered. For one thing, industrial nations, even where there is some consensus as to desirable family size, have had notoriously little success in influencing personal decisions about child-bearing. For another, Italy has traditionally exported people. Under the Schengen agreement, it is part of a Europe with free movement of people, and the net flow of people within Europe is unpredictable. For a third, it has yet to be established whether the movement across borders can be controlled in the face of intense migratory pressures generated by the gulf between industrial nations and most of the third world. In Japan, perhaps yes; in Europe, maybe not. Finally, there is no more evidence of a consensus about population policy in Europe than in the United States.

Nevertheless, if they want to preserve viable societies, Italy (and all of Europe and Japan) have every reason to look with hope, not despair, at the prospect of smaller populations. They need to manage the transition. Given the difficulties I have cited in engineering population change, that management process is far more complex than Peterson has described, but that—and not the single issue of fiscal solvency—is the overriding issue facing Europe and, eventually, all nations where population growth has come to a halt.

NOTES:

1. A note on definitions: Peterson defines "developed countries" as the members of the Organization for Economic Cooperation and Development (OECD), consisting of the European countries (excluding those which were Communist) plus Japan, Canada, the United States, Australia, New Zealand and now Mexico. For statistical purposes, we both use "Western Europe" in the popular sense, i.e. roughly the UN's "Northern, Southern and Western Europe."

THE GROWTH MANAGEMENT DELUSION

Gabor Zovanyi

October 1999

INTRODUCTION

During the 1960s and 1970s an ideological shift occurred in America with respect to the value of further growth. The traditional association of population, economic, and urban growth with societal progress began giving way to a new and more skeptical view. This ideological shift did not come easily; conventional thinking had historically associated ongoing growth with a range of benefits, including stronger local economies, higher personal incomes, lower taxes, greater upward economic mobility for the poor, and a wider range of lifestyle choices for consumers. Despite these supposed benefits, increasing numbers of Americans were rejecting the view that growth was only beneficial during this period. Their personal experiences led them to associate growth with overcrowded schools, tax increases, rising crime rates, physical blight, traffic congestion, the loss of open space, the destruction of a way of life, and increasing air and water pollution.

This ideological shift in American attitudes toward growth began to affect popular perceptions regarding land development. Uses of land were increasingly being linked to a number of specific societal problems during this period. Growth, as manifested in the development of land, was being blamed for such diverse problems as the costly and destructive development pattern associated with urban sprawl, the loss of prime agricultural land, an inefficient provision of public facilities and services, escalating housing prices, pervasive environmental degradation, and the loss of community character. Growth management suggested an avenue for addressing these ill effects.

The growth management movement that emerged during the late 1960s and early 1970s reflected a direct response to this new ideological position. Most participants in the movement had come to think of growth as something to be managed, regulated, or controlled, rather than simply promoted as in the past. Different conventional definitions of growth management refer to governmental programs that influence, guide, channel, redistribute, regulate, or control future growth. Embedded in these definitions is the belief that it is possible to accommodate ongoing growth in a responsible fashion if we merely manage the amount, rate, location, and quality of future development. What is missing from the literature on growth management is a definition of management activity directed at a deliberate attempt to stop growth. This omission reflects the fact that the growth management movement has not entertained the possibility of a no-growth focus for growth management efforts. The movement has instead been directed at making ongoing growth possible and acceptable. In order to consider a case against the growth-accommodation focus of current growth management in the United States, one must first appreciate the degree to which growth management represents continuing support for the growth imperative that pervades U.S. social and political structures.

THE CURRENT NATURE OF GROWTH MANAGEMENT IN THE UNITED STATES

Since the 1970s there has been widespread experimentation with growth management by cities and counties in the United States. These local governments have utilized their authority to plan and regulate the use of land to further growth management ends. In some instances they have actually limited the amount of future growth by downzoning land, that is, by reducing the permitted intensity of use on specific parcels of land. However, downzoning has typically been accompanied by increasing density allowances on other parcels deemed more suitable for development. In a minority of cases, communities moved to introduce rate controls, attempting to gain control over the timing of future development by limiting the annual number of building permits. These rate controls were assumed to buy time to respond to concerns about the availability, quality, and financing of public facilities and services, and to slow growth sufficiently to allow it to be absorbed without destroying community character or a current way of life. The majority of local growth management programs have, however, focused on directing the location of future growth. Many programs have assumed that containing new growth within designated growth boundaries would further a number of desired public ends, such as holding down facility and service costs, conserving resource lands, and protecting environmentally-sensitive lands from sprawl development. Other communities have emphasized the role that adequate facilities and services play in ensuring quality development, making development permission contingent on the availability of public facilities and services, and requiring developers to share the cost of providing that infrastructure. In the end, growth management programs have been deployed to manage all of the principal attributes of growth: amount, rate, location, and quality.

Although growth management on the part of local governments has represented increased regulation of private property in the United States, it has not served to stop or significantly slow ongoing growth. Even where management programs have deployed rate controls to slow growth, new annual growth allotments effectively permitted growth to continue. With most management activity directed at influencing the location and quality of development, rather than its amount or rate, growth management has been able to maintain an allegiance to the growth imperative. One survey of city and county management programs during the mid-1970s claimed it had been unable to detect a single program directed at stopping growth (Finkler and Peterson, 1974). Another survey of 586 growth management measures through 1989 similarly documented the growth-accommodation bias of city and county growth management activities (Glickfeld and Levine 1991). While 17 percent of those 586 measures temporarily limited the amount of growth by imposing annual caps on growth, 83 percent of the measures managed growth by geographically redistributing it using infrastructure requirements and urban limit lines. That practice has not changed during the 1990s. Most local management programs seek to reduce neither the overall amount or rate of growth, and instead reflect the belief that growth can be accommodated if its location is properly planned and its most obvious negative effects appropriately mitigated. Whether local governments are managing growth in the absence of state legislation directing that activity, or managing growth under the guidelines of a statewide growth management law, the overwhelming majority of local management programs have played an active role in accommodating ongoing growth.

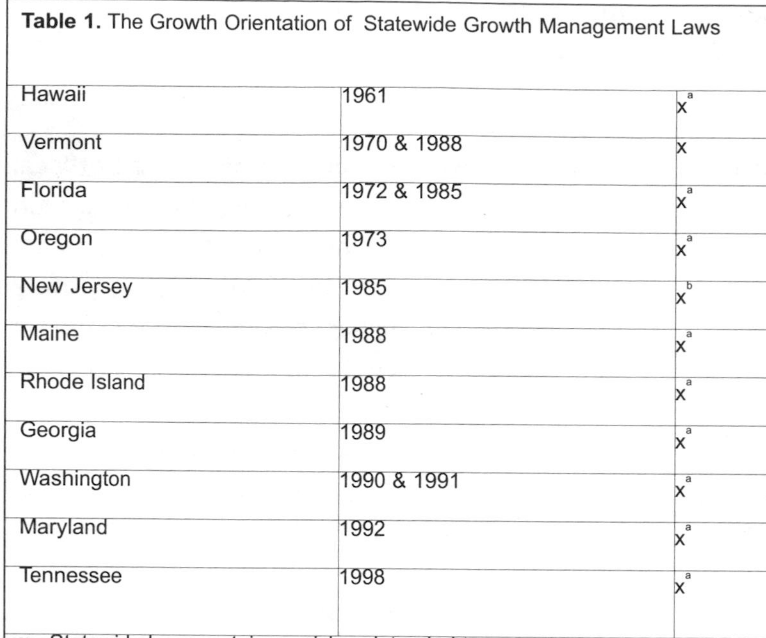

Table 1. The Growth Orientation of Statewide Growth Management Laws

Hawaii	1961	x[a]
Vermont	1970 & 1988	x
Florida	1972 & 1985	x[a]
Oregon	1973	x[a]
New Jersey	1985	x[b]
Maine	1988	x[a]
Rhode Island	1988	x[a]
Georgia	1989	x[a]
Washington	1990 & 1991	x[a]
Maryland	1992	x[a]
Tennessee	1998	x[a]

x Statewide laws contain provisions intended to promote ongoing growth.

x[a] Legislative provisions actually mandate growth accommodation measures on the part of local governments.

x[b] Acknowledges limits for further growth within specific locations within the state, but maintains traditional accommodative stance for the remainder of the state.

Although local governments are the principal players in implementing growth management programs in the United States, some state governments have passed laws asserting a state role in growth management activity. At present, eleven states have statewide growth management laws: Hawaii (1961), Vermont (1970 & 1988), Florida (1972 & 1985), Oregon (1973), New Jersey (1985), Maine (1988), Rhode Island (1988), Georgia (1989), Washington (1990 & 1991), Maryland (1992), and Tennessee (1998). These enabling acts specify what local governments are required to do, and what they may elect to do, as they engage in growth management activity. In many respects these statewide laws have addressed the same concerns that many local governments had attempted to address prior to the passage of state enactments governing growth management. The state laws universally contain provisions for protecting the environment. Most have elements intended to conserve resource lands. Many include containment components designed to achieve compact growth patterns and combat sprawl. Some of the state laws have sections to ensure "concurrency," or the provision of facilities and services at the time development occurs. Most have features that promote economic development in response to declining federal revenues under the new federalism, and features intended to balance development and environmental protection. However, the state laws have extended beyond matters previously addressed by local growth management efforts implemented in the absence of statewide guidelines.

Statewide growth management laws all contain provisions requiring local management programs to be consistent with specified state goals and policies. These provisions have provided a form of mandated direction for local management programs that did not exist prior to the passage of the state laws. Some of the state enactments have also required local governments to regulate land in a manner consistent with previously adopted local comprehensive plans, which has served to grant legal status to local land-use plans and reduce the possibilities for arbitrary and capricious regulatory behavior by local governments. Some of the statewide laws additionally required local governments to plan for controversial land uses such as affordable housing and factious public facilities like prisons. What all the statewide growth management laws have in common, however, is their continued commitment to preserving the growth imperative. All of the statewide management laws passed to date contain provisions intended to promote ongoing growth, and in eight of the eleven states the laws actually mandate ongoing growth accommodation by local governments. In the state of Washington, for example, local urban growth boundaries are required to be adjusted every ten years to accommodate the next twenty years of state-projected growth. All statewide growth management laws therefore reinforce the accommodative nature of the majority of local management programs implemented to date.

The growth management movement in America must be recognized for what it really is: an institutionalized form of support for the growth imperative. Most growth management programs are directed at a "managing to grow" option, rather than toward actual efforts to limit or stop future growth. The movement can, therefore, be criticized as representing little more than ongoing development facilitation. Spokespersons for the movement continue to defend the view that ongoing growth and environmental protection represent equally legitimate objectives, and that a "balance" can be achieved between these ends without compromising either. They also advocate the oxymoronic ideas of "sustainable growth" and "smart growth" at a time when ongoing growth is revealing itself to be lethal to other species and natural ecosystems. Even though current ecological realities clearly indicate that just managing ongoing growth is an insufficient response to the escalating nature of growth-induced environmental problems, the growth management movement remains wedded to accommodative management practices.

INADEQUACY OF THE "MANAGEMENT" RESPONSE TO GROWTH

As this century comes to a close, evidence mounts that we have gone beyond ecological limits to growth. Even the present scale of the human enterprise has effected ozone depletion and global climate change. By the 1990s researchers were making a case that even present rates of resource extraction and pollution emission were environmentally unsustainable (Meadows et al., 1992). In the same period other researchers were detailing the nature of pervasive environmental constraints to further growth: diminished fertility of existing agricultural lands, overgrazed grasslands, overharvested fisheries, depleted and polluted water sources, and truncated natural forests (Brown et al., 1994). During the 1990s other assessments indicated humans were losing ground in feeding an expanding global population (Brown and Kane, 1994). The decade also witnessed researchers arguing that even the current human population is living off the planet's capital rather than its income, and that living on that capital was producing serious environmental deterioration (Ehrlich and Ehrlich, 1991). Underlying virtually all of these arguments for current limits to growth is the recognition that the present scale of the human enterprise is threatening the planet's life-support systems.

The planet's ecosystems constitute humanity's life-support apparatus. All life is utterly dependent on these ecosystems to support it, and the continued existence of our species, economy, and civilization is not exempt from such dependency. For ecologists the entire biosphere constitutes an ecosystem, as do the innumerable local biotic communities and the physical environments with which the organisms in these communities interact. Natural ecosystems provide a wide variety of essential services that are delivered free. These ecosystems maintain a benign mix of atmospheric gases, regulate the hydrologic cycle, purify air and water, generate and maintain fertile soils, dispose of wastes, recycle nutrients, provide pest control and pollination services, supply forest products and food from the oceans, and create and maintain biodiversity (Ehrlich and Ehrlich, 1991). As the unrelenting expansion of the human enterprise takes over more and more of the natural landscapes, which comprise ecosystems, we lose both physical environments and biodiversity, and in the process diminish the very life-support functions on which we depend.

Evidence of the extent to which our species is eliminating the world's ecosystems and thereby reducing their vital services is revealed by the increasing resources we are required to commit to such things as sewage treatment, air purification, flood control, pest control, restoration of soil nutrients, and the preservation of species. Another indicator of the extent to which humans are converting natural ecosystems to human-dominated ones, and thereby diminishing their vital services, comes from research into how much of the biological activity of the planet has been appropriated for the use of human beings. Research has investigated the extent of this appropriation by assessing human impact on the planet's total supply of energy produced by photosynthesis, that is global net primary production (NPP). Global net primary production is the total amount of solar energy converted into biochemical energy through plant photosynthesis minus the energy used by plants for their own processes. NPP represents the basic food source of all life, and research published in 1986 revealed our species had already commandeered about 40 percent of all potential NPP generated on land (Vitousek et al., 1986). This 40 percent appropriation of NPP directly correlates with estimates of the global level of land use by humans: humanity's use of nonpolar land for settlements, crops, permanent pastures, and woodlands now amounts to people already using at least 40 percent of the planet's land surface intensively.

As our species appropriates more and more of the planet, taking ever higher percentages of NPP and land area for its own use, the consequences for many other species is clear: extinction. It has been estimated that 15 to 20 percent of species have been eliminated during the last two decades of this century. Most of that loss is directly attributable to habitat destruction. Based on current and accelerating trends, estimates are that we may well see 50 percent of the remaining species on the planet disappear by 2050. In the 1990s the World Conservation Union's *Red Data Book* paints a sad picture for the world's animals, providing figures that illustrate how many already face threatened or near threatened status: birds (20 percent), mammals (39 percent), reptiles (26 percent), amphibians (30 percent), and fish (39 percent). The *Red Data Book* notes that one-third of all plants on the planet are currently threatened with extinction. This sorry state of the world's fauna and flora is not limited to areas outside of the United States. The Nature Conservancy currently tells its members that one-third of all plants and animals in America are facing extinction. This ongoing loss of life on the planet is directly attributable to the growth of the human enterprise.

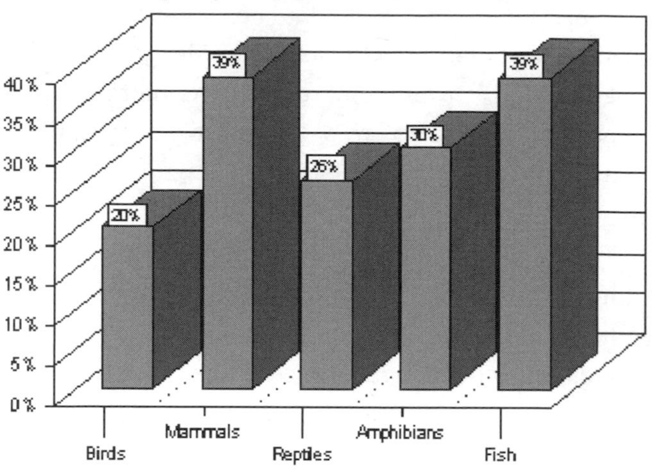

Figure 1.

As long as the growth imperative spins off population, economic, and urban growth at exponential rates, it will displace natural ecosystems at exponential rates, and in turn push the number of extinctions to increase exponentially. Life on this planet simply cannot sustain the expansion of the human enterprise experienced during recent decades. Global population that was increasing by some 42 million people a year in 1950 jumped up to an annual increase of about 82 million a year by the latter 1990s. Global population increased by 112 percent during that forty-year period (from 2.5 to 5.3 billion), and the 2.8 billion added in that mere four decades surpassed the 2.5 billion reached in the prior 3 million years. While population increased by 112 percent, global industrial output increased five-fold. From an annual production of some 10 million motor vehicles a year in 1950, the number exploded to over 50 million vehicles a year in the 1990s. In terms of urban growth, the United Nations estimates that from 20 to 30 million people a year now stream off the rural landscape into the urban centers of developing countries, adding to the significant natural increases occurring in these cities.

While most of the aforementioned growth has occurred outside the United States, the degree of growth here has nevertheless been substantial. From 1950 to 1990 the population of America increased from some 150 million to about 250 million. Over 10 million of the 50 million vehicles produced annually are produced in the United States. And in terms of urban growth, the current annual increase of at least 2.5 million people a year translates into twenty-five cities of 100,000 every twelve months. Attempting to maintain these rates of growth will certainly occur at the expense of other life forms. In California, population increased from 10 million in 1950 to almost 30 million in 1990. The impact of that past growth on plants and animals in that state is reflected by the fact there are more threatened and endangered species listed federally there than in any other state. California's population is projected to increase to 64 million by 2040, and it is time to concede that mere "management" of such ongoing growth will not stop it from being lethal for many species that still struggle to survive there. The 25 million Americans added during the last decade of this century are stressing habitats and eliminating species nationwide, and the projected increase to almost 400 million Americans by 2050 will certainly eliminate significant biodiversity in the United States.

The fact that even the present scale of the human enterprise is serving to kill off a sizable portion of the nonhuman life on the planet, and in the process acting to degrade the life-support systems needed to sustain our own species, provides proof of the unsustainable nature of growth at the end of this century. It is time to recognize that the pursuit of physical growth has now become an obsolete and lethal ideology, and that we must abandon the growth imperative if we are to survive. Mere management of ongoing growth must be acknowledged to be an insufficient response to the ecological realities of the late twentieth century. Those realities dictate that humans must shift their emphasis from the current ongoing growth accommodation advanced by the growth management movement to a new focus on overseeing the required downsizing and redesigning of the human enterprise to a level and form that is ecologically sustainable.

A NEW ECOLOGICAL FOCUS FOR GROWTH MANAGEMENT

Ecologists refer to the present as an Era of Impoverishment. They describe what our species is doing to the natural world as "a global biological holocaust of unthinkable proportions" and "biological meltdown." Based upon these revelations we must concede that a point in history has been reached where the continued elimination of species and ecosystems must be condemned by all reasonable persons as insane behavior. From an ecological perspective, which in the long run is the only one that matters, our behavior is simply unsustainable. Humanity's war on the community of life and the habitats that support it must end if our species hopes to experience an indeterminate future. In order to keep that option open, ecological sustainability must become the primary focus of both the growth management movement and society at large.

An ecological focus suggests a few key operational measures for directing the transition to a state of ecological sustainability. Since preserving the diversity of life is a necessary condition for ecological sustainability, actions that serve to reduce biodiversity are by definition ecologically unsustainable. The first operational measure of ecological sustainability is therefore clear: no further loss of biodiversity due to anthropogenic causes. Since maintaining the integrity of ecosystems is also a necessary condition for ecological sustainability, actions that serve to reduce the number or integrity of ecosystems are by definition ecologically unsustainable as well. This reasoning yields another operational measure of ecological sustainability: no further loss of ecosystems or impairment of their continued productivity and functioning due to anthropogenic causes. Since even the current scale of the human enterprise is eliminating species and ecosystems, further growth in that scale is also by definition ecologically unsustainable. The last operational measure of ecological sustainability is therefore clear: an ongoing reduction in the scale of the human enterprise to a level capable of being supported indefinitely without eroding biodiversity or the integrity of ecosystems.

If progress is to be made in realizing these operational measures our species will have to abandon the growth imperative and adopt an alternative: the imperative of ecological sustainability. As the unequivocal primacy of ecological sustainability is accepted, the necessity of rejecting the growth imperative will become increasingly self-evident. It must be recognized that our species can persist without growth, but not without sustainable ecosystems. If people can accept this obvious truism, the requisite transition from the artificial growth imperative to the indispensable ecological imperative can finally occur.

At present the growth management movement impedes the essential transition from the growth imperative to the ecological imperative. The overwhelming majority of management programs have allowed, facilitated, or actually mandated ongoing growth accommodation. The movement remains committed to the assumed wisdom of future growth, and has evidenced no receptivity to the idea that management efforts might legitimately be directed at stopping growth. A no-growth option for management programs has, in fact, been written off by members of the movement, repeatedly being characterized as inefficient, unjust, and irresponsible. Even management programs that have sought only to limit future growth, as an alternative to actually stopping it, have been attacked by members of the movement and referred to as the worst, unenlightened, unrealistic, immature, and improperly defined programs. The growth management movement, in short, represents a wholehearted endorsement of ongoing growth accommodation (Zovanyi, 1998).

Members of the movement continue to defend "balanced growth," "smart growth," and "sustainable growth" at a time when escalating growth-induced problems increasingly demonstrate the irresponsible nature of ongoing growth accommodation practices. If the growth management movement is to become relevant to the needs of the current era, it will have to abandon the delusional position that it will be possible to protect the environment under ongoing growth. Psychiatrists define delusion as a false, persistent belief maintained in spite of evidence to the contrary. The growth management movement represents continued support of ongoing growth in spite of mounting evidence that growth no longer represents a viable policy option or survival strategy. A point has been reached in human history where further population, economic, and urban growth must be rejected if we are to preserve the biodiversity that sustains us. If growth management is unable to undergo a paradigm shift based on a rejection of the growth imperative, it will loose its social relevance and be replaced by activity more in tune with needs of the current era. The movement's present focus on ongoing growth accommodation is both irrelevant and irresponsible, and its mission must become one of stopping the growth that is dismantling the web of life on this planet.

Transforming growth management into a no-growth endeavor will not come easily. The federal government has abstained from entering the growth management arena, and its endorsement of ongoing growth for the country makes it an unlikely advocate of actions intended to stop growth at any point in the foreseeable future. Statewide growth management laws passed to date have tended to mandate ongoing growth accommodation, and in the short term other states might be expected to copy these existing pro-growth statutes. Only local governments appear likely candidates for experimenting with growth management efforts designed to stop growth. In local settings, advocates of a no-growth position can lobby to change the growth accommodation biases of comprehensive land-use plans and regulation that make ongoing growth both possible and inevitable. While changing these land-use documents to reflect no-growth ends will undoubtedly be difficult, they will have to be changed if we are to create a sustainable future.

NOTES:

1. Brown, Lester R., Alan Durning, Christopher Flavin, Hilary Frency, Nicholas Lenssen, Marcia Lowe, Ann Misch, Sandra Postel, Michael Renner, Linda Starke, Peter Weber, and John Young. 1994. *State of the World*. Worldwatch Institute. New York: WW Norton.
2. Brown, Lester R., and Hal Kane. 1994. *Full House: Reassessing the Earth's Population Carrying Capacity*. New York: WW Norton.
3. Ehrlich, Paul R., and Anne H. Ehrlich. 1991. *Healing the Planet: Strategies for Resolving the Environmental Crisis*. New York: Addison-Wesley.
4. Finkler, Earl, and David L. Peterson. 1974. *Nongrowth Planning Strategies: The Developing Power of Towns, Cities, and Regions*. New York: Praeger Publishers.
5. Glickfeld, Madelyn, and Ned Levine. 1991. *Growth Controls: Regional Problems—Local Responses*. Cambridge, Massachusetts: Lincoln Institute of Land Policy.
6. Meadows, Donella H., Dennis L. Meadows, Jorgen Randers. 1992. *Beyond the Limits: Confronting Global Collapse, Envisioning a Sustainable Future*. Post Mills, Vermont: Chelsea Green Publishing Company.
7. Vitousek, Peter M., Paul R. Ehrlich, Anne H. Ehrlich, and Pamela A. Matson. 1986. "Human Appropriation of the Products of Photosynthesis." *BioScience*. 36,6: 368–73.
8. Zovanyi, Gabor. 1998. *Growth Management for a Sustainable Future: Ecological Sustainability as the New Growth Management Focus for the 21st Century*. Westport, Connecticut: Praeger Publishers.

ENDING ILLEGAL IMMIGRATION: MAKE IT UNPROFITABLE

David Simcox

March 1999

However insensitively named, *Operation Wetback* in 1953 and 1954 was the United States' last, and only truly successful, effort to root out illegal immigration. Using extensive sweeps across the southwest, the U.S. Immigration and Naturalization Service (INS) achieved the Eisenhower administration's goals. Some 2.1 million, mostly Mexican, illegal aliens were removed between 1953 and 1955. While abuses marred the effort, illegal immigration stayed under control for more than a decade.

Notwithstanding its excesses, *Operation Wetback* left one clear lesson: with political will illegal immigration can be controlled. It showed how a display of firmness could persuade illegals to go home voluntarily and deter others abroad from coming. The lesson is still valid.

ILLEGAL IMMIGRATION'S POPULATION EFFECTS

But too much has changed for the strategy of episodic mass roundups to work in the nation's current immigration crisis. Such a strategy would be inefficient as well as politically questionable. Thirty years of government neglect of our borders and ports of entry has created a radically new situation. Illegal alien workers are no longer concentrated in agriculture in a few southwestern states, but are in most nooks of the economy. The permanent pool of illegal aliens is now between 5.0 million and 6.0 million and was growing by 300,000 yearly or more, according to a 1994 INS estimate[1].

Since 1960, illegal immigration has added more than 10 to 12.5 million to the U.S. population, including an estimated 3.5 million U.S.-born minor children of present and former illegals[2] in 1996. The illegal settlers are no longer overwhelmingly Mexican, most don't work on farms, and, according to INS[3], more than half don't enter by sneaking across the border, but come in as "nonimmigrants" (temporary visitors) and then overstay.

Vested interests in illegal immigration have also become more rooted in the last thirty years. Important constituencies must now be reckoned with: low-wage employers; providers of public services and education; landlords and realtors; churches; ethnic lobbies and politicians; human rights and immigrant advocates; and kinship networks.

WITHOUT ACTION, ILLEGAL IMMIGRATION TO SWELL

The collective pursuit of these lobbies of their particular interests adds up to a tenacious social structure committed to encouraging and legitimizing illegal settlement. This structure finds fertile ground in the larger American culture, which regards all growth as good and sees population growth as both validation and sustenance of the U.S. market economy. For many businessmen and their political spokesmen, the U.S. economic boom and tight labor market of the 1990s have made illegal immigration a virtue that knows no excess.

Conditions portend steady growth of illegal immigration in the coming decades. The world's pool of candidates for illegal entry swells as a function of the 40 million annual increase of the third world's largely underemployed labor force. In the United States, many employers are showing a preference for young foreign workers, whatever their status, over an aging American labor force with its rising health insurance costs and higher wage expectations.

Overcoming these pressures and curbing illegal immigration effectively will require firm political will and a range of responses that are more finely tuned than the broad axe methods of *Operation Wetback*. While variants of some of the proposals discussed here have been enacted by Congress, many of the remaining proposals have poor prospects in the present climate. They are offered for consideration if the political will for action should emerge.

This study is not about eliminating the "root causes" of illegal immigration. Before proceeding, we discard the cherished but spurious "remedies" to illegal settlement that are often put forth by those really favoring delayed action or no action at all.

Spurious Remedy No. 1: Curing the "Push" Factors—Economic stagnation, rapid population growth, and random disasters in the third world are a given. Trade and aid schemes to help immigrant-sending countries may be worth doing for sound economic and humanitarian reasons, but they have only a remote effect on migration—indeed they may stimulate more of it.

More often, quixotic trade and aid schemes are advanced to avoid the tough choices facing this country. Their implicit logic is that the United States must literally rebuild the third world before managing its own borders. But the reality of mass immigration, fed by world population growth, is right now. Continued delay in acting is setting the United States on an inalterable demographic spiral downward toward lower living standards and environmental degradation.

Spurious Remedy No.2: Defining Illegal Immigration Away—Since immigration's population effects are a prime concern, this analysis also rejects proposals that would simply redefine illegal immigrants as legal. Amnesties, temporary worker and humanitarian arrangements such as temporary protected status or "deferred enforced departure" are seductive redefinitions. They customarily lead to permanent settlement, produce more chain migration and further raise immigration expectations abroad.

FIGHTING ILLEGAL IMMIGRATION ON THREE FRONTS

Determination and Focus in Washington—Washington must strengthen and expand external and, particularly, internal enforcement with increased authority and resources, more and tougher penalties, new deterrents, and overall better management. It must face up to the fact that successful enforcement will offend powerful political clusters and resolve to resist the backlash. While removing the political hobbles from enforcement agencies, our leaders must rid a confused immigration system of its built-in incentives to illegal entry.

All levels of government must look more carefully at the market incentives for illegal immigration: the implicit subsidies to privileged groups, the profit opportunities for business with the socialization of the costs, and the inviting prospect to the would-be illegals of low risks and high returns. These market incentives can be dampened by shifting the costs of immigration to the immigrants themselves and to their employers and sponsors, and away from the taxpayers.

The specific action proposals we summarize here comprise three interrelated lines of action:

1. More efficient enforcement and deterrence;
2. Shifting the costs of immigration management to its beneficiaries, and
3. Turning off the magnets in the legal immigration system.

Each strategy is examined in more detail.

TIGHTENING INTERNAL AND EXTERNAL ENFORCEMENT

The U.S. government defines two main sources of illegal immigrants:

A) Entry Without Inspection (EWI), meaning those who bypass legal border entry points and sneak into America; and

B) visa abuse, referring to those who come in properly documented for temporary visits and then don't leave. These two modes of entry are not exhaustive. Many ostensibly legal entries involve fraud, imposture and misrepresentation, such as false claims of U.S. citizenship, a common option given the poor security of U.S. vital records. INS estimated in 1994 that 53 percent of the 300,000 illegal aliens they estimate have settled yearly since 1988 are visa abusers.

External Enforcement—Build up at the Border— The Clinton Administration since 1992 has increased the Border Patrol from about 4,300 to an expected 9,000 by mid-1999, thanks in large part to the 1996 Illegal Immigration Reform and Immigrant Responsibility Act of 1996 (IIRIRA). The country clearly needs the full 10,000 border patrol officers envisaged in the 1996 law to turn back the estimated four million to five millions trying to slip in each year. Concentration of border patrol forces at main crossing areas around El Paso, Texas and San Ysidro, California, along with triple fencing, new barriers, better lighting and high-tech detective devices at high traffic border areas have shown promise. But even the enlarged border patrol is still stretched thin and now faces new spillover pressures at more isolated Mexican border sectors, at the Canadian border and on the maritime frontiers.

Even as it enlarges the Border Patrol, Washington must use military and state national guard units and their equipment in critical areas during high-traffic periods. The rise of sea-borne alien smuggling argues for more funding for the Coast Guard and U.S. Customs Service. It is not necessary here to prescribe specific border control strategies. The problem has never been that the Departments of Justice, Treasury and Transportation do not know what needs to be done. The positive enforcement lessons of *Operation Hold the Line* in El Paso and subsequently *Operation Gatekeeper* in the San Diego border sector must be applied at all crossing points. Interdiction at sea must be increased, adding U.S. Navy support and state maritime police forces to the efforts of INS, U.S. Customs and the Coast Guard.

Internal Enforcement: Derailed by Political Ambivalence—Congress has tended to stress border enforcement in recent years because it has been politically unassailable. Since the late 1980s, Washington has enthusiastically appropriated funds for round up and removal of criminal aliens. With funds for deportation more than doubling between 1995 and 1998, deportations have risen from 50,400 to 171,000 in the same period. Although removal of criminal aliens has been the political cover, now about 70 percent of removals are non-criminal illegal aliens.

The effort has made voluntary departures of illegals rise as well. A bottleneck to even larger deportations is the availability of detention spaces, now limited to about 14,000. INS officials estimated that it could remove every criminal alien if it had 21,000 more

detention spaces and 1,500 more employees. The required increase of $652 million in the detention and deportation budget would be easily amortized by savings on the costs of crime and incarceration and other public services to illegal aliens.[4]
When it comes to enforcement at the workplace, lawmakers are far more ambivalent about making the employer sanctions they themselves have legislated really work. This attitude has been the single greatest obstacle to internal enforcement in the 1990s. Congress' loyalty to employers of illegals and underlying resistance to more regulation of business continues to saps the integrity of enforcement and restricts funding for employer sanctions investigators to just 300 nationwide, despite rapid growth of other INS enforcement personnel.

Washington's tepid support for workplace enforcement appeared to be weakening more in 1998 and 1999. The Labor Department put limits on the information it will give INS on suspected illegals gained from its own workplace inspections. INS workplace raids continued to decline and INS planners, beset by enforcement funding shortages and employer ill-will, were considering a new enforcement strategy that would eliminate them altogether.[5] Without determined alternate enforcement measures, INS withdrawal will signal "anything goes" to illegal aliens and their prospective employers. Jobs remain the major magnet for illegal immigrants. Until Washington rigorously bars ineligible aliens from working here, there can be no victory over illegal immigration.

The 1986 employer sanctions law recognized that a better worker identification system might be needed rather than reliance on fraud-prone civil documents. The Commission on Immigration Reform in 1995 called for a phone-in system for employers to match job applicants against a national database of social security and INS information[6]. President Clinton began a pilot program on verification of workers in 1995, a delay of nine years since the project was authorized by Congress. In 1996 Congress considered, but rejected, a national electronic verification program. Such a system is essential to making employer sanctions a true deterrent.

Fraud-resistant identification is vital to good internal enforcement. The technological options for better controls now exceed the political will to use them. Ineligible aliens, rarely challenged by complacent employers, have effectively nullified employer sanctions with an avalanche of fraudulent work eligibility documents. Now, employers have little to gain—and risk penalties for discrimination—by examining ID documents more carefully. The burden of verification must be lifted from employers.

Better Identification and Personal Data on Aliens—The INS must end the gaps and imperfections in its own existing alien database and expand it to include all recipients of visas and border crossing cards and all illegal aliens discovered in the country. Vast technological progress in automated fingerprint identification systems (AFIS) now allows high speed enrollment of masses of persons, cataloging and storage, and prompt retrieval of prints for electronic matching.

INS has used AFIS to record prints of as many as 1.5 million illegal entrants caught in some border areas—a practice that should be generalized. Renewing the requirement abandoned in 1981 that all aliens in the United States report their whereabouts annually would strengthen the INS database.

The two databases of Social Security accounts and INS's central index of aliens are powerful tools for confirming work eligibility, tracking and verifying departures of temporary entrants, and monitoring illegal immigrants, particularly criminals and repeat offenders. Measures in the 1996 law facilitate the use of this data for enforcement and prepares the way for use of digitized fingerprints or other biometrics in all individual data files. But the immigrant rights and privacy lobbies will stall these identification measures unless there is determined leadership from Washington.

The 1996 act mandates that the driver's license for all states meets federal security standards and contains the social security number. It also bars illegal aliens from receiving driver's licenses and professional and occupational licenses. The support of the states is essential for these initiatives, and for others, such as barring illegals from purchasing or renting real estate. An up-to-date and secure verification system is critical to make these restrictions work.

Tracking Visa Abusers—Coming and Going— Temporary admission to the United States involves a "two-key" system. The prospective foreign visitor must first convince a U.S. Consular officer abroad that he or she does not intend to overstay. Those receiving visas are "inspected" again on entry by INS officials.

With seven to eight million applicants for visas a year, the time available to Consuls for each individual screening continues to shrink. Consular staffing must be increased and readiness, accuracy and volume of background data on applicants must be improved. More fundamental is the de-politicizing of the State Department's management of visa issuance and insistence on strict interpretation of the law's criteria of eligibility.

There should be more use of INS "pre-inspection," as the 1996 IIRIRA promises, of U.S.-bound travelers at major international airports abroad. It is far more effective to stop overstayers, terrorists, or frivolous asylum seekers before they reach U.S. soil. U.S. law now permits waiver of visas for visitors from countries that have low overstay rates. Inverting this approach would be effective: suspend issuance of all discretionary, temporary visas for countries whose overstay rates exceed a certain threshold.

Finding Overstayers in the U.S.—The State Department and INS must cooperate closely in developing a secure system for tracking nonimmigrant visitors from the receipt of their visa abroad. Individual case files should include personal data, the visa holder's declared personal, family, school or business contacts in the United States and travel arrangements.

Automated fingerprinting, which is non-invasive, should be required for most non-diplomatic and official visa applicants everywhere, and certainly for travelers from countries with a high incidence of overstaying. Overstays could be investigated here by matching personal and biometric data on suspected visa recipients against social security rolls, driver's license issuances, tax and criminal records, U.S. Post Office address files, and records of gun purchasers (federal prohibitions on gun ownership by illegal aliens are not being enforced). Nonimmigrant aliens in the United States three months or more should be required to report their whereabouts to the Justice Department at least yearly. As both a deterrent and as a source of revenue, the State Department and INS should make much more frequent use of departure bonds and non-refundable round-trip air tickets for high-risk visa holders.

Here again, Congress has blown hot and cold on reducing visas overstays. After legislating a major INS program in 1996 to track the entry and exit of foreign visitors, in 1998 Congress delayed the program for two and a half years at border ports of entry because of complaints from local civic and business leaders.

INS must improve its spotty record of acting on leads supplied by other agencies and concerned citizens.

Worth a try would be a well advertised twenty-four-hour 1-800 hotline available for interested citizens to report suspected immigration violations. The agency should provide frequent, widely disseminated reports on the use of these leads.

SHIFTING THE COSTS: MAKING ILLEGAL IMMIGRATION UNPROFITABLE

Paying for Better Immigration Control—The task is to mount and maintain the political will to deploy—and pay for—the people, technology and barriers known to be effective. The build up of these enforcement agencies is expensive. Far more of the rising costs of immigration regulation must be borne by the beneficiaries of immigration: the legal and illegal immigrants themselves, their families, employers and labor contractors, and ethnic advocacies.

While this principle may seem mercenary to some, INS has increasingly applied it in recent years. In 1994, 43.8 percent of the agency's operating budget came from fees for immigration benefits, user fees, fines, confiscations and bond forfeitures. The amount now collected, nearly $800 million, could be readily doubled in two or three years with more realistic fees for underpriced services, and with heftier and better collected fines and forfeitures. INS moved in the right direction in 1998 by increasing its fees to immigrants and their sponsors from as little as $20 to as much as $250 for 27 different services, such as petitions, waivers, permits, ID and travel documents and naturalization. Worth reviving is the White House's unsuccessful February 1995 proposal for a border crossing fee to raise $400 million a year for immigration control. INS was also on the right track in 1994 in proposing, unsuccessfully, a new fee of $130 to apply for political asylum.

Residence in the United States is one of the world's most valuable privileges. Yet U.S. taxpayers now pay for much of the cost of granting it, when the country should share in the large increase in lifetime earnings most immigrants will realize. Enlightened but unsuccessful legislation in 1989, for example, proposed a 15 percent tax on salaries paid by employers to temporary foreign workers. The Commission on Immigration Reform (CIR) in 1995 recommended a similar levy. Lawmakers endorsed the concept in 1998 by imposing a $500 fee on employers for each foreign worker beyond a certain threshold imported in the expanded H1-B temporary skilled worker program. A similar tax should be applied to employers of illegal aliens. More recovery for the Treasury of a portion of immigrants' and employers' windfalls from immigration, and more sharing of it with state and local governments would encourage their support for enforcement, help cover their large hidden social costs, and dampen the hyper-demand for U.S. residence.

The Informal Economy, Magnet and Sustenance for Illegal Immigrants—The underground, or "informal," economy interacts with and supports the formal U.S. economy in intimate and often pernicious ways, from low cost subcontracting of production of name-brand items, to the semi-peonage system of farm labor contractors in perishable crop agriculture, to industrial home work and street vending.

Findings of a 1992 Labor Department review indicate that the informal economy in 1994 cost the country about $110 billion in lost revenue[7]. An INS survey of former illegal aliens confirms their heavy presence in the informal sector. Fully 10.0 percent of them claimed to have worked for less than the legal minimum wage, compared to 2 percent of the overall U.S. labor force, and 13 percent were not paid for all hours worked, according to surveys of former illegal aliens done by INS in 1989 and 1992.

Combating the informal economy calls for more resources and backing for the labor and safety compliance agencies, more cooperation among them and with INS, and more involvement of state and local agencies in immigration enforcement. State and federal labor agencies must have the power, now held only by INS, to impose fines on employers of illegal aliens. Fines should be increased and collected more diligently. Cooperating state and local agencies should share in the fines and forfeitures from delinquent employers to defray the cost of this additional mission. The Labor Department's authority to sequester goods produced under flagrant violations of the Fair Labor Standards Act should be extended to egregious immigration violations.

Shared Liability between Firms and Contractors—A serious deterrent to labor and immigration violations would be to make contracting firms or farmers share liability for the violations of their contractors. The exposure of those firms to fines and the shame of big-name marketers of garments, electronics, furniture and processed meats being publicly linked with sweatshop conditions and exploitation would be important deterrents.

Congress bowed to the powerful farm lobby in 1986 by barring the INS from entering open fields without a warrant to check for unlawful workers. Since then, arrests of illegals on farms have fallen by 75,000 a year and the percentage of the paid farm workforce that is illegal has risen from 9 percent to 42 percent[8]. INS must be re-authorized to enter open fields without warrants as needed, and farmers in violation should share the sanctions imposed on their labor contractors.

Private Sector Help for a Swamped INS—Washington over time has seriously degraded INS's effectiveness by heaping new obligations on it without a comparable increase in support. Policy makers have overlooked that the agency's core missions have ballooned with the tripling of the immigrant population in the last quarter century. Even if INS is able to recover from its chronic administrative disarray, the agency on its own will not have the resources to end illegal immigration.

Privatizing some of the record-keeping and monitoring aspects of immigration enforcement is a way out, one that also transfers some of the costs of enforcement to illegal immigrants and their patrons. Reliance on the private sector in this field is not new: Internal Revenue Service and other government agencies now use private collection agencies. Prisons are operated by private firms. And private bonding companies now use bounty hunters to bring in fugitive deportable aliens to INS. The 1986 amnesty for aliens was administered by private nonprofit entities.

A major potential deterrent and market dampener would be legislation making employers who knowingly hire illegal aliens liable for at least one-half the cost of the public assistance and services those aliens and their dependents receive during their period of employment. Using INS lists of employers in violation, private collection agencies, law firms, or other private contractors would determine the amount of the firm's liability for restitution and proceed through negotiation, administrative action or litigation to recover that amount for the state or federal government on contingency. Successful privatization here could open the door for private sector supervision of other temporary categories, such as tourists, students, "temporary protected status," and temporary workers.

REFORMING LEGAL IMMIGRATION TO TURN OFF ILLEGAL ENTRY

By making family reunification, humanitarian concern, and—most recently—"diversity" sacrosanct, the

U.S. ideology of legal immigration provides both a motivation and a means for illegal immigration. The promise to new immigrants of ultimate reunification of their families here has created high expectation of resettlement. While 3.5 million family members are nominally required to wait for periods up to twenty years for rationed immigration visas, a feeling of entitlement leads many to enter illegally and do their waiting here. The existence of this massive backlog nurtures illegal settlement, and invites quick fixes by politicians under pressure by ethnic lobbies to end family separations. An example was Washington's willingness in 1988 to exempt from deportation scores of thousands of undocumented dependents of amnestied illegal aliens, later blessed by law in 1990.

Annual immigration lotteries since 1986 have created expectations among millions of applicants abroad. A portentous measure of the pent-up demand for resettlement in the United States is the 1994 lottery, which drew 7.5 million applicants for 55,000 slots.

Real or prospective amnesties, group waivers of deportation, or special temporary protection arrangements for presumably endangered national groups also stimulate illegal immigration. An estimated 500,000 to 600,000 aliens, mostly ineligible farm workers, entered the United States in 1987 and 1988 to fraudulently claim amnesty under the 1986 Immigration Reform and Control Act. In early 1999, Washington's decision to respond to Central America's 1998 hurricane disaster with "temporary protected status" for Central Americans illegally in the country stimulated an even larger influx from that region.

Family Chains as Magnets—The opening of more doors to the logic of family reunification, creates new flows of legal and illegal immigrants in the future. Illegal immigration would be chilled by:

- Sizable reductions of immigrant and refugee admissions—now approaching 1.0 million yearly;
- Limiting family reunification to spouses and minor children of citizens;
- Ending immigration lotteries and phasing out the 4.0 million-person worldwide waiting list in favor of one-time, simultaneous admission of eligible immediate family groups.

Political Asylum an Unintended Lure—The most idealistic, impractical, and reckless feature of the legal immigration structure, is political asylum—a critical magnet for illegal immigration. NPG's proposals for reform of the philosophy and process of political asylum appear in the 1995 NPG Forum paper: "Political Asylum: Achilles Heel of Immigration Control." Its key proposals are: 1) making asylum temporary only, ending it when the conditions improve in the asylees' source countries; and 2) rejecting all asylum claims from persons who are citizens or residents of states deemed by the U.S. government to have adequate human rights conditions.

CONCLUSION: CHOOSE OR BE CHOSEN

The record of three-decades of mounting illegal immigration points to some sobering conclusions. Turning it around will take a degree of political will and perseverance that has been lacking so far in all Washington administrations since Eisenhower. Even a massive, coordinated and well-funded effort involving federal and local agencies and private sector contractors will need five years or more to make major reductions in the inflow and the size of the resident illegal population.

The rising numbers of visa overstayers demands more rigorous overseas selection and far more active internal enforcement than the United States has exerted so far. The budget increases INS has gained since 1994 must be maintained and extended to those deliberately starved functions, such as worksite enforcement, that powerful economic interests see as threatening. Such progress will not come easily in today's tight labor markets and deep ideological divisions about the civic responsibilities of business.

But efforts of emasculate immigration control in the guise of "reorganizing" the INS must be resisted. However effective, INS cannot do it alone. New monitoring and enforcement arrangements involving a much wider range of public and private sector participants must be developed. To overcome bureaucratic inertia and turf-protection and special interest tinkering will require a firm and persistent national political commitment to the task as a priority interest.

All of this is a tall order for a U.S. political system with a notoriously short attention span. But the alternative is unacceptable. Inaction has meant growing flows of illegal immigration. If not closely regulated, millions of aliens and their smugglers and patrons will make momentous decisions about America's demographic, social and environmental future that the nation as a whole deserves to make for itself.

NOTES:

1. Robert Warren (1994). *"Estimates of the Unauthorized Immigrant Population Residing in the United States, by Country of Origin and State of Residence: October 1992,"* Washington: Immigration and Naturalization Service.
2. David Simcox (1994). "INS Estimates 4.0 million Illegals Present in 1994: Estimate Seen as Low." *Immigration Review*. No. 18, Summer 1994.
3. Based on an estimate of 8 million persons in the U.S. in 1994 whose presence here was made possible by an initial illegal entry. Further assumed is that 40 percent of this population are women of child-bearing age present in the United States for an average of ten years with an average annual birth rate of ninety-three per 1000. This yields an estimate of 3 million U.S.-born children in 1996.
4. Robert Warren (1994).
5. *New York Times*, December 15, 1998
6. "INS is Scaling Back its Workplace Raids." *Chicago Tribune*, January 17, 1999.
7. Ibid.
8. U.S. Commission on Immigration Reform. *U.S. Immigration Policy: Restoring Credibility—A Report to Congress*. Washington: GPO, 1994.
9. David Simcox. "Immigration and the Informalization of the Economy." *Population and Environment*, January, 1997.
10. *Rural Migration News*, January 16, 1999.

A TALE OF TWO FUTURES: CHANGING SHARES OF U.S. POPULATION GROWTH

Ed Lytwak

March 1999

U.S. POPULATION GROWTH 1950 TO 1996, IN PERSPECTIVE

The second half of the twentieth century was a period of unprecedented and remarkable population growth in the United States. By 1950, the U.S. population had grown from the nearly four million people enumerated in the nation's first census (in 1790) to over 151 million. In less than fifty years, from 1950 to 1996, the population of the United States exploded to 268 million. This increase of over 116 million people represented the largest population growth of any fifty year period in U.S. history and more than all population growth in the first one hundred and fifty years of the nation's history. The 116 million new Americans added between 1950 and 1996 were 41 million more than the 75 million Americans added to the population in the previous fifty years, as well as 41 million more than the entire U. S. population at the beginning of the twentieth century.

The second half of the twentieth century also saw a remarkable shift in the demographic shares accounting for most of the growth. During this relatively short time, the driving force behind U.S. population growth dramatically shifted from native-born natural increase to immigration, both directly and indirectly through births to immigrant women living in the U.S. The period began with a baby boom and bust during which U.S. total fertility fell from an average of 3.5 births per woman to below replacement level (the average 2.1 births per woman necessary to replace the mother and father) in less than one decade. The boom and bust was followed by a sustained period of sub-replacement fertility by the native-born population, which continues today.

At the very time that the great majority of native-born Americans were voluntarily choosing to limit their family sizes to levels which could have led to the end of U.S. population growth, Congress was making changes in immigration policy which has ensured ever more growth. The result of these changes was the highest sustained immigration and greatest population growth in U.S. history—population growth which shows no sign of ending as the U.S. prepares to enter the twenty-first century. Ironically, were it not for the dramatic increase in immigration, this extraordinary period of population growth would have been a prelude to the end of U.S. population growth in the first part of the twenty-first century.

BOOM AND BUST: U.S. POPULATION GROWTH 1950 TO 1970

In many ways, the 1950s and early 1960s were typical of population growth patterns throughout U.S. history. Natural increase of the native-born population was the primary component of growth. Net immigration, which during this period averaged about 240,000 annually, also approximated traditional historic averages. Somewhat atypically, natural increase attributable to immigrants, was actually negative. That is, deaths outnumbered births to immigrants, a reflection of the fact that many foreign born had entered the U.S. during the great wave of immigration from 1896 to 1915. As a result, immigration's overall share (net immigration plus natural increase attributable to immigrants) of U.S. growth during the 1950s was small, less than 4 percent. By the 1960s, however, increased immigration began to push this share gradually upward, more than doubling it to 9 percent during the decade 1961 to 1970.

Nonetheless, the primary demographic force during the 1950s and '60s was the Baby Boom. The Baby Boom was a post-World War II period of high domestic fertility, during which American women gave birth to some 76 million babies from 1946 to 1964—the largest generation in U.S. history. Almost all population growth during the 1950s was attributable to births to U.S. born women with annual population growth rates peaking in 1957 when the U.S. population grew by 1.8 percent.

By the mid 1960s, however, two events occurred which were to have profound long-term consequences for the United States' demographic future. First, the Immigration and Nationality Act Amendments of October 3, 1965 marked a major shift in U.S. immigration policy. Although the impact was gradual at first, the change in emphasis (from a policy based on national quotas and labor market needs to one based on family reunification), resulted in dramatically increased immigration. By the 1980s and 1990s, immigration swelled to the highest sustained levels in U.S. history.

The second major event was a sudden and remarkable drop in U.S. fertility. At the end of the Baby Boom (1960–1964), the Total Fertility Rate (TFR) stood at 3.5. By the end of the 1960s that rate had fallen to 2.6 (1965–69) and by the early 1970s (1970 to 1974) was at replacement level, the average of 2.1 births per woman necessary for a biologically stationary population. From boom to bust, this extraordinary drop in fertility served to set the stage for the unprecedented shift in the shares of U.S. population growth that was to occur in the next three decades.

DIVERGING DEMOGRAPHIC FUTURES: U.S. POPULATION GROWTH 1971 TO 1980

The 1970s were a demographic watershed for several reasons. First, in 1972, the U.S. TFR went below replacement level for the first time since the 1930s, an astounding event considering that just over ten years earlier the United States had experienced record numbers of annual births. Another milestone, occurred just two years later, when, for the first time in the second half of the twentieth century, births to the foreign born began to outnumber foreign-born deaths. In the next two decades these two divergent trends would continue. As native-born fertility remained at sub-replacement levels and dropped as a share of total U.S. population growth, direct immigration and births to the foreign born began to rapidly increase their shares of U.S. population growth.

The remarkable drop in native-born fertility continued throughout the 1970s, with the U.S. TFR reaching a historic low of 1.7 in 1976. This marked the beginning of a sustained period of sub-replacement level fertility, which continued into the 1990s. Overall, U.S. TFR remained at sub-replacement levels throughout the 1970s and 1980s: 1975–79, 1.8; 1980–84, 1.8; 1985–88, 1.9. Although the overall TFR has since risen back to replacement level (largely due to the higher fertility and growing number of foreign-born women in the U.S.), the native-born population has continued to maintain below replacement fertility of about 1.9.

Table 1. Components of U.S. Population Growth By Decade 1951-1996

Decade	1951–60	1961–70	1971–80	1981–90	1991–96
Total Growth (% of Total)	27,664,479 -100%	22,493,591 -100%	19,974,785 (100%)	24,828,693 (100%)	16,751,176 -100%
Native-Born Share[1]	26,610,726 (96%)	20,466,805 (91%)	13,001,265 (65%)	14,206,174 (57%)	7,040,510 -42%
Net Immigration	2,224,479 (8%)	2,597,677 (11%)	6,297,314 (32%)	8,349,062 (33%)	6,638,213 -40%
Foreign-Born Natural Increase[2]	-1,170,726 (-4%)	-570,891 (-2%)	376,206 (2%)	2,573,457 (10%)	3,072,453 -18%
Immigration's Share[3]	1,053,753 (4%)	2,026,786 (9%)	6,673,520 (34%)	10,922,519 (43%)	9,710,666 -58%

Notes: 1. Natural increase attributable to the U.S. born population minus after 1970 emigration of U.S. born persons estimated at 48,000 annually. 2. Natural increase attributable to immigration, that is births to foreign-born women minus deaths of the foreign born. 3. Net immigration plus natural increase attributable to immigrants.

Had immigration remained at replacement level (in and out migration equal) after 1970, this sustained period of sub-replacement level fertility would have resulted in the U.S. population peaking at about 250 million around the year 2030.[1] Assuming that domestic fertility remained at about 1.9 births per woman and immigration remained at replacement levels, the U.S. population would have then begun a very gradual transition to a smaller and ultimately optimum population. This was the demographic future that the majority of American families have, since the 1970s, chosen.

By the 1970s, however, another demographic future—this one chosen for the American people by the politicians in Washington—was beginning to take shape. With the chain migration provisions of the 1965 amendments kicking in, legal immigration during the decade rose to nearly 5 million, more than double the annual average of the previous four decades[2]. Illegal immigration also significantly increased with an estimated net three million illegals establishing permanent residence in the U.S. from 1971 to 1980. The rapidly growing number of immigrants was also reflected in the growing stock of foreign born in the U.S. which rose from slightly over 10 million (4.9 percent of the total population) in 1971 to more than 14 million (6.2 percent of the total population) in 1980.

As a result, the 1970s saw immigration's total share of U.S. growth dramatically increase. In 1970, immigration (net immigration plus the net natural increase of the foreign born) accounted for 280,949 (13 percent) of total U.S. growth that year (2,111,281). By 1980 immigration's contribution had tripled to 897,965 or 38 percent of total annual population growth. Most of this growth in immigration's share of U.S. growth was due to rapidly increasing levels of immigration. Net foreign-born migration for the decade totaled 6,297,314 and accounted for 34 percent of total growth. Because of the age structure and relatively small size of the foreign born population in the U.S., natural increase attributable to immigration (births to foreign-born women minus deaths to the foreign born) was still minor, only 376,206, or 2 percent of total U.S. growth for the decade (19,974,785). When combined with net migration, however, immigration accounted for fully one-third of all U.S. growth for the decade 1971 to 1980 (6,673,520 or 34 percent). Astoundingly, this was over eight times immigration's growth share from the 1950s and more than triple the contribution of immigration to U.S. growth in the previous decade, the 1960s.

SHIFTING SHARES: U.S. POPULATION GROWTH IN THE 1980S

The dual trends, of rapidly increasing immigration and a growing number of births to immigrants already in the country, greatly intensified in the 1980s. The latter 1970s marked the beginning of a prolonged period that saw the highest sustained immigration in United States' history. According to INS figures, from 1977 until 1996 15,566,019 immigrants were granted legal permanent residency in the U.S. This is more than the 14,818,902 immigrants who entered during what had, until recently, been the historic period of highest immigration, the twenty-year period 1896 to 1915. This figure also does not include the estimated 5.5 million illegal immigrants added to the U.S. population from 1977 to 1996 (illegal immigration was not a significant factor around the turn of the century).

After tripling in the 1970s, immigration's share of annual U.S. population growth was on the path to double again. In 1981 immigration accounted for 881,886, 38 percent of annual U.S. growth. By 1990 that share would grow to 2,068,828–58 percent of all U.S. population growth. Directly, this radically changing share of growth was due to very high levels of legal immigration. Indirectly, however, as the total number of foreign-born women permanently residing in the U.S. rapidly grew, so too did the number of births attributable to immigrants. The growth in total numbers of foreign-born women was compounded by the much higher fertility of large segments of the foreign-born population. A 1995 Census Bureau report has confirmed that foreign-born women had fertility one-third higher than that of native-born women of childbearing age.[3] Women born in Mexico, who comprise one-third of all foreign-born women of childbearing ages, had fertility two-thirds higher.

While direct immigration was the most obvious contributor to U.S. population growth, the full importance of the indirect component, births to immigrants living in the U.S. has largely gone unrecognized. It was only recently, that the Census Bureau finally acknowledged that, "most of the importance of net migration in understanding population growth is the natural increase of the population it adds.[4]" Of all the components of U.S. growth, natural increase attributable to the foreign born was the fastest growing, nearly tripling (a 178 percent increase) between 1981 and 1990 (from 157,286 to 436,945). The decade of the 1980s, also saw births to the foreign born jump from 10 percent to 15 percent, of total births as did the foreign born share of total natural increase, which rose from 9 percent to 22 percent. Likewise, the share of foreign-born natural increase as a percentage of total growth, increased from 7 percent to 12 percent. These figures are all the more remarkable considering that the foreign born were still a relatively small fraction of the total U.S. population, 6 percent in 1981 and 7 percent in 1990.

Overall, the numbers for the decade 1981 to 1990 clearly substantiate these trends, especially when compared to the earlier decades. For the 1980s, immigration's share increased to 10,922,519 or 43 percent of total U.S. population growth (24,828,693) for the decade. The enormous number of new immigrants entering the U.S. were likewise reflected in the rapidly shifting shares which included natural increase attributable to the foreign born of 2,573,457 (10 percent of total growth) and net immigration of

Table 2. Contribution of Foreign-Born Births to U.S. Population Growth

Year	Total Foreign- Born Population (% Total Population)	Births to Foreign-Born Women (% Total Births)[1]	Percentage of U.S. Natural Increase[2]	Immigration's Share of Total Growth[3]
1950	10,347,000 (6.9%)	103,578 (3.4%)	-7%	1%
1960	9,661,000 (5.4%)	150,498 (4.2%)	-4%	5%
1970	9,740,000 (4.8%)	222,642 (5.9%)	-1%	13%
1980	14,080,000 (6.2%)	335,358 (9.3%)	+7%	38%
1990	19,767,000 (7.9%)	645,589 15.5%)	+22%	58%
1996	25,208,604 (9.5%)	747,167 (19.2%)	+34%	61%

Notes: 1. Births to foreign-born (immigrant) women permanently residing in the United States. 2. Foreign-born natural increase (foreign-born births minus foreign-born deaths) as a percentage of U.S. natural increase. 3. Net foreign-born migration and foreign-born natural increase as a percentage of total U.S. population growth.

8,049,062 (32 percent of total growth). From 1981 to 1990, immigration's annual share of total U.S. growth increased an astonishing 152 percent.

IMMIGRATION: DRIVING 1990's POPULATION GROWTH

Two further changes in immigration policy, helped to accelerate this shift from native-born births to immigration as the driving force behind U.S. population growth. The 1986 Immigration Reform and Control Act (IRCA) not only gave permanent legal status to some three million illegal aliens, but more importantly, made them eligible to bring additional family members into the country under the generous family reunification provisions of current law. Second, the 1990 Immigration Act directly increased total legal immigration by about 35 percent.

During the 1990s, these two changes worked together to solidify immigration's role as the primary component of U.S. growth. Including the IRCA legalizations, the nearly two million—1,827,167—legal immigrants granted permanent residency in the U.S. in 1991 marked the highest annual level of immigration in U.S. history. This was over 42 percent higher than the previous record for annual immigration, 1907, when 1,285,349 immigrants entered the country.

Natural increase of native-born Americans has continued to play an important role accounting for 48 percent of total U.S. population growth in the 1990s. Much of that growth, however, was population momentum from pre-1970 fertility, that is, births to the Baby Boom generation. Although women from the Baby Boom generation have averaged less than two births each, population momentum dictates that their total births will outnumber the total of people dying, most of whom are from earlier and smaller generations. Thus, Baby Boom population momentum was essentially predetermined population growth that could not be changed. By the 1990s most of the women from that generation had already completed their families or were nearing the end of their child-bearing years (fifteen to forty-four) and their population momentum was, likewise, nearing its end.

While Baby Boom population momentum has been winding down, births to the foreign born have continued their remarkable and steady rise as a percentage of total U.S. births. In the relatively short period from 1991 to 1996, foreign-born births (as a percentage of total U.S. births) increased from 16 percent to 19 percent, and natural increase attributable to immigration (births to immigrant women minus deaths of immigrants) increased from 25 percent to 35 percent. These figures are even more remarkable given the fact that the foreign born still comprised less than 10 percent of the total population during this time.

The growing number of foreign-born births combined with high immigration were clearly evident in immigration's share of U.S. population growth which totaled almost 10 million (9,710,666), or 58 percent, for the entire period 1991–96 (16,751,176). For the last year in which full data is available, 1996, the foreign born population in the U.S. was 25,208,604, or 10 percent of the total U.S. population. Yet, births to the foreign born totaled 747,167, 19 percent of total births. Likewise, 34 percent of all natural increase (1,576,804) and 21 percent of total U.S. growth (2,524,704) was due to immigration. Similarly, net immigration was extraordinarily high, approaching one million (995,900) and accounting for 39 percent of total U.S. population growth in 1996. Taken together, direct immigration and births to immigrants accounted for more than 1.5 million, or 61 percent, of total U.S. population growth.

U.S. POPULATION GROWTH: THE PAST, PRESENT AND FUTURE LINKED

The rapidly shifting shares of population growth in the second half of the twentieth century were unprecedented in U.S. history. Also without parallel was the extent that a single federal government policy—immigration—has fostered continued population growth. By the 1970s, most Americans were voluntarily choosing to limit their families to a size which would have stopped population growth. Contrary to the direction native-born fertility was taking, the U.S., Congress raised immigration to the highest sustained levels in U.S. history.

While the direct impact of immigration was important, the indirect effect of immigration, births to the foreign born, quickly became an increasingly powerful engine of additional population growth. Immigration policy dramatically increased the total number of U.S. births in two ways. First, it greatly increased the total number of women giving birth in the U.S. Second, the total fertility of most immigrant women has been substantially higher than the native-born population. Currently, immigrants account for about 10 percent of the total U.S. population, yet contribute well over one-third of U.S. biologic growth.

The last twenty years of high immigration has also created tremendous population momentum, which will drive U.S. population growth far into the next century. Due in large part to immigration, the Census Bureau now projects that "beginning in 2012, the number of births each year will exceed the highest annual number of births ever achieved in the United States[5]." The full extent of immigrant driven population momentum and the consequences of continuing current immigration policy are provided in projections done by the Census Bureau and confirmed in a study by the National Research Council[6].

According to the Census Bureau middle series projections, which assume net immigration of 820,000 a year, immigration will boost U.S. population growth by almost 80 million (61 percent of all growth) between 1995 and 2050[7]. That is, the U.S. population will be 393 million rather than the 314 million if there was no immigration.

Because of population momentum, U.S. immigration policy has already determined a demographic future of continued growth through 2050—even if immigration were stopped today. Rather than a population that would have peaked at 250 million and begun a transition to an optimum and sustainable level, the U.S. is now committed to a growing population of at least 314 million[8]. Americans and our political leaders can, however, still choose a demographic future different from the one that current high levels of immigration are taking us toward. The tale of America's demographic future in the twenty-first century is being written today in annual levels of immigration and the family size choices of all Americans. The choice between our two possible futures is clear: continued growth, environmental degradation, and a declining quality of life or population reduction and long-term sustainability.

NOTES ON SOURCES AND METHODOLOGY

This NPG Forum was adapted from a longer study analyzing the changing shares of U.S. population growth from 1950 to 1996. Unless otherwise noted, the source for all figures mentioned in the report are published birth, death, immigration and population data (or direct derivations from that data) provided by the National Center for Health Statistics, the Census Bureau and the Immigration and Naturalization Service (INS). Where reliable data is simply not available, such as estimates of emigration and illegal immigration, figures are taken directly from Census Bureau or INS estimates or derived by comparing available data and estimates from both government and private analyses. A complete listing of sources and references is available in the full study.

Immigration's share of total population growth was determined by looking at both its direct and indirect contributions. The direct component is simply the net addition of those who immigrate into the country and establish permanent residence minus the foreign born who permanently leave—net immigration. Immigration's indirect impact on population growth is determined by subtracting annual deaths of permanent resident immigrants from annual births to immigrant women, that is, the natural increase attributable to immigration.

It should also be noted that this methodology for calculating immigration's share of growth underestimates the long-term impacts of immigration on population growth. In limiting immigration's share to direct immigration and births to immigrant women, the broader impacts of generation after generation of immigrant descendants are not included. A full discussion of the methodology behind the figures, is also available in the full study.

The full demographic analysis from which this Forum was adapted, "The Changing Shares of U.S. Population Growth: 1950 to 1996," is available from Negative Population Growth.

NOTES:

1. If U.S. immigration had remained at replacement level after 1970, U.S. population growth would have peaked around 2030 at about 247 million. Based on projections done by demographer Leon Bouvier in Roy Beck, "Immigration No. 1 in U.S. Growth." *The Social Contract*, Vol. 2, No. 2, Winter 1991–92.

2. The INS lists total immigration between 1931 and 1970 at 7,400,626, an annual average of 185,016 and a decade average of 1,850,157.
3. U.S. Census Bureau, *Current Population Reports*, Series P20-499, "Fertility of American Women: June 1995." Forthcoming.
4. U.S. Census Bureau, *Current Population Reports*, Series P23-194, "Population Profile of the United States: 1997." U.S. Government Printing Office, Washington, D.C., 1998, p.9.
5. U.S. Census Bureau, *Current Population Reports*, Series P23-194, "Population Profile of the United States: 1997." U.S. Government Printing Office, Washington, D.C., 1998, p.9.
6. Smith, James P., and Barry Edmonston, Editors. 1997. *The New Americans: Economic, Demographic, and Fiscal Effects of Immigration*. National Academy Press, Washington, D.C.
7. U.S. Census Bureau, *Current Population Reports*, Series P25-1130, "Population Projections of the United States by Age, Sex, Race, and Hispanic Origin: 1995 to 2050." U.S. Government Printing Office, Washington, D.C., 1996.
8. Bouvier, Leon. 1998. "The Impact of Immigration on United States' Population Size: 1950 to 2050." *NPG Forum*, Negative Population Growth, Washington, D.C.

THE ENVIRONMENTAL FUTURE HOW DO WE GET THERE FROM HERE?

Gaylord Nelson

October 2000

Forging and maintaining a sustainable society is The Challenge for this and all generations to come. At this point in history, no nation has managed to evolve into a sustainable society. We are all pursuing a self-destructive course of fueling our economies by drawing down our natural capital—that is to say, by degrading our resource base—and counting it on the income side of the ledger. This, obviously, is not a sustainable situation over the long term.

EARTH DAY AND SUSTAINABILITY

Thirty years ago on April 22, 1970, Earth Day burst onto the political scene. Twenty million people demonstrated their concern over what was happening to the natural world around them—polluted rivers, lakes, trout streams, ocean shores, the air we breathe and much more. The people cared, but the political establishment seemed oblivious to it all. The specific objective on Earth Day was to stir up a public demonstration big enough to shake up the establishment and force the environmental issue onto the national political agenda. Earth Day was a truly astonishing grassroots explosion. It achieved everything I had hoped for. At long last, the environment was on the national agenda, where it will remain as a constant reminder for this and future generations.

This brief essay speaks to the fundamental issue of our time—forging a sustainable society. A sustainable society may be described in several ways: a society whose activities do not exceed the carrying capacity of its resource base; or a society that manages its environmental and resource systems so that their ability to support future generations is not diminished. Every nation on the planet faces the same challenge.

Since the first Earth Day, we have tried a lot of things. We have learned a lot, and we have achieved a lot. It has been a kind of piecemeal approach to the environmental challenge. We tackled the most obvious and threatening problems—air pollution, water pollution, etc. Even after thirty years there is still much to do in these areas. We have learned that almost all environmental problems are either preventable—or at least manageable. With this new knowledge we now stand at the threshold of a "Golden Opportunity" to change the course of history. We can do it by turning away from the uneconomic practice of fueling our economy by consuming our natural capital. Forging an economically sustainable society is the practical and profitable alternative. We know all we need to know to launch a long-term program that will lead us to sustainability.

After three decades of discussion, debate, legislation and education, there has evolved a new level of understanding and concern over what is happening around us. The public is prepared and, in the end, will support those measures necessary to forge a sustainable society if the President and the Congress present a well-documented and convincing case. Failing to achieve sustainability is not an acceptable option. That would be a disaster for future generations.

POLITICAL LEADERSHIP: THE ONLY DIRECT PATH TO SUSTAINABILITY

The presidency and the Congress are the political institutions with the position and authority to take advantage of this opportunity before it is too late.

- **The President** must jump-start the move to sustainability if we are to get this enterprise off the ground in a timely fashion. He can do so by delivering to Congress the first State of the Environment message in the history of our nation. That will be front-page news across the nation. The message should come this spring or early summer. It is important that sustainability become an active issue in politics if we are to get this matter on the national agenda.
- **The Congress**—Congressional hearings on sustainability are a critical part of the process. These hearings will need to cover the whole spectrum of environmental problems and extend over a period of several years. Public understanding of the issues is the key to broad support for doing what is necessary to achieve sustainability.
- **The National Academy of Sciences** would serve as consultant and make annual recommendations to the President and Congress on environmental problems and priorities.

YOUTH INVOLVEMENT

Message to the Youth of America—Because this is the future of our country, the campaign for sustainability will rely heavily on youthful participation and enthusiasm. Grade school, high school, and college students furnished much of the energy that invigorated Earth Day in 1970. We welcome your participation again.

I also suggest you get involved in the campaign for sustainability. This is a non-partisan issue, not a Republican or Democratic issue. Make your voices heard—you will have to live with the result.

Write letters to your candidates for Congress and the candidates for President asking their views on sustainability. Specifically, ask the candidates for Congress whether they will actively support Congressional hearings on sustainability and the candidates for President whether they, if elected, would submit an annual State of the Environment address to the Congress.

Sustainability must become an important part of the debate along with every other issue. Indeed, sustainability is more significant for the future of the nation than any other issue that will be raised during the 2000 election campaign.

FURTHER THOUGHTS ON SUSTAINABILITY

We have finally come to understand that the real wealth of a nation is its air, water, soil, forests, minerals, rivers, lakes, oceans, scenic beauty, wildlife habitats and biodiversity. Take this resource base away, and all that is left is a wasteland. That's the whole economy. That is where all the economic activity and all the jobs come from. These biological systems contain the sustaining wealth of the world. All around the planet these systems are under varying degrees of stress and degradation in almost all places, including the United States. As we continue to degrade them, we are consuming our capital. And, in the process, we erode living standards and compromise the quality of our habitat. We are veering down a dangerous path. We are not just toying with nature; we are compromising the capacity of natural systems to do what they need to do to preserve a livable world. We can—and must—forge a sustainable society, but it will take more vigorous leadership in the future. Fortunately, the ranks of the concerned and committed are rapidly expanding. The ultimate goal is to nurture a society imbued with a guiding environmental ethic. That ethic has been evolving, and ultimately, it will save us from many costly blunders. The British jurist, Lord Moulton, summarized the matter in one sentence—"The measure of a civilization is the degree of its compliance with the unenforceable." That is our goal.

Scientists and Sustainability—In a dramatic and sobering joint statement (1992), the United States National Academy of Sciences and the Royal Society of London, two of the world's leading scientific bodies, addressed the state of the planet in the following words:

"If current predictions of population growth prove accurate and patterns of human activity on the planet remain unchanged, science and technology may not be able to prevent either irreversible degradation of the environment or continued poverty for much of the world . . .

. . . Sustainable development can be achieved, but only if irreversible degradation of the environment can be halted in time . . ."

Late in the day, it has finally dawned on the political establishments around the world that environmental deterioration threatens both economic and environmental stability. This prompted the international community to organize two conferences on sustainability: 1992 in Rio and 1994 in Cairo. Next was the International Conference on Global Warming. These conferences were the first formal manifestations of serious international concern over the challenge of sustainability.

Global Warming—The Transition from Fossil Fuels—We can begin the process of forging a sustainable society now. We can begin the long and necessary transition from fossil fuels to solar energy; we can reduce air and water pollution to a level that is easily managed by nature; we can stop over-drafting the supply of ground waters, depleting our fisheries, deforesting the land, poisoning the land with pesticides, eroding the soil, degrading the public land, urbanizing farm lands, and destroying wetlands.

We can do this and much more. One thing is certain—we cannot afford to delay fixing problems here at home while we wait for the rest of the world to act. We can help, but we cannot wait. As a nation we have it in our power to do most things necessary to achieve sustainability, but the longer we delay, the more we undermine the livable quality of the environment and the resource base that undergirds the economy.

How Do We Transition to Sustainability?—The President and the Congress have the key leadership roles, while the public has the key support role. The failure of any one of these elements spells failure of the enterprise. The challenge is to forge a society that is economically and environmentally sustainable. Since this is primarily a political challenge, we start with those two political institutions, which share the key to the whole enterprise. Success or failure will turn on what kind of leadership comes from the President and the Congress. To be successful, their joint leadership must be vigorous and sustained over a period of several years.

THE PRESIDENCY

To crank up the political machinery for a move down the path to sustainability, someone has to spark the engine. The President is in the best position to do that. He owns the bully pulpit; he is the chief educator of the nation, the superstar, the only one who can command top billing in the papers and on television and radio, whenever he wishes.

We have come a long way in the past thirty years. Opinion polls show upwards of eighty percent (80 percent) of the U.S. population is concerned about the state of the environment. It is now time for the key political leadership, the President and the Congress, to join a non-partisan effort to design a plan of action for the future. It took three decades of effort to get where we are and it will take a least that long to get to where we want to go. An annual State of the Environment address to the Congress, coupled with regular Congressional hearings on sustainability, would inspire the kind of public dialogue that must precede major decisions on controversial matters.

While there is a well-established tradition of an annual message to the Congress on the State of the Union, there is no tradition of a message on the State of the Environment. This, despite the face that the actual "State of the Union" is totally dependent on the state of the environment and its resource base.

Presenting the Congress with a State of the Environment message on sustainability would set a powerful precedent that would be difficult, if not impossible, for future candidates and presidents to ignore. That would be a proud legacy for any president to leave to the nation.

THE CONGRESS

Education and Legislation—The Congress is the other key player. Its primary and critical role will be a combination of education and legislation. Public opinion polls show overwhelming concern for the environment and support for whatever measures may be required to maintain a clean environment. However, what particular measures may be required is not broadly understood. Until it is, the public won't support—and the Congress won't pass—the necessary legislation. This means several years of hearings, debate and legislative enactments involving the broad spectrum of issues that must be addressed on the way to sustainability. In many ways, this may appear to be an onerous and intimidating challenge because it will extend over considerable time and involve much debate and controversy. However, the only rational choice is to begin the process without delay.

To make this undertaking succeed will require a cooperative non-partisan effort unlike any other in our peacetime history. The state of the environment, and its impact upon the economy and the quality of life, needs to be much better understood. This is the function of the hearings, which should be held at least once or twice a month over the next several years, preferably by a joint Congressional committee. This would require about four to eight hours a month—certainly not a burdensome task. For example, during the ten-year period between 1969 and 1979, the Senate Small Business Committee conducted 135 hearings on prescription drugs—their pricing, uses and abuses. The hearings were newsworthy and regularly covered by the press and network TV. The famous Truman Committee conducted even more extensive hearings. Both of these sets of hearings had a significant impact on public policy.

Of necessity, sustainability hearings must range over all significant issues on the environmental spectrum. That will include exploring: how we make a transition from our overwhelming reliance on fossil fuels to a significant reliance on solar energy; how we move to restore ocean fisheries; how we reduce air and water pollution to a level manageable by nature; how we preserve our magnificent heritage of public lands; how we shrink our excessive reliance on herbicides and pesticides; how we stop over-drafting ground water, reduce soil erosion; and how we preserve wetlands, forests and biodiversity.

Congressional Hearings on Sustainability— Congressional hearings on sustainability could start almost any place. My choice would be public lands because almost everyone has some familiarity with National Parks, National Forests, wildlife refuges or Bureau of Land Management (BLM) lands. These lands are a rare heritage of almost one million square miles totaling about twenty-six percent of the U.S. landmass. No other nation on Earth preserved such a vast mosaic of mountains, wetlands, lakes, rivers, seashores, islands, plains, forests, grasslands and deserts. Within these bounds, a sample of almost every major American landform is represented. These are the only large expanses of natural areas left in the lower forty-eight states. Here are lands that would be recognized by our forefathers, lands inhabited by wildlife that cannot survive elsewhere, a rare condition of quiet undisturbed by man-made noises, and immense vistas of scenic beauty that cannot be found any other place. If this is not a rare asset deserving our most caring attention, then there is no such place.

PUBLIC LANDS

National Parks: The Best Idea We Ever Had— Early in the twentieth century, when the national park system was new in this country and unknown in any other, James Bryce, an Englishman, characterized it as "the best idea America ever had." Yellowstone National Park was created in 1872, the world's first national park. Since then, more than one hundred countries have established national parks. The national park system was formally established by the 1916 Organic Act and now encompasses some 80 million acres. The Organic Act specified that parks be managed with the purpose of conserving—

" . . . the scenery and the natural and historic objects and the wildlife therein and to provide for the enjoyment of the same in such manner and by such means as will leave them unimpaired for the enjoyment of future generations."

What a wonderful thing it would be if the park system were managed in compliance with the spirit and letter of the law. Sadly, it is not. Over many years, a succession of presidents and Congresses have defaulted in their responsibilities and permitted all kinds of incompatible activities to proliferate, much to the detriment of the system. Obviously, those activities that adversely affect wildlife, pollute the air, destroy the peace and quiet of the parks, and otherwise degrade the enjoyment of these special places, violate the mandate to leave these parks "unimpaired for the enjoyment of future generations.

The Best Idea We Ever Had Is Rapidly Falling Apart—The whole national park system is in varying degrees of serious decline. Park visitations have ballooned from 30 million in 1950 to almost 300 million today, resulting in traffic and noise pollution. Automobile traffic should be drastically reduced or eliminated in most parks. Snowmobiles are causing air pollution and noise pollution in Yellowstone National Park. At Yosemite, several thousand visitors stay in cabins and tents, creating a virtual city that has been described as "looking like downtown Los Angeles at midnight." In Grand Canyon National Park, 100,000 commercial tourism flights a year fly down the canyon, disturbing wildlife and the peace and quiet of that special place. In 1985, then-Governor Bruce Babbitt of Arizona testified that the noise in the canyon is "equivalent to being in downtown Phoenix at rush hour . . . and that's not what a national park is for." Contrast this with what Zane Gray wrote on the Grand Canyon in 1906: "One feature of this ever changing spectacle never changes: its eternal silence."

This is just a quick peek at what is happening to the crown jewels of our public land system. At the current rate of degradation, the National Parks as we know them will be gone within thirty years. They will be modified theme parks or Disneylands. The same thing is happening to our National Forests and the Bureau of Land Management lands—only much worse because they don't have the legal level of protection that the National Parks do. These lands are being degraded by all kinds of four-wheel drive vehicles, motorcycles, snowmobiles, jet skis, and more.

Doesn't all this degradation at least justify extensive hearings to inform the Congress and the public what is happening to twenty-six percent of the United States' land base? It is my view that the use of off-road vehicles on public lands should be phased out and that cattle grazing should be re-evaluated and reduced or phased out wherever it is compromising the resource base. This is controversial stuff and begs for public discussion.

HEARINGS ON POPULATION

What will America look like and be like when the population doubles from about 265 million to 520 million within the next seventy-five to eighty years? If we permit that to happen, it will have a dramatic and pervasive impact on almost all aspects of our living condition. Indeed, the Rockefeller Report to the President and the Congress in 1972 concluded that there would be no benefit to the country from further population growth and recommended that we move to stabilize our population. Since that report, the United States' population has ballooned by another 70 million.

If stabilization is to be achieved, it will require a substantial reduction in the immigration rate, and that is attacked as racist by some pro-immigration groups. This has silenced almost everyone, including many distinguished newspapers and other journals of opinion. Joseph McCarthy, from my state of Wisconsin, used exactly the same tactics—it is now called McCarthyism.

Since population density affects all aspects of our lives in quite significant ways, it should not be driven out of the market place of public discussion by McCarthyism or any other demagogic contrivance. Surely, this is an issue that ought to be explored in public hearings.

THE OPPORTUNITY FOR LEADERSHIP

This generation of political leaders has a golden opportunity to launch a program that will reverberate through history.

There have been two international conferences on sustainability during the past eight years. Finally, the international political community has come to recognize the threat of environmental deterioration. This is an important step. However, we cannot afford to delay addressing our own environmental problems while we wait for the international community. Now that we know that forging a sustainable society is the key to our future well-being, and that of succeeding generations, where and how do we start? That is simple enough: it must all start with the President and the Congress because the legal authority is in their hands alone.

Most of us have many chances to do the right thing during our lives, but very few among us are afforded the opportunity to be key players in launching a program that will reverberate down through history as an act of vision and statesmanship. The President and this Congress have that chance.

This is that Golden Opportunity for the President and the Congress to heed Bismarck's elegant observation "The best a statesman can do is listen to the rustle of God's mantle through history and try to catch the hem of it for a few steps."

THE FATE OF AMERICA

Tim Palmer

2000

AMERICA'S CHANGING LANDSCAPE

From one shining sea to another, well-known places in the United States are becoming unrecognizable. Home towns, rural countrysides, mountain retreats, the borders of our national parks, and the sprawling belts around our cities illustrate the rapid-change-scenario that leaves old identities in the dust, or more literally, under the asphalt. And beyond that strange twist of cultural and geographic destiny, the land is failing to function, failing to support us. The flood damages grow worse, the hurricane disasters more severe, the water more toxic with pesticide residues, and the soil saturated with chemicals that debilitate it as a source of life. Alarmed at these changes, I set out to write a book about the American landscape at the turn of the twenty-first century. I investigated mountains, forests, grasslands, deserts, rivers, lakes, wetlands, and seashores. I sought to document the changes, to understand the reasons for them, and to learn how people are responding.

Verification of a vast and troubling litany of loss is easily found: up to ninety-eight percent of the old-growth forest has been cut, less than four percent of the tallgrass prairie remains, a third of our waters are unfit for use, a third of our native plant and animal species could face extinction, mountaintop removal decapitates whole topographies in the Appalachians, and sprawl consumes three million acres a year-more than double the rate experienced as recently as the 1980s. Provoked by all of this-necessitated by it and motivated by it-people everywhere are taking new responsibility for stewardship of their homelands. They're forming land trusts, watershed associations, study groups, educational programs, and political campaigns for future-looking public officials. These people are the heroes and heroines of my book, *The Heart of America.*

Because of their work, the curve of protection activity and effectiveness has gone up dramatically since my youth in the 1950s. But the curve of destruction is still climbing steeper. The reforms that people are striving toward are utterly essential for the health of our land. But no mater what all these people do-even if they are successful with progressive new directions in the difficult arena of land-use planning and sustainability-population growth still renders the finest efforts futile unless our country comes to grip with the fundamental force of population growth now responsible for liquidating so much of the natural wealth of the continent.

RAMPANT POPULATION GROWTH

Nearly doubling in the past half-century, the American population has reached 275 million and is increasing by more than two-and-a-half million a year. At the current rate, another 35 million people will be added to the Untied States by the year 2010—the equivalent of another New Jersey every three years. In January 2000, the U.S. Census

Bureau projected that our population would reach 404 million by the year 2050 and 571 million by the end of the twenty-first century. "High estimates" considered possible by the Bureau foresee a population of 553 million by the year 2050 and 1.2 billion by the year 2100.

With such growth, one might expect that everything man-made has also doubled in the past half-century or so, from houses and cars to garbage, asphalt, and streetlights dimming the stars at night. But while the population has swollen, each person's consumptive capacity has also increased by two times, causing total consumption to boom by 400 percent in only fifty-eight years. Between just 960 and 1987, the urbanized acreage doubled. And aside from the increase in new dwellings, the size of the average house jumped 25 percent during the 1980s though the size of families did not grow. Each year, highway departments paved 11,200 more miles of road.[1] The number of motor vehicles grew at twice the rate of population growth from 1970 to 1995, and the number of miles driven per vehicle also increased 20 percent. These trends continue. Even if they didn't, a reduction in per capita consumption would only buy time to allow an increasing population to eventually reach the same high levels of impact on the earth.

For most people, population growth is not a distant problem but one that affects them directly, in their own communities, every day. Crime increases with population. Anybody from a small town or rural area will unhesitatingly confirm this fact after visiting a large city, but statistics bear the trend out as well.[2] Taxes also increase with population. This, too, is obvious to anyone who has paid taxes in a rural community and then moved to an urban or suburban one. In Louden County, Virginia, economists found that for every $1.00 in tax revenues collected, $1.28 in services were required for residential land uses, while only $0.11 was required for farmland. And the more a community grows, the more expensive it becomes to maintain basic services. In the early 1990s, roads, water lines, sewers, and parkland needed for each new home in booming Portland, Oregon, cost $28,500-an expense that had to come from taxes.[3] According to author William Ashworth in his book on economics, "The biggest creators of new taxes are not the tax-and-spend welfare Democrats in Congress, but the economic development committees of the Chamber of Commerce."[4]

Housing costs likewise increase with population growth, as comparison of most small-versus-large communities will show. When Portland grew by 35,000 people per year between 1991 and 1995, housing costs jumped 32 percent. But median income rose on 8 percent; many local families found themselves priced out of the market.

In the face of current population growth, open lands all across America are threatened, and hard-earned environmental gains of the past will be wiped out. For example, through vigorous conservation measures, per capita use of energy barely increased from 1970 to 1990, but total energy use still rose 36 percent, with nine-tenths of the increase from population growth.[5] This affects mountaintop removal for coal in the Appalachians, gas drilling on the eastern front of the Rockies, hydropower dams on salmon streams of the Northwest, and the threatened status of the last great wilderness on the Arctic Coastal Plain in Alaska. For a time, the perceived quality of life in some communities may go up with more population, but most of our towns, cities, and states passed that point long ago. Now, with a more crowded land, the quality of life goes down, and the liberties we enjoy and cherish as a birthright are eroded by the pressures of scarcity, competition, and the regulation that goes with overcrowding.[6]

After looking at what's happening to the American land, I can see that all the current talk of personal freedom-from libertarians claiming sovereignty in Montana to the Republican Congress voting for deregulation in Washington, D.C.-fails to grapple with the real cause of eroding liberties. The culprit is not a mindless bureaucracy but rather growing numbers of people whose needs and conflicts require that we have fees for building permits, high-rise apartment buildings even for people who don't want to live in them, restricted entry at the most popular national parks, and two-hour tow-away zones designed simply to give someone else a chance to park their car. We didn't have or need these things when our population was small.

OVERCOMSUMPTION OF RESOURCES

Studies have shown that in North America, at current rates of consumption, each person requires 12.6 acres of land for support.[7] A city of 1 million thus requires 12.6 million acres for its support in living space, food processing, commodity production, and waste disposal. And that assumes "productive" land. With these figures in mind, America is not nearly as spacious as it might seem, even beyond the sprawl of the cities.

A phenomenon I call the "delusion of open space" occurs when flying over the United States. I think everybody experiences this: I look out the window and see a lot of "empty" land. But when I consider the facts that water must be available for people to live, that those 12.6 productive acres are needed by each person, that substantial acreage in areas such as flood plains must be available for the earth's built-in maintenance program to function, that habitat must be shared with other forms of life if natural systems are to survive and we're not to be alone in this world, and that a bottomless deficit is accumulating every day because we consume massive amounts of non-renewable resources just to sustain the population we already have-when I consider all that, I can only conclude that America is full. Indeed, it's over-full, whether I see "empty" land out the window or not.

Looking at this question in a far more systematic way back in 1972, the Rockefeller Commission concluded that there was not benefit to further population growth in America. In 1980 the Global 2000 Report to President Reagan agreed. But neither study had much affect on national policy.[8] By the time the 1990s era of rapid economic growth and runaway materialism rolled around, it became more and more evident that we were consuming the resources of the earth and of future generations as if the monetary wealth of today's people was the only thing that mattered.

Our current population subsists to a large degree on non-renewable resources, principally fossil fuels, which will someday run out. This exhaustion of our capital extends to prime farmland, soil, forest productivity, ocean fisheries, groundwater, and minerals.[9] Once these things are gone, how will people live? Renewable resources such as solar power and well-managed forests offer us an answer to this conundrum and a path to the future, but it's not the path we're on. Economist Robert Costanza reported that a U.S. population of 85 million could exist on renewable resources at current per capita consumption levels; with half our current rate of consumption, which is how we lived in 1950, renewable resources could support 170 million people-still only 63 percent of our current number.[10] Costanza concluded that a reduced population should be our goal. Otherwise, with unlimited numbers of people vying for limited resources on earth, a drastic lowering of the standard of living emerges as the only future in sight.[11] This scenario is graphically seen in the swarming capital city of our next-door neighbor, Mexico, where a quarter of the 16 million residents live in extreme poverty without adequate shelter.[12] Scarcity, inflation, poverty, regulation, fatal levels of pollution, and an erosion of freedom are unavoidable consequences of an ever-increasing population.

A stable population would mean little additional loss of open space from mountains to seashore and all across the landscapes of America. While conventional wisdom holds that we must grow, more and more people now wonder why. The population of Pittsburgh, Pennsylvania, declined by nearly half since 1950 and in the process the city was transformed from a deadly exemplar of pollution and urban decay to the "most livable city in America" with an unemployment rate of only 4.3 percent. Meanwhile, high-growth cities such as Los Angeles and Miami only got worse.

A goal of stabilizing population does not mean we cannot grow. Free of the struggle to simply accommodate more and more people and free of the all-absorbing efforts to cope with the challenges of an ever-larger population-whether this means building a larger church or finding another landfill-people could turn their energies to growth of other kinds: greater meaning in our work, more time for the family, better education, added opportunities to learn and explore, more exercise for recreation and health, a strengthening of friendships, a heightened sense of community, more closeness to each other and to the earth. Every person can add to this wish-list of what could be growing instead of traffic jams, taxes, and the size of prisons.

Even in today's picture-one that history may regard as a depiction of madness-there could be hope, because, driven by new cultural desires, by education, by economic imperatives, and by safe, reliable, and accepted methods of contraception, the birth rate among established Americans is quite low. The fertility rate in 1990 hovered at about two children per woman-up from 1.8 in 1976, and higher than in Europe, though still at a level that would result in a plateau of population fairly early in the twenty-first century.[13] But that's not going to happen.

IMMIGRATION: CULPRIT OF POPULATION GROWTH

The birth rate of established Americans is low, but because of immigration, the national growth rate continues to soar. According to Census data, 62 percent of the increase from now until the year 2050 will come from immigration along with the high birth rates among new immigrants.[14] The National Research Council predicted that two-thirds of the growth to 2050 will result from immigration.[15] Much of this growth owes directly to Congress, which in 1990 increased legal immigration rates by 35 percent, raising it to the highest level in history-an immigration rate exceeding that of any other nation.[16]

If immigration continues at a high level, the rapid rate of population growth will not subside. The Census Bureau's medium estimate calls for 404 million people.[17] And that's only until 2050. At that point, much of the United States will look more like the crowded island of Japan than the America we know. Choosing to have virtually no immigration, the Japanese population, in fact, is expected to shrink while ours increases with no bounds.[18]

Of course, almost all Americans today are descended from immigrants. But consider, as well, that most of those people came when there was space and resources for them (native Americans certainly disagree, but still, there was clearly more space for immigrants in the past than there is today). Now the situation has changed. Though space and resources are now scarce, an estimated 1 million legal and illegal immigrants move here each year.[19]

It's not fair that my ancestors made it into America unrestricted but that today, people from other countries cannot, but neither was it fair that my parents' generation had to deal with both the Great Depression and World War II. Runaway population growth, quite simply, is the great challenge of our time. And many people are aware of this.

A Roper poll in 1997 found that 54 percent of Americans, including majorities of Latinos, supported a reduction of immigration to 100,000 or fewer people per year-one tenth the 1997 rate. Seventy percent supported a limit of 300,000 or less-a number that could still allow for needs such as unification of nuclear families. In a 1999 poll contracted by Negative Population Growth, Florida voters by a 2:1 margin supported the reduction of immigration levels. And regarding overall population, Americans by a seven-to-on margin thought there were already too many people-a view shared widely across lines of race, income, region, and education.[20] This landslide of public opinion should come as no surprise. It's evident in people's choice of living space: we move to the suburbs and spacious neighborhoods for more room. We resettle in less-crowded regions such as the Northwest and Rocky Mountains, we vacation where there's open space, and we try to avoid rush hour. We're dismayed when the Saturday night movie is sold-out, or when we have to wait in line for anything.

While many regard population as an issue that we can do nothing about-beyond the important personal response of having fewer children-that's not true. A single act of legislation could lower the legal immigration rate and set America on the course of population stability. Of all the factors in population growth, legal immigration is the one we should most be able to control. We could address the substantial humanitarian obligations tied up in this issue by helping other countries attain population stability and helping them improve their quality of life. This can be done by educating women, which has dramatic spin-off effects though cultures.[21] We could work toward reducing the "push" for immigration by supporting family planning worldwide, reducing resource depletion, and encouraging respect for human rights.[22] A restricted immigration quota should be coupled with U.S. reforms and aid programs toward these ends with the result of really helping the other countries rather than just providing an escape valve so that Los Angeles becomes like Mexico City, so that Sacramento becomes like Los Angeles, and so that Boise, Idaho becomes like Sacramento.

Some people with humanitarian conscience believe that we cannot solve our own population problem until we solve the population problems of the world. But most countries have eschewed that view and adopted low immigration quotas. More important, considering the magnitude of global population growth, many people believe that worldwide overcrowding cannot be solved in time to preserve anything of much value in America if growth continues as it is. They agree that we must do everything we can to find global solutions. But in the meantime, our first responsibility is not for the islands of Tonga-just one of scores of overcrowded countries whose people want to come to America-but for our own country and for the livability, health, and sustainability of our own communities and our own generations to come. They ask, Without saving ourselves, how can we save anyone else?

Many programs worldwide have effectively and voluntarily lowered birth rates; sixty-three nations have adopted some kind of policy to lower fertility (America is not among them).[23] For example, a program in the Philippines encouraging "small, happy families" strives to improve education on the issue. Supporting such programs (which do not include the string-armed model of China) may be a far better investment than trying to accommodate the virtually unlimited numbers of people who want to emigrate to the United States from overpopulated countries. Recently in New York City, I hailed a taxicab driven by a fine and thoughtful immigrant from Bangladesh. I asked, “Do other people in your country want to come to America?” Without hesitation he responded, “Everybody in Bangladesh wants to come to America.” Even if his statement was rhetorical, consider that the population of his country-of-origin is 135 million. Even if we opened the floodgates of immigration to the U.S., we would scarcely put a dent in the demand form regions such as Central America alone.[24]

In spite of a global situation in which there is little hope of stabilizing population in time to protect America from enormous amounts of immigration and the attendant effects of rapid growth, some environmental groups, such as the Sierra Club and National Audubon Society, have declined to take a position on the issue. “Immigration is an extremely divisive topic,” explained Pat Waak, director of Audubon’s population program. “We prefer to work on creating a broad constituency. Half the pregnancies in the U.S. Are unintended, and that alone presents a huge mission.”

THE NEED FOR NEGATIVE POPULATION GROWTH

Some people still argue that unlimited population growth will serve us well by offering cheap labor, more consumers, and cultural diversity. But by looking deeply at the land, by striving t understand its workings and meanings, I can draw only one conclusion: the earth is finite, and unlimited numbers of people cannot live on a limited earth.

Our population doubled in the last fifty-eight years, as it will likely double again in the twenty-first century, and this process of doubling needs to be understood as the virtual exponential growth that it is . Biologists, who see this kind of thing often in experiments, use this analogy: If duckweed on a pond doubles every week, and only one square foot is now covered on a 100-acre pond, when will the whole pond be covered? It will take only twenty-six weeks. That’s fast. But the real lesson for our society is this: in the twenty-fifth week, the pond will be only half covered. At that point there will appear to be plenty of open water. Yet in fact, the pond will be completely covered only one week later. If America does not already appear to be full, it certainly seems to be half full, which allows us only one more doubling cycle to bring about change and take responsibility for our numbers.

Otherwise, what will happen? According to demographic analyst Lindsey Grant, at recent growth rates it would take only 600 years for the world’s human population to reach the absurdity of one person on each square meter of ice-free land.[25] Obviously that won’t happen. A mass die-off from disease, starvation, or warfare over scarce resources will intervene, likely with unparalleled horror in human suffering. So, if adjustments are to be made, why not make them now, before the level of suffering escalates? Why not now, while we still have something of value left in America?

NOTES:

1. U.S. Department of the Interior, U.S. Fish and Wildlife Service, *Restoring America’s Wildlife, 1937–1987*, ed. Harmon Kallman (Washington, D.C.: U.S. Fish and Wildlife Service, 1987).
2. Claude Fischer, *The Urban Experience* (New York: Harcourt Brace Javanovich, 1980).
3. Gregory R. Nokes and Gail Kinsey Hill, “The Faster the growth, the faster the tab mounts,” *Portland Oregonian,* 24 Oct. 1995.
4. William Ashworth, *The Economy of Nature* (Boston: Houghton Mifflin, 1995), 169.

5. Mark W. Nowak, *Immigration and U.S. Population Growth* (Washington, D.C.: Negative Population Growth, 1997), 7.
6. Lindsey Grant, ed. *Elephants in the Volkswagen: Facing the Tough Questions About Our Overcrowded Country* (New York: W. H. Freeman, 1992); Leon F. Bouvier, *Americans Have Spoken: No Further Population Growth* (Washington, D.C.: Negative Population Growth, 1997), 2.
7. Mathis Wackernagel and William Rees, *Our Ecological Footprint* (Philadelphia: New Society Publishers, 1996).
8. Grant, 237.
9. Paul R. Ehrlich and Anne H. Ehrlich, "The Most Overpopulated Nation," in *Elephants in the Volkswagen.*
10. Robert Costanza, "Balancing Humans in the Biosphere," in *Elephants in the Volkswagen.*
11. David Pimentel and Marcia Pimentel, "Land, Energy and Water," in *Elephants in the Volkswagen.*
12. Alan Riding, *Distant Neighbors: A Portrait of the Mexicans* (New York: Vintage, 1984), 254.
13. Grant, 225.
14. Leon Bouvier and Roy Beck, "Immigration Number One in U.S. Growth," *The Social Contract,* winter 1991–1992; Negative Population Growth, "Florida Voters Support Limits on Population Growth," *Population and Resource Outlook,* Jan. 2000.
15. National Research Council, *The New Americans: Economic, Demographic, and Fiscal Effects of Immigration* (Washington, D.C.: the Council, 1997).
16. Vernon M. Briggs, Jr., "Political Confrontation with Economic Reality," in *Elephants in the Volkswagen*; Nowak.
17. U.S. Bureau of the Census, *Population Projections of the United States by Age, Sex, Race, and Hispanic Origin 1995 to 2050,* by Jennifer Cheesman Day (Washington, D.C.: the Bureau, 1996).
18. Meredith Burke, *Uncoupling Growth from Prosperity: the U.S. Versus Japan* (Washington, D.C.: Negative Population Growth, 1997).
19. Leon F. Bouvier, *Peaceful Invasions: Immigration and changing America* (Washington, D.C.: Center for Immigration Studies, 1991).
20. Bouvier, *Americans have Spoken*; Tim Palmer, *California's Threatened Environment* (Washington, D.C.: Island Press, 1993), 31.
21. Al Gore, *Earth in Balance* (Boston: Houghton Mifflin, 1992), 311.
22. Frank Sharry, "Immigration and Population in the United States," in *Beyond the Numbers*, ed. Laurie Ann Mazue (Washington, D.C.: Island Press, 1994), 387.
23. John R. Weeks, "How to Influence Fertility," in *Elephants in the Volkswagen,* 188.
24. Robert W. Fox, "Neighbors' Problems, Our Problems," in *Elephants in the Volkswagen.*
25. Grant, 143.

GROWTH MANAGEMENT STRATEGIES FOR STOPPING GROWTH IN LOCAL COMMUNITIES

Gabor Zovanyi

2000

Gabor Zovanyi's 1998 book, Growth Management for a Sustainable Future: Ecological Sustainability as the New Growth Management Focus for the Twenty-First Century, *exposes the growth-accommodation bias of current growth management practices and makes a case for redirecting management efforts to a no-growth end based on ecological considerations. In his 1999 NPG Forum publication* The Growth Management Delusion, *Dr. Zovanyi argued that growth management must abandon its support for the growth imperative, reject the false belief that management will make environmentally-benign growth possible, and accept the need for basing future growth management activity on the imperative of ecological sustainability. In this Forum, Dr. Zovanyi presents arguments for debunking traditional pro-growth mythology, techniques for stopping growth in local communities, and suggestions for countering claims that local governmental actions to stop growth are illegal.*

HYPERACTIVE GLOBAL GROWTH FROM 1950 TO 2000

The last five decades of the twentieth century represented a period of unprecedented growth in the scale of the human enterprise. Between 1950 and the year 2000 the human population increased from 2.5 billion to 6 billion. The addition of 3.5 billion people surpassed the total increase over all of human history prior to 1950. From a growth of some 42 million people a year in 1950, the annual increase jumped to around 80 million a year by 2000. In that same period the global economy expanded from some $5 trillion to over $30 trillion. In the first half of the 1990s it expanded by more than $5 trillion, matching the growth from the beginning of civilization to 1950. The dramatic nature of the growth from 1950 to 2000 may also be illustrated by the striking growth of giant urban centers during that period. In the developing countries, the world went from having to contend with only one city of more than 5 million in 1950 to forty-six cities topping 5 million by 2000.

The planet's carrying capacity has already been stressed by the hyperactive demographic, economic, and urban growth of the past five decades. If one defines human carrying capacity as the maximum rate of resource consumption and waste discharge that can be maintained indefinitely without impairing the functional integrity and productivity of the planet's global ecosystem, then a case can easily be made for the claim that natural limits to growth have already been exceeded on this planet. One may, for example, argue existent limits to growth based on human biomass appropriation, global warming, and the rupture of the ozone shield; land degradation as indicated by accelerated soil erosion, salination, and desertification; and the loss of biodiversity (Goodland 1992). Current limits to growth of the human enterprise are also being revealed by the depletion of an one-time inheritance of natural capital in the form of croplands, rangelands, forests, fisheries, and groundwater.

Further evidence that we have surpassed the carrying capacity of the planet comes from research on the ecological footprint of the human enterprise (Wackernagel and Rees 1995). This method measures the area of land and water required to provide consumption-related resource flows and waste sinks for the human enterprise, with the ecological footprint being the total area appropriated from nature to support all human activity. Ecological footprint analysis shows the area appropriated by industrialized nations, representing less than 20 percent of the world population, is larger than all the available ecologically-productive land on Earth, and that if the planet's current population were to live at present North American ecological standards it would take an additional two planet Earths to accommodate the increased ecological load. These ecological realities, as revealed by the destruction of ecosystems and biodiversity, clearly indicate that growth of the human enterprise must cease. If the richness of life on Earth is to be preserved, the growth imperative driving current human behavior must be replaced with the imperative of ecological sustainability.

RUNAWAY GROWTH IN THE UNITED STATES FROM 1950 TO 2000

By growing from 150 million people in 1950 to 275 million in 2000, the United States added 125 million Americans, far surpassing the 74 million added during the first fifty years of the past century. The census bureau predicts we will match the 100 million Americans added in the forty years between 1950 and 1990 in the four decades between 1990 and 2030. If the economic growth rate of 6.5 percent for the final quarter of 1999 were to be maintained, the enormous American economy would double in just over ten years. The magnitude of economic expansion during recent years may be illustrated by the growth rate of automobiles in America. In 1998 the number of registered vehicles topped 200 million for the first time, with 15.29 million new vehicles registered and 12.51 million used vehicles scrapped. At that annual growth rate of 2.78 million vehicles, the total number of registered cars in the country would increase to 255 million vehicles by 2020, putting 55 million additional vehicles in 2 decades on roads that are already experiencing gridlock in many of the country's metropolitan areas. In terms of urban growth, the annual population increase of 2.5 million Americans translates into the equivalent of twenty-five cities of 100,000 people every 12 months.

Runaway demographic, economic, and urban growth is taxing the natural carrying capacity of the U.S. in the same manner that the planet's carrying capacity is being stressed by global growth. As early as the 1980s an assessment of the carrying capacities of the four renewable resource systems of fisheries, forests, croplands, and rangelands concluded those systems were being exploited beyond their natural capacities of renewal in the United States (Webb and Jacobsen 1982). Topsoil, for example, is being lost at a rate approximately twenty times faster than it is being replenished. Environmental organizations report we have already lost over 50 percent of our original wetlands, more than 90 percent of our old growth forests, and fully 99 percent of the country's native prairies. Some sense of the extent of ecosystem disruption associated with ongoing growth is illustrated by a 1987 study which reported that of twenty-three ecosystem types that once covered about 50 percent of the coterminous United States, those ecosystems now cover only about 7 percent of the country's land area. Expansion of the human enterprise in America is eliminating natural ecosystems and killing off other life forms here as it is elsewhere on the planet. The scope of the destruction of biodiversity is revealed by a recent estimate that put at least 4,000 domestic species at risk of extinction. All of these indicators reveal that the pursuit of physical growth has now become an obsolete and lethal ideology, and that we are well past the point of having to abandon the growth imperative. Rather than seeking to maintain the unsustainable behavior of continued physical growth, current ecological realities domestically and globally demand that we proactively undertake actions to stop growth.

THE INADEQUATE GROWTH MANAGEMENT RESPONSE TO GROWTH

The phenomenal growth in the United States during the latter half of the twentieth century produced an ideological shift in public perceptions regarding the value of further growth. During the 1960s and 1970s an increasing number of Americans began to question the merit of continued growth. Rather than automatically associating it with traditionally-assumed benefits like higher personal incomes and prospects for spreading an increasing tax burden over a growing number of residents, many started to view it as the cause of problems like overcrowded schools, traffic congestion, the loss of open space, and worsening environmental conditions. At the same time, increasing public opposition to ongoing land development surfaced as one expression of a new mindset on the phenomenon of physical growth. Land development, as one of the most obvious indicators of growth in local communities, started to be blamed for problems like the costly and destructive development pattern of urban sprawl and an inefficient provision of public facilities and services. The growth management movement that emerged during the late 1960s and early 1970s was a direct response to this new ideological position on growth. Growth management suggested a relatively painless avenue for addressing any and all ills associated with future growth and its accompanying land development.

Growth management embodies the idea that growth needs to be managed, regulated, or controlled, rather than simply promoted as in the past, but it also maintains a decidedly pro-growth posture. As practiced in the United States, it assumes the possibility of accommodating ongoing growth in a responsible fashion if local communities merely manage its amount, rate, location, and quality. In reality, however, few communities have attempted to control the amount or rate of growth because of ongoing allegiance to the growth imperative, and have instead focused their attention on influencing its location and quality. The overwhelming majority of local growth management programs implemented to date clearly reflect continued growth accommodation (Zovanyi 1998). All eleven statewide growth management laws passed to date contain provisions intended to promote ongoing growth, and eight of the eleven laws actually mandate continued growth accommodation by local governments. Rather than conceding that growth itself represents the major problem of the current era, the growth management movement represents an institutionalized form of support for the growth imperative that pervades all aspects of our national culture.

Spokespersons for the growth management movement affix a number of adjectives to growth in order to justify its continuance. They speak of "inevitable, normal, reasonable, proper, realistic, sensible, responsible, and legitimate growth." They also refer to "balanced growth," arguing that a balance can be achieved between ongoing growth and environmental protection without compromising either. Most recently they have become advocates of "smart growth," extending the realm of management concerns beyond containment of sprawl, efficient provision of facilities and services, conservation of resource lands, and environmental protection, to such things as affordable housing, public transit, restoration of urban cores, maintenance of open space, protection of rural lifestyles, and the creation of livable communities in efforts to counter or offset the negative effects of growth. Defenders of the movement's current growth accommodation focus even suggest the possibility of "sustainable growth," when growth is by definition unsustainable and showing itself to be lethal to the community of life on this planet. Rather than recognizing the idiotic nature of the oxymoronic term sustainable growth, management advocates maintain their allegiance to the growth imperative. As supporters of ongoing growth they even condemn the idea that management activity might legitimately be directed at efforts to stop growth, asserting this would represent inefficient, unjust, and irresponsible behavior. This position has not, however, stopped all efforts to remake growth management into something other than ongoing development facilitation. An increasing number of Americans are contesting any expansion of their local communities, and by doing so they are expressing opposition to the growth accommodation bias of current growth management activity. Part of their hostility to new development of any kind is based on direct attacks on the assumed merit of continued growth.

CHALLENGING PRO-GROWTH MYTHS

Those who have come to reject the wisdom of further growth have recently been afforded new arguments for challenging continued growth. An excellent overview of some of these arguments is provided in Eben Fodor's book *Better Not Bigger: How to Take Control of Urban Growth and Improve Your Community* (Fodor 1999). In that work he provides evidence debunking the mythology associated with the assumed benefits of growth. With respect to the myth that growth provides needed tax revenues, Fodor points to research showing that new development tends to increase property taxes for existing property owners, and that communities with the most rapid growth tend to experience the greatest tax increases. As for the myth that we have to grow to provide jobs for people in the community, he cites national research indicating no statistical correlation between the growth rate and the unemployment rate across twenty-five of the fastest and slowest growing cities in the U.S. With regard to the myth that housing and land prices will shoot up if a community tries to limit growth, Fodor notes research showing that housing is more affordable in some growth-control cities than in comparable cities with rapid growth, and research that land prices are rising faster in some cities without growth boundaries, such as Oklahoma City, Salt Lake City, and Houston, than in a city like Portland with an urban growth boundary. Fodor's book debunks twelve such growth myths, and in the process provides sound rationales for questioning the growth accommodation practices of local governments.

Fodor's book also provides some surprisingly counterintuitive insights regarding the cost implications of land development. In contrast to the widely held assumption that development of vacant land will improve the fiscal standing of a local government, he points to studies in Maine, New Hampshire, New Jersey, New York, Alabama, and California showing that it would be cheaper for local governments to buy undeveloped land rather than allow it to be developed and have to pay the increased costs of providing infrastructure and services. In his treatment of the cost of public facilities for a single new house in Oregon, he counters the conventional view that new development is a fiscally sound proposition by revealing local communities there subsidize new development to the tune of about $25,000 for each new house. This represents off-site costs for schools, sanitary sewerage, transportation, water systems, parks and recreation, fire protection, and stormwater facilities, and does not include the local streets and utility connections that are part of a subdivision's internal development costs. These financial revelations provide further rationales for abandoning the ongoing growth accommodation of present growth management actions. For some they represent motivations for curbing the role of local governments in the urban growth machine that perpetuates growth in communities across America.

ALTERING THE ROLE OF LOCAL GOVERNANCE IN THE URBAN GROWTH MACHINE

Fodor's book points out the most consistent theme in American local governance has been the pursuit of growth. As Fodor explains, local elected officials have historically been key players in a powerful pro-growth alliance that serves to maintain growth. The business and professional groups that have a common economic interest in promoting local growth fund candidates for political office who are sympathetic to a pro-growth agenda. Once elected, these officials advance land development through growth-stimulating activities that include supportive land-use regulations, investments in infrastructure required by development, economic development programs that court outside investors, new business subsidies, tax waivers, and a general subsidy of ongoing land development. If growth is to be restrained, Fodor suggests these growth incentives and subsidies will need to be reduced or eliminated. This would require changing economic subsidies, tax subsidies, below cost services, free infrastructure provisions, favorable or relaxed land-use regulations, and other pro-growth policies practiced by local governments.

Changing the growth-promotion focus that represents the essence of local government, according to Fodor, will require that local governments adopt growth-neutral policies in place of their current growth-inducing incentives and subsidies that stimulate growth. As examples of growth-neutral policies he proposes impact fees to recover the full cost of public infrastructure, fees that recover the full cost of all development services, requiring that development pay for growth-related planning activities, and the application of local land-use regulations in a manner that does not promote growth. Fodor concedes, however, that these policies would only get local governments out of the business of stimulating growth, and would not necessarily guarantee growth would actually slow or stop. To achieve a sustainable state of nongrowth, local governments would have to execute a number of specific strategies.

STRATEGIES FOR STOPPING GROWTH IN LOCAL COMMUNITIES

For those communities willing to go beyond the use of rate controls to slow growth, a number of strategies would have to be implemented to stop growth.

Strategy #1: *Eliminate the growth-promotion focus of local government by election or initiative.*

The best way to eliminate the growth-promotion focus of a local community would be to elect local officials willing to support a no-growth agenda. Where the strength of the local urban growth machine makes this impossible, an alternative approach would be to force a no-growth agenda on reluctant or unwilling local officials with a public initiative. The initiative could require local elected officials to fund research to determine the natural limits to growth in an area. Once that research identifies limits based on considerations like sustainable water yield from an aquifer or the ability to maintain biodiversity in local habitats, programs to cap growth within established ecological limits could be implemented. The initiative could also require the establishment of growth threshold standards (Fodor 1999: 117) that would preserve or improve an existing quality of life in a local setting, and thereby serve to stop growth in many communities. These standards would prohibit any deterioration, or require improvements, in things like environmental quality (e.g., air or water quality), community service (e.g., police or fire protection, library capacity), or travel times on a community's road network (e.g., congestion levels). In many local settings the cost of overcoming constraints established by these standards would effectively serve to shut down further growth. Under inevitable legal challenges to capping growth in a local community these documented natural limits or growth threshold standards would be extremely important, because courts would insist on justifiable rationales for stopping growth. For example, an appellate court in Florida showed a willingness to accept a cap on growth in the community of Hollywood, where studies showed the cap was warranted to protect public health, safety, and general welfare, as opposed to invalidating a cap set by public vote without supportive studies in the city of Boca Raton (Zovanyi 1998: 129–30). Once a community established a cap on further growth based on ecological limits or growth threshold standards it would have to implement the cap, which would require executing a number of other specific strategies.

Strategy #2: *Establish a moratorium on processing development permits until the community's comprehensive land-use plan and land-use regulations are amended to reflect the research-based cap on growth.*

In the absence of a moratorium, land developers would be able to impose considerable additional growth on a community by vesting their right to develop under existing lax land-use regulations that typically embody tremendous potential for growth. Courts have allowed moratoria to block development during the time required to amend plans or regulations, when ongoing development would defeat the stated intent of revising these public documents in response to an emergency consisting of threats to a community's health, safety, and general welfare.

Strategy #3: *Amend the community's comprehensive plan and land-use regulations so as to close out options for further growth.*

During the period of the moratorium the comprehensive plan and land-use regulations would be changed to eliminate prospects for continued growth. Traditional comprehensive land-use plans for local communities reflect a decidedly pro-growth bias. In a growing number of states, local communities would have to change these comprehensive land-use plans in a fashion that eliminates options for growth before modifying their land-use regulations, because many states now require regulatory changes in permitted uses of land to be consistent with previous planning reflected in comprehensive plans. In these states, comprehensive land-use plans will have to be changed to reflect the studies justifying a cap on growth before regulatory actions, like downzoning and plat vacations that eliminate existing subdivisions of land, can be legally undertaken to curb land development. Once comprehensive plans have been changed to reflect a no-growth end, a community could legally change the zoning and subdivision ordinances that currently ensure ongoing growth.

Most of America's cities and counties are vastly overzoned and overplatted. Their existing zoning districts and previously approved subdivisions of land represent enormous unrealized capacity for future land development. The absurdity of the growth potential embodied in existing community plans and land-use regulations was illustrated by a 1999 report in Florida. That report revealed city and county plans and associated zoning would permit the state to grow from its current 15 million to over 100 million under development based on the highest density permitted by those documents (Howard 1999). In order to stop growth, local communities must downzone land and vacate previously approved subdivisions, because overzoning and overplatting of land guarantee ongoing land development. Downzoning rural land from five-acre hobby farms to viable large agricultural parcels is legally defensible if the land can be viably farmed. Similarly, downzoning residential land holdings from one-acre lots to forty-acre parcels is legal if the action is required to protect a community's aquifer or other environmentally-sensitive lands. An existing subdivision of land that permits twenty single-acre lots on a twenty acre land holding, with associated zoning that allows densities ranging from one to twenty housing units per twenty acres, may in a like fashion be vacated to allow only a single house on the twenty acre land holding if the action is based on justifiable health, safety, and general welfare rationales embodied in a community's comprehensive plan. While these reductions in permitted intensities of use on undeveloped land, and the associated reductions in land value accompanying downzoning and plat vacation actions, will be opposed by defenders of the urban growth machine and by private property rights advocates, both actions are clearly legal if they can be justified based on a need to protect and promote the health, safety, and general welfare of a community (Zovanyi 1998: 112–3). However, in most cities and counties in America, changes in comprehensive plans and regulatory changes, like downzoning and plat vacations, will represent insufficient acts to completely shut down further growth. Local communities will need to reinforce these changes in their local plans and land-use regulations with other strategies.

Strategy #4: *Terminate public investments in capital facility programs that make ongoing growth possible.*

Without public investments in roads, sewers, and other public infrastructure, land development could not continue to sprawl across America's local landscapes. Historically, local governments have extended these capital facilities in support of the urban growth machine. If local officials change the way they use a community's spending power for infrastructure so as to reduce development options on the landscape, further progress will be made toward the end of stopping growth. At the same time a community changes its capital improvements program in order to stop supporting outward expansion of the community, it can also reinforce its objective of blocking further extension of its built environment by executing a related containment strategy.

Strategy #5: *Create a permanent urban growth boundary to physically limit further growth in the form of sprawl.*

While downzoning to lower densities can block upward expansion within a community, a permanent urban growth boundary would eliminate prospects for growing outward. The permanence of the boundary could in turn be furthered by establishing a greenbelt of protected land around the community. This greenbelt could be created by regulatory techniques like exclusive agricultural zones, large parcel zoning with associated clustering of any limited development, and land-use regulations used in conjunction with techniques such as conservation easements. In many communities regulatory actions alone will not suffice to stop growth, and communities will have to supplement changes in land-use regulations with the strategy of public land acquisition.

Strategy #6: *Take private land out of development by acquiring it and holding it in public trust.*

With recent research showing land purchases may save a community money over the cost of providing infrastructure and ongoing services to new development, these purchases appear to represent a fiscally sound option for local communities in the present era. Purchasing open space outside of urban growth boundaries represents a vehicle for closing out development options within a permanently designated greenbelt surrounding a community. Purchasing private land holdings may also provide the only feasible way of stopping the development of certain commercial and industrial properties where the character of surrounding land uses makes downzoning to less intensive uses difficult to justify. In these instances public acquisition would prevent more commercial and industrial development where downzoning of these properties was not practical and thereby advance yet another strategy for stopping growth.

Strategy #7: *Stop the job formation that fuels further growth.*

Growth management experts have long conceded that control of future growth requires management actions that go beyond controlling new residential starts to managing the creation of new employment. In order to stop the job creation that fuels ongoing growth, communities must close out development options for new commercial and industrial enterprises. At some locations, communities may be able to eliminate commercial and industrial developments by downzoning properties to uses that do not generate new jobs. In other instances the only practical recourse would be to purchase these properties and thereby stop the new job formation that drives growth.

If local communities pursue these seven strategies they can quickly move a community to a state of nongrowth. However, even consideration of these growth-termination strategies is certain to illicit a strong response from defenders of the urban growth machine and private property rights advocates. That response will, in turn, undoubtedly contain claims that governmental actions to stop growth are illegal. Proponents of the no-growth agenda will therefore bear the burden of countering such claims.

COUNTERING CLAIMS THAT GOVERNMENTAL ACTIONS TO STOP GROWTH ARE ILLEGAL

Claims of the illegality of stopping growth can be expected to reference a few principal arguments (Zovanyi 1998: 124–29).

Argument #1: *No-growth programs would impose unconstitutional regulatory restrictions on private property.*

Advocates of private property rights would certainly claim the dramatic reductions in use and value associated with no-growth regulations represent illegal "regulatory takings." However, as long as implemented regulations allow some remaining economically viable use of a private land holding, the courts will tolerated extreme reductions in use and value if the regulations are reasonably related to important health, safety, and general welfare considerations. A forty-acre parcel subdivided into one-acre lots can, for example, be legally returned to a single parcel allowing only 1 residence by changing land-use regulations, if the action can be justified on legitimate grounds such as protecting a community's sole-source aquifer.

Regulatory takings assessments also involve the "whole parcel rule," which examines the impact of a regulation on an entire landholding, and which permits the denial of all use to a portion of an owner's land as long as some reasonable use remains for the entire property. This rule allows regulators to prohibit development of environmentally-sensitive portions of individual landholdings even when these constitute the majority of the whole private parcel. If 75 percent of a property holding is comprised of wetlands, for example, a community can legally use its land-use regulations to deny all use of that portion of the property, as long as the owner is left with some economically viable use of the remaining 25 percent.

Furthermore, communities interested in implementing a no-growth program could still allow economically viable uses of land other than the commercial and industrial uses that generate growth through expanding employment opportunities or the residential uses that serve to house a growing population. There are, for example, a number of income-producing agricultural and recreational uses that are capable of representing economically viable uses without forcing endless growth on a community. While Supreme Court standards for deciding regulatory taking claims do not allow a denial of "all use," "economically viable use," or "all economically beneficial or productive use," there are allowable uses that may be permitted with less potential for generating further growth. Most regulatory taking claims are resolved by focusing on the remaining uses that regulations permit. Communities must therefore devise no-growth programs that still permit economically viable uses of private land, but they have no legal obligation to allow the most profitable use of any particular property. Where the desired use restrictions on individual properties could only be achieved by land-use regulations that deny economically viable uses, a community would have to abandon the regulatory approach and acquire these properties to advance its end of stopping growth.

Argument #2: *No-growth programs would impose unconstitutional restrictions on the fundamental right to travel.*

Opponents of no-growth strategies would also be apt to claim these actions would violate Americans' fundamental right to travel and settle in communities of their choice. This argument may be countered by pointing out that this right is not absolute, and that courts will tolerate interference with fundamental rights if the regulatory body can justify the interference based on compelling state interests. One might assume that certain environmental rationales, such as an inability to provide sustainable groundwater supplies for a growing population, would be accepted as compelling grounds for stopping in-migration to a local community.

Argument #3: *No-growth programs would violate statewide growth management statutes.*

In states with statewide growth management laws that mandate ongoing growth accommodation, defenders of the growth imperative would certainly argue no-growth strategies were precluded by state law. However, this claim is complicated by the existence of other state laws that may require local actions quite different from, and potentially in conflict with, continued growth accommodation. Many state environmental laws, for example, direct local governments to protect the environment. When environmental protection is compromised by ongoing growth the courts would have to resolve the conflict between state laws, and one can hope they would exempt specific local settings from further growth if it could be shown to harm the community's health, safety, and general welfare. In the end, local governments have a right and an obligation to protect and promote the health, safety, and general welfare of their residents. If these ends cannot be achieved under continued growth, local communities must be assumed to have the legal right to stop growth within their political jurisdictions.

TRANSFORMING GROWTH MANAGEMENT FOR NO-GROWTH ENDS

Growth management as practiced in the United States seeks to accommodate growth in ways that minimize its negative effects. The practice assumes ongoing growth is possible if the land development that occurs represents "smart growth." However, "smart growth" will eventually produce the same intolerable conditions as dumb growth. Physical growth of human populations, their economies, or their settlements represents unsustainable behavior in the current era. To pretend that growth can be made sustainable by planning it well represents as false a belief as the traditional view that there is nothing wrong with the dumb and unsustainable growth of past decades. Instead of "smart growth" many communities desperately need to reach a state of no growth if they are to move toward sustainable behavior. In fact, stopping growth represents the top priority among a long list of necessary actions required to make the transition to sustainable behavior. Local governments are in the unique position of being able to initiate this critical societal transition to a state of no growth by stopping the growth of local communities and beginning the process of transforming all our cities and counties into sustainable, nongrowing communities. A limited number of progressive communities must establish the precedent and begin the inevitable process of reinventing growth management to serve no-growth ends. For if communities do not stop growth by deliberate governmental actions, growth will certainly be stopped over time by intolerable environmental conditions.

THE REQUISITE GROWTH MANAGEMENT AGENDA FOR AMERICA

The transition to a state of nongrowth in America will clearly require changes beyond implementation of the seven noted strategies for stopping growth in local communities. If growth is to be stopped in the United States, the federal and state governments will have to change numerous laws that currently serve to perpetuate growth. At the federal level, an example of a critically needed statutory revision would be a shift in current immigration laws. In 1986 the federal government initiated a series of changes to immigration laws that increased the annual number of legal immigrants from 400,000 a year to over 800,000 a year, and during a few years of the early 1990s the annual number permitted entry exceeded 1 million. The implications for future population growth have been noted by demographers, who point out that up to 70 percent of the 100 million people expected to be added to the United States between 1990 and 2030 will be immigrants and their descendants (Bouvier 1998). While stopping population growth nationally will also require policy changes directed at nonimmigrants, the role of immigrants in fueling future growth makes revisions to existing immigration laws a vital component of any national strategy for halting growth in America.

At the level of the states, one urgently needed revision in existing laws would be changes to statewide growth management enactments that mandate ongoing growth accommodation by all local governments. To date, eleven states have passed statewide growth management enactments that promote growth, and in 8 of the states the statutes actually mandate continued growth accommodation by all cities and counties (Zovanyi 1999). In order to stop growth, these laws will have to be revised to allow local communities to opt out of further growth accommodation if local health, safety, or general welfare considerations warrant shutting down additional expansion. Part of the associated strategy for stopping growth through state actions would require opposing the adoption of further accommodative growth management laws in states that enact statewide growth management statutes in the future.

While federal and state governments would obviously have to become participants in any meaningful effort to achieve a national state of nongrowth, the short-term prospects for such participation are not good. The federal government continues to endorse ongoing growth and its adherence to the growth imperative makes it an unlikely advocate of any growth management actions to impede growth in the foreseeable future. The states that have enacted growth management laws to date have evidenced their commitment to continued growth by passing acts that either promote or mandate future growth. It is only at the local level that serious questioning of the merit of further growth has occurred. In local communities the negative effects of growth are causing increasing opposition to growth, and it is in these settings that one can hope for experimentation with implementing no growth strategies. The focus on local strategies for stopping growth presented here is based on the view that local governments represent the best route for initiating a societal transition to a state of nongrowth. If a growing number of progressive communities implement strategies to stop growth in their locales over time, it will inevitably force a response by the federal and state governments that will bring about the needed rejection of growth as a viable policy option or survival strategy.

Once local communities stop growth they will be able to redirect their attention from coping with the negative effects of growth to creating livable and sustainable communities. However, this new focus will undoubtedly introduce challenges beyond those represented by the barriers to implementing strategies to stop growth. In many community settings, historic violations of local carrying capacities will require achieving and then maintaining a period of negative growth until populations and their associated economies reach a level that can be maintained indefinitely (sustained) without impairing the functional integrity and productivity of local ecosystems (Bartlett 1994). This new focus on downsizing and redesigning local communities to an ecologically sustainable level and form will represent an even more daunting task than stopping growth, but the alternative of maintaining growth is not a sustainable option.

Growth of the human enterprise does not represent sustainable behavior. No amount of wishful thinking or elaborate management will serve to make it sustainable. In the end, "smart growth" is just as unsustainable as dumb growth. America's current population growth rate of about 1 percent per year represents a doubling time of approximately seventy years, and if that rate were maintained for 312 years the country's present population of 275 million would match the current global population of some 6 billion before it doubled for the fifth time. The country's economic growth rate of almost 7 percent during the final quarter of 1999 represents a doubling time of about ten years, and ten such doublings over a century would produce a national economy 1000 times larger than its current level. These examples clearly illustrate the unsustainable nature of demographic and economic growth. As an alternative to such unsustainable activity, communities in the United States can take the first step toward the inevitable process of moving the country to a state of sustainable behavior by implementing strategies to stop growth. Rather than pursue the false end of "smart growth," local jurisdictions must act to stop growth before they can hope to attain and then maintain livable and sustainable communities.

NOTES:

1. Bartlett, A.A. 1994. "Reflections on Sustainability, Population Growth, and the Environment." In *The Carrying Capacity Briefing Book*. Washington, DC: Carrying Capacity Network.
2. Bouvier, Leon F. 1998. "The Impact of Immigration on United State's Population Size: 1950 to 2050. *NPG Forum*. Washington, DC: Negative Population Growth, Inc.
3. Fodor, Eben. 1999. *Better Not Bigger: How to Take Control of Urban Growth and Improve Your Community*. Gabriola Island, BC: New Society Publishers.

4. Goodland, Robert. 1992. "The Case That the World Has Reached Limits: More Precisely That Current Throughput Growth in the Global Economy Cannot be Sustained." *Population and Environment*. 13,3: 167–82.
5. Howard, Peter E. 1999. "Report Warns of State Growth to 101 Million." *The Tampa Tribune*. Friday, April 2: A2.
6. Wackernagel, Mathis, and William E. Rees. 1995. *Our Ecological Footprint: Reducing Human Impact on the Earth*. Gabriola Island, BC: New Society Publishers.
7. Webb, Maryla, and Judith Jacobsen. 1982. *U.S. Carrying Capacity: An Introduction*. Washington, DC: Carrying Capacity, Inc.
8. Zovanyi, Gabor. 1999. "The Growth Management Delusion." *NPG Forum*. Washington, DC: Negative Population Growth, Inc.
9. Zovanyi, Gabor. 1998. *Growth Management for a Sustainable Future: Ecological Sustainability as the New Growth Management Focus for the 21st Century*. Westport, Connecticut: Praeger Publishers.

A NO-GROWTH, STEADY-STATE ECONOMY MUST BE OUR GOAL

Donald Mann, President

Negative Population Growth, Inc.

August 2002

SUMMARY:

1. *Economic growth in a finite world, which is the only world we have, is not sustainable. Sustainable economic growth is an oxymoron, a contradiction in terms.*
2. *In order to create a sustainable economy we must first discard the goal of macro economic growth and replace it with the goal of a no-growth, steady-state economy.*
3. *Even a steady-state economy, however, would need to be of a size relative to our ecosystem that would allow it to be in balance with our resources and environment, and thus be sustainable indefinitely.*
4. *Even if growth were halted now, the size of our present economy is too large to be sustainable. The scale of our economy needs first, therefore, to be reduced to a sustainable size and then maintained at that level.*
5. *The only way to reduce the size of our macro (aggregate, overall) economy while maintaining or even increasing per capita income is by a reduction in our numbers to an optimum, sustainable level. An optimum population size might be defined as that level which would permit the creation of a sustainable steady-state economy with an adequate standard of living for all.*
6. *Macro economic growth requires a growing labor force so that GNP can increase constantly. A growing labor force is only possible if population grows, and population growth in the U.S. depends largely on massive immigration. It is highly unlikely, therefore, that we will ever reduce immigration drastically (which we urgently need to do in order to achieve a smaller population) until we renounce the goal of economic growth and replace it with the goal of a steady-state economy.*

In this paper I will argue that in order to create a sustainable economy, and thus prevent the destruction of our environment and resources, and a drastic reduction in per capita income and our standard of living, we must renounce and discard the goal of macro economic growth (as distinct from per capita income). Even a steady-state economy, however, in order to be sustainable indefinitely, would need to be of a size relative to our ecosystem that would allow it to be in balance with our resources and environment.

We at NPG are convinced that such a steady-state U.S. economy, in order to be sustainable, would need to be far smaller than today's, which is clearly far too large to be sustainable for the long run. In order to reduce the size of our economy to a sustainable level (while at the same time maintaining or even increasing per capita income) we would need to reduce our U.S. population to a size far smaller than today's, and then stabilize it at that smaller level. A reduction in population would have the effect of reducing the size of our economy proportionately.

The size of our population and the size of our economy go hand in hand, since the latter is a function of numbers of people times per capita consumption. For example, with a U.S. population of 144 million (half our present size of 288 million) our economy, with the same per capita income, would be only half as large as today's. Our impact on our resources and environment would, of course, be only half as large as well, and so would our nation's emissions of the heat-trapping gases that cause global warming.

Furthermore, urban sprawl and traffic congestion would be much alleviated, and would not be the steadily worsening major problems that they are today.

With a present population of 288 million (following an unprecedented increase of 33 million in the decade of the '90s) our nation is already vastly overpopulated in terms of the long-range carrying capacity of its resources and environment. Our continued population growth, which shows no signs of abating, is driving us rapidly down the road to both environmental and economic disaster.

The Census Bureau "middle series" projects a 40 percent increase in U.S. population by 2050, and a doubling by 2100. Most of that enormous and disastrous increase will be because of post-2000 immigration. The Census Bureau "high projection" which is more likely if the present level of immigration is allowed to continue, is 1.2 billion in 2100, more than four times the size of our present population.

While massive immigration is the driving force behind our U.S. population growth, the fact that economic growth is our top-priority goal is the fundamental, underlying cause. That is because, according to the conventional wisdom, unending population growth is necessary in order to fuel perpetual material economic growth. Population growth, and with it the growth of our labor force, are looked on as indispensable to macro economic growth, as expressed by the Gross National Product (GNP). In the United States massive immigration is looked on as necessary for population growth.

It follows that we will never make a serious and sustained effort to halt our population growth—much less to halt and then reverse it—until we have renounced the goal of economic growth and replaced it with the goal of a steady-state economy.

The same holds true for immigration. We will never reduce legal immigration drastically, and halt illegal immigration completely, until we have discarded the goal of economic growth.

The growth of our economy, which is driven primarily by our population growth, is rapidly destroying our ecosystem and will, if left unchecked, eventually destroy the economy itself, since our economy is a subset of the ecosystem and dependent on it for its very existence. Without the ecosystem and the materials, energy and services it provides, our economy could no longer exist.

The conventional wisdom with respect to our U.S. economic growth can be described as follows: We need economic growth in order to improve our standard of living and the quality of our lives. A growing population is needed to fuel economic growth, and mass immigration is necessary in order to fuel population growth. It follows, therefore, that immigration is good because it is necessary for economic growth, the supreme good toward which we all must strive.

The following two excerpts from recent newspaper articles reflect that view:

In an article in the *New York Times* (February 16, 2001) commenting on the Bush-Fox meeting in

Mexico the following statement was made without attribution: "An estimated 150,000 undocumented Mexican immigrants enter the United States each year. Their labor—in Florida orange groves, Georgia onion fields, Las Vegas hotels and Oregon nurseries—has fueled growth in many parts of the American economy."

In an article in the *New York Times* (April 11, 2001) the following statement was made without attribution: "The new illegal workers have helped sustain the state's buoyant economy, and economists and demographers acknowledge that without them, that economy and those of many other states could not have grown so fast." (The sub-title of the article, about Arizona, is "Illegal Immigration, Unrelenting, Has Put a Strain on Services.")

The largely unchallenged assumption, therefore, is that economic growth is good and that faster economic growth, forever and ever, is even better. We in the United States (along with the rest of the world) worship macro economic growth, the world's great secular religion. We worship it because we strongly, and wrongly, believe that such growth is necessary in order to improve our standard of living and the quality of our lives.

If a sustainable steady-state economy with a U.S. population of not over 150 million (as opposed to our present 288 million heading rapidly toward 400 million and more) were our top priority goal, we as a nation would be adamantly opposed to any increase in our population and there would be overwhelming support for a reduction in immigration to some small fraction of the present over one million each year. Immigration would be clearly seen for what it is—an impediment and an obstacle to achieving a smaller population and a sustainable steady-state economy, and with it an adequate and sustainable per capita income for all.

The balance of this paper will be divided into two sections. In the first section, on economic growth, I will try to examine what I believe to be the principal defects of the concept of economic growth. In the second section, on a steady-state economy, I will try to describe the benefits of a steady-state economy, and how we could achieve it.

I. ECONOMIC GROWTH

Terms defined: When speaking of economic growth I refer to macro economic growth; that is, the growth of the total over-all economy usually defined as Gross National Product (GNP) as opposed to per capita economic growth, or per capita income. We believe the two opposing goals—growth of GNP and per capita economic growth—are inherently incompatible and inimical.

One of our basic themes is that macro economic growth, if left unchecked, will eventually diminish and then destroy the only thing that counts for each individual—per capita income. That is because macro economic growth will eventually destroy the very life support systems of our planet, upon which all economic activity is totally dependent.

A. The Unacceptably High Cost of Economic Growth

All human economic activity is destructive of the environment because of its inevitable and unavoidable by-products: resource depletion and production of waste and pollution. Those by-products can be mitigated, but not eliminated, by science and technology. The evidence is overwhelming that our economy is already far too large to be sustainable for the long run, and that further economic growth will only serve to lead us to disaster sooner rather than later.

For example, according to a World Wildlife Fund

study published in October 2000 the natural wealth of the world's ecosystems has declined by a third over the past thirty years.

With our economy at its present size, we are in the process of destroying our ecosystem. The obvious and only solution is to reduce the over-all economy to a size that will be sustainable indefinitely and then stabilize it at that point so that it would become transformed into a non-growing, steady-state economy. Such an economy would require an optimum population size much smaller than today's, and would allow per capita income to be maintained, or continue to grow.

B. Macro Economic Growth Is Not Sustainable

The most obvious, and telling, criticism of the concept of perpetual economic growth is that it is simply an impossibility. Economic growth, in fact all economic activity, even in the age of information technology, requires inputs of materials and energy, and results in outputs of waste and pollution.

A simple concept—that of exponential growth and doubling times ñ proves that any material growth in a closed system (which is the finite planet we live on) cannot long continue. The concept shows clearly that no resource, regardless of how vast, can withstand more than a very few doublings (Bartlett, 1978).

Exponential growth can be described as the result of a constant annual growth rate applied to a constantly increasing base. Interest on a savings account is a good example. One of the characteristics of exponential growth is that, at a given rate of growth, the time it would take anything (e.g. money, energy use, the economy) to double in size can be fairly accurately calculated by dividing the constant annual growth rate into seventy.

If our economy, and the input of materials and energy, and the output of waste and pollution required to support it, is growing at the rate of three percent annually, it would double in roughly twenty-three years (seventy divided by three). It would take, therefore, only 115 years to have doubled five times and be (if the world's resources and environment could possible allow such growth) a staggering thirty-two times larger than it is today!

Another five doublings would result in the absurdity of an economy over 1,000 times larger than today's. The assertion that no resource can possibly withstand more than a very few doublings cannot be successfully refuted, it can only be ignored and swept under the rug. The belief that economic growth can long continue flies in the face of logic, reason and common sense.

C. How Can Per Capita Income Be Maximized and Made Sustainable?

Only the creation of a steady-state economy will allow per capita income to be maximized and made sustainable indefinitely. In the world we live in, which is a world of limits, macro economic growth cannot possibly maximize per capita income in such a way that it will be sustainable indefinitely. That goal can only be achieved by a negative rate of population growth so that our economy can shrink to, and then be stabilized at, a size that will be sustainable indefinitely, and allow the creation of a steady-state economy.

Lindsey Grant (2000) has given us the formula for maximizing per capita income in a world of limits:

> "The only way to reconcile the economic objective with the environmental constraint is to keep total economic activity within tolerable environmental limits. That is, decide first how large a pie the environment can tolerate. Then decide how big the individual slices (the standard of living) should be. Then divide the pie by the size of each slice. The result is the number of slices (the population) the system can support."

TO SUM UP THE CHARGES AGAINST ECONOMIC GROWTH

I have argued that the cost of economic growth is unacceptably high because it is destroying our ecosystem, and it is not sustainable. Economic growth cannot possibly achieve what should be its central objective and raison d'etre—the maximization of per capita income in a way that would make it sustainable indefinitely. We turn now to the alternative to macro economic growth, the non-growing Steady-State economy.

II. THE STEADY-STATE ECONOMY

Introduction—Since the publication of his book titled Toward a Steady-State Economy *in 1973 economist Herman Daly, has been the leading theorist of the steady-state economy. In this section I will quote extensively from his works. He is now Professor at the University of Maryland in College Park, MD.*

In contrast to classical economics, the concept of the steady-state economy recognizes that the economy is a sub-set of our ecosystem, and that our ecosystem is finite and non-growing. Again in contrast to classical economic theory it recognizes that there is an optimal scale for human economic activity, which must not exceed a size that will be sustainable indefinitely. It recognizes that there is an optimum size population, which cannot be exceeded in order for a sustainable steady-state economy to be created.

These concepts—our economy as a totally dependent sub-set of our finite ecosystem, an optimum scale of human economic activity, an optimum population size, and sustainability—which are some of the most important intellectual underpinnings of the concept of the steady-state economy, are totally foreign to classical economics with its curious belief in perpetual and unlimited economic growth.

Professor Daly writes (1996): "Sustainability has had a hard time breaking into economic theory because the economics of the past fifty years has been overwhelmingly devoted to economic growth. The term "economic growth" has in practice meant growth in gross national product. All problems are to be solved, or at least ameliorated, by an ever-growing GNP. It is the only magnitude in all of economics that is expected to grow forever—never to reach an economic limit at which the marginal costs of further growth become greater than the marginal benefits. In microeconomics every enterprise has an optimal scale beyond which it should not grow. But when we aggregate all microeconomic units into the macroeconomy, the notion of an optimal scale, beyond which further growth becomes antieconomic, disappears completely!"

In this paper I will try to address only what I consider to be two of the central questions with regard to a steady-state economy:

How big should our macro economy (GNP) be relative to our ecosystem in order to be sustainable indefinitely, or for the very long term, while affording an adequate per capita income for all?

How could we go about creating such an economy?

HOW BIG SHOULD OUR ECONOMY BE?

How big should a U.S. steady-state economy be in order to be sustainable indefinitely, or for the very long term? It should not exceed a size that allows it to meet the following criteria, as set forth by Professor Daly (1990):

Output rule: Waste outputs should be within the natural absorptive capacities of the environment.

Input rules: (a) For renewable inputs, harvest rates should not exceed regeneration rates (nondepletion of the source services of natural capital). (b) For non-renewable inputs the rate of depletion should not exceed the rate at which renewable substitutes can be developed.

Those are indeed rigorous criteria, but sustainability could not be achieved with anything less demanding. It is clear that the present level of economic activity cannot long be sustained without causing permanent and irreparable damage to our environment and resources.

The preponderance of evidence clearly indicates that the size of our economy, in order to be sustainable, would need to be substantially smaller than its present size. The direction we need to move in, therefore, is clear, even if a specific numerical target cannot be defined with scientific precision.

In fact a scientifically precise calculation that would pinpoint with absolute certainly a sustainable size for either the economy or for population may well be unattainable. Fortunately, we do not need scientific precision before taking action. In most social and political areas we must make decisions based on imperfect knowledge, while applying the rule of prudence. The same holds true for economics and population.

HOW COULD WE CREATE A SUSTAINABLE STEADY-STATE ECONOMY?

I have argued that a sustainable U.S. economy would need to be far smaller than our present one, in order to be sustainable indefinitely. In theory, such a smaller economy could be achieved in only one of two ways, since only two variables are involved: numbers of people (population size) and per capita consumption. One or the other, or some combination of the two, would have to be reduced.

Let us suppose that there is a national consensus that our GNP would need to be reduced by half in order to achieve sustainability. How could that reduction be achieved?

We could maintain the size of our population, and reduce per capita income by 50 percent.

We could reduce the size of our population so that per capita income could be maintained, or even increased.

Assuming that we chose to maintain per capita income at the present level and reduce our population size by roughly half in a gradual, orderly way, would that be feasible? Yes, it would be. We would only need to reduce immigration to not over 100,000 a year, together with a moderate reduction in our fertility, for our population to soon stop growing and begin a slow decline. It would probably take a century or so for our U.S. population to be reduced to not over 150 million, a size that we at NPG judge might well be sustainable indefinitely.

SUMMING UP

The central arguments I have tried to present in this paper are as follows:

In a world of limits, macro economic growth, if left unchecked, will continue to do irreparable damage to our environment, and diminish or destroy its capacity to provide the sinks, materials, energy and services necessary to support an industrial society. Economic growth is not sustainable.

Since we live in a world of limits, macro economic growth cannot possibly maximize per capita income in a way that would be sustainable. On the contrary, in the long run it would surely greatly diminish or even utterly destroy per capita income, the very thing that, to maximize, is its very raison d'etre. The only way to maximize per capita income and make it sustainable is to create a steady-state economy by reducing population to a sustainable level. Population size is, without any question, the key variable.

Mainstream economic theory is directly responsible for our disastrous population growth. That is because of its core beliefs that economic growth is necessary for the growth of per capita income, that population growth and the growth of the labor force are necessary for macro economic growth, and that massive immigration is necessary for the continued growth of our population and labor force.

NOTES:

1. Bartlett, Albert A. (1978). Forgotten Fundamentals of the Energy Crisis. *American Journal of Physics, Volume 46, September 1978, pages 876 to 888.*
2. Daly, Herman E. (1996). *Beyond Growth.* Boston, MA: Beacon Press.
3. Daly, Herman E, (1990). Toward Some Operational Principles of Sustainable Development, *Ecological Economics*, 2, 1–6.
4. Grant, Lindsey (2000). *Too Many People*. Santa Ana, CA: Seven Locks Press.

AMNESTY:OVERPOPULATION BY FIAT

David Simcox

November 2002

SUMMARY

Political and diplomatic promises made by both parties make it likely that the Bush White House and the new 108th Congress, despite public opposition, will take up the nagging issue of amnesty for as many as six million illegal immigrants before the 2004 national elections. Amnesty, as now envisioned by both parties, has the potential over the next decade and a half to endow as many as forty million persons abroad with family preference entitlements for immigration to the U.S. The higher fertility of these added legal residents and their families, and the resulting millions of new migration chains have the potential to accelerate America's population growth to the "highest" and, until now, "least likely" level projected by the Census Bureau. Immigration-fed population momentum could produce a U.S. population of 550 million by mid-century, reaching the one billion mark in the 2080s.

The nation's experience with amnesties, as with the sweeping liberalization of immigration of 1965, shows that the numbers ultimately admitted will be considerably higher than political leaders will acknowledge. Overruns are built into the process. Inherent in amnesties have been high fraud and lax adjudication, intent-altering court decisions, stimulation of added legal and illegal immigration, and the piecemeal "creep" of amnesty to ineligible groups.

The Bush administration's offer of "earned legalization" for some 3.5 million Mexican illegals counts on Mexico's cooperation in discouraging future illegal immigration. But the Mexicans have ruled out blocking the outflow of their own people and are stymied by internal corruption from effective cooperation against smuggling and trafficking. North of the border, U.S. low-wage employers are unlikely to end their preference for plentiful and compliant illegal alien workers.

Amnesties have no place in effective immigration control. A workable alternative is first to stop any further growth of the illegal population by tighter border and visa controls. Stepping up deportations from around 180,000 a year to at least 250,000 would stimulate more voluntary departures and could reduce the unreplenished illegal population by as much as 4.0 million over a decade.

Sometime after the seating of the 108th Congress in early 2003, Capitol Hill and the White House will set about in their confounding way to make a truly epochal decision of population policy—whether to legalize the presence in the U.S. of upwards of 6 million unlawful immigrants and their families. This amnesty, along with the related immigration changes now under consideration by both major political parties, such as guest worker programs and expedited family reunification, could lock in millions of current illegal immigrants and add tens of millions of new residents and their U.S.-born children to this country over the next decade and a half.

The portentous choices to be made on amnesty are already being rationalized as matters of national security, economic development, civil rights or human rights. They are not discussed or even acknowledged as matters of population policy. Washington's population policy now as most often in the past is simply "*More*." And its outlook in the charged political ambiance can be summed up as "*immigration is pork*."

Scornful of limits and absorbed in the short term view, America's political leaders have historically made fateful demographic decisions with little consideration for the future consequences of the growth, composition and distribution of the population for society and the environment. Reminiscent of what was once said of Britain's acquisition of an empire, the U.S. has put itself on track to a one-half billion population "in a fit of absent-mindedness."

THE "GRAND BARGAIN"—BLESSING THE FLOW FROM MEXICO

Since taking power, the Bush administration, utterly pro-business and pro-populationist, has leaned toward a package deal with Mexico that would amnesty illegal Mexican aliens putatively here at least five years. Since public opinion remains hostile to "amnesties," the administration would rename it "earned legalization" and create a "temporary worker" status for working illegal aliens as a transition to full legal residence. Washington would also increase regular Mexican immigration ceilings to allow reunification of families originally divided by acts of illegal immigration. This package deal—called the "grand bargain" by U.S. and Mexican negotiators—may also include Mexican commitments to restrain illegal immigration from or through its territory.[1]

These proposed concessions to Mexico have won considerable interest group support in the U.S. from business, the once immigration-shy labor movement, the churches and ethnic lobbies. Bush's own personal interest and his desire to placate Mexican President Vicente Fox have given the deal impetus. The September 11 attacks soured the general public's receptiveness to major immigration initiatives. Even so, mindful of the GOP's need for Latino votes, Bush has remained supportive of an immigration deal of some sort. Some observers prematurely declared the grand bargain dead after September 11.[2] More likely it will lie comatose until 2003.

If the 2002 elections produce turnout for the GOP that promises the party more success among Latinos in 2004, the Bush administration would be encouraged to press ahead for the immigration deal, particularly if job growth picks up. While Bush has focussed only on Mexicans in the U.S., he has not ruled out extending amnesty to other nationalities.

DEMOCRATS UP THE BIDDING

According to House Democratic minority leader Richard Gephardt, his party favors an "earned" amnesty for all illegal aliens of any nationality with at least five years in the country—an estimated 5.8 million people.[3] Gephardt tossed off this massive, nation-transforming proposal with no more solemnity than if he were announcing a new bridge for his Missouri congressional district. Senate Democratic leader Tom Daschle has echoed his zeal.

In October, 2002, Gephardt followed up on his pledge by introducing HR 5600, the "*Earned Legalization and Family Reunification Act of 2002*." The bill came out early enough to improve Democratic chances in the then impending November 5 elections, but too late to get serious consideration by the lame duck 107th Congress. The Democratic bill would grant legal residence to those here five-years and who have worked at least two years, unless they were not of working age.

Spouses and children of eligible aliens would be admitted.

The bill would further expand the numbers by offering permanent residence to legal temporary sojourners, such as those in parole, deferred departure and temporary protected status, and to undocumented students in grades seven through college. Applicants must pay all taxes owed (IOUs are acceptable) and have "minimal" understanding of English and the history and government of the U.S. To ensure their prompt entry on the voter rolls, satisfaction of the "minimal" understanding requirement will be considered as satisfying a similar requirement for naturalization.

Buoyed by its success in marginalizing the Republican party in California by recruiting immigrants, the Democratic party now accepts high immigration as its default position. A large turnout for Democrats among Latinos and the foreign-born in November 2002 will increase the appeal of a broad amnesty before the 2004 presidential elections.

HOW MANY ELIGIBLE FROM MEXICO? FROM THE WORLD?

Best estimates are that under what is known of the Bush proposal as many as 3.5 million Mexican illegal aliens would meet the five-year presence requirement.[4] No specific numbers have been proposed for increasing Mexico's regular immigration quota, already the world's highest with an average of some 150,000 a year in the late 1990s. Neither have negotiators yet specified any target numbers for guest workers, or whether they contemplate recruiting additional guest workers now living in Mexico. The agriculture, construction and restaurant lobbies are pressing for such an arrangement.

With polls consistently showing most Americans opposed to increased immigration, it is not surprising that both parties are vague about how many new residents their plans would bring. The Administration and the Democrats have emphasized "earned legalization" as promoting the values of family reunification, fairness and compassion, along with the nation's presumed need for the additional workers. Curiously, employment while in illegal status will be considered as a meritorious concession to the country rather than a violation of law still on the books.

In defending "earned" legalization, proponents try to reassure the public by claiming that the number of new immigrants will not be large, since those to be legalized are "already here, and they are not going home." Similarly, public concerns about guest workers and higher immigration quotas are often dismissed with such fatalistic contentions as "they'll come anyhow, so it's better if they come legally." A related argument tailored for post-September 11 anxieties and used by U.S. and Mexican proponents alike is that the mass legalizations will enhance national security by bringing the illegal population into the light of day where it can be identified and counted.[5] Such Washington disingenuousness on the real population effects of major immigration liberalizations, such as past amnesties and the 1965 law easing the quota system, is traditional.

THE AMNESTY "ECHO:" NEW AND BIGGER MIGRATION CHAINS

The current arguments are no less disingenuous and manipulative. Experience with amnesties shows that all concessions in the "grand bargain" so far considered will end up importing more migrants than acknowledged. Those concessions and incentives are likely as well to reduce the repatriation rate of the illegal population already here and stimulate added legal and illegal immigration at the outset and well into the future. The Democrats' amnesty bill offering permanent residence even to adult college students and legal sojourners shows how easily such legislation can abandon its original intent and become a migration "Christmas tree."

A substantial literature on the late 1980s' general and farm worker amnesties of 1.7 million and 1.1 million illegal aliens respectively shows the potential for immense follow-on immigration of relatives and friends of the amnestied population. A study done for the U.S. Commission on Immigration Reform (USCIR—the Jordan Commission) studied 1.58 million of those beneficiaries and concluded that they had 8.0 million relatives living abroad who would become eligible for a U.S. immigration benefit—5.2 overseas relatives per amnestied alien. This discussion assumes the same 5.2 to 1 ratio for the 1.2 million amnestied persons not addressed in the USCIR report. That report, based on a 1992 Immigration and Naturalization Service survey of the legalized population, estimated that about 25 to 30 percent of overseas relatives (2.0 to 2.5 million) would immigrate.[6]

However, a subsequent interpretation of the 1992 legalization data done by the author of the USCIR report upped the estimate of the number of relatives abroad of the 1.58 million amnestied aliens to 9.6 million, 20 percent more than the number estimated for the USCIR report.[7]

Note that the large retinues of entitled relatives estimated in these studies were for a relatively small anchor population of legalized aliens compared to the current prospects. The Mexican undocumented population alone now eligible under a five-year residency rule is estimated at 3.5 million. Using the ratios implied by the 1994 USCIR report, they would have some 18.2 million relatives abroad.[8] Applying USCIR's restrained estimates, "only" about 30 percent (about 5.5 million), would use their family reunification preference to come here.

Proponents of amnesty dismiss such concerns with the claim that much of the prospective family immigration is limited by quotas that tightly limit annual admissions. So, most eligibles would wait for years to cash in their family preferences. It is precisely that long wait for what is seen as a U.S. commitment that encourages illegal immigration and boosts pressures for amnesties and other circumvent ions of the waiting period. Also, many overseas relatives would become legally eligible to come with little delay once the legalized alien sponsor gains citizenship. .

DATA FROM MEXICO ON FAMILY CHAINS

Another assessment of the family immigration liability attending the amnesties of the 1980s, done by American scholar Douglas Massey and Mexican expert Jorge Durand, and based on surveys in Mexico, supported similar conclusions. It found that each of the 2.3 million Mexican legalized in the late 1980s had an average of four relatives who qualified for a preference, thus creating 9.2 million additional immigration entitlements.

Massey and Durand also highlight the multiplying effect that naturalization of the legalized aliens, and the resulting removals of limits on the numbers of certain relatives would have on future immigration. They conclude that the IRCA amnesty and the subsequent naturalizations of Mexican aliens induced by U.S. policy through 1998 had created 11.5 million potential new immigrants subject to numerical limits and another 10.5 million subject to no limits at all.[9]

Worth noting is that these large numbers grew from a root population of only 2.3 million amnestied Mexicans.

If, however, as the Democrats prefer, all illegals and some legal temporary sojourners residing for five years become eligible regardless of nationality, the projected numbers jump smartly. The amnesty-eligible population in the U.S. rises to 5.8 million, with more than 35 million relatives abroad. Even if only 30 percent of them actually immigrates, the U.S. would still receive 10.5 million more newcomer relatives in a few years to join the nearly six million newly legalized in this country—adding up to 16.5 million newcomers able to petition to start their own family chains.

Under Massey and Durand's reckoning, and assuming naturalization rates comparable to the earlier amnesty, a Democratic party-style amnesty would ultimately create quota-limited immigration entitlements for 29 million persons abroad and unrestricted immigration privileges for more than 26 million. There is some overlap between the quota-limited and unrestricted family populations. Naturalization of the anchor immigrant moves some overseas relatives from quota-limited categories to unrestricted ones, while creating new eligibilities for siblings. Even so, the size of the potential worldwide immigration liability is mind-numbing.

The following table presents 1) estimates of preference-eligible family members abroad per legalized alien derived from three studies of the 1987–90 amnesties: Woodrow 1995, USCIR, and Massey/Durand; and 2) the estimates of the total number of family members abroad who would become eligible for family preference visas under the three scenarios in a Mexico-only amnesty and a worldwide amnesty.

Even these formidable numbers may understate the prospects. The studies cited above are based

Table 1. Estimates of Family Preference Immigration Candidates Resulting from Current Amnesty Proposals

SOURCE:	Woodrow 1995	USCIR 1994	Massey/Durand 2002
Overseas Relatives Per Alien Amnestied Under 1986 IRCA	6.1	5.2	4
Estimated Eligibles for Amnesty under 5-Yr Residence Rule Mexico Only	3.5 million	3.5 million	3.5 million
Total Eligible for Family Visa - Mexico Only	21.35 million	18.2 million	14.0 million
Estimated Eligibles For Amnesty - 5 yrs Worldwide	5.8 million	5.8 million	5.8 million
Total Eligible for Family Visa - Worldwide	35.4 million	30.2 million	23.2 million
Total Worldwide: Legalized + Family	41.2 million	36.0 million	29.0 million

largely on the demographics of migration from Mexico, where population growth is slowing and immigration demand has been somewhat attenuated. What can be expected in follow-on immigration from the 1.8 million amnesty candidates who are non-Mexican? Many illegal aliens are from nations such as China, India, Pakistan and Bangladesh, where populations are huge and immigration demand explosive.

Neither does the table estimate added illegal immigration, which increased measurably because of the 1986 amnesty. Massey and others concluded from the Mexican surveys in 1997 that

> *. . . Being in a household in which someone had been legalized under IRCA (the 1986 Amnesty statute) increased the likelihood of migrating illegally by a factor of almost nine, raising it from .04 per year to .35 per year.*[10]

A heavy share of those household members determined by Massey to be more likely to migrate illegally are spouses and minor children of the newly legalized aliens. This illustrates another trap of the amnesty concept—the subsequent pressure to expand and extend privileges to presumed hardship groups, and the growth of those hardship groups through marriage and childbirth. The USCIR study showed that in 1992—four years after the amnesty and after a considerable number of "family fairness" admissions—the 1.58 million amnestied Mexican aliens studied still had 484, 000 spouses and children abroad who intended to come, implying a total immediate family population in waiting of 850,000 in just Mexico.

THE FAMILY UNITY COMPULSION AND "AMNESTY CREEP"

Masses of ineligible family members become poster children for special exceptions and, ultimately, demands for new amnesties. Their ineligibility to legally join their family member in the U.S. because of quota limits was deplored by humanitarian groups and resulted in legal and ad hoc administrative measures to let them come anyway. Among those measures were 120, 000 additional quota numbers under "family fairness," and de facto acquiescence in considerable illegal presence. Since 1994 there has been 245 (i), a provision granting legal permanent residence on payment of $1000 to hundreds of thousands of illegals here awaiting approval of family or employer petitions (8USC1255(i)(I)). As often the case, 245 (i) originated as a time-limited special relief measure, but has become a de facto rolling amnesty of its own with repeated extensions. INS likes the extra money and Congress likes the patronage.

A downstream population effect of "amnesty creep" has been the spiraling rise in post-amnesty legal immigration of Mexicans from 90,000 yearly in 1995 to 207 thousand in 2001. More than two-thirds of 2001 Mexican immigrants—20 percent of all U.S. legal immigration—were family sponsored and about two-thirds were already living in the United States.

Unlike in the 1986 amnesty, the present lawmakers would simply capitulate in advance to the sanctity of family reunification. They would provide for otherwise ineligible immediate family members by adding more quota numbers for family reunification or, in the generosity of the Democrats' HR 5600, grant virtually automatic legalization to spouses and children of applicants.

AMNESTY FRAUD—RISKY POPULATION WILD CARD

America could expect up to 35 million additional immigrants over a decade and a half if all features of the proposed amnesties were enacted. But this estimate rests on optimistic assumptions—that the amnesty would have unambiguous and politically-backed rules, would be rigorously adjudicated and reasonably fraud-free, and would not be expanded or liberalized by court decisions. Our previous amnesty experiences suggest that these outcomes are most unlikely.

Fraud abounds in all U.S. government immigration benefit programs, where time-short adjudicators must deal with dubious foreign documents, often counterfeit or altered U.S. documents, and the vestigial identity of petitioners and beneficiaries. INS is hampered in fighting fraud by wavering support from Congress and the White House, chronically shortages of manpower and time, and an awareness that denials of applicants are more politically and judicially risky than rubber-stamp approval. A 2002 General Accounting Office report finds that 20 percent to 30 percent of applications for benefits in some places are fraudulent. In one desirable visa category, an examination of a sample of 5000 applications found that 90 percent were fraudulent.[11]

Mexico's own culture of corruption will plague administration of legalization and guest worker programs. A Mexico-only amnesty would make "proofs" of Mexican identity and presence in the U.S. highly valuable commodities throughout Latin America. The Mexican bureaucracy will be hard pressed to resist this opportunity for quick and easy enrichment. Flourishing private immigration document counterfeiters in the U.S. and abroad are also likely to equip clients with Mexican documentation. Already demand for counterfeit Mexican birth certificates is rising because of the increasing number of U.S. jurisdictions and businesses willing to honor ID cards issued by Mexican consulates. Without the most exacting scrutiny—which a swamped INS is unable to give—a Mexico-only amnesty could yield substantial numbers of non-Mexican newcomers.

About half of the successful applications for amnesty in the 1986 Special Agricultural Workers (SAW) legalization in California were fraudulent, allowing in up to one-half million ineligible aliens.[12] It is hardly surprising that the 1986 amnesties were fraud-ridden and lenient. The primary vetting of applications was done largely by "Qualified Designated Entities (QDE's)"—non-governmental civic, religious and ethnic volunteer groups that openly favored "generosity."

Mushy legal language and regulations and some court decisions created presumptions in favor of the applicants or otherwise eased the rules. That legal battle continues. Various court rulings since the IRCA amnesty, culminating in a 1993 Supreme Court decision (*Reno v. Catholic Social Services, Inc. 509* U.S. *43*) have overturned INS amnesty rules and opened the way for legalization of up to 350,000 more illegal residents previously denied. In another display of "amnesty creep," the 2000 "LIFE" Act legislated relief for the appellants and other ineligible family members.[13]

With INS manpower now heavily committed to border security, the country will likely have to again place adjudication of millions of legalization requests in the hands of QDE's. Congress' continuing ambivalence about immigration is likely to produce legislative ambiguities on eligibility, putting key policy decisions again in the hands of sympathetic private screeners or judges bent on "fairness."

"NOTHING IS SO PERMANENT AS A TEMPORARY WORKER"

Farm interests, seasonal employers, and their congressional tribunes want the "grand bargain" to include a guest worker program that will not lead to permanent residence. Past experience in the U.S. and Europe with "braceros" and other temporary worker programs hold out little hope that this is doable.

The pull of life in the U.S. is too strong and the opportunities for better jobs as a longstayer are seductive. Spouses and children acquired while in the U.S. will remain a powerful fixative. And the U.S. is unlikely to police labor standards enough to ensure employers meet the terms of their guest workers' contracts.

The likely continued availability to employers of more compliant illegal immigrants will undermine guest worker labor standards. Effective management of a guest worker program would demand effective use of employer sanctions, which have become a dead letter. The risk is high that a guest worker program will rapidly become a conduit for permanent settlement in the U.S., with regular intake from Mexico or other sending countries and little return flow.

LITTLE MEXICAN RECIPROCITY IN THE "GRAND BARGAIN"

What the United States seemingly hopes to gain from these sweeping agreements is, in the President's words, immigration that is "orderly, safe, humane and legal." and Mexico's cooperation in bringing it about. But so far in the negotiations, Mexico's prospective concessions to make the immigration agreement work have been timid and shifting. Early on, Mexican Interior Minister Santiago Creel made it clear that there would be no efforts to restrict Mexicans' movements, as it would supposedly violate Mexico's constitution.[14]

Thus, the one Mexican concession that would have brought balance to the "grand bargain" is not even on the table. Instead, there are Mexican promises to discourage emigration by cracking down on the pervasive alien-smuggling industry and curbing the flow of transiting migrants from Central American. Also mentioned have been possible Mexican incentives to ensure guest workers comply with the terms of their admission. Results from previously agreed cooperative efforts against smugglers, document forgers, and transiting third-country aliens have been unspectacular.

Expert U.S. analysts of Mexico are skeptical that the Mexican government can deliver even on these modest deterrents. Robert Leiken, a Brookings Institution scholar, says President Fox's good intentions would be defeated ". . . at the street level because the culture in law enforcement circles is so corrupt." DeLal Baer of Washington's Center for Strategic and International Studies, warned that cooperation against smuggling runs up against the same obstacles that have undercut U.S.-Mexican cooperation on environmental protection and curbing the drug trade.[15]

On the U.S. side, hundreds of thousands of private sector employers dependent on cheap and vulnerable foreign workers will have a major say in whether illegal immigration diminishes. Past performance is not encouraging. Labor-intensive industries such as agriculture continued preferring illegal workers during the Bracero program and following the 1987–1990 amnesty's legalization of 1.1 million purported farm workers.

Illegal immigration for low-wage employers fills a critical perceived need. Guest worker programs, to the extent they uphold basic wages and conditions, eliminate important advantages for such employers—making guest workers a distant second choice. The stand down of INS internal enforcement and sanctions against employers in the roaring '90s demonstrates the political clout of employers of illegals—clout the laissez-faire, business-friendly Bush administration is unlikely to challenge.

AMNESTY: TENS OF MILLIONS MORE STRAWS ON THE CAMEL'S BACK

The average American shows little concern for devastating population outcomes that may be decades away. But he or she can see some of the effects of it now year by year. The largest ever intercensal growth of the foreign born population, 13 million between 1990 and 2000, was an eye-opener for many. And the link is evident between that exuberant growth and pervasive school crowding and shortages of affordable housing.

An amnesty in the next few years will bring even more rapid growth in the foreign-born population, the foreign stock, and the nation. This growth would be appreciably higher if the proposed amnesty is extended to all nationalities. The forty million persons ultimately qualifying for legalization or family preferences would implant myriad new immigration ladders in troubled and crowded countries now low on links here.

The 2000 Census showed the greatest population surge for any decade—32 million additional residents in just ten years. The Census Bureau consistently underestimates immigration in projecting the U.S. population, producing population projections for 2000 that were 7 million too low. Immigrants and their U.S.-born children now account for 60 percent of U.S. population growth. About 20 million of the new residents were either immigrants or the 7 million children born to immigrants. Each expansion of already high immigration adds to the momentum that is leaving far behind the limits that an environmentally safe and sustainable U.S. population demands. That upper limit of sustainability was breached about 1970 when population passed 200 million and the National Commission on Population and the American Future recommended that immigration go no higher.

If immigration-based population growth, now about 1.4 million annually, continues its upward trend of the 1990s, the U.S. could well be headed for a mid-century population of 550 million, not the 404 million deemed the "most likely" outcome by Census in its 2000 projections. With the booster fuel of massive amnesties and guest worker programs, and the consequent opening of new immigration channels to heavily population nations, annual immigration is likely to rise to Census' "highest" projection of 2.2 million by 2025.[16]

With the Census' highest projection of immigration now increasingly plausible, and with the heavy influx of higher fertility nationalities, the U.S. population will reach the half-billion mark in 2044 with considerable built-in momentum. A stable population at a sustainable level will have become a a distant dream. Continued growth on this trajectory after 2044 would have the U.S. joining China and India in the dubious "one billion member club" by 2088, just one lifetime from now.

AN ALTERNATIVE TO AMNESTY: HOLD THE LINE, LET ATTRITION WORK

In the debate leading up to the 1986 amnesty some legislators held out for regaining control of our borders first—then amnesty. Though they were unsuccessful, it is still good advice. Stopping now the yearly net flow of some 400, 000 unlawful migrants with tougher border controls and internal enforcement would end further growth of the illegal population. Then the numbers would begin to fall through attrition and by legalization of those here now and genuinely entitled under existing laws. Now, about 200,000 one-time illegals and overstays are legalized in this fashion each year. That number would decline as tighter immigration controls took hold.

Another 180,000 illegal aliens now are removed from the country every year. The number of removals with modest effort could realistically be expanded by at least another 50,000 to 75,000 yearly. More determined deportation efforts would also stimulate an even higher level of voluntary departures. If new cohorts of illegals were blocked, one could expect an annual decline in the illegal population, now eight to ten million, to fall by as much as 4 million in a decade.[17]

Whatever the strategy, Americans must recognize the high long-term environmental and social costs to U.S. society of another mass amnesty. The immigration laws are complex, malleable and mystifying. Only an alert and determined public can mount the informed resistance needed to thwart further mass immigration in both its overt and stealthy forms.

NOTES:

1. Marcus Stern, "Phased-in Access": is not like amnesty or a guest worker program," *San Diego Union Tribune*, August 12, 2001. "Phased-in access," like "earned legalization," is one of several euphemisms used by Washington spokesman to avoid or soften the politically unpopular term, "amnesty." For a Mexican view of the Grand Bargain see Francisco Alba, Colegio de Mexico, "Mexico: A crucial crossroads," *Migration Policy Institute*, July 1, 2002.
2. Jose Luis Cubria, "Analysts say there is no chance for a Mexico-U.S. immigration accord," Mexico City *News*, August 7, 2002
3. Estimates of Mexican and general illegal populations here at least five years from: Lindsey Lowell and Roberto Suro, *How Many Undocumented*, Pew Hispanic Center, March 21, 2002 Lowell and Suro
4. Ronald Brownstein, "Immigration Reform on House Democrats' Minds," *Los Angeles Times*, July 23, 2002.
5. Karen A. Woodrow-Lafield (1994), *Potential Sponsorship by IRCA-Legalized Immigrants*, U.S. Commission on Immigration Reform
6. Woodrow-Lafield (1995), *Post-Legalization Household Changes and Potential Family Reunification* (Revised version of paper presented at the 1994 annual meeting of the Population Association of America, Miami.)
7. Woodrow-Lafield (1994), pp. 12, 39
8. Douglas S. Massey and Jorge Durand (2002); *Beyond Smoke and Mirrors: Mexican Immigration in an Era of Economic Integration. New York: Russel Sage Foundation*. Pp 138–139.
9. Massey and Durand, p. 140
10. "Report by GAO cites INS on Benefit Fraud," *Washington Post*, February 15, 2002
11. Philip L. Martin, "Good Intentions Gone Awry: IRCA and U.S. Agriculture." *Annals of the American Academy of Political and Social Sciences*, July 1994 Public Law 106-553
12. "Mexico proposes immigration pact to cut down third-country passage." *Washington Post*, April 5, 2001.
13. "Mexico pledges to get tough on smugglers," *Arizona Republic*, February 23, 2002; "Personal de Aduana y de la PFP, coluidos con polleros," *Milenio*, October 3, 2002
14. Population Division, Bureau of the Census: "Annual Projections of the Total Resident Population as of July 1: Middle, Lowest, Highest and Zero International Migration Series, 1999 to 2100" (NP-T1) And: "Projected Migration by Race and Hispanic Origin, 1999–2100 (NP-T7-C).
15. Comments on Steven Camarota at panel on "Mexican Immigration after 9/11: New and Old Challenges," The Nixon Center, Washington, DC, August 6, 2002

DIVERGING DEMOGRAPHY, CONVERGING DESTINIES: GROWTH, INTERDEPENDENCE, MIGRATION AND WORLD INSTABILITIES

Lindsey Grant

January 2003

The past half century was marked by unprecedented population growth, driving fundamental environmental changes, and by dramatic growth in interdependence among nations for the necessities of life. The next half century will be shaped in considerable measure by the enormous differences in fertility and population growth between the developed and developing worlds. The resulting instabilities will be magnified by the extent to which open trading systems have made nations interdependent, but the instabilities have their origin in demographic change. They can be avoided or at least ameliorated if population growth in the less developed world (the LDCs) and the United States is halted and reversed. Despite its appearance of awful inevitability, that growth can be reversed, but it will require a new mindset that recognizes continuing population and economic growth as a threat rather than a blessing.

DEMOGRAPHY BY ACCIDENT

Much of human activity can be characterized as accidental experiments. It is a useful metaphor. We do things to our environmental support systems without realizing it—or indeed much caring. The growth of human populations and consumption in the past two generations, the transformation of agriculture, the multiplication of new chemicals, and the growth of fossil energy use are all interconnected. They have not been seen as a whole, and they are not sustainable.

The vastest of these experiments gathered force in the 1950s. Modern medicine and public health practices sharply reduced mortality in the poor countries. The motive was humane. We all can applaud a reduction of mortality. But when we tampered with one side of a natural equation without changing the other side, we generated a fundamental imbalance. Efforts to address human fertility were delayed, timid and faltering. Consequently, the world's population grew much more in the following two generations than it had in all previous human history. The poorer, less developed countries (LDCs) nearly trebled from 1.7 billion in 1950 to 4.9 billion in 2000. The United States' population, driven increasingly by immigration, nearly doubled from 151 million to 281 million. The rest of the industrial world (DCs) grew by 37 percent, to 910 million. (UN2000)

Concurrently, there has been a consumption boom unparalleled in human history. The combination has led to hitherto unknown pressures on resources and productive systems. For the first time, humans now dominate most ecosystems and affect all of them.

I hope that readers will ask the question, as they address the issues below: was this problem driven by population growth? Would it be less difficult to resolve if populations were smaller?

SUBSIDIARY EXPERIMENTS

Food and Water: Pushing the Limits.

The population growth was made possible by fundamental changes in agriculture. We now use roughly six times as much commercial fertilizer as we did in 1950. Human activity puts nitrogen, potassium, phosphates, and sulfates into the environment faster than natural processes produce them. We know this input causes damage to farmland, degrades wetlands and estuaries, contributes to the decline of fisheries and the appearance of the "dead zone" in the Gulf of Mexico, "brown slime" in the Adriatic and the "mahogany tide" in the Chesapeake, but we don't know the full range of consequences. And we don't know what will happen if this goes on for very long, but we cannot simply stop the experiment, because without commercial fertilizers, literally billions of people would starve (Smil, 1991).

We would have drowned in the nitrogen if it were not being processed back into its inert atmospheric state by some helpful microbes. We don't know much about those microbes, but we are changing their environment and thereby testing how much abuse they can take. If we learn the answer to that unintentional experiment, it may be too late, because our lives depend on them. (President's Acid Rain Review Committee, 1983)

The "green revolution" crops provide more food but they demand more fertilizer and more pesticides. Traditional crops developed defenses against pests through generations of seed selection. The miracle crops do not have that defense. We are introducing new pesticides and thereby inadvertently promoting the evolution of our opponents into more formidable adversaries. The mutant pests can handle the pesticides, so we invent something nastier, in an ongoing and dubious war. For example, bacterial blight thrives on the heavy nitrogen applications demanded by "miracle rice." Now, scientists are experimenting with new bacterial-resistant rice strains, over the opposition of farmers who demand a return to traditional rice varieties even if yields are lower. (ENS 2000)

The new crops also require much more water, and irrigation has doubled, but the era of rising irrigation has ended. Now, arid regions are running out of water, and scarcities are appearing even in moist areas, including the eastern and central United States. (As this is written, Frederick, Maryland—with a population growing nearly 3 percent a year—has had to start importing water by truck.) It takes about a thousand tons of water to grow a ton of corn. The supply of available fresh water is basically static. When the areas with enough rainfall are already in use, when farmers have bought whatever water is available and have mined the aquifers, the price of water skyrockets. Water-rich nations (such as Canada) are showing themselves unwilling to export water.

Desalination is no solution. With the best available technologies, and with energy prices at present levels, it costs about $2 to $3 to desalinate 1000 gallons of seawater—delivered at the seashore, not the farm. That works out to about $14 to $21, plus transportation, for the water to raise a bushel of corn that presently fetches about $2.00–$2.50. Desalinating brackish inland groundwater is not a solution, because the question arises: what do you do with the waste brine? Desalination for irrigation is simply out of sight unless food prices multiply. And only the rich can afford that.

Farmers won't recycle the water by building huge greenhouses. That is possible for specialty crops such as tomatoes for the prosperous. But as a way of providing basic food for six billion people, and rising, the cost would be prohibitive.

Mankind's demand for food is outrunning our ability to produce it. Worldwide grain production rose 2.7 percent annually in the 1960s and 1970s, and 2.5 percent in the 1980s, but only 0.5 percent in the 1990s (FAOSTATS)—much less than population growth.

As yields rise, it takes more and more fertilizer to gain another increase in yield. The response curve flattens out, and eventually there is no benefit from adding more fertilizer. The developed world has reached that point; fertilizer use has declined sharply in Europe and Japan, and somewhat less dramatically in the United States. Some LDCs such as China are approaching that point. Perhaps that is a blessing in disguise. I have pointed out the penalties of excessive use of commercial fertilizer. The fertilizer is made from petroleum and natural gas, and we are exhausting those resources. But it means that we cannot count on fertilizer to produce much higher yields.

What is possible? Nobody really knows. Total grain production in the developed countries has been stagnant for twenty years—despite recurrent news stories about new miracles. But corn and wheat yields in the United States were somewhat higher in the 1990s than ever before. Industrial countries' yields per hectare are 35 percent higher than in the poor countries. The optimist would say: "look, there is plenty of room for growth." More realistically, the poor countries will have trouble maintaining present food production—to say nothing of accommodating their anticipated population growth—in the face of land erosion, loss of arable land, intensifying water shortages, fertilizer shortages, and the prospect of a hotter and more volatile climate. And the United States, as I will later show, is not a reliable long-term residual supplier.

There is a furious debate about genetic modification (GM), but no assurance that it can bring back the growth of the 1960s–1970s. Moreover, it is another of those unplanned experiments whose potential consequences we see only dimly. In a recent study, wild sunflowers' seed production rose by 50 percent after they acquired a gene for pest protection from adjacent genetically modified domesticated sunflowers. (ENS 2002) The prospect of more prolific weeds is only one potential consequence. For years, the dream of GM has been to instill nitrogen-fixing capabilities into grain crops. If we succeed, but the gene escapes into wild grasses, we may dramatically increase the worldwide release of nitrogen and thereby intensify a problem we have already created.

We should proceed much more deliberately when we modify natural systems. We should understand the consequences before we propagate experiments. With smaller populations, or just an end to growth, the pressure to apply the experiments to feed more people would no longer drive our behavior.

Then why not farm the oceans? The answer is that we are already over-fishing them. Theoretically, we could raise yields by fertilizing them, as we do the land. In particular, spreading iron in the sea in very small concentrations would lead to increased phytoplankton production and larger fish harvests. Experiments have been tried, and their proponents want to extend them. More phytoplankton might also sequester more atmospheric carbon dioxide and thus mitigate climate warming. Speculative companies have been created, hoping to make a profit from a potential world market in credits for carbon sequestration.

The problem here is that the proposal would transform the sea and the climate in ways we cannot predict. It would be another unplanned experiment with the Earth, this one on a scale so vast as to make our fertilizer experiment on land seem picayune. The proponents are, in effect, proposing a very dangerous "solution" to two perceived problems, in an effort to avoid the one thing we must do: limit the demand side.

The Energy Transition: the Twilight of Fossil Fuels. The modern world is dependent upon fossil energy, which itself is a profound disturbance to the ecosystem. We move carbon—and with it sulphur and mercury and other incidental substances—from the lithosphere into the biosphere and then the atmosphere, at a rate and scale unlike any natural processes.

We worry about the threat of terrorism to petroleum supplies, but the supply will decline, anyway. That will be an environmental boon but an economic disaster unless we have prepared for it. Estimates of remaining world resources range around two trillion barrels. The U.S. Geological Survey estimate is among the highest at about 2.2 trillion barrels. (USGS 2000) World consumption presently runs at roughly 68 million barrels a day, and rising, but world production will soon begin to decline, perhaps within this decade (Deffeyes 2001; Duncan 2001), probably in twenty years or less (Kerr1998). The International Energy Agency thinks that non-OPEC production has already peaked. (IEA 1998) Not a very long future. The United States has already consumed about 70 percent of the petroleum we started with.

When world petroleum production passes its peak, competition will intensify and prices will rise sharply. Users are already turning increasingly to natural gas, but gas resources are limited, too. Coal is more abundant, but it is a dirty fuel. Some of the pollution could be controlled, but the cost is very high. (Coal is very unevenly distributed, world wide, like petroleum—but the United States has the largest share.)

Growth apologists, faced with those calculations, look for panaceas. Oil sands are offered as an energy source, but their processing is environmentally destructive and they may demand more energy to exploit than they can produce. Ocean methane from the continental slopes is suggested as a possibility, but the environmental consequences could be frightening. We might release the methane without capturing it, thus further warming the climate and triggering undersea mudslides and tsunamis. (Normile 1999) Biomass is not a solution; its production competes with human food needs.

Nothing can replace fossil fuels' versatility, their usefulness for purposes as diverse as powering airplanes and providing feedstock for chemical plants. Wind and photovoltaics can, however, supply electricity. For peaking power, wind energy is nearly as cheap as fossil fuels, right now—and probably much cheaper if we could figure in the environmental costs of fossil fuels. (Economists periodically try to make that calculation, but one cannot put a price on the destruction of the only environment we have.) For reliable base power, however, wind and solar energy are likely to be much more expensive than fossil fuels are now, because of the problem of storing the energy until it is needed. (Grant 2000)

The world is headed into a rapid energy transition. The rising costs and dislocations will threaten the world economies. We would be much better off if there were fewer people, demanding less energy, than if nations must finance the energy transition on top of the costs of accommodating rising populations.

The Human Effect on Climate. Fossil energy is the principal cause of anthropogenic climate warming. The decline of fossil fuels will eventually make that problem obsolete—after the damage is done. Meanwhile, the Intergovernmental Panel on Climate Change (IPCC) in 1995 estimated that it would take an immediate reduction in carbon emissions to 30 to 50 percent of present levels to hold the human impact on climate even at its present levels. In the face of that calculation, the modest reductions proposed in the Kyoto protocols are largely symbolic.

The experts did not address population size at Kyoto, but it must be addressed if we are to come close to the 30 to 50 percent goal. To visualize that point, apply current (2000) per capita carbon emissions to the 1950 population base. Total U.S. emissions would be 54 percent of the present level of 1.57 billion metric tons. Emissions by the rest of the industrial world would be 73 percent of 2.34 billion tons. The LDCs' emissions would be 35 percent of 2.53 billion tons. Totaled, world emissions from fossil energy would be 53 percent of the present 6.44 billion tons. (EIA 2000) Moreover, destruction of tropical forests adds roughly 20 percent to world greenhouse gas emissions. (Science 2002) The data are very fuzzy, but this source of carbon emissions has undoubtedly multiplied since 1950, as LDC populations have exploded.

In sum, with populations at 1950 levels, we would be close to or within the IPCC's 30 to 50 percent target, even without reducing present per capita emissions. That is a ballpark calculation, but it suggests the importance of population growth in climate warming.

THE REVOLUTION IN MAN-MADE CHEMICALS.

Most of our unplanned experiments involve chemicals, many of them developed to serve agriculture. The American Chemical Society's worldwide registry in 1999 contained 22 million chemicals (including DNA biosequences). Three-fourths of them are new since 1980. The National Academy of Sciences (NAS) in 1983 sampled a tiny fraction of the 75,000 or so chemicals then in commercial use and found that very few of them had been tested for their direct health effects. I know of no comparable study since then, or of any systematic effort to understand the secondary effects as they move through the environment and are transformed by chemical and microbial action.

This unmonitored proliferation of chemicals is particularly disturbing because medical science is learning the role of even trace chemicals in human life processes. For one example: organochlorides include PCBs, DDT, and dioxin, and perhaps 11,000 other compounds. Their commercial production dates only from the 1940s but already they are found in living organisms everywhere. We worry about human health, but far more important to the biosphere is what they may be doing to the microbial world on which we depend but which we do not understand.

It took forty years from the introduction of chlorofluorocarbons (CFCs) before two scientists discovered that they were attacking stratospheric ozone and leading to increased ultraviolet (UV) radiation on Earth, which causes human cancers and—more important—kills the plankton that form the base of the marine food chain. Fortunately, that one case was manageable and clear. CFCs are being phased out. The broader point, however, is that we must take the time to understand the consequences before we propagate new chemicals—and we are falling farther and farther behind.

The Endangered Biosphere. Human activities, including the proliferation of chemicals, have become the principal driver of species extinction and the unwitting architect of evolution. If we disturb the balance enough, as we may with nitrogen-processing bacteria or other microbes, we may imperil ourselves.

Humans have assumed an immense role on Earth. By the most detailed and most quoted estimate, we are appropriating about 40 percent of all terrestrial photosynthetic productivity. (Vitousek 1986) This understates our disturbance, since it ignores the human role in disturbing chemical balances throughout the biosphere, described above.

ATTEMPTED SOLUTIONS

We can no longer behave like other animals, oblivious to the consequences of our activities. We have learned to change the Earth, but not to manage it. We cannot put the genie back in the bottle. We must learn to control it.

Efforts to deal with the unintended byproducts of our experiments have focused on mitigating the consequences of rising human activity. We have tried to solve growing problems with ever more ingenious and costly technological remedies. And those remedies have generated about as many problems as solutions.

Some of the measures have helped. Current industrial processes were generally not developed with the environment in mind, and there is room for more benign alternatives. But the cheaper and easier improvements come first. Witness air pollution in the United States: the biggest gains were made soon after passage of the Clean Air Act of 1970. G Aggregate emissions have actually risen since 1995. (USEPA 2002)

Technological solutions should indeed be sought to specific problems, but they should not be seen as a substitute for a population policy. Organic agriculture—a decidedly low-tech idea—minimizes artificial chemical inputs. It restores the soil. It sometimes increases farmers' net income. But it does not maximize current yields. Reverting to organic agriculture, globally, would raise the question: where do you get all that natural compost? Traditional agriculture could feed two billion people, but probably not six billion, and certainly not the ten billion or more toward which the world may be heading.

THE SOLUTION ON THE DEMAND SIDE

We need to turn the problem around. Reduce our demands upon the system, and the remedies become unnecessary.

Managing Consumption. It is fashionable to decry present consumption levels. That criticism is legitimate in the United States, but hardly in Bangladesh. The poorest countries would love to be richer, and with reason. World wide, lowering consumption would be a cruel "solution."

Population and Sustainability. To those concerned with equity, I offer an interesting statistic. How many people could live sustainably at a decent standard of living at the present global level of economic activity? As a rough measure of such a standard, let us use the average per capita GDP (gross domestic product) of the World Bank's forty-four "high income" nations, which China and India see as their goal.

The answer: 1.06 billion people. (World Bank 1996) One sixth of the present population. A crude indicator, indeed. It assumes that the current level of activity is sustainable, which it is not. GDP is not necessarily the measure of well-being. Income disparities within nations are ignored. The richest nations would hardly choose to level downward. But it does make a point: the poor countries' dreams of prosperity are imaginable only if their populations are much smaller. The present effort to achieve such living standards for growing LDC populations will generate pressures on the environment that will make our present problems seem trifling.

Or take food. Per capita grain production in the less developed countries is one third that in the industrial countries, and population growth is widening the disparity. I think the discussion above should make clear that the gap will narrow only if LDC populations are much smaller than they are now.

In short, a reversal of the experiment in population growth is essential to any prospect of creating a viable and prosperous world.

INTERDEPENDENCE AND CONFLICT

Dependence on foreign sources can have advantages and disadvantages. Economically, it promotes efficiency and cheaper goods, and it enables importing countries' economies to expand beyond the limits of indigenous resources. Politically, it gives nations a stake in each others' stability. Beyond that point, however, such trade can be disruptive. It can destroy existing producers. Farmers in Mexico have been demonstrating against the threat of cheap grain from the United States under NAFTA. American and European workers are beginning to realize that free movement of capital and goods, organized usually by the multinational corporations (MNCs), tends to drive the returns to labor down toward the lowest level, anywhere.

International trade has become a major distributor of food and energy. The growth in trade is in part a product of the MNCs' search for larger markets and higher profits, but there are more fundamental drivers. Expanding LDC populations need food. Growing industrial economies need energy.

In the 1950s, international trade in grains consisted largely of shipments from North America to Europe. The less developed countries were largely self-sufficient, though often at subsistence levels. By 2000, world grain production had more than doubled. Exports were 13 percent of total production—and they were going largely to the less developed world, where they have become a critical addition to diets with little margin above subsistence.

Petroleum trade is even more dramatic, but here the industrial countries are the vulnerable ones. International shipments by sea have reached 1.66 billion tons annually, which is about 46 percent of total production and nearly half of all ocean trade. (*Times* 2002)

Interdependence entails dependence on distant and uncertain sources for food to eat and energy to keep warm. It can force conflict. The Gulf War demonstrated that nations will go to war if they believe that their supply of energy is threatened.

The intensifying competition for water is another growing source of conflict, which becomes international when rivers or aquifers cross national boundaries.

Growth has led to this interdependence, which in turn breeds instability as the world faces the waning years of the Big Bonanza in food and energy production. The consequences will intensify with future growth and its uneven distribution. I will spell out that argument in the next section.

THE AGE OF MIGRATIONS

Three very different demographic trends are intersecting in the world today. The poor countries are growing, most of the industrial world is beginning to shrink, and the United States is growing rapidly largely because of immigration. Those trends, and the way they may intersect, pose very different issues in the three areas. I will address the three trends and then suggest policies whereby the United States may contribute to managing the problems being generated by the interplay of those mighty vectors.

THE POOR COUNTRIES

The United Nations Population Division expects the "less developed countries" (i.e. LDCs, or poor countries) to grow by two thirds by 2050—from 4.9 to 8.1 billion. This is despite some encouraging signs of fertility decline in most of those countries. (UN 2000; there will be a new, probably somewhat lower estimate in 2003).

Africa alone is projected to grow from 794 million to 2 billion. I don't think it will get there. It must import nearly 30 percent of the grain it consumes now, (FAOSTATS) and its growing population must compete for tightening world food supplies. Moreover, AIDS and the resurgence of diseases such as malaria and drug-resistant tuberculosis are raising death rates in the less developed world. The very improvements in health services that started the population explosion are being undermined. People have been flooding into third world cities that have grown six fold since 1950 and are now growing faster than ever. Those cities' services are breaking down.

Whatever the growth curve, there are already, probably, more than a billion people desperate to leave home and find work, with more to come. And, there or here, they are ready to work hard for almost any wage that keeps them alive.

Turmoil and Terrorism. We are preoccupied with terrorism and its sources right now. Its origins lie in population growth, and the future looks worse if that growth continues.

How can people become so angry they will destroy themselves to destroy others? Most people tend to be friendly when they are not threatened. Tensions grow and hostilities mount when they are competing for scarce goods and resources. The Middle East is mostly desert, with few natural resources except petroleum and gas. By and large, the populations in 1950 were living at subsistence level within those constraints. The oil boom and the population boom changed all that. Since then, Saudi Arabia has gone from three to 22 million people, the United Arab Emirates from 70,000 to 2.6 million (most of them foreigners). Jordan, without oil resources, has five million inhabitants now; it had fewer than 500,000 then. Most of the countries in the region have trebled.

Israel, at the center of the powder keg, has gone from 1.3 to six million. It is growing 2.4 percent each year. There are 900,000 Arabs in Israel and 3.2 million in Palestine, which is growing 3.83 percent per year—doubling in18 years. With few jobs and almost no resources, young Arabs are probably at a stage of anger we can hardly imagine.

Jobless college graduates in Egypt or Saudis with declining incomes find it hard enough to be poor. It is intolerable to be poor and see immense wealth around them, to have no job or any sense of purpose other than that provided by fundamentalist destroyers such as bin Laden.

The minuscule supply of water in that region has not increased, so per capita supplies are declining accordingly. The oil-rich can desalinate seawater for their own use, at a very high price. The poor do not have that luxury. As competition for water intensifies, so do the international tensions. The Jews are sequestering water supplies at the expense of the Palestinians, but the Palestinian West Bank is the source of the aquifers on which Israel depends. Aquifers in the Gaza Strip are turning saline. Water is a major issue between Israel and Syria, and with Jordan. The Turks have been putting dams on the Tigris and the Euphrates, threatening Syrian supplies and Iraq's irrigation systems.

The Middle East requires more and more imported food. In historical perspective, the oil boom is a transient affair. What will support them when the boom runs down?

The Arab world is the slowest of all regions, except Africa, to adopt family planning. That means that the poverty, the inequities and the shortage of water are going to become even more galling. Most poor countries would welcome more help in bringing human fertility under control (Statement 1995), but probably not in the Middle East. They are locked into their antagonisms, and family planning is a victim of competitive breeding.

Without a reversal of population growth, there is trouble ahead for all of us in that troubled region. An increasingly desperate populace, led by fanatics who still have access to oil wealth, is hardly a recipe for peace in an interconnected world.

We are coming to the end of the petroleum era, and terrorism will not change that, but it may make the process much more abrupt. Even a fanatic would probably want to sell oil, because his followers would need food and necessities. The more likely danger is that turmoil would interrupt the oil supplies on which the industrial world depends. During Desert Storm, the Iraqi Army managed to torch the oil wells in its path even when it was in full retreat. Japan, with almost no indigenous energy sources, is the most immediately vulnerable, but a significant interruption of oil from the Persian Gulf would create worldwide economic pandemonium.

Fundamentalism and Fanaticism. Terrorism is an extreme form of fundamentalism, which is naturally hostile to all non-believers. Neither science nor history offers much help in trying to understand why aggressive fundamentalist movements wax and wane and are now very much on the rise. Common sense suggests that they flourish when pragmatism seems to be failing to provide answers to the secular problems we face.

The LDCs may be in one of those turning points, now. Population growth is beginning to reverse the gains in income and nutrition of recent decades, and it is multiplying the competition for water, space and other necessities. The urbanized villager is deracinated, living outside traditional village ethics. He lives under worsening conditions, buffeted by forces he cannot understand or control. He may be jobless. His food and fuel arrive, uncertainly, from far away. These growing stresses and doubts may well turn their victims toward some oracular leader who offers answers and promises solutions, in this world or the next, in exchange for obedience.

THE RICH COUNTRIES

The industrial countries—except for the United States—have grown very modestly, and most are now beginning to decline. The United Nations Population Division guesses they will decline 13 percent by 2050, to 784 million, about where they were in 1970 (UN2000).

In itself, this decline would be a good thing. The European Union is relatively secure in its food supply. It is a net exporter of grains, but that security was achieved at very high cost. Food prices are artificially high to encourage production, which has led to extremely heavy use of manufactured fertilizers and pesticides. Indeed, European agriculture has reached the plateau I described earlier, and Europe is fortunate to look forward to a decline in its food needs, because a further increase in production is questionable.

Freed from the need to feed a growing population, the European Union is beginning to experiment with "extensive agriculture," cutting the subsidies to intensive agriculture. Perhaps lower food prices will hasten the trend to decreasing fertilizer use.

Japan, with an unfavorable food trade balance, has even heavier food subsidies and higher food prices than Europe. A declining population should encourage it to move in the same direction.

Both Europe and Japan are energy-short, but both are beginning the move away from fossil fuels toward nuclear and more benign energy sources.

Such trends are desirable, but the decline must stop. Those countries are being reshaped by a phenomenon that we did not anticipate. Women are enjoying their new independence. They have nearly stopped having children. Europe and Japan must decide how small they want to be and how they can stabilize at about that level. If they cannot raise fertility, they will face a Hobson's choice between immigration so massive that it will replace the existing stock, or the prospect of simply fading away. A functioning society is a complex thing. Can those civilizations survive massive demographic replacement?

Current experience suggests that they cannot. Migration into Europe has risen sharply since World War II. The European elites by and large welcomed the migrants, expecting them to meld into the society. That did not happen. The migrant groups, instead of integrating, created enclaves. Particularly for Islamic migrants, this segregation was fed by the gulf between their mores and customs and those of their hosts.

Resentment has been rising among the common folk of Europe who are affected and displaced by the migrants, and that resentment has been exploited by populist politicians. The current tensions are probably simply a harbinger of the tensions that would result from a systematic immigration program to compensate for low fertility.

Italy provides an extreme case. Italian women are averaging just 1.2 children. If their fertility does not rise, the population will plummet 87 percent in this century alone, passing below eight million by 2100, absent immigration. With a quick return to replacement level fertility (2.05 children) by 2020, the population would eventually stabilize at less than half its present level—which in itself would be an attractive prospect if Italy were not in an overpopulated world where population decline invites immigration.

If they try to supplement fertility with immigration, most Italians will eventually be "new Italians." However, replacement is likely, despite the tensions it will generate. There will be a vacuum as populations decline. Throughout the industrial world, a push/pull process is already driving immigration. Poor foreigners are desperate to come. They can see the attractions of the developed countries on TV; and modern transportation facilitates their movement. Businessmen want the cheap labor. Political leaders in aging countries will want workers.

Free trade will be a casualty if the industrial countries seek to restrict immigration and thus protect their workers' earnings, because their high priced labor already finds it hard to compete against poor countries' low wage labor, usually organized and trained by multinational corporations.

The industrial world may well wonder why nobody looked ahead and warned that we ourselves might be so profoundly affected by the poor countries' demographic explosion that we helped to start.

Where will fertility go? Young women are becoming a powerful group in the industrial countries, as political leaders beg and bribe them to have children. Will the leaders succeed? History suggests they will not. Pro-fertility policies in Europe have had very little success. Will women generally decide on their own to have more children, again? It is one of the great demographic unknowns of our era.

The present fertility decline will affect the more successful developing countries, too. A few, such as South Korea and Singapore, are already facing the same issues. However, population growth itself keeps the poorest countries from enjoying the general prosperity that has led to very low fertility.

The forces driving migration will continue and probably intensify over the next two generations—even if disease and hunger eventually stop population growth in the poor countries—unless the energy transition or some other crisis makes the industrial countries unattractive to migrants.

The overwhelming questions for Europe and Japan are, can they raise their own fertility? And can they control migration? Nations are used to dealing with migration, but not with fertility. Most women in history have probably seen their fertility as something that just happened. As they learned they can control it, they have been using that ability to achieve personal goals, not social ones. The idea that women's fertility is a social issue is rather new in human affairs.

THE PROFLIGATE GIANT

The United States is starting to resemble India and China in numbers, in the extreme inequalities between rich and poor, and eventually in its food balance. We are creating a future that we never debated. Our population—now about 293 million—is growing nearly four million per year, because immigration is running about 1.3 million per year and because the phenomenon of "shifting shares" drives fertility upward—i.e. overall fertility is rising, and the composition of the populace is changing, as more fertile groups come to constitute a larger fraction of the total population. Most immigration to the United States is coming from traditionally high fertility societies.

The Census Bureau middle population projection is 404 million in 2050 and 571 million in 2100, (Census 1999) but the 2000 census showed that growth is running ahead of the official estimates and puts us on the track of the high projection—1.2 billion by 2100—the present population of China. China is trying to stop growth, while we are not. How big we get depends largely on how long the migratory pressures continue and how the country responds to them.

Food Scarcity at Home? The United States is still the residual grain supplier to the world—we provide one-third of all the grain entering international trade—but before long we will need the grain we now export. Right now, we export about 26 percent of the grain we produce (FAOSTATS). If yields and our consumption habits stay as they are, we will need that grain ourselves in one generation (assuming the Census high projection) or two (assuming the middle projection). It will take a remarkable increase in grain yields, plus a dramatic dietary shift away from meat, to feed our own growing population through this century, to say nothing of exporting grain. And such increases in yields seem most unlikely in the face of the constraints I described earlier.

If there is free trade, world prices will rise, and the poorest will suffer, worldwide. With restrictions on U.S. exports (which we imposed once before on soybeans in the face of one poor harvest), the food deficit nations will face starvation and the United States will eventually face hunger. If we run out of food, there is no country that can supply our needs.

The world has an interest in the United States' ability to produce food. Simply hoping that we can return to the rising yields of a generation ago is a frail basis for policy. If we could stop population growth, we would have some confidence in our continuing ability to supply ourselves and others. If we could reverse our population growth, we would need less food and could turn to a more benign agriculture less dependent on artificial fertilizers, pesticides and technological innovations.

The Energy Trap. U.S. crude oil extraction continues its ineluctable downward course, from 9.637 million barrels per day in 1970 to 5.834 million in 2000 (USDOE/EIA 2000). We depend on imports for 62 percent of our crude oil. But President Bush's energy policy relies on more drilling to find more oil in the U.S. It is perhaps the most short-sighted energy policy imaginable. He dismisses his own experts' predictions of the drawdown of crude oil resources, he rejects the scientific consensus that fossil fuel burning is contributing to global warming, and he favors growth in Americans' already high consumption levels. He has thus condemned the world to faster and more devastating warming; and he has encouraged American industry to continue its energy-intensive ways, which will be thoroughly uneconomic in a world with rising energy prices.

Trifling With The Biosphere. Even more fundamental, the United States is the world's biggest single consumer and polluter. I have suggested that the growing human role in Earth's ecosystem threatens other organisms now and is beginning to threaten our own well-being and perhaps eventually our existence. The United States must bring its population growth and consumption levels under control if mankind is to reverse that trend.

THE WAY OUT OF THE TRAP

There is no reliable substitute for a decline in population and food demand, in the poor countries and in the United States.

A sane energy policy requires a prompt decrease in U.S. dependence on others and a fundamental shift from fossil energy to more benign sources. Both objectives would be served by reversing our population growth.

We need to act with other nations to bring some order to the introduction of chemicals into the biosphere. What should the United States do?

We should, belatedly, promote population planning assistance from a stepchild of our foreign aid program to its central feature. It would help the poor countries and offer us an eventual amelioration of migratory pressures. We should be urging other industrial countries to help the poorer countries stop their population growth. In effect, reverse our present national aid policies.

We must address an immigration policy gone out of control.

As to U.S. fertility: we must assure that all American women have access to family planning and an interest in limiting their family size. To simplify: go for the two-child family and net annual immigration in the 200,000 range, and population growth will gradually turn around. (Grant 1994)

At a more fundamental level, we should reexamine our national faith in growth, demographic and economic. We must ask ourselves: what are the consequences of our present courses of action?

Proponents justify growth by the need to accommodate the needs of expanding populations for food and jobs and a decent living. The argument is circular. If we did not need to provide for more people, the only justification for economic growth would be to improve the lot of the poor. And that could best be achieved if there were fewer of them. Western Europe and Japan show that population growth is not a prerequisite for prosperity.

In the United States, we are afraid to address fertility because one faction gets it entangled with the abortion argument and another faction sees it as "interference with women's right to control their own bodies." We are afraid to address immigration because for some it is a convenience and because some moralists see an obligation to give the stranger the opportunities we have had.

If we do not develop a vision of our future, and act on it, we may get where we are presently heading.

NOTES:

1. Census 1999. United States Census Bureau, Department of the Interior, Population Projections Branch, *Population Projections of the United States, 1999 to 2100*. Issued online December 1999 to January 2000; at http://www.census.gov.
2. Deffeyes 2001. Kenneth S. Deffeyes, *Hubbert's Peak: The Impending World Oil Shortage* (Princeton: Princeton University Press, 2001)
3. Duncan 2001. Richard C. Duncan, "World Energy Production, Population Growth, and the Road to the Olduvai Gorge," in *Population and Environment*, May 2001, pp. 503–522.
4. EIA 2000. U.S. Department of Energy, Energy Information Administration, *International Energy Annual 2000*, Table H1.
5. ENS 2000. Environmental News Service, 8-17-2000.
6. ENS 2002. Environmental News Service, 8-9-2002.
7. FAOSTATS. Food and Agriculture Organization, United Nations, FAOSTATS, no date (on-line statistical series at http://www.statistics.fao.org).
8. Grant 1994. Grant, L., "The Two Child Family," NPG FORUM (Washington: Negative Population Growth, Inc., May 1994.)
9. Grant 2000. Grant. L., *Too Many People: The Case for Reversing Growth*. USA, Santa Ana, CA, Seven Locks Press, 2000, pp. 36–42.
10. IEA 1998. International Energy Agency (IEA), Organization for Economic Cooperation and Development (OECD), quoted in Kerr (q.v.)
11. Kerr 1998. Kerr, Richard A., The Next Oil Crisis Looms Large—and Perhaps Close. *Science,* August 21, 1998, pp. 1128–1131.
12. Normile 1999. Normile, Dennis, Ocean Project Drills for Methane Hydrates. *Science,* November 19, 1999, p. 1456.
13. President's Acid Rain Review Committee, 1983. Executive Office of the President, Office of Science and Technology, news release June 28, 1983.
14. Science 2002. Jocelyn Kaiser, "Satellites Spy More Forest Than Expected," in *Science*, 8–9-2002, p. 919.
15. Smil 1991. Smil, Vaclav, Population Growth and Nitrogen: An Exploration of a Critical Existential Link. In: *Population and Development Review,* December 1991, pp.569–601.
16. Statement 1995. Statement on Population by World Leaders, signed by seventy-five heads of government and presented to the
17. United Nations Secretary General by Indonesian President Soeharto in October 1995. See Grant, L., *Juggernaut: Growth on a Finite Planet.* USA, Santa Ana, CA: Seven Locks Press, 1996, p. 150.
18. *Times* 2002. *Times Shipping Journa*l, 11-30-02.
19. UN 2000. United Nations, Department of Economic and Social Affairs, Population Division, *World Population Prospects: The 2000 Revision.* New York: United Nations, 2001.
20. U.S./DOE/EIA 2000. United States Department of Energy, Energy Information Administration, *Annual Energy Review 2000.* Washington: U.S. Department of Energy, 1999. Table 5-2.
21. USEPA 2002. United States Environmental Protection Agency (EPA), *Air Trends. Six Principal Pollutants, Graph "Comparison of Growth Areas and Emissions."* (www.epa.gov/airtrends/sixpoll.html, updated 9-12-02). See also *National Air Pollution Emission Trends, 1900–1998*, 3-2000, Chapter 3.
22. USGS 2000. United States Geological Survey, United States Department of the Interior, "USGS Reassesses Potential
23. World Petroleum Resources: Oil Estimates Up, Gas Down." Press release March 22, 2000. From *USGS World Petroleum Assessment 2000,* Online at http://energy.usgs.gov.

24. Vitousek 1986. Vitousek, Peter M., Ehrlich, A., Ehrlich, P., Human Appropriation of the Products of Photosynthesis. In *Bioscience*, June 1986, pp. 368–373.
25. World Bank 1996. Based on data from the *World Bank Atlas, 1996. p.20*.

FORECASTING THE UNKNOWABLE: THE U.N. "WORLD POPULATION PROSPECTS: THE 2002 REVISION"

Lindsey Grant

2003

The United Nations Population Division has put the highlights of its new population estimates and projections onto the Web.[1] Present world population is 6.3 billion. It is projected to rise to 8.9 billion by 2050, a number almost identical to the 1998 projection but 400 million below the 2000 version and slightly below the U.S. Census Bureau projection of 9.079 billion. The projection reflects (1) the expectation that fertility is heading below 2.1 in all but the poorest less developed countries (LDCs) and (2) the growing seriousness of AIDS.

The new report represents an ongoing effort to bring the projections into line with recent experience. That process is still incomplete. Uncertainties internal and external to the calculations raise several questions:

- *Will European fertility rise as anticipated?*
- *Will mortality continue to decline, particularly in the least developed countries, or will it rise and thus eventually bring population growth to a stop through the grim process of rising death rates rather than the benign process of reduced fertility?*
- *Do the projections still understate U.S. fertility and population growth?*

The report makes no effort to analyze the external forces that will affect mortality and migration.

THE NUMBERS

Population is expected to decline substantially in Europe and Japan.

The "least developed countries" will double. Africa, where most of them are located, is expected to double to 1.83 billion. The question arises; can they really get there?

The "medium" projection is the one the Population Division considers most likely and is the one discussed in this paper. The "high" and "low" projections reflect arbitrary average fertility levels one-half child higher and lower, respectively, than the "medium" projection, keeping the same assumptions about mortality and migration. The "constant" projection is a reminder of what would happen if fertility in all the world's countries should stay where it is now, instead of continuing to drop as it has been doing in most countries.

The world total for 2050 is 400 million less than was projected in 2000. Of the 400 million decline, about half reflects lower fertility expectations and half reflects the impact of AIDS. (Incidentally, the new total is almost identical to the one projected in 1998. The projections fluctuate as the authors' expectations change, and the projections were raised in 2000 because fertility, particularly in India, was not declining as anticipated.)

The report says that half of world population growth between now and 2050 will be in India, Pakistan, Nigeria, the United States, China, Bangladesh, Ethiopia and the Democratic Republic of the Congo, in that order. The United States is a member of that unhappy club—and not the least—because of migration.

Population growth is continuing to slow down in most of the world. This is some comfort for those of us who believe that world population is already too large. However, the world may already be at that grim point where growth will be constrained by ever-tighter resource and environmental problems. The Population Division—in all four projections—changes its fertility assumptions but assumes that mortality will continue to decline. I will suggest that mortality may play a greater role.

The Division's estimates of present population are a valuable compilation of world data, but they are not immune from error. Even in an industrial nation such as the United States, there is intense disagreement as to the accuracy of our Census counts. Population counts in the LDCs can be very casual and may be subject to differing political pressures. Nigerian population, for instance, has in the past been inflated by tribal efforts to multiply their population count to increase their power. In China and some other countries, the ratio of boy to girl babies is suspiciously high. Some of that difference may reflect lingering infanticide as families seek to have boy children, but more of it probably reflects under reporting of girl babies. (There is anecdotal evidence of that practice.) We should recognize that the real world numbers are far less precise than the detailed figures produced by the computers.

The projections are even more chancy—as areany projections of an unknowable future. The numbers simply encapsulate the Population Division's assumptions about trends in fertility, mortality and migration. The Division is engaged in a continuing but still incomplete adjustment of those assumptions to bring them into line with recent experience. The projections still do not completely reflect recent realities. And there is a

TABLE 1. ESTIMATED AND PROJECTED POPULATION OF THE WORLD, MAJOR DEVELOPMENT GROUPS AND MAJOR AREAS, 1950, 2000, 2003 AND 2050 ACCORDING TO FERTILITY VARIANT

	Estimated Population (millions)			*Population in 2050 (millions)*			
Major Area	*1950*	*2000*	*2003*	*Low*	*Medium*	*High*	*Constant*
World	2519	6071	6301	7409	8919	10633	12754
More developed regions	813	1194	1203	1084	1220	1370	1185
Less developed regions	1706	4877	5098	6325	7699	9263	11568
Least developed countries	200	668	718	1417	1675	1960	3019
Other less developed countries	1505	4209	4380	4908	6025	7303	8549
Africa	221	796	851	1516	1803	2122	3279
Asia	1398	3680	3823	4274	5222	6318	7333
Latin America and the Caribbean	167	520	543	623	768	924	1032
Europe	547	728	726	565	632	705	597
Northern America	172	316	326	391	448	512	453
Oceania	13	31	32	40	46	52	58

Source: Population Division of the Department of Economic and Social Affairs of the United Nations Secretariat (2003). *World Population Prospects: The 2002 Revision. Highlights.* New York: United Nations.

fundamental conceptual question: will the real world continue to behave as it has in recent decades?

FERTILITY

In the 1990s, the Statistical Division (with decreasing confidence) based its medium projection on the assumption that average fertility everywhere will arrive by 2050 at a level that would eventually stabilize population numbers. At the very low mortality levels we presently enjoy in the industrial world, that "replacement fertility" level is about 2.1 children per woman. It would lead to population stability (or, technically, "stationarity.") It portrays a serene future, without runaway growth or decline, in a prosperous, industrialized world.

There is no basis in demography for assuming that fertility will arrive at that level, or stay there. Fertility may gravitate toward a different level. More likely, it will fluctuate in decades to come, and between countries, as it has in the past. Replacement fertility is a mythical goal, better explained by psychological and political needs than by demographic logic. In a profoundly unstable world, we seek stability.[2]

The 2002 projection still seems to reflect a doomed effort to preserve some vestige of the dream of "replacement level fertility" while recognizing that there are wide disparities and that it doesn't fit the observed facts. Worldwide fertility in 2045–2050 is projected at 2.02, down from the previous projection of 2.15. The country-by-country fertility projections generally arrive at 1.85 (give or take a percentage point) except for those countries to which it is clearly inapplicable. This in effect substitutes a 1.85 target for 2.1.

Countries with 84 percent of the world's population are projected to be below replacement fertility level by 2050.

The Industrial World. For Europe, the "replacement fertility" fixation for years led the Population Division to underestimate population decline. It simply ignored the implications of declining European fertility, choosing instead to project a turnaround to 2.1 by 2045–2050. Probably it did so because, like most demographers, they simply could not believe that Europe was on a demographic path to extinction.

That convention has been progressively modified. Starting in 1998, the Division recognized that European and Japanese fertility levels were not on course toward 2.1 by 2050. In the new projection, rising fertility is still projected for Europe, but now it stops at 1.84. That projection still reflects hope rather than experience. European fertility was 1.41 in 1995–2000 and still falling.

For the whole industrialized world, fertility is projected to rise to 1.85 in 2045–2050, even though it has been low and declining for decades and is now at 1.58. (Those figures include the United States, which is sui generis. I will discuss it later.)

The LDCs. Fertility is projected at 2.04 in 2045–2050, down from the previous projection of 2.17. Excluding the least developed countries, LDC fertility is predicted at 1.90. The adjustment of future fertility results not so much from any dramatic recent evidence as from the realization that in many LDCs fertility is on a trajectory taking it below replacement level, as happened in the industrial world.

The "least developed countries." At the demographic extreme, the Division in 2000 belatedly recognized that the forty-eight (now forty-nine) poorest countries—with current fertility at 5.46—are most unlikely to reach 2.1 by 2050. It pegged their 2045–2050 fertility at 2.51—which in itself would be a remarkable decline. In 2002, the projection has been lowered very slightly, to 2.47.

Demographically, this fertility distribution is less arbitrary than a universal target of 2.1, and closer to current trends. Its implications, however, are much more complex and perhaps less reassuring.

On the plus side, the projected fertility levels would lead to a declining world population at the end of this century. That would bring human numbers into a better balance with the Earth?s support system. If population declines sufficiently, per capita incomes in most of the world can improve, and the present terrible imbalance between living standards in the industrialized countries and the LDCs can be ameliorated. A declining population generates its own problems, but it offers the hope of a better world.

However, with fertility of 1.85 in the industrial world and 1.90 among the more prosperous LDCs, the poorest will inherit the Earth. Having abandoned the myth of a universal convergence at replacement level, the Population Division now recognizes that differential fertility will be with us indefinitely, which brings us face to face with the phenomenon known as “shifting shares.” In the midst of a general population decline, those countries with fertility above replacement level will grow and replace less fertile groups. Theoretically, at some distant time, if they stay above replacement level, they will raise world fertility and even world population again.

Is that possible? Within the conceptual limits of demography, it is almost inevitable. The new report notes that the thirty-eight countries with fertility above 2.1 in 2050 will constitute 16 percent of the world’s total population at that time, up from their present eight percent. This is the statistical result of “shifting shares.”

That distant and frightening threat may, however, evaporate. It can disappear happily if the most fertile come to recognize that they are being kept poor by their own fertility, or grimly if the conditions in the poorest countries reach the point where mortality rises enough to outweigh their fertility. I will later suggest that mortality in the poorest countries may not decline according to the U.N. expectations. If it actually rises, replacement level fertility will rise with it. (After all, replacement level fertility was probably more than four children in the United States when the Republic was founded.) Their population growth may thus slow down and eventually be stopped by the resource constraints I will describe below, but their people may, in desperation, emigrate in increasing numbers.

There is no really satisfactory way to predict fertility. Unlike mortality, it does not respond predictably to changes in conditions. Trends change. One cannot safely project current fertility, nor can one graph a curve of past fertility changes to predict the future, because the curves lead quickly to absurdities. Perhaps the safest approach is an empirical one, taking account of current trends but making value judgments as to when they must flatten out or reverse. This approximates the U.S. Census Bureau?s approach. It works fairly well but, like all projections, it requires constant adjusting.

A final note on the fertility projections: the Population Division is well aware that its projections depend on world efforts to address fertility. It warned that the medium projection for the LDCs is unrealistic unless there are continuing efforts to provide family planning.

MORTALITY

The Population Division has long assumed that life expectancy will rise (and mortality will decline) indefinitely. That has been true almost everywhere in recent generations, but perhaps a closer look is needed at the happy assumption that it will continue.

The report raises worldwide life expectancy at birth from sixty-five years in 1995–2000 to seventy-five years in 2045–2050. The developed countries go from seventy-five to eighty-two years. The LDCs go up from sixty-three to seventy-three, and within that group the least developed countries go from forty-nine to sixty-six. Those last two projections are somewhat lower than two years ago, suggesting that the Division is becoming a bit less sanguine.

Still, the dramatic longevity projection for the poorest countries seems to defy the evidence of worsening conditions in those countries. The report itself noted that sub-Saharan Africa saw a decline of life expectancy from forty-nine to forty-seven years during the 1990s. It attributed that decline to AIDS, but other diseases and hunger may have played a role. Faced with such numbers, one wonders how the Population Division arrived at a 35 percent increase in the least developed countries' longevity by 2050.

To dramatize my point, look at two specific countries.

- Bangladesh is projected to grow from a crowded 142 million now (in which perhaps 20 percent live in flood-prone, typhoon-prone disaster areas) to 255 million in 2050—in a country smaller than Wisconsin. The growth will happen despite a sharp fertility decline from 3.5 to 1.85. Life expectancy is expected to rise from sixty-one years to seventy-five years. Is that projection credible?
- Ethiopia, with 71 million people now, is projected to rise to 171 million in 2050, even though fertility (which has not changed significantly since records have been kept) is expected to decline from 6.1 to 2.55. Life expectancy is projected to rise from forty-six to sixty-one years. That projection—to be charitable—is at the outside edge of the credible, for a country already suffering serious and rising food deficits even in good years, and with famines a regular occurrence. It becomes incredible in the "high" projection, which leads to a population of 198 million, and absurd in the "constant fertility" projection, which is 324 million.

Such projections are simply an act of faith. It would be more reasonable to expect that mortality will skyrocket and population growth will stop and perhaps reverse. It is a chilling prospect.

The projections ignore multiple changes occurring in the world—including the consequences of population growth itself. They will affect mortality. The Division periodically convenes groups of experts to examine its assumptions. The problem is that the experts are all demographers, and demographers as a group tend to be insensitive to the forces that drive mortality and migration. Perhaps the Division should include some public health specialists, urban sociologists, environmental biologists, agronomists, air and water specialists and climatologists in its meetings.

Health. The U.S. Surgeon General in 1969 told Congress "The war against infectious diseases is effectively finished."

In 2000, a generation later, Dr. James Hughes, Director of the National Center for Infectious Diseases at the Centers for Disease Control and Prevention (CDC), said that "The microbes are challenging us in ways we wouldn't have imagined ten years ago and for which we're not prepared."[3]

The quotations stand for themselves. We have learned that we are not in command, as we thought we were. The microbes have regrouped and counterattacked.

The Population Division has addressed AIDS. In the new report, it has studied the 53 most severely afflicted countries and calculated that their population will be 480 million smaller in 2050 than it would have been without AIDS. But it concludes that the epidemic will be brought under control by 2010 and that only lingering pockets will remain in 2050. The optimism seems questionable.

The report does not foresee any epidemics beyond AIDS, but the World Health Organization (WHO) has identified several major diseases that constitute a greater threat, such as (1) the new drug-resistant strains of tuberculosis, or (2) malaria, which is estimated to attack some 500 million people a year, mostly African children, and to cause some 2.5 million deaths.[4] And new threats constantly appear, such as the lethal new epidemic SARS.

The American Chemical Society's worldwide registry of chemicals listed 22 million chemicals in 1999, four times the number in 1980. Some of them are medicines and presumably good for our health, but others are known to be dangerous. Few of them have been systematically tested for direct health effects, and almost none have been tested for secondary effects on health or the environment. We are multiplying the environmental sources of illness, even as we learn that minute quantities of chemicals can affect human health.[5]

Crowding. The health problem is compounded by rapid urbanization, particularly of the LDCs, where cities have exploded from 300 million to 2.2 billion since 1950 and are expected to grow by another 1.6 billion by 2030. Urban services have not kept pace, and it is a tribute to modern medicines that epidemics have so far been kept fairly well under control.

Water. Growing shortages of water compound the problems of providing water and sanitation in those exploding cities.

WHO predicts that by 2025 some 2.7 billion people "will face severe shortages of fresh water" and five billion will face shortages, in "a looming crisis that overshadows nearly 2/3rds of the Earth's population."[6] That threat is not just to human health. Irrigation takes over 70 percent of human water consumption, and shortages mean less food.

Food. World agricultural production in the past half century experienced a rise unlike anything in human history. That growth has been the principal support for a near trebling of human numbers. There was a 15 percent increase in cultivated acreage, more than a doubling of irrigated acreage, a six fold increase in the use of commercial fertilizers, a bigger increase in chemical pesticides, and a remarkable propagation of improved crop varieties.[7]

Those sources of growth of food production are tapering off or finished. Grain yields grew faster than population growth from the 1950s until the 1980s, but much slower in the 1990s. Cultivated acreage is decreasing in the industrial world and stagnant in the LDCs. Irrigated acreage, worldwide, has almost stopped growing, and it is constrained by the accumulation of salts in irrigated soils, and of course by the tightening competition for water. The United States and China, and probably many other countries, are diverting water from irrigation to urban needs. Commercial fertilizer use in the industrialized world has been declining since the 1980s, because heavy use did not produce enough food to pay for itself. There are hopes that genetic modification will reinvigorate plant breeding, but the technique is still unproven, chancy, and bitterly resisted in many quarters.

Commercial farming itself is under attack for the disturbance to environmental systems caused by its release of chemicals and pesticides, its damage to soils, and the intense pollution generated by operations like factory hog and poultry farms.

The basic sources of food are arable land, range fed livestock, and wild fishery. Expedients such as aquaculture actually compete with traditional crops for grains and arable land, and are extremely polluting to boot. The three sources are already being overexploited, and there are no magic solutions in sight to enable the world to continue the dramatic growth in production that has supported population growth.

The European Union is actually trying to scale back intensive commercial agriculture, but the growing populations of the LDCs do not have that option. They need all the food they can get. Contrary to popular wisdom, the LDCs have become net food importers. Some are totally dependent on imports, or nearly so. Africa, and the least developed countries generally, are in the worst shape. The industrialized regions (except Japan) are exporters, on balance. The United States provides some 26 percent of all the grains entering the world market. U.S. population is growing fast, and—barring a remarkable increase in U.S. grain production or a renunciation of our meat diet—that source will be drying up as our own consumption increases.

The demographers should meet the agronomists. Anybody who projects rising life expectancy in coming generations needs to answer the question: what will they eat?

Climate. There is very little doubt now that human activities are warming the climate, though there is much to learn about the details and the regional changes. There is a debate as to the net effect of climate warming on food production in middle and northern latitudes, because increasing carbon dioxide tends to promote plant growth (within limits), while droughts, floods and heat waves do not—and climate warming means more such weather. There is no real disagreement among the experts that climate warming is making agriculture more perilous in the lower latitudes where most of the world's population lives.

That calculation should be factored into expectations of future human mortality. It adds force to the question I asked above: what will they eat?

Aging. The report points out that "In more developed regions, the population aged 60 or over currently constitutes 19 percent of the population; by 2050 it will account for 32 percent of the population. In the less developed regions, the proportion of the population aged 60 or over will rise from 8 percent in 2000 to close to 20 percent in 2050." Here, from within the demographers' own precinct, comes another warning. The aged are a particularly vulnerable group. If an effort is made to maintain health services for this growing population, the services will be spread increasingly thin. If the effort is not made, the mortality of the aged presumably will rise. The sheer magnitude of the problem, and the intergenerational conflict posed by the needs of the aged, make one wonder whether they will continue to get the resources they now receive.

The Impact of Growth Itself. In the U.N. projections, population growth has no effect on mortality. All the projections assume that life expectancy in the LDCs will be 16 percent higher in 2045–2050 than in 1995–2000, even though (for example) water resources per capita—the mirror image of population growth—will be down 23 percent in the low projection, 37 percent in the medium projection, 47 percent in the high projection and 58 percent in the constant fertility projection. (Those figures are optimistic, because deforestation, urbanization, and the draw down of groundwater reserves will presumably reduce total available water supplies.) It is hard to believe that mortality will be the same for all the projections, or that any of them will lead to rising longevity.

Tropical forest resources are being cut down at a rising rate. We are running out of the petroleum/gas era and must find other sources of ***energy and chemical feedstocks***, which will necessarily impose some very difficult stresses and adjustments, and probably armed conflicts.

In Sum . . . Taken together, this is an impressive set of trends that will raise mortality, or at least forestall the predicted gains. The Population Division mortality projections rely on some unexplained deus ex machina, medical or technological, which is not identified. They do not deal with the looming realities. We cannot predict what the numbers will be, but we have reason to believe that population growth will be constrained more by mortality levels than the Division predicts.

It would be difficult for the Population Division to incorporate all these issues into its projections, simply because they are so complex and unpredictable, and because of the controversy that would attend any estimate. On the other hand, the Division is in fact taking a position on all of them by assuming that they are not serious enough to diminish the anticipated improvement in mortality.

Perhaps the most prudent projection would take note of those other experts' testimony and assume that those problems may stop or dramatically slow down the recent improvement in mortality.

MIGRATION

Until the early 1990s, the UN simply ignored international migration. Then it introduced migration into the projections but made the assumption that it would soon taper off and stop. In 2000, for the first time, the projections suggested that it would continue. The new study projects the major flows at their current rate through 2050. Net immigration into the United States is estimated at 1.1 million annually. For Germany, the figure is 211,000, for Canada 173,000, for the United Kingdom 136 thousand, and Australia 83 thousand. The major net senders are identified as China at 303,000, Mexico at 267,000, India at 222,000, the Philippines at 184,000 and Indonesia at 180,000. There are other, lesser flows, including those between poorer and richer LDCs.

The migration projections approximate the present realities. The receiving countries are not effectively controlling immigration, their businesses like the cheap labor, political leaders in aging societies will welcome new workers, and sending countries regularly promote emigration as a way of easing their population pressures. The working age population (fifteen to sixty-four) in the LDCs is expected to grow by 1.8 billion by 2050, and there is little hope that there will be enough jobs for them in their home countries. On the other hand, migration is creating growing political resentment among working people in Europe and—to judge by the polls—in the United States.[8]

In short, although the present projection is an improvement over the earlier practice, international migration will be perhaps the most volatile and unpredictable demographic vector for the foreseeable future. It will particularly affect the industrial countries because it is larger relative to their total population than it is for the LDCs. And it is already profoundly affecting the United States, because migration presently drives our population growth.

"SHIFTING SHARES" IN THE U.S.

The U.N. statistics treat each country as a single demographic entity. The U.S. Bureau of the Census runs separate projections for different racial and ethnic groups in the United States and then combines those projections.[9] It can thereby chart the relative size of those groups as time passes. Its methodology predicts "shifting shares" within the country, not just among countries.

The U.N. has chronically underestimated U.S. growth, both by underestimating future immigration and failing to take account of "shifting shares." In 1998, it thought U.S. population would reach 348 million by 2050. In 2000, it recognized that immigration is unlikely to stop, and it raised the projection to 397 million. In 2002, the projection is 409 million. It predicts that U.S. fertility will be down to 1.85 in 2045–2050, well below the current 2.1.

The Census Bureau also has tended to underestimate U.S. population growth, because it has underestimated current immigration. Its methodology does, however, incorporate the impacts of "shifting shares" as more fertile groups multiply and become a larger share of the population. For 2050, overall fertility in its Middle series is 2.219, raised primarily by the growing Hispanic population, which has a current fertility of 3.0. Its Middle estimate of total population in 2050 has tentatively been raised to 420 million. It will probably be raised again, because new data show that the Hispanic population is larger than expected, and growing faster, and its fertility is rising rather than falling.

The Population Division might consider using the Census Bureau's methodology for countries with distinct ethnic groups with markedly different fertility rates. As the Census calculations suggest, domestic as well as international "shifting shares" raise the growth projections.

CONCLUSIONS

The doubts I have raised would push the projections in different directions. If European fertility stays where it is, Europe will be growing smaller, faster. If LDC fertility does not drop so far, it will speed their population growth and the world's. External forces may drive mortality upwards and population growth downwards, particularly in the poorest countries. The United States is growing faster than either the Statistical Division or the U.S. Census Bureau expected, and growth projections will have to be raised again.

Those adjustments may balance each other out in some ways. They may well lead to a 2050 world population somewhere around nine billion, or less, but it would be a very different world. Forecasting is an elusive art. Demographic projections often seem to be immune from the fluctuations of real life. The questions that will shape our demographic futures are being asked mostly by non-demographers. Will there be enough water and enough food for rising populations? Will epidemics and the proliferation of chemicals be counterbalanced by the continuing advance of medical knowledge? Will climate change diminish the support capacity of world ecosystems and reduce population growth within the time period under review? Or later?

We may never have all the answers to those questions in advance, but we would come closer if we began to integrate our demographic projections with the findings that are being made in other disciplines.

For anybody with a sense of humanity, it is an agonizing time. The issue has long been—not whether population growth will go on forever—but whether it will be brought to a stop by nature and the rise of mortality or by the more benign path of conscious human decisions to limit fertility. The choice is stark: Europe and Japan have opted for the benign alternative. For the LDCs, and particularly for the poorest, the chance to make that choice is ebbing away. The numbers I have cited for Bangladesh and Ethiopia make that point. And the rich countries will not escape the consequences of their desperation. I think the U.N. statisticians implicitly recognize those realities. Perhaps they should spell them out.

NOTES:

1. See www.un.org/esa/population/unpop.htm for the Highlights and Annex Tables. Nation-by-nation figures are not systematically included in this preliminary report, but can be accessed by punching the "data" button at the website. The complete printed text is scheduled for publication during 2003.
2. Lindsey Grant, *Juggernaut: Growth on a Finite Planet* (Santa Ana, Seven Locks Press, 1996, pp. 10–11.)
3. Associated Press 4-27-2000.
4. World Health Organization, quoted by Environmental News Service E-Wire 11-29-2000. The U.S. National Institutes of Health offers a less precise estimate embracing the same numbers, and adds that global warming threatens to spread the disease more widely in the southern United States. Environmental News Service, 8-2-2001.
5. For an extended treatment of recent evidence supporting the statements in this entire section, see Lindsey Grant, *Too Many People: The Case for Reversing Growth* (Santa Ana: Seven Locks Press, 1996) and *Diverging Demography*, Converging Destinies (NPG FORUM, January 2003).
6. AP 3-22-2002, "UN Warns of Severe Water Shortages."
7. These numbers are approximate. The 1950 base is extrapolated from 1961, when the Food and Agriculture Organization (FAO) FAOSTAT data series start.
8. In a Roper Poll on 3-7-2003, 76 percent of the respondents thought immigration should be less than one million and 85 percent considered illegal immigration to be a "serious problem."
9. See the international population projections revised on 10-10-2002 at www.census.gov /ipc/www/idbnew.html.

IT'S THE NUMBERS, STUPID!

Lindsey Grant

November 2003

In 1992, Candidate Bill Clinton's election campaign manager is said to have tacked a paper to the bulletin board with the slogan: "It's the economy, stupid!" I will borrow that blunt but effective message for this paper. From coast to coast, crowding has become a central issue at the local level, but—almost universally—the issue is argued without any recognition of the force that drives it: national population growth, which in turn is driven by immigration and by the high fertility of many of the immigrants. Only Congress can get at the fundamental cause of the crowding. The unhappy victims of crowding should direct their fire, not at their neighbors but at Congress.

THE PROBLEMS OF CROWDING

There is an intensifying conflict between people whose lives are being made worse by crowding and the developers and entrepreneurs who seek to profit from growth. From NPG and elsewhere, I have collected over 1500 news stories during the past three years about crowding in growth areas of the United States. The range of issues is enormous: rising housing prices and the displacement of the less prosperous; urban sprawl, stalled traffic and the "transportation crisis"; infrastructure costs and rising taxes; the deterioration of public and social services; the impact of massive housing developments; rising school populations and inadequate schools; worsening local air quality; the polarization of local politics and the deadlock of government; rising unemployment in some areas and the dislocations caused by new industry in others; the spread of paving and the attendant problems of runoff and flooding; the failure of water supplies; the destruction of woodlands, farmland and natural landscapes; the sense of a lost quality of life and the feeling that growth has somehow gone bad.

Those articles deal exhaustively with the proximate sources of the complaints—such as a new development or shopping center, rising school populations, the construction of superhighways (or the lack of them), diminishing rivers and aquifers. They are all silent about the underlying driving force. A conservation group announces that excessive consumption is draining rivers across the country—and it blames "U.S. irrigation habits, urban sprawl, increased groundwater pumping and loss of wetlands . . . more often than not government policies . . ." and excessive municipal consumption.[1] Not a word about population growth.

National population growth is driven largely by high levels of migration and by the high fertility of some of the immigrants. International migration generates internal migration as people seek to escape the problems of the cities, creating successive waves of movement.

TEMPORIZING WITH GROWTH

The slogan "smart growth" has become fashionable among planners. The idea is that sprawl can be averted, and more people accommodated, and rural space can be protected, if we can simply persuade people to live more densely packed. Efficient, yes. It permits more people to be accommodated at a lower direct and social cost, and it slows the loss of farmlands and forests. Moreover—although its proponents seldom notice this advantage—it prepares us for the end of the petroleum era, when automobiles will probably become a prohibitively costly way for most people to shop and commute.

However, efficiency is not necessarily happiness. Americans tend to like to have space around them, and that gets harder as population grows. Japanese in their tiny apartments—or chickens in a modern chicken factory—are paradigms of efficient housing, but they don't much like it. In the long term, "smart growth" simply accommodates more growth and rising tensions if we do not turn off the engines that drive growth.

And "smart growth" is not benign even in the short term if it facilitates growth. As one study noted, "smart growth" aggravates the pollution problems of the Chesapeake Bay because more people, moving into new urban settlements, generate more piped sewage which, in turn, increases the flow of nitrogen into the Bay.[2]

THE SOURCE OF GROWTH

The population of the United States grew by 32.7 million between the 1990 and 2000 Censuses, the largest growth decade in our history. The rate of growth was 1.28 percent per annum, a higher rate than any since the 1960s. Numerically, we added another California in ten years.

The Role of Immigration. The Census Bureau thinks that net annual immigration has averaged 976,000 since 1996—about one-third of total growth. The U.N. Population Division puts the level at 1.1 million. A private research group puts it at "more than 1.2 million."[3]

The numbers are remarkably fuzzy, because:

- Many de facto immigrants are admitted on temporary visas, and little or no effort is made to learn whether they ever leave.
- Illegal immigrants have reason to avoid being counted.
- We gave up trying to count emigrants in 1957.
- Legal immigration is in part the regularization of illegal migrants who were already part of the population for Census purposes—if we could count them.

Whatever the number, that is only a partial figure. The demographic impact of immigration includes both the immigrants and their descendants. The Census Bureau does a Middle projection of U.S. population and then runs a Zero Net Migration series (which is the Middle projection without any migration after 1999). By 2050, the Middle projection is 404 million. The Zero Net Migration projection is 328 million—a difference of 76 million in fifty years. In other words, 62 percent of the projected growth is the consequence of new immigration. Those projections are conservative because they were based on underestimates of recent immigration and immigrant fertility; they are being revised upward.

The Middle projection for 2100 is 570 million, and it too will have to be revised. We are moving toward population levels we used to associate with China and India. Is that where we want to go?

Fertility and Shifting Shares. Though the statistics on migration flows are fuzzy, we can get some sense of the impact by studying what is happening to different ethnic groups and their fertility.

Fertility among non-Hispanic White women has been well below replacement level since the 1970s. Their total fertility rate (TFR) is now at 1.84 children per woman, just about what it was in 1990, and the total number of children born to them each year has declined, because the population is aging. Among non-Hispanic Blacks, the TFR has declined by a dramatic 18 percent since 1990. It now stands exactly at replacement level, 2.1 children. The experience among American Indian women is even more startling. Their fertility has fallen by 20 percent since 1990 and now stands at 1.75, which is well below the fertility of non-Hispanic Whites—although poor populations such as the AmerIndians traditionally have higher fertility than the rich and educated.

At those rates, U.S. population growth would stop and turn around in a few years without immigration.

The situation of our Hispanic population is dramatically different. It has almost trebled from 14.6 million in 1980 to 38.8 million today, making it the largest minority. (As a percentage of the total population, it has risen from 6.4 to 13.4.) Part of that growth is immigration. Part of it is high fertility. In 2001, Hispanic fertility in the United States was 2.7 children—higher than Mexican fertility, and far above replacement level. It had declined only 7 percent since 1990, and it has been flat or slightly rising in the past three years.[4]

About half of all immigration is Hispanic. Some other sources of migration such as Africa, the Philippines and the Arab world also have high fertility, but we do not have the data to run a similar analysis on them.

The Census Bureau thought that the fertility of immigrants' descendants would descend to the overall U.S. level. That has not been happening. In fact, convergence is working the other way. As the immigrants become an increasing part of the U.S. population, they pull overall U.S. fertility upward.

To limit immigration is not to demand that it stop. It plays useful roles in an interdependent modern world. "It's the numbers, stupid." If non-Hispanic White and Black and American Indian fertility stay as low as they are, and if Hispanic fertility can be brought down to those levels, we could welcome 200,000 or so immigrants each year and still enjoy a slow population decline to more reasonable levels.

Will Hispanic fertility decline? The U.S. Government has long encouraged lower fertility in less developed countries, but not at home. Ideally, it should embrace a policy of "Stop at two," and it should adopt nondiscriminatory incentives and disincentives to encourage women and families to do so. Such a policy is hardly on the political horizon.

Hispanic fertility in this country is unique in the industrial world. Elsewhere—including Roman Catholic Spain, Italy and Quebec—fertility plummeted far more than would be needed here, as women on their own addressed the penalties imposed by large families. Perhaps some such change will occur among Hispanic women here. Perhaps.

REPUBLOCRATS VS. THE PEOPLE

The Odd Couple. There is an odd alliance setting immigration policy. Business wants cheap and docile labor. Some idealistic people do not want to limit immigration because "they should have the same chance we did." Having those idealists on their side is a great convenience for business interests because it provides the moral justification for a policy that serves their pocketbooks.

The Persistence of an Unpopular Policy. Immigration is not popular. For years, opinion polls have regularly shown a large majority of the respondents favoring lower immigration levels, but they have not had a perceptible influence on Congress.[5]

Hispanic Opinion and Political Misperceptions. The Hispanic population size has achieved a critical mass, and both parties now court the Hispanic vote. The problem is that the parties are listening to the self-proclaimed Hispanic leaders—whose own interests are advanced if Hispanic populations grow—rather than to the Hispanic public. I know of only two serious in-depth opinion studies analyzing Hispanic attitudes on immigration, and both date from the early 1990s. They found that some 60 percent to 80+ percent of Hispanics from different national origins wanted immigration reduced.[6] One can understand why Hispanics felt that way. Many of them are unskilled or semi-skilled workers, and they compete directly with new immigrants.

Class and Attitude. The divergence between elite and public attitudes is not limited to the Hispanics. There is a remarkable difference between the way that immigration is viewed by the elite and by the general public. The Chicago Council on Foreign Relations for years has sponsored a unique Gallup poll comparing attitudes of "the public" with the views of the business, political and intellectual "leaders" on foreign policy issues. In 1995, 84 percent of the public but just 51 percent of the leaders saw the preservation of American jobs as an important foreign policy objective. Immigration and refugees were seen as "a critical threat" by 74 percent of the public but only 31 percent of the leaders. Controlling illegal immigration was seen as "a very important goal" by 73 percent of the public but only 28 percent of the leaders. A subsequent poll in 2002 found that the present level of immigration was seen as a critical threat by 60 percent of the public but only 13 percent of the leaders. The sense of threat has receded somewhat, but the gap between public and leadership attitudes has widened.[7]

The upper middle-class people who lead many moral crusades tend to be silent on this one, because they can find cheap and compliant labor among the immigrants, particularly the illegal ones. They enjoy the low prices resulting from cheap labor. The immigrants they see are likely to be pleasant and likeable and no threat to them.

The Politics of Money. According to the adage, politicians' first responsibility is to get elected. They need money to get elected, and generally they respond more to money and to those who have it than to the popular will. The Center for Immigration Studies cites the decision to expand the H-1b visa program, which allows companies to replace high-priced American technicians with cheaper foreign technicians, mostly from India. Rep. Tom Davis, one of the sponsors, admitted candidly that "This is not a popular bill with the public. It's popular with the CEOs . . . This is a very important issue for the high-tech executives who give the money."[8] The bill passed the Senate 96-1, even though Sen. Bob Bennett observed that many senators supported it only because they were "tapping the high-tech community for campaign contributions."

Democrat legislators tend to score better than Republicans when rated by environmental groups, but an end to population growth is the starting point for environmental improvement, and Democrats do even worse than Republicans if one tallies their votes on legislation that affects immigration and child-bearing.[9]

There is trouble ahead when our elected officials respond to money rather than to the people. In Europe, popular frustration with the unwillingness of governments to address immigration has led to the rise of populist demagogues taking extreme anti-immigrant positions. The political landscape in this country may shift, regrettably, in that direction.

CAN THE POPULAR WILL CHANGE THE POLITICS?

The current political scene is no cause for optimism. The people who suffer most from population growth are poor and unskilled. Money talks. The political calculus may change if unemployment continues to rise and begins to hurt the more prosperous (as it already hurts engineers and computer programmers). The complaints may become more insistent, and Congress may begin to hear them.

But we don't need to wait for a depression to address the problem. The crowding that afflicts suburban and exurban America is a problem of the prosperous, but most of them do not see its source. The message to those people is: You are hacking at the branches, not the root. Your problem starts, not with the shopping mall or rising local taxes or water shortages, but with the population growth that drives those symptoms. The population growth is a function of migration. Immigration policy is made by Congress. State and local governments could do much more than they now do to encourage and help the federal government to enforce the immigration laws we now have, but the fundamental decisions rest with Washington. Take your problem to your senators and congressman. You cannot solve it locally.

NOTES:

1. American Rivers, "America's Most Endangered Rivers," quoted in Environmental News Service, 4-10-03.
2. Larry Carson, "Control of Growth vs. Harm to Environment. Sewage: Smart Growth's Success Could Add to Nitrogen Problems in the Chesapeake Bay" (Baltimore Sun, 6-4-01).
3. U.S. Bureau of the Census, www.census.gov/population/projections/nation/summary/up-t6-a.txt. U.N. Statistical Division, *World Population Prospects: the 2002 Revision*. Steven A. Camarota, "Immigrants in the United States –2000" (Washington: Center for Immigration Studies, January 2001)
4. National Center for Health Statistics, "National Vital Statistics Reports," Vol. 51, No.4, 2-6-2003, Table 2 and Figure 1. Final data for 2001. Fertility rates have been revised to reflect the discovery in Census 2000 that U.S. population growth, particularly of Hispanics, had been substantially underestimated.
5. For example, Roper ASW "Immigration Perceptions," March 7–9, 2003, sponsored by NPG, reported that 67 percent of the respondents thought that immigration should be less than 600,000 per year, 85 percent of respondents regarded illegal immigration as a serious problem, and 67 percent said that Congress should set a goal of reducing it to near zero. The numbers are similar to Roper Poll results going back to the 1970s.
6. *Latino National Political Survey Report*, "Latinos Speaking in Their Own Voices" (Released 12-15-1992 by a multi-university consortium sponsored by the Ford, Rockefeller, Spencer and Tinker Foundations), table 7.24. A parallel Ford Foundation study found majorities of 66 percent (Cuban) to 79 percent (Puerto Rican) favoring reduced immigration.
7. John E. Reilly, Ed., "American Public Opinion and U.S. Foreign Policy" (Chicago Council on Foreign Relations, 1995) and www.worldviews.org/dailyreportsusreport/html/ch5s5.html for the 2002 study.
8. Mark Krikorian, "The Year In Immigration" (Washington: Center for Immigration Studies. 2001).

9. For a systematic tally of Congressional votes on environment and population issues in 2000–2001, see Comprehensive U.S. Sustainable Population (CUSP), "Scorecard for the 107th Congress." On the web at www.uscongress-enviroscore.org. Or contact CUSP President Alan Kuper, 216-229-2413, cuspscore@earthlink.net.

HUMANITARIAN IMMIGRATION: THIRD WORLD "PERSECUTION" SWAMPS THE WEST

David Simcox

January 2004

EXECUTIVE SUMMARY

Humanitarian-induced immigration, in its many diverse channels, has grown to account for an estimated 20 percent of the 1.3 million foreign born now settling in the U.S. each year. Other democratic industrial nations of the West face even greater flows relative to their smaller populations. The power of the refugee lobby, rising migration hunger overseas, and ever more generous readings of refugee law portend rapid future growth. For three decades the U.S. has compensated for the overtaxed formal refugee and asylee pipeline with a series of measures to allow in far more humanitarian claimants for ostensibly "temporary" forms of protection, such as Temporary Protected Status (TPS), or by disguised amnesties.

The U.S. asylum system has become the "hole in the fence" for millions of dubious claimants—and a major immigration magnet in itself. For patronage-hungry legislators in an age of ethnic identity politics, humanitarian admissions are choice pork. Vague legislation and aggressive litigation by the human rights bar, feminists and gays have persuaded the courts to open asylum to new victim groups. If the U.S. is to meet legitimate demands for protection without accepting population-swelling mass settlement, much tougher screening is needed, such as rigorously limited temporary stays; offshore protection of claimants; tight limits on appeals; and narrower definitions of persecution.

Former Senator Alan Simpson called it "compassion fatigue."

The one-time Chair of the Senate Immigration subcommittee was describing the American public's weariness with the seemingly unending arrival of waves of refugees and asylees on our shores needing acceptance and public support. The term captures the fatigue many feel toward a demanding task one can never finish, one can't quit, and one didn't ask for—a task that seems to grow, not diminish, with each wave of new demands met.

HAS INTERNATIONAL REFUGEE LAW OUTGROWN THE WEST?

Arrivals of new immigrants and births to children of immigrants already here now account for about two-thirds of America's population growth. The U.S. added nearly 33 million people in the decade of the '90s and 20 million were immigrants or their U.S. born children.

Formal admissions of refugees and asylees, which is only a fraction of overall humanitarian entries, came to about 105,000 in 2002, about 11 percent of all legal immigration. Between 1945 and 2001, 3.6 million refugees and asylees were formally settled in the U.S. These numbers, though an important force in postwar U.S. population growth, are probably about half of the actual influx of humanitarian or humanitarian-induced immigration since the 1980s. How did it get to be this way?

The U.S. signed the Universal Declaration of Human Rights of 1948, which ambitiously proclaims in Article 14 the right of every person in the world to "seek *and to enjoy* in other countries asylum from persecution."[1] Despite the wording of the article, the U.S. has consistently held that the "right" in question is to apply for asylum, not to receive it. The Universal Declaration is just that, a declaration, not a binding treaty.

Article 14 was a remarkably generous and innocent international undertaking in a world that was radically different from today's. In 1950, there were only a few more than fifty independent nations; today there are nearly 200. World population in 1950 was just 2.5 billion, compared to today's 6.4 billion. Most of that growth has, and will continue to come from the world's poorest areas where misery and restlessness are greatest. The less developed countries have increased in population from 1.7 billion in 1950 to 4.9 billion in 2000.

The region most prone to send migrants to the U.S., nearby Latin America, tripled its population in that half century to 523 million. The era of mass, inexpensive international air travel did not dawn until 1952 with the use of the first commercial passenger jets. Now, some 70 million passengers from abroad arrive in the U.S. by air each year—two-thirds of them aliens. The United Nations High Commission on Refugees (UNHCR) estimates that almost 200 million of the globe's people are international migrants and now about 35 million of those would like to move from the places they are now. Those numbers grow briskly.

The spread of literacy in the third world and the view provided by mass media to hundreds of millions there of the blandishments of life in the industrialized world have spawned ubiquitous yearnings to emigrate. One striking measure of this wanderlust is the annual U.S. "visa lottery," which in 2003 saw almost 8 million apply for only 50,000 immigrant visas. And the visa lottery accepted no applications from citizens from Mexico, China or the other top exporter nations of immigrants to the U.S. It is the studied blindness of Washington policy makers to this worldwide ravenous immigration demand that puts the nation's population and resource future at greatest risk.

The politics of densely populated Western Europe have been transformed by its massive surge of asylum seekers in the past two decades, as right-wing, anti-immigrant parties have burgeoned. Germany, once Europe's preferred target for asylum hopefuls, saw asylum applications rise nearly eleven-fold between 1982 and 1992, peaking then at 438,000. This population-asylum ratio for the United States would mean 1.5 million applicants for the U.S. Under intense political pressure, the German government in 1993 amended its laws and its constitution to restrict asylum. Applications now are back down to less than 100,000 a year.

To the chagrin of the careerists of UNHCR, many other western European nations have followed suit, some of the smaller countries (Denmark, Netherlands, Austria) imposing even more severe restrictions. Britain, having now replaced Germany as Europe's most popular asylum target, with applications exceeding 100,000 in 2003, introduced further tough legislation in 2003 with the goal of reducing applications by half.

Faced with rising "on-shore" asylum applications, and a surge of boat people beginning in 1999, Australia enacted tough restrictions in 2001. But like the United States, many of these countries have temporary protection or other quasi-asylum laws that help keep overall humanitarian immigration high. In a number of western nations the rising sense of loss of control over entries has sparked serious debate about reinterpreting, amending, or even withdrawing from the 1951 Geneva Convention of Refugees and its 1967 Protocol.[2] But Europe's opponents of tighter asylum controls argue that these restrictions will only increase illegal immigration, which figures suggest is on the rise.[3]

U.S. POSTWAR REFUGEE POLICY: FROM CAUTIOUS TO PRODIGAL

In the immediate postwar decades of the '40s, '50s, and '60s the U.S. was more selective than now about humanitarian immigration. The U.S. declined until 1968 to sign-on to the 1951 Geneva Convention, which bound states to a broader definition of refugees and asylees. U.S. refugee policy until then stressed its own national interest in stabilizing an impoverished and war-ravaged Europe by resettling displaced persons, combating the Soviet cold war threat, and affirming its anti-communism. Intake in this period was modest by today's standards.[4]

Refugee and asylum admissions subsequently began to mount in the '70s—to over a million in each of the last two decades. In the three decades since the end of the Vietnam war 1.5 million Indochinese received shelter in the U.S.—and they continue to come as refugees a generation after the end of the war. These are just the formal admission numbers. Off-the-books admissions through humanitarian parole or through loosely defined "special entrant" categories or bureaucratic sleight of hand to avoid deportations such as "extended voluntary departure" or "cancellation of suspension of removal" have swelled the numbers.

The figures for 2002 are fairly typical. During that year the U.S. was host to some 527,000 entrants whose claims for asylum or other relief were pending before immigration officials or immigration judges. Another 21,000 were persons granted temporary protected status (TPS) in that year, joining the estimated 410,000 TPS holders already accumulated here. Still another 150,000 Colombians not included above were living in the U.S. in refugee-like circumstances, while Congressional action to grant them TPS too is under consideration.[5] In addition more than 40,000 persons were admitted provisionally to the U.S. under "humanitarian parole"—a broad discretionary authority of the Executive Branch. As many as 25,000 persons who were denied formal asylum were allowed to remain in the U.S. anyway under other forms of bureaucratic relief such as special "adjustments of status" that were disguised amnesties.

HIGHER NUMBERS OF HUMANITARIAN—RELATED MIGRANTS AHEAD

Humanitarian-induced immigration is now a major U.S. population booster, implanting many new migration chains for future flows. It directly or indirectly brings the entry of all humanitarian-induced migrants to at least twice the 100,000 or so annually acknowledged in formal immigration statistics. A goodly share is persons who originally entered illegally and were allowed to remain without formal decisions on asylum, or who entered and sought asylum and, when denied it, went underground—"absconded," in the jargon of immigration officials.

These high numbers are likely to go higher. Of all forms of humanitarian intake, only the flow of officially-selected overseas refugees is reasonably controllable. The U.S. has demonstrated its control by reducing the annual flow from 100 thousand yearly in the 1990s to 70,000 a year in the late '90s. Fraud, however, is rife. Identities of presumptive refugees and their follow-on dependents are elusive. The Director of the State Department's refugee office estimated that 40 percent to 60 percent of claims for family reunification with settled refugees are fraudulent.[6]

Since September 11, 2001, Washington has further cut the projected inflow of refugees by sixty percent for security or workload reasons. A government-subsidized U.S. refugee lobby of churches and ethnic resettlement organizations is demanding a restoration of 100,000 refugees yearly as a minimum, regardless of human rights circumstances abroad.

NOT SO "TEMPORARY" PROTECTED STATUS

Washington legislated TPS in 1990, to provide a cheaper alternative to formal asylum and to provide a legal basis for questionable bureaucratic ad hoc arrangements then used to let people stay here. TPS expanded the intent of humanitarian immigration law by "temporarily" harboring those fleeing not the targeted persecution envisaged in the refugee convention, but generalized violence and natural disasters abroad. Most often the temporary relief becomes permanent. Washington lacks the political will or enforcement resources to ensure the departure of its hundreds of thousands of beneficiaries here when things improve in their host countries. Since 1990 some 430,000 aliens from sixteen countries have been granted TPS. El Salvador alone has some 285,000 mostly illegal TPS aliens here. Illustrating the creeping permanence of TPS, Salvadorans have had their temporary stays repeatedly extended since 1990. Many of those once covered by TPS have become legal permanent residents.

A dismaying lesson of TPS is that most of the world's poor and troubled states do not want their citizens to come home, but work aggressively for more of them to find a foothold in the U.S. With overseas remittances of immigrants in the U.S. reaching $44 billion in 2003, this is not surprising. Acentral foreign policy goal of El Salvador, Honduras, Guatemala and Nicaragua, which have sent the vast majority of the temporarily protected, is to pressure Washington for amnesties or, failing that, repeated extensions of stay for their TPS clients and expansion of the privilege to cover later arrivals.

THE ASYLUM SYSTEM: AN ENTITLEMENT FOR THE RESTLESS

Unlike refugee selection, the asylum process has virtually no safeguards against masses of "spontaneous arrivals." Asylum claims are unilateral choices of aliens in the U.S. or at the ports of entry who are impelled at times by genuine fear of persecution, but more often by the hope of evading U.S. immigration limits and partaking of state subsidies to asylees. Estimates of the portion of individual claims that are meritless run as high as 90 percent. Denial of those asylum claims is often academic in the U.S. and other receiving nations since there is little capability or willingness to find and remove those refused.

The asylum adjudication system itself in the U.S. and western countries is stacked in favor of the frivolous applicant. The asylum seeker makes claims of persecution or mistreatment at home by government officials (often local officials) or, increasingly, by their own family members. On-site verification of those claims by asylum officials here is out of the question. Indeed, asylum advocates oppose any inquiry to the applicants' home governments as a violation of "privacy." Short-staffing and heavy case loads of adjudicators encourage rubber-stamping. Credibility determinations are largely intuitive. Pro-asylum advocacies and most of the U.S. press routinely presume that all claims are valid and denounce efforts to get at reality as "heartless" or contrary to the Refugee convention. Increasingly, professional people-smugglers have mastered using national asylum systems to get their client migrants in.

Receiving governments are expected by refugee legalists to disregard questions of numbers entering when judging asylum claims.[7] They argue that the commitment of states under refugee treaties to protect endangered individuals is an obligation that trumps states' need to control immigration numbers.

The prospect of asylum or some other form of humanitarian admission to the U.S. is a powerful invitation to the world's troubled, ambitious or opportunistic. A claim for asylum is a ticket to either, in the best case, legal residence, or at worst a foothold here among the country's teeming irregular population. U.S. immigration officials have estimated that eighty percent of all those applying for asylum end up remaining in the U.S., whatever the outcome of their claims.

BIG NUMBERS THROUGH A TATTERED ASYLUM SCREEN

Those numbers add up. Between 1973 and 2002 the U.S. had received some 1.53 million applications for asylum, representing nearly two million persons, if applicants' dependents are factored in. Applying the 80 percent rule of thumb, some 1.6 million have stayed on here. Even though rarely more than 30 percent of those applicants received formal asylum, many others have remained illegally, or with some other temporary form of relief, or by winning legal resident status through family connections or amnesties, overt or disguised.

A large number of those two million applicants are persons who, aware of the weakness of their cases, used the application process to gain work authorization and then "absconded" before their claims could be heard. Many others advanced asylum claims to delay deportation until something would turn up, like an amnesty.

With those odds it does not surprise that the number of asylum claimants has surged. In 1980 when Congress enacted the present asylum system in the Refugee Act (PL 96-212), government witnesses testified there would be a maximum of 5000 applicants annually. Instead, applications soared to nearly a 150,000 a year by the mid-nineties.[8] This cascade led to changed INS procedures and restrictive measures such as "expedited removal" in 1996 (Public Law 104–208) that by 2002 had brought annual applications back down to 66,000.

Despite optimistic projections of slowing global population growth, the worldwide pool of candidates to immigrate to the U.S. will keep growing for the foreseeable future—through natural population increase, through the bulge in third world working age populations, and because of rising education levels, inadequate job creation, and rejection of traditional societies abroad. Immigration begets more immigration. As America's foreign-born population grows, so does its power to influence immigration policy and its propensity to lure more immigrants of the same kinship group, nationality or ethnicity.

HUMANITARIAN ADMISSIONS AS OFF-BUDGET PATRONAGE

For many Washington leaders immigration is a particularly useful form of patronage at a time when tight budgets limit other giveaways. The legal immigration system is severely overcommitted, with years of waiting the norm in many family reunification categories (viz. the Philippine's waiting list for admission of siblings of U.S. citizens is twenty-two years; India's is thirteen years). The public has become more resistant to higher ceilings or legislative legerdemain to "clear backlogs." Immigration is most salable politically when clothed in humanitarian garb.

Congress is increasingly prone to legislate special humanitarian admissions programs for particular ethnic or gender constituencies. The spread of identity politics in the U.S. has reinforced this tendency. Also still at work is Congress' penchant to use refugee policy to somehow fight unpopular ideologies, "embarrass" authoritarian regimes, and otherwise influence events abroad. Still other special legislative concessions are forced on Congress and the Executive by court decisions which overrule executive branch refusals of some categories of asylum seekers.

The lobby for humanitarian immigration is strong and well armored by the righteousness of its cause. It's hard for legislators to say no to admitting the ostensibly afflicted. Churches and synagogues, bar associations, and human rights and ethnic protective groups loom large in keeping the refugee and asylum valves open and in ensuring ample Federal and local government funds for their clients—often channeled through nonprofit bureaucracies operated by the major refugee/asylee lobbies themselves. Full involvement of pro bono lawyer groups has sparked heavy litigation, which successfully has expanded the definitions of persecution and persecuted groups.

Congress's production of ad hoc refugee and asylum programs in recent decades for ethnic special interests are remarkably profuse and diverse. With pressures from so many interest groups, the legislative record of humanitarian immigration in the '80s and '90s is the specter of a Christmas tree for persistent constituencies. Consider just a few of them:

The Cuban Adjustment Act of 1966 (PL 89-732) granted parole to all Cubans, probably the most coddled constituency of all, who can reach the U.S. and permanent resident status after one year. In 1986 and 1996 laws Washington further eased Cuban resettlement rules. An egregious example of exile grievances driving refugee policy, the Cuban Adjustment Act manifests Congress's need to affirm anti-communism, appease a demanding ethnic lobby, and to use refugee admissions to somehow "weaken" Cuba's Marxist Castro regime, still solidly in power after forty-four years. The executive branch does not escape this illusion. As recently as October 10, President Bush marked a Cuban-American holiday at the White House by promising increases in Cuban immigration numbers and renewed efforts to inform would-be Cuban refugees of the "many routes to safe and legal immigration into the U.S." Meanwhile, Washington's pandering to the Cuban lobby has triggered "me too" demands from Haitians and other ethnic advocacies.

The **Lautenberg Amendment** to refugee enabling legislation since 1989 has granted virtual automatic refugee status to some 400,000 Jews, Evangelicals and a few other religious minorities in former Soviet nations. Showing membership in these religious groups is enough to qualify; applicants are not required to show a well-founded fear of persecution required by the Geneva Convention. Lautenberg keeps being quietly reenacted year after year, even as the Russian Republic has become more open and democratic.

The **International Religious Freedom Act (HR 2431 and PL 106-55)**, passed in 1998 under intense lobbying by conservative Christian groups, is designed to produce higher refugee and asylum admissions for overseas believers. It mandates special indoctrination of adjudicators on the nature and extent of religious persecution abroad and on making refugee guidelines more sensitive.

The **Nicaraguan Adjustment and Central American Relief Act (NACARA—PL 105-100 of 1997) and the Haitian Refugee Immigrant Fairness Act (HRIFA—PL 105-277 of 1998)** were enacted to comply with a court decision reversing the executive branch's denial of humanitarian relief to certain asylum seekers from those nations. NACARA became a Christmas tree—a *de facto* amnesty, granting ultimate permanent residence status to nearly one million Nicaraguans, Salvadorans, Guatemalans, Cubans, and citizens of former Soviet bloc countries in irregular status.

HRIFA offered similar benefits to certain Haitians here by 1995. Some 125,000 Haitians gained permanent residence. Predictably, Congress is under heavy pressure to extend the benefit to Haitians now specifically excluded.[9]

The **Torture Victims Relief Act (PL 105-320) of 1998** implemented the U.S. ratification of the United Nations Convention against Torture, which bars the deportation of anyone to a country where he is likely to face torture. The Act is now commonly invoked as a delaying tactic among failed Asylum seekers. Nearly 800 aliens have avoided deportation under this policy—more than a third of them hardened criminals. In what seems like a contradiction, others protected by the act are themselves former torturers in their homelands.[10] Inexplicably, the U.S. has at times dealt with human rights-deficient countries (such as Haiti and El Salvador, Guatemala, Somalia and Ethiopia) by sheltering both the persecuted and their persecutors.

The **Chinese Student Protection Act of 1992 (PL 102-404)** In response to the Tianamen Square massacre in Beijing, the act granted permanent legal residence to Chinese temporarily in the U.S. between June 1989 and April 1990. An estimated 80,000 Chinese earlier given temporary protection under a 1990 executive order were made permanent residents.[11]

1996 legislation on **Persecution for Resistance to Coercive Population Control (PL 104-208)**. This law mandated that forced abortion or sterilization (principally in China) or a well-founded fear of such coercive population control measures were grounds for asylum.

Domestic repugnance toward China's population control measures illustrates the difficulty of consistent asylum standards when overseas conditions become enmeshed with such volatile domestic issues as "right to life." From 1989 to 1994 the Board of Immigration Appeals regarded China's population control laws as "social policy" applicable to all, not "persecution." A federal court ruled otherwise in 1994. Ironically, the Chinese Government, in dealing with the U.S. government on steps to stop Chinese alien smuggling, has suggested that less magnetic asylum opportunities in the U.S. would help slow the flow.

The foregoing are but a sample of some of the immense variety of victim groups Washington has responded to. Others would include Syrian Jews, Iraqi Kurds and Christians, Soviet scientists, victims of human trafficking, unemployed Northern Irish, volcano-struck Monserratans, Indochinese children of American soldiers, Bosnians, Croats and Kosovars, and if Congress has its way North Korean refugees in China and Japan.

CONCLUSION

If a sustainable, stationary U.S. population is to be achieved, sizable cuts in all forms of immigration are a must. Despite its inflated moral claims to exception, Humanitarian immigration, because of its egregious political manipulation and the carelessness in its application, must be a candidate for major pruning. Alarm over its abuse and its likely future trajectory, has led the U.S. and a number of western nations to consider or even adopt hardheaded measures to block mass population transfers to their soil under a presumed entitlement to protection. Many of the measures that would have been unthinkable in the West when innocence prevailed and the numbers were low (interdiction at sea, offshore protection, limited temporary protection only), have become a reality. But restrictive laws will provide little relief until western nations—the U.S.

included—accept the need for close and continuous tracking of their non-citizen populations to identify and promptly remove the uninvited. A forthcoming NPG Forum paper will examine the options for remedying a broken humanitarian system and the institutional misperceptions and flaws that nurture it.

NOTES:

1. Universal Declaration of Human Rights, Article 14, paragraph 1
2. (a) Adrienne Milbank (2001), Australia and the 1951 Refugee Convention, *People and Places*, Vol. 9, no 2; (b) *Migration Watch UK: Asylum Laws: a Way Forward (2003)*—www.migrationwatchUK.org/bulletinNo6.htm
3. Harald Lederer (1998). *Illegal Immigration: Why Does it Exist and What do We Know about the Numbers and Trends? European Forum for Migration Studies, Bamberg, EFMS Paper No. 19*
4. Gil Loescher and John A. Scanlan (1986): *Calculated Kindness: Refugees and America's Half-Open Door—1945 to the Present*, New York: The Free Press.
5. U.S. Committee for Refugees, *World Refugee Report –2002*
6. Mark Fritz, "U.S. admits record low number of refugees," *Associated Press*, September 21, 2003
7. American Baptist Churches v Thornburg (760 F Supp ND Cal 1991)
8. Federation for American Immigration Reform (2003): "Asylum Reform," www.fairus.org/htm104106303.htm
9. Estimates of NACARA and HRIFA amnesty beneficiaries from NumbersUSA www.numbersusa.com/interest/amnesty_print.html, and from General Accounting Office, Annual Reports to Congress on HRIFA, 2001, 2002.
10. "Lawmakers attack use of anti-torture law to block immigrants' deportation." *New York Times*, July 12, 2003
11. Mark Krikorian, *Past Grants of Temporary Protection*, Testimony Prepared for the U.S. House of Representative, Committee on the Judiciary, Subcommittee on Immigration, March 4, 1999

THE NEW AMERICAN CENTURY?

Lindsey Grant

June 2004

In 1997, a small group of neo-conservatives organized the Project for the New American Century (PNAC) and published a Statement of Principles. The organization's name describes its state of mind. Its philosophy is perhaps most succinctly expressed in a short quotation from the Principles:

> "We need to accept responsibility for America's unique role in preserving and extending an international order friendly to our security, our prosperity, and our principles. Such a Reaganite policy of military strength and moral clarity may not be fashionable today. But it is necessary if the United States is to build on the successes of this past century and to ensure our security and our greatness in the next[1]."

Among the signers of that declaration were our present Vice President, Secretary of Defense and Deputy Secretary of Defense Paul Wolfowitz. The group is proud to claim parentage of the administration's Iraq strategy. Its views are reflected in the White House position that there is "a single sustainable model for national success: freedom, democracy and free enterprise . . . These values of freedom are right and true for every person, in every society . . . and the duty of protecting these values against their enemies is the common calling of freedom-loving persons across the globe and across the ages[2]." Condoleezza Rice called this our "moral mission," and it was cited as an argument for invading Iraq

The Project believes that "a cheap energy policy will lead to sustained, rapid, long-term economic and employment growth[3]." The Bush administration agrees. Under Secretary of State Alan Larsen in April 2003 told the Senate Foreign Relations Committee that the United States must have access to energy "on terms and conditions that support (our) economic growth and prosperity," and that we require "improved investment opportunities" in the energy producing regions of the world.[4] It would, as the saying goes, be nice if you can do it, but Mr. Larson has his work cut out for him, as I will demonstrate later.

The neo-conservatives have belatedly learned that petroleum is indeed finite, and that we are running out of it. The Iraq invasion bears all the marks of a deliberate, and failed, policy to take political control of a country in the middle of the oil patch so as to assure our future oil supplies. If free trade and investment are a mask for taking control of the resources we want, it will encounter mounting resistance from others, such as the recent riots in Bolivia that forced the government to back out of a contract to sell gas to the United States.

Even Canada may begin to wonder whether, in a world increasingly desperate for fresh water, the U.S. may eventually demand a share of Canadian water resources—despite the Canadian policy prohibiting the bulk export of water.

The assertion that we must assure our access to others' resources runs in uneasy harness with the belief in growth. President Bush (like other presidents before him) has called for faster economic growth. In a bid for the Hispanic vote (perhaps a misdirected bid), he has proposed a program to legalize illegal immigrants and to allow businesses to import more labor when they claim to need it, both of which will dramatically accelerate U.S. population growth—and our appetite for resources. And the Democrats are trying to outbid him.

Taken together, the assertion of our moral rectitude, our right to impose our values on the world, the desirability of continuing growth, and our right to support that growth with access to others' resources constitutes a sweeping assertion of our rights and power that seems a bit ambitious for a country with annual budgetary and foreign trade deficits of about $500 billion. Foreigners are financing that trade deficit—more than $1 billion a day—and buying out our businesses, while U.S. capital investments abroad decline dramatically. But there are bigger problems than that.

In this paper, I will argue that the coming century is more likely to be a debacle than an American hegemony unless we curb our spendthrift ways, stop and reverse U.S. population growth and help others to control theirs.

GROWTHMANIA: THE DURABLE BUBBLE

Before the 1300s, the idea of unlimited growth hardly figured in human thinking. Then came the Renaissance, which led to the Age of Exploration to the new world and new wealth. It started the agricultural and industrial revolutions and set in motion a worldwide scientific enterprise that is still accelerating. It began a period of enrichment and growth without parallel in human history.

The period has lasted, with minor interruptions, for six centuries. That success led gradually to a widespread conviction that growth is the natural and desirable order of things, and forever benign. Enter the Romantic Era and its sense of limitless horizons, and the "Age of Exuberance" (to borrow William Catton's term). Western civilization is still in that mode and is teaching it to the East and South.

It is a formidable belief system, but its proponents have forgotten that its origins were not in population growth, but in the Black Death, the most widespread and severe population collapse in human history. Brutally, it readjusted the ratio of people to land. The surviving peasants found themselves with more farmland and more wealth. New wealth flowed into the depopulated cities. The institutional constraints of Feudalism were swept away and replaced by the system now identified with capitalism[5]. The subsequent Age of Exploration further improved the ratio of land to people by opening access to the new world, which has more than quadrupled the arable land available to Europeans[6].

THE GROWTH MACHINE

One legal innovation, the limited liability corporation, was fundamental in promoting and shaping the age of growth. It changed the calculus of risk. If you succeed, unimaginable wealth. If you fail, you lose only the money you had put in the company. It was an immense inducement to risk-taking, an astonishing engine of growth, and the vehicle for the rise of capitalism.

Capitalism is uniquely the system for the entrepreneur, the risk taker, the business adventurer. It serves the successful. So do its theoreticians. Conventional current economics is grounded in the expectation of endless growth. Economic growth, for more profits. Population growth for more markets and cheap labor. (Not economic growth per capita, which would be more reasonable.) The economists' other myths and simplifications—economic man, infinite substitutability, comparative advantage, free trade and investment—all justify the freedom of action of the corporation.

The "economic man" hypothesis assumes that people displaced by change will find other and probably better employment. The overwhelming current evidence is to the contrary. "Infinite substitution" is regularly argued but never proven. It justifies the faith that growth can go on forever. (Right now, with an accelerating fresh water crisis, one may reasonably ask: what is your proposed substitute for water?)

Free trade is said to maximize efficiency through comparative advantage. It also widens the playing field for the TNC (trans national corporation), as does the prospect of unfettered investment and movement of capital.

The Austrian-American economist Joseph Schumpeter recognized that there is much suffering as old arrangements are swept aside, but he characterized it ingeniously as "creative destruction"—the old must be swept away to make room for the new and efficient. It is devil take the hindmost, unless it is controlled by social restraints, which themselves may be blocked by the financial and political power of capital.

Politicians respond to the siren song, and so do investors. Even now, as the world and the country try to shake off a recession, investors do not ask "were we on the wrong course" but rather "is the slump over? Can we start coining money again?"

THE MIGHTY ENGINE WITH NO BRAKES

In the twentieth century, modern medicine and public health programs lowered mortality in the poorer countries, and modern agriculture fed the rising numbers, but too little was done, too late, to lower fertility. That created a fundamental demographic imbalance. The resulting population growth has dwarfed all previous human experience. World population quadrupled in one century, a change so astonishing that it has altered—or should have altered—our assumptions as to the human connection with the rest of the planet. Are we plunging toward a collapse because of that very success? Philosophers since John Stewart Mill have warned against the illusion of perpetual growth. Endlessly growing numbers cannot enjoy endlessly growing consumption. There is a mathematical platitude that post-Keynesian economists ignore: material growth at some point becomes a logical impossibility on a finite planet. When?

John Maynard Keynes is something of a demigod to conventional modern economists. When the machine stopped in the Great Depression, Keynes offered a way to start it again. However, Keynes was not as wedded to growthmania as his followers. He raised serious questions: Can growth go on indefinitely? Would it be desirable[7]? Is market capitalism—motivated by greed—a sound moral basis for society[8]? Those doubts were swept aside in the rush to profit.

Herman Daly, considered a renegade by conventional macroeconomists, makes a point his colleagues ignore: the economy is a subset of the environment; it is not independent. The Earth is not simply a source of resources and a sink for the waste products—the principal products—of economic activity. It is the matrix that sustains life, including human life, and we must ask whether human economic activity is degrading that matrix.

Two hundred years ago, Thomas Malthus worried (perhaps prematurely) about how many people the

Earth could support, but he did not ask the next question: what will increasing human numbers do to the Earth? George Perkins Marsh in 1864 was the first to systematically address that question.[9] Science has been describing the impacts ever since. In 1992, the Presidents of the U.S. National Academy of Sciences and the British Royal Society adopted a joint statement (later adopted by the world's major national scientific societies) that "If current predictions of population growth prove accurate and patterns of human activity on the planet remain unchanged, science and technology may not be able to prevent either irreversible degradation of the environment or continued poverty for much of the world."[10] If expanding populations and growing consumption impose unbearable strains on the ecosystems that support us, we must learn to identify the turning point and ask, what population is sustainable?

Population growth is not necessary for well-being. Japan and Europe, with stable or declining populations, show a vitality that belies the common wisdom. A Brookings Institution study examined cities' growth and prosperity in depth. It concluded that "we have punctured one important piece of conventional wisdom: the idea that achieving income growth in a metropolitan area requires population growth.[11]" Various other studies have shown that the residents in stable cities are likely to be better off than those in rapidly growing ones, both by economic measures and quality of life indicators. Pittsburgh, PA, long the epitome of the "rust belt," ranks at or near the top on both scales, despite two generations of population decline—and despite its wretched weather. And taxes tend to rise with urban growth.

The literature challenging growthmania has itself been growing, documenting the charge that the benefits of growth have gone to the entrepreneurs rather than to the mass of working people, and that the growth of the human economic enterprise has run down the natural capital of the Earth—which does not appear in GNP statistics[12].

Mainstream economics has ignored that literature. In the pursuit of growth, it has brushed aside every doubt.

The enthusiasm for population growth is hardly universal. President Nixon asked whether it was a good thing. He persuaded Congress to create the Commission on Population Growth and the American Future (the "Rockefeller Commission"), which concluded that it could see no advantage in further growth of the American population. Unfortunately, President Nixon shelved it for political reasons (and so have all subsequent presidents). That was thirty-two years ago. We have added 86 million people since then.

Polls suggest that the American public is not enamored of further population growth, but there is a virtual political taboo. Almost nobody mentions the demographic consequences when politicians discuss policies such as increasing immigration that generate population growth, because the pro-growth argument is endorsed by the powerful.

Nevertheless, growth must stop. The question is when and where will it stop?

THE MEASUREMENT OF OPTIMUM POPULATION

NPG examined the concept of optimum population fifteen years ago, in a series of FORUM papers. Populations, U.S. and worldwide, have grown substantially since then, as has the addiction to growth among our political leaders. Perhaps it is time to revisit the concept in the light of developments in recent years.

The effort to define "optimum population" challenges the prevailing economic and political wisdom that growth is by definition a good thing. So be it. The challenge itself is at least as important as the number that we may eventually assign to optimum population.

Maximum population is simply an estimate of how many people can be supported at a given time. Sustainable population is the population that can be supported, indefinitely, without degrading the ability of the ecosystem to support it. Optimum population extends that idea; it undertakes to describe a population level that could live a comfortable life within those resource and environmental constraints. It is the antithesis of current economic goals, but it should be congenial with the economic aspirations of all but the greedy. And it is a vision of a future without the threat of collapse.

Putting numbers on optimum population is a mix of science, value judgements and outright guessing. How do we decide whether further population growth is bad and what numbers would serve humanity better? I will briefly identify a few such yardsticks below[13].

Food. World food production kept ahead of population growth in the 1960s and 1970s, stayed just ahead in the 1980s, and fell behind in the 1990s. Grain production has been stagnant since the mid-1990s, and even that may not be sustainable. Our hope for higher yields now rests mostly on genetic modification (GM), itself a dangerous project.

The other sources of rising yields are beginning to fail. Chemical fertilizers produce less and less additional food as yields rise. Eventually the added fertilizer does not pay for itself. The developed world has passed that point, and China is approaching it.

Modern agriculture depends on petroleum and gas to run its heavy machines and provide feedstock for fertilizer plants, and we are approaching an era when both fuels will be in short supply.

Arable acreage is declining and topsoils are eroding. As a result of population growth and urban sprawl, arable land per capita has declined since 1970 by one-third, to 0.16 hectares, in the less developed countries. It has declined by one-fifth, to 0.2 hectares, in Europe, and by one-third, to 0.63 hectares in the United States. In only thirty years.

That acreage figure for the United States points to a subsidiary lesson. We still have more room than most countries. But our rapid growth narrows the advantage. We supply one-third of the grain that enters international trade, but if yields and our consumption habits stay as they are, we will need that grain ourselves in one generation (assuming the Census high projection) or two (assuming the middle projection). It will take a remarkable increase in grain yields, plus a dramatic dietary shift away from meat, to feed our own growing population through this century, to say nothing of exporting grain. And such increases in yields seem most unlikely in the face of the constraints I described earlier.

The chemical industry will compete for more and more land as it turns to cellulose to replace hydrocarbons as feedstock, and as crops are engineered through GM to produce pharmaceuticals and other chemicals.

Irrigated land now produces 40 percent of the world's crops, but salinization is lowering yields in perhaps one-third of world irrigated cropland. Irrigation uses about 70 percent of human fresh water consumption, but we are running out of water. Rivers are going dry and water tables are declining in China, India, Pakistan, the Middle East, Mexico and the American West. Even moister regions are feeling the pinch. Freshwater data are notoriously inexact, but a United Nations study in 2003 found that global per capita water supplies declined by one-third between 1970 and 1990 and are likely to decline by another one-third in the next twenty years, and very little is being done about it.

Climate change threatens food production (see below).

The world has run through the windfalls provided successively by the Black Death and the opening of the new world. Much smaller populations, with more land per capita, would provide a cushion against the threats to food production.

Modern agriculture is itself destructive. The world now uses about six times as much commercial fertilizer as it did in 1950, and twenty-five times as much chemical pesticide. Human activities put nitrogen compounds, potassium, phosphates, and sulfates into the environment faster than natural processes produce them, and we are just beginning to understand the consequences. Monocultures and high-yielding "green revolution" crops demand more water and more pesticides. New pesticides are introduced as pests develop resistance to the old ones. It is a squirrel cage, and experts differ as to whether it has reduced the proportion of the crops that are lost to pests.

World food production could be sustained at roughly half its present level with a judicious combination of organic manures and chemical fertilizers. (Before the reliance on commercial fertilizer, U.S. corn yields were about 40 percent of current yields.) We would need to change our ways and utilize more natural manures from livestock and, indeed, from humans, but that in itself would solve some serious pollution problems. Very roughly, half the production would support half the present population, and it would be much less damaging agriculture.

Health. The proliferation of chemicals is not just an agricultural problem. There are four times as many chemicals in the world chemicals registry as there were in 1980. We all carry hundreds of those new chemicals in our bodies. Some of them are known sources of cancer, endocrine disruption, immune system suppression, falling sperm counts and infertility, and learning disabilities in children. And most of them have not been tested for their impact on health or the environment.

The urban population in the less developed world (LDCs) was 300 million in 1950. By 2000, it had reached two billion, propelled largely by desperate peasants moving to cities to stay alive. Water supplies, sewage services and electric supplies have lagged far behind, and it is remarkable that the crowded slums have not generated more epidemics than they have. With the public health measures that kicked off the population explosion now in disarray, rising mortality may forestall the United Nations' (UN) projection that LDCs' urban population will reach four billion by 2030.

The growth of cities and growing water shortages mean that city residents in the less developed countries re-use sewage, with disastrous health effects. Even in the industrial world, sewage plants filter out the solid wastes and kill the microbes but usually leave the nitrogen in the water; and we have not started to try to filter out the many drugs that people take and then pass on to others. They can be detected even in rivers below the sewage outfalls.

It would be a happier world with fewer chemicals and better water.

The Microbial World. This chemical assault affects other animals. It may be endangering the microbes that we depend upon but cannot see. For one example: earth microbes have so far converted nitrogen fertilizers back into inert molecular nitrogen fast enough to keep us from swamping the Earth in nitrogen compounds, yet we don't know how much of a chemical load the microbes can tolerate.

Human population growth drives chemical production both by keeping up the pressure for more food production and by increasing the demand for nonagricultural chemicals. A much smaller population would lead to a reduction in the introduction of chemicals into an environment which we are changing but do not really understand.

Fisheries. Worldwide marine fish production rose from 20 to over 70 million tons from 1950 to the late 1980s, but has stuck there. Then came a soaring growth in aquaculture, which pollutes the water, competes with livestock for feed, and concentrates the harmful chemicals we are putting into the environment. (The Environmental Protection Agency recommends eating one serving or less of farmed salmon per month.)

It would be a better world if human demand for fish and the pollution we put into the ocean were both closer to the 1950 level.

The Energy Transition. Fossil energy is a profound disturbance to the ecosystem. It moves carbon—and sulphur, arsenic, mercury, chromium, lead, selenium, and boron—from the lithosphere into the biosphere and the atmosphere, at a rate and scale greater than all natural processes. We worry about the threat of terrorism to petroleum supplies, but the supply will decline, anyway. That will be an environmental boon but an economic disaster unless we have prepared for it.

Estimates of the world's remaining petroleum resources range around two trillion barrels.[14] World consumption is presently about 28 billion barrels a year. Dividing the estimated resources by current annual consumption, it is commonly (and erroneously) said that about seventy to eighty years' supply remains, but consumption is rising fast, as China and India industrialize.[15] Not a very long future.

United States crude oil and natural gas production peaked over thirty years ago. The country now produces 40 percent less crude oil and 13 percent less gas than it did then. U.S. petroleum imports account for 62 percent of our consumption now, and the proportion is rising.[16] With less than 5 percent of the world's population, we consume 26 percent of world petroleum production. The share is going down as others, including the rising giants China and India, compete for a larger share.[17] China is moving into a stronger bidding position than ours, because it is not saddled with massive trade deficits. Under Secretary Larsen's vision of the United States moving in to exploit others' petroleum resources may be an anachronism.

Those who expect continuing growth in petroleum consumption ignore petroleum geologists' warnings that world production will begin to decline, probably in less than twenty years. Extracting the remaining petroleum will become more costly, competition for petroleum will intensify, and prices will rise sharply. Gas will follow petroleum. Not a happy prospect for a nation that is already by far the biggest importer and wants to import more.

Repeated military interventions to secure oil will become less and less effective, because of mounting resistance abroad and rising discontent in this country over the financial and moral burdens and the military appropriation of civilian oil supplies. A vast and sophisticated military that has to fight abroad for the oil it needs to operate is a costly and uncertain tool.

American politicians have regularly talked of "energy independence" even as we have grown more and more dependent on foreign sources. (Who wants to be dependent on the unstable Persian Gulf?) We won't get back to the good old days in petroleum, even if we get population growth under control, but it would help our adjustment to a new and leaner energy mix.

Coal is more abundant, and much of it is in the United States, but it is a dirty fuel. Some of the pollution could be controlled at a high cost, but the carbon dioxide, and its effect on climate, is a particular problem.

Growth apologists look for panaceas. They suggest oil sands and shales, but processing them is environmentally destructive and may demand more energy than they would yield. Ocean methane from the continental slopes is suggested, but the environmental consequences could be frightening.[18] The activity might release the methane without capturing it, thus further warming the climate and triggering undersea mudslides and tsunamis.

Biomass is a very limited solution because its production competes for land with rising human needs for food and wood.

Wind and photovoltaics can only supply electricity, while petroleum has been used for everything from airplane fuel to chemical feedstock. For peaking power, wind energy is nearly competitive right now, and much more benign than fossil fuels. For reliable base power, however, wind and solar energy will be much more expensive than fossil fuels are now, because of the problem of storing the energy until it is needed.

The world is headed into an energy transition, probably toward a mix of coal, nuclear and more benign renewable power. The rising costs and dislocations will threaten the world's economies. A saner U.S. policy would stop the effort to monopolize other countries' oil supplies and instead look toward reducing our demand for petroleum and gas. We must phase out our current waste and, more fundamentally, we must stop and reverse current population growth. A smaller population would make the energy transition easier, but demographics move slowly.

Climate Change. Fossil fuels generate climate change, which is beginning to reduce crop yields, especially in the poorer countries. It is already raising sea levels and generating more extreme weather: floods, droughts, extreme hot or cold spells. The impacts are likely to worsen for centuries. So far, the human race is doing very little about the problem it has created.

The Intergovernmental Panel on Climate Change (IPCC) in 1995 estimated that it would take an immediate reduction in carbon emissions to 30 to 50 percent of present levels to hold the human impact on climate even at its present levels. In the face of that calculation, the modest reductions proposed in the Kyoto protocols are largely symbolic.

Population size must be addressed if we are to come close to the 30 to 50 percent goal. With populations at 1950 levels, the world would have been within that range even with present per capita emissions[19]. Whatever we can gain in energy efficiency would be lagniappe.

Technology, the Headstrong Servant. Modern Americans expect technology to solve our environmental problems, but it actually generated most of them. It can be of help. When the United States Government passed the Clean Air Act in 1972, technical fixes reduced some of the principal pollutants. Technology has its limits, however, and overall air pollution has been rising again for several years. Technology can be part of the solution, but not all of it. Lower numbers and lower demand are central to reducing pollution.

In one respect, technology has betrayed the progrowth economists. They call for economic growth to provide jobs for growing populations. But technology has driven productivity up. Economic growth is not necessarily job-connected any more, as we have been learning in recent years. Businesses can turn to automation, instead. The solution for unemployment and low wages is fewer workers competing for jobs. Proponents of more immigration, take note.

Social Equity and Human Numbers. China and India explicitly seek to raise per capita income to the present average level in the industrial world, and most poor nations would probably agree. The effort to get rich has created horrendous pollution problems in China. If the poor countries are to get as rich as they hope, without increasing gross world economic activity and further damaging the world's environment, world population would have to be not much over one billion.

Non-linearities. My analysis so far has been linear, i.e. so much more of a given input produces a comparable change in the impact. In fact, nature is seldom linear. In the study of climate change, for example, scientists are regularly identifying non-linearities—feedback loops that may intensify the prospective problems—from alterations in ocean currents which could alter weather worldwide and make Europe's climate like Labrador's, or the warming effect of diminishing ice and snow fields, to the release of stored methane from the ocean and carbon dioxide from Arctic tundra.

Prudence would suggest that we not press our present systems to the limit, so that we may have space to maneuver if unexpected changes reduce the productive capacity of our support systems.

Crowding and the Intangibles. I was told of a kid from the New York City ghetto who was sent to a city-owned summer camp in the hills. The bus arrived after dark, and when the kid stepped out, he looked up and said, "What are all them little white things up there?" He had never seen the stars. That, I submit, is deprivation. It is getting worse as cities grow and the sky gets murkier.

The kid was hardly unique. There are literally thousands of newspaper stories about the strains of increasing crowding in the United States.[20] In some degree, they result from our insistence on a costly and inefficient life style, but they are even more fundamentally the product of population growth. We don't like to be crowded, nor do the people of more crowded lands who have become resigned to it. The search for optimum population should include the calculation: how much room do we like?

THE BOTTOM LINE

The United States' power and well-being rest on flimsier footings than the Administration and the New American Century members seem to believe. Our balance of payments deficit is chronic and worsening. If foreigners turn away from the United States as the residual safe repository for their funds, it will drive the dollar down, fast and far. That might encourage what exports we have left, but it would generate massive cost-push inflation. Our budgetary deficit contributes to such a scenario. The current decline of the dollar may be a harbinger.

Those problems would be manageable, if the United States had the discipline and the will. The issues of food, water, energy, health, climate and crowding are more fundamental and can be addressed only if we abandon our fixation on growth and address the demand side rather than denying it is a problem. Each of those issues can be resolved only if we move toward a smaller population.

My fellow writers on optimum population would probably agree that for the United States, optimum may be something like the numbers we passed around 1950: 150 million (half the present 293 million), give or take a half.

It is much harder to put a number on optimum world population, because an outsider can hardly determine what consumption level might seem "comfortable" for the billions of people who are presently at or close to the margin of survival, and we cannot know what tradeoffs countries will choose between prosperity and pollution. Perhaps the 1950 figure of about 2.5 billion (40 percent of the present 6.4 billion) would be an upper limit. I have pointed out that, for everybody to achieve something like the average consumption level of the industrial world without vastly increasing pollution, world population would have to be in the vicinity of one billion.

The poor countries arrived too late to join the feast. Most of them have little or no fossil fuel and no hope of enjoying a boom period based on the rapid drawdown of a one-time energy source, such as the industrial world enjoyed. Their arable land is overused and deteriorating. They suffer the most from water shortages and climate change. The problems of poverty and the competition for resources are producing tensions and conflict, whether they take the form of intensified migration to the West, or terrorism, or rogue states or interminable local wars and insurrections. For them, a future with far fewer people and more resources per capita would be a much happier future. Again, I think of the unexpected results of the Black Plague, though I would hope for a more benign process.

The less developed world has grown by two-thirds since 1950—and they were poor in 1950. The need for a fundamental shift in the ratio of resources to people in the poor countries may itself justify an optimum world population figure of one billion. Barring a catastrophe, it might take centuries to reach such figures, even with a determined worldwide effort.

Europe and Japan are already on the way to lower populations and must face the question, where should they stop? I'll come back to that.

WHY SUCH ROUND NUMBERS?

Those are hardly rigorous calculations. There are too many horseback calculations and value judgements. What living standard is "comfortable"? There will be unpredictable technological changes, and continuing environmental degradation will almost certainly diminish the Earth's support capability.

But then again, when do we know the exact consequences of any major decision? They are all made on the basis of partial information, and they can be refined only as we go along and learn more. Precision is not required here. If the weight of evidence suggests that a population should be smaller than it is now, the policy implications are similar, whether the gap is 100 million or 200 million. The important thing is to ask the question, in one context after another, would this problem be more easily solved with a smaller population or a larger one? I think the examples above provide the answer.

WHY TRY TO ESTIMATE OPTIMUM POPULATION?

We need to show that human numbers matter in order to illuminate the flaws in growthmania. When I point out that a given policy will lead to more population growth, a typical reaction is "so what." The present debates about immigration, welfare and tax policies ignore their demographic impact and thus dismiss the future.

Defining a desirable population level is one step toward a more stable and less uncertain future. It sets the stage for the next necessary step: putting policies in place that will move human numbers in the right direction.

RESTORING A FLICKERING VISION

A vision flickered briefly in the 1960s and 1970s: it should be possible to combine modern technology with population stability, and thereby create a world in which all can live well. Modern productivity would replace the arduous physical toil whereby the poor labored to support the rich. That vision is being eroded because, in much of the world, economic growth is being absorbed by population growth that eventually eats up the gains.

Salvation may come from an unexpected source: young women with jobs and their own income and control over their decisions about child-bearing. They have learned to practice family planning. In theory, that offers a way to regulate the balance between people and resources humanely, rather than through the grim operation of mortality as happened in the Black Death. In fact, women's choices have been based mostly on personal considerations, not on social or demographic grounds.

So far, in Europe, Japan, South Korea, Taiwan and Singapore and among non-Hispanic Whites in the United States, women have chosen to have far fewer children than would be necessary to replace themselves. In none of them has the fertility decline yet brought population down to optimum levels, but there are dramatic population declines in prospect if fertility does not soon rise to replacement levels. In many less developed countries, fertility is also declining, but not so far. It is not happening in Africa or the Middle East.

The world is tending to divide into two different demographic regions. In one of them, there is a real option of consciously managing population levels, but a need to define optimum population as a social goal and to enlist young women's participation in pursuing that goal. In the other, population growth is on a path that will stop and turn around only through catastrophe, hunger and rising mortality.

HOW FEW IS TOO FEW?

For those countries poised at the edge of population decline, the question arises: how far? Who will support the aged? Is free trade a serious possibility when wealthy and aging countries' labor faces the competition from overpopulated poor countries, working for a fraction as much money? What does women's independence bode for the traditional conjugal family? (More than half of Swedish children are now born out of wedlock, and other European countries are not far behind.)

There are answers to those questions, but the more fundamental question is one of numbers. Italy's population will be eight million and still declining in 2100 if present fertility levels persist. If fertility should come back to replacement level by 2020—70 percent above present fertility—population would stabilize at 25 million, about 43 percent of the present level. Environmentally, it might be a good level. Practically, there are problems. Will Italian women fit their child-bearing to social needs? If not, how much immigration can Italy sustain? Genetically, Italians would progressively disappear, to be supplanted by the descendants of the immigrants. In the absence of action on fertility and migration, Italy could simply be overwhelmed by illegal migration from desperate countries to the south.

Population writers have yet to address the question, what is a desirable lower limit to optimum? Certainly, one cardinal rule is that fertility must at some point come back up to replacement level.

THE IMMEDIATE TASK

The more pressing task is to define and popularize the idea of an upper limit, and to act on it. For the United States, that would mean limiting immigration and persuading mothers to stop at two children, at least until growth turns around. We should return to the policies—largely abandoned during the Reagan administration and this one—of helping the poor countries to stop growth, which most of them want to do. They would be better off, and so would we, if they were not made desperate by growing idle and hungry populations.

Most poor countries know they are already too big, though none have adopted a target for optimum population. The United States is unique. Facing undiminished population growth driven mostly by immigration, we do not recognize the problem. We need to help the poor countries to accomplish their demographic revolution—and to apply the lesson to the United States.[21]

NOTES:

1. www.newamericancentury.com
2. "National Security Strategy of the U.S.A.," transmitted by President Bush to Congress on 9-18-2002.
3. Lewis E. Lehrman, Co-Chairman of PNAC, "Energetic America," in the *Weekly Standard*, September 23, 2003. See PNAC website Note 1.
4. Environmental News Service, 4-8-2003; full text at www.state.gov.
5. David Herlihy, *The Black Death and the Transformation of the West* (Cambridge, MA: Harvard University Press, 1997.)
6. Data from U.S. Department of Agriculture, *World Agriculture*, Statistical Bulletin 861, November 1993. In the "new world," I include the Western hemisphere, Australia and New Zealand. "Europe" excludes Russia.
7. "A great transition in human history will have begun when civilized man endeavors to assume conscious control (of population growth) in his own hands, away from the blind instinct of mere predominant survival." J.M. Keynes, Preface to Harold Wright, *Population* (London: Harcourt Brace, 1923.)
8. Keynes' famous statement that "Avarice and usury and precaution must be our gods a little longer still." is quoted in E.F. Schumacher, *Small is Beautiful: Economics as if People Mattered* (London: Blond and Briggs, 1973, reprints by Harper & Row, New York, 1975 to 1989; p.24.)
9. George Perkins, *Marsh, Man and Nature, Or, Physical Geography as Modified by Human Action* (originally published 1864. Reprinted Cambridge: Harvard University Press, 1965.)
10. Joint Statement by the Presidents of the U.S. National Academy of Sciences and the British Royal Society, released February 26, 1992, by the National Research Council, Washington.
11. Paul D. Gottlieb, "Growth Without Growth: An Alternative Economic Development Goal for Metropolitan Areas" (Washington: Brookings Institution Discussion Paper, February 2002, p.25).
12. Most famous is E.F. Schumacher, *Small is Beautiful (op cit)*. The evidence that the working classes have enjoyed little or, in some periods, none of the benefits of growth has been assembled by Richard Douthwaite in *The Growth*

Illusion (Tulsa, OK: Council Oak Books, 1993; originally published in Great Britain by Green Books, 1992.)

13. For citations and a much fuller exploration of these limits, see Lindsey Grant et al, *Elephants in the Volkswagen* (New York: W.H. Freeman, 1992), Lindsey Grant, *Juggernaut: Growth on a Finite Planet* (Santa Ana: Seven Locks Press, 1996), *Too Many People: The Case for Reversing Growth* (Seven Locks Press, 2000) and "Diverging Demography, Converging Destinies" (Alexandria, VA: Negative Population Growth, Inc. FORUM series January 2003; also at www.npg.org.)
14. The U.S. Geological Survey estimates remaining world resources at 2269 billion barrels. (USGS, Digital Data Series DDS-60.) It is one of the more optimistic projections.
15. The EIA, in its *International Energy Outlook 2003*, projects world oil demand to rise by 41 million barrels per day—53 percent—by 2025, and 15 million barrels of that growth will be in developing Asia.
16. *U.S. Statistical Abstract 2001*, Table 877.
17. U.S. Department of Energy, Energy Information Administration (EIA), "Monthly Energy Review, March 2004," Table 11.2.
18. Walter L. Youngquist, GeoDestinies (Eugene, OR: National Book Company, 1997, Chapter 13). Richard A. Kerr, "Gas Hydrate Resource: Smaller But Sooner," *Science*, Vol. 303, 2-14-04, pp.246–247.)
19. With the lower populations of 1950, total U.S. emissions would be 54 percent of the present 1.57 billion metric tons. Emissions by the rest of the industrial world would be 73 percent of 2.34 billion tons. Developing country emissions would be 35 percent of 2.53 billion tons. Totaled, world emissions from fossil energy would be 53 percent of the present 6.44 billion tons. (Data from U.N. Population Division and U.S. Department of Energy, Energy Information Agency, *International Energy Annual*, 2000.) Moreover, lower populations would mean less destruction of tropical forests, which presently add roughly 20 percent to world greenhouse gas emissions.
20. I treat this phenomenon at length in "It's the Numbers, Stupid!" NPG FORUM September 2003. See www.npg.org.
21. The discussion of optimum population in this paper expands on an article titled "Optimum Population: How Many Is Too Many?" scheduled for publication in the August-September 2004 issue of FREE INQUIRY, the *Journal of the Council for Secular Humanism.*

ABOUT THE AUTHORS

(Data as of the time of their contribution)

BARTLETT, DR. ALBERT

Albert A. Bartlett is Professor Emeritus of Physics at the University of Colorado in Boulder. A distinguished and dedicated educator and widely published author, Dr. Bartlett recently received the first George Gamow Memorial Lecture Award in recognition of his "most significant contribution to the public's understanding of science." Besides an illustrious career as a physicist, educator, and activist for stopping population growth, Dr. Bartlett is perhaps best known for his lecture, "Arithmetic, Population, and Energy: The Forgotten Fundamentals of the Energy Crisis," which has been given over a thousand times, including repeat performances to members of Congress at the U.S. Capitol. NPG is honored to have Dr. Bartlett as one of our Board of Advisors.

BECK, ROY

Roy Beck is the Executive Director of NumbersUSA and has authored several books, including, *The Case Against Immigration: The moral, economic, social and environmental reasons for reducing immigration back to traditional levels* (W.W. Norton & Co., 1996).

BERMINGHAM, JOHN R.

John R. Bermingham, a retired lawyer, is a long time activist. He served in the Colorado State Senate from 1965 to 1973, successfully sponsoring much population and environmental legislation. He has served as Chairman of the Colorado Land Use Commission and President of CSOC, the forerunner of today's Colorado Environmental Coalition. Currently he is President of the Colorado Population Coalition.

BINKIN, MARTIN

Mr. Binkin is a senior fellow in the Foreign Policy Studies program at the Brookings Institution, currently on sabbatical, serving as the Secretary of the Navy Fellow in the Economics Department United States Naval Academy. He has written extensively on defense manpower issues.

BOUVIER, LEON

Dr. Leon Bouvier is currently a visiting professor at Old Dominion University in Norfolk, Virginia and adjunct professor of Demography at Tulane University. Dr. Bouvier is former Vice President of the Washington-based Population Reference Bureau and has served as the demographic advisor to the U.S. House of Representatives Select Commission on Immigration and Refuge Policy. With a Ph.D. in sociology from Brown University, Dr. Bouvier currently serves as Senior Advisor to NPG.

BRECHER, JOSEPH

Mr. Brecher is an attorney in private practice in Oakland, California, specializing in environmental law. Before establishing his practice in 1975, he worked for the Native American Rights Fund.

BRIGGS JR., VERNON
Dr. Briggs is Professor of Human Resource Economics at the New York State School of Labor and Industrial Relations of Cornell University. He has written extensively on the subject of immigration policy and the U.S. labor force. He is a former Chairman of the National Council on Employment Policy.

BROWNRIDGE, DENNIS
Dr. Brownridge teaches at The Orme School in Arizona and writes on Western resource and environmental issues. He formerly taught geography at the University of California at Santa Barbara.

BURKE, B. MEREDITH
B. Meredith Burke, a demographer and economist, is a Visiting Scholar at the Hoover Institution at Stanford University and has served as a senior fellow of Negative Population Growth. Dr. Burke has also served as a consultant to the World Bank, U.S.A.I.D. and the U.N. Development Program.

CATTON, WILLIAM
William R. Catton, Jr. is Professor of Sociology Emeritus, Washington State University. A distinguished educator, he has taught courses in sociology and human ecology at universities in the U.S., Canada and New Zealand. Dr. Catton has authored or co-authored over 100 articles in journals or as chapters of books and four books on sociology, the environment and human ecology, including his 1980 classic *Overshoot: The Ecological Basis for Revolutionary Change.*

COSTANZA, ROBERT
Dr. Costanza is an Associate Professor at the University of Maryland's Chesapeake Biological Laboratory. He is the chief editor of the new journal *Ecological Economics.* He is also President and co-founder (with Herman Daly) of the International Society for Ecological Economics.

EHRLICH, PAUL AND ANNE
Paul Ehrlich is Bing Professor of Population Studies, Stanford University, and author or co-author of many articles and books, including *The Population Explosion.* Among his many awards are the Crafoord Prize of the Royal Swedish Academy of Sciences (given in lieu of a Nobel Prize in areas where the Nobel is not given), a MacArthur Prize Fellowship, the United Nations' Sasakawa Environment Prize, the Eminent Ecologist Award of the Ecological Society of America, and the Distinguished Scientist Award of the American Institute of Biological Sciences.

Anne Howland Ehrlich is a senior research associate in biology and associate director of the Center for Conservation Biology at Stanford. She has written or co-authored many technical and popular articles and books on issues such as population control, environmental protection and environmental consequences of nuclear war. She is the recipient of many honors, including selection for the United Nations' Global 500 Roll of Honour for Environmental Achievement.

FOX, ROBERT
Mr. Fox has been on the staff of the Organization of American States and the Inter-American Development Bank. He is presently co-authoring a series of reports that capture world population growth issues in three dimensional computer graphics and text.

GIAMPIETRO, MARIO
Mario Giampietro is a senior researcher at the Istituto Nationale della Nutrizione, Rome, and presently a visiting scholar at Cornell University, where David Pimentel is a professor in the College of Agriculture and Life Sciences.

HUDDLE, DONALD
Dr. Huddle is Professor of Economics at Rice University.

JENKS, ROSEMARY
Rosemary Jenks is Director of Policy Analysis at the Center for Immigration Studies, a Washington DC-based immigration think-tank.

KEYFITZ, NATHAN
Dr. Keyfitz is one of the "grand old men" of American demography. During a long and distinguished career, he has been chairman of the Sociology Department at the University of Chicago, Professor of Demography at the University of California, Berkeley, Andelot Professor and Chairman of the Department of Sociology at Harvard. He is presently at the International Institute for Applied Systems Analysis, Laxenburg, Austria.

LIND, MICHAEL
Michael Lind is a freelance writer who writes about environmental and population matters.

LYTWAK, ED
Ed Lytwak is a former research director of NPG. A long-time environmental and population activist, his articles on U.S. population issues and immigration have appeared in journals such as *Wild Earth* and *Population and Environment.*

MANN, DONALD
Donald Mann is the founder and President of Negative Population Growth Inc., a national public interest membership organization working to educate the American people on population, immigration and environmental policies.

Mr. Mann is a graduate of Wesleyan University, and has studied at Columbia University and the University of Paris (l'Institut d'Etudes Politiques). He has also served in the U.S. Navy.

After a successful career in international business, Mr. Mann founded NPG in 1972. He is frequently quoted in print, radio and television, and has authored many publications, including; *Why We Need a Smaller U.S. Population and How We Can Achieve It*, *The Case for Reducing Immigration from Over One Million to 100,000 a Year*, *The Costs of Overpopulation*, *The Cairo Conference on Population and Development* and *Immigration and the U.S. Energy Shortage.*

NELSON, GAYLORD
Gaylord Nelson is a former U.S. Senator from Wisconsin, an early environmentalist in the Senate, the originator of the first Earth Day in 1970, and one of the most distinguished names in environmentalism. He is now Counselor to The Wilderness Society. We reprint here, slightly abridged, the text of his statement for the thirtieth Earth Day.

PALMER, TIMOTHY
Tim Palmer is the author of twelve books on the American landscape, its rivers, and the environment. *The Fate of America* is adapted from his latest book, *The Heart of America: Our Landscape, Our Future*, recently published by Island Press.

PIMENTEL, DAVID & MARCIA
David Pimentel is a professor in the College of Agriculture and Life Sciences at Cornell University. He has published extensively and has chaired panels dealing with food, energy, population and natural resources, for the National Academy of Sciences, the American Association for the Advancement of Science and the U.S. Department of Energy.

Marcia Pimentel is Senior Lecturer (retired), Division of Nutritional Sciences in the College of Human Ecology at Cornell. She has authored a book and several papers dealing with nutrition and human populations.

SIMCOX, DAVID

David Simcox is a Senior Advisor of NPG. He is also a Senior Fellow of the Center for Immigration Studies, Washington, D.C., a non-profit research and policy analysis group that study the effects of immigration on broad national social, demographic and environmental interests of the United States. From 1985 to 1992, he was the Center's executive director.

From 1956 to 1985, Simcox was a career diplomat of the U.S. Department of State, with service in diplomatic posts in Latin America, Africa, Europe, and in Washington. His diplomatic assignments involved formulation of policy for labor, population and migration issues in such countries as Mexico, Panama, Dominican Republic, Brazil and the nations of Indo-China.

Simcox is a frequent contributor on population, immigration and Latin American matters to national newspapers and periodicals and has testified on several occasions before congressional committees on immigration, labor and identification policies.

He holds degrees from the University of Kentucky, American University and the National War College. Simcox is a veteran of the U.S. Marine Corps and saw service in the Korean conflict.

SMAIL, J. KENNETH

J. Kenneth Smail is a Professor of Anthropology Department of Anthropology/Sociology at Kenyon College, Gambier, Ohio.

SMITH, ANTHONY WAYNE

Anthony Wayne Smith is Special Counsel to NPG, and is one of the founders of the population stabilization movement in the United States. He served as a Fellow of the Population Reference Bureau at the time Robert C. Cook was reorganizing it in 1948. Beginning even earlier, he was associated with William Vogt, Fairfield Osborne, and Hugh Moore, particularly with respect to the environmental; aspects of the population explosion.

As President of the National Parks and Conservation Association from 1958 to 1980 Mr. Smith brought the population issue into its programs and wrote extensively on population in its magazine.

SPEARE, DR. ALDEN

Dr. Speare is Professor of Sociology at Brown University. His research interests are in the areas of internal migration and population aging. He has recently authored (with William Frey) a 1980 census monograph, *Regional and Metropolitan Growth and Decline in the United States.*

STYCOS, J. MAYONE

J. Mayone Stycos is Director of the Cornell University Population and Development Program, and the author of books and papers on population problems in Latin America and the Middle East.

TENNENBAUM, STEPHEN

Stephen E. Tennenbaum has a master's degree in environmental engineering from the University of Florida and is presently engaged in doctoral study on spatial ecosystem modeling at the University of Maryland, with Dr. Costanza.

WEEKS, JOHN

Dr. Weeks is Professor of Sociology and Director of the International Population Center at San Diego State University. He is the author of the text *Population: An Introduction to Concepts and Issues* (Belmont: Wadsworth), now in its fourth edition. Currently he is completing a federally funded research project on infant health outcomes among low-income immigrants in California.

WHITE, DR. MICHAEL

Dr. White is Associate Professor of Sociology at Brown University. His current research is in the areas of internal migration and U.S. immigration. He is author of the 1980 census monograph *American Neighborhoods and Residential Differentiation*.

ZOVANYI, GABOR

Gabor Zovanyi is Professor of Urban Planning, Eastern Washington University. He has taught growth management courses at Eastern Washington University, California Polytechnic University, Worcester Polytechnic Institute, and the University of Washington. His experience with growth management also includes years of employment as an urban planner with city, county, and federal agencies, as well as work as a private consultant on growth management projects. Dr. Zovanyi's current interest and research focus on assisting local governments in overcoming the obstacles to using growth management to stop growth. His book *Growth Management for a Sustainable Future* identifies the legal obstacles to stopping growth in local communities, but argues that these obstacles are not insurmountable.